# CHI 2014
## One of a CHInd

## Conference Proceedings

Toronto, Canada | April 26 – May 1, 2014

Association for Computing Machinery

SIGCHI

The 32nd Annual ACM Conference on Human Factors in Computing Systems

Association for Computing Machinery

*Advancing Computing as a Science & Profession*

**The Association for Computing Machinery**
**2 Penn Plaza, Suite 701**
**New York, New York 10121-0701**



**ISBN:** 978-1-4503-2473-1 (Digital)

**ISBN:** 978-1-4503-3287-3 (Print)

Additional copies may be ordered prepaid from:

**ACM Order Department**
PO Box 30777
New York, NY 10087-0777, USA

Phone: 1-800-342-6626 (USA and Canada)
+1-212-626-0500 (Global)
Fax: +1-212-944-1318
E-mail: acmhelp@acm.org
Hours of Operation: 8:30 am – 4:30 pm ET

Printed in the USA

# Welcome to CHI 2014!

CHI is more than a conference, it is an international community of researchers and practitioners who want to make a difference. Everything we do is focused on uncovering, critiquing and celebrating radically new ways for people and technology to evolve together. People in their everyday contexts, in diverse regions of the world, from very different backgrounds, with alternative outlooks on life drive this innovation. As you take part in the conference sessions we really hope you will experience how powerful this people-centred approach to technological transformation can be. CHI as a conference is now in its 32nd year and has grown to become the premier international forum on human-computer interaction, gathering us all to share innovative interactive insights that shape people's lives. CHI draws together a multidisciplinary community from around the globe.

Our great strength is our ability to bring together students and experts, researchers and practitioners, scientists, designers and engineers, drawing from their rich perspectives to create new visions of humancomputer interaction. This year's conference theme is One of a CHInd. We chose this nearly two years ago as we began planning for this event. It has helped us focus our efforts and we hope you will use it to keep your eyes open to the bigger picture amongst all the excitement, range of presentations and activities at the conference.

CHI 2014 is One of CHInd because it is a celebration of the conference's one of a kind diversity; from the broad range of backgrounds of its attendees, to the diverse spectrum of communities and fields that the conference and its research have an impact on. CHI 2014 will take place at the Metro Toronto Convention Centre in Toronto, Canada, a city itself known for its one of a kind cultural diversity. But, CHI 2014 is more than a celebration of the diversity of our community and conference setting.

We hope that this year's event, more than anything, reminds you that the "people," "participants," "users" or "humans" that you hear described throughout this week are actually uniquely wonderful individuals full of hopes, concerns, joys and frustrations. CHI is here to serve all of these one of a kinds.

CHI 2014 features two outstanding keynote speakers: Booker prize winning author, Margaret Atwood and leading UX designer, Scott Jenson.

New for CHI 2014, we have Provoke! Wisdom! Impact! plenary talks first thing each morning on Tuesday, Wednesday and Thursday. Come along, join the crowd and be energised by our speakers who will each bring in their experience of the Big Picture to inspire us. The talks will be short - twenty minutes - and then the rest of the day's programme will begin.

We are also delighted to host a timely retrospective exhibition on wearable technology curated by Thad Starner and Clint Zeagler. CHI 2014 also includes two days of focused workshops and four days of technical content, including CHI's prestigious technical program, with 16 parallel sessions of rigorously reviewed research Papers, engaging Panels, Case Studies and Special Interest Groups (SIGs), an extensive Course program and invited talks from SIGCHI's award winners: Steve Whittaker, Gillian Grampton Smith and Richard Ladner.

We also host student research, design, and game competitions, provocative alt.chi presentations and last-minute SIGs for discussing current topics. Interactivity hands-on demonstrations showcase the best of interactive technology. We also highlight over 241 Work-In-Progress posters: this year we have added some features to these sessions to better help you get the most out of the exciting, early stage work on show; do go along and engage with the authors about their work. Evening events include the CHI 2014 conference reception, Sponsors and University events, local performances and the Job Fair.

We received over 3200 submissions and accepted nearly 1000 that will appear in the ACM Digital Library. To help you navigate through this immense program, there are a number of online and digital resources from the conference website to our mobile apps. You can also browse the videos, papers and extended abstracts on the CHI 2014 USB Key. But, CHI 2014 is about being in Toronto so perhaps the best way to select from and experience the event is by asking for pointers and chatting with your fellow attendees, our wonderful student volunteers, the information desk helpers or any of this year's committee.

We are all here to make your experience as useful and enjoyable as possible. We are deeply indebted to our vast number of volunteers, without whom CHI 2014 would not be possible, including over 3800 reviewers, over 180 senior members of the program committee, nearly 100 members of the CHI 2014 conference committee and, of course, the more than 180 student volunteers. We thank you all! We are honored and excited by the opportunity to host CHI 2014 and wish you a productive and enjoyable stay in Toronto!

**Matt Jones,**
*Swansea University, Wales, UK*
CHI 2014 General Conference Co-Chair

**Albrecht Schmidt**
*University of Stuttgart, Germany*
CHI 2014 Technical Program Co-Chair

**Philippe Palanque**
*Université Paul Sabatier*
CHI 2014 General Conference Co-Chair

**Tovi Grossman**
*Autodesk Research, Canada*
CHI 2014 Technical Program Co-Chair

# From ACM SIGCHI's President and Vice President for Conferences

SIGCHI is proud to sponsor the premier annual conference in the field of human-computer interaction. We are extremely grateful to the CHI 2014 Conference Chairs Matt Jones and Philippe Palanque , to Technical Program Chairs Albrecht Schmidt and Tovi Grossman, and to their wonderful crew, who succeeded to build an impressive program and experience.

CHI 2014 is back in Toronto, Canada, returning to the same location of CHI 1987, 5 years after the first conference, on Human Factors in Computer Systems, in Gaithersburg, MD, March 1982. That first conference in Gaithersburg drew over 900 attendees, and since then CHI, with the official name: "ACM Conference on Human Factors in Computing Systems", has continued to grow and broaden its range of topics and contributing disciplines: the founding psychologists and software engineers began to meet new visions from ethnography, sociology, communication sciences and arts, among others. Relevant industries, as well as research institutes and academia, showed an increasing - and often long-lasting - interest and involvement (through volunteers and through sponsorship for conference expenses).

CHI is an ideal forum for people to meet formally as well as informally, to exchange knowledge and views, to share experiences, and to learn. The CHI conference brings together professionals from research and practice; people from industry, academia, and from government; long-term veterans of HCI, young professionals and students; all in an environment designed to encourage interaction. We invite you to actively participate in that interaction: introduce yourself to people, interact with presenters and speakers, renew old friendships and make new ones.

CHI is organized on behalf of ACM's Special Interest Group on Computer-Human Interaction (SIGCHI), an international community of professionals who share an interest in the many diverse facets of HCI. SIGCHI is committed both to advancing the field of HCI, to facilitate exchange of information within the SIGCHI community, and to support students to enter the domain.

The CHI conference is arguably the single most visible activity of SIGCHI, but we also sponsor and support a wide range of specialized conferences and workshops in areas ranging from interactive systems design to user interface technology to computer-supported cooperative work to "intelligent" user interfaces. Visit the SIGCHI website at **http://www.sigchi.org** to find our conference schedule, listing upcoming as well as past conferences.

SIGCHI and ACM produce some of the most respected publications in the field. All members receive interactions, a highly-acclaimed magazine covering the broad field of HCI and user interface design. ACM Transactions on Computer-Human Interactions (ToCHI), now in its 21st year, is our flagship journal - a quarterly publication with the top-quality archival research aimed at researchers and those translating research into practice.

SIGCHI is truly an international organization, with over 30 local chapters and 3 student chapters in 25 countries on 6 continents. We encourage all SIGCHI members to join their local chapter - or if there isn't one in your area, we would love to help you create one. And don't forget virtual communities! SIGCHI hosts dozens of electronic mailing lists on topics ranging from HCI and the Web, to HCI educations, to public policy and beyond. Those lists range from dozens of subscribers to thousands, and are an excellent way to keep up with the field and with friends and colleagues.

Finally, on behalf of ACM SGICHI, we again want to thank the conference committee and all of the hundreds of volunteers who make this conference possible. Their work makes this a rewarding experience for all of us.

**Gerrit C. van der Veer**
SIGCHI President

**John "Scooter" Morris**
SIGCHI Vice-President for Conferences

# CHI 2014 Papers and Notes Chairs' Welcome

The CHI Papers and Notes programme is continuing to grow and this year we received more than 2000 submissions for the first time. We are pleased that CHI is still the leading conference for research in humancomputer interaction.

CHI 2014 continued the use of subcommittees to manage the review process. Authors selected the subcommittee they believed was best qualified to review their work: Due to the changing pattern of submissions we split some subcommittees into more manageable sizes and coalesced others. We are pleased with the subcommittee process: By dividing the work, each paper received much more careful discussion than would otherwise have been possible.

This year we considered 2036 submissions, including 1428 papers and 608 notes, representing a 4% growth over last year. We accepted 465 submissions (23%): 382 papers and 83 notes.

The CHI review process demands a tremendous amount of work from all areas of the human computer interaction community. As co-chairs of the process, we are amazed at the ability of the community to organize itself to accomplish this task. We would like to thank the 2866 individual reviewers for their careful consideration of these papers. We also deeply appreciate the huge amount of time donated to this process by the 205-member program committee, who paid their own way to attend the face-to-face program committee meeting, an event larger than the average ACM conference.

We are proud of the work of the CHI 2014 program committee and hope that you enjoy these papers and notes, which represent the best research in human-computer interaction.

**Stephen Brewster**,
*Glasgow University*
CHI 2014 Papers and Notes Chairs

**Andy Cockburn**,
*University of Canterbury*
CHI 2014 Papers and Notes Chairs

# Table of Contents



## April 28th, 2014 – Volume 1

### Visualization and Aesthetics



### Stress



### Social Local Mobile



### Coordination and Collaboration

## Activity Recognition



## Managing Income



## Designing and Understanding Visualizations



## Crowdfunding and Crowd Storage



## Novel Approaches to Navigation



## Interfaces for Care and Support

## April 29th, 2014 – Volume 2a

### Interactive Visualization and Visual Elements



### Understanding and Designing Games



### Personal Values and Preferences

# April 29th, 2014 – Volume 2b

## Learning and Education

Session Chair: Deborah Tatar , *Virginia Polytechnic Institute and State University*



# April 30th, 2014 – Volume 3a

## Telepresence and Connecting over Video

Session Chair: Kori Inkpen , *Microsoft Research*



## Exergame Design

Session Chair: Sean Munson , *University of Washington*

## Designing and Modeling GUIs

Session Chair: Michael Nebeling , *ETH Zurich*



## Health and Everyday Life

Session Chair: Maria Wolters , *University of Edinburgh*



## Text Entry and Evaluation

Session Chair: Antti Oulasvirta , *Max Planck Institute for Informatics*



## Emotions and Mobiles

Session Chair: Antonio Krüger , *DFKI Saarbrücken*



## Privacy

Session Chair: Sameer Patil , *Helsinki Institute for Information Technology HIIT / Aalto University*

## Shape-Changing Interfaces

Session Chair: Abhijit Karnik , *Lancaster University*



## Touch Input

Session Chair: Daniel Wigdor , *University of Toronto*



## Risks and Security

Session Chair: Alexander De Luca , *University of Munich*



## CHI for Social Development

Session Chair: Nithya Sambasivan , *University of California*

# April 30th, 2014 – Volume 3b

## Lost and Found in Translation
Session Chair: Tiago Guerreiro , *University of Lisbon*



## Participatory Design
Session Chair: Mona Leigh Guha , *University of Maryland*



## Brain Computer Interfaces
Session Chair: Lynne Baillie , *Glasgow Caledonian University*



## 3D Printing and Fabrication
Session Chair: Alex Olwal , *Google [x]*

# CHI 2014 Conference Organization

| | |
|---|---|
| **General Chair:** | Matt Jones, *Swansea University, Wales, UK*<br>Philippe Palanque, *Université Paul Sabatier, France* |

## Technical Program

| | |
|---|---|
| **Technical Program Co-Chairs:** | Albrecht Schmidt, *University of Stuttgart , Germany*<br>Tovi Grossman, *Autodesk Research, Canada* |
| **Technical Program Chair Assistant:** | Michael Glueck, *Autodesk Research, Canada* |
| **Papers and Notes:** | Stephen Brewster, *University of Glasgow, UK*<br>Andy Cockburn, *University of Canterbrury, New Zealand* |
| **Panels:** | Gillian Hayes, *University of California, Irvine, USA*<br>Khai Truong, *University of Toronto, Canada* |
| **Case Studies:** | Jonathan Arnowitz, *Google, USA*<br>DJ Hoets, *SAP, USA*<br>Michael Arent, *Rivendel Consulting, USA*<br>*KAIST, Republic of Korea* in Henderson, *Flipside, The Netherlands* |
| **Courses:** | Regina Bernhaupt, *Ruwido, France*<br>Elizabeth Churchill, *eBay Research Labs, USA* |
| **Interactivity:** | Steven Benford, *University of Nottingham, UK*<br>Julie Rico Williamson, *University of Glasgow, Scotland, UK* |
| **Video Showcase:** | Jinwook Seo, *Seoul National University, Korea*<br>Nicolas Roussel, *INRIA, France* |
| **SIGs:** | Enrico Rukzio, *Ulm University, Germany*<br>Henry Duh, *University of Tasmania, Australia* |
| **Doctoral Consortium:** | Manfred Tscheligi, *University of Salzburg, Austria*<br>Katherine Isbister, *New York University, USA* |
| **Workshops:** | Nadir Weibel, *University of California, San Diego, USA*<br>Juergen Steimle, *Max Planck Institute, Germany* |
| **Works in Progress:** | Shelly Farnham, *Microsoft, USA*<br>Shamsi Iqbal, *Microsoft, USA*<br>Shaun Lawson, *University of Lincoln, USA* |
| **Student Research Competition:** | Celine Latulipe, *UNC Charlotte, USA*<br>Floyd Muller, *University in Melbourne, Australia* |
| **Student Design Competition:** | Thecla Schiphorst, *Simon Fraser University, Canada*<br>Youn-Kyung Lim, *KAIST, Korea* |

**Student Game Competition:** Seth Cooper, *University of Washington, USA*
Alessandro Canossa, *Northeastern University, USA*

**alt.chi:** Daniela Rosner, *University of Washington, USA*
Lilly Irani, *UC San Diego, USA*

**TOCHI Papers:** Jeffrey Nichols, *IBM Research, USA*

**Best of CHI Awards:** Daniel Wigdor, *University of Toronto, Canada*
Karyn Moffatt, *McGill School of Information, Canada*

## Spotlights

**Spotlights Chairs:** Kristina Höök, *Royal Institute of Technology, Sweden*
Ed Chi, *Google Research, USA*

**Games & Entertainment:** Magy Seif El-Nasr, *Northeastern University, USA*
Heather Desurvire, *Behavioristics, Inc, USA*
Lennart Nacke, *University of Ontario, Canada*

**HCI For Development (HCI4D):** Melissa Densmore, *Microsoft Research, USA*
Matthew Kam, *Carnegie Mellon University, USA*
Ban Al-Ani, *University of California, Irvine, USA*

**Interaction Science:** Andrew Howes, *University of Birmingham, UK*
Benjamin R. Cowan, *University of Birmingham, UK*
Stephen J. Payne, *University of Oxford, UK*
Paul Cairns, *University of York, UK*
Christian P. Janssen, *The Smith-Kettlewell Eye Research Institute, USA*
Anna L Cox, *University College London, UK*
Anthony J. Hornof, *University of Oregon, USA*
Peter Pirolli, *Palo Alto Research Center (PARC), USA*

**Making Cultures:** Jeffrey Bardzell, *University Bloomington, USA*
Shaowen Bardzell, *Shaowen Bardzell, USA*
Carl DiSalvo, *Georgia Institute of Technology, USA*
Ann Light, *Northumbria University, UK*
Daniela Rosner, *University of Washington, USA*

**Art and Interaction:** David England, *John Moores University, UK*
Joceyn Spence, *University of Surrey, UK*

## Operations

**Student Volunteer Coordinators:** Lindsay Reynolds, *Cornell University, USA*
Jon Haber, *University of Calgary, Canada*

**Technology Liaisons:** Scooter Morris, *University of California, San Francisco, USA*
Sara Drenner, *University of Minnesota-Twin Cities, USA*

**Webmaster:** Liam Betsworth, *Swansea University, Wales, UK*

| | |
|---|---|
| **Social Media:** | Max Wilson, *Nottingham University, UK*<br>Katie Panciera, *University of Minnesota, USA* |
| **Proceedings:** | Marco Winckler, *Université Paul Sabatier, France*<br>Yann Riche, *Microsoft, USA*<br>Stéphane Conversy, *ENAC, France* |
| **Infrastructure Accessibility Chair:** | Jennifer Rode, *Drexel University, USA* |
| **Digital Accessibility Chair:** | Jonathan Lazar, *Towson University, USA* |
| **Community Sourcing & Scheduling:** | Paul André, *Facebook, USA*<br>Anant Bhardwaj, *MIT, USA*<br>Lydia Chilton, *University of Washington, USA*<br>Juho Kim, *MIT, USA*<br>Steven Dow, *Carnegie Mellon University, USA*<br>Rob Miller, *MIT, USA*<br>Haoqi Zhang, *Northwestern University, USA* |
| **Mobile Apps:** | Stephen Oney, *Carnegie Mellon University, USA*<br>Eiji Hayashi, *Carnegie Mellon University, USA*<br>Jason Wiese, *Carnegie Mellon University, USA*<br>Célia Martinie, *Université Paul Sabatier, France* |
| **Video Previews:** | Gene Golovchinsky *[in memory]*<br>Gonzalo Ramos, *University of Toronto, Canada*<br>Fanny Chevalier, *INRIA, France* |
| **Conference Management:** | Janeé Pelletier, *Conference & Logistics Consultants, USA*<br>Allison Perrelli, *Conference & Logistics Consultants, USA* |
| **Sponsors, Exhibits & Recruitment:** | Carol Klyver, *Foundations of Excellence, USA* |
| **Registration:** | Yvonne Lopez, *Executive Events, Inc. USA*<br>Brooke Daley, *Executive Events, Inc. USA* |
| **PCS Liaisons:** | Max van Kleek, *University of Southampton, UK*<br>Carol Klyver, *Foundations of Excellence, USA*<br>Scooter Morris, *University of California, San Francisco, USA* |
| **Women's Breakfast Event:** | Allison Druin, *University of Maryland, USA* |

## CHI 2014 Papers and Notes Subcommittee & Associate Chairs

**Subcommittee Chairs:**

Mark Ackerman, *University of Michigan, USA*
Victoria Bellotti, *Xerox PARC, USA*
Laura Dabbish, *Carnegie Mellon University, USA*
Stephen Fairclough, *Liverpool John Moores University, UK*
Steven Feiner, *Columbia University, USA*
Jon Froelich, *University of Maryland, USA*
Vicki Hanson, *IBM Research, USA*
Jettie Hoonhout, *Philips Research, The Netherlands*
Hilary Hutchinson, *Google Research, USA*
Shahram Izadi, *Microsoft Research, UK*
David Kirk, *Newcastle University, UK*
Antonio Krueger, *DFKI, Germany*
Myriam Lewkowicz, *Université de Technologie de Troyes, France*
Youn-Kyung Lim, *KAIST, South Korea*
Joanna McGrenere, *University of British Columbia, Canada*
Bilge Mutlu, *University of Wisconsin-Madison, USA*
Fabio Paterno, *CNR ISTI, Italy*
Wanda Pratt, *University of Washington, USA*
mc schraefel, *University of Southampton, UK*
Sriram Subramanian, *University of Bristol, UK*
Bill Thies, *Microsoft Research, India*
Manfred Tscheligi, *CURE, Austria*
Ron Wakkary, *Simon Fraser University, Canada*
John Zimmerman, *Carnegie Mellon University, USA*

**Associate Chairs:**

Eytan Adar, *University of Michigan, USA*
Jason Alexander, *Lancaster University, UK*
Paul André, *Carnegie Mellon University, USA*
Judd Antin, *Yahoo! Research, USA*
Alissa Antle, *Simon Fraser University, Canada*
Paul Aoki, *Intel Labs, USA*
Daniel Ashbrook, *Nokia Research Center Hollywood, USA*
Gabriela Avram, *University of Limerick, Ireland*
Brian Bailey, *University of Illinois, USA*
Lynne Baillie, *Glasgow Caledonian University, UK*
Ravin Balakrishnan, *University of Toronto, Canada*
Jeffrey Bardzell, *Indiana University Bloomington, USA*
Richard Beckwith, *Intel Research, USA*
Hrvoje Benko, *Microsoft Research, USA*
Timothy Bickmore, *Northeastern University, USA*
Jeffrey Bigham, *Carnegie Mellon University, USA*
Mark Blythe, *Northumbria University, UK*
Alexander Boden, *University of Siegen, Germany*
Sebastian Boring, *University of Copenhagen, Denmark*
Duncan Brumby, *University College London, UK*
A.j. Brush, *Microsoft Research, USA*
Andreas Bulling, *Max-Planck Institut Für Informatik, Germany*
Daniela Busse, *Samsung Research America (SRA), USA*
Andreas Butz, *Ludwig-Maximilians-Universität München, Germany*
John Canny, *UC Berkley, USA*
Xiang Cao, *Lenovo Research & Technology, China*
Erin Carroll, *University of Rochester, USA*
Nicholas Chen, *University of Maryland, UK*
Yunan Chen, *University of California, USA*
Coye Cheshire, *UC Berkeley, USA*
Fanny Chevalier, *University of Toronto, Canada*
Keith Cheverst, *Lancaster University, England, UK*
Luigina Ciolfi, *Sheffield Hallam University, UK*
Rob Comber, *Newcastle University, UK*
Lorrie Cranor, *Carnegie Mellon University, USA*
Scott Davidoff, *Jet Propulsion Laboratory, USA*
Antonella de Angeli, *University of Trento, Italy*
Alexander de Luca, *University of Munich, Germany*
Rogerio de Paula, *IBM Research, Brazil*
Marco de Sá, *Facebook, USA*
Morgan Dixon, *University of Washington, USA*
Steven Dow, *Carnegie Mellon University, USA*
Pierre Dragicevic, *INRIA, France*
Mark Dunlop, *University of Strathclyde, Scotland, UK*
Darren Edge, *Microsoft Research Asia, China*
Serge Egelman, *University of California, USA*
Niklas Elmqvist, *Purdue University, USA*
Ylva Fernaeus, *KTH, Sweden*
Clifton Forlines, *Draper Laboratory, USA*
Jodi Forlizzi, *Carnegie Mellon University, USA*
Zhiyong Fu, *Information Art and Design Department, China*
Dominic Furniss, *University College London, UK*
Susan Fussell, *Cornell University, USA*

**Associate Chairs:**

Krzysztof Gajos, *Harvard University, USA*
Luciano Gamberini, *University of Padova, Italy*
David Geerts, *KU Leuven, Belgium*
Darren Gergle, *Northwestern University, USA*
Jennifer Golbeck, *University of Maryland, USA*
Judith Good, *University of Sussex, UK*
Ning Gu, *Fudan University, China*
Tiago Guerreiro, *University of Lisbon, Portugal*
Mona Leigh Guha, *University of Maryland, USA*
Carl Gutwin, *University of Saskatchewan, Canada*
Mark Hancock, *University of Waterloo, Canada*
Beverly Harrison, *Yahoo! Labs, USA*
Steve Harrison, *Virginia Tech, USA*
Mike Hazas, *Lancaster University, UK*
Otmar Hilliges, *ETH Zurich, Switzerland*
Eve Hoggan, *Aalto University, Finland*
Jonathan Hook, *Newcastle University, UK*
Kasper Hornbæk, *University of Copenhagen, Denmark*
Eva Hornecker, *Bauhaus Universität Weimar, Germany*
Gary Hsieh, *University of Washington, USA*
Elaine Huang, *Georgia Institute of Technology, USA*
Jina Huh, *Information Studies, USA*
Faustina Hwang, *The University of Reading, UK*
Kori Inkpen, *Microsoft Research, USA*
Lilly Irani, *University of California, USA*
Pourang Irani, *University of Manitoba, Canada*
Petra Isenberg, *INRIA, France*
Michal Jacovi, *IBM Research Lab In Haifa, Israel*
Giulio Jacucci, *Aalto University, Finland*
Wendy Ju, *California College of the Arts, USA*
Evangelos Karapanos, *Madeira Interactive Technologies Institute, Portugal*
Abhijit Karnik, *University of Bristol, UK*
Judy Kay, *University of Sydney, Australia*
Patrick Gage Kelley, *Carnegie Mellon University, USA*
Aisling Kelliher, *Carnegie Mellon University, USA*
Julie Kientz, *University of Washington, USA*
David Kim, *Newcastle University, UK*
Jesper Kjeldskov, *Aalborg University, Denmark*
Predrag Klasnja, *University of Michigan, USA*
Per Ola Kristensson, *University of St Andrews, UK*
Effie Law, *ETH Zurich, UK*
Christopher Le Dantec, *Georgia Institute of Technology, USA*
Joonhwan Lee, *Seoul National University, South Korea*
Yang Li, *Google Research, USA*
Silvia Lindtner, *University of California, USA*
Kris Luyten, *Hasselt University - Tul - Iminds, Belgium*
Kent Lyons, *Yahoo, USA*
Nicolai Marquardt, *University College London, UK*
Paul Marshall, *University College London, UK*
Michael Massimi, *Microsoft Research, UK*
Marilyn Mcgee-Lennon, *University of Glasgow, UK*
David Mcgookin, *Heriot-Watt University, Scotland, UK*
Helena Mentis, *University of Maryland, USA*

**Associate Chairs:**

Natasa Milic-Frayling, *Microsoft Research Ltd, UK*
Robert Miller, *The Pennsylvania State University, USA*
Karyn Moffatt, *McGill University, Canada*
Tom Moher, *University of Illinois at Chicago, USA*
Wendy Moncur, *University of Dundee, Scotland,*
Dan Morris, *Microsoft Research, USA*
Tomer Moscovich, *INRIA, France*
Ingrid Mulder, *Delft University of Technology, The Netherlands*
Michael Muller, *Alexander Von Humboldt Institute for Internet and Society, USA*
Jörg Müller, *University of Arts, Berlin, Germany*
Sean Munson, *University of Washington, USA*
Lennart Nacke, *University of Ontario Institute of Technology, Canada*
Michael Nebeling, *ETH Zurich, Switzerland*
Carman Neustaedter, *Simon Fraser University, Canada*
Jeffrey Nichols, *IBM Research, USA*
Ian Oakley, *Ulsan National Institute of Science and Technology, South Korea*
Marianna Obrist, *Newcastle University, UK*
William Odom, *Carnegie Mellon University, USA*
Amy Ogan, *Carnegie Mellon University, USA*
Patrick Olivier, *Newcastle University, UK*
Alex Olwal, *Royal Institute of Technology (KTH), USA*
Claire O'malley, *University of Nottingham, UK*
Antti Oulasvirta, *Max-Planck Institut Für Informatik, Germany*
Andrea Parker, *Northeastern University, USA*
Sameer Patil, *Aalto University, Finland*
Mark Perry, *Brunel University, UK*
Christopher Power, *University of York, UK*
Aaron Quigley, *University of St. Andrews, UK*
Chris Quintana, *University of Michigan, USA*
Emilee Rader, *Michigan State University, USA*
David Randall, *University of Siegen, UK*
Pei-Luen Patrick Rau, *Tsinghua University, China*
Stuart Reeves, *University of Nottingham, England*
Katharina Reinecke, *Harvard University, USA*
Anne Roudaut, *University of Bristol, Germany*
Mark Rouncefield, *Lancaster University, UK*
Daniel Russell, *Google, USA*
Nithya Sambasivan, *University of California, USA*
Corina Sas, *Lancaster University, UK*
Martina Angela Sasse, *University College London (UCL), UK*
Christina Satchell, *The University of Melbourne, Australia*
James Scott, *Microsoft Research, UK*
Andrew Sears, *Rochester Institute of Technology, USA*
Abigail Sellen, *Microsoft Research, UK*
N. Sadat Shami, *IBM Research, USA*
Rajinder Sodhi, *University of Illinois at Urbana-Champaign, USA*
Erin Solovey, *Drexel University, USA*
Danae Stanton Fraser, *University of Bath, UK*
Jürgen Steimle, *Massachusetts Institute of Technology, USA*
Wolfgang Stuerzlinger, *York University, Canada*
Hironobu Takagi, *IBM Research, Japan*
Yuichiro Takeuchi, *Sony Computer Science Laboratories, Japan*
Deborah Tatar, *Virginia Tech,*

**Associate Chairs:** Jaime Teevan, *Microsoft Research, USA*
John Thomas, *IBM T.J. Watson Research Center, USA*
Melanie Tory, *University of Victoria, Canada*
Zachary Toups, *New Mexico State University, USA*Deborah Tatar, *Virginia Tech*
Elise Van Den Hoven, *University of Technology Sydney, Australia*
John Vines, *Newcastle University, UK*
Daniel Vogel, *University of Waterloo, Canada*
Amy Voida, *Indiana University, USA*
Annalu Waller, *University of Dundee, Scotland, UK*
Hao-Chuan Wang, *National Tsing Hua University, Taiwan*
Nadir Weibel, *University of California San Diego, USA*
Daniel Wigdor, *University of Toronto, Canada*
Lauren Wilcox, *Georgia Institute of Technology, USA*
Maria Wolters, *University of Edinburgh, UK*
Volker Wulf, *University of Siegen and Fraunhofer FIT, Germany*
Sarita Yardi Schoenebeck, *University of Michigan, USA*
Svetlana Yarosh, *AT&T Research Labs, USA*
Thorsten Zander, *TU Berlin, Germany*
Shengdong Zhao, *National University of Singapore, Singapore*
Michelle Zhou, *IBM Research - Almaden, USA*
Xiaomu Zhou, *Rutgers University, USA*

## CHI 2014 Papers and Notes Reviewers

Konstantin Aal, *University of Siegen, Germany*
Parham Aarabi, *University of Toronto, Canada*
Francisco Abad, *Universitat Politècnica de València, Spain*
Julio Abascal, *University of the Basque Country, Spain*
Evgeniy Abdulin, *Texas State University, USA*
Saeed Abdullah, *Cornell University, USA*
Troy Abel, *Virginia Tech, USA*
Gregory Abowd, *Georgia Institute of Technology, USA*
Alessandro Acquisti, *Carnegie Mellon University, USA*
Lada Adamic, *University of Michigan, USA*
Anne Adams, *UCL Interaction Centre, USA*
Anne Adams, *Simplec, UK*
Dustin Adams, *University of California, USA*
Kim Adams, *University of Alberta, Canada*
Phil Adams, *Cornell University, USA*
Idris Adjerid, *Carnegie Mellon University, USA*
Rachel Adler, *Northeastern Illinois University, USA*
Tamara Adlin, *USA*
Daniel Afergan, *Tufts University, USA*
Ana Afonso, *Universidade de Lisboa, Portugal*
Stefan Agamanolis, *Akron Children's Hospital, USA*
Maneesh Agrawala, *University of California, USA*
David Ahlström, *Alpen-Adria Universität Klagenfurt, Austria*
Salman Ahmad, *Stanford University, USA*
Teemu Ahmaniemi, *Nokia Research Center, Finland*
June Ahn, *University of Maryland, USA*
Aino Ahtinen, *VTT Technical Research Centre, Finland*
David Akers, *Stanford University, USA*
Devdatta Akhawe, *UC Berkeley, USA*
Abdullah Al Mahmud, *Delft University of Technology, Netherlands*
Vicent Alabau, *Universidad Politécnica de Valencia (UPV), Spain*
Amro Al-Akkad, *Fraunhofer Institute for Applied Information Technology (FIT), Germany*
Gazihan Alankus, *Washington University In St. Louis, USA*
Turadg Aleahmad, *Coursera, USA*
Saleem Alhabash, *Michigan State University, USA*
Abir Al-Hajri, *UBC, Canada*
Dzmitry Aliakseyeu, *Philips Research, The Netherlands*
Doris Allhutter, *Institute of Technology Assessment, Austria*
Sonya Allin, *University of Toronto, Canada*
Norman Alm, *University of Dundee, UK*
Abdullah Al-Mahmud, *Delft University of Technology, The Netherlands*
Omar Alonso, *Microsoft, USA*
Basak Alper, *University of California Santa Barbara, USA*
Mohammad Al-Smadi, *Tallinn University, Estonia*
Florian Alt, *University of Munich, Germany*
Bashar Altakrouri, *University of Luebeck, Germany*
Reem Alzahabi, *Michigan State University, USA*
Saleema Amershi, *Microsoft Research, USA*

Morgan Ames, *Stanford University, USA*
Oliver Amft, *TU Eindhoven, Netherlands*
Farshid Amirabdollahian, *University of Hertfordshire, UK*
Swamy Ananthanarayan, *University of Colorado, USA*
Margarita Anastassova, *CEA, France*
Nazanin Andalibi, *Drexel University, USA*
Erik Andersen, *University of Washington, USA*
Fraser Anderson, *University of Alberta, Canada*
Ken Anderson, *Intel Corporation, USA*
Nazareno Andrade, *Universidade Federal de Campina Grande, Brazil*
Adrienne Andrew, *University of Washington, USA*
Christopher Andrews, *Virginia Polytechnic Institute and State University, USA*
Sean Andrist, *University of Wisconsin--Madison, USA*
Marvin Andujar, *Clemson University, USA*
Leonardo Angelini, *University of Applied Sciences Western Switzerland, Svizzera*
Michelle Annett, *University of Alberta, Canada*
Craig Anslow, *Victoria University of Wellington, New Zealand*
Lisa Anthony, *University of Florida, USA*
Thomas Apperley, *The University of New South Wales, Australia*
Caroline Appert, *Université Paris-Sud, France*
Bruno Araujo, *INESC-ID, Portugal*
Daniel Archambault, *Swansea University, UK*
Carmelo Ardito, *University of Bari, Italy*
Ahmed Arif, *Ryerson University, Canada*
John Arnott, *University of Dundee, UK*
Rosa Arriaga, *Georgia Institute of Technology, USA*
Kate Arrington, *Lehigh University, USA*
Thierry Artieres, *Université Pierre Et Marie Curie, France*
Mariam Asad, *Georgia Institute of Technology, USA*
Chieko Asakawa, *IBM Research - Tokyo, Japan*
Felix-Robinson Aschoff, *University of Zurich, Switzerland*
Debi Ashenden, *Cranfield University, UK*
Maryam Ashoori, *IBM, Canada*
Ilhan Aslan, *Universität Salzburg, Austria*
Zeina Atrash, *Northwestern University, USA*
Alan Au, *University of Washington, USA*
Anne Aula, *Google, USA*
Hane Aung, *University College London, UK*
Nikolaos Avouris, *University of Patras, Greece*
Daniel Avrahami, *Intel, USA*
Katerina Avramides, *London Knowledge Lab, UK*
Yuji Ayatsuka, *Koozyt, Japan*
Matthew Aylett, *Cereproc Ltd., UK*
Ruth Aylett, *Heriot-Watt University, UK*
Mobolaji Ayoade, *Glasgow Caledonian University, UK*
Phillip Ayoub, *Pennsylvania State University, USA*
Yadid Ayzenberg, *MIT, USA*
Shiri Azenkot, *University of Washington, USA*
Maryam Azh, *National University of Singapore, Singapore*
Tamara Babaian, *Bentley College, USA*
Chris Baber, *The University of Birmingham, UK*

Benjamin Bach, *INRIA, France*
Paula Bach, *The Pennsylvania State University, USA*
Myroslav Bachynskyi, *Max-Planck Institut Für Informatik, Germany*
Jonathan Back, *University College London, UK*
Maribeth Back, *FX Palo Alto Laboratory, USA*
Norm Badler, *University of Pennsylvania, USA*
Sangwon Bae, *Yonsei University, Seoul*
Seok-Hyung Bae, *KAIST, Republic of Korea*
Ronald Baecker, *University of Toronto, Canada*
Naveen Bagalkot, *IT University of Copenhagen, Denmark*
Zhen Bai, *University of Cambridge, UK*
Gilles Bailly, *CNRS, France*
Ryan Baker, *Teachers College, USA*
Suzanne Bakken, *Columbia University, USA*
Saskia Bakker, *Eindhoven University of Technology, The Netherlands*
Eytan Bakshy, *Facebook, USA*
Madeline Balaam, *Newcastle University, UK*
Aruna Balakrishnan, *Google, USA*
Guha Balakrishnan, *MIT, USA*
Matthias Baldauf, *FTW Telecommunications Research Center, Austria*
Rebecca Balebako, *Carnegie Mellon University, USA*
Elizabeth Bales, *University of Washington, USA*
Robert Ball, *Stephen F. KAIST, Republic of Korea in State University, USA*
Stinne Ballegaard, *KORA, Denmark*
Till Ballendat, *University of Munich, Germany*
Liam Bannon, *University of Limerick, Ireland*
Nikola Banovic, *Carnegie Mellon University, USA*
Francesco Banterle, *ISTI-CNR, Italy*
Xuan Bao, *Duke University, USA*
Evan Barba, *Georgetown University, USA*
Simone Barbosa, *Pontifical Catholic University of Rio de Janeiro (PUC-Rio), Brasil*
Jakob Bardram, *IT University of Copenhagen, Denmark*
Shaowen Bardzell, *Indiana University Bloomington, USA*
Javier Bargas-Avila, *Google, Switzerland*
Louise Barkhuus, *Stockholm University, Sweden*
Connelly Barnes, *Princeton University, USA*
Douglas Barnes
Pippin Barr, *University of Malta, Malta*
Barbara Barricelli, *University of West London, UK*
Barbara Barry, *MIT Media Lab, USA*
Tom Bartindale, *Newcastle University, UK*
Christoph Bartneck, *University of Canterbury, New Zealand*
Thomas Bartoschek, *University of Münster, Germany*
Lyn Bartram, *Simon Fraser University, Canada*
Santosh Basapur, *Illinois Institute of Technology, USA*
Rahul Basole, *Georgia Institute of Technology, USA*
Arianna Bassoli, *London School of Economics, UK*
Archer Batcheller, *University of Michigan, USA*
Scott Bateman, *University of Prince Edward Island, Canada*
Oliver Bates, *Lancaster University, UK*
Agathe Battestini, *Nokia, USA*
Olivier Bau, *Samsung Research America, USA*
Patrick Baudisch, *Hasso Plattner Institute, Germany*

Christine Bauer, *Vienna University of Economics and Business, Austria*
Jared Bauer, *University of Washington, USA*
Lujo Bauer, *Carnegie Mellon University, USA*
Eric Baumer, *Cornell University, USA*
Gordon Baxter, *University of St Andrews, UK*
Philip Beaman, *University of Reading, UK*
David Beattie, *Glasgow Caledonian University, Scotland, Uk*
Michel Beaudouin-Lafon, *Université Paris-Sud, France*
Elke Beck, *University of Salzburg, Austria*
S. Ann Becker, *Florida Tech, USA*
Benjamin Bederson, *University of Maryland, USA*
Roman Bednarik, *University of Eastern Finland, Finland*
Jenay Beer, *University of South Carolina, USA*
Andrew Begel, *Microsoft Research, USA*
Marios Belk, *University of Cyprus, Cyprus*
Rachel Bellamy, *IBM Research, USA*
Francesco Bellotti, *University of Genoa, Italy*
Raquel Benbunan-Fich, *Baruch College, USA*
Peter Benda, *The University of Melbourne, Australia*
Zinaida Benenson, *University of Erlangen-Nuremberg, Germany*
Steve Benford, *University of Nottingham, UK*
Mike Bennett, *Microsoft, USA*
Peter Bennett, *University of Bristol, UK*
Frank Bentley, *Motorola Mobility Inc., USA*
David Benyon, *Edinburgh Napier University, UK*
François Bérard, *CLIPS-IMAG, France*
Bettina Berendt, *KU Leuven, Belgium*
Alistair Beresford, *University of Cambridge, England*
Ofer Bergman, *Bar-Ilan University, Israel*
Kirsten Bergmann, *Bielefeld University, Germany*
Shane Bergsma, *Johns Hopkins University, USA*
Joanna Bergstrom-Lehtovirta, *Helsinki Institute for Information Technology HIIT, Finland*
Shlomo Berkovsky, *NICTA, Australia*
Gunilla Berndtsson, *Ericsson AB, Sweden*
Regina Bernhaupt, *IRIT, France*
Olav Bertelsen, *Aarhus University, Denmark*
Florent Berthaut, *INRIA, France*
Andrew Besmer, *UNC Charlotte, USA*
Michael Best, *Georgia Institute of Technology, USA*
Katrien Beuls, *Vrije Universiteit Brussel, Belgium*
Chris Bevan, *University of Bath, UK*
Nigel Bevan, *Professional Usability Services, UK*
Anastasia Bezerianos, *Université de Paris-Sud, France*
Konstantin Beznosov, *University of British Columbia, Canada*
Anant Bhardwaj, *Massachusetts Institute of Technology, USA*
Samit Bhattacharya, *IIT Guwahati, India*
Xiaojun Bi, *Google, USA*
Andrea Bianchi, *KAIST, Republic of Korea*
Nadia Bianchi-Berthouze, *University College London, UK*
Peter Bibby, *University of Nottingham, UK*
Nicola Bidwell, *CSIR-Meraka, South Africa*
Gerald Bieber, *Fraunhofer IGD, Germany*

Ralf Biedert, *German Research Center for Artificial Intelligence (DFKI), Germany*
Jacob Biehl, *FX Palo Alto Laboratory, USA*
Matthew Bietz, *University of California, USA*
Lukas Biewald, *CrowdFlower, USA*
Ali Bigdelou, *Technical University of Munich, Germany*
Dania Bilal, *University of Tennessee, USA*
Mark Billinghurst, *University of Canterbury, New Zealand*
Dorrit Billman, *NASA Ames, USA*
Jens Binder, *University of Manchester, UK*
Jon Bird, *City University London, UK*
Max Birk, *University of Saskatchewan, Canada*
Jeremy Birnholtz, *Northwestern University, USA*
Walter Bischof, *University of Alberta, Canada*
Pradipta Biswas, *University of Cambridge, England*
Staffan Björk, *University of Gothenburg, Sweden*
Pernille Bjorn, *IT University of Copenhagen, Denmark*
Alan Blackwell, *University of Cambridge, UK*
Rachel Blagojevic, *University of Auckland, New Zealand*
Renaud Blanch, *Université Grenoble I, France*
Ann Blandford, *University College London, UK*
Benjamin Blankertz, *Berlin Institute of Technology, Germany*
Eli Blevis, *The Hong Kong Polytechnic University, USA*
Brett Bligh, *Lancaster University, UK*
Jan Blom, *Nokia Research Center, Switzerland*
Katherine Blondon, *University of Washington, USA*
Marco Blumendorf, *Yetu AG, Germany*
Susanne Bødker, *Aarhus University, Denmark*
Mads Boedker, *Copenhagen Business School, Denmark*
Kirsten Boehner, *Cornell University, USA*
Cristian Bogdan, *KTH, Sweden*
Matthias Böhmer, *German Research Center for Artificial Intelligence (DFKI), Germany*
Susanne Boll, *University of Oldenburg, Germany*
Albertus Bongers, *University Technology Sydney, Australia*
Joe Bonneau, *USA*
Matthew Bonner, *Georgia Institute of Technology, USA*
David Bonnet, *Université Paris-Sud & CNRS, France*
Elizabeth Bonsignore, *University of Maryland, USA*
Kellogg Booth, *University of British Columbia, Canada*
Jan Borchers, *RWTH Aachen University, Germany*
Silvia Bordin, *TrentoRise, Italy*
Marcela Borge, *Penn State, USA*
Michelle Borkin, *Harvard University, USA*
Alan Borning, *University of Washington, USA*
Nis Bornoe, *Aalborg University, Denmark*
Gaetano Borriello, *University of Washington, USA*
Brennon Bortz, *Virginia Polytechnic Institute and State University, USA*
Nathan Bos, *University of Michigan, USA*
Claus Bossen, *University of Aarhus, Denmark*
Paolo Bottoni, *University of Rome - 'la Sapienza', Italy*
Matt-Mouley Bouamrane, *University of Glasgow, UK*
Stephane Bouchard, *Université Du Quebec En Outaouais, Canada*
Andy Boucher, *Goldsmiths College, UK*

Nadia Boukhelifa, *INRIA Saclay, France*
Anders Bouwer, *University of Amsterdam, Netherlands*
Judy Bowen, *The University of Waikato, New Zealand*
Chris Bowers, *University of Birmingham, UK*
John Bowers, *Newcastle University, UK*
Geoffrey Bowker, *UC Irvine, USA*
Doug Bowman, *Virginia Polytechnic Institute and State University, USA*
John Boyd, *Google, Na*
Erin Bradner, *Autodesk, USA*
Erin Brady, *University of Rochester, USA*
Andrew Bragdon, *Microsoft, USA*
Jonathan Bragg, *University of Washington, USA*
Giorgio Brajnik, *University of Udine, Italy*
Pedro Branco, *University of Minho, Portugal*
Joel Brandt, *Adobe Research, USA*
Stacy Branham, *Virginia Tech, USA*
Tone Bratteteig, *University of Oslo, Norway*
Cristian Bravo-Lillo, *Carnegie Mellon University, USA*
Matthew Brehmer, *University of British Columbia, Canada*
Margot Brereton, *Queensland University of Technology, Australia*
Robert Brewer, *University of Hawaii at Manoa, USA*
Jo Briggs, *Northumbria University, UK*
Pam Briggs, *Northumbria University, UK*
Willem-Paul Brinkman, *Delft University of Technology, The Netherlands*
Katie Brittain, *Newcastle University, UK*
Juliana Brixey, *UT Health Science Center at Houston, USA*
Anke Brock, *IRIT, France*
Eric Brockmeyer, *Disney Research, USA*
Gregor Broll, *DOCOMO Euro-Labs, Germany*
Geert Brone, *University of Leuven - Campus Antwerp, Belgium*
Jonas Brönstrup, *Technical University of Berlin, Germany*
Andy Brooks, *University of California, USA*
Mark Brosnan, *University of Bath, UK*
Ryan Brotman, *Intel Corporation, USA*
Anne-Marie Brouwer, *TNO Human Factors, Netherlands*
Barry Brown, *University of California San Diego, USA*
Deana Brown, *Georgia Institute of Technology, USA*
Michael Brown, *The University of Nottingham, UK*
Jed Brubaker, *University of California, USA*
Amy Bruckman, *Georgia Institute of Technology, USA*
Gerd Bruder, *University of Würzburg, Germany*
Pascal Bruegger, *University of Applied Sciences, Switzerland*
Clemens Brunner, *Graz University of Technology, Austria*
Miguel Bruns Alonso, *Eindhoven University of Technology, The Netherlands*
Anders Bruun, *Aalborg University, Denmark*
Nick Bryan-Kinns, *Queen Mary, UK*
Martin Brynskov, *Aarhus University, Denmark*
Michael Brzozowski, *Google, USA*
George Buchanan, *City University London, UK*
Sarah Buchanan, *University of Central Florida, USA*
Karolina Buchner, *Yahoo! Labs, USA*
Elizabeth Buie, *Northumbria University, UK*
Andrea Bunt, *University of Manitoba, Canada*

Cody Buntain, *University of Maryland, USA*
Judee Burgoon, *University of Arizona, USA*
Stefano Burigat, *University of Udine, Italy*
Moira Burke, *Facebook, USA*
Gary Burnett, *University of Nottingham, UK*
Margaret Burnett, *Oregon State University, USA*
Jesse Burstyn, *Queen's University, Canada*
Chris Burton, *University of Edinburgh, UK*
Jerry Busby, *Lancaster University, UK*
Marc Busch, *CURE - Center for Usability Research & Engineering, Austria*
Georg Buscher, *Microsoft, USA*
Monika Buscher, *Lancaster University, UK*
Stefano Bussolon, *Università di Trento, Italy*
Brian Butler, *UMD, USA*
D. Alex Butler, *Microsoft Research, UK*
Fabio Buttussi, *University of Udine, Italy*
Ayse Buyuktur, *University of Michigan, USA*
Daragh Byrne, *Arizona State University, USA*
Michael Byrne, *Rice University, USA*
Béatrice Cahour, *CNRS Télécom Paristech, France*
Kelly Caine, *Clemson University, USA*
Paul Cairns, *University of York, UK*
Maya Cakmak, *University of Washington, USA*
Jeffrey Calcaterra, *IBM Corporation, USA*
Roberto Calderon, *University of British Columbia, Canada*
André Calero Valdez, *RWTH Aachen University, Germany*
Janko Calic, *CVSS, UK*
Chris Callison-Burch, *Johns Hopkins University, USA*
Gaelle Calvary, *Grenoble Institute of Technology, France*
Licia Calvi, *NHTV Breda University of Applied Sciences, The Netherlands*
L Jean Camp, *Indiana University, USA*
Jose Campos, *Universidade do Minho, Portugal*
Heloisa Candello, *University of Brighton, UK*
Angelo Cangelosi, *Plymouth University, UK*
Cristina Cannone, *Università degli Studi di Milano, Italy*
Robert Capra, *University of North Carolina at Chapel Hill, USA*
Baptiste Caramiaux, *Goldsmiths College, London*
Giuseppe Carenini, *University of British Columbia, Canada*
Stefan Carmien, *University of Colorado, Spain*
Davide Carneiro, *University of Minho, Portugal*
Sheelagh Carpendale, *University of Calgary, Canada*
Luis Carriço, *University of Lisbon, Portugal*
John Carroll, *The Pennsylvania State University, USA*
Scott Carter, *FX Palo Alto Laboratory, USA*
Thomas Carter, *University of Bristol, UK*
Samuel Carton, *Northwestern University, USA*
Mark Cartwright, *Northwestern University, USA*
Géry Casiez, *University of Lille & INRIA Lille, France*
Alvaro Cassinelli, *University of Tokyo (todai), Japan*
Steven Castellucci, *York University, Canada*
Marcelo Cataldo, *Carnegie Mellon University, USA*
Grevet Catherine, *GVU Center, USA*
Abigail Cauchi, *Swansea University, UK*

Marc Cavazza, *University of Tesside, UK*
James Caverlee, *Texas A&M University, USA*
Melissa Cefkin, *IBM Research, USA*
Robert Cercos, *RMIT University, Australia*
Daniel Cernea, *University of Kaiserslautern, Germany*
Matteo Cesana, *Politecnico di Milano, Italy*
Pablo Cesar, *CWI, The Netherlands*
Ruy Cevantes, *UC Irvine, USA*
Elizabeth Cha, *Personal Robotics Lab, USA*
Samidh Chakrabarti, *Google, USA*
Matthew Chalmers, *University of Glasgow, UK*
Teresa Chambel, *University of Lisbon, Portugal*
Alan Chamberlain, *The University of Nottingham, UK*
Erik Champion, *Curtin University, Australia*
Deborah Chan, *University Health Network, Canada*
Joel Chan, *University of Pittsburgh, USA*
Liwei Chan, *Academia Sinica, Taiwan*
Angela Chang, *MIT Media Lab, USA*
Keng-Hao Chang, *University of California, Berkeley*
Remco Chang, *Tufts University, USA*
Peter Chapman, *University of Nottingham, UK*
Olivier Chapuis, *Université Paris-Sud, France*
Catherine Chase, *Carnegie Mellon University, USA*
Duen Horng (polo) Chau, *Georgia Institute of Technology, USA*
Beenish Chaudry, *Indiana University, USA*
Fang Chen, *Tsinghua University, Spain*
Gaowei Chen, *Pittsburg University,*
Hsiang-Ting Chen, *University of Tokyo, Taiwan*
Jay Chen, *New York University, USA*
Jilin Chen, *IBM Research, USA*
Judy Chen, *University of California, USA*
Liming Chen, *University of Ulster, UK*
Monchu Chen, *University of Madeira, Portugal*
Xiang 'Anthony' Chen, *Carnegie Mellon University, USA*
Yi-Shin Chen, *National Tsing Hua University, Taiwan*
Britte Cheng, *SRI International, USA*
Kai-Yin Cheng, *Microsoft Research Asia, Taiwan*
Lung-Pan Cheng, *National Taiwan University, Germany*
Shiwei Cheng, *Zhejiang University of Technology, China*
Mauro Cherubini, *Telefonica Research, Italy*
Marshini Chetty, *University of Maryland, USA*
Gifford Cheung, *University of Washington, USA*
Ed Chi, *Google, USA*
Pei-Yu Chi, *University of California, USA*
Sonia Chiasson, *Carleton University, Canada*
Mark Chignell, *University of Toronto, Canada*
Parmit Chilana, *University of Waterloo, USA*
Lydia Chilton, *MIT CSAIL, USA*
Alvin Chin, *Nokia Research Center, China*
George Chin, *Pacific Northwest National Laboratory, USA*
Clark Chinn, *Rutgers University,*
Winyu Chinthammit, *University of Tasmania, KAIST, Republic of Korea*
Eun Kyoung Choe, *University of Washington, USA*
Erik Choi, *Rutgers University, USA*

Ming Ki Chong, *Lancaster University, UK*
Wen Huei Chou, *Yunline University of Science and Technology, Taiwan*
Tanzeem Choudhury, *Dartmouth College, USA*
Ellen Christiansen, *Mads Clausen Institute, Denmark*
Georgios Christou, *Cyprus College, Cyprus*
Hao-Hua Chu, *National Taiwan University, Taiwan*
Jason Chuang, *University of Washington, USA*
Tyng-Ruey Chuang, *Academia Sinica, Taiwan*
Chia-Fang Chung, *University of Washington, USA*
Eunki Chung, *Carnegie Mellon University, USA*
Karen Church, *Telefonica Research, Spain*
Elizabeth Churchill, *eBay Research Lab, USA*
Marcelo Cicconet, *New York University, USA*
Jesse Cirimele, *Stanford University, USA*
Gabriel Cirio
Adrian Clark, *University of Canterbury, New Zealand*
Alan Clark, *Northwestern University, USA*
Lillian Clark, *University of Portsmouth, UK*
Rachel Clarke, *Newcastle University, UK*
James Clawson, *Georgia Institute of Technology, USA*
Adrian Clear, *Lancaster University, UK*
Tamara Clegg, *University of Maryland, USA*
Torkil Clemmensen, *Copenhagen Business School, Denmark*
Sue Cobb, *University of Nottingham, UK*
Michael Coburn, *RMIT University, Australia*
Gilbert Cockton, *Northumbria University, UK*
Gabe Cohn, *University of Washington, USA*
Marisa Cohn, *University of California Irvine, USA*
Michael Cohn, *Compukol Communications LLC, USA*
Jared Cole, *Carnegie Mellon University, USA*
Heather Cole-Lewis, *Columbia University, USA*
Lizzie Coles-Kemp, *Royal Holloway, UK*
Christopher Collins, *University of Ontario Institute of Technology, Canada*
Kevyn Collins-Thompson, *University of Michigan, USA*
Sébastien Combéfis, *Université Catholique de Louvain, Belgium*
Cristina Conati, *University of British Columbia, Canada*
Karin Coninx, *Hasselt University, Belgium*
Kay Connelly, *Indiana University Bloomington, USA*
Sunny Consolvo, *Google, USA*
Stéphane Conversy, *ENAC, France*
Gregorio Convertino, *Xerox Research Center Europe, Italy*
Perry Cook, *Princeton Computer Science, USA*
Michael Cooke, *Trinity College Dublin, Ireland*
Kovila Coopamootoo, *Newcastle University, UK*
Seth Cooper, *University of Washington, USA*
Andrew Cordar, *University of Florida, USA*
Raymundo Cornejo, *CICESE, Mexico*
Nicola Corradi, *Università di Padova, Italy*
Dan Cosley, *Cornell University, USA*
Joao Costa, *University of Ontario Institute of Technology, Canada*
Marc Cavazza, *University of Tesside, UK*
Gennaro Costagliola, *University of Salerno, Italy*
Enrico Costanza, *University of Southampton, UK*
James Coughlan, *Smith-Kettlewell Eye Research Institute, USA*

Tim Coughlan, *The University of Nottingham, UK*
Paul Coulton, *Lancaster University, UK*
Scott Counts, *Microsoft Research, USA*
Céline Coutrix, *Université Joseph Fourier, France*
Lynne Coventry, *University of Northumbria, UK*
Benjamin Cowan, *University of Birmingham, UK*
Anna Cox, *University College London, UK*
David Coyle, *University of Bristol, UK*
Michael Crabb, *University of Dundee, Scotland, UK*
Claire Craig, *Sheffield Hallam University, UK*
Scotty Craig, *Arizona State University,*
Henriette Cramer, *Yahoo! Labs, USA*
Meg Cramer, *UC Irvine, USA*
Angela Crandall, *iHub, Kenya*
Justin Cranshaw, *Carnegie Mellon University, USA*
Charles Crook, *University of Nottingham, UK*
Andrew Crossan, *University of Glasgow, UK*
R. Jordan Crouser, *Tufts University, USA*
Kevin Crowston, *Syracuse University, USA*
David Crundall, *University of Nottingham, UK*
Weiwei Cui, *Microsoft Research Asia, China*
Yanqing Cui, *Nokia Research Center, Finland*
Franco Curmi, *Lancaster University, UK*
Simone Cutini, *Università di Padova, Italy*
Edward Cutrell, *Microsoft Research India, India*
Chandrika Cycil, *Brunel University, UK*
Allen Cypher, *IBM Research - Almaden, USA*
Mary Czerwinski, *Microsoft Research, USA*
Alexei Czeskis, *Google, USA*
Raimund Dachselt, *Technische Universität Dresden, Germany*
Palle Dahlstedt, *Chalmers,*
Peng Dai, *Google, USA*
Florian Daiber, *DFKI German Research Center for AI, Germany*
Peter Dalsgaard, *Aarhus University, Denmark*
Ruth Dalton, *Northumbria University, UK*
Sashikanth Damaraju, *Texas A&M University, USA*
Chi Tai Dang, *University of Augsburg, Germany*
Andreea Danielescu, *Arizona State University, USA*
Darcy Dapra, *Google, USA*
Sauvik Das, *Carnegie Mellon University, USA*
Jennifer Davidson, *Oregon State University, USA*
Nigel Davies, *Lancaster University, UK*
James Davis, *UC Santa Cruz, USA*
Janet Davis, *Grinnell College, USA*
Katie Davis, *University of Washington,*
Richard Davis, *Singapore Management University, Singapore*
Rahmad Dawood, *Universitas Syiah Kuala, Indonesia*
Munmun de Choudhury, *Microsoft Research, USA*
Tjerk de Greef, *Delft University of Technology, The Netherlands*
Edward de Guzman, *Autodesk, USA*
Martin de Jode, *University College London, UK*
Daniele de Massari, *Fondazione Ospedale San Camillo, Italy*
Clarisse de Souza, *PUC-Rio, Brazil*

Cleidson de Souza, *Universidade Federal do Pará, Brazil*
David Dearman, *Twitter, USA*
Rob Deline, *Microsoft Research, USA*
Nicola Dell, *University of Washington, USA*
Robert Deloatch, *University of Illinois at Urbana-Champaign, USA*
Cagatay Demiralp, *Stanford University, USA*
Carrie Demmans Epp, *University of Toronto, Canada*
Nick Depalma, *Massachusetts Institute of Technology, USA*
Jan Derboven, *IBBT-KU Leuven, Belgium*
Katie Derthick, *University of Washington, USA*
Parag Deshpande, *Umeå Institute of Design, Sweden*
Audrey Desjardins, *Simon Fraser University, Canada*
Heather Desurvire, *Behavioristics, USA*
Sebastian Deterding, *Hans Bredow Institute for Media Research, Germany*
Laura Devendorf, *UC Berkeley, USA*
Guy Dewsbury, *Gdewsbury, UK*
Anind Dey, *Carnegie Mellon University, USA*
Barbara di Eugenio, *University of Illinois, USA*
Nicholas Diakopoulos, *Rutgers University, USA*
E.ilana Diamant, *University of Pittsburgh, USA*
Michael Dickard, *Ohio University, USA*
Margaret Dickey-Kurdziolek, *Virginia Tech, USA*
Sarah Diefenbach, *Folkwang University of the Arts, Germany*
Paul Dietz, *Microsoft, USA*
Tawanna Dillahunt, *Carnegie Mellon University, USA*
Jill Dimond, *Sassafras Tech Collective, USA*
Christian Dindler, *Aarhus University, Denmark*
Xianghua Ding, *Fudan University, China*
Abdigani Diriye, *Carnegie Mellon University, USA*
Betsy Disalvo, *Georgia Institute of Technology, USA*
Carl Disalvo, *Georgia Institute of Technology, USA*
Anke Dittmar, *University of Rostock, Germany*
Stephen Diverdi, *Adobe Systems Inc, USA*
Alan Dix, *Lancaster University, UK*
Sidney D'mello, *University of Notre Dame, USA*
Chuong do, *Coursera,*
Gavin Doherty, *Trinity College Dublin, Ireland*
Lynn Dombrowski, *University of California Irvine, USA*
Judith Donath, *MIT, USA*
Tao Dong, *University of Michigan, USA*
Birsen Donmez, *University of Toronto, Canada*
Marco Donnarumma, *Goldsmiths College, UK*
Jonathan Donner, *Microsoft Research India, USA*
Mira Dontcheva, *Adobe Research, USA*
James Doodson, *University of Leicester, England, UK*
Tanja Döring, *University of Bremen, Germany*
Marian Dörk, *Newcastle University, UK*
Brian Dorn, *University of Nebraska at Omaha, USA*
Michael Dorsch, *University of Michigan, USA*
Afsaneh Doryab, *Carnegie Mellon University, USA*
Jakub Dostal, *University of St Andrews, UK*
Wenwen Dou, *University of North Carolina at Charlotte, USA*
Andre Doucette, *University of Saskatchewan, Canada*

Audubon Dougherty, *MIT, USA*
Mark Doughty, *University of Lincoln, UK*
Paul Dourish, *University of California, USA*
John Downs, *The University of Melbourne, Australia*
Julie Downs, *Carnegie Mellon University, USA*
Toby Dragon, *Ithaca College, USA*
Christoph Draxler, *LMU München, Germany*
Martha Driessnack, *Oregon Health & Science University, USA*
Laurie Dringus, *Nova Southeastern University, USA*
Milena Droumeva, *Simon Fraser University, Canada*
Steven Drucker, *Microsoft Research, USA*
Allison Druin, *University of Maryland, USA*
Honglu Du, *Palo Alto Research Center, USA*
Ruofei Du, *Microsoft Research Asia, China*
Tina Du, *University of South KAIST, Republic of Korea ralia, Australia*
Carlos Duarte, *Universidade de Lisboa, Portugal*
Luís Duarte, *University of Lisbon, Portugal*
Emmanuel Dubois, *University of Toulouse, France*
Nicolas Ducheneaut, *Palo Alto Research Center, USA*
Andrew Duchowski, *Clemson University, USA*
Tobias Duckworth, *University of Salford, UK*
Casey Dugan, *IBM, USA*
Geoffrey Duggan, *University of Exeter, UK*
Susan Dumais, *Microsoft Research, USA*
Bruno Dumas, *Vrije Universiteit Brussel, Belgium*
Sean Duncan, *Indiana University, USA*
Lucy Dunne, *University College Dublin, Ireland*
Paul Dunphy, *Newcastle University, UK*
Andreas Dünser, *CSIRO - CCI, Australia*
Sophie Dupuy-Chessa, *University of Grenoble, France*
Shree Durga, *University of Wisconsin, USA*
Abigail Durrant, *Newcastle University, UK*
Erik Duval, *KU Leuven, Belgium*
Tim Dwyer, *Monash University, Australia*
Jason Dykes, *City University London, UK*
James Eagan, *Télécom-Paristech, France*
Sarah Eagle, *University of Bristol, UK*
David Ebert, *Purdue University, USA*
Florian Echtler, *Siemens Corporate Technology, Germany*
Dean Eckles, *Stanford University, USA*
Ernest Edmonds, *De Montfort University, UK*
Alistair Edwards, *University of York, UK*
Keith Edwards, *Georgia Institute of Technology, USA*
Kate Ehrlich, *IBM, USA*
Michael Eisenberg, *University of Colorado, USA*
Inger Ekman, *Aalto School of Economics, Finland*
Rana El Kaliouby, *University of Cambridge, UK*
Irene Eleta, *University of Maryland, USA*
Gunnar Ellingsen, *University of Tromsø, Norway*
Dan Ellis, *Columbia University, USA*
Geoff Ellis, *Lancaster University, UK*
Nicole Ellison, *University of Michigan, USA*
Lia Emanuel, *University of Bath,*
Bernadette Emsenhuber, *Johannes Kepler University of Linz, Austria*

Alex Endert, *Pacific Northwest National Laboratory, USA*
Klaus-Peter Engelbrecht, *Telekom Innovation Laboratories, Germany*
David England, *Liverpool John Moores University, UK*
Arvid Engström, *Mobile Life @ Stockholm University, Sweden*
Johan Engström, *Volvo Group Trucks Technology, Sweden*
Barrett Ens, *University of Manitoba, Canada*
Clayton Epp, *University of Saskatchewan, Canada*
Daniel Epstein, *University of Washington, USA*
Sheena Erete, *Northwestern University, USA*
Ingrid Erickson, *Rutgers University, USA*
Thomas Erickson, *IBM Research - T. J. Watson, USA*
Elina Eriksson, *KTH, Sweden*
Eva Eriksson, *Chalmers University of Technology, Sweden*
Lizbeth Escobedo, *Universidad Autonoma de Baja California, Mexico*
Parisa Eslambolchilar, *Future Interaction Technologies Lab, UK*
Sergio Espana, *Universitat Politecnica de Valencia, Spain*
Augusto Esteves, *University of Madeira, Portugal*
Michael Evans, *British Broadcasting Corporation, UK*
Vanessa Evers, *University of Twente, The Netherlands*
Marc Fabri, *Leeds Metropolitan University, UK*
Jerry Fails, *Montclair State University, USA*
Shamal Faily, *University of Oxford, UK*
Anthony Faiola, *Indiana University (IUPUI), USA*
Fiona Fairlie, *Glasgow Caledonian University, UK*
Majdi Faleh
Josef Faller, *Graz University of Technology, Austria*
Daniel Fallman, *Umeå University, Sweden*
Min Fan, *Simon Fraser University Surrey, Canada*
Xianyong Fang, *Anhui University, China*
Jill Fantauzza, *Georgia Institute of Technology, USA*
Jan Erik Farbrot, *Institute for Energy Technology / OECD Halden Reactor Project, Norway*
Elisabetta Farella, *DEIS - University of Bologna, Italy*
Shelly Farnham, *Microsoft Research, USA*
Umer Farooq, *The Pennsylvania State University, USA*
Karen Farris, *University of Michigan, USA*
Michael Farrugia, *UCD Dublin, Luxembourg*
Rosta Farzan, *University of Pittsburgh, USA*
Haakon Faste, *California College of the Arts, USA*
Andrew Faulring, *Carnegie Mellon University, USA*
Stu Favilla, *Swinburne University of Technology, Australia*
Melanie Feinberg, *University of Texas at KAIST, Republic of Korea in, USA*
Jean-Daniel Fekete, *INRIA, France*
Niels Feldmann, *Karlsruhe Institute of Technology (KIT), Germany*
Karla Felix Navarro, *University of Technology Sydney, Australia*
Deborah Fels, *Ryerson University, Canada*
Sidney Fels, *University of British Columbia, Canada*
Adrienne Felt, *Google, USA*
Jinjuan Feng, *University of Maryland, USA*
Robert Ferguson, *McGill University, Canada*
Jennifer Fernquist, *Google,*
Denzil Ferreira, *University of Oulu, Finland*
Pedro Ferreira, *Mobile Life @ KTH, Sweden*

Gabriele Ferri, *Indiana University, USA*
Brian Ferris, *University of Washington, USA*
Francesco Ferrise, *Politecnico di Milano, Italy*
Bruce Ferwerda, *Johannes Kepler University, Austria*
Mirko Fetter, *University of Bamberg, Germany*
Stephen Few, *Perceptual Edge, USA*
Christos Fidas, *University of Cyprus, Cyprus*
Rebecca Fiebrink, *Princeton University, UK*
Daniel Filonik, *Queensland University of Technology, Germany*
Leah Findlater, *University of Maryland, USA*
Thomas Finholt, *University of Michigan, USA*
Julia Fink, *Ecole Polytechnique Fédérale de Lausanne (EPFL), Switzerland*
Janet Finlay, *Leeds Metropolitan University, UK*
Andrew Fiore, *Facebook, USA*
Joel Fischer, *The University of Nottingham, UK*
Brian Fisher, *Simon Fraser University, Canada*
Danyel Fisher, *Microsoft Research, USA*
Stephen Fitchett, *University of Canterbury, New Zealand*
Daniel Fitton, *University of Central Lancashire, UK*
Elizabeth Fitzgerald, *The Open University, UK*
George Fitzmaurice, *Autodesk, Canada*
Geraldine Fitzpatrick, *Vienna University of Technology, Austria*
Zachary Fitz-Walter, *Queensland University of Technology, Australia*
Steve Flaherty, *Northeaster University, USA*
David Flatla, *University of Dundee, UK*
Ivan Flechais, *University of Oxford, England, UK*
Rowanne Fleck, *University College London, UK*
Scott Fleming, *University of Memphis, USA*
Martin Flintham, *The University of Nottingham, UK*
John Flowers, *University of Nebraska -- Lincoln, USA*
Allen Flynn, *University of Michigan, USA*
Brynn Flynn, *Carnegie Mellon University, USA*
James Fogarty, *University of Washington, USA*
Bj Fogg, *Stanford University, USA*
Sean Follmer, *MIT, USA*
Eelke Folmer, *University of Nevada, USA*
Peter Forbrig, *University of Rostock, Germany*
Alain Forget, *Carleton University, Canada*
Azadeh Forghani, *Simon Fraser University, Canada*
Laura Forlano, *Parsons The New School for Design, USA*
David Forsyth, *University of Illinois at Urbana-Champaign, USA*
Andrea Forte, *Drexel University, USA*
Jutta Fortmann, *University of Oldenburg, Germany*
Lesley Fosh, *The University of Nottingham, UK*
Elizabeth Foss, *University of Maryland, USA*
Derek Foster, *University of Lincoln, UK*
Stephen Foster, *UC San Diego, USA*
Marcus Foth, *Queensland University of Technology, Australia*
Brooke Foucault, *Northwestern University, USA*
Adam Fourney, *University of Waterloo, Canada*
Adam Fouse, *University of California, USA*
Allan Fowler, *Waiariki Institute of Technology, New Zealand*
Sarah Fox, *University of Washington, USA*

Suely Fragoso, *Federal University of Rio Grande do Sul (UFRGS), Brazil*
Anders Frank, *Swedish National Defence College, Sweden*
Mario Frank, *UC Berkeley, Germany*
Mike Fraser, *University of Bristol, UK*
Christopher Frauenberger, *University of Sussex, UK*
Dustin Freeman, *University of Toronto, Canada*
Euan Freeman, *University of Glasgow, Scotland, UK*
Andre Freire, *Universidade de Lisboa, Brazil*
Luanne Freund, *University of British Columbia, Canada*
Jill Freyne, *CSIRO, Australia*
Sarah-Christin Freytag, *Berlin Institute of Technology, Germany*
Enrique Frias-Martinez, *Telefonica Research, Spain*
Adrian Friday, *Lancaster University, UK*
Doron Friedman, *The Interdisciplinary Center, Israel*
Mathias Frisch, *MID Gmbh, Germany*
Chris Frisina, *Virginia Tech, USA*
Jonas Fritsch, *Aarhus University, Denmark*
Mario Fritz, *MPI Informatik, Germany*
Thomas Fritz, *University of Zurich, Switzerland*
Bernd Froehlich, *Bauhaus Universität Weimar, Germany*
Jon Froehlich, *University of Maryland, USA*
David Frohlich, *University of Surrey, UK*
Peter Fröhlich, *FTW Telecommunications Research Center, Austria*
Erik Frøkjær, *Københavns Universitet, Denmark*
Mads Frost, *IT University of Copenhagen, Denmark*
Wai-Tat Fu, *University of Illinois at Urbana-Champaign, USA*
Georg Fuchs, *Fraunhofer Institute Intelligent Analysis and Information Systems IAIS, Germany*
Johannes Fuchs, *University, Germany*
Verena Fuchsberger, *ICT&S Center, Austria*
Kaori Fujinami, *Tokyo University of Agriculture and Technology, Japan*
Kentarou Fukuda, *IBM Research - Tokyo, Japan*
Benjamin Fung, *McGill University, Canada*
Mathias Funk, *Eindhoven University of Technology, The Netherlands*
Silvia Gabrielli, *Create-Net, Italy*
Hind Gacem, *Télécom-Paristech, France*
Martin Gaedke, *Technische Universität Chemnitz, Germany*
Andrea Gaggioli, *Catholic University of Milan, Italy*
Sarah Gallacher, *UCL, UK*
Teresa Galvão, *Universidade do Porto, Portugal*
Maribeth Gandy, *Georgia Institute of Technology, USA*
Eva Ganglbauer, *Vienna University of Technology, Austria*
Ge Gao, *Cornell University, USA*
Ruth García-Gavilanes, *Universitat Pompeu Fabra, Spain*
Simson Garfinkel, *MIT, USA*
R. Kelly Garrett, *Ohio State University, USA*
Daniel Gartenberg, *George Mason University, USA*
Franca Garzotto, *HOC-Politecnico di Milano, Italy*
Nadia Gauducheau, *ICD-CNRS, France*
Steffen Gauglitz, *University of California, USA*
Paul Gault, *University of Dundee, UK*
William Gaver, *Goldsmiths College, UK*
Tom Gedeon, *KAIST, Republic of Korea ralian National University, Australia*

Nils Gehlenborg, *Harvard Medical School, USA*
Sven Gehring, *German Research Center for Artificial Intelligence (DFKI), Germany*
Johanna Gelderblom, *University of Pretoria, South Africa*
Hans Gellersen, *Lancaster University, UK*
Aaron Genest, *University of Saskatchewan, Canada*
Kallirroi Georgila, *University of Southern California, USA*
Elizabeth Gerber, *Northwestern University, USA*
Peter Gerjets, *Knowledge Media Research Center*
Jens Gerken, *ICT Innovative Communication Technologies AG, Germany*
Kathrin Gerling, *University of Lincoln, UK*
David Gerritsen, *Carnegie Mellon University, USA*
Paul Gestwicki, *Ball State University, USA*
Luc Geurts, *KU Leuven, Belgium*
Werner Geyer, *IBM Research - T. J. Watson, USA*
Giuseppe Ghiani, *ISTI-CNR, Italy*
George Ghinea, *Brunel University, UK*
Emilien Ghomi, *Université Paris-Sud, France*
Maysam Ghovanloo, *Georgia Institute of Technology, USA*
Alicia Gibb, *Nycresistor, USA*
Lorna Gibson, *University of Dundee, UK*
Eric Gilbert, *Georgia Institute of Technology, USA*
Kathleen Gilbert, *Indiana University, USA*
Alastair Gill, *University of Surrey, UK*
Kiel Gilleade, *Liverpool John Moores University, UK*
Nicholas Gillian, *MIT Media Lab, USA*
Stephen Gilroy, *Teesside University, UK*
Shuli Gilutz, *Interdisciplinary Center (IDC) Herzliya, Israel*
Shiry Ginosar, *University of California, USA*
Jeffrey Girard, *University of Pittsburgh, USA*
Audrey Girouard, *Carleton University, Canada*
Voula Gkatzidou, *Brunel University, UK*
Dylan Glas, *ATR, Japan*
Marie Glasemann, *Aalborg University, Denmark*
Michael Glueck, *University of Toronto, Canada*
Janet Go, *Autodesk, USA*
Kentaro Go, *University of Yamanashi, Japan*
Fernand Gobet, *University of Liverpool, UK*
Mayank Goel, *University of Washington, USA*
Anja Goeritz, *University of Freiburg, Germany*
Sean Goggins, *University of Missouri, USA*
Wooi Boon Goh, *Nanyang Technological University, Singapore*
Sergio Goldenberg, *Georgia Institute of Technology, USA*
Scott Golder, *Cornell University, USA*
Ilya Goldin, *Carnegie Mellon University, USA*
Dan Goldman, *Adobe, USA*
David Golightly, *Experian UK, UK*
Connie Golsteijn, *Eindhoven University of Technology, Netherlands*
Evan Golub, *University of Maryland, USA*
Richard Gomer, *University of Southampton, UK*
Antonio Gomes, *Queen's University, Canada*
Rafael Gomez, *Queensland University of Technology, Australia*
Steven Gomez, *Brown University, USA*

Jorge Goncalves, *Instituto Superior Técnico, Finland*
Daniel Gonçalves, *University of Oulu, Portugal*
Tiago Gonçalves, *FCUL, Portugal*
Nan-Wei Gong, *Massachusetts Institute of Technology, USA*
Amy Gonzales, *Indiana University, USA*
Berto Gonzalez, *University of North Carolina at Charlotte, USA*
Victor Gonzalez, *University of Manchester, UK*
Walkyria Goode, *SPARK Experience, USA*
Elizabeth Goodman, *UC Berkeley, USA*
Paul Gorman, *Oregon Health & Science University, USA*
Sandy Gould, *University College London, UK*
Rúben Gouveia, *University of Madeira, Portugal*
Nitesh Goyal, *Cornell University, USA*
Kazjon Grace, *UNC Charlotte, USA*
Michele Graffeo, *University of Trento, Italy*
Connor Graham, *National University of Singapore, Singapore*
Martin Graham, *Napier University, UK*
Nicholas Graham, *Queen's University, Canada*
Klaus Gramann, *Berlin Institute of Technology, Germany*
Dimitris Grammenos, *Foundation for Research and Technology - Hellas, Greece*
Sukeshini Grandhi, *Eastern Connecticut State University, USA*
Laura Granka, *Google, USA*
Raphael Grasset, *Graz University of Technology, Austria*
Colin Gray, *Indiana University, USA*
Rebecca Gray, *Michigan State University, USA*
David Green, *Newcastle University, UK*
Keith Green, *Clemson University, USA*
Michael Greenberg, *Northwestern University, USA*
Saul Greenberg, *University of Calgary, Canada*
Chris Greenhalgh, *The University of Nottingham, UK*
Peggy Gregory, *University of Central Lancashire, UK*
Catherine Grevet, *Georgia Institute of Technology, USA*
Harry Griffin, *University College London, UK*
Erin Griffiths, *University of Virginia, USA*
Thomas Grill, *University of Salzburg, Austria*
Rebecca Grinter, *Georgia Institute of Technology, USA*
Laurent Grisoni, *University Lille, France*
Alex Groce, *Oregon State University, USA*
Georg Groh, *TU Muenchen, Germany*
Diane Gromala, *Simon Fraser University, Canada*
Kaj Grønbæk, *University of Aarhus, Denmark*
Erik Grönvall, *IT University of Copenhagen, Denmark*
Mark Gross, *Carnegie Mellon University, USA*
Shad Gross, *Indiana University Bloomington, USA*
Tom Gross, *University of Bamberg, Germany*
Jens Grossklags, *The Pennsylvania State University, USA*
Jens Grubert, *University of Technology Graz, Austria*
Shion Guha, *Cornell University, USA*
Yves Guiard, *Télécom-Paristech CNRS, France*
François Guimbretière, *Cornell University, USA*
Rebecca Gulotta, *Carnegie Mellon University, USA*
Hatice Gunes, *University of Technology, Australia*
Philip Guo, *Stanford University, USA*

Ankit Gupta, *University of Washington, USA*
Sidhant Gupta, *University of Washington, USA*
David Gurzick, *Hood College, USA*
Sean Gustafson, *Hasso Plattner Institute, Germany*
Mattia Gustarini, *University of Geneva, Switzerland*
Francisco Luis Gutiérrez Vela, *University of Granada, España*
Ricardo Gutierrez-Osuna, *Texas A&M University, USA*
Mark Guzdial, *Georgia Institute of Technology, USA*
Tajin Ha, *KAIST, S. Korea*
Joerg Haake, *Fernuniversitaet Hagen, Germany*
Eija Haapalainen Ferreira, *University of Oulu, Finland*
Eben Haber, *IBM Research - Almaden, USA*
Jonathan Haber, *University of Calgary, Canada*
Martin Hachet, *Labri-INRIA University of Bordeaux, France*
Mieke Haesen, *Hasselt University - Tul - Iminds, Belgium*
Joshua Hailpern, *Hewlett Packard, USA*
Oliver Haimson, *University of California, USA*
Julia Haines, *University of California, USA*
Maria Håkansson, *Chalmers University of Technology, Sweden*
David Hakken, *Indiana University Bloomongton, USA*
Jonna Hakkila, *University of Oulu, Finland*
Jonna Häkkilä, *Soul4design, Finland*
Jukka Häkkinen, *Aalto University School of Science and Technology, Finland*
Timothy Hale, *Partners Healthcare Inc., USA*
Aaron Halfaker, *University of Minnesota, USA*
Joseph Hall, *The Center for Democracy & Technology, USA*
Michael Haller, *University of Applied Sciences Upper KAIST, Republic of Korea ria, Austria*
Lars Hallnäs, *Chalmers University of Technology, Sweden*
John Halloran, *Coventry University, UK*
Kim Halskov, *Aarhus University, Denmark*
Christine Halverson, *IBM Research - T. J. Watson, USA*
Tim Halverson, *Air Force Research Laboratory, USA*
Martin Halvey, *Glasgow Caledonian University, UK*
Perttu Hämäläinen, *Aalto University, Finland*
William Hamilton, *Texas A&M University, USA*
Jessica Hammer, *Carnegie Mellon University, USA*
Nils Hammerla, *Newcastle University, UK*
Tracy Hammond, *Texas A&M University, USA*
Jaehyun Han, *KAIST, Republic of Korea*
Jeonghye Han, *Computer Education, Republic of Korea*
Kyungsik (keith) Han, *The Pennsylvania State University, USA*
Teng Han, *University of Bristol, China*
Jeff Hancock, *Cornell University, USA*
Mark Handel, *The Boeing Company, USA*
Alina Hang, *University of Munich, Germany*
Benjamin Hanrahan, *Virginia Polytechnic Institute and State University, France*
Derek Hansen, *Brigham Young University, USA*
John Paulin Hansen, *IT University of Copenhagen, Denmark*
Kotaro Hara, *University of Maryland, USA*
Mona Haraty, *University of British Columbia, Canada*
Marian Harbach, *Leibniz University Hannover, Germany*

Gunnar Harboe, *University of Zurich, Switzerland*
Ellie Harmon, *UC Irvine, USA*
Morten Harning, *Dialogical ApS, Denmark*
Franklin Harper, *University of Minnesota, USA*
Richard Harper, *Microsoft Research, UK*
Simon Harper, *University of Manchester, UK*
Erik Harpstead, *Carnegie Mellon University, USA*
Rikard Harr, *Umeå University, Sweden*
Chris Harrison, *Carnegie Mellon University, USA*
Daniel Harrison, *University College London, UK*
Lane Harrison, *University of North Carolina at Charlotte, USA*
Jennefer Hart, *Lancaster University, UK*
Casper Harteveld, *Northeastern University, USA*
Björn Hartmann, *University of California, USA*
Mark Hartswood, *University of Edinburgh, UK*
Andrea Hartzler, *University of Washington, USA*
Catherine Harvey, *University of Nottingham, UK*
Khalad Hasan, *University of Manitoba, Canada*
Chelsea Hash, *Polytechnic Institute of NYU, USA*
Mitsuyo Hashida, *Soai Uiversity, Japan*
Marc Hassenzahl, *Folkwang University of the Arts, Germany*
Doris Hausen, *University of Munich, Germany*
Sabrina Hauser, *Simon Fraser University, Canada*
Kirstie Hawkey, *Dalhousie University, Canada*
Eiji Hayashi, *Carnegie Mellon University, USA*
Gillian Hayes, *University of California, USA*
Helen He, *University of Calgary, Canada*
Marti Hearst, *UC Berkeley, USA*
Brent Hecht, *University of Minnesota, USA*
Per-Olof Hedvall, *Lund University, Sweden*
Jaimee Heffner, *Fred Hutchinson Cancer Research Center, USA*
Tomi Heimonen, *University of Tampere, Finland*
Eric Hekler, *Arizona State University, USA*
Robert Held, *University of California, USA*
Bradley Hemminger, *University of North Carolina, USA*
Niels Hendriks, *University of Leuven, Belgium*
David Hendry, *University of Washington, USA*
Fabian Hennecke, *University of Munich, Germany*
Nathalie Henry Riche, *Microsoft Research, USA*
Niels Henze, *University of Stuttgart, Germany*
Cormac Herley, *Microsoft Research, Ghjhj*
Hamilton Hernandez, *Queen's University, Canada*
Davinia Hernandez-Leo, *Universitat Pompeu Fabra, Spain*
Marc Herrlich, *University of Bremen, Germany*
Morten Hertzum, *University of Copenhagen, Denmark*
Philipp Herzig, *SAP Research CEC Dresden, Germany*
Phil Heslop, *Newcastle University, UK*
Luke Hespanhol, *University of Sydney, Australia*
Jan Hess, *University of Siegen, Germany*
Susan Hessey, *Brithish Telecom, UK*
Wilko Heuten, *OFFIS - Institute for Information Technology, Germany*
Clint Heyer, *IT University of Copenhagen, Denmark*
Nadja Heym, *University of Nottingham, UK*

Jutta Hild, *Fraunhofer IOSB, Germany*
Benjamin Mako Hill, *University of Washington, USA*
Serena Hillman, *Simon Fraser University, Canada*
Juan David Hincapié-Ramos, *IT University of Copenhagen, Canada*
Ken Hinckley, *Microsoft Research, USA*
Jon Hindmarsh, *King's College London, UK*
Uta Hinrichs, *University of St Andrews, UK*
Sen Hirano, *University of California, USA*
Matthew Hirsch, *MIT Media Lab, USA*
Tad Hirsch, *University of Washington, USA*
Leanne Hirshfield, *Hamilton College, USA*
Chaya Hiruncharoenvate, *Georgia Institute of Technology, USA*
Christina Hochleitner, *CURE - Center for Usability Research & Engineering, Austria*
Nadia Hocine, *Montpellier 2 University, France*
Duncan Hodges, *University of Oxford, UK*
Gray Hodgkinson, *Massey University, New Zealand*
Orland Hoeber, *University of Regina, Canada*
Jesse Hoey, *University of Waterloo, Canada*
Guy Hoffman, *IDC Herzliya, Israel*
Bernie Hogan, *University of Toronto, Canada*
Trevor Hogan, *Cork Institute of Technology, Ireland*
Andrew Hogue, *University of Ontario Institute of Technology, Canada*
James Hollan, *UCSD, USA*
Simon Holland, *The Open University, UK*
Tobias Hollerer, *University of California, USA*
Nic Hollinworth, *University of Reading, UK*
Caitlin Holman, *University of Michigan, USA*
David Holman, *Queen's University, Canada*
Hrönn Holmer, *Cornell University, USA*
Stefan Holmlid, *Linköpings universitet, Sweden*
Lars Erik Holmquist, *Indep. Consultant, USA*
Kenneth Holmqvist, *Lund University, Sweden*
Bree Holtz, *Information Studies and Media, USA*
Christian Holz, *Yahoo! Labs, USA*
Andreas Holzinger, *Graz Medical University, Austria*
Hwajung Hong, *Georgia Institute of Technology, USA*
Jason Hong, *Carnegie Mellon University, USA*
Jin-Hyuk Hong, *Carnegie Mellon University, USA*
Lichan Hong, *Google, USA*
Kristina Höök, *KTH, Sweden*
Mohammed Hoque, *University of Rochester, USA*
Michael Horn, *Northwestern University, USA*
John Horton, *Harvard University, USA*
Matthew Horton, *Child Computer Interaction Group, UK*
Simo Hosio, *University of Oulu, Finland*
Steven Houben, *IT University of Copenhagen, Denmark*
Kirralie Houghton, *Queensland University of Technology, Australia*
Robert Houghton, *The University of Nottingham, UK*
Juan Pablo Hourcade, *University of Iowa, USA*
Rachid Hourizi, *University of Bath, UK*
Aaron Houssian, *Philips Research, The Netherlands*
Andrew Howes, *University of Manchester, UK*

James Howison, *Carnegie Mellon University, USA*
Kate Howland, *University of Sussex, UK*
Iris Howley, *Carnegie Mellon University, USA*
Idris Hsi, *Microsoft, USA*
Yi-Ta Hsieh, *University of Helsinki, Finland*
Chang Hu, *Microsoft, USA*
Jun Hu, *Eindhoven University of Technology, Netherlands*
Mengdie Hu, *Georgia Institute of Technology, USA*
Y. Charlie Hu, *Purdue University, USA*
Yuheng Hu, *Arizona State University, USA*
Chung-Ching Huang, *Indiana University, USA*
Haosheng Huang, *Research Group Cartography, Austria*
Jeff Huang, *University of Washington, USA*
Kevin Huang, *Georgia Institute of Technology, USA*
Shih-Wen Huang, *University of Washington, USA*
Jochen Huber, *MIT Media Lab, USA*
Bernardo Huberman, *HP Labs, USA*
Matthew Hudson, *The University of York, UK*
Scott Hudson, *Carnegie Mellon University, USA*
David Huffaker, *Google, USA*
Amanda Hughes, *Utah State University, USA*
Julie Hui, *Northwestern University, USA*
Alina Huldtgren, *Delft University of Technology, Germany*
Jessica Hullman, *University of Michigan, USA*
Shah Rukh Humayoun, *University of Kaiserslautern, Germany*
Seth Hunter, *MIT Media Lab, USA*
Stephane Huot, *Université Paris-Sud, France*
Annika Hupfeld, *University of Nottingham, UK*
Amy Hurst, *Carnegie Mellon University, USA*
Wolfgang Hürst, *Utrecht University, The Netherlands*
Christophe Hurter, *University of Toulouse, France*
Heinrich Hussmann, *Ludwig-Maximilians-Universität München, Germany*
Dugald Hutchings, *Elon University, USA*
John Hutchinson, *Lancaster University, UK*
C.j. Hutto, *Georgia Institute of Technology, USA*
Luke Hutton, *University of St Andrews, UK*
Ebba Thora Hvannberg, *University of Iceland, Iceland*
Inseok Hwang, *KAIST, South Korea*
Sungjae Hwang, *KAIST, South Korea*
Aulikki Hyrskykari, *University of Tampere, Finland*
Ioanna Iacovides, *UCL, UK*
Djilali Idoughi, *University A. Mira of Bejaia, Algeria*
Takeo Igarashi, *The University of Tokyo, Japan*
Klas Ihme, *University of Leipzig, Germany*
Masahiko Inami, *KMD, Japan*
Todd Ingalls, *Arizona State University, USA*
Stephen Intille, *Northeastern University, USA*
Alexandra Ion, *University of Applied Sciences Upper KAIST, Republic of Korea ria, Austria*
Iulia Ion, *Google, USA*
Panos Ipeirotis, *New York University, New York*
Shamsi Iqbal, *Microsoft Research, USA*
Ellen Isaacs, *PARC, USA*

Katherine Isbister, *Polytechnic Institute of New York University, USA*
Tobias Isenberg, *INRIA, France*
Kentaro Ishii, *The University of Tokyo, Japan*
Poika Isokoski, *University of Tampere, Finland*
Ali Israr, *Disney Research, USA*
Howell Istance, *De Montfort University, UK*
Yuichi Itoh, *Osaka University, Japan*
Bret Jackson, *University of New Mexico, USA*
Daniel Jackson, *Newcastle University, UK*
Steven Jackson, *Cornell University, USA*
Tanner Jackson, *Princeton, USA*
Robert Jacob, *Tufts University, USA*
Mattias Jacobsson, *Mobile Life @ SICS, Sweden*
Nassim Jafarinaimi, *Georgia Institute of Technology, USA*
Nils Jäger, *University of Nottingham, UK*
Mohit Jain, *University of Toronto, Canada*
Sharad Jaiswal, *Bell Labs India, India*
Timo Jakobi, *University of Siegen, Germany*
Mikkel Jakobsen, *University of Copenhagen, Denmark*
Hamid R. Jamali, *Kharazmi University, Iran*
Anthony Jameson, *German Research Center for Artificial Intelligence (DFKI), Germany*
Jacek Jankowski, *Digital Enterprise Research Institute, France*
Maddy Janse, *Philips Research, The Netherlands*
Bernard Jansen, *The Pennsylvania State University, USA*
Yvonne Jansen, *Université Paris-Sud, France*
Christian Janssen, *Smith-Kettlewell Eye Research Institute, USA*
Joris Janssen, *Eindhoven University of Technology, The Netherlands*
Ryan Janzen, *University of Toronto, Canada*
Tim Jay, *University of Bristol, UK*
K. Neil Jenkings, *Newcastle University, UK*
Tom Jenkins, *Georgia Institute of Technology, USA*
Carlos Jensen, *Oregon State University, USA*
Jennifer Jenson, *York University, Canada*
Seokhee Jeon, *ETH Zurich, Switzerland*
Jin-Woo Jeong, *Hanyang University, Republic of Korea*
Hans-Christian Jetter, *University of Konstanz, UK*
Jiepu Jiang, *University of Massachusetts Amherst, USA*
Nan Jiang, *Bournemouth University, UK*
Marina Jirotka, *University of Oxford, UK*
Kazuhiro Jo, *IAMAS, Japan*
Bonnie John, *IBM Research, USA*
Andrew Johnson, *University of Illinois at Chicago, USA*
Gabe Johnson, *Blank Slate Systems, USA*
Jeff Johnson, *UI Wizards, USA*
Kimberly Johnson, *Google, USA*
Maritza Johnson, *University of California, USA*
Mikael Johnson, *Helsinki University of Technology, Finland*
Steven Johnson, *Temple U., USA*
Aditya Johri, *Virginia Tech, USA*
Tero Jokela, *Nokia Research Center, Finland*
Brett Jones, *University of Illinois at Urbana-Champaign, USA*
J. Adam Jones, *University of Southern California, USA*

Malcolm Jones, *Northumbria University, UK*
Matt Jones, *Swansea University, Wales, UK*
Steve Jones, *University of Waikato, New Zealand*
William Jones, *University of Washington, USA*
Martin Jonsson, *Södertörn University, Sweden*
Sergi Jorda, *Universitat Pompeu Fabra, Spain*
Joaquim Jorge, *INESC-ID, Portugal*
Rui Jose, *Universidade do Minho, Portugal*
Anirudha Joshi, *Indian Institute of Technology, India*
Neel Joshi, *Microsoft, USA*
Ricardo Jota, *University of Toronto, Portugal*
M.-Carmen Juan, *UPV, Spain*
Oskar Juhlin, *Mobile Life @ Stockholm University, Sweden*
Satu Jumisko-Pyykkö, *Tampere University of Technology, Finland*
Heekyoung Jung, *University of Cincinnati, USA*
Malte Jung, *Cornell University, USA*
Tzyy-Ping Jung, *UCSD, USA*
Yumi Jung, *Michigan State University, USA*
Beyerer Jürgen, *Karlsruhe Institute of Technology (KIT), Germany*
Marko Jurmu, *University of Oulu, Finland*
Mike Just, *Glasgow Caledonian University, UK*
Antti Jylhä, *University of Helsinki, Finland*
Dennis Kafura, *Virginia Tech, USA*
Anne Kaikkonen, *Nokia Corporation, Finland*
Sanjay Kairam, *Stanford University, USA*
Yasuaki Kakehi, *Keio University, Japan*
Matthew Kam, *American Institutes for Research, USA*
Noreen Kamal, *University of British Columbia, Canada*
Alexander Kan, *The University of Melbourne, Australia*
Sean Kandel, *Stanford University, USA*
Eser Kandogan, *IBM, USA*
Bridget Kane, *Trinity College Dublin, Ireland*
Shaun Kane, *University of Maryland Baltimore County, USA*
Ruogu Kang, *Carnegie Mellon University, USA*
Marije Kanis, *Brunel University, UK*
Gopinaath Kannabiran, *Indiana University, USA*
Anne Marie Kanstrup, *Aalborg University, Denmark*
Ashish Kapoor, *Microsoft Research, USA*
Dennis Kappen, *University of Ontario Institute of Technology, Canada*
Evangelos Kapros, *Trinity College Dublin, Ireland*
Maurits Kaptein, *Eindhoven University of Technology, The Netherlands*
Victor Kaptelinin, *Umeå University, Sweden*
Mustafa Karagozler, *Disney Research, USA*
Karrie Karahalios, *University of Illinois, USA*
Amela Karahasanovic, *SINTEF ICT, Norway*
John Karat, *IBM Research - T. J. Watson, USA*
David Karger, *MIT, USA*
Thorsten Karrer, *RWTH Aachen University, Germany*
Christos Katsanos, *Hellenic Open University, Greece*
Brian Katz, *LIMSI-CNRS, France*
Larry Katz, *University of Calgary, Canada*
Andrea Kavanaugh, *Virginia Tech, USA*
Fahim Kawsar, *Phd Candidate, Japan*

Matthew Kay, *University of Waterloo, Canada*
Joseph 'jofish' Kaye, *Nokia, USA*
Gabriella Kazai, *Microsoft Research, UK*
Konstantinos Kazakos, *Newcastle University, UK*
Rubaiat Habib Kazi, *National University of Singapore, Canada*
Elizabeth Kaziunas, *University of Michigan, USA*
Wendy Keay-Bright, *University of Wales Institute, Wales, UK*
Daniel Keefe, *University of Minnesota, USA*
Brian Keegan, *Northeastern University, USA*
Flavius Kehr, *University of Koblenz-Landau, Germany*
Caitlin Kelleher, *Washington University, USA*
Wendy Kellogg, *IBM Research - T. J. Watson, USA*
Diane Kelly, *University of North Carolina, USA*
Ryan Kelly, *University of Bath, UK*
Logan Kendall, *University of Washington, USA*
Denisa Kera, *National University of Singapore, Singapore*
Dagmar Kern, *Bertrandt Ingenieurbüro Gmbh, Germany*
Andruid Kerne, *Texas A&M University, USA*
Andreas Kerren, *Linnaeus University, Sweden*
Karina Kervin, *University of Michigan, USA*
Cem Keskin, *Microsoft Research, UK*
Rilla Khaled, *University of Malta, Malta*
Mohammadreza Khalilbeigi, *Darmstadt University of Technology, Germany*
Vassilis-Javed Khan, *NHTV Breda University of Applied Sciences, The Netherlands*
Ahmed Kharrufa, *Newcastle University, UK*
Rohit Khot, *RMIT University, Australia*
Vera Khovanskaya, *Cornell University, USA*
Emre Kiciman, *Microsoft Research, USA*
Wolf Kienzle, *Microsoft Research, USA*
Johan Kildal, *Nokia, Finland*
Dongwhan Kim, *Seoul National University, Republic of Korea*
Hyang-Sook Kim, *St. Norbert's College, USA*
Hyung Nam Kim, *Northwestern University, USA*
Joy Kim, *Stanford University, USA*
Juho Kim, *Massachusetts Institute of Technology, USA*
Ju-Whan Kim, *KAIST, Republic of Korea*
Kibum Kim, *Kochi University of Technology, Japan*
Seung Wook Kim, *Samsung R&D Center Silicon Valley, USA*
Seungjun Kim, *Carnegie Mellon University, USA*
Si Jung Kim, *University of Central Florida, USA*
Sung-Hee Kim, *Purdue University, USA*
Sunyoung Kim, *Carnegie Mellon University, USA*
Taemie Kim, *Sociometric Solutions, USA*
Kenrick Kin, *University of California, USA*
Jennifer King, *University of California, USA*
Michael Kipp, *Augsburg University of Applied Sciences, Germany*
Reuben Kirkham, *Nottingham University, England*
Iacovos Kirlappos, *University College London, UK*
Alex Kirlik, *University of Illinois at Urbana, USA*
Ben Kirman, *University of Lincoln, UK*
Paul Kirschner, *Open Universiteit, Nederland*
David Kirsh, *University of California, USA*

Christopher Kirwan, *Parsons The New School for Design, USA*
Yoshifumi Kitamura, *Tohoku University, Japan*
Kris Kitani, *Carnegie Mellon University, USA*
Aniket Kittur, *Carnegie Mellon University, USA*
Funda Kivran-Swaine, *Rutgers University, USA*
René Kizilcec, *Stanford University, USA*
Scott Klemmer, *UC San Diego, USA*
Jayne Klenner, *King's College, USA*
Clemens Klokmose, *Aarhus University, Denmark*
Eric Klopfer, *MIT, USA*
Jarrod Knibbe, *University of Bristol, UK*
Bart Knijnenburg, *University of California, The Netherlands*
Cory Knobel, *University of California, USA*
Hendrik Knoche, *EPFL, Switzerland*
Bran Knowles, *Lancaster University, UK*
Masatomo Kobayashi, *IBM Research - Tokyo, Japan*
Michael Koch, *Bundeswehr University Munich, Germany*
Kenneth Koedinger, *Carnegie Mellon University, USA*
Lone Koefoed Hansen, *Aarhus University, Denmark*
Christian Koehler, *Carnegie Mellon University, USA*
Hyunseung Koh, *Indiana University, USA*
Kyle Koh, *Seoul National University, South Korea*
Hideki Koike, *University of Electro-Communications, Japan*
Mario Kolberg, *University of Stirling, UK*
Boriana Koleva, *The University of Nottingham, UK*
Beth Kolko, *University of Washington, USA*
Jon Kolko, *Frog Design, USA*
Thomas Költringer, *Ventum Consulting, Austria*
Steven Komarov, *Harvard University, USA*
Anita Komlodi, *University of Maryland, USA*
Andreas Komninos, *University of Strathclyde, UK*
Joseph Konstan, *University of Minnesota, USA*
Matthias Korn, *Aarhus University, Denmark*
Oliver Korn, *University of Applied Sciences Esslingen, Germany*
Gerd Kortuem, *The Open University, UK*
Robert Kosara, *Tableau Software, USA*
Timothy Koschmann, *Southern Illinois University, USA*
Ilpo Koskinen, *University of Art and Design Helsinki, Finland*
Vassilis Kostakos, *University of Oulu, Finland*
Ilkka Kosunen, *University of Helsinki, Finland*
Theodora Koulouri, *Brunel University,*
Matthias Kovatsch, *ETH Zurich, Switzerland*
Yong Ming Kow, *University of California Irvine, Hong Kong Sar*
Nicole Kraemer, *University of Duisburg-Essen,*
Adam Kramer, *Facebook, USA*
Jan-Peter Krämer, *RWTH Aachen University, Germany*
Matthias Kranz, *University of Passau, Germany*
Sven Kratz, *University of Munich, Germany*
Robert Kraut, *Carnegie Mellon University, USA*
Christian Kray, *University of Münster, Germany*
Shivsubramani Krishnamoorthy, *Amrita University, USA*
Ernst Kruijff, *Graz University of Technology, Austria*
John Krumm, *Microsoft Research, USA*
Erin Krupka, *University of Michigan, USA*

Ravi Kuber, *UMBC, USA*
Sebastien Kubicki, *CERV - Centre Européen de Réalité Virtuelle, France*
Alex Kuhn, *University of Michigan, USA*
Kai Kuikkaniemi, *Helsinki Institute for Information Technology HIIT, Finland*
Sari Kujala, *Aalto University, Finland*
Tuomo Kujala, *University of Jyväskylä, Finland*
Hannu Kukka, *University of Oulu, Finland*
Anand Kulkarni, *University of California, USA*
Chinmay Kulkarni, *Stanford University, USA*
Anuj Kumar, *Carnegie Mellon University, USA*
Arun Kumar, *IBM Research, India*
Neha Kumar, *University of California, USA*
Ranjitha Kumar, *Stanford University, USA*
Santosh Kumar, *University of Memphis, USA*
Ponnurangam Kumaraguru, *IIIT-Delhi, India*
Andrew Kun, *University of New Hampshire, USA*
Andreas Kunz, *Swiss Federal Institute of Technology Zurich, Switzerland*
Kai Kunze, *Osaka Prefecture University, Japan*
Liisa Kuparinen, *University of Jyväskylä, Finland*
Sri Kurniawan, *University of California, USA*
Gordon Kurtenbach, *Autodesk, Canada*
Arma an Kuru, *Middle East Technical University, Turkey*
Raja Kushalnagar, *Rochester Institute of Technology, USA*
Diana Kusunoki, *Drexel University, USA*
Kari Kuutti, *University of Oulu, Finland*
Stacey Kuznetsov, *Carnegie Mellon University, USA*
Youngshin Kwak, *Ulsan National Institute of Science and Technology, South Korea*
Bum Chul Kwon, *University of Konstanz, Germany*
Gyu Hyun Kwon, *Virginia Polytechnic Institute and State University, USA*
Jarmo Laaksolahti, *Swedish Institute of Computer Science, Sweden*
Richard Ladner, *University of Washington, USA*
Ben Lafreniere, *University of Waterloo, Canada*
Carl Lagoze, *University of Michigan, USA*
Susan Lai, *San Jose Gateway, Canada*
Denis Lalanne, *University of Fribourg, Switzerland*
Mary Lalomia, *Philips Medical, USA*
Shyong Lam, *Google, USA*
Anthony Lamarca, *Intel Research Seattle, USA*
Kristin Lamberty, *University of Minnesota, USA*
Cliff Lampe, *University of Michigan, USA*
Airi Lampinen, *Helsinki Institute for Information Technology HIIT, Finland*
James Landay, *University of Washington, USA*
Richard Landers, *Old Dominion University, USA*
Monica Landoni, *University of Lugano, Switzerland*
Pascal Landry, *Universitat Pompeu Fabra, Spain*
Steven Landry, *Purdue University, USA*
Peter Landwehr, *Carnegie Mellon University, USA*
Nicholas Lane, *Microsoft, China*
Patrick Langdon, *University of Cambridge, UK*
Marc Langheinrich, *Università Della Svizzera Italiana, Switzerland*
Joel Lanir, *University of Haifa, Israel*

Edward Lank, *University of Waterloo, Canada*
Rosa Lanzillotti, *Università di Bari, Italy*
Astrid Larssen, *Ashesi University College, Ghana*
Walter Lasecki, *University of Rochester Computer Science, USA*
Nancy Latham, *Boston University School of Public Health, USA*
Thomas Latoza, *UC Irvine, USA*
Celine Latulipe, *University of North Carolina at Charlotte, USA*
Manfred Lau, *Lancaster University, UK*
Felix Lauber, *University of Munich, Germany*
Carolyn Lauckner, *Michigan State University, USA*
Gael Laurans, *Delft University of Technology, The Netherlands*
Eric Laurier, *University of Edinburgh, UK*
Yann Laurillau, *University of Grenoble, France*
Debra Lauterbach, *Google, USA*
Joseph Laviola Jr., *University of Central Florida, USA*
Joseph Lawrance, *Oregon State University, USA*
Shaun Lawson, *University of Lincoln, UK*
Shawn Lawson, *Rensselaer Polytechnic Institute, USA*
Amanda Lazar, *University of Washington, USA*
Jonathan Lazar, *Towson University, USA*
Marco Lazzari, *University of Bergamo, Italy*
Lucian Leahu, *SICS, Sweden*
Alex Leavitt, *University of Southern California, USA*
Eric Lecolinet, *Télécom-Paristech, France*
Kerstin Leder Mackley, *Loughborough University, UK*
David Ledo, *University of Calgary, Canada*
Bongshin Lee, *Microsoft Research, USA*
Charlotte Lee, *University of Washington, USA*
Geehyuk Lee, *KAIST, Korea*
Joon Suk Lee, *Virginia Tech, USA*
Joyce Lee, *University of Michigan, USA*
Matthew Lee, *Philips Research, USA*
Michael Lee, *University of Washington, USA*
Min Kyung Lee, *Carnegie Mellon University, USA*
Stephanie Lee, *University of Washington, USA*
Uichin Lee, *KAIST, South Korea*
Young Lee, *Motorola Research, USA*
Colby Leider, *University of Miami, USA*
Darren Leigh, *USA*
Iolanda Leite, *Instituto Superior Técnico, Portugal*
Daniel Leithinger, *Massachusetts Institute of Technology, USA*
Luis A. Leiva, *Universitat Politècnica de València, Spain*
Eva Lenz, *Folkwang University of the Arts, Germany*
Pedro Leon, *Carnegie Mellon University, USA*
Chiara Leonardi, *Fondazione Bruno Kessler, Italy*
Stefania Leone, *University of South Carolina, USA*
Tuck Leong, *University of Technology, Australia*
George Lepouras, *University of Peloponnese, Greece*
Gilly Leshed, *Cornell University, USA*
Catherine Letondal, *ENAC, France*
Rock Leung, *University of British Columbia, Canada*
Vincent Levesque, *Immersion, Canada*
Peter Levin, *Intel Corporation, USA*

Vincent Lewandowski, *KTH, Sweden*
Clayton Lewis, *University of Colorado, USA*
Caroline Leygue, *University of Nottingham, UK*
Ian Li, *Carnegie Mellon University, USA*
Karen Li
Na Li, *Pennsylvania State University, USA*
Nan Li, *EPFL, Switzerland*
Wei Li, *Autodesk Research, Canada*
Hai-Ning Liang, *Xi'an Jiaotong-Liverpool University, China*
Rung-Huei Liang, *National Taiwan University of Science and Technology, Taiwan (r.o.c.)*
Fotis Liarokapis, *Coventry University, UK*
Ilaria Liccardi, *INRIA Paris, France*
Henry Lieberman, *Massachusetts Institute of Technology, USA*
Michael Liegl, *Lancaster University, UK*
Ann Light, *Northumbria University, UK*
Lassi Liikkanen, *Helsinki Institute for Information Technology HIIT, Finland*
Brian Lim, *Fraunhofer Center for Sustainable Energy Systems, USA*
Sohye Lim, *Ewha Womans University, Republic of Korea*
James Lin, *Google, USA*
Jialiu Lin, *Carnegie Mellon University, USA*
Min Lin, *Samsung Electronics, P. R. China*
Per Linde, *Malmö University,*
Robert Lindeman, *Worcester Polytechnic Institute, USA*
Rhema Linder, *Texas A&M University, USA*
Gitte Lindgaard, *Carleton University, Canada*
Siân Lindley, *Microsoft Research, UK*
Janne Lindqvist, *Rutgers University, USA*
Stephen Lindsay, *Swansea University, Wales, UK*
Conor Linehan, *University of Lincoln, UK*
Jessica Lingel, *Microsoft Research, USA*
Heather Lipford, *University of North Carolina at Charlotte, USA*
Roman Lissermann, *Technische Universität Darmstadt, Germany*
Eden Litt, *Northwestern University, USA*
Greg Little, *Massachusetts Institute of Technology, USA*
Linda Little, *Northumbria University, UK*
Jin Liu, *Cornell University, USA*
Leslie Liu, *University of Washington, USA*
Tracy Liu, *University of Michigan, USA*
Wei Liu, *Delft University of Technology, Netherlands*
Yefeng Liu, *Waseda University, Japan*
Ying Liu, *Charles Sturt University, Australia*
Ying Hsang Liu, *Intel, China*
Yun-En Liu, *University of Washington, USA*
Zhicheng Liu, *Georgia Institute of Technology, USA*
Zhicheng Liu, *Georgia Institute of Technology, USA*
Mark Livingston, *Naval Research Laboratory, USA*
Avishay Livne, *The University of Michigan, USA*
Sara Ljungblad, *LOTS Design AB, Sweden*
Markus Löchtefeld, *German Research Center for Artificial Intelligence (DFKI), Germany*
Dan Lockton, *University of Warwick, UK*

Thomas Lodato, *Georgia Institute of Technology, USA*
Courtney Loder, *UC Irvine, USA*
Sebastian Loehmann, *University of Munich, Germany*
Steffen Lohmann, *University of Stuttgart, Germany*
Benjamin Lok, *University of Florida, USA*
Lian Loke, *University of Sydney, Australia*
Derek Lomas, *Carnegie Mellon University, USA*
Benjamin Long, *Bristol University, UK*
Kiel Long, *Lancaster University, England, UK*
Chee Kit Looi, *NTU, Singapore*
Jack Loomis, *UCSB, USA*
Arminda Lopes, *Instituto Politecnico de Castelo Branco, Portugal*
Pedro Lopes, *Hasso Plattner Institute, Germany*
Fabien Lotte, *INRIA Bordeaux Sud-Ouest, France*
Danielle Lottridge, *San Francisco State University, USA*
Sandy Louchart, *Heriot-Watt University, Scotland, UK*
Oriana J Love, *Pacific Northwest National Laboratory, USA*
Hao Lu, *Intel, USA*
Hong Lu, *IBM Research, USA*
Jie Lu, *Samsung, USA*
Mei Lu, *CUNY Graduate Center, USA*
Pengfei Lu, *Fudan University, USA*
Tun Lu, *University of Washington, China*
Hao Lü, *Google, USA*
Andrés Lucero, *Nokia Research Center, Finland*
Bernd Ludwig, *University of Regensburg, Germany*
Patrick Lühne, *Hasso Plattner Institute, Germany*
Rowena Luk, *AMITA Telemedicine, Canada*
Kristian Lukander, *Finnish Institute of Occupational Health, Finland*
Jonathan Lukens, *University of Tennessee, USA*
Stephan Lukosch, *Delft University of Technology, The Netherlands*
Jay Lundell, *Intel Research, USA*
Kurt Luther, *Carnegie Mellon University, USA*
Wayne Lutters, *UMBC, USA*
Marianne Lykke, *Aalborg University, Denmark*
Peter Lyle, *Queensland University of Technology, Australia*
Leilah Lyons, *University of Illinois at Chicago, USA*
Michael Lyons, *Ritsumeikan University, Japan*
Heikki Lyytinen, *University of Jyväskylä, Finland*
Xiaojuan Ma, *Noah's Ark Lab, Hong Kong, China*
Catriona Macaulay, *University of Dundee, UK*
Craig Macdonald, *Pratt Institute, USA*
Carolyn Macgregor, *University of Waterloo, Canada*
Cristiano Maciel, *Universidade Federal de Mato Grosso, Brazil*
Giuliano Maciocci, *Qualcomm Research Cambridge, UK*
Wendy Mackay, *INRIA, France*
Scott Mackenzie, *York University, Canada*
Allan Maclean, *Image Semantics Ltd, UK*
Karon Maclean, *University of British Columbia, Canada*
Christopher Maclellan, *Carnegie Mellon University, USA*
Andrew Macvean, *Heriot-Watt University, Edinburgh*
Rui Madeira, *ESTSetúbal/IPS, Portugal*
Pattie Maes, *Massachusetts Institute of Technology, USA*

Rachel Magee, *Drexel University, USA*
Charlotte Magnusson, *Lund University, Sweden*
Mary Lou Maher, *University of Sydney, Australia*
Jalal Mahmud, *IBM Research - Almaden, USA*
Nasim Mahmud, *Hasselt University - Tul - IBBT, Belgium*
Angela Mahr, *German Research Center for Artificial Intelligence (DFKI), Germany*
Scott Mainwaring, *Intel Research, USA*
Julie Maitland, *Populus Global Solutions Inc., Canada*
Päivi Majaranta, *University of Tampere, Finland*
Yasutoshi Makino, *Keio University, Japan*
Sylvain Malacria, *University of Canterbury, France*
Miguel Malheiros, *University College London, UK*
Alessio Malizia, *University 'la Sapienza' of Rome, Italy*
Lone Malmborg, *IT University of Copenhagen, Denmark*
Lena Mamykina, *Columbia University, USA*
Hiroyuki Manabe, *NTT DOCOMO, Japan*
Clara Mancini, *The Open University, UK*
Regan Mandryk, *University of Saskatchewan, Canada*
Jennifer Mankoff, *Carnegie Mellon University, USA*
Daniela Mapelli, *Università di Padoa,*
Valérie Maquil, *Public Research Center Henri Tudor, Luxembourg*
Gabriela Marcu, *Carnegie Mellon University, USA*
Adam Marcus, *MIT CSAIL, USA*
Georgios Marentakis, *Institute for Electronic Music and Acoustics - Graz, Austria*
Gloria Mark, *University of California, USA*
Anders Markussen, *University of Copenhagen, Denmark*
Thomas Markussen, *Kolding School of Design, Denmark*
Jennifer Marlow, *Carnegie Mellon University, USA*
Elena Márquez Segura, *Uppsala University, Sweden*
Gary Marsden, *University of Cape Town, South Africa*
Andrea Marshall, *Drexel University Ischool, USA*
Catherine Marshall, *Microsoft, USA*
Joe Marshall, *University of Nottingham, UK*
Mark Marshall, *Sheffield Hallam University, UK*
Stuart Marshall, *Victoria University of Wellington, New Zealand*
Jean-Bernard Martens, *Eindhoven University of Technology, The Netherlands*
Stefan Marti, *Harman International, USA*
Anna Lisa Martin, *Zurich University of the Arts, Switzerland*
Aqueasha Martin, *Clemson University, USA*
Benoît Martin, *Université de Lorraine, France*
David Martin, *Xerox Research Center Europe, France*
Taylor Martin, *USU, USA*
Sarah Martindale, *The University of Nottingham, UK*
Diego Martinez Plasencia, *University of Bristol, UK*
Célia Martinie, *University Toulouse 3, France*
Misa Maruyama, *University of Hawaii at Manoa, USA*
Sergio Mascetti, *University of Milan, Italy*
Afra Mashhadi, *Alcatel-Lucent, Ireland*
Mikhil Masli, *Grouplens Research, USA*
Winter Mason, *Stevens Institute of Technology, USA*
Justin Matejka, *Autodesk, Canada*

Anijo Mathew, *Illinois Institute of Technology, USA*
Akhil Mathur, *University of Toronto, Canada*
Ben Matthews, *The University of Queensland, Australia*
Mark Matthews, *Cornell University, USA*
Tara Matthews, *IBM Research - Almaden, USA*
Denys Matthies, *University of Munich, Germany*
Frank Maurer, *University of Calgary, Canada*
Max-Emanuel Maurer, *University of Munich, Germany*
Deborah Maxwell, *University of Edinburgh, UK*
Aaron May, *Simon Fraser University, Canada*
Simon Mayer, *ETH Zurich, Switzerland*
Christopher Mayhorn, *North Carolina State University, USA*
Walterio Mayol-Cuevas, *University of Bristol, UK*
Oscar Mayora, *ITESM Cuernavaca, Mexico*
Rene Mayrhofer, *Lancaster University, UK*
Ali Mazalek, *Georgia Institute of Technology, USA*
Melissa Mazmanian, *University of California, USA*
Michelle Mazurek, *Carnegie Mellon University, USA*
Emanuela Mazzone, *University of Central Lancashire, Spain*
Victoria Mcarthur, *York University, Canada*
Simon Mccallum, *Gjøvik University College, Norway*
John Mccarthy, *University College Cork, Ireland*
Scott Mccrickard, *Virginia Tech, USA*
Sean Mcdirmid, *Microsoft Advanced Technology Center, Peoples Republic of China*
David Mcdonald, *University of Washington, USA*
Nora Mcdonald, *Drexel University, USA*
Mary F Mcdonough
Daniel Mcduff, *MIT Media Lab, USA*
Gregor Mcewan, *University of Saskatchewan, Canada*
Daniel Mcfarlane, *Lockheed Martin Advanced Technology Laboratories, USA*
Kevin Mcgee, *National University of Singapore, Singapore*
Mark Mcgill, *University of Glasgow, UK*
William Mcgrath, *Stanford University, USA*
Joanna Mcgrenere, *University of British Columbia, Canada*
Michael Mcguffin, *École de Technologie Supérieure, Canada*
Ross Mclachlan, *University of Glasgow, Scotland, UK*
Ryan Mcmahan, *University of Texas at Dallas, USA*
Donald Mcmillan, *SICS, Sweden*
Indrani Medhi-Thies, *Microsoft Research, India*
Richard Medland, *Queensland University of Technology, Australia*
Ben Medler, *EA, USA*
Elisa Mekler, *University of Basel, Switzerland*
Volkamer Melanie, *TU Darmstadt, Germany*
David Mellis, *Massachusetts Institute of Technology, USA*
Gustavo Mello Machado, *University of Stuttgart, Germany*
Nemanja Memarovic, *Universita Della Svizzera Italiana, Switzerland*
Maria Menendez, *University of Trento, Italy*
Sarah Mennicken, *University of Zurich, Switzerland*
Rachel Menzies, *University of Dundee, UK*
Emma Mercier, *University of Illinois at Urbana-Champaign, USA*
David Merrill, *Massachusetts Institute of Technology, USA*
Ronald Metoyer, *Oregon State University, USA*

Johanna Meurer, *University, Germany*
Jochen Meyer, *OFFIS - Institute for Information Technology, Germany*
Miriah Meyer, *University of Utah, USA*
Haipeng Mi, *Tsinghua University, China*
Nicholas Micallef, *Glasgow Caledonian University, UK*
Martin Mihajlov, *Ss. Cyril and Methodius University, Macedonia*
Silvia Miksch, *Vienna University of Technology, Austria*
David Millen, *IBM Research, USA*
Andrew Miller, *University of British Columbia, USA*
Gregor Miller, *Massachusetts Institute of Technology, Canada*
Scarlett Miller (herring), *Georgia Institute of Technology, USA*
Michael Minge, *Berlin University of Technology, Germany*
Aliaksei Miniukovich, *University of Trento, Italy*
Andrea Minuto, *University of Twente, The Netherlands*
Pejman Mirza-Babaei, *University of Ontario Institute of Technology, Canada*
Sonali Mishra, *University of Michigan, USA*
Taniya Mishra, *AT&T, USA*
Alex Mitchell, *National University of Singapore, Singapore*
Tanushree Mitra, *Georgia Institute of Technology, USA*
Tracy Mitzner, *Georgia Institute of Technology, USA*
Takahiro Miura, *The University of Tokyo, Japan*
Takashi Miyaki, *Inria, France*
Bart Moens, *Ghent University, Belgium*
Andrew Molineux, *Lancaster University, England*
Andreas Möller, *Technische Universität München, Germany*
Max Möllers, *RWTH Aachen University, Germany*
David Molyneaux, *Microsoft Research, England, UK*
Arthur Money, *Brunel University, UK*
Andrew Monk, *University of York, UK*
Andres Monroy-Hernandez, *Massachusetts Institute of Technology, USA*
Toni-Jan Keith Monserrat, *National University of Singapore, Philippines*
Kyle Montague, *University of Dundee, Scotland, UK*
Bob Moore, *PARC, USA*
Simone Mora, *Norwegian University of Science and Technology, Norway*
Stuart Moran, *University of Nottingham, UK*
Neema Moraveji, *Microsoft Research Asia, China*
Guillaume Moreau, *Ecole Centrale de Nantes, France*
Lourdes Moreno, *Universidad Carlos III de Madrid, Spain*
Jonathan Morgan, *University of Washington, USA*
Giulio Mori, *ISTI-CNR, Italy*
Joji Mori, *The University of Melbourne, Australia*
Carlos Morimoto, *University of Sao Paulo, Brazil*
Janine Morley, *Lancaster University, UK*
Fabio Morreale, *University of Trento, Italy*
Patricia Morreale, *Kean University, USA*
Margaret Morris, *Intel Corporation, USA*
Meredith Morris, *Microsoft Research, USA*
Ann Morrison, *Aalborg University, Denmark*
Cecily Morrison, *Microsoft Research, UK*
Richard Mortier, *The University of Nottingham, UK*
Lee Morton, *Glasgow Caledonian University, UK*
Christiane Moser, *ICT&S Center, Austria*
Vicki Moulder, *Simon Fraser University, Canada*

Christos Mousas, *University of Sussex, England, UK*
Mu Mu, *Lancaster University, UK*
Omar Mubin, *University of Western Sydney, Australia*
Christian Muehl, *Inria Bordeaux, France*
Florian "Floyd" Mueller, *Exertion Games Lab, Australia*
Stefanie Mueller, *Hasso Plattner Institute, Germany*
Christian Mueller-Tomfelde, *CSIRO ICT Centre, Australia*
Max Mühlhäuser, *TU Darmstadt, Germany*
Adiyan Mujibiya, *The University of Tokyo, Japan*
Heiko Müller, *IBM Research, Germany*
Gernot Müller-Putz, *Graz University of Technology, Austria*
Alessandro Mulloni, *Qualcomm Research KAIST, Republic of Korea ria, Austria*
Cosmin Munteanu, *National Research Council Canada, Canada*
Helmut Munz, *RMIT University, Austria*
Martin Murer, *University of Salzburg, Austria*
Dianne Murray, *Indep. Consultant, UK*
Ildar Muslukhov, *University of British Columbia, Canada*
Mirco Musolesi, *University of Birmingham, UK*
Brad Myers, *Carnegie Mellon University, USA*
Elizabeth Mynatt, *Georgia Institute of Technology, USA*
Mor Naaman, *Cornell University, USA*
Miguel Nacenta, *University of St Andrews, UK*
Frank Nack, *University of Amsterdam (uva), The Netherlands*
Till Nagel, *University of Applied Sciences Potsdam, Germany*
Tobias Nägeli, *ETH Zurich, Switzerland*
Hideyuki Nakanishi, *Osaka University, Japan*
Kevin Nam, *University of Michigan, USA*
Suranga Nanayakkara, *Singapore University of Technology and Design, USA*
Mathieu Nancel, *University of Canterbury, France*
Nitya Narasimhan, *edupreneur, USA*
Bonnie Nardi, *University of California, USA*
Amani Naseem, *RMIT University, Australia*
Chris Nash, *University of Cambridge, UK*
Meena Natarajan, *UC Berkeley, USA*
Lisa Nathan, *University of British Columbia, Canada*
David Navarre, *IRIT, France*
Elena Nazzi, *IT University of Copenhagen, Denmark*
Mark Neerincx, *TNO Human Factors, Netherlands*
Michael Neff, *UC Davis, USA*
Paolo Negri
Matei Negulescu, *University of Waterloo, Canada*
Matti Nelimarkka, *Helsinki Institute for Information Technology HIIT, Finland*
Les Nelson, *PARC, USA*
Cornelius Neufeldt, *University of Siegen, Germany*
Alena Neviarouskaya, *University of Tokyo, Japan*
Alan Newell, *Dundee University, Scotland, UK*
Mark Newman, *University of Michigan, USA*
Victor Ng-Thow-Hing, *Honda Research Institute USA, USA*
David Nguyen, *Nokia Research Center, USA*
Duyen Nguyen, *Cornell University, USA*
James Nicholson, *Northumbria University, England, UK*

Hugo Nicolau, *University of Dundee, UK*
Lene Nielsen, *IT University of Copenhagen, Denmark*
Gerrit Niezen, *Swansea University, UK*
Femke Nijboer, *University of Twente, The Netherlands*
Valentina Nisi, *University of Madeira, Portugal*
Xi Niu, *Indiana University, USA*
Sylvie Noël, *Universita di Trento, Italy*
Pedro Nogueira, *LIACC - Artificial Intelligence and Computer Science Laboratory, Portugal*
A. Imran Nordin, *University of York, UK*
Mie Nørgaard, *Aarhus School of Architecture, Denmark*
Francesco Nori
Maria Normark, *Södertörn University, Sweden*
Lauren Norrie, *University of Glasgow, Scotland, UK*
Chris North, *Virginia Polytechnic Institute and State University, USA*
Oded Nov, *Polytechnic Institute of New York University, USA*
Laurie Novak, *Vanderbilt University, USA*
Francisco Nunes, *Vienna University of Technology, Austria*
Petteri Nurmi, *Helsinki Institute for Information Technology HIIT, Finland*
Andreas Nürnberger, *Otto-Von-Guericke-University Magdeburg, Germany*
Stina Nylander, *Swedish Institute of Computer Science, Sweden*
Heather O'brien, *University of British Columbia, Canada*
Marita O'brien, *University of Alabama-Huntsville, USA*
Brendan O'connor, *Carnegie Mellon University, USA*
Lora Oehlberg, *INRIA, USA*
Anne Oeldorf-Hirsch, *University of Connecticut, USA*
Eyal Ofek, *Microsoft Research, USA*
Corinna Ogonowski, *University of Siegen, Germany*
Alice Oh, *KAIST, Republic of Korea*
Jonghwan Oh, *Seoul National University, Republic of Korea*
Kenton O'hara, *Microsoft Research, UK*
Harri Oinas-Kukkonen, *University of Oulu, Finland*
Aisling O'kane, *University College London, UK*
Bugra Oktay, *University of Nevada, USA*
Patrick Oladimeji, *Swansea University, UK*
Halla Olafsdottir, *Université Paris-Sud, France*
Erica Olmsted-Hawala, *U.S. Census Bureau, USA*
Dan Olsen, *Brigham Young University, USA*
Gary Olson, *University of California, USA*
Judith Olson, *U of Michigan, USA*
Katherine Olson, *Georgia Institute of Technology, USA*
Thomas Olsson, *Tampere University of Technology, Finland*
Sile O'modhrain, *University of Michigan, USA*
Jacki O'neill, *XRCE, France*
Stephen Oney, *Carnegie Mellon University, USA*
Wei Tsang Ooi, *National University of Singapore, Singapore*
Elisa Oreglia, *University of California Berkeley, USA*
Tihomir Orehovacki, *University of Zagreb, Croatia*
Eleanor O'rourke, *University of Washington, USA*
Valeria Orso, *University of Padova, Italy*
Martin Ortlieb, *Google, Switzerland*
Keith Ostfeld, *Children's Museum of Houston, USA*
Nuno Otero, *Linnæus University, Sweden*
Tom Ouyang, *MIT, USA*

Derya Özçelik, *Eindhoven University of Technology, The Netherlands*
Jeni Paay, *Aalborg University, Denmark*
Tyler Pace, *Indiana University Bloomington, USA*
Tim Paek, *Microsoft Research, USA*
Michel Pahud, *Microsoft Research, USA*
Helen Pain, *University of Edinburgh, UK*
Drew Paine, *University of Washington, USA*
Aditya Pal, *IBM Research - Almaden, USA*
Philippe Palanque, *ICS-IRIT, France*
Leysia Palen, *University of Colorado, USA*
Henri Palleis, *Ludwig-Maximilians-Universität München, Germany*
Susan Palmiter, *Design Technologies, USA*
Viktoria Pammer, *Know-Center, Austria*
Yingxin Pan, *IBM Research - China, China*
Yue Pan, *Indiana University Bloomington, USA*
Zhengzheng Pan, *Facebook, USA*
Katherine Panciera, *University of Minnesota, USA*
Sabrina Panëels, *McGill University, France*
Carolyn Pang, *Simon Fraser University, Canada*
Saurabh Panjwani, *Microsoft Research India, India*
Katrina Panovich, *MIT, USA*
Nadia Pantidi, *The University of Nottingham, UK*
Caroline Pantofaru, *Willow Garage, USA*
Eleftherios Papachristos, *University of Patras, Greece*
Savvas Papaioannou, *University of Oxford, UK*
Joseph Paradiso, *MIT Media Laboratory, USA*
Aditya Parameswaran, *Stanford University, USA*
Zachary Pardos, *UC Berkeley, USA*
Pablo Paredes, *University of Berkeley, USA*
Narcis Pares, *Universitat Pompeu Fabra, Spain*
Tapan Parikh, *UC Berkeley, USA*
Minsu Park, *KAIST, South Korea*
Souneil Park, *Univ. of Michigan, USA*
Sun Young Park, *University of California, USA*
Taiwoo Park, *KAIST, South Korea*
Young-Woo Park, *KAIST, South Korea*
Chris Parnin, *Georgia Institute of Technology, USA*
Kurt Partridge, *Google, USA*
Gaurav Paruthi, *University of Michigan, USA*
Marco Pasch, *University of Lugano, Switzerland*
Gert Pasman, *Delft University of Technology, The Netherlands*
Jerome Pasquero, *Research In Motion Limited, Canada*
Kayur Patel, *University of Washington, USA*
Nirmal Patel, *Georgia Institute of Technology, USA*
Rupa Patel, *University of Washington, USA*
Rupal Patel, *Northeastern University, USA*
Shwetak Patel, *University of Washington, USA*
Jessica Pater, *Georgia Institute of Technology, USA*
Andrew Patrick, *Carleton University, Canada*
Donald Patterson, *University of California Irvine, USA*
Sharoda Paul, *GE Global Research, USA*
Eric Paulos, *University of California, USA*
Dana Pavel, *University of Essex, UK*

Ioannis Pavlidis, *University of Houston, USA*
Andriy Pavlovych, *York University, Canada*
Stephen Payne, *University of Bath, UK*
Jennifer Pearson, *Swansea University, UK*
Fabrizio Pece, *University College London, UK*
Evan Peck, *Tufts University, USA*
Sonja Pedell, *Swinburne University of Technology, Australia*
Sonjs Pedell, *Swinburne University of Technology, Australia*
Esben Pedersen, *University of Copenhagen, Danmark*
Thomas Pederson, *IT University of Copenhagen, Denmark*
Peter Peltonen, *University of Helsinki, Finland*
Jorge Peña, *University of California, USA*
Wei Peng, *Information Studies, USA*
Gerald Penn, *University of Toronto, Canada*
Kylie Peppler, *Indiana University, USA*
Lucas Pereira, *Madeira Interactive Technologies Institute, Portugal*
Adam Perer, *IBM Research, USA*
Manuel Perez-Quinones, *Virginia Tech, USA*
Charles Perin, *INRIA Saclay, France*
Trevor Pering, *Intel Research, USA*
Ken Perlin, *New York University, USA*
Simon Perrault, *National University of Singapore, Singapore*
Daniel Perry, *University of Washington, USA*
Florian Perteneder, *University of Applied Sciences Upper KAIST, Republic of Korea ria, Austria*
Marianne Graves Petersen, *Aarhus University, Denmark*
Daniela Petrelli, *Sheffield Hallam University, UK*
Helen Petrie, *University of York, UK*
Tamara Peyton, *Penn State University, USA*
Laura Pfeifer Vardoulakis, *Google, USA*
Max Pfeiffer, *Leibniz Universität Hannover, Germany*
Thies Pfeiffer, *Bielefeld University, Germany*
Bastian Pfleging, *University of Stuttgart, Germany*
Martin Pielot, *Telefonica Research, Spain*
James Pierce, *Carnegie Mellon University, USA*
Jeffrey Pierce, *Samsung UX Innovations Lab, USA*
Emmanuel Pietriga, *INRIA, France*
Mary Pietrowicz, *National Center for Supercomputing Applications, USA*
Thomas Pietrzak, *University of Lille, France*
Hannah Pileggi, *Georgia Institute of Technology, USA*
Clément Pillias, *CNAM, France*
Laura Pina, *'UCSD' As In University of California at San Diego, USA*
Fabiano Pinatti, *Institute of Design and Assessment of Technology, Austria*
Kathleen Pine, *University of California, USA*
Claudio Pinhanez, *IBM Brazil, Brazil*
Volkmar Pipek, *University of Siegen, Germany*
Anne Marie Piper, *Northwestern University, USA*
Michael Pirker, *Ruwido KAIST, Republic of Korea ria Gmbh, Austria*
Peter Pirolli, *PARC, USA*
Catherine Plaisant, *University of Maryland, USA*
Andreas Pleuss, *University of Limerick, Ireland*
Bernd Ploderer, *The University of Melbourne, Australia*
Thomas Ploetz, *Newcastle University, UK*

Barry Po, *HSBC, Canada*
Henning Pohl, *University of Hannover, Germany*
Margit Pohl, *Vienna University of Technology, Austria*
Anna Pohlmeyer, *Delft University of Technology, Netherlands*
Ioannis Politis, *Eindhoven University of Technology, Netherlands*
John Pollak, *Cornell University, USA*
Marc Pomplun, *University of Massachusetts Boston, USA*
Heather Pon-Barry, *Informatics, USA*
Suporn Pongnumkul, *University of Washington, USA*
Erika Poole, *Penn State University, USA*
Alan Pope, *NASA Langley Research Center, USA*
Ana-Maria Popescu, *Pinterest, USA*
Leslie Poppe, *University of Washington, USA*
Kristi Potter, *University of Oregon, USA*
Tania Pouli, *Technicolor, France*
Ivan Poupyrev, *Disney Research, USA*
Sören Preibusch, *Microsoft Research, UK*
Chris Preist, *University of Bristol, UK*
Nora Presson, *University of Pittsburgh, USA*
Mike Preuss, *WWU Münster, Germany*
Blaine Price, *The Open University, UK*
Sara Price, *Institute of Education, UK*
Reid Priedhorsky, *Los Alamos National Laboratory, USA*
Rafael Prikladnicki, *Pucrs, Brazil*
Michael Prilla, *University of Bochum, Germany*
Suzanne Prior, *Media and Computer Games, UK*
Kathrin Probst, *University of Applied Sciences Upper KAIST, Republic of Korea ria, Austria*
Jason Procyk, *Simon Fraser University, Canada*
Halley Profita, *University of Colorado, USA*
Sebastian Prost, *CURE - Center for Usability Research & Engineering, Austria*
Janna Protzak, *Berlin Institute of Technology, Germany*
Emily Provost, *University of Michigan, USA*
John Pruitt, *Microsoft, USA*
Larissa Pschetz, *Microsoft Research Asia, Midlothian*
Deborah Ptak, *University of Toronto, Canada*
Pearl Pu, *EPFL, Switzerland*
Andreas Pusch, *Julius-Maximilians-Universität, Germany*
Cynthia Putnam, *Depaul University, USA*
Pardha Pyla, *Virginia Tech, India*
Huamin Qu, *HKUST, Hong Kong*
Novi Quadrianto, *University of Cambridge, UK*
Daniele Quercia, *Yahoo! Research, UK*
Whitney Quesenbery, *Whitney Interactcive Design, USA*
Alexander Quinn, *University of Maryland, USA*
Philip Quinn, *University of Canterbury, New Zealand*
Pablo-Alejandro Quinones, *University of Michigan, USA*
Andrew Quitmeyer, *Georgia Institute of Technology, USA*
Pernilla Qvarfordt, *FX Palo Alto Laboratory, USA*
Daphne Raban, *University of Haifa, Israel*
Mashfiqui Rabbi, *Cornell University, USA*
Robert Racadio, *University of Washington, USA*
Irene Rae, *University of Wisconsin, USA*

Matthew Rafalow, *University of California Irvine, USA*
Nikunj Raghuvanshi, *Microsoft Research, USA*
Tauhidur Rahman, *Cornell University, USA*
Kari-Jouko Räihä, *University of Tampere, Finland*
Andrew Raij, *University of South Florida, USA*
Roope Raisamo, *University of Tampere, Finland*
Eeva Raita, *Helsinki Institute for Information Technology HIIT, Finland*
Mikko Rajanen, *University of Oulu, Finland*
Thusha Rajendran, *UK*
Nitendra Rajput, *IBM Research, India*
Ismo Rakkolainen, *University of Tampere, Finland*
Raf Ramakers, *Hasselt University - Tul - Iminds, Belgium*
Ernesto Ramirez, *University of California, USA*
Gonzalo Ramos, *Microsoft, USA*
Adriane Randolph, *Kennesaw State University, USA*
Nimmi Rangaswamy, *Microsoft Research India, India*
Juhi Ranjan, *University of Virginia, USA*
Dimitrios Raptis, *Aalborg University, Denmark*
Umar Rashid, *University of Kent, UK*
Kirsten Rassmus-Gröhn, *Lund University, Sweden*
Rabindra Ratan, *Information Studies, USA*
Matt Ratto, *University of Toronto, Toronto*
Martina Rau, *University of Wisconsin, USA*
Janet Read, *University of Central Lancashire, England*
Kyle Rector, *University of Washington, USA*
Madhu Reddy, *Penn State University, USA*
Fiona Redhead, *Queensland University of Technology, Australia*
Johan Redström, *Umeå Institute of Design, Sweden*
Darren Reed, *University of York, UK*
Robert Reeder, *Google, USA*
Sarah Reeder, *Indiana University, USA*
Tim Regan, *Microsoft, UK*
Holger Regenbrecht, *University of Otago, New Zealand*
Derek Reilly, *Dalhousie University, Canada*
Peter Reimann, *University of Sydney, Australia*
Bryan Reimer, *MIT, USA*
Sofia Reis, *Universidade Nova de Lisboa, Portugal*
Wolfgang Reitberger, *Vienna University of Technology, Austria*
Harald Reiterer, *University, Germany*
Thomas Reitmaier, *UCT Centre In ICT4D, South Africa*
Jun Rekimoto, *University of Tokyo / Sony CSL, Japan*
Christian Remy, *University of Zurich, Switzerland*
Gang Ren, *University of Bath, UK*
Xiangshi Ren, *Kochi University of Technology, Japan*
Yuqing Ren, *Carnegie Mellon University, USA*
Karen Renaud, *University of Glasgow, UK*
Christian Rendl, *University of Applied Sciences Upper KAIST, Republic of Korea ria, Austria*
Stefan Rennick-Egglestone, *The University of Nottingham, UK*
Ronald Rensink, *University of British Columbia, Canada*
Paul Resnick, *University of Michigan, USA*
Glenda Revelle, *University of Arkansas, USA*
Gabriel Reyes, *Georgia Institute of Technology, USA*
Lindsay Reynolds, *Cornell University, USA*

Mark Rice, *Institute of Infocomm Research, Singapore*
Alex Richardson, *The KAIST, Republic of Korea ralian National University, Australia*
Alexander Richter, *Unibwm, Germany*
Jochen Rick, *Saarland University, Germany*
Angela Riechers, *School of Visual Arts, USA*
Jens Riegelsberger, *University College London, UK*
Soo Young Rieh, *University of Michigan, USA*
Andreas Riener, *Johannes Kepler University, Austria*
Alexander Rind, *Vienna University of Technology, Austria*
Lazlo Ring, *Northeastern University, USA*
Mikko Rissanen, *Move Correctly, Singapore*
Tobias Ritschel, *MPI Informatik, Germany*
Giuseppe Riva, *Università Cattolica Del Sacro Cuore, Italy*
Christopher Roast, *Sheffield Hallam University, UK*
Lionel Robert, *University of Michigan, USA*
Jonathan Roberts, *Bangor University, UK*
Judy Robertson, *Heriot-Watt University, UK*
Scott Robertson, *University of Hawaii at Manoa, USA*
Toni Robertson, *University of Technology, Australia*
Jeffrey Robins, *Google, USA*
Simon Robinson, *Swansea University, UK*
Carsten Röcker, *RWTH Aachen University, Germany*
Tom Rodden, *University of Nottingham, UK*
Edgar Rodriguez, *Wellington, New Zealand*
David Roedl, *Indiana University, USA*
Yvonne Rogers, *University College London, UK*
Daniel Roggen, *Newcastle University, UK*
Markus Rohde, *International Institute for Socio-Informatics, Germany*
Michael Rohs, *University of Hannover, Germany*
Daniel Romero, *Northwestern University, USA*
Mario Romero, *Delft University of Technology, Sweden*
Natalia Romero Herrera, *KTH, The Netherlands*
John Rooksby, *University of St Andrews, UK*
Chris Rooney, *Middlesex University, UK*
Carolyn Rose, *Carnegie Mellon University, USA*
Asta Roseway, *Microsoft Research, USA*
Joel Ross, *University of California, USA*
Chiara Rossitto, *Stockholm University, Sweden*
Mattias Rost, *Mobile Life @ SICS, Sweden*
Robert Roth, *University of Wisconsin-Madison, USA*
Virpi Roto, *University of Helsinki, Finland*
Nicolas Roussel, *Inria, France*
Maria Roussou, *Makebelieve Design & Consulting, Greece*
Debjani Roy, *IIT Bombay, India*
Quentin Roy, *CNRS LTCI UMR 5141, France*
Agata Rozga, *Georgia Institute of Technology, USA*
Elisa Rubegni, *Universita Della Svizzera Italiana, Switzerland*
Steve Rubin, *University of California, USA*
Michael Rubinstein, *MIT, USA*
Stefan Rüger, *The Open University, UK*
Jaime Ruiz, *Colorado State University, USA*
Enrico Rukzio, *Lancaster University, Germany*

Sonja Rümelin, *University of Munich, Germany*
Tuukka Ruotsalo, *Aalto University, Finland*
Derek Ruths, *McGill University, Canada*
Kimiko Ryokai, *MIT Media Laboratory, USA*
Jeffrey Rzeszotarski, *Carnegie Mellon University, USA*
Daniel Saakes, *Delft University of Technology, The Netherlands*
Selma Sabanovic, *Indiana University, USA*
Andreas Sackl, *FTW Telecommunications Research Center, Austria*
Ramik Sadana, *Georgia Institute of Technology, USA*
Alireza Sahami Shirazi, *University of Stuttgart, Germany*
Arnaud Sahuguet, *Google, USA*
Alan Said, *CWI, The Netherlands*
Daisuke Sakamoto, *The University of Tokyo, Japan*
Mona Sakr, *Institute of Education, UK*
Ben Salem, *Northumbria University, UK*
Pascal Salembier, *University of Technology of Troyes, France*
Mariana Salgado, *Laurea University of Applied Sciences, Finland*
Guarionex Salivia, *Minnesota State University, USA*
Eva Lotta Sallnäs Pysander, *Royal Institute of Technology, Sweden*
Katri Salminen, *University of Tampere, Finland*
Antti Salovaara, *Aalto University, Finland*
Anastasia Salter, *University of Baltimore, USA*
Frode Sandnes, *Oslo University College, Norway*
Aditya Sankar, *University of Washington, India*
Vagner Santana, *State University of Campinas, Brazil*
Pedro Santana-Mancilla, *University of Colima, Mexico*
Carmen Santoro, *ISTI-CNR, Italy*
T. Saponas, *Microsoft Research, USA*
Aleksandra Sarcevic, *Drexel University, USA*
Makoto Sasaki, *Iwate University, Japan*
Daisuke Sato, *IBM Research - Tokyo, Japan*
Munehiko Sato, *Disney Research, USA*
Yoichi Sato, *The University of Tokyo, Japan*
Debra Satterfield, *Iowa State University, USA*
Allison Sauppé, *University of Wisconsin-Madison, USA*
Valkyrie Savage, *University of California, USA*
Nadav Savio, *Google.org, USA*
Pete Sawyer, *Lancaster University, UK*
Walt Scacchi, *University of California, USA*
Christopher Scaffidi, *Carnegie Mellon University, USA*
Joey Scarr, *University of Canterbury, New Zealand*
Christopher Schaefbauer, *University of Colorado, USA*
Patricia Schank, *SRI International, USA*
Raimund Schatz, *Forschungszentrum Telekommunikation Wien (ftw.), Austria*
Florian Schaub, *Carnegie Mellon University, USA*
Benjamin Scheibehenne, *University of Basel, Switzerland*
Jesse Schell, *Carnegie Mellon University, USA*
Ansgar Scherp, *Business Informatics and Business Mathematics, Germany*
Gianluca Schiavo, *University of Trento & FBK, Italy*
Markus Schilling, *Simon Fraser University, Canada*
Thecla Schiphorst, *Simon Fraser University, Canada*
Steven Schirra, *Massachusetts Institute of Technology, USA*
Chris Schmandt, *Massachusetts Institute of Technology, USA*

Dominik Schmidt, *Hasso Plattner Institute, Germany*
Holger Schnädelbach, *University of Nottingham, UK*
Jodi Schneider, *National University of Ireland, Ireland*
Guy Schofield, *Newcastle University, UK*
Jean Scholtz, *Pacific Northwest Laboratory, USA*
Johannes Schöning, *Hasselt University - Tul - Iminds, Belgium*
Marén Schorch, *University of Siegen, Germany*
Falk Schreiber
Ronald Schroeter, *Queensland University of Technology, Australia*
Kai Schubert, *University of Siegen, Germany*
Daniel Schultheiss, *Ilmenau University of Technology, Germany*
Timothy Schultz, *Drexel University, USA*
Victoria Schwanda Sosik, *Cornell University, USA*
Tobias Schwartz, *Fraunhofer FIT, Germany*
Julia Schwarz, *University of Washington, USA*
Lauren Scissors, *Northwestern University, USA*
Stacey Scott, *University of Waterloo, Canada*
Peter Scupelli, *Carnegie Mellon University, USA*
Sue Ann Seah, *University of Bristol, UK*
A. Fleming Seay, *Carnegie Mellon University, USA*
Michael Sedlmair, *University of Vienna, Austria*
Magy Seif El-Nasr, *Northeastern University, USA*
Julian Seifert, *Ulm University, Germany*
Susanne Seitinger, *MIT Media Lab, USA*
James Self, *UNIST, South Korea*
Kate Sellen, *OCAD University, Canada*
Katherine Sellen, *University of Toronto, Canada*
Bryan Semaan, *University of Hawaii at Manoa, USA*
Shilad Sen, *University of Minnesota, USA*
Phoebe Sengers, *Cornell University, USA*
Sepandar Sepehr, *McMaster University, Canada*
Marcos Serrano, *IRIT, France*
Lauren Sessions Goulet, *Facebook, USA*
Leslie Setlock, *Cornell University, USA*
Burr Settles, *Carnegie Mellon University, USA*
Teddy Seyed, *University of Calgary, Canada*
Aviv Shachak, *University of Toronto, Canada*
Orit Shaer, *Tufts University, USA*
David Shaffer, *University of Wisconsin, USA*
Chirag Shah, *Rutgers University, USA*
Priti Shah, *University of Michigan, USA*
Qonita Shahab, *Eindhoven University of Technology, The Netherlands*
Noor Shaker, *IT University of Copenhagen, Denmark*
David Shamma, *Yahoo!, USA*
Ben Shapiro, *Tufts,*
Ehud Sharlin, *University of Calgary, Canada*
Moushumi Sharmin, *University of Memphis, USA*
Sarah Sharples, *University of Nottingham, UK*
Wes Sharrock, *Manchester University, UK*
Aaron Shaw, *Northwestern University, USA*
Richard Shay, *Carnegie Mellon University, USA*
John Shearer, *Newcastle University, UK*
Mohamed Sheik-Nainar, *Synaptics Inc, USA*
Chia Shen, *Harvard University, USA*

Dawei Shen, *Massachusetts Institute of Technology, USA*
S. Andrew Sheppard, *University of Minnesota, USA*
Yuanchun Shi, *Tsinghua University, China*
Patrick Shih, *The Pennsylvania State University, USA*
Choonsung Shin, *Carnegie Mellon University, USA*
Hiroyuki Shinoda, *The University of Tokyo, Japan*
Frank Shipman, *Texas A&M University, USA*
Sajad Shirali-Shahreza, *University of Toronto, Canada*
Mariya Shiyko, *Northeastern University, USA*
Buntarou Shizuki, *University of Tsukuba, Japan*
Irina Shklovski, *IT University of Copenhagen, Denmark*
Garth Shoemaker, *Google, USA*
Milad Shokouhi, *Microsoft Research, UK*
Jamie Shotton, *Microsoft Research Cambridge, UK*
Mark Shovman, *Yahoo! Inc., Israel*
George Siemens, *Athabasca University, Canada*
Beat Signer, *Vrije Universiteit Brussel, Belgium*
Six Silberman, *Bureau of Economic Interpretation, USA*
Elizabeth Sillence, *Northumbria University, UK*
Liz Sillence, *Northumbria University, UK*
Paula Alexandra Silva, *University of Hawaii at Manoa, Portugal*
Johanna Silvennoinen, *University of Jyväskylä, Finland*
Adalberto Simeone, *Lancaster University, UK*
David Simmons, *University of Glasgow, UK*
Ian Simon, *University of Washington, USA*
Judge Simon, *RAT Group, UK*
Laurent Simon, *University of Cambridge, UK*
Jolynna Sinanan, *The University of Melbourne, Australia*
Leif Singer, *University of Victoria, Canada*
Karan Singh, *University of Toronto, Canada*
Supriya Singh, *Royal Melbourne Institute of Technology, Australia*
Vikash Singh, *University of North Carolina at Charlotte, USA*
Valentina Sintsova, *EPFL, Switzerland*
Behzod Sirjani, *Northwestern University, USA*
David Sirkin, *Stanford University, USA*
Daniel Sjölie, *Umeå University, Sweden*
Mikael B. Skov, *Aalborg University, Denmark*
Marjorie Skubic, *University of Missouri, USA*
Roger Slack, *Bangor University, Wales, UK*
Bernhard Slawik, *University of Munich, Germany*
Manya Sleeper, *Carnegie Mellon University, USA*
Karin Slegers, *KU Leuven, Belgium*
James D. Slotta, *University of Toronto, Canada*
Petr Slovák, *Vienna University of Technology, Austria*
Jan Smeddinck, *University of Bremen, Germany*
Joshua Smith, *University of Washington, USA*
Madeline Smith, *Cornell University, USA*
Matthew Smith, *Leibniz Universität Hannover, Germany*
Ross Smith, *University of South KAIST, Republic of Korea ralia, Australia*
Thomas Smith, *Newcastle University, UK*
Michael Smyth, *Edinburgh Napier University, UK*
Jaime Snyder, *Syracuse University, USA*
Timothy Sohn, *Google, USA*
Tomas Sokoler, *IT University of Copenhagen, Denmark*

Jacob Solomon, *Michigan State University, USA*
Andreas Sonderegger, *University of Fribourg, Switzerland*
Hyunyoung Song, *University of Maryland, USA*
Junehwa Song, *KAIST, Korea*
Yale Song, *MIT CSAIL, USA*
Diane Sonnenwald, *UCD, Ireland*
Daniel Sonntag, *DFKI German Research Center for AI, Germany*
Vladimir Soroka, *IBM Haifa Research Lab, Israel*
Alexander Sorokin, *CrowdFlower, USA*
Iris Soute, *Eindhoven University of Technology, The Netherlands*
Caleb Southern, *Georgia Institute of Technology, USA*
Michiel Sovijärvi-Spape, *Aalto University, Finland*
Anna Spagnolli, *University of Padova, Italy*
Oleg Spakov, *University of Tampere, Finland*
Lucio Davide Spano, *University of Cagliari, Italy*
Mirjana Spasojevic, *Nokia, USA*
Chris Speed, *Edinburgh College of Art, UK*
Tess Speelpenning, *Philips Research, The Netherlands*
Wolfgang Spiessl, *BMW Research and Technology, Germany*
Tasos Spiliotopoulos, *Madeira Interactive Technologies Institute, Portugal*
Martin Spindler, *University of Magdeburg, Germany*
Adam Sporka, *Czech Technical University In Prague, Czech Republic*
Mary Ann Sprague, *Xerox, USA*
Srinath Sridhar, *Max-Planck Institut Für Informatik, Germany*
Saurabh Srivastava, *IBM India Research Laboratory, India*
Robert St. Amant, *North Carolina State University, USA*
Tad Stach, *Queen's University, Canada*
Frank Stajano, *University of Cambridge, UK*
Jeannie Stamberger, *Carnegie Mellon University, USA*
Brodie Stanfield, *University of Ontario Institute of Technology, Canada*
Kevin Stanley, *University of Saskatchewan, Canada*
Pieter Jan Stappers, *Delft University of Technology, The Netherlands*
Kate Starbird, *University of Washington, USA*
Thad Starner, *Georgia Institute of Technology, USA*
John Stasko, *Georgia Institute of Technology, USA*
Bogdan State, *Stanford University, USA*
Ian Stavness, *University of Saskatchewan, Canada*
Anthony Steed, *University College London, UK*
Ann Steele, *The University of Texas at KAIST, Republic of Korea in, USA*
Daniel Steffen, *German Research Center for Artificial Intelligence (DFKI), Germany*
Ben Steichen, *University of British Columbia, Canada*
Martin Stein, *University of Siegen, Germany*
Sebastian Stein, *University of Dundee, Scotland, UK*
Fabius Steinberger, *University of Technology, Australia*
Thomas Steiner, *Hamburg, Germany*
Aaron Steinfeld, *Carnegie Mellon University, USA*
Frank Steinicke, *University of Würzburg, Germany*
Sophie Stellmach, *Technische Universität Dresden, Germany*
Amanda Stent, *Yahoo! Labs, USA*
William Steptoe, *UCL, UK*
Sarah Stevenage
Gunnar Stevens, *University of Siegen, Germany*
Craig Stewart, *University of Glasgow, Scotland, UK*

Michael Stewart, *Virginia Polytechnic Institute and State University, USA*
Rainer Stiefelhagen, *Universität Karlsruhe (TH), Germany*
Jeremiah Still, *Missouri Western State University, USA*
David Stillwell, *University of Nottingham, UK*
Greg Stoddard, *Northwestern, USA*
Erik Stolterman, *Indiana University Bloomington, USA*
Margaret-Anne Storey, *University of Victoria,*
Cristiano Storni, *University of Limerick, Ireland*
Steven Strachan, *CEA, France*
Daniel Strazzulla, *INRIA, France*
Yolande Strengers, *AHURI-RMIT Research Centre, Australia*
Dagny Stuedahl, *University of Oslo, Norway*
Simone Stumpf, *City University London, UK*
Christian Sturm, *Hamm-Lippstadt University of Applied Sciences, Germany*
Norman Su, *University College Dublin, Ireland*
Ozge Subasi, *Vienna University of Technology, Austria*
Sriram Subramanian, *University of Bristol, UK*
Yusuke Sugano, *The University of Tokyo, Japan*
Masanori Sugimoto, *Hokkaido University, Japan*
Bongwon Suh, *Seoul National University, Republic of Korea*
Hyeon-Jeong Suk, *KAIST, South Korea*
Piyawadee Sukaviriya, *IBM Research - T. J. Watson, USA*
Gita Sukthankar, *University of Central Florida, USA*
Evan Suma, *University of Southern California, USA*
Chengzheng Sun, *Nanyang Technological University, Singapore*
David Sun, *UC Berkeley, USA*
Huatong Sun, *University of Washington Tacoma, USA*
Xiao Hua Sun, *IBM Research China, China*
Hari Sundaram, *Arizona State University, USA*
Petra Sundström, *Mobile Life @ SICS, Sweden*
Ja-Young Sung, *Georgia Institute of Technology, USA*
Siddharth Suri, *Microsoft Research, USA*
Alistair Sutcliffe, *The University of Manchester, UK*
Dag Svænes, *NTNU, Norway*
David Swallow, *University of York, UK*
Colin Swindells, *University of Victoria, Canada*
Cristina Sylla, *University of Minho, Portugal*
Anna-Liisa Syrjänen, *University of Oulu, Finland*
Daniel Szafir, *University of Wisconsin, USA*
Agnieszka (aga) Szostek, *Warsaw School of Social Psychology, Poland*
Gerd Szwillus, *Universität Paderborn, Germany*
Aurélien Tabard, *University of Munich, Germany*
Leila Takayama, *Willow Garage, USA*
Justin Talbot, *Stanford University, USA*
Chek Tien Tan, *University of Technology, Australia*
Hong Tan, *Microsoft Research Asia, China*
Kumiko Tanaka-Ishii, *University of Tokyo, Japan*
Joshua Tanenbaum, *Simon Fraser University, Canada*
Karen Tanenbaum, *Simon Fraser University, USA*
Anthony Tang, *University of Calgary, Canada*
Charlotte Tang, *University of British Columbia, Canada*
John Tang, *Microsoft Research, USA*
Stefano Targher, *University of Trento, Italy*
Andrea Tartaro, *Furman University, USA*

Craig Tashman, *Georgia Institute of Technology, USA*
Dan Tasse, *Carnegie Mellon University, USA*
Sarah Tausch, *University of Munich, Germany*
Alex Taylor, *Microsoft Research, UK*
Nick Taylor, *University of Dundee, UK*
Robyn Taylor, *Newcastle University, UK*
Stuart Taylor, *Microsoft Research, UK*
Robert Teather, *McMaster University, Canada*
Kimberly Tee, *SMART Technologies, USA*
Daniel Teibel, *Cassia, USA*
Paul Tennent, *The University of Nottingham, UK*
Monica Tentori, *UABC, Mexico*
Leong-Hwee Teo, *Carnegie Mellon University, Singapore*
Lucia Terrenghi, *Google, Switzerland*
Michael Terry, *University of Waterloo, Canada*
Loren Terveen, *University of Minnesota, USA*
Ambuj Tewari, *University of Michigan, USA*
Anuj Tewari, *UC Berkeley, USA*
Anja Thieme, *Newcastle University, UK*
Harold Thimbleby, *University of Swansea, Wales, UK*
Elizabeth Thiry, *Pennsylvania State University, USA*
Jennifer Thom, *Amazon, USA*
Katherine Thomas, *University of North Texas, USA*
Edison Thomaz, *Georgia Institute of Technology, USA*
Bart Thomee, *Yahoo Labs, Spain*
Robin Thompson, *Newcastle University, UK*
Feng Tian, *Chinese Academy of Sciences, P.r. China*
Lorenza Tiberio, *National Research Council of Italy (CNR), Italia*
Rob Tieben, *Eindhoven University of Technology, Netherlands*
Janko Timmermann, *OFFIS - Institute for Information Technology, Germany*
Nava Tintarev, *University of Aberdeen, Scotland, UK*
Mike Tissenbaum, *University of Toronto, Canada*
Hiroaki Tobita, *Sony CSL Paris, Tokyo*
Eran Toch, *Tel Aviv University, Israel*
Lisa Tolentino, *Arizona State University, USA*
Konrad Tollmar, *KTH, Sweden*
Peter Tolmie, *University of Nottingham, UK*
Catalina Toma, *University of Wisconsin-Madison, USA*
Christian Tominski, *University of Rostock, Germany*
Martin Tomitsch, *Vienna University of Technology, Australia*
Bill Tomlinson, *University of California, USA*
James Tompkin, *MPI Informatik, Germany*
*KAIST, Republic of Korea* in Toombs, *Indiana University Bloomington, USA*
Mercan Topkara, *IBM Research, USA*
Tammy Toscos, *Indiana University-Purdue University, USA*
Chad Tossell, *Rice University, USA*
W. Ben Towne, *Carnegie Mellon University, USA*
Cuong Tran, *University of California, USA*
Minh-Triet Tran, *University of Science, Vietnam*
Matthias Treder, *Technische Universität Berlin, Germany*
Jeffrey Treem, *Northwestern University, USA*
Shari Trewin, *IBM Research - T. J. Watson, USA*

Ha Trinh, *University of Dundee, UK*
Giovanni Maria Troiano, *Universitat Pompeu Fabra, Spain*
Khai Truong, *University of Toronto, Canada*
Janice Tsai, *Microsoft Research, USA*
Theophanis Tsandilas, *Inria, France*
Jason Tsay, *Carnegie Mellon University, USA*
Edward Tse, *SMART Technologies, Canada*
Nikolaos Tselios, *University of Patras, Greece*
Yuan-Chi Tseng, *National Cheng Kung University, Taiwan*
Jessica Tsimeris, *KAIST, Republic of Korea ralian National University, Australia*
Gill Tsouri, *Rochester Institute of Technology, USA*
Katherine Tsui, *University of Massachusetts Lowell, USA*
Oren Tsur, *Harvard University, USA*
Huawei Tu, *Swansea University, UK*
Alexandre Tuch, *University of Basel, Switzerland*
Zeynep Tufekci, *University of North Carolina, USA*
Kathleen Tuite, *University of Washington, USA*
Marcello Turconi, *University of Trieste, Italy*
Jayson Turner, *Lancaster University, UK*
Thea Turner, *USA*
Lisa Tweedie, *Tweedie Consulting, UK*
Michael Twidale, *University of Illinois at Urbana-Champaign, USA*
George Tzanetakis, *University of Victoria, Canada*
Brygg Ullmer, *Louisiana State University, USA*
Kent Unruh, *University of Washington, USA*
Connor Upton, *Intel Labs Europe, Ireland*
Blase Ur, *Carnegie Mellon University, USA*
Dina Utami
Stephen Uzor, *Glasgow Caledonian University, UK*
Kaisa Väänänen-Vainio-Mattila, *Tampere University of Technology, Finland*
Heli Väätäjä, *Tampere University of Technology, Finland*
Philip Vahey, *SRI International, USA*
Rajan Vaish, *University of California, USA*
Consuelo Valdes, *Wellesley College, USA*
Dimitar Valkov, *University of Muenster, Germany*
Anna Vallgårda, *IT University of Copenhagen, Denmark*
Philip Van Allen, *Art Center College of Design, USA*
Bram Van de Laar, *University of Twente,*
Robin Van Den Akker, *Belgium*
Jan Van Den Bergh, *Hasselt University - Tul - Iminds, Belgium*
Bart Van Den Hooff, *VU University Amsterdam, The Netherlands*
Janet Van Der Linden, *The Open University, UK*
Jelle Van Dijk, *Eindhoven University of Technology, Netherlands*
Aart Van Halteren, *Philips Research, Netherlands*
Frank Van Ham, *IBM Research, USA*
Nancy Van House, *University of California, USA*
Max Van Kleek, *MIT, UK*
Kristof Van Laerhoven, *TU Darmstadt, Germany*
Jos Van Leeuwen, *University of Madeira, Portugal*
Christof Van Nimwegen, *Utrecht University, The Netherlands*
Paul Van Schaik, *Teesside University, UK*

Peter Van Waart, *Rotterdam University of Applied Sciences, The Netherlands*
Davy Vanacken, *Hasselt University - Tul - Iminds, Belgium*
Jeroen Vanattenhoven, *KU Leuven, Belgium*
Andrew Vande Moere, *KU Leuven, Belgium*
Jean Vanderdonckt, *Université Catholique de Louvain (UCL), Belgium*
Kami Vaniea, *Carnegie Mellon University, USA*
Elina Vartiainen, *Nokia Research Center, Sweden*
Asimina Vasalou, *University of Birmingham, UK*
Radu-Daniel Vatavu, *University Stefan Cel Mare of Suceava, Romania*
Yolanda Vazquez-Alvarez, *University of Glasgow, UK*
Eduardo Veas, *Graz University of Technology, Austria*
Rajesh Veeraraghavan, *UC Berkeley, USA*
Laurian Vega, *Virginia Tech, USA*
Tiffany Veinot, *University of Michigan, USA*
Eduardo Velloso, *Lancaster University, UK*
Gina Venolia, *Microsoft Research, USA*
Colin Venters, *University of Huddersfield, UK*
Nervo Verdezoto, *Aarhus University, Denmark*
Arnold Vermeeren, *Delft University of Technology, The Netherlands*
Amber Vermeesch, *Michigan State University, USA*
Jo Vermeulen, *Hasselt University - Tul - Iminds, Belgium*
Frederic Vernier, *Université Paris XI, France*
Keith Vertanen, *Montana Tech, USA*
Roel Vertegaal, *Queen's University, Canada*
Janet Vertesi, *Princeton University, USA*
Carla Verwijs, *In Transition, Canada*
Chi Vi, *University of Bristol, UK*
Melodie Vidal, *Lancaster University, UK*
Timothy Vidas, *Carnegie Mellon University, USA*
Sarah Vieweg, *Qatar Computing Research Institute, Qatar*
Markel Vigo, *University of Manchester, UK*
Nicolas Villar, *Microsoft Research, UK*
Vinayak, *Purdue University, USA*
Jussi Virkkala
Jessica Vitak, *University of Maryland, USA*
Lisa Vizer, *University of Maryland, USA*
Vasillis Vlachokyriakos, *Newcastle University, UK*
Simon Voelker, *RWTH-Aachen University, Germany*
Christian Vogler, *Gallaudet University, USA*
Stephen Voida, *Indiana University, USA*
Martin Voigt, *TU Dresden, Germany*
Dirk Vom Lehn, *King's College London, Great Britain*
Ulrich Von Zadow, *Archimedes Exhibitions Gmbh, Germany*
Emanuel Von Zezschwitz, *University of Munich, Germany*
Mihaela Vorvoreanu, *Purdue University, USA*
Hana Vrzakova, *University of Eastern Finland, Finland*
Romain Vuillemot, *Harvard University, USA*
Dhaval Vyas, *University of Twente, The Netherlands*
Katarzyna Wac, *Carnegie Mellon University, USA*
Chat Wacharamanotham, *RWTH Aachen University, Germany*
Juan P. Wachs, *Purdue University, USA*
Greg Wadley, *The University of Melbourne, Australia*

Johanna Wagner, *Graz University of Technology, Austria*
Julie Wagner, *INRIA, Germany*
Patrick Wagstrom, *Carnegie Mellon University, USA*
Shahtab Wahid, *Virginia Tech, USA*
Brendan Walker, *The University of Nottingham, England, UK*
Bruce Walker, *Georgia Institute of Technology, USA*
Erin Walker, *Arizona State University, USA*
I Walker, *University of Bath, UK*
Lorna Wall, *UCL, UK*
Steven Wall, *System Concepts Ltd, UK*
James Wallace, *University of Waterloo, Canada*
Jayne Wallace, *University of Dundee, UK*
Guenter Wallner, *University of Applied Arts Vienna, Austria*
Jagoda Walny, *University of Calgary, Canada*
Greg Walsh, *University of Maryland, USA*
Tanja Walsh, *Tampere University of Technology, Finland*
Robert Walter, *Telekom Innovation Laboratories, Germany*
Lin Wan, *University of Siegen, Germany*
Chaoli Wang, *Michigan Technological University, USA*
Fei Wang, *IBM Research - Almaden, USA*
Jing Wang, *The Pennsylvania State University, USA*
Jingtao Wang, *University of Pittsburgh, USA*
Liang Wang, *Microsoft, USA*
Robert Wang, *Massachusetts Institute of Technology, USA*
Rongrong Wang, *Samsung Research America, USA*
Xiaoyu Wang, *University of North Carolina at Charlotte, USA*
Yang Wang, *Syracuse University, USA*
Yi-Chia Wang, *Carnegie Mellon University, USA*
Yuchen Wang, *University of Alberta, Canada*
Colin Ware, *University of New Hampshire, USA*
Andrew Warr, *Google, USA*
Rick Wash, *Michigan State University, USA*
Gloria Washington, *Clemson University, USA*
Takayuki Watanabe, *Tokyo Woman's Christian University, Japan*
Kari Watkins, *Georgia Institute of Technology, USA*
Diane Watson, *University of Waterloo, Canada*
Martin Wattenberg, *IBM Research, USA*
Leon Watts, *University of Bath, UK*
Jenny Waycott, *The University of Melbourne, Australia*
Kimberly Weaver, *Georgia Institute of Technology, USA*
Gerhard Weber, *Technische Universität Dresden, Germany*
Michael Weber, *University of Ulm, Germany*
Ina Wechsung, *TU Berlin, Germany*
Rina Wehbe, *University of Ontario Institute of Technology, Canada*
Xuetao Wei, *University of Cincinnati, USA*
Anne Weibert, *University of Siegen, Germany*
Christian Weichel, *Lancaster University, UK*
Karl-Heinz Weidmann, *Fachhochschule Vorarlberg, KAIST, Republic of Korea ria/Europe*
Alexandra Weilenmann, *IT-University of Göteborg, Sweden*
Tino Weinkauf, *Max-Planck Institut Für Informatik, Germany*
Astrid Weiss, *Vienna University of Technology, Austria*
Stephan Wensveen, *Eindhoven University of Technology, The Netherlands*

Elizabeth Wenzel, *NASA Ames Research Center, USA*
Wayne Westerman, *Apple, USA*
Adam Westerski, *Universidad Politecnica de Madrid, Spain*
Tara Whalen, *Dalhousie University, Canada*
Joseph Wherton, *Barts and The London School of Medicine and Dentistry, UK*
Brandyn White, *University of Maryland: College Park, USA*
Kevin White, *University of Maryland Baltimore County, USA*
Sean White, *Nokia, USA*
Anthony Whitehead, *Carleton University, Canada*
Michael Whitney, *University of North Carolina at Charlotte, USA*
Steve Whittaker, *University of California Santa Cruz, USA*
Jon Whittle, *Infolab21, UK*
Mikael Wiberg, *Umeå University, Sweden*
Hadley Wickham, *Rstudio, USA*
Josef Wiemeyer, *Sport Science, Germany*
Jason Wiese, *Carnegie Mellon University, USA*
Alexander Wiethoff, *University of Munich, Germany*
Andrea Wiggins, *University of New Mexico, USA*
Danielle Wilde, *Rmit University, Australia*
Erik Wilde, *UC Berkeley, USA*
Oliver Wilder-Smith, *Northeastern University, USA*
David Wilfinger, *University of Salzburg, Austria*
Wesley Willett, *INRIA, France*
Amanda Williams, *Wyld Collective Ltd., Canada*
Amanda Marisa Williams, *University of California, Canada*
Joseph Williams, *Stanford University, USA*
Kaiton Williams, *Cornell University, USA*
John Williamson, *University of Glasgow, UK*
Julie Williamson, *University of Glasgow, UK*
Andrew Wilson, *Microsoft Research, USA*
Graham Wilson, *University of Glasgow, Scotland, UK*
Mathew Wilson, *Swansea University, UK*
Max Wilson, *Swansea University, UK*
Raphael Wimmer, *University of Munich, Germany*
Marco Winckler, *ICS-IRIT, France*
Christian Winkler, *Ulm University, Germany*
Sarah Wiseman, *University College London, UK*
Pamela Wisniewski, *The Pennsylvania State University, USA*
Jason Wither, *Microsoft, USA*
Jens Witkowski, *Albert-Ludwigs-Universität Freiburg, Germany*
Dan Witzner Hansen, *IT University of Copenhagen, Denmark*
Jacob Wobbrock, *University of Washington, USA*
Jill Woelfer, *University of Washington, USA*
Donghee Yvette Wohn, *Northwestern University, USA*
Katrin Wolf, *Deutsche Telekom Laboratories, Germany*
Peter Wolkerstorfer, *CURE - Center for Usability Research & Engineering, Austria*
B.l. William Wong, *Middlesex University, UK*
Nelson Wong, *University of Saskatchewan, Canada*
Krist Wongsuphasawat, *University of Maryland, USA*
Gavin Wood, *Newcastle University, UK*
Simon Wood, *ABC, Australia*
Emma Woodberry, *Addenbrooke's Hospital, UK*

Rob Woodbury, *Simon Fraser University, Canada*
Allison Woodruff, *Intel Research, USA*
Kirk Woolford, *University of Surrey, UK*
Marcel Worring, *University of Amsterdam, The Netherlands*
Rita Wouhaybi, *Intel Corporation, USA*
Julie Wright, *Umass Boston, USA*
Michael Wright, *University of Bath, UK*
Peter Wright, *Newcastle University, UK*
Andy Wu, *Georgia Institute of Technology, USA*
Anna Wu, *Pennsylvania State University, USA*
Jiayu Wu, *Tsinghua University, China*
Mike Wu, *The University of Toronto, Canada*
Shaomei Wu, *Information Science, USA*
Yu Wu, *The Pennsylvania State University, USA*
Daniela Wurhofer, *University of Salzburg, Austria*
Susan Wyche, *Michigan State University, USA*
Peta Wyeth, *Queensland University of Technology, Australia*
Ruth Wylie, *Arizona State University, USA*
Lonce Wyse, *National University of Singapore, Singapore*
Robert Xiao, *Carnegie Mellon University, USA*
Xiao Xiao, *Massachusetts Institute of Technology, USA*
Xing Xie, *Microsoft Research Asia, China*
Anbang Xu, *University of Illinois at Urbana-Champaign, USA*
Heng Xu, *The Pennsylvania State University, USA*
Yan Xu, *Intel Labs, USA*
Kota Yamaguchi, *University of Tokyo, Japan*
Katsu Yamane, *Disney Research, USA*
Naomi Yamashita, *NTT Communication Science Laboratories, Japan*
Hirotake Yamazoe, *Osaka University, Japan*
de-Nian Yang, *Academia Sinica, Taipei*
Huahai Yang, *IBM Research - Almaden, USA*
Jiang Yang, *University of Michigan, USA*
Rayoung Yang, *University of Michigan, USA*
Rui Yang
Stephen Yang, *SUNY Cortland, USA*
Xing-Dong Yang, *University of Alberta, Canada*
Koji Yatani, *Microsoft Research Asia, China*
Yina Ye, *Helsinki Institute for Information Technology HIIT, Finland*
Nick Yee, *PARC, USA*
Tom Yeh, *University of Colorado, USA*
Yeliz Yesilada, *University of Manchester, UK*
Jude Yew, *National University of Singapore, Singapore*
Samantha Yglesias, *Virginia Tech, Montgomery*
Ji Soo Yi, *Purdue University, USA*
Emine Yilmaz, *University College London, UK*
Langxuan Yin, *Northeastern University, USA*
Ming Yin, *Harvard University, USA*
Jason Yip, *University of Maryland, USA*
Salu Ylirisku, *Aalto University, Finland*
Christian Yoder, *University of California, USA*
Daisy Yoo, *Carnegie Mellon University, USA*
Hyoseok Yoon, *KAIST, Korea*
Chuang-Wen You, *Academia Sinica, Taiwan*

Alyson Young, *UMBC, USA*
James Young, *University of Manitoba, Canada*
Chun Yu, *Tsinghua University, China*
Lixiu Yu, *Carnegie Mellon University, USA*
Michael Yu, *Carnegie Mellon University, USA*
Neng-Hao Yu, *National Taiwan University, Taiwan*
Zhiwen Yu, *School of Computer Science Xi'an, China*
Chien Wen Yuan, *Cornell University, USA*
Nicholas Yuan, *Microsoft Research Asia, China*
Beste Yuksel, *Tufts University, USA*
Stanislaw Zabramski, *Uppsala University, Sweden*
Lisl Zach, *Drexel University, USA*
Jose Zagal, *Georgia Institute of Technology, USA*
Panagiotis Zaharias, *Athens University of Economics and Business, Greece*
Bieke Zaman, *IBBT-KU Leuven, Belgium*
Massimo Zancanaro, *FBK-Irst, Italy*
Richard Zanibbi, *Rochester Institute of Technology, USA*
Michael Zarro, *Drexel University, USA*
Polle Zellweger, *Maczell Consulting, USA*
Shumin Zhai, *Research @ Google, USA*
Cheng Zhang, *Georgia Institute of Technology, USA*
Haimo Zhang, *National University of Singapore, Singapore*
Haoqi Zhang, *Harvard University, USA*
Pei Zhang, *Carnegie Mellon University, USA*
Tao Zhang, *North Carolina State University, USA*
Yan Zhang, *University of Texas at KAIST, Republic of Korea in, USA*
Yanxia Zhang, *Lancaster University, UK*
Chen Zhao, *Alibaba International UED, USA*
Dejin Zhao, *PSU, USA*
Jian Zhao, *University of Toronto, Canada*
Xuan Zhao, *University of Michigan, USA*
Bin Zheng, *University of Alberta, Canada*
Yangshuo Zheng, *Tsinghua University, China*
Jia Zhou, *Chongqing, China*
Lina Zhou, *University of Maryland, USA*
Yajin Zhou, *Raleigh, USA*
Bin Zhu, *Microsoft Research Asia, China*
Haiyi Zhu, *Carnegie Mellon University, USA*
Mengxiao Zhu, *Rutgers University, USA*
Zhigang Zhu, *The City College of New York, USA*
Martina Ziefle, *Rwth Aachen University, Germany*
Juergen Ziegler, *University of Duisburg-Essen, Germany*
Caroline Ziemkiewicz, *Brown University, USA*
Roshanak Zilouchian Moghaddam, *University of Illinois at Urbana-Champaign, USA*
Ryder Ziola, *University of Washington, USA*
Miriam Zisook, *Northeastern University, USA*
Hadar Ziv, *University of California, USA*
Goranka Zoric, *Stockholm University, Sweden*
Jo Zucco, *University of South KAIST, Republic of Korea ralia, Australia*
Sacha Zyto, *MIT, USA*

Special thanks for the financial support provided by the following sponsors:

CHI Champion Sponsors

AUTODESK.

Bloomberg

Google

Graphisme, animation et nouveaux médias
GRAND
Graphics, Animation and New Media

Microsoft

NAVER

Computer Science
UNIVERSITY OF TORONTO

CHI Contributing Sponsors

facebook.

NSF

YAHOO! LABS

Friends of CHI

Disney Research    Newcastle University

Printed on Rolland Enviro 100
100% post-consumer fiber
Certified EcoLogo
Processed chlorine free
Manufactured using biogas energy
Printed using soy-based inks

# Visualizing Dynamic Networks with Matrix Cubes

**Benjamin Bach**
INRIA
benjamin.bach@inria.fr

**Emmanuel Pietriga**
INRIA & INRIA Chile (CIRIC)
emmanuel.pietriga@inria.fr

**Jean-Daniel Fekete**
INRIA
jean-daniel.fekete@inria.fr

## ABSTRACT

Designing visualizations of dynamic networks is challenging, both because the data sets tend to be complex and because the tasks associated with them are often cognitively demanding. We introduce the *Matrix Cube*, a novel visual representation and navigation model for dynamic networks, inspired by the way people comprehend and manipulate physical cubes. Users can change their perspective on the data by rotating or decomposing the 3D cube. These manipulations can produce a range of different 2D visualizations that emphasize specific aspects of the dynamic network suited to particular analysis tasks. We describe Matrix Cubes and the interactions that can be performed on them in the *Cubix* system. We then show how two domain experts, an astronomer and a neurologist, used Cubix to explore and report on their own network data.

### Author Keywords

Dynamic Networks; Information Visualization; Interaction; Metaphors; Multiple Views

### ACM Classification Keywords

H.5.2 [Information Interfaces and Presentation]: User Interfaces - Graphical user interfaces.

### General Terms

Human Factors; Design

## INTRODUCTION

Network structures exist in many domains, including social networks, neural signaling networks in the brain, and ad-hoc networks of computers and mobile devices. To understand and analyse these networks, it is important to be able to visualize them in a comprehensible way. Yet, designing network visualizations that effectively support users in their exploration and analysis tasks is quite challenging. Moreover, many networks are actually dynamic, and their topology as well as the attributes associated with nodes and edges can vary over time. This additional level of complexity often leads to more complicated visual interfaces with larger numbers of views and more widgets to adjust parameters of the visualizations. This is a significant issue, as above a certain level of complexity, users are less able to learn – or less willing to take the time to learn – the system.


*CHI 2014*, April 26 - May 01 2014, Toronto, ON, Canada
Copyright 2014 ACM 978-1-4503-2473-1/14/04...$15.00.
http://dx.doi.org/10.1145/2556288.2557010

One of the main goals of human-computer interaction is to improve the tradeoff between power and simplicity in interfaces [3]. In this paper we introduce the *Matrix Cube*, an easy-to-understand yet powerful approach to representing dynamic networks. Matrix Cubes result from stacking adjacency matrix representations of the network at each time step, forming a space time cube. Compared to node-link diagrams, adjacency matrices are better suited to the visualization of dense networks. With the Matrix Cube, we explore their applicability to the visualization of dynamic networks.

The Matrix Cube representation and associated interactions are inspired by the way people comprehend and manipulate physical cubes. Users can change their perspective on the data by rotating and projecting the 3D cube, or decomposing it using operations such as slicing and filtering. These operations lead to various 2D visualizations, that offer a set of coherent, easy-to-relate views on the data. The 3D view of the cube provides an overview of the data, as well as a visual model for understanding transitions and pivots between views. Meanwhile, the 2D views derived from the cube support more detailed analysis of specific aspects of the network and entities that constitute it.

In this paper, we first review related work on visualizing dynamic networks and introduce the concept of Matrix Cubes. When then present *Cubix*, an interactive system that uses Matrix Cubes to support the visualization and analysis of large, dense dynamic networks. Finally, we describe how two domain experts—an astronomer and a neurologist—used Cubix to analyze dense dynamic network data from their own work.

## BACKGROUND

We define a dynamic network as $G = (V, E, T)$ where $V$ is the set of all vertices, $E$ the set of all edges, and $T$ the set of discrete time steps. Edges can have attributes associated with them, such as a weight. Attributes can vary between time steps. A time step $G_t = (V_t, E_t)$ of $G$ consists of the vertices and edges present in the network at time step $t \in T$.

### Node-link diagrams

Most techniques for exploring dynamic networks visualize them using node-link diagrams. Any static network tool can be used to create an image per time step. These diagrams can then be displayed one after the other (time-multiplexed), or side by side (juxtaposed). Animations between individual images, as in Ahn *et al.* [1] and Marey [16], can make it easier to recognize changes and better track moving nodes and edges when the graph layout is not stable. But showing images in a sequence can increase users' cognitive load by forcing them to remember the network's state when navigating between time steps. This is especially problematic for networks with many time steps. Alternatively, individual images can be shown side-by-side as in Ploceus [25]. The amount of screen real-estate dedicated to each time step depends on their number. This has a direct impact on the amount of detail that can be displayed. While these side-by-side images provide a quick overview of the network's evolution, they make it hard to track individual graph elements across steps, or directly compare distant images, especially for dense graphs.

Changes in time-multiplexed or juxtaposed representations are not visualized explicitly, which makes them difficult to identify. Events such as the addition or removal of a node or edge can be explicitly encoded in a single image using color, as in Gevol [11] or Donatien [21]. However, these visual variables are no longer available to encode information about the network, such as edge weight [2].

Dynamic networks can be decomposed not only along time, but also based on their topology. *Dynamic ego-networks* representations show the evolution of a node's neighborhood using other approaches (e.g. a node-link diagram that maps time to concentric circles as in Farrugia *et al.* [14], or a timeline as in Shi *et al.* [29]). Ego-networks make it easier to observe specific nodes, but do not help identify and understand the more general evolution of trends over the network. Other techniques represent the entire network along a single timeline using a spatial mapping that makes it possible to describe locations and distances between time points. Using this approach, the challenge is to represent the topology using the only remaining spatial dimension. Reda *et al.* [27], as well as Sallaberry *et al.* [28], represent bundles of clusters or communities along a timeline. Parallel edge splatting [7] shows time steps as vertical lines and places network links between slices. Such timeline visualizations can show temporal trends, but fail to show the network's topology.

### Adjacency Matrices

Adjacency matrices provide an alternative to node-link diagrams that is particularly effective when visualizing dense graphs [2, 18, 22]. Furthermore, matrix cells provide better opportunities than the lines or curves of a node-link diagram to visually encode information about the corresponding edges. However, only a few projects have investigated the use of matrices to visualize dynamic networks. TimeMatrix [31] displays a temporal bar chart in each matrix cell to show the evolution of edge weights. Brandes and Nick [6] use *gestalt-lines*, to represent changes of bi-directed edge weights over time. Another way to encode edge value changes over time is to use brightness changes on space-filling curves in matrix cells [30]. In addition to matrices, Netvisia [20] uses a heatmap, where one dimension is time and the other contains the vertices. Similar to FlowStrates [5], cells in the heatmap encode the value of one particular vertex attribute in the corresponding time step.

Each of these techniques emphasize some aspects of dynamic networks at the expense of others. Common tradeoffs include visualizing the network's topology vs. encoding time, providing overview vs. detail, and showing many time steps with few details vs. fewer ones with more detail.

### The Space-Time-Cube Metaphor

Metaphors are used frequently in interface design to help users understand a new or unknown system or object by referring to existing systems with which they are already familiar. This provides a mental model of the system's functionality that helps users to understand the *current state* of the system and to *anticipate interactions* that might change its state. For example, both ScatterDice [13] and GraphDice [4] use a rotating cube metaphor to convey changing dimensions in scatterplots and multivariate graphs, respectively.

A space-time cube is a representation that maps data onto two dimensions, while time is shown as a third spatial dimension. Space-time cubes are able to show both spatial *and* temporal information simultaneously [17, 23, 24]. However, those representations face several common problems encountered when showing 3D models on a 2D screen: more complex navigation, reduced depth perception, and visual occlusion. To address the latter problem, GeoTime [23] provides an additional view that shows trajectories as projections on the landscape. While space-time cubes in geographic information systems are often sparse, time cubes for video analysis, resulting from the alignment of all video frames, are fully filled. To explore their interior, Fels et al. [15] allow users to freely cut the video cube. Cassinelli et al. [10] interactively distort the cube. Carpendale investigated several ways to explore dense time cubes using geometric distortion [9], cutting planes, and filtering techniques [8].

Brandes and Corman [6], as well as Dwyer and Gallagher [12], represent dynamic networks as space-time cubes by extruding nodes from 2D node-link diagrams to 3D columns and "worms". Edges become bridges between extruded nodes. However, node-link diagrams become unreadable above a certain (very low) network density threshold and stacking them in 3D introduces even more line crossings due to perspective overlap. Interactive 3D rotation or temporal coloring fail to fully address these issues. In addition, projection and decomposition of these diagrams is not straightforward, which makes visual exploration and analysis difficult.

## THE MATRIX CUBE

The *Matrix Cube* is a representation of dynamic networks based on the space-time cube metaphor. It is created by stacking adjacency matrices in chronological order, one for each time step (Figure 1-a and 1-b). The cube consequently has two vertex dimensions which are colored red, and one time dimension which is colored blue. A *cell* $c_{vwt} \in (V \times V \times T)$ exists for each edge $e_{vwt}$ between vertices $v$ and $w$ at time $t$. Along the time dimension, the cube contains *time slices* (adjacency matrices) that show the time steps of $G$ at time t (Figure 1-a). Slicing the cube along one of its vertex dimensions yields *vertex slices*, one for every vertex (Figure 1-c). Rows in a vertex slice correspond to the network's vertices $V$ and columns correspond to time steps in $T$. Vertex slices show the dynamic ego-network of each node; a cell in the vertex slice for vertex $v$ indicates an edge between $v$ and the vertex indicated by the row the cell belongs to, at the time indicated by the cell's column. Since the Matrix Cube comprises two vertex dimensions, there are potentially two different types of

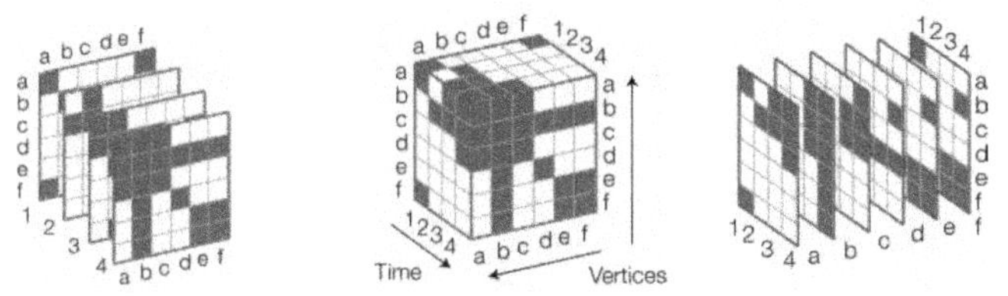


(a) Adjacency Matrices (b) Matrix Cube (c) Vertex Slices

**Figure 1. The Matrix Cube. (a) Each time step of the network (1,2,3,4), is represented as an adjacency matrix. (b) The Matrix Cube results from stacking those matrices. Red edges of the cube hold nodes and correspond to the rows and columns of the constituent adjacency matrices; blue edges of the cube hold time steps. (c) Slicing the cube along one of the vertex dimensions yields *vertex slices*.**

vertex slices. We focus on undirected networks, where both types of vertex slices contain the same information.

Cells in the same row and column across all matrices form a *time vector* that describes the evolution of the connectivity between two vertices. In a similar way, cells in the same row or column in one time slice form a *neighborhood vector* that describes the neighborhood of a single vertex at the time corresponding to this slice.

To make topological patterns visible in adjacency matrices as well as in matrix cubes, rows and columns (vertex slice) can be reordered using one of four methods: alphabetical, reverse Cuthill-McKee, TSP, and optimal leaf-ordering of a hierarchical clustering technique.

## CUBIX

Cubix is an interactive system for the visualization of large, dense dynamic networks represented using matrix cubes. It lets users navigate in the data by manipulating the cube interactively, thus deriving meaningful 2D views that emphasize particular dimensions of the data. Orientation in, and navigation between, views is facilitated by the *Cubelet*, a small widget that represents the current view configuration and all possible manipulations. Cubix animates the 3D representation of the cube to smoothly pivot between views, illustrating the operations performed during the transitions and helping users maintain perceptual continuity across multiple views.

Cubix is based on the following design principles:

1. **3D as a pivot** — As discussed earlier, 3D representations are hard to visualize on two-dimensional screens. Cubix focuses on the 2D visualizations that can be derived from the cube. Still, explicitly showing the 3D cube has advantages: 1) it explicitly conveys the cube-based model to the user, 2) it provides an overview of the data along all dimensions, and 3) it serves as a pivot visualization when switching between views.
2. **Animated transitions** — Changes between views on the cube are smoothly animated, providing a good level of perceptual continuity during transitions, which helps users to understand the relationship between views as well as track elements across them.
3. **Limited number of views** — The number of views that can be derived by decomposing the cube and arranging its parts is potentially infinite. In Cubix, we constrain the set of operations that users can perform on the cube, in order to keep navigation simple and manageable.
4. **Easy navigation** — Some views require multiple operations. For instance, laying out slices side-by-side requires specifying the slicing direction (time slices or vertex slices), and moving them to their appropriate position in 3D space. The cubelet allows users to quickly navigate between most predefined views, which are also accessible via keyboard shortcuts.

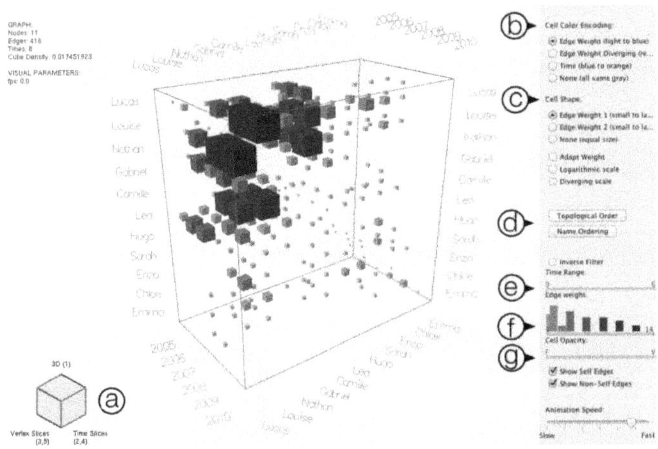

**Figure 2. Cubix UI screenshot. a) Cubelet Widget, b) Cell color encoding, c) Cell shape encoding, d) Vertex ordering, e) Time range slider, f) Cell weight filter with histogram indicating edge weight distribution, g) Cell opacity.**

We illustrate Cubix using a simple research collaboration network. This network contains one time step per year. Researchers correspond to vertices, and connections between vertices indicate a co-authorship relation on at least one publication during that year. Self-edges correspond to publications by a single author. Edge weights represent the number of papers between any two authors for a given year.

### Matrix Cube Overview

Figure 2 shows the default view for this co-authorship network. The main interface components include: the Matrix Cube in the center, the Cubelet widget for rapid view switching (a), and control widgets on the right-hand side to parameterize the visualization (b-g).

For this dataset, the cube's axes are labeled with author names and dates. By default, cell size and color indicate the number of publications per year (edge weight). Color ranges from light gray for low edge weight, to dark blue for high edge weight (*value encoding*). Edges with high values stand out across the entire cube while smaller cells make it possible to see through the cube. While freely rotating the cube can give an overview of the data, it is often difficult to locate particular cells of interest, and to situate them along the time dimension. To tackle this problem, we can redundantly encode time by switching to a cell color mapping (*time encoding*, Figure 2-b) that uses a gradient ranging from blue (early time steps) via violet to orange (later time steps).

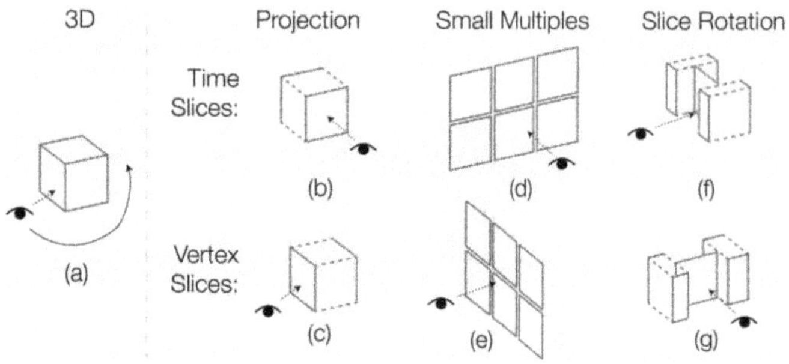


Figure 3. Cubix View design space. Columns indicate operations applied to the cube. Rows indicate operations applied to time (red × red) and vertex slices (blue × red), respectively. (a) 3D view, (b) time-projection view, (c) vertex-projection view, (d) time small multiples, (e) vertex small multiples, (f) time-slice-rotation, and (g) vertex-slice-rotation.

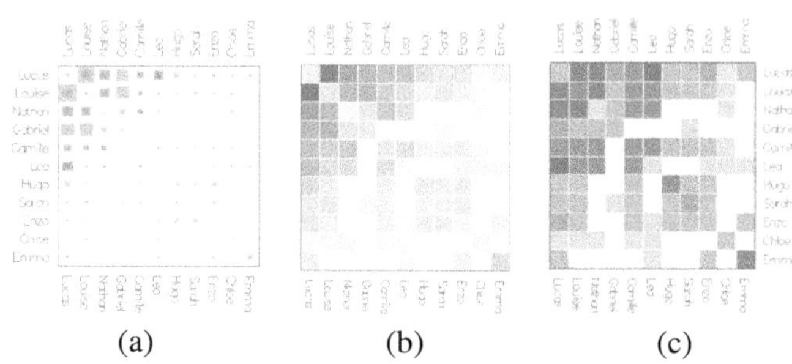


Figure 4. Cell color and size mappings in Time-projection view. (a) Cell color is mapped to time, and cell size to edge weight. (b) Constant cell size, with color mapped to edge weight shows accumulated edge weight over time. (c) Constant cell size and same color (gray) for all cells gives an idea of the number of edges in time vectors, independent of weight.

By looking at the cube in 3D, one can get an overview of the data, including the number of vertices in the network (rows and columns), the number of time steps, the number and density of edges (cells), and the distribution of edges over time. Rotating the cube gives a better impression of particular cells' location, and helps identify sparse and dense areas. From Figure 2 we can notice a spatio-temporal cluster that features a dense core of high-weight edges and a wide range of somewhat lower-weight edges. A significant number of smaller cells exist, almost equally distributed across the cube.

While the 3D view shows the entire dataset, it only shows the most obvious patterns. Other views can be derived from this default representation, which emphasize specific aspects of the network. Cubix currently implements seven predefined views, illustrated in Figure 3. Slice and camera positions are predefined, as well as the projection method (perspective projection for the 3D view, orthogonal projection in all other cases). Each view provides specific interaction capabilities, such as slice rotation or free camera rotation.

### View Navigation with the Cubelet Widget

Quick navigation between views is enabled by an interactive overview widget called the *Cubelet* (Figure 2-a). The Cubelet is a static 2D-isometric abstraction of the Matrix Cube that indicates the current view of the Matrix Cube. It uses the same color coding for the cube's dimensions as the actual Matrix Cube: blue for time, red for nodes. The Cubelet's left face corresponds to vertex slices (red × blue), the right face to time slices (red × red). Clicking on one of these faces transitions to the corresponding projection view. During the transition, the Matrix Cube smoothly rotates to show the selected side. In any of the projection views, the corresponding face of the Cubelet is highlighted. Dragging the mouse on the cube's faces transitions to the corresponding small-multiples view. When this happens, the Cubelet also changes its appearance, to make it look like if it were sliced. Clicking on the Cubelet's top face animates back to the 3D pivot.

### Exploring the Network's Aggregated Topology

Clicking on the Cubelet's right face rotates the cube to the time-projection view shown in Figure 4-a. Cubix switches from a perspective projection to an orthogonal projection. Consequently, all cells corresponding to the same edge over time become aligned (all cells in the same time vector become superimposed), and the topological structure of the network becomes clearly visible. The opacity slider (Figure 2-g) can be used to adjust cell translucency. Using the time color mapping, cells that are predominantly purple indicate an edge weight that decreases over time, while those that are predominantly orange indicate an increasing one.

Superimposed cells of different sizes appear nested inside of one another. A higher number of nested squares indicates more weight variability. Figure 4-c demonstrates an alternative cell color-and-size mapping that makes use of translucency, enabling users to evaluate how often an edge is present between two nodes over time. Darker cells indicate a longer presence or higher overall weight, which in this case translates to a larger number of co-publications between these two authors.

### Temporal Trends

Clicking on the Cubelet's left side rotates the Matrix Cube by 90 degrees to the right (Figure 5). In this view, we can see a heat-map with one column per time step (left to right). Rows still represent the network's vertices, showing the aggregated connectivity for each vertex (neighborhood vector), for every year. As illustrated in Figure 5, the general trend in this research group is towards more publications and collaboration (darker cells due to superimposition of translucent elements), except in 2008. We can further compare the connectivity over time for each vertex by comparing rows in this view. We can see that some authors always collaborated and did so increasingly over time (Lucas, Louise, Nathan), while others joined the team later (Gabriel, Hugo, Sarah, Enzo), or collaborated less frequently (Chloe).

### Topology of Individual Time steps

We can use the time range slider to change the set of time slices that are visible (Figure 2-e). A list next to the cube in the time-projection view shows the labels of elements in the projected dimension (Figure 5-b). Hovering over a label in this list shows only the corresponding slice.

This allows for quick navigation to, and between, time slices. If we want to see the different stages of topology evolution at-a-glance, dragging the mouse on the Cubelet's right face

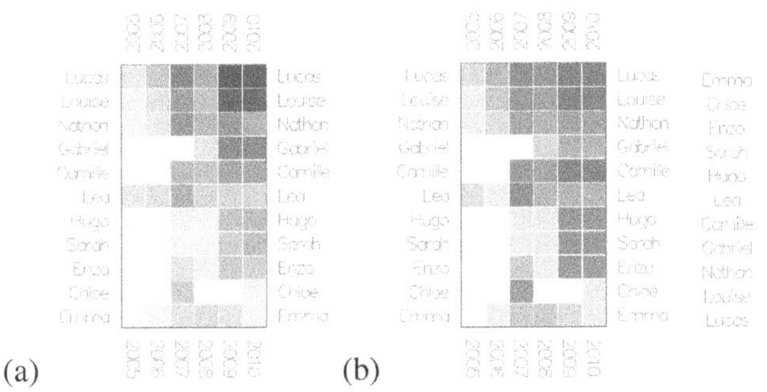


Figure 5. Temporal trends in the vertex-projection view

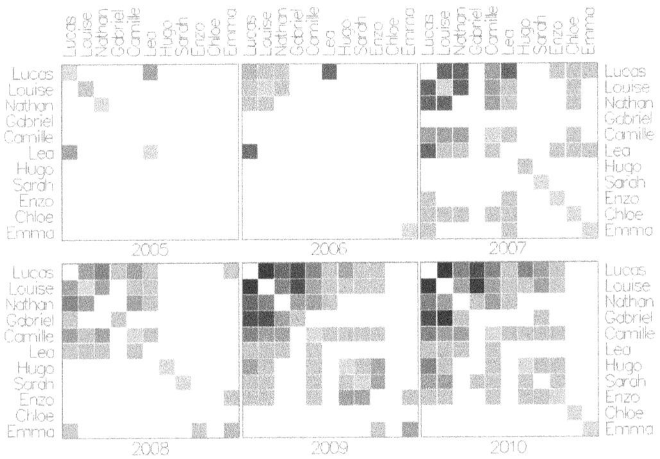


Figure 6. Time slices juxtaposed in the time-slices view. Darker cells correspond to more publications between people.

triggers an animation that decomposes the cube into individual time slices. Switching back to the edge-weight-to-color visual mapping, Figure 6 reveals four characteristic topological configurations, that explain the different patterns observed in Figure 5. Year 2007 seems to contain meaningful patterns, that the default reordering of rows and columns, computed globally over all time slices, fails to show (Figure 6). When only a subset of time steps are selected, asking for a new reordering takes only those steps into account, potentially yielding more meaningful visual patterns.

### Slice Rotation

Brushing through slices using the list displayed on the right-hand side in both projection views makes it possible to quickly browse through them one-at-a-time. However, all information about other slices is hidden. Projected slices (orthogonal to the camera) can be rotated 90 degrees, as illustrated in Figure 7 (cf. Figure 3-b and Figure 3-c), thus creating a focus+context view. Users can rotate as many slices as they want simultaneously. In a rotated slice, columns correspond to those of the projected dimension. Rows are still horizontally aligned with those of the projected slices. For example, the rotated slice in Figure 7 reveals that Camille collaborated with three people from the core cluster (Lucas, Louise, Nathan) over four consecutive years (2007-2010).

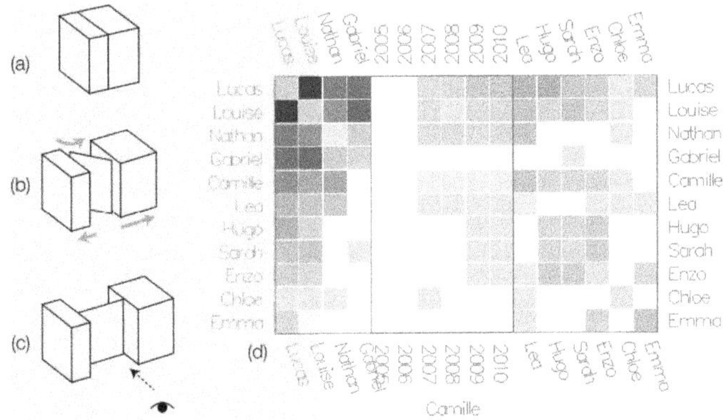


Figure 7. Rotation of a vertex slice. (a-c) schematic representation of the operation, (d) resulting focus+context visualization.

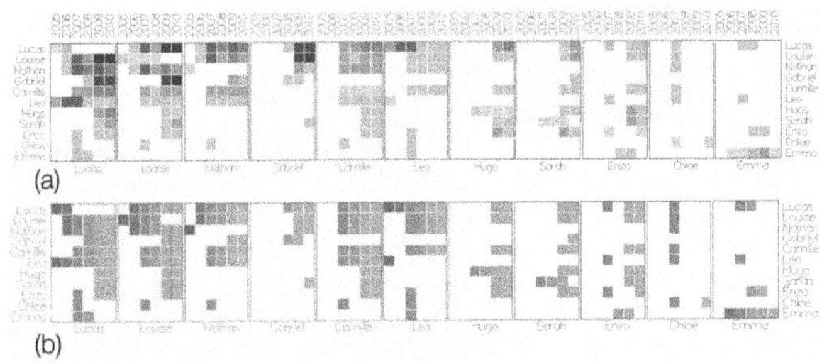


Figure 8. Vertex Small multiples view illustrating both color mappings. (a) Cells are colored according to edge weight, highlighting differences in weight across slices. (b) Mapping color to time-index facilitates topological comparisons across slices.

### Individual Collaboration Behavior

Switching to the vertex small-multiples view lets us compare all collaboration patterns across group members (Figure 8-a). The overview on all vertex slices reveals who has been most active and for what period of time. Slices for Hugo, Sarah and Enzo show very similar patterns. The same is true for Lucas, Louise and Camille. Switching to the time-index color mapping (Figure 8-b) makes it easier to compare ego-network topologies for a given time step.

### Cell Filtering

Cubix offers multiple filtering methods that let users specify what cells should be shown or hidden in the cube (and thus across all views). (i) Selecting one or more slices, by right clicking slice labels in the 3D view, automatically hides all others. If both horizontal and vertical slices are selected, only the cells at the intersection of all selected slices remain visible. Hovering over a hidden slice's label temporarily reveals that slice. (ii) Clicking a cell once hides all slices but those that contain this cell. Clicking it twice hides all cells but those that belong to the same time and neighborhood vectors. (iii) The edge weight range slider makes it possible to hide edges whose weight is below or above some thresholds, which is especially useful when the cube is complete. Cells filtered out using one of these methods can be made translucent instead of completely invisible, so that some context is retained. Finally, individual slices can be painted with a custom color, making them easier to keep track of across views.

## VALIDATION WITH EXPERTS

Visualizing dense, weighted dynamic networks is a problem in multiple application domains. For this first evaluation of matrix cubes, we contacted two researchers that face the issue of visualizing dynamic networks: an astronomer and a neurologist. We wanted to focus on the overall usefulness of Matrix Cubes and usability of Cubix through an open-ended evaluation using real data, so as to answer questions such as: Is the metaphor understandable? How well do experts manage to manipulate the cube and interpret the views? Can they gain insights about their data from this visualization?

### General Methodology

Both experts were approached independently and asked if they would be interested in trying to visualize their data with Cubix. We demonstrated Cubix using the co-authorship network described earlier in this paper. In both cases, the experts' feeling was that the approach had potential, and they agreed to provide us with actual data. Once their data had been imported in Cubix, we met again with each of the two experts for a longer session, walking them through the different views and features based on a sample of their own data. Experts then took control, looking at their data in more detail by themselves under our guidance as detailed below.

## ALMA

The Atacama Large Millimeter/submillimeter Array [26] is a state-of-the-art radio-telescope composed of 66 high-precision *antennas* currently under construction in the Chilean Andes. Observations are based on the principle of interferometry: a source in the sky is observed by a subset of 12-to-50 of those antennas, called an *array*. In a given array, all antennas are connected to the other ones in a pairwise manner, thus forming a fully-connected network. Edges of this network, called *baselines*, have several quantitative time-dependent variables associated with them, which astronomers are interested in looking at.

Astronomers currently use a tool developed in-house to plot these variables as scatterplots or line charts. While these charts may be able to produce legible visualizations for antenna-based variables, they do not scale to the number of baselines in an array (typically 1225 for 50 antennas). Still, astronomers need to either monitor in real-time or analyze a posteriori those data over numerous time steps.

Following the general methodology described above, we approached an ALMA astronomer. The session consisted of two parts. We used one of the four baseline-based variables available in the data he had provided (see below) for the walk-through. Then the astronomer took control of the computer, and visualized all four datasets, commenting on his findings and insights, and asking for help to get to a particular view when stuck (he was told that he could freely ask for our assistance). These two phases lasted 22 and 45 minutes, respectively. The entire session lasted 1.5 hours, including preliminary explanations and post-hoc discussions. We recorded the session and took pictures of meaningful views on the data for analysis once back in our lab.

#### *Data*

The dataset corresponds to a calibration, used to compute very precisely the (x,y,z) geographical position of antennas. For this, antennas point at a series of quasars that act as reference sources. Quasars are pointed at, one after another, by all antennas simultaneously. Each quasar represents one of the 34 time steps in the data. The data consists of four variables, each visualized independently in a separate cube: DELAY, Amplitude (AMP), Amplitude RMS (RMS), and signal-to-noise ratio (SNR). All are measured for 42 antennas, i.e., 861 baselines, for one particular baseband and one polarization only. Each cube thus consists of $42 \times 42 \times 34 \approx 60{,}000$ cells (see Figure 9-a).

#### *Usage Scenario*

We first provide a summary of the visual exploration process over the entire session, focusing on the main steps related to the key findings which are discussed afterwards.

We used the RMS data to give a walkthrough to the astronomer. Straight from the 3D overview, four time slices stood out, featuring larger values than other time steps, as illustrated in Figure 9-a. After briefly showing the time-projection view, we quickly switched to the vertex-projection view at the expert's request, as he was interested in getting a better look at the evolution of values over time (Figure 9-b). From this view, he confirmed his intuition that the four time slices spotted in the 3D overview were quasars that were too weak and should probably be removed from the catalogue of sources used for calibration. Based on the visual appearance of the four columns in the vertex-projection view, he further inferred that these four time steps might actually correspond to the same quasar observed 4 times, or to 2 quasars observed twice each. At the expert's request, we filtered out higher values corresponding to the weak sources, so as to be able to better compare the cells from other time steps visually (the value-to-color mapping adjusts cell color dynamically as higher-value cells get filtered out). The result looked homogeneous, leading the astronomer to the conclusion that there was no antenna-based problem, which would have appeared visually as one-or-more entire rows of cells with high values. We then finished the walkthrough by explaining both time and vertex small-multiples views, illustrating features such as brushing.

Now familiar with Cubix's main features, the astronomer started exploring the data on his own, switching to DELAY. In this data, he was looking for baselines whose delay varies over time, as this was not supposed to happen (delay should be more or less constant). He switched to the vertex-projection view, which shows time steps as columns. However, as all vertex slices were superimposed, it was difficult to spot specific baselines that would feature significant variability. The expert realized this, and decided to switch to the time-projection view. Some rows and columns stood out, indicating possible antenna-based problems. From there, he asked that we switch to the view that shows vertex slices as small multiples, as he wanted to get an overview of what particular antennas feature higher variability, something that can easily be seen in this view by visually scanning the whole

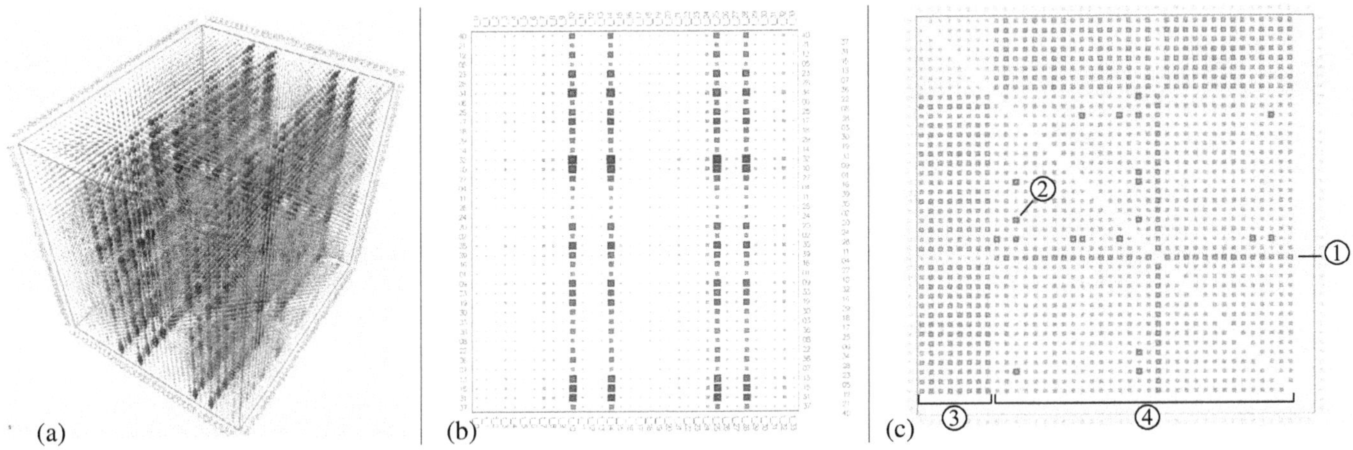


**Figure 9. ALMA dataset. (a) Overview of RMS in which four time steps seem to stand out. (b) The vertex-projection view of RMS confirms this and provides additional detail. (c) The time-projection view on AMP, showing an abnormal behavior of one specific antenna ①, various baseline specific outliers such as ②. A different behavior of the first eight antennas compared to the other ones is clearly visible: ③ vs. ④.**

set of small multiples (Figure 10). This view revealed another pattern: for some antennas, roughly half of the baselines had much larger delays than the other half. The astronomer switched back to stacked vertex slices to quickly brush through the slices in more detail. There was no clear explanation for this observation, which requires further investigation by looking at additional data not available here. We then switched to AMP data. The astronomer was very interested in the time-projection view, as the two main types of problems were readily apparent. First, antenna-based problems affect all baselines that connect to it, which visually translates into the corresponding row/column featuring a lot of variability (see ①). Second, problems affecting a single baseline, possibly due to, e.g., atmospherical changes, which visually translate into isolated cells featuring a lot of variability (see ②). Another pattern that clearly stood out in this view is the difference between the eight left-most columns ③ and the following ones ④, attributed to the different types of antennas that compose ALMA[1]. Finally, the astronomer looked at SNR data, identifying similar visual patterns, and then finished the session.

### Brain Function Activity

The second expert, a researcher in neurology, studies signal patterns between regions of the brain under different stimuli, collected using EEG-correlated fMRI [19]. He is interested in identifying time steps that feature a high activity level overall, connectivity patterns that reoccur over time, and which regions are active at specific moments. All of these can then be compared across different stimuli.

The neurologist currently uses spatial brain maps to explore his data, but the physical position of brain regions is not important when analyzing this type of dataset: maps do not properly convey the network's topology. Currently, no visualization faithfully represents his data since node-link diagrams fail to provide a legible view of such dense networks.

[1]We discussed the possibility that the antenna in ① could belong to group ③. This was ruled out because of the way the data was generated, with antennas sorted alphabetically, and thus by type.

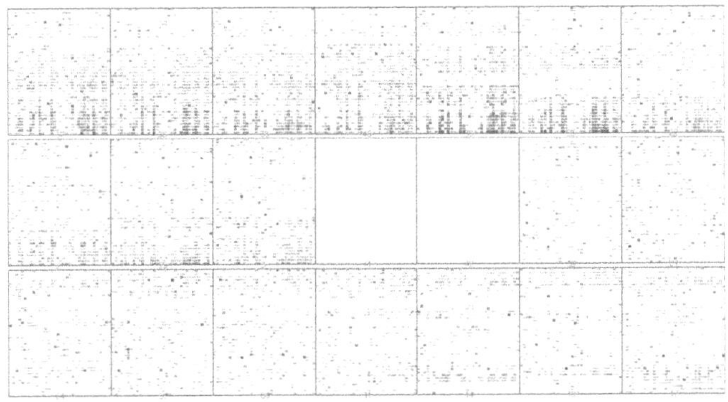

**Figure 10. ALMA DELAY data: vertex slices as small multiples. View cropped to show only 21 out of 42 slices. Similar patterns (reversed) appear in the lower half.**

Therefore, just like the astronomy expert, neurologists typically look at time-series for each region of the brain, without any visual feedback about the topology.

The methodology employed for the neurologist was slightly different than for the first expert. The neurologist was located on another continent, and thus sessions were conducted remotely using a videoconferencing tool. The neurologist was provided with the Cubix software; the system ran simultaneously on both ends, with screen sharing enabled. We conducted two sessions, with one day in-between the two. After looking at the data and explaining to us what it was about, the neurologist asked for a few changes to the visual representation to reflect domain-specific information. We planned for the second session to implement the requested changes and give him time to explore his data with the adapted version of Cubix. The second session was conducted under the same conditions, using the new visual representation.

#### *Data*

We obtained data about three different regions of the brain from multiple subjects, observed under 3 different stimuli. For each of these regions, signals for 50 different frequencies in 8-to-16 subregions were recorded. Several measures are used to characterize connectivity, such as Granger causal-

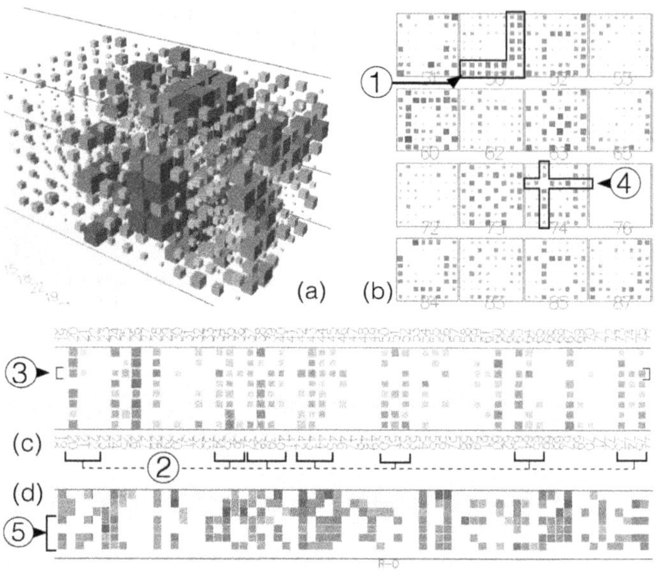

Figure 11. Brain connectivity data. 8 regions over a sample of 15 time steps. (a) Overview reveals that some time steps are more active than others. (b) Detailed view of 16 time slices. (c) Vertex-projection view, showing activity patterns and revealing one region more active than the others. (d) Individual vertex slice sending more than it receives.

ity, and we can only show one dynamic network at a time from this rich dataset in a matrix cube. The networks visualized in Cubix consist of 8 or 16 vertices over 150 time steps (5 minutes of recorded brain activity at a 2-second sampling frequency). Measures exist between any two regions, meaning that networks are fully-connected, the corresponding matrix cubes containing from $8 \times 8 \times 150 = 9600$ to $16 \times 16 \times 150 = 38400$ cells. Figure 11-a shows 15 out of 150 time steps for a network of 8 regions.

During the first session, the neurologist explained that edge weights have normalized values in $[-1.0, 1.0]$, and that edges of interest are those near the extrema. We added an additional color scale and mapping, emphasizing those values, as illustrated in Figure 11: 1.0 gets mapped to red, 0 to light gray, and $-1.0$ to blue. A new mapping of edge weight to cell size was also added, assigning smaller sizes to edges with lower absolute values. The range slider used to filter out edges based on their weight now features an option to invert the selection, so as to remove values in-between the two knobs rather than those outside the corresponding range.

### *Usage Scenario*

Data visualized during the first session corresponded to a resting phase (no visual stimulus, subjects' eyes closed). At the neurologist's request, the second session focused on data observed during a phase featuring visual stimuli. Using the new color and size mappings revealed the symmetric distribution of red and blue cells in the 3D overview (Figure 11-a). Several time steps also stood out as significantly denser than others, distributed over time. Switching to time-projection view made it possible to get a clear look at the denser time-slices, confirming the symmetry between red (sending) and blue (receiving) edges. Beyond symmetry, one pattern appeared consistently across all slices that feature a high level of activity, made even more apparent when reordering rows and columns based on their similarity: two or three regions received from exactly four other regions (blue cells in the same row) while sending signals to the remaining four regions (red cells in the same row, ①). Sending and receiving regions were the same. However, one of the two active regions also sent to the other one, not receiving any signal from it.

Switching to the vertex-projection view (Figure 11-c), salient patterns could be observed when looking at the temporal distance between highly-active time steps. The neurologist indicated again that edges with low absolute values were irrelevant; those got removed accordingly, keeping cells whose absolute value was larger than $|0.5|$ only. We adapted translucency as illustrated in Figure 11-b. Rotating some time slices in-place enabled the neurologist to recognize the topological patterns previously spotted in the time-projection view. Temporal patterns seemed randomly distributed but occurred in intervals of 3 or 4 time steps ②. As illustrated in Figure 11-c, one region was more active than the others ③. Switching to time small multiples (Figure 11-b) confirmed that region R-4 was indeed active in many time slices, and was often among the most active ones ④. Switching to the vertex small multiples, the neurologist found two regions that were more active than the others, one of them ⑤ sending more often than it received, and almost always sending to the same regions (Figure 11-d).

### Key Findings

**The cube metaphor was quickly understood. It helped, along with animated transitions, to switch between views.** Right from the start, both experts understood what the cube was about, as well as the views that were derived from it. For instance, as the view was animating from the 3D cube to the time-projection view, the astronomer made the following comment: *"Ah! ok, now you are stacking time."* Once he took over, he always managed to switch between views without assistance, sometimes hitting the wrong key but quickly recognizing that this was not the view he wanted. The neurologist used both the Cubelet and keyboard shortcuts. There was only a bit of confusion for the astronomer the first time we switched to the view that shows vertex slices as small multiples, but that view was then well understood and used, though the astronomer asked for assistance to go back to this particular view from the time-projection view. It is worth noting that he knew exactly what view he wanted; his problem was that he did not remember how to get there. Further evidence of the experts' understanding of the matrix cube comes from a comment the astronomer made as he was looking at DELAY data in the time-projection view. As he was looking for baselines featuring significant variability, i.e., squares within squares in a given cell, he realized on his own that for a given baseline, larger cells earlier-in-time would hide smaller cells that were behind them in this particular view, thus masking some types of variability patterns. This is indeed true; we then explained how to overcome this limitation in Cubix by, e.g, adjusting cell translucency to see through them, or by switching to another view. The astronomer also took for granted that cells filtered out in one view would still be hidden when transforming the cube to another view, without us mentioning this at all. We interpret this as further evidence that the cube was well-understood as a model/pivot view.

**Filtering, brushing and linking were useful.** To look at individual slices, the astronomer used the slice list on the right side in vertex- and time-projection views. Sometimes he looked at one particular antenna he had identified in another view, sometimes he browsed through slices to find antennas with particular characteristics hinted at by the default view, which shows all slices stacked. Filtering was also found useful, and the astronomer understood on his own that filtering was happening on the cube as an object, not on a particular view of it. He made one request: in addition to being able to select what slices to show, he wanted to select which slices to hide (which was at the time only possible by selecting all slices not to hide). The astronomer also mentioned that brushing and linking in the small multiple views was very helpful to compare particular values across slices.

**Cell color was always mapped to edge value.** The neurologist asked specifically for a new edge-weight-to-color mapping and used it exclusively. The astronomer was told about both original color mappings: time and value. He immediately stated that redundantly encoding time with color was of no interest to him, instead, he wanted cell color to reflect the associated edge value. The fact that most of the walkthrough was performed with cell size set to its maximum value for all edges (i.e., not reflecting the associated value) might have played a role in this, as there was then no other way in this configuration to visualize edge value.

**Row and column reordering are useful, but can be confusing.** Rows and columns of matrices can be either sorted alphabetically or reordered based on their similarity, so as to make some visual patterns such as clusters more apparent. By default, users are presented with the latter option. The astronomer had not realized the type of ordering, which was confusing to him at first, as he is used to looking at matrices sorted alphabetically, by antenna type and name. As a result, he was not expecting to see some of the visual patterns that appeared, and was instead expecting individual, isolated rows and columns to stand out. He realized this when we switched to *name ordering* while discussing possible differences due to antenna type. This alphabetically-sorted view felt much more familiar to him, as the visual patterns of clusters were no longer there to *"prevent him from seeing individual rows and columns."* However, the neurologist specifically requested that rows be reordered based on similarity when looking for patterns in the time-projection view.

**Matrix Cubes succeeded in providing a legible visualization where other approaches had failed so far.** Astronomers currently visualize data using line charts and scatterplots. While this worked fine during the early construction phase of the observatory with only a few antennas available, this solution clearly does not scale to the over a thousand baselines now formed by the almost full complement of 66 antennas. What the astronomer appreciated with Cubix was that he could clearly see patterns at once, such as antenna-based problems, without having to select and plot specific antenna pairs as he has to do now, and which is very tedious: *"With Cubix, you visualize it instantaneously. It is much faster."* He also enjoyed the fact that he could smoothly transition from one view to another. In the same vein, the neurologist commented: *"With your tool you just load the data and you see it [...] It is a very nice piece of work."* At the time of writing, both experts expressed interest in exploring their data further with Cubix. The astronomer is currently preparing additional datasets that he would like to explore with our system. The neurologist also stated that he wanted to further use Cubix in the coming weeks. The data he looked at was the result of a recent experiment, and he wanted to spend more time exploring it as to become more familiar with it.

## CONCLUSION AND FUTURE WORK

We introduced Matrix Cubes, a novel representation for dynamic weighted networks. We described how Cubix, our interactive system for the exploration of Matrix Cubes, can be used to visualize such networks by decomposing the cubes into meaningful 2D views. The design decisions made in Cubix were primarily aimed at making the cube model – and the associated interactions for manipulating it – both simple to understand and consistent across views on the data, so as to provide users with an effective metaphor.

The feedback we got from the two experts was encouraging: they both understood the cube metaphor and to navigate between views, which enabled them to make interesting observations about their data. Furthermore, the two experts stated that Cubix was the first system that actually gave them the opportunity to look at their data in an effective way. Both of them expressed interest in using it further to explore additional data in the future. However encouraging, this evaluation is only a first step and we need to further evaluate the Matrix Cube . A limitation of the study is that it only involved two domain experts. While they were from two very different domains (astronomy and neurology), Cubix should be evaluated with more experts to check that our results generalize across additional domains. Controlled experiments involving low-level network exploration and analysis tasks will also help identifying the strengths and weaknesses of the Matrix Cube approach compared to other dynamic network visualization approaches.

The Matrix Cube model is an effective metaphor that opens up a rich design space for complex data structure visualization. While the current model only supports undirected networks, we believe that it can be adapted to other data visualization problems and application domains. Possible extensions include support for multi-variate networks, as requested by one of the experts; directed networks and support for larger graphs by allowing users to interactively collapse and expand individual slices and cells.

Cubix is implemented in Java using OpenGL and is available for download at `http://www.aviz.fr/Research/Cubix`

## ACKNOWLEDGMENTS

We wish to thank the experts who used Cubix and gave us feedback: Denis Barkats from the Joint ALMA Office, National Radio Astronomy Observatory; Stephane Sockeel and

Habib Benali from the Laboratoire d'Imagerie Fonctionnelle, Université Pierre et Marie Curie Paris VI.

## REFERENCES


1. Ahn, J., Taieb-Maimon, M., Sopan, A., Plaisant, C., and Shneiderman, B. Temporal Visualization of Social Network Dynamics: Prototypes for Nation of Neighbors. In *Proc. Social Computing, Behavioral-Cultural Modeling and Prediction conference* (2011), 309–316.
2. Alper, B., Bach, B., Henry Riche, N., Isenberg, T., and Fekete, J.-D. Weighted Graph Comparison Techniques for Brain Connectivity Analysis. In *Proc. CHI*, ACM (2013), 483–492.
3. Beaudouin-Lafon, M. Designing interaction, not interfaces. In *Proc. AVI*, ACM (2004), 15–22.
4. Bezerianos, A., Chevalier, F., Dragicevic, P., Elmqvist, N., and Fekete, J. Graphdice: A system for exploring multivariate social networks. *Computer Graphics Forum 29*, 3 (2010), 863–872.
5. Boyandin, I., Bertini, E., Bak, P., and Lalanne, D. Flowstrates: An approach for visual exploration of temporal origin-destination data. *Computer Graphics Forum 30*, 3 (2011), 971–980.
6. Brandes, U., and Corman, S. R. Visual unrolling of network evolution and the analysis of dynamic discourse. *Information Visualization 2*, 1 (2003), 40–50.
7. Burch, M., Vehlow, C., Beck, F., Diehl, S., and Weiskopf, D. Parallel edge splatting for scalable dynamic graph visualization. *IEEE TVCG 17*, 12 (2011), 2344–2353.
8. Carpendale, S., Cowperthwaite, D. J., Tigges, M., Fall, A., and Fracchia, F. D. The Tardis: A Visual Exploration Environment for Landscape Dynamics. In *Proc. SPIE Conference on Visual Data Exploration and Analysis VI* (1999), 110–119.
9. Carpendale, S., Fall, A., Cowperthwaite, D., Fall, J., and Fracchia, F. Case study: visual access for landscape event based temporal data. In *Proc. Visualization*, IEEE (1996), 425–428.
10. Cassinelli, A. The Khronos Projector, June 2005. `http://www.k2.t.u-tokyo.ac.jp/members/alvaro/Khronos/`.
11. Collberg, C., Kobourov, S., Nagra, J., Pitts, J., and Wampler, K. A system for graph-based visualization of the evolution of software. In *Proc. SoftVis*, ACM (2003), 77–86.
12. Dwyer, T., and Gallagher, D. R. Visualising changes in fund manager holdings in two and a half-dimensions. *Information Visualization 3*, 4 (2004), 227–244.
13. Elmqvist, N., Dragicevic, P., and Fekete, J.-D. Rolling the dice: Multidimensional visual exploration using scatterplot matrix navigation. *Proc. InfoVis 2008 14*, 6 (2008), 1141–1148.
14. Farrugia, M., Hurley, N., and Quigley, A. Exploring temporal ego networks using small multiples and tree-ring layouts. In *Proc. ACHI*, IARIA (2011).
15. Fels, S., Lee, E., and Mase, K. Techniques for interactive video cubism. In *Proc. Multimedia (poster session)*, ACM (2000), 368–370.
16. Friedrich, C., and Eades, P. The marey graph animation tool demo. In *Proc. Graph Drawing*, Springer-Verlag (2001), 396–406.
17. Gatalsky, P., Andrienko, N., and Andrienko, G. Interactive analysis of event data using space-time cube. In *Proc. Information Visualization*, IEEE (2004), 145–152.
18. Ghoniem, M., Fekete, J.-D., and Castagliola, P. On the readability of graphs using node-link and matrix-based representations: a controlled experiment and statistical analysis. *Information Visualization 4*, 2 (2005), 114–135.
19. Goldman, R. I., Stern, J. M., Engel, J., and Cohen, M. S. Acquiring simultaneous EEG and functional MRI. *Clinical Neurophysiology 111*, 11 (2000), 1974– 1980.
20. Gove, R., Gramsky, N., Kirby, R., Sefer, E., Sopan, A., Dunne, C., Shneiderman, B., and Taieb-Maimon, M. NetVisia: Heat Map and Matrix Visualization of Dynamic Social Network Statistics and Content. In *Proc. SocialCom/PASSAT* (2011), 19–26.
21. Hascoët, M., and Dragicevic, P. Interactive graph matching and visual comparison of graphs and clustered graphs. In *Proc. AVI*, ACM (2012), 522–529.
22. Henry, N., and Fekete, J.-D. MatrixExplorer: a Dual-Representation System to Explore Social Networks. *IEEE TVCG 12*, 5 (2006), 677–684.
23. Kapler, T., and Wright, W. GeoTime information visualization. *Information Visualization 4*, 2 (2005), 136–146.
24. Kraak, M. J. The Space-Time Cube revisited from a Geovisualization Perspective. *Proc. International Cartographic Conference* (2003), 1988–1996.
25. Liu, Z., Navathe, S., and Stasko, J. Ploceus: Network-based visual analysis of tabular data. In *Proc. VAST*, IEEE (2011), 41–50.
26. Pietriga, E., Cubaud, P., Schwarz, J., Primet, R., Schilling, M., Barkats, D., Barrios, E., and Vila Vilaro, B. Interaction Design Challenges and Solutions for ALMA Operations Monitoring and Control. In *Proc. Astronomical Telescopes and Instr.*, SPIE (2012).
27. Reda, K., Tantipathananandh, C., Johnson, A., Leigh, J., and Berger-Wolf, T. Visualizing the evolution of community structures in dynamic social networks. In *Proc. EuroVis*, Eurographics Assoc. (2011), 1061–1070.
28. Sallaberry, A., Muelder, C., and Ma, K.-L. Clustering, visualizing, and navigating for large dynamic graphs. In *Proc. Graph Drawing*, Springer (2013), 487–498.
29. Shi, L., Wang, C., and Wen, Z. Dynamic network visualization in 1.5D. In *Proc. PacificVis*, IEEE (2011), 179–186.
30. Stein, K., Wegener, R., and Schlieder, C. Pixel-oriented visualization of change in social networks. In *Proc. Int. Conf. on Advances in Social Networks Analysis and Mining*, IEEE (2010), 233–240.
31. Yi, J.-S., Elmqvist, N., and Lee, S. TimeMatrix: Visualizing Temporal Social Networks Using Interactive Matrix-Based Visualizations. *IJHCI 26*, 11-12 (2010), 1031–1051.

# À Table! Improving Temporal Navigation in Soccer Ranking Tables

**Charles Perin**
INRIA, Univ. Paris-Sud &
CNRS-LIMSI
Bat. 660, Univ. Paris-Sud,
91405 Orsay, France
charles.perin@inria.fr

**Romain Vuillemot**
Harvard University
Cambridge, MA, USA
romain_vuillemot@hks.harvard.edu

**Jean-Daniel Fekete**
INRIA
Bat. 660, Univ. Paris-Sud,
91405 Orsay, France
jean-daniel.fekete@inria.fr

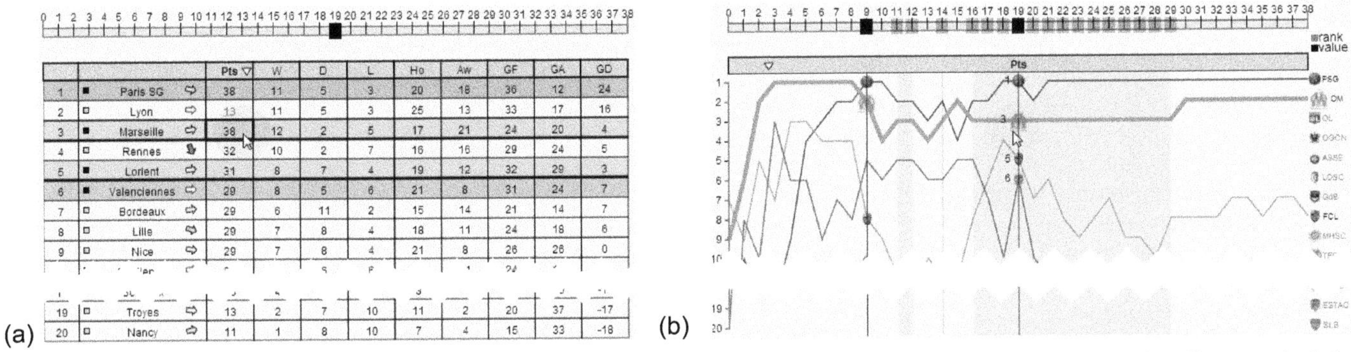


**Figure 1. (a) Drag-Cell and (b) Viz-Rank, two novel temporal navigation techniques for ranking tables. Drag-Cell is a direct manipulation technique to browse values over time by dragging them; Viz-Rank uses transient visualization (line chart) to show the values of cells over time. For both techniques, the temporal slider on the top provides feedback on the current temporal navigation.**

## ABSTRACT

This article introduces *À Table!*, an enhanced soccer ranking table providing temporal navigation by combining two novel interaction techniques. Ranking tables order soccer teams represented as rows, according to values of columns containing attributes *e. g.,* accumulated points, or number of scored goals. Because they represent a snapshot of a championship at a time $t$, tables are regularly updated with new results. Such updates usually change the rows order, which makes the tracking of a specified team over time difficult. We observed that the tables available on the web do not support tracking such changes very well, are generally hard to read, and lack interactions. This contrasts with the extensive use of comments on temporal trends found in soccer analysts articles. To better support such analyzes, the two interactive techniques presented allow exploration of time, and are designed to preserve users' flow: Drag-Cell is based on direct manipulation of values to browse ranks; Viz-Rank uses a transient line chart of team ranks to visually explore a championship. An on-line evaluation with 143 participants shows that each technique efficiently supports a set of important temporal tasks not supported by current ranking tables. This paves the way for introducing efficient advanced visual exploration techniques to millions of soccer enthusiasts who use tables everyday.


*CHI 2014*, April 26–May 1, 2014, Toronto, Ontario, Canada.

http://dx.doi.org/10.1145/2556288.2557379

### Author Keywords
Ranking Tables; Soccer; Temporal Navigation; Visualization

### ACM Classification Keywords
H.5.m. Information Interfaces and Presentation (e.g. HCI): Miscellaneous

## INTRODUCTION

Every day, millions of soccer enthusiasts study web sites, newspapers, or other media to learn about their favorite team's current ranking and how it compares historically. One way to present this information is to use ranking tables. Soccer ranking tables show results for a given championship, at a given day. Rows are teams, and columns are statistics. Column types include, for example: the total points per season, number of wins, draws, and lost games. Tables are updated once a round of games is over, and can become quite large. Assuming a championship with 20 teams, a table will be updated 38 times since each team plays against each other twice.

We conducted an empirical study of 51 articles (weekly and monthly summaries of soccer championships) from major soccer websites, and collected 44 pseudo-interactive soccer tables to investigate how they support temporal tasks. Our first observation was that ranking tables are not designed for comparison, despite the need for analysts and the existence of guidelines [21, 15]. Furthermore, 77.3% of tables do not implement column sorting, and 73% of them do not provide any aid for temporal navigation although it may be useful for interactive exploration [15, 9]. Finally, we did not observe any use of visualization, however it provides compact representation for multidimensional data [15, 9] and displays trends over long time periods with line charts [13, 17].

We present *À Table!*, an enhanced ranking table combining two novel temporal navigation techniques. DRAG-CELL is a direct manipulation technique to browse values over time by dragging them into the *Value* domain; VIZ-RANK uses a line chart to show the values of cells over time, in the *Time* domain. Both techniques follow Bederson [4] principles to preserve users' flow, to focus on tasks and prevent interruptions.

We conducted an on-line evaluation to assess how standard interactions with ranking tables (sorting and changing time with a slider), along with the two novel techniques, DRAG-CELL and VIZ-RANK, can be effective for temporal tasks. Our evaluation shows that the novel techniques efficiently support temporal tasks, which are currently not supported by ranking tables. We discuss the design implications of our improvements and give some scenarios to apply *À Table!* to other domains of application.

The contributions of this paper are as follows:

1. A Domain description and task analysis for temporal navigation techniques.
2. Two new techniques for temporal navigation in ranking tables, one in the value domain (DRAG-CELL) and one in the time domain (VIZ-RANK).
3. A crowdsourced evaluation of the two techniques along with standard navigation techniques; we then discuss which technique is well suited to which task according to the results and present the main takeaways from the experiment.

Such results provide a framework for further experiments with temporal tasks, and the design of novel navigation techniques in both the *Value* domain and the *Time* domain. Numerous application areas where ranking tables are important would benefit from these results.

## BACKGROUND AND RELATED WORK

Soccer ranking tables (Figure 2) are standard ranking tables, *i. e.* tabular data vertically ordered according to values in *one* column. Ranking tables have been extensively explored using summarization, interaction and visualization techniques. As far as we know, temporal exploration in tables has never been investigated in a comprehensive way.

A rank is an ordering technique taking as input a set of items $S$ (*e. g.,* teams) and provides a permutation of these items according to one dimension (*e. g.,* points, goals scored). A rank is a function $\text{RANK} : S \rightarrow 0, ..., |S|-1$, that generates up to $|S|!$ permutations, *i. e.* the number of ways the items in the set can be uniquely ordered [11]. Ranks apply to dimensions (columns) $D$, $|D| > 0$. Finally, a rank can be applied to *temporal* values, where $t \in T$, with $T$ a set of discrete events (*e. g.,* games in a championship). $S_{d_i,t_j}$ is the ranking table,

Rank according to number of points
Number of points
Dimensions to compute the number of points

| | | Team | Pts | W | D | L | Ho | Aw | GF | GA | GD |
|---|---|---|---|---|---|---|---|---|---|---|---|
| 1 | — | Paris-SG | **83** | 25 | 8 | 5 | 43 | 40 | 69 | 23 | 46 |
| 2 | — | Marseille | **71** | 21 | 8 | 9 | 40 | 31 | 42 | 36 | 6 |
| 3 | — | Lyon | **67** | 19 | 10 | 9 | 37 | 30 | 61 | 38 | 23 |
| 4 | ▲ | Nice | **64** | 18 | 10 | 10 | 38 | 26 | 57 | 46 | 11 |
| 5 | ▼ | Saint-Etienne | **63** | 16 | 15 | 7 | 37 | 26 | 60 | 32 | 28 |
| 6 | ▼ | Lille | **62** | 16 | 14 | 8 | 34 | 28 | 59 | 40 | 19 |
| 7 | ▲ | Bordeaux | **55** | 13 | 16 | 9 | 32 | 23 | 40 | 34 | 6 |
| 8 | ▼ | Lorient | **53** | 14 | 11 | 13 | 36 | 17 | 57 | 58 | -1 |
| 9 | ▼ | Montpellier | **52** | 15 | 7 | 16 | 38 | 14 | 54 | 51 | 3 |
| 10 | — | Toulouse | **51** | 13 | 12 | 13 | 28 | 23 | 49 | 47 | 2 |
| 11 | ▲ | Valenciennes | **48** | 12 | 12 | 14 | 33 | 15 | 49 | 53 | -4 |
| 12 | — | Bastia | **47** | 13 | 8 | 17 | 30 | 17 | 50 | 66 | -16 |
| 13 | ▼ | Rennes | **46** | 13 | 7 | 18 | 23 | 23 | 48 | 59 | -11 |
| 14 | — | Reims | **43** | 10 | 13 | 15 | 31 | 12 | 33 | 42 | -9 |
| 15 | — | AC Ajaccio | **42** | 9 | 15 | 14 | 26 | 16 | 39 | 51 | -12 |
| 16 | ▲ | Sochaux | **41** | 10 | 11 | 17 | 23 | 18 | 41 | 57 | -16 |
| 17 | ▼ | Evian-TG | **40** | 10 | 10 | 18 | 25 | 15 | 46 | 53 | -7 |
| 18 | ▲ | Nancy | **38** | 9 | 11 | 18 | 20 | 18 | 38 | 58 | -20 |
| 19 | ▼ | Troyes | **37** | 8 | 13 | 17 | 26 | 11 | 43 | 61 | -18 |
| 20 | — | Brest | **29** | 8 | 5 | 25 | 18 | 11 | 32 | 62 | -30 |

Last team evolution
Team logo

**Figure 2. Illustrative example of a "complete" table at time $t$, featuring the most frequent designs and embedded visualizations. Pts: number of points; W, D, L: number of Wins, Draws, Losses; Ho, Aw: number of points at Home and Away; GF, GA, GD: Goals For (scored), Against (conceded), Difference (GF-GA).**

which is a *snapshot* of a championship, ranked according to a dimension $d_i$ at a time $t_j$.

A soccer ranking table usually has the following properties: $|S| = 20$ teams; $|D| = 10$ dimensions; $|T| = (|S| - 1) \times 2$, *i. e.* $|T| = 38$ games; $0 \leq t \leq 38$. An important property of permutations in soccer championships is that the higher $t$ is, the less the teams' permutation amplitude is important because teams tend to have high points difference.

Ranking tables display tabular data and their visual design normally obey to guidelines. Tufte [21] suggests that minor visual improvements, such as vertical alignment of characters and row coloring with zebra patterns, enable comparison tasks and reduce errors. Interacting with the rank *order* help users perform some tasks (*e. g.,* finding maximum or minimum values) faster, without scanning all the rows. Many software packages, such as spreadsheets, implement ranking interactions. They also provide formulas to summarize rows for more compact representations with *Pivot tables* [23] by computing counts or totals. The same principles can be applied to columns with statistics such as averages of multiple columns or min/max values to provide other ranking mechanisms [15].

Summarization of tables is an important challenge because rankings are often longer than the screen. Visualization techniques can provide compact representation of cells. TableLens [15] represents tables using Focus+Context principles, collapsing rows to their minimum size or up to a pixel. This enables representing large tables on one screen as long as the number of rows is less or equal than the number of pixels. However, one row is always expanded as a focus and the

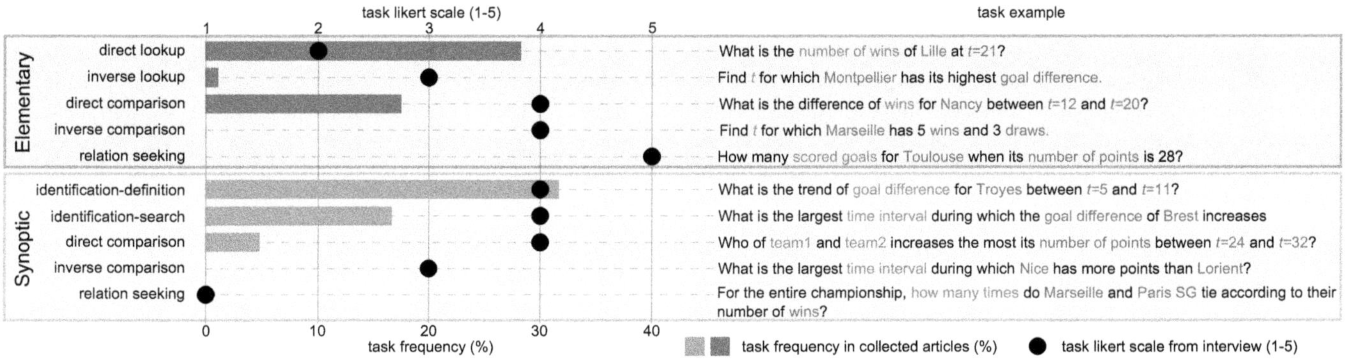


**Figure 3. Extracted task categories mapped to Andrienko et al. task taxonomy for temporal data, in percent of the collected articles. Black dots indicate how a soccer expert analyst estimates each category's relevance on a Likert scale from 1 (not relevant at all) to 5 (highly relevant). On the right are exemplary tasks for the categories. Red words are the unknown variable, blue words are the known variables.**

content of the cells is visible. LineUp [9] also uses nested compact visualizations in tables, but for headers showing the distribution of values contained in the rows beneath.

Ranking also plays an important role in discovery, particularly when tables are represented as a grid layout where visual variables such as color encode values. It results in heatmap-like representations [20], and ranking becomes the primary interaction for finding patterns [16]. Such tables may become very large and require space transformation techniques, such as zooming or space folding techniques [8] to bring rows and columns back together for comparison.

Visualization techniques to display ranks are mainly inspired by line charts [13], and are also called *bump charts* because of the visual effect that permutations provide. Slope Graph [21] plots items' *values* on two vertical axis—one for each time $t_1$ and $t_2$—and connects similar items from one axis to another with a line. The slope of the line is a visual cue that conveys the importance of the items' value change. However, some empty space may appear within the chart and elements may overlap. Several recent attempts produced compact charts reducing the amount of space and overlapping, while handling scalability. RankExplorer [17] shows items ranking as a flow, with glyphs wherever two items swap their ranks, or when an item has a particular increase in rank. Generally, visualization techniques are low-dimensional projections of data, that do not keep the original multidimensional flavor and interactivity of tables. They may also break users' flow [4] because tabular layouts are too different from line charts, which require a cognitive overhead for users to connect both.

In summary, existing table improvements tackle the challenge of better sorting, summarizing, and visualizing tables. These techniques are usually not trivial for a non-expert, which may explain why we did not find any in our empirical study. Another reason might be that techniques are not specifically tailored for temporal navigation, as time is usually a tricky dimension that requires specific attention.

## EMPIRICAL STUDY OF SOCCER RANKING TABLES

We conducted an empirical study to better understand current soccer ranking tables design practices. Over the 44 tables we collected, we observed that temporal navigation is rarely supported, unless the table uses non-dynamic drop-down lists. We also investigated the use of time in soccer newspapers by collecting 51 articles. We realized that they constantly refer to temporal trends or team performances during a time period, that current table designs do not support well.

### Time in Soccer Articles

We collected and analyzed 51 soccer articles, mainly from two highly influential and visited websites: L'équipe[1] (70%) weekly summaries for the entire 2012/2013 Ligue 1 Championship in France; and premierleague.com[2] (20%) monthly summaries of the 2012/2013 Premier League Championship in the UK. This was completed with articles from Yahoo sports, Wikipedia and other soccer websites (10%). The articles we collected outlined main events of the week or month, and illustrated them with statistics.

Out of the articles, we extracted up to 33 different tasks the journalists had to perform to write these summaries. Then, we grouped similar tasks into *generic* categories. For example, both tasks *"What is the number of points of Paris SG at week 17?"* and *"How many goals has Marseille scored until week 5?"* are subtasks of the generic category *"What is the* `VALUE` *of* `TEAM` *at* $t$*?"*, where `TEAM` and `t` are the two known variables and `VALUE` the unknown one. This grouping resulted in 18 generic task categories.

We observed that all the tasks categories are temporal. Indeed, even the most basic task, such as *"What is the* `VALUE` *of* `TEAM`*?"* implies knowing when to look at the value. When $t$ is not explicitly written, it is implicitly the latest week of the championship. We also observed that the most important column for ranking tables is the number of points of a team, determining its rank in the championship. However, the other dimensions also occur, to improve the summary details and analysis. For example, analysts often report: the number of scored goals or wins for the last $n$ games of a team; the team's performances at home; or a series of consecutive games with the same result (*e. g.,* 5 losses in a raw).

To structure our analysis, we mapped the categories to the task taxonomy for temporal data by Andrienko et al. [3]. Figure 3 illustrates the mapping and provides examples. They classify

[1] `http://www.lequipe.fr`
[2] `http://www.premierleague.com/`

the tasks into two categories. 1) *Elementary tasks* are *local* tasks where the object of interest is a given value or a given time. For example, such tasks are value estimation (*e. g.*, finding extrema [1]), comparison of values at different times and time retrieval according to a given value. 2) *Synoptic tasks* are *global* tasks involving the user to take into account a set of values or a time interval. For example, such tasks are trend estimation, trend comparison, and finding time intervals with a given trend. Both categories contain *direct* and *inverse* tasks. Direct tasks consist of estimating a value or a trend according to a given time or time interval. Inverse tasks consist of estimating the time or time interval for which a dimension has a given value or trend. Finally, *relation-seeking* tasks consist of finding relations between dimensions, values and time. For example, such a task consists of comparing the value of a dimension for one team with the value of another dimension of another team, at different times.

We also conducted an interview with a soccer analyst in charge of an influential French web site[3] and asked him to evaluate the fitness of each task category for soccer (Figure 3, Likert scale values). One interesting result is that the expert considers some *categories* to be important, despite not found in articles (*e. g.*, elementary relation-seeking tasks), suggesting that those tasks are probably unconsciously in the head of our expert but that he can not perform them with his current tools.

The expert and the task analysis together legitimate the tasks that we classified in the taxonomy. The tasks our expert mentioned are, according to him, difficult to perform. In particular because they involve ranks that change over time, which are difficult to track with series of static tables. This suggests that journalists have important questions that they are not easily able to answer. Consequently, we focus on supporting tasks and analysis questions that occur in this particular domain (i.e. temporal navigation in ranking tables) in the rest of the paper.

### Soccer Ranking Tables Visual and Interactive Design

We collected a series of 44 ranking tables for soccer, from UK (39%), France (35%), Spain (11%), Argentina (9%), Brazil and US (3% each). We extracted and ranked the visual features of the collected tables, such as colors and decorations.

An example of an important feature in soccer tables is the background color for the top-$k$ ranks, such as the top-3 ranks that qualify for the Champion's League. Or the bottom-$k$ that indicates which team will downgrade to a minor league. Such an apparently small visual aid is actually very useful, to immediately know which team will earn additional revenues with Champion's Leagues games, or will lose revenues by playing in a less popular league the next year.

For the top-3 rank, we found that only 50% of the tables highlight the corresponding areas, and their design is inconsistent (*e. g.*, icons, colored rows, bold/dashed separators, colored text, and gray scale). Tables also make use of Zebra (50%) and embed visualizations: 27.3% show team logos, 29.5% add an icon encoding the latest ranking evolution, and 13.6% represent the latest results using colored circles. As a reference, Figure 2 shows a *full* table, with the most frequent features.

[3] `http://www.cahiersdufootball.net/`

One of the main takeaways from our findings is that interaction is rarely available. At best, the table provides the most common column sorting (for 22.7% of analyzed ranking tables). At times, the table provides widgets to interact with the temporal dimension: dropdown lists (11%), range selection (6.8%), next/previous arrows (4.5%), discrete slider (2.3%). However, it usually triggers a page reload, making the tracking of changes between the two tables difficult.

We also observed an interesting type of ranking table mapping rows on an absolute scale (linear scale of values, in this case points) rather than the relative scale (linear scale of ranks). It is referred as *Absolute scale rank*. Similarly as for Slope Graph [21], it gives a better idea of the team's distribution at a given time. However, it requires more space as the count of rows for such a table is not the number of teams, but the difference of points between the first and the last team.

### Time Navigation

Only 27% (12/44) of the tables implement temporal navigation while both soccer ranking tables and analyst tasks heavily rely on time. When available, changing $t$ is usually cumbersome, with standard widgets—certainly because implemented in every GUI—such as:

- Drop-down lists to directly jump to a specific time. They cannot be used to dynamically browse a time interval but are very efficient to select a particular time.
- Arrow widgets to jump to previous or next tables, with some shortcuts to the beginning or the end of the championship. They are efficient to navigate sequentially, step by step.
- Range slider for 6.8% (3/44), to select the data in $[t_i, t_j]$ and compute the cell values between these two times.
- slider for 2.3% (one table) to support temporal navigation, similarly to a seeking bar to scrub videos.

The results from our study highlight the lack of temporal navigation mechanisms, and only one table featured a slider which would be recommended as an efficient way to explore such a quantitative data space [19]. We are not able to give any explanation. From a technical perspective, standard widgets are implemented in `<HTML>` and the data to compute ranking tables are relatively small and freely available. From a user perspective, we showed a dynamic slider to our soccer expert and he found it of great value, wondering himself why he does not provide one on his website.

## IMPROVING TEMPORAL NAVIGATION

*À Table!* is an advanced ranking table that includes current ranking table practices (Figure 4), with two novel techniques for temporal navigation: DRAG-CELL is based on direct manipulation of values to browse ranks; VIZ-RANK uses a transient visualization of team ranks (line chart) to explore a championship. Those techniques aim at improving the support of temporal tasks we introduced in Figure 3.

### Features from Current Ranking Tables

*À Table!* is a ranking table, along with the following features:

- *Temporal Slider* to give both an overview of the championship, and to provide a continuous temporal navigation.

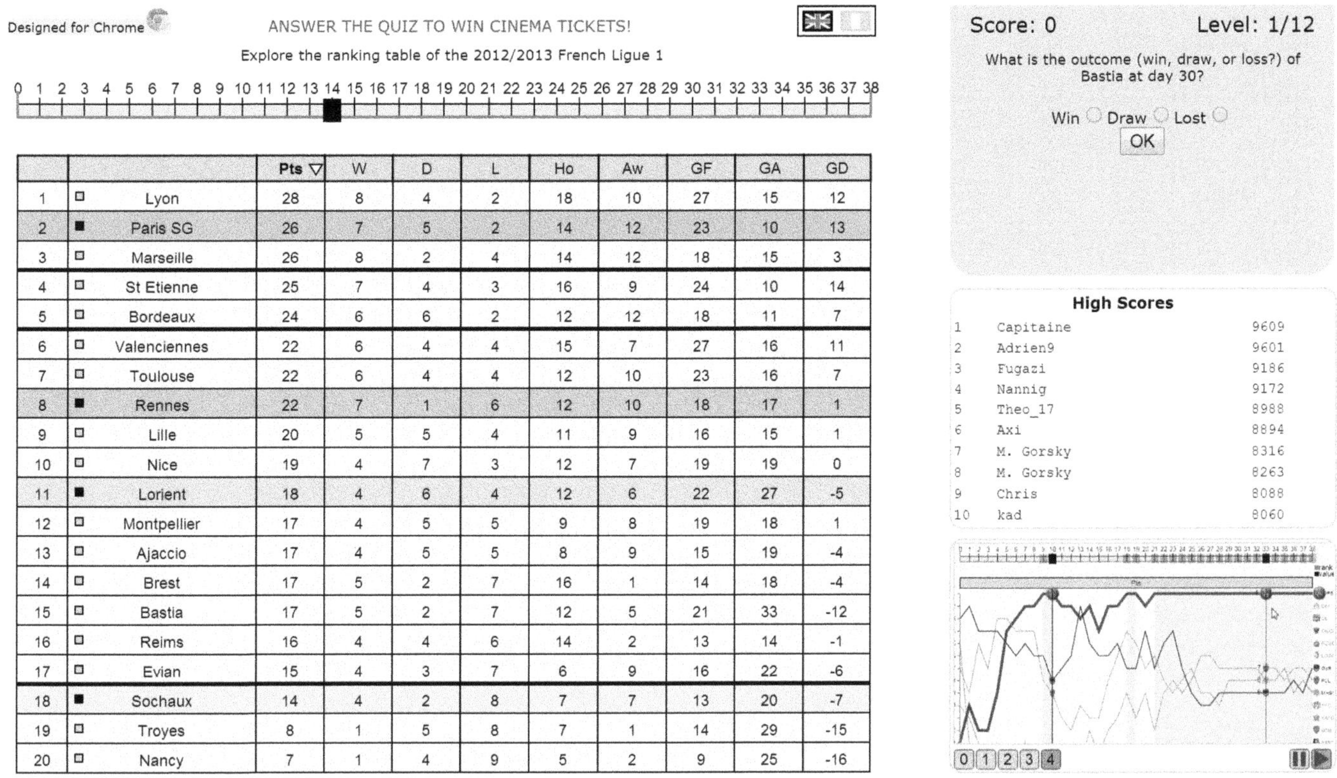


| | | | Pts ▽ | W | D | L | Ho | Aw | GF | GA | GD |
|---|---|---|---|---|---|---|---|---|---|---|---|
| 1 | □ | Lyon | 28 | 8 | 4 | 2 | 18 | 10 | 27 | 15 | 12 |
| 2 | ■ | Paris SG | 26 | 7 | 5 | 2 | 14 | 12 | 23 | 10 | 13 |
| 3 | □ | Marseille | 26 | 8 | 2 | 4 | 14 | 12 | 18 | 15 | 3 |
| 4 | □ | St Etienne | 25 | 7 | 4 | 3 | 16 | 9 | 24 | 10 | 14 |
| 5 | □ | Bordeaux | 24 | 6 | 6 | 2 | 12 | 12 | 18 | 11 | 7 |
| 6 | □ | Valenciennes | 22 | 6 | 4 | 4 | 15 | 7 | 27 | 16 | 11 |
| 7 | □ | Toulouse | 22 | 6 | 4 | 4 | 12 | 10 | 23 | 16 | 7 |
| 8 | ■ | Rennes | 22 | 7 | 1 | 6 | 12 | 10 | 18 | 17 | 1 |
| 9 | □ | Lille | 20 | 5 | 5 | 4 | 11 | 9 | 16 | 15 | 1 |
| 10 | □ | Nice | 19 | 4 | 7 | 3 | 12 | 7 | 19 | 19 | 0 |
| 11 | ■ | Lorient | 18 | 4 | 6 | 4 | 12 | 6 | 22 | 27 | -5 |
| 12 | □ | Montpellier | 17 | 4 | 5 | 5 | 9 | 8 | 19 | 18 | 1 |
| 13 | □ | Ajaccio | 17 | 4 | 5 | 5 | 8 | 9 | 15 | 19 | -4 |
| 14 | □ | Brest | 17 | 5 | 2 | 7 | 16 | 1 | 14 | 18 | -4 |
| 15 | □ | Bastia | 17 | 5 | 2 | 7 | 12 | 5 | 21 | 33 | -12 |
| 16 | □ | Reims | 16 | 4 | 4 | 6 | 14 | 2 | 13 | 14 | -1 |
| 17 | □ | Evian | 15 | 4 | 3 | 7 | 6 | 9 | 16 | 22 | -6 |
| 18 | ■ | Sochaux | 14 | 4 | 2 | 8 | 7 | 7 | 13 | 20 | -7 |
| 19 | □ | Troyes | 8 | 1 | 5 | 8 | 7 | 1 | 14 | 29 | -15 |
| 20 | □ | Nancy | 7 | 1 | 4 | 9 | 5 | 2 | 9 | 25 | -16 |

**Figure 4. *À Table!* integration into a web page for on-line evaluation. The interactive table along with the temporal slider is on the left; the quiz, the high scores and navigable animated GIFS as explanations on the right.**

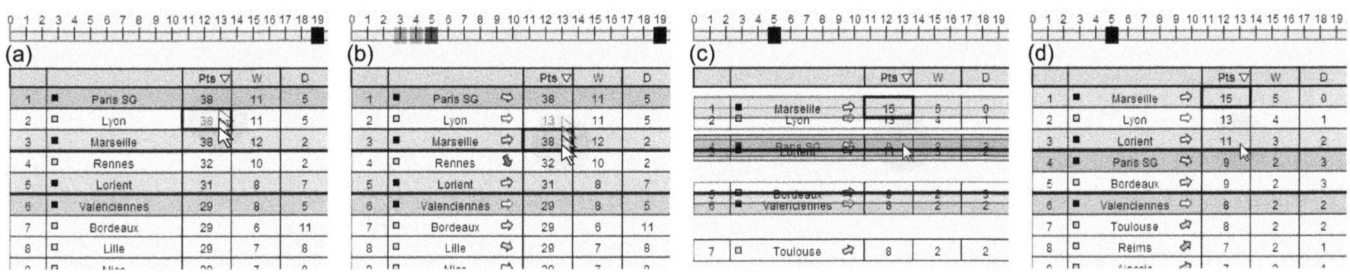

**Figure 5. DRAG-CELL: (a) dragging up and down the value of a cell (in this case, Points of Team Lyon) makes this value change (b) for the set of values it can have, and colored arrows indicate how teams would behave if the drag was released (green to red arrows). (c-d) Releasing the drag animates the rows to their new position.**

The slider is also synchronized with the two new interaction techniques we describe below to convey visual feedback.

- *Multiple teams selection* by clicking on team names to select and highlight their row, to facilitate their tracking over time.
- *Column sorting* by clicking on the table's headers to apply the `rank` function over a specific dimension.

## Design Philosophy for the Novel Techniques

We designed DRAG-CELL and VIZ-RANK with the challenge of preserving users' flow. We followed Bederson [4] principles by supporting both novice and experts with the same display. While tabular display remains the default view, novel techniques are activated with specific mouse interactions and new representations are animated to prevent users' interruptions. User is always in control with incremental actions and a visual feedback to constantly show what he is doing.

Because the design space for novel techniques is important, we decided to focus on two techniques which support specific temporal tasks that ranking tables or standard widgets do not currently support: DRAG-CELL lets the user interact in the *value domain* and VIZ-RANK in the *time domain*.

## Novel Technique 1: Direct Manipulation of Values

From the task analysis, we observed that the expert estimated as important several inverse tasks which were not frequent in journalist articles. Inverse tasks are challenging to perform using standard tables and it may explain why journalists avoid these tasks. We designed DRAG-CELL to make easier to perform these difficult tasks by interacting with cell values directly (*e. g.,* the number of points of a team): the user manipulates the *value domain* instead of the *time domain*, unlike standard navigation techniques such as a temporal slider. Typically, DRAG-CELL allows users to quickly find if

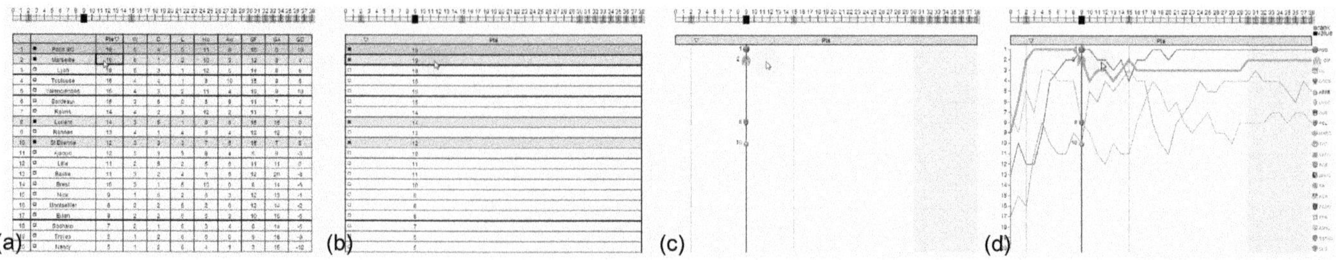

Figure 6. Table to VIZ-RANK: (a) clicking on a cell of a team for a dimension makes (b) the dimension's column grow horizontally, stretching the other columns until they disappear; then (c-d) the cells fade out and the time series of the cell's value for the team fades in. Line charts with a thinner stroke shows previously selected teams' line charts.

and when a value was reached. For example, a frequent task consists of finding the time when a team reaches 42 points; this specific value being the theoretical minimum number of points a team needs to be safe from the downgrade area.

DRAG-CELL follows the principle of direct manipulation [18], with teams as objects of interest and is inspired by Tangle [22]. The visual instance of teams are rows, and each cell can be dragged to explore the values of the cell itself over $t$ (Figure 5). Releasing the drag changes the value of $t$ for the table to the local $t_c$ of the cell. The user's flow is as follows:

1. **Start:** DRAG-CELL is activated by a mouse *drag* on a cell.
2. Then by dragging the mouse up and down, the cell value changes for all possible values for this cell.
3. Arrows indicate the preview of each team's behavior over time if the drag was released: the arrows range from pointing down and red (*e. g.,* the team is going down a lot) to heading up and green (*e. g.,* the team is going up a lot).
4. Additionally, the temporal slider displays a visual feedback as a preview of the current $t_c$.
5. **End:** Once the drag is released, $t_c$ is applied to the table. Rows permute with animation to their new rank position.

### Novel Technique 2: Line Charts as Transient Objects

VIZ-RANK displays a temporary or *transient* line chart when a user clicks on a cell (Figure 7). This line chart displays the teams' ranks over the whole championship. The user can click on one point on the chart and $t$ is set according to the corresponding value. The user's flow is as follows:

1. **Start:** VIZ-RANK is activated by a mouse *click* on a cell.
2. Then, an animated staged transition [10] transforms the table into a time-line format by successive widening of columns and rows (Figure 6).
3. A line chart is displayed with the X-axis encoding the whole championship time range and the Y-axis the dimension of the cell the user clicked on. Each team line is encoded with Semantically-Resonant Colors [12] that matches teams' logo (which is also displayed at the end of the lines).
4. The line chart displays by default the ranks, but the Y-axis can also encode the absolute values (Figure 7).
5. A visual feedback displays a vertical bar at the current mouse position to enable comparison. The team associated to the cell the user clicked on is highlighted.
6. **End:** When clicking on the chart, it is animated back to its table form with $t$ corresponding to the click $x$ coordinate.

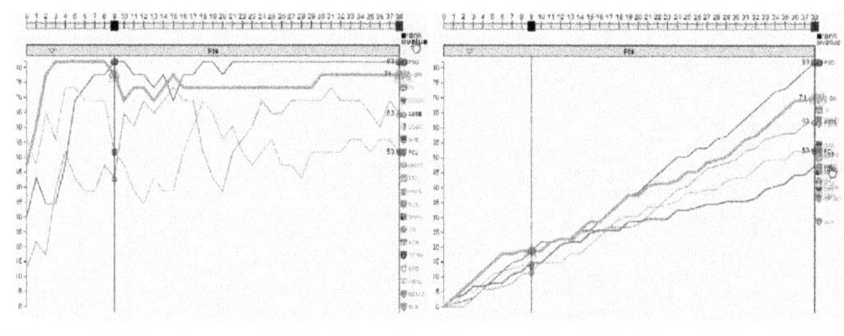
Figure 7. The two available line chart types: Rank (left) or Value (right). A click on a team's name or logo on the right selects the team.

The staged transitions are similar to the ones from the table to the line chart, but in reverse order.

## CROWDSOURCED EVALUATION

We conducted an evaluation to assess how standard interactions, along with DRAG-CELL and VIZ-RANK, can be effective for temporal tasks. We also expect to identify which task categories discriminate the techniques.

### Methodology

We released *À Table!* on the web during a 3-week period, for a crowdsourced evaluation. *Crowdsourcing* is the use of an unknown public to perform simple tasks [14]. Participants (workers) are usually recruited through online markets (*e. g.,* Amazon's Mechanical Turk) and paid to obtain results of quality. We crowdsourced the evaluation because the target user is specific (soccer enthusiast with interest in statistics) and to keep unaltered their environment (they usually browse specialized websites) without paying them. We also picked up this evaluation method because existing tables do not support dynamic temporal navigation and have very inconsistent designs, thus a traditional lab experiment with a baseline comparison would not be appropriate.

We evaluated participants' performance using a quiz (Figure 4, top right). We designed the quiz's questions based on the extracted tasks for soccer analysis (similar as the examples in Table 3). We also displayed the quiz high scores as an incentive to engage visitors.

### Implementation

*À Table!* is implemented using JavaScript and *D3* [5] to run in any modern web browser. The web page is available in English and French at `https://github.com/charlesperin/atable`. We implemented the table and the temporal slider on the left; the quiz and the high scores on the right (Figure 4).

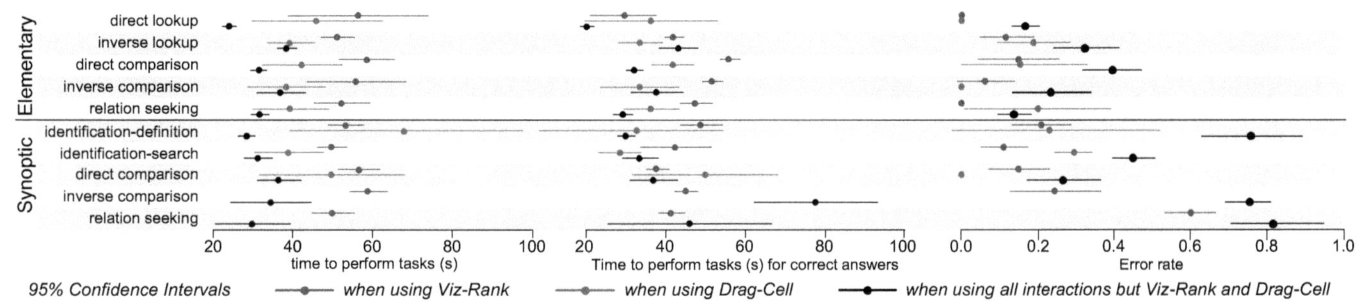


**Figure 8. Time and Error for each task category, by performed interactions.**

We also added a tutorial as instructions for the novel techniques on the bottom right, using a slide-show of animated GIFs. A help button at the bottom opened a help page on how to use the table. The experimental setting is available at `http://charles.perin.free.fr/atable`. We collected feedback from participants with an on-line questionnaire, reached either by clicking on a feedback button or once the quiz is completed. We used the data from the French Ligue 1 2012/2013 championship.

## Hypotheses

Our hypotheses for the experiment are as follows:

- **H1**: side tutorials will help users to activate and learn the novel techniques, even without visual cues or affordances on the table.
- **H2**: the temporal slider will be faster for elementary direct lookup/comparison because these tasks only require changing $t$ and browsing the table.
- **H3**: DRAG-CELL will be the fastest for elementary inverse lookup/comparison tasks, tasks it was designed for.
- **H4**: VIZ-RANK will be errorless for synoptic tasks because it expresses best the temporal evolution of values over the whole time span.
- **H5**: VIZ-RANK will be slower for all tasks because the mental representation of the teams for users changes.

## Tasks

Participants performed tasks issued from each category (Figure 3) using our previously set of 33 tasks. We equally distributed elementary and synoptic tasks. Task variables were randomly generated with some constraints to avoid trivial tasks where the participant's knowledge of the data would be enough to answer. Participants had to answer 36 questions correctly to complete the quiz.

## Participants

We recruited participants by advertising the web page URL using social networks, mailing lists and soccer forums, to select appropriate participants interested in soccer and statistics.

*Incentive Impact:* after two weeks, among the 141 visitors who resulted in 242 tasks performed, only **one** fully completed the quiz and answered the questionnaire. We observed the following recurring pattern: most visitors interacted with the table, answered a few questions and then dropped out without finishing the quiz. To encourage visitors to answer more questions and eventually complete the quiz, as an incentive we advertised free cinema tickets to participants with the highest scores. This immediately resulted in a stronger engagement from the participants.

*Demography:* we extracted the following informations from Google Analytics: most of the visitors were from France (60.5%), then United States (17.4%), United Kingdom (4.9%) and Canada (3%). 53.1% used French and 46.9% English.

## Participation Logs

We logged all participants' interactions, such as: column sorting, team highlighting, slider navigation, DRAG-CELL and VIZ-RANK interactions. We recorded the following values for each quiz answer: quiz session, question number, id, and category; time to perform the task; participant's answer; correct answer; associated interactions ids.

## Results

Over a 3-week period, we registered 1292 visits and 648 visitors performed at least one task. We discarded the data for participants who performed less than 10 tasks and the 239 answers longer than 120 seconds. 143 performed more than 10 tasks (*G1*), 62 participants completed the quiz (*G2*) and 34 filled the questionnaire. Only participants who completed the quiz filled the questionnaire. This results in 6693 tasks performed and 185 636 interaction logs.

*Quantitative results:* participants used VIZ-RANK for 31% of their answers, DRAG-CELL for 9%, and exclusively the other features for 60%. We performed the quantitative analysis using *G1* results—the larger dataset—because we did not find any significant difference between *G1* and *G2*. Figure 8 shows the time and error for all task categories according to performed interactions. We grouped the answers from participants using VIZ-RANK and other interactions into *VR*, DRAG-CELL and other interactions into *DC*, and other interactions (exclusively) into *O*. When both DRAG-CELL and VIZ-RANK were triggered, we counted the last interaction as the one that led to the answer. We performed Anovas when the data had a normal distribution (we applied a log transform to the measures of time) and when the analysis of variance allowed it (Bartlett's K-squared). We used a Welsh two-sample t-test (unequal sample size and variance) for pairwise means comparison. We report significant results only in Table 1.

*Interactions:* Figure 9 shows which interactions were performed, for correct and incorrect answers: all the interactions have a higher percentage of use for correct answers than for

| Factor | Task category | F | p | Pairwise mean comparisons | Mean | | |
|---|---|---|---|---|---|---|---|
| | | | | | *DC* | *VR* | *O* |
| *Error* | elementary inverse lookup | $F_{3,401} = 3$ | * | $DC < O$ & $VR \ll O$ | 0.19 | **0.11** | 0.34 |
| | synoptic identification-definition | $F_{3,406} = 3$ | * | $DC < O$ & $VR \lll O$ | 0.22 | **0.21** | 0.75 |
| | synoptic identification-search | $F_{3,423} = 5$ | ** | $VR \lll O$ | 0.28 | **0.11** | 0.45 |
| | synoptic inverse comparison | $F_{2,143} = 27$ | *** | $VR \lll O$ | / | **0.25** | 0.77 |
| | synoptic relation seeking | $F_{2,186} = 6$ | ** | $VR \ll O$ | / | **0.61** | 0.82 |
| *Time* (correct answers) | elementary direct lookup | $F_{2,337} = 9$ | *** | $O \ll DC$ & $O \ll VR$ | 38s | 33s | **19s** |
| | elementary inverse lookup | $F_{3,241} = 5$ | *** | $DC \ll VR$ | **36s** | 43s | 45s |
| | elementary direct comparison | $F_{3,206} = 21$ | *** | $O \lll VR$ | 42s | 58s | **33s** |
| | elementary inverse comparison | $F_{3,74} = 6$ | *** | $DC \ll VR$ & $O < VR$ | **36s** | 51s | 39s |
| | elementary relation seeking | $F_{3,261} = 12$ | *** | $DC \ll VR$ & $O \lll VR$ | 35s | 48s | **30s** |
| | synoptic identification-definition | $F_{3,226} = 22$ | *** | $O \lll VR$ | 32s | 49s | **31s** |

* for $p \leq 0.05$, ** for $p \leq 0.01$, *** for $p \leq 0.001$; Welsh two sample t-test: $x < y$, $x \ll y$, $x \lll y$.

**Table 1. Significant results for answers based on DRAG-CELL (*DC*), VIZ-RANK (*VR*), and exclusively other interactions (*O*). We analyzed the *Error* for all tasks and the *Time* for correct answers only.**

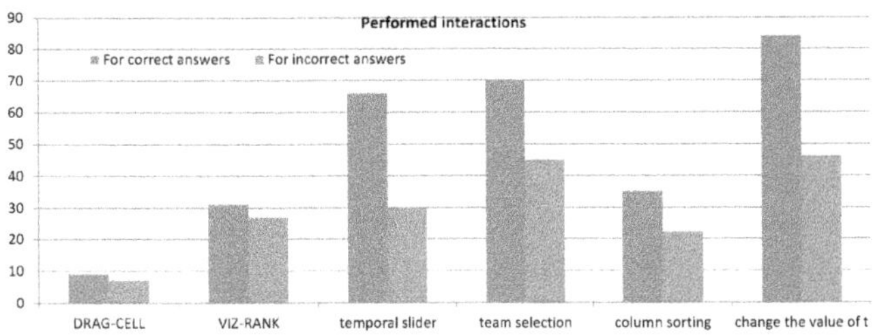


**Figure 9. Percent of answers for which interactions were performed at least one time, for correct and incorrect answers.**

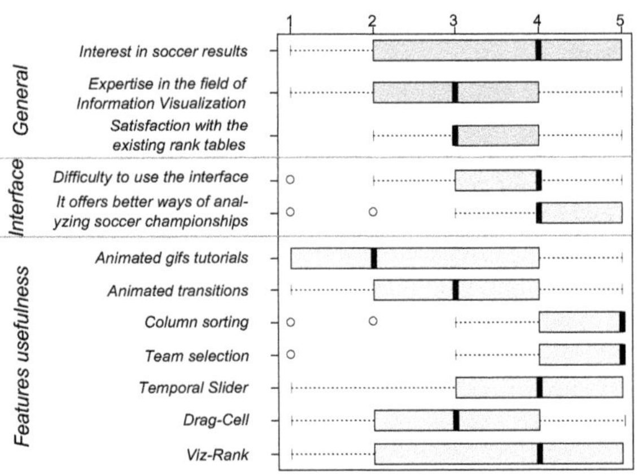


**Figure 10. Answers to the questionnaire, on Likert scales [1-5].**

incorrect ones. The most frequent interaction is changing the value of $t$ (for more than 80% of correct answers) and was triggered most using the temporal slider, then VIZ-RANK and DRAG-CELL. Participants used the team selection for 70% of the tasks, and column sorting for a third.

*Qualitative Results:* Figure 10 shows the participant's scores on Likert scales for their background, questions on the interface and more specific questions about *À Table!* features. The main observation is that participants' satisfaction with existing ranking tables is low: 91% (31/34) of the participants would like to have access to such an interactive table on their favorite soccer website. Indeed, they estimate it offers better ways to analyze soccer championships (74% of the participants discovered unknown information during the quiz). Interestingly, they scored the team selection, the column sorting and the temporal slider as the most useful features. However, none complained that the novel techniques were distracting, or that they were disturbing obstacles to perform the tasks.

## DISCUSSION

### Observations from Experiment and Main Findings

Soccer enthusiasts with heterogeneous backgrounds in Information Visualization discovered and performed *À Table!* interactions. Our investigation confirms **H1**, although users rated the interface as difficult to use. We also had to provide an incentive in order to engage participants and make them complete all the tasks.

Some participants commented that it was difficult to discover the interactions. For example, one participant wrote: *"I think it has a low discoverability for the graph and the drag in the cell"*. DRAG-CELL and VIZ-RANK are relatively advanced techniques, performed directly on the table, to let users focus on their task. For such techniques, discoverability is a well known problem (as noted by Bederson [4]). We provided a side tutorial for beginners to learn by example. However, the results showed that almost all participants discovered both techniques by exploring the table, without using this side tutorial and they often accidentally triggered the interactions the first time. In fact, both DRAG-CELL and VIZ-RANK appear to be quite discoverable without specific affordance.

Answers to the questionnaire confirm the interest from soccer enthusiasts for *À Table!*: 74% of them discovered new information and 31/34 participants gave a score higher than 3 on the 1-5 Likert scale to rate how *À Table!* offers better ways of analyzing soccer championships. For example, one participant wrote: *"wish I had it for my own championship (UK)"*.

*O* is faster than *VR* for both elementary direct lookup and comparison. This is explained because choosing the appropriate value for $t$ is enough to perform the task well and using VIZ-RANK makes the user waste time. *O* is also faster than *DC* for elementary direct lookup, so we partially confirm **H2**.

For both elementary inverse lookup and comparison, *DC* has the lowest mean time and is significantly faster than *VR* and we partially confirm **H3**. We also note that for inverse lookup tasks, we did not find any significant difference between *DC* and *O* because the standard deviation for *O* was too high, although it was the slowest technique overall. DRAG-CELL was rarely used, but when it was, participants performed tasks faster and with fewer errors. These results confirm that DRAG-CELL is efficient to perform the tasks it was designed for.

For four synoptic tasks (identification definition, identification search, inverse comparison, and relation seeking) *VR* has significantly less error than *O*, participants making respectively 3.6, 4.1, 3.1 and 1.3 times less error using VIZ-RANK. We did not find any significant difference between *DC* and *VR* for these tasks but the mean error is the smallest for *VR* and we partially confirm **H4**. We also note that *DC* has less error than *O* for the identification definition task.
*VR* is the slowest for five out of the six tasks for which we were able to analyze time, with *VR* being almost twice as long as *O* for several tasks. For half the tasks with significant difference, *VR* is slower than both *DC* and *O* and we partially confirm **H5**. We explain this result because participants may not be familiar with line charts. However, it is not clear if this is a general issue, if this is in the context of rank visualization or because of the short apparition of the chart.
Participants used VIZ-RANK for complex synoptic and relation-seeking tasks that are extremely painful to perform without a dedicated technique. The technique involves fewer errors but requires more time. However, because journalists cannot afford to publish incorrect data, the technique must be accurate, even at the cost of a slight increase in completion time; comparing time between techniques makes sense when the techniques have similar error rates, which is not the case.

The main takeaways from our experiment are as follows:

- *Basic interactions remain essential, fast to operate and easy to learn for basic tasks.* However, some tasks are almost impossible to perform using only these features (up to 82% of error) and advanced interaction techniques are required.
- *Interactive techniques are crucial to explore temporal ranking tables.* The more interactions are used, the more the task is performed correctly (Figure 10).
- DRAG-CELL *is fast and error-less for the tasks it was designed for (inverse tasks)* but almost never used for other task categories.
- VIZ-RANK *is accurate and well-suited to synoptic tasks and all tasks can be performed using it.* However, it is slow to operate and requires user's basic knowledge in Information Visualization.

Finally, both DRAG-CELL (for elementary inverse lookup and comparison) and VIZ-RANK (for four out of the five synoptic tasks categories) makes it easier to perform the tasks they were designed for. Moreover, several of these tasks were almost absent from the task analysis from soccer articles but were estimated as highly relevant by the expert. We may expect that by providing such interaction techniques as DRAG-CELL and VIZ-RANK, the analysts will be able to perform tasks they can not perform today and therefore enhance the quality of the insights and statistics they can retrieve from the data.

## Applicability Beyond Soccer and Limits

*À Table!* is seamlessly applicable to other sport ranking tables showing team statistics. We now describe *À Table!* applicability to two types of ranking tables from different domains and discuss possible issues and limits.

### Academic Rankings

Since 2003, the Shanghai University [6] publishes every year an updated Academic Ranking of World Universities. It ranks the top $|S| = 500$ institutions, with $|D| = 6$ dimensions. The main rank is computed on the number of Nobel Price or Fields Medal winners from the institution, among other criteria. Top institutions like Harvard and MIT are respectively ranked first and second, and tracking them over time can be done visually. *À Table!* would be efficient to browse the top-$k$, $k = 20$ ranks for which permutations are important but mostly remain on the same screen. However, some issues occur for ranks lower than 100 which are not all visible without scrolling and contain ties. Furthermore, it only ranks the top-500 universities every year, meaning that new institutions may appear or disappear over time, making their tracking difficult.

### Sorting Algorithms Execution

Sorting algorithms, such as quicksort or bubble sort, perform many permutations until they end in a final result. The number of permutations varies according to the size of the dataset $|S|$. The type of permutations varies according to the algorithm itself. Existing works already explored the visualization of execution steps[4] which enable a non-expert to grasp the underlying sorting strategy. *À Table!* would be useful to inspect executions and to reach a specific execution step or time. Such an investigation of algorithms—or any ordered dynamic process—can be used in a variety of contexts, ranging from educational purpose to algorithms optimization.

### Limits

Some real-life rankings may not be immediately compatible with current *À Table!* design. It is already challenging to visualize and interact with rankings with partial ranks, missing data during time intervals, new dimensions, etc. In contrast, tables do justice to such rankings by creating empty rows or additional columns to represent missing data. It may not be optimal but it has the merit of being a consistent representation.

## Design Implications

Adding novel interactive techniques to legacy techniques, such as ranking tables, implies many design considerations. We only scratched the surface of making them fully effective, and we share some lessons we learned on their discover-ability and learn-ability. Discover-ability is mainly connected to the affordance of the first interaction to **start** the technique. We did not use any for simplicity, and considered natural to change values by dragging them up and down. Some codes for affordance are already available, such as Bret Victor's [22] use of dashed lines to show draggable values. Learn-ability can

[4] `http://www.youtube.com/watch?v=m1PS8IR6Td0`

be supported in many ways. The tutorial we provided during our experiment was probably not sufficiently contextualized, explaining why most of the participants discarded it. It seems that it was natural for users to click and drag cells as they are their primary interest. They may have acquired this knowledge elsewhere and applied it to *À Table!* by associativity [2]. Line charts provide visual guides, but require space and time to appear. Exploring hybrid features, such as dragging values with a visual overlay showing upcoming and past values, might be the best of the two worlds but needs more investigation. Still, regular dragging can be left as an expert-feature [4].

## CONCLUSION AND FUTURE WORK

This paper presented *À Table!*, an enhanced ranking table with improved temporal navigation, by combining two novel interaction techniques. Initially, our goal was to better support ranking tables interactivity and representation of time, as the temporal dimension is crucial to understand soccer championships. We designed novel interactions following Bederson [4] principles to preserve user's flow, to focus on tasks and prevent interruption. Our evaluation shows that the techniques efficiently support temporal tasks, currently not supported by ranking tables, while not breaking user flow. This paves the way for efficiently introducing advanced visual exploration techniques to millions of soccer enthusiasts who use tables everyday, as well as other application domains which use ranking tables.

We also thought to design novel navigation techniques to include in *À Table!*. One of them is using a table cube metaphor, with a transient 3D animation similar as Rolling the Dice [7], to change a time $t$ or a dimension $d$ step-by-step. This type of transition provides a consistent temporal navigation paradigm—adequate with tables which are also squared—and perfectly fits in table boundaries.

## ACKNOWLEDGMENTS

We thank Jérôme Latta, our journalist expert; Jeremy Boy for his help with the design of the table; Lora Oehlberg for her help on the paper and her delightful voice on the video; and Petra Isenberg, Pascal Goffin and Sarah Hopkinson for proofreading the paper.

## REFERENCES

1. Amar, R., Eagan, J., and Stasko, J. Low-level components of analytic activity in information visualization. In *Proc. INFOVIS'05*, IEEE (2005), 15.
2. Anderson, J. R. *Learning and memory*, vol. 86. John Wiley New York, 2000.
3. Andrienko, N., and Andrienko, G. *Exploratory Analysis of Spatial and Temporal Data: A Systematic Approach*. Springer, Dec. 2005.
4. Bederson, B. B. Interfaces for staying in the flow. *Ubiquity 2004*, September (2004), 1–1.
5. Bostock, M., Ogievetsky, V., and Heer, J. $D^3$ data-driven documents. *TVCG 17*, 12 (2011), 2301–2309.
6. Consultancy, S. R. Academic ranking of world universities 2013. *Shanghai: Center for World Class Universities and Institute of Higher Education of Shanghai Jiao Tong University 66* (2013), 2013–06.
7. Elmqvist, N., Dragicevic, P., and daniel Fekete, J. Rolling the dice: Multidimensional visual exploration using scatterplot matrix navigation visualization. *TVCG* (2008).
8. Elmqvist, N., Henry, N., Riche, Y., and Fekete, J.-D. Melange: space folding for multi-focus interaction. In *Proc. CHI'08*, ACM (2008), 1333–1342.
9. Gratzl, S., Lex, A., Gehlenborg, N., Pfister, H., and Streit, M. Lineup: Visual analysis of multi-attribute rankings. *TVCG 19*, 12 (2013), 2277–2286.
10. Heer, J., and Robertson, G. G. Animated transitions in statistical data graphics. *TVCG 13*, 6 (2007), 1240–1247.
11. Kreher, D. L., and Stinson, D. R. Combinatorial algorithms: Generation. *Enumeration, and Search* (1999).
12. Lin, S., Fortuna, J., Kulkarni, C., Stone, M., and Heer, J. Selecting semantically-resonant colors for data visualization. *Computer Graphics Forum (Proc. EuroVis)* (2013).
13. Playfair, W. *Playfair's commercial and political atlas and statistical breviary*. Cambridge University Press, 2005.
14. Quinn, A., and Bederson, B. Human computation: a survey and taxonomy of a growing field. In *Proc. CHI'11*, ACM (2011), 1403–1412.
15. Rao, R., and Card, S. K. The table lens: merging graphical and symbolic representations in an interactive focus+ context visualization for tabular information. In *Proc. CHI'94*, ACM (1994), 318–322.
16. Seo, J., and Shneiderman, B. A rank-by-feature framework for interactive exploration of multidimensional data. *Information Visualization 4*, 2 (2005), 96–113.
17. Shi, C., Cui, W., Liu, S., Xu, P., Chen, W., and Qu, H. Rankexplorer: Visualization of ranking changes in large time series data. *TVCG 18*, 12 (2012), 2669–2678.
18. Shneiderman, B. 1.1 direct manipulation: a step beyond programming languages. *Sparks of Innovation in Human-Computer Interaction* (1993), 17.
19. Shneiderman, B. Dynamic queries for visual information seeking. *Software, IEEE 11*, 6 (1994), 70–77.
20. Sopan, A., Freire, M., Plaisant, C., Golbeck, J., and Shneiderman, B. Distribution column overviews in tabular visualizations. Tech. rep., HCIL, 2010.
21. Tufte, E. R., and Graves-Morris, P. *The visual display of quantitative information*, vol. 2. Graphics press Cheshire, CT, 1983.
22. Victor, B. Tangle: a javascript library for reactive documents, 2013. `http://worrydream.com/Tangle/`.
23. Wikipedia. Pivot table, 2013. `http://en.wikipedia.org/wiki/Pivot_table`.

# Kinetica: Naturalistic Multi-touch Data Visualization

**Jeffrey M. Rzeszotarski, Aniket Kittur**
Human-Computer Interaction Institute, Carnegie Mellon University, Pittsburgh, PA, USA
{jeffrz, nkittur}@cs.cmu.edu

**ABSTRACT**
Over the last several years there has been an explosion of powerful, affordable, multi-touch devices. This provides an outstanding opportunity for novel data visualization techniques that leverage new interaction methods and minimize their barriers to entry. In this paper we describe an approach for multivariate data visualization that uses physics-based affordances that are easy to intuit, constraints that are easy to apply and visualize, and a consistent view as data is manipulated in order to promote data exploration and interrogation. We provide a framework for exploring this problem space, and an example proof of concept system called Kinetica. We describe the results of a user study that suggest users of Kinetica were able to explore multiple dimensions of data at once, identify outliers, and discover trends with minimal training.

**Author Keywords**
Visualization, multivariate data, multi-touch, physics

**ACM Classification Keywords**
H.5.m. Information interfaces and presentation: Misc.

## INTRODUCTION

The ways in which people consume information and make decisions is changing rapidly, with a rise in powerful, affordable, multi-touch devices that support a wide range of interactions and applications. A 2013 Pew Research survey estimated that one third of American households owned a tablet computer [40], a number double that of the previous year. There has also come a bevy of collaborative surfaces, interactive whiteboards, and touch-enabled traditional PCs. These devices create an opportunity for developing natural user interfaces (NUIs) that are grounded in naturalistic human ways of interacting with real things [12].

However, despite the crucial importance of interpreting and understanding complex data in nearly any personal or business setting [31], existing information visualization techniques have largely failed to make effective use of the multi-touch, direct manipulation capabilities of these new, ubiquitous devices [23]. Instead, techniques remain primarily within the realm of traditional, directed interactions using WIMP metaphors. Lee et al. employed the terms *post-WIMP* and *post direct manipulation* to describe the rich area of research currently filling this gap [23]. Such techniques that move towards gestures and naturalistic interactions may have benefits for information literacy and awareness. For exploratory data visualization, post-WIMP approaches have the potential to preserve users' growing mental model of an information space as they explore it, and help them interact with more variables more fluidly than traditional interfaces. This might help them understand the structure and distributions of data even without significant training or statistical expertise by leveraging their models of the physical world [18].

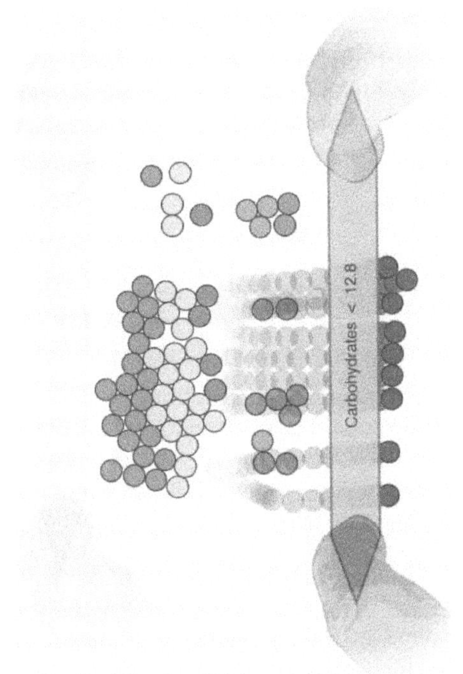


**Figure 1: A user drags a two finger semi-permeable filter across some data. Points that meet its criteria collide and are pulled with it to the right, passing over unfiltered points.**

In this paper we explore how post-WIMP interactions might improve exploratory data visualization through the introduction of physics-based affordances and multi-touch interaction techniques. Grounding data exploration in a physics-based metaphor may have a number of benefits, including supporting richer mental models of an information space by keeping data salient and fluidly tracking their locations over time; providing better awareness of amounts and distributions; making outliers



*CHI 2014*, April 26 - May 01 2014, Toronto, ON, Canada

ACM 978-1-4503-2473-1/14/04...$15.00.
http://dx.doi.org/10.1145/2556288.2557231

stand out over the course of exploration; and augmenting working memory through visual traces. It may also minimize training time and participation barriers by tapping into users' knowledge of the physical world, their own bodies, their surroundings, and their social context [18]. We describe a proof of concept system, Kinetica, and use it to demonstrate some of the benefits of this approach through a comparative user study. We find that physics-based interactions help users explore multiple dimensions at once, make more descriptive and comparative findings about their data, and develop a more holistic understanding of a dataset. We also present a generative framework for naturalistic multi-touch visualization that may help to inspire future work in this space. Finally, we consider limitations and discuss areas for future work.

## RELATED WORK

Below we briefly discuss some of the most relevant related work covering different aspects of post-WIMP information visualization and systems for exploring data.

### Multi-touch and Gestural Interaction

Gestures, multi-touch, and physical interactions are key components of NUIs regardless of the particular application. Keefe and Isenberg [20] highlight some of the major interest areas for natural interaction in data visualization. Foremost are actual ways of interacting with data, which Isenberg and Isenberg [17] break down into the relationship between data representation and interaction technique. What are the interaction primitives one uses, and how do we bind them to data visualization operations? RoomPlanner [38] used physical actions like cupping a hand and transparency to make data easy to explore on a DiamondTouch surface, and Wilson et al. explored a wide variety of game physics-based interactions [35]. These interactions have the benefit of both ease of use and the ability for users to improvise new ones based on their experiences in the real world. Wobbrock et al. [36] take this idea further, allowing users to build their own gestures.

Moving towards more structured interaction techniques, NEAT and interactive grids [9,10] provide a set of pen and touch primitives to align and locate data on a field. This can be critical given the imprecision that can accompany touch interaction. TouchWave [3] displays stacked hierarchical graphs much in the way a WIMP application might, but uses drags and swipes to scale and separate overlaps naturalistically. Schmidt et al. [28] treat graph edges and nodes like beads on strings that can be gathered and stacked. SketchInsight and SketchStory [24,34] combine interactive sketching with dynamically constructed traditional charts for didactic presentations. Some approaches even employ physical objects. Senseboard [19] places pucks on a grid to organize and manipulate information, while Ullmer et al. [33] use physical tokens to control and visualize database queries.

Another crucial component Isenberg and Isenberg identify is evaluation. Drucker et al. [6] provide one such example. They use a grounded methodology to study user preference and effectiveness in different visualization prototypes in comparison, findings NUIs to be effective but at times constraining when people already knew what to do.

### Multivariate Data Visualization

Wong and Bergeron provide a good summary of the history of multivariate visualization [37]. Early examples such as starfield visualizations [2], brushing [26], and dynamic querying [30] permit similar interactions, allowing users to filter different dimensions with active feedback. To visualize complex or categorical data, techniques such as parallel coordinates [16] and parallel sets [22] offload multivariate relationships onto a visual field, highlighting outliers and trends. DataMeadows [7] and Jigsaw [32] all use multiple techniques in tandem to represent trends or clusters within multiple dimensions.

One highly relevant inspiration for our line of work is that of Yi et al.'s Dust & Magnet [39], which used a magnet physical metaphor to visualize multivariate data. By allowing users to place and move magnets, attracting points, users could discover trends among their data. We build on the idea of using physics and interaction to compress the dimensionality of multivariate data, but generalize to a wider set of physics-based techniques.

### Physics and Interactivity

One avenue for intuitive, interesting interactions cited by Jacob et al. [18] is the introduction of physical metaphors. Bumptop [1] shows one such example in a general computing context. Files become physics objects that can be pinned to walls and moved around in an environment. This has the benefit of requiring minimal training, since people already intuit that objects fall and pins stick things to walls. North et al. [27] extend this sort of physics approach into data sorting in comparison with a traditional WIMP system. People readily adapted to physical models, outperforming those using a mouse. Force-based graph layouts use attraction and repulsion, which people naturally intuit, to make graph exploration easier [11]. Sticky tools make touch manipulations of objects more naturalistic and therefore easier [13]. Visual sedimentation metaphors use the buildup of material to analogize the aggregation of time-series data in an easily comprehensible way [15].

Klemmer, Hartmann, and Takayama [21] suggest a more general explanation of this sort of effect. The *tangibility* of an artifact, or how naturally it maps actions to physical reality can greatly influence the performance of a system. While closer mappings to reality may come with additional constraints and limitations, they also provide benefits for training and understanding, especially for inexpert users. This might extend beyond just NUIs. The description of post-WIMP possibilities that Jacobs et al. provide and the design considerations of Lee et al. [23] still might work within traditional mouse-and-keyboard computers. While they may not be quite as *tangible* as if one were touching

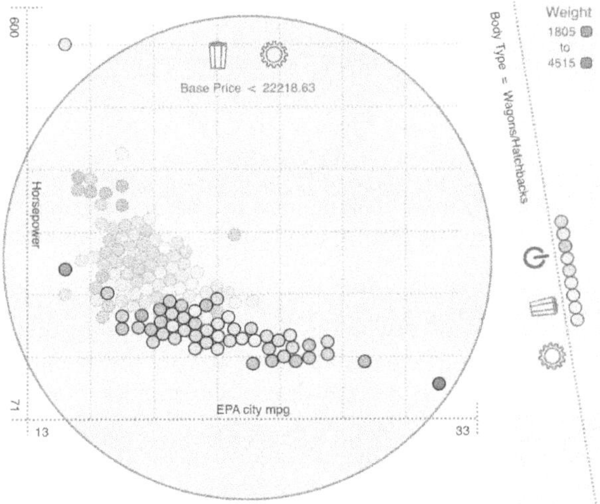


**Figure 2: A user explores car model data using Kinetica. She cares about mileage and power, so she placed the points into a scatterplot. She doesn't like wagons, so she used a wall to filter. Finally, she added a lens to highlight cheaper vehicles.**

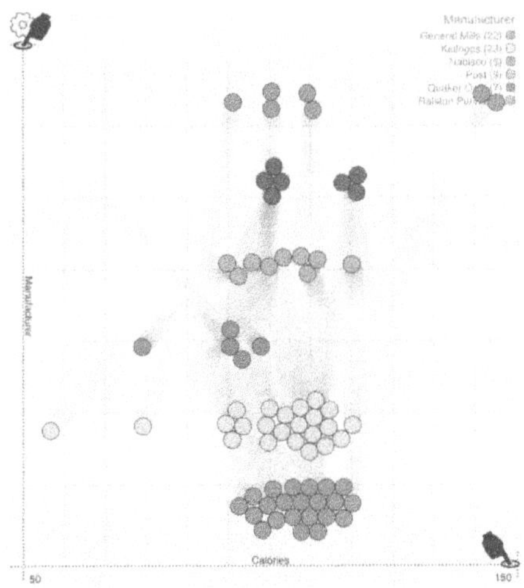


**Figure 3: A user can draw a scatterplot using two fingers, one at each corner. When they place the scatterplot, the points feel a pull towards their proper place on the chart. They move towards their location, forming clumps if the points are concentrated in a certain range of values.**

the screen, the interactions and feedback may nonetheless remain physically grounded and beneficial.

## KINETICA

To explore the benefits of physics-based affordances and multi-touch interactions for data visualization and to understand the technical challenges of implementing such techniques, we developed a proof of concept application called Kinetica. For our proof of concept, we used a tablet computer because it occupied the physical space of the user, could be twisted and turned, and was responsive to touch. We decided to use an iPad due to the convenience and general availability of the device, though we hope to extend Kinetica to more systems in the future.

We implemented Kinetica using Objective C, and make use of an MIT licensed physics library called Chipmunk Physics [25] to handle forces and collisions. This library makes use of multiple CPU cores to improve efficiency. Indeed, the most computationally costly portion of the prototype was actually the rendering loop.

We adopted an iterative strategy in developing the physics-based interactions in Kinetica. Initially we encoded data into circles colliding in a sandbox, implemented a touch-responsive magnet tool much like Dust & Magnet [39], and added gravity based on device orientation. This prototype by itself was evocative. By tilting the device so gravity took hold and pulling points with a magnet such that the forces balanced each other, data readily sorted itself and separated, highlighting outliers. We embarked in a process of loading different canonical multivariate datasets into the program and exploring them. We used datasets of cereal and car brands to explore comparisons and decision making. We used datasets of Titanic shipwreck passengers and Pittsburgh census demographics to explore how one might generate and test hypotheses about trends in the data.

As we felt a desire to interact with the data in a way not yet written into the program, we implemented new features. When an affordance went unused or superseded, we removed it. Over many successive passes, we designed two primary types of tools based on the affordances we explicated earlier: manipulative tools and interrogative tools. Manipulative tools alter points' locations, or move them around the sandbox. Interrogative tools change the appearance of a point or its interactivity. A mix of these tools can be layered to explore multiple dimensions at once, and the tools leave traces on the sandbox field so users can see what is affecting points.

In the following sections we describe the physics-based tools implemented in Kinetica through two use cases based on participants' explorations during our user study.

### Use Case 1 - Choosing a Car

Margaret would like a new car, but does not know which model to buy. There are many on sale, and each car has a dozen or so different columns of statistics, including weight, fuel economy, and manufacturer. She loads a database of car models into Kinetica, and begins exploring.

She wants a vehicle that is somewhat powerful but uses little fuel. To help answer questions like this, we combined physics-based forces with traditional multivariate charts: histograms and scatterplots. *Histograms* pull points to their proper place on a number line or categorical division. If there are a lot of points in a particular part of the distribution, they will bunch up and visually consume more area. *Scatterplots* functioned similarly, pulling points based on their values in 2D. We initially had concerns of points blocking one another, leading to data being located in an incorrect position on a histogram. To help avoid this overconstraint, we temporarily disable point collision until the data settle down into the proper locations. While this

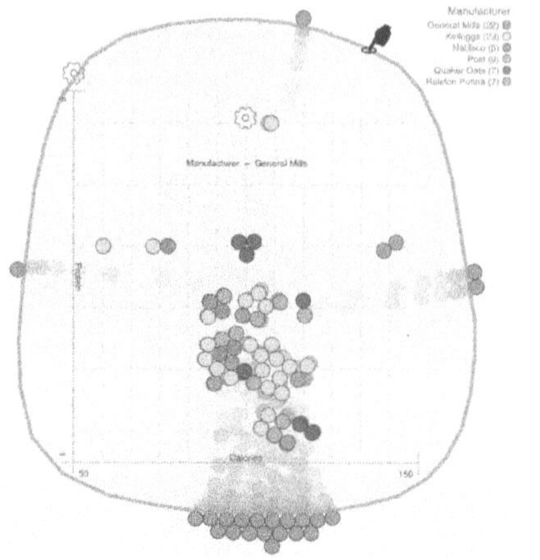

**Figure 4: Instead of pulling a barrier across points, a user can also draw a region that filters points. Here a user has chosen to filter points from a region that includes a chart. Once they finish drawing, the points are immediately pushed outwards..**

breaks with the physical model, it makes the resulting visualization more accurate and produces a satisfying "settling" effect for the points.

Margaret places a scatterplot that graphs horsepower and mileage, watching as the points are pulled into the chart (Figure 2). Because she sees the points moving, she has an implicit awareness of the action she just made, and can attribute the motion of the data to a specific operation (Figure 3). She sees a big clump of cars with moderate horsepower and mileage as expected, and a longer tail or low horsepower, high mileage cars. Because the points collide, she can interpret their distribution at a glance, and she easily spots the super high efficiency outlier in the lower right corner because it is so visually distinct.

She sees several good candidates in the lower right corner of the chart, but she would like to filter hatchbacks cars. For filtering actions, one could imagine simply removing the points from the screen. However, we wanted to maintain users' mental model of the data landscape, and simply removing points entirely would break it, leading to uncertainty. Instead, we implemented a *semi-permeable barrier* that could be dragged over points or placed onto the field. The points build up against the barrier, showing just how much has been filtered (Figure 1).

We implemented a collision layering system so that points that should pass through do not get mired in the pile of points backing up against the barrier. Each barrier adds a bit to a bitmask, with points permitted to pass the barrier assigned a 1. When points collide, they compare their bitmasks. If they are the not the same, the points can pass through one another. So if there are two barriers, points that can pass through both form one "layer" of collisions, points that can pass through exclusively one barrier form another "layer", and so forth. This creates some edge cases where collision should happen but does not, such as when barriers are nested. In the future we would like to incorporate regions of space into the algorithm to solve this issue.

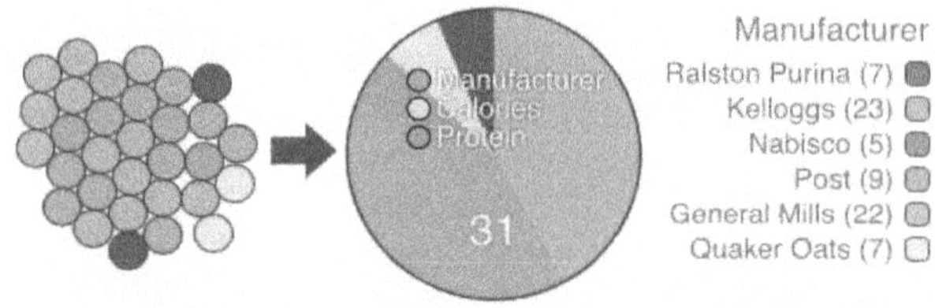


**Figure 5: A set of datapoints can become a group. The pie chart updates dynamically to show distributions.**

Margaret drags a wall across the scatterplot, picking up filtered points as she drags. She finally taps to make the wall permanent, separating them off to the right of her screen (Figure 2). As she drags, she notices most of the points she picks up come from the middle of the distribution, leading her to believe most hatchbacks had moderate horsepower and efficiency. The process of filtering not only moves the points away, but also provides insight into relationships between variables and data.

Margaret also has a budget, so she needs to filter expensive cars. However, she doesn't want to move the points since she already know where most of her candidates lay in the sandbox. For this situation, we developed a movable *lens* (Figure 2) that highlights points that match a criterion, performing an analogous, non-manipulative role to the barrier. The lens also can optionally affect the physics within its area, only allowing points that meet its criteria to accept interactions.

Finally, Margaret is ready to investigate individual points. Because all of the tools she used left traces in the sandbox, it is easy for her to backtrack and find the points she remembered were interesting candidates. She uses a double tap to access a *detail view* to explore them. We wanted to avoid occlusion, so the taps place a static magnification glass and show the details of the points within in the glass with labels to help pick out the right one.

### Use Case 2 - Titanic Shipwreck

After watching a movie, Margaret is interested in the survivors and victims of the Titanic shipwreck. She is curious if the old adage "women and children first" actually bears out in the data. To test her hypothesis, she loads the data up into Kinetica (see Figure 6). She begins by *coloring* the points based on survival. We implemented separate, color-blind friendly scales for both continuous and nominal values, and also allow users to scale points' size by value.

Margaret now charts the passengers based on gender and cabin class. With a quick glance it is obvious more women than men survived due to the coloring (Figure 6). To investigate how children fared, she draws a semi-permeable barrier around the data, which pushes out points whose age is less than 18. Because the points still feel a pull to their place in the chart, this has the emergent property of keeping the filtered points separated into gender/class groups. From this new chart she makes the conclusion that indeed most children survived, though male children in the third class still faced poor odds.

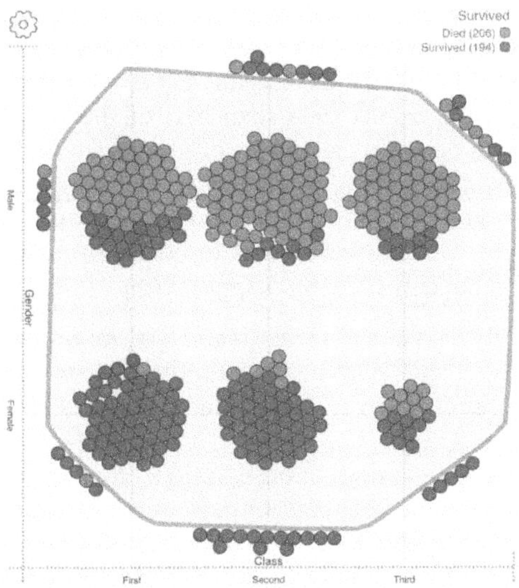


**Figure 6: 400 randomly shown passengers are colored by whether they survived (blue) or died (red), and are charted by cabin class (x) and gender (y). Note many more women (top) survived. A filter (green) pushes all passengers under 18 years of age to the outside. Because they still feel a pull to their place on the chart, they separate into class/gender groups. Note third class boys (upper right) still had poor survival odds.**

An issue with large datasets is screen real estate. To increase scalability and provide the ability to categorize data, we added a *grouping* function (Figure 5). Users may select a region of points or manually choose points to incorporate into groups. These groups express the characteristics of their constituents, obeying forces as if they are a point whose data is the average of their members.

### Gestures and Combinations

For each of the tools we developed, we initially assigned unique gestures and numbers of fingers. For example, to create a barrier, the user would put down four fingers along the contour, while creating a line histogram required only two. This proved cumbersome and confusing. Instead, we adopted gestures that used either one or two fingers. Two fingers define two control points allowing for a histogram between fingers, a bounding box for scatterplots, a barrier between fingers, a lens spanning fingers, or a group that floats between fingers (to avoid occlusion) which selectively consumes points. On the other hand, one finger gives us one control point, which allows for drawing actions. This permits freehand drawn histograms, drawn areas that permit/deny points, drawn lenses, and selecting specific points to form a group.

In testing, we observed several interesting combinations of tools. A scatterplot that bunched points into categorical clusters could be enhanced with a histogram that pulled points into sorted order. Each cluster still felt a pull towards its group, but also self-assembled into sorted order within the cluster thanks to the influence of the histogram. Similarly, drawing an area or barrier that rejected a subset of points while a scatterplot was present meant that even the filtered points still felt a pull to their proper locations, albeit stopped by the barrier. This meant that they still took the form of clusters against the barrier. In practice through techniques like this we could effectively layer 5 dimensions of data within the iPad screen sandbox.

## USER STUDY

To evaluate Kinetica, we invited participants to use the software for 45 minutes in a lab study. As a comparison case, we also invited another group of participants to follow the same study protocol using Excel rather than the application. We considered incorporating exploratory visualization suites such as Tableau, Many Eyes, or infogr.am, however we were concerned that training would consume too much time in comparison to Kinetica, especially considering novice computer users. We recruited from a campus participant pool, and scheduled sessions over the course of two days, one for each technique.

We solicited samples for 16 participants in each condition, however one Kinetica participant did not complete the study protocol and their submission was excluded. 15 participants identified as male, and 16 as female. Their average age was 28.9 years. 20 participants reported as using statistical software like Excel at least once a month, and all but one reported having used spreadsheets to analyze data at least once. 11 out of 15 Kinetica users reported having used a tablet, though only 5 owned an iPad. Excel was the only tool participants identified as a way to explore tabular, multi-dimensional data, and all but 2 participants had used it before.

At the start of the study participants received either an iPad with Kinetica loaded or a preloaded instance of Excel with study data present and a populated example chart and pivot table. The study first provided five minutes of basic training. In the case of Kinetica, participants followed a built-in tutorial that goes over each tool with a use case example. For the Excel participants, the study observer presented two well-viewed YouTube video tutorials on Excel and pivot tables/charts. In both conditions study participants were informed that their interface actions were being logged, and an observer watched during the study.

After training, participants were asked to look at a dataset of 73 different brands of cereal containing nutritional information (see Figures 3, 5). They had 10 minutes to use their respective tools to answer a set of 5 basic questions of increasing difficulty/dimensionality. These ranged from "What cereal has the most calories," to "Of cereals with more than 2g of protein and less than 160mg of sodium which has the most fat?" This also functioned as additional training, and the observer was available to answer questions about how to use the software, but not give hints about the questions themselves. Participants averaged 3.4 questions correct, and there was no difference between conditions. This suggests that perhaps neither condition benefitted more from training, or that the choice of software did not affect participants' basic statistical ability.

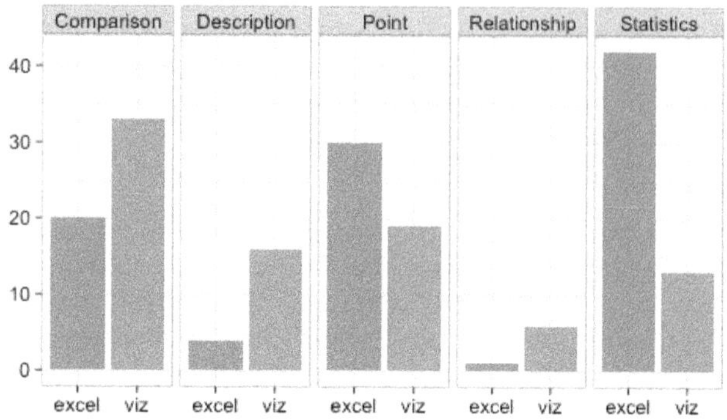


**Figure 7: Coded Titanic findings made during user studies**

Following the cereal question period, we asked users to pick a car they would like to buy from a dataset of 133 car models with specifications. Purchasing decisions often require people to balance multiple different kinds of data, making them well suited for multivariate visualizations. We first asked users to write down the criteria they would use for buying a car to make them to think about different dimensions of the data. Participants commonly reported considering multiple dimensions at once, including cost, horsepower, gas mileage, and car body type. Afterwards, they used Excel or Kinetica to pore through the data and pick a car they liked. All participants were able to identify at least one car to buy. Kinetica participants used a variety of tools to complete this task. Some plotted points out, then used barriers to filter points. Others layered multiple lenses onto a field, manually pushing points from criterion to criterion. The Excel participants used tools such as charts and pivot tables. Every participant considered at least 2 dimensions of data, with some Kinetica participants considering 4 or 5. This suggests that Kinetica might help participants consider more dimensions of data at once. We will investigate this more quantitatively in the next task.

In the final 15 minutes, we gave participants a dataset containing a random sample of 200 passengers on the Titanic. Since they now had experience with the software, we gave them an open ended prompt. There were to make as many findings as they could in the time limit using the data. For instance, they might identify who the youngest passenger was, or see a relationship between cabin class and passenger survival. Excel participants made on average 5.1 findings, and Kinetica participants made on average 5.5 findings (the difference is not significant). The Kinetica participants' findings generally encoded more dimensions per finding than Excel participants (M:1.74 vs. M:1.38; repeated measures $F(1,164)=17.67$, $p<0.001$).

We were especially interested in whether the nature of participants' findings would differ by condition. In particular, we hypothesized that physics-based affordances would grant participants a more holistic understanding of the data, increasing their awareness of trends and distributions and enabling them to layer and investigate multiple dimensions at once. To investigate this we had two coders classify each of the findings made by participants into five types: *point* findings that discussed a particular row of data (youngest passenger), *statistical* findings that gave summary statistics (mean age), *descriptions* that capture general trends (less than half of the people lived), *comparisons* between categories or groups (more third class passengers died), and *relationships* between dimensions (the older you were, the more likely you were in a high class cabin). Coders were blind to condition and had high interrater reliability (N=186, kappa=0.96).

Interestingly, Kinetica users made far more descriptive, comparative, and relationship findings than their Excel peers who almost always made point or statistical findings (Figure 7; $c^2(5)=31.3$, $p<0.001$). Thus while they do not make as many quantitative observations, they demonstrate a greater awareness of distribution and multidimensional trends. This suggests that physics-based affordances may be helping users build a more holistic understanding of data.

### Qualitative Responses

The qualitative responses during the survey suggest a similar trend. On 7-point Likert scales, Kinetica participants reported that the tool was fairly easy to learn (M:5.53), made it easy to explore data (M:6.0), was fun to use (M:6.07), was fairly easy to use (M:5.07), and that they would use it again (M:6.0). They identified the scatterplots and lenses as especially useful (M:6.2, M:6.47), and groups as less useful (M:4.93), perhaps because they broke with the force-based tools that comprised most of the interface by absorbing points rather than moving/altering them.

After the study, a participant reported that Kinetica was, "… so much better than Excel. I can see when my sort isn't quite right because a point will be where it shouldn't be. It's visual." This points to both the visual memory and process benefits of physics affordances. Another reported, "I like it 'cuz you could just compare things because they were right there. You didn't have to look between rows or anything." In written free response sections, a participant wrote "The scatterplot allows you to visualize your most important priorities [then] …The lens helps you narrow down scope & they can be layered on top of each other," identifying how the layering of physics constraints matched their internal exploration process. Other participants identified ludic elements, stating Kinetica "allows you to "play" around with the data," "makes seeing the data fun and interesting," and "fluidity made it engaging." One participant reacted strongly after the car portion of the study, saying aloud "You can [use Kinetica to]… make really informative decisions on what you purchase in your everyday life."

Participants also had some issues using Kinetica. One participant complained that it was hard to get exact numbers for things. While the interface was well suited for qualitative findings, the participant had to tap three times to see numeric details for a point. Interface limitations did not help, as configuration sliders could not always provide enough granularity to participants so that they could set

| | Forces | Layouts | Mutations | Barriers | Filters | Queries & Overlays |
|---|---|---|---|---|---|---|
| **Forces** | ***Magnets*** Points are pulled to a finger | | | | | |
| **Layouts** | ***Force plots*** Points are pulled to their place in a chart | ***Fixed charts*** Points snap to their place on a chart | | | | |
| **Mutations** | ***Group by vector*** Group points that are moving similarly | ***Group by layout*** Group points by their place in a chart | ***Groups*** Put points into abstract groups | | | |
| **Barriers** | ***Jelly walls*** Points need an extra push to pass a wall | ***Layout walls*** As points pass, put them into a layout | ***Collision to data*** Points that hit a wall are assigned values | ***Walls*** Block points from a region of space | | |
| **Filters** | ***Query magnet*** Attract points that meet specific criteria | ***Detail view*** See point details in a layout popup | ***Group by filter*** Group points based on specific criteria | ***Sieves*** Walls only permit certain points | ***Show/hide*** Display points by criteria | |
| **Queries & Overlays** | ***Query fields*** Visualize the pull of different forces | ***Area details*** See details for points that meet criteria | ***Group zoom*** Zoom in and manipulate points | ***Lens*** Highlight certain points in a region | ***Selective overlay*** Highlight/select points by criteria | ***Overlays*** Color/scale points by data dimensions |

**Forces** - Act on points to move, attract, or accelerate
**Layouts** - Place points into meaningful locations
**Mutations** - Mutate, combine, or change points
**Barriers** - Prevent points from occupying a region
**Filters** - Selectively include or exclude based on criteria
**Queries** - Change the display appearance of points

**Table 1: Generative framework that combines different physics-based affordances to generate new tools/interactions**

exact filtering criteria they wanted for lenses and barriers. Kinetica did not have an undo action implemented, and some participants complained that they wanted to go back, but had already moved data around since then. This raises an interesting question of what undo operations mean in this space. Kinetica also used basic on-screen controls rather than gestures (see buttons in Figure 2). This meant that they sometimes got in the way, annoying users. Of all the tools, participants voiced the magnet as being the least useful, primarily because its one-dimensional force was subsumed by histogram charts whose behavior was clearer.

## GENERATIVE FRAMEWORK

Our initial work in Kinetica points to a fertile new area for exploration in data visualization. Physics-based visualization affordances make use of the inherent expertise users have based on their experiences in the everyday world in order to help them develop an understanding of data. These techniques are different from traditional visualization approaches, and, in light of users' desire at times for more familiar controls, may work well in concert. However, because they are different from traditional approaches, it is not always easy or intuitive to create new interactions.

As we explored physics-based visualization techniques in Kinetica, we developed a framework to generate potential affordances. From our development, we propose the following set of physics-based affordance primitives to enhance interactive multivariate data visualization:

- **Data** are represented as physical points that have associated physical properties that correspond to their values in different dimensions
- Data occupy a **sandbox** that contains them and allows for interaction. Interactions with the sandbox change the physical arrangement of the data, and leave traces of their activities.
- The user can employ **forces** to act on physical points either independently or as a result of their unique data. For instance, a magnet may repulse points with low values in a particular dimension.
- The user may use **layout** tools to force points into strict, meaningful locations, breaking with the physics metaphor when necessary (such as when allowing points to pass over or under others to avoid being trapped).
- The user can **mutate** points, for instance combining multiple points into one group so as to observe more points at once or see larger trends.
- The user may place **barriers** that block or selectively block points based on criteria.
- The user can employ **filters** to selectively include or exclude points to help avoid overload or choose only a small subset of interest.
- The user may use **queries and overlays** to change the appearance or behavior of points on the screen.

We imagine these affordances could work in a variety of contexts and situations. They could be used in 2D, which may be easier to interact with (as Sedlmair, Munzner, and Tory [29] suggest in the context of scatterplots), or in 3D where there is a richer space of interactions and there is room for more dimensions. Likewise, they can function using a keyboard, mouse or multi-touch.

Furthermore, these primitives could be combined to generate a much richer set of potential physics-based affordances. Mixing these different techniques together can provoke new ways to augment data visualizations with physics. Table 1 provides some examples of different tools that can come out of a combinatorial brainstorming on these primitives. For instance, combining a barrier that blocks points with a selective filter could generate Kinetica's permeable barrier. Combining forces with a scatterplot layout could create a force-based plot that pulls points to their proper location, and might work in concert with other barriers and forces. We found this framework useful for building the specific physics-based interaction methods we instantiated into Kinetica. We hope it will be useful for future researchers and practitioners in generating even more interaction types that can promote effective physics-based interactions with data.

## DISCUSSION AND LIMITATIONS

In this paper we introduced a general set of physics-based affordances for multivariate data visualization. These affordances come with both benefits and costs. For example, on one hand, tools that are easy for users to intuit and interpret might make exploring data easier. On the other hand, constraint-based systems may produce output whose causes are difficult to interpret. In this section we explore these benefits and costs through the lens of Kinetica and more generally, and describe future work that may help to make physics-based affordances more versatile.

### Potential Limitations

*Scalability.* Because of the iPad's limited computational resources and screen real estate, it is hard to analyze more than 500 points without either the rendering being sluggish or the screen filling. While making points smaller and simpler helps, the device itself is a limitation. This hearkens back to the more general scalability limitation of physics-based affordances: some devices, sizes, and interfaces are more suited to certain amounts of data and ways of interacting, and cognitive or attentional resources may be constrained to smaller amounts of data onscreen. While it might only be possible to render 200-500 points on an off-the-shelf iOS, Windows, or Android tablet, those 200 points could be abstract representations of thousands of points. Users might zoom in and out of different levels of detail (or infinite levels of detail [4]), especially given systems that help users make approximate queries and abstractions [8]. As devices grow in power and can render more points, this need may diminish, though the constraints of human visual attention and sensemaking might still suggest limiting the number of points shown.

Another possibility is to use different devices for different purposes. While a large surface may display all points, a smaller device in tandem might help users explore a smaller subset using more detail-oriented interactions. The large- and small-scale tools may not even need to share the same tool set because of their different needs. Instead of using differently sized displays, one might also employ collaboration. One user might take one section of a larger continuous physics environment, handling a certain kind of points, while another manages a different area.

*Effect attribution.* Participants in the study also expressed several situations where they had a hard time attributing effects. If they placed too many force-based plots on the screen, it became a mess of points that was hard to interpret. This is a general problem inherent in physics-based affordances. As more constraints and forces interact in the sandbox, it becomes harder to attribute them to specific causes. In the case of Kinetica, participants quickly found a solution: using the visual traces of what forces are currently in use to backtrack until the sandbox made sense again. It is possible that more feedback could help solve this issue, but could necessitate a tradeoff with increased clutter. For example, in a case where three forces are interacting on a small set of points all at once, perhaps each force could produce waves or lines of force that indicate their effects on the point.

*Expert usability and overload.* A few participants voiced concerns similar to Drucker et al. [6], where their expertise and familiarity with traditional WIMP statistical tools made them want quantitative tools like means or the ability to draw traditional bar charts. This is also suggested by Excel participants' ability to make more point-specific or quantitative findings compared to Kinetica. In principle such statistics could be added to a physics-based visualization, for example in a panel, though again tradeoffs in terms of training and screen real estate may be incurred.

*Overconstraining.* One risk in any constraint-based system is that points become trapped by the constraints such that the visualization does not faithfully represent the underlying relationships in the data. We tried very hard to eliminate such situations during the design of Kinetica. We introduced measures that broke with physical consistency as needed, allowing points to pass through one another to avoid bunching up at permeable barriers. If points are being pulled into a sorted order, then we once again disable collision temporarily to prevent mis-sorts. While such breaks with physical models could reduce the consistency of the visualization interactions, they represent a tradeoff between usability and data faithfulness. This is a general problem that may affect physics-based affordances as they are developed further, exacerbated by the difficulty of predicting what minima or overconstrained situations might occur in practice.

### Potential Benefits

*Minimal training.* Participants approached our novel interface, some never having used a touch device or tablet before, and were able within ten minutes to explore and generate findings from data they had never seen before. As Jacob et al. [18] mention, users already have an intuitive awareness of physics and their surrounding environment. As a result, many of these primitive affordances are in a sense already "trained" [27]. Users know that a magnet pulls objects towards it even if they do not know about magnetic forces and inverse square decay. This minimal barrier to entry surprised participants. One suggested that these approaches may be useful for teaching data literacy to young students or visual learners.

*Outlier detection.* Participants regularly spotted outliers in the data because they were in unusual locations, had different colors than the points near them, or moved unlike the rest of their nearby points. These properties emerged out of their general use of physics-based tools, and spatial correlations and groupings often make identifying outliers easier [14]. Participants felt encouraged to explore these points and try and explain why they were different, generating stories and expressing surprise.

*Awareness of distribution.* Kinetica participants made more descriptive and comparative findings, describing amounts of points and using words like *more* or *less*. Because data in a physics-based visualization are treated as physical objects, they can bunch up and form salient visual patterns. Imagine a histogram or scatterplot where points collide with each other (see Figure 2). Places where there is higher density of data are inherently more bunched together. This fits users' intuitions, and gives an implicit, visual depiction of data distribution without a need to chart frequencies. However, this qualitative understanding may come at the expense of the quantitative, point-by-point understanding that Excel can provide. A hybrid of these approaches, with more quantitative analytical techniques stepping in when a user is ready to focus on a small subset of data might give users a satisfying middle ground.

*Understanding process.* Kinetica participants also cited a better understanding of process in their qualitative responses. They mentioned fluidity and how everything was "right there" when they needed it on the screen. When participants used Kinetica to explore their data, the physics interactions unfolded in front of them, with points moving to their proper places on charts and gathering behind permeable barriers. These small changes, over time, helped them to interpret the end state of an operation and gave them new ideas for future hypotheses to explore. This may be a more general property of physics-based affordances, since as groups of points move together and possibly share visual features, people can gain a summary/qualitative understanding of their data [14].

*Augmenting working memory.* Participants in the Kinetica case also generated findings that made use of more dimensions than their Excel peers. This may be because of an ability to consider and keep track of more dimensions. As a user combines interactions in the process of exploring multivariate data, they leave traces of their explorations encoded onto the sandbox. For example, if a user uses a barrier to separate points based on one dimension, then the barrier remains as visual element, and the points are physically separated into two different areas of the sandbox. Because each of the tools leaves traces in the sandbox (see Figures 2, 3), it is easy to trace back what sorts of dimensions are at play. Further, because the user has been slowly moving points and arranging the field, the sandbox encodes contextual cues for the user which can improve their memory of the current state of the data and their past actions [5].

### Future Work

Kinetica only took a small slice of the physics-based affordances we generated using our framework. It could make use of many more, perhaps solving some user concerns in the process. In its current state, Kinetica does not do any layout computations. Everything is force directed, which runs the risk of local minima or overconstrained blocking. Layout algorithms that put points into predefined, semantically meaningful configurations might help users make sense of new data and also help solve some overload. For instance, points could be forced into clusters decided by k-means clustering, or pushed into tabular rows that are easy to manipulate along side a richer query language. Other than just filtering points by a simple </=/> criterion, barriers might employ complex logic or themselves push points that pass through into layouts.

More generally, physics-based affordances are not an end-all solution for multivariate data visualization. In Kinetica we mixed in traditional scatterplots because they were so familiar and so useful. Such affordances probably work best in a hybrid situation. If there are millions of points, maybe a WIMP technique on a computer is best for a first pass. Even within a system like Kinetica there also may be a need for traditional visualizations like parallel coordinates and plots. While this may break the consistency of the data-to-point physics model, it may improve user capabilities, especially if they already have expertise.

## CONCLUSION

In this paper we contributed an outline of physics-based affordances to augment multivariate data visualization. Using this outline, we developed a generative framework for ideating new interactions and affordances in this space. We instantiated some of these different affordances in the form of an iPad application, and conducted a comparative study between the physics-based visualization tool and a traditional WIMP spreadsheet tool with charts and pivot tables. In general the physics-based tool was more satisfying for participants, and led them to a more holistic understanding of the data they were exploring. Although this work is only one step towards a future of enhanced data interaction, we hope that in the future an interdisciplinary group of interface, information visualization, human factors, and other researchers will generate new and exciting approaches for exploring data that harness the growing tide of new devices and new ways of interacting.

## ACKNOWLEDGMENTS

This work was supported by NSF grants IIS-1149797, IIS-1217559, IIS-0968484, IIS-1111124, and Microsoft.

## REFERENCES

1. Agarawala, A. and Balakrishnan, R. Keepin'it real: pushing the desktop metaphor with physics, piles and the pen. *CHI*, (2006).
2. Ahlberg, C. and Shneiderman, B. Visual information seeking: Tight coupling of dynamic query filters with starfield displays. *CHI*, (1994), 313.

3. Baur, D., Lee, B., and Carpendale, S. TouchWave: kinetic multi-touch manipulation for hierarchical stacked graphs. *ITS*, (2012).
4. Bederson, B. and Hollan, J. Pad++ : A Zooming Graphical Interface for Exploring Alternate Interface Physics. *UIST*, (1994).
5. Chun, M. and Jiang, Y. Contextual cueing: Implicit learning and memory of visual context guides spatial attention. *Cognitive psychology 36*, 1 (1998), 28–71.
6. Drucker, S., Fisher, D., Sadana, R., and Herron, J. TouchViz: a case study comparing two interfaces for data analytics on tablets. *CHI*, (2013).
7. Elmqvist, N., Stasko, J., and Tsigas, P. DataMeadow: a visual canvas for analysis of large-scale multivariate data. *Information Visualization 7*, 1 (2008), 18–33.
8. Fisher, D., Popov, I., Drucker, S., and Schraefel, M. Trust me, i'm partially right: incremental visualization lets analysts explore large datasets faster. *CHI*, (2012).
9. Frisch, M., Kleinau, S., Langner, R., and Dachselt, R. Grids & guides: multi-touch layout and alignment tools. *CHI*, (2011).
10. Frisch, M., Langner, R., and Dachselt, R. Neat: a set of flexible tools and gestures for layout tasks on interactive displays. *ITS*, (2011).
11. Fruchterman, T., and Reingold. E. "Graph drawing by force-directed placement." *Software: Practice and experience* 21, 11 (1991), 1129-1164.
12. Goth, G. Brave NUI world. *Communications of the ACM*, (2011).
13. Hancock, M., Cate, T., and Carpendale, S.. "Sticky tools: full 6DOF force-based interaction for multi-touch tables." *ITS*, (2009).
14. Haroz, S. and Whitney, D. How Capacity Limits of Attention Influence Information Visualization Effectiveness. *IEEE Transactions on Visualization and Computer Graphics 18*, 12 (2012), 2402–2410.
15. Huron, S., Vuillemot, R., and Fekete J. "Visual Sedimentation." *IEEE Transactions on Visualization and Computer Graphics*19.12 (2013): 2446-2455.
16. Inselberg, A. and Dimsdale, B. Parallel coordinates: a tool for visualizing multi-dimensional geometry. *IEEE Transactions on Visualization and Computer Graphics*, (1990), 361–378.
17. Isenberg, P. and Isenberg, T. Data Visualization on Interactive Surfaces : A Research Agenda. *IEEE Computer Graphics and Applications*, April (2013).
18. Jacob, R., Girouard, A., Hirshfield, L., et al. Reality-based interaction: a framework for post-WIMP interfaces. *CHI*, (2008).
19. Jacob, R.J.K., Ishii, H., Pangaro, G., and Patten, J. A tangible interface for organizing information using a grid. *CHI*, 1 (2002), 339.
20. Keefe, D. and Isenberg, T. Reimagining the Scientific Visualization Interaction Paradigm. *Computer*, May (2013), 51–57.
21. Klemmer, S., Hartmann, B., and Takayama, L. How bodies matter: five themes for interaction design. *DIS*, (2006).
22. Kosara, R., Bendix, F., and Hauser, H. Parallel sets: interactive exploration and visual analysis of categorical data. *IEEE Transactions on Visualization and Computer Graphics 12*, 4 (2006), 558–68.
23. Lee, B., Isenberg, P., Riche, N.H., and Carpendale, S. Beyond Mouse and Keyboard: Expanding Design Considerations for Information Visualization Interactions. *IEEE Transactions on Visualization and Computer Graphics 18*, 12 (2012), 2689–2698.
24. Lee, B., Kazi, R., and Smith, G. SketchStory: Telling More Engaging Stories with Data through Freeform Sketching. *IEEE Transactions on Visualization and Computer Graphics*, August (2013).
25. Lembcke, S. Chipmunk Physics. www.chipmunk-physics.net.
26. Martin, A. and Ward, M. High Dimensional Brushing for Interactive Exploration of Multivariate Data. *VIZ*, (1995).
27. North, C., Dwyer, T., Lee, B., and Fisher, D. Understanding multi-touch manipulation for surface computing. *INTERACT*, (2009), 236–249.
28. Schmidt, S., Nacenta, M., Dachselt, R., and Carpendale, S. A set of multi-touch graph interaction techniques. *ITS*, (2010), 113.
29. Sedlmair, M., Munzner, T., and Tory, M. Empirical Guidance on Scatterplot and Dimension Reduction Technique Choices. *IEEE Transactions on Visualization and Computer Graphics*, August (2013).
30. Shneiderman, B. Dynamic queries for visual information seeking. *IEEE Software*, (1994), 1–18.
31. Spitzer, K., Eisenberg, M., and Lowe, C. Information Literacy: Essential Skills for the Information Age. *DESIDOC Journal of Library & Information Technology 28*, 2 (1998), 39–47.
32. Stasko, J., Goerg, C., and Liu, Z. Jigsaw: Supporting Investigative Analysis through Interactive Visualization. *Information Visualization 7*, 2 (2008), 118–132.
33. Ullmer, B., Ishii, H., and Jacob, R. Tangible query interfaces: Physically constrained tokens for manipulating database queries. *INTERACT*, (2003).
34. Walny, J., Lee, B., Johns, P., Henry Riche, N., and Carpendale, S. Understanding Pen and Touch Interaction for Data Exploration on Interactive Whiteboards. *IEEE Transactions on Visualization and Computer Graphics 18*, 12 (2012), 2779–2788.
35. Wilson, A., Izadi, S., Hilliges, O., Garcia-Mendoza, A., and Kirk, D. Bringing Physics to the Surface. *UIST*, (2008).
36. Wobbrock, J.O., Morris, M.R., and Wilson, A.D. User-defined gestures for surface computing. *CHI*, (2009), 1083.
37. Wong, P. and Bergeron, R. 30 Years of Multidimensional Multivariate Visualization. *Scientific Visualization : Overviews, Methodologies, and Techniques*, (1994), 3–33.
38. Wu, M. and Balakrishnan, R. Multi-finger and whole hand gestural interaction techniques for multi-user tabletop displays. *UIST*, (2003), 193–202.
39. Yi, J.S., Melton, R., Stasko, J., and Jacko, J. a. Dust & Magnet: multivariate information visualization using a magnet metaphor. *Information Visualization 00*, April (2005), 1–18.
40. Zickuhr, K. *Pew Report: Tablet Ownership 2013.*

# Traffigram: Distortion for Clarification via Isochronal Cartography

**Sungsoo (Ray) Hong[1], Yea-Seul Kim[1], Jong-Chul Yoon[2], Cecilia R. Aragon[1]**

University of Washington[1]
428 Sieg Hall, Box 352315
Seattle, WA 98195, USA
{rayhong, yeaseul.kim, aragon}@uw.edu

Kangwon National University[2]
245-711 Jungang-ro Samcheok-si,
Gangwon-do, Republic of Korea
media19@kangwon.ac.kr

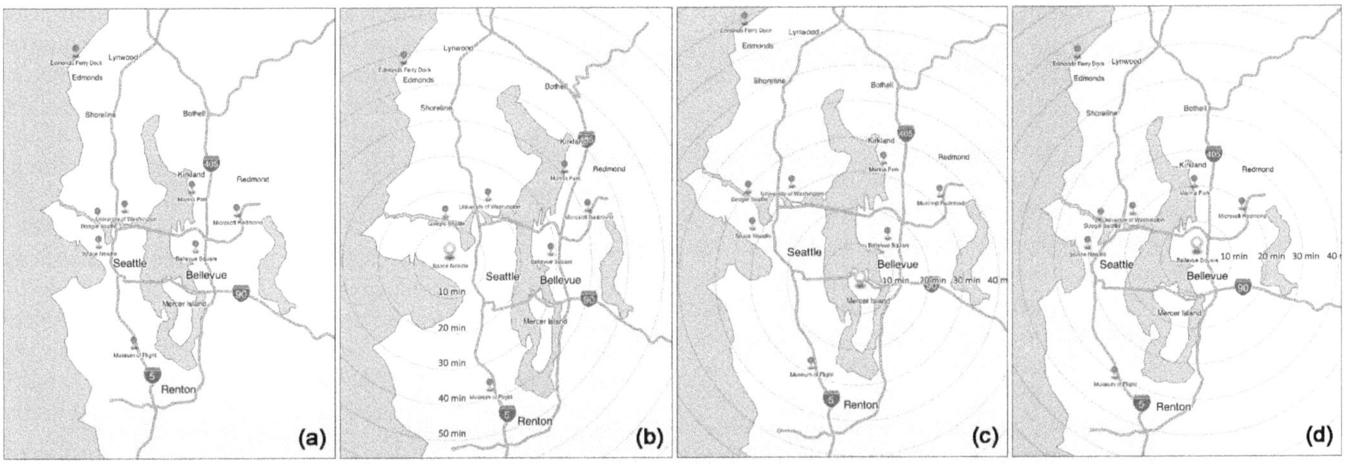


**Figure 1. Traditional map and Traffigram results warped from three different places in the Seattle area at 4:00 p.m., 26th of February 2013: (a) Traditional map; (b) From the Space Needle; (c) Mercer Island; (d) Bellevue square.**

## ABSTRACT

Most geographic maps visually represent physical distance; however, travel time can in some cases be more important than distance because it directly indicates availability. The technique of creating maps from temporal data is known as isochronal cartography, and is a form of distortion for clarification. In an isochronal map, congestion expands areas, while ideal travel conditions make the map shrink in comparison to the actual distance scale of a traditional map. Although there have been many applications of this technique, detailed user studies of its efficacy remain scarce, and there are conflicting views on its practical value. To attempt to settle this issue, we utilized a user-centered design process to determine which features of isochronal cartography might be most usable in practice. We developed an interactive cartographic visualization system, Traffigram, that features a novel combination of efficient isochronal map algorithms and an interface designed to give map users a quick and seamless experience while preserving geospatial integrity and aesthetics. We validated our design choices with multiple usability studies. We present our results and discuss implications for design.


*CHI 2014*, April 26–May 1, 2014, Toronto, Ontario, Canada.

ACM 978-1-4503-2473-1/14/04...$15.00.
http://dx.doi.org/10.1145/2556288.2557224

### Author Keywords

Isochrones; time-space map; information visualization; geographic visualization; map user interface; map usage

### ACM Classification Keywords

H.5.0. Information interfaces and presentation: General

## INTRODUCTION

Maps provide a simple, yet powerful visualization method for representing geospatial reality [9]. Many maps are constructed to representationally reflect geospatial dimensions. Since they reflect real-world geography (or attempt to reflect, as effectively as possible, the three-dimensional Earth as a two-dimensional construct), individuals can intuitively estimate the distance between two points on a map by measuring the distance between them. However, physical proximity may not always most effectively predicate accessibility. Urban travel is fraught with traffic congestion and uncertainty; the variable nature of the time between two points in urban areas regularly distresses people because geospatially representative maps may fail to represent realistic accessibility of any given point on the map.

Meanwhile, various digital map solutions and widely used devices (including mobile) have led people to use digital maps more frequently in complex contexts. Compared to traditional map usage, which is primarily focused on understanding geography, users of digital maps may wish to select a place to live based on travel times from their workplace, evaluate the traffic situation downtown at a particular time, or select a branch bank in an unfamiliar area. One critical aspect of knowledge often sought by digital map users is temporal information, because it helps users choose when and where to move during increasingly busy lives. Travel time between two points is easy to display, but it is not so obvious how to effectively present multiple travel times to a variety of potential destinations. Limitations in human working memory must be addressed [21]. Additionally, presenting travel times in a traditional "static" equidistant map is a challenging task. This is because, first, there may be an intrinsic discrepancy between spatial distance and spatial accessibility. Second, travel time information is based on specific locations (origins) and is always changing [2, 3].

Isochronal cartography is an intuitive visualization technique to represent temporal information. This cartography aligns every point on the map with isochrones, or temporally equidistant contours, from the origin. Studies have shown that humans most efficiently glean quantitative information from spatial position [14]. Thus, by using position to represent travel time from the origin, a user can directly compare travel times to multiple points. However, there are several barriers to implementing such an interface, including the difficulty of collecting, managing, and dealing with discontinuities in travel time data and presenting them in a usable interface, and the relative lack of usability studies of isochronal cartography [7].

This paper's contributions are the following:

- Traffigram, a novel web-based map visualization for users in areas of high and variable traffic congestion.
- An optimized isochronal warping algorithm and database designed to present a seamless map user experience (within a second per user query). Our database is extensible across dimensions of both time and space. We resolve the challenge of efficiently and usably presenting dynamic geotemporal information within a traditionally geospatial construct (there is a complex set of visual discontinuities that must be resolved).
- A usability study consisting of four user scenarios and one survey supporting our work's applicability in real world settings. We focus on how effectively a geotemporal cartogram aids people in recognizing temporal accessibility and present a set of design guidelines for this type of isochronal cartography.

For the project, we utilized real-time traffic data from the Seattle metropolitan area. This region includes areas of heavy traffic, bridges, and a large number of corporate businesses including Microsoft, Boeing, Amazon, Starbucks, and others. Fig. 1 depicts an example Traffigram screenshot. On the left is (a) the traditional cartographic representation. The three visualizations on the right show the Traffigram result on February 26, 2013 at 4:00 p.m. from three separate origins: from left to right, (b) the Space Needle, (c) Mercer Island, and (d) Bellevue Square. In Fig. 1(b) it is easy to see the easterly/westerly expansion of the landmass just north of Seattle indicating the slower roads and increased traffic in that direction at that time of day coming from the Space Needle; at the same time, Fig. 1(b) reveals an east/west narrowing in Bellevue, indicating easy access in that direction coming from the Space Needle.

## RELATED WORK

### Simplification and Abstraction in Map Design

For many years, researchers have attempted to understand how mapmakers can produce effective, visually esthetic, cognitive, and communicative visual designs. This is a challenging problem because the associated data is complex and has many dimensions. Even with meaningful information, the expression of these data is a difficult task. To manage these data, it is best to capitalize on the human faculty for processing visual information, thereby improving comprehension, memory, and inference. [1]. Designers put considerable effort into the selection of data to represent in their visualization and how to visualize it in order to aid human perception [12]. Harry Beck's map of the London Underground is a stellar example of such design practice. He introduced the pivotal idea of mapping by simplification when he reduced the complex London subway system to the renowned representational London Subway Map of 1933. This visualization did not reflect geographical reality, but it helped people in London use the complex subway with ease and comfort. Kopf et al. [10] also used simplification to abridge complex route information thereby aiding users' cognition on understanding routes to their destinations through a cartographic visualization. Traffigram builds on these visualizations by reducing the complexity of a traditional map to isochrones. Thus by sacrificing the accurate representation of geographical reality and by focusing on the selective representation of information, users gain a greater understanding of temporal accessibility.

### Time-space Maps and Isochronal Cartography

Adding temporal information to maps has been investigated for several decades [11], and time-space maps or isochronal cartography has been developed as one solution. Shimizu's approach is one of the earliest time-space cartography examples [17]. He proposed the term "time-space map", and cartographically represented a major Japanese city with elapsed train travel time. Shimizu minimized the discrepancy between travel time and actual distance between connected points by using optimization to preserve spatial integrity [18, 19]. His approach does not include a user origin or isochrones, so the user may have difficulty in extracting exact travel time from one point to another. Lightfoot and Steinberg's travel-time map of Great Britain utilized colored isochrones to represent train travel time [13]. This work successfully preserved travel time without distorting geography by using color, but multi-layered color along with other information can render this solution illegible in some cases. Karlin redesigned the London underground map around the time it takes to travel between specific points [8]. Inspired by this work, Carden created an interactive web application of Karlin's London underground map [20]. This application uses an interlaced circular background to represent travel times. Bies upgraded the time-space map to a more user-centric formulation via triangulation [2]. Her approach lets users select an origin and shows the travel time to other areas of the map. Chen proposed subjective cartography to present various contexts including travel time [3]. Despite the multiplicity of approaches to time-space cartography, few usability studies have been conducted [21], and Kaiser pointed out that further usability studies are needed to verify the effectiveness of this technique [7]. Many of these approaches focused on entities with scheduled temporal patterns, such as trains. However, automobile traffic conditions are unscheduled. To address this situation, Traffigram utilizes a traffic anticipation model which will be described in more detail in the Algorithm section.

### Quantitative Presentation in Cartogram: Linear vs. Area

For anyone who has explored the many different projections of the Earth, it is easy to understand the difficulty of the cartographer's task of reducing three dimensions to two [6]. While there are challenges associated with people realizing that the landscape is not "accurate" as represented on a traditional map, it is important to realize that cartographers have been wrangling with this issue perhaps since Anaximander the ancient Greek cartographer, who first scribed such representations over 2500 years ago. With these efforts, many researchers have attempted unique geo-visualization methodologies to convey more insightful context to people and to enhance human perception and cognition. Linear and area cartogram methods have both advantages and limitations. Linear cartograms use position to present quantitative data. As Mackinlay noted [14], position is the most powerful method to present quantitative information; thus it is generally used to represent travel time or positional relationships in cartograms. Beck's [1] and Carden's [20] London underground maps are examples of linear cartograms. Area is not as visually effective for presenting quantitative data than position, but it is frequently used in cartography when time or distance is already represented by linear position because people's background knowledge of the map's contour and position help them to understand the secondary information. Worldmapper [5] is a geo-visualization system that presents statistical data such as national population and wealth around the world by using a value-by-area technique. Newman's work with election maps also uses an area cartogram technique to reveal real voting power that might be obscured by geographic area data [15]. In general, linear cartograms are effective at visualizing quantitative metrics, but excessive warping may impact geographical integrity, perception, and usability.

## TRAFFIGRAM

### Algorithm

To address the issues mentioned above, we developed a novel combination of warping and shortest-path algorithms to display isochronal maps interactively. Traffic information has two important characteristics; it is direction-dependent and ever-changing. These aspects require two user inputs to our system; an origin (initial user position) and a specific time of day/date. With these inputs, we describe the four steps of the Traffigram algorithm: traffic network construction [Fig. 2(a)], real traffic data acquisition [Fig. 2(b)], isochronal contour generation based on shortest path analysis [Fig. 2(c)], and thin-plate spline (TPS) based warping [Fig. 2(d)].

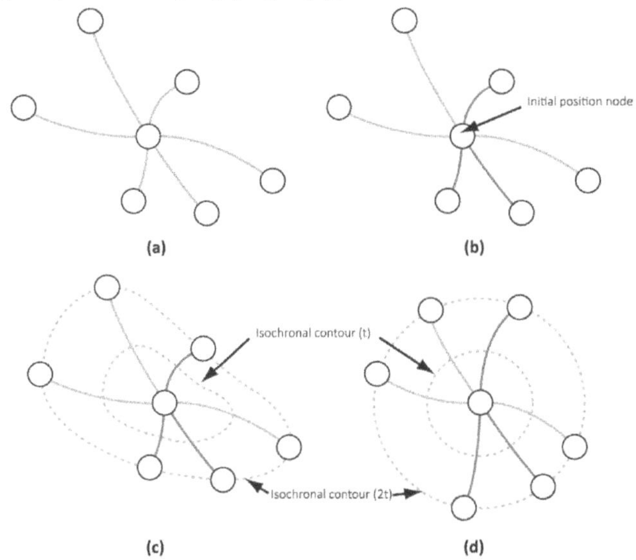


**Figure 2. Traffigram algorithm: (a) Traffic network construction; (b) Traffic data acquisition; (c) Isochronal contour generation; (d) TPS warping**

*Traffic Network Construction*

The first step in the construction of Traffigram is developing a directional network structure (i.e. directionally-weighted graph) that reflects an existing road infrastructure in the Seattle area. This task is accomplished by overlaying a network structure onto a traditional spatial-based map. The traffic network functions as a skeleton; this structure must accurately represent the real road infrastructure and general traffic information. In our system, every node represents a geographical point; node data includes longitude and latitude. In practice, we have two types of nodes: one, a crossroad with geographic significance and above a certain threshold of traffic. The other type is a point on a highway related to an entrance, exit, or fork. Every edge represents a road that connects two nodes; the presence of an edge means two nodes are geographically adjacent and physically connected. Our system contains crossroad/crossroad edges, highway/ crossroad edges (highway exit), crossroad/highway edges (highway entrance) and highway/highway edges. Fig. 3(a) depicts the traffic network structure of Traffigram applied to the Seattle area. The challenge of structuring this network lies in applying the following factors: occasional one-way traffic, numerous highway entrances/exits, and complex connections related to inter-highway junctions. As a result, we simplified the metropolitan Seattle area road infrastructure by representing it with 107 nodes and 435 edges. We considered the following aspects when sampling for traffic network construction. First, we evenly distributed every node and edge in our coverage area considering population and traffic issues. Second, we represented existing routes to preserve geospatial realism. Third, we focused on building an interactive warping and construction system to provide a faster, more responsive user interface.

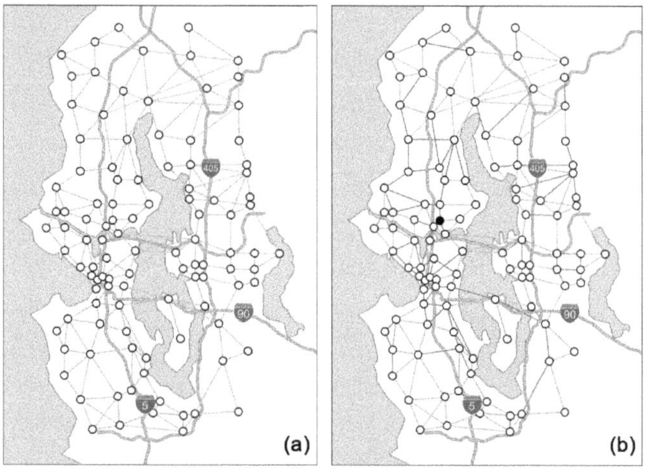

**Figure 3. Network construction and data acquisition: (a) Traffic network structure; (b) Congestion factor from black node: green Cij=1, yellow 1< Cij <2 and red 2≤ Cij**

*Real Traffic Data Acquisition*

The second phase involves the gathering of information on traffic conditions. In our optimized traffic network structure, we weighted every edge with real travel time. Different types of temporal traffic information are available; data might be aggregated from individuals (i.e. observed on a highway) or collected from a public data center. We chose to use the Bing map API and data since publicly-available sources in the Seattle area currently only address primary arterial routes. Traffigram gathers travel time data every 30 minutes. Upon user request with a specific time and origin, Traffigram fetches weekly periodic data and presents the weighted mean value to the user. Utilizing periodic traffic data to estimate traffic flow is a classic and broadly-adopted technique and with this approach, the database delivers a meaningful and concrete estimation model to a user. We then calculated a congestion factor for every edge by dividing the actual travel time (with traffic) by the baseline time (without traffic). Fig. 3(b) illustrates one snapshot of our data. The roads depicted in red show congestion while those in green are clear or uncongested. Fig. 3(b) depicts a visualization of the congestion factor of the network. The congestion factor $C_{ij}$ from node $i$ to $j$ is encoded as edge color in this figure. A value of 1 is green, $1< C_{ij} <2$ yellow and $2 \leq C_{ij}$ red.

*Isochronous Contour Generation*

Traffigram then calculates every node's shortest route from the origin via Dijkstra's shortest path algorithm [4]. In our network, the system automatically generates one virtual edge if the user's chosen origin is not the same as the representative, predefined node; the virtual edge links the user-selected origin and the "adjacent node" that has a minimum geospatial Euclidean distance from the origin. Based on the shortest path analysis, Traffigram creates isochrones by connecting all points that are equitemporally distant from the origin; i.e. all points on a given contour are an equal amount of time away from the origin. Fig. 4 depicts this process. With the shortest path analysis, Traffigram gathers travel time information [Fig. 4(a)]. In Fig. 4(b), we can see the disparity of several contour intervals by comparing the three double-headed arrows. For each arrow, a traveler spends the same amount of time to traverse the varying distances. Thus, the lengths of these arrows are inversely proportional to the degree of congestion. The route through downtown Seattle is highly congested (the shortest arrow), Bellevue (to the right of the bay) is less congested, and Northgate (north of the center contour) is the least congested.

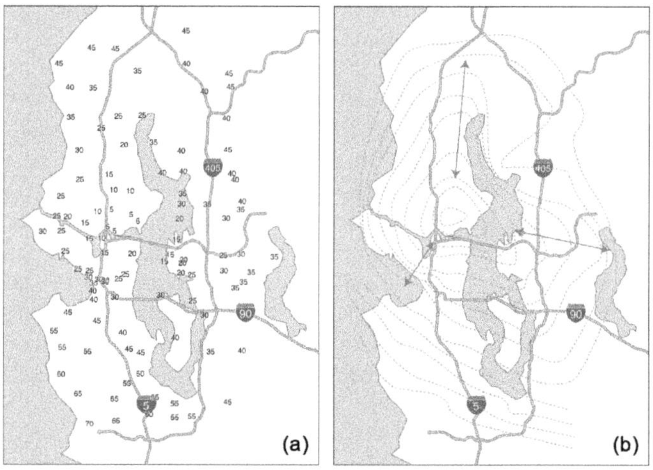

**Figure 4. Isochrone generation: (a) Shortest path analysis; (b) Isochrone construction; length of double headed arrows represents congestion**

*TPS Warping*

For the final step, we warped the equidistant map to generate an isochronal cartogram, using thin-plate spline warping (TPS). TPS is a well-known algorithm that has been widely used as a non-rigid transformation model in image alignment and shape matching [23]. TPS was chosen since it has two important merits. First, the algorithm provides closed-form solutions for interactive warping and thus enables fast computation. This feature fits well with the goal of Traffigram since the system should generate an isochronal map within a second to provide a seamless map usage experience to a user. Furthermore, TPS can generate smooth map results while preserving the source among several smoothing techniques; TPS is known as one of the most robust-toward-outlier solutions [23]. We begin by generating a sparse vector map [Fig. 5(a)] that illustrates the displacements necessary to align isochronous nodes into circular shapes. The red and blue vectors visualize the gap between geospatial accessibility and actual geography. With this sparse vector map, we interpolate a TPS surface and apply it to create a final result. Fig. 5(b) shows a warped map; note that the landmass located west of the bay (downtown Seattle and the University District) is largely expanded while the landmass located east of the bay (Bellevue/Newcastle) is condensed compared with Fig. 5(a).

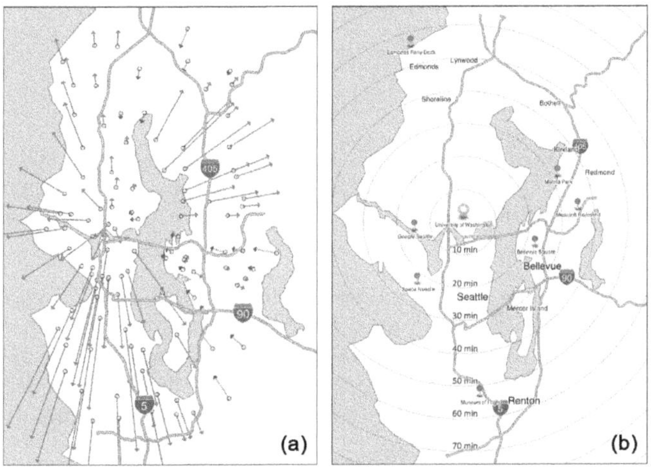


**Fig. 5. TPS warping: (a) Sparse vector map, red vectors denote expansion (congestion) while blue indicates shrink (nearly ideal condition); (b) Warped Traffigram result**

### Design Variations

Even though the algorithm created an efficient isochronal cartogram, the result needs to be visually recognizable to users to allow them to rapidly obtain the actual information they want. During our ideation phase, we considered the following questions: What are the cognitive processes involved with "consuming" the information presented on a map? What roles do maps play in embodied experience? How do cartographers convey physical constructs to a map user and how might a distorted map advance this conveyance? After the development of numerous low-fidelity prototypes, we produced a set of what we believed were functionally useful, cognitively efficient, and aesthetically appealing results based on Mackinlay's graphical representation theory [14]. We evaluated them via a usability study, which will be described in more detail in the user research method section. Fig. 6(a) shows the basic warping result without additional visual cues. Fig. 6(b) was designed to maximize the power of "position" in Mackinlay's theory by placing 10-minute band circular isochrones. We combined color information in an interlaced manner in 6(c) to enhance the recognizability of each band, as used in Carden's visualization [20]. In figure 6(d) and 6(e), we offered a grid and city boundary respectively in order to present users with a sense of geographical spatiality by utilizing "area". The grid gives users a visual cue for physical distance; each grid has 1.5-mile length and height. 6(e) gives users geographical information via city boundaries, often used in area cartograms. This visualization is useful if excessive warping is present. We also added a color scheme in figure 6(e) for each city we covered. Seattle shows the most congestion. Cities adjacent to Seattle, such as Shoreline, Bellevue, Kirkland, Burien and Edmond have a congestion factor between 1.00 and 2.00. The other cities have minimal traffic issues. In Fig. 6(f), we added vectors whose lengths represent expansion or shrinking based on the current traffic situation.

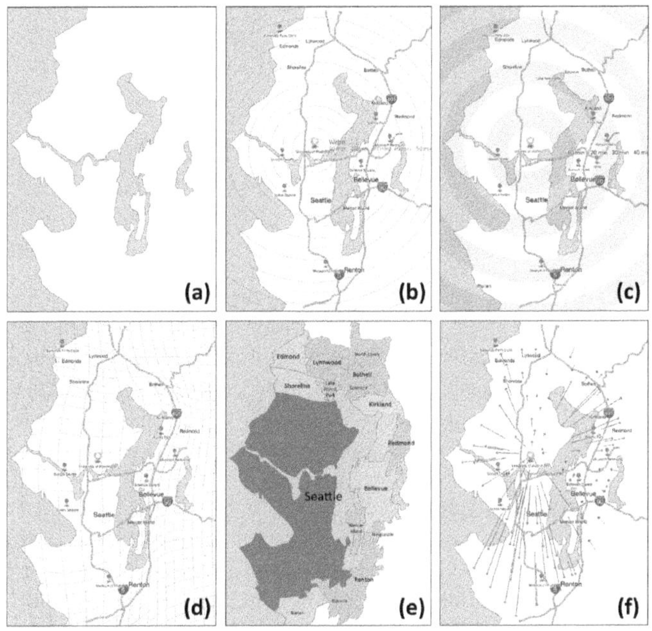


**Figure 6. Design Variations: (a) Warped map; (b) Con-centric circular view; (c) Color-interlaced concentric circular view; (d) Grid view; (e) City view; (f) Vector view**

### Traffigram User Interface

We recorded users' comments and opinions about their needs and expectations of isochronal cartography, that is, if the service might be helpful in their daily lives. Specifically, we gathered feedback about which functionalities they found helpful, and which interfaces they preferred. We discuss this further in the user research section. Fig. 7 presents a Traffigram screenshot. Users can input their origin as text (i.e. address), or can drag and drop the cursor in the map display area. Equidistant and isochronal maps are presented simultaneously and are synchronized as the user pans. (Zoom in/out is not available in this version.) At the bottom, a user can select time. Drop box input allows the user to select from Monday to Sunday, or "now". If users select one day of the week, the time setting is enabled, and users may choose a specific time. In that case, the average travel time for that specific timeframe is retrieved from the database and the isochronal map is updated.

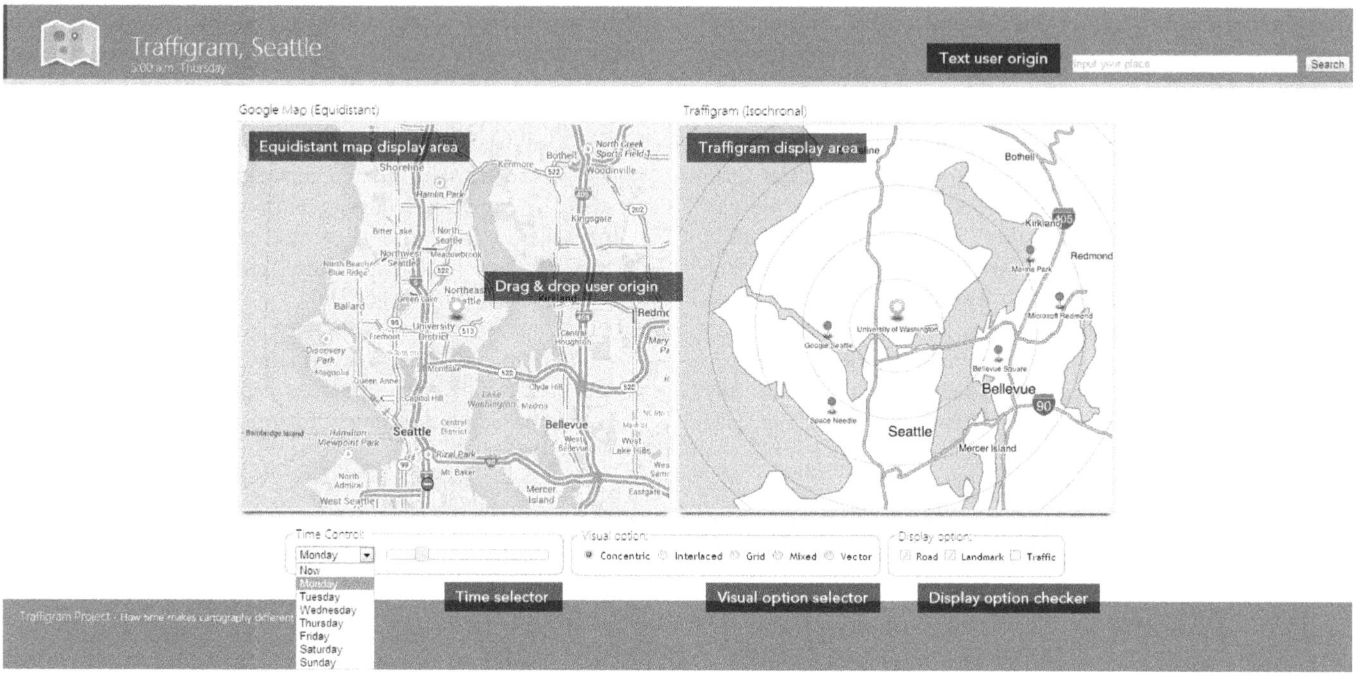


**Figure 7. Traffigram User Interface**

If user selects the "now" option, the system fetches the most recent travel time information. As we described, the database automatically gathers the travel time information every 30 minutes. Users can select design variations via a radio button interface, and also can select visual components (i.e. road, landmark, or traffic information).

## USER RESEARCH

We conducted a usability test to evaluate how Traffigram might be perceived and used in daily life. We recruited 25 participants (19 male), 12 in the USA and 13 in South Korea, via e-mail to student mailing lists. All participants were university students. Prior to each session, we briefly explained Traffigram to participants verbally. After participants felt comfortable with the main purpose of Traffigram, we conducted the session. Participants completed four tasks and one design preference survey. After the survey, we inquired about their perceptions of the Traffigram user interface. Participants were tested with several visualizations generated by Traffigram via a think-aloud protocol. All images used in the study were displayed on a computer monitor. Twelve subjects lived in the Seattle area were familiar with the area that Traffigram covers. In contrast, the 13 participants from South Korea had never been in Seattle and had little knowledge of the area. None of the subjects dropped out throughout the tasks and analysis was performed on all responses (n=25). The orders of every comparative analysis (i.e. task 2 and task 4) were generated using a Latin square to counterbalance carryover effect.

### Task 1: Landmark Matching

We designed this task to understand the effect of distortion on map recognizability. We presented two images to participants on the same screen. One of the images showed a non-distorted map containing area, district, and freeway information with seven different landmarks. The other image showed a distorted Traffigram visualization with the same seven landmarks. Participants were asked to move seven pin icons in the distorted map to where they thought each landmark belonged. There is a possibility that geotemporal disparities (such as a congested route or speed limits) may cause the isochrones to contort in a highly eccentric manner; in this case, the distortion will obviously break spatial integrity. For more realistic applicability however, Traffigram must provide information without hampering readability. We used one of the most distorted results to make the experiment more challenging and to account for this possibility. Figure 9 shows the test result. The average time on the task was 66.7 sec. (SD = 31.0). Fig. 8 depicts a result of this task. Magenta circles represent a 1.5-mile spatial radius for each landmark. To analyze task error, we used average Euclidian distance of discrepancy between user's selected point and actual point. In this task, we hoped to avoid the issue that smaller less-congested grid areas might be harder to identify with their icons. Interestingly, we found that this was not the case, since we observed the highest user errors for the Museum of Flight, which was only the fifth most congested area out of seven spots, which in part, seems to dismiss our rationale. These errors may be due to the fact that there are very few visual references (coastlines, crossings, bridges, etc.) by the museum. In contrast, Bellevue Square has the second smallest grid area, but none of the participants identified the place incorrectly. The proximity of the city name may also have helped in this case.

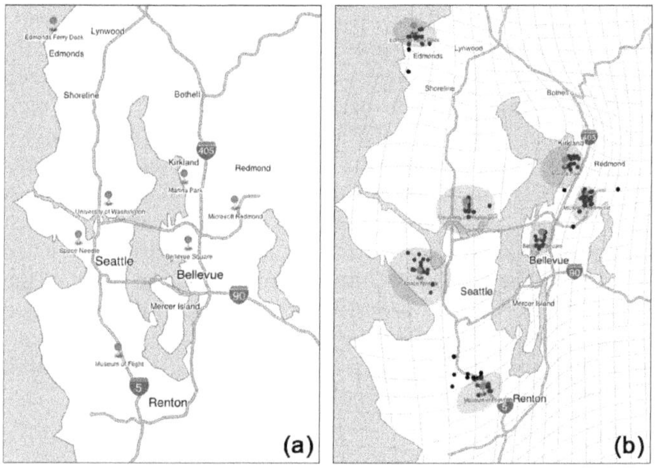


**Figure 8. Landmark matching: (a) Reference map; (b) Landmark matching result**

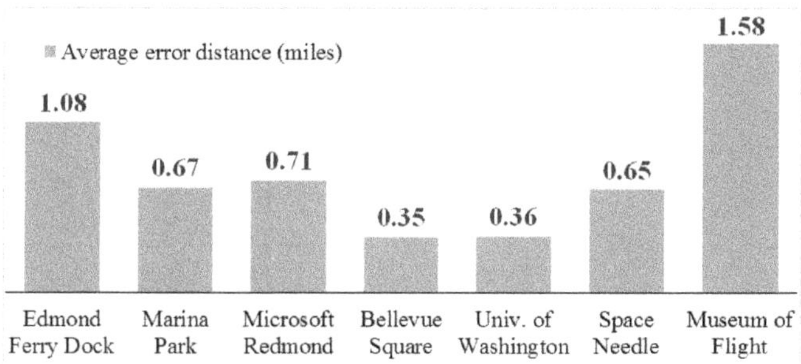


**Figure 9. Average error distance on Task 1**

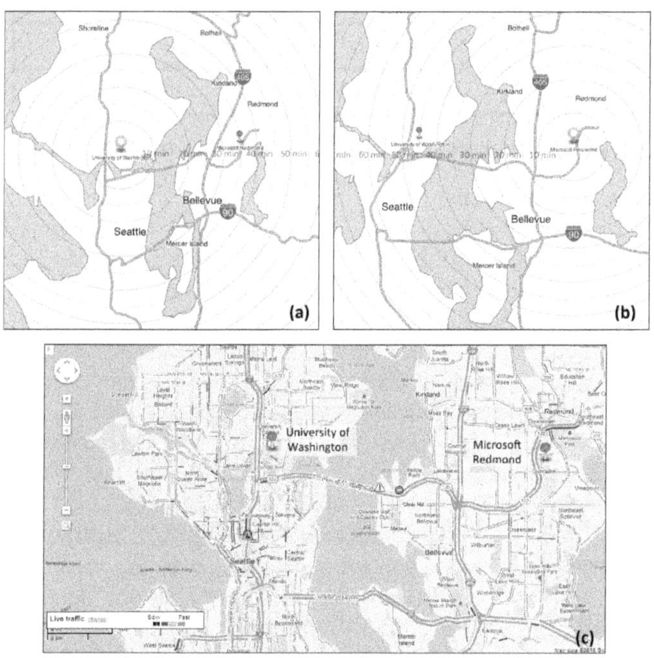


**Figure 10. Where do we meet?: (a) Warped from University of Washington; (b) Warped from Microsoft Redmond; (c) Google map traffic visualization**

**Task 2: Where do we meet?**

In task 2, we studied how efficiently Traffigram provides directions when two or more people have different initial positions, yet want to know the traffic situation for a given time. Our hypothesis was that users would recognize traffic situations more easily with Traffigram than with a traditional map utilizing a traffic color metaphor. The scenario was presented to the subject as follows: one person is at the University of Washington, and one person is at Microsoft in Redmond, and they want to meet on Wednesday at 4:00 p.m. at whichever place is closest (temporally) to the other. We then presented two Traffigram visualizations with origins at, respectively, the University of Washington [Fig. 10(a)] and Microsoft Redmond [Fig. 10(b)] and Google Maps' traffic view [Fig. 10(c)] in rotation. Google Maps depicts an asymmetric traffic condition; the bridge connecting the two areas has different amounts of congestion depending on the direction of travel. Participants were asked to determine which commute was shorter based on time and relevant traffic issues. This task illustrated the degree to which Traffigram aided the correct decision (meeting in Redmond) and how efficiently it led to understanding compared to the use of a traditional traffic visualization. Table 1 relays the experiment results. Time-on-task between Google Maps and Traffigram were significantly different ($t=-3.06$, $p<0.05$) and the correct answer ratio of Traffigram (96%) was also higher than Google Maps (72%). The time on Google Maps and Traffigram between American and Korean was not significant ($F(1,23) = 1.46$, n.s.) The participants understood the concept of Traffigram as they counted rings on the map or estimated length between two places to answer quickly. However, it may have been burdensome for the user in that Traffigram uses two images while Google Maps uses only one.

| Tool | Average time on task | Correct Answer Ratio |
|---|---|---|
| Google Maps | 25.3 sec. | 72% |
| Traffigram | 14.3 sec. | 96% |

**Table 1. Time on task and correct answer ratio on Task 2**

**Task 3: When should I head home?**

Even when the origin does not change, traffic is a time-dependent metric. The third experiment was devised to evaluate whether Traffigram could enable people to understand ever-changing traffic information. In this experiment, participants were asked to decide when they would like to return home from work. On a computer screen, we presented one traditional map [Fig. 11(a)] and three Traffigram visualizations centered on their fictional work location of Google Seattle in Fremont from 4:30 p.m., 4:45 p.m., and 5:00 p.m. [Fig. 11(b-d)]. We then asked participants which departure time minimizes their time on the road. 23 out of 25 participants (92%) provided the correct answer of 4:30 p.m.

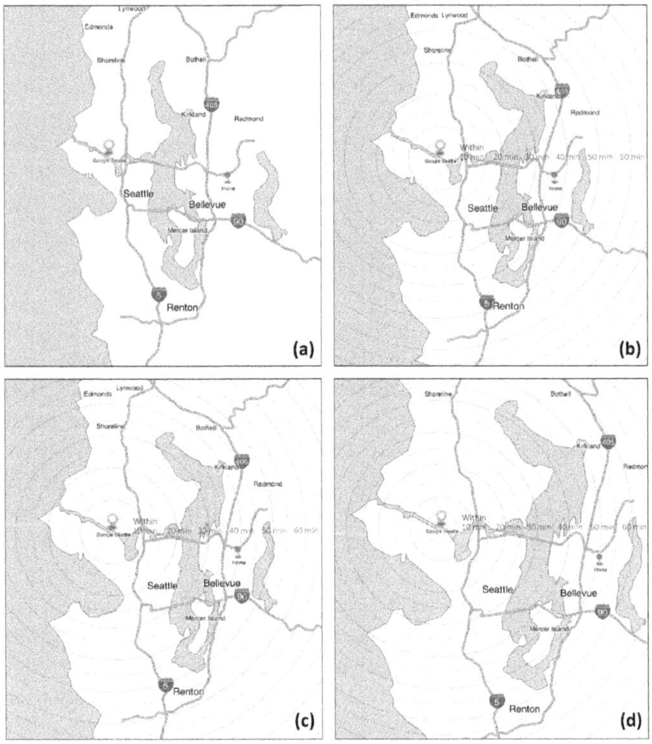


**Figure 11. When should I head home?: (a) Equidistant map; (b) Warped at 4:30 p.m.; (c) Warped at 4:45 p.m.; (d) Warped at 5:00 p.m.**

The difference between American and Korean was not significant (F(1,23) = 1.92, n.s.). We evaluated the learnability of Traffigram through this task as well, as the average time-on-task decreased 38% compared to Task 2, even though this task involved an additional image. (On the previous task, participants spent on average 14.3 seconds, and for this task, 8.9 seconds.) 24% of the participants chose their answer within 6 seconds. 52% of participants stated they found this task the most useful among all the tasks they had conducted.

### Task 4: Pizza delivery

In this experiment, our main purpose was to understand Traffigram's utility when a user is considering multiple potential destinations. A fictional pizza restaurant owner runs a delivery service near the University of Washington. He has to decide which pizzas to make first since his customers are spread out across the Seattle area and he has a 40 minute delivery policy. In order to make sure he meets the deadline, he queues his orders appropriately. In practice, this task is somewhat artificial since an algorithm could easily sort the orders. However, we wanted to test the situation where users were selecting from among multiple destinations visually. (A better task, and one to be studied in future work, would be to select from multiple rental homes assuming a fixed work location. In that case, the context of each location is important and a list would be insufficient.) After explaining the scenario, we asked participants to sort pizza orders from longest to shortest travel time using two different visualizations; Traffigram map [Fig. 12(left)], and list view with address [Fig. 12(right)]. The difference between the task times presented in Table 2 is statistically significant (p < 0.0001). The time difference between American and Korean participants was not significant (F(1,23) = 0.03, n.s.). Participants completed the task 1.7 times faster with Traffigram. We also asked the participants how stressed they were during each sub-task using a Likert scale from no stress to highly stressed and 88% of participants answered Traffigram was less stressful. Even though Traffigram lacked the capacity to inform users of the exact travel time, participants still felt less stressed completing the task with the visualization. Thus Traffigram could potentially be a useful solution when user is located in one spot and (s)he has multiple choices of destination.

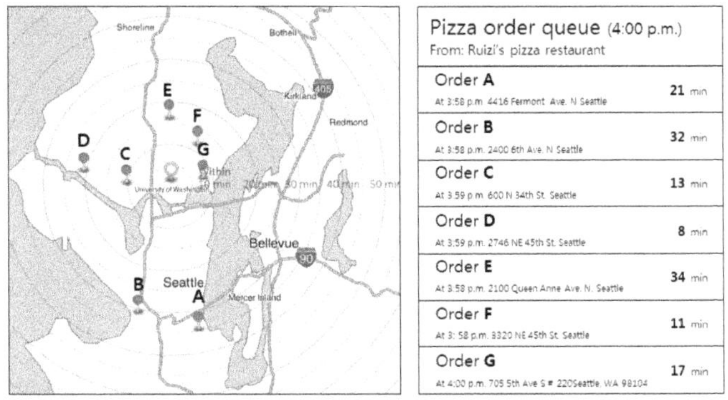


**Figure 12. Perception test: Traffigram pizza order result (left); List view of pizza order (right)**

| Tool | Average time on task | Correct Answer Ratio |
|---|---|---|
| List View | 36.7 sec. | 92% |
| Traffigram | 21.9 sec. | 96% |

**Table 2. Time on task and correct answer ratio on Task 4**

### Post-task survey

After completing four experiments, we surveyed participants' design preference from among variations Fig. 6(b) - Fig. 6(f). We asked participants to choose one or two design variations that were visually intriguing. After that, we asked them to select the most practical design variation. The result of this preference survey and some of their insights are listed in Table 3. Fig. 6(c) received the highest number of votes for both criteria; several subjects mentioned that 6(c) clearly explains travel time and is easy to recognize. Furthermore, many subjects mentioned that they found 6(c) to be aesthetically beautiful. Meanwhile, many participants responded negatively to design variations 6(e) and 6(f). Responses included: 6(e) is not detailed; difficult to recognize the difference between normal maps. One subject mentioned that he couldn't find any information he wanted to know in 6(e). Three participants remarked they didn't prefer 6(f) because it was visually too busy. For the aesthetic criterion, survey results depicted participants' varied preferences compared to the practical criterion; many people had difficulty deciding among 6(b) through 6(d). From the aesthetic perspective, people mentioned that colored circles are clear, easy to perceive, and more attractive than interlaced thick and thin lines. Some people remarked that 6(d) has potential because it supports their need for a sense of distance. For the practical criterion, more than 50% of participants chose 6(c). Many remarked that the power of Traffigram lay in enabling people to understand the variation in travel time from their place of origin to their destination. Participants felt that concentric circles (i.e. isochrones) helped achieve this goal. Interestingly, in both groups, participants suggested a new design variation; combining 6(c) and 6(d), so that users can perceive travel time and distance concurrently.

| | 6(b) | 6(c) | 6(d) | 6(e) | 6(f) |
|---|---|---|---|---|---|
| Aesthetic | 17% | 39% | 28% | 11% | 4% |
| Practical | 20% | 52% | 20% | 0% | 8% |

**Table 3. Design preference (Voting portion)**

## DISCUSSION

### Implications for Design

Based on our experience, we suggest the following usability principles for developers of isochronal cartography:

- *Present equidistant map and isochronal map simultaneously*: Seven participants mentioned that Traffigram would be more useful if an equidistant map is placed next to the isochronal map so that the user has a sense of both distance and time, and two subjects mentioned their worry about the possibility of illegibility caused by severe distortion. We believe this design decision could relieve that problem.
- *Provide easy-to-use time and origin setting*: Five subjects mentioned preferences for inputting position or time. Two of them proposed a specific user interface. To accommodate these needs, Traffigram provides text based input (i.e. address) and drag-and-drop based input in map display area for origin setting, and day selection dropbox and time setting slider bar for time selection. In the day selection dropbox, users can select the day from Monday to Sunday, or select "now". They also can modify the time that they want to see with a slider bar.
- *Interactivity and seamless experience*: Five subjects were concerned about the loading time and interactivity of the map if they were to frequently change user origin and time information. Our algorithm (including TPS and database design to gather travel time information), displays results within a second, which appears to be acceptable for map usage [16].
- *Consider aesthetics and practicality*: Users preferred 6(b): concentric circular view, 6(c): color-interlaced concentric circular view and 6(d): grid view. Table 3 shows the sums of 85% for aesthetic and 92% for practical reasons in the post-task survey.
- *Present proper complexity in isochronal cartograms*: One of the participants said that "Google Maps gives me too much information while showing routes. It makes me think too much." Three subjects described the visual complexity of maps they ordinarily use; this is a very important issue in map design [10]. Providing too much information on a distorted map (including visual cues) may disrupt understanding. Thus, Traffigram provides minimal, user-selectable information on top of isochronal cartography, including the main roads, city name, landmarks, and visual cues.

### Real-World Applicability of Traffigram

According to an annual study of national driving patterns, US residents have wasted $121 billion due to traffic congestion in 2011, and this number is rising. We believe that a tool for understanding traffic patterns could have a positive impact on sustainability. Our user study focused on the potential applicability of Traffigram in real life situations. Participants stated Traffigram could be a practical tool when users want to choose departure time or location based on traffic conditions. The variable nature of the time between urban locations regularly frustrates travelers. Traffigram could assist in clarifying this traffic uncertainty. Traffigram could be especially useful when users have to select one destination from among multiple choices; for example, recently-hired employees looking for a place to live in their new community or people selecting a restaurant during rush hour. Commonly-used maps utilizing equidistant cartography are not optimal for presenting multiple destinations and travel times simultaneously.

Additionally, our study suggests that isochronal cartography might offer an improvement over the traditional stoplight-colored (red/yellow/green) traffic presentation. The method is used in major digital map services such as Google, Bing Maps and government services such as WSDOT (Washington State Dept. of Transportation). It has two main characteristics; it uses two lines to present directional traffic information and utilizes colors for traffic flow. In the context of understanding temporal information, this method has the following problems. First, the method indicates direction by using two lines, but some people have difficulty detecting which line denotes which direction. During our user study, many subjects did recognize the asymmetric traffic flow by focusing on color, but they had difficulty determining the direction, and we believe this frequently happens in ordinary life for many users. Second, color can represent a sense of temporal information, but fails to present the actual travel time. Thus, an auxiliary user step, such as inputting the destination, is needed to get an accurate and usable travel time from the origin to the destination. Lastly, this scheme is not suitable for colorblind users [22].

Finally, our method is not limited to human automobile traffic. It could be applied to any geographically-based map where travel time is potentially variable, including applications as diverse as air traffic, cargo shipping, network routing, packet switching, or other any situation where entities must travel between multiple discrete points.

## CONCLUSIONS AND FUTURE WORK

Although the initial implementation of Traffigram appears to be successful, there is much more room for additional features and improvements. First, more precise traffic network construction is needed. Realistic (un-simplified) traffic networks entailing millions of nodes and edges would provide greater real-time complexity to our experiment. Due to this complexity, sampling is required. Traffigram would benefit from a more robust network construction algorithm that seamlessly yields real time results that represent geospatial reality evenly by minimizing the difference between actual travel time and the shortest path analysis. Second, Traffigram needs more coverage and scalability. Current digital map users zoom in and zoom out, and systems powered by AJAX provide results within a very short amount of time. This scalability lets users browse the world – literally – very easily. We intend to implement these techniques in Traffigram by expanding the hierarchical traffic network structure. Additionally, further usability studies of isochronal cartography are needed. Broader coverage may eventually compromise geographic integrity [2], and there are few studies on how impaired geospatial integrity affects the recognizability of isochronal cartography. We intend to continue developing Traffigram to reach these goals.

In one of the first studies investigating the usability of isochronal cartograms, we developed a novel traffic visualization system, Traffigram, and validated our design with usability tests. Our research led to several principles for developing usable isochronal maps. Isochronal cartography appears to be a practical technique that may have many future applications and uses.

## ACKNOWLEDGMENTS

We thank Ben Samples, Karin Hellman, Carin Fishel, Wiley Bennett, Sean Mitchell, and the anonymous reviewers for their helpful contributions and suggestions.

## REFERENCES

1. Agrawala M., Li W. Berthouzoz, F. 2011. Design principles for visual communication. *Communications of the ACM*, 54(4), 60-69.
2. Bies S., Van Kreveld M. 2013. Time-Space Maps from Triangulations. *In Proc. International Symposium on Graph Drawing 2013*, LNCS 7704, 511-516.
3. Chen X. 2011. *Seeing Differently – Cartography for Subjective Maps Based on Dynamic Urban Data*. MIT SMArchS Thesis, MA, USA.
4. Dijkstra E.W. 1959. A Note on Two Problems in Connection with Graphs. *Numerische Mathematik* 1:269-271.
5. Dorling D., Barford A., Newman M. 2006. Worldmapper: The world as you've never seen it before. *IEEE TVCG* 12(5), 757-764.
6. Jenny B. 2012. Adaptive Composite Map Projection. *IEEE TVCG* 18(12), 2575-2582.
7. Kaiser C., Walsh F., Farmer C. J. Q., Pozdnoukhov A. 2010. User-Centric Time-Distance Representation of Road Networks. *In Proc. GIScience 2010*, LNCS 6292, 85-99.
8. Karlin O. 2005. Time Travel. http://oskarlin.com/2005/11/29/time-travel
9. Kimerling A.J., Buckley A.R., Muehrcke P.C., Muehrcke J.O. 2011. *Map Use: Reading, Analysis, Interpretation*. Esri Press, California
10. Kopf J., Agrawala M., Salesin D., Bargeron D., Cohen M. F. 2010. Automatic Generation of Destination Maps. *In Proc. SIGGRAPH Asia 2010*, 158:1 – 158:12.
11. Kraak M.-J., Ormeling F. 2003. *Cartography: Visualization of Geospatial Data*. Longman, UK
12. Kramer J. 2007. Is Abstraction the Key to Computing? *Communications of the ACM*, 50(4), 36-42.
13. Lightfoot C., Steinberg T. 2006. Travel-time Maps and their Uses. http://www.mysociety.org/2006/travel-time-maps.
14. Mackinlay J. 1986. Automating the Design of Graphical Presentations of Relational Information. *ACM TOG* 5.2. 110-141.
15. Newman M. 2012. Maps of the 2012 US presidential election results. http://www-personal.umich.edu/~mejn/election/2012
16. Nielsen, J. 1993. *Usability Engineering*. AP Professional, UK.
17. Shimizu E. 1992. Time-space Mapping Based on Topological Transformation of Physical Map. In Proc. of WCTR 6th. 219-230.
18. Shimizu E., Inoue R. 2003. A Generalized Solution of Time-space Mapping. *In Proc. CUPUM 2003* (CD-ROM). Vol 11.
19. Shimizu E., Inoue R. 2009. A New Algorithm for Distance Cartogram Construction. *International Journal of GIS* 23.11(2009): 1453-1470
20. Carden T., London Tube map. http://www.tom-carden.co.uk/p5/tube_map_travel_times/applet
21. Ullah R., Kraak M.-J., Van Elzakker, C. 2013. Using cartograms to explore temporal data: Do they work? http://www.geomatik-hamburg.de/geoviz/online/Ullah_slides.pdf
22. VanBuskirk, J., Harper, J. S. 2012. Traffic Lighting: The Next Generation. *In Proc. SAS Global forum*, 282-2012.
23. Wahba, G. 1990. *Spline Models for Observational Data*. Society for Industrial and Applied Mathematics, Philadelphia.

# Understanding Procedural Content Generation: A Design-Centric Analysis of the Role of PCG in Games

**Gillian Smith**
Northeastern University
Playable Innovative Technologies Group
Boston, Massachusetts, USA
gillian@ccs.neu.edu

## ABSTRACT
Games that use procedural content generation (PCG) do so in a wide variety of ways and for different reasons. One of the most common reasons cited by PCG system creators and game designers is improving replayability—by providing a means for automatically creating near-infinite amounts of content, the player can come back and replay the game and refine her strategies over a long period. However, this notion of replayability is both overly broad and incomplete as a motivation. This paper contributes an analytical framework and associated common vocabulary for understanding the role of PCG in games from a design standpoint, with an aim of unpacking some of the broad justifications for PCG use in games, and bringing together technical concerns in designing PCG systems with design concerns related to creating engaging playable experiences.

### Author Keywords
Procedural content generation; game AI; MDA framework; game design; game design theory.

### ACM Classification Keywords
H.5.m. Information Interfaces and Presentation: Miscellaneous; I.2.1 Artificial Intelligence: Applications and Expert Systems—Games

## INTRODUCTION
Procedural content generation (PCG) is a growing area of research and practice in game design. Researchers in artificial intelligence are creating more efficient and more expressive methods for having a computer create levels, weapons, terrain, and even game rules [17,56]. Simultaneously, game designers from both industry and research backgrounds are increasingly turning to the computer to create massive, varied worlds for players to explore, at a fraction of the cost of human authorship [10]. Furthermore, recent work at the intersection of HCI and AI has been examining using PCG to create intelligent user interfaces for game designers, while lacking a design vocabulary for how PCG can be used [25,47,52].



*CHI 2014,* April 26 - May 01 2014, Toronto, ON, Canada
Copyright is held by the owner/author(s). Publication rights licensed to ACM.
ACM 978-1-4503-2473-1/14/04...$15.00.
http://dx.doi.org/10.1145/2556288.2557341

In order for further advancements in PCG research to be made, it is vital that both AI researchers and designers have a common vocabulary for understanding not just what PCG is but how it can be used to induce particular experiences and what it uniquely offers to game design. Thus, what is needed is a framework for understanding and communicating about how PCG is taking a role in game design. This framework needs to address both the ways in which the PCG system works to create content, which is of primary concern to the PCG researcher, and the experience the player (or user, in the case of AI-based tools) has that is shaped by that system, which is of primary concern to a game designer [19,42]. The framework presented in this paper was created by analyzing several PCG games and research projects through the lens of the Mechanics, Dynamics, and Aesthetics (MDA) framework [19].

PCG is used in a variety of ways in games, with the common justifications of replayability (as described in [56]) and tailoring content for an individual player. The promise of personalized content generation is especially compelling for educational and training games (e.g. [48]). This paper argues that "replayability", in particular, is a nuanced concept that requires unpacking through an examination of the designs of both the PCG system and the game that the system is embedded within. This overly-broad justification is examined more deeply through a design-centric analysis of how PCG has been used in games thus far. While the framework introduced in this paper focuses largely on PCG's implementation in game design, it is also important to note that the representation and mechanics portions of the framework can also be used to describe the role that PCG can play in game design tools, offering more detail than previous work in PCG design metaphors [23].

This paper has two main contributions. First, a conceptual framework for analyzing the role of PCG in game design (both for games and for game design tools), and second, a resulting vocabulary for both practitioners and researchers—from both artificial intelligence and game design—to discuss the affordances of PCG. The framework is illustrated using examples from several games, design tools, and research projects, and a longer worked example is also provided. However, this is not intended to be a full survey of PCG, and only illustrative examples are used. Finally, the paper closes with a discussion of future work and a reflection on the unique experiences that can come from incorporating PCG in a game's design.

## BACKGROUND

This section begins with an overview of technical approaches to procedural content generation and their design-relevant tradeoffs, then discusses the background in the two main contribution areas.

### Approaches to Procedural Content Generation

There are many different approaches taken in procedural content generation, each with different affordances and tradeoffs for design. All approaches can be used in both a game and design tool setting. The five main categories that a content generator can fall into are: generation as **optimization**, generation as **constraint satisfaction**, generation with **grammars**, generation as **content selection**, and generation as a **constructive** process.

#### *Optimization*

Optimization approaches to content generation treat the design process as a search for the combination of elements that best fit some criteria, which can be either specified mathematically by the system creator, or judged and curated by a human. Optimization-based generators explicitly and externally model the desired qualities of generated content. A great deal of research in PCG uses evolutionary algorithms (this is sometimes referred to as "search-based PCG" [56]), which is an optimization approach. Optimization approaches to PCG are often (though not always) computationally expensive, making it difficult to use them in games that require a highly responsive PCG system. They are often used with a human-in-the-loop for the evaluation function [16,38,43] and to create personalized content [45] offline.

#### *Constraint Satisfaction*

This approach involves the declarative specification of properties of and constraints on the content that will be created. For example, levels in the math education game *Refraction* are generated by searching for solutions for a set of design constraints [48]. Declarative representations have the strength that a designer can specify knowledge about how the content should appear without needing to specify how the underlying search algorithm should perform. The challenge with constraint-based approaches comes largely in determining an appropriate representation for facts about the generated content, and with debugging a set of complex, interrelated constraints. This approach has been used extensively in tools for designers [4,46,52].

#### *Grammars*

These systems involve the specification of a grammar that the algorithm should expand upon to create content. These are not simply representational grammars used by an optimization-based generator (e.g. [44]). Grammars can be used purely as production rules to drive generation, without any regard for an external measure of the quality of the level. In such cases, level quality is implicitly baked into the grammar based on how the production rules are authored. Grammar-based methods attempt to strike a balance between designer-specified rules for how content components should fit together and computer exploration of the design space through expanding the grammar. Grammars have been used in offline content generation for games [8,51] and in tools for designers [30].

#### *Content Selection*

There is some contention about whether or not selecting content from a library to piece it together is complex enough to qualify as content generation [54,55]. This paper takes the position that content selection, however simple, is a form of PCG when it is used to procedurally create an environment for the player to explore or content for the player to experience within the context of different mechanics. Content selection is a very simple form of PCG that is susceptible to players recognizing large-scale patterns; however, it is also one of the fastest methods for generating content and is typically used in games where the generator must run during play time, such as "endless runner" games [1,41].

#### *Constructive*

A constructive generator is one that builds content in an ad-hoc manner by piecing together customized building blocks (see next section). It typically has all of its design knowledge baked into the algorithm; while it may perform some amount of search internally, it does not test the results of the level against some external heuristic to help guide the search process. Constructive generators are often quite game-specific. Examples of constructive generators are those used in *Rogue*-like games [39]. Constructive generators can be seen as content selection-based generators that use smaller pieces of content.

### What is Procedural Content Generation?

There are two main survey and taxonomy papers for PCG in games. The first, from Togelius et al., focuses on the technical approaches to creating optimization-based generators, written from the perspective of PCG researchers for readers with a background in AI [56]. The search-based PCG taxonomy does identify two design-relevant characteristics of PCG systems, however: 1) necessity, and 2) whether the generator runs offline or online. The first of these characteristics is not discussed in this paper, as the "necessity" of generated content for the player to complete the game is not relevant to how the player experiences the content. The second property also appears in our framework as a property of the game's mechanics, in terms of how the user or player has control over the generator. This taxonomy also mentions a scale of directness-of-representation, as we do, but only in the context of evolutionary approaches to content generation. The second survey focuses on the granularity of the content being created—from textures and small "game bits" to NPC behaviors and entire rulesets—and the maturity of the AI techniques used to create them [17]. It does not address issues of player experience or how the player interacts with the content generator within the game.

Togelius et al. have also written on what exactly constitutes PCG, and where the line can be drawn between randomness, player-generated content, and procedurally-generated content [55]. They concluded that PCG is defined as "the algorithmic creation of game content with limited or indirect user input". This paper takes a somewhat broader view of content generation, classifying games that do not provide any user input over the generator as still containing PCG, and also contributes a more nuanced set of attributes for how to describe the role of PCG in games.

Finally, Khaled et al. have written on creating "design metaphors" for PCG systems, to make PCG research from the AI community more accessible to those in HCI and design communities [23]. Their metaphors—which include considering the system as a *tool*, *material*, *designer*, and *domain expert*—all are broad categories for how a PCG system can be seen by a designer. This paper has similar goals in its aim to identify design-relevant properties of PCG systems and better understand the role that PCG can play in a game's design, but takes a more detailed look at the way the systems are used.

### Frameworks for Game Design

Doug Church, in his call for more work in creating "formal abstract design tools", stated that "the primary inhibitor of design evolution is the lack of a common design vocabulary" [5]. Since this call for a genre-agnostic design language, there have been several attempts at creating languages and frameworks for understanding a game's design, the framework in this paper being among them.

One thread of design vocabulary research is in game design patterns (e.g. [2,18,28]). The framework contributed in this paper can also be considered as a set of "design patterns" for the role of PCG in games. Bjork and Holopainen's work is among the most comprehensive of these efforts, and includes a pattern for "Procedurally Generated Game Worlds" [3], but does not offer detail into the role that these worlds play in the player's experience, or different ways that they might be implemented in the game's rules.

Other efforts for building a design vocabulary include building languages to describe specific aspects of game design, such as Dan Cook's work on skill atoms [6] or Joris Dormans's "machinations" framework for abstractly representing and prototyping game mechanics [9]. These two frameworks sit at opposite ends of a spectrum of formality. Cook's framework, which focuses on designing for player learning and progression, is not at all formally defined. Dormans's framework, on the other hand, is a highly formalized, computational model for expressing game mechanics and subsystems. The framework presented in this paper aims to sit closer to the middle of this spectrum: it is not formal or detailed enough to be used to immediately synthesize a new game, but offers a strong enough vocabulary and set of examples that it can be easily used by designers to describe and guide the design of their own games.

Hunicke et al.'s MDA framework is another example of a language for describing and designing games [19], and forms the foundation of the analysis presented in this paper. In this framework, the design of a game is split into three main components: 1) the mechanics, or rules and systems in terms of algorithms and representation; 2) the dynamics, which are interactions between mechanics and the player's input; and 3) the aesthetics, or the "desirable emotional responses" that are experienced by the player. The framework is useful for the analysis performed in this paper because of its dual focus on design and experience. In order to understand the role that PCG takes in different games, it is crucial to understand it from both the system designer's perspective and the player's perspective.

## UNDERSTANDING PCG IN GAMES

This section describes each aspect of the framework for understanding the role of PCG in games, categorizing each property by whether or not it is related to the game's mechanics, dynamics, or aesthetics. Each category in the framework is illustrated with an example from either a game or research project. It is important to note that aspects and properties in the framework are **not** intended to be mutually exclusive from each other—for example, a game might provide multiple kinds of control over its PCG system in different contexts.

### Mechanics

There are four main mechanical aspects of the PCG system that are considered in this framework, summarized in Table 1. These aspects were chosen as a combination of concerns of the AI programmer (how the generator works) and concerns of the game designer (how the generator is used). Each of these mechanical aspects can be used to describe the role that a PCG system plays in a game design tool, as well as in games themselves.

#### *Building Blocks*

How design knowledge is represented to the generator is a crucial aspect of procedural content generation, impacting the range of content that can be produced. This framework contains four different categories for the building blocks used by generators: **experiential chunks**, **templates**, **components**, and **subcomponents**. These categories are actually discrete points on what is close to a continuous spectrum, from highest to lowest authorial burden.

**Experiential Chunks**. Experiential chunks are large building blocks for content that are designed by a human and are sufficiently large that, standing on their own, they can be experienced by the player. An example of these

| Building Blocks | Game Stage | Interaction Type | Player Experience |
|---|---|---|---|
| *Experiential Chunk*<br>Large, human-authored | *Offline*<br>Before game | *None*<br>No human influence | *Indirect*<br>No direct experiential control |
| *Template*<br>Computer fills in blanks | *Online*<br>During game | *Parameterized*<br>Indirect, human sets values | *Compositional*<br>Human influences available components |
| *Component Pattern*<br>Small, human-authored | | *Preference*<br>Human selects good products | *Experiential*<br>Human influences player experience |
| *Subcomponent*<br>Internal representation | | *Direct Manipulation*<br>Human manipulates product | |

**Table 1. Summary of the mechanical aspects of PCG. Each aspect has several potential values it can take on.**

chunks include the rhythm groups that are stitched together by the *Polymorph* level generator [21][1].

**Templates.** Templates are a generalized form of experiential chunk; a human has still authored a great deal of the content, enough to dictate the kind of experience that will be had by a player, but has left some "blanks" (which may be further constrained) for the computer to fill in. Examples of these include the quest templates used in the *Scriptease* authoring tool [7].

**Component Patterns.** Component patterns are patterns that are large enough to be identifiable as human-designed in the game, but small enough that, on their own, they do not greatly dictate the experience a human will have. For example, patrolling enemies in platformer levels (e.g. Goombas in the *Infinite Mario Bros.* generator [34]) have a general behavior dictated by the human designer, but that behavior is meaningless to the player unless it is placed in context alongside other level components.

**Subcomponents.** Generators that operate at the subcomponent level are using the same building blocks as a human designer would if she were designing the content herself. Subcomponents exist at the layer of how the game is represented internally, such as individual tiles within a tile grid. *Galactic Arms Race* [16] operates at this layer, with it constructing weapon behavior to guide individual particles along a path.

### *Stage of Game*
Togelius et al. make the distinction between generation that happens offline vs. online [56]; that distinction is continued here. Note that it is possible for a game to incorporate both kinds of content generation, if the game begins with some generated content, but that content might be procedurally altered or added to during play (e.g. *Galactic Arms Race* weapon generation).

**Offline**. Offline content generation happens before a unit of play experience begins. Thus, the generator used in *Civilization IV* [13] is classified as an offline generator, as the entire map is created before the main game activity begins. It is important to note that level generation in *Rogue* [57] is also considered to be offline—even though new maps are generated when the player progresses to the next level, the entire dungeon is created before the player begins exploring it and does not base generation on prior player behavior.

**Online.** Online content generation happens during the play experience, optionally in response to how the player is acting. Examples of online content generation include *Canabalt*'s placement of level chunks in front of the player just off-screen, or *Endless Web*'s [50] generation of new level geometry whenever the player alters a parameter to the underlying generator.

### *Player Interaction with Generator*
In most games, the player interacts exclusively with the generated content, just as if it were created by a human designer. However, there are some games that offer the player the ability to interact with the generator itself: directly or indirectly requesting new content. Thus, it is useful to understand the different ways that a player can exert control over the generator.

**None.** With no control, the player interacts solely with the generated content and has no influence whatsoever over the kind of content that will be created by the generator. Examples of games that give the player no control over the generator include *Rogue*-like games [39], "endless runner" games, and *Minecraft* [35].

**Parameterized**. Parameterized control is a form of indirect control, where the player can provide the value for some set of parameters that influence the content the generator creates. For example, the player is able to manipulate parameters for the *Civilization IV* level generator [13] at the beginning of the game, to request the generator create a particular kind of map (e.g. one with no oceans, or a single large continent surrounded entirely by ocean).

[1] These chunks are, themselves, generated and ranked offline by the Launchpad level generator [51]; however, who owns authorship for those chunks is irrelevant to the Polymorph game and its generator, thus it is classified as a generator that uses experiential chunks.

**Preference.** Preference control is another form of indirect control, where the system is set so that the player can state (intentionally or implicitly) preferences about the content they are seeing. This form of control typically comes in the form of the player evaluating content that has already been generated to give feedback to the generator and help guide its future decisions. For example, *Galactic Arms Race* [16] uses player preferences, inferred from player behavior, to guide the next generation of evolved weapons.

**Direct Manipulation**. Direct manipulation involves the player actively altering the generated content to provide additional constraints to the generator. This form of manipulation is more commonly seen in PCG-enabled design tools [46,52], rather than games themselves. The *Spore Creature Creator* [26], a design tool offered as part of the game *Spore* [27], offers this kind of interaction.

### *Awareness of Player Experience*

Some generators are designed simply to piece together content haphazardly and let player experience emerge from the results, while others are designed for crafting particular kinds of player experiences. In the case of generators that can be controlled by the player, it is also worth discussing whether or not the player's control extends to all aspects of how the generator designs for player experiences. There are three different ways a generator constructs content to produce an experience.

**Indirect**. All content generators, by their very definition, impact player experience somehow—it is simply a matter of understanding how intentional the impact is. Generators that exhibit indirect control over desired player experience are ones that do not have any intent baked into their design. For example, the gun generation system in *Borderlands* [14] is simply a matter of combinatorics—new guns are made by compositing different hand-authored gun properties. There is no desire to create specific kinds of guns for specific kinds of players, or even to limit the combinations that can be made based on game constraints.

**Compositional.** Compositional control involves influencing the appearance of particular components in the content being created, but not directly having experiential control over what is made. For example, *Endless Web* [50] requires players to manipulate parameters that control the frequency of different level components appearing in the generated geometry, but does **not** offer control in the form of demanding a particular difficulty or pattern for pacing. While the configuration of components does lead to a particular kind of experience, compositional control does not let a player explicitly control for experience, it must be left to emerge from the composition.

**Experiential**. Experiential control means that the generator can directly control for the kind of experience the player will receive from the content generator, and that (optionally) the player can interact with the generator at the experiential level. Yannakakis and Togelius attempt to directly model and capture player experience in their work on experience-driven procedural content generation [58]. A non-optimization based approach to experiential control comes in the game *Warning Forever* [33], in which the player's actions when attacking the boss directly influences how the boss evolves over time.

## Dynamics

The results of these kinds of mechanics are several dynamics—ways in which the rules interact with each other and the player during play (see Table 2). When considering how PCG enables these dynamics, it is helpful to compare a game with PCG to a game with similar mechanics that does not have PCG. By doing so, it is possible to see what the unique dynamics are that are brought out by the incorporation of the PCG system, and how the mechanics related to the generator contribute to these dynamics.

### *PCG Relationship to Other Mechanics*

First, in order to understand how the PCG system is situated within the game and the dynamics that emerge from it, it is helpful to think about how the player will be interacting with the generated content and the extent to which the generated content will influence the player's overall game experience.

**Core.** These games use the procedurally generated content as a core part of the player's experience. For example, *Infinite Mario Bros.* relies entirely on the generated content for the player to be able to experience the game; platformers are heavily reliant on level design to dictate the aesthetic experiences that are core to the game.

**Partial framing.** These are games that use procedurally generated content to frame some aspect of the player's experience, but it does not make up the entirety of that experience. For example, *Civilization [13]* is a game where map generation heavily influences early stage exploration and decisions about where to build cities, but there are so many other mechanics in the game that the player can build strategies around that, by the later stages of the game, the fact that the map was procedurally generated is far less important.

**Decorative**. There are many games that use PCG to create content that is intended to be purely decorative; this is especially common in computer graphics, where a concern is how to generate reasonable textures, vegetation, and decorative façades for city buildings [11,20,30]. While this distinction between "decorative" and the other two categories might be seen as similar to Togelius et al.'s declaration that some content is "unnecessary", that is *not* the intent with this category. All content in a game makes up a part of the player's experience, even if it is not directly interacted with, and thus there is no "unnecessary" content from a dynamics point of view.

### *Memorization vs. Reaction*

Games that are heavily dependent upon PCG for their core play, and that use either online or offline generation of

| Other Mechanics | Memorization vs. Reaction | Strategizing | Searching | Practicing | Interacting |
|---|---|---|---|---|---|
| *Core*<br>Reliant on PCG<br>*Partial Framing*<br>Partial player experience<br>*Decorative*<br>Not core to game experience | *Memorization*<br>Testing player memory<br>*Reaction*<br>Reacting to unforeseen circumstances | Player builds strategies for influencing the content generator | Player seeks out new content in a vast world | Player practices game mechanics in new settings | Communities of players discuss differences in game experiences |

**Table 2. Summary of the dynamics aspects of PCG. There are six dynamic aspects, two of which can take on different values, while the others are properties that games using PCG might have.**

content with no direct control from the player are games that are about **reacting to unforeseen circumstances**. Sometimes this reaction must come very quickly, in the case of endless runner games like *Robot Unicorn Attack* [1]. Other times, the reaction may be related to exploring an unfamiliar space, as in the platformer *Spelunky* [59].

In contrast, games such as these that do not have PCG and instead simply have static, pre-authored content tend to lead to dynamics of the player memorizing paths through a level (e.g. *Sonic the Hedgehog* [53]) or where items are hidden (e.g. *Donkey Kong Country 2* [36]), with the player's goal on replay being to beat her best score or test her memory.

It is important to note that the dynamic of reaction emerges simply from the use of randomness; it is possible for generators that perform content selection from a library of experiential chunks or templates to produce these experiences; there is no need for sophisticated generators that incorporate experiential design. Indeed, the dynamic of reaction vs. memorization arises in games without any PCG at all, but that include a random element, such as match-three games. Such games would be drastically different were the gem ordering to be deterministic; players would be able to memorize sequences of moves and practice moves that lead to optimal play.

Further, it is plausible that a similar experience about reacting to unforeseen circumstances could be crafted through crowdsourcing level designs from a large pool of users, such that each time the game is played, the player sees content from a different user. Without any input or control from the player, the role of the computer is to be an on-demand, highly productive replacement for a human designer.

### *Building Generator Strategies*

Online, controllable content generators can lead to a dynamic in which the player builds strategies around the generator. This leads to a cycle in which the player informs the generator what should be created next, and the content presented in response informs the next decision that the player will make. Examples include *Warning Forever* [33] and *Endless Web* [50], which is described later in the paper.

There is no clear analog to this dynamic when considering games with static, human-authored content. Building a strategy around the generator is, clearly, only possible with an actual content generator that can respond believably to human input. In fact, generators that have only indirect control over player experience are not as suitable for producing this dynamic, as the player needs to have a mapping between action and generator reaction in order to learn how the system works and build a strategy.

### *Searching a Vast World*

This dynamic arises from a generator's ability to create vast, varied spaces that could never be reasonably made by a single author. Generators that produce this dynamic are those that work either offline or online, at the level of components or subcomponents (experiential chunks and templates have patterns that can be quite easy for players to detect), create either core or framing content, and do not necessarily require any player control over the generator but can design for experience either directly or through components. There are several examples of games that use this dynamic, including *Minecraft* [35], the academic project *Charbitat* [32], and *Inside a Star-Filled Sky* [40].

The key here is that the generator produces content that is somehow surprising to the player as they explore the space. For example, the *Borderlands* [14] weapon generator produces a vast array of guns that the player can be surprised by, but the player might be searching for a particular kind of gun as they hunt through the space.

In order to produce this dynamic in games without content generation, it would require a large authorial burden on a team of human designers. However, there are games that show that this level of authoring is plausible; for example *Animal Crossing: New Leaf* [31] is a game that has a huge cast of characters, each of whom have item preferences, unique home layouts, one of several kinds of personality, and unique verbal cues. It has a large catalog of items for the player to purchase and search for over the course of play. While the physical space of the game is a small town, there is still a massive amount of designed content in the game that produces a similar dynamic of searching and discovering a vast, designed space.

### *Practicing in Different Environments*

There are also games that use content generation to frame choices made by the player, where content is generated offline with or without control from the player. The dynamic that emerges from this form of generation is an ability for the player to practice game strategies in a variety of different environments. *Civilization IV* [13] is an example of a game that allows the player to exert parameterized control over the generator, in order to help guide the environment they will be playing and practicing in. *Diablo 3* [37] does not give the player control over the generator, but still allows the player to practice different combat strategies or character classes in different worlds.

In comparison, games that have only a single environment to play in do not achieve the same sort of dynamic. For example, *Professor Layton and the Curious Village* [24] is a game where the player must progress through a series of hand-authored puzzles. If the player is stuck on a particular puzzle, there are no options other than to ask for hints or seek the solution from another player. The incorporation of procedurally generated puzzles would allow the player to practice different solving strategies in a variety of related contexts. On the other hand, there are puzzle games such as *Picross* [22] which do allow the player to practice and improve upon their overall puzzle solving strategy simply through practicing on a large set of hand-authored levels at increasing difficulty. It is plausible for human-created content to compensate for the content-generator.

### *Interaction with a Community of Players*

The final dynamic identified in this framework is that of how PCG impacts the community of players surrounding a game. Gee describes this community as the "external semiotic domain" for games, and as an area where players engage in a great deal of learning and reflection while talking to each other about game strategies [15]

PCG researchers typically focus on crafting an experience for individual players, only within the game's internal semiotic domain. However, there is evidence that the incorporation of PCG into a game prompts communication about the underlying system and its impact on the play experience within a community of players. For example, *Civilization IV* players engage in long discussions about how different map generation options work, how they impact strategies, and why they prefer certain options [29]. In a point-and-click adventure game that incorporated offline content generation to produce a unique set of puzzles for each player, the designer noticed that players who typically rush to post a walkthrough for adventure games worked together to figure out how the underlying content generator was working [12].

Understanding the community that surrounds games that use PCG is an area ripe for future research, both from a PCG AI point of view (how do we create generators that target a community of players?) and an HCI/game design point of view (how do communities of players communicate about PCG?). There is also an opportunity to study how PCG impacts player learning in games [49].

## Aesthetics

The design choices made for the PCG system, in concert with the mechanics of the game, lead to unique dynamics. These dynamics then act in support of several different aesthetic experiences. The three aesthetics mentioned below are among the eight "kinds of fun" identified by Hunicke et al. in the original MDA framework paper [19].

### *Discovery*

PCG acts in support of discovery by providing new environments for the player to explore or new procedural systems for the player to learn about over time. This aesthetic is supported by the dynamics of *Searching a Vast World* and *Building Generator Strategies*. In the first case, discovery comes simply through exploring a large, unknown environment. In the second case, discovery is also cast as a form of exploration for the game's *generative* space.

### *Challenge*

PCG acts in support of challenge through the dynamics of *Memorization vs. Reaction*, *Building Generator Strategies*, and *Practicing in Different Environments*. Again, each of these dynamics leads to a different form of challenge. Games that use PCG to force the player to react quickly are providing a form of twitch challenge, where the player must make moment-to-moment decisions based on a world unfolding in front of them. Whereas games that use PCG to force the player to react, but not necessarily in a time-sensitive way, offer challenge in that the exact content being experienced has not been seen before by the player. Similarly, *Practicing in Different Environments* allows the player to experience new challenges (though, the same *kind* of challenges) through playing the same game in several different environments.

We can also consider dynamic difficulty adjustment as related to the *Memorization vs. Reaction* dynamic, in which the player is not consciously making a decision about how to guide the generator, but nonetheless is influencing how the generator will mete out challenges over the course of the game, thus altering the player's path and making it impossible for them to memorize what will come next.

When *Building Generator Strategies*, the game has added challenge through the layer of strategic play that comes in learning how the generator works, what it can create, and how to use that knowledge to the player's advantage.

### *Fellowship*

PCG acts in support of fellowship through creating an emergent system that encourages player communication outside of the game environment, via the *Interaction with a Community of Players* dynamic. Not only does PCG seem to encourage player discussion, but it also shapes the ways that players talk about the game, including discussing general strategies for different kinds of content configurations.

## WORKED EXAMPLE

This section provides a worked example, illustrating how the framework can be used as a language for describing the combination of PCG system and game.

### Endless Web

*Endless Web* has been used as a motivating example for several of the framework options thus far. It is a PCG-based game [50], designed intentionally so that its mechanics, dynamics, and aesthetics are heavily interdependent with the PCG system, and where the PCG system and game were iteratively co-designed. *Endless Web* uses a generator called Launchpad. It is a 2D platforming game that uses entirely procedurally generated content; players are tasked with exploring Launchpad's generative space while simultaneously exploring physical pace.

#### *Mechanics*

The Launchpad generator is a *grammar-based* generator. It provides *parameterized* control over both *compositional* and *experiential* aspects of content. The generator uses a *component* representation—it knows about individual level components and some constraints on how they fit together (e.g. enemies walk on top of platforms), but does not know about larger-scale common patterns of geometry. The generator's experiential control comes in the form of being able to manipulate level pacing *parameters*, by specifying a length of time and frequency/pattern of actions that the player takes during that time. Launchpad is used to perform *online* level generation; new level segments are generated whenever the player makes a choice that influences the generator, and in front of the player while she is running through the world. *Endless Web* can theoretically produce an infinite world for the player to explore.

#### *Dynamics*

As a platformer, the generated levels make up a *core* aspect of the way players interact in the game. There are two main dynamics that emerge from this combination of mechanics: *Searching a Vast Space*, and *Building Generator Strategies*. By being given control over the generator's content composition, the player is exploring both a physically infinite space and a very large (though not infinite) generative space. She is tasked with searching for specific goals that are hidden at different configurations of this generative space, so she must manipulate the generator to find these goal points over the course of the game. This goal-oriented play also contributes to the dynamic of *Building Generator Strategies*. The player will have to experiment with different configurations of generation parameters that are at an acceptable difficulty level, and can choose to push the generator in different directions to find power-ups that can help through more difficult generated content. Thus, the player is expected to form strategies around which goal to search for next, and which directions to push the generator to both maintain an appropriate difficulty level and move towards the next goal point.

#### *Aesthetics*

These two dynamics lead to two aesthetics for the game. The primary aesthetic is *discovery*, brought about by the fact that the game actively encourages the player to search a generative space as well as physical space. The game is about the wonder and confusion of exploring a constantly changing space, which the PCG contributes to heavily. A secondary aesthetic is *challenge*, which emerges from the strategies that the player needs to form and, to a lesser extent, from the platforming challenges themselves.

## CONCLUSIONS

This paper has presented a framework for analyzing and discussing the role of PCG in game design and PCG-based design tools. The framework has been illustrated with numerous examples from both industry games and academic research projects, and has helped uncover nuances in the motivations for using PCG in game design, and how the style of control a user has over the PCG system influences their experience.

One of the goals of this research was to unpack the concept of "replayability" and critically examine how PCG is used to impact play experience. The framework has uncovered three primary dynamics that lead to different kinds of replayability: 1) reacting in a surprising environment, 2) building generator strategies, and 3) practicing in different environments. The first of these dynamics leads to replayability in that the entire purpose of the game is to play different content on each attempt, typically in order to beat a high score or progress further than in prior attempts. The third leads to replayability by providing content that supports replay of more traditional mechanics as a way to practice in different scenarios. Both the first and third dynamics could be plausibly attained through the use of large amounts of human-authored content. While the second dynamic does lead to replayability (through experiencing different content on each play through and having the opportunity to build strategies around the generator), it is also a kind of game dynamic that is unique to what PCG can offer.

It is important to note that there are some aspects of how the player controls the content generator that are not prioritized in the framework. In particular, no difference is explicitly drawn between intentional and unintentional control over how the generator is being controlled, it simply provides a language for the style of control from the generator's point of view. Whether or not the player is explicitly provided with control over generated content is a matter for how the game is designed, and irrelevant to the generator. The distinction was not made more explicit because it does not drastically impact game dynamics and overall play experience; in cases such as *Galactic Arms Race* [16], where the player is (supposedly) unintentionally influencing the next generation of weapons, the dynamic of *building generator strategies* is still present as the player still takes actions that rely upon the PCG's existence and ability to be directed by the player. One might think that intentional control might be required for a PCG-enabled game design tool, and certainly some aspects of control must be intentional—however, one of the goals of using PCG in design tools is to help the designer brainstorm different design variants, where lack of intention in control and resulting surprise over produced content is a benefit.

The presented framework finds broader relevance in the area of AI-enabled creativity and design support tools outside of the domain of games. For example, the Picbreeder [43] tool for cooperating with a computer to create 2D evolutionary art can be described using the same set of "mechanics" aspects: patterns emerge from the underlying *subcomponent* representation that is not expected to be recognizable to the creator (our "player"), is performed *online* in that creators are building upon each others' work, uses a *preference*-based interaction type, and allows users to exert *compositional* control over its output. In future work, I intend to perform a broader survey of existing computationally creative tools to see how well the framework extends, as well as use the framework as a basis for exploring new potential tools, games, and research projects that use unique—or even undiscovered—forms of mechanical control to create new kinds of user experiences.

## REFERENCES


1. [adult swim games]. *Robot Unicorn Attack (PC Game)*. 2010.
2. Bjork, S. and Holopainen, J. *Patterns in Game Design (Game Development Series)*. Charles River Media, 2004.
3. Bjork, S. Procedurally Generated Game Worlds. *Game Design Patterns 2.0.* http://gdp2.tii.se/index.php/Procedurally_Generated_Game_Worlds.
4. Butler, E., Smith, A.M., Liu, Y.-E., and Popovic, Z. A Mixed-Initiative Tool for Designing Level Progressions in Games. .
5. Church, D. Formal Abstract Design Tools. *Gamasutra [Online]*, 1999. http://www.gamasutra.com/view/feature/3357/formal_abstract_design_tools.php.
6. Cook, D. The Chemistry Of Game Design. *Gamasutra*, 2007. http://www.gamasutra.com/view/feature/129948/the_chemistry_of_game_design.php.
7. Cutumisu, M., Onuczko, C., McNaughton, M., et al. ScriptEase: A generative/adaptive programming paradigm for game scripting. *Science of Computer Programming 67*, 1 (2007), 32–58.
8. Dormans, J. Adventures in Level Design: Generating Missions and Spaces for Action Adventure Games. *Proceedings of the 2010 Workshop on Procedural Content Generation in Games (co-located with FDG 2010)*, (2010).
9. Dormans, J. Engineering Emergence: Applied Theory for Game Design. 2012.
10. Doull, A. The Death of the Level Designer: Procedural Content Generation in Games. *ASCII Dreams: A Roguelike Developer's Diary*, 2008. http://roguelikedeveloper.blogspot.com/2008/01/death-of-level-designer-procedural.html.
11. Ebert, D.S. *Texturing & Modeling: A Procedural Approach*. Morgan Kaufmann, 2003.
12. Fernández-Vara, C. Personal communication, creator of Symon game. (2012).
13. Firaxis Games. *Civilization IV (PC Game)*. 2K Games, 2005.
14. Gearbox Software and Feral Interactive. *Borderlands (XBox 360)*. 2K Games, 2009.
15. Gee, J.P. *What video games have to teach us about learning and literacy*. Palgrave Macmillan, New York, NY, 2003.
16. Hastings, E.J., Guha, R.K., and Stanley, K.O. Automatic Content Generation in the Galactic Arms Race Video Game. *IEEE Transactions on Computational Intelligence and AI in Games 1*, 4 (2009), 245–263.
17. Hendrikx, M., Meijer, S., Van der Velden, J., and Iosup, A. Procedural Content Generation for Games: A Survey. *ACM Transactions on Multimedia Computing, Communications and Applications*, (2011).
18. Hullett, K. and Whitehead, J. Design Patterns in FPS Levels. *Proceedings of the 2010 International Conference on the Foundations of Digital Games (FDG 2010)*, (2010).
19. Hunicke, R., LeBlanc, M., and Zubek, R. MDA: A Formal Approach to Game Design and Game Research. *Proceedings of the 2004 AAAI Workshop on Challenges in Game Artificial Intelligence*, AAAI Press (2004).
20. Interactive Data Visualization Inc. *SpeedTree (PC Software)*. Lexington, SC, 2010.
21. Jennings-Teats, M., Smith, G., and Wardrip-Fruin, N. Polymorph: A Model for Dynamic Level Generation. (2010).
22. Jupiter. *Picross DS (Nintendo DS)*. Nintendo, 2007.
23. Khaled, R., Nelson, M.J., and Barr, P. Design metaphors for procedural content generation in games. *Proceedings of the SIGCHI Conference on Human Factors in Computing Systems*, (2013), 1509–1518.
24. Level-5. *Professor Layton and the Curious Village (Nintendo DS)*. Nintendo, 2008.
25. Liapis, A., Yannakakis, G.N., and Togelius, J. Sentient sketchbook: Computer-aided game level authoring. *Proceedings of ACM Conference on Foundations of Digital Games*, (2013).
26. Maxis. *Spore Creature Creator (PC Game)*. Electronic Arts, 2008.
27. Maxis. *Spore (PC Game)*. Electronic Arts, 2008.
28. McNaughton, M., Cutumisu, M., Szafron, D., Schaeffer, J., Redford, J., and Parker, D. ScriptEase:

Generative design patterns for computer role-playing games. *Automated Software Engineering, 2004. Proceedings. 19th International Conference on*, (2004), 88–99.

29. Mortac. The Complete Guide to Map Generation. *Civ Fanatics Forums*, 2007. http://forums.civfanatics.com/showthread.php?t=246788&s=b667c50191bb40c93402f38a7560b7ac.
30. Müller, P., Wonka, P., Haegler, S., Ulmer, A., and Van Gool, L. Procedural Modeling of Buildings. *ACM Transactions on Graphics 25*, 3 (2006), 614–623.
31. Nintendo EAD. *Animal Crossing: New Leaf (Nintendo 3DS)*. Nintendo, 2013.
32. Nitsche, M., Ashmore, C., Hankinson, W., Fitzpatrick, R., Kelly, J., and Margenau, K. Designing Procedural Game Spaces: A Case Study. *Proceedings of FuturePlay 2006*, (2006).
33. Ohkubo, H. *Warning Forever (PC Game)*. Hikware, 2003.
34. Persson, M. *Infinite Mario Bros! (PC Game)*. http://www.mojang.com/notch/mario/, 2008.
35. Persson, M. *Minecraft (PC Game)*. 2011.
36. Rareware. *Donkey Kong Country 2: Diddy's Kong Quest (Nintendo DS)*. Nintendo, 1995.
37. Regier, J. and Gresko, R. Random Asset Generation in Diablo 3. *Invited Talk, UC Santa Cruz*, (2009).
38. Risi, S., Lehman, J., D'Ambrosio, D.B., Hall, R., and Stanley, K.O. Combining Search-Based Procedural Content Generation and Social Gaming in the Petalz Video Game. *Proceedings of the 2012 Conference on Artificial Intelligence and Interactive Digital Entertainment*, (2012).
39. Rogue Basin. Articles on Implementation Techniques. http://roguebasin.roguelikedevelopment.org/index.php?title=Articles#Implementation.
40. Rohrer, J. *Inside a Star-Filled Sky (PC Game)*. 2011.
41. Saltsman, A. *Canabalt (PC Game)*. Adam Atomic, 2009.
42. Schell, J. *The Art of Game Design: A book of lenses*. Morgan Kaufmann, 2008.
43. Secretan, J., Beato, N., D'Ambrosio, D.B., et al. Picbreeder: a case study in collaborative evolutionary exploration of design space. *Evolutionary Computation 19*, 3 (2011), 373–403.
44. Shaker, N., Nicolau, M., Yannakakis, G., Togelius, J., and O'Neill, M. Evolving Levels for Super Mario Bros Using Grammatical Evolution. *IEEE Transactions on Computational Intelligence and Games (CIG)*, (2012).
45. Shaker, N., Yannakakis, G.N., and Togelius, J. Towards Automatic Personalized Content Generation for Platform Games. *Proceedings of the Sixth Artificial Intelligence in Interactive Digital Entertainment Conference (AIIDE10)*, (2010).
46. Smelik, R., Galka, K., de Kraker, K.J., Kuijper, F., and Bidarra, R. Semantic constraints for procedural generation of virtual worlds. *Proceedings of the 2nd International Workshop on Procedural Content Generation in Games*, ACM (2011).
47. Smelik, R.M., Tutenel, T., de Kraker, K.J., and Bidarra, R. Integrating Procedural Generation and Manual Editing of Virtual Worlds. *Proceedings of the 2010 Workshop on Procedural Content Generation in Games (co-located with FDG 2010)*, (2010).
48. Smith, A.M., Andersen, E., Mateas, M., and Popovic, Z. A Case Study of Expressively Constrainable Level Design Automation Tools for a Puzzle Game. *Proceedings of the 2012 Conference on the Foundations of Digital Games*, (2012).
49. Smith, G. and Harteveld, C. Procedural Content Generation as an Opportunity to Foster Collaborative Mindful Learning. *Workshop on Games and Learning, co-located with Foundations of Digital Games 2013*, (2013).
50. Smith, G., Othenin-Girard, A., Whitehead, J., and Wardrip-Fruin, N. PCG-based Game Design: Creating Endless Web. *Proceedings of the International Conference on the Foundations of Digital Games*, ACM (2012), 188–195.
51. Smith, G., Whitehead, J., Mateas, M., Treanor, M., March, J., and Cha, M. Launchpad: A Rhythm-Based Level Generator for 2D Platformers. *IEEE Transactions on Computational Intelligence and AI in Games (TCIAIG) 3*, 1 (2011).
52. Smith, G., Whitehead, J., and Mateas, M. Tanagra: Reactive Planning and Constraint Solving for Mixed-Initiative Level Design. *IEEE Transactions on Computational Intelligence and AI in Games (TCIAIG), Special Issue on Procedural Content Generation 3*, 3 (2011).
53. Sonic Team. *Sonic the Hedgehog (Genesis)*. SEGA, 1991.
54. Sullivan, A. Content Selection vs. Content Generation. *Expressive Intelligence Studio*, 2010. http://eis-blog.ucsc.edu/2010/06/content-selection-vs-content-generation/.
55. Togelius, J., Kastbjerg, E., Schedl, D., and Yannakakis, G.N. What is procedural content generation?: Mario on the borderline. *Proceedings of the 2nd International Workshop on Procedural Content Generation in Games*, (2011), 3.
56. Togelius, J., Yannakakis, G.N., Stanley, K.O., and Browne, C. Search-Based Procedural Content Generation: A Taxonomy and Survey. *Computational Intelligence and AI in Games, IEEE Transactions on 3*, 3 (2011), 172 –186.
57. Toy, M., Wichman, G., Arnold, K., and Lane, J. *Rogue (PC Game)*. 1980.
58. Yannakakis, G.N. and Togelius, J. Experience-Driven Procedural Content Generation. *IEEE Transactions on Affective Computing 2*, 3 (2011), 147–161.
59. Yu, D. *Spelunky (PC Game)*. 2009.

# A Systematic Review of Quantitative Studies on the Enjoyment of Digital Entertainment Games

**Elisa D. Mekler, Julia Ayumi Bopp, Alexandre N. Tuch, Klaus Opwis**
University of Basel, Department of Psychology, Center for Cognitive Psychology & Methodology
Missionsstrasse 62a, 4055 Basel, Switzerland
elisa.mekler@unibas.ch, j.bopp@stud.unibas.ch, a.tuch@unibas.ch, klaus.opwis@unibas.ch

## ABSTRACT
Enjoyment has been identified as a central component of the player experience (PX), but various, overlapping concepts within PX make it difficult to develop valid measures and a common understanding of game enjoyment. We conducted a systematic review of 87 quantitative studies, analyzing different operationalizations and measures of game enjoyment, its determinants, and how these were related to other components of PX, such as flow, presence and immersion. Results suggest that game enjoyment describes the positive cognitive and affective appraisal of the game experience, and may in part be associated with the support of player needs and values. Further, we outline that enjoyment is distinct from flow in that it may occur independently of challenge and cognitive involvement, and argue that enjoyment may be understood as the valence of the player experience. We conclude with a discussion of methodological challenges and point out opportunities for future research on game enjoyment.

### Author Keywords
Digital Games; Enjoyment; Player Experience; Flow

### ACM Classification Keywords
K.8.0 Personal Computing: Games; J.4 Social and Behavioral Sciences: Sociology, Psychology

## INTRODUCTION
Digital games offer some of the most intense, rich and engaging experiences of all interactive products. Not only are they steadily increasing in popularity [1], but their growing importance as a medium for education, persuasion, and self-expression [12], as well as the different cultural practices that have formed around them (e.g., let's play videos, modding, game journalism, etc.) make games an immensely fascinating topic for the HCI community to study.

People play games for the experience they create [47]. However, the experience of being entertained through games is not well understood yet from a psychological perspective [83, 89]. Various concepts have been discussed, such as immersion [39], flow [59] or presence [78], making it difficult to decide upon which psychological concepts are best suited to study the player experience (PX) [8]. Meanwhile, enjoyment has been characterized as the core experience of all entertainment media [83] and games in particular [58, 77], and has previously been identified as a key motive for why people play games (for an overview refer to [13]).

Unfortunately, the definition of game enjoyment is fuzzy [77] and not well differentiated from other potentially related psychological components of PX, such as flow [58]. This raises the issue of how the experience of playing digital games can be effectively operationalized and measured [16, 89]. Moreover, many models of PX often neglect previous findings and/or are based on little empirical grounding [58, 89]. For these reasons, a common terminology for discussing and measuring PX and game enjoyment is still lacking, making it difficult to compare study findings and assess which factors contribute most to enjoyable game experiences.

Synthesizing and building upon existing knowledge on game enjoyment may improve the validity of measures, which in turn strengthens our understanding of what makes games so enjoyable. Hence, the present paper aims to provide a comprehensive review of previous quantitative research on game enjoyment. We take stock of the different conceptualizations and operationalizations of game enjoyment currently employed, in order to gain a clearer understanding of how the experience of enjoyment when playing digital games may be adequately measured. We also investigate how other psychological components of PX relate to game enjoyment, in order to further clarify the concept. Finally, we identify and categorize relevant determinants of game enjoyment and uncover opportunities for further research. We believe that by elaborating what constitutes game enjoyment, we may not only get more insights on how to properly measure the construct, but also gain a clearer understanding of the overall player experience.

## RELATED WORK
Enjoyment describes an individual's positive response towards media technology and its content [83] and has become a central concept within HCI research [11], as well as one of the most frequently assessed dimensions of user experience [5]. The enjoyment of websites, for instance, has already been well conceptualized and operationalized [49], but may not be readily applicable to assess players' enjoyment of digital games, as websites generally serve some utilitarian goal, whereas the *single most important goal of games* is enjoyment [77].


*CHI 2014*, April 26 - May 01, 2014, Toronto, ON, Canada.

http://dx.doi.org/10.1145/2556288.2557078

Similarly, Boyle et al. [13] distinguish between different stages of the engagement process in digital games and consider the subjective experience of enjoyment key to engagement. They define the subjective experience as moment-to-moment feelings of enjoyment that players experience while gaming. In contrast, enjoyment as a motive for playing games denotes the more enduring reason to play. In other words, people are motivated to play games, because they wish to experience enjoyment.

Many models and concepts have been proposed to explain this subjective experience of enjoyment in games (for an overview see [78]). For instance, game enjoyment has often been equated with the experience of flow [77, 85]. Flow describes the subjective experience of engaging in challenging, yet manageable activities (e.g., digital games), further characterized by complete cognitive absorption, time distortion and enjoyment [61]. But some argue that flow is too restrictive, as it is only concerned with extreme experiences [39, 78] and may not adequately cover more casual experiences of enjoyment, such as gaming on the phone while waiting for the bus. And indeed, Nakamura and Csikszentmihalyi have shown that enjoyment may occur independently of the flow experience [61].

Others still, consider flow and enjoyment distinct concepts. The Game Experience Questionnaire (GEQ), for instance, defines enjoyment as a multi-dimensional construct, made up of challenge, competence, (minimal) frustration and positive affect, whereas flow constitutes part of the involvement construct, which also includes immersion and (lack of) boredom [29]. In contrast, Jennett et al. [39] define immersion as the key component of good game experiences. However, in one experiment involving a non-game task they found that high immersion could also be accompanied by anxiety and negative affect, which makes it difficult to infer whether the task was not enjoyable or whether participants simply felt tense due to the task's increasing challenge. In short, these inconsistent, often overlapping conceptualizations make it difficult to form a common definition of game enjoyment, which poses serious challenges to effectively measuring the construct, thereby hampering our understanding of PX [16, 58, 89].

## METHOD

The aim of this paper is to clarify the concept of *game enjoyment*, in order to better understand how the construct may be operationalized and measured. To do so, we analyzed 87 quantitative studies measuring game enjoyment. The selection of the publications was done according to an adapted QUOROM procedure, which has previously been employed by Bargas-Avila and Hornbæk for their review on empirical studies in user experience research [5].

### Data collection

*Source selection.* Relevant publications on PX are spread across multiple scientific journals and conferences, so we chose not to limit our search to a pre-defined set of venues, lest relevant sources be missed. Instead, the following three publication databases were searched: ACM Digital Library (DL), ScienceDirect (ScD) and ISI Web of Knowledge (WoK). A time frame of five years (2008 to 2012) was set to restrict the search and because research on PX grew considerably in the last few years [89].

*Search procedure.* In all three databases, the terms *game* and *enjoyment* were combined to search all publications. Although many different terms, such as *liking*, *fun* or *preference*, are used synonymously for *enjoyment*, it has been argued that the aforementioned terms do not cover the exact same meaning [11, 57]. *Liking*, for instance, reflects reactions to the media message only, whereas enjoyment reflects reactions to both the media message and the media experience (i.e., the situation and context in which the media message was received) [57]. Similarly, Blythe and Hassenzahl [11] consider *fun* and *pleasure* two distinct forms of enjoyable experiences (i.e., enjoyment in terms of distraction or absorption respectively). We argue that games may provide both absorbing experiences and be played for distraction, and thus settled for the general term *enjoyment*. The search resulted in a total of 3'036 publications (DL=977, ScD=1'716, WoK=343).

*Screening criteria.* Four screening criteria were defined to narrow the entries: The papers had to be about (1) digital games and (2) more specifically, about entertainment games, that is, games, whose "only" intended purpose is to generate enjoyment [58, 77]. Enjoyment is without doubt crucial for games with specific purposes, such as serious games or exergames (e.g., [53]), but – for the sake of manageability, – they are beyond the scope of this review. Similarly, papers studying pervasive and augmented reality games were not taken into account, because it has been suggested that they differ from more "traditional" digital entertainment games in several dimensions and thereby require their own criteria for enjoyment [38]. Lastly, the publications included for analysis had to be (3) original full papers and (4) written in English.

Note that these categories are not mutually exclusive – as exclusion criteria the first obvious category was chosen. The screening was done in entirety by the first author. To control for interrater effects, an independent rater performed the same categorization using 20% of the entries. Interrater reliability was found to be Kappa = 0.928 ($p < .001$), 95% CI (0.788, 1.067). A Kappa value of .8 and higher is considered *almost perfect*.

#### *Selection criteria for inclusion in the final analysis*

As we were concerned with the conceptualization and subsequent operationalization of game enjoyment, it had to be measured in some form. For this reason, papers that did not contain quantitative empirical user data (e.g., theoretical papers) were excluded. Furthermore, only publications in which the authors explicitly mention that they measured enjoyment were included. Concepts such as *liking* or *fun* were only included, if the authors explicitly equated them with enjoyment (e.g., [76]). Exceptions were made if a study employed the GEQ [29] or based its questionnaire on the GameFlow model [77], as the original authors explicitly link these to game enjoyment. Lastly, only studies about the subjective experience of enjoyment were considered for analysis, resulting in a final sample of 68 publications.

Again, the screening was done by the first author and an independent rater. The interrater reliability was found to be Kappa = 0.873 ($p < .001$), 95% CI (0.701, 1.045). Then, all papers were coded in terms of aim of the study, measures, results, measuring times, study designs, participants, game genre, duration of gameplay, and if provided, definition of enjoyment. Note that some papers contained two or more studies, each containing measures of enjoyment. In this case, we treated those experiments as individual studies. Thus, a total of 87 studies were included in the final analysis. A table containing the collected data for each study is available online at ACM Digital Library `http://dx.doi.org/10.1145/2556288.2557078`.

## RESULTS

In the following, the results of the analysis of the 87 studies are reported. Due to the current lack of a common terminology for game enjoyment research, we structured the results section into general methodological observations, followed by a more in-depth look at the measures employed. Next, we summarize the current state of research on determinants of game enjoyment and compare how enjoyment has been operationalized in relation to other PX components.

### General methodological observations

*Purpose of the studies.* The majority of studies analyzed specific determinants of game enjoyment (n=49). Seventeen studies were about the evaluation of a particular game and 15 studies developed or compared methods for assessing game enjoyment and/or the overall player experience. The remaining studies were concerned with other aspects of gaming, such as the impact of violence on aggressiveness (e.g., [4]).

*Participants.* In more than half of the studies (n=44), participants' mean age ranged between 20 and 29 years, whereas in 14 studies participants were 19 years or younger. There were only 3 studies, where the mean age lay above 40 years. Moreover, 7 studies provided only the range of participants' age and 19 studies did not state any information on participants' age. Most studies (n=56) featured students as participants. Regarding gender distribution, the majority of studies had more female than male participants, apart from 10 studies where only male participants were present.

Most studies (n=52) did not assess game expertise in any form. Twenty-three studies asked players about the frequency of game-play, 2 studies let participants rate their expertise and 10 studies used other methods (e.g., Fang et al. [27] assessed the number of years participants have been playing digital games).

*Games and Genre.* First-person shooter games were by far the most frequently studied genre (n=22), followed by racing (n=13) and sports games (n=12, including bowling, boxing, football and tennis games). These three genres represent more than a half of the entries (n=47). Twenty-four studies did not provide any explanation on why they chose a certain game title or genre for their study.

*Study setting, gameplay duration and game metrics.* The time participants spent playing a game ranged between 2 to 60 minutes, with a median of 10 minutes. Apart from the online surveys, only 3 studies investigated game enjoyment outside of the lab setting [56, 63, 66]. Out of the 87 studies, 26 looked at game metrics, that is, the quantified measures of in-game data (e.g., time spent playing, actions taken by the player).

*Measuring point of enjoyment.* More than half the studies (n=46) assessed enjoyment after participants interacted with the game. Twelve studies measured enjoyment in-between the different gaming sessions or experimental conditions and 8 studies measured enjoyment during game-play. Thirteen studies did not provide any information on the time of measurement.

### Measurement of enjoyment

*Techniques used to measure enjoyment.* Overall, three groups of measures were identified: Subjective self-reports in the form of questionnaires (n=82), physiological measures (n=11) and other (n=2), which includes one study which let participants rank the games they played according to their preference [9] and another study that observed the amount of player behavior that expressed enjoyment [74]. We categorized the latter along with physiological measures as a more objective means to assess game enjoyment, seeing how participants have less direct control over their responses compared to self-reports [55, 60]. Most studies employed only subjective measures (n=75), 4 studies used only objective techniques, and 8 studies employed both subjective and objective measures to assess game enjoyment.

The most frequently used standardized questionnaires were the Intrinsic Motivation Inventory (IMI; n=15), the GEQ (n=8, including iGEQ) and the self-assessment manikin scale (SAM; n=2) [66, 82]. Several studies referenced and adapted other questionnaires (e.g., [20, 75]. Except the GEQ and the scale developed by Fang et al. [27], all questionnaires were uni-dimensional. Out of 82 studies that used questionnaires to assess game enjoyment, only 31 provided psychometric properties. As illustrated in Table 1, most studies (n=29) that investigated determinants of game enjoyment utilized self-developed questionnaires.

We also took account of the individual items used to measure game enjoyment. As seen in Table 2, *enjoy* was by far the most frequently used term. Strictly speaking, items measuring the subjective experience of enjoyment were the most common (n=54; e.g., "I enjoyed playing Madden very much" [73]), the remaining items measured the "enjoyability" of the game itself (e.g., "The game was enjoyable" [69]) or some individual aspect of it (e.g., "This interface made the game play more enjoyable" [19]).

There were some differences when comparing subjective and objective measures. Overall, facial electromyography (EMG) corresponded the most to subjective reports [18, 59, 66, 82], as game enjoyment was associated with an increase in activation of the zygomaticus major, orbicularis oculis and decrease in activation of the corrugator supercilii region. Other physiological measures, such as electrodermal activity, electrocar-

Table 1. Enjoyment measures employed by study purpose

| | | | | self-developed | | | | |
|---|---|---|---|---|---|---|---|---|
| Purpose | IMI | GEQ | referenced other | single item | items unknown | all listed | partly listed | objective measures |
| Determinants of enjoyment | 15 | 2 | 6 | 12 | 6 | 6 | 5 | 3 |
| Game Evaluation | – | 1 | 2 | 6 | – | 3 | 1 | 3 |
| Method Validation | – | 3 | – | – | – | 7 | 1 | 4 |
| Other | 1 | 2 | 6 | 6 | 1 | 3 | – | 2 |
| **Total** | 16 | 8 | 14 | 24 | 7 | 19 | 7 | 11 |

Note. Data do not sum up to 87 because some studies use more than one measure or serve more than one purpose.

Table 2. The 11 most frequent terms used to measure game enjoyment.

| Term | Examples and sources | N |
|---|---|---|
| Enjoyable, Enjoying | "How much did you enjoy the game?" [30] | 77 |
| Fun | "Playing the game was fun" [81] | 30 |
| Interesting | "I thought playing Madden was interesting" [73] | 17 |
| Good | "I felt good" [18] | 17 |
| Future play intent | "Would you like to play the game again?" [39] | 16 |
| Boring | "I thought the game was boring" [67] | 13 |
| Happy | "I feel happy when playing this game" [27] | 11 |
| Frustrating | "I felt frustrated" [60] | 10 |
| Challenge | "I felt challenged" [29] | 10 |
| Entertaining | "This game was entertaining" [80] | 9 |
| Irritating | "I felt irritable" [71] | 9 |

diography or electroencephalography were not as clearly related to game enjoyment, even though they correlated significantly with different dimensions of the GEQ [18, 24, 45, 60].

## Determinants of game enjoyment

We grouped the factors that potentially predict game enjoyment broadly into game system, player and context variables, as suggested by Nacke and Drachen [58].

*Game System.* Challenge was the most frequently examined factor (n=21) and was found to be an important determinant of game enjoyment, although this effect was further determined by player skills [3, 41] and motives [76]. Game outcome yielded mixed results, as some studies showed that winning a game increased enjoyment [41, 65], whereas others did not [3, 48, 75]. However, winning only by a bit was experienced as particularly enjoyable [3, 65]. Intuitive control schemes facilitated feelings of being in-control and self-efficacy [48, 72, 81], which in turn also contributed to game enjoyment. This was further reflected in some of the evaluation studies, as players enjoyed interfaces that were easy to control and allowed for best performances the most [15, 42, 51].

Quick et al. [68] found that fantasy was an important determinant of game enjoyment, and several studies confirm this notion, as narrative [64], avatar resemblance [23], as well as identification with the avatar [44, 50] and other playable characters [22] all significantly contributed to enjoyable game experiences. Sound and music also enhanced enjoyment to a certain degree [17, 60].

Of the 12 studies that examined violence in games, most found that violent game content did not or only marginally enhance enjoyment (e.g., [6]). In fact, there was some evidence that players enjoy games less, when they contain violence against humans, as they cause moral distress [30]. However, players that were already familiar with a violent game experienced less guilt and negative affect, as well as more enjoyment [34].

*Player.* Player types and motives were important determinants of game enjoyment [2, 21, 68, 76]. Similarly, personality traits, such as sensation seeking and self-forgetfulness were found to correlate positively with enjoyment of games [28]. Mental imagery capability had no influence on enjoyment [88]. Two studies found that game enjoyment of certain genres was dependent on the player's gender [48, 50].

Various psychological outcomes were also associated with enjoyable game experiences, such as feelings of being in-control, self-efficacy and need satisfaction [67, 79, 80]. Further, Downs and Sundar [23] found a strong positive correlation between winning, ego-enhancement and game enjoyment. Similarly, Reinecke et al. [69, 70] found that enjoyment was significantly related to mood repair and recovery experience, that is, allowing for the satisfaction of psychological needs that were previously thwarted. On the other hand, there were some indications that feelings of guilt are negatively correlated with enjoyment [34, 50].

*Context.* Context factors were rarely examined (n=5) and yielded mixed results. For instance, there was no clear indication that the co-presence of other players increases enjoyment (e.g., [35]). Lack of communication between players had little impact on enjoyment [9], as did location (i.e., playing at home vs. in a laboratory) [18].

## Enjoyment in relation to other PX components

Twenty-four studies measured flow in some form (Abuhamdeh and Csikszentmihalyi never mention "flow" and refer to "optimal experience" instead [2, 3]), with varying definitions of how enjoyment and flow relate to each other. Some use the terms "flow" and "enjoyment" interchangeably (e.g., [40]), a notion which was further reflected by the activation of reward-related midbrain structures during flow experiences [43].

Others [21, 51] refer specifically to the GameFlow model of player enjoyment [77], whereas studies that rely on the GEQ argue that flow is a dimension of player involvement rather than enjoyment (e.g., [29]). Lastly, some state that the two constructs share similarities and that enjoyment results from the flow experience (e.g., [86]).

These inconsistent definitions stem largely from the different aspects of flow that the studies chose to focus on. Several studies associate flow with focused attention [40, 85] and the balance of skill and challenge [41, 43, 59]. However, Shim et al. [76] found that the balance of skill and challenge – arguably a defining factor of flow – did only partially account for game enjoyment on its own. Rather, this was further dependent on players' motivations for game-play. In contrast, Limperos et al. [48] found that the experience of control – an aspect also associated with flow – was related to players' enjoyment, but not to other characteristics of flow.

Notably, several studies found a strong positive relation between presence and flow [40, 59, 87]. While presence seemed not to affect enjoyment directly [72, 86], Weibel et al. found that it increased enjoyment indirectly through flow. They concluded that being immersed in a virtual environment may facilitate cognitive involvement and subsequently, enable the experience of flow.

Similarly, Jennett et al. [39] consider immersion key to a good gaming experience, characterized by real world dissociation, as well as cognitive and emotional involvement. Unfortunately, although their measure of immersion also includes enjoyment as a subconstruct, they do not report how it relates to the aforementioned aspects. In contrast, Nacke and Lindley [59] offer an alternative definition of immersion in terms of the sensory experience that a game provides and found that immersive level design was associated with positive affect and feelings of competence, most likely due to providing a sense of spatial presence.

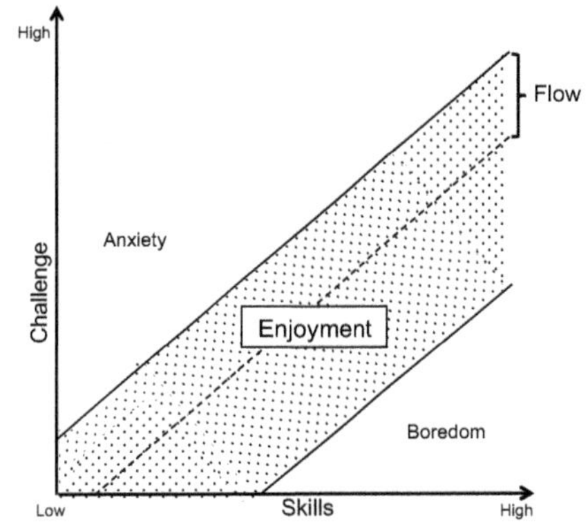


**Figure 1. Flow results from the balance of game challenge and player skills. Less challenging gameplay may still be experienced as enjoyable.**

## DISCUSSION

On the basis of the 87 studies reviewed, we compare the various operationalizations of game enjoyment and differentiate it from related constructs, in order to establish a working definition of the concept and consider its relevance for PX. Moreover, we discuss what implications our results have for future PX research.

### Conceptualizing game enjoyment

As illustrated in Table 2, game enjoyment was frequently associated with fun and interest, as well as being the opposite of boredom, especially in studies that operationalized enjoyment as intrinsic motivation and hence employed the IMI (e.g., [67, 73]). This is in line with previous conceptualizations of enjoyment as a positive cognitive appraisal of media [57, 83]. Game enjoyment was also operationalized as positive affect, using both self-reports and biometrics (e.g., [66]). However, only Fang et al. [27] attempted to distinguish between affective and cognitive aspects of enjoyment. Notably, all studies that employed measures of frustration either assessed it as a separate dimension of game enjoyment, or acknowledged that it should not be considered the antipode of enjoyment [23], because even though many games provide moments of frustration, the overall experience may still be enjoyable.

Interestingly, game enjoyment was often associated with feelings of being in-control (e.g., [72]), competence (e.g., [41]) and improved mood after game-play, due to to the satisfaction of psychological needs [70]. It has been stated that need satisfaction may in part explain how game enjoyment comes into being [67, 79]. In fact, several of the reviewed studies indicated that this aspect of enjoyment is more pronounced for games than for non-interactive media [69, 70, 80]. Concurrently, game enjoyment was to certain degree negatively correlated with feelings of guilt [34, 50], and Gollwitzer and Melzer even operationalized it as the opposite of moral distress [30]. This was further reflected in some of the items used to measure enjoyment, such as in the instrument developed by Fang et al. [27] ("The activities in this game [...] are respectable"). It seems that – beyond 'mere' fun, – game enjoyment not only denotes a positive cognitive and affective appraisal of the gaming experience, but is in part also characterized by certain psychological outcomes, namely need satisfaction and the absence of guilt. This recalls the concept of serious fun proposed by Lazzaro [47], which suggests that players experience enjoyment when a game reflects their values (e.g., the absence of guilt) and positively affects their thoughts and feelings (e.g., through need satisfaction).

This raises some interesting research questions. For instance, whether it is more enjoyable if a game, albeit less challenging, provides ample opportunities for competence need satisfaction, or whether players experience more enjoyment when they achieve a rare moment of triumph in an extremely challenging game, and how this differs with regards to player motives. On the other hand, researchers may look into how games that were intentionally designed as non-enjoyable – such as *Torture Game 2*, which seeks to elicit disinterest by "allowing" players to commit atrocities [12], – induce guilt, and compare them to popular (i.e., enjoyable), albeit controversial games, such as *Grand Theft Auto V*, in order to clarify the relationship between need satisfaction, identification, guilt and enjoyment.

#### *Relationship between enjoyment and other PX components*

Presence did not impact game enjoyment directly, but facilitated flow experience, which itself gave rise to enjoyment [40, 86]. Arguably, game enjoyment shares many similarities with flow. But even though enjoyment is a crucial aspect of the flow experience [61], they still differ in specific ways: It seems that the experience of challenge, enjoyment and deep concentration are the main characteristics of flow (e.g., [43]), while other aspects, such as a sense of control, facilitate flow and make games more enjoyable, but do not trigger flow by themselves [48]. Put differently, flow encompasses both enjoyment and involvement, triggered by the optimal balance of challenging gameplay and player skills [41], but players may experience enjoyment independently of flow [48, 76], if their skills exceed the challenges posed by the game [59, 61] (see Figure 1). Therefore, we conclude that limiting game enjoyment to the experience of flow would fail to account for the variety of enjoyable experiences that games may provide. Nevertheless, more empirical research is required to further probe under what circumstances game enjoyment and flow occur and whether the flow experience is characterized by particularly deep enjoyment.

This conceptualization of game enjoyment has some potential theoretical implications for PX research, namely that game enjoyment may be understood as the valence of the player experience. In contrast, the intensity of the player experience may perhaps be best represented by players' immersion, involvement or engagement, that is, the extent to which players's attention is held by gameplay challenges and the game environment (i.e., presence) [14, 39]. Put differently, the more immersive a game, the more intense the player experience, eventually culminating in cognitive absorption and time distortion. While it is beyond the scope of the present paper to establish a working definition of this concept, flow may thus be explained in terms of a very intense, yet positive experience (see Figure 2).

This framework supports previous conceptualizations of flow as effortless attention [16] and immersion as a graded experience [39]. However, more research is needed to empirically assess its validity. For instance, whether a non-intense gaming experience may be just as enjoyable as an intense one, and how the valence and the intensity of the player experience relate to each other. Moreover, in order to deepen our understanding of PX, it is necessary to consider how the intensity of the player experience can be operationalized and measured, how it is affected by challenge and presence and how this relates to need satisfaction, as well as to cognitive and affective aspects of game enjoyment. Unraveling this issue is especially relevant in light of the increasing realism of digital games, the upcoming resurgence of VR technology, such as the Oculus Rift, and for research on the negative effects of gaming [14].

### Methodological challenges

Our review uncovered some methodological issues currently present in research on game enjoyment. Firstly, few studies employed standardized questionnaires, although validated and standardized questionnaires are easier to compare and may be taken with more confidence [36]. As illustrated in Table 1, many studies on the determinants of game enjoyment relied on self-developed scales, which makes it difficult to compare results and also adds to the problem of distinguishing the different components of PX. Additionally, many studies omitted item descriptions, as well as information on the reliability and validity of the scales. To facilitate interpretation of study results and advance PX research, future studies on game enjoyment would be well advised to provide as much information as possible on the measures used.

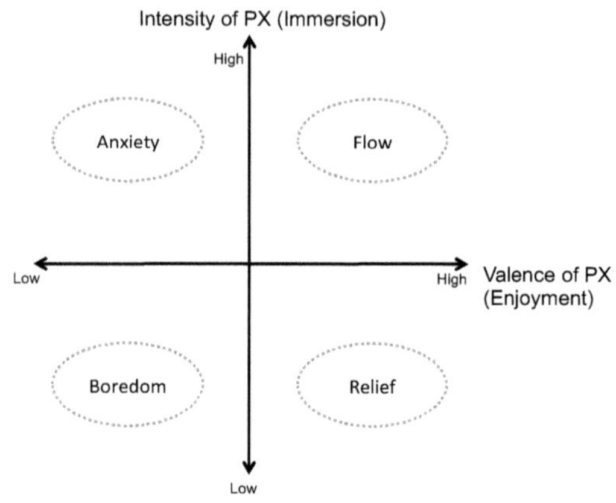


**Figure 2. Valence and intensity of PX framework. Enjoyment describes the valence of the player experience, whereas immersion may denote its intensity.**

Interestingly, physiological measures seem to be more common in the study of PX than in user experience research [5]. However, apart from EMG, physiological measures yielded mixed results with regards to game enjoyment. But due to the low number of studies, it would be foolhardy to dismiss physiological measures as not suitable, as they show a lot of promise, given that they allow the objective measure of player experience without interrupting the player-game interaction.

Next, the majority of studies recruited students between 20 and 29 years, although this represents only around a third of the gaming population [1]. And even though game expertise and familiarity has been found to affect enjoyment (e.g., [34]), most studies (n=52) did not take this into account. Notably, FPS games were the most frequently studied genre, even though they are mostly popular with the 21 - 29 year old male demographic [26], while other popular genres, such as casual or computer role-playing games [1] were underrepresented. To establish a more comprehensive understanding of game enjoyment, it would be beneficial to study a wide spectrum of game genres and player demographics.

Lastly, as of now, there is scant quantitative evidence on what characterizes long-term game enjoyment, as well as how players experience games before actually engaging with them [16, 58]. Seeing how some players are willing to invest hundreds of hours into a game, it would be interesting to study what aspects of the player, game system or context determine game enjoyment, how it changes over time and how this affects other components of PX.

### Further research

Strikingly, although the importance of the context surrounding the player experience has been emphasized time and again [35, 58], only little attention has been paid to how contextual factors affect game enjoyment. Yet many players enjoy gaming with others [1], indicating that social aspects are indeed an important determinant of game enjoyment [47].

Moreover, Lazarro's 4 keys to fun model [47] associates many of the aforementioned determinants with particular emotions, such as challenge and *fiero* (i.e., pride). Further research on how aspects of the game system, player and context elicit these emotions, and how this impacts overall game enjoyment, would benefit both game designers and PX researchers alike. Also, many recent games strive to provide more complex experiences than mere "fun". Seeing how previous research on non-interactive media showed that sad or frightening media content is often experienced as enjoyable [57], future studies should look into games that, for instance, inspire negative affective experiences, such as when the plot of a game demands for the death of a character, in order to study how these affect players' overall experience of enjoyment, whether they impact the cognitive and affective aspects of enjoyment differently, and how they relate to need satisfaction and player values.

Finally, it has been argued that enjoyment may facilitate media effects such as learning, aggressiveness or behavior change [57]. Not only is more research necessary to examine how game enjoyment and the intensity of the player experience are linked to negative effects, such as aggressiveness or addiction [14], but in light of the steadily increasing interest in games as a medium for expressing ideas, teaching and behavior change [12, 53], it would be especially valuable to study in what ways game enjoyment is related to these beneficial outcomes of game-play.

### Limitations of the present paper

The present paper features several shortcomings. First, while our review procedure attempted to cover the gamut of quantitative studies on game enjoyment, we might have missed out on relevant studies that studied enjoyment under another term (e.g., fun). Secondly, we solely focused on studies that employed quantitative measures. For a more comprehensive understanding of enjoyable game experiences, it is necessary to also consider qualitative studies – which may in turn inform the development of quantitative measures [16], – and multi-method approaches [16], such as the biometric user studies conducted by Mirza-Babaei et al. [55]. Also, we only included studies examining "traditional" entertainment games. More research is required to find out whether the present findings may be extended to serious games and pervasive games. Thirdly, due to the nature of the review, we discussed a wide array of studies, but as a consequence, discussed individual studies only briefly. Finally, although our conclusions were founded on substantial amounts of empirical data, they in turn await empirical scrutiny.

## CONCLUSION

This paper sought to investigate the concept of game enjoyment and its various operationalizations and measures. Based on the review of 87 recent quantitative studies, we found that game enjoyment is commonly understood as the positive cognitive and affective appraisal of the game experience, and is in part associated with need satisfaction and the absence of guilt. Moreover, we provide a clearer outline of how enjoyment, flow, immersion and presence differ and interrelate, and suggest that the player experience may be studied in terms of its valence, that is, how enjoyable it is. Correspondingly, we discuss the strengths and shortcomings of both objective and subjective means by which the extent of game enjoyment can be measured. More research is needed to tackle the challenge of further disentangling the different psychological components of PX, especially immersion, and elaborating upon how other relevant components, such as need satisfaction and affect relate to game enjoyment and the overall player experience.

## ACKNOWLEDGEMENTS

We would like to thank the reviewers for their very helpful comments. Special thanks to Florian Brühlmann.

## REFERENCES

1. Essential facts about the computer and video game industry. Tech. rep., Entertainment Software Association, 2013. Retrieved June 1, 2013 from `http://www.theesa.com/facts/pdfs/ESA_EF_2013.pdf`.
2. Abuhamdeh, S., and Csikszentmihalyi, M. Intrinsic and extrinsic motivational orientations in the competitive context: An examination of person–situation interactions. *Journal of personality 77*, 5 (2009), 1615–1635 *.
3. Abuhamdeh, S., and Csikszentmihalyi, M. The importance of challenge for the enjoyment of intrinsically motivated, goal-directed activities. *Personality and Social Psychology Bulletin 38*, 3 (2012), 317–330 *.
4. Anderson, C. A., and Carnagey, N. L. Causal effects of violent sports video games on aggression: Is it competitiveness or violent content? *Journal of Experimental Social Psychology 45*, 4 (2009), 731–739 *.
5. Bargas-Avila, J. A., and Hornbæk, K. Old wine in new bottles or novel challenges: a critical analysis of empirical studies of user experience. In *Proc. CHI '11*, ACM (2011), 2689–2698.
6. Bastian, B., Jetten, J., and Radke, H. R. Cyber-dehumanization: Violent video game play diminishes our humanity. *Journal of Experimental Social Psychology 48*, 2 (2012), 486–491 *.
7. Bateman, S., Doucette, A., Xiao, R., Gutwin, C., Mandryk, R. L., and Cockburn, A. Effects of view, input device, and track width on video game driving. In *Proc. GI '11*, Canadian Human-Computer Communications Society (2011), 207–214 *.
8. Bernhaupt, R. User experience evaluation in entertainment. In *Evaluating User Experience in Games*. Springer, 2010, 3–7.
9. Beznosyk, A., Quax, P., Coninx, K., and Lamotte, W. The influence of cooperative game design patterns for remote play on player experience. In *Proc. APCHI '12*, ACM (2012), 11–20 *.
10. Bharambe, A., Douceur, J. R., Lorch, J. R., Moscibroda, T., Pang, J., Seshan, S., and Zhuang, X. Donnybrook: enabling large-scale, high-speed, peer-to-peer games. In *Proc. SIGCOMM '08*, vol. 38, ACM (2008), 389–400 *.

11. Blythe, M., and Hassenzahl, M. The semantics of fun: Differentiating enjoyable experiences. In *Funology*. Springer, 2005, 91–100.
12. Bogost, I. *How to Do Things with Video Games*. University of Minnesota Press, 2011.
13. Boyle, E. A., Connolly, T. M., Hainey, T., and Boyle, J. M. Engagement in digital entertainment games: A systematic review. *Computers in Human Behavior* (2011).
14. Brockmyer, J. H., Fox, C. M., Curtiss, K. A., McBroom, E., Burkhart, K. M., and Pidruzny, J. N. The development of the game engagement questionnaire: A measure of engagement in video game-playing. *Journal of Experimental Social Psychology 45*, 4 (2009), 624–634.
15. Browne, K., and Anand, C. An empirical evaluation of user interfaces for a mobile video game. *Entertainment Computing 3*, 1 (2012), 1–10 *.
16. Calvillo-Gámez, E. H., Cairns, P., and Romero, P. Catching the game: multi-method approaches to understanding gaming experiences. In *Game User Research Workshop CHI '12* (2012).
17. Cassidy, G., and MacDonald, R. A. The effects of music on time perception and performance of a driving game. *Scandinavian journal of psychology 51*, 6 (2010), 455–464 *.
18. Chanel, G., Kivikangas, J. M., and Ravaja, N. Physiological compliance for social gaming analysis: Cooperative versus competitive play. *Interacting with Computers 24*, 4 (2012), 306–316 *.
19. Charbonneau, E., Miller, A., Wingrave, C., and LaViola Jr, J. J. Understanding visual interfaces for the next generation of dance-based rhythm video games. In *Proc. Sandbox '09*, ACM (2009), 119–126 *.
20. De Simone, J., Verbruggen, T., Kuo, L.-H., and Mutlu, B. Is cheating a human function? the roles of presence, state hostility, and enjoyment in an unfair video game. *Computers in Human Behavior* (2012), 2351–2358 *.
21. Dias, R., and Martinho, C. Adapting content presentation and control to player personality in videogames. In *Proc. ACE '11*, ACM (2011), 18 *.
22. Dimas, J., Pereira, G., Santos, P. A., Prada, R., and Paiva, A. I'm happy if you are happy.: a model for emotional contagion in game characters. In *Proc. ACE '11*, ACM (2011), 2 *.
23. Downs, E., and Sundar, S. S. "we won" vs."they lost": Exploring ego-enhancement and self-preservation tendencies in the context of video game play. *Entertainment Computing 2*, 1 (2011), 23–28 *.
24. Drachen, A., Nacke, L. E., Yannakakis, G., and Pedersen, A. L. Correlation between heart rate, electrodermal activity and player experience in first-person shooter games. In *Proc. Sandbox '10*, ACM (2010), 49–54 *.
25. Duh, H. B.-L., Yew Yee, S. L. C., Gu, Y. X., and Chen, V. H.-H. A narrative-driven design approach for casual games with children. In *Proc. Sandbox '10*, ACM (2010), 19–24 *.
26. Elliott, L., Golub, A., Ream, G., and Dunlap, E. Video game genre as a predictor of problem use. *Cyberpsychology, Behavior, and Social Networking 15*, 3 (2012), 155–161.
27. Fang, X., Chan, S., Brzezinski, J., and Nair, C. Development of an instrument to measure enjoyment of computer game play. *Intl. Journal of Human–Computer Interaction 26*, 9 (2010), 868–886 *.
28. Fang, X., and Zhao, F. Personality and enjoyment of computer game play. *Computers in Industry 61*, 4 (2010), 342–349 *.
29. Gajadhar, B. J., Nap, H. H., de Kort, Y. A., and IJsselsteijn, W. A. Out of sight, out of mind: co-player effects on seniors' player experience. In *Proc. FnG '10*, ACM (2010), 74–83 *.
30. Gollwitzer, M., and Melzer, A. Macbeth and the joystick: Evidence for moral cleansing after playing a violent video game. *Journal of Experimental Social Psychology* (2012), 1356–1360 *.
31. Gualeni, S., Janssen, D., and Calvi, L. How psychophysiology can aid the design process of casual games: A tale of stress, facial muscles, and paper beasts. In *Proc. FDG '12*, ACM (2012), 149–155 *.
32. Gürkök, H., Hakvoort, G., Poel, M., and Nijholt, A. User expectations and experiences of a speech and thought controlled computer game. In *Proc. ACE '11*, ACM (2011), 53 *.
33. Hagelbäck, J., and Johansson, S. J. Measuring player experience on runtime dynamic difficulty scaling in an rts game. In *Proc. CIG '09*, IEEE (2009), 46–52 *.
34. Hartmann, T., and Vorderer, P. It's okay to shoot a character: Moral disengagement in violent video games. *Journal of Communication 60*, 1 (2010), 94–119 *.
35. Heeter, C., Sarkar, C. D., Palmer-Scott, B., and Zhang, S. Engineering sociability: Friendship drive, visibility, and social connection in anonymous co-located local wi-fi multiplayer online gaming. *Intl. J. of Gaming and Computer-Mediated Simulations 4*, 2 (2012), 1–18 *.
36. Hornbæk, K. Current practice in measuring usability: Challenges to usability studies and research. *Intl. journal of human-computer studies 64*, 2 (2006), 79–102.
37. Jefferson, C., Moncur, W., and Petrie, K. E. Combination: Automated generation of puzzles with constraints. In *Proc. SAC '11*, ACM (2011), 907–912 *.
38. Jegers, K. Pervasive game flow: understanding player enjoyment in pervasive gaming. *Computers in Entertainment 5*, 1 (2007), 9.

39. Jennett, C., Cox, A. L., Cairns, P., Dhoparee, S., Epps, A., Tijs, T., and Walton, A. Measuring and defining the experience of immersion in games. *Intl. journal of human-computer studies 66*, 9 (2008), 641–661 *.

40. Jin, S.-A. A. "i feel present. therefore, i experience flow:" a structural equation modeling approach to flow and presence in video games. *Journal of Broadcasting & Electronic Media 55*, 1 (2011), 114–136 *.

41. Jin, S.-A. A. "toward integrative models of flow": Effects of performance, skill, challenge, playfulness, and presence on flow in video games. *Journal of Broadcasting & Electronic Media 56*, 2 (2012), 169–186 *.

42. Jörg, S., Normoyle, A., and Safonova, A. How responsiveness affects players' perception in digital games. In *Proc. SAP '12*, ACM (2012), 33–38 *.

43. Klasen, M., Weber, R., Kircher, T. T., Mathiak, K. A., and Mathiak, K. Neural contributions to flow experience during video game playing. *Social cognitive and affective neuroscience 7*, 4 (2012), 485–495 *.

44. Klimmt, C., Hefner, D., Vorderer, P., Roth, C., and Blake, C. Identification with video game characters as automatic shift of self-perceptions. *Media Psychology 13*, 4 (2010), 323–338 *.

45. Kuikkaniemi, K., Laitinen, T., Turpeinen, M., Saari, T., Kosunen, I., and Ravaja, N. The influence of implicit and explicit biofeedback in first-person shooter games. In *Proc. CHI '10*, ACM (2010), 859–868 *.

46. Lai, J.-H., Chen, C.-L., Wu, P.-C., Kao, C.-C., and Chien, S.-Y. Tennis real play: an interactive tennis game with models from real videos. In *Proc. MM '11*, ACM (2011), 483–492 *.

47. Lazzaro, N. The four fun keys. *Game Usability: Advancing the Player Experience (K. Isbister and N. Schaffer, Eds.). Burlington: Elsevier* (2008), 315–344.

48. Limperos, A. M., Schmierbach, M. G., Kegerise, A. D., and Dardis, F. E. Gaming across different consoles: exploring the influence of control scheme on game-player enjoyment. *Cyberpsychology, Behavior, and Social Networking 14*, 6 (2011), 345–350 *.

49. Lin, A., Gregor, S., and Ewing, M. Understanding the nature of online emotional experiences: a study of enjoyment as a web experience. In *Proc. ICEC '09*, ACM (2009), 259–268.

50. Lin, S.-F. Gender differences and the effect of contextual features on game enjoyment and responses. *Cyberpsychology, Behavior, and Social Networking 13*, 5 (2010), 533–537 *.

51. Macret, M., Antle, A. N., and Pasquier, P. Can a paper-based sketching interface improve the gamer experience in strategy computer games? In *Proc. IHCI '12*, IEEE (2012), 1–6 *.

52. Maruyama, Y., Masoodian, M., and Rogers, B. A survey of japanese gamers' ratings of experience elements for different game genres. In *Proc. ACE '11*, ACM (2011), 47 *.

53. Mellecker, R., Lyons, E. J., and Baranowski, T. Disentangling fun and enjoyment in exergames using an expanded design, play, experience framework: A narrative review. *GAMES FOR HEALTH: Research, Development, and Clinical Applications* (2013).

54. Merritt, T., McGee, K., Chuah, T. L., and Ong, C. Choosing human team-mates: perceived identity as a moderator of player preference and enjoyment. In *Proc. FDG '11*, ACM (2011), 196–203 *.

55. Mirza-Babaei, P., Nacke, L. E., Gregory, J., Collins, N., and Fitzpatrick, G. How does it play better?: exploring user testing and biometric storyboards in games user research. In *Proc. CHI '13*, ACM (2013), 1499–1508.

56. Moser, C., Fuchsberger, V., and Tscheligi, M. Rapid assessment of game experiences in public settings. In *Proc. FnG '12*, ACM (2012), 73–82 *.

57. Nabi, R. L., and Krcmar, M. Conceptualizing media enjoyment as attitude: Implications for mass media effects research. *Communication Theory 14*, 4 (2004), 288–310.

58. Nacke, L., and Drachen, A. Towards a framework of player experience research. In *EPEX '11* (2011).

59. Nacke, L., and Lindley, C. A. Flow and immersion in first-person shooters: measuring the player's gameplay experience. In *Proc. Future Play '08*, ACM (2008), 81–88 *.

60. Nacke, L. E., Grimshaw, M. N., and Lindley, C. A. More than a feeling: Measurement of sonic user experience and psychophysiology in a first-person shooter game. *Interacting with Computers 22*, 5 (2010), 336–343 *.

61. Nakamura, J., and Csikszentmihalyi, M. The concept of flow. *Handbook of positive psychology* (2002), 89–105.

62. Obaid, M., Han, C., and Billinghurst, M. Feed the fish: an affect-aware game. In *Proc. IE '08*, ACM (2008), 6 *.

63. Obrist, M., Igelsböck, J., Beck, E., Moser, C., Riegler, S., and Tscheligi, M. Now you need to laugh!: investigating fun in games with children. In *Proc. ACE '09*, ACM (2009), 81–88 *.

64. Park, N., Min Lee, K., Jin, S.-A. A., and Kang, S. Effects of pre-game stories on feelings of presence and evaluation of computer games. *Intl. journal of human-computer studies 68*, 11 (2010), 822–833 *.

65. Piselli, P., Claypool, M., and Doyle, J. Relating cognitive models of computer games to user evaluations of entertainment. In *Proc. FDG '09*, ACM (2009), 153–160 *.

66. Poels, K., Hoogen, W. v. d., Ijsselsteijn, W., and de Kort, Y. Pleasure to play, arousal to stay: The effect of player

emotions on digital game preferences and playing time. *CyberPsychology, Behavior, and Social Networking 15*, 1 (2012), 1–6 *.

67. Przybylski, A. K., Ryan, R. M., and Rigby, C. S. The motivating role of violence in video games. *Personality and Social Psychology Bulletin 35*, 2 (2009), 243–259 *.
68. Quick, J. M., Atkinson, R. K., and Lin, L. Empirical taxonomies of gameplay enjoyment: Personality and video game preference. *Intl. Journal of Game-Based Learning 2*, 3 (2012), 11–31 *.
69. Reinecke, L., Klatt, J., and Krämer, N. C. Entertaining media use and the satisfaction of recovery needs: Recovery outcomes associated with the use of interactive and noninteractive entertaining media. *Media Psychology 14*, 2 (2011), 192–215 *.
70. Reinecke, L., Tamborini, R., Grizzard, M., Lewis, R., Eden, A., and Bowman, N. D. Characterizing mood management as need satisfaction: The effects of intrinsic needs on selective exposure and mood repair. *Journal of Communication* (2012), 437–453 *.
71. Schild, J., LaViola, J., and Masuch, M. Understanding user experience in stereoscopic 3d games. In *Proc. CHI '12*, ACM (2012), 89–98 *.
72. Schmierbach, M., Limperos, A. M., and Woolley, J. K. Feeling the need for (personalized) speed: How natural controls and customization contribute to enjoyment of a racing game through enhanced immersion. *Cyberpsychology, Behavior, and Social Networking* (2012), 364–369 *.
73. Schmierbach, M., Xu, Q., Oeldorf-Hirsch, A., and Dardis, F. E. Electronic friend or virtual foe: Exploring the role of competitive and cooperative multiplayer video game modes in fostering enjoyment. *Media Psychology 15*, 3 (2012), 356–371 *.
74. Seif El-Nasr, M., Aghabeigi, B., Milam, D., Erfani, M., Lameman, B., Maygoli, H., and Mah, S. Understanding and evaluating cooperative games. In *Proc. CHI '10*, ACM (2010), 253–262 *.
75. Shafer, D. M. Causes of state hostility and enjoyment in player versus player and player versus environment video games. *Journal of Communication* (2012), 719–737 *.
76. Shim, K. J., Srivastava, J., and Hsu, K.-W. An exploratory study of player performance, motivation, and enjoyment in massively multiplayer online role-playing games. In *Proc. PASSAT SocialCom '11*, IEEE (2011), 135–140 *.
77. Sweetser, P., and Wyeth, P. Gameflow: a model for evaluating player enjoyment in games. *Computers in Entertainment (CIE) 3*, 3 (2005), 3–3.
78. Takatalo, J., Häkkinen, J., Kaistinen, J., and Nyman, G. Presence, involvement, and flow in digital games. In *Evaluating user experience in games*. Springer, 2010, 23–46.
79. Tamborini, R., Bowman, N. D., Eden, A., Grizzard, M., and Organ, A. Defining media enjoyment as the satisfaction of intrinsic needs. *Journal of Communication 60*, 4 (2010), 758–777 *.
80. Tamborini, R., Grizzard, M., Bowman, N. D., Reinecke, L., Lewis, R. J., and Eden, A. Media enjoyment as need satisfaction: The contribution of hedonic and nonhedonic needs. *Journal of Communication 61*, 6 (2011), 1025–1042 *.
81. Trepte, S., and Reinecke, L. The pleasures of success: game-related efficacy experiences as a mediator between player performance and game enjoyment. *Cyberpsychology, Behavior, and Social Networking 14*, 9 (2011), 555–557 *.
82. van den Hoogen, W., Poels, K., IJsselsteijn, W., and de Kort, Y. Between challenge and defeat: Repeated player-death and game enjoyment. *Media Psychology 15*, 4 (2012), 443–459 *.
83. Vorderer, P., Klimmt, C., and Ritterfeld, U. Enjoyment: At the heart of media entertainment. *Communication theory 14*, 4 (2004), 388–408.
84. Weaver, A. J., and Lewis, N. Mirrored morality: An exploration of moral choice in video games. *Cyberpsychology, Behavior, and Social Networking 15*, 11 (2012), 610–614 *.
85. Weber, R., Tamborini, R., Westcott-Baker, A., and Kantor, B. Theorizing flow and media enjoyment as cognitive synchronization of attentional and reward networks. *Communication Theory 19*, 4 (2009), 397–422 *.
86. Weibel, D., and Wissmath, B. Immersion in computer games: The role of spatial presence and flow. *Intl. Journal of Computer Games Technology* (2011), 6 *.
87. Weibel, D., Wissmath, B., Habegger, S., Steiner, Y., and Groner, R. Playing online games against computer-vs. human-controlled opponents: Effects on presence, flow, and enjoyment. *Computers in Human Behavior 24*, 5 (2008), 2274–2291 *.
88. Weibel, D., Wissmath, B., and Mast, F. W. Influence of mental imagery on spatial presence and enjoyment assessed in different types of media. *Cyberpsychology, Behavior, and Social Networking 14*, 10 (2011), 607–612 *.
89. Wyeth, P., Johnson, D. M., and Sweetser, P. Conceptualising, operationalising and measuring the player experience in videogames. In *Extended Proc. FnG '12*, IRIT Press (2012), 90–93.
90. Yun, C., Shastri, D., Pavlidis, I., and Deng, Z. O'game, can you feel my frustration?: improving user's gaming experience via stresscam. In *Proc. CHI '09*, ACM (2009), 2195–2204 *.

* Denotes a reference among the reviewed studies.

# The Effectiveness (or Lack Thereof) of Aim-Assist Techniques in First-Person Shooter Games

**Rodrigo Vicencio-Moriera[1], Regan L. Mandryk[1], Carl Gutwin[1], Scott Bateman[2]**

[1]University of Saskatchewan
Saskatoon, SK, S7N 5C9
firstname.lastname@usask.ca

[2]University of Prince Edward Island
Charlottetown, PEI, C1A 4P3
sbateman@upei.ca

## ABSTRACT

Aim-assistance techniques have been shown to work for player balancing in 2D environments, but little information exists about how well these techniques will work in a 3D FPS game. We carried out three studies of the performance of five different aim assists in an Unreal-based game world. The assists worked well in a target-range scenario (study 1), but their performance was reduced when game elements were introduced in a walkthrough map (study 2). We systematically examined the relationships between realistic game elements and assist performance (study 3). These studies show that two techniques – bullet magnetism and area cursor – worked well in a wide variety of situations. Other techniques that worked well were too perceptible, and some previously-successful techniques did not work well in any game-like scenario. Our studies are the first to provide empirical evidence of the performance of aim assist techniques in 3D environments, and the first to identify the complexities in using these techniques in real FPS games.

## AUTHOR KEYWORDS

Aim assistance; first-person shooter games; game balancing

## ACM Classification Keywords

H.5.m. Information interfaces and presentation (e.g., HCI).

## INTRODUCTION

3D First Person Shooter (FPS) games are one of the most popular genres in computer gaming [10]. FPS games are complex and fast paced – this is especially true in multiplayer matches, where players need considerable skill to effectively navigate through a 3D environment, target opposing players, and avoid obstacles. FPS games take time to learn, resulting in a wide range of skill levels; experts are often vastly better at controlling the game than novices.

In many FPS scenarios, expertise is an important part of the experience: for example, some games have tournaments and rankings (e.g., Battlefield 3, Counter Strike, Call of Duty[1]). However, expertise differences also reduce the possibility of playing with others who have a different skill level; if skills differ greatly, the game is not fun for anyone [11].

Aiming is a critical component of FPS games, and aiming speed and accuracy is often a main differentiator between experts and novices. To improve novice targeting ability, *aim assistance* could be used. Aim assistance improves the accuracy and speed of target acquisition by manipulating factors such as the size of the target in motor space. Aim assistance techniques have been shown to improve targeting in 2D shooting games [4]. Aim assistance in these 2D situations led to closer matches between pairs and increased enjoyment, and the effects were not highly perceivable. Therefore, 3D versions of these aim-assistance techniques hold promise for assisting novices in FPS games.

Little information is available, however, about the use of these techniques in 3D FPS environments. Commercial games such as Halo appear to implement various forms of aim assist and previous work has shown that Fitts's law holds in 3D aiming tasks [19], so it is likely that applying aim assist techniques should help to improve performance in a 3D FPS. However, previous research has also shown that adding even simple game elements to a 2D aiming task can significantly change target acquisition time [14]. The complexity of a 3D FPS game environment (e.g., moving while aiming, moving targets, multiple targets, targets that shoot back, etc.) may interfere with the potential benefits of aim assist techniques, ultimately reducing their efficacy.

To investigate whether aim assist techniques are effective in 3D FPS games, we implemented five techniques (target lock, bullet magnetism, area cursor, sticky targets, and gravity) in a custom game environment and carried out three performance studies. In the first study (S1), we set up a simple 3D shooting range that was similar to the 2D games used in past evaluations of aim assistance. In the second study (S2), we created a realistic game level where players moved through a map with a number of computer-controlled players (bots). To begin teasing out the effects of realistic game elements, we carried out a third study that systematically varied two specific factors from S2: the effect of distractor targets, by removing friendlies from the map (S3A), and the effect of having more precise weapons, by switching to a semi-automatic sniper rifle (S3B).


*CHI 2014*, April 26–May 1, 2014, Toronto, Ontario, Canada.
Copyright © 2014 ACM 978-1-4503-2473-1/14/04..$15.00.
http://dx.doi.org/10.1145/2556288.2557308

[1] battlefield3tournament.com, definitive-leagues.com, eswc.com

Our results showed that although all techniques worked well in S1, the presence of realistic game elements compromised the efficacy of most techniques – sticky targets and target gravity in particular. However, bullet magnetism and area cursor worked well in several settings, and were not highly perceptible. These two techniques are interesting in that they both change the targeting process *after* the user has completed their aiming motion and pressed the trigger; in contrast, the two worst techniques (gravity and sticky targets) both adjust the user's crosshairs during the aiming action. We speculate that there is value in letting the user plan and execute their own aiming motions, and only adjusting the shot during the flight of the bullet.

Our work is the first to explore the complexities of aim assistance in 3D environments, and the first to provide an analysis of real-game factors that can affect assistance. We also identify two successful candidate techniques that show potential for use in player balancing for FPS games.

## RELATED WORK: GAME BALANCING

*Flow* describes a state where people are engaged and interested in their tasks without being overly anxious [8]. In order to provide players with a state of flow, game designers try to balance the level of challenge [11]. Striking the right balance is important, because a player's desire or willingness to play depends on whether the game is enjoyable [22, 24]. Unbalanced game elements may cause players to become frustrated or unengaged because they find the game too difficult or too easy [22]. For this reason, the game industry makes use of simulations and extensive play testing to discover unbalanced game elements [6].

To maintain flow in multi-player games, players' abilities to compete must be balanced. This means that players of equal skill should have an equal opportunity to win [1]. However, it can be difficult to balance the performance of different players [1] because people's abilities are based on many factors including their experience, reaction times, and skill [23]. Many games rewards skill, and newer or less-skilled players can have difficulty playing with more experienced players. Despite the difficulties in balancing competition in games, it has an important impact on player experience; a recent study demonstrated that balancing play of differently skilled players increases enjoyment for all [4].

Through our literature review and examination of games, we have identified four primary balancing approaches:

*1. Difficulty Adjustment*: Difficulty adjustment is one of the most common ways to allow users to adjust the level of challenge in a game. Many games allow players to explicitly select a difficulty setting, whereas others use dynamic difficulty adjustments, which change game elements based on in-game performance [17]; e.g., Left 4 Dead increases challenges if players do well. Dynamic adjustments in competition can lead to frustration if experienced players feel cheated [22], and can result in players feeling their achievements are meaningless [6].

*2. Matchmaking:* Many multiplayer online games use elaborate ranking systems that aim to group players with others of a similar skill level to ensure that the level of competition is balanced [22]. These work in a manner similar to ladders for sports like squash or tennis at sports clubs, and are important parts of Halo [16] and StarCraft 2.

*3. Asymmetric Roles:* In many games, players can take on different roles that suit their abilities or level of skill. For example, in Team Fortress 2, successful teams are composed of several different roles (e.g., spy, sniper, medic). This is analogous to real world sports teams, where players have very different roles (e.g., offense or defense).

*4. Aim Assistance:* Aim assistance facilitates the basic skills used in games that involve shooting, by making it easier to select on-screen targets. A recent study showed that aim assistance was an effective mechanism for balancing a simple 2D shooting-gallery game [4]. Players with less skill were able to improve and better compete with more skilled partners, and players reported having more fun when the competition was tighter. Further, participants did not notice that aim assistance was being given. However, there is little information about whether or not aim-assistance techniques would be effective in FPS games, which take place in a 3D environment and involve navigating an avatar through the space. Below we provide an overview on work in aim assistance and its use in video games.

## RELATED WORK: AIM ASSISTANCE

Many aim assistance techniques have been devised to allow people to select on-screen targets quickly and accurately. Aim-assistance techniques are based on an understanding of aimed movements as modeled by Fitts's Law [13]. Fitts's Law states that the time to aim to a target is determined by the distance to reach the target (*amplitude*) and the size of the target (*width*). The smaller the amplitude and the larger the width, the easier and faster it is to point to a target. Aim-assistance techniques work in digital environments to facilitate pointing tasks using a device like a mouse or game pad by artificially manipulating amplitude and width [3]. Three general approaches for doing this are to reduce the distance to the object (amplitude manipulation), increase the width of the object in visual or motor space (width manipulation), or both [3]. There have been many aim-assistance techniques proposed (e.g., [4,5,7,9,12,15,18,20]). We refer the reader to a recent review (see [3]) for an overview, and we present individual techniques in the context of those implemented for the studies.

While work in aim assistance has been focused on its use in traditional 2D GUI pointing, a recent study has shown that Fitts's law also holds in a 3D FPS environment [19]. This suggests that aiming assistance techniques that have been developed in 2D should also work in 3D environments.

## RELATED WORK: AIM ASSISTANCE IN GAMES

There are many genres where shooting (aim and select a target) is a core game element. Many are console games and use gamepads as input. Gamepads, where thumbsticks are used for aim, are not as precise as mice [21], so several aim-assistance techniques have emerged in FPS games that work similarly to techniques used in 2D GUI pointing. Our review identified three common approaches for aim assistance in games: bullet magnetism, target lock, and gravity. We discuss each of these in the next section.

## TECHNIQUES CHOSEN FOR COMPARATIVE STUDIES

We chose to include five aim assist techniques in our work.

### Target Lock

The Target Lock method (Lock) moves the crosshairs of the player to the closest target's head; Lock was activated when players pressed a button on the mouse (determined through pilot studies) The player's pitch and yaw were manipulated to make them face the closest opponent when the lock was activated. To vary the level of assistance, we varied the time to move the crosshairs to a target's head. At the lowest levels it was possible for an opponent to outrun being locked on to. At the highest level the crosshairs would be on the target virtually instantly. It took approximately 0.5s to lock on to a stationary target 90 degrees away at level 1 (roughly 7 degrees per tick) and 0.15s at level 10 (roughly 12 degrees per tick). In terms of Fitts's law, Lock reduces targeting time by reducing the distance between the pointer and the location of the target.

Target lock is not commonly used in FPS games but is popular in other genres. Games like Grand Theft Auto, Red Dead Redemption, and the 3D games in the Legend of Zelda series have used locking. This method is also based on the "object pointing" interaction technique, which tries to reduce empty space between targets by moving between selectable targets [15]. Lock may seem ideal for reducing targeting time but has drawbacks that may make it not viable in an FPS: distractor targets may compromise the performance of Lock; Lock requires explicit activation by the player; and Lock is obvious so players in competitive situations players may not enjoy it [2].

### Bullet Magnetism

Bullet Magnetism (Bullet) "bends" bullets towards the closest target if a target is within the activation range (see Figure 1). The bullets in the game are instant shots, thus each bullet fired is described by a vector. When an enemy is within range (defined by 160 UDK units * Level, where $1 \leq \text{Level} \leq 10$), then Bullet adjusts this vector towards the closest opponent when the player fires and before the bullet collision logic. The higher the level of assistance, the farther away the effect begins and the more it corrects.

Bullet is not based on existing aim-assistance research but is present in games like Halo and Gears of War 3. It is exclusive to shooting games because of the presence of bullets. Bullet Magnetism adjusts the flight path of bullets once they leave the gun, and was implemented to mimic the way that bullet magnetism works in Halo. The closer the player is to a target when shooting, the more the bullet is attracted to the target. The end effect is similar to the area cursor method (described next) because it allows players to hit targets without perfect aiming, essentially increasing the target's width. We applied magnetism towards the body of the enemy if the crosshair was off the target and to the head of the enemy if the crosshair was already over a target. Assistance level was varied by the amount of magnetism applied. Bullet does not move the crosshair or change the CD ratio so may be less intrusive than other methods. However, Bullet may have issues if distractor target are present as it may be attracted to the wrong opponent.

### Area Cursor

Area cursor (Area) follows the original implementation [18], but is adjusted to work in a 3D environment. Normally when a shot is made in the game a zero extent trace is used to determine if a target has been hit. When the area cursor method is active, a rectangle (non-zero extent) is projected into space and used to test intersection. On screen, the regular crosshair radius is 10px. With assistance, the physical size of the crosshair changes as the activation area changes, as seen in Figure 1. The size is calculated as 10px+(5px*Level), where $1 \leq \text{Level} \leq 10$.In terms of Fitts's law, area cursors essentially increase the width of the target [18], as such bigger cursors lower the index of difficulty. Assistance level is varied by varying activation area sizes.

Area cursor was chosen because it had the best performance results when compared with sticky targets or the gravity method in a 2D environment [4]. Additionally, Area has improved targeting for older adults [26] and users with motor impairments [12]. One advantage of Area is that it should still be effective with moving targets; however, sloppy targeting behavior may appear with players who get accustomed to the extra activation area [7], and distractor targets will affect Area. Our implementation handles multiple targets inside the activation area by choosing the target closest to the center of the crosshairs to be hit. Finally, we chose that our implementation would not directly help players get headshots; to score a headshot the center of the crosshair must be over the target's head.

### Sticky Targets

The sticky targets method (Sticky) works by changing the control-to-display (CD) ratio when the crosshairs are over a target. The lower CD ratio results in a pseudohaptic effect of stickiness when over a target [7]. In our case, the amount of movement is divided by (Level + 4), where $1 \leq \text{Level} \leq 10$. In terms of Fitts's law, this method increases the width of the target in motor space [5] by affecting the second phase of pointing where corrective actions are taken. Once the player gets to the target and the stickiness kicks in they can position the cursor on the opponent more precisely due to the bigger size in motor space.

Sticky is used in games like Halo, Modern Warfare 2, and Red Dead Redemption (called reticule magnetism), and is generally applied on console games. We include Sticky because previous studies have shown that low levels of

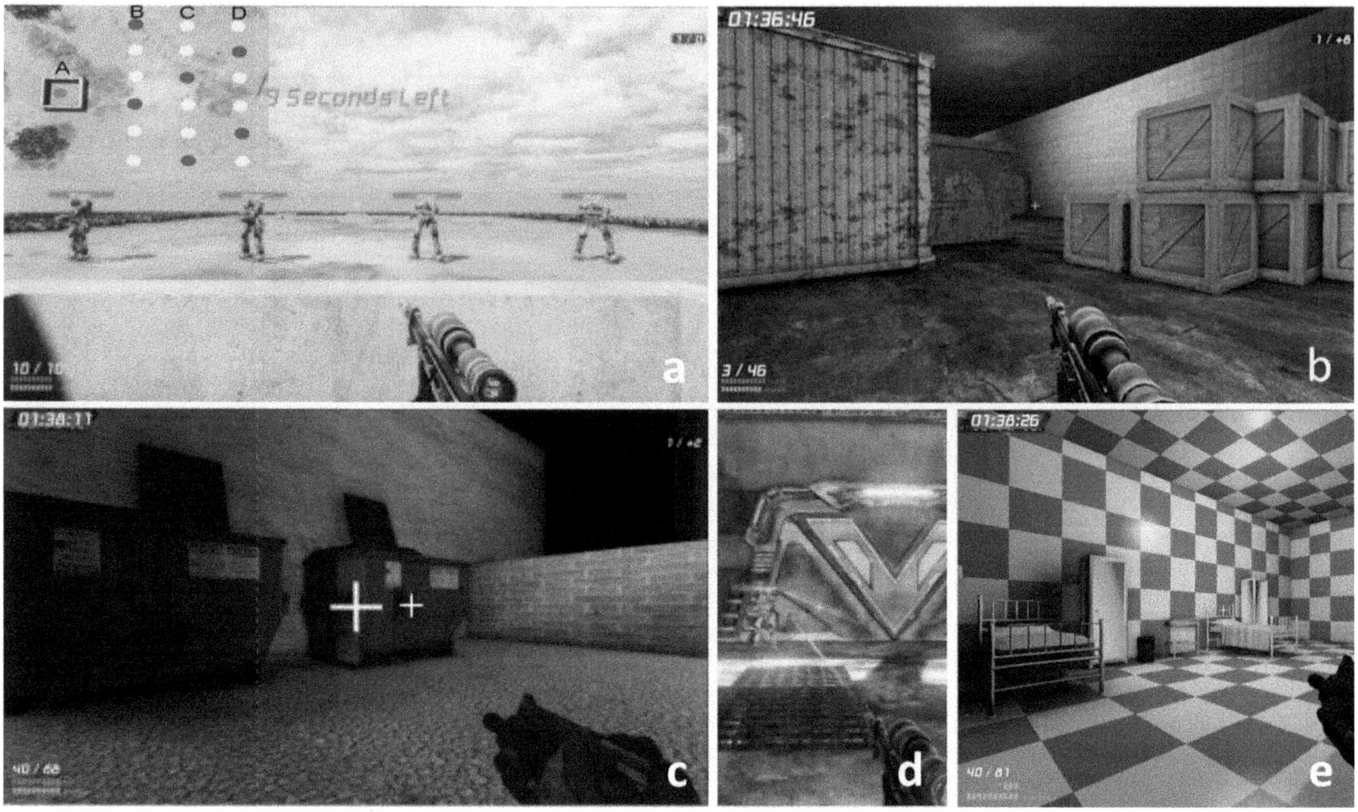


**Figure 1. Images from the FPS environment. a) the player view of the shooting gallery; player and enemy locations are inset top-left; b) the realistic walkthrough; c) reticule showing low and high levels of Area Cursor; d) Bullet warping the hit location away from the crosshairs and toward enemy target; e)hospital room in the walkthrough.**

stickiness are difficult to perceive [20]. Informal studies have also suggested that subjects are more accurate in a 3D FPS environment with CD adaptation than without [9]. However, distractors could be an issue with Sticky, compensation may lead to overshooting [20], and studies have suggested that this method might not be useful for moving targets [4]. Games like Call of Duty tend to move the cursor along with a target to mitigate the moving target problem; however, we did not implement this feature to better mirror the 2D version used in prior research.

### Target Gravity

The target gravity method (Gravity) gives each target an attractive force that results in a player's crosshairs being dragged towards targets. In terms of Fitts's Law, Gravity reduces the distance to the target. There are several different ways of implementing target gravity; however, we transferred the 2D algorithms [4] directly into the 3D environment. The gravity is calculated by first identifying all targets within the player's line of sight. For these $n$ targets, let $p_1, p_2,..p_n$ be the position of the targets, $p_0$ be the position of the player in the 3D space, and $p_w$ be the warped position. G is the gravitational constant. For each target, the target weight is calculated with Equation 1. Then the warped position in 3D space is calculated with Equation 2.

$$w_i = \frac{G}{|p_0 - p_i|^2 + 1} \quad (1) \qquad p_w = \frac{\sum_{i=1}^{n} w_i p_i}{\sum_{i=1}^{n} w_i} \quad (2)$$

Equation 2 gives a position in the 3D environment that is the weighted average of all attractive forces. Because our 3D crosshairs do not have an actual position in the world (as opposed to the 2D implementation), we have to anchor the gravity effect. We calculate the current direction of the player and the direction of the warped position. The crosshair is then moved. A lower level of assistance moves the crosshairs more slowly than a higher level.

Gravity was included because of its strong performance in previous studies of 2D games [4]. Commercial games that use gravity, (e.g., console Call of Duty) try to only apply gravity effects on the closest target. In our implementation, we only activate gravity if the mouse is moved toward the warped position. If the mouse is not moved, or is moved away from the warped position, no effect is applied on the crosshairs. In addition, we implemented gravity to be attracted to the head of enemy targets to assist players with headshots. Gravity is subject to distractors, potentially moving the crosshairs when a player is aiming at another target.

## STUDY DESCRIPTIONS

To test aim assist in FPS games, we conducted three studies.

### Common Apparatus across Studies

We developed an FPS game using the Unreal Development Kit (UDK) to test the performance of the aim-assistance methods. The game was developed in UnrealScript, using

Visual Studio 2010 with the Nfringe add-on by PixelMine. The system ran on a Windows 7, Intel Core 2 Quad machine and an Acer 24-inch, 1920x1080 LCD monitor with a 60 Hertz refresh rate. Each participant set a comfortable sensitivity level for the Logitech G5 gaming mouse during the training round, and could not change it once the training rounds were complete. Logging of in-game actions was done on a Microsoft Sql Server 2008 R2 database. A C# console was written to receive logging messages from game clients and write them to the database.

Targets were shot by placing the center of the crosshairs on the target and left-clicking the mouse. The targets in S1 were stationary. In S2, the enemies moved in a random pattern when the player was in the enemy's line of sight. A random spot was chosen (within 300 UDK units from the current position) and the enemy began to move to that location while shooting at the player. Once the spot was reached, a new random location was chosen; this was repeated until the enemy was dispatched. The movement was limited so the enemies could not wander out of their rooms or move to the location of another enemy.

In both studies the player movement was controlled with a standard WASD scheme. Aim assistance levels were determined through pilot tests, and were custom-made. The walkthrough level was split into a hospital-themed area and a warehouse area. Both areas were linear so that the player could not explore, affecting the time measure. In the hospital area, enemies were placed in rooms along with friendlies. The warehouse area was darker and the enemies and friendlies were encountered as the player moved up. The locations of the enemies can be seen on the map in (Figure 2). The shooting gallery level was a simple outdoor environment. The player was confined to a square and the targets appeared in front of the player in several waves.

Participants were told that they would be testing several implementations of aiming assistance and that some rounds would have assistance, whereas some would not. Participants were unique to each study, which were all approved by the research ethics board.

### Study 1 – Shooting Gallery

Study 1 (S1) extended previous work on modeling Fitts's Law in 3D FPS environments [19] and quantifying targeting assistance in 2D shooting games [4] with a shooting gallery-style task and 5 types of aim assist. User movements and enemy actions were constrained and the task focused on control rather than realism. The purpose of the study was to determine if the aiming assistance techniques that proved effective in 2D [4] transfer to 3D.

#### Task

Study 1 (S1) was a shooting-range-style level that was modeled after the level in the FPS Fitts's Law study by Looser et al. [19]. Participants used the sniper rifle (scope disabled), which took two body shots or one head shot to "kill" a target. The study consisted of one training round (no assistance), followed by the six technique rounds. In each round, there were seven waves of enemies. Each wave consisted of six targets; players tried to shoot as many as possible in 10 seconds. Waves 1 and 4 were close to the player; 2 and 5 were at a middle distance; 3 and 6 were farthest. In wave 7, enemies were placed in varying locations at the three distances, as shown in Figure 1.

In each of the six rounds, one type of aim assist was used: Bullet Magnetism, Area Cursor, Sticky Targets, Gravity, and Lock, all with the high level of assistance, and no assist (Control); a Latin Square balanced the presentation order.

#### Participants and Procedure

We recruited 12 players (11 male) to participate in S1. Three participants identified themselves as novices at FPS games, 5 as intermediate players, and 4 as experts. The experiment took 20 minutes to complete. After providing informed consent, participants completed the experimental task. Participants were compensated with $5.

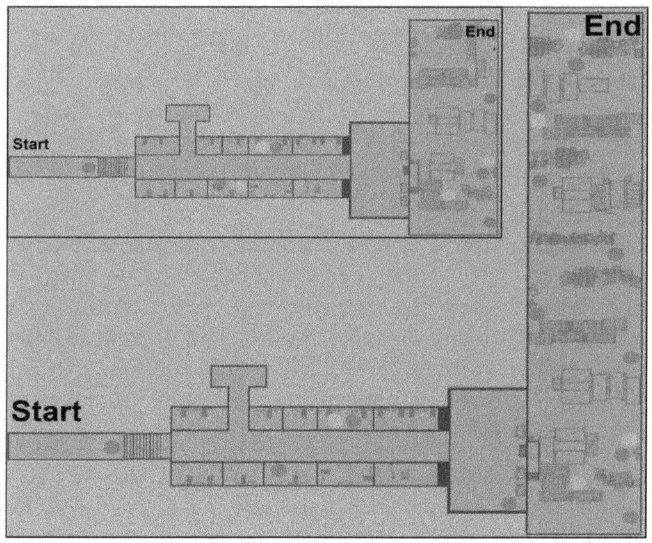


**Figure 2. Walkthrough Maps: Grey Background–Full (S2); Inset Blue Background–Modified (S3). Red dots represent enemies; green dots represent friendly targets.**

### Study 2 – Full Walkthrough

Study 2 (S2) investigated the same 5 aim assist techniques in a realistic walkthrough task, complete with enemy targets who fired at the player and friendly targets that were to be avoided. Common features in FPS games (e.g., rifle scope) were implemented as we focused on game realism over control. The purpose of the study was to determine if the techniques that worked in the simple 3D environment would hold in a more complex "game-like" environment.

#### Task

S2 was a full game-like walkthrough level set in an abandoned warehouse (see Figure 2). The level contained 12 enemy bots and 8 friendly turtles that acted as distractor targets. Participants were equipped with an assault rifle and a pistol. The assault rifle had a higher rate of fire than the sniper rifle and did less damage with each hit. It took roughly 10 body shots or 5 head shots to kill a target with the assault rifle. The pistol had a slower rate of fire than the assault rifle, but did more damage per bullet (roughly five body shots or three head shots to kill a target). The level was complete with visual effects (e.g., lighting effects, glass shattering) to look and feel like a realistic FPS game.

Participants played the custom level 14 times. The first two rounds were used as training to familiarize players with the controls and locations of enemies and friendlies. The remaining 12 rounds consisted of one round with each of the six aim methods at low (Level 2) and high (Level 8) assistance and an additional two control rounds. At the end of each round, players completed a survey. Participants were instructed to avoid shooting the friendly turtles.

#### Participants and Procedure

We recruited 16 players (10 male) to participate in S2. Eight participants identified themselves as FPS novices and eight as experts. The same procedure as for S1 was used, except that due to the longer experiment time (between 80 min and 2 hours), participants were compensated with $15.

### Study 3 – Full Walkthrough 2

Study 3 systematically varied two of the factors in Study 2 – presence of friendlies (S3A) and weapon type (S3B) – to quantify their relative effects on performance.

#### Task

Participants played two versions of the same map as S2 that was reduced in distance by half and contained six enemies (see Figure 2). The first version (S3A) used an assault rifle and had no friendly distractor targets. The second version (S3B) used a sniper rifle (scope disabled) and four friendly turtles. S3A and S3B omitted the Lock method and used only high (Level 8) assistance.

Participants went through the level 12 times. The first two rounds were training; the first was training for S3A and the second for S3B. The remaining ten rounds consisted of running through the control, bullet magnetism, area cursor, sticky targets, and gravity rounds in S3A and then repeating the process in S3B. The order of presentation of assistance types was balanced with a Latin Square. Half of the participants started with S3A and half started with S3B.

#### Participants and Procedure

We recruited 15 players (14 male) to participate in S3. Six participants identified themselves as FPS novices, five as intermediates, and four as experts. S3 used the same procedure as S2; participants were compensated with $10.

### Dependent Measures

The same dependent measures were collected for each of the three studies, except there are no survey data for S1. **Accuracy:** *Hit Ratio* presents the number of hits over the number of shots fired, representing targeting efficiency. *Headshot Ratio* presents the number of headshots over the total number of hits, representing targeting quality. Subjective *Accuracy Rating* was provided by participants on a 21-pt scale (-10=least accurate to 10=most accurate). **Speed:** *Time* measured the elapsed time to complete the task. Subjective *Speed Rating* was provided by players on a 21-pt scale (-10=slowest to 10=fastest). **Outcome:** *Deaths* is the number of times a player was killed by an enemy. In S1, there were no enemies, thus *Kills* (the number of enemies killed) is used to reflect outcome (in S2 and S3, the player had to kill all enemies, thus there was no variance in kills). Subjective *Performance Rating* was provided by players on a 21-pt scale (-10=worst to 10=best). **Perception:** The *Perceptibility* of the assist technique was rated by players on an 11-pt scale (0=lowest, 10=highest).

### Data Analyses

For each of the four data sets, we conducted RM-ANOVAs with Assist Technique as a within-subjects factor on all dependent measures. In S1 and S2 there were six levels of Aim Assist Technique (Control, Lock, Bullet Magnetism, Sticky Target, and Gravity); in S3A and S3B, there were five levels (no Lock). In S2, S3A, and S3A, we also included Expertise (novice or expert) as a between-subjects factor). Finally, S2 had an additional within-subject factor: level of Technique Strength (low or high).

Data violating the sphericity assumption had the degrees of freedom adjusted using the Huynh-Feldt method. Type 1 error was prevented by using the Bonferroni adjustment on all pairwise comparisons. $\alpha$ was set at 0.05 for all effects.

## RESULTS

For all studies, statistical test results are shown in Table 1 and means and variances are shown in Figure 3. To improve readability, we summarize only main results here.

### S1 – Shooting Gallery

**Accuracy.** All of the techniques improved the Hit Ratio over Control, except Gravity. Lock and Bullet also improved Headshot Ratio. **Outcome.** Lock, Bullet, and Area improved Kills over Control (and Gravity).

#### Summary of S1 Results

Gravity did not improve over Control on any measure. Sticky improved on Hit Ratio; Area improved on both Hit Ratio and Kills. Lock and Bullet improved on Hit Ratio, Headshot Ratio, and Kills. There were differences between the techniques as well, with Bullet and Lock beating the other techniques for Headshot Ratio and Kills.

### S2 – Full Walkthrough

In S2, there were main effects of Technique Strength (level); the higher level resulted in a higher Headshot Ratio ($F_{1,14}$=14.9, p=.002, $\eta^2$=.52) and greater Perception ($F_{1,14}$=6.8, p=.021, $\eta^2$=.33). Because level produced few systematic differences, we present results for the higher level of aim assist only in S2 to correspond to the high level that was used in S1 and S3 (also in Table 1 and Figure 3).

#### Differences in Aim Assist Techniques

**Accuracy.** Lock and Area had higher Hit Ratios than Gravity. Lock and Bullet had higher Headshot Ratios than others. **Outcome.** Bullet and Lock resulted in fewer Deaths than Control. **Perception.** Lock was most noticeable.

**Table 1. RM-ANOVA main effects for aim assist technique across all four data sets (columns) and measures (rows). Significant pairwise comparisons are shown (C=Control, B=Bullet Magnetism, A=Area Cursor, S=Sticky Targets, G=Gravity, L=Lock).**

| | Measure | S1 – Target Range | S2 – Realistic Level | S3A – No Friendlies | S3B – Sniper Rifle |
|---|---|---|---|---|---|
| Accuracy | Hit Ratio | $F_{5,55}=23.3, p\approx.000, \eta^2=.68$<br>$L, B, A, S > C^{\ddagger}, G^{\ddagger}$ | $F_{5,70}=7.7, p\approx.000, \eta^2=.35$<br>$L > C^{*}, G^{*}$<br>$A > G^{*}$ | $F_{4,52}=14.5, p\approx.000, \eta^2=.53$<br>$B > C^{\ddagger}, S^{\dagger}, G^{\dagger}$<br>$A > C^{\ddagger}, S^{*}$ | $F_{4,52}=9.4, p\approx.000, \eta^2=.42$<br>$A > C^{\ddagger}, G^{\ddagger}$ |
| | Headshot Ratio | $F_{5,55}=31.1, p\approx.000, \eta^2=.74$<br>$L, B > A^{\ddagger}, C^{\ddagger}, S^{\ddagger}, G^{\ddagger}$ | $F_{5,70}=53.5, p\approx.000, \eta^2=.79$<br>$L, B > A^{\ddagger}, C^{\ddagger}, S^{\ddagger}, G^{\ddagger}$<br>$G > A^{\dagger}$ | $F_{4,52}=60.0, p\approx.000, \eta^2=.82$<br>$B > A^{\ddagger}, C^{\ddagger}, S^{\ddagger}, G^{\ddagger}$<br>$G > A^{\dagger}, C^{*}$ | $F_{4,52}=64.6, p\approx.000, \eta^2=.83$<br>$B > A^{\ddagger}, C^{\ddagger}, S^{\ddagger}, G^{\ddagger}$<br>$G > S^{\dagger}$ |
| | Accuracy Rating | N/A | $F_{5,70}=7.8, p\approx.000, \eta^2=.36$<br>$L > C^{*}, S^{*}, G^{*}$<br>$B > G^{*}$ | $F_{4,52}=3.27, p=.019, \eta^2=.20$<br>No pairwise differences | $F_{4,52}=4.8, p=.002, \eta^2=.27$<br>$B > S^{\dagger}$ |
| Speed | Time | $F_{5,55}\approx0.0, p\approx1.00$<br>(Controlled) | $F_{5,70}=7.8, p\approx.000, \eta^2=.36$<br>$L < C^{*}, G^{*}$ | $F_{4,52}=9.48, p\approx.000, \eta^2=.42$<br>$B < C^{\dagger}, A^{\dagger}, S^{*}, G^{*}$ | $F_{4,52}=6.1, p\approx.000, \eta^2=.32$<br>$B < C^{*}$<br>$A < C^{*}, S^{*}, G^{*}$ |
| | Speed Rating | N/A | $F_{5,70}=3.7, p=.007, \eta^2=.21$<br>$L > S^{*}$ | $F_{4,52}=3.23, p=.019, \eta^2=.20$<br>$B > C^{*}$ | $F_{4,52}=7.7, p\approx.000, \eta^2=.37$<br>$B > A^{*}, S^{\dagger}, G^{\ddagger}$ |
| Performance | Deaths (Kills-S1) | $F_{5,55}=84.7, p\approx.000, \eta^2=.89$<br>$L, B > A^{\ddagger}, C^{\ddagger}, S^{\ddagger}, G^{\ddagger}$<br>$A > C^{*}, G^{\ddagger}; C > G^{*}$ | $F_{5,70}=7.9, p\approx.000, \eta^2=.36$<br>$B < C^{\dagger}, S^{\dagger}, G^{*}$<br>$L < C^{*}$ | $F_{4,52}=10.3, p\approx.000, \eta^2=.44$<br>$B < C^{\dagger}, A^{*}, S^{\ddagger}, G^{\dagger}$ | $F_{4,52}=8.7, p\approx.000, \eta^2=.40$<br>$B < S^{*}, G^{*}$<br>$A < S^{\ddagger}, G^{*}$ |
| | Performance Rating | N/A | $F_{5,70}=5.3, p=.003, \eta^2=.28$<br>$L > C^{\dagger}, S^{\dagger}$ | $F_{4,52}=4.6, p=.003, \eta^2=.26$<br>$B > C^{*}, S^{\dagger}$ | $F_{4,52}=4.9, p=.002, \eta^2=.27$<br>No pairwise differences |
| Perception | Perception Rating | | $F_{5,70}=8.1, p\approx.000, \eta^2=.37$<br>$L > B^{*}, A^{\dagger}, C^{\ddagger}, S^{\ddagger}$ | $F_{4,52}=4.8, p=.002, \eta^2=.27$<br>$A^{\dagger}, S^{*} > C$ | $F_{4,52}=2.7, p=.041, \eta^2=.17$<br>$B > C^{*}$ |

$^{*}p<.05$, $^{\dagger}p<.01$, $^{\ddagger}p<.001$

There were Expertise effects: novices took more Time ($F_{1,14}$=28.2, p≈.000, $\eta^2$=.67), had more Deaths ($F_{1,14}$=10.3, p=.006, $\eta^2$=.42), and a lower Hit ($F_{1,14}$=6.3, p=.025, $\eta^2$=.31) and Headshot Ratio ($F_{1,14}$=31.1, p≈.000, $\eta^2$=.69); however, there were no differences in technique based on expertise.

### *Summary of S2 Results*

In general, players noticed the Lock method, and perceived that it aided their speed, accuracy, and overall performance. In terms of objective differences only Lock showed systematic improvements over Control in improved Time, Hit Ratio, and Headshot Accuracy, and fewer Deaths. Bullet magnetism also improved Headshot Ratio and Deaths over control, but there were no other improvements offered by the aim assist techniques over Control and differences between the assist techniques were minimal.

### S3A – Assault Rifle, No Friendlies

**Accuracy.** Bullet and Area had higher Hit Ratios than Control or Sticky (Bullet higher than Gravity). Bullet and Gravity improved Headshot Ratio over Control and Area (Bullet higher than Sticky, Gravity). **Speed.** Bullet reduced Time over others. **Outcome.** Bullet reduced Deaths over others. **Perception.** Area and Sticky most perceptible.

There were no main effects of Expertise for any of the measures and no systematic differences between the aim assist techniques depending on expertise.

### *Summary of S3A Results*

When friendlies were removed Bullet is the clear winner in terms of improved Hit Ratio, Headshot Ratio, Time, and Deaths. Interestingly, players did not notice Bullet, making it both effective and subtle. Other techniques also improved aspects: Area improved Hit Ratio but was perceived; Gravity improved Headshots and wasn't perceived; Sticky had no effect on performance, but was perceived.

### S3B – Sniper Rifle

**Accuracy.** Area increased Hit Ratio over Control and Gravity. Bullet increased Headshot Ratio over all others. **Speed.** Area reduced Time over Control, Sticky, and Gravity. Bullet reduced Time over Control. **Outcome.** Bullet and Area reduced Deaths over Sticky and Gravity. **Perception.** Area and Sticky were more perceptible.

There were no main effects of Expertise for any of the measures; however, an interaction of Expertise and Aim Assist on Time ($F_{4,52}$=3.0, p=.027, $\eta^2$=.19) shows that experts took significantly less time than novices in the Bullet (p=.019) and Area (p=.001) conditions.

### *Summary of S3B Results*

When the sniper rifle was used the techniques improved aiming differently. Area improved the Hit Ratio, whereas Bullet improved the headshot ratio. Both Bullet and Area reduced Deaths and the Time taken over the other approaches. In terms of noticeability, Area was perceived, whereas Bullet was not. Gravity had an elevated Headshot Ratio but no other differences, and Sticky resulted in no improvements, but was perceived.

### Comparison of Techniques across Studies

The techniques differentially improved performance over Control under the various experimental conditions. **Gravity** underperformed across the board, and was the only approach that did not improve hit ratio in S1. **Sticky** helped with Hit Ratio in S2 but did not improve performance on any measure in the walkthrough tasks. Sticky only helps with targeting when the avatar and the enemies are both

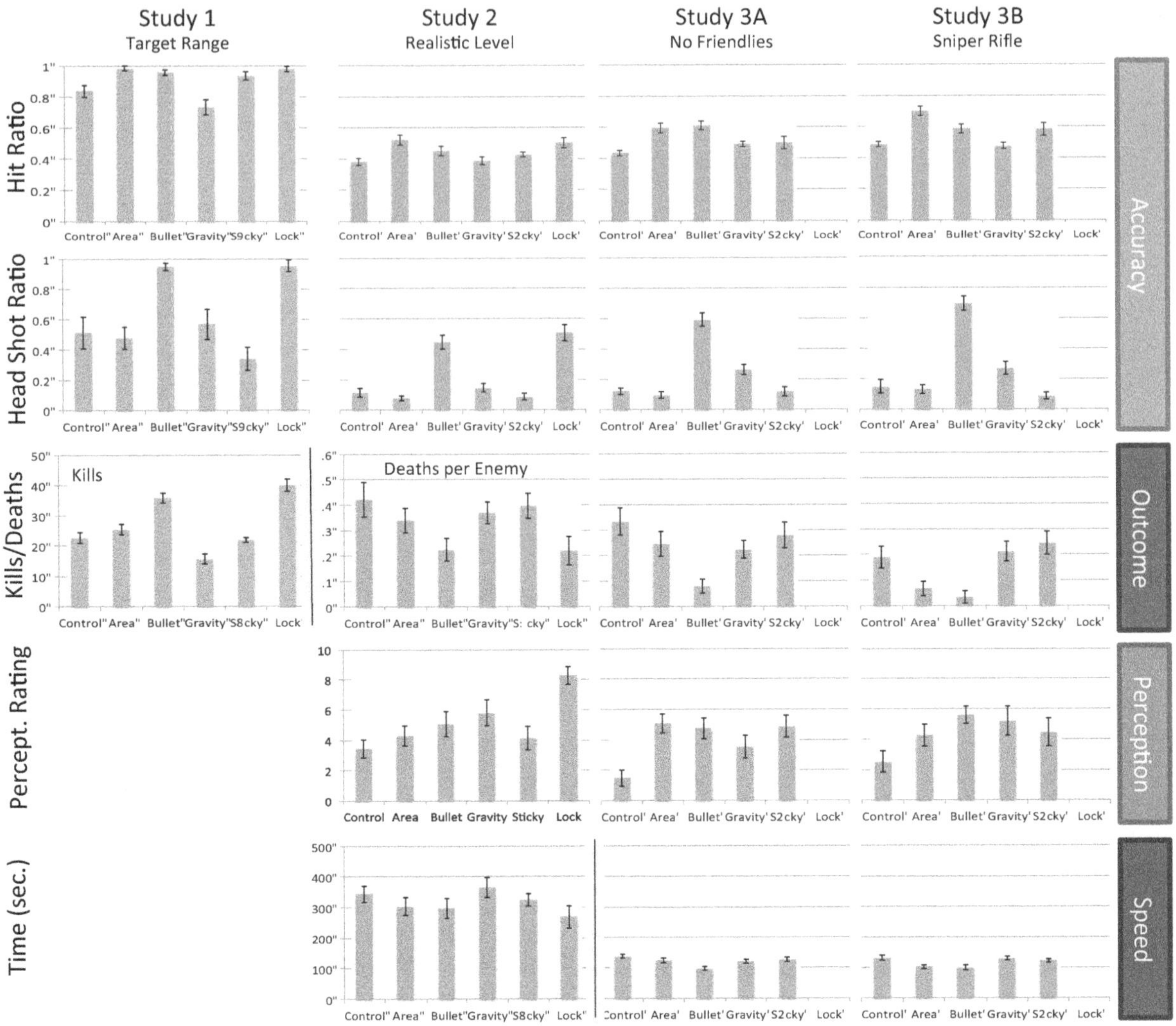


Figure 3. Means (±SE) from Studies 1 - 3. Vertical separators are used where comparison between studies is not possible. Line charts are used for a categorical x-axis to clearly show trends.

standing still. **Area cursor** improved Hit Ratio in S1, S3A, and S3B, but not S2. Area also improved kills/deaths in S1 and S3B, but did not work as well when the assault rifle was primarily in play (S2, S3A). **Bullet magnetism** worked well on all measures in S1, S3A, and S3B, but only worked for Headshot Ratio and Deaths in S2. **Lock** was only used in S2, and improved over Control on all objective measures.

## DISCUSSION

The main findings from our studies are:

- Realistic game elements such as moving and aggressive targets, distractor friendlies, multiple-shot weapons, and lighting effects dramatically altered which aim assist techniques worked well in the 3D FPS;
- In our least-constrained game environment (S2), only target lock consistently outperformed the control condition (but was highly perceptible); bullet magnetism worked well for deaths and headshots;
- In the single-issue manipulations of study 3, bullet magnetism and area cursor performed well; gravity and sticky targets performed poorly;

### Why did bullet magnetism and area cursor work well?

The bullet magnetism technique attracts a fired bullet, by a certain amount, to a point on the nearest target's head (if shooting at them) or body (if not shooting at them). Using the head as an attraction point is a clear explanation for this technique's success on the headshot measure; even when targeting the body, bullet magnetism could still bend the bullet's trajectory upwards to the enemy's head. Bullet magnetism also worked well both with a higher-precision weapon and with fewer distractor targets. These results are likely due to the technique's limited manipulation of trajectory: if the player can get the targeting reticule close to the intended enemy then the assist will improve targeting performance without causing errors.

Area cursor also performed well for several measures; this technique essentially shoots a larger bullet, increasing the target size. This effect worked particularly well with the higher-precision rifle – because there is no alteration to the aiming action, higher precision appeared to allow players to make faster use of the larger targets. Area cursor did not do well on the headshots measure, likely because of our implementation – unlike Bullet, if a user targeted the body with Area, the shot would hit the body, even if the area cursor's rectangle intersected the enemy's head.

It is interesting that both bullet magnetism and area cursor alter the targeting process only *after* the player has carried out their aiming action. These techniques do not change the user's control over moving their view, and do not attempt to 'decide' which target the user is aiming for. It is possible that magnetism and area cursor worked well because they caused less conflict with the user's control actions.

### Why did gravity and sticky targets perform poorly?

Gravity and Sticky performed badly on almost all measures in all studies. Observations and player comments suggest that these techniques had problems because they change the movement of the reticule *while* a player is aiming, and this may cause conflicts with the user's intentions.

The gravity technique could drag the player's crosshairs to the wrong target (e.g., a friendly, or a different enemy than the user intended), and this would result in the user fighting against the assist. The gravity algorithm is attracted to the nearest target, but this may sometimes be at odds with where a user is trying to aim. This behavior may be specific to FPS games where a player plans to hit targets in a certain order – in contrast, in the 2D shooting gallery game where gravity worked well, targets were equally desirable and it mattered little if the technique hit the wrong target; the user could simply target the desired target on the next shot.

Sticky targets encountered similar problems – player ability to control an aiming movement was hampered by the assist because it manipulates the 'user movement phase' of targeting rather than the 'bullet travel' phase.

### How can the effectiveness of techniques be judged?

In previous work in aim assistance for 2D pointing, and in applying aim assistance in a 2D game [4], hit ratio (i.e., a reduced error rate) was a primary metric for assessing success. This was the approach we initially used in judging our techniques in S1. However, with S2, it became clear that Bullet and Lock were the most effective techniques – participants died fewer times while completing the level, even though the hit ratio of Bullet was worse than other techniques that performed poorly in terms of outcome. Furthermore, Bullet was effective at increasing the number of headshots; because headshots are so important in Unreal, scoring a few headshots has more impact than scoring many body shots. When considering assistance techniques, designers should not focus only on hit ratio, but also be aware of key game mechanics, such as the importance of where hits register. While we expected that hit ratio would be the most important metric, it turned out to be only part of the larger picture when evaluating a complex game.

### Practical Significance and Limitations

Our study looks at only how players respond when first using aim assistance (i.e., the early effects) and does not address what might happen after long-term repeated use (i.e., the long term effects). However, we feel that these early effects are more important to understand because the goal is for the techniques to be applied in a multiplayer environment to help weaker players compete. Balancing play actually *requires* early effects – the techniques have to work well for people who have not used them before. In addition, the weaker player will in all likelihood have less experience, and thus is it critical that the techniques work in unfamiliar environments with imperfect handling of the controls; realistically, novice players cannot anticipate enemies and may not be familiar with a certain game map.

The long-term effects are also important, which even our 2-hour study cannot assess. However, we have some guidance because half of our participants were FPS experts (and thus very familiar with the type of control and environment); the other half were novices. There were no systematic differences in the efficacy of the techniques depending on expertise. This is important because regardless of whether a novice is playing against an expert or an expert is playing against a professional, certain techniques will be more effective. So although we cannot predict the effects of long-term usage of the techniques themselves, we can assume that long-term usage of the general controls and environment do not affect technique efficacy.

The application of our results is limited to aiming in 3D games – our work is the first to investigate aim assistance in this realistic scenario, and generalizing to all 3D aiming is premature. However, this is not a niche topic – these games have huge player numbers and represent a massive industry that historically has not been guided by HCI research.

There are also aspects of our work that may apply beyond 3D FPS. The trend that post-aim techniques work better might be interesting to designers of other realistic and time-constrained systems (e.g., safety-critical or medical), whereas the controlled nature of S1 means that our results are of interest to others who study 3D aiming (e.g., VR).

### Future Work

Our future work in this area will follow three directions. First, we will explore additional game factors– such as player movement, cost functions associated with shooting (e.g., in situations of limited ammunition), or additional precision (e.g., with a scope sight), and the role of lighting. Second, we will investigate the use of bullet magnetism and area cursor for balancing multiplayer games, using the modified Unreal system that we built for these studies. Third, we will further consider the way that the 3D environment itself affects assistance techniques, in terms of the user's movements in the X-Y plane versus the bullet's movement in all three dimensions – a characterization that has not been applied before to aim assistance techniques.

## CONCLUSION

Aim-assistance techniques have been shown to work for player balancing in 2D studies, but little information exists about how well these techniques could work in a 3D FPS game. We carried out three studies to examine the performance of five different aim assists. Although the assists worked well in a target-range scenario, their performance was reduced when real-game elements were introduced. We examined the relationships between game elements and assist performance by manipulating specific game elements; we found that two techniques – bullet magnetism and area cursor – worked well in a wide variety of situations. In addition, we found that some techniques that worked well (i.e., target lock) were too perceptible to be successful for balancing, and that some previously-successful techniques (gravity and sticky targets) worked poorly throughout. Our studies provide initial insight into how game factors affect aim assistance, and identify techniques that show potential for player balancing.

## ACKNOWLEDGMENTS

We thank our CHI reviewers, Jared Cechanowicz, the Interaction Lab, and NSERC and GRAND for funding.

## REFERENCES

1. Adams, E. Fundamentals of Game Design. New Riders, 2010.
2. Adams, E. Difficulty Modes and Dynamic Difficulty Adjustment. *Gamasutra: The Art & Business of Making Games Blog*. Published May 2008, gamasutra.com/view/feature/3660/the_designers_notebook_.php
3. Balakrishnan, R. "Beating" Fitt"s law: virtual enhancements for pointing facilitation. IJHCS, 61, (2004), 857-874.
4. Bateman, S., Mandryk, R.L., Stach, T. and Gutwin, C. Target assistance for subtly balancing competitive play. In CHI 2011, 2355-2364.
5. Blanch, R., Guiard Y., and Beaudouin-Lafon, M. Semantic Pointing: Improving Target Acquisition with Control-Display Ratio Adaptation. In CHI 2004, 24-29.
6. Bostan, B., and Öğüt, S. Game challenges and difficulty levels: lessons learned From RPGs. In International Simulation and Gaming Association Conference, 2009.
7. Cockburn, A, and Firth, A. Improving the Acquisition of Small Targets. In HCI03 Conference on People and Computers XVII, 2003. 181-196.
8. Csíkszentmihályi, M. Flow: The Psychology of Optimal Experience. Harper and Row, 1990.
9. Elmqvist, N., and Fekete, J. Semantic Pointing for Object Picking in Complex 3D Environments. In GI 2008, 243-250.
10. Entertainment Software Association. *2013 Essential Facts About the Computer and Video Game Industry* www.theesa.com/facts/pdfs/ESA_EF_2013.pdf
11. Falstein, N. Understanding fun – the Theory of Natural Funativity. In Introduction to Game Development, Rabin, S. (ed.), 71-98. Charles River Media, 2005.
12. Findlater, L, Jansen, A., Shinohara, K., Dixon, M., Kamb, P., Rakita. J., and Wobbrock, J.O. Enhanced Area Cursors Reducing Fine Pointing Demands for People with Motor Impairments. In UIST 2010, 153-162.
13. Fitts, P.M. (1954). The information capacity of the human motor system in controlling the amplitude of movement. J.Exp. Psych., 47, 381-391.
14. Flatla, D., Gutwin, C., Nacke, L.E., Bateman, S., and Mandryk, R.L. Calibration Games: Making Calibration Tasks Enjoyable by Adding Motivating Game Elements. In UIST 2011, 403-412.
15. Guiard, Y., Blanch, R., and Beaudouin-Lafon, M. Object pointing: a complement to bitmap pointing in GUIs. In GI 2004, 9-16.
16. Herbrich, R., Minka, T., and Graepel, T. TrueSkill(TM): A Bayesian skill rating system. In Advances in Neural Information Processing Systems, 20, 569-576, 2007.
17. Hunicke, R. The case for dynamic difficulty adjustment in games. In ACE 2005, vol. 265, 429-433.
18. Kabbash, P. and Buxton, W. The "Prince" Technique: Fitts' Law and Selection Using Area Cursors. In CHI 1995, 273-279.
19. Looser, J., Cockburn, A. and Savage, J. On the Validity of Using First-Person Shooters for Fitts' Law Studies. In HCI 2005, 33-36.
20. Mandryk, R.L., Gutwin, C. Perceptibility and Utility of Sticky Targets. In GI 2008, 65-72.
21. Natapov, D., Castellucci, S. J., and MacKenzie, I. S. (2009). ISO 9241-9 evaluation of video game controllers. In GI 2009. 223-230.
22. Newheiser, Mark. Playing Fair: A Look at Competition in Gaming. *Strange Horizons*, www.strangehorizons.com/2009/20090309/newheiser-a.shtml
23. Sweetser, P. and Wyeth, P. GameFlow: a model for evaluating player enjoyment in games. Computers in Entertainment, 3, 3-3, 205.
24. Vorderer, P., Hartmann, T., and Klimmt, C. Explaining the enjoyment of playing video games: the role of competition. In Entertainment Computing'03, 1-9.
25. Wobbrock, J.O., Fogarty, J., Liu, S., Kimuro, S., Harada, S. The Angle Mouse: Target-Agnostic Dynamic Gain Adjustment Based on Angular Deviation. In CHI 2009, 1401-1410.
26. Worden A, Walker N, Bharat K, Hudson S. Making Computers Easier for Older Adults to Use: Area Cursors and Sticky Icons. In CHI 1997, 266-271
27. Youssef, A. and Cossell, S. Thoughts on adjusting perceived difficulty in games. In Australasian Conference on Interactive Entertainment, 1-4, 2009.

# Design Tactics for Authentic Interactive Fiction: Insights from Alternate Reality Game Designers

**Elizabeth Bonsignore[1], Vicki Moulder[2], Carman Neustaedter[2], Derek Hansen[3], Kari Kraus[1], and Allison Druin[1]**

[1]Human-Computer Interaction Lab, University of Maryland College Park, MD, USA {ebonsign,kkraus, allisond@umiacs}@umd.edu

[2]School of Interactive Arts & Technology Simon Fraser University, Surrey, BC, CA V3T 0A3 {vmoulder,carman_neustaedter}@sfu.ca

[3]School of Technology Brigham Young University Provo, UT, USA dlhansen@byu.edu

## ABSTRACT

This paper presents insights from designers of Alternate Reality Games (ARGs) regarding the design tactics they employ to integrate participatory storytelling and "authentic fiction" into the transmedia experiences they create. Our approach was motivated by recent efforts in HCI to more closely align the development of interaction design theory to the craft knowledge and experiences of designers themselves. The resulting insights enhance our understanding of design approaches that a diverse group of ARG producers follow to create interactive, participatory narratives. We outline narrative-specific themes to support designers who craft similar interactive experiences.

### Author Keywords

Alternate reality games; transmedia; narrative design.

### ACM Classification Keywords

J.5 Arts and Humanities; K.4.0 Computers and Society: General; K.8.0 Personal computing: Games.

## INTRODUCTION

An ARG is a genre of transmedia storytelling [13], comprised of interactive elements that are scattered and hidden in websites, books, phone and text messages, movie trailers, and even billboards [14,16]. To engage with an ARG, players collaboratively solve puzzles and share clues to reassemble the fragments of a story that has spilled out into their everyday world. But the designers' initial storyline is not the only story told through ARG gameplay. Any overarching narrative sketched out by designers at a game's outset is subject to change, because players have a central role in assembling the story world as they collect, connect, and make sense of its distributed bits. As players weave their own hypotheses, interpretations, and extensions into gaps they perceive in the unfolding storyline, the ARG effectively becomes a collective narrative. ARG designers monitor player response in real-time and often modify the storyline based on player speculations [8,14,16,17]. Ongoing summaries that players compile on "the story so far" act as a guide for new audiences and a ready reference for existing players and even designers [8,14]. Indeed, ARGs represent a participatory culture, where players "actively participate in the creation and circulation of new content" [13, p.207].

Players may traverse an ARG's narrative using everyday communications tools, but the interaction design challenges are not an everyday process. Designers must create and connect story bits across multiple media (video, audio, text) and multiple platforms (phones, computers, physical spaces). They must engage players to access and follow various story paths, as well as afford players opportunities to add their own voices. How do ARG designers and producers manage these interleaving storylines? How do they determine the essential elements of the story to start with? What design considerations guide their decisions about how, where, and when to distribute these nodes across their planned story network?

This paper explores these issues through the perspectives of designers themselves. Our approach is motivated by recent efforts in HCI to develop "theories of interaction design practice that resonate with practitioners themselves" [10], based on systematic compilation and synthesis of craft knowledge [3,10]. We adhere to the philosophy of gleaning design theories from designers' own experiences and "appreciation systems" [12,20]. From this grounding, we focused on the following questions: *How do ARG designers perceive transmedia narrative formats, and how does this inform their design approaches? How do they incorporate narrative hooks that invite potential audiences to play?*

We have synthesized insights from a diverse set of ARG designers. Some of them have been producing ARGs for over a decade; others have only created one ARG. Since 2001, when *The Beast* was first launched as a promotional vehicle for the movie, *A.I.*, ARGs have been developed by expansive production crews [16] and crafted by small teams of educators [6]. They have been commissioned as marketing campaigns, designed in educational contexts and


*CHI 2014*, April 26 - May 1 2014, Toronto, Ontario, Canada

http://dx.doi.org/10.1145/2556288.2557245

for social engagement in environmental topics such as climate change [5,6,11]. That ARGs and similar transmedia experiences are now being developed across a wide variety of domains underscores [3]'s prediction that "where experimental artists lead, the cultural mainstream often follows" [p.717]. This paper distills craft knowledge beyond that of professional artists to encompass a wide range of practitioners (e.g., educators, museum curators).

## INTERACTIVE, PARTICIPATORY NARRATIVE DESIGN

Narrative is a fundamental element of human experience. Whether they were etched on cave walls 40 millennia ago or stained glass windows 500 years ago; inscribed in print or embedded in multiple media across multiple hyperlinks; encapsulated in 140 characters or in petabytes of data — we encounter stories everywhere, in every aspect of our lives [2,20]. Narrative can also be a highly interactive experience [1]. Over the past few decades, the growth of digital media and mobile technologies has enabled increasingly interactive narrative formats that not only invite, but also require reader/audience participation [4,23]. Researchers and designers across a wide range of disciplines, such as artificial intelligence, humanities, game studies, and performance art, are exploring design strategies for immersive stories that people can play [4]. In game design research and in the gaming industry, there persists a theoretical and practical interest in analyzing the relationship between game and narrative [19,23]. The core interaction mechanism in ARGs is a distributed, transmedia story. Thus, ARG designers must devise ways to: 1) lead players across media and platforms that contain interactive story fragments [16], and 2) support player efforts to add to the collective experience with their own interpretations and contributions to the evolving storyline [8,14,17].

## METHODS

We interviewed a diverse set of 18 game designers and researchers who have experience producing ARGs and similar new media immersive artworks. Most of our participants (n=10) are established professionals in the entertainment industry (transmedia writers, producers, and designers). Three participants are games studies and new media scholars; two have produced ARGs specifically for undergraduate-level educational environments; and two have designed ARGs to support informal learning and cultural institutions (libraries and museums). An interactive art director/freelance illustrator who designed the artwork for an ARG rounds out the group. Of note, our inclusion of eight designers *outside* of the entertainment industry spotlights the potential value of their practices beyond highly professional contexts like [3,12]. In addition, all of the authors of this paper have designed at least one ARG. While we do not include ourselves in the interview sample, our own ARG experiences guided our analysis. We refer to our designers by number (e.g., D#3) to maintain anonymity.

Our interviews followed a semi-structured format [15]. As these interviews are part of a larger series of studies aimed at developing a design framework for ARG praxis and production, we covered several topics regarding ARG design, such as: the overall design process; the challenge of recruiting a cadre of players to a genre that prides itself in being hidden; and challenges of preserving narratives that cross multiple platforms and timeframes. We used a qualitative approach inspired by [7] to analyze all interview transcripts. Given the range of production contexts of our interviewees, our goal was to glean commonalities among the ways in which they employed a variety of media and platforms "to enact a network...binding separate content into whole, coherent expressions" [18, p.283]. During open coding, we noted a consistent emphasis on the primacy of story, along with tactics for structuring narrative "through-lines" (D#18) across media and platforms. To glean common story-specific design strategies, codes were compared and refined iteratively by multiple authors, then constantly compared across designer transcripts [7].

## FINDINGS

The story-specific themes we uncovered include 1) options for narrative structure and 2) tactics for active participation.

### *Narrative Structure/Form*

All designers contrasted ARG narratives against "deeply-architecturally-sophisticated" content that designers "build in, like books or films" (D#7). Instead, ARG narratives are unique structures that "leave space for the player to feel that their choices make a difference" (D#7), or motivate the player community to "make sense between subplots, and make linkages...to the main story" (D#11). These views establish a narrative ecology with two main story types: the designer's macro-story and the players' collective micro-stories. From the perspective of ARG designers, the macro-stories they orchestrate can be situated along a continuum, with two distinct structures at each end: an open-ended, "thinly" plotted spine versus a close-ended, "thickly" plotted graph-like network.

The narrative structure of thickly plotted narratives resembles a dense graph of story elements. The term "close-ended" emphasizes that much of the macro-story is crafted *pre*-game, with ARG designers orchestrating players' progression toward a preconceived endgame. Player interaction is driven by puzzle-solving and sense-making activities. In "closed/thick" ARGs, the narrative goal is collective re-construction of the macro-story, driven by individual player interpretations (micro-stories) of the distributed transmedia fragments. In contrast, a single "*What if?*" theme drives player interaction in open-ended ARGs. Designers for *World Without Oil* (*WWO*, http://worldwithoutoil.org) asked players to simulate 32 weeks of a global oil crisis, inviting them to share personal stories about how their lives would change in such a world. In these participatory storytelling systems, the motivating theme acts as a single ("thin") central thread about which players weave their own meaningful micro-stories. The shared, emergent narrative is directly co-created by the player community. At both ends of the spectrum, designers must devise ways to balance authorial intent and player contributions: "it's a continuously important issue with ARGs. How do you make people feel they have an impact and voice without letting them say Hamlet would be way better if it had a happy ending?" (D#10).

Figure 1 depicts this ARG narrative design continuum. The horizontal axis reflects the close- to open-ended narrative design dimension. The vertical axis reflects narrative scope, or levels of player interaction (e.g., number and types of transmedia elements, puzzles/clues, etc.). For example, Fourth Wall Studio's *RIDES* (http://rides.tv/about-rides/) are highly orchestrated transmedia narratives. Player interaction is scripted and fairly passive (e.g., reading an incoming text message). *RIDES* were conceived as the "album" solution to elaborate, live, "rock-concert" ARGs, and are intended as a "product that is *not* ephemeral...a replayable, single player cross-platform" experience" (D#10). In contrast, *WWO* was very open-ended, allowing each player to contribute to the story in her own way; using whatever media she was comfortable with. *The Beast* and *I Love Bees* contained many transmedia story elements (high player interaction required) and played out toward a preconceived endgame with a balance of scripted and player-enacted plot points.

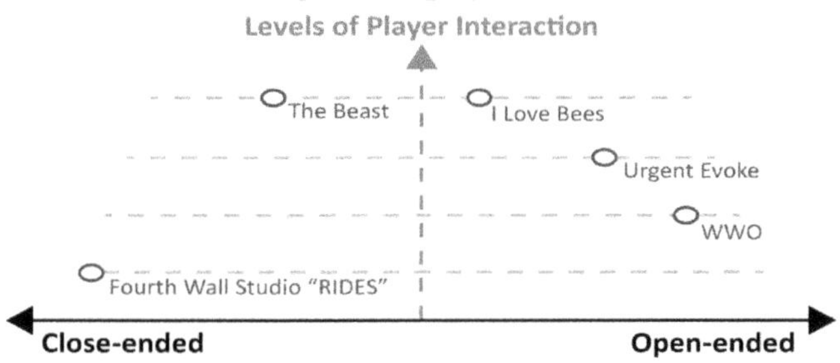


**Figure 1: ARG Narrative Design Dimensions**

*Tactics for engagement: points of convergence and "gaps"*

All the designers emphasized embedding actionable tasks into the macro-story to promote active player engagement. Many of their tactics can be described as *points of convergence* where distributed narrative elements and game mechanics intersect. Based on our interviews, the most important approaches to narrative design revolved around the following questions:

- *What action-oriented tropes can be embedded in the story to help players see themselves as active participants?* "Secret societies" were used to motivate players to "join" the game, and to reinforce required actions, such as decrypting codes. An in-game character asking players for help and providing expository information is another oft-used narrative convention (Designers #2,5-12,14).
- *How can we bring the real-world into the story in an authentic way?* Several designers highlighted the need to integrate real world constructs and social contracts, such as connecting players to the micro-stories in a museum repository through missions (Designers#4-6,14). They expressed a need for players to role-play for "real", such as having an urban planner evaluate player plans or guild members meeting up at a specific location to complete a mission (Designers#2,7,12,14). As D#14 noted: "We incorporated bits of our museum's history. It made it so much more real to people... That's where you really succeed in blurring that line."
- *What are essential nodes that must be traversed?* Regardless of whether they produced close-ended or open-ended ARGs, all designers highlighted a need to help players find a consistent "through-line" (Designer#18), or "ways to define [stable] islands of stuff that you're sure of – and other assets that you can create and destroy very, very fast" (Designer#10).

In addition to these points of convergence, designers noted that *gaps*, or *absence of narrative information* were important, and especially critical in open-ended ARGs, whose emergent storylines rely on inciting player contributions. Such gaps can be described as counterfactual design, a mechanism that motivates players to imagine "what if" scenarios to fill in gaps in close-ended narratives or add nodes to open-ended ones [5]. For example, D#13 noted, "What is the vacuum I create that allows the story to be told?" For D#12, the vacuum that could compel players to contribute to an ARG narrative was embodied in counterfactual gaps in history [5]: "every time historians say, we don't know how this happened or we really can't explain this, I would mark it" as an inflection point ripe for player intervention. Such tactics reflect the evocative power of ambiguity for interactive designs [13].

Several designers also noted that the points at which they left gaps in their narrative proved to be an incentive for players to document the macro-story for others, or to enrich it with their own micro-stories: "If you have a sufficiently large audience, they will filter and do quality control. The players do it for you; they do it better; and they are infinitely more painstaking and careful assembling and documenting how well the pieces go together" (D#10). Indeed, [10] showed that player productions are often more popular to broader audiences than designer macro-stories. This suggests a potential touch-point for future designs that can enable players to participate in the production and preservation of their own participant trajectories, thereby increasing the community archival power for an interactive art form that has been heretofore largely ephemeral.

## CONCLUSIONS AND CONTRIBUTIONS

ARG design and production involves the dynamic coordination of multiple narrative and ludic components that play out across space and time. Over the past decade, designers from a variety of contexts have tackled these ARG design challenges. In this paper, we drew from their experiences to tease out key themes that can support the development of theories for interactive narrative design. We have proposed an ARG narrative design framework that is a continuum from close-ended, designer-orchestrated transmedia structures to open-ended, emergent stories co-created by players/designers. Our analysis extends [3]'s trajectories framework, which describes user experiences of performance artworks as designer-orchestrated journeys. While [3] acknowledges that a player's journey is "shaped by narratives that are embedded into spatial, temporal, and performative structures by authors" [p.712], it does not explicitly unpack how designers can embed and distribute narrative elements to invite active story input from players in authentic ways. Many existing game designs offer players optional paths to change their gameplay experience [19]; however, our ARG designers sought ways for players to incorporate *new* content into the macro-narrative frame. These approaches complement [3]'s examples that explicitly had players add their own micro-stories to the orchestrated narrative (e.g., Thrill Lab). Our emphasis on participatory storytelling also acts as a foil to [3]'s framework. ARG designer tactics underscore the allure of gaps and ambiguity to inspire players to contribute to a collective story, not just interact with it. This insight may be unique to ARGs in that it overtly allows for players to subvert the hierarchy of authority that [3] suggests with its language of "canonical" vs. "participant" trajectories.

We also identified three key questions that should be addressed by designers of interactive narratives like ARGs to engage players. These questions go beyond existing tropes because they demonstrate ways to 1) map physical artifacts and places scattered across multiple, everyday media and platforms into a macro-story (e.g., stories about objects in a museum repository, gaps in historical records); and then 2) incite players to share their interpretations in the same way: "The little narratives of our lives may not seem like much—but the cautionary tale my friend tells me is much more likely to persuade me of something than anything James Cameron will produce. I try to create a space that encourages people to make these stories they find meaningful – that's what authentic fiction is about" (D#13).

### ACKNOWLEDGMENTS
We thank our interviewees, and research funding from NSF IIS-0952567, GRAND NCE Canada, and SSHRC Canada.

### REFERENCES
1. Aarseth, E. J. *Cybertext*. Balto., MD: JHU Press, 1997.
2. Barthes, R., & Duisit, L. An Introduction to the Structural Analysis of Narrative. *New Literary History, 6*(2), (1975), 237–272.
3. Benford, S., Giannachi, G., Koleva, B., & Rodden, T. From interaction to trajectories: designing coherent journeys through user experiences. *In Proc. CHI 2009*, ACM Press (2009) 709–718.
4. Bizzocchi, J., Lin, M. A. B., & Tanenbaum, J. Games, narrative and the design of interface. *Int'l Journal of Arts and Technology, 4*(4), (2011), 460–479.
5. Bonsignore, E., Kraus, K., Visconti, A., Hansen, D., Fraistat, A., & Druin, A. Game design for promoting counterfactual thinking. In *Proc CHI2012*, ACM Press (2012), 2079–2082.
6. Bonsignore, E., Hansen, D., Kraus, K., & Ruppel, M. ARGs as Platforms for Practicing 21st-Century Literacies. *IJLM, 4*(1), (2012), 25–54.
7. Charmaz, K. (2006). *Constructing grounded theory*. Thousand Oaks, CA: Sage Publications.
8. Dena, C. Emerging Participatory Culture Practices: Player-Created Tiers in Alternate Reality Games. *Convergence, 14*(1), (2008), 41–57.
9. Gaver, W. W., Beaver, J., & Benford, S. Ambiguity as a resource for design. In *Proc CHI 2003*, ACM Press, (2003), 233–240.
10. Goodman, E., Stolterman, E., & Wakkary, R. Understanding interaction design practices. In *Proc. CHI 2011*, ACM Press, 2011, 1061–1070.
11. Hansen, D., Bonsignore, E., Ruppel, M., Visconti, A., & Kraus, K. Designing reusable alternate reality games. In *Proc. CHI2013*, ACM Press, (2013), 1529–1538.
12. Isbister, K., Flanagan, M., & Hash, C. Designing games for learning: insights from conversations with designers. In *Proc. CHI 2010*, ACM Press (2010), 2041–2044.
13. Jenkins, H. *Convergence culture: where old and new media collide*. NY: New York Univ. Press, 2006.
14. Kim, J. Y., Allen, J. P., & Lee, E. Alternate reality gaming. *Commun. ACM*, 51(2), (2008), 36–42.
15. Lazar, J., Feng, J. H., & Hochheiser, H. *Research methods in HCI*. West Sussex, UK: Wiley, 2010.
16. Martin, A., Thompson, B., & Chatfield, T. ARG White Paper: IGDA ARG SIG. 2006. http://bit.ly/18rxSWX.
17. McGonigal, J. Why I Love Bees: A Case Study in Collective Intelligence Gaming. In K. Salen (Ed.), *The Ecology of Games*. Cambridge, MA: MIT Press, 2008.
18. Ruppel, M. Narrative Convergence, Cross-Sited Productions and the Archival Dilemma. *Convergence, 15*(3), (2009), 281–298.
19. Salen, K., & Zimmerman, E. *Rules of play: game design fundamentals*. Cambridge, MA: MIT Press, 2003.
20. Schön, D. *The Reflective Practitioner*. New York, NY: Basic Books, 1984.
21. Seely-Brown, J., Denning, S., Prusak, L., & Groh, K. *Storytelling in organizations*. Boston: Elsevier, 2004.
22. Van Dam, A., Balsamo, A., Brinkman, D., & Watrall, E. Big Heritage, Big Quilts & Big Canvases. *SXSW Interactive Panel*, 2013. http://bit.ly/16aBpIj
23. Wardrip-Fruin, N., & Harrigan, P. (Eds.). *First person: new media as story, performance, and game*. Cambridge, MA: MIT Press.

# Jump and Shoot! - Prioritizing Primary and Alternative Body Gestures for Intense Gameplay

**Chaklam Silpasuwanchai**
Kochi University of Technology, Kochi, Japan
ren.xiangshi@kochi-tech.ac.jp

**Xiangshi Ren**
Kochi University of Technology, Kochi, Japan
ren.xiangshi@kochi-tech.ac.jp

## ABSTRACT
Motion gestures enable natural and intuitive input in video games. However, game gestures designed by developers may not always be the optimal gestures for players. A key challenge in designing appropriate game gestures lies in the interaction-intensive nature of video games, i.e., several actions/commands may need to be executed concurrently using different body parts. This study analyzes user preferences in game gestures, with the aim of accommodating high interactivity during gameplay. Two user-elicitation studies were conducted: first, to determine user preferences, participants were asked to define gestures for common game actions/commands; second, to develop effective combined-gestures, participants were asked to define possible game gestures using each body part (one and two hands, one and two legs, head, eyes, and torso). Our study presents a set of suitable and alternative body parts for common game actions/commands. We also present some simultaneously applied game gestures that assist interaction in highly interactive game situations (e.g., selecting a weapon with the feet while shooting with the hand). Interesting design implications are further discussed, e.g., transferability between hand and leg gestures.

### Author Keywords
Games; interactivity; motion gestures; concurrent gestures; user-defined approach.

### ACM Classification Keywords
H.5.m. Information Interfaces and Presentation (e.g. HCI): Miscellaneous.

### General Terms
Human Factors; Design.

## INTRODUCTION
The introduction of Kinect-based interaction has enabled more natural and intuitive input for video games. However, game gestures designed by developers may not always be the most suitable for players. Indeed, players have reported difficulties in playing some motion-based games, particularly in interaction-intensive games (e.g., First Person Shooters/Action/Adventure) where several actions/commands have to be executed at or nearly at the same time (e.g., [4]). Thus one key challenge in game gestural interfaces lies in defining suitable gestures that enable players to effectively perform multiple game actions/commands simultaneously and with ease.

Several full-body gesture studies have been conducted [1, 5, 10, 11], but still little study has been conducted considering the dynamic nature of game environments in general. When a player's hand is occupied with "Shooting Zombies", it is not known which other body parts and gestures players might prefer to perform simultaneous actions such as "Use First Aid Kit" or "Viewpoint Change". Since a literal "Jump" or "Climb" action can be tiring, we need to consider whether users might prefer less tiring gestures. We would also do well to ask what gestures veteran gamers and non-gamers devise or envisage to enhance their interaction experiences.

To investigate these potentials, this study analyzes how users define gestures for common game actions. In addition, we identify a set of alternative body parts and game gestures that facilitate the high amount of interaction experienced in games. Last, we highlight important design implications.

## RELATED WORK
Several works regarding full-body game interaction have been conducted, e.g., how emotions, role-play, and social expressions interplay with body movement [1, 6]; how motivation affects the player's use of gestures [10]; factors affecting player engagement in body interaction [11]; naturalistic full-body gestures in public spaces [3, 8]; accommodating variability of same gesture execution [2]. Yet, the simultaneous use of gestures in video games has remained largely unexplored.

One recent approach to design suitable gestures is the user-elicitation methodology, originally based on the guessability technique [9, 12], where participants were asked to define gestures for commands/actions. Indeed, Morris et al. [7] suggested that a user-defined approach can produce more preferable gestures, compared to interactions designed by HCI experts who are likely to develop more "physically and conceptually complex gestures than end-users". Many works have been conducted using a user-defined approach, e.g., gestures for surface computing [13]; full-body interactions for older adults [5]. Leveraging this approach, we were motivated to design gestural interfaces that consider the dynamic, interaction-intensive nature of video games, or in a broader sense, to explore gestural interfaces in a highly interactive, fast-paced environment.

## GAME GESTURE STUDY
We conducted two user-elicitation studies. First, participants were asked to define single gestures for each common game actions/commands. Agreement scores, frequency of use of body parts, gesture types, and subjective assessment were analyzed. In the second study, participants were asked to define several gestures for each actions/commands using each body part (one and two hands, one and two legs, head, eyes, torso). This second study is intended to help designers consider a set of suitable and alternative body parts for each game action/command. In addition, we aimed to uncover simultaneous game gestures that can promote higher interactivity in game situations.

## EXPERIMENT I: ANALYZE USER PREFERENCES
### Participants
Twelve university students (all males, M=22.1 years) were recruited. Five of the participants regularly played games


http://dx.doi.org/10.1145/2556288.2557107

everyday with more than 15 game hours per week (veteran gamers). Five reported to have no experience with Kinect and motion game gestures. All participants were right-handed and each was paid $10.

### Events

Thirty-two actions and commands were derived from typical interactions in video games. The complete set of events[1] includes adventure/role-playing actions (Climb, Walk, Stop Walking, Run, Jump, Stealth Walking, Steal, Open Chest, Open Door, Pick Item, Use Item, Push Box, Shake Item), sport/fighting actions (Hitting Baseball, Catch Ball, Throw Ball, Row Boat, Roll Bowling, Racket Hitting, Kick, Guard), first person shooters actions (Shoot, Reload Gun, Slash, Viewpoint Change), racing actions (Drive, Accelerate, Shift gear), and system commands (Zoom-In, Zoom-Out, Open Menu, Select Menu Item).

### Procedure

At the start of the experiment, participants were asked to define game gestures for 32 game events. Each event was displayed along with the name of the event and a target scene on a large display. Target scenes were created by using Visual Studio 3D Toolkit to represent an effect (e.g., a treasure chest being opened, an opponent being slashed), and participants were asked to perform gestures to cause (trigger) the effect. Target scenes were not taken from animated screenshots of any existing video games, as we tried to keep the target scenes independent of any particular game, which might otherwise influence the resulting gesture. Some target scenes were not animated, e.g., stealth walking, as these scenes require the participants to see the actors in third-person view to show the effect clearly, which may influence participant's defined gestures; so we simply communicated the effect using instructions along with the name of the events. A think-aloud protocol was used where participants indicated the start and end of their performed gesture and described the corresponding rationale. Participants stood approximately 1.8 meters away from the display while performing gestures. A camera was set in front of the participant to record the performed gesture for later analysis. As with common elicitation studies, we did not want participants to take recognizer issues into consideration, i.e., to remove the *gulf of execution* between the user and the device, and to observe the users' best possible gesture without users being affected by the recognition ability of the system - similar to the rationale described in [13]. Participants evaluated the gestures immediately after each performed gesture to assist recall efforts. A similar evaluation method to that of [13] was used: "The gesture I performed is a good match for its purpose"; "The gesture I performed is easy to perform"; "The gesture I performed is tiring". The questionnaire followed a 7-point Likert scale style with 7 as "strongly agree". The experimental session took around 1-hour.

### Results

Agreement scores, frequency of use of body parts, gesture types, and subjective assessment were analyzed. Total of 384 gestures were collected.

#### *Agreement score*

Wobbrock et al's method [13] was used to investigate the degree of consensus for each game event. The calculation of agreement score is as follows (see equation 1):

$$A_r = \sum_{Pi} \left( \left| \frac{P_i}{P_r} \right| \right)^2 \quad (1)$$

[1]For simplicity, the term *"events"* will be used in place of *"actions and commands"* throughout this paper.

$Pr$ represents all gestures performed for event $r$ and $Pi$ is a subset of identical gestures from $Pr$. $Ar$ ranges 0 to 1.

Figure 1 shows the agreement score for each game event. Two gestures were considered identical if they have similar trajectories and poses. The overall agreement score was 0.37, which is slightly higher than Wobbrock et al. (0.32 and 0.28)[13]. The high agreement score was due to participants mimicking their daily life gestures for performing some game actions. Regardless of the high overall agreement score, system commands including "Open Menu", "Zoom-In", "Zoom-Out" achieved relatively low overall agreement scores (0.126).

#### *Use of body parts and gesture types*

Figure 2 shows the use of body parts. It is not surprising that one handed gestures were the most preferred (40%), followed by two handed (35%), one leg (16%), two legs (4%), torso movement (3%), and head (2%). However, this pattern was not the same across all actions. For navigational actions such as "Run", "Walking", "Stop Walking", most participants preferred leg gestures. For the "Viewpoint Change" action, participants preferred head input with a few using the torso. For the commands "Select Menu Item" and "Open Menu", many participants preferred hands, however head input was used by some.

Regarding gesture types, we feel it is important to highlight the difference in gesture preferences between veteran gamers and normal/non-gamers. We classified the defined gestures into four broad types [13]: physical (direct manipulation), symbolic (making an "OK" gesture), metaphorical (using a foot to "double click" items), and abstract (arbitrary mapping). As shown in Figure 2, most defined gestures resembled daily life gestures (physical gestures). On the other hand, non-physical gestures were mostly performed by veteran gamers, e.g., for the action "Jump", non-gamers tend to prefer using an actual "Jump" action while veteran gamers preferred a less tiring gesture (e.g., raising a leg slightly above the ground).

#### *Subjective assessment*

Participants evaluated their defined gestures based on the Likert 7-scale rating (7 as strongly agree). The mean value is "The gesture I performed is a good match for its purpose?" (5.84); "The gesture I performed is easy to perform" (5.90); and "The gesture I performed is tiring" (5.51). The correlation between participants' good match ratings and agreement scores was found to be significant ($r$=0.746, $p$<0.01), suggesting that a good match rating is a good indicator of the consensus between users on the gestures performed.

## EXPERIMENT II: ACCOMMODATING INTERACTIVITY

In Experiment 1, we were able to better understand user preferences in game gestures. However, the experiment revealed two remaining gaps: (1) the suitability of alternative body parts for each game event was not adequately explored in cases where the preferred body part was occupied with the task at hand. (2) Few possible simultaneous game gestures were discovered, i.e., participants mostly defined gestures based on their daily life actions but such actions may not always be applicable in highly interactive game situations and gestures more applicable to digital gaming might thus be overlooked. Thus, in Experiment II, we asked participants to define possible gestures using each of body parts and to rate their suitability.

### Participants

Another twelve university students (1 female, M=22.4 years) were recruited. Six were veteran gamers. Four reported to have no experience with Kinect and motion game gestures. All were right-handed. They were paid $10. The only female participant had no experience in video games. In our study, we did not observe any gender-specific differences between the female participant and other male non-gamer participants.

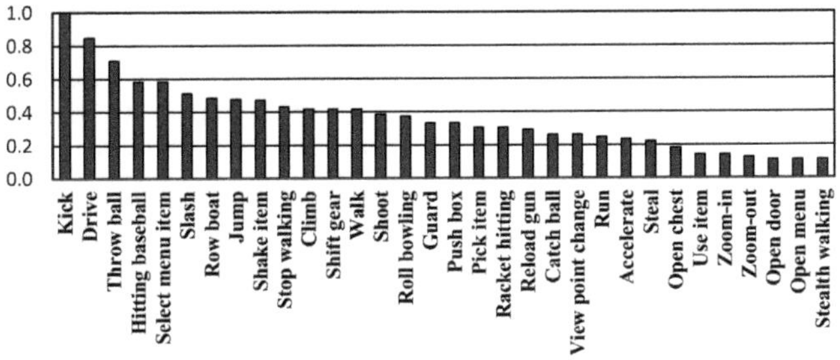


**Figure 1. Overall agreement scores for events sorted in descending order.**

## Events

For better coverage, 8 more game events were added for analysis including adventure/role-playing actions (Crawl, Roll Body), sport/fighting actions (Dodge, Headbutt, Punch), racing actions (Break, Boost), first person shooters actions (Hide).

## Procedure

Participants were asked to define possible game gestures for 40 game events, using each body part (one and two hands, one and two legs, head, eyes, torso). Regarding the use of eye(s), we instructed participants that eye gestures could be any interaction performed using eye movements or fixations. Participants were allowed to skip when they felt that no suitable gestures could be performed using a particular body part. There was a 3-minute break between each body part testing session. The setting was similar to that used in experiment 1. Regarding subjective assessment, an additional item was added - "The body part I used is suitable".

## Results

The results of suitable and alternative body part sets and possible simultaneous game gestures were analyzed and reported.

### *Suitable and alternative body parts*

We analyzed the most suitable body parts and alternatives based on the participants' subjective assessments of "The body part I used is suitable". The most suitable body part for each event was selected based on the highest mean score. We also analyzed alternative body parts in case the most suitable body part was already occupied with the task at hand. Alternative body parts were selected on the grounds that they did not conflict with the most suitable body part and they presented with the highest mean score among all the alternatives. In cases where two body parts achieved equivalent highest mean scores and posed no conflict in body part usage, both were highlighted as the most suitable body part and no alternative was highlighted (e.g., Roll body). Figure 3 shows the suitable and alternative body parts for each game event.

### *Simultaneous game gestures*

We found potentially useful game gestures with simultaneity as the main criteria. We also considered gesture combinations that are anatomically and kinetically feasible. **Shooting-** "Shoot" action was most preferably performed using one-hand mimicking a gun-gesture. Simultaneously, players were able to perform the "Reload" action by stamping one foot into the 12 o'clock position. Players could also simultaneously perform the "Use item" action by "double clicking" (tapping) one foot on the floor. Head movement was most preferable for "View point change", but in cases when the head input was already assigned,"View point change" could also be optionally performed using eye movement or 1-hand movement as a cursor indicating the point of view. "Hide" could be performed by moving the whole body (torso) down. In some cases when "Shoot" action could not be performed by the hands (e.g., when the hands were already assigned for "Slash"), the "Shoot" action could be optionally performed with a kicking gesture.

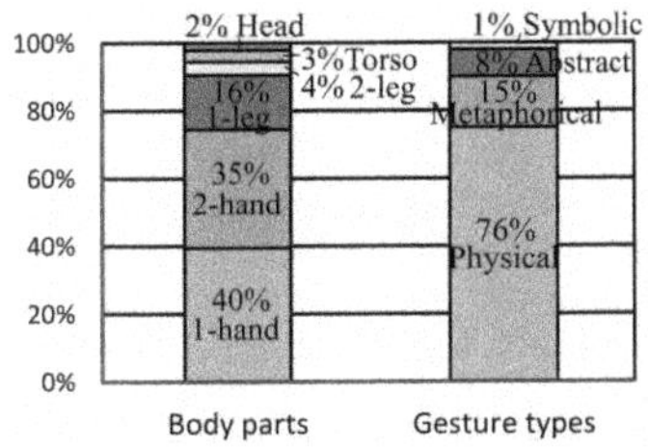


| | Normal/ non-gamers | Veteran gamers |
|---|---|---|
| Physical | 66% | 34% |
| Metaphorical | 32% | 67% |
| Abstract | 40% | 60% |
| Symbolic | 0% | 100% |

**Figure 2. The proportion of body parts used and gesture types (left) and veteran gamers vs. non/normal gamers (right).**

| | | Suitability of body part | | | | | | |
|---|---|---|---|---|---|---|---|---|
| No. | Events | 1-hand | 2-hand | 1-leg | 2-leg | Head | Eye | Torso |
| 1 | Accelerate | 2.75 | 2.75 | 4.75 | 1 | 1 | 1 | 1 |
| 2 | Boost | 6.75 | 3.5 | 1.75 | 1 | 1 | 1 | 1 |
| 3 | Break | 2.75 | 1.75 | 6.25 | 1 | 1 | 1 | 1 |
| 4 | Catch ball | 4 | 6.5 | 1 | 1 | 1 | 1 | 1.25 |
| 5 | Climb | 1 | 6.5 | 1 | 2.5 | 1 | 1 | 1 |
| 6 | Crawl | 3.5 | 2.5 | 1 | 2 | 1 | 1 | 1 |
| 7 | Dodge | 1 | 1 | 1 | 1 | 1 | 1 | 6.5 |
| 8 | Drive | 6.25 | 6.75 | 1 | 1 | 1 | 1 | 2.25 |
| 9 | Guard | 5.5 | 6.75 | 4 | 1 | 1 | 1 | 1 |
| 10 | Headbutt | 1 | 1 | 1 | 1 | 7 | 1 | 1 |
| 11 | Hide | 2 | 2.5 | 1.25 | 2.5 | 1.75 | 1 | 6.25 |
| 12 | Hitting baseball | 4.5 | 4 | 1.75 | 1 | 1 | 1 | 1 |
| 13 | Jump | 1.75 | 1 | 3 | 5.5 | 1 | 1 | 1 |
| 14 | Kick | 1.75 | 2.25 | 7 | 2.75 | 1 | 1 | 1 |
| 15 | Open chest | 5.25 | 4.25 | 3.25 | 2.5 | 1 | 2 | 1 |
| 16 | Open door | 6.25 | 3.25 | 4.75 | 1 | 1 | 2 | 1 |
| 17 | Open menu | 3.75 | 6.25 | 2 | 1.75 | 1.75 | 1 | 1 |
| 18 | Pick item | 6.5 | 5.25 | 1.75 | 1 | 1 | 2.25 | 1 |
| 19 | Punch | 7 | 6.5 | 1.75 | 2.25 | 1 | 1 | 1 |
| 20 | Push box | 6.25 | 6.25 | 3.25 | 1 | 2 | 1 | 1 |
| 21 | Racket hitting | 5.75 | 4 | 1.75 | 1 | 1 | 1 | 1 |
| 22 | Reload gun | 4.75 | 5.75 | 2.25 | 1 | 1 | 1 | 1 |
| 23 | Roll body | 2.5 | 2 | 1 | 2.5 | 1 | 1 | 1 |
| 24 | Roll object | 6 | 6.25 | 3.25 | 1 | 2 | 1 | 1 |
| 25 | Row boat | 5.25 | 6.25 | 1.75 | 1 | 1 | 1 | 1 |
| 26 | Run | 1 | 3.5 | 2 | 5.5 | 1 | 1 | 1 |
| 27 | Select menu item | 5.5 | 4 | 3 | 2 | 1 | 2.25 | 1 |
| 28 | Shake item | 6.5 | 6 | 1 | 1 | 1 | 1 | 1 |
| 29 | Shift gear | 6.5 | 2.25 | 3.25 | 1 | 1 | 1 | 1 |
| 30 | Shoot | 5.75 | 5 | 1.5 | 1 | 1.25 | 1 | 1 |
| 31 | Slash | 6.25 | 5 | 2.5 | 1 | 1.75 | 1 | 1 |
| 32 | Steal | 6.5 | 3.25 | 1 | 1 | 1 | 1 | 1 |
| 33 | Stealth walking | 1 | 1.25 | 1 | 5.5 | 1 | 1 | 1 |
| 34 | Stop walking | 6 | 2.75 | 3.75 | 1.5 | 1 | 1 | 1 |
| 35 | Throw ball | 6.25 | 2.75 | 1 | 1 | 1 | 1 | 1 |
| 36 | Use item | 5.75 | 5.5 | 2 | 1.75 | 2 | 1 | 1 |
| 37 | View point change | 3.5 | 1 | 2.25 | 1 | 6.5 | 5 | 1.75 |
| 38 | Walk | 1.25 | 3.5 | 2 | 5.5 | 1 | 1 | 1 |
| 39 | Zoom-in | 4.5 | 5.75 | 2.5 | 1 | 2.25 | 1 | 1 |
| 40 | Zoom-out | 4.25 | 5.25 | 2.5 | 1 | 2 | 1 | 1 |

Most suitable body part
Most suitable alternative body part

**Figure 3. A set of suitable and alternative body part (7 as most suitable).**

**Racing-**"Drive" was most preferably performed using two-hands mimicking a driving-wheel gesture. Simultaneous actions such as "Shift gear" could be performed by stamping one foot to the left or right (shifting the gears up and down), "Break" and "Accelerate" by stamping the foot to 12 o'clock or 6'clock, and "Boost" by double-tapping one foot on the floor. **Adventure/Role-Playing-**Our participants preferred using the legs for navigation and head movement for "View point change". A palm gesture or a kick gesture could be used for the "Open Chest" and "Open Door" actions. "Pick Item" action could be optionally performed by staring with the eyes at a target for a short period of time (our participants recommended around 2-3 seconds), when a hand was not available. "Crawl" action could be performed by performing a continuous snake-like gesture with one hand. **Navigation-**"Walk", "Run", and "Stealth Walking" actions were most preferably performed using both legs. Simultaneously, other leg-preferred navigational actions including "Jump" and "Roll Body" could be performed using 1-hand. "Jump" could be simultaneously performed by facing a palm up and raising the hand, and "Roll Body" by facing a palm down and lowering the hand. Sometimes, depending on certain game situations, the use of body parts could possibly be swapped around, i.e., "Walk", "Run", and "Stealth Walking" actions could be optionally performed using two-hands on the sides of the body swinging back and forth, with the swinging velocity determining the different actions. At the same time, "Jump" action could be simultaneously performed by slightly raising one leg above the ground, and "Roll-Body" action could be performed by lowering the body by bending the knees. **System Commands-**During gameplay with certain body parts being occupied, "Zoom-in/out" action could be performed using either a hand or a leg; a clenched fist could indicate "Zoom-in" and an open palm can indicate "Zoom-out" or, alternatively, raise a foot to 45 degrees to indicate "Zoom-out" and lower the foot for "Zoom-in". "Open menu" could be performed by making a camera gesture (imitating a photo-taking gesture by having thumb and index finger of each hand resembling an L-shape sign, combining both hands to form a rectangle) or by dragging one foot from 12 o'clock to 6 o'clock or by performing a rotating movement with the head. "Select menu item" could be performed using a hand or the eyes to move the cursor, or by moving the legs to a different position (up, down, left, right) of the clock (three o'clock, six o'clock etc).

## DISCUSSION AND FUTURE WORK

Our results present a set of most suitable and alternative body parts for affecting game events. We found an interesting and potentially useful result, i.e., most of hand gestures can be achieved using similar leg gestures and vice versa, suggesting possible gesture transferability between hand and leg. This can significantly expands the bandwidth of interactions in gaming. Furthermore, one participant suggested the possible gesture transferability between left and right hands in cases where one hand is already assigned. As for leg gestures, our study indicates that the assignment of one leg is more preferable than the assignment of two legs, with participants commenting that two-leg gestures can be difficult to execute and can cause the gamer to lose body balance. Similar trends for hand gestures were found. "View Point Change" is largely limited to head with eye control as the most promising alternative. Torso action was the only and thus preferred body part for torso gestures. Eye input was promising for acquisition tasks.

Our work indicates that as gamers grow in experience they are inclined to develop a less literal, more symbolic, and more efficient unique gesture vocabulary. One possible reason is that veteran gamers tend to play games for longer periods of time and thus do not want to expend their energy on over-complicated gestures. Another possible explanation is that veteran gamers are more motivated to achieve challenges in games, thus they prefer more efficient gestures [10, 11]. Last, it may simply be due to the greater experience and understanding of video games in general of veteran gamers. Designers might well consider designing full-body game interfaces that accommodate varying levels of fatigue, player motivation and expertise. This might also imply that the same gesture may not be valid for all users, places [3, 8], or situations (e.g., gamepad might be preferred over a very long session of gameplay).

Designers may need to pay attention to system commands such as "Zoom-In/Out" and "Open Menu". Significantly, these abstract actions achieved low agreement scores, suggesting the need for new gestures for similar commands. These system commands might possibly suffer from a larger degree of freedom when compared to 2D interaction settings, thus resulting in diverse gesture preferences. However, this large degree of freedom also provides players with a greater array of potential input combinations. It may be beneficial to investigate methods to incorporate the variability of players' gestures (e.g., [2]) and to investigate the right degree of freedom for system commands and common game actions.

Our results posed learnability implications for game gestural interfaces. We conducted a follow-up informal interviews with three of our six veteran gamers regarding the resulting set of simultaneous gestures. Our veteran gamers commented that the proposed alternative body parts and gestures are essential for more effective, fast action gameplay but that they also require some time to learn and master. To assist learnability, it might be beneficial for designers to use the most suitable body parts and gestures for crucial game events (e.g., shoot), while using alternative body parts for the less important events (e.g., use item). Crucial game events are usually determined by designers as the most exciting or climactic actions, but game events may also be considered crucial because they are simply the most frequently used actions.

In future work we will comprehensively evaluate the proposed set of combined gestures. Other possible future works include an investigation of the human capacity to perform simultaneous gestures and an investigation of the simultaneous use of gestures in different types of games and contexts (public vs. non-public places).

## ACKNOWLEDGMENTS

We thank the members of RenLab, and thank the anonymous reviewers for their insightful comments.

## REFERENCES

1. Bianchi-Berthouze, N. Understanding the role of body movement in player engagement. *Human Computer Interaction 28*, 1 (2013), 40–75.
2. Fothergill, S., Mentis, H., Kohli, P., and Nowozin, S. Instructing people for training gestural interactive systems. In *Proc. CHI 2012*, ACM (2012), 1737–1746.
3. Freeman, D., LaPierre, N., Chevalier, F., and Reilly, D. Tweetris: A study of whole-body interaction during a public art event. In *Proc. C&C 2013*, ACM (2013), 224–233.
4. Gamespot. Rise of Nightmares Review, 2011. `http://www.gamespot.com/rise-of-nightmares/reviews/`.
5. Gerling, K., Livingston, I., Nacke, L., and Mandryk, R. Full-body motion-based game interaction for older adults. In *Proc. CHI 2012*, ACM (2012), 1873–1882.
6. Isbister, K., and DiMauro, C. Waggling the Form Baton: Analyzing Body- Movement-Based Design Patterns in Nintendo Wii Games, Toward Innovation of New Possibilities for Social and Emotional Experience. In *Whole Body Interaction*, Springer (2011).
7. Morris, M. R., Wobbrock, J. O., and Wilson, A. D. Understanding users' preferences for surface gestures. In *Proc. GI 2010*, CIPS (2010), 261–268.
8. Müller, J., Walter, R., Bailly, G., Nischt, M., and Alt, F. Looking glass: A field study on noticing interactivity of a shop window. In *Proc. CHI 2012*, ACM (2012), 297–306.
9. Nielsen, M., Störing, M., Moeslund, T. B., and Granum, E. A procedure for developing intuitive and ergonomic gesture interfaces for hci. In *Gesture-Based Communication in Human-Computer Interaction*, vol. 2915, Springer (2004), 409–420.
10. Nijhar, J., Bianchi-Berthouze, N., and Boguslawski, G. Does movement recognition precision affect the player experience in exertion games? In *Proc. INTETAIN 2011*. Springer, 2012, 73–82.
11. Pasch, M., Bianchi-Berthouze, N., van Dijk, B., and Nijholt, A. Movement-based sports video games: Investigating motivation and gaming experience. *Entertainment Computing 1*, 2 (2009), 49–61.
12. Wobbrock, J. O., Aung, H. H., Rothrock, B., and Myers, B. A. Maximizing the guessability of symbolic input. In *Proc. CHI EA 2005*, ACM (2005), 1869–1872.
13. Wobbrock, J. O., Morris, M. R., and Wilson, A. D. User-defined gestures for surface computing. In *Proc. CHI 2009*, ACM (2009), 1083–1092.

# KnowMe and ShareMe: Understanding Automatically Discovered Personality Traits from Social Media and User Sharing Preferences

**Liang Gou**
IBM Research - Almaden
San Jose, CA, USA
lgou@us.ibm.com

**Michelle X. Zhou**
IBM Research - Almaden
San Jose, CA, USA
mzhou@us.ibm.com

**Huahai Yang**
IBM Research - Almaden
San Jose, CA, USA
hyang@us.ibm.com

## ABSTRACT
There is much recent work on using the digital footprints left by people on social media to predict personal traits and gain a deeper understanding of individuals. Due to the veracity of social media, imperfections in prediction algorithms, and the sensitive nature of one's personal traits, much research is still needed to better understand the effectiveness of this line of work, including users' preferences of sharing their computationally derived traits. In this paper, we report a two-part study involving 256 participants, which (1) examines the feasibility and effectiveness of automatically deriving three types of personality traits from Twitter, including Big 5 personality, basic human values, and fundamental needs, and (2) investigates users' opinions of using and sharing these traits. Our findings show there is a potential feasibility of automatically deriving one's personality traits from social media with various factors impacting the accuracy of models. The results also indicate over 61.5% users are willing to share their derived traits in the workplace and that a number of factors significantly influence their sharing preferences. Since our findings demonstrate the feasibility of automatically inferring a user's personal traits from social media, we discuss their implications for designing a new generation of privacy-preserving, hyper-personalized systems.

## Author Keywords
Personality traits, Big 5 personality, basic values, fundamental needs, privacy, social media

## ACM Classification Keywords
H.5.2 Information Interfaces and Presentation : User Interfaces - evaluation/methodolody, theory and methods, K.4.1 Computers and society: Public policy issues - privacy

## INTRODUCTION
Numerous studies from Psychology to Behavioral Economics have shown that *personality*, which is an *"individual characteristic pattern of thought, emotion, and behavior, together with the psychological mechanisms–hidden or not–behind those patterns"* [12][1], influences a person's behavior and performance in the real world, including occupational proficiency (e.g., [3]) and economic decisions (e.g., [11]). Traditionally, standard psychometric tests (e.g., Big 5 personality inventory) are used to gauge one's personality, which however is impractical in many real world situations. For example, it would be difficult for a business to ask millions of its customers to take a personality test so they could receive more personalized services. Moreover, standard tests or surveys may not even exist for deriving certain personality traits, such as fundamental needs [11].

On the other hand, advances in Psycholinguistics have shown that it is feasible to *automatically* infer personality traits from one's linguistic footprints [39, 34]. In addition, the emergence of social media has prompted hundreds of millions of people to leave their linguistic footprints on the internet. A number of research efforts have already begun to utilize these footprints to acquire a deeper understanding of individuals, including inferring their demographics and political orientation [27], Big 5 personality [13], and task fitness [21].

Inspired by these works, we are developing a system that uses one's social media footprints (e.g., tweets) to automatically derive her personality traits. Instead of inferring personality traits based on people's online social activities, e.g., number of posts and votes, ours analyzes the language choices in their

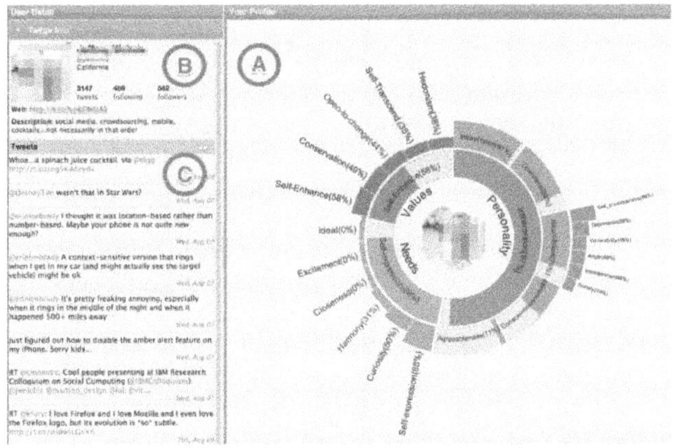


**Figure 1. User interface of the experimental system, KnowMe.**

[1]By this definition, personality traits include one's motivation and needs. In this paper, we use "personality", "personality traits", and "personal traits" interchangeably to refer to three types of traits, Big 5 personality, basic values, and fundamental needs.


*CHI 2014*, April 26 - May 01 2014, Toronto, ON, Canada

ACM 978-1-4503-2473-1/14/04$15.00.
http://dx.doi.org/10.1145/2556288.2557398

posts. Specifically, we develop a lexicon-based approach that predicts personality traits based on individual word choices in written samples. Our current model automatically computes three basic types of personality traits: Big 5 personality [15], fundamental needs [11], and basic values [29]. Figure 1 shows the portrait of an individual, including the three types of personality traits derived from the person's tweets. Table 1 lists all three traits and their factors.

Due to the veracity of social media, imperfections in computational inference, and the sensitive nature of one's personality traits, we are piloting our system with a limited group of users within our company. The main purpose is to answer two sets of questions about our system:

- How accurate are our system-derived personality traits?
  - How well do the derived traits match with the psychometric test scores?
  - How well do the derived traits match with our users' perception about themselves?
- Whether and how would users like to use/share the derived personality traits with others in an enterprise context?
  - What and with whom users would like to share the derived traits?
  - What are the perceived benefits and risks of sharing?
  - What factors affect users' sharing preferences of personality traits?

To answer these two sets of questions, we have designed and conducted a two-part study involving 256 participants from our company. In the first part, we derived participants' three types of traits from their tweets and compared them with their psychometric test scores. We also solicited the participants' perception of the derived traits. In the second part, we designed a questionnaire inquiring a participant's preferences and concerns of sharing her derived personality traits. We then analyzed how various factors influence their preferences.

Findings from our study are interest-provoking and promising. First, our findings show that the trait of basic human values derived from Twitter show correlation of marginal significance with the participants' psychometric test scores, and outperforms the models of Big 5 personality and fundamental needs. This demonstrates the feasibility of automatically deriving one's personality traits from social media with various factors, such as data variety and culture difference, impacting the accuracy of models. Second, over 61.5% participants are willing to share their derived traits in workplace. However, a number of factors, including the type of trait to be shared and the trait value, significantly influence their sharing preferences. This bears important implications for designing privacy-preserving, hyper-personalized systems that adapt to a user's personality traits and privacy preferences.

## RELATED WORK

### Personality Modeling and Computation

Our work on personality modeling is grounded in Psychology and Behavioral Economics (e.g., [15, 11, 29]). For example, our needs model is based on Psychology [23] and Marketing [11]. While we leverage existing psychological findings to identify personality traits to model, we build computational models to automatically infer these traits from a person's social media footprints.

| Trait | Definition |
|---|---|
| Big5 | *Openness-to-experience (+)*: the extent to which a person is open to experience a variety of activities |
| | *Conscientiousness (+)*: a tendency that a person acts in an organized or spontaneous way |
| | *Extraversion (+)*: a tendency to seek stimulation in the company of others |
| | *Agreeableness (+)*: a tendency to be compassionate and cooperative towards others |
| | *Neuroticism (-)*: the extent to which a person's emotion is sensitive to the environment |
| Basic Values | *Self-transcendence (+)*: showing concern for the welfare and interests of others |
| | *Conservation (-)*: emphasizing conformity, tradition, security |
| | *Self-enhancement (+)*: seeking personal success for oneself |
| | *Openness-to-change (+)*: emphasizing stimulation, self-direction |
| | *Hedonism (-)*: seeking pleasure and sensuous gratification for oneself |
| Needs | *Ideals (+)*: a desire for perfection |
| | *Harmony (+)*: appreciating other people, their feelings |
| | *Closeness (+)*: being connected to family and setting up home |
| | *Self-expression (+)*: discovering and asserting one's own identity |
| | *Excitement (+)*: upbeat emotions, and having fun |
| | *Curiosity (+)*: a desire to discover and grow |

**Table 1. Three types of personality traits to share. + and - indicate a trait positively or negatively perceived in the Western Culture [20, 11, 29].**

Our approach of inferring personality traits from text builds on existing work in psycholinguistic analysis (e.g., [39, 34]). However, we extend the existing work by constructing our own psycholinguistic dictionaries to derive traits that have not been computationally modeled before, such as fundamental needs and basic human values.

Our work is related to many efforts on inferring people's traits from various digital footprints. They include predicting Big 5 personality from essays and conversation scripts [22] and emails [30], and inferring political orientation[27] and emotional states [8] from Twitter.

Closest to ours, Golbeck et al. use psycholinguistic analysis to predict Big 5 personality from social media (e.g., from Facebook [14] and from Twitter [13]). However, we go beyond Big 5 personality to derive two additional traits, basic values and fundamental needs, which have not been computed before. Because of our extended computational capability, our study also aims at understanding how our users would use different types of traits in their lives and the implications of such use (e.g., further loss of privacy).

### Privacy, Contextual Integrity, and Personality

There has been extensive research on understanding users' privacy preferences regarding to different types of personal data in HCI [17]. Lots of efforts focus on personal data involving personal communications (e.g. email and social media) [25, 31], and mobile and location-based activities [19]. However, few have examined people's privacy and sharing preferences about their own personality traits. In contrast, our study here is on investigating users' privacy and sharing preferences of personality traits.

Another related thread of research investigates how people's traits impact their privacy concerns. For example, Smith [32] found people's privacy concerns are related to their trust and risk propensity. Research also shows that certain dimensions of Big Five personality traits influence one's privacy concerns [20]. Compared to these works, ours specifically studies how a number of factors, beyond Big 5 personality, influence one's privacy preferences of their own personality traits.

In this paper, our study design on understanding users' privacy concerns is rooted in the contextual integrity theory [24]. This theory examines users' privacy concerns from the violations and changes of context, actors, attributes, and transmission principles, and has been employed to examine information privacy in HCI (e.g., [2, 31]). Similar to these works, our design explicitly investigates users' privacy around the four aspects: context (e.g., benefits and risks in workplace), actors (who have access to the traits), attributes (personality traits and their properties), and transmission principles(tratis granularity). However, unlike other privacy studies, ours specifically focuses on soliciting and analyzing users' opinions on revealing and sharing their own personality traits.

## METHOD

### Experimental System: KnowMe

We have built an experimental system, *KnowMe*, which allows a user to login with his twitter ID, collects the user's most recent 200 public tweets, and automatically derives three types of personality traits from the tweets: Big 5 personality, basic values, and fundamental needs. Our system uses only 200 tweets, since they provide a reasonably representative sample that can produce within 10% rank of the results obtained using the person's thousands of tweets.

The three models (Big 5, basic values, and fundamental needs) use a lexicon-based analysis by calculating correlations between personal traits and the usage of certain words or word categories. For example, if a person uses lots of words of 1st person plural , such as "we" and "us", this person tends to have high agreeableness of Big 5 and high self-transcendence of basic values. In particular, our Big 5 personality and basic values [6] use words and word categories derived from the LIWC dictionary [39, 34], and our needs model [38] uses a custom dictionary. Each trait is associated with a collection of words identified in the dictionaries.

To develop a custom dictionary, we used a hybrid empirical and computational approach. First, we designed and conducted large-scale, psychometric studies on Amazon Mechanical Turk to collect training data. For each needs dimension, we designed an item-based survey that collects a person's psychometric scores describing his needs along that dimension. In the survey, we also collected participant-generated text describing a specific need. We collected the survey results from over 5000 turkers. Second, based on the collected data, we analyzed how the set of words extracted from participant-generated text are positively or negatively correlated with each needs dimension. As a result, we constructed a custom dictionary. We then built a statistical model that uses the dictionary to predict needs scores along each dimension.More details can be found in [38, 6]. With the dictionaries and their correlation with personality traits, we can derive people's traits from their writings by calculating the use of words.

Our system allows a user to interactively examine the derived personality. Figure 1 shows the system interface with three areas: three types of derived traits (panel A), twitter profile (panel B), and tweets used to derive the traits (Panel C).

### Participants

We first identified 1325 colleagues in our company who have Twitter presence and also produced at least 200 tweets. We invited each of them via email to participate in our study. 625 of them responded to our invitation, among which 256 completed the study. The high incompletion rate (369 out of 625 started but did not complete) is mainly due to the lengthy survey. Among the people who completed the study, almost half of them were from the United States (42.0%), with the rest of them from Europe (32.1%) and other parts of the world (25.9%), ranging from 30 to 45 in age, which is representative of our company or alike, i.e. the target population of the study.

### Overall Study Design

To answer the two sets of questions posed in our Introduction, we designed and conducted a two-part study. In this study, we asked each participant to use our experimental system (KnowMe) and complete a two-part online survey. In the first part, our goal is to collect "ground truth" of the three types of personality traits through psychometric tests. The second part is to elicit users' privacy and sharing preferences of their personality traits. On average, the whole study took about 45 minutes for a participant to complete.

### Part I. Assessing Automatically Derived Personality Traits

This study was designed to gauge the accuracy of our system-derived personality traits from Twitter, which was assessed from two aspects: comparing the derived traits with psychometric test scores and with users' perception.

***Psychometric Tests.*** We asked each participant to take three sets of psychometric tests: 50-item Big 5 personality test (adopted from www.ipip.ori.org), 21-item basic values test (adopted from [29]), and 52-item fundamental needs test developed by us as described above.

***Perception of Derived Traits*.** Each participant was first given a video tutorial on how to use our experimental system. The participants were then asked to login with their Twitter ID and interactively explore their own personal traits derived from their tweets. Our system also provided detailed explanation for each trait. While examining the derived traits, they were also asked to rate *how well* each type of the derived trait matched with their perceptions of themselves on a five-likert scale (1 being "not at all" and 5 being "perfect"). In our study, the participants were never given their psychometric test scores and asked to rate their scores shown in the system to avoid the interaction effect of psychometric tests.

### Part II. Understanding Trait Sharing Preferences

Guided by the framework of contextual integrity [24], we designed a set of questions to investigate users' privacy preferences around the four key aspects: attributes, actors, context and transmission principles.

***Attributes of information.*** The *Attributes* dimension defines the type of information to be shared. In our context, we hypothesized that *trait type, trait value*, and *trait accuracy*, all impact users' sharing preferences.

*Trait type.* Since the three types of personality traits reveal a person's characteristics from different aspects, we hypothesize that people would have different privacy concerns for different traits:

- **H1a**. People have different preferences for sharing three types of personality traits.
- **H1b**. Within each type of trait, people also have different sharing preferences for its sub-traits.

*Trait value.* We also hypothesize that *trait value* would impact sharing behavior, since people may be more willing to reveal their "positive" (e.g., friendliness) but not the negative traits (e.g., emotional unstability):

- **H2a**. The values of personality traits affect people's sharing preferences.
- **H2b**. People are likely to share more high-value positive traits.

*Trait accuracy.* Previous study shows that people have shown a high privacy concern about inaccurate information of themselves [33], and have less confidence in sharing such information. We thus hypothesize:

- **H3a**. The accuracy of traits impacts people's sharing behavior.
- **H3b**. People tend to share traits that are accurate.

***Actors.*** One important factor concerning privacy is with whom the information to be shared. We hypothesize that users' willingness to share information especially their personal trais may vary depending on the recipients of the information [4, 25]:

- **H4a**. People have different preferences about sharing their personality traits with different audience.

For each type of traits, we asked users' sharing preferences with four groups: "public", "distant colleagues", "management", and "close colleagues" [25].

Since previous work shows that certain dimensions of Big 5 personality influence one's privacy concerns [18, 20], we also examined the participants' own characteristics, specifically, their three types of personality traits: Big 5, basic values and needs. We hypohypothesize:

- **H4b**. Users' three types of personality traits impact their sharing behavior.

Moreover, we investigated the impacts of their general disposition towards privacy and adoption of new technologies [26]. In particular, we used five questions, including three items of Disposition to Value Privacy (DTVP) [36], and two items of Technology Innovativeness (INNV) [1].

***Context.*** Context also influences people's privacy preferences [24]. Our context was users' perceived benefits and risks of sharing their personality traits in an enterprise. We hypothesize that people would balance the benefits and risks when assessing privacy concerns [37]. To do so, we asked the participants to state the expected benefits and risks for sharing each type of personality trait in the work place.

***Transmission Principles.*** Transmission principles indicate the types of constraints imposed on the information flow from senders to recipients. One such constraint is the granularity of information to be shared, which often impacts people's sharing preferences [19, 10]. To test this aspect, we asked users' preference of sharing their personality traits at three levels: "none", "range" (ordinal scale), and "numeric" (precise score). We also sought participants' input on desired controls for sharing their personality traits.

## RESULTS AND ANALYSES

Among 650 invited participants, 256 of them completed our study, and 224 provided complete answers to all questions. Here we report our findings to answer the two sets of questions raised in the Introduction.

### Accuracy of Personality Traits from Social Media

To answer the first set of questions, we compared the system-derived personality traits from Twitter with those from psychometric tests. We also gathered the participants' perception about their derived traits.

#### *Comparing Derived Traits with Psychometric Scores*

Correlational analyses were performed to compare the derived traits and the psychometric measures. One straightforward approach is to calculate the correlation coefficients for all individual factors of all the traits. The resulting coefficients were in the range of $0.05 < r < 0.2$, consistent with the findings from previous work of this nature [13, 6]. Because all of our traits (personality, needs and values) are multiple dimensional constructions, we would like to use a measure that takes into account the multi-dimensionality and structure of the traits. For example, the factors of a trait often correlate each other: within Big 5, *extroversion* and *agreeableness* are highly correlated ($r$=0.36, $p$=0.001); within basic values, *conservation* and *open to change* are negatively correlated ($r$=-0.24, $p$=0.003), and so on. In addition, a single correlation measure gives a sense of overall confidence on the models, and is easier to interpret than a multitude of correlation coefficients. To this end, we used RV-coefficient [28] to examine the overall correlation between derived traits and the corresponding psychometric scores. RV coefficient is a multi-variate generalization of squared Pearson correlation coefficient, and it measures the closeness of two sets of points in a multiple dimensional space.

Over the entire sample ($N$=224), our analyses showed that the RV-coefficient tests for three models were not significantly strong and varied from model to model. Specifically, the model for human basic values showed a marginal significance ($rv$=0.026, $p$=0.06), and the scores were not significant for Big 5 ($rv$=0.006, $p$=0.83) and fundamental needs ($rv$=0.013, $p$=0.61). A power analysis was also conducted because of small effect size here. Since there is no existing tool to conduct power analysis for RV-coefficient correlation, we used a power analysis for general correlation analysis [7]. We selected the trait feature with best correlation in each category for our power analysis, because we are estimating power of the models in the best case. To reach .05 significance level for correlations, the power is $\beta$=0.43 for human basic values model (using the feature of *Open-to-Change*, $r$=0.119), and $\beta$=0.40 for Big 5 model (using *Agreeableness*, $r$=0.115) and $\beta$=0.58 for fundamental needs model (using *Harmony*, $r$=0.144). This indicates that there is insufficient statistical power to detect the small correlations due to the relative small sample size. It is difficult to collect real world data such as ours in an enterprise setting. Even with the relative small sample size, the correlation is still close to be significant for the basic values model. With a much larger sample size, it is reasonable to assume that the correlations would be better for all three models.

The results suggest some interesting observations. It first shows the feasibility of automatically deriving one's personality traits from Tweets even with lots of noises (such as short posts, slang and abbreviations) in a real world. Secondly, in terms of effectiveness and accuracy, there are several possible factors with large impact identified from this study. For example, people often maintain multiple personalities through different channels: twitter might be used for professional and work purpose, and facebook reveal more personal life [14]; western and eastern culture have different value systems [35] and so on. The details are presented in discussion section.

### Comparing Derived Traits with User Perception

Each participant rated how accurate they *thought* the derived traits were. Figure 2 shows that the means of all ratings are above 3 ("somewhat") out of 5 ("perfect"), with 3.4 ($sd$ = 1.14), 3.13 ($sd$ = 1.17), 3.39 ($sd$ = 1.34) for Big 5 personality, values, and needs, respectively. Although subjective, the ratings suggested that the system-derived traits somewhat matched with users' own perception. We consider this aspect important since people often behave based on their perception (e.g., deciding on whether to share a trait depending on its accuracy).

## R2. Users' Sharing Preferences of Personality Traits

We analyzed the effects of various factors by estimating the sharing preferences with a generalized linear mixed model with Poisson log link function. The measurement is the participants' disclosed preference ("none", "range value" and "numeric value") on each type of trait.

| Factor | Level Comparision | Hypo. |
|---|---|---|
| $Trait\ Type^{***}$ | $PD(Values) < PD(Big5)^{***}$<br>$PD(Values) < PD(Needs)^{***}$ | $H1a$:+ |
| $Big5^{***}$ | $PD(Neuro.) < PD(Open.)^{***}$<br>$PD(Neuro.) < PD(Consci.)^{**}$<br>$PD(Neuro.) < PD(Extr.)^{*}$<br>$PD(Neuro.) < PD(Agrb.)^{*}$ | $H1b$:+ |
| $Values$ | $N/A$ | $H1b$:− |
| $Needs$ | $N/A$ | $H1b$:− |

**Table 2. Main effects of traits on sharing preferences ($PD(*)$ is probability of information disclosure. * p<0.05, ** p<0.01, *** p<0.001)**

- Trait type to be shared (Big 5, basic values, and needs)
- Trait value to be shared (coded "low", "medium", and "high" based the ranked percentile in the sample population)
- Perceived trait accuracy (5 levels of user ratings)
- Recipient ("public", "distant colleagues", "management", and "close colleagues")
- Users' personality traits (Big 5, basic values, and needs)

Since our analysis did not identify any significant effects of the participants' general disposition to privacy and technology innovativeness over their sharing preferences, we dropped these two factors. The final model shows adequate fitness with 1.7 DevianceValue/DevianceDF ratio (as a thumb of rule, a good ratio is approximately 1).

### Effects of Traits

We analyzed the effects of trait type, value, and perceived accuracy on users' sharing preferences.

*Effects of trait type.* The type of traits impacts participants' sharing preferences in multiple ways (Table 2). First, the type of traits has significant effect on user's sharing preferences ($p$-$value$<0.001). Our participants prefered to share their values trait *the least*, compared to the other two types of traits, with needs ($\beta$=-0.065, $p$-$value$<0.005) and Big 5 ($\beta$=-0.08, $p$-$value$<0.001). Our hypothesis **H1a** is thus supported. Such findings were corrobrated by the participants' comments on the risks of sharing one type of trait. For example, one participant stated "*(values) seems VERY personal information, as it goes to the heart of what makes someone "tick". I think most people would feel very vulnerable if this information were shared in a work environment*". In addition, some were less willing to share traits that could not be easily observed, "*A few of these (needs) traits may not be easily observed in a work setting (e.g., curiosity, ideal)*".

Certain trait dimensions also impact the sharing preferences (Table 2). In Big 5, *neuroticism* has a significantly lower probability to be shared compared with other four dimensions ($PD(*)$ indicating the expressed probability of sharing a trait). However, we did not observe any differences among trait dimensions in basic values or needs. Hypothesis **H1b** is thus supported for the Big 5 trait, but not for the other two.

*Effects of trait value.* The effects of trait value is only observed for basic values ($p$-$value$= 0.001), but not for Big 5

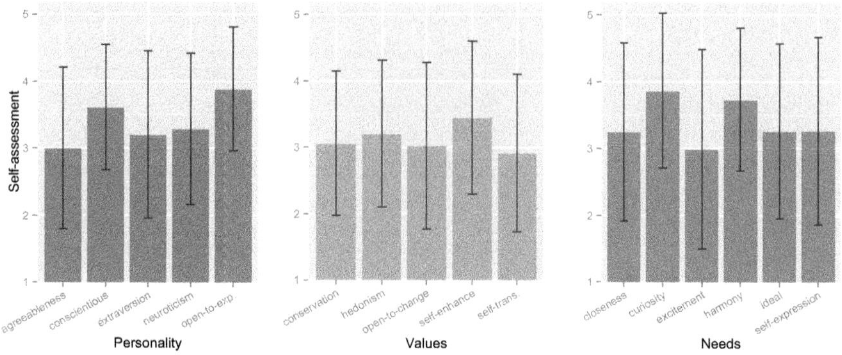


Figure 2. Average self-assessment ratings for traits of personality, values and needs.

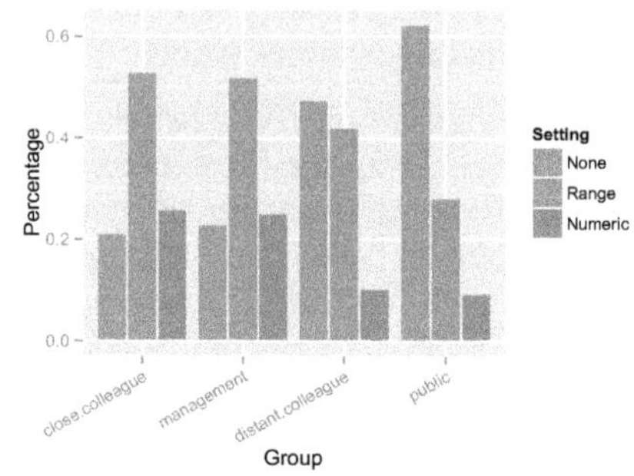


Figure 3. Overall sharing setting for four recipient groups.

| Type | Trait | Interaction with Score |
|---|---|---|
| Big 5 | Openness (+) | $PD(High) > PD(Low)^{**}$ |
| | Conscientiousness (+) | $PD(High) > PD(Low)^{*}$ |
| | Agreeableness (+) | $PD(High) > PD(Low)^{**}$ |
| | Neuroticism (-) | $PD(High) < PD(Low)^{**}$ |
| Values | Conservation (-) | $PD(High) < PD(Low)^{*}$ |
| | Hedonism (-) | $PD(High) < PD(Low)^{*}$ |
| Needs | Ideal (+) | $PD(High) > PD(Low)^{\circ}$ |
| | Self-Expression (+) | $PD(High) < PD(Low)^{\circ}$ |

**Table 3. Interaction among trait value and type over sharing perferences ($PD(*)$ is probability of information disclosure. ○ p<0.1, * p<0.05, ** p<0.01, *** p<0.001)**

| Factors | | Types of Trait to Be Shared | | |
|---|---|---|---|---|
| Type | Trait | Big 5 | Values | Needs |
| Big 5 | Openness-to-exp. | **-.075*** | **-.061** | **-.0072*** |
| | Conscientiousness | **-.081*** | **-.110*** | **-.0039** |
| | Extraversion | **.094*** | .032 | **.0011*** |
| | Agreeableness | -.031 | -.038 | -.0021 |
| | Neuroticism | -.016 | -.018 | -.0034° |
| Values | Hedonism | .042° | **.103*** | **.0081*** |
| | Open-to-change | .041° | .005 | .0020 |
| | Conservation | .041° | .035 | -.0029 |
| | Self-transcendence | .050° | .051° | -.0086 |
| | Self-enhancement | **-.065** | **-.086*** | **-.0058** |
| Needs | Ideals | **-.116*** | **-.132*** | **-.0011*** |
| | Harmony | **.062*** | .040 | .0044° |
| | Closeness | **.110*** | **.085*** | **.0075*** |
| | Self-expression | **-.062*** | -.051° | .0034 |
| | Excitement | .038 | **.158*** | .0049° |
| | Curiosity | .022 | **.058*** | .0010 |

**Table 4. Impacts of participants' personality traits from psychometric tests over sharing preferences (showing $\beta$ scores in the model. ° p<0.1, * p<0.05, ** p<0.01, *** p<0.001)**

nor needs. Table 3 shows the interactions among the type of trait and trait value. For Big 5, our participants prefered to disclose high *Openness, Conscientiousness*,and *Agreeableness*, but *not* to share high *Neuroticism*. For basic values, people preferred not to share high *Conservation* and *Hedonism*. For needs, people were willing to reveal high *Ideals*. In summary, both hypotheses **H2a** and **H2b** are partially supported: trait value affects people's sharing preferences but their preferences vary by the type of trait.

*Effects of perceived trait accuracy*. We also observed significant effects of the participants' perceived accuracy of the derived traits on their sharing preferences across all three types of traits (all *p-values*<0.001). Our analyses showed that the participants prefered to share traits they perceived "perfect", compared with other perceived accuracy levels (all $\beta > 0$ and *p-values*<0.01). The preference of sharing inaccurate traits ("not at all") is low, compared with other accuracy levels (all $\beta < 0$ and *p-values*<0.05). This suggests that the participants were highly sensitive to the accuracy of the derived traits because inaccuracy could cause potential misunderstanding. Hypothesis **H3a** and **H3b** are thus supported.

### Effects of Actors

*Effects of Recipient Type*. Figure 3 shows the participants' sharing preferences over different groups of recipients. Among all the participants, 61.5% of participants were willing to disclose their traits and share more with close colleagues and management than with others. Such sharing differences are statistically significant: ($\beta_{\{close|management\} vs. \{distant|public\}} < 0, p < 0.001$). However, there was no significant difference among sharing with management and close colleagues. We did not find any interactions among the recipient factor and other factors. This suggests that the participants' sharing preferences for different recipients were consistent across all three types of traits. Thus, hypothesis **H4a** is partially supported: recipient has main effects on people's sharing preferences, but has no influence on the type of trait to be shared.

*Effects of Users' Personality Traits*. We found that the participants' personality traits also have an impact on their sharing preferences. Table 4 shows the regression coefficients ($\beta$) measuring the effects of their personality traits. As shown, certain dimensions of the participants' personality traits significantly impact their sharing preferences. For example, *extrovertion* positively impacts one's sharing preferences for Big 5 and needs, but not for basic values. Certain dimensions consistently influences the three types of traits to be shared. For example, *conscientiousness* negatively impacts the participants' sharing preferences of all three types of traits. The hypothesis **H4b** is thus supported.

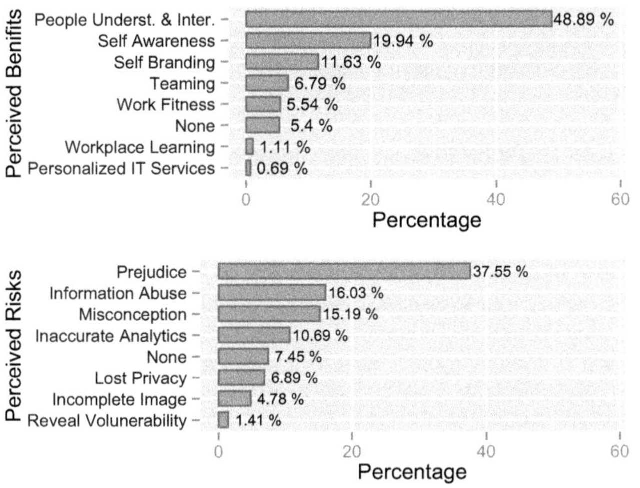


**Figure 4. Distribution of the perceived benefits and risks for sharing three types of traits.**

## Perceived Benefits and Risks

Our participants voiced a variety of benefits and risks of sharing their personality. Two coders independently read all completed responses ($225 \times 3 \times 2 = 1344$) and categorized the benefits and risks. After several iterations of discussion, two coders achieved an inter-coder reliability with Cohen's Kappa = 0.94 and 0.95 for benefits and risks, respectively.

Figure 4 shows the distribution of expected benefits and risks over three types of traits. Eight types of benefits and eight types of risks were extracted. Among the benefits, the top one was *People Understanding and Interaction* (48.89%). They mentioned that sharing personal traits would help "people understand each other, facilitate communication and collaboration", and "motivating or rewarding people". *Self awareness*(19.94%) and *Self-Branding* (11.63%) were also among the top-rated benefits. By *Self-awareness*, participants talked about "understanding my strength and weakness", while *Self branding* were meant for building one's own brand to gain recognition. Other interesting benefits included *Teaming* (6.79%) and *Work Fitness* (5.54%).

For perceived risks, participants frequently mentioned about their concerns of *Prejudice*(37.55%). Participants stated the risk of "being pigeon-holed with stereotypes, and assumptions". With the risk of *Information Abuse*(16.03%), participants were afraid that others might use their personal traits to manipulate them or management misuses their personal traits for performance assessment. Participants also mentioned other types of potential risks, including *Misinterpretation*(15.19%) referring to the potential misunderstanding of traits due to a lack of knowledge. Interestingly, only a small portion of participants mentioned the potential risk of "Loss of Privacy (6.89%)".

## Preferred Control Mechanisms

We also asked participants' suggestions about desired features and methods to control the sharing of personal traits. The coded results included eleven categories of desired con-

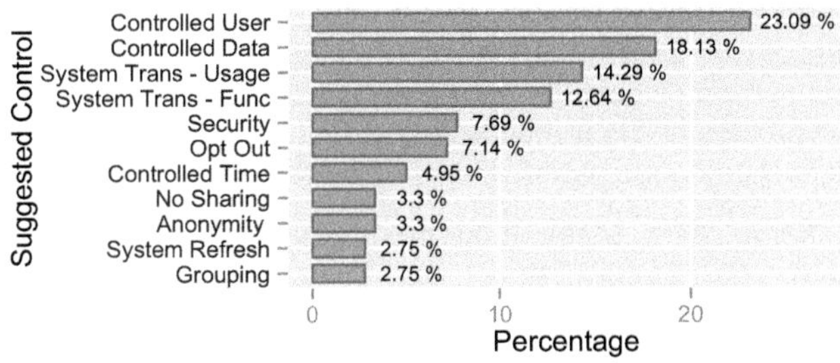


**Figure 5. Suggested controls for sharing personality traits.**

trols(Cohen's Kappa = 0.93), as shown in Figure 5. The top suggested feature was (23.09%) to support *Controlled Users*, "fully control of who can access their personal traits", "sharing traits with selected people", and etc. *Controlled Data* was recommended by 18.13% participants, including updating, editing, and deleting user data. The rest also mentioned desire functions to provide with *System Transparence* in terms of its functions(14.29%) and its usage (12.64%).

As discussed below, the participants' suggestions provided a basis for designing a privacy-preserving, personalized system.

## IMPLICATIONS

The findings from our study present several important implications for designing a new generation of *hyper-personalized* systems, which are capable of acquiring a much deeper understanding of users based on their personal traits, and tailoring the interactions to the users based on their personality.

### Support of System Transparency

Since personality uniquely distinguishes one individual from another, many of our participants considered it very personal information. On the other hand, the participants also wished to learn about the personality of their own and others to help improve self awareness and branding, and workplace collaboration. To make such a system effective and prevent its potential abuse, our participants voiced the desire of system transparency from two main aspects: system usage and function.

First, usage wise, the system should clearly explain the meaning of each trait and intended use. For example, one participant desired *"Existence of a clear legend that states exactly what do those characteristics refer to. It might happen that people could understand something else from the name... and this should be explained very carefully"*. Users also desire concrete usage examples, *"Give some examples how others can use of misuse/misinterpret the data. Good examples with benefits and risk (as you are researching) are key"*.

Second, functionally, the system should be prescriptive and clearly states what it is capable of and its limitations. For example, one participant indicated the system's *"ability to mark that certain attributes are inaccurate conveying the inability of system to gauge them properly."*. As another commented, *"I consider to be important to inform how many entries were taken into consideration for having such results"*, the system should also be able to explain where the results are derived from to make the results more trustworthy.

#### Mixed-Initiative Privacy Preserving

Many participants (61.5%) indicated their willingness to share their personality traits with others if their privacy could be protected. Their input suggests that both users and the system should take initiatives to protect the users' privacy.

*What to share.* Many of our participants explicitly stated that they want to control the granularity of personality traits to be shared. For example, one commented *"In this system maybe being able to switch off sections of information - maybe to allow sharing of values but not personality and needs"*. On the other hand, some participants wished the system to assess the risk of sharing certain types of information. Specifically, they want the system to provide *risk ratings* of sharing different types of traits based on *"analysis of how traits are perceived by others and the impact sharing this information might have"*. Based on the findings presented in the previous section, we believe that a system should be able to recommend proper privacy settings based on the users' concerns (e.g., trait type and value).

*Whom to share with.* The second most voiced concern is the recipient of the information. Participants wished to specify the recipient themselves and to *"approve explicitly the list of people who will receive this information. In that way I will validate the impact of sharing the information"*.

It is interesting to note that quite a few participants wanted to be alerted or know when someone is accessing their profiles. One wished to *"see who is watching / visiting my profile"*; the other stated *"a social listening feedback loop that might be able to show a person what others might perceive or be able to derive about you from your semi-public disclosure of information. This would allow someone to be aware of what is being shared with others, and managed that as appropriate"*. While knowing who are accessing the information might provide a sense of protection for the information owners, it may violate the privacy of those who do not wish their system usage to be monitored and publicized. As a compromise, the system could recommend to a user with a list of potential people whom to share information with, and explain the risks and benefits of sharing information with these people.

*When to share.* Quite a few participants voiced the importance of controlling *when* to share their personality traits. For example, one participant stated *"when to share is key. We do not want to show to the new manager that I am a liberal, future thinking and creative mind if he do not appreciate that behavior. We may need to set up the background personally prior to share such results"*. The ability to control when to share also provides users a sense of protection especially when they feel volunerable: *"want to decide whether continue or stop sharing information from specific times in your life, so you can protect insights from tough personal times"*. In addition to timing, participants also want to control *sharing frequency*–how often to share, an important parameter in protecting privacy. From the system standpoint, it could help a user automatically track her "downtime" and reminds the user to readjust the sharing preferences. *Where to share.* Participants also wish to control the channel where to share their personality traits. They suggested a number of channels, from paper printout, to email, to online sharing, depending on the context. Similar to deciding on other factors, it would be helpful for the system to assess the risks of each channel and help users make informed decisions.

#### User-Assisted Personality Discovery

In our study, it took our participants about 40 minutes on average to complete the three psychometric surveys. Our *automated* computational approach to deriving one's personality traits reduces users' manual efforts on taking the surveys. However, our computational models have limitations due to many factors, e.g., analytic inaccuracy, data quality, and culture influences (see Discussion section). For example, one participant stated *"My values in this field I believe is totally wrong I have always seen myself being open to change and self enhancement"*. To compensate for the imperfections in analytics, we believe it is critical to allow users to interactively amend and mark the derived results. Recent research has found that such an approach is feasible and effective, since users are willing and able to correct system mistakes and improve the quality of the system over time [16].

Based on our participants' input, we have summarized several approaches for a system like ours to allow users to help improve automated personality discovery. First, the system should allow users to amend inaccurate analysis results. As our participants stated, they want the *"ability to adjust the results where you feel the system has given you an inaccurate score"*. In this case, user amendaments, especially collective amendaments from multiple users, will help the system learn about its weaknesses and improve these areas. Second, the system should allow users to *"comment on areas where I disagree with the results.... and let others draw a more true and pure conclusion"*. Such user agreements and disagreements will help the system learn what is/is not working. Third, the system should allow users to select the data for deriving their personality traits. For example, one participant stated *"You should be able to specifically exclude specific tweets from the calculation, you might have had a tweet that was accidental or not reflective of your personality"*. As indicated by the findings in [16], the "power" given to users may cause potential system abuse, where some users might manipulate the results and data for their own personal advantages (e.g., purposefully portraying a false personality). In such cases, a system must be able to detect and prevent potential misuses.

### DISCUSSION

#### Data Variety and Model Effectiveness

To contain the scope of our study, we have applied psycholinguistic analysis to a person's tweets to derive his three types of personality traits: Big 5, human values, and fundamenal needs. Although separate efforts have shown that Big 5 can be derived from different data sources, including essays [22], emails [30], and social media [14], it is unknown as which data sources would be most effective in deriving one's Big 5, let alone the other two types of traits in our model.

Since a person often produces different types of linguistic footprints (e.g., tweets, emails, and forum posts), a natural extension of our work is to investigate the use of different data sources in personality analysis. This is however a non-trivial task as there are many nuances in one's verbal communications depending on the context. For example, one participant in our study considered Twitter a branding channel and expresses only work-related content, *"I desire to keep my personal and professional lives separate.... and thus only share work-related content on twitter. This maintains the 'brand' image I've cultivated for years."*. To make it more challenging, people's certain personality, e.g., motivations and needs, may change triggered by significant life events (e.g., becoming a parent) [11]. This implies that new data should be used to derive one's up-to-date personality. Morever, some people maintain "multiple personalities" even using the same communication channel: *"I have been concerned though that my Work Twitter account is seperate from my personal Twitter account and how would the system understand me fully? "*. People may also intentionally mask their own identity, *"My twitter account is used to promote my company - I try not to put my own values or views in it"*.

To gain a deeper understanding of different data sources, we see several interesting research topics. One is to collect a person's linguistic footprints from multiple sources and characterize the data by multiple dimensions (e.g., availability, veracity, and life span). We can then apply our model to collected data to test the capability of different data sources. Another interesting topic is how to consolidate multiple personalities derived from different data sources. This may require a hybrid approach where both users and systems provide input to reconcile the differences in derived personalities.

### Cultural and Language Influence

Our current personality model is based on well-known psychological models developed under the Western culture. For example, our needs model is based on Maslow's hierarchy of needs, which reflects the values of twentieth-century Western middle-class males and is hardly culture neutral. In addition, our current model can only process English input. As seen from the demographics of our participants, most of them (74.1%) were rooted in the Western culture. It is thus unknown whether and how well our current work is applicable to individuals under other cultures especially a vastly different culture (e.g., Chinese).

There are numerous research efforts in investigating cultural influences on personality [35]. The findings from our current study also suggest possible cultural influences on our results. For example, our participants' personality-sharing preferences reflected cultural influence, as they prefered to share individualist traits valued by the Western culture [35], such as openness and idealism. Moreover, some of our participants voiced how the interpretation of each trait may be influenced by culture. One participant commented " *The term 'Family' for instance has very different meaning between people of different cultures and you can't expect universal understanding or acceptance of the terms*". To truely understand cultural influences on our model, further studies are needed. One is to extend our current study to a population under a different culture (e.g., Chinese).

Besides cultural influences, language proficiency also influences the derived personality. As suggested by previous effort [9], we will need language-specific personality models instead of just translating a reference model (American English) into a destination language (e.g., Dutch). Second, we can also "culturize" our existing personality model by incorporating culture-specific personality factors (e.g., Chinese personality factors in [5]).

## CONCLUSION

In this paper, we presented a two-part study that examined (1) the accuracy of three types of personality traits derived from Twitter and (2) how users would prefer to share these traits in an enterprise setting. In the first part of study, our findings show there is small effect size for the correlation among the personality trait scores derived from Tweets and psychometric tests, and the model of basic values outperforms the models of Big 5 personality and fundamental needs. This demonstrates the potential feasibility of automatically deriving one's personality traits from social media with various factors impacting the accuracy of models. In the second part of the study, our results indicate that over 61.5% users are willing to share their derived traits in the workplace, and a number of factors, including the users' own personality and the perceived benefits/risks, significiantly influence the users' sharing preferences. Distilled from these findings, important implications have also been discussed for guiding the design of a new generation of privacy-preserving, hyper-personalized systems.

## ACKNOWLEDGEMENT

We would like to thank the reviewers for their invaluable comments, and all participants for their contributions to this study. We also want to thank Dr. Heng Xu and Ms. Na Wang for their suggestion on this study.

## REFERENCES

1. Agarwal, R., Ahuja, M., Carter, P., and Gans, M. Early and late adopters of IT innovations: extensions to innovation diffusion theory. In *Proc. DIGIT '98* (1998), 1–18.
2. Barkhuus, L. The mismeasurement of privacy: using contextual integrity to reconsider privacy in HCI. In *Proceedings of the SIGCHI Conference on Human Factors in Computing Systems*, CHI '12, ACM (New York, NY, USA, 2012), 367376.
3. Barrick, M. R., and Mount, M. K. The big five personality dimensions and job performance: a metaanalysis. *Personnel psychology 44*, 1 (1991), 1–26.
4. Bellotti, V., and Sellen, A. Design for privacy in ubiquitous computing environments. In *Proc. ECSCW '93* (1993), 77–92.
5. BOND, M. H. Localizing the imperial outreach the big five and more in chinese culture. *American Behavioral Scientist 44*, 1 (2000), 63–72.
6. Chen, J., Hsieh, G., Mahmud, J., and Nichols, J. Understanding individuals personal values from social media word use. In *To appear in CSCW '2014* (2014).

7. Cohen, J. *Statistical power analysis for the behavioral sciencies*. Routledge, 1988.
8. De Choudhury, M., Counts, S., and Horvitz, E. Predicting postpartum changes in emotion and behavior via social media. In *Proc. CHI'2013* (2013), 3267–3276.
9. De Raad, B., Perugini, M., Hrebckov, M., and Szarota, P. Lingua franca of personality taxonomies and structures based on the psycholexical approach. *Journal of Cross-Cultural Psychology 29*, 1 (1998), 212–232.
10. Eriksson, E., Artman, H., and Swartling, A. The secret life of a persona. In *Proc. CHI' 2013* (2013), 2677–2686.
11. Ford, J. K. *Brands Laid Bare*. John Wiley & Sons, 2005.
12. Funder, D. C. *The personality puzzle*. WW Norton & Co, 1997.
13. Golbeck, J., Robles, C., Edmondson, M., and Turner, K. Predicting personality from twitter. In *Proc. SocialCom' 2011* (2011), 149–156.
14. Golbeck, J., Robles, C., and Turner, K. Predicting personality with social media. In *CHI'11 Extended Abstracts* (2011), 253–262.
15. Goldberg, L. R. The development of markers for the big-five factor structure. *Psychological Assessment 4*, 1 (1992), 26.
16. Hu, M., Yang, H., Zhou, M., Gou, L., Li, Y., and Haber, E. OpinionBlocks: a crowd-powered, self-improving interactive visual analytic system for understanding opinion text. In *Proc. INTERACT '2013* (2013), 116–134.
17. Iachello, G., and Hong, J. End-user privacy in human-computer interaction. *Foundations and Trends in Human-Computer Interaction 1*, 1 (2007), 1–137.
18. Junglas, I. A., Johnson, N. A., and Spitzmller, C. Personality traits and concern for privacy: an empirical study in the context of location-based services. *Euro. J. of Info. Sys. 17*, 4 (2008), 387–402.
19. Knijnenburg, B., Kobsa, A., and Jin, H. Preference-based location sharing: are more privacy options really better? In *Proc. CHI '2013* (New York, NY, USA, 2013), 2667–2676.
20. Korzaan, M., Brooks, N., and Greer, T. Demystifying personality and privacy: An empirical investigation into antecedents of concerns for information privacy. *Journal of Behavioral Studies in Business 1* (2009), 1–17.
21. Mahmud, J., Zhou, M., Megiddo, N., Nichols, J., and Drews, C. Recommending targeted strangers from whom to solicit information on social media. In *Proc. IUI '2013* (2013), 37–48.
22. Mairesse, F., Walker, M. A., Mehl, M. R., and Moore, R. K. Using linguistic cues for the automatic recognition of personality in conversation and text. *J. Artif. Intell. Res.(JAIR) 30* (2007), 457–500.
23. Maslow, A., Frager, R., and Fadiman, J. *Motivation and personality*, vol. 2. Harper & Row New York, 1970.
24. Nissenbaum, H. *Privacy in context: Technology, policy, and the integrity of social life*. Stanford Uni. Press, 2009.
25. Olson, J., Grudin, J., and Horvitz, E. A study of preferences for sharing and privacy. In *Proc. CHI '2005 EA*, ACM (2005), 1985–1988.
26. P&AB, C. P. A. A major shift since 2000 and why. *Privacy & American Business Newsletter 10*, 6 (2003).
27. Pennacchiotti, M., and Popescu, A.-M. A machine learning approach to twitter user classification. In *ICWSM* (2011).
28. Robert, P., and Escoufier, Y. A unifying tool for linear multivariate statistical methods: The RV- coefficient. *Applied Statistics 25*, 3 (1976), 257.
29. Schwartz, S. H. *Basic human values: Theory, measurement, and applications*. Revue francaise de sociologie, 2006.
30. Shen, J., Brdiczka, O., and Liu, J. Understanding email writers: Personality prediction from email messages. In *Proc. UMAP '2013*. Springer, 2013, 318–330.
31. Shi, P., Xu, H., and Chen, Y. Using contextual integrity to examine interpersonal information boundary on social network sites. In *Proc. CHI' 2013* (2013), 35–38.
32. Smith, H. J., Dinev, T., and Xu, H. Information privacy research: An interdisciplinary review. *MIS quarterly 35*, 4 (2011), 989–1016.
33. Smith, H. J., and Milberg, S. J. Information privacy: measuring individuals' concerns about organizational practices. *MIS Q. 20*, 2 (June 1996), 167–196.
34. Tausczik, Y. R., and Pennebaker, J. W. The psychological meaning of words: LIWC and computerized text analysis methods. *Journal of Language and Social Psychology 29*, 1 (2010), 24–54.
35. Triandis, H. C., and Suh, E. M. Cultural influences on personality. *Annual review of psychology 53*, 1 (2002), 133–160.
36. Xu, H., Dinev, T., Smith, J., and Hart, P. Information privacy concerns: linking individual perceptions with institutional privacy assurances. *Journal of the Association for Information Systems 12*, 12 (2011), 1.
37. Xu, H., Teo, H.-H., Tan, B. C., and Agarwal, R. The role of push-pull technology in privacy calculus: the case of location-based services. *Journal of Management Information Systems 26*, 3 (2009), 135–174.
38. Yang, H., and Li, Y. Identifying user needs from social media. *IBM Tech. Report* (2013).
39. Yarkoni, T. Personality in 100,000 words: A large-scale analysis of personality and word use among bloggers. *J. research in personality 44*, 3 (2010), 363–373.

# Faces Engage Us: Photos with Faces Attract More Likes and Comments on Instagram

**Saeideh Bakhshi**
Georgia Tech
sbakhshi@cc.gatech.edu

**David A. Shamma**
Yahoo Labs
aymans@acm.org

**Eric Gilbert**
Georgia Tech
gilbert@cc.gatech.edu

## ABSTRACT
Photos are becoming prominent means of communication online. Despite photos' pervasive presence in social media and online world, we know little about how people interact and engage with their content. Understanding how photo content might signify engagement, can impact both science and design, influencing production and distribution. One common type of photo content that is shared on social media, is the photos of people. From studies of offline behavior, we know that human faces are powerful channels of non-verbal communication. In this paper, we study this behavioral phenomena online. We ask how presence of a face, it's age and gender might impact social engagement on the photo. We use a corpus of 1 million Instagram images and organize our study around two social engagement feedback factors, *likes* and *comments*. Our results show that photos with faces are 38% more likely to receive likes and 32% more likely to receive comments, even after controlling for social network reach and activity. We find, however, that the number of faces, their age and gender do not have an effect. This work presents the first results on how photos with human faces relate to engagement on large scale image sharing communities. In addition to contributing to the research around online user behavior, our findings offer a new line of future work using visual analysis.

## Author Keywords
mobile; photo; Instagram; faces; face detection; engagement; age; demographics; gender; content; image; social media; image sharing community

This material is based upon work supported in part by the Defense Advanced Research Projects Agency (DARPA) under Contract No. W911NF-12-1-0043. Any opinions, findings and conclusions or recommendations expressed in this material are those of the authors and do not necessarily reflect the views of DARPA or the U.S. Government. The views and conclusions contained in this document are those of the authors and should not be interpreted as representing the official policies, either expressly or implied, of the Defense Advanced Research Projects Agency or the U.S. Government.


CHI 2014, April 26May 1, 2014, Toronto, Ontario, Canada.
Copyright 2014 ACM 978-1-4503-2473-1/14/04..$15.00.
http://dx.doi.org/10.1145/2556288.2557403

## ACM Classification Keywords
H.5.m. Information interfaces and presentation (e.g., HCI): Miscellaneous.

## INTRODUCTION
Even as babies, humans love to look at faces; infants, barely minutes old, turn toward faces, sensing that they are important [39]. It is widely accepted in neuroscience that face perception is perhaps the most highly developed human visual skill [26]. Faces are also powerful channels of nonverbal communication [45]. We constantly monitor faces because they provide vital clues in an impressive variety of contexts: attraction, the complexity of emotions, identity, age, humor, and a person's regional and national background [24].

Many of the faces we see everyday now have an online presence. Photo sharing communities such as Instagram have made it possible to communicate with large groups of distributed people through an image—be it a picture of whats for dinner or a selfie—perhaps more easily than through words alone. As Kelsey puts it, "we are moving away from photography as a way of recording and storing the past, and instead turning photography into a social medium in its own right" [35].

Online photo sharing communities have grown at an impressive pace. At the time of this writing, Instagram users upload 55 million photos a day to the site[1]. This presents a key research challenge for photo sharing communities like Instagram (cf. Flickr, Imgur, Tumblr): how do we discover the mechanisms by which users communicate around visual content and engage with such content. In other words, since engagement is vital to photo sharing communities, it is critical to understand what form of content drives engagement. While several research studies have focused on how users engage with textual content [6, 9, 11, 12, 31, 38], there are few studies on what makes visual content socially engaging online. To investigate this, we ask the following research questions in this paper, driven by social psychology work on face perception:

**RQ1:** Do photos with faces differ in online engagement compared to photos without them?

**RQ2:** If so, how do characteristics of the image subject, such as gender and age, affect engagement?

[1] `http://instagram.com/press` (Accessed 9/2013)

We use Instagram to answer our research questions. Instagram has over 150 million active monthly users who collectively generate 1.2 billion likes per day. There are two social aspects of engagement here: the number of likes and the number of comments on the Instagram image [2]. Using a corpus of 1 million images from the community, we find that on an average a photo that contains a face receives 38% more likes and 32% more comments compared to a photo that does not contain any faces (even after controlling for user activity levels and social network reach). Further, we find that the number of faces in the photo, their age and their gender do not impact engagement.

To our knowledge, our study is one of the first to show, systematically and at scale, how photos with faces drive online social engagement. In addition to contributing to the ongoing research conversation surrounding engagement, we believe that these findings create a path for future work, not only to uncover the impact of faces on other aspects of online user behavior, but also to use computer vision techniques to discover other antecedents of engagement. For example, we may be able to apply vision techniques to relate facial *expressions* of emotion to social behavior.

We begin with a review of related research on content and face perception, and a summary of the Instagram community. Next, we introduce the corpus we collected from Instagram and describe the statistical methods we used to isolate the effect of faces on likes and comments. Finally, we interpret our findings within the frame of existing work, both in theory and in practice.

## LITERATURE REVIEW

In this section, we describe related work on role of content in engagement, face perception theories and HCI studies of faces. We then summarize the media community of our study, Instagram.

### Role of Content on User Engagement

As Ellison and colleagues note, "the primary function of these [social network] sites is to consume and distribute personal content about the self" [22]. Sharing content can in turn ensure that users remain engaged and committed in the future visits [13, 47]. On the other hand, users have diverse motivations to share content on social network sites. For example, users may share useful content to appear knowledgeable or simply to help out [50]. Not only the content of posts, but also the emotional valence behind it can drive its usage. For example, in a recent study, researchers used New York Times articles to examine the relationship between the emotion evoked by content and its virality [9], finding that that there is a direct relationship.

Much research attention has gone into investigating what makes content in an online community interesting to its members. In a series of studies conducted on Usenet newsgroups, researchers investigated properties that influenced the likelihood of reply, a measure of the community's engagement. Explicit requests, personal testimonials relating one's connection to the group, and staying on-topic increased the probability of receiving a reply. Newcomers to a group were less likely to receive a reply than veterans [6]. Following up on this work, Burke et al. studied the role of self-disclosing introductions, mentions of the poster's age, and an acknowledgment that this is the poster's first post; these factors were found to increase reply probability [11]. In another study, Burke and Kraut, studied the effect of the politeness of a post, finding that politeness leads to more replies in certain types of groups, while in other types of groups, rudeness actually increases replies [12]. On Twitter, researchers have used retweeting as a measure of community interest/engagement, and have investigated the features that predict retweeting. Suh et al. found that the presence of URLs and hashtags in tweets predicted more retweeting, as did a richer connection with the community [44]. In a recent work, Gilbert et. al. studied Pinterest- a social networking site based on images- and found that which properties of an image makes the content more interesting to users [23]. The properties used in this work are based on meta data and not the content of images.

As far as we know, however, we have no such similar line of work on how image content can affect different aspects of online behavior, such as engagement, diffusion or link formation. In our work, we intend to provide an understanding of image engagement by looking at the photo content.

### Face perception

One of the common types of photo content shared on social networking sites is the photos of people or the ones with human faces in them. Through daily experience, we know that human faces are readily distinguishable. People tend to find faces in unexpected scenes and photographs even where faces do not exist. For example, the 1976 Viking 1 prob photographed a shadowed region on Mars' northern planes that resembled a face. While higher resolution imagery has shown the region to actually be a mesa, the face on Mars remains a pop icon and the source of many books, TV shows, and films [40].

Faces have long been a source of scientific interest in a wide range of disciplines. In recent years, this breadth of interests, approaches and expertise has led directly to rapid advances in our understanding of many different aspects of how we perceive and process faces [10]. The human brain has evolved to recognize faces within hours after birth [33]. Human infants only minutes old attend particularly to face-like stimuli relative to equally complicated non-face stimuli [10, 30]. We prefer to look at faces from that early age and thereafter, often opting to spend more time looking at faces than any other type of object [53]. By the age of two months, infants begin to differentiate specific visual features of the face [39] and process facial expressions [20]. Our brains have a specific region, Fusiform Face Area (FFA), that is specialized for facial recognition [34, 41]. Faces are important for social cognition as well, not only because we are able to recognize them earlier than other objects, but also because they display our feelings about past, current and future events through expressions [17,

[2] We use the terms image and photo interchangeably throughout this paper to refer to the images on Instagram.

21]. This can be highly important to very practical concerns: faces, particularly attractive ones, are found to be effective in improving consumer responses to advertisements [7].

Our research examines the presence of this phenomena online, by analyzing the effect of having faces in engaging users on Instagram.

### Faces and HCI research

In HCI research, there is a great deal of work exploring the benefits of using face icons and faces in interfaces [36, 43, 45, 49]. Walker et al. [49] studied how having faces and facial expressions for a computer application affects users' performance and productivity. They compared subjects' responses to an interview survey under three conditions: questions spoken by a synthesized face with neutral expressions, spoken by a face with stern expressions, or text only. Subjects who responded to the spoken face made more effort to answer the questions by spending more time, writing more comments and making fewer mistakes. They reported that having a face is engaging and takes more effort and attention from the user.

Takeuchi et al. [46] compared users' impressions of an agent which helped them to win a card game. The agent was represented either as an arrow or a face. They showed that users respond differently to systems having a face than to those without. The arrow was recognized as useful and reliable, while the face was rated as fun and entertaining. They conclude that a face in an interface captures more attention and people try to interpret the meaning behind the expression.

Studies on embodied interfaces showed similar results. Agents are visual digital representations of a computer interface often in the form of human-like faces [15]. In a review study of embodied agents [18], authors reported that adding an embodied agent to an interface made the experience more engaging.

### Role of Age and Gender

Age and gender have been studied extensively as factors affecting social media use [8, 16, 27, 28]. Recent data[3] shows that women form a majority of Facebook and Twitter users, as well as dominating Pinterest; however, men are the majority of users on Google+ and LinkedIn. In a recent study Gilbert et. al. [23] found that females are more likely to receive repins and fewer followers than males on Pinterest. Moreover, Pew Internet Research [4] ran a survey to give marketers a clearer picture of who they can expect to reach on Instagram. According to the source, 28% of U.S. internet users aged 18 to 29 snapped and posted photos on the network in December 2012. 14% of those aged 30 to 49 did the same, and very few users older than 50 participated in any way on Instagram.

Inspired by previous research on disparities in internet usage and social network audience, we used age and gender variables to investigate whether they affect the number of likes and comments on photos.

### Instagram

Instagram is a social network site designed around photo- and video-sharing. It enables users to take photos and videos with their mobile devices, apply digital filters to them and share them on variety of social networking services, such as Facebook, Twitter, Tumblr and Flickr [2], all of which are social media sites in their own right. Instagram has rapidly gained popularity with over 100 million active users as of April 2012 [19]. The total number of photographs uploaded recently exceeded one billion [1, 3].

Instagram accounts are public by default, unless users elect to create a private account; there is no tier privacy photo by photo. To add a photo, users can take a photo from inside the app. It is also possible to choose a photo from an existing album on the mobile device to share with Instagram followers. Instagram users can apply filters on their photos. An Instagram filter is a digital layer that when added to a photo, gives it the appearance of stylistic editing. Some filters enhance the colors in a photo, while others dull the light to a soft glow for an aged, vintage appearance.

Despite the popularity of Instagram, there is little scholarly work on it. In a recent piece, Hochman et al. [29] analyzed colors in photos uploaded from two different cities of New York and Tokyo and found differences across the two locations. For instance, hues of pictures in New York were mostly blue-gray, while those in Tokyo were characterized by dominant red-yellow tones.

## METHODS

We take a quantitative approach in this paper to investigate the relationship between faces and engagement. While engagement can be quantified in various ways, we use two essential aspects of content on Instagram that can signal for engagement: likes and comments. The number of likes signals for the extent to which the content is interesting to users and the number of comments quantifies the level of discussion on the social network. In this section, we describe the data we collected from Instagram and how we detected faces and their age and gender; followed by clarifying our statistical methods and analysis process.

### Face detection

Face detection and recognition from images or video is a popular topic in vision research and it has received lots of attention [48, 51]. A general statement of the problem of machine recognition of faces is usually formulated as follows: given still or video images of a scene, identify or verify one or more persons in the scene using a stored database of faces or facial features. The solution to the problem involves segmentation of faces (face detection) from cluttered scenes and extraction of features from the face.

While the current state of the art in face detection and recognition is highly accurate [32], we did not have access to an implementation that can work for large scale image analysis. We therefore used a publicly available face detection API developed by Face++ [5]. We only use the detection modules, as the goal of this paper is to find relationship between existence of faces and the social engagement. Face++ provides a set of compact, powerful, and cross-platform vision services,

[3] `http://mashable.com/2012/07/04/men-women-social-media/` (Accessed 9/2013)

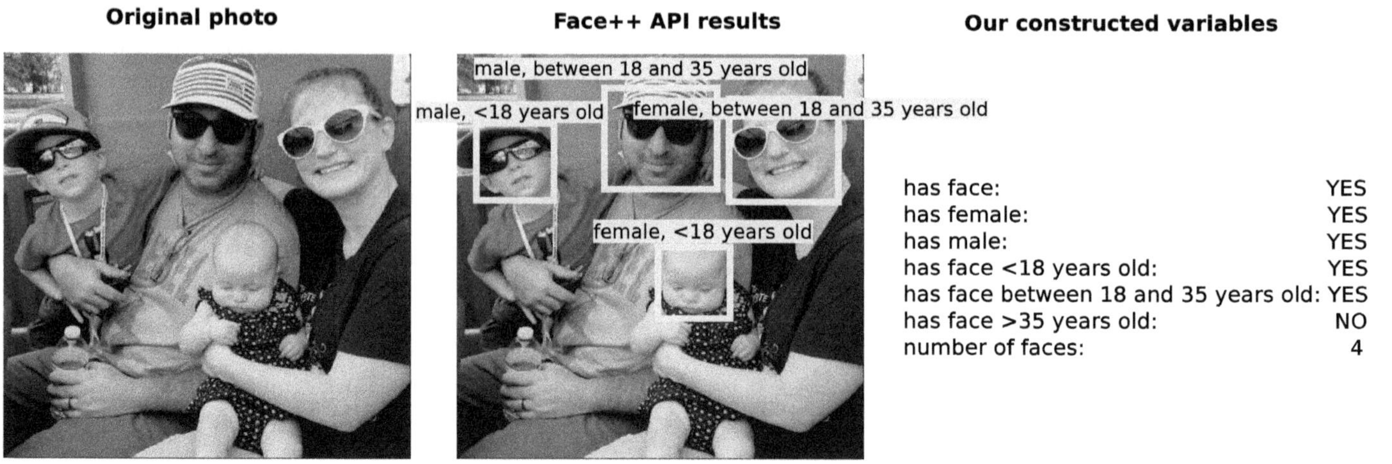


**Figure 1. Example Face++ face detection and how we construct our variables. The photo used in this example is a photo under Creative Commons license from Flickr.**

which enabled us to use cutting-edge vision techniques. The API does not provide us with an estimation of accuracy, so we turn to a crowd-sourced validation method to confirm the accuracy of our face detector described later in the validation section.

Face++ provides us with an API that accepts the URL of an Instagram image and returns information about detected faces. This information includes the position of the face in the image, as well as the detected gender and age range of all faces. We then reduce the dimensionality of data by converting the results into a binary space, where we mark only when there is a face in an image. We also identify whether any of the faces in the image belong to certain age ranges. The three age ranges we consider in this paper are (1) children and teens- younger than 18, (2) young adults- faces with age between 18 and 35, and (3) older adults- older than 35. To evaluate the role of gender, we construct another binary feature which determines whether at least one female or one male face is in the image. Figure 1 shows an example Face++ detection and how we construct our variables.

## Data

Our goal is to obtain a random sample of photos from Instagram. Even though Instagram provides us with a publicly available API, gathering a random subset of photos is a challenging task. We can either search for photos by location or query on the list of most recent popular photos. We opted to start with a set of 2,000 popular Instagram photos, collected on November 2012. We then used snowball sampling [25] to collect the users and their followers as well as a random set of their photos. Our dataset consists of 23 million Instagram photos and over 3 million Instagram users. To soften biases due to snowball sampling, we randomly selected 1.1 million photos from this data set. The snowball sampling method was necessary because Instagram does not provide any mechanism by which to monitor the global stream of photos. Figure 2 shows a detailed flowchart of data collection, evaluation and analysis processes.

### *Response variables (dependent measures)*

Our goal in this paper is to investigate the role of photos in predicting user engagement on Instagram. We chose number of likes and number of comments as two features that represent fundamental aspects of engagement on the site. An overview of each of these variables is provided in Table 1.

**Likes:** Number of likes is a measure of engagement for the photo. It quantifies the number of distinct users who liked the photo. Like is a strong social signal on Instagram that demonstrates the extent to which users liked the photo.

**Comments:** Number of comments is another measure of engagement, or as Yew and Shamma [52] note, a measure of explicit action on the content. The number of comments is the number of distinct comments posted on the photo. The number of comments determines the extent to which users discussed the photo and hence it can be considered as measure of discussion.

### *Predictor variables*

In this paper, we use two major control variables to adjust for the impact of social network reach and a user's activity.

**Control: user's followers count.** An Instagram photo is posted by an Instagram user. The nature of relationship on Instagram is follower/following. Users form a social network based on "follow" relationships. When *A* follows *B*, *B*'s photos will show up in *A*'s photo-stream. The number of followers signals the social network reach. The more number of followers, the more people can see the photo and there is presumably a higher chance of receiving likes and comments.

**Control: user's photo count.** Photo count is the feature we use to quantify a user's activity on the site. It represents the number of photos on a user's profile. The larger values of photo count show the user has shared more content on the site; in other words the user is more active.

As we discussed in related work section, faces are found to be effective stimuli [10, 30] in attracting people's attention. We use a binary variable as our predictor to account for presence of a face in the photo.

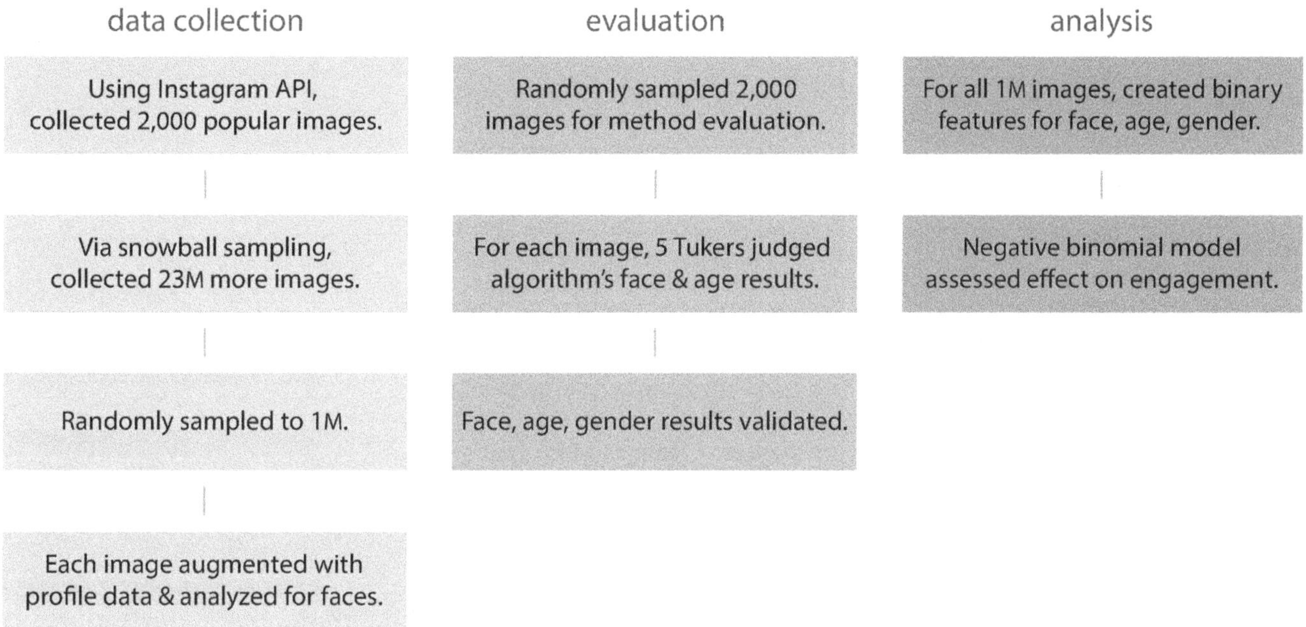


**Figure 2. An overview of the steps taken in this paper for collection, evaluation and analysis of the data.**

**Has face.** For each Instagram photo, we determine whether at least one human face exists in the photo. This is a binary feature; when it is set to 1, there is at least one face in the image, otherwise it is set to 0.

Other than presence of faces, we consider variables identifying age and gender of them. Our age and gender variables are derived using face detection method.

**Has children and teens- has face $<$ 18 years old.** We use a binary feature to determine whether the photo has any faces in the age group $<$18 years old. The variable is set to 1 when at least one of the identified faces in the image appears to be younger than 18 years old, and set to 0 otherwise.

**Has young adults- has face $>$ 18 and $<$ 35 years old.** This is another age feature that is set to 1 when at least one of the identifies faces in the image appears to be between 18 and 35 years old, and it is set to 0 otherwise.

**Has older adults- Has face $>$ 35 years old.** Our final age feature is to identify presence of older adults in the image. If at least one of the faces in the image appears to be older than 35 years old, this variable is set to 1, 0 otherwise.

**Has female face.** This feature is a binary feature reflecting whether there is a female face in the photo. When the variable is set to 1, the image has at least one female face, and it is set to 0 otherwise.

**Has male face.** This feature is a binary feature reflecting whether there is a male face in the photo. When the variable is set to 1, the image has at least one male face, and it is set to 0 otherwise.

The distribution and short summary of each of these features is provided in Table 1.

### Statistical methods

Next, we present statistical methods we used to model our two dependent variables, number of likes and number of comments. Both dependent variables are *count* variables. We model the number of likes and the number of comments using negative binomial regression, on two classes of independent variables: the control variables (followers count and photos count) and our variables of interest (related to existence of a face, age group of the face and gender of the face). Negative binomial regression is well-suited for *over-dispersed* distributions of *count* dependent variable [14]. We use negative binomial regression instead of Poisson regression since the variance of the dependent variable is larger than the mean for both likes and comments. We use over-dispersion to test whether Poisson or negative binomial regression should be used. This test was suggested by Cameron and Trivedi [14], and involves a simple least-squares regression to test the statistical significance of the over-dispersion coefficient.

The regression coefficients $\beta$ allow us to understand the effect of an independent variable on the number of likes and comments (note that to be able to compare coefficients, we z-score all numerical variables before performing regression). For the variables with heavy tail distribution, such as followers count and photos count, we log transformed the variables before performing regression. We use Chi-squared statistics to find the statistical significance of our regression models, computing the reduction in deviance as compared to a null model.

| Type | Variable | Description | Distribution |
|---|---|---|---|
| Engagement | likes* | Number of likes on each photo. |  |
| | comments* | Number of comments on each photo. |  |
| Audience & Activity | followers* | Number of users who follow the photo's owner. |  |
| | photos* | Number of photos shared by photo's owner. |  |
| Faces | has face | 1 if the photo contains a face, 0 otherwise. | 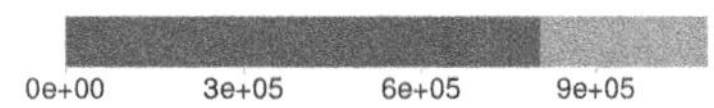 |
| | has face $<$ 18 years old | 1 if there is at least one face younger than 18, 0 otherwise. |  |
| | has face $\in$ [18, 35] years old | 1 if there is at least one face with age between 18 and 35, 0 otherwise. |  |
| | has face $>$ 35 years old | 1 if there is at least one face older than 35, 0 otherwise. |  |
| | has female face | 1 if there is at least one female face in the photo, 0 otherwise. |  |
| | has male face | 1 if there is at least one male face in the photo, 0 otherwise. | 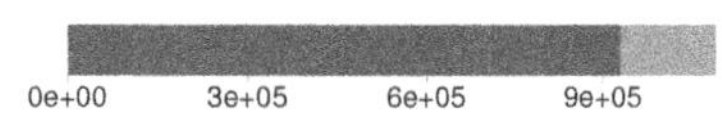 |

**Table 1. Distributions of quantitative and binary variables used in this paper. Variables marked with '*' are log-transformed. The red and blue lines identify mean and median of the distribution, respectively. Orange refers to 1's in the bar graphs. The engagement variables are our dependent measures. Audience and activity variables are used as controls, and faces variables are the focal point of this study.**

## FACE DETECTION VALIDATION

As we mentioned in the previous section, we use Face++ API to detect faces in Instagram photos. Even though the currently used face detection mechanisms are high in accuracy (over 95%), we undertake an additional evaluation step to validate and confirm the accuracy of our methods. For this purpose, we crowd-source a random sample of photos from our dataset to Mechanical Turkers in order to verify the results of API.

The validation process is as follows: we select a random sample of 2,000 images from our dataset. We then create tasks on Mechanical Turk, where the image is shown to five different Turkers. We ask questions regarding the faces they see in the image. They answer the questions about each image by identifying how many human faces they see in the image, how many of them are female and how many are male. We then ask Turkers to categorize the faces into different age groups and report the number of people in each age group. We specifically ask Turkers to only report the human faces and avoid reporting the people they see in the picture if the faces are not visible.

We take the majority votes on each image and the results of Mechanical Turkers evaluations are in agreement with API output $97\% \pm 0.75\%$ of the time. $93\% \pm 1.11\%$ of the Turker evaluations are in agreement in detecting faces with age range under 18, $96\% \pm 0.86\%$ in age range agreement between 18 and 35, and $99\% \pm 0.44\%$ in detecting ages over 35. Overall the evaluation of our face detecting API shows high accuracy.

The results of the human validation are summarized in Table 2.

## RESULTS

We use negative binomial regression to model the number of likes and comments on photos. The results of the regression are presented in Table 3. We use the Chi-squared Test to find the significance of the regression model, by computing the reduction in deviance from a null model. For our likes model, we find reduction in deviance of $\chi^2 = (5.2M - 1.2M)$, or 76%, on 8 degrees of freedom. The test rejected the null hypothesis of a null model ($p < 10^{-15}$); hence, the model is well-suited to characterize the effects of the described variables.

For our comments model, the reduction in deviance is $\chi^2 = (1.79M - 1.1M)$, or 38%, on 8 degrees of freedom. The test rejected the null hypothesis of a null model ($p < 10^{-15}$). The model for comments is also well-suited to characterize the effects of the independent variables.

We test coefficients of all independent variables for the null hypothesis of a zero-valued coefficient (two-sided) and find that the test rejects the null hypothesis ($p < 10^{-5}$) in all cases.

### Effect of control variables

We use number of followers and number of photos as our control variables. As expected, the followers count has a large positive effect on the number of likes and comments. This

| Validation test | Accuracy | Margin of error |
|---|---|---|
| has face | 97% | 0.75% |
| has female face | 96% | 0.86% |
| has male face | 96% | 0.86% |
| has face < 18 years old | 93% | 1.11% |
| has face between 18 and 35 years old | 96% | 0.86% |
| has face > 35 years old | 99% | 0.44% |

**Table 2. Results of Mechanical Turk evaluation for our face detection approach. Margin of Error is computed for 95% confidence. Our face detector works correctly $97\% \pm 0.75\%$ of the time.**

means the higher the number of followers, the more likely it is for the photo to receive likes and comments. The higher number of followers guarantees a larger audience and so the photo is expected to be seen by more number of people, increasing the likelihood of receiving likes and comments.

On the other hand the number of photos shared by user shows a negative effect on both likes and comments. The number of photos is an indicator of activity on Instagram. As we can see in our results (Table 3) the higher activity (number of photos), the lower chances of receiving likes and comments. This might also be interpreted another way: the more photos a user has, the lower probability any single one has of being liked or commented on.

### Effect of faces

All other predictors in our model come from the face detection results. We are interested in quantifying the effect of faces and their comparative importance on social engagement. We use a binary variable that reflects the existence of a face in the image. We can see in Table 3 that number of likes and comments are significantly higher when there is at least one face in the image ($\beta_{likes} = 0.32$, $\beta_{comments} = 0.28, p < 10^{-15}$). This means that photos with faces are 38% more likely ($IRR = 0.38$) to receive likes and 32% more likely ($IRR = 0.32$) to receive comments[4].

We also check the effect of number of faces on engagement and find that while existence of a face positively correlates with the number of likes and comments, the number of faces does not particularly change this effect. Regardless of whether it is a group photo or a single person's photo, the fact that a face is in the image significantly impacts the number of likes and comments. It does not matter how many faces are in the image. We did not include the number of faces in the final model to avoid co-linearity of the predictor variables.

### Effects of age and gender

To test whether the demographic of users [4] biases toward photos with younger face groups, we considered using three binary variables each identifying the age of a face. Table 3 shows that the age group of the faces are generally not strong predictors for the number of likes. In case of number of comments the photos with adult age groups negatively affects the number of comments. This could be related to lower presence of older age groups in the social network of Instagram.

[4]We use IRR to refer to *Incidence Rate Ratio*. We compute IRR for a categorical independent variables $x$ as the ratio of amount of change in the dependent variable (outcome) for $x$ relative to a reference level of $x$.

Gender of the faces in the image does not show any strong effect on the image's engagement. Table 3 shows that the $\beta$ coefficients for gender variables are of negligible size compared to some other features such as existence of a face.

## DISCUSSION

Using Instagram as our research context, we set out to investigate how photos with faces relate to engagement, as measured as the number of likes and comments, compared to those without. We considered presence of a face in a photo, it's gender and age as predictors, controlling for social network reach and activity. From this we asked two research questions: are photos with faces more engaging than those without and if so how do the characteristics of a face in a photo affect engagement?

As expected, we find that among the factors we measured, the number of followers is the main driver of engagement for both likes and comments on the photo. The number of followers is a proxy for the size of a user's audience. Having a larger audience increases the likelihood of a like or comment, a common sense fact realized in our models. Furthermore, we find that activity level is negatively correlated with likes and comments. The more photos a user posts, the less likely it is that her photos receive likes and comments. As we mentioned earlier, this most likely represents the intuition that the more photos a user posts, the less likely any one of them is to be highly liked or commented.

### Faces engage us

The major finding of this paper is that the existence of a face in a photo significantly affects its social engagement. This effect is substantial, increasing the chances of receiving likes by 38% and comments by 32%. We also find that number of faces in the image does not have significant impact on engagement. Having a photo with a face, regardless of how many faces are in the photo, increases the likelihood of receiving likes and comments. Our findings connect to the findings from offline studies in psychology, marketing and social behavior, as well as qualitative studies of HCI, confirming that people engage more with photos of faces.

### Age and gender do not impact engagement

Our results show that the age and gender of faces in the photo does not seem to drive or hinder it's engagement values. This is a surprising finding, given the bias of demographics using the site and the general belief that photos of kids or female faces may get more attention. For comments, we see in the results that there is a small negative effect of older adult photos. Since the comments are mostly related to the extent to which a photo is discussed, the lower number of comments on this type of photos can be related to the lower demographics of older adults on Instagram. Future work can look at effect of similar factors on other photo sharing communities such as Pinterest with biased gender demographics.

### Implications and future work

This work raises many fundamental questions about the nature of social interaction around multimedia content. We believe that this is an initial step and there is a rich landscape

| Variable | $\beta$ | Std.Err | $p$ |
|---|---|---|---|
| number of followers | 1.32 | 0.00 | $< 10^{-15}$ |
| number of photos | -0.21 | 0.00 | $< 10^{-15}$ |
| has face | 0.32 | 0.01 | $< 10^{-15}$ |
| has face <18 years old | 0.02 | 0.01 | $< 10^{-15}$ |
| has face >18 and <25 | -0.03 | 0.01 | $< 10^{-15}$ |
| has face >25 years old | -0.03 | 0.01 | $< 10^{-15}$ |
| has female face | -0.04 | 0.01 | $< 10^{-8}$ |
| has male face | -0.02 | 0.01 | $< 10^{-3}$ |
| (Intercept) | 3.47 | 0.00 | $< 10^{-15}$ |
| Null deviance | | | 5208940 |
| Residual deviance | | | 1227787 |

| Variable | $\beta$ | Std.Err | $p$ |
|---|---|---|---|
| number of followers | 0.97 | 0.00 | $< 10^{-15}$ |
| number of photos | -0.12 | 0.00 | $< 10^{-15}$ |
| has face | 0.28 | 0.00 | $< 10^{-15}$ |
| has face <18 years old | -0.01 | 0.01 | $< 10^{-15}$ |
| has face >18 and <25 | -0.07 | 0.01 | $< 10^{-15}$ |
| has face >25 years old | -0.04 | 0.01 | $< 10^{-15}$ |
| has female face | -0.01 | 0.01 | $< 10^{-4}$ |
| has male face | -0.02 | 0.01 | $< 10^{-6}$ |
| (Intercept) | 3.47 | 0.00 | $< 10^{-15}$ |
| Null deviance | | | 1790136 |
| Residual deviance | | | 1105145 |

**Table 3. Results of negative binomial regression with number of likes (left) and number of comments (right) as dependent variable.**

of research directions and open questions in this area. Future work can look at other visual characteristics of multimedia and study their impact on online behavior. Here we find that faces might have an impact on engagement, but faces are just one visual feature. Other signals can be gathered from people in photos, including facial expression, gaze direction, as well as, body posture and movement. Although facial expressions reliably signal the so-called basic emotions such as fear or happiness, human viewers are also surprisingly adept at making reliable judgments about social information from impoverished stimuli, such as faint changes in facial expressions [30]. Emotional expressions in faces are known to activate several areas of the brain [24]. Future work can look at emotional expressions of faces and explore the effects on user behavior. For example, are we more likely to comment on wry smiles or broad grins?

Our quantitative results illuminate what is the response to the photos with faces, but not why users behave this way or what kind of connections they make with such photos. Additional work, particularly using qualitative methods, is needed to answer these questions. Some of the most compelling questions concern the person in the photo; for example, are users engaging with faces as generic objects or are they connecting with the face as a person they know.

As our work is based on quantitative studies and observational data, we cannot make any strong causal claims. We find that photos with faces have higher chances of being liked and commented on, but we don't know if faces are the exact cause of this. More experimental work needs to corroborate these findings. Further, the statistical methods we used examine only a small segment of behavior on the site.

Faces and their presence connect to psychological studies of human behavior, and emphasize the importance of engaging our unconscious perceptual biases—instantiated in this work as face perception. Future work can investigate the relationship between face perception theories and other aspects of online user behavior. For example are faces effective when it comes to spreading the content on the social network? Are photos or topics, accompanied by human faces more/less persuasive in terms of delivering the content?

The context in which faces appear also invites interesting questions about individual and group behavior. Are photos of friends group more/less popular than the family ones? What about selfies and people's reaction to self portraits? It is worth studying the cultural impacts on photo sharing, say for example are group photos more engaging in collectivism cultures rather than individualistic ones?

Camera-phones and mobile photo capture has changed how we perceive photo-work in the academic community. This work takes one of the first steps into understanding modern photo capture and consumption through the study of Instagram. That said, Instagram is one online ecosystem and it has been claimed that perception and semantics in social media sites is a construction of the community on that site [42]. For example, Instagram is a people-centric site and the influence of faces might be different in a product-centric site such as Pinterest. On the other hand a community such as Instagram, which is strongly based on social connections might react differently to faces than a professional photography community such as Flickr.

The practical implication of social engagement in online photo sharing lies strongly in search and recommendation. Knowing photos with faces increase engagement suggests one could increase their search ranking to keep people on site and active. Our results highlight the importance of effective methods that take advantage of presence of faces in photos for personalization of site content. Additionally, while we have seen face finding applications for social media sites [37], these tools have been designed for the utility of retrieval and not for conversation and comments.

For designers, the present findings may shed light on how to filter, prioritize and highlight photos from the global image stream, especially ones that have just been submitted and therefore haven't had time to accumulate very many likes and comments.

## CONCLUSION

Faces are shown to be powerful visual tool used in human non verbal communication. With the widespread use of image sharing communities, most of which are on top of social platforms, a key challenge in research community is to understand the role of the image content in online user behavior. In this paper, we took a first step toward uncovering an important feature of some of images, the human faces. We find that photos with faces are 38% more likely to be liked and 32% more likely to be commented on. Our results, however, show that number of faces, their age and gender do not have significant impact. In addition to speaking to the ongoing studies in online user behavior and social engagement, our findings open a new thread of future work, suggesting research in visual analysis.

## REFERENCES


1. 150,000,000 photos. `http://blog.instagram.com/post/8758450298/150-000-000-photos`, August 2011.
2. Here's how to use instagram. `http://www.businessinsider.com/instagram-2010-11?op=1`, May 2011.
3. Testing, testing... `http://blog.instagram.com/post/8758396471/testing-testing`, July 2011.
4. A demographic portrait of users of various social media services. `http://pewinternet.org/Reports/2013/Social-media-users/Social-Networking-Site-Users/Demo-portrait.aspx`, 2013.
5. Face++. `http://en.faceplusplus.com/`, 2013.
6. Arguello, J., Butler, B. S., Joyce, E., Kraut, R., Ling, K. S., Rosé, C., and Wang, X. Talk to me: foundations for successful individual-group interactions in online communities. In *Proceedings of the SIGCHI conference on Human Factors in computing systems*, ACM (2006), 959–968.
7. Baker, M. J., and Churchill J., G. A. The impact of physically attractive models on advertising evaluations. *Journal of marketing research* (1977), 538–555.
8. Beckwith, L., Kissinger, C., Burnett, M., Wiedenbeck, S., Lawrance, J., Blackwell, A., and Cook, C. Tinkering and gender in end-user programmers' debugging. In *Proceedings of the SIGCHI conference on Human Factors in computing systems*, ACM (2006), 231–240.
9. Berger, J., and Milkman, K. L. What makes online content viral? *Journal of marketing research 49*, 2 (2012), 192–205.
10. Bruce, V., and Young, A. *In the eye of the beholder: the science of face perception.* Oxford University Press, 1998.
11. Burke, M., Joyce, E., Kim, T., Anand, V., and Kraut, R. Introductions and requests: Rhetorical strategies that elicit response in online communities. In *Communities and Technologies 2007*. Springer, 2007, 21–39.
12. Burke, M., and Kraut, R. Mind your ps and qs: the impact of politeness and rudeness in online communities. In *Proceedings of the 2008 ACM conference on Computer supported cooperative work*, ACM (2008), 281–284.
13. Burke, M., Marlow, C., and Lento, T. Feed me: motivating newcomer contribution in social network sites. In *Proceedings of the SIGCHI conference on human factors in computing systems*, acm (2009), 945–954.
14. Cameron, C. A., and Trivedi, P. K. *Regression analysis of count data (econometric society monographs).* Cambridge university press, September 1998.
15. Cassell, J., et al. Nudge nudge wink wink: elements of face-to-face conversation for embodied conversational agents. *Embodied Conversational Agents* (2000), 1–27.
16. Cunha, E., Magno, G., Almeida, V., Gonçalves, M. A., and Benevenuto, F. A gender based study of tagging behavior in twitter. In *Proceedings of the 23rd ACM conference on Hypertext and social media*, ACM (2012), 323–324.
17. Darwin, C. *The expression of the emotions in man and animals.* Oxford University Press, 1998.
18. Dehn, D. M., and Van Mulken, S. The impact of animated interface agents: a review of empirical research. *International journal of human-computer studies 52*, 1 (2000), 1–22.
19. Desmarais, C. Facebook's instagram says it has 90 million monthly active users, February 2013.
20. Diener, E., Fraser, S. C., Beaman, A. L., and Kelem, R. T. Effects of deindividuation variables on stealing among halloween trick-or-treaters. *Journal of personality and social psychology 33*, 2 (1976), 178.
21. Ekman, P., and Friesen, W. *Pictures of facial affect.* consulting psychologists press, 1975.
22. Ellison, N., Steinfield, C., and Lampe, C. Connection strategies: social capital implications of facebook-enabled communication practices. *New media & society 13*, 6 (2011), 873–892.
23. Gilbert, E., Bakhshi, S., Chang, S., and Terveen, L. I need to try this?: a statistical overview of pinterest. In *Proceedings of the SIGCHI conference on human factors in computing systems*, ACM (2013), 2427–2436.
24. Goldman, A. I., and Sripada, C. S. Simulationist models of face-based emotion recognition. *Cognition 94*, 3 (2005), 193–213.
25. Goodman, L. A. Snowball sampling. *The Annals of Mathematical Statistics 32*, 1 (1961), 148–170.
26. Haxby, J., Hoffman, E., and Gobbini, M. The distributed human neural system for face perception. *Trends in cognitive sciences 4*, 6 (2000), 223–233.
27. Herring, S. C. Gender and power in on-line communication. *The handbook of language and gender* (2008), 202.

28. Herring, S. C., Kouper, I., Scheidt, L. A., and Wright, E. L. Women and children last: The discursive construction of weblogs. In *Into the blogosphere: Rhetoric, community, and culture of weblogs*, Citeseer (2004).
29. Hochman, N., and Schwartz, R. Visualizing instagram: Tracing cultural visual rhythms. In *Proceedings of the workshop on social media visualization (socmedvis) in conjunction with the sixth international AAAI conference on weblogs and social media (ICWSM-12)* (2012).
30. Iacoboni, M., Koski, L., Brass, M., Bekkering, H., Woods, R., Dubeau, M., Mazziotta, J., and Rizzolatti, G. Reafferent copies of imitated actions in the right superior temporal cortex. *Proceedings of the national academy of sciences 98*, 24 (2001), 13995–13999.
31. Jamali, S., and Rangwala, H. Digging digg: comment mining, popularity prediction, and social network analysis. In *International Conference on Web Information Systems and Mining, 2009. WISM 2009*, ieee (2009), 32–38.
32. Jenkins, R., and Burton, A. M. 100% accuracy in automatic face recognition. *Science 319*, 5862 (2008), 435.
33. Johnson, M. H., Dziurawiec, S., Ellis, H., and Morton, J. Newborns' preferential tracking of face-like stimuli and its subsequent decline. *cognition 40*, 1 (1991), 1–19.
34. Kanwisher, N., McDermott, J., and Chun, M. M. The fusiform face area: a module in human extrastriate cortex specialized for face perception. *The Journal of Neuroscience 17*, 11 (1997), 4302–4311.
35. Kelsey, R. E., and Stimson, B. *The meaning of photography*. Clark Art Institute, 2008.
36. Laurel, B. Interface agents: Metaphors with character. *Human values and the design of computer technology* (1997), 207–219.
37. Lei, Y.-H., Chen, Y.-Y., Iida, L., Chen, B.-C., Su, H.-H., and Hsu, W. H. Photo search by face positions and facial attributes on touch devices. In *Proceedings of the 19th ACM international conference on Multimedia*, MM '11, ACM (New York, NY, USA, 2011), 651–654.
38. Millen, D. R., and Patterson, J. F. Stimulating social engagement in a community network. In *Proceedings of the 2002 ACM conference on Computer supported cooperative work*, ACM (2002), 306–313.
39. Morton, J., and Johnson, M. H. Conspec and conlern: a two-process theory of infant face recognition. *Psychological review 98*, 2 (1991), 164.
40. Phillips, T. Unmasking the face on mars. new high-resolution images and 3d altimetry from nasa's mars global surveyor spacecraft reveal the face on mars for what it really is: a mesa. `http://science.nasa.gov/science-news/science-at-nasa/2001/ast24may_1/`, May 2001.
41. Sergent, J., Ohta, S., and Mdonald, B. Functional neuroanatomy of face and object processing: a position emission tomography study. *Brain 115*, 1 (1992), 15–36.
42. Shamma, D. A., Shaw, R., Shafton, P. L., and Liu, Y. Watch what i watch: using community activity to understand content. In *MIR '07: Proceedings of the international workshop on Workshop on multimedia information retrieval* (2007), 275–284.
43. Sproull, L., Subramani, M., Kiesler, S., Walker, J. H., and Waters, K. When the interface is a face. *Human-Computer Interaction 11*, 2 (1996), 97–124.
44. Suh, B., Hong, L., Pirolli, P., and Chi, E. H. Want to be retweeted? large scale analytics on factors impacting retweet in twitter network. In *2010 IEEE Second International Conference on Social Computing (SocialCom)* (2010), 177–184.
45. Takeuchi, A., and Nagao, K. Communicative facial displays as a new conversational modality. In *Proceedings of the INTERSECT'93 and CHI'93 conference on human factors in computing systems*, ACM (1993), 187–193.
46. Takeuchi, a., and naito, t. Situated facial displays: towards social interaction. In *Proceedings of the SIGCHI conference on human factors in computing systems*, acm press/addison-wesley publishing co. (1995), 450–455.
47. Vasalou, A., Joinson, A., and Courvoisier, D. Cultural differences, experience with social networks and the nature of true commitment in facebook. *International journal of human-computer studies 68*, 10 (2010), 719–728.
48. Viola, p., and jones, m. j. Robust real-time face detection. *International Journal of Computer Vision 57*, 2 (2004), 137–154.
49. Walker, J. H., Sproull, L., and Subramani, R. Using a human face in an interface. In *Proceedings of the SIGCHI conference on human factors in computing systems*, ACM (1994), 85–91.
50. Wojnicki, A., and Godes, D. Word-of-mouth as self-enhancement. *HBS marketing research paper*, 06-01 (2008).
51. Wright, J., Yang, A., Ganesh, A., Sastry, S., and Ma, Y. Robust face recognition via sparse representation. *Pattern analysis and machine intelligence, IEEE Transactions on 31*, 2 (2009), 210–227.
52. Yew, J., and Shamma, D. A. Know your data: Understanding implicit usage versus explicit action in video content classification. *IS&T/SPIE Electronic Imaging (January 2011)* (2011).
53. Young, A., Mcweeny, K., Hay, D., and Ellis, A. Matching familiar and unfamiliar faces on identity and expression. *Psychological research 48*, 2 (1986), 63–68.

# Photo Sharing of the Subject, by the Owner, for the Viewer – Examining the Subject's Preference

**Auk Kim**
Korea Advanced Institute of Science and Technology
Daejeon, South Korea, 305-701
kimauk@kaist.ac.kr

**Gahgene Gweon**
Korea Advanced Institute of Science and Technology
Daejeon, South Korea, 305-701
ggweon@kaist.ac.kr

## ABSTRACT
Photo sharing activities on social networking sites concern not only the person sharing the information (owner) and the person receiving the information (viewer) but also the person who is in the photo (subject). In our exploratory lab study, we asked 29 participants about their comfort level in allowing a photo owner to share a picture containing both the participant (subject) and the owner. Our results show that the photo subject feels more comfortable in sharing a photo when i) the "closeness between the subject and the owner (SO closeness)" is higher, and ii) the "closeness between the subject and the viewer (SV closeness)" is higher. In addition, we observed that both SV and SO closeness are important in determining the subject's picture sharing preference level.

## Author Keywords
Information sharing preference; closeness

## ACM Classification Keywords
H.5.m [Information Interfaces and Presentation]: MISCELLANEOUS

## INTRODUCTION
Photo sharing helps create and maintain social relationships, and is becoming part of our daily lives [1, 9]. For example, in Facebook, 25 million photos are uploaded and shared between Facebook users every day [5]. Additionally, many other social networking services (SNS) are incorporating photo-sharing features, allowing users to instantly broadcast daily activities and interests. However, some of these photos are undesirable digital traces. While many people spend time uploading and tagging photos that are taken with others, many others spend time un-tagging some of those photos [1]. There appears to be a gap between the sharing preferences of a person who uploads a photo ("owner") and the person in the photo ("subject").

Such a gap between a photo owner and a subject exists, because a photo uploaded by the owner reveals information about both the owner and the subject in the photo, but the owner and the subject may have different photo sharing preferences depending on who the "viewer" is. Figure 1 shows the relationship between the three parties involved. In our paper, we study interpersonal relationships between each party involved, in terms of closeness, and examine how the strength of interpersonal relationships affects the photo sharing preference of the subject. We will refer to the level of closeness between photo subject and photo owner as "subject-owner (SO) closeness" and to the level of closeness between photo subject and photo viewer as "subject-viewer (SV) closeness". Note that although our study examines the effect of closeness on the photo sharing preference, other variables such as the nature of an event (e.g. drinking event) or the characteristics of the parties involved (e.g. ex-girlfriend) are also important. In our study, we carefully selected images with neutralized content to minimize the impact of these other variables. As shown in Figure 1, the pictures shown in the study were taken in an office environment, and the two people in the picture are standing next to each other, facing the camera.

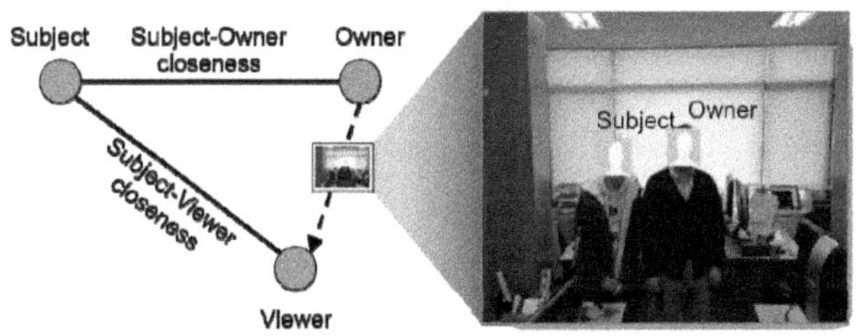


**Figure 1. Three types of parties involved in sharing a picture**

The effect of strength of interpersonal relationships on information sharing preferences has been demonstrated in previous research [3, 10]. For example, Wiese and his colleagues have examined how tie strength, expressed as closeness, relates to a person's willingness to share information [10]. Insights from such research on how social relationships affect sharing preferences can be used to inform policies for managing photos / information on diverse SNS systems. However, although researchers have examined the relationship between the information sharer (owner) and the receiver (viewer) and how the relationship affects their information sharing preference, the preference of the *subject* in the picture has not been discussed extensively. Therefore, in this paper, we examine the photo subject's information


*CHI 2014,* April 26 - May 01, 2014, Toronto, ON, Canada.

http://dx.doi.org/10.1145/2556288.2557247

sharing preferences, a topic that has received little attention thus far.

The remainder of this paper is organized as follows. We begin by introducing three research questions that deal with two types of closeness influencing a subject's photo sharing preferences. In the next sections, we present the details of our study. Then the results and discussion about the study are presented, followed by the conclusion.

## RESEARCH QUESTIONS ON CLOSENESS AND PHOTO SHARING PREFERENCE

In this section, three research questions on closeness with respect to a photo subject and his photo sharing preferences are discussed. Sharing one's own photo is, in a broader sense, an act of self-disclosure because photos contain information about the people in it. Research shows that the degree of self-disclosure in a relationship is affected by the strength of the relationship [4], which is measured by closeness in our study. In addition, research shows that the higher the relationship strength, the higher the trust [6, 7]. Similarly, Weise and his colleagues showed that a higher level of closeness is associated with a higher degree of willingness to share [10].

From a photo subject's perspective, these results suggest that if the degree of closeness between the subject and a photo viewer is high, then the probability of the subject's picture sharing preference with the viewer will be greater due to higher degree of self-disclosure and trust. Extending these results further, we hypothesize that if closeness between a subject and a viewer is already high, then the subject will be comfortable with a friend (owner) sharing a picture because in such a case the owner is just a medium for sharing. Therefore, we present our hypothesis as follows.

*Hypothesis 1: If subject-viewer (SV) closeness increases, a subject's picture sharing preference for an owner to share their personal picture with a viewer will also increase.*

Another type of closeness that we are interested in is the relationship between a photo subject and an owner (SO closeness), who shares their personal photo. The effect of this relationship on a subject's photo sharing preference can be inferred from previous work that shows when a person has a shared acquaintance, he is more trusting of that acquaintance [11]. In our study, that shared acquaintance is the owner. In addition, literature shows that even without any communication, seeing a person in an online group repeatedly can be a precursor to forming personal attachment [8]. This work suggests that having a common friend (owner) with a high degree of closeness increases the likelihood of seeing that friend's friend (viewer) online, for example, on the owner's Facebook timeline. Therefore, our second hypothesis is summarized as follows.

*Hypothesis 2: If subject-owner (SO) closeness increases, a subject's picture sharing preference for an owner to share their personal picture with a viewer will also increase.*

In addition to the independent effect of SV closeness and SO closeness on a photo subject's sharing preference, we hypothesize that there will be an interaction effect between the two types of closeness. More specifically, we hypothesize the following.

*Hypothesis 3: As subject-viewer (SV) closeness increases, relationships with higher subject-owner (SO) closeness will have a stronger impact than relationships with lower SO closeness on a subject's picture sharing preference for an owner to share their personal picture with a viewer.*

Partial support for our reasoning comes from previous research, which shows that people increasingly disclose their inner thoughts and feelings in greater frequency and depth and in a wider range of topics as relationships develop over time [1]. Therefore, we expect that if a photo subject feels close to both an owner and a viewer, the two types of closeness can have a synergy effect, similar to the increasing level of self-disclosure that develops over time.

## THE EXPERIMENTAL STUDY

The goal of our study was to examine a person's (subject) picture sharing preferences when his friend (owner) shares a picture that shows both the subject and the owner, to a friend of the owner (viewer).

### Participants

We recruited 29 participants by posting ads on a campus online community bulletin board. To participate in the study, a participant had to be a member of Facebook and have at least 70 Facebook friends. The average number of Facebook friends of participants was 435.1 (SD = 220.8). Fifteen participants were female, and fourteen were male. The average participant age was 22.8 (SD = 2.5).

### Measurements

#### *Closeness*

Closeness measures the degree of intimacy in interpersonal relationships. As used in previous research by Weise and his colleagues [10], we asked our participants the following question: "How close do you feel to X?". Participants rated two groups of people. The first is a list of their Facebook friends (photo owner), and the second is a list of their Facebook friend's friends (photo viewers), who will view photos uploaded by photo owners. To rate photo owners, a Likert scale with five levels of closeness (1: very distant, 3: neither distant nor close, 5: very close) was used. For rating photo viewers, a scale of six levels of closeness ranging from 0 to 5 was used. A rating of "0: do not know" was added because the participant may not know the photo viewer.

#### *Picture Sharing Preference*

We also measured picture sharing preference, which is the degree of comfort level that a participant feels towards a photo sharing activity. We asked the participant, "How comfortable do you feel about <photo owner> sharing this picture with <photo viewer>?". We used a five level Likert scale (1: definitely not comfortable, 3: no preference, 5: definitely comfortable) to measure the participant's comfort levels for photo disclosure.

### Method

We conducted a laboratory study, which lasted about 60 – 90 minutes depending on how quickly the participants answered questions. After signing a consent form for the study, each participant was first asked to login to his Facebook account so that our system can have access to the participant's Facebook friends. Next, the participant answered a brief questionnaire consisting of background questions such as gender and age. The following three steps describe the procedure used to collect our data.

*Step 1. Rating Photo Owners in terms of Closeness and Generating a Photo Owner List*

In step 1, a participant was asked to rate the closeness between him and his friend, who was selected randomly by our system from the participant's Facebook friends. This friend is the "photo owner" and the participant is the "photo subject" in our study. Since we wanted photo owners from all five levels of closeness, our system randomly selected a Facebook friend until it collected at least one photo owner friend per closeness category. For example, after rating five friends, if the participant rated friend #1 as closeness 2, friend #2 as closeness 3, friend #3 as closeness 5, friend #4 as closeness 1, and friend #5 as closeness 4, then this participant satisfied the requirement of having at least one friend in each closeness category. Therefore, the participant would be done with rating photo owners. However, after rating 5 friends, if the participant rated friend #1, #2, and #3 as closeness 3, and friend #4, and #5 as closeness 1, then the participant has to keep rating friends until he satisfied our requirement. On an average, a participant rated forty Facebook friends before satisfying our requirement, and took about twenty minutes to complete this task. Once the participant satisfied the requirement of having at least one photo owner friend per closeness category, we randomly selected one person from each closeness category to generate a "photo owner list" for each subject.

*Step 2. Rating Photo Viewers in terms of Closeness and Generating a Photo Viewer List*

Next, the participant was asked to rate a photo owner's randomly selected Facebook friend (photo viewer) in terms of closeness. As in step 1, the system presented a photo viewer until the participant identified at least one viewer for each of the six closeness categories for the selected owner from the photo owner list. Once the participant satisfied this requirement, we randomly selected one person from each closeness category to generate a "photo viewer list". This list consists of thirty viewers (five photo owners * six closeness levels). On an average, the participant rated 22 Facebook users before identifying at least one user per category.

*Step 3. Rating the Picture Sharing Preference*

In this step, we asked a participant to indicate their comfort level towards a photo owner's act of sharing a picture. In addition to the question, a modified version of the photo shown in Figure 1 was presented. The participant/ subject and the owner's faces shown in the photo were replaced with their Facebook profile images. We told the participant that the photo was taken from an event for the owner, e.g. owner's birthday.

## RESULTS AND DISCUSSION

We conducted a mixed model analysis of variance (multi-level model) predicting picture sharing preference as the outcome variable. Each column in table 1 shows the five regression models predicting the sharing preferences using a different set of predictors. Because we had 30 ratings per participant, we included the participant in all five models as a random effect to control for non-independence of the data.

| n = 870 | Sharing preference, M = 3.44 (1.17) | | | | |
|---|---|---|---|---|---|
| age | | -0.09* | -0.10* | -0.10* | -0.10* |
| gender = male | | -0.22 | | | |
| SV closeness | | | 0.30** | | 0.20** |
| SO closeness | | | | 0.28** | 0.19** |
| SV x SO close | | | | | 0.04** |
| Intercept | 3.44** | 5.63** | 4.87** | 4.79** | 4.30** |
| Conditional $R^2$ | 0.18 | 0.18 | 0.38 | 0.30 | 0.51 |
| Model name | User | Age | Viewer | Owner | All |

**Table 1. Multi-level Regression models sharing preference, controlling for each participant. The data in each cell are non-standardized β, except for last row which is conditional $R^2$. Significance: *p<0.05; **p<0.001**

The second column (model name = User, $R^2$ = 0.18) shows a model that only has the effect of the participant, which accounts for individual differences. Data shows that 18% of variance is due to individual differences. The third column (model name = Age, $R^2$ = 0.18) shows the participant-level effect of gender and age. Only the effect of age was statistically significant. Participants were less comfortable with an owner sharing photos as they get a year older (2% less preference in sharing per year, $\beta$ = -0.09, $p < 0.01$). However, this result many not hold for the general population since our user population is limited in terms of age, ranging from 19 to 32. Given the significant effect of age from this model, we included age as a fixed effect for the rest of the models.

Next, we examined how well the two different closeness types (SV and SO) predicted the picture sharing preference as stated in hypotheses 1 and 2. For hypothesis 1, as hypothesized, the effect of SV closeness on picture sharing preference was statistically significant. The fourth column of table 1 (model name = Viewer, $R^2$ = 0.38) shows that subjects feel more comfortable when their personal photos are shared by an owner whom they are closer to ($\beta$ = 0.30, $p < 0.01$). A one-point gain in SO closeness accounts for a 6% increase in sharing preference. Similarly, for RQ2, the effect of SO closeness on picture sharing preference was statistically significant. The fifth column of table 1 (model name = Owner, $R^2 = 0.30$) shows that a one-point gain in SO closeness accounts for a 5.6% increase in sharing preference ($\beta = 0.28$, $p < 0.01$).

When comparing the conditional $R^2$ values of the viewer and the owner models, one can see that SV closeness is a better predictor than SO closeness when explaining a subject's picture sharing preference. This result is not surprising, because SV closeness is a direct measure of relationship strength between a subject and a viewer and the owner acts like a medium for sharing a photo. However, although SO closeness is a more indirect measure compared to SV closeness, it still explains much of the variance ($R^2 = 0.30$) and is potentially a useful measure. Furthermore, the beta coefficients associated with the two predictors are similar ($\beta = 0.30$ vs. $0.28$), thus suggesting that both types of closeness can account for changes in picture sharing preference at a similar level.

For hypothesis 3, we wanted to examine the relationship between SV closeness and SO closeness in a subject's picture sharing preference. The last column of table 1 (model name = All, $R^2$=0.51) shows a model that uses SV closeness, SO closeness, and the interaction of these two types of closeness. Our data shows that in addition to SV closeness and SO closeness, the interaction between the two is also significant. Namely, the effect of SV closeness on the picture sharing preference of a subject is greater for relationships that have higher SO closeness than for relationships with lower SO closeness ($\beta = 0.04$, $p < 0.01$). In this model, the beta coefficients for SV closeness and SO closeness are similar in value (0.20 and 0.19 respectively), suggesting that they are both important factors in predicting a subject's picture sharing preference. In addition, the model that uses both SV closeness and SO closeness as predictors ($R^2$=0.51) is better than a model that uses only one of the closeness types ($R^2$=0.30 or 0.38).

## CONCLUSION

As support for photo sharing activities increases in SNS systems, privacy concerns emerge as well. This paper presents our preliminary study on a photo *subject*'s sharing preferences. Our results show that the photo subject feels more comfortable in sharing a photo when i) the SV closeness is higher, and ii) the SO closeness is higher. In addition, we observed that both SV and SO closeness are important in determining the subject's picture sharing preference level.

Currently, most SNS systems allow photo owners to post pictures to viewers and leave the photo subject's picture sharing preference at the total discretion of the owners. Results from our study can be used in supplementing these SNS systems so that the photo sharing preferences are recommended automatically or semi-automatically. However, our main findings on SV and SO closeness on the photo sharing preference may not hold when additional factors, which were controlled for in this study, are considered. For example, although SV closeness may be high between family members, if the event in which the photo was taken is not neutral in nature (e.g. drinking event), the sharing preference may not be as high as what's predicted from our study. Nevertheless, by examining a photo subject's sharing preference in a neutral setting, our study presents a first step towards improving the experience of sharing. Another limitation of our study is that the data used in the study are self-reported, and thus some of the answers may not be as accurate as hard data. In addition, the study results may not generalize, given that our user population is limited in terms of demographics, such as age and background diversity. As a next step, we plan to explore more complex scenarios, such as how different types of pictures affect sharing preferences.

## ACKNOWLEDGEMENT

This research was supported by Basic Science Research Program through the NRF of Korea, funded by the Ministry of Science, ICT & Future Planning (2013R1A1A1013319).

## REFERENCES


1. Altman, I., and Taylor, D. *Social Penetration: The Development of Interpersonal Relationships*, Holt, Rinehart & Winston, Dalmas, 1973.
2. Besmer, A., and Lipford, R. H. Moving Beyond Untagging: Photo Privacy in a Tagged World. In *Proc. CHI 2010*, ACM Press (2010), 1563–1572.
3. Consolvo, S., et al. Location Disclosure to Social Relations: Why, When, & What People Want to Share. In *Proc. CHI 2005*, ACM Press (2005), 81–90.
4. Duck, S. *Human Relationships*. SAGE Publications Limited, 2007.
5. Ebersman, D.A. Facebook, Inc Registration Statement on Form S-1. *Securities and Exchange Commission*. 1, (2012).
6. Ganovetter, M.S. "The strength of weak ties." *American Journal of Sociology* (1973), 1360-1380.
7. Marsden, P., and Campbell, K. E. "Measuring Tie Strength." *Social Forces* 63.2 (1984): 482-501.
8. Milgram, S. The Familiar Stranger: An Aspect of Urban Anonymity. *The Individual in a Social World: Essays and Experiments*. Longman, 1977.
9. Sleeper, M., Balebako, R., Das, S., McConahy, A. L., Wiese, J., and Cranor, L. F. The Post that Wasn't: Exploring Self-censorship on Facebook. In *Proc. CHI 2013*, ACM Press (2013), 793–802.
10. Wiese, J., et al. Are you Close with Me? Are you Nearby?: Investigating Social Groups, Closeness, and Willingness to Share. In *Proc. UbiComp 2011*, ACM Press (2011), 197–206.
11. Yuki, M., Maddux, W., Brewer, M., and Takemura, K. Cross-Cultural Differences in Relationship- and Group-Based Trust." *Personality and Social Psychology Bulletin* 31,1 (2005), 48-62.

# Does Content Determine Information Popularity in Social Media?

## A Case Study of YouTube Videos' Content and their Popularity

**Flavio Figueiredo**[1], **Jussara M. Almeida**[1], **Fabrício Benevenuto**[1]
[1]Department of Computer Science, UFMG, Brazil
{flaviov,jussara,fabricio}@dcc.ufmg.br

**Krishna P. Gummadi**[2]
[2]MPI-SWS, Germany
gummadi@mpi-sws.org

### ABSTRACT
We here investigate *what drives the popularity of information on social media platforms*. Focusing on YouTube, we seek to understand the extent to which content by itself determines a video's popularity. Using mechanical turk as experimental platform, we asked users to evaluate pairs of videos, and compared users' relative perception of the videos' content against their relative popularity reported by YouTube. We found that in most evaluations users could not reach consensus on which video had better content as their perceptions tend to be very subjective. Nevertheless, when consensus was reached, the video with preferred content almost always achieved greater popularity on YouTube, highlighting the importance of content in driving information popularity on social media.

### Author Keywords
Content popularity; social media; user study

### ACM Classification Keywords
H.5.4 Hypertext/Hypermedia: User issues.

### INTRODUCTION
*What drives the popularity of information in social media?* Recently, this question has attracted a lot of research attention as social media sites become increasingly popular. An unresolved part of this question is about the relative roles of two primary forces that drive the popularity of a piece of information: (i) its content, i.e., the interestingness, topicality, or quality of the information *as perceived by users*, and (ii) its dissemination mechanisms, such as propagation by word-of-mouth, blogs or mass media channels. It stands to reason that both factors matter, but the extent to which they impact the popularity of a piece of information remains an open issue.

Many previous studies on how information becomes popular in social media sites focused on dissemination related factors (e.g, social influence, mechanisms that expose content to users, time of upload) [2, 4, 7, 9, 10], ignoring the role of the content itself. Other efforts, instead, analyzed social media content focusing on data mining tasks such as popularity prediction [11] and video classification [5], analyzing popularity differences in content duplicates [2], and exploring content importance as parameter of popularity evolution models [8]. In this paper we take a different and complementary approach, focusing on understanding the extent to which content matters for popularity of videos on YouTube.

Our methodology attempts to assess *users' relative perceptions* of the contents of pairs of videos through user surveys conducted over Amazon mechanical turk. Users in our experiments are exposed only to the video content, and are not subjected to other factors (inherent to the YouTube site) that may impact their perceptions of content (e.g., user comments, social links, appearance of content in external sites). Specifically, we present to users pairs of videos from the same major topic and uploaded around the same date, and ask them to choose which one: (1) *they enjoyed more*, (2) *they would be more willing to share with friends*, and (3) *they predicted would become more popular on YouTube*. These questions target the user's individual perception of content interestingness and of the interests of her social circle (and thus the chance of the content spreading through it), as well as the user's expectations on a global scale. Our goals are to assess, for each of these questions, whether users reach consensus, and, when there is consensus, whether user perceptions match the relative popularity achieved by the videos on YouTube.

We find that users could not reach consensus in many evaluations, even when the popularity (on YouTube) of the evaluated videos differs by orders of magnitude. The lack of consensus is more striking for sharing and liking choices. It also depends on the video topic. This suggests that users' perceptions about content are quite subjective and that content may not be the most important factor that drives popularity in many cases. However, whenever participants reached consensus, their choices mostly match the video with largest popularity on YouTube, suggesting that, in these cases, content has a significant impact and predictive power on video popularity.

The goals of our study complement previous work. In particular, Salganik *et al.* [9] also relied on a user study to understand popularity dynamics. However, they focused on the impact of social influence on popularity, whereas we focus on the role of content and rely on users to evaluate the content in a setup that is isolated (to the extent possible) from dissemination mechanisms that might influence popularity. To our knowledge, the human perceptions of content and how they correlate to popularity in a social media site have not been

**Acknowledgments:** Research supported by InWeb - Institute of Science and Technology for Web Research and by individual grants from CNPq, Capes and Fapemig.


*CHI'14*, April 26–May 1, 2014, Toronto, Canada.
Copyright © 2014 ACM ISBN/14/04...$15.00.
http://dx.doi.org/10.1145/2556288.2557285

previously analyzed. Thus, this work is a first step towards assessing the role of content in determining popularity of a piece of information, and our proposed experimental methodology, discussed next, is a key contribution towards that goal.

## EXPERIMENTAL METHODOLOGY

Our study is guided by two questions: *[Q1] Given a pair of videos with similar topic, can users reach consensus on their relative popularity? [Q2] When users reach consensus, does the preferred video match the most popular one on YouTube?*

Question Q1 is focused on the collective notion of popularity reported by the users in our experiment, who are subject only to the content itself. This notion relates to whether a user likes and/or would be willing to share a video more than the other, and also whether a user, despite personal tastes, believes one video would become more popular than the other. Question Q2 aims at comparing this notion with the popularity achieved by the videos on YouTube, measured by the total number of views at the time we collected the videos, which can be affected by various factors, other than content alone.

### Datasets

In order to identify videos with similar topic, we used Freebase[1], a collaborative semantic knowledge database covering over 30 million topics. We crawled YouTube for videos indexed under the same Freebase topic on its API, focusing on 2 topics that span diverse user interests and are neither too specific nor too broad: *major league baseball* and *music videos*.

We crawled YouTube on August 2013, focusing on videos that were uploaded from the US on April 2012. By studying videos of similar topic and uploaded from the same country, we factored out the notion of popularity due to latent social, cultural and psychological issues (e.g., soccer is less popular than baseball in the US). By focusing on videos uploaded around the same time, we factored out popularity variations due to first mover advantage [2] and upload date [7]. We also downloaded only videos considered safe by YouTube's safe search, limiting the chance of users finding a video offensive, and that could be embedded in external sites. The latter is to allow user evaluations to be done outside YouTube, and thus be unaffected by the other pieces of information (e.g., number of views, user comments) available on a video's page.

We also defined three ranges of YouTube popularity values: *low*, with number of views between 10 and 100; *medium*, from 1,000 to 10,000 views; and *high*, from 100,000 to 1,000,000 views. For each topic, we chose 3 videos of each range, each video having from 4 to 6 minutes of duration.

### Human Intelligence Tasks

We ran our user experiments on Amazon mechanical turk (MT), recruiting as participants of our task only master workers (i.e., the best workers as ranked by MT) based on the US.

The first step was to build, for each topic, all 36 pairings for the 9 selected videos. These pairs were assigned to 9 *folds*, so as to have only unique videos in each fold, and deployed on a web application built by us, called YouRank. YouRank assigns one fold (4 video pairs) to each user following a round-robin schedule. It shows to the user only the embedded video streams, hiding any other video metadata kept by YouTube.

[1] `http://www.freebase.com`

| S1. How old are you?<br>S2. Are you a male or a female?<br>S3. How often do you watch a video on YouTube?<br>S4. How often do you share YouTube videos with friends or colleagues?<br>S5. How often do you share any kind of online content with friends or colleagues? | E1. Which video did you enjoy watching more?<br>E2. Which video you would be most willing to share with a friend or group of friends?<br>E3. Which video do you predict will be more popular on YouTube?<br>E4. Did you already know (watched previously) one of these videos? |
|---|---|
| **(a) Demographic Survey** | **(b) Video Evaluation Form** |

**Figure 1: YouRank Forms**

After logging in, each user was first asked to answer the demographic survey in Figure 1a. For questions S3 to S5, the possible answers were: 1) never; 2) rarely (few times a year); 3) occasionally (few times a month); 4) often (few times a week); 5) very often (once or more daily).

Next, the user was asked to watch 4 video pairs, and, for each pair, answer the form shown in Figure 1b picking one of four options: a) Video 1 (left); b) Video 2 (right); c) Both; d) Neither. Thus, two neutral options (c-d) were available in case the user could not choose one video. The user could also provide feedback in free text form for each pair. We asked users not to visit the video page on YouTube, and to indicate whether they had watched any of the videos in the past. To avoid bias due to user fatigue, the pairs of a fold were randomized whenever a new user was assigned to the fold. A user was expected to take roughly 45 minutes to evaluate 4 pairs of videos, each one from 4 to 6 minute long. Thus, upon task completion, each user was paid 4.50 US dollars, which is consistent with the MT suggested hourly rate of 6 US dollars. In practice, the users took on average 44.8 minutes to complete the task, although some evaluations were disregarded (see below).

### Evaluation Metrics

To tackle question Q1, we measured consensus for each video pair using the Fleiss' Kappa ($\kappa$) score of agreement [6]. This score varies from -1 to 1, while values above .4 are interpreted as fair to good agreements, and above 0.75 as very good agreements [6]. We determined that consensus was reached if the null hypothesis of negative or no agreement ($\kappa \leq 0$) could be rejected. The same score was achieved regardless of whether the neutral responses c, d, were included. Thus, we computed it over all responses. We also applied Bonferroni correction to rule out significance due to random chance [3].

To answer Q2, we focused only on pairs of videos for which consensus was reached and computed the fraction $\hat{p}$ of those pairs for which the preferred video matches the one with larger popularity on YouTube. We then used an exact binominal sign test based on Clopper-Pearson confidence interval [6], which is suitable to small samples (as our case), to test whether $\hat{p}$ is above random chance (i.e., $\hat{p} > 0.5$).

## RESULTS

We now discuss the results of two rounds of MT experiments, one for each chosen topic. We ran each round until 72 users

| | Major League Baseball | | | Music Videos | | |
|---|---|---|---|---|---|---|
| | S3 | S4 | S5 | S3 | S4 | S5 |
| Never | 0% | 4% | 1% | 0% | 1% | 0% |
| Rarely | 0% | 18% | 12.5% | 0% | 22% | 13% |
| Occasionally | 8% | 39% | 28% | 21% | 45% | 32% |
| Often | 48% | 29% | 37.5% | 39.5% | 28% | 37% |
| Very Often | 44% | 10% | 21% | 39.5% | 4% | 18% |

**Table 1: Answers to S3, S4 and S5 in the demographic survey (Fig. 1a).**

| p-value | | Major League Baseball | | | Music Videos | | |
|---|---|---|---|---|---|---|---|
| | | E1 | E2 | E3 | E1 | E2 | E3 |
| .05 | $\%(\kappa > 0)$ | 25% | 13% | 52% | 11% | 2.7% | 13% |
| | Avg. $\kappa$ | .68 | .64 | .74 | .63 | .53 | .65 |
| .01 | $\%(\kappa > 0)$ | 19% | 8% | 41% | 8% | 2.7% | 11% |
| | Avg. $\kappa$ | .75 | .76 | .78 | .63 | .53 | .69 |
| .001 | $\%(\kappa > 0)$ | 16% | 5% | 36% | 5% | 2.7% | 8% |
| | Avg. $\kappa$ | .79 | .76 | .83 | .65 | .62 | .86 |

**Table 2: Percentage of video pairs that rejected the Fleiss' Kappa null hypothesis of $\kappa \leq 0$ and the average level of agreement $\kappa$ for those cases. The columns correspond to the questions in Figure 1b.**

had finished their tasks. However, in both rounds, some users refused the task after logging in. Also, we disregarded evaluations in which the users reported they: (1) were unable to watch a video, 2 cases, or (2) had watched at least one of the videos before (5% and 8% of the cases for the major league baseball and music video experiments, respectively). The latter was done to avoid a bias due to prior knowledge. We were then left with 6 to 10 evaluations per pair (8 on average). We summarize the answers to the demographic survey next, and afterwards we discuss the results for our two driving questions based on the answers to the form in Figure 1b.

### Demographic Survey

On MT, we required all users to be from the US. Moreover, 53% and 42% of the them (of 72 per round) were males in the baseball and music experiments, respectively, whereas in both rounds, most (57%) had from 20 to 45 years of age, and only 5% were under 20 years old. The answers of users regarding their viewing and sharing habits (S3-S5 in Figure 1a) are summarized in Table 1. Note that participants of both rounds of experiments are avid YouTube viewers: they watch videos at least occasionally, and most of them do it often (39.5-48%) or very often (39.5-44%). Also, most users share YouTube content occasionally (39-45%) or often (28-29%), whereas only 22% of the users in both rounds share YouTube videos only rarely or never. Finally, in both rounds, users tend to share online content in general more often, as expected.

### Q1: Can users reach consensus?

Table 2 shows, for both video topics, the percentage of pairs in which users reached consensus, (i.e., pairs for which the null hypothesis of $\kappa \leq 0$ can be rejected). It also shows the average $\kappa$ scores for *those pairs that rejected the null hypothesis*. Results are shown separately for each question in Figure 1b, and for different significance levels (p-values).

In general, for any considered significance level, and for both topics, the fraction of pairs that passed the test tends to be very small (with few exceptions). The fraction is larger when users were asked which video they predicted would be more popular (E3). Thus, user agreement is easier when it comes

| | Baseball | Music |
|---|---|---|
| E1 | 100%** | 75% |
| E2 | 100%* | 100% |
| E3 | 84%** | 100%* |

**Table 3: Percentage of pairs (with consensus) that match YouTube popularity. * (**) indicate above random chance p-val=.05 (.01)**

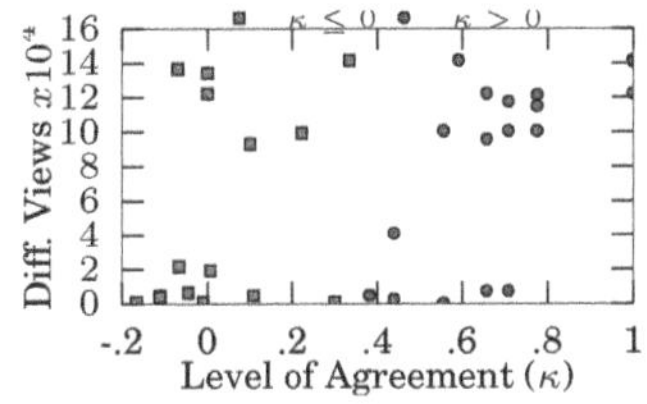


**Figure 2: $\kappa$ vs popularity gap**

to the collective knowledge of popularity. However, this happened in at most 52% of the pairs (p-value=0.05). Users agreed less often when asked which video they enjoyed the most (E1), reflecting a natural heterogeneity of user interests. The consensus was even rarer for sharing patterns (E2), possibly reflecting heterogeneity in terms of social activities and users' perceptions of the interests of their social networks. This is reflected by the number of times users chose a neutral answer. For E2 this occurred from 40% (baseball) to 52% (music) of the evaluations. For both topics and the other questions, less than 20% of the evaluations used a neutral choice. Finally, we show that when consensus was reached, the agreements were on average good ($\kappa$>0.4) or very good ($\kappa$>0.75).

To illustrate these findings, note the divergence in opinions in the following feedbacks on the same music video:

U1: the girl in the video 2 was stunningly beautiful so i would share that one

U2: Video 2 was sad and dark and I didn't like the girl's voice.

U3: I secretly like Evanescence but I would never let my friends know.

U4: The video on the left was much better music for my tastes

The divergence in opinions reveals the more egocentric notions of liking/sharing content. U2 dislikes the video because it was sad, and U4 likes it because of her personal musical taste. U1 would share the video because of the girl in it, while U3 would not share it because she secretly likes the band.

Recall that users evaluated pairs of videos that covered a wide range of popularity values on YouTube. Thus, one may ask whether users could reach consensus more often for pairs of videos with a larger gap in their relative popularity. Surprisingly, we found no strong trend towards that, as illustrated in Figure 2 for E3 in the major league baseball experiments (p-val = .05). Very low $\kappa$ values were obtained even for videos which differ in popularity by hundreds of thousands views.

Table 2 also shows that the agreements are more common for major league baseball videos than for music videos. While this may be related to a more diverse range of personal interests for music videos (e.g., U4's feedback), it may also relate to promotional campaigns for this kind of content. Such campaigns may cause videos to be popular for a short while, regardless of user tastes. As an example, we could note case of music videos that experienced a burst in popularity, possibly caused by promotion (professional or amateur such as in a blog) but was unable to remain popular over time.

Nevertheless, there are many cases of lack of consensus. One example is a pair of baseball videos, where one of them has over 100 times more views than the other, and remains more popular throughout the monitored period. Yet, the users of our experiment could not reach consensus in none of the questions. Further investigating these videos, we noted that the most popular video has a watermark that affected user opinions in our experiment, as indicated by the feedback: "The watermark on video 2 ruins it". This suggests that other latent factors may play a role on driving the popularity of social media.

**Q2: Does consensus match the popularity on YouTube?** Considering only pairs for which consensus was reached (p-value=0.05), Table 3 shows the fraction of pairs in which the video preferred by MT users has higher popularity on YouTube. Note that, whenever consensus is reached, user preferences match YouTube's popularity in almost all cases. This result is above random chance (p-value=0.05) in most cases, except when the number of pairs with consensus is too small. Thus, if users can reach consensus on their opinions, the preferred video is likely to become more popular.

## DISCUSSION

In the traditional media (e.g., newspapers, TV), dissemination mechanisms are closely tied to the content generators. Content is traditionally generated or selected by professionals on behalf of organizations that have vested interest and ability to promote their content (e.g., ad campaigns). Differently, social media is dominated by content generated by ordinary users, and the key dissemination mechanisms are (i) crowd-endorsements: information "liked" by crowds is promoted in search results and recommendation tools, and (ii) viral propagation over a social network: anyone who finds the information content interesting can "share" it with friends. Thus, the dissemination mechanisms are democratized and only loosely coupled with the content generators. This democratization offers the hope that information popularity would be driven to a larger extent by its content (i.e., how users perceive or like it) than it is in traditional media. In this paper we give the first step towards understanding the extent to which this is true.

To that end, we relied on user evaluations of pairs of YouTube videos of similar topic, factoring out dissemination related factors. We found that users' perception of content is very subjective, as users often could not reach consensus at which video they liked or would share more, or predicted would become more popular. This result indicates the difficulty in determining the role of content in driving popularity, and complements previous observations that users cannot estimate the extent of visibility of their content [1]. However, whenever there was consensus, the preferred video almost always matched the one with higher popularity on YouTube, highlighting the key role played by content in those cases.

From a social media research perspective, this finding emphasizes the need to account for content in studies of popularity. From a media site operator's or viral marketer's perspective, it has implications for popularity prediction. For example, it can be leveraged by marketers or advertisers to compare new videos against old ones with known popularities to define which one has more chance of attracting viewers. It also motivates future studies on how a site operator can design a scalable way for gathering users' feedback to predict which of newly uploaded videos are more likely to become popular.

We note that representativeness is an important but challenging issue in any empirical study, as ours. We here designed an experimental methodology that is as thorough as possible, given our practical constraints. We chose one of the most popular social media sites, YouTube, and recruited only master MT workers, who are known to perform better tasks. Given our budget, we carefully chose the videos of our dataset, covering three popularity levels, with multiple videos per level. To avoid extraneous factors, we only compared videos of the same topic and similar age, and only used evaluations of users who had not seen the video before. To ensure that our sample sizes are not too small to draw conclusions, we applied conservative and exact statistical tests, adequate for them, presenting results for various significance levels. Thus, our setup was designed to yield the most accurate and representative results, within our constraints[2].

However, we acknowledge that it is impossible to generalize our findings without future studies. We hope that this work will encourage future efforts to apply our methodology across various applications and over more content instances.

## REFERENCES


1. Bernstein, M. S., Bakshy, E., Burke, M., and Karrer, B. Quantifying the Invisible Audience in Social Networks. In *Proc. CHI* (2013).
2. Borghol, Y., Ardon, S., Carlsson, N., Eager, D., and Mahanti, A. The Untold Story of the Clones: Content-Agnostic Factors that Impact YouTube Video Popularity. In *Proc. KDD* (2012).
3. Bretz, F., Hothorn, T., and Westfall, P. *Multiple Comparisons Using R*, 1 ed. CRC Press, 2010.
4. Figueiredo, F., Benevenuto, F., and Almeida, J. The Tube Over Time: Characterizing Popularity Growth of YouTube Videos. In *Proc. WSDM* (2011).
5. Filippova, K., and Hall, K. B. Improved Video Categorization from Text Metadata and User Comments. In *Proc. SIGIR* (2011).
6. Fleiss, J. L., and Levin, B. *Statistical Methods for Rates and Proportions*, 3 ed. Wiley-Interscience, 2003.
7. Lakkaraju, H., McAuley, J., and Leskovec, J. What's in a Name? Understanding the Interplay between Titles, Content, and Communities in Social Media. In *Proc. ICWSM* (2013).
8. Matsubara, Y., Sakurai, Y., Prakash, B. A., Li, L., and Faloutsos, C. Rise and Fall Patterns of Information Diffusion. In *Proc. KDD.* (2012).
9. Salganik, M., Dodds, P., and Watts, D. Experimental Study of Inequality and Unpredictability in an Artificial Cultural Market. *Science 311*, 5762 (2006), 854–856.
10. Shamma, D. A., Kennedy, L., and Churchill, E. F. Peaks and Persistence: Modeling the Shape of Microblog Conversations. In *Proc. CSCW* (2011).
11. Yano, T., and Smith, N. A. Whats Worthy of Comment? Content and Comment Volume in Political Blogs. In *Proc. ICWSM* (2010).


[2] In favor of reproducibility, our source code and our datasets are available at: `http://github.com/flaviovdf/yourank`

# You Read What You Value: Understanding Personal Values and Reading Interests

**Gary Hsieh**
Human Centered Design & Engineering
DUB group, University of Washington
garyhs@uw.edu

**Jilin Chen, Jalal Mahmud, Jeffrey Nichols**
IBM Almaden Research Center
650 Harry Road, San Jose, CA 95120, USA
{jilinc, jumahmud, jwnichols}@us.ibm.com

## ABSTRACT
This paper presents an experiment on the relationship between personal values and reading interests of online articles. Results suggest that individuals' values can predict their topical interests. For example, holding stronger universalism values predict interests towards environmental articles, whereas holding stronger achievement values predict interest towards work-related articles. Findings demonstrate the possibility of targeting based on individuals' personal values, but also highlight certain challenges and limitations when applying this approach for online content.

### Author Keywords
Personal values; reading interest; Twitter; content targeting

### ACM Classification Keywords
H.5.3. Group and Organizational Interfaces: Computer-supported cooperative work.

## INTRODUCTION
Personal values convey what is important to us. By definition, they are "deeply rooted, abstract motivations that guide, justify or explain attitudes, norms, opinions and actions" [5]. They underlie and influence individual behaviors, from choice of college major, consumer decisions, religiosity, etc (see Schwartz et al. [5]). More recently the study of values and behaviors have also been extended to the online context, where values have been shown to predict word usage in online posts [1].

In this work, we aim to build on this body of research by exploring whether values may also influence the types of textual content that we are interested in consuming online. If demonstrated, the influence of personal values on an individual's topical interests could contribute to valuable applications such as online content recommendation, where existing techniques (e.g. content similarity, collaborative filtering and social network structure, see Jannach et al. [2] for a review) are mostly agnostic about people's deeper motivations.


*CHI 2014*, April 26 - May 01 2014, Toronto, ON, Canada.

ACM 978-1-4503-2473-1/14/04…$15.00.
http://dx.doi.org/10.1145/2556288.2557201

Existing research on personal values suggest that upholding certain values motivate people to seek certain types of information when making a decision, as values have been found to direct attention. Verplanken and Holland demonstrated that when the universalism value (i.e. pursuing the welfare of all people and for nature) was first primed in an unrelated task, students who strongly endorsed the value sought twice as much information about environmental impacts of TV sets as sought by students who did not endorse such value [7].

However, there are two limitations with prior work. First, Verplanken and Holland studied how individuals' values influence their decision process when there is a clear objective, but online content consumption is not always driven by goals. When individual are not seeking information in order to make a decision, are their topical interests and reading behaviors still influenced by values? Second, and perhaps more importantly, existing research has only shown a link between the universalism value and consumption of environmental information. If values do influence content consumption, then other types of values should also induce interests in other types of information. Without additional research, we lack the practical knowledge of what topics map onto which values.

## VALUES AND TOPICAL INTERESTS
As with prior work by Verplanken and Holland, we use the value dimensions in the Theory of Basic Values by Schwartz et al., which were developed through surveys of people across 67 countries and are well studied and tested [5]. Schwartz derived 10 basic values, which map onto 5 higher-level value dimensions [4]. In addition to being well studied and tested, Schwartz's values are also appropriate for this work as they discriminate among individual people instead of national cultures and that they are not limited to work but also include values from different life domains. As represented in Figure 1, the circumflex structure in Schwartz' Value Theory indicates relations of conflict and congruity across values. The closer any two values are to one another, the more similar their underlying motivations. For scope, we focus on three specific value dimensions: universalism, achievement, and hedonism.

First, given the aforementioned prior work [7], we hypothesize a link between universalism and environment related content. By definition, those who value universalism care about preserving and enhancing the welfare of all people and for nature.

**H1. Stronger universalism value predicts stronger interest in content about the environment.**

Opposing universalism is achievement. Instead of focusing on others, self-enhancement values focus on individuals' own wellbeing. Those who value self-enhancement emphasize in personal advancement and desire prestige, social status, and demonstrating competence. Recent research showed that these values correlate with the use of work-related words in an online community [1]. Here, we hypothesize a positive link between achievement value and work/career related content.

**H2. Stronger achievement value predicts stronger interest in content about the work/career.**

Lastly, we hypothesize a positive relationship between hedonism values and leisure content. Hedonism refers to the pursuit of pleasure and sensuous gratification for oneself. It is about seeking pleasure, enjoying life and self-indulgence. Individuals who value hedonism may then strive to maximize pleasure online.

**H3. Stronger hedonism values predict stronger interest in content about leisure.**

Besides establishing a more comprehensive relationship between values and topical interests, we also aim to answer a practical question: would targeting content based on individual's values actually work? Values do not force behaviors, but merely "induce" [7]. It is possible then that values themselves are not strong influencers when it comes to article reading. Hence, in our study, we test the potential of article targeting in the context of Twitter. Twitter is a microblogging service that is heavily used to share and re-share content online [3].

**RQ. Are people more likely to read an article on Twitter that is targeted to their value orientation?**

## METHODS

The goal of this study is to test whether certain values may predict interest in reading certain types of articles. To explore the feasibility of content targeting, we focused on a concrete reading scenario: article reading on Twitter.

Participants were asked to rate and read three articles, one on each of our three topical foci: Environment, Work, and Leisure. They were then asked to report their general interests in reading articles on each topic category.

### Procedure and Measures

This experiment used Twitter as the media backdrop for content targeting. Participants were told that they were participating in a study about reading articles through Twitter. They were first asked to verify whether they had a Twitter account via the Twitter API. Then, they were asked to complete the Portrait Value Questionnaire, which provided a measure for their value orientations [5].

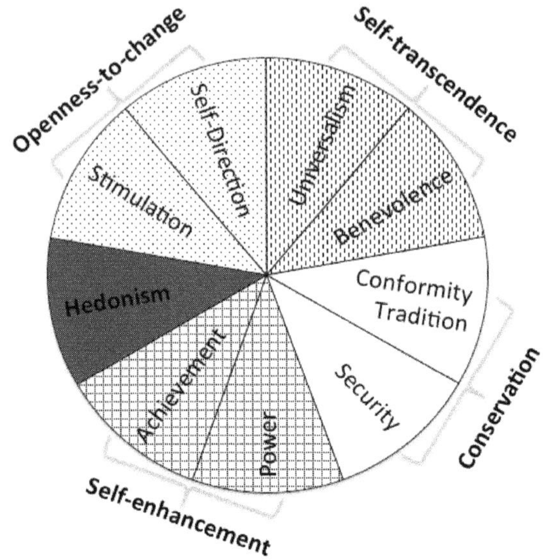


**Figure 1. Schwartz' Values**

Participants were presented with three articles serially, randomly selected from each of the three topic categories. All nine articles were from Lifehacker, a popular weblog. We chose Lifehacker as our source of articles, because it publishes news feeds on many manually categorized topics (known as tags), and is a popular source of news and tips on Twitter. Our articles were chosen using the "environment" tag for Environment, "work" and "jobs" tags for Work, and "fun" tag for Leisure.

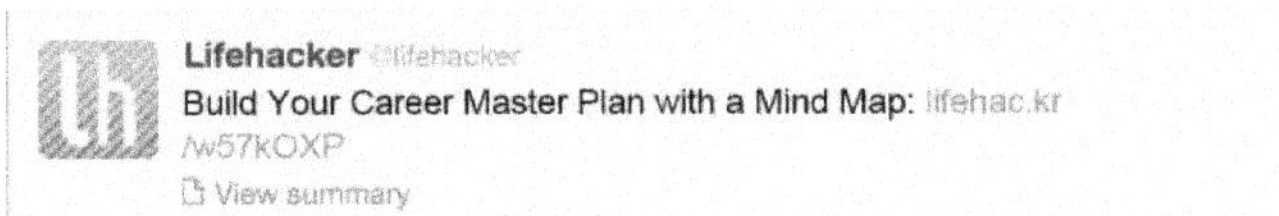


**Figure 2. Example Screenshot of Tweet Used in Study (Work)**

For our research question on article interest on Twitter, 3 measures were collected. To mimic a typical Twitter reading experience, for each article, participants were given a screenshot of a tweet with the title of the article first (Figure 2). They were then asked to rate their likelihood to click on the link and read the article on a Likert scale ("after reading the tweet, how are you to click on the link to read this article?"). Then, regardless of their ratings, they were directed to a screenshot of the article, and asked to read the article's content. After the article was read, two separate measures were collected: "found the article to be worth reading", and "would re-tweet the article." This experimental design enables us to collect both interest ratings before and after exposure to the article content. Amongst these three measures, the correlation between the two post-reading measures was the strongest at 0.75, with the other pairwise correlations at around 0.55.

At the end of the study, participants were asked to provide basic demographic information and to rate, using Likert scales, their interests in reading articles about the "environment" (M=3.41, SD=1.10), "work/career"

| | Openness-to-Change | | Self-Transcendence | | Conservation | | | Self-Enhancement | | Hedonism |
|---|---|---|---|---|---|---|---|---|---|---|
| | Sti. | S.D. | Uni. | Ben. | Con. | Tra. | Sec. | Pow. | Ach | Hed. |
| Environment | 0.03 | 0.09 | **0.46***** | 0.20** | 0.03 | -0.04 | -0.10 | -0.29*** | -0.25** | -0.18* |
| Work | -0.04 | 0.03 | -0.08 | -0.04 | -0.02 | -0.07 | -0.03 | 0.20** | **0.23***** | -0.15* |
| Leisure | -0.07 | -0.11 | -0.02 | 0.09 | 0.07 | -0.08 | -0.03 | -0.02 | 0.07 | **0.13**† |

**Table 1. Correlations Between Values and Topical Interests. Note: *p < 0.05, **p < 0.01, ***p < 0.001, †p = 0.07**

(M=3.24, SD=1.09), and "leisure" (M=3.66, SD=0.95). This latter measure was introduced to test our three hypotheses on general topical interests.

### Participants

Participants were recruited from Amazon's Mechanical Turk. Participation was limited to United States residents to ensure sufficient English language proficiency. In addition, as we are interested in exploring the practical challenges of article targeting on Twitter, the study required participants to be Twitter users who have submitted at least 10 tweets and had created the account more than 4 weeks prior.

202 responses were collected, of which 17 were removed from analysis due to inconsistent responses and no variance in scale ratings. Of the 185 used for analysis, about half were female (93) with the average age of 30 (median 28). Respondents on average posted 1008 tweets (median 377).

## RESULTS

To test our three hypotheses on the links between values and topical interests, we examined the correlations between individuals' value ratings with their self-reported interest in article topics. Results are shown in Table 1. H1 and H2 were both supported. There is a strong correlation between universalism value and interests in reading environment related content (r(183)=0.46, p<0.001), and a moderate correlation between achievement value and work-related content (r(183)=0.26, p<0.001). However, the correlation between hedonism and leisure content was much weaker (H3) with only a weak to negligible relationship between the two (r(183)=0.13, p=0.07). As we will elaborate in the discussion, this weak link between hedonism and leisure articles may be because reading may not be considered a hedonic activity, no matter the topic of the article.

To answer our research question, multiple regression models were built. For each set of articles, we used the hypothesized value as the independent variable (e.g. universalism value for Environment). Article id, modeled as a random effect, is used as a control variable. The results are shown in Table 2.

| | Interest when reading given article title in a tweet (β) | Worth reading after reading the article (β) | Likely to retweet after reading the article (β) |
|---|---|---|---|
| Universalism Value for Environment | 0.11 | **0.37***** | **0.35***** |
| Achievement Value for Work | **0.24*** | 0.15 | 0.08 |
| Hedonism Value for Leisure | **0.16**† | 0.10 | -0.05 |

**Table 2. Regression Coefficients Between Values and Interests on Articles of Corresponding Topics.**
**Note: *p < 0.05, **p < 0.01, ***pc< 0.001, †p = 0.10**

For Environment, universalism was not a predictor of participants' interest in reading the article when presented with the tweet (β=.11, p=0.30). However, after reading the article, participants report a significantly higher likelihood to find the article worth reading (β=.37, p<.001) and re-tweeting (β =.35, p<.001). For Work, achievement was shown to be significant predictor of participants' interest in reading the article when presented with the tweet (β=.24, p=.03), but did not influence their likelihood to find the article worth reading (β=.15, p=.12) or re-tweeting (β=.08, p=.43). Lastly, for Leisure, there was a weak relationship between hedonism and interests in reading leisure articles (β=.16, p=.10), and no relationship with participants' likelihood to find the article worth reading (β=.01, p=.91) or re-tweeting (β=-.05, p=.60).

## DISCUSSION AND LIMITATIONS

This study explores the use of personal values and reading interests. From a theoretical perspective, our findings extend existing research and demonstrate that, in addition to the other influences, values also influence what we choose to read. From a practical perspective, our exploration demonstrates the feasibility of value-based content targeting, but also highlight challenges.

### Link Between Values and Topical Interests

Our findings (Table 1) demonstrate that universalism values predict interests in reading about the Environment and achievement values predict interests in reading about Work. This result advances prior work on the value-behavior link by demonstrating that values also influence our reading interests. More importantly, this exploratory work calls for a more comprehensive examination of values and topical interest, beyond the three chosen for this study.

It is important to note that in comparison to the effects of universalism and achievement, the link between hedonism value and Leisure is negligible to weak. We believe that this is because the reading activity in itself may not be considered by many to be a hedonistic activity. This suggests that a more accurate model for the value-reading interest should include a moderating variable. Future work should consider measuring individual's interests in the activity as a moderating variable, as e.g., value's influence on topical interests for reading may be different from value's influence on topical interest for movies.

### Feasibility and Challenges of Value-Based Targeting

Our exploration also demonstrates the feasibility of using personal values to target content to an online audience. Testing article targeting in the Twitter context using Lifehacker's categorization of articles, we found that participants' personal values can influence their interest and evaluation of the articles. Specifically, achievement and hedonism values predicted participants' likelihood to read the Work and Leisure articles, respectively, when presented with tweets containing the titles. In addition, universalism value predicted participants' positive evaluation of the Environment articles, post-reading.

However, there were discrepancies in our results. For *Environment* articles, participants' interest were affected by universalism values *only* after they read the article content, while for *Work* and *Leisure* articles, the result is opposite. In that case, personal values affected interests initially, right after reading the tweet, but not their general evaluation of content after reading. One likely explanation is that the articles' title and content may not hold the same appeal-strength. For example, all of the Environment articles were tagged as "environment" on Lifehacker and while these articles have content appealing those with universalism values, the titles (e.g. "easy ways to live greener") seem to often be less direct and less clearly associated with that value. In contrast, our Work articles seem to often have titles explicitly appealing to the motivating values (e.g. "build your career master plan with a mind map"), while their actual content may be mediocre and less effective in advancing one's career. This explanation concurs with Templeton et al. [6], who argued that personal values' effect depends on how well the writing appeals to readers' values.

These results highlight an inherent challenge in targeting content on Twitter. Given that the titles of the articles are often the only text communicated in the tweet, the titles need to be carefully crafted to appeal to the targeted value-orientation. Otherwise, valuable and desirable content may be easily overlooked.

While our findings have demonstrated the feasibility of using value-based targeting, just how useful is it? How could personal values contribute to existing approaches in content targeting and recommendation, such as topic similarity and collaborative filtering [2]?

For topic modeling, because one value can correspond to many topics, personal values may help by associating online posts of seemingly unrelated topics. For a topic modeling algorithm, three online posts may appear unrelated because their topic foci, for example school, work, and career advancement, appear to be different. However, a value-based algorithm may be able to associate these posts due to their common relationship to achievement values. Based on this association, we may be able to predict a person to receive career articles positively despite a lack of data directly linking to career-oriented content, because she has previously reacted positively to achievement-related articles in other topics.

For collaborative filtering, personal values may alleviate the common "cold-start" problem. While effective collaborative filtering requires sufficient rating and/or feedback data for each new problem domain, personal values do not have such a requirement at all. In fact, because values have 10 fixed dimensions and are stable across time and context, we could expect to model a user's values once and use them repeatedly. As such, personal values could serve as a powerful tool for bootstrapping targeting efforts in new unknown domains. As prior work has demonstrated possibility to derive personal values from text [1,6], future work could explore content targeting using not topics but values derived from text.

## CONCLUSION

Prior research suggests that personal values can influence the type of information sought when making a choice. This current research builds on prior work by demonstrating that our values also influence our general reading interests. Our findings further demonstrate the feasibility of using values to support content targeting.

## ACKNOWLEDGEMENTS

Funding for the first author, Gary Hsieh, was provided by NSF grant #1348542. This research was sponsored by the U.S. DARPA under the SMISC program, Agreement Number W911NF-12-C-0028. The views and conclusions contained in this document are those of the author(s) and should not be interpreted as representing the official policies, either expressed or implied, of the U.S. Defense Advanced Research Projects Agency or the U.S. Government. The U.S. Government is authorized to reproduce and distribute reprints for Government purposes notwithstanding any copyright notation hereon.

## REFERENCES

1. Chen, J., Hsieh, G., Mahmud, J., Nichols, J. To appear. Understanding Individuals' Personal Values from Social Media Word Use. *Proc. of CSCW*.
2. Jannach, D., Zanker, M., Felfernig, A., & Friedrich, G. 2010. *Recommender systems: an introduction*. Cambridge University Press.
3. Java, A., Song, X., Finin, T., and Tseng, B. 2007. Why we twitter: understanding microblogging usage and communities. In *Proc. of the WebKDD and SNAKDD Workshop on Web Mining and Social Network Analysis*, 56-65.
4. Schwartz, S. H. 1994. Are There Universal Aspects in the Structure and Contents of Human Values? *Journal of Social Issues*, 50(4), 19-45
5. Schwartz, S. H. 2002. A Proposal for Measuring Value Orientations across Nations. Chapter 7 in the *Questionnaire Development Package of the European Social Survey*.
6. Templeton, T. C., Fleischmann, K. R., & Boyd-Graber, J. 2011. Simulating audiences: Automating analysis of values, attitudes, and sentiment. In *Proc. Of PASSAT/SocialCom*, pp. 734-737
7. Verplanken, B., Holland, R. W. 2002. Motivated decision making: Effects of activation and self-centrality of values on choices and behavior. *Journal of Personality and Social Psychology*, 82(3) 434-447

# Gaining Empathy for Non-Routine Mobile Device Use Through Autoethnography

**Aisling Ann O'Kane**
UCL Interaction Centre
University College London
London, United Kingdom
a.okane@cs.ucl.ac.uk

**Yvonne Rogers**
UCL Interaction Centre
University College London
London, United Kingdom
y.rogers@ucl.ac.uk

**Ann Blandford**
UCL Interaction Centre
University College London
London, United Kingdom
a.blandford@ucl.ac.uk

## ABSTRACT
In this paper, we report on autoethnography as a method to access non-routine usage of mobile devices, such as during business trips, vacations, etc. Autoethnography, a self-study method with the researcher as participant, was employed for the evaluation of a wrist blood pressure monitor used by people with conditions such as hypertension. The findings from the study were surprising, especially with respect to the environmental and social impact on the use of the technology. Although the autoethnographic method can be disruptive for the researcher, it enables them to understand and empathize with the experiences mobile device users can face in difficult to access contexts. This method allows HCI researchers to better understand user experiences with mobile devices, including mobile medical technology, especially during non-routine times that can be difficult to study in-situ with traditional user studies.

### Author Keywords
Autoethnography; context; empathy; mobile; healthcare.

### ACM Classification Keywords
H.5.m. Information interfaces and presentation (e.g., HCI): Miscellaneous.

## INTRODUCTION
Mobile devices can be difficult to study in context as found in a number of situated studies in HCI [14]. They can be carried and used in a wide range of situations, which of course can be hard to capture with methods such as observation. Other methods such as diary studies and the experience sampling method may be used, but there are times when users may not be amenable to participating in this type of study, including when they are travelling, on holiday, or attending celebrations. These non-routine times can be difficult to study because of their infrequency and because of possible intrusiveness in participants' lives.

This is a particular concern for studying mobile medical technologies, used by people for the care or maintenance of a health condition. Such devices are becoming increasingly popular based on the financial need to move healthcare outside of clinical settings, enabling patients to live more independently [9]. Because it is difficult to observe interactions in these non-routine contexts, nuances of the interaction that influence the adoption and use of these medical devices are not captured. Without a rich understanding of the interactions, it is difficult to have empathy with users and this may influence the quality of both the design and evaluation of mobile technology.

In this paper, we report on a study that explores the potential value of autoethnography for evaluating mobile medical devices in-situ. A study was conducted using autoethnography, a method of self-observation with the researcher as participant [7], to experience aspects of using a mobile medical device during routine and non-routine times. Although the method was personally disruptive and could not capture the whole user experience, it revealed subtleties in the interactions that influenced the adoption and use of the device, providing the researcher with more empathy for situations mobile medical device users experience, particularly during non-routine usage.

## AUTOETHNOGRAPHY AND EMPATHY
Empathy is an important resource for design and evaluation [15]. A goal of much HCI design, evaluation, and research is to understand the user [16]. Wright and McCarthy propose that this should be extended to understanding what it *feels like to be a user*, influenced by what they call a pragmatist approach: the felt and valued response from the researcher's point of view to the separate and unique user. For HCI researchers and practitioners, they propose that this can be achieved through dialogue, narratives, and 'the imagined other' [16]. Gaining empathy with users through 'the imagined other' involves researchers personally in the use of technology and includes various forms of self-study.

Self-study is not new in HCI; for example, in the 1990s, Jeff Hawkins carried a block of wood in his pocket to simulate what a Palm Pilot would feel like to actually carry around and use all the time [3]. Methods of qualitative self-


*CHI 2014,* April 26 - May 01 2014, Toronto, ON, Canada

*ACM 978-1-4503-2473-1/14/04...$15.00.*
http://dx.doi.org/10.1145/2556288.2557179

study arose in the social sciences [2]. One of these, autoethnography, is a form of ethnography where the researcher adopts the role of participant. It has been used in a wide range of HCI studies, allowing researchers to gain empathy with users of various types of technology (e.g. [10]), including a similar technique used for design - experience prototyping - in the medical domain [6]. In a review of eleven researchers who had used autobiographical design, a self-study method for exploring design prototypes, for over a year, it was found that the method uncovered the 'big effects' on usage, surprising usage practices, and "detailed, subtle understandings that [...] might have seemed unremarkable" [11:31]. The self-study method's popularity in HCI can be attributed to the need to conduct ethnography-light studies, as "spending twenty-four hours over several weeks with the participants is just not feasible" [7:2]. Self-study can be used to explore 'the imagined other' [16] in a less time consuming and resource demanding way during the evaluation of mobile devices.

As such, autoethnography has potential for revealing user experiences when using mobile medical devices in context. The importance of understanding context has been recognized by the medical usability standards that are used for the design and evaluation of mobile medical devices [1,8]. However, recommended methods for addressing contextual factors all require some level of observation that may not be possible with mobile medical devices used by patients. One standard [8] explicitly states that designers should not participate in user studies.

In this paper, we report and reflect on the use of autoethnography for the evaluation of a mobile blood pressure monitor. We explore the use of autoethnography to gain access to non-routine situations that might not be available to researchers conducting traditional user studies. During travel, business trips, celebrations and other non-routine times, users can be in unusual situations and may use their mobile devices in different ways [13]. However, these are the very times that users might be reluctant to disrupt for researchers using other HCI methods, such as diary studies or observation. Alternatively, researchers can become participants, and in doing so, disrupt their own holidays and celebrations to experience the use of such technologies in context. The autoethnographic self-study of a mobile medical device presented below discusses the challenges and opportunities for gaining insights into the non-routine contexts of use not easily captured with user studies.

## METHOD

In order to explore various contexts of use for mobile medical devices, the first author (O'Kane) conducted an autoethnography study covering normal routine and non-routine usage. During this study, O'Kane had planned a number of non-routine events, including visiting family overseas, going to a wedding, attending an academic conference, and having visitors stay in her shared apartment, together with her usual daily routine activities as a PhD student in a major city (studying, eating, meeting friends, bicycling, using public transport, etc.). Using information from discussions with mobile medical device users, an autoethnography study was planned to emulate some of the conditions they reported experiencing, using a non-invasive wrist blood pressure monitor as the device to be evaluated.

The test was taken twice a day using the Omron R7 monitor [12] and O'Kane was reminded to test through a mobile phone alarm. The study was conducted over three months and O'Kane recorded her use of the device using a mobile phone diary keeping technique [4], capturing photos of the context and optional text descriptions. An iterative and open thematic analysis [5] of diary entries, personal reflection, and discussion with other researchers, suggests that autoethnography is particularly well suited for uncovering insights concerning the context of use during non-routine times and also with mobile medical devices.

## FINDINGS

The findings from the study are discussed in terms of social and environmental factors, highlighting the most unusual and influential contexts of use.

### Unexpected Environmental Influences

During a number of discussions with mobile medical device users, it became apparent that non-routine times sometimes led to using the devices in unfamiliar places. During O'Kane's use of the wrist blood pressure monitor through non-routine times, she often found herself using a washroom stall or a more private area to conduct the testing alone. The earlier interviews prepared O'Kane for these situations at an abstract level, but the subtleties of these experiences were not fully comprehended until she experienced them herself.

What stood out for her were the noises the device makes during the testing procedure. This was an issue in public washrooms that O'Kane often used in unfamiliar places - where the noises could be a great source of embarrassment. When the user adjusts their arm towards the proper angle for testing, there is feedback in the form of beeps to indicate when the angle of the device is getting closer to the proper testing angle. In addition, the device has to inflate around a user's wrist in order to test blood pressure, which causes a flowing air sound. Although this sound is not particularly loud, it is quite distinct and cannot be silenced. O'Kane also found that the noises could cause embarrassment elsewhere, including during unusual times at home.

*A friend of my flatmate is staying with us [...] im a little worried she heard it.* (Diary Entry on June 19)

Other than the noises it caused, physical features of the device seemed to be designed for ideal conditions that did not allow for variations in the environment. This was very clear when O'Kane was in a conference restaurant with colleagues, and used the washroom to conduct the test, only to encounter poor lighting for reading the results of the test.

As well as problems with illumination, the device design imposed other unexpected demands on the user. The testing process requires a person to rest for about 5 minutes before taking the test whilst sitting. This frequently caused disruptions to normal activities, but the need to rest was particularly hard to accommodate in non-routine situations. This issue came up at the conference venue washrooms, which did not have seats on their toilets. As there was no other easy location to conduct the test, she tried to perch on the toilet paper dispenser, which of course caused tension in her legs producing an error message on the device (see Figure 1). Although this was only encountered once, having found that the conference centre washrooms could not be used, O'Kane had to more carefully plan her activities to have easy access to a suitable place to conduct the testing.

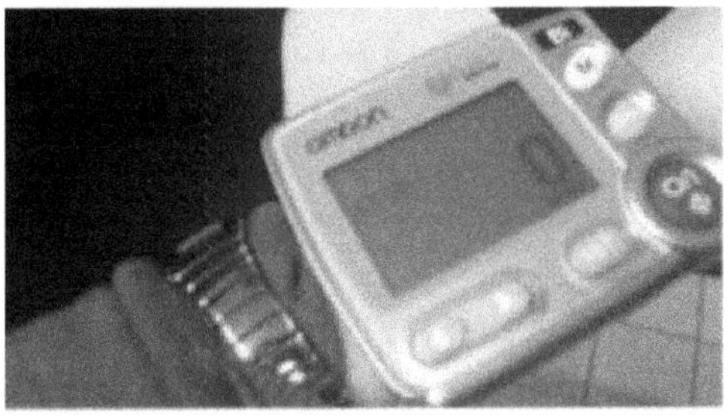


**Figure 1: Wrist blood pressure monitor showing an error**

The preparatory dialogues with mobile medical device users were very helpful in planning the self-study, but these conversations did not give a thorough understanding of the physical constraints of the environment in which these devices were used, as was experienced by O'Kane when sitting in a public washroom stall for too long with the device making beeping noises. O'Kane experienced the subtleties and nuances of using the device in environments that she could not control during non-routine times. Although it was awkward to conduct the self-study when visiting family or during an academic conference, these inconvenient times highlighted how the design features could create embarrassment in uncontrolled environments and how these negative experiences guided the way she used the device.

### Unexpected Social Situations

Based on the interviews and the dialogues O'Kane had had with medical device users, she had expectations as to what it was like to try to adapt quickly to unfamiliar social situations. It was only through experiencing the testing that she was made aware of the significant impact the medical aesthetic of the device had.

In public settings, it was sometimes not possible to go to a washroom for privacy during non-routine times. These were generally times when O'Kane had belongings that she was not able to take with her to a washroom stall easily or that could not be left in public as she went to a washroom stall. When she was away from her office and working on her laptop in coffee shops, O'Kane did not want to close her laptop, unplug her phone, pack up her bag, give up her seat, and take her coat to the washroom, just to unpack everything again once she had completed the test. She experienced something similar while waiting in an airport alone. Both times, she chose to use the device in front of strangers, but tried to diminish the attention it received.

*I did hide the device slightly behind my hair whilst doing the actual test and didn't look up to make eye contact. [...] Not that embarrassed, but maybe because I felt if anyone did pay too much attention to me they would be in the wrong judging someone with a health issue.* (Diary Entry on May 2)

Like anyone visiting family or attending a conference, O'Kane had many social engagements and was regularly carrying the device with her. Often, this would put her in a situation where she was rushing to complete the test as she felt social pressure to not keep people waiting. Also, if the alarm went off during a conversation or social interaction, O'Kane would have to interrupt that interaction to take the test. In some circumstances during non-routine times, she chose not to explain these disruptions to her companions, as she did not know them well enough to feel comfortable in doing so. One instance of this was at a friend's wedding where O'Kane only knew a handful of other guests. After being delayed in the testing because of speeches, and in the middle of a polite conversation with someone at her table, she excused herself to conduct the test in the washroom, as she did not want to pull out a medical device that might gain attention. Additionally, O'Kane had to find an evening purse large enough to accommodate the device, so as not to attract attention. This bag was a striking orange colour, meaning she had to match her entire outfit to the only large purse she possessed that could carry the device.

*Had to wait until dinner was served and then also a speech so I'm late. [...] I'm in the washroom trying to be silent but also quick so that my table doesn't notice. Also. The device hardly fit in the only purse that matched my dress and it is quite chunky looking.* (Diary Entry on April 28)

Funny anecdotes of awkward social interactions had been brought up in conversations with mobile medical device users, but many of these instances were not amusing to the device user at the time; O'Kane got to experience some of these types of interactions. She was able to attain empathy with users who need to carry devices with them at all times, through having to alter a wedding outfit and also interrupt conversations to conduct tests. She got to experience what variables influenced her to conduct the test away from others, such as embarrassment with acquaintances, or to test in front of others, such as not caring what strangers thought. Although the social influences on her use would not be the same as someone with an actual health condition, O'Kane got closer to what it feels like to use mobile health technology during non-routine times.

## DISCUSSION AND CONCLUSIONS

O'Kane experienced a range of interactions with a mobile medical technology and was able to gain insight into the influence of contextual factors by actually using the device herself, especially during non-routine times. We found that autoethnography allows the researcher to comprehend the experience of using the device during times not normally available to them during other kinds of user studies, such as when devices are used on vacation. Instead of putting users in inconvenient situations, the researcher can try using them during their own vacation and other non-routine times so as to actually experience some of the awkward situations that can occur when using mobile interactive technology.

What we found was consistent with the literature: namely that self-study allows practitioners to capture some of the subtleties and nuances of those contexts that can influence the adoption and use of a device not easily achieved without experiencing them [11]. In addition, we found it to be a lightweight yet powerful tool compared to time-consuming user studies [7]. We propose that this method is additionally useful for accessing non-routine times not easily captured through user studies. For example, during holidays, conferences, and celebrations, users may not be able to control where and when they use their devices, influencing their use and adoption of them. This is particularly important for healthcare technologies that require regular interaction for personal health and yet may be designed for more stable contexts. Hence, the self-study method can be useful for the evaluation of mobile medical devices, despite its absence from medical usability standards.

As this is the case, autoethnography should be considered as an additional method that designers, evaluators, and researchers of mobile interactive technology could employ to understand better non-routine user experiences. This method could be particularly useful as a first step in user research, to inform the design of user studies, and to be used as a lightweight method throughout an iterative design cycle. Despite the disruptiveness of the method and how subjective and personal the results can be, if a HCI practitioner keeps these concerns in mind, their reflections on the results and discussions with other researchers can produce interesting insights on the use of mobile technologies, particularly in unusual contexts. Although this method should not replace standardized usability methods, for non-routine times it is an insightful method for challenging assumptions, gaining empathy with user experiences, and planning future user studies, including with mobile medical technologies.

## ACKNOWLEDGEMENTS

We would like to thank our reviewers for their comments and the UK EPSRC CHI+MED interactive medical device safe use project [EP/G059063/1] for their support.

## REFERENCES

1. ANSI. Medical devices - Application of usability engineering to medical devices. *ANSI/AAMI/IEC 62366:2007*, 2007.
2. Banks, S.P. and Banks, A. Reading "the critical life": Autoethnography as pedagogy. *Communication Education 49*, 3 (2000), 233–238.
3. Bergman, E. Designing the PalmPilot: a conversation with Rob Haitani. *Information appliances and beyond: interaction dsign for consumer products, Morgan Kaufmann, San Francisco, CA*, (2000), 81–102.
4. Brandt, J., Weiss, N., and Klemmer, S.R. txt 4 l8r: lowering the burden for diary studies under mobile conditions. *Ext. Abstracts CHI 2007*, ACM Press (2007), 2303–2308.
5. Braun, V. and Clarke, V. Using thematic analysis in psychology. *Qual. Res. in Psych. 3*, 2 (2006), 77–101.
6. Buchenau, M. and Suri, J.F. Experience prototyping. *Proc. DIS 2000*, ACM Press (2000), 424–433.
7. Cunningham, S.J. and Jones, M. Autoethnography: a tool for practice and education. *Proc. OZCHI 2005*, ACM Press (2005), 1–8.
8. FDA. Draft Guidance for Industry and Food and Drug Administration Staff - Applying Human Factors and Usability Engineering to Optimize Medical Device Design. 1757 (2011).
9. Graham, F. MHealth: Mobile technology brings healthcare home. 2010. http://www.bbc.co.uk/news/business-12068754.
10. Höök, K. Transferring qualities from horseback riding to design. *Proc. NORDCHI 2010*, ACM Press (2010), 226–235.
11. Neustaedter, C. and Sengers, P. Autobiographical design: what you can learn from designing for yourself. *Interactions 19*, 6 (2012), 28–33.
12. Omron. R7 (HEM-637-E7). 2012. http://www.omron-healthcare.com/en/product/blood_pressure_monitors/All/HEM-637-E.html.
13. Owen, T., Buchanan, G., and Thimbleby, H. Understanding user requirements in take-home diabetes management technologies. *Proc. BCS People and Computers*, BCS Press (2012), 268–273.
14. Rogers, Y. Interaction design gone wild: striving for wild theory. *Interactions 18*, 4 (2011), 58.
15. Segal, L.D. and Suri, J.F. The empathic practitioner: Measurement and interpretation of user experience. *Proc. HFES 2007*, (1997), 451–454.
16. Wright, P. and McCarthy, J. Empathy and experience in HCI. *Proc. CHI 2008*, ACM Press (2008), 637–646.

# Designing For Movement: Evaluating Computational Models using LMA Effort Qualities

**Diego Silang Maranan, Sarah Fdili Alaoui, Thecla Schiphorst, Philippe Pasquier, Pattarawut Subyen, Lyn Bartram**
School of Interactive Arts and Technology, Simon Fraser University
102 Avenue, Surrey, British Columbia, V3T 0A3, Canada
{diegom, sfdilial, thecla, pasquier, psubyen, lyn}@sfu.ca

## ABSTRACT
While single-accelerometers are a common consumer embedded sensors, their use in representing movement data as an intelligent resource remains scarce. Accelerometers have been used in movement recognition systems, but rarely to assess expressive qualities of movement. We present a prototype of wearable system for the real-time detection and classification of movement quality using acceleration data. The system applies Laban Movement Analysis (LMA) to recognize Laban Effort qualities from acceleration input using a Machine Learning software that generates classifications in real time. Existing LMA-recognition systems rely on motion capture data and video data, and can only be deployed in controlled settings. Our single-accelerometer system is portable and can be used under a wide range of environmental conditions. We evaluate the performance of the system, present two applications using the system in the digital arts and discuss future directions.

## Author Keywords
Movement recognition; Movement analysis; Laban Effort analysis; Movement analysis; Movement-based interaction.

## ACM Classification Keywords
I.5.1 Pattern Recognition: Models; H.1.2 Models and Principles: User/Machine Systems.

## INTRODUCTION
Within Human Computer Interaction (HCI) movement was originally understood as a functional component of interaction. This design approach reflects the task-oriented focus of early HCI research, which was preoccupied with ergonomics and efficiency as exemplified. Yet, movement is not solely functional, it is also highly expressive and experiential. Our research articulates higher-level semantics of human movement qualities, which exploits the language of Laban Movement Analysis (LMA) as a model for describing movement expressivity for the design of novel, nuanced and meaningful movement-based interaction.


*CHI 2014,* April 26–May 1, 2014, Toronto, Ontario, Canada.

ACM 978-1-4503-2473-1/14/04...$15.00.
http://dx.doi.org/10.1145/2556288.2557251

Movement analysis systems such as LMA have a rich epistemological history particularly in the domains of dance, non-verbal communication, psychoanalysis and psychology providing rigorous explanatory models for the description of movement [16], its function and its expression. LMA has been used in previous computational systems, to interpret the physical movements of robot agents as outward manifestations of internal emotional states [2], to generate physically expressive animated characters [8], support social intimacy by interpreting qualities of touch applied to networked, tactile interfaces [25], and classify activities such as walking and running [14]. Yet, within HCI, the application of LMA theories, principles and models remains marginal and most of the time incomplete or compressed.

The general goal of our research is to explore how movement expertise from LMA can lead to the design and integration of more richly articulated human movement knowledge within movement-based interaction. In particular, we are interested in the notion of "movement qualities" (MQs) that practitioners and theorists of movement define as the qualitative characteristics defining the manner in which a movement is executed. LMA formalizes MQs into the Effort category (the other categories being Body, Space, and Shape). Laban describes the movement's Effort according to four factors: Space, Time, Weight, and Flow. Each factor has two elements (Space: Direct/Indirect, Time: Sudden/Sustained, Weight: Light/Strong, Flow: Bound/Free) that can be understood as two ends of a continuum in which the movements can vary and thus reveal different qualities or "Effort qualities". Laban considers the Effort qualities as expressive attributes of movement produced by dynamics. Although MQs are a central notion that conveys movement expressiveness, they haven't been explored in designing and evaluating Human-Computer Interactions until lately [9,11,17,27]. We believe that because MQs reveals movement expressiveness, their use has strong potential for movement-based interaction with applications in the arts, digital media, entertainment, education, or rehabilitation. Precisely, our work aims at designing and evaluating interactive systems where the notion of MQs is central, and that provide feedbacks that can inform users about their MQs. Our systems include MQ analysis (motion capture, feature extraction, and real-time recognition), synthesis and control through for example sound or visual feedback (given the extracted MQs).

In this paper, we present the design and evaluation of a prototype of MQs analysis system called EFFORTDETECT that uses a single-accelerometer data fed to Machine Learning software to recognize in real-time and classify Laban Effort qualities. We also present two artistic applications that use EFFORTDETECT to capture MQs and integrate it as an interaction modality. They demonstrated the system's applicability in the performing Arts and in particular in two successful dance performances and an interactive installation venue.

While most of the MQs recognition techniques rely on motion capture or video data, which require careful positioning of a subject and cameras, our system is based on a single-accelerometer to perform continuous MQs classifications. The advantage of using accelerometers is that they are small and thus highly portable, and can be used under a wide range of environmental conditions including interactive installations targeting general public audience, interactive performances or mobile applications. In such conditions, a compelling feature of single-accelerometer systems is their pervasive ability to pragmatically 'hand over' interaction capability between users. Our approach to selecting single-accelerometer systems emphasizes the often precarious and critical temporal transactions between users. Interaction designers may trade-off the recognition accuracy from multiple accelerometers systems for the ease and simple handing over of one accelerometer between users. This is a key pervasive feature for Art settings, as well as mobile device uses. In addition, accelerometer data are directly linked to movement dynamics that produce MQs, and thus offer a coherent alternative to positional data when feeding the recognition process. Moreover, single-accelerometers are among the most common embedded sensor in popular consumer mobile technologies. Accelerometer data abounds in everyday contexts through rapidly growing access to consumer products such as mobile phones, accelerometer wristbands and game controllers. The embedded single-accelerometer remains a common-denominator in this large range of consumer sensor devices. Yet, representing movement data as an intelligent resource remains scarce. How can we expand the affordances of single-accelerometer applications to include MQs? Our research in articulating a language of human movement is based on higher-level semantics that computationally describe MQs, utilizing LMA as a stable and replicable model that can be directly applied to a wide variety of single-accelerometer consumer platforms. Our contribution to HCI is targeting mobile applications based on data from personal devices with single-accelerometers.

## LABAN MOVEMENT ANALYSIS

In this section, we present the LMA system in order to clarify how we use it to define a framework for MQs recognition and evaluation. LMA looks at movement through four different categories of Body, Space, Effort, and Shape [16] that comprise a rigorous and systematic framework for understanding and categorizing movement. The Effort component describes human MQs using four Factors: Space, Time, Weight, and Flow. Observable qualities of Effort mark the outer manifestation of an inner attitude. Each of the Effort Factors is a continuum bounded by two extreme values or elements (Space: Direct/Indirect, Time: Sudden/Sustained, Weight: Light/Strong, Flow: Bound/Free) in which movement can vary and thus reveal different qualities or "Effort qualities". One of the values is the result of "Indulging" through the Effort, while the other extreme value is the result of "Fighting" through the Effort [15]. Space is related to the subject's attention to the surrounding environment. Time is related to the subject's sense of urgency. Weight is related to the subject's impact upon the world. Flow is related to the subject's attitude towards bodily control. Table 1 lists the Indulging and Fighting Effort elements and their related internal attitudes.

| Factor | Indulging element | Fighting element |
|---|---|---|
| Space | **Indirect**<br>flexible, meandering, wandering, multi- | **Direct**<br>single focus, channeled, |
| Weight | **Light**<br>buoyant, delicate, overcoming gravity | **Strong**<br>powerful, having an impact |
| Time | **Sustained**<br>lingering, leisurely | **Sudden**<br>hurried, urgent |
| Flow | **Free**<br>uncontrolled, abandoned, unable to | **Bound**<br>controlled, restrained, able to stop |

**Table 1. The Effort Factors and their Indulging and Fighting elements.**

| Basic Effort Action | Space Factor | Time Factor | Weight Factor |
|---|---|---|---|
| **Press** | Direct | Sustained | Strong |
| **Glide** | Direct | Sustained | Light |
| **Punch** | Direct | Sudden | Strong |
| **Dab** | Direct | Sudden | Light |
| **Wring** | Indirect | Sustained | Strong |
| **Float** | Indirect | Sustained | Light |
| **Slash** | Indirect | Sudden | Strong |
| **Flick** | Indirect | Sudden | Light |

**Table 2. The BEAs of Laban Action Drive.**

Not all the Effort Factors play a significant role at all times. One or more of the Efforts may be attenuated in movement. Laban denotes by *Action Drive*, actions with MQs where Flow Effort is not emphasized. To delimit the *Action Drive*, he combines the extreme values of Space, Time, and Weight Effort into what he calls the eight Basic Effort Actions

(BEAs). The BEAs, outlined in Table 2, are not movement *per se*. When waving one's hand goodbye, for example, the movement could have either a *punching* or a *floating* quality. The BEAs can thus be treated as qualitative descriptors of movement that combines three Effort Factors. Because these actions are prevalent in daily activity and because they cover a large range of Efforts, qualities and dynamics, we chose to train EFFORTDETECT computational model to recognize and classify them in real time.

## BACKGROUND

In this section, we review computational approaches to Laban Efforts recognition as well as the literature on the use of accelerometers for movement recognition to provide the context for EFFORTDETECT's model of MQs recognition.

### Computation Models of Laban Efforts

The rich framework of MQs provided by LMA contributes to its appeal in the field of Computer Science. Indeed, most models that incorporate MQs analysis and/or synthesis rely on the Effort and Shape categories of LMA [20,22,24,29,32]. Some of the earliest work taking MQs into account in computer animation comes from Norman Badler's research group. They developed the EMOTE system to animate a 3D character using Laban's Effort and Shape qualities in order to produce more expressive and natural simulated movements [8]. They also developed movement segmentation techniques along the Laban Effort Factors, using high-level movement descriptors inspired by the eight Effort elements [7]. LMA Shape qualities were exploited by Swaminathan et al. and used to train dynamic Bayesian networks for MQs recognition [29].

In Human-Computer Interaction, some remarkable systems have been exploring MQs [11]. Laban Effort qualities inspired a theoretical framework for the design of "graceful" movement-based interactions proposed by Hashim et al [12]. Schiphorst uses the eight BEAs defined by Laban that convey different combinations of Effort qualities, in order to enhance the aesthetic appreciation of digital art by better involving the body of the user in the experience of interacting with digital media [26]. Schiphorst et al. also use the BEAs to interpret qualities of touch applied to networked, tactile interfaces [25]. More recently, Mentis and Johanson proposed a study that aims to situate the perception of MQs, in ones own movement and in another's movements [18]. For this purpose they built a Kinect-based system for an improvisational dance performance where audience members MQs as defined by Laban Efforts, are used to influence the music.

Most of the existing approaches of Effort recognition use positional data taken either from motion capture systems or video data. These require the subject to be positioned in a constrained way in relation to a camera or to a motion capture setup. Additionally, these approaches require the movement to be a priori partitioned into discrete segments before the classification is performed. Bindiganavale delimits the segment boundaries by computing the zero-crossings of acceleration data and detecting local velocity extrema [5]. Zhao extracts a curvature feature from motion capture data and segments movement where extreme changes in the curvature are accompanied by zero-crossings in the acceleration data [32]. These approaches to motion segmentation presume that motion is a series of discrete segments and each segment embeds an independent set of Laban Effort qualities. Our approach doesn't require segmenting the movement and thus maps to movement theories articulated by Laban, Bergsen, Sheets-Johnstone, and other movement philosophers who understand movement as continuous and nondiscrete [4,28].

### Accelerometer-based Movement Recognition

Accelerometers built into mobile phones and gaming devices such as the Nintendo Wii Remote have popularized mobile applications that rely on movement recognition. Accelerometers have been mostly used for tasks such as navigation [1], pointing [31], gesture-based authentication [10], or text input [13]. These single-accelerometer systems usually include movement properties such as its contours [1], orientation, tilt and direction [6], but only few of them take into consideration the dynamical or temporal component of movement by including for instance variation of speed and acceleration (which are crucial to the notion of MQs) [27]. However, some accelerometer-based systems have explored aspects of MQs for example, when recognizing semaphoric signals such as shakes, whacks, or bumps [6], which all have Direct and Sudden qualities. Roudaut *et al.* incorporate aspects of MQs in their design of the TimeTilt system, which differentiates between smooth and jerky tilting of their accelerometer-equipped device [23]. Khoshhal *et. al.* use a system of six accelerometers to extract Time Effort, but no other Factor of MQs [14]. Our prototype is the only portable, single-accelerometer-based system that is designed to recognize a wide range of MQs including three of Laban Effort Factors. It can be ported to existing mobile devices by using the mobile device's built-in accelerometer and interfacing it with an application that can process the acceleration data.

## SYSTEM DESIGN

We designed the EFFORTDETECT system based on the knowledge and embodied practice provided by the LMA system.

### Wearable Accelerometer

EFFORTDETECT uses data from a single wearable accelerometer. Although acceleration can be derived from positional data, collecting acceleration data is a more natural fit to motion dynamics and thus MQs recognition than capturing positional information. More generally, LMA analyses human movement as the *process of change*, any change of Body Effort Shape or Space, rather than the positions within the trajectories traced by a movement [3]. Moreover, the use of a single accelerometer is consistent with the practice & observation of LMA Basic Effort

Actions (BEAs) that are performed using a dominant body part leading the movement. In most of the cases, the hand and arm is the body segment leading the BEA. We chose a wrist-mounted accelerometer to detect the BEAs led by the dominant arm. This could also be replicated in consumer use by holding a mobile device such as a smart-phone or wearing an accelerometer wristband or a watch.

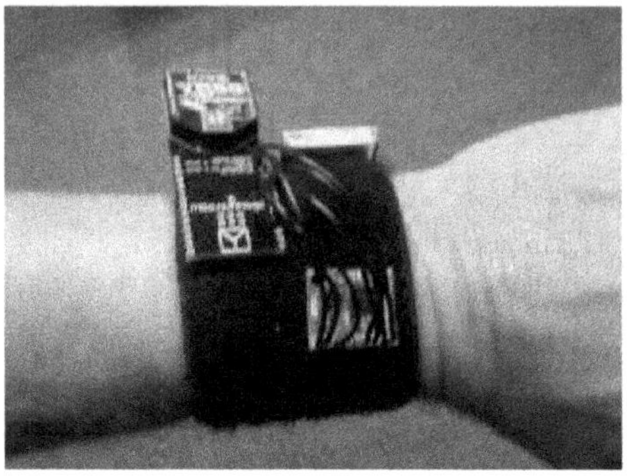

**Figure 1. The Wearable Acceleration Unit**

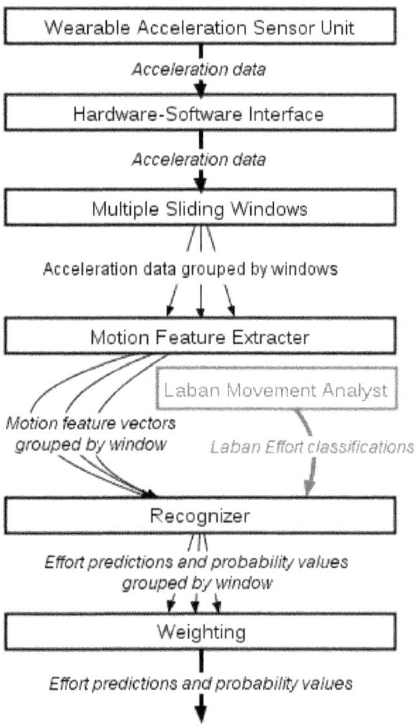


**Figure 2. The architecture of EFFORTDETECT. Components in red are active in the training phase.**

Technically, our Wearable Acceleration Sensor Unit is composed of a wireless transmitter and a 5DOF accelerometer sensor mounted on a microcontroller and powered by a 3.7-volt battery. The sensors transmit acceleration data from the x, y, and z-axes as well as pitch and roll acceleration data. The wireless transmitters send the acceleration data to the Hardware-Software Interface once every 10 milliseconds. A Wearable Acceleration Sensor Unit is sewn into a 4-inch wide elastic fabric band that is attached to the dancer's right arm, as shown in Figure 1.

EFFORTDETECT's use of wireless transmitters and acceleration sensors implies that the system can be used in low-light situations where a computer vision-based method would perform poorly. Our wearable hardware system prevents from body part occlusion witch is a concern in both computer vision-based tracking and in passive and active IR tracking. While occlusion is not a problem with magnetic motion tracking systems, the need of both IR and magnetic tracking to process the data from multiple moving bodies are cost-prohibitive compared to EFFORTDETECT [21]. Moreover, computer vision-based methods often rely on multiple viewing angles for greatest accuracy, making these methods unsuitable in situations where ideal lines-of-sight cannot be established, such as spaces that contain obstacles, *e.g.* furniture, or outdoor spaces that do not allow cameras to be placed in optimal locations. Furthermore, EFFORTDETECT's hardware subsystem allows the computers processing the motion data to be located a long distance away from the moving bodies.

### Multiple Sliding Time Windows

Because we consider human movement as a dynamic, continuous flux [19], we designed the EFFORTDETECT system using multiple sliding time windows approach rather than an a priori motion segmentation approach. EFFORTDETECT adapts a sliding window system first described by Widmer and Kubat [30] and analyzes movement data incrementally by examining it in context across three time scales. Each time scale view is a sliding time window, where the incoming data displaces the oldest data in a circular buffer. We define three windows, $w_{L,i}$, $w_{M,i}$, $w_{S,i}$ to represent a large window containing $L$ samples, a medium window containing $M$ samples, and a small window containing $S$ samples, respectively, where $L > M > S$. These three sets of motion samples are passed on to the Motion Feature Extractor (see next section); at time $t_{i+1}$, we generate windows $w_{L,i+1}$, $w_{M,i+1}$, and $w_{S,i+1}$, which discards the earliest sample in each window and appends a new sample to each window. We note that in our implementation, we find that at a sampling rate of 100 samples per second, $L = 200$, $M = 150$, and $S = 50$ produce good results.

### Motion Features

The Motion Feature Extractor examines the data in each time window and produces motion feature vectors, one per window, which summarizes the character of the motion within the time scale of each window. For every window $w_{n,i}$ of size $n$, we compute a *motion feature vector collection* $M_{n,i} = \{ X_{n,i}, Y_{n,i}, Z_{n,i}, P_{n,i}, R_{n,i} \}$, where $X_{n,i}, Y_{n,i}, Z_{n,i}, P_{n,i}, R_{n,i}$ are *motion feature vectors* associated with window $w_{n,I}$, composed of 9 real-numbered *motion features*. The motion features are normalized. Since every motion feature is associated with a particular degree of freedom, for a particular window, for a particular sensor, for a particular

| Profile number | Dab conf | Flick conf | Float conf | Glide conf | Press conf | Wring conf | Slash conf | Punch conf | 1st-dominant *BEA* ($e_{m,1}$) | 2nd-dominant *BEA* ($e_{m,2}$) |
|---|---|---|---|---|---|---|---|---|---|---|
| 1 | 0.035 | 0.442 | 0.025 | 0. | 0. | 0.006 | 0. | 0.451 | Punch | Flick |
| 2 | 0.040 | 0.392 | 0.025 | 0. | 0. | 0.008 | 0. | 0.377 | Flick | Punch |
| ... | ... | ... | ... | ... | ... | ... | ... | ... | ... | ... |
| 99 | 0.226 | 0.101 | 0.052 | 0.006 | 0. | 0.006 | 0. | 0.451 | Punch | Dab |
| 100 | 0.181 | 0.034 | 0.063 | 0.023 | 0. | 0.007 | 0. | 0.451 | Punch | Dab |

**Table 3. Example of *BEA* profile stream for a 1-second gesture (target *BEA* = Punch) determining the 1st and 2nd dominant *BEA* using profile-centered analysis**

time step, we generate 9 motion features x 5 motion feature vectors x 3 motion feature vector collections x 3 sensors = 405 motion features per time step.

To describe the nine motion features we extracted, we present as an example a time window, $w_{n,i}$, of size $n$ at time step $i$, and motion sample $x_i$ along the x-axis from the window. A similar analysis can be made for motion samples in the $y$, $z$, $p$, and $r$ axes.

1. We compute a current difference feature as the signed difference in value between the current motion sample value, xi, and the one immediately preceding it, xi-1.
2. The average difference is the mean of all the current differences in the window. We compute the ratio of the current and average difference features
3. We define the trajectory of xi to be the slope of the line determined by the line passing through xi and xi-1, and the current trajectory to be a value associated with the current time step.
4. The average trajectory is defined as the average of the trajectories of all n samples within the current time window. We compute the ratio of the current trajectory on the average trajectory.
5. The number of direction changes describes the number of times where the motion switches direction along the axis. We compute the ratio of the number of direction changes per number of samples in window and per duration of the window.
6. Finally, we define a threshold value determined by recording the x value of the accelerometer at rest, below which we consider the sensor to be still. We compute the ratio of stillness to overall motion given by the number samples that represent the sensor at rest divided on the number of samples that represent the sensor in motion.

### Recognition Process

EFFORTDETECT is based on a supervised learning system built using Max/MSP and Java and using a classifier implemented in Weka[1], an open source collection of data mining and Machine Learning algorithm. The stream of incoming feature vectors are fed to a classifier that operates in a training phase and a performance phase. During the training phase, an expert Laban Certified Movement Analyst (CMA) from the dance department of the University of Illinois recorded examples of the BEAs. During the performance phase, the recognition process would evaluate other dancers execution of the BEAs. Based on the examples recorded during the training, the recognition process is able, during the performance phase, to estimate in real-time the similarities between the BEAs performed by the user and the pre-recorded examples and decide on the BEA that is most likely to be performed by the user. Precisely, during the performance phase, the system outputs a continuous stream of classifications, which we call the BEA profile stream i.e. recognition rates or confidence values associated with each of the eight *BEAs*, rated from 0 to 1, for each of the time windows. Figure 2 shows the subsystems and the data they generate. The system examines the motion at all time scale windows and combines them to produce a single *BEA* profile stream. Depending on the target *BEA* under consideration, the system weights the output from different time scale windows. For example, quick *BEAs* such as Punch may occur within half a second or less, but they would be lost in the context of a five-second window. To detect the occurrence of these quick motions, we give heavier weight to the results of the shortest time window than of the longest time window. This approach supports continuous analysis of motion over time, and allows us to examine complex composite motion (interesting combinations and sequences of motion) over a variety of time scales.

## SYSTEM EVALUATION

### Experimental Procedure

We conducted an evaluation session with a dancer who has studied LMA as part of her university-level dance training and a Certified Laban Movement Analyst (CMA). The evaluation session was structured into several components. We organized an *LMA knowledge exchange session* where the movement analyst worked with the dancer to ensure that the dancer was performing the *BEAs* to a degree that was legible to the analyst. We then recorded the dancer

[1] Weka Software http://www.cs.waikato.ac.nz/ml/weka/

performing eight *BEAs* ten times, in random sequence, while the analyst confirmed the legibility of each performance. Finally, we did an *open-ended interview* where we encouraged the dancer and the CMA to share observations and provide feedback on EFFORTDETECT and any aspect of the evaluation session itself. We would like to emphasize that although the evaluation uses only one dancer and one CMA, these two participants are experts, highly trained in the Laban Movement Analysis system. When movements that exhibit the eight BEAs are performed, certified analysts can unambiguously and consistently recognize their presence and with little variation in performance. In other words, the categories are consistently identified. Our expert review of the system relies on the connoisseurship that is developed and refined by movement experts, and on which previous LMA-recognition research has also relied.

### Data Collected

We collected 80 profile streams that we recorded using a custom tool built in Max/MSP to assess quantitatively the performance of the EFFORTDETECT system.

## RESULTS AND DISCUSSION

### Data Analysis

In this evaluation, we measure the *accuracy* of the recognition (i.e., how accurately the system chooses the dominant *BEA* in a movement from the eight possible *BEAs*) and the *confidence* of that recognition. Consider a BEA representing a Punch performed over the duration of 1 second. Since EFFORTDETECT produces a *BEA* profile every 10 ms, it generates 100 Effort profiles for the gesture over 1 second. To assess the accuracy and the confidence of the recognition for a profile stream with respect to the target effort, we compute a profile-centered analysis that determines the *nth*-dominant *BEA* (denoted $e_{m,n}$) as the effort in profile $m$ that has the $nth$ highest confidence (denoted $p_{m,n}$). The *nth*-dominant *BEA* for the stream (denoted $E_n$) is the *BEA* that appears most frequently in $\{e_{1,n}, e_{2,n}, e_{3,n}, \ldots, e_{M,n}\}$, where $M$ is the number of profiles in the stream. The *nth*-dominant recognition confidence for the stream (denoted $C_n$) is the mean of all $c_{m,n}$ assigned to $e_{m,n}$ where $e_{m,n} = E_n$ for $1 \le m \le M$. Table 3 summarizes these measures for the profile streams of a punch; due to space constraints, we show only the first two and the last two profiles.

### Analysis of Accuracy

We compute the accuracy value of the system by analyzing whether the target BEA is recognized or not. We define $r_{m,n}$ to be the Boolean value associated with $e_{m,n}$ (the $n$th-dominant *BEA* in profile $m$), where $r_{m,n} = 1$ if $e_{m,n}$ is the target BEA and $r_{m,n} = 0$ if otherwise. We define $R_n$ to be the accuracy value of the $n$th-dominant *BEA* in the entire profile stream, and is computed as the average of $r_{m,n}$ for $1 \le m \le M$. The average of the simple accuracy values, as well as the average of the 1st-dominant recognitions for all profile streams is summarized in the confusion matrix in Figure 3.

Because of the different number of profiles we used for each target effort, we express the entries of the matrix in percent, computed by using the column sum as 100%. For example, 10 of the 14 gestures that were performed with the target effort of Dab were classified as a gesture with a 1st-dominant *BEA* of Dab; hence, the value in the Dab/Dab entry is 71.43%. The size of the squares is scaled to match the numerical values in the entries, while the opacity represents the average confidence associated with the recognition. The notable results shown in Figure 3 include high accuracy and confidence values for Punch and Glide recognition, a strong tendency to confidently misclassify Slash as Punch, and strong Dab and Wring recognition accuracy but with low confidence.

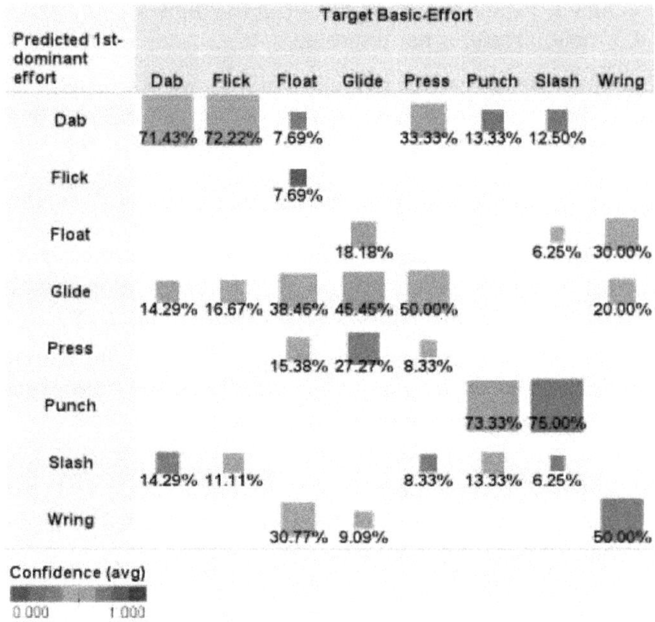


**Figure 3. Modified confusion matrix using a simple, profile-centered interpretation of profile streams.**

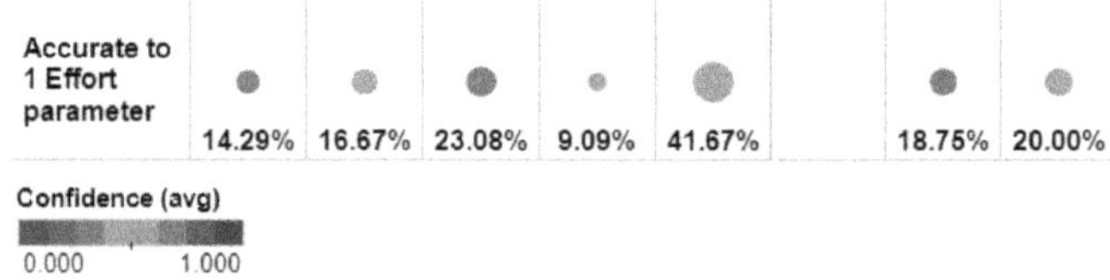


**Figure 4. LMA-adjusted accuracy for 1st-dominant *BEA* recognitions.**

### LMA-adjusted Analysis of Accuracy

A simple analysis of accuracy ignores the fact that the eight *BEAs* have fundamental similarities. For instance, Dab (*Light, Direct, Quick*) and Flick (*Light, Indirect, Quick*) differ only in their Space Factor. In contrast, Dab and Slash (*Heavy, Indirect, Quick*) differ by two Effort Factors. Figure 3 indicates that EFFORTDETECT often mistook a Flick for Dab (72.22%). However, the results of the interviews of the CMA contrasted this, since she stated that these variations were consistent with her experience of LMA highlighting the degree of movement variability and complexity that occurs within movement streams, but that certain other kinds of classifications would not be as admissible. *For instance, it would make little sense if Dab were classified as Wring (*Heavy, Indirect, Sustained*), and even less sense if Dab were classified as Slash (*Heavy, Indirect, Quick*).*

Following the movement analyst's observations, we propose an *LMA-adjusted analysis* of accuracy that appropriately weights the contribution of each predicted 1st-dominant *BEA* within a profile when calculating the 1st-dominant *BEA* for the profile stream. Instead of a confusion matrix, a comparison of LMA-adjusted accuracy values—averaged across profile streams and grouped by target Effort—is more appropriate. Figure 4 graphs the distribution of LMA-adjusted accuracy values across the eight-targeted *BEAs*. Profile streams associated with Glide and Wring targets demonstrate complete Effort parameter accuracy more than 45% of the time (Glide: 45.45%; Wring: 50%), and accuracy to within two Effort parameters at least 30% of the time (Glide: 45.45%, Wring: 30%). Profile streams associated with Dab and Punch targets are accurate to within all Effort parameters more than 70% of time (Dab: 71.43%; Punch: 73.33%). Profile streams associated with Flick, Float, and Slash targets are accurate to within two Effort parameters at least 75% of the time. Figure 4 also reveals that no profile stream was *inaccurate* by all three Effort parameters.

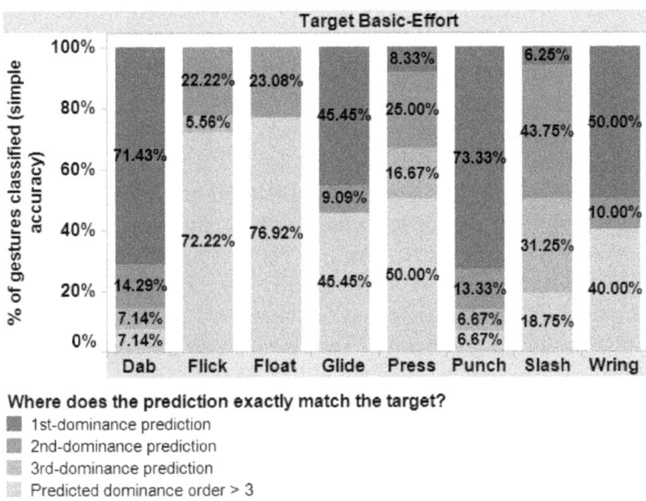


**Figure 5. Simple accuracy by dominance order.**

### Dominance Order Analysis

Figure 4 shows that 1st-dominance matching for Flick, Float, and Slash targets is inaccurate by a degree of only one Effort parameter between 75% and 83% of the time. This finding suggests another line of inquiry: at which dominance levels are these *BEAs* exactly recognized? Figure 5 visually charts the answer and reveals that profile streams for the Slash target exactly matches all Effort parameters in the predicted 2nd-dominant *BEA* 44% of the time. This shows that though the system is often (75%) confident that Punch is present in a Slash-based movement, the system's next best guess is more accurate 43.75% of the time

## COMPARISON WITH EXISTING SYSTEMS

We would like to emphasize that while EFFORTDETECT does not outperform LMA-based recognition systems described in the literature, we stress the significance of the results given that the data comes from a single accelerometer attached to only one body part, unlike the systems reported by Zhao and Badler (seven body parts) [32], Rett *et al.* (two body parts) [22], and Santos *et al.* (three body parts) [24]. Indeed, Zhao and Badler [32] used magnetic trackers and video and reported a recognition rate of about 90% for Weight, Time, and Flow Efforts. Rett *et al.* [22] use Bayesian reasoning to perform continuous classification on video data to detect Time and Space Efforts, but not Weight Effort. They report success rates between 75% to 92% in distinguishing between the four *BEAs* with Light Weight: Flick, Dab, Glide, and Float. Santos *et al.* [24] achieved recognition rates between 58.7% and 97.1% for Space, Weight, and Time Efforts.

To compare EFFORTDETECT's performance with other LMA systems, we compute a weighted overall detection accuracy as *(rate of perfect parameter matching + 2/3*(rate at which two out of three parameters are matched) + 1/3*(rate at which one out of three parameters are matched)* at the 1st-dominance recognition level, as summarized in Table 4.

In this paper, our main contribution is not the movement recognition system itself. We do not claim that EFFORTDETECT outperforms other LMA-based recognition systems. Rather, we believed that a significant amount of MQs information can be recognized from a computationally efficient, real-time single accelerometer-based sensor that is readily wearable and deployable.

| Basic Effort Action | Weighted accuracy |
|---|---|
| **Dab** | 80.97% |
| **Flick** | 61.11% |
| **Float** | 58.97% |
| **Glide** | 78.78% |
| **Press** | 55.55% |
| **Punch** | 91.11% |
| **Slash** | 62.5% |
| **Wring** | 76.67% |
| **Average** | **70.71%** |

**Table 4. Accuracy for *1st*-dominant recognition**

## APPLICATIONS IN HCI AND DIGITAL PERFORMANCE

EFFORTDETECT system was successfully used in applications in digital performances and interactive installations and has future potential to be expanded into the greater HCI applications for health and well-being, gaming, visual analytics for the quantitative self, pedagogical and locative media, and large scale public entertainments platforms such as interactive urban screens.

Our contribution is to design for MQs as an interaction modality. For this purpose, we represent movement as a higher level semantic, which can map to human expression, affect and psychological factors. We utilize a stable and replicable system such as LMA that can be directly applied to HCI applications exploiting single-accelerometer consumer platforms. Thus, EFFORTDETECT can be incorporated in applications using the ubiquitous single-accelerometer consumer-devices for movement-based interaction, including hand-held mobile phone, game controllers, wrist-mounted accelerometers as well as wearable on-body devices embedded in clothing or accessories. Our system enables these applications to integrate users' MQs and thus expand the affordances of single-accelerometers beyond current uses such as the orientation of a browser page (a choice between portrait or landscape mode), or tilting a screen-based sprite. While our system utilizes a wrist-mounted accelerometer it can be ported to existing mobile devices by transmitting its accelerometer data as input to our Effort detection engine and mapping Effort recognition to higher-level movement semantics used by the application.

We have demonstrated the system's applicability in the performing Arts and in particular its use in two successful dance performances. Our system was also tested in a public context where participants collaboratively interacted through their MQs. We are currently expanding the use of our system in a large public interactive urban screen setting using mobile phones.

### Astral Convertible

EFFORTDETECT's system was successfully used in a live restaging of choreographer Trisha Brown's Masterpiece, *Astral Convertible* (shown in Figure 6), at the Krannert Center for the Performing Arts at the University of Illinois at Urbana Champaign. Dancers performed choreographic material that was accurately recognized by software built on the same backend as EFFORTDETECT [21]. The recognized Efforts from the performers' acceleration data was used to trigger changes in aesthetic effects in the performance environment including light, sound, and projection. The use of EFFORTDETECT system in restaging the piece of Trisha Brown, valued the new perspectives that constantly emerge from the intersection of movement studies, Dance and more generally the Arts, with the field of HCI and movement-based interaction design. Moreover, this artistic production demonstrated the EFFORTDETECT system's applicability in the field of Dance and Performing Arts.

**Figure 6. Image of Trisha Brown's piece, Astral Convertible. ©Guy Garnett, MovingStories Partnership.**

### EMVIZ Visualization

In the fields of human movement analysis, artistic visualization, and interactive dance performance, EFFORTDETECT has also been used in the EMVIZ visualization system[2] (shown in Figure 7) to explore visual metaphors by mapping movement qualities, in the form of Laban BEAs to parameterized abstract visualizations.

The motivation for EMVIZ project comes from the interest and expertise about human movement in the field of contemporary dance performance and artistic visualization. The visualization system places attention on aesthetics, provides real-time response through models from expertise-based knowledge on properties of movement. EMVIZ uses metaphoric mappings that rely on artistic interpretation of human MQs to generate visual forms, and illustrate the creative design process for communicating expert knowledge around movement. EMVIZ was also used in an interactive art installation during which the audience interacted with the visuals. Audience provided feedback regarding their response to the aesthetic and communicative properties of the visualizations. They reported the system's capacities to support their ability to become aware of, engaged in, differentiate and furthermore, appreciate various MQs based on the changes in their own or alternatively in a dancer's movement, with the aid of EMVIZ.

[2] EMVIZ system http://metacreation.net/index.php?s=projects#top

**Figure 7. (a) EMVIZ used in a Dance performance, (b) EMVIZ used in a public interactive installation at Simon Fraser University Open House Event 2011. ©Pattarawut Subyen, MovingStories Partnership**

## CONCLUSION

EFFORTDETECT is a single-accelerometer system that recognizes in real-time Laban eight Basic Effort Actions and can be used under a wide range of environmental conditions. In designing and evaluating the EFFORTDETECT model, we applied quantitative approaches to assess the accuracy of our computational system to match our conceptual and epistemological goals. Its form factor makes it an ideal candidate for use in mobile and handheld devices. The analysis of the data indicates that the model recognizes MQs to various degrees of accuracy and confidence, and that in most cases both the systems level of accuracy and performance could be described and rationalized by the LMA analyst.

The main contribution of this paper is our approach to using expertise in planning and carrying out an evaluation for movement recognition systems rather than proposing a new movement recognition system. This, we argue, is of significant interest to the HCI community. As an additional contribution of our paper, we also aimed to illustrate in general the utility of acceleration as primary data when looking at movement quality. We believe that this is particularly relevant to the HCI field because of increasing use of accelerometers in mobile devices and proliferation of mobile applications that take advantage of acceleration-based data.

As perspectives of our study, we are currently applying the results of the evaluation of the EFFORTDETECT presented in this paper, to the iterative design and development of the system. We are experimenting with variations of the underlying recognition model by generating new types of training data while actively using movement expertise to inform the process. For instance, we initially trained the system with movement corresponding to the eight *BEAs*; we are pursuing this work by generating training data that correspond to qualities that interpolate between *BEAs*, e.g., movements that have qualities somewhere between Dab and Punch, or Slash and Wring. However, instead of controlling only the outer form of the expression by simply directing the dancer to move "slower" or "more lightly", the dancer develops an inner image (such as "digging a shallow trench in the sand" or "closing a 6-foot high wooden gate") that aids them in performing the movement. Our future work is being explored across each level of the data stream: sensor data acquisition, categorizing and modeling low-level motion features, iterating the movement recognition and analysis model, and multi-modal representation of movement recognition data.

## ACKNOWLEDGMENTS

We thank Kristin Carlson, Cheryl Prophet, and the members of the Expressive Motion Research Project, and the Performance-Research Group in the School of Interactive Arts and Technology at Simon Fraser University. We thank our international collaborators at the Institute for Advanced Computing Applications and Technologies at the University of Illinois Dance Department. We also thank our funders MITACS, and the New Media Initiative funded through the Canada Council for the Arts (CCA) and the Natural Sciences Engineering Research Council (NSERC).

## REFERENCES

1. Amstutz, R., Amft, O., French, B., Smailagic, A., Siewiorek, D., and Troster, G. Performance Analysis of an HMM-Based Gesture Recognition Using a Wristwatch Device. *Proceedings of the International Conference on Computational Science and Engineering. (CSE)*, IEEE (2009), 303-309.
2. Barakova, E.I. and Lourens, T. Expressing and interpreting emotional movements in social games with robots. *Proceedings of the Personal Ubiquitous Comput. 14*, 5 (2010), 457–467.
3. Bartenieff, I. and Lewis, D. *Body Movement: Coping with the Environment*. Routledge, 1980.
4. Bergson, H. *Matter and Memory*. Zone Books, New York, 1988.
5. Bindiganavale, R.N. *Building parameterized action representations from observation*. Doctoral dissertation University of Pennsylvania Philadelphia, PA, USA, 2000.

6. Bott, J.N., Crowley, J.G., and LaViola,Jr., J.J. Exploring 3D gestural interfaces for music creation in video games. *Proceedings of the 4th International Conference on Foundations of Digital Games*, ACM (2009), 18–25.
7. Bouchard, D. and Badler, N. Semantic segmentation of motion capture using Laban Movement Analysis. *Proceedings of the international conference on Intelligent Virtual Agents*, Springer (2007), 37-44.
8. Chi, D., Costa, M., Zhao, L., and Badler, N. The EMOTE model for Effort-Shape. *Proceedings of the conference on computer graphics and interactive techniques*, ACM (2000), 173–182.
9. Djajadiningrat, T., Matthews, B., and Stienstra, M. Easy doesn't do it: skill and expression in tangible aesthetics. *Personal and Ubiquitous Computing 11*, 8 (2007), 657-676.
10. Farella, E., O'Modhrain, S., Benini, L., and Riccó, B. Gesture Signature for Ambient Intelligence Applications: A Feasibility Study. In K.P. Fishkin, B. Schiele, P. Nixon and A. Quigley, eds., *Pervasive Computing*. Springer Berlin Heidelberg, 2006, 288-304.
11.Fdili Alaoui, S., Caramiaux, B., Serrano, M. and Bevilacqua, F., Dance Movement Quality as Interaction Modality. *Proceedings of the International Conference on Designing Interactive Systems (DIS),* ACM (2012) 761-769.
12. Hashim, W.N.W., Noor, N.L.M., and Adnan, W.A.W. The design of aesthetic interaction: towards a graceful interaction framework. *Proceedings of the International Conference on Interaction Sciences: Information Technology, Culture and Human*, ACM (2009), 69–75.
13. Jones, E., Alexander, J., Andreou, A., Irani, P., and Subramanian, S. GesText: accelerometer-based gestural text-entry systems. *Proceedings of the International Conference on Human Factors in Computing Systems (SIGCHI),* ACM (2010), 2173–2182.
14. Khoshhal, K., Aliakbarpour, H., Quintas, J., Drews, P., and Dias, J. Probabilistic LMA-based classification of human behaviour understanding using Power Spectrum technique. *Proceedings of the 13th Conference on Information Fusion (FUSION)*, IEEE (2010), 1-7.
15. Laban, R. and Lawrence, F.C. *Effort: Economy of Human Movement.* Macdonald and Evans, Plymouth, 1974.
16. Laban, R. *Effort*. Macdonald & Evans, London, 1947.
17. Loke, L., Larssen, A.T., Robertson, T., and Edwards, J. Understanding movement for interaction design: frameworks and approaches. *Personal and Ubiquitous Computing 11*, (2007), 691-701.
18. Mentis, H., and Johansson, C. Seeing movement qualities. *Proceedings of the International Conference on Human Factors in Computing Systems (SIGCHI),* ACM (2013), 3375-3384.
19. Moore, C.L. and Yamamoto, K. *Beyond Words: Movement Observation and Analysis*. Gordon & Breach Science Publishers, New York, U.S.A, 1988.
20. Nakata, T., Mori, T., and Sato, T. Analysis of impression of robot bodily expression. *Journal of Robotics and Mechatronics 14*, 1 (2002), 27-36.
21. Pietrowicz, M., Garnett, G., McGrath, R., and Toenjes, J. Multimodal gestural interaction in performance. *Proceedings of the International Conference on Human Factors in Computing Systems (SIGCHI),* ACM (2010).
22. Rett, J., Dias, J., and Ahuactzin, J.-M. Bayesian reasoning for Laban Movement Analysis used in human-machine interaction. *International Journal of Reasoning-based Intelligent Systems 2*, 1 (2010), 13-35.
23. Roudaut, A., Baglioni, M., and Lecolinet, E. TimeTilt: Using Sensor-Based Gestures to Travel through Multiple Applications on a Mobile Device. *Proceedings of INTERACT International Conference on Human-Computer Interaction,* Springer-Verlag (2009), 830–834.
24. Santos, L., Prado, J.A., and Dias, J. Human Robot interaction studies on Laban human movement analysis and dynamic background segmentation. *Proceedings of the IEEE/RSJ international conference on Intelligent robots and systems* (2009), 4984-4989.
25. Schiphorst, T., Nack, F., KauwATjoe, M., et al. PillowTalk: can we afford intimacy? *Proceedings of the 1st international conference on Tangible and embedded interaction*, ACM (2007), 23–30.
26. Schiphorst, T. Self-evidence: applying somatic connoisseurship to experience design. *Proceedings of the International Conference on Human Factors in Computing Systems (SIGCHI),* ACM (2011), 145–160.
27. Scoditti, A., Blanch, R., and Coutaz, J. A novel taxonomy for gestural interaction techniques based on accelerometers. *Proceedings of the 16th international conference on Intelligent user interfaces*, ACM (2011), 63–72.
28. Sheets-Johnstone, M. *The Primacy of Movement*. John Benjamins Publishing Company, Amsterdam, 1999.
29. Swaminathan, D., Thornburg, H., Mumford, J., Rajko, S., James, J., Ingalls, T., Campana, E., Qian, G., Sampath, P., Peng, B., A dynamic Bayesian approach to computational Laban shape quality analysis. *Advances in Human Computer Interaction*, (2009), 1-17.
30.Widmer, G., Kubat, M., Learning in the presence of concept drift and hidden contexts, *Machine Learning, 23, 1 (1996),* 69-101.
31. Wilson, A. and Shafer, S. XWand: UI for intelligent spaces. *Proceedings of the International Conference on Human Factors in Computing Systems (SIGCHI),* ACM (2003), 545–552.
32. Zhao, L. and Badler, N. Acquiring and validating motion qualities from live limb gestures. *Graphical Models 67*, 1 (2005), 1-16.

# The Vocal Chorder – Empowering Opera Singers with a Large Interactive Instrument

**Carl Unander-Scharin**
KTH Royal Institute of Technology, CSC/MID
10044 Stockholm, Sweden
carl.unander-scharin@telia.com

**Åsa Unander-Scharin**
Luleå University of Technology
97187 Luleå, Sweden
asa.scharin@ltu.se

**Kristina Höök**
Mobile Life @ KTH
100 44 Stockholm, Sweden
khook@kth.se

## ABSTRACT
With *The Vocal Chorder*, a large interactive instrument to create accompaniment, opera singers can get more power over the performance. The device allows performers to interactively accompany themselves through pushing, leaning on and bending steel wires. The design was guided by the unique needs of the solo-singer, explored through autobiographical design and material explorations, some on stage, and later tested by other singers. We discuss how designing for opera and for the stage requires extraordinary durability and how opera performances can change with a bodily-oriented instrument such as The Vocal Chorder. Through a designerly exploration, we arrived at a device that offered (1) a tool for singers to take control over the rhythmical pace and overall artistic and aesthetic outcome of their performances, (2) an enriched sense of embodiment between their voice and the overall performance; and (3) a means to empower opera singers on stage.

## Author Keywords
Opera; Autobiographical design; Interactive instruments; embodiment; empowerment; appropriation

## ACM Classification Keywords
H.5.m

## INTRODUCTION
We aim to describe a designerly exploration (following the terminology of Zimmerman and colleagues [38]) leading to the creation of a novel, interactive instrument for the opera – the Vocal Chorder. As opera is a highly physical art form, taking quite some space on stage, we built a large artifact that would allow singers to accompany their own voices through bodily interaction. The device is designed to endure the demands that are typical for the stage: reliability, repeatability and stamina. Whereas opera originally constituted an innovative cultural movement where singers fully participated in the artistic processes, contemporary opera productions have become increasingly hierarchical and singers' influence on the creative process is becoming more and more limited – both off and on stage. This is what we set out to address with our device.


*CHI 2014*, April 26 - May 01 2014, Toronto, ON, Canada
Copyright 2014 ACM 978-1-4503-2473-1/14/04…$15.00.
http://dx.doi.org/10.1145/2556288.2557050

### Designing for Empowerment
By designing for empowerment through putting the control of the accompaniment in the hands of the singer, we, in a sense, link our research to early operatic practices. As design for the opera is a novel domain for interaction design, we will provide a brief background to opera and discuss some of the particular challenges of this design space. We will focus on describing how opera started out as an exploratory art form and how our designerly explorations in that sense reconnect to the early developments of opera.

**Figure 1. The Vocal Chorder**

Given this background, we will then move on to describe some of the designerly explorations, lasting over several years, that resulted in this particular instrument. We will focus on four cases of interactions and performances we engaged in. In particular, the first author of this paper, who is an opera singer and composer, used himself as both subject and object of our design inquiry – a method referred to as autobiographical design [27]. Our work with The Vocal

Chorder is therefore an example of research *through* art and design, as opposed to research *for* or *into* art and design, as differentiated by Frayling [8]. Our findings add on to a historical context of searching new expressions through exploring the art form opera with new works and technologies. We end by discussing how our insights are relevant beyond developing the operatic art proper, in particular for other on-stage settings.

## RELOCATING CONTROL IN PERFORMANCES

We are not the first to explore the topic of empowerment in on-stage performance. There are several examples where the audience can partake directly in the performance through various interactive technologies. For example, in the humanaquarium musicians were placed in a large interactive glass box in public places and people walking by could change their performance through touching the glass box [30]. There are also numerous examples of how to use movement sensors to allow audiences to influence both music and imagery, see e.g. [13, 17, 29]. On stage, digital interactivity in different forms have been introduced to put artists, musicians and singers, in charge of the overall aesthetic form of their performance, see e.g. [1, 11, 35]

More specifically, in the opera context, there has been many fertile encounters between electroacoustic music and vocal performances both on and off the stage since the birth of Elektronische musik [4] and Musique Concrète [25] in the 1940s and 50s. Through the appearance of computerized interactive musical instruments, around 1990 and onwards, we got works like Machover and Paradiso's *Brain Opera* that explored opera on-line [18], Waiswisz's interactive interface *The Hands* for controlling sounds through gestures [34], and Manoury's *K...* [20], where interactive technologies aim to liberate the singers on stage. Composers such as Stockhausen, Nono, Berio, Ligeti, Cage, Wishart, Adams and Saariaho have incorporated electronic processing of voices in their operas and vocal music[1]. Research institutes where vocal music and various forms of interactivity has been developed in particular are STEIM in the Netherlands [13, 17, 34, 35], IRCAM in France [1, 20, 29], and Opera for the Future Lab at MIT in the US [11, 18]. An interactive gesture controller was created by Park and colleagues [19], allowing singers to generate additional vibrato and other vocal effects through embedded sensors. In the opera *Death and the powers* [11] various real-time interactive technologies were deployed to create a "disembodied performance" in order to portray a dystopic scenario. In the opera *The Crystal Cabinet* [33], singers and dancers functioned as joysticks. Entering "The Charged Room", they scratched their sounds through altering their positions, letting the resulting sounds feed back into the performance, thereby creating new movements and new sounds. Moreover, the research around *The Throat III* [5, 6, 31] revolves around embodiment of singers' voices in relation to an interactive hand-held instrument for vocal manipulation. With The Throat III, the control of the performance resides in a glove put on the singer's right hand. It modifies the singer's voice to artistically portray and embody the disformed voice of *The Elephant Man.*

### Long-term changes in power hierarchies in opera

But apart from our own work on *The Throat III*, to our knowledge, none of these projects have aimed to create interactive instruments that can both empower opera singers at the same time as they improve and extend on the aesthetic and experiential qualities of the whole performance.

There is an incongruity between the aura around famous opera-singers, "divas", supposedly mastering the end-result of their performances and the reality where the contemporary opera singer have little influence over the essential creative process. It has been argued that the opera-world of today is "the age of the producer" and that sequentially the ages of the poet, the singer, the composer, and the conductor have passed by [14]. According to this viewpoint, singers' influence decreased already at the end of the 18th century when composers' influence increased. They, in turn, lost power in favor of the conductors during early 20th century. Finally, the producers (agents, casting directors, and others) of opera today excel the main authority over artistic decisions. Accordingly, this ongoing change in power hierarchies continuously changes the conditions for the singers.

## OPERA AND INNOVATION

Opera was born at the end of the 16th century when a group of artists, the Camerata Florentina, were searching for new expressivity that would help them re-create what they understood as the antique drama [23]. In this double procedure of both looking backward to a presumably forlorn art and at the same time envisioning something new, the art form we now refer to as opera was born. In early opera, the solo-singer was commonly accompanied by only one instrument – a harp or a lute – creating a rhythmical and harmonic grounding on top of which the singer performed the vocal lines with a large amount of improvisation. Singers developed virtuosity both in a technical sense, and in an aesthetic sense, adding flavor and personality to the performance within the boundaries that composers and authors had set in the score. In the very early days, there seems to have been less demarcation between creating and performing opera. It has been reported that Jacopo Peri, composer of the very first opera *Daphne* in 1597, accompanied himself on the lute whilst singing [2, 22]. This practice then became less and less common throughout the history.

However, the innovative and creative search for new expressions continued in opera. For example, as a result of the focus on vocal performance, the particular singing tech-

[1] E.g. Karl-Heinz Stockhausen: *Gesang der Jünglinge* 1956 and *Stimmung* (1968); Luigi Nono: *A floresta é jovem e cheja de vida* (1966); Luciano Berio: *Coro* (1976); György Ligeti: *Le Grand Macabre* (1977); John Cage: *Roaratorio* (1979), Trevor Wishart: *Anticredos* (1980), John Adams *Nixon in China* (1987), and Kaija Saariaho: *From the grammar of dreams* (2002).

nique evolved which constitutes what we today understand as operatic singing, *Bel Canto* [2, 22, 28]. In short it means that a singer through years of study acquires loudness, a homogenous sound in all registers and stamina to withstand a whole performance. On top of that the performer integrates singing with acting and drama.

### Orchestral Instruments Changing Singer Conditions

At the end of the 19th century the romantic orchestra had reached its full power, often numbering over 100 persons, each playing on instruments that constantly were developed to gain more loudness. We see this for example, in how the gut strings of the violin were replaced by strings made of steel during the late 17$^{th}$ century, empowering the violin section with a much louder volume. In parallel, the wooden flute evolved to a metallic version, and brass instruments such as the trumpet and the trombone improved likewise. These ongoing modifications in the orchestra required changes in vocal practice. One example is when the tenor Gilbert-Louis Duprez invented a means to sing the "high c" with a full voice in 1837. Earlier, high tones in the tenor voice were managed through singing with the so-called "head voice", whereas Duprez introduced his new technique to bring also the "chest voice" up to the high pitches [3], enabling louder and more heroic singing. In parallel, the vocal parts created by composers such as Wagner, Berlioz and Verdi were stretching the boundaries of the human voice. In order to find and train singers that could manage the high-strung vocal parts, such as Wagner's *Tristan* – by contemporaries deemed as "unsingable" [12] – the German *Fach-system* emerged [16]. According to this now internationally established practice, an opera-singer's vocal career is structured in accordance with the available repertory, allowing the artist to perform a rather narrow range of roles supposedly fitting for each type of voice. This system has evolved in order to provide singers to the opera houses, but has detrimental consequence such as that it tends to narrow the individual artistic freedom for singers and even has negative impact on their health [22, 24, 28].

### Composers Stretching Boundaries

Thus, the specific way of utilizing operatic voices, as we know it today, evolved throughout the centuries in a history of innovations, co-evolving with the repertory and the orchestra. Composers have continuously been exploring the human voice as well as making use of novel instruments in order to enhance expressivity and create novel artworks. Many of the canonical composers were in fact singers themselves, e.g. C. Monteverdi and G. Rossini. Moreover, composers of opera have often merged newly invented instruments in their orchestras, as was the case when Kastner, for example, introduced the saxophone and Messiaen utilized the synthesizer *Ondes Martenot* in their operas[2].

[2] Jean-Georges Kastner: *Le dernier Roi de Juda* (opera, 1844); Olivier Messiaen: *Saint-François d'Assise* (opera, 1975-83)

### Questioning a Traditional Framework through Design

The artistic framework and possible ways of interpreting a particular opera are in most parts predetermined even before rehearsals start, as most operas in the common repertory have been staged many times before. Moreover, as the music in most cases was composed a long time ago, there is little room for the singers to partake in the overall compositional decisions. Albeit there are numerous examples of influential contemporary singers (notably Cathy Berberian, herself a composer, and groups such as The King's Singers and Electric Phoenix) that have been muses for the creation of important vocal works, it is rare for singers to have influence on the musical foundations – nor has technology seldom afforded feedback to the performers themselves. The singers that took part in our work all expressed a wish of participating more in the aesthetic shaping of their art form. Acknowledging opera-singers through designing an interactive instrument for them challenges century-old power structures in opera through letting singers actively taking part in shaping the performance.

## A DESIGNERLY APPROACH TO DESIGN OF MUSICAL INSTRUMENTS FOR THE OPERA

The Vocal Chorder introduced here, is part of a larger research *program* aiming to open and populate a new *design space* [36] in opera. According to Redström [21] a research program in an interactive design research setting consists of three steps: (1) formulation of a program, often starting through extensive exploration of the aesthetic qualities of the material at hand – be it electricity, interactive textiles or, as in this case, opera, (2) realization of the program through design experiments – *exemplars*, and (3) finally articulation of the experiments through reflection. The latter often leads to reformulation of the overall program. Redström has used this framing of design research to open design spaces such as "slow technology", interactive textiles or aesthetic ways to communicate energy consumption in the home [9, 21]. Of key importance in a designerly research exploration is to let the particular exemplars both explore possibilities and inform the overall research program. That is to say, through the actual design process, the key knowledge is gained [10].

Through our work with the *exemplars* The Vocal Chorder, reported here, The Charged Room [33] and The Throat III [5, 6, 31] we are taking our first steps towards the articulation of a research program investigating new aesthetic expressions for opera. A main defining property of exemplars in this design space is emancipation of the artist through the use of an interactive instrument. To explain what we mean by this, let us go into a quite detailed account of how the Vocal Chorder emerged.

## THE VOCAL CHORDER DESIGN PROCESS

Drawing on autobiographical design procedures [27] that *"rest(s) on the user's genuine need for the system"*, and that allows for *"a much tighter coupling between user input and implementation"*, we departed on an intense journey of material explorations (here we follow on the materiality strand in HCI [7, 37] that we will account for below. As the first author is an opera singer and composer, the early explorations built to a large extent on his own needs.

After describing his explorations and needs, we turn to performances by other opera singers reporting on their experiences of performing with the device.

The outcome of this process was not only an interactive instrument, The Vocal Chorder, but in fact several different versions of the instrument as well as range of performances with operatic music composed specifically to enhance experiential and aesthetic qualities of the artifact.

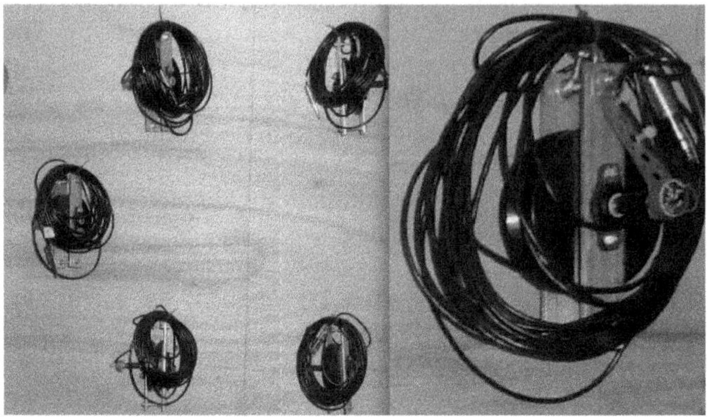

**Figure 2. Sensors consisting of wheels, housing, cabling and potentiometers (in blue in the upper right corner detail)**

### Starting the Material Explorations

When computers started to encompass real-time audio processing, performing with laptops on stage became more and more common. Around 1999, laptop computers were powerful and stable enough to allow for using them live whilst performing music. A few years later, around 2003, they could also process images and video in real-time. On the one hand, this opened up for performing in novel ways in "laptop performances". On the other hand, this would normally mean that artists were constantly sitting behind computer screens during concerts and shows. At the time, however, new technologies such as sensors and wireless connectivity were becoming more commonplace, providing a new material that could be used to design novel interactive instruments. Many different ideas for how to create a bodily instrument allowing for interactions with sensors and wireless connectivity were discussed and dismissed before we arrived at the design we describe below, where we finally arrived at a solution that let performers immerse in the interface while performing.

### Choosing our Components

We set out on our explorations with the wish that the design should dodge the need to be monitored from the outside by an artist sitting behind a computer screen. Rather, the performance should arise as an autonomous activity by the interactions with and through the instrument. This wish for an emancipating instrument on stage placed strong demands on robustness and reliability of the components and in the overall design of the artifact as well as in the software. We could not risk designing an instrument where singers would not be able to fulfill a whole performance on stage. To feel secure on stage, performers need to rest assured that the instrument and all the components will endure the physical demands on stage and will not let them down while performing. We can simplify what is needed into three sets of components: *hardware, software* and *music*. The hardware consists of all the physical parts we needed to place on stage, which in the end became a combination of sensors, steel wires, cabling, computers, two projectors and a synthesizer. The software had to process and remap incoming signals to outgoing sound and visuals. And finally, we needed new music that would thrive on the particulars of the artifact.

#### *Hardware*

Musical Instrument Digital Interface (MIDI) is a standard for communication between digital musical instruments and computers. In order to transform movement to electric signals, we used a so-called voltage-to-midi-converter[3]. The converter had eight inputs where eight independent streams of variable electric current could be transformed to MIDI. In order to produce the currents, eight *potentiometers* were used (see upper right detail in Figure 2). A potentiometer is a simple device where turning a knob changes the amount of voltage that is allowed to pass through it. By turning the knob, the changes in current would occur that we wanted to transform to MIDI and later to music and visuals. To find means to twist the potentiometers we needed to transform movement from the body in space to the turning of the knob. The most straightforward way to do this would perhaps have been to mount larger knobs on the potentiometers, but we wanted to achieve a larger interaction that would allow the performer to inflict changes with bodily movements. We tried various ways of turning the knobs with cords that were wrapped around them. But the need for more performativity led us to try steel wires leading from the floor to the ceiling, enabling the performer to stand when pushing and pulling them over the potentiometers. The potentiometers where therefore mounted in the ceiling on wheels made of styrene which were mounted in metallic housings enabling the steel wires to roll them back and forth. Thereby the wires influenced the eight potentiometers (see Figure 3).

[3] Rolls MP-2884, Voltage to Midi Converter.

Figure 3. Potentiometers mounted in styrene wheels, allowing the flexibility of rubber to roll them via the wires

As we wanted the movements of the performer to be large and even allow the artist to lean on the wires, we needed a construction that would endure the weight of a person. Therefore, thick rubber bands were fixed at the end of each wire. The rubber bands allowed for flexibility that let the wires roll over the wheels to twist the potentiometers with large pressure. Moreover, a physical housing was built, enabling the performer to step into the artifact in order to interact with it from within, see Figures 5 + 6. The whole construct was 3.5 high and the surface measured 2*4 meters.

*Software*

To be able to remap incoming MIDI-data originating from the potentiometers to sounds and visuals, we used the software Max/MSP/Jitter (Figure 4). This programming environment enables simultaneous processing of MIDI, audio and visual data[4]. The software had to map the eight separate incoming streams of data into both music and in visuals. It enabled the movements of the performer via the wires to simultaneously inflict changes in sound and vision. As can be seen in Figure 5, two projectors showed an interactive pyramid, which was rendered with Max/MSP/ Jitter. The music that was composed for The Vocal Chorder, was inspired by a short story by Ray Bradbury, "Tomorrow's Child", that revolves around a child that was born in another dimension. The story opens with the line *"He didn't want to be the father of a small blue pyramid"* and we wanted to convey this emotion in the performance. Through the performers interactions, the pyramid responded to the movements of the singer that at the same time created accompaniment for the voice in the music.

[4] www.cycling74.com

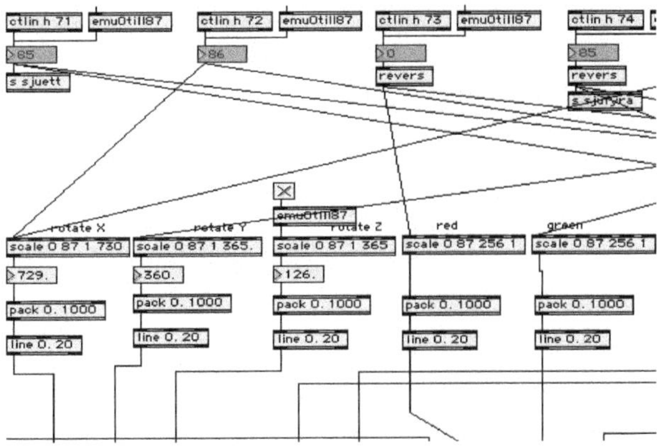


Figure 4. Detail from a patch in Max/MSP/Jitter showing mapping of parameters from incoming data to audio & visuals

*Music*

In parallel to these material exploration processes, music that would thrive on the artifact's particulars was devised. To be able to use The Vocal Chorder for accompaniment, music that could be performed via the wires was needed. This called for a particular solution in the musical structure and in the resulting composition. Most music can be analyzed and subsequently parsed into a block of tones that sound simultaneously, called a *chord*. Normally a chord is played by a guitarist or pianist using both hands.

Figure 5. Singer interacting with sound and visuals

Here, we wanted to simplify this so that a singer could interact with the artifact without being an instrumentalist. We realized that if we could alter the playing of chords so that they could be forwarded one at a time, the performer would control the ongoing pace of the music. To achieve this, the device was equipped with a chord-forwarding feature – a dedicated wire operated by the singer that would forward one chord at a time when pushed over a preset break point. When a row of chords is at hand, they constitute a *chord sequence*. We devised a long chord sequence that would allow the composition to be forwarded by the performer by bending one of the strings. The bending of the strings in order to advance the chord sequence became an important building block for both the design of the artifact as well as for the music composed for it as it emancipated the singer.

### *Allocating wires to different components of the performance*

The other wires were allocated to change the sound of the synthesizer as well as modifying the interactive visuals projected by the two projectors, as seen in Figure 5. For example, bending wire number three would inflict changes in the sound of the chord and at the same time make the pyramid turn slowly in space. Likewise, bending wire number five would change the volume of the chords, and at the same time alter the colors and patterns of the projections.

### *Sensory Digital Intonation*

At this point, having carefully explored and then subsequently chosen our materials and constructing the artifact, it was time to prepare our first public performances with it. In order to fine-tune a multi-faceted digital instrument as this, a procedure where *"artistic intuition and experience continuously influence the technical development and vice versa"* and *"that has similarities to what musicians call intonation"* [32] takes place. This is, in short, the procedure where precise considerations regarding the aesthetics within the interaction is undertaken. For example, carefully judging how far the wires are to be bent before a chord is sounding, or setting how multiple parameters that are inflicted by the same wire interplay with each other in an aesthetically pleasing way. Using *Sensory Digital Intonation* we finetuned the artifact towards performing with it, balancing the many parameters in the software against one another, as seen in Figure 4.

But this design did not come about without involving singers in the design process. Let us now turn to four example performances with the instrument, at different stages of the instrument development, influencing the design.

## PERFORMING WITH THE VOCAL CHORDER

The first incarnation of the Vocal Chorder had as its main goal to enable the first author of this paper to establish an autonomous, interactive embodied performance, where visuals and accompaniment came together in a homogenous gestalt. As mentioned above, a design process where the user and the designer are one and the same, constitutes what Sengers refers to as *autobiographical design* [27]. Thus, the account will hereinafter use the first-person noun "I" when personal accounts by the first author are cited.

### Case 1: Autobiographical Performance

In my working diary I wrote that one of my outsets was to *"develop a new bodily interface and to integrate it in an operatic context"*. Now, having carefully prepared the artifact, it was time to perform with it. In opera, repeatability is a core feature, as the repertory is rehearsed over and over again in order to reach a point when it can be presented for an audience. Our procedure followed this pattern, with one week of intense rehearsals before the audience came, during which the overall aesthetic concept emerged in dialogue with technological fine-tuning.

As we had chosen the materials in the hardware carefully, few if any problems with wires, rubber bands, styrene wheels or mechanical housing showed up during this time. However, other unforeseen technological challenges surfaced in the software. The at the time novel Mac OSX (10.2) turned out to have a fairly unreliable MIDI communication. I wrote in my diary *"the performances were completely governed by the technical conditions"*.

When performing, it is very frustrating not to be able to rely on the supporting structures of the performance, be it an orchestra playing out of tune, or as in this case, an unreliable digital instrument. I realized that the data communication was the problem rather than how the processing of that same data was done. I had to come up with a solution to stabilize the communication. In my diary I wrote:

*"I have had similar technical problems before and I have learned that you have to consider your technological tools as acoustical instruments - i.e. you must treat them with care and in the same way every time you use them. In practice this means that I have to start different devices in the same order each day (or search for other arrangements if something is not working/communicating), and then launch each piece of software in the same order as well. This procedure materializes almost as a ritual. Then and only then, technology behaves predictably"*.

This is a lived experience of the reflective conversation with the materials that Schön refers to when he talks about the *reflective practitioner* [26]. We managed to rectify the problems through a careful procedure for starting up the ingoing computers, synthesizers, projectors and most particularly the software. Thus, the rehearsals could lead up to four public performances. In a review it was reported that: *"The result comes forward as well worth seeing, even cool, considering that it results from experimenting without a preset libretto [...]"*[5].

From this response and others that also mentioned that the performance had liberating qualities, we understood that we had found something interesting, taking us closer to the kinds of experiences we were seeking.

### Case 2: Explorations of Durability and Embodiment

Our next iteration of the artifact was an audience-interactive version. In this phase, The Vocal Chorder was touring as part of an interactive exhibition where audiences were invited to perform with it. We encouraged the audiences to be rather playful in their interactions with the artifact, allowing us to explore the durability of the materials. In order to do this, the second author of this paper – who is a professional

[5] Review by Thomas Michelsen in "Politiken", March 25, 2004. Translated from Danish.

dancer – demonstrated the stamina of the artifact, pushing the limits of the construction in order for the audience to dare to be playful and perform extreme movements with it.

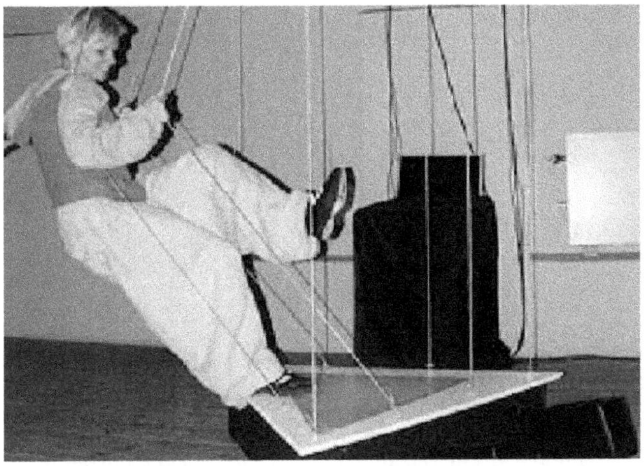

**Figure 6. The demands for durability were probed.**

Inspired by how the wires of The Vocal Chorder has similarities with human vocal chords we now wanted to incorporate vocal sounds in the artifact itself, transferring the manipulation of the wires to direct playback of prerecorded sounds of the human voice. This made The Vocal Chorder accessible to the public who are not trained opera singers.

**Figure 7. Vocal Sound used in case 2, 3 and 4. The movements of the performer in the artifact scratched playback of the sound.**

By this change, we also wanted to explore the feeling of embodying the voice with the movements in the artifact. The sensory setup was aiming at affording a playful but deep interplay between voice, body and machine. In a newspaper article a journalist who got to try the Vocal Chorder during its tour expresses his experience as:

*"It is not some orgiastic technology. The sensory interplay between people, dancers and things lets something deeply human and lively emerge. In this interaction liveness is born"* [6].

We feel that he his pinpointing something important here: when the singing, movements and the forwarding of chords come together in a live real-time performance, it is not a mechanical pushing of strings that the singer experiences, but a living experience that is created. While it may take some time to learn an instrument, the end goal is to become *one* with the instrument – embodied – allowing for an immediate sensation of both performing and experiencing at the same time.

### Cases 3 and 4: External Singers in The Vocal Chorder

In the third iteration of the instrument, we shifted away from the general public, back to professional singers to test and further develop the instrument. But this time, it was not only the first author of this paper who got to interact and work with the instrument, but instead two professional sopranos. They participated in a course in Extended Opera at The University College of Opera in Stockholm.

In this iteration, we wanted to return to letting performers accompany themselves through forwarding of chords. The music we chose for this iteration was a composition by 17th century composer Orlando Gibbons, called *The Silver Swan.* The singers first learnt to sing the song with normal piano accompaniment, and then they were introduced to a reduced score for The Vocal Chorder with only seven chords. These chords were recorded by the singers themselves, and implemented in the software (see Figure 7). We allocated the strings to one pre-recorded chord each, summing up to seven chords. One of the strings was now used as a *disturber,* a string that did not have a sound of its own but that would disturb the sound of the other strings, allowing more variation in the accompaniment. The sounds were allocated along the wires so that the chords were not triggered on a specific break point as earlier. Rather, the sounds were scratched by precise interaction by the user carefully pushing and stretching the wires of the artifact. This gave the performer a sense of *connecting* with the vocal sounds by carefully listening to the response of the artifact, whilst performing the aria along the accompaniment created by themselves by leaning, stretching and pulling the wires from within the large bodily interface.

One of the singers later reports on this experience:

*"I was asked to improvise with The Vocal Chorder* in A Silver Swan *by Gibbons, and noticed that this was a task I had to consider carefully. Not because others judged my performance, or me, but because I noticed that I did that myself, and therefore felt unfree even if the intention was the opposite. Beforehand, I did not think it would be problematic, I've been doing some improvisation before but it was many years ago and I had perhaps forgotten how one gets into it, and I noticed more prestige in that I did not want to do something that might sound silly, or was not good enough. [...] I do not mean that we should go on to make the mistake of not singing properly, but music is a living art form and the music needs to breathe. No appearance is exactly like the next, it is not natural for us humans. It was interesting that this appeared to me to while working with The Vocal Chorder."*

[6] Article by Calle Pauli in DN På Stan, May 20, 2005. Translated from Swedish.

**Figure 8. The first external singer in The Vocal Chorder**

The solo singer is here relating to a holistic and relational experience of her voice that arouse from performing with the artifact. In The Technology as Experience framework, McCarthy and Wright [15] refers to this kind of experience as *sense making*. They propose six different strands of sense making. One of them is *interpreting*. According to them, interpreting is characterized as *"an unfolding experience [that] involves discerning the narrative structure"*. Here the solo-singer was uncovering the hidden narrative structures in her own professional practice – the narrative that says that an opera-singer cannot improvise, cannot become part of the "living art form".

Furthermore, McCarthy and Wright discuss sense-making as a process of *reflection*: *"make[-ing] judgments about the experience as it unfolds"*. By making the performance a real-time synchronization between voice and accompaniment, we are allowing the singer to make their own judgments come into play: not sounding silly, choosing the tempo that expresses the sentiments they want to express, and so on. One year later, another singer was introduced to the same setup. In her reflections both *connecting* and *interpreting* is reported:

*"I pretty quickly got a feeling for the instrument. One of the major challenges consisted of getting a flow in the style and voice in combination. An additional challenge was that things happened with technology at times and it was challenging to try to stay in the moment and find a flow in the performance and not be disturbed by technological hassle."*

In order to comply with the unforeseen obstacles that interacting with the device offers, the performer realizes that connecting with it, and staying in the moment helps to overcome the challenges. The singer then relates to the bodily experience with the artifact:

*"There was also a strong and nice experience to see how it became like dance and choreography of the various arias we did together with technical instruments, how the instruments, in combination with us, gave the music form and life in unexpected ways*.". We see this as evidence of how the instrument opened up for different forms of sense making through performing interactively with it.

**Figure 9. The second singer in The Vocal Chorder**

The first singer continues:

*"We got to play in a way opera singers rarely get the chance to do; exploring movement and playing with sounds, everything did not necessarily have to be beautiful or perfect [...]. It was much more like a theater monologue than a regular song. As I got to know Vocal Chorder and felt confident in improvisation, I got a completely different relationship to it, and when we came to the last concert I felt really totally free."*

These two singers both relate to processes of becoming more and more embodied with the instrument. It is not a one-step process, but something that requires some work before arriving at the experience of being "totally free". The use of the artifact offered new perspectives on experiencing their own voices and performances, as phrased by the first singer: *"I had no other accompaniment than myself and did thus not need to be clearly and correctly relating to another human being in order for the music to work, I was in charge of time and could take breaks too"*. Interacting with the instrument had a noticeable positive impact on her vocal performance, offering a new freedom and adding new flavours to her voice, and she continues:

*"As regards to singing technique, I tried to keep it much more naked than I otherwise would have sung in school, it felt like the right thing in the face of this piece. How good it was, it is still difficult for me to judge, but I'm at least less afraid of going to be in this situation again, and I stretched a little on the old boundaries."*

The second singer concludes, referring to her colleagues that performed with other interactive instruments during the course:

*"Another thing that was so interesting and nice was to follow the development of others with both their arias and their work with the technical instruments they had been assigned. How it from the first tentative meeting with the*

*new technology changed to almost becoming part of the person who performed with it."*

When it comes to our aim – the empowerment of opera singers – the following quote indicates that we accomplished that: *"I learned that there is more to opera than just learning a score, showing up to a rehearsal and singing it – we are musicians".*

## CONCLUSIONS

Through our designerly exploration, lasting over several years, several incarnations of the instrument, we arrived at a device that offered (1) a tool for singers to appropriate and take control over the rhythmical pace and overall artistic and aesthetic outcome of their performances, (2) an enriched sense of embodiment between their voice and the overall performance; and (3) a means to empower opera singers on stage.

The bodily experiences and sensory engagements that have been accounted for here have materialized alongside the artifact itself. In a quite surprising way, power hierarchies and the history of opera have been explored through this design procedure. We did not expect that performing with the instrument would lead to the kinds of reflections reported by the singers who discussed how the instrument made the innate power structures in opera came to the fore for them. Another of our singers reasons around empowerment and her change in opinion after working with our interactive instruments: *"I thought at the time that I wanted to 'play by the rules' and succeed in opera through more typical pathways. After this semester I have come to realize that there is no* one *path to success, and that I need to follow my instinct to create, and see where that takes me, instead of waiting for someone else to give that to me. What a gift that is, and what an experience this has been."*

There are lessons learnt in our design process that are applicable not only to our research program for opera, but possibly to other on-stage interactive technologies: to explore robustness and durability, aesthetic expression through bodily movement, and how to create tools for empowerment.

### Material Explorations and Durability on Stage

We explored the many ingoing components by designing for the extreme requirements that follow from putting an interactive device on stage. We found that an almost ritual approach when handling materials such as computers, software and sensors was essential. As opera normally is rehearsed meticulously before the audience meets it, a rehearsal is in fact an inquiry into the endurance of the materials. The repetitions of rehearsals call for stamina in the performers as well as in the instruments in the orchestra, the scenography and the scaffolding.

In addition, when a performer meets an audience, the robustness of the design is tested under somewhat extreme conditions – not only in terms of physical robustness but also in terms of robustness in delivering an aesthetic experience, shaped in the moment between singer and instrument.

### Bodily Expression and Voice

As can be seen in Figures 8 and 9, the singers are not only singing and pushing the strings, they are at the same time engaged in a on-stage performance. Their movements within the instrument are expressive and aesthetically startling for the audience. Here, it was important to strike a balance between the complexity of learning the instrument, the expressivity of the instrument and the requirements on both singing and manipulating the instrument at the same time.

### An Instrument for Empowerment

In our work, we enabled opera singers to perform in ways that were, in some respects, quite the opposite of what they typically do. The Vocal Chorder became a tool for empowerment. When singers took the demand over crucial musical and visual elements in the performance, while interacting with the device, it not only changed their performance, but it also led to reflections on their profession. Through the creation of this new interactive instrument, we aim at opening a new design space and at the same time uncover hidden assumptions while re-activating traditions in a stagnating and overly hierarchical practice, opera.

## REFERENCES

1. Bonardi, A. and Rousseaux, F. Composing an Interactive Virtual Opera: The Virtualis Project. *Leonardo 35*, 3 (2002), 315–318.
2. Celletti, R. and Fuller, F. *A history of bel canto.* Clarendon press, 1991.
3. Diday, P. and Pétrequin, D.J.P.É. *Mémoire sur une nouvelle espèce de voix chantée.* Félix Malteste et Cie, 1840.
4. Eimert, H. and Humpert, H.U. *Das Lexikon der elektronischen Musik.* G. Bosse, 1977.
5. Elblaus, L., Hansen, K.F., and Unander-Scharin, C. Exploring the Design Space: Prototyping "The Throat v3" for The Elephant Man Opera (2011). *Proceedings of the Sound and Music Computing Conference*, Padova University Press (2011), 141–147.
6. Elblaus, L., Hansen, K.F., and Unander-Scharin, C. Artistically directed prototyping in development and in practice. *Journal of New Music Research 41*, 4 (2012), 377–387.
7. Fernaeus, Y. and Sundström, P. The material move how materials matter in interaction design research. *Proceedings of the Designing Interactive Systems Conference*, ACM (2012), 486–495.
8. Frayling, C. *Research in art and design.* Royal College of Art London, 1993.

9. Hallnäs, L. and Redström, J. Slow technology–designing for reflection. *Personal and ubiquitous computing 5*, 3 (2001), 201–212.

10. Höök, K. and Löwgren, J. Strong concepts: intermediate-level knowledge in interaction design research. *ACM Transactions on Computer-Human Interaction (TOCHI) 19*, 3 (2012), 23.

11. Jessop, E., Torpey, P.A., and Bloomberg, B. Music and Technology in Death and the Powers. *New Interfaces for Musical Expression*, (2011), 349–354.

12. Kloiber, R., Konold, W., and Maschka, R. *Handbuch der Oper*. Deutscher Taschenbuch Verlag, 2002.

13. Krefeld, V. and Waisvisz, M. The hand in the web: An interview with Michel Waisvisz. *Computer music journal 14*, 2 (1990), 28–33.

14. Littlejohn, D. *The ultimate art: essays around and about opera*. Univ of California Press, 1992.

15. McCarthy, J. and Wright, P. *Technology as experience*. MIT Press, 2004.

16. McGinnis, P.Y. *The Opera Singer's Career Guide: Understanding the European Fach System*. Scarecrow Press, 2010.

17. Norman, S.J., Waisvisz, M., and Joel, R. Touchstone. *Catalogue to the first STEIM Touch-Exhibition* (1998).

18. Paradiso, J.A. The brain opera technology: New instruments and gestural sensors for musical interaction and performance. *Journal of New Music Research 28*, 2 (1999), 130–149.

19. Park, Y., Heo, H., and Lee, K. VOICON: An Interactive Gestural Microphone For Vocal Performance, *Proceedings of the 2012 Conference on New Interfaces for Musical Expression, Univ. of Michigan* (2012)

20. Ramstrum, M. and Lemouton, S. Realtime Performance Strategies for the Electronic Opera K.... *Proceedings of the... International Computer Music Conference*, International Computer Music Association (2003), 139.

21. Redström, J. Designing everyday computational things. *rapport nr.: Gothenburg studies in Informatics*, 20 (2001).

22. Rosselli, J. *Singers of Italian opera: the history of a profession*. Cambridge University Press, 1995.

23. Sadie, S.E. *The new Grove dictionary of music and musicians*. Macmillan, London, 1980.

24. Sandgren, M. *Becoming and being an opera singer: Health, personality and skills*. Stockholm Univ. 2005.

25. Schaeffer, P. *Traité des objets musicaux: essai interdisciplines*. Éditions du seuil, 1977.

26. Schön, D.A. Designing as reflective conversation with the materials of a design situation. *Knowledge-Based Systems 5*, 1 (1992), 3–14.

27. Sengers, P. Autobiographical design. *CHI 2006 Workshop on Theory and Method for Experience-Centred Design*, (2006).

28. Stark, J. *Bel canto: a history of vocal pedagogy*. University of Toronto Press, 2003.

29. Tanaka, A. Musical Performance Practice on Sensor-based Instruments. *Trends in Gestural Control of Music*, Ircam - Centre Pompidou (2000), 389–405.

30. Taylor, R., Schofield, G., Shearer, J., Boulanger, P., Wallace, J., and Olivier, P. humanaquarium. *Proceedings of the 2010 Conference on New Interfaces for Musical Expression, Sydney, Australia*, (2010), 440–443.

31. Unander-Scharin, C., Höök, K., and Elblaus, L. The throat III: disforming operatic voices.. *CHI'13 Extended Abstracts on Human Factors in Computing Systems*, ACM (2013), 3007–3010.

32. Unander-Scharin, C. & Å. Sensory Digital Intonation. *Carpa 3, vol 43, Artistic Research in action.* (2013).

33. Unander-Scharin, Å. *Three Interactive Scenes of The Crystal Cabinet.* Brunel Univ, London, 2011.

34. Waisvisz, M. The hands. *Proceedings International Computer Music Conference*, 313–318.

35. Waisvisz, M. Crackle history. *STEIM. Retrieved November 21*, (2004)

36. Westerlund, B. *Design Space Exploration: co-operative creation of proposals for desired interactions with future artefacts.* KTH, Stockholm, 2009.

37. Wiberg, M., Ishii, H., Dourish, P., et al. Material interactions: from atoms & bits to entangled practices. *CHI'12 Extended Abstracts on Human Factors in Computing Systems*, ACM (2012), 1147–1150.

38. Zimmerman, J., Stolterman, E., and Forlizzi, J. An analysis and critique of Research through Design. *Proceedings of the 8th ACM Conference on Designing Interactive Systems*, ACM (2010), 310–319.

# Let me catch this! Experiencing Interactive 3D Cinema through Collecting Content with a Mobile Phone

**Jonna Häkkilä[1], Maaret Posti[1], Stefan Schneegass[2], Florian Alt[2,3], Kunter Gultekin[1], Albrecht Schmidt[2]**

[1]University of Oulu
CIE
Pentti Kaiteran katu
90014 Oulu, Finland
firstname.lastname@cie.fi

[2]University of Stuttgart
VIS
Pfaffenwaldring 5a
70569 Stuttgart, Germany
firstname.lastname@vis.uni-stuttgart.de

[3]University of Munich
Media Informatics Group
Amalienstraße 17
80333 München, Germany
florian.alt@ifi.lmu.de

## ABSTRACT
The entertainment industry is going through a transformation, and technology development is affecting how we can enjoy and interact with the entertainment media content in new ways. In our work, we explore how to enable interaction with content in the context of 3D cinemas by means of a mobile phone. Hence, viewers can use their personal devices to retrieve, for example, information on the artist of the soundtrack currently playing or a discount coupon on the watch the main actor is wearing. We are particularly interested in the user experience of the interactive 3D cinema concept, and how different interactive elements and interaction techniques are perceived. We report on the development of a prototype application utilizing smart phones and on an evaluation in a cinema context with 20 participants. Results emphasize that designing for interactive cinema experiences should drive for holistic and positive user experiences. Interactive content should be tied together with the actual video content, but integrated into contexts where it does not conflict with the immersive experience with the movie.

### Author Keywords
Interactive cinema; mobile phone interaction; 3D; user studies; user experience.

### ACM Classification Keywords
H.5.m. Information interfaces and presentation: Miscellaneous.

## INTRODUCTION
During the past few years, new technologies and services have emerged around the entertainment industry, including the rise of 3D movies and an ever-increasing number of movie-related extra content available online. In the era of the mobile Internet, mobile apps, and social media services, extra content related to the movie can be searched, accessed, and discussed easily, virtually anywhere. In this paper, we look beyond the conventional experience of watching a movie and explore the concept of interactive 3D cinemas.


*CHI 2014*, April 26–May 1, 2014, Toronto, Ontario, Canada.

ACM 978-1-4503-2473-1/14/04 ...$15.00.
http://dx.doi.org/10.1145/2556288.2557187

Figure 1: Interactive 3D cinema: We conducted a user study in a real cinema to explore the concept of interactive 3D cinema, focusing on the impact on user experience.

Capturing and assessing interaction around TV and cinema content has so far been possible through Twitter, Facebook, or tailored mobile apps [25]. These interactions are particularly valuable for several reasons. On one hand, they could be used to implicitly identify interesting parts of the content, for example, those that trigger most discussion. This may help producers to enhance the story of future episodes or also provide an automatically created summary, for example, of a sports game. On the other hand, this is interesting for merchandising. While the merchandising industry currently mainly targets the after-movie experience through selling products to fan communities, our approach can complement the instant experience and trigger sales already during the movies.

At the same time, with the rise of mobile apps and social media, we see 3D content becoming more popular – both in cinemas and at home. This allows more immersive experiences to be created by having an additional dimension for information placement. Today, this dimension is used to create special effects and, thus, intensify the user's experience.

The use case for our work is an interactive movie that could be shown in a cinema. In this movie users can collect different items by catching them through mobile phone based interaction techniques. The main focus of our work is on understanding the UX aspects of interactive 3D cinema. Particularly, we chart what kind of user experiences and preferences different interaction and visualization methods provoke. In order to do so, we compare different concepts, namely

- catching interactive elements in a competitive vs. informative condition,
- touch vs. shake gestures on mobile phones, and
- different types of interactivity cues.

The novelty of our work lies in presenting the first study on interactive S3D cinema where users interact with their mobile phones to collect content and in conducting the study in a real cinema. While our study is artificial in that we used customized, short movie clips, we made the experiment as realistic as possible by conducting it in an authentic environment. We assessed our research questions through logging, questionnaires, and interviews.

The contribution of this work is twofold. First, we investigate the requirements for interaction with 3D content, including means to communicate the interactivity of particular screen elements and suitable interaction techniques to retrieve the content. Second, we evaluate the influence on UX. Our work provides information for future researchers and practitioners who want to create interactive cinema experiences. Particularly, we (a) identify preferred input modalities, (b) show design solutions for presenting the interactive content, and (c) report on user perceptions and lessons learnt on the concept of collecting items in an informative and competitive manner.

## RELATED WORK

Our work draws from several areas of related work. Particularly we revisit work on experience with new (S3D) media, interactive cinema and TV and interaction with large screens.

### Experiencing New (S3D) Media

Along with the fast development in media technologies as well as communication and social media services, the culture of consuming media content and activities around it have changed compared to conventional practices. Mobile devices in the form of smart phones and pads have liberated the access to media content [6], social media services increased the opportunities to immediately share and discuss the experiences [25], and new technologies such as S3D have emerged and are seeking to provide better and more immersive experiences for people [11]. Nakatsu et al. describe that in the age of rapidly developing technologies, we witness the development of new media, characterized by (a) new types of experiences, (b) active instead of passive experiences, and (c) integration of spatial, social, mental, and physical presence [18].

User experience (UX) has gained an increasing amount of attention in HCI and design communities. Although there is hardly a unified definition for UX [15, 16], it is widely agreed that UX goes beyond usability and instrumental aspects [16]. A definition presented in [9] describes UX as "a momentary, primarily evaluative feeling (good-bad) while interacting with a product or service". UX includes both a utilitarian and a hedonic aspect [10], which affect the holistic experience when using a product. Forlizzi and Batterbee have formulated a UX framework around user-product interaction, and distinguish between fluent, cognitive, and expressive interactions [7].

When comparing the UX of a 3D media installation to a conventional 2D presentation, Karukka et al. reported that user perception with 3D is more conspicuous, interesting, and visually attractive, whereas 2D was perceived more serene, basic, and matter-of-fact like [12] . In the context of auto-S3D mobile phones, it has been pointed out that S3D UI design concentrates on impressive visual effects, but utilitarian value for using 3D in the UI is largely missing [27].

Whereas our research focuses on interaction, earlier research has mostly concentrated on the viewing experience. Stereoscopic screens have been found to have benefits in encoding large amounts of data due to the additional degree of freedom, separation of details, compensation of poor image quality, and in catching the user's attention [13, 17]. However, there are also challenges. The use of S3D can cause fatigue, eyestrain, and headache [13]. The brain combines depth information from multiple cues to form an understanding of a 3D image [14]. This processing of the stereoscopic images requires mental effort. Creating optimal visual ergonomics and viewing experience is challenging and has been addressed in several studies [5, 15, 20]. When studying interaction with 3D content, the use cases so far have been quite different from our work. Prior art focused on investigating 3D object manipulation and touch-screen based interaction (see [26, 28]), whereas 3D cinema is a novel study context.

### Interactive Cinema and Interactive TV (iTV)

Interaction in cinemas has recently gained popularity. In the horror movie "App", users were encouraged to interact with the mobile phone[1]. Interaction was triggered by the use of inaudible sounds that a mobile phone app could detect. With Disney's Second Screen[2], children are able to interact with content as they watch a movie. Finally, Cinime[3] is a mobile application that focuses on entertaining users, primarily before and after the movie. Despite these first commercial attempts that did not include any scientific evaluation, attention from an HCI perspective has been rather scarce. Häkkinen et al. have investigated people's focal attention wtowards S3D movies using eye tracking [8]. When comparing the S3D and 2D versions of the movies, they found out that whereas in 2D movie viewers tend to focus quickly on the actors, in the S3D version the eye movements were more widely distributed among other targets [8]. Pölönen et al. studied on user perceptions related to two S3D films, the science fiction movie Avatar and the music documentary U2 3D [21]. They report that the genre of the film has a significant effect on the viewers' opinions and sense of presence, and that previous experience with S3D significantly reduces the amount of

[1]App Website: http://appdefilm.nl
[2]Disney Second Screen Website: http://disneysecondscreen.go.com
[3]Cinime Website: http://www.cini.me

**Figure 2: Example screenshots of the commercial (left) and the movie (right), both including interactive items.**

inconvenience related to eyestrain and weight of the viewing S3D glasses [21]. These early attempts on interactive cinema encouraged us to scientifically investigate this concept. Our work expands the boundaries or prior art by focusing new interactivity concepts and 3D content.

Interactive TV (iTV) has received considerable attention in the past. In contrast to our approach, however, iTV follows a broadcast distribution model, making collaboration and competition scarce (e.g., WorldCupinion [25]). Furthermore, the interactive cinema setting fundamentally differs in that it targets a large co-located audience, making it likely for the experience to be different from iTV, which mainly occurs in home settings with few people present.

### Mobile Interaction with Large Screens

Our research utilizes two main technologies – large displays used to render 3D content, and mobile devices, which are used for interacting with the content. In earlier research, interaction with pervasive displays has been addressed in several studies summarized by Alt et al. [2]. In this work, the authors explored different interaction techniques for public displays, and report that preferred interaction techniques depend, for example, on the user and their context when interacting with the display. In general however, mobile phone interaction is preferred over public display input with people on the move, tech savvy youngsters, and privacy-aware users [2]. Gesture interaction with a mobile phone has been found to provoke reactions related to social acceptability and making large gestures can be perceived as distracting or odd looking [23]. However, gesture input with the mobile device in hand has the benefits of eyes free interaction. Particularly with touch screen equipped smart phones, eyes free interaction is difficult as the touch screen input does not provide haptic cues similar to hard keys.

Kauko et al. compared two interaction techniques, distal and proximal selection, when interacting with a large screen with a mobile phone [22]. Whereas proximal selection, where items are selected on the phone screen, was found to be faster for complex tasks, distal selection, where selecting the targets is done by pointing at them on the large screen, was as fast for simple tasks and perceived more fluent, as it does not require switching the attention from the large screen. In the context of cinema, the interaction design should not require the viewer to switch attention from the movie screen to the mobile phone. Prior work showed that interaction also has a positive effect on cognition. In particular, users that interacted with content on public displays could afterwards recall significantly more content compared to users that only passively observed the same content [1].

### Positioning of Our Research

We draw on research from different areas, mainly interaction with mobile phones and user experience. At the same time, our work has novelty in several aspects. It goes beyond the prior art, focusing on the interactive movie concept rather than the viewing experience of static 3D [8, 21]. The context of use (i.e., a movie theatre) has hardly received attention in HCI research and, again, interactive cinema is a rather unexplored field. Earlier research on interactive cinema has addressed alternative narrative structures and steering of plots [3, 29], whereas we look at the mobile phone based interaction with the movie screen to collect digital extra content from the movie screen.

## INTERACTIVE 3D CINEMA

Our concept for interactive 3D cinema is focused on showing interactive 3D content on the cinema screen. The interactive objects are integrated into the commercials and the movie clips, and are shown for a limited period of time. The users can then catch these interactive objects with their mobile phones by performing a gesture, and the collected items are stored on the mobile phone application – either for the purpose of an interactive game or for later use. We explore two different concepts:

- Competition, where users compete against each other in trying to catch as many interactive objects as possible, integrated with a commercial video clip.
- Collecting informative content items, where each user can collect any interesting interactive items without any competition, integrated in a movie clip.

Screenshots of the clips with interactive content are depicted in Figure 2.

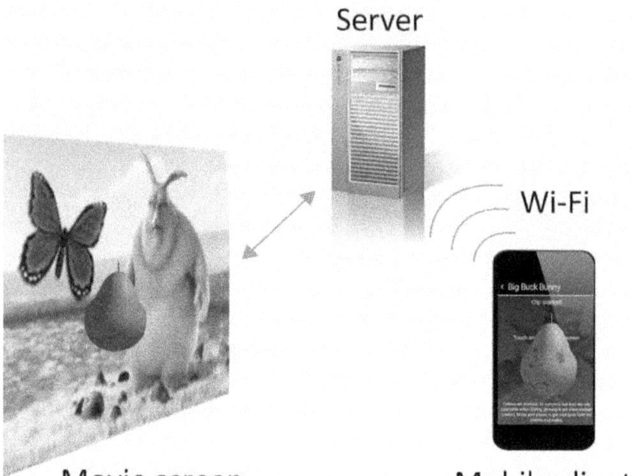


**Figure 3: Illustration of the main components of the test setup. Server and client are connected via Wi-Fi.**

We explore two different interaction techniques for mobile phone interaction for catching the interactive objects – tapping the touch screen and gesture input (shake). The technical set-up and mobile phone application are explained in more detail in the following sections.

### Technical Prototype

We developed a prototypical system using a client-server architecture (see Figure 3).

#### *Server*

The server consists of a game engine (Panda3D[4]) that is responsible for displaying the movie as well as rendering the 3D objects in real time and a component that handles client interactions over HTTP. The client mobile application (see next section) requests the state of the clip currently being run and communicates back any user interaction (tap or shake). Success of the interaction, i.e., whether a user managed to catch an item, is then calculated on the server side and the result responded back to the client software.

Since client and server are in the same local Wi-Fi network, the use of HTTP does not introduce a significant latency and the interaction appears to be almost instantaneous. To be able to handle numerous Wi-Fi connections within the same room without causing delays, two commodity wireless access points are configured on the same network. Operating two distinct channels allows for distributing clients evenly between the access points and, thus, balance the load.

#### *Mobile Application*

A mobile app enables users to interact with 3D content by retrieving content items as they appear on the screen. Retrieval of content can be triggered (a) by tapping the phone screen, or (b) by performing a catching gesture with the phone.

[4]Website: http://www.panda3d.org

**Figure 4: Screenshot of the mobile phone application in the interactive 3D cinema study. Interactive icons could be obtained from the movie by tapping the smart phone screen, where the icon appeared after the capture.**

For the client software, we use an Android app that communicates with the communication server to get the state of the clip running and indicating an interaction (tap or shake). For the tap interaction, we used the entire screen of the phone to provide an easy and eyes-free interaction. For the shake interaction we used the accelerometer data and simply detect shake gestures by defining a certain threshold (i.e., more than $25\, m/s^2$ acceleration). Success of the interaction is calculated on the server and responded back to the client. The phone then displays the caught item for 1 second and vibrates for 2 seconds to provide feedback to the users.

The mobile app currently supports two different modes: a competitive mode and an informative mode. In the competitive mode, content items can be collected. This mode is mainly meant for games, for example, in the form of commercials, where the audience can compete for an incentive (e.g., an ice cream) by collecting as many items as possible. For each collected item a symbol is shown on the screen. Depending on the game setting (server), only the first n users to perform the interaction as content items appear will collect the item. In the informative mode, people can retrieve meta-information. This mode is means to be used during motion pictures to enable viewers to retrieve information on actors, the name of the song currently playing, or a screenshot of the current scene as a background image. In this mode, each user performing the interaction will receive the information. The UI when collecting an interactive item is shown in Figure 4.

### The Movies

#### *Interactive Items*

During the evaluation we were particularly interested in how interactivity of an item within 3D clips could be communicated to the user, and how users would perform using the mobile phone interaction techniques, tapping and gesture. We use three interactivity cues: 1) glow, 2) particles flying from the object, and 3) no additional visual cues but depth. The interactivity cues are presented in Figure 5.

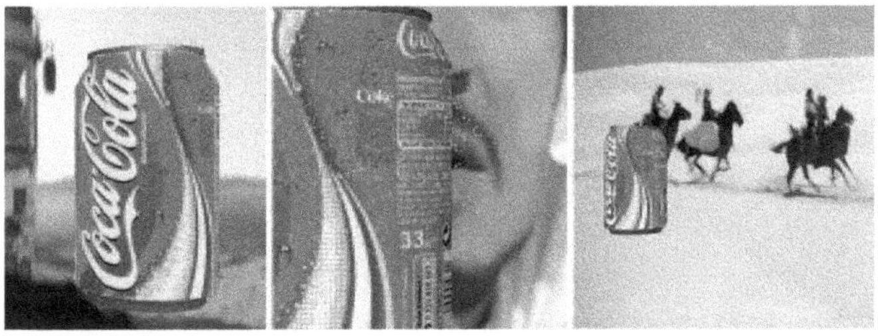


**Figure 5: Examples of interactivity cues applied to a can and used in the study (from left); glow, particles, and depth (movement towards the user along the z axis).**

The depth only cue was included as a baseline condition, as we were first interested whether using depth only would be perceived as a sufficient cue to indicate interactivity. Hence, in this condition, we simply let interactive items float towards the user. In prior art, glow has been found to be a visual effect that is perceived particularly well when it comes to indicating interactive items in 3D virtual world user interfaces [19]. Finally, small particles emitted from the object are selected as the third cue, as this visualization has been earlier used in computer games. Note, that glow and particles are used in combination with depth. In the commercial clip, the we also add a movement of the object towards the viewer.

Only one interactive item appears at a time on the cinema screen with one cue applied. The overall number of interactive items was 30 per clip for the competition case (10 for each visualization technique) and 30 per clip for the informative content item collection. The fraction of the screen space taken by an appearing collectable item is approximately 2% in both cases. Each item is shown for approximately 8 seconds – although in practice the time was shorter in the competitive mode, since catching the item causes it to disappear from the movie screen.

We prepared different pieces of interactive 3D content (Figure 2). A professional designer created all content in Blender.

### *Commercial*

For the competition concept, we use a commercial video clip (appr. 1 min), which was edited to be approximately 6 minutes long by repeating it over. During the commercial, we show altogether 30 interactive items (soft drink cans) that users can catch with their mobile phone. The items utilize three different visualization techniques (10 items with each interactivity cue), and their order is randomized. All items are shown as moving towards the audience, and they become interactive approximately two seconds after their appearance on the screen. When the first user catches the item, it disappears from the screen and is shown on the mobile phone of the "winner". As we have two interaction techniques, tapping and gesture, we created two randomized clips.

### *Movie*

For the informative content collection concept, we chose the "Big Buck Bunny" movie, an open movie created with Blender. We augmented the movie with certain items, which, if caught by the viewer, would transfer meta-content of the movie (e.g., information on the characters, a soundtrack, background images) to the mobile phone of the user. Altogether, 30 interactive content items appear during the 10-minute movie clip. We created two versions of the interactive movie – one with glow and sparkle effects (no movement), and the other one with interactive items that move towards the audience. This decision to include less content items compared to the commercial was made to leave more space for the immersive experience with the movie, as we found approaching items to be quite dominating when testing.

**Figure 6: Participants of group 1 answering the questionnaire in between the video clips.**

## EVALUATION

In the following, we describe the evaluation of our concept in a cinema setting, using the technical prototype described in the previous section.

### Procedure

For the purpose of the study we rented a commercial movie theater with 45 seats (Figure 1). The dimensions of the screen are 4.5 m x 2.5 m. People were recruited in the days prior to the study via mailing lists, Facebook, and a local online forum. Participants were offered a movie ticket for their participation. When recruited, participants were told that they could use their own mobile phone (Android 2.2, 2.3, or 4.x) or they were provided with a phone for the duration of the study. We run two user study sessions (with 11 and 9 users), each lasting for an hour. Two study sessions were organized to counterbalance between the different interaction techniques and movie visualizations.

As participants arrived at the cinema, we briefed them about the purpose of the study and had them sign a consent form and background questionnaire on demographics and earlier experience with 3D. Following the briefing, researchers helped them to install the mobile application on their phone. After that, participants were handed out anaglyph glasses and questionnaires for the study. Then the participants were asked to take a seat in the theater (Figure 6). Here, we observed people sitting both alone and in the groups of 2-3 people.

The actual study consisted of the following steps:

- Stereovision test
- Commercial, clip A (group 1: tapping; group 2: shaking)
- Commercial, clip B (group 1: shaking, group 2: tapping)
- Movie (group 1: clip A with glow and sparkles; group 2: clip B with objects moving towards audience)
- Movie (group 1: clip B; group 2: clip A)

After each step, the participants had to fill in a questionnaire. Questions concerned the interaction techniques (tap and gesture), the interaction cues (glow, particles and depth only) and a comparison of the two presented concepts. The steps in the test procedure are described in more detail in the following paragraphs. The stereo vision test consisted of three images (stereoscopic photos of camera, car, and flowers) and participants were asked to describe what they see and whether seeing the photos is easy, hard, or impossible.

We then moved on with the first part of the study where we showed participants a set of commercials. We told the participants that several items in the commercials were interactive and could be caught by means of the smartphone. We explained them both the tap and the gesture interaction and told them that at the beginning of each commercial there would be an indicator, which interaction technique to use. However, we neither told them which items were interactive nor revealed how they could determine the interactive items. Additionally, we told that only the first person to execute the interaction would receive the item and that the person who at the end of the session collected most items would receive two free movie tickets. After that we played the video clip repeating the commercial 6 times (6 minutes in total), each with a different combination of interactivity cues. After the commercials we provided the users another questionnaire that asked them to answer a set of questions on the interaction techniques and interactivity cues.

After that we proceeded with the main movie. We told the participants that during the movie several interactive items would be shown that would provide them meta-content of the movie. We told them that they could collect items upon interest and that there would be no competition among the viewers. During the instructions, we also showed them the interactive items and their meaning (i.e. extra information on the characters, concurrent movie scene, or music). To interact with the movie, only one interaction technique was available (tapping). After the movie we provided them a final questionnaire assessing the user experience.

### Participants

Altogether 20 subjects participated in the study, aged from 20 to 29 years ($M = 25.7$, $SD = 3.10$). In total, 7 out of 20 were female. The majority (14/20) visits a cinema theater approximately 2-3 times a month. 15/20 participants do not have 3D gadgets at home to watch 3D content. Altogether 7/20 do not use any vision aids, whereas the rest of the participants reported wearing glasses or contact lenses. The stereovision test revealed that 19 out of 20 are able to easily see stereoscopic content on the movie theater screen. One participant with glasses had some difficulties due to the anaglyph glasses she had to wear on top of her own glasses. None of the participants reported suffering from color vision deficiency.

| Adjective | Chosen by n participants |
|---|---|
| Responsive | 8/19 |
| Playful | 7/19 |
| Visually pleasant | 7/19 |
| Easy to use | 6/19 |
| Approachable | 6/19 |

**Table 1: The five most frequent terms describing the overall interaction experience with 3D movie and objects, n=19 (one participant excluded for not completing the task)**

### Data Collection

The written survey consisted of open-ended questions, ratings on Likert scales, and word picking tasks adapted from Microsoft Product Reaction Cards (PRC) methods [4]. With PRC, participants selected five words of the provided list of 52, which consisted of 26 pairs (e.g., inspiring, uninspiring). In addition to the written survey, we logged the user interaction with the interactive items during the user study. For each user we recorded the time between the appearance of an interactive item and the execution of the catching interaction. In addition, we logged the items that were collected.

## RESULTS

### Interactive 3D Cinema Concept

The words describing the experience with interactive 3D cinema concept collected with PRC method [4] after the study are presented in Table 1. Overall, seeing and interacting with 3D objects during the movie is perceived as a positive experience according to participants. Open feedback responses from 6/20 participants indicate that interactive 3D content takes attention away from the actual video clip (see Figure 7). Two participants (#1, #20) want to see interactive content follow more the actual story line. *"It would be great, if the objects would appear according to the plot of the movie."* (participant #20). Due to its occupying nature, users suggest 3D object interaction to be used in short clips and commercials. *"Good for commercials and short clips, but not for the whole movie"* (participant #8).

### Competing Against Other Viewers

The two different interactive cinema concepts (i.e. competition and informative item collecting) received both positive and negative comments. According to open text responses, 13/20 participants appreciate the opportunity to compete against the other viewers and win something. Competition occupies focus and concentration efficiently and results in immersive experiences. *"I liked the competition, but once I got excited with the game, I couldn't concentrate on the clip at all."* (participant #1). On the downside, failure in the competition results in negative feelings afterwards. *"I like winning. I could catch only one can which reduced the enjoyment of the game."* (participant #10). During the four competition sessions, on average 6/20 participants per group managed to catch cans. Each can could be collected only once.

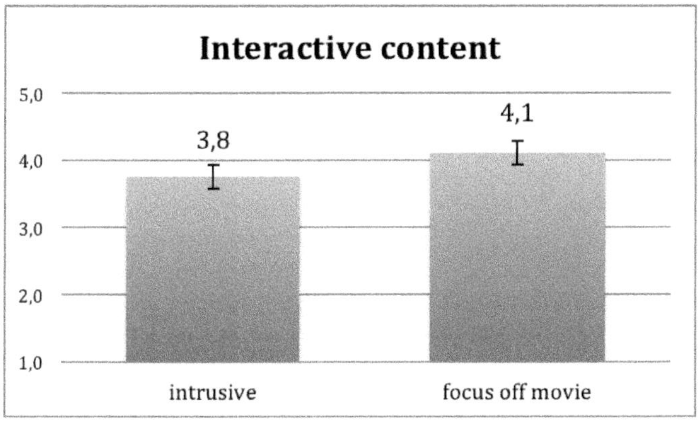


**Figure 7: User perceptions of the interactive content (intrusive, focus off the movie) in the scale 1-5. Error bar describes the standard deviation.**

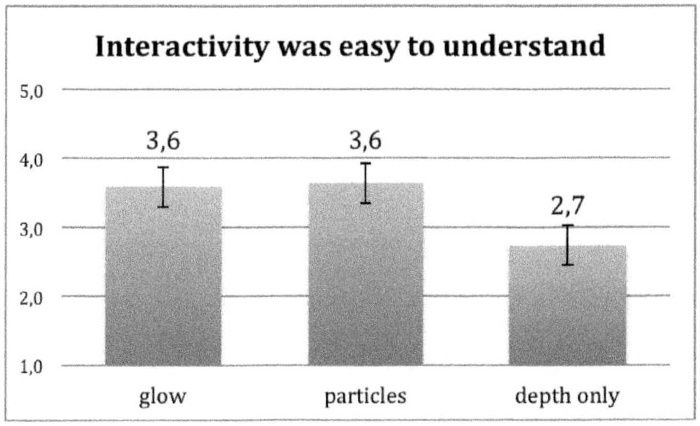


**Figure 8: Participants' perceptions on how well the effect represented interactivity. Error bar describes the standard deviation. Results show no statistical differences.**

### Collecting Informative Items

In the collection mode, viewers were able to collect the items they wanted. Thus, they did not have to catch all the objects shown in the movie. Gathering specified items from the movie is experienced as a personal activity; the selected items reflect participant's own personal preferences and interests. *"I liked the idea that I can collect objects that interest me personally. This made the experience more pleasant and less stressful than during the competition."* (participant #7). The open-ended results show that the possibility to get extra information about the movie by collecting items is regarded as a useful function by 11/20 participants. *"This would be a good way to learn about characters and movie scenes."* (participant #4). Interestingly, we received quite strong feedback from participants who feet disappointed with their performance with the competition, but who like collecting the informative items from the movie. This is demonstrated e.g. in the following comments: *"I liked the collection part of the study. I was happy I could collect the items I wanted. During competition I felt frustrated since I couldn't catch anything."* (participant #8), and *"I was able to actually get the icons which was better than in the coke clip."* (participant #19).

Participants collected in total 458 items ($M = 11.73$ per session, $SD = 5.12$) in all four sessions. Thus, on average each participant collects roughly 39.1% of the items shown on the screen.

### Tapping vs. Gesture Interaction

During the commercial clips, participants were able to test and compare tapping and gesture their smart phones for catching 3D content. The questionnaire results show that nearly half of the audience preferred tapping (9/20) and half gesture (11/20). PRC frequencies show that tapping was most commonly described as easy to use (5/19), simple (4/19) but also dated (3/19) way to use the phone for interaction. Gesture was evaluated as playful (7/19), novel (6/19) and easy to use (5/19). Following responses indicate a feeling of immersion with gesture. *"(The gesture creates a) better feeling for playing, and it was exciting (participant #11). Gesture was more physical. There was more action than in tapping?"* (participant #2). Interestingly, we did not receive any feedback on gesture interaction to be socially awkward, even though people were sitting in the movie theater among strangers. Quite the opposite, seeing others shake their phones as well was reported to create a feeling of social activity. *"It was nicer to compete when you could see others shake their phones as well."* (participant #6). An example of participant doing a shake gesture is illustrated in Figure 9.

In the commercial clip tasks, we evaluated the time needed to catch an interactive item presented within the main content. Therefore, we analyzed both interaction techniques. Participants caught the items faster with the tap ($M = 3.17\,s$, $SD = 0.74$) than with the gesture ($M = 3.56\,s$, $SD = 0.90$). We performed a two-way analysis of variance (ANOVA). The ANOVA shows statistically significant differences for the reaction time in the interaction technique, $F(1, 112) = 6.542$, $p = .012$, $r = .232$. This shows that the interaction by tapping the phone is faster than gesture.

### Interactivity Cues

Glow and particles were subtle but perceived as sufficient enough indicators of interactivity during the clips (see Figure 8). The depth only cue, where the interactive items were moving towards the audience, was reported to take too much screen space and interfere the movie experience.

The emergent results of the interactivity cues indicate that particles ($M = 3.26\,s$, $SD = 0.72$) performed best, followed by glow ($M = 3.30\,s$, $SD = 0.95$) and no depth cue ($M = 3.54\,s$, $SD = 0.84$) at all. Analyzing the interactivity cues, the ANOVA shows no statistically significant differences, $F(1, 112) = 1.350$, $p = .264$, $r = .105$.

### Placing the Content

Most participants (15/20) stated that general information about the movie (e.g., music and background image) should be placed in the corners of the screen. More content-related information (e.g., information about a certain actor or product seen in the scene) should be placed next to the subject in matter according to 10/20 participants. In general, the idea of receiving useful and interesting information already during

Figure 9: A participant performing the gesture input with his phone.

the movie obtained twofold opinions. 35% of the respondents do not want to have any extra material during the movie and feel that extra content rather limits the experience. The rest (65%) argues that relevant and interesting information during the movie can enhance the overall experience, if the interaction design is well executed.

## DISCUSSION

### Experiencing Interactive 3D Cinema

Based on our study, the interactive cinema concept, where people interact to collect items into their personal repository, does provide an interesting potential for the future development. In general, the competition concept is perceived as rewarding and playful, whereas collecting informative items is perceived as useful and personal. The interest and positive comments left us with an encouraging overall perception about the concept of interactive 3D cinema. However, there are a number of findings that should be carefully considered before designing such an application or service.

As movie experience is very much content-driven, it is crucial to avoid breaking the immersion or disturbing the movie. Hence, participants want interactive items to be integrated contextually with the actual media content shown on the theater screen. Additionally, extra content should appear close to the objects (e.g., actor) they relate to. An ideal solution to combine these two design requirements would be to use the interactive items in places where they do not interfere with the movie experience – commercials, trailers, or end scripts.

In terms of Forlizzi 's UX framework [7], our concept of interactive cinema provides means to shift the balance from cognitive towards expressive user experience. Whereas the cinema experience is still essentially linked to the action and duration of watching the movie in the theater, i.e., cognitive interactions, there are already elements which extend the experience before and after the theater, such as trailers, advertisements and discussion forums. The approach of collecting and retrieving items and extra content, adds to the existing means and fosters a more personal relationship with the product (i.e., the movie), thus forming an expressive user experience. Roto highlights, how user experience extends also to the time after use [24], and collecting movie related items and take them away, either as information or as tokens, has the potential to further prolong this connection. In addition, the collective information about the audience can offer interesting reflections. For instance, a ranking list of the most commonly collected information items can support the perception of a shared experience. Interestingly, interactions themselves are not regarded as socially unacceptable, which was somewhat surprising given prior work on interaction with public displays [23]. This may be partly due the context, as people are sitting in a dark room, where the visibility towards other viewers is limited. Also, it may have been the case that our participants were immersed with the content of the film and, hence, paid less attention to their surroundings.

### Design Considerations

Our study revealed several findings regarding designing for a competition in the interactive cinema. The feedback on collecting the items should be very clear, and it should preferably be designed to create feelings of excitement, delight, and playfulness. To achieve this, one potential option is to use some special effects in the interactive items. In our study, the glow and sparkle effects were well received, but additional effects could be added, e.g., on how the interactive item appear or disappear on the screen. Here, the graphics and animation design could also be matched to reflect the movie genre. Also, in the competition, participants want to know more about their fellow competitors, not just their own performance. The opportunity to know something about the rest of the audience, for example, winning scores shown on the large cinema screen, would create a common experience and the feeling of being together in the common place.

Another important thing to consider relates to the overall user experience with movies. People often go to the cinema to relax and feel good, or to immerse themselves with emotional or exciting scenes, and it is important to design for such an experience. In the context of competition, this means that the interaction should provide positive experiences to avoid situations, as in our study, where some participants felt very disappointed about not catching interactive items even though they thought they were doing well. A possible solution to this is to reward not just one person but for example the first 30% of the users that catch an item, or provide them with other inspiring or positively surprising UI feedback. In the middle of a (supposedly) relaxing and refreshing situation (the cinema), the user should be able to achieve positive experiences, and not feel ignored or disappointed.

From a design perspective, presenting interactive items in a sequence, i.e., not several items simultaneously, was a good solution, as it did not require switching attention from the movie screen to the mobile phone – tapping anywhere on the touch screen would suffice.

### Limitations

Our study has several limitations. First, the sample size was small ($n = 20$), but we believe to have tested the concept with a sufficiently large sample to gather early insights.

Second, the movie experience was different from a "real" visit to the cinema, and although we wanted to study an as authentic environment as possible, we acknowledge that the study setting was artificial. While we believe the commercial task to be quite realistic, the main movie clip lasting approximately for 10 minutes was rather short. We deliberately decided to limit the length of the videos for not making the study too long (1.5 h). This also ensured that participants optimally remembered their impressions when interacting with the system. Consequently, the length of the clips corresponds rather with trailers and ads shown before the main movie. Nevertheless we believe that the movie clip was long enough for the users to give an initial perception of the overall experience. In addition, it should be noted that the design of graphics and animation elements should preferably be aligned with the movie genre. Our study was limited to a cartoon style movie, but alternative effects should be explored for different movies genres, for example, for action or horror. While showing a full-length movie would be very interesting, we think that this should be subject to a separate study planned for the future. For future work we aim to test full movies and take into consideration how interactive elements should be integrated unobtrusively.

Third, in our study, we opted to let participants use their own phones since (a) an unfamiliar phone may have had a positive or negative influence on the experience (form factor, distraction, etc.) and (b) in this way we expected the external validity of the results to increase. During the development, we tested the software on different phone models, and in addition, on every participant‘s phone. Since all participants connected to the same WiFi hotspot, we expect differences for technical reasons to be minimal. All 20 participants collected interactive items during the study, reflecting the successful technical implementation. Given our data we did not find any evidence that different sensors influenced our results.

## CONCLUSION

In this paper we have investigated the concept of interaction with 3D cinema content. We explored collaborative as well as competitive forms of interaction. Our results show that people engage themselves with both the content and extra material related to the actual movie. We envision the popularity of such applications to further increase as means are provided for the viewer to retrieve information on the main actor or buy the current soundtrack by just one click during watching the movie or while they play a game prior to the movie.

The finding that interaction was sometimes perceived to be distracting suggests that interaction should be realized in a simple and unobtrusive way that does not negatively influence the cinema experience. For example, retrieved content could be stored for later use and then be brought to the attention of the user as the movie is over. Our findings indicate also that the concept of interactive cinema provides means to enhance both individual and communal experiences in the cinema. Whereas collecting items to your personal devices makes the experience more personal and lasting, the design of interactive games can be used to create the perception of a shared experience. Our findings also emphasize that designers of interactive cinema concepts should pay particular attention to create positive experiences and reward the users, as feeling good or exited is an inseparable part of the overall movie experience and motivation to attend the theater.

## ACKNOWLEDGEMENTS

We thank the staff at Valve cinema for their help in conducting the study. The research has partly received funding from the European Union Seventh Framework Programme ([FP7/2007-2013]) under grant agreement no 600851.

## REFERENCES

1. Alt, F., Schneegass, S., Girgis, M., and Schmidt, A. Cognitive effects of interactive public display applications. In *Proceedings of the 2nd ACM International Symposium on Pervasive Displays*, PerDis '13, ACM (New York, NY, USA, 2013), 13–18.
2. Alt, F., Shirazi, A. S., Kubitza, T., and Schmidt, A. Interaction techniques for creating and exchanging content with public displays. In *Proceedings of the SIGCHI Conference on Human Factors in Computing Systems*, CHI '13, ACM (New York, NY, USA, 2013), 1709–1718.
3. Atkinson, S. Crossed lines. In *Proceedings of the 3rd International Conference on Digital Interactive Media in Entertainment and Arts*, DIMEA '08, ACM (New York, NY, USA, 2008), 537–538.
4. Benedek, J., and Miner, T. Measuring desirability: New methods for evaluating desirability in a usability lab setting. *Proceedings of Usability Professionals Association 2003* (2002), 8–12.
5. Broy, N., Alt, F., Schneegass, S., Henze, N., and Schmidt, A. Perceiving layered information on 3d displays using binocular disparity. In *Proceedings of the 2Nd ACM International Symposium on Pervasive Displays*, PerDis '13, ACM (New York, NY, USA, 2013), 61–66.
6. Finamore, A., Mellia, M., Munafò, M. M., Torres, R., and Rao, S. G. Youtube everywhere: Impact of device and infrastructure synergies on user experience. In *Proceedings of the 2011 ACM SIGCOMM Conference on Internet Measurement Conference*, IMC '11, ACM (New York, NY, USA, 2011), 345–360.
7. Forlizzi, J., and Battarbee, K. Understanding experience in interactive systems. In *Proceedings of the 5th Conference on Designing Interactive Systems: Processes, Practices, Methods, and Techniques*, DIS '04, ACM (New York, NY, USA, 2004), 261–268.
8. Häkkinen, J., Kawai, T., Takatalo, J., Mitsuya, R., and Nyman, G. What do people look at when they watch stereoscopic movies? In *IS&T/SPIE Electronic Imaging*, International Society for Optics and Photonics (2010), 75240E–75240E.

9. Hassenzahl, M. User experience (ux): Towards an experiential perspective on product quality. In *Proceedings of the 20th International Conference of the Association Francophone D'Interaction Homme-Machine*, IHM '08, ACM (New York, NY, USA, 2008), 11–15.

10. Hassenzahl, M., and Tractinsky, N. User experience-a research agenda. *Behaviour & Information Technology 25*, 2 (2006), 91–97.

11. Jumisko-Pyykkö, S., Weitzel, M., and Strohmeier, D. Designing for user experience: What to expect from mobile 3d tv and video? In *Proceedings of the 1st International Conference on Designing Interactive User Experiences for TV and Video*, UXTV '08, ACM (New York, NY, USA, 2008), 183–192.

12. Karukka, M., Nisula, P., Häkkilä, J., and Kangasoja, J. Charting the audience perceptions of projected 3d media installations. In *Proceedings of the 11th International Conference on Mobile and Ubiquitous Multimedia*, MUM '12, ACM (New York, NY, USA, 2012), 48:1–48:2.

13. Kooi, F. L., and Toet, A. Visual comfort of binocular and 3d displays. *Displays 25*, 2 (2004), 99–108.

14. Lambooij, M. T., IJsselsteijn, W. A., Heynderickx, I., et al. Visual discomfort in stereoscopic displays: a review. *Stereoscopic Displays and Virtual Reality Systems XIV 6490*, 1 (2007).

15. Law, E., Roto, V., Vermeeren, A. P., Kort, J., and Hassenzahl, M. Towards a shared definition of user experience. In *CHI '08 Extended Abstracts on Human Factors in Computing Systems*, CHI EA '08, ACM (New York, NY, USA, 2008), 2395–2398.

16. Law, E. L.-C., Roto, V., Hassenzahl, M., Vermeeren, A. P., and Kort, J. Understanding, scoping and defining user experience: A survey approach. In *Proceedings of the SIGCHI Conference on Human Factors in Computing Systems*, CHI '09, ACM (New York, NY, USA, 2009), 719–728.

17. Mizobuchi, S., Terasaki, S., Häkkinen, J., Heinonen, E., Bergquist, J., and Chignell, M. The effect of stereoscopic viewing in a word-search task with a layered background. *Journal of the Society for Information Display 16*, 11 (2008), 1105–1113.

18. Nakatsu, R., Rauterberg, M., and Vorderer, P. A new framework for entertainment computing: From passive to active experience. In *Proceedings of Entertainment Computing*, ICEC 2005. Springer Berlin Heidelberg, 2005, 1–12.

19. Pakanen, M., Arhippainen, L., Vatjus-Anttila, J., and Pakanen, O.-P. Visual indication while sharing items from a private 3d portal room ui to public virtual environments. In *Proceedings of INTERACT 2013*. Springer Berlin Heidelberg, 2013, 737–744.

20. Pölönen, M., Järvenpää, T., and Bilcu, B. Stereoscopic 3d entertainment and its effect on viewing comfort: Comparison of children and adults. *Applied Ergonomics 44*, 1 (2013), 151 – 160.

21. Pölönen, M., Salmimaa, M., Takatalo, J., and Häkkinen, J. Subjective experiences of watching stereoscopic avatar and u2 3d in a cinema. *Journal of Electronic Imaging 21*, 1 (2012), 011006–1.

22. Rashid, U., Kauko, J., Häkkilä, J., and Quigley, A. Proximal and distal selection of widgets: Designing distributed ui for mobile interaction with large display. In *Proceedings of the 13th International Conference on Human Computer Interaction with Mobile Devices and Services*, MobileHCI '11, ACM (New York, NY, USA, 2011), 495–498.

23. Ronkainen, S., Häkkilä, J., Kaleva, S., Colley, A., and Linjama, J. Tap input as an embedded interaction method for mobile devices. In *Proceedings of the 1st International Conference on Tangible and Embedded Interaction*, TEI '07, ACM (New York, NY, USA, 2007), 263–270.

24. Roto, V. Temporal and granular nature of user experience. In *Proceedings of the Nordic Conference on Experience* (2008).

25. Sahami Shirazi, A., Rohs, M., Schleicher, R., Kratz, S., Müller, A., and Schmidt, A. Real-time nonverbal opinion sharing through mobile phones during sports events. In *Proceedings of the SIGCHI Conference on Human Factors in Computing Systems*, CHI '11, ACM (New York, NY, USA, 2011), 307–310.

26. Strothoff, S., Valkov, D., and Hinrichs, K. Triangle cursor: Interactions with objects above the tabletop. In *Proceedings of the ACM International Conference on Interactive Tabletops and Surfaces*, ITS '11, ACM (New York, NY, USA, 2011), 111–119.

27. Sunnari, M., Arhippainen, L., Pakanen, M., and Hickey, S. Studying user experiences of autostereoscopic 3d menu on touch screen mobile device. In *Proceedings of the 24th Australian Computer-Human Interaction Conference*, OzCHI '12, ACM (New York, NY, USA, 2012), 558–561.

28. Teather, R. J., and Stuerzlinger, W. Pointing at 3d target projections with one-eyed and stereo cursors. In *Proceedings of the SIGCHI Conference on Human Factors in Computing Systems*, CHI '13, ACM (New York, NY, USA, 2013), 159–168.

29. Verdugo, R., Nussbaum, M., Corro, P., Nuñnez, P., and Navarrete, P. Interactive films and coconstruction. *ACM Trans. Multimedia Comput. Commun. Appl. 7*, 4 (Dec. 2011), 39:1–39:24.

# Coding Livecoding

**Ben Swift**
R.S. Computer Science, CECS
Australian National University
ben.swift@anu.edu.au

**Andrew Sorensen**
Inst. Future Environments
Queensland University of Technology
a.sorensen@qut.edu.au

**Michael Martin**
R.S. Finance, Actuarial Studies and Applied Statistics
Australian National University
michael.martin@anu.edu.au

**Henry Gardner**
R.S. Computer Science, CECS
Australian National University
henry.gardner@anu.edu.au

## ABSTRACT
Livecoding is an artistic programming practice in which an artist's low-level interaction can be observed with sufficiently high fidelity to allow for transcription and analysis. This paper presents the first reported "coding" of livecoding videos. From an identified corpus of videos available on the web, we coded performances of two different livecoding artists, recording both the (textual) programming edit events and the musical effect of these edits. Our analysis includes a novel, transition-matrix visualisation of the textual and musical dimensions of this data to create a "performer fingerprint". We show how detailed transcriptions of livecoding videos can be made which, we hope, will provide a foundation for further research into describing and understanding livecoding.

### Author Keywords
Creativity Support Tools; End-user Programming

### ACM Classification Keywords
H.5.2 Information Interfaces and Presentation: User Interfaces – Evaluation/methodology

## INTRODUCTION
Livecoding is a "new direction in electronic music and video" [1] in which the performer(s) write computer code in front of an audience to generate music and visuals in real time. The act of programming is part of the performance, and performers are exhorted to "show us your screens... code should be seen as well as heard" [1]. Academic treatments of livecoding can be found in [3, 2, 8] and elsewhere.

In spite of its revolutionary manifesto, livecoding is now well over a decade old and has become part of the establishment of computer music. Allied forms of musical performance are electronic music, minimalist music, and jazz. Modern, software-enabled DJ/VJ performance is a more mainstream relative of livecoding, and there has been recent interest in the "top-down" HCI design of software interfaces for DJ/VJ and other similar artistic practices [4, 5]. In contrast to these interfaces, the genesis of livecoding was as a reaction against the strictures of "designed" interfaces. In the words of Collins et. al: "Not content to submit meekly to the rigid interfaces of performance software... (livecoding artists) work with programming languages, building their own custom software, tweaking or writing the programs themselves as they perform." [3]

The documentation and sharing of livecoding performances takes the form of performance videos, together with (often indistinct) images of projected computer screens. A few artists have taken to producing direct-feed screencasts of livecoding performances, whose quality is sufficiently high to permit manual 'coding' of these performances after the fact. The existence of these higher-quality videos motivates the following questions:

1. Can a "bottom-up", edit-level analysis of livecoders' activity reveal insights into the into the way that livecoding performances evolve in real time as the artists write computer code to create and manipulate music and video?
2. Are there ways in which differences in "musical style" between different artists can be represented from this interaction data?

## PROCEDURE
In this note we describe a systematic study of a collection of livecoding videos, each of which was manually annotated to produce a time-stamped transcript. Each video in our corpus satisfied the following requirements:

- We restricted ourselves to complete, musical livecoding pieces rather than shorter 'tech-demo' style videos. This also ruled out livecoding videos where the artistic outcome was visual, rather than auditory, a choice which was made not as a value judgement but rather to simplify the comparisons between pieces in our analysis.
- One norm in livecoding is to start performances from a blank editor screen [7]. We restricted our focus to livecoding videos that started in this way for the sake of bringing out common aspects of these performances. This restriction meant that the start-up phases of the videos contained


*CHI 2014*, April 26–May 1, 2014, Toronto, Ontario, Canada.

http://dx.doi.org/10.1145/2556288.2557049

a large number of insertion events.

- To look for elements of style across multiple works by the same artist, we required that the artist have at least four eligible videos to be included in the corpus.

Identifying a comprehensive corpus of livecoding videos is a challenge in its own right. While livecoding has a semi-official home at **toplap.org**, there is no canonical list of videos there. There are other websites[1] which attempt to maintain curated lists of livecoding videos, but none of these lists are comprehensive. In the end, our list of potential videos was assembled from livecoding artists' individual websites, Google, YouTube, and from our knowledge of the TOPLAP community. Our restrictions meant that our videos were direct screen recordings.

We selected the videos of two artists: Andrew Sorensen[2] (AS) and Ben Swift[3] (BS), who between them made up approximately three quarters of all the videos which met the criteria described above. In addition, both of these artists used the Scheme-based livecoding software environment Impromptu [8]. This allowed for a simplified coding schema and facilitated an easy comparison between the two artists. In the end our dataset comprised 13 livecoding videos, with a total running time of approximately three hours. A full list (including URLs) of the videos analysed to produce the final dataset is given in Table 1.

### Coding

Each of the selected videos was analysed frame by frame to produce a series of time-stamped event codes[4] describing the activity of the livecoder. We chose an event-level granularity for these codes, since the framerate of the videos did not always allow us to delineate individual keystrokes. Event boundaries were determined by the times at which the source code was syntactically correct. For example, if the livecoder started to write a new function, that event was considered to last until the function was complete (i.e. callable). When editing existing code, smaller events were possible, such as the changing of a literal value or the addition of a new clause to a `case` statement.

Our coding schema had the following fields:

- **timestamp**: the *start* time of an event (in seconds), and (optionally) the *end* time of that edit, for edit events longer than one second.
- **textual meaning**: was an event an *insertion*, *deletion* or *evaluation*, or was it a *quick edit*, (such as changing an integer literal `60` to `70`)?
- **musical meaning**: did an edit affect the *pitch*, *rhythm*, *dynamics* or *timbre* of the music, or *all* of the above (as in the introduction of a new instrument)?
- **instrument**: in most cases it was possible to delineate different musical instruments/voices in the piece (e.g. *bass*, *drums*, *piano melody*, *piano accompaniment*).
- **comment**: a free-form text field for any salient features of the edit which were not captured in the other fields.

[1] such as **http://livecoding.co.uk/doku.php/videos**

[2] **http://vimeo.com/andrewsorensen**

[3] **http://vimeo.com/benswift**

[4] In this paper we use the term "code" to describe both the textual source code of a program and the (event code) label given to a particular event in the "coded" transcript.

The rationale for this coding schema was to keep the cardinality of each coding "dimension" as small as possible, and to allow the interactions of these dimensions (4 textual codes $\times$ 6 musical codes) to provide richness and complexity in the data.

Event coding was completed by a professional composer, with tertiary degrees in both music composition and computer science. Although this person had some livecoding experience, they were not the creator of any of the pieces studied. While determining the textual meaning of each edit was fairly straightforward, the musical and instrument fields required subjective judgements, and we also provided a free-form "comment" field to enable notes to be recorded about possible ambiguities and other issues. It was possible to provide *multiple* musical or instrumental codes for a given textual edit, e.g. when the modification of a global parameter affected both the pitch and dynamics of the piece.

## RESULTS

In total, 2577 edit events were recorded in the dataset, with an average of 15 edits/min. Figure 1 shows the way that the distribution of these events changed over the course of each piece by breaking each piece into three equal segments: the beginning (first third), middle (middle third) and end (final third) of each piece.

In the textual dimension data exhibits a shift from having a large number of insertion events (writing new code) at the beginning of each piece towards primarily evaluation and quick edit events at the end of the piece. Both artists exhibited this trend. Musically, however, there are different edit proportions between the artists: AS favoured dynamic (loudness) edits, while BS preferred rhythmic ones and edits which affect whole instruments (the "all" musical category).

Figure 2 shows the frequency of some of the different edit types between pieces, separated into the beginning-middle-end time chunks. This figure shows the same trends as Figure 1, with code insertion events early in the piece and evaluations and quick edits in the latter stages. AS makes noticeably more dynamic (musical) edits in the latter stages of his pieces—a trend not evident for BS.

### Transition matrices

Transition matrices (Figure 3) can help us look for "signatures" of artists in terms of their edit *transitions* (the sequence of edit events) in both the textual and musical dimensions. This is a new contribution of this work which expands on the use of transition matrices for chord sequences by Nichols et. al. [6]. A key aspect of our approach is the creation of a temporal sequence (beginning-middle-end) of transition matrices to show the evolution of an artist's activity within their pieces.

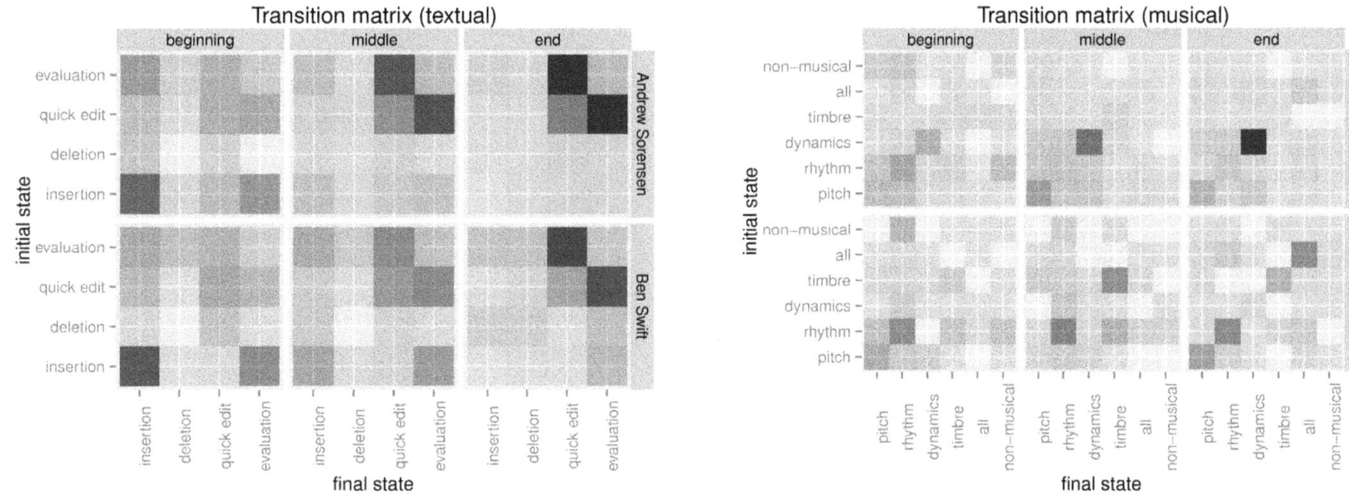


**Figure 3. Transition matrices for both the *textual* and *musical* dimension of each edit event. A darker cell in the matrix indicates a more common transition (initial state → final state) in the dataset.**

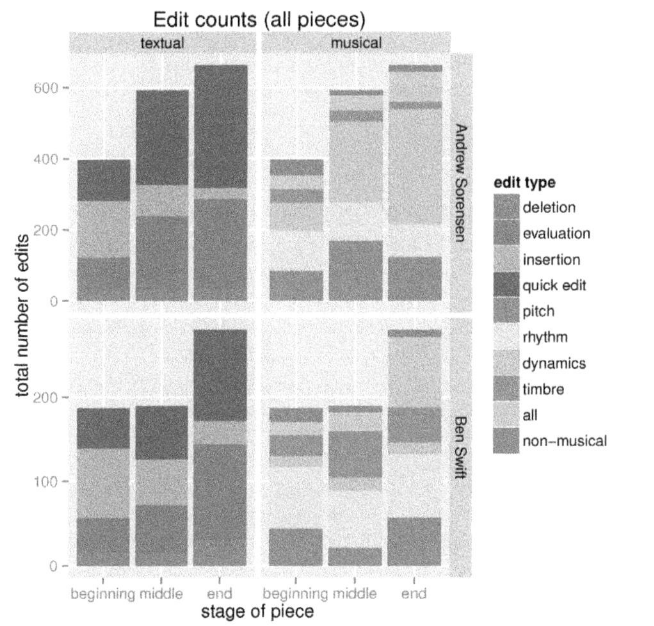


**Figure 1. Total number of edits across the dataset. The y-axis scale is different between artists due to the fact that each artist had a different number of pieces in the dataset. There is a trend towards a greater number of edits toward the end of a piece, as well as a general shift in proportions of the edit types (both textually and musically) across the different stages of each piece.**

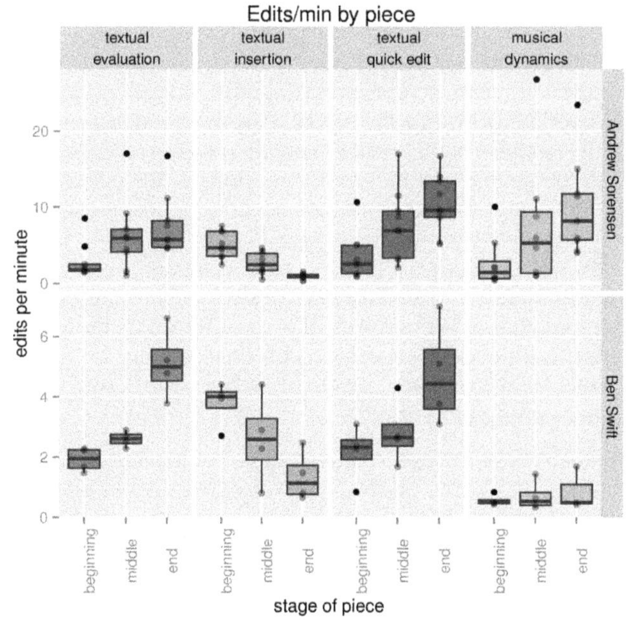


**Figure 2. The edits/minute activity across pieces, broken down by artist and both the textual and musical meaning of their edits. Since the pieces are different lengths, we have used an edits/min variable instead of a total edit count to facilitate comparisons between pieces (and piece segments) of differing lengths. The raw values for each piece are shown with black dots, overplotted with box plots to show the distribution. These boxplots may be misleading in the bottom row (artist BS) due to the small number of pieces ($n = 4$ for BS, while $n = 9$ for AS). Note also that the y-axis scale is different for each row—in general AS (top row) makes more edits per minute than BS.**

Figure 3 (left-hand side) shows the textual transition matrices for each artist. Both artists exhibit a progression from insertion events (bottom left-hand corner) to quick edits and evaluations (top right-hand corner) as each piece develops. Also visible in the transition matrix is the 'quick edit → evaluation' (and back again) loop in state space. This suggests that the quick edit and evaluation events in the latter stages of a piece tend to alternate, rather than being contiguous in time. This observation makes sense given the nature of the Impromptu software environment, in which changes to the source code must be evaluated before they take effect.

Figure 3 (right-hand side) shows the same transition matrices, but this time from a musical perspective. Interestingly, there is much less similarity between the artists. Over time, AS's transition matrix becomes increasingly dominated by 'dynamic edit → dynamic edit' self-transitions, while BS's matrix remains diffuse, even in the later stages of his pieces. This suggests that, from a musical perspective, AS starts out making code edits which affect many different aspects of the music, but in the later stages of his pieces he 'zooms in' on dynamic edits, adjusting the already-running musical voices up and down in dynamic range as dictated by his aesthetic goals. In contrast, BS continues to jump around more in the musical nature of his edits, although there seems to be a slight trend towards the on-axis (i.e. self-transitions) values in the transition matrix in the final third of his pieces.

## DISCUSSION

Figures 1, 2 and 3 all show visible differences in edit activity over the course of the pieces. The most interesting aspect of the analysis is that while there are recognisable patterns in both the textual and musical dimensions of the edits, only in the musical dimension do there seem to be recognisable differences *between* the artists (see Figure 3). While it might seem, on the surface, that a textual programming language may provide too broad an interface to the musical power of the computer, it is interesting that the differences between the artists are not so visible based on their activity on a purely textual level, but come out clearly when considering the musical meaning of their edits.

A potential future use for the sequence of local transition matrices is the detection of natural change points in live-coded pieces, through both the textual and the musical activity of the livecoder.

## CONCLUSION

This paper has presented the first reported coding and event-level analysis of a decade-old artistic endeavour which is centred around programming at a computer interface. Although our data set is small, being limited by the available web presence of livecoding, we have examined the works of two different livecoding artists with a one second temporal resolution along both the programming (text editing) and musical dimensions. We have also demonstrated the utility of transition matrices for visualising stylistic differences between artists.

The possibilities of this data collection approach are exciting, and we acknowledge that this note presents only a preliminary exploration of these possibilities. Future work could extend our study through the instrumentation of the programming interface to enable automatic data collection, refining the coding scheme (e.g. breaking "quick edit" into subtypes), exploring the relationship between the textual and musical dimensions of the scheme, and also to examine and contrast livecoding with other source code editing activities. As more data is collected, we hope to be able to answer with more confidence questions about the nature of style and the specific patterns of interaction which characterise livecoding.

## ACKNOWLEDGEMENTS

The authors would like to thank Matt Rankin for his contribution to this work.

| Artist | Title | Vimeo ID |
|---|---|---|
| AS | Strange Places | 2503257 |
| AS | Dancing Phalanges | 8732631 |
| AS | A Study in Keith | 2433947 |
| AS | Jazz Ensemble Study | 15679078 |
| AS | Variations on a Christmas Theme | 18008372 |
| AS | A Christmas Carol | 8364077 |
| AS | Day of the Triffords | 2735394 |
| AS | Orchestral | 2579694 |
| AS | Antiphony | 2503188 |
| AS | A Study in Part | 2434054 |
| BS | I am an Elder Brother | 7525775 |
| BS | Archtop | 6940393 |
| BS | A Few Days Late | 7196155 |
| BS | Fear of Sucking | 7039223 |

**Table 1. The livecoding videos which were coded for analysis. Each video can be seen online at `https://vimeo.com/<VimeoID>`**

## REFERENCES

1. *TOPLAP Manifesto.* `http://toplap.org/wiki/ManifestoDraft`.
2. Blackwell, A., and Collins, N. The programming language as a musical instrument. *Proceedings of PPIG05 (Psychology of Programming Interest Group)* (2005).
3. Collins, N., McLean, A., Rohrhuber, J., and Ward, A. Live coding in laptop performance. *Organised Sound 8*, 03 (2003), 321–330.
4. Hook, J., Green, D., McCarthy, J., Taylor, S., Wright, P., and Olivier, P. A vj centered exploration of expressive interaction. In *Proceedings of the SIGCHI Conference on Human Factors in Computing Systems*, ACM (2011), 1265–1274.
5. Hook, J., McCarthy, J., Wright, P., and Olivier, P. Waves: exploring idiographic design for live performance. In *Proceedings of the SIGCHI Conference on Human Factors in Computing Systems*, ACM (2013), 2969–2978.
6. Nichols, E., Morris, D., and Basu, S. Data-driven exploration of musical chord sequences. In *IUI '09: Proceedings of the 14th international conference on Intelligent user interfaces*, ACM Request Permissions (Feb. 2009).
7. Nilson, C. Live coding practice. *Proceedings of the 7th international conference on New interfaces for musical expression* (2007), 112–117.
8. Sorensen, A., and Gardner, H. Programming with time: cyber-physical programming with impromptu. In *OOPSLA '10: Proceedings of the ACM international conference on Object oriented programming systems languages and applications* (2010), 822–834.

# Exploring Percussive Gesture on iPads with Ensemble Metatone

**Charles Martin, Henry Gardner, Ben Swift**
Research School of Computer Science, CECS
Australian National University, Canberra, ACT, 0200, Australia
{charles.martin, henry.gardner, ben.swift}@anu.edu.au

## ABSTRACT
Percussionists are unique among western classical instrumentalists in that their artistic practice is defined by an approach to interaction rather than their instruments. While percussionists are accustomed to exploring non-traditional objects to create music, these objects have yet to encompass touch-screen computing devices to any great extent. The proliferation and popularity of these devices now presents an opportunity to explore their use in combining computer-generated sound together with percussive interaction in a musical ensemble.

This paper examines Ensemble Metatone, a group formed to explore the "infiltration" of iPad-based musical instruments into a free-improvisation percussion ensemble. We discuss the design approach for two different iPad percussion instruments and the methodology for exploring them with the group over a series of rehearsals and performances. Qualitative analysis of discussions throughout this process shows that the musicians developed a vocabulary of gestures and musical interactions to make musical sense of these new instruments.

### Author Keywords
music; expression; multitouch; gesture; percussion; user experience

### ACM Classification Keywords
H.5.2. Information Interfaces and Presentation (e.g. HCI): Evaluation/methodology

## INTRODUCTION
Percussion is a musical practice more defined by the methods of interacting with instruments rather than the instruments themselves. Percussionists perform by "striking, scraping, brushing, rubbing, whacking, or crashing any... available object" [11]. These percussive gestures are used to coax wide varieties of timbres and musical gestures from simple instruments. For percussionists, free improvisation is often a process of gestural exploration, discovering new sounds from traditional and non-traditional instruments and responding to other sounds in an ensemble. Like some percussion instruments, touch-screen computing devices can be rubbed, scraped, and struck with fingers and hands. While it is well established that popular touch-screen devices can be used to make music, mainstream creative frameworks for their use (tapping virtual piano keys, for instance) are limited. The percussive affordances of these devices motivates an exploration of their use in a modern percussion ensemble to establish more varied modes of interaction that could be used in app-design, for musical composition, and other applications.

**Figure 1. Ensemble Metatone performing with iPads and percussion instruments.**

HCI studies of gestures on touch screens have been conducted for tasks such as activating a shortcut in a smartphone [10, 1], manipulating virtual objects on a table-based interface [7] and controlling a video performance [9]. Many of these studies have characterised gestures that emerged as part of users' interactions with a touch interface. In a similar way, the work described in this paper examines touch-screen gestures that emerge when iPads are introduced into a modern, free-improvisation percussion ensemble. Qualitative analysis of a series of the group's rehearsals and discussions reveals a vocabulary of new gestures invented by the musicians. These gestures were used by the musicians to creatively interact-with, and expand the power of, two specially-designed iPad percussion apps. Unlike other studies such as Wobbrock et al [12], the gestures we observed are generally two-handed and combine many touches over a number of seconds to express sustained musical ideas. Our study also yields a refined concept of how iPad based instruments fit into a percussive


*CHI 2014*, April 26–May 1, 2014, Toronto, Ontario, Canada.

ACM 978-1-4503-2473-1/14/04..$15.00.
http://dx.doi.org/10.1145/2556288.2557226

artistic practice and how these instruments can contribute to the musical structure of a free-improvisation.

### Ensemble Metatone

Ensemble Metatone was brought together to explore the "infiltration" of iPad-based musical instruments into a percussion ensemble through free-improvisation. The members of the group, Charles Martin (CM - one of the authors of this paper), Christina Hopgood (CH), Jonathan Griffiths (JG), and Yvonne Lam (YL), had previously studied and worked together as professional musicians. CM was the designer of the iPad instruments and facilitator of the group's rehearsals and performances. Over four studio sessions and two live concerts, two different performance paradigms were explored: in the first paradigm, only iPads were used; in the second, the performers each played a setup which included a number of percussion instruments of their own choosing as well as an iPad.

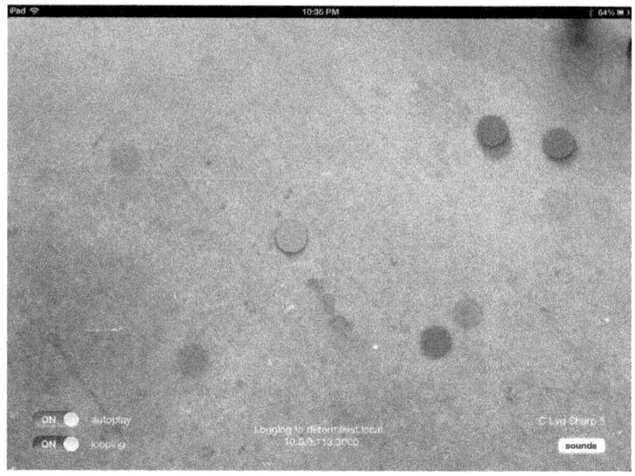


**Figure 2. Screenshot of the MetaLonsdale app. The green circle denotes the user's touch point while red circles show delayed notes. The delay and auto play functions are controlled by switches on the lower left and the button on the lower right changes the sounds that can be played.**

## DESIGNING TABLET INSTRUMENTS

While the field of computer music abounds with creative examples of touch-sensor-based instruments, the goals of this project placed constraints on what could practically be used within the percussion group: the touch-screen devices needed to be self-contained, durable, and easy to provision with software updates. Many tablet computing devices meet these requirements, but Apple iPads were chosen as the computer instrument in the ensemble because of their widespread adoption and established development frameworks for musical applications. Even though iPad touch screens have drawbacks such as a lack of pressure sensitivity or physical feedback, their physical dimensions mimic that of some simple percussion instruments such as the woodblock or tambourine. Despite their limitations, the study described below shows that they can be played musically and expressively, particularly in setups of multiple percussion instruments.

Two apps were produced for the group: MetaTravels and MetaLonsdale (shown in Figure 2). Both apps used the same interaction scheme and both allowed access to pitched percussive sounds and field recordings. In both apps, the majority of the iPad screen was a performance surface and there were few graphical UI elements. Tapping the screen produced short sounds at a pitch determined by the location of the tap. Swiping triggered continuous field recordings with the velocity of the swipe directly mapped to the volume of the field recording. Both apps featured simple delay functions, that repeated tapped notes, and switchable auto-play features, that algorithmically produced background sounds. These features were activated by switches in the user interface. A button on both apps allowed the performer to shuffle the available sounds.

While the functionality of the two apps was similar, the sound palette was different. MetaTravels used field recordings from around the world, with chromatically-tuned pitches, while MetaLonsdale featured field recordings from a particular location (a coffee shop and gallery in Canberra, Australia) and diatonically-tuned pitches selected from three different scales. An additional network feature in MetaLonsdale ensured that all iPads in the ensemble had the same scale. Finally, both apps allowed logs of performances to be captured by sending OSC messages of each touch event to a server.

## DEVELOPING AN ENSEMBLE "VOICE"

Our approach for studying the emergence of "expressive interaction" [8] of the performers with the iPad instruments followed common methods for collaboratively developing a musical performance. The process for creating the performance was collaborative amongst all four musicians with free-improvisation leading to collective decisions about stucturing the work both in rehearsal and in performance [6]. The rehearsal process followed Cahn's concept of "Creative Music Making" [3] with a series of freely-improvised performances that were recorded, played back and discussed. These rehearsals were facilitated by CM who, as noted above, was the app developer and one of the authors of this paper. Similar to video-cued recall [5], the listening stage of this process allowed the performers to articulate their musical intentions and discuss the structure of the pieces in context.

Following a public concert, the three other musicians participated in an open-ended interview with CM concerning the techniques they had developed for performing with the iPads and how they had used them to shape the performances over the whole process. Video and multi-channel audio recordings were made of all the rehearsals and the final performance. The performers' touch interactions with the iPads were logged and visualised into recreations of the performances that were incorporated into the video record.

The rehearsal discussions and interview, a corpus of over six hours of video (see Table 1), were transcribed and coded using Thematic Analysis [2]. The coding focussed on the the performers' articulations of gestures they used on the iPads, their understanding of the iPads in relation to percussion instruments and how the iPad instruments influenced the structure of the improvisation. The codes followed the gestures available in the app: taps, swipes and combinations of the two.

| Date | Type | Duration | id |
|---|---|---|---|
| 13-04-20 | iPads only | 1H16M | |
| 13-04-20 | iPads only | 40M | ifgC_KnauOs |
| 13-04-21 | iPads only | 46M | 5OmUnKYcaL4 |
| 13-04-27 | iPads only | 1H | x1SwCVfqLQU |
| 13-05-04 | iPads & percussion | 54M | |
| 13-05-04 | iPads & percussion | 1H8M | RqLfsBCE3mM |
| 13-08-04 | interview | 29M | |

**Table 1. The corpus of rehearsal and interview recordings used in this study. Selected performances are available online at `http://youtu.be/id`**

## RESULTS

The qualitative analysis of interview and recording transcripts revealed a vocabulary of gestures developed by the group to express musical ideas in the rehearsals and performances. The gestures embrace the affordances of the iPad instrument but also reflect the group's training and experience with percussion. The study produced a refined concept of the relationship between the iPads and percussion and how the performers used these instruments to structure improvisation.

### Taps

By their own admission, the pitched percussion sounds that could be created with taps on the iPad were well understood by the performers. As described below, over the rehearsals they used the iPads to create unique interpretations of these sounds.

#### *Fast Taps*

The performers used fast tapping and the delay function to create a continuous, pitched sound. Fast Taps were generally not used in precise rhythms but in a single stroke roll where continuous fast attacks created the illusion of a continuous sound [4]. When this was performed with low pitches, the attacks blended together and created an "organ" or "bass" sound which was used as a "pedal point", or continuous low-pitched drone. High-pitched Fast Taps were a very distinctive sound that encouraged imitation among the group while Fast Taps used on field recordings created soft underlying textures. The performers commented on the experience of filling up the delay function's buffer with fast taps: "setting it going and just watching it for a while" (JG).

#### *Slow Taps*

Very slow taps were associated with low-pitched sounds from the performers and were used with and without the delay function to create a slow, but measured, rhythm.

#### *Random Phrases*

YL demonstrated a "capricious" sound using multiple fingers in quick succession to tap all over the iPad screen. Unlike the fast and slow tap, these random phrases grouped a small number of taps into a short gesture.

### Swipes

Swiping, moving a finger across the iPad screen, produced continuous field recording sounds with volume directly controlled by the velocity of the movement. The performers used this control of volume (or "dynamics" in musical terminology) to express rhythm and to accompany performers using other gestures.

#### *Short Swipes*

Short swipes had a distinct beginning and end and were usually performed in a straight line across the iPad screens. The end of short swipes was often more striking than the beginning due to the sudden stop in sound when the performer lifted their finger from the screen. Performers emphasised this contrast by accelerating their movement at the end of the gesture producing a loud sound and then silence. This gesture was rhythmically clear, CH remarked that it was: "more defined, I can make rhythms that way".

#### *Swirls*

A continuous swiping sound could be achieved by moving continually back and forth across the iPad screen. While large circular motions could be made slowly or quickly to form soft or loud dynamics, the performers often used small swirls for softer sounds and larger swirls for accents and loud continuous sounds. This gesture mimics snare-drum brush-technique where wire brushes are swept across a rough drumskin in patterns of large and small swirls to create rhythms [4]. A very slow movement across the iPad screen was used to produce a very quiet but continuous sound in a long, focussed gesture.

### Combinations

Two gestures were discussed that used combinations of taps and swirls. In the first, a small swirl in one hand was used as an underlying sound for phrases of taps in the other. The second combination-gesture used taps with a distinctive pitched sound followed by a short swipe.

### Volume control

The iPads' volume control was used performatively throughout the improvisations. While the performers would use the hardware volume control to balance their sound with the rest of the group, they also used it to fade continuous sound in and out, especially those created with the delay function. CH used quick changes to the "mute" volume setting to produce a sense of space and rhythm in her phrases.

### Relationship between iPads and percussion

Performers commented that the iPad instruments afforded less control over sound than percussion instruments and, in response, they developed gestures that emphasised rhythmic playing and dynamics. The performers did, however, acknowledge features of the iPad instruments that were not available in percussion instruments. The field recordings were "something we can't replicate" (JG) and the network feature that matched the scale of pitched notes across the ensemble "made everyone sound more cohesive" (CH). When matched with percussion instruments, the iPad became "just another instrument" (CH) in multi-instrument setups. In this situation, CH commented that she "really wanted to play the iPad with sticks", but also acknowledged that she would sometimes play her regular percussion instruments with her fingers. In this way, the gestural vocabulary of iPad performance had influenced her approach to the percussion setup.

### Structuring an Improvisation

Rather than using the app to create melodies and rhythmic accompaniments, the performers acknowledged that they were instead creating "textures" (YL, JG) or layerings of timbrally diverse sounds. While performers frequently imitated each other, responding with similar gestures, they also developed a sense of their own style over the rehearsals, for example, YL used "the ideas I was doing yesterday". They also had moments of introversion, "I wasn't listening to anybody, just having fun" (JG).

The performers were conscious of creating an aesthetically pleasing structure in their performances and were more successful after a number of improvisation sessions together. At the end of the series of rehearsals, YL commented that "we're really developing a sense of... motion. There's definitely parts of it where... we're definitely now in a new section". Given the ease of creating continuous sounds with the iPads, the performers appreciated moments of silence or "space" (YL) in between musical ideas. When discussing the goal of playing longer performances, the performers noted they would need to continue developing confidence pursuing particular musical ideas. YL commented "we'd have to be comfortable sitting on one idea for longer" and JG suggested "getting used to... the really gradual shift" of musical ideas.

## CONCLUSIONS

We have described the findings of a qualitative study of gestures used by a group of percussionists on new iPad instruments. The main contribution of this research is a vocabulary of expressive gestures that emerged from the group to communicate musical ideas and to overcome some of the perceived limitations of the apps. The performers borrowed from their percussion backgrounds to create distinctive gestures using one or both hands: fast, slow and random phrases of taps; short swipes; fast and slow swirls; combinations of swirls and taps; single handed extension of taps with a swipe; and combinations of these gestures with the iPad's volume control.

The performers used these gestures to express rhythm and dynamics and to explore timbres from outside the design-intentions of the apps. While the "organ" sound of continually delayed fast taps was not foreseen in the design of the app, this became a key motif in performances. Our vocabulary of touch gestures can be used for composition or music-education with the apps, as a design framework for expanding the expressive possibilities of future touch-screen based instruments, or even other non-musical touch-screen applications.

We have also discussed the group's understanding of how the iPads fitted into their existing percussive artistic practice and how they used the iPads to give structure to an improvisation. While the performers felt the touch-screen provided less control than percussion instruments, they used the non-percussive sounds from the apps to augment the traditional percussion in their setups. Even though they were equipped with identical iPad instruments, the performers developed their own styles over the rehearsals. In each improvisation they were conscious of carefully pacing their performance and using space between phrases and ideas. The group used ensemble interactions such as imitation as well as introverted explorations of particular gestures.

This work demonstrates that expressive gestures can be used to expand the power of musical touch-screen apps and create compelling performances. In future work, our results could be used to iterate the design of iPad percussion instruments so that they fit more easily within percussion setups. Our findings could also be useful for training other musicians or students in the use of iPad percussion instruments.

## REFERENCES


1. Bragdon, A., Nelson, E., Li, Y., and Hinckley, K. Experimental analysis of touch-screen gesture designs in mobile environments. In *Proc. CHI 2011*, ACM Press (2011), 403–412.
2. Braun, V., and Clarke, V. Using thematic analysis in psychology. *Qualitative Research in Psychology 3*, 2 (2006), 77–101.
3. Cahn, W. L. *Creative Music Making*. Routledge, 2005.
4. Cook, G. *Teaching Percussion*. Schirmer Books, 1997.
5. Costello, B., Muller, L., Amitani, S., and Edmonds, E. Understanding the experience of interactive art: Iamascope in beta_space. In *Interactive Entertainment 2005*, Creativity & Cognition Studios Press (2005), 49–56.
6. Hayden, S., and Windsor, L. Collaboration and the composer: Case studies from the end of the 20th century. *Tempo 61*, 240 (2007), 28–39.
7. Hinrichs, U., and Carpendale, S. Gestures in the wild: studying multi-touch gesture sequences on interactive tabletop exhibits. In *Proc. CHI 2011*, ACM Press (2011), 3023–3032.
8. Hook, J., Green, D., McCarthy, J., Taylor, S., Wright, P., and Olivier, P. A vj centered exploration of expressive interaction. In *Proc. CHI 2011*, ACM Press (2011), 1265–1274.
9. Hook, J., McCarthy, J. C., Wright, P., and Olivier, P. Waves: exploring idiographic design for live performance. In *Proc. CHI 2013*, ACM Press (2013), 2969–2978.
10. Ouyang, T., and Li, Y. Bootstrapping personal gesture shortcuts with the wisdom of the crowd and handwriting recognition. In *Proc. CHI 2012*, ACM Press (2012), 2895–2904.
11. Schick, S. *The Percussionist's Art: Same Bed, Different Dreams*. University of Rochester Press, 2006.
12. Wobbrock, J. O., Morris, M. R., and Wilson, A. D. User-defined gestures for surface computing. In *Proc. CHI 2009*, ACM Press (2009), 1083–1092.

# How Carat Affects User Behavior: Implications for Mobile Battery Awareness Applications

Kumaripaba Athukorala ‡§ Eemil Lagerspetz ‡§ Maria von Kügelgen ‡§
Antti Jylhä ‡§ Adam J. Oliner † Sasu Tarkoma ‡§
Giulio Jacucci ¶§

‡ Helsinki Institute for Information Technology HIIT, University of Helsinki, † UC Berkeley
§ Department of Computer Science, University of Helsinki
¶ Helsinki Institute for Information Technology HIIT, Aalto University
§ first.last@helsinki.fi, † oliner@eecs.berkeley.edu

## ABSTRACT

Mobile devices have limited battery life, and numerous battery management applications are available that aim to improve it. This paper examines a large-scale mobile battery awareness application, called Carat, to see how it changes user behavior with long-term use. We conducted a survey of current Carat Android users and analyzed their interaction logs. The results show that long-term Carat users save more battery, charge their devices less often, learn to manage their battery with less help from Carat, have a better understanding of how Carat works, and may enjoy competing against other users. Based on these findings, we propose a set of guidelines for mobile battery awareness applications: battery awareness applications should make the reasoning behind their recommendations understandable to the user, be tailored to retain long-term users, take the audience into account when formulating feedback, and distinguish third-party and system applications.

### Author Keywords

user retention; user behavior; smartphone; energy awareness

### ACM Classification Keywords

H.5.m. Information Interfaces and Presentation (e.g. HCI): Miscellaneous; H.1.2. User/Machine Systems: Human Factors

## INTRODUCTION

Mobile devices have limited battery life, sometimes requiring a recharge more than once per day. Rapid energy drain may be caused by extensive use of resources (e.g., the network, CPU, or GPS) by running applications or the device operating system, itself. Poor battery life contributes negatively to user experience [21].


*CHI'14*, April 26–May 1, 2014, Toronto, ON, Canada.
Copyright © 2014 ACM 978-1-4503-2473-1/14/04$15.00.
http://dx.doi.org/10.1145/2556288.2557271

To automatically increase battery life or help users manage power consumption (a.k.a. *battery awareness*), numerous battery-saving applications have come to application markets [4, 15, 16, 25]. Although these applications can improve battery life, the automated solutions do not typically give users a direct indication of the concrete actions that make the battery last longer. Such applications, therefore, tend not to guide user behavior towards battery-saving choices.

There is prior work on the effect on user behavior of household energy awareness applications [1, 3] and mobile battery level indicators [20, 22]. However, we are not aware of any user behavior studies in the context of mobile battery awareness applications.

In this paper, we examine users of Carat, a community-based mobile battery-awareness application deployed worldwide to more than 670,000 devices. We conducted a survey of over 1,000 Carat users and analyze their responses along with data automatically gathered by Carat. Prior work on the Carat logs has shown not only that the application recommendations improve battery life (11% after 10 days and 40% after 90 days, on average), but that there is a positive correlation between the duration of using the application and the extent of the improvement [15]. One question we examine in this work is what distinguishes these long-term users from short-term users that might explain the difference in battery life improvement.

The contributions of this work are as follows:

- Elucidates the relationship between mobile battery awareness applications and user behavior;
- Examines two classes of users, distinguished by duration of use of the application, with distinct behaviors;
- Articulates lessons learned in the form of actionable guidelines for future battery awareness applications.

## RELATED WORK

There is a growing body of literature on improving the battery life of mobile devices. The majority of this work consists of technical solutions, not intended for novice users [12, 16]. Other work provides suggestions or guidelines to users on how to reduce battery consumption [6, 14, 15]. There is another line of research on Human-Battery Interaction (HBI) that focuses on user interaction with different battery indicators. Understanding the battery charging behavior and users' knowledge of power-saving features has been the subject of some HBI studies [2, 7, 20, 22]. In the domain of household energy awareness, there has been research on user behavior changes [1, 3]. We are not aware of any user behavior studies in the context of mobile battery awareness applications. As the goal of this research is to understand how mobile battery awareness applications change behavior, this section mainly considers work related to such applications, human-battery interaction, and behavior studies in the domain of household energy awareness.

### Mobile Battery Awareness Applications

The primary goal of mobile battery awareness applications is to make the user aware of what consumes energy. The Android operating system has a built-in energy profiler that shows statistics about battery use on the device. This can be accessed from the battery option in the settings on most devices. Early consumer tools for energy awareness on smartphones include the Nokia Energy Profiler [4], which runs in the background, recording phone subsystem use, and later reports the energy use (in watts) over time. A more recent profiler is PowerTutor for Android [25], which shows energy use similarly to Android's built-in profiler but broken down by resource (e.g., CPU, WiFi, and the screen) and by category (e.g., by application or system component).

Carat is the first collaborative approach to mobile battery awareness, which allows it to perform diagnoses which would be impossible on a single device [15]. For example, although the tools discussed in this section are able to obtain accurate energy consumption profiles on a device, they cannot determine whether the amount of energy used by an application or device is normal. With a community of hundreds of thousands of client devices, Carat identified applications that consume abnormally large amounts of energy compared with other applications as well as instances of indiviual applications that consume abnormally large amounts of energy on only a subset of devices.

### Human Battery Interaction (HBI)

Some work in HBI considers how users deal with limited mobile battery life. Banerjee et al. [2] studied phone battery-charging behavior and identified two categories of users: those who charge their phones regularly regardless of the remaining battery level and those who charge based on battery status indicators. Furthermore, there was usually a significant amount of power left in the battery when it was charged, even for users who charge based on the battery status indicator. There is also research on how battery-use feedback in mobile phones affects behavior [20, 22]. Studies revealed that some battery charging habits can reduce battery lifetime [7]. We extend these lines of inquiry by studying how mobile battery awareness applications affect behavior.

### Behavior Change in Energy Awareness Applications

Literature on feedback for energy conservation spans several decades and includes work from several disciplines, including the behavioral sciences. This literature mostly considers domestic settings [18]. Although battery awareness applications address a different problem from domestic energy consumption feedback, there are similiarities. One key difference for mobile battery management is that power conservation is motivated by extending use time, while in domestic settings motivations are environmental or monetary.

Carat follows some of the key principles proposed in the energy consumption feedback literature; it provides actionable feedback, rewards users to keep them motivated, and avoids information overload. A solution tailored to individual users facilitates the job of persuading users to take the suggested actions, as each behavior has its own personalized reasons and constraints [1, 3].

Effective feedback should be real-time [3] and actionable, demonstrating a way to fill the gap between current actions and desired goal state [13]. The goal should always be clear to the user and be accompanied by instructions on how to achieve it.

Sustained involvement requires interfaces that evolve, rewarding improvements to keep the user motivated after the initial curiosity drops [11]. Recent work proposed a three-stage approach for feedback including the following: raise awareness, inform complex changes, and maintain sustainable routines [23].

There are a variety of other principles (e.g., format of feedback [9, 17, 19]), but the ones above are the most relevant for the case of battery awareness applications. Most available applications only provide simple feedback [23] ranging from power measures to monetary charges to carbon footprints. By themselves, such numbers do not suggest clear actions to take. Like recent energy consumption solutions that include contextually triggered advice [10], Carat provides concrete, actionable suggestions to users to improve battery life.

## INTRODUCTION TO CARAT

Carat [15] uses a collaborative black-box method for diagnosing anomalies on mobile devices. Carat is an application on both the iOS and Android platforms.

The client application sends intermittent, coarse-grained measurements to a server. The server correlates running applications, device model, operating system, and other features with energy use. The system generates actions that the user could take to improve battery life. The amount of improvement error, and confidence of the suggestions given by Carat is presented to the user along with the actions. Carat has been installed on more than 670,000 devices.

On a single device, it is not possible to diagnose all types of abnormal energy use, because it could result from device or user-specific factors. A collaborative approach is required to diagnose energy bugs of this kind. Carat achieves this by using a community of devices.

### Carat in Action

To walk through the features of Carat, we use the following scenario. John is a smartphone user with battery life issues. He starts by installing Carat on his phone. At first, when John

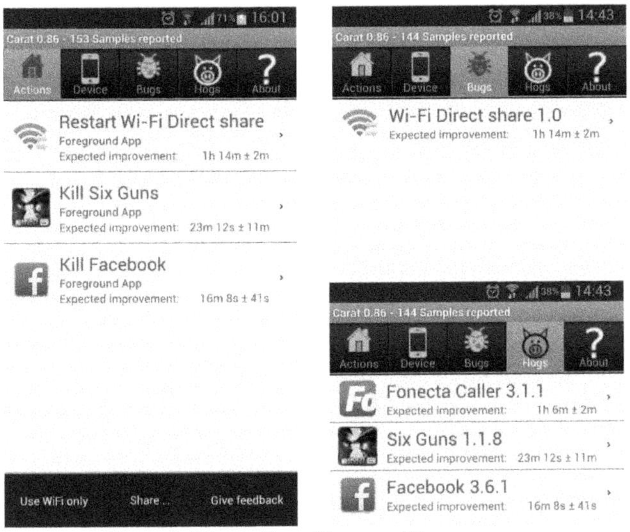


**Figure 1. The Actions, Hogs, and Bugs screens**

opens Carat, the system has no data on his device. However, he may see suggestions based on his currently running applications that are known anomalous energy consumers in the Carat community.

To calculate results for John's phone, Carat needs data from that phone. Carat application gathers intermittent measurements of the running applications, battery level, and other device features. When John opens Carat, it sends these data, referred to as samples, gathered so far to the server. John needs to open Carat regularly, preferably at least once a day, to receive personalized results as quickly as possible. He can see the number of sent samples in the top bar of the Carat application (Figure 1).

### *Actions*

After about a week, John receives his first results. On the opening screen of Carat, the "Actions" tab, he sees suggestions given by Carat (Figure 1). There are usually two types of suggestions: "Kill application X" or "Restart application Y". Carat also shows how much the battery life is expected to increase if these applications were not used. If John wishes to kill or restart these applications, he can click on the corresponding item, and Carat will show a screen with instructions on how the application can be killed. Most of the time, John can kill an application just by clicking a button on this Carat screen, and Carat provides alternative instructions in case that fails. Sometimes, killing an application on Android does not succeed, because the application's background service restarts it right after it has been killed. Applications that behave like this can be *force killed* through the Task Manager, accessible from the same screen of Carat. However, doing this for applications required by the system can lead to instability, and often there is not much the user can do about them.

### *Bugs and Hogs*

John can also see the applications mentioned in the "Actions" screen on the "Bugs" and "Hogs" tabs (See Figure 1). There might be other applications listed in those tabs as well, since actions are suggested only for the applications that are running on the users phone at that moment. On these tabs John sees lists of applications that he has been using after installing Carat that have been classified as *bugs* or *hogs*.

Hogs are applications that use more energy than an average application in the Carat community. Typically hogs require more energy for normal function; examples of this are VoIP, Internet radio, navigation, and camera applications. However, hogs can also result from a widespread problem with an application's energy use.

If the application is not a hog, it can still be a bug. A bug is an application that, for some reason, uses more battery than average on a specific device. For example, the Kindle application uses less energy, on average, than the average application, so it is not a hog. However, as reported in [15], some versions of the Kindle application had a bug which caused it to use more energy when connected via a mobile network. This made Kindle show up as a bug for Carat users who preferred mobile networks over WiFi. How hogs and bugs are calculated is described in detail by Oliner et al. [15].

The actions along with the hog and bug reports help John understand which applications are draining the battery faster than others, but also which of these applications are often running when the user opens the Carat application. He can use the actions screen to kill or restart running applications, and from hogs and bugs screens he can gain wider knowledge about applications that lower his battery lifetime and that of the other users in the Carat community.

### *J-Score and Other Information about Battery Life*

After getting to know the energy efficiency of his applications better, John starts to get more interested in how well his battery lasts compared to other people. On the "Device" tab (see Figure 2) he sees a value called the J-Score. The J-Score tells him the percentage of devices in the Carat community that have a worse battery life than his phone. Underneath the J-Score is the expected active battery life calculated by Carat. This shows how long the battery would last if the device was used in the way that John has been using it since he started using Carat.

### *Other Features of Carat*

John also sees some basic information about his phone on the "Device" tab: the operating system version, the device model, and information about the memory use of his phone. He can also look at a list of all the currently running applications by clicking the button "View Process List".

## METHOD

We collected data from the existing Carat users by following two data collection methods: survey and system logs of Carat.

### User Survey

Our first goal was to identify how different features of Carat affect user behavior. Therefore, we constructed a questionnaire and placed a link to it on the opening screen of Carat. The link was published to all Carat Android users. The survey was open for two weeks starting from August $12^{th}$, 2013.

**Figure 2. The Device screen and the process list**

### *Survey Questionnaire*

The questionnaire was composed of 16 questions plus optional free-text fields to express any additional comments regarding Carat application use experience and suggestions for improvement. All the questions were multiple choice, except for questions 8, 9, and 12, which were 7-point Likert scale. The full questionnaire with the multiple choice answer options can be found on the Carat website[1]. The following questions were asked in the questionnaire:

1. How long have you been using Carat?
2. What kind of device are you using now?
3. Do you use external batteries for this device?
4. How often do you charge the battery on this device?
5. On how many devices do you use Carat?
6. What is your main reason for using Carat?
7. Why did you choose Carat (instead of some other energy saving app)?
8. How well do you understand how Carat works?
9. Are you interested in knowing how Carat works?
10. What is the main reason for opening the Carat app?
11. Which of the following things do you do most times when you open Carat?
12. How often do you kill or restart an app when Carat suggests it?
13. What are the reasons why you don't kill an app when Carat suggests it?
14. How often have you opened Carat during the past month?
15. In what kind of situation do you usually open Carat?
16. In what ways has using Carat changed the way you use your device?

### *Response Statistics*

A total of 1,140 valid responses were received from dozens of countries covering many of the regions with Carat users. Among the respondents 16% had been using Carat for over a year, while 40% had been using Carat for less than three months. Most of the respondents (93%) had been using Carat on their mobile devices while few of them had been using Carat on tablet devices. Around 26% of the respondents had been using Carat on more than one mobile device. 89% of the respondents were male, and the average age of respondents was 37 years. We are aware of the limitations of self-reporting, and we discuss them in the Limitations section.

[1]`http://carat.cs.berkeley.edu/chi/Carat-usage.html`

| Samples | Reports |
|---|---|
| user id | average battery life (h) |
| date and time | hogs, the date they were found |
| battery level | bugs, the date they were found |
| running applications | list of applications the user has run |

**Table 1. Contents of Carat logs.**

### Carat Logs

In addition to the survey responses we also used automatically gathered Carat usage logs like Carat *samples* and *reports* of the users who answered the survey. The Carat application sends data to the servers in the form of samples. Each sample contains information about application use and battery life. After enough samples have been collected, Carat generates reports about users and applications. These reports are not available on the mobile client. These include details about the user's average battery life, the most battery-consuming applications that have been running on their device (hogs), and any applications that use more energy on their device than in the rest of the community (bugs). In this research we used these samples and reports to quantify user behavior. The contents of the two types of data used in this paper are detailed in Table 1. The logs give us important information, such as when a problematic application was reported to the user by Carat, and how that changed the behavior of the user in terms of running that application.

## RESULTS

This section discusses the responses of the questionnaire and results of Carat log data analysis. To quantify differences and correlations in our results, we use two statistical tests. When comparing beginners and advanced users, we apply the Mann-Whitney U test; when discussing correlation, we use Kendall's tau ($\tau$).

### Beginners and Advanced Users

Prior work shows that there is a positive correlation between duration of Carat use and battery life [15]. In this paper we examine what are the reasons for this, and what features of Carat and user behaviors cause this positive correlation.

We found a significant positive correlation between the responses to *"How long have you been using Carat?"* and *"How well do you understand how Carat works?"* (seven-point Likert Scale where 1 = not at all, 7 = very well), $r_\tau(N = 1,140) = .13, p < .001$. There was also a significant positive correlation between the responses *"How long have you been using Carat?"* and *"On how many devices do you use Carat?"*, $r_\tau(N = 1,140) = .26, p < .001$. These results suggest that long-time Carat users believe that they

| Definition of beginner | $U(Z)$ | p | $r$ |
|---|---|---|---|
| $<$ 1 month | 81,027(-4.324) | $p < .01$ | -.128 |
| $<$ 3 months | 132,180(-4.396) | $p < .01$ | -.130 |
| $<$ 6 months | 136,352(-3.688) | $p < .01$ | -.109 |
| $<$ 1 year | 71,478(-4.150) | $p < .01$ | -.123 |

**Table 2. Results of Mann-Whitney U test conducted among the two groups of Carat users (classified as beginners according to the given definition) on how well they understand how Carat works. Each classification scheme defines advanced users as those who have used longer than beginners.**

| Group Characteristics | Advanced Users | Beginners |
|---|---|---|
| Number of Respondents | 689 | 451 |
| Duration of Carat Use | >90 days | <90 days |
| Gender | male = 620<br>female = 58<br>other = 11 | male = 389<br>female = 60<br>other = 2 |
| Mean age in years | 38 | 36 |

**Table 3. Primary characteristics of the two groups of Carat users.**

better understand how Carat works and have it installed on many devices.

We compared the responses to the question *"How long have you been using Carat?"* with the length of Carat usage logs from the device that was used to answer the questionnaire. The two are significantly correlated ($r_\tau(N = 1,072) = .357, p < .001$. The Carat logs underestimate actual duration of use because re-installation of the application or migration to a new device is recorded as a new user. The true correlation is therefore likely to be higher. In light of this limitation in the Carat log data, we use the questionnaire responses as a proxy for how long the respondents have used Carat.

Behavioral studies conducted with users of energy awareness applications have found that habits formed over three months are likely to stick with users [5]. We analyzed the survey responses to investigate the validity of this finding in the context of mobile battery awareness applications. First, we classified the respondents as beginners and advanced users by using each of the five options we gave them in the questionnaire (Less than a month, 1-3 months, 3-6 months, 6-12 months, and over year) as the threshold value. Next, for each classification we separately conducted a Mann-Whitney U test on how well they believe they understand how Carat works. A summary of the results is given in Table 2. According to the results, all the four classification schemes result in a significant difference between beginners and advanced users ($p < .01$). However, when we classify those who have been using Carat for less than three months as beginners, the relationship between the duration of use of Carat and how well they believe they understand it is stronger than in others ($r = -.130$). Based on these results and the importance of the three-month milestone in previous work [5], we use that as the classification threshold in this paper. Table 3 summarises the characteristics of these two groups.

### Why Users Open Carat

In the survey, we asked the respondents to select from a list of options the main reason for opening Carat. We provided

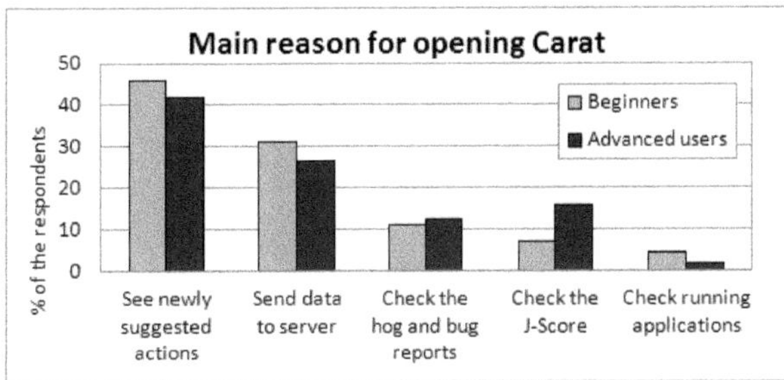


**Figure 3. The main reason for opening Carat.**

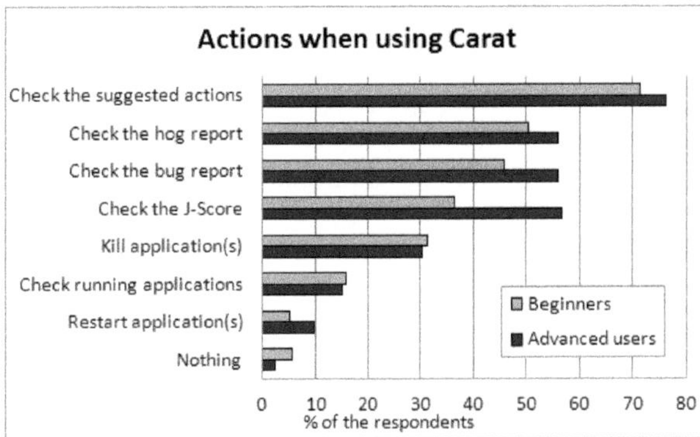


**Figure 4. The actions performed when Carat is open.**

the primary features of Carat as the options: send data to server, see newly suggested actions (kill or restart an application), check the reports (bugs and hogs), check the J-Score, and check running applications. Figure 3 summarizes the responses.

The majority of respondents (44%) mainly open Carat to see if any actions are suggested for them, and according to Figure 3 it is clear that nearly a similar proportion of beginners and advanced users have selected this reason. Group-wise analysis shows that for both beginners and advanced users, sending data to the server is the second-most-popular reason (27% of all the respondents selected this). Advanced users (16%) were more interested in checking the J-score than beginners (7%). The respondents were also asked which actions they perform most times when they open Carat (Figure 4). 71% of the beginners and 76% of the advanced users mentioned that they check the suggested actions. About half of all the users check the hog and bug reports, advanced users slightly more often than the beginners. The majority (57%) of the advanced users check the J-Score, but only 36% of the beginners are interested in it. A bit less than a third of the users kill applications most times they open Carat. The running applications are checked by 15% of the users, and applications are restarted by less than 10% of the users. Some users stated that they do nothing most of the time when they open Carat. The percentage of these users is higher among beginners (5.5% compared to 2.5% in the advanced users' group), probably because Carat does not give results to the user during the first week after installing Carat, so there is not much to do at that point.

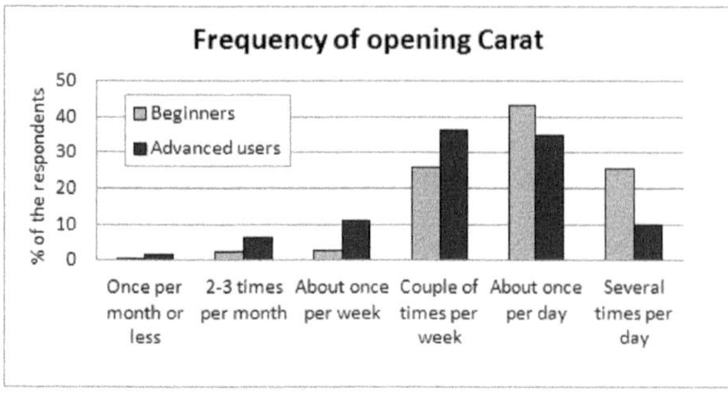


Figure 5. Summary of responses to the survey question "How often have you opened Carat during the past month".

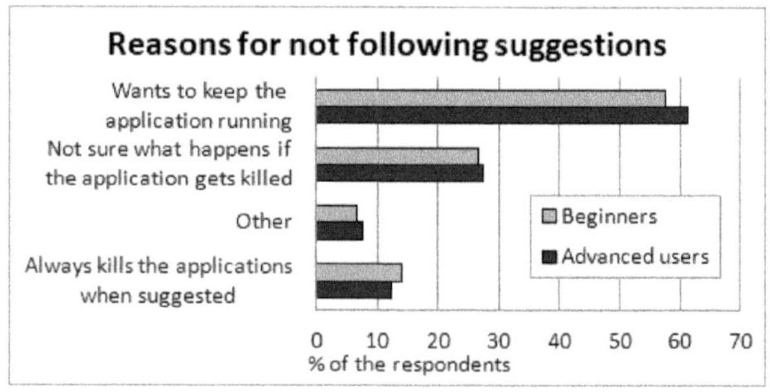


Figure 6. The reasons why users ignore suggestions to kill applications.

The primary reason for opening Carat and the most common actions performed after opening Carat do not vary much across beginners and advanced users. However, features like J-Score are more popular among advanced users. Based on these findings, we suggest that advanced users enjoy functions that support comparing against others in the Carat community.

### How Often Users Open Carat

We asked the respondents to rate how often they have opened Carat during the past month. Beginners open Carat significantly more frequently than the advanced users. Figure 5 summarizes the responses to this question.

Beginners and advanced Carat users differ in their responses to the question *"How often have you opened Carat during the past month?"* (Figure 5 contains the options), ($U = 107,132, p < .001, r = .28$). Advanced Carat users had an average rank of 500 (Mdn = 4, SD = 1.08), while beginners had an average rank of 677 (Mdn = 5, SD =.95 ).

We infer that the suggestions provided by Carat are more useful to the beginners, and over time users learn to manage their battery without repeatedly checking Carat. These findings further suggest that the Carat use behavior changes over time, and the user's knowledge about how to improve battery life also grows with use of Carat.

### Who Follows Suggestions and What They Gain

We asked the respondents to rate how often they kill or restart an application when Carat suggests it (seven-point Likert Scale where 1 = never and 7 = always). Most respondents follow application kill or restart suggestions (mean = 4.39) and beginners and advanced users follow Carat suggestions equally often. However, the users who claim to understand better how Carat works, charge their devices less often and follow Carat suggestions more often.

The difference between beginners (Mdn = 4, SD = 1.91) and advanced Carat users (Mdn = 5, SD = 1.76) on how often they follow Carat suggestions was not significant ($U = 155,203, p = .975, r = .0009$), suggesting that the two groups are similar in how often they kill or restart an application that Carat suggests.

There was a significant negative correlation between the responses to the questions "How well do you understand how Carat works?" and "How often do you charge the battery" ($r_\tau(N = 1,140) = -.084, p < .01$). Further, we also found a significant positive correlation between how often users kill or restart an application that Carat suggests, and how well user believe that they understand how Carat works ($r_\tau(N = 1,140) = .071, p < .01$). This suggests that even though the duration of use of Carat does not affect how often users follow Carat suggestions, how well the user understands how Carat works has an effect.

Statistical comparison between beginners and advanced Carat users on the percentage of battery life improvement (collected from Carat logs) after using Carat was significant ($U = 15,200, p < .05, r = -.102$). Advanced Carat users had an average rank of 227 (Mdn = .011, SD = 10.2), while beginners had an average rank of 196 (Mdn = -.53, SD = 10.1). In agreement with prior work [15], we found that duration of use correlates positively with battery life improvement.

All these results suggest that Carat fosters learning, and as a result of that users learn to manage their battery better with long-term use. This encourages the users to stick with Carat. We conclude that energy awareness applications should make the logic behind their suggestions understandable to the users in order to support learning, and encourage them to follow the suggestions and use the application for long.

### Why Users Ignore Suggestions

The users of energy awareness applications do not always follow the suggestions provided to them. In order to find why Carat users sometimes ignore the suggestions, we asked the respondents to select from a list of options all the reasons for not killing an application suggested by Carat. The options were: I want to keep it running, I'm not sure what happens if I kill it, I always kill the application when suggested, and a free text field to provide other options. Figure 6 provides a summary of responses. The main reason for ignoring the suggestions to kill applications is that the user wants to keep that application running (58% of the beginners and 61% of the advanced users) regardless of its high power consumption. Some of the respondents provided further justifications for this option in the free text field. According to them, one of the most common reasons that eight beginners and 18 advanced users stated was that some applications cannot be killed. Thirteen advanced users and two beginners stated that they check the estimated battery improvement provided by Carat, and if it's too low they do not kill the suggested application. Seven

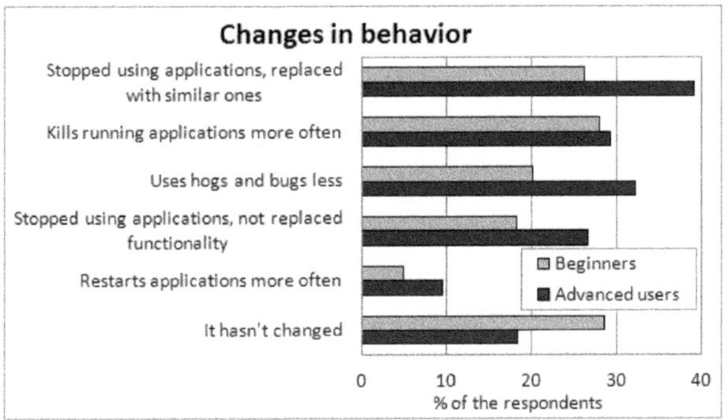


**Figure 7. Summary of responses to the survey question "In what ways using Carat has changed the way you use your device?".**

advanced users and one beginner mentioned that sometimes Carat suggests to kill system applications. Eight beginners also stated that they have heard that killing applications in Android is bad.

We conclude that suggestions to kill system applications and regularly used applications are not very useful to the user. However, the estimated battery life improvement number provides additional information for the user to decide whether to kill an application or not.

### How Carat Changes Device Use

To understand how Carat has influenced the mobile device use behavior, we asked the respondents to select all the relevant options from a list of user behavior changes that we expected Carat to cause. Responses revealed that Carat has caused behavioral changes especially in advanced Carat users. Figure 7 provides a graphical illustration of the list of given options and the percentage of users selected each option.

Carat did not affect the mobile device use behavior of 29% of the beginners. However, 39% of advanced users agreed that Carat has made them stop using some applications and replace them with similar ones. The second most common change that Carat has caused in 28% of beginners and 29% of advanced users is killing running applications more often. Advanced Carat users agreed on all the behavioral changes more than the beginners.

These results suggest that Carat has a bigger impact on the mobile device use behavior of advanced users, and it takes time for new users to adapt these new habits. This further explains why initial performance analysis indicated that the battery life of Carat users improves gradually over time [15].

### Who Kills Bugs, Hogs, and Other Applications

From the Carat logs, we learned that beginners reduced the use of 64.3% of their hogs and bugs on average when they were first reported. All hogs were reduced by 36.5% and bugs by 23% on average. Advanced users reduced the use of 67.2% of their hogs and bugs, hogs by 46% and bugs by 30%. Table 4 shows these reduction ratios.

Furthermore, we compared how much beginners and advanced Carat users reduce the use of hogs and bugs. The difference for hogs was significant ($U = 58,369, p < .001, r = .17$). Advanced Carat users had an average rank of 427 (Mdn = 45, SD = 23) while beginners had an average rank of 345 (Mdn = 36, SD = 25). These results indicate that advanced users reduce the use of hogs significantly more than the beginners. This can be one of the reasons why advanced users improve battery life better than the beginners. However, the test for bugs was not significant $U = 12,995, p = .189, r = .07$, indicating that both the beginners (Mdn = 27 , SD = 38) and advanced users (Mdn = 33, SD = 39) have equally reduced the use of bugs. We also calculated the reduction in use of other applications that have not been reported as hogs or bugs. Here we considered actions, such as starting to use new applications, abandoning old ones, and killing applications for battery saving. Beginners have reduced use of these other applications by 11.51% and advanced users by 24.14%. Since the percentage of reduction in use of other applications was normally distributed, we conducted an independent T-test on this data and found that the advanced users (M=17.9%, SD=1.99) have reduced the use of other applications significantly more than the beginners (M=5.81%, SD=1.86); $t(851)=-8.88$, $p < .001$. These results along with our previous findings that show that advanced users open Carat less often, yet have better battery life suggest that advanced users have learned to better manage their battery with less help from Carat. Given below is how bugs, hogs, and other application reduction percentages are calculated.

#### *Calculation of Application Use Reductions*

We examined the Carat samples and the Carat log reports of the survey respondents. For each user, we obtained the total number of samples $u_t$ they reported to Carat. For the first hog or bug report of each application $z$ for each user $u$, we split $u_t$ into the samples before the report $u_b$ and after $u_a$. We took the subset of samples that contained $z$, before $z_{ub}$ and after $z_{ua}$ the report. Finally, we only considered the samples before the report from the point that $z$ was first run $t_{uz1}$ by $u$ to avoid diluting the ratio: $u_{z1} = u_b|\text{time} >= t_{uz1}$. Then we compared the ratio of running the application before the report, to after it, and obtained the reduction ratio $r$:

$$r = 1 - \frac{z_{ua}/u_a}{z_{ub}/u_{z1}}. \tag{1}$$

Note that if the user increased the ratio of running the application, then $r < 0$. We then calculated the averages of decreasing application use for all $u$ in each category, and all $z$ for all the reports that we had obtained from Carat:

$$a = \frac{\sum_u^n \sum_z^m r}{n \times m}. \tag{2}$$

### The Respondents' Comments on Carat

We asked the respondents to comment on what they specifically like about Carat, and provide suggestions for improvement. This was an optional part of the survey. Hence only 20.6% of the respondents provided comments. The advanced

| Category | % of Hogs/Bugs affected | Hog % reduced | Bug % reduced |
|---|---|---|---|
| Beginners | 64.3 | 36.50 | 23.48 |
| Advanced users | 67.2 | 46.35 | 30.12 |

**Table 4. The percentage of Hogs/Bugs that the users reduced the use of, and the reduction percentages, the first time a user gets a report on them.**

users provided more suggestions for improvement than beginners, which is natural since they have more experience with Carat.

### *Most Liked Features of Carat*

We received comments about preferable features of Carat from 6.4% of the beginners and 8.6% of the advanced users. Most of the comments were not addressing any specific features, but rather stating general interest in Carat.

The hog and bug reports were positively acknowledged by 12 beginners and 13 advanced users in their comments: *"I really like how [Carat] tells you about buggy [applications] and [...] hogs."*

23 advanced users stated that they like the J-Score the most: *"The J-Score is a great way for comparing battery life with other devices."* However, only four beginners expressed their interest in J-Score. This is in line with our previous findings about the advanced users being more interested in the J-Score.

14 advanced users and 7 beginners admired non-functional features of Carat, such as reliability, usability, and low battery consumption: *"[Carat] just works without being a hog itself."*, *"[Carat] works very well and is very simple to use."* Respondents also mentioned using Carat because it does not kill applications by itself but gives control to the user.

Another feature that was mentioned in many comments was the actions tab, and the fact that other applications can be killed directly through Carat. This also gave users information about applications that restart right after killing them: *"I have found it useful to see which [applications] [...] are constantly restarted by built-in [...] software."*

### *Suggestions for Improvement*

8.5% of the beginners and 18% of the advanced users made suggestions for improvement. Figure 8 provides a summary of these suggestions. Many of the suggestions were about additional features such as automatic collection of samples, but a significant number of respondents also requested more information about current features. 27 advanced users and five beginners suggested that Carat should send samples automatically or show periodic reminders to open Carat often enough. We also received comments requesting more information about hogs and bugs. Among them we identified three types of problems concerning the actions suggested by Carat: insufficient information about applications reported as hogs/bugs, system applications are suggested for killing, and no solution for applications that reopen immediately after killing. Three beginners and 17 advanced users stated that they would like to have more information about applications that are suggested to be killed, such as what it does, and suggestions for substitute applications. 12 advanced users stated that Carat is

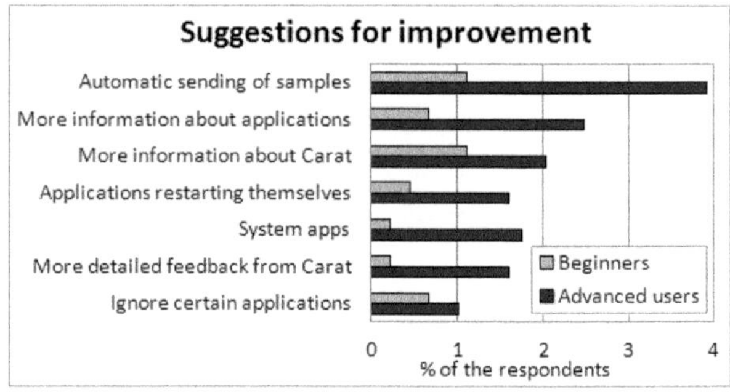


**Figure 8. Types of suggestions for improvement**

suggesting them to kill system applications: *"[...] sometimes [the applications suggested for killing] seem like system [applications] or important services."*. Respondents also stated that they would like Carat to detect applications that reopen immediately after killing, and make alternative suggestions for them. Furthermore, seven advanced users and three beginners stated that sometimes Carat suggests them to kill applications that they use regularly. They prefer a way to hide hogs and bugs that they want to use: *"Having a way to ignore some [applications] would be great."*

Five beginners and 14 advanced users commented that they need more information about how Carat works. Beginners stated more directly that they do not understand how Carat works. However, advanced users stated that they misinterpreted some features of Carat, or the feature that the user needed more information about was often specified: *"[I] wish I understood what expected improvement means."*

## LIMITATIONS

The limitations of self-reporting are well-known. Since the survey respondents were a group of self-opted volunteers among all Carat users, this group might be more interested in features of Carat than the other users. In addition, subjects may, intentionally or not, provide inaccurate or imprecise responses. To address this, we combined Carat log data with user-reported data where possible. However, some aspects cannot be corroborated with Carat log data, such as gender and understanding how Carat works. Since the majority of the respondents were male (89%) the results may not generalize so well to female users and we have no ability to compensate for potential gender biases or incorrect user beliefs on their understanding of how Carat works. For the purpose of our discussion we assume that the gender of respondents is not correlated with the features of interest such as how much their battery life improved.

There could be other external factors such as users' long term experience with smart phones that could have influenced the battery management skills of users. However, we assume the duration of Carat use is the dominant factor, because previous Carat studies showed that not only does user battery life improve over time, but that this improvement is much stronger for users who receive suggestions from Carat compared with those who do not [15], and also literature [5] suggests that the users form habits with long-term use of energy awareness applications.

Our results track groups, not individual users, and their behavior. In future work, we will conduct longitudinal studies with Carat users and analyze their behavior in more detail.

## DISCUSSION AND CONCLUSIONS

We discovered features of Carat that influence user behavior and how behavior changes with long-term use of the application. The findings deepen our knowledge on how to improve community-based battery awareness applications to better support both new and long-term users.

We conducted a survey with existing users of the application, and analyzed their interaction logs from Carat. With the help of these quantitative and qualitative data, we compared the behavior of two types of users, beginners and advanced, to better understand why the latter group enjoys a greater improvement to battery life. Our results revealed that advanced users open Carat less frequently than beginners. However, Carat has considerably changed the mobile device use behavior of advanced users. They have stopped using some applications and replaced them with alternatives, have gained better battery life, charge their devices less frequently, kill reported hogs and bugs more often, and have learned to better manage their battery without the help of Carat. These findings suggest that Carat has changed user behavior while helping users learn to identify applications that drain the battery quickly. Building on these observations, we propose a set of guidelines applicable to the design of battery-awareness applications.

### First Guideline: Show Your Work

Carat has succeeded in changing behavior by combining crowdsourcing with explicit instructions that are missing in many similar battery awareness applications [8, 16]. Carat provides explicit information about which applications are draining the battery abnormally quickly through its action list, and the bug and hog reports help the user understand how these applications are affecting the broader community. These are primary features of Carat that enhance user knowledge. Furthermore, information about expected battery life improvement helps users learn how killing an application actually affects the battery life. Our findings indicate that advanced users get into the habit of checking expected battery life improvement before killing applications, and that such features foster learning about mobile battery life and application behavior. In household energy awareness systems, it was recommended to provide feedback to support learning [5]. Our results also suggest that users are not interested in blindly following instructions, but seem to follow Carat suggestions more often when they understand how it works. This understanding helps the user trust the recommendations and possibly learn enough to make similar diagnoses on their own in the future. According to these findings we propose our first guideline: *Expose to the user not just recommendations, but also the reasoning or data behind them.*

### Second Guideline: Retain Long-Term Users

If the goal of battery awareness applications is to improve users' knowledge of the device and increase battery life, then prolonged use should result in increasingly better battery life. In Carat, this effect is amplified by increasingly accurate recommendations as Carat learns more about the user's device. However, our findings also suggest that there is a tendency for long-term users to leave Carat once they have learned to manage their battery without the help of the application. Tailoring features for different types of users has been a challenge in domestic energy awareness research [1, 3]. Community-based mobile battery awareness systems that learn from their users should also be tailored to retain long-term users. The J-Score feature in Carat tries to achieve this retention through community engagement. Advanced Carat users are more interested in the J-Score, and the competitive environment it creates. According to these results, we propose our second guideline: *Tailor community-based battery awareness applications to retain long-term users.*

### Third Guideline: Give Clear, Action-Oriented Instructions

Providing effective feedback on resource consumption is a key challenge in household energy awareness systems [24]. It is important to give feedback in way that is easy for users to grasp; the instructions should be unambiguous and action-oriented. As shown in Figure 4, the most popular feature of Carat was the "actions" tab. These suggested actions were more popular than the hogs or bugs, even though they simply tell users to "kill" or restart running applications on the hogs and bugs lists. However, in our study we found that the term "killing" an application was misinterpreted by some users, since they feared that killing would result in data loss. The term was chosen to represent permanently closing an application and keeping it closed. Unfortunately, some applications automatically restart when killed, for example Facebook on Android restarts unless "Force Closed" through the Application Manager. Based on these findings we propose our third guideline: *Take into account the audience when formulating feedback to convey precisely what is intended. Provide the user with clear, action-oriented instructions for improving battery life.*

### Fourth Guideline: Distinguish System Components

System components pose a problem for Carat, as they are sometimes difficult to distinguish from third-party applications and require different treatment with respect to kill/restart recommendations. Carat maintains a list of system applications in order to mitigate this problem. However, with new versions of mobile operating systems and custom Android versions, maintaining an up-to-date list is a difficult task. Android provides a flag that indicates whether an application is part of the pre-installed image on a device, yet many service providers include applications that can be safely killed such as Facebook and Twitter in the pre-installed applications. This problem can be addressed through crowdsourcing by allowing users to flag suspected system applications. We propose our fourth guideline based on this example: *Distinguish system components from third-party applications when making diagnoses and recommendations.*

The findings presented in this paper provide suggestions for the improvement of mobile battery awareness applications. The guidelines above target community-based mobile battery awareness applications. Single-device applications can take advantage of all but the second guideline.

## REFERENCES


1. Abrahamse, W., Steg, L., Vlek, C., and Rothengatter, T. The effect of tailored information, goal setting, and tailored feedback on household energy use, energy-related behaviors, and behavioral antecedents. *J. Environmental Psych. 27*, 4 (2007), 265–276.
2. Banerjee, N., Rahmati, A., Corner, M. D., Rollins, S., and Zhong, L. Users and batteries: Interactions and adaptive energy management in mobile systems. In *Proc. UbiComp 2007*. Springer, 2007, 217–234.
3. Chetty, M., Tran, D., and Grinter, R. E. Getting to green: understanding resource consumption in the home. In *Proc. UbiComp*, ACM (2008), 242–251.
4. Creus, G., and Kuulusa, M. Optimizing mobile software with built-in power profiling. In *Proc. Mobile Phone Programming*, F. Fitzek and F. Reichert, Eds. Springer Netherlands, 2007, 449–462.
5. Darby, S. The effectiveness of feedback on energy consumption. *A Review for DEFRA of the Literature on Metering, Billing and direct Displays 486* (2006), 1–21.
6. Datta, S. K., Bonnet, C., and Nikaein, N. Minimizing energy expenditure in smart devices. In *Proc. ICT*, IEEE (2013), 712–717.
7. Ferreira, D., Dey, A. K., and Kostakos, V. Understanding human-smartphone concerns: a study of battery life. In *Proc. Pervasive Computing*. Springer, 2011, 19–33.
8. Ferreira, D., Ferreira, E., Goncalves, J., Kostakos, V., and Dey, A. K. Revisiting human-battery interaction with an interactive battery interface. In *Proc. UbiComp*, ACM (2013).
9. Froehlich, J., Findlater, L., and Landay, J. The design of eco-feedback technology. In *Proc. CHI*, ACM (2010), 1999–2008.
10. Gamberini, L., Spagnolli, A., Corradi, N., Jacucci, G., Tusa, G., Mikkola, T., Zamboni, L., and Hoggan, E. Tailoring feedback to users actions in a persuasive game for household electricity conservation. In *Persuasive Technology. Design for Health and Safety*. Springer, 2012, 100–111.
11. Henryson, J., Håkansson, T., and Pyrko, J. Energy efficiency in buildings through information–swedish perspective. *J. Energy Policy 28*, 3 (2000), 169–180.
12. Liu, X., Shenoy, P., and Corner, M. Chameleon: application level power management with performance isolation. In *Proc. Intl. Conf. on Multimedia*, ACM (2005), 839–848.
13. Midden, C. J., Meter, J. F., Weenig, M. H., and Zieverink, H. J. Using feedback, reinforcement and information to reduce energy consumption in households: A field-experiment. *J. Econ. Psych. 3*, 1 (1983), 65–86.
14. Oliner, A., Iyer, A., Lagerspetz, E., Tarkoma, S., and Stoica, I. Collaborative energy debugging for mobile devices. *Proc. USENIX HotDep* (2012).
15. Oliner, A. J., Iyer, A. P., Stoica, I., Lagerspetz, E., and Tarkoma, S. Carat: Collaborative energy diagnosis for mobile devices. In *Proc. SenSys* (2013).
16. Pathak, A., Hu, Y. C., and Zhang, M. Where is the energy spent inside my app?: fine grained energy accounting on smartphones with eprof. In *Proc. European Conf. on Computer Systems*, ACM (2012), 29–42.
17. Pierce, J., Fan, C., Lomas, D., Marcu, G., and Paulos, E. Some consideration on the (in) effectiveness of residential energy feedback systems. In *Proc. DIS*, ACM (2010), 244–247.
18. Pierce, J., and Paulos, E. Beyond energy monitors: interaction, energy, and emerging energy systems. In *Proc. CHI*, ACM (2012), 665–674.
19. Pierce, J., Schiano, D. J., and Paulos, E. Home, habits, and energy: examining domestic interactions and energy consumption. In *Proc. CHI*, ACM (2010), 1985–1994.
20. Rahmati, A., Qian, A., and Zhong, L. Understanding human-battery interaction on mobile phones. In *Proc. MobileHCI*, ACM (2007), 265–272.
21. Rahmati, A., Tossell, C., Shepard, C., Kortum, P., and Zhong, L. Exploring iphone usage: The influence of socioeconomic differences on smartphone adoption, usage and usability. In *Proc. MobileHCI*, ACM (2012), 11–20.
22. Rahmati, A., and Zhong, L. Human–battery interaction on mobile phones. *J. Pervasive and Mobile Comp. 5*, 5 (2009), 465–477.
23. Riche, Y., Dodge, J., and Metoyer, R. A. Studying always-on electricity feedback in the home. In *Proc. CHI*, ACM (2010), 1995–1998.
24. Rodgers, J., and Bartram, L. Exploring ambient and artistic visualization for residential energy use feedback. *J. IEEE Trans. Visualization and Comp. Graphics 17*, 12 (2011), 2489–2497.
25. Zhang, L., Tiwana, B., Qian, Z., Wang, Z., Dick, R. P., Mao, Z. M., and Yang, L. Accurate online power estimation and automatic battery behavior based power model generation for smartphones. In *Proc. Int. Conf. on Hardware/Software Codesign and System Synthesis*, ACM (2010), 105–114.

# EnergyBugs: Energy Harvesting Wearables for Children

**Kimiko Ryokai**
UC Berkeley
kimiko@berkeley.edu

**Peiqi Su**
NYU ITP
ps2409@nyu.edu

**Eungchan Kim**
UC Berkeley
chan@ischool.berkeley.edu

**Bob Rollins**
Park Day School
bob.rollins@parkdayschool.org

**ABSTRACT**

EnergyBugs are energy harvesting wearables with features that invite children to move their bodies to generate tiny, yet usable amounts of electricity. EnergyBugs not only convert children's kinetic energy into usable electrical energy, but also let children power a specially designed LED lamp with the energy the children have personally harvested. EnergyBugs therefore turn the electrical energy into a tangible object that children can manipulate and think with. Two studies of EnergyBugs with 34 elementary school children have revealed that children carefully observed and negotiated the use of personally harvested energy with their classmates, as well as developed emotional connections to energy. In particular, moving their own bodies to generate energy led the children to more actively ask questions about energy from new perspectives. We report our iterative design process and discuss the implications of our results for HCI.

**Author Keywords**

Energy harvesting; children; wearable; kinetic energy; human-powered microgeneration; tangible UIs.

**ACM Classification Keywords**

H.5.m. Information interfaces and presentation.

## INTRODUCTION

Sustainability and energy-conscious technologies are growing topics for HCI research. The field is concerned with the design and evaluation of systems that enable people to be more aware of their daily energy consumption habits in a variety of contexts, from personal home [e.g., 29] to workplace [e.g., 12] to public [e.g., 18], as well as how such feedback systems may lead to behavioral changes to conserve energy [e.g., 4,5]. HCI research involving energy is also explored in a variety of scales from an individual [e.g., 20], to household [e.g., 21], to city [e.g., 9].

Within this growing research area in HCI, we focus on technologies that invite people to interact with *tiny energy* (up to 3mJ per second), which can be generated by the motions of a human body. Such "human-power microgeneration" [25] produces enough energy to light up an LED for a short period of time (as with a hand cranked flashlight), but cannot power products such as a laptop. With microgeneration, the focus of interaction shifts from how


*CHI 2014,* April 26–May 1, 2014, Toronto, Ontario, Canada.
ACM 978-1-4503-2473-1/14/04.
http://dx.doi.org/10.1145/2556288.2557225

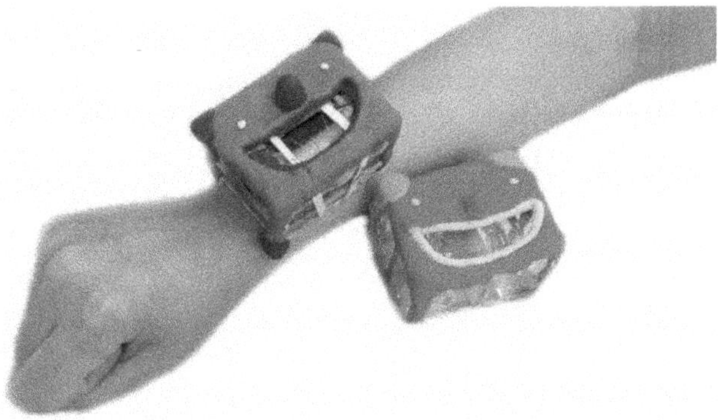

**Figure 1. EnergyBugs' energy harvesting Bugs.**

much energy we *use*, to *how much energy* we can *produce* with our body. It also shifts how people understand energy from something that simply arrives from some distant source and reliably flows from the wall outlet, to something that could be "handmade" [25,24] and stored in a container. With such a shift in perspective, one may begin to (re)consider the value of energy and how one relates to energy. In particular, we see *educational* potential for engagement with microgeneration as children actively participate in the generation of their own energy and interpret their activities.

We introduce *EnergyBugs*, an experimental system consisting of a set of wearable energy-generating devices and a specially designed lamp that demonstrates how tiny, yet usable energy can be harvested from physical motion. The EnergyBugs system combines both tactile and visual engagements. Visually, the system demonstrates the energy harvesting process in real-time, and dynamically displays how kinetic energy is turned into electrical power. Through bodily and tactile engagement, we are presenting new ways for children to experience, engage with, and think about energy based on a more direct, physical, and concrete connection to the production of energy. In line with a constructionist approach of learning through construction and manipulation of personally meaningful projects [22,28], the EnergyBugs system turns *energy into tangible representations children can directly manipulate, personally relate to, talk about, and think with.*

We present our iterative design process, evaluations, and discuss implications for HCI.

## BACKGROUND

In response to climate change, pollution, and natural resource depletion, the HCI community has responded with a variety of approaches to address sustainability issues [14]. The majority of HCI research thus far has focused on systems that provide electricity consumption feedback [5,20,11], often intended to persuade users to behave in a more sustainable way [7].

Recent efforts have moved beyond persuasion. Dourish [8] has argued that sustainable HCI's focus on shaping individual choices to reduce energy consumption (electrical or otherwise) can inadvertently rely on guilt around consumption as a (de-)motivating factor. Taking up Dourish's point, we argue that a crucial foundation for sustainable design lies less in prompting guilt than in prompting questions about energy as "an entity within our world, and in understanding how we use it, how we relate to it, and how we live with it" [29].

In order to understand our relationship with energy, Pierce and Paulos [25,24] have argued that we must explicitly define what we mean when we talk about energy. HCI can play an important role in prototyping future energy applications, visualizing invisibles and enabling interaction with intangibles. Yet conceptualizing *what energy means to us in our everyday context* can be difficult because energy is generally invisible and intangible. Pierce and Paulos argued that HCI and interaction design have not significantly and explicitly engaged with energy and materiality. They have suggested a variety of techniques and designs to *materialize* energy, turning energy into a material form so that we can relate to and even develop playful and emotional connections to it [e.g., 13,25,24]. Interaction with energy need not only be about utility, but may also be about critical reflection through objects at hand [1]. Our research builds on such conceptualization of energy as a physically instantiated "thing" [25,24]. Here we apply the concept in the context of children's interaction with energy.

We also draw inspiration from recent research, which suggests that interactions and experiences which require *less* energy can be more pleasurable, enjoyable, and meaningful. For example, Håkansson and Sengers [16] studied families who have voluntarily chosen to "live simple" and found that families were not driven by details about *how much* energy they consume in everyday life, but positively motivated, by being satisfied with what is *enough.*

In particular, Pierce and Paulos' work on "human-power microgeneration" has inspired our research. Pierce and Paulos [25] introduced the term "human-power microgeneration" to designate the microgeneration of electrical energy from human energy sources, with an emphasis on bodily, kinetic energy. Human-powered microgeneration is energy generation at its smallest and most personal scale (up to 75W = 1 human unit of power [25]): electricity that can be generated *by hand.* Through their design explorations, Pierce and Paulos described a variety of human-electricity relations and explored diverse elements of energy consumption as an intentional, embodied entity. However, it is important not to confound human-powered devices as a reliable solution to world-wide energy depletion. For example, Wyche and Murphy [33] illuminated a mismatch between the real-world conditions of developing countries and Western designers' good intentions. Many of the HCI human-powered electricity design explorations are not meant to effectively bridge the electricity gap between the affluent urban energy consumers and that of rural areas. The primary goal of these design explorations is to investigate educational and transformative aspect of human-power microgeneration.

Epistemologically, making energy "by hand" and thinking about the very act, fit well with the constructionist tradition of learning by doing. In the constructionist approach, learning happens when a person is actively engaged in construction of meaningful objects in the real world [23,22,28]. Knowledge is not transmitted, but rather (re)constructed through active involvement. We see human-powered microgeneration as a constructionist educational opportunity. Materializing energy in a tangible form allows children to actively engage in the making process, and think about what they are doing as they do it. Rather than informing children how energy *is* or *should be* used, turning energy into a *manipulable* material invites them to take ownership over the concept through personal, engaged reflection.

### Technologies for Children to Learn about Energy

While the constructionist approach has been applied to many different types of tangible educational tools in HCI [e.g., 28,26,35, just to name a few], applying tangibles to children's interaction with energy within HCI is a relatively new area [e.g., 6,15]. Exceptions are the games by Johansson et al. [17] and Zhang et al. [34]. In both games, children explore different types of energy and energy consumption through their embodied performances tracked by body-worn motion sensors. However, both games are educational simulations; they do not actually harvest kinetic energy from children's physical movement.

Outside of HCI, hands-on museums such as San Francisco's Exploratorium host exhibits that demonstrate kinetic energy interactively. Our work builds on such interactive exhibits, but makes the activities even more personal by creating wearables that can exist in children's personal environments. Our research involves treating actual energy as a personal manipulable. The focus is on creating a tangible artifact for the *quantity* of energy, not just the flow of energy, and not through simulation, but through actual energy generation and use of energy.

### Related Technologies

We have reviewed different types of human motion based energy harvesting technologies. "Parasitic Power Shoes" [30] is a classic example that uses piezoceramic composite material to generate electrical energy "parasitically" while walking. Paradiso and his colleagues have also created a version with a shoe-mounted rotary magnetic generator [19]. Today, we see efforts to turn these research prototypes into commercial products. For example, *SolePower* [31] aims to manufacture waterproof shoe insoles with energy harvesting mechanical links and crank-style generators inside. *ReRev* [27] is a commercial service that retrofits exercise equipment (such as elliptical machines) into electricity generating machines. *Fenix International* [10] sells bicycle attachments for a portable energy generator set designed for use in developing nations. One hour of pedaling generates approximately 45 watt-hours. The Figure 2 compares our technology to other energy harvesting technologies.

In contrast to these commercial products, our contribution is not aimed at efficient energy harvesting technology. Rather, we are designing technology to support energy generation at its smallest and most personal scale, through a small object children can hold in their hands (c.f., Villar & Hodge's Peppermill [32], Badshah et al.'s InGen [2], and Pierce & Paulos' Energy Memento [24]). We ask how such human-powered microgeneration influences the relationship children may have with energy.

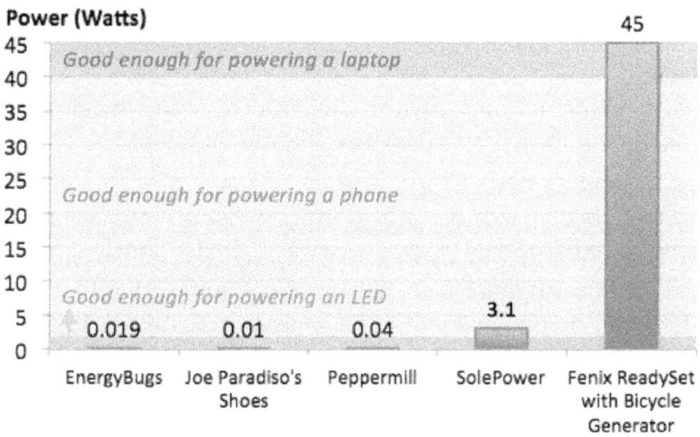


**Figure 2. Graph showing where our technology places in the landscape of other energy harvesting technologies.**

## ENERGYBUGS

We created the *EnergyBugs* system to invite children to directly engage with and to be the creators/generators of personal energy. The goal is to make the interaction with energy 1) *bodily* and *tactile*, 2) *portable* (so that they can take it anywhere) and 3) *visible* (the connection between the bugs and the lamp is made visible as are the energy resources and the energy flow).

The EnergyBugs system has two parts: the energy harvesting "Bugs" and the "Lamp" that can be powered by the harvested energy from the Bugs (Figure 3). The *Bugs* are wireless self-powering units with dual energy generators inside. Each time a Bug is physically shaken, a magnetic cylinder in the Bug moves back and forth causing the outer coil to generate energy. When piezoceramic disks on each end contact the magnetic cylinder, they generate additional energy upon impact. Vigorous shaking results in a fast charge and gentle shaking results in a slow charge. The harvested energy is used to power the Lamp as well as to power the Bug itself. For example, if a child shakes the Bug for one minute, the Bug generates approximately 0.66J, which is enough to power the Lamp for 50 seconds as well as to power the microprocessor inside for 180 seconds. Data regarding how much energy harvested relative to how much the Bug was shaken is also recorded, enabling kids to track how much energy they have collected over time. This analytic data and energy can be transferred when the Bug is connected to the Lamp's base station. We describe the technical implementation further in the following section.

**Figure 3. EnergyBugs system with energy harvesting Bugs, display, and the Lamp.**

The *Lamp* is powered only by energy from one or more EnergyBugs. When the Bugs are connected to the Lamp's base station, the display shows how much energy each Bug has harvested as well as how long the harvested energy can power the Lamp. (Figure 3 & 4) When the energy from the Bug runs out, the Lamp goes dark. The more energy is harvested, the longer the Lamp remains lit. The Lamp also has dimmers, allowing children to vary the levels of brightness. The dimmers demonstrate in real time that a brighter light consumes more electricity. The display also shows the countdown to give children the sense of energy "burn rate." For example, at full brightness, the energy is used at 45mJ/second, while at the mid brightness it is only 11.25mJ/second. The display shows the number of seconds left before the energy is expended.

In our current system, up to 6 Bugs can be plugged into the Lamp simultaneously. When the Bug is shaken while it is plugged into the Lamp, the display shows the harvested energy value in real time. When the Bug is disconnected, the value is stored inside the Bug and shown when it is plugged into the Lamp.

The Bugs are color coded red, green, and blue (RGB). All Bugs function identically, except at the Lamp base station the Lamp illuminates with the Bug's corresponding color (i.e., the red Bug turns the Lamp red). Three dimmers at the base of the Lamp (Figure 3) control the intensity of individual colors in order to mix them.

## Design and Technical Implementation

### *Bugs*

The Bug implements two energy harvesting methods: 1) the electromagnetic method and 2) the piezoelectric method in collecting kinetic energy.

*The Electromagnetic Energy Harvesting Subsystem* of each Bug houses a rare-earth magnet (neodymium magnet) inside a clear acrylic tube in the middle of the box. Each tube has two 1500-turn coils: one is for generating usable energy to power the lamp; the other is to power the whole circuit (Figure 4). One coil with a 5494 surface Gauss neodymium magnet generates approximately 9.5 mW when users shake the bug. This energy, stored in a 0.6 Farah super capacitor, powers the lamp. Stored in a 0.4 Farah super capacitor, it powers the circuit. Customized hardware minimizes both the energy consumption of the circuit and the size of the Bug.

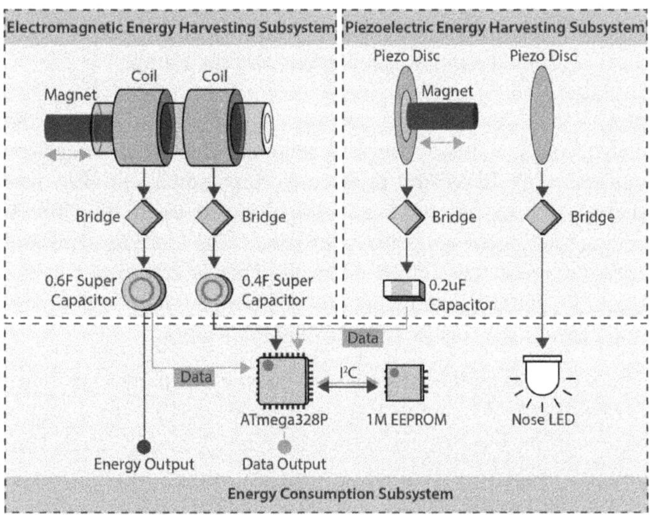


**Figure 4. EnergyBugs' dual energy harvesting system.**

*The Piezoelectric Energy Harvesting Subsystem* contains two piezo discs that serve as sensors. The voltage output of one disc triggers a 10mm white LED (the Bug's "nose"), while the other senses user movement data (Figure 4). As a user shakes a Bug, the magnet first hits one piezo disc to flash the nose LED, then hits the disc on the opposite side to generate a voltage reading which is logged into the EEPROM. The system can then visualize this movement data later.

We designed the box of the Bugs to be transparent so that children can see the inner mechanisms of the generator and other electronics. To make it look friendly, we dressed up one side of the box with a character face. The mouth of the Bug acts as a window enabling children to see the mechanisms inside. A blinking "heart beat" LED, visible through the Bug's transparent body, indicates that the system is on. The Bugs are small and they are wireless so children may run around without any tether. In wireless mode, a modified *GoPro* wristband attaches the Bug to an arm or leg.

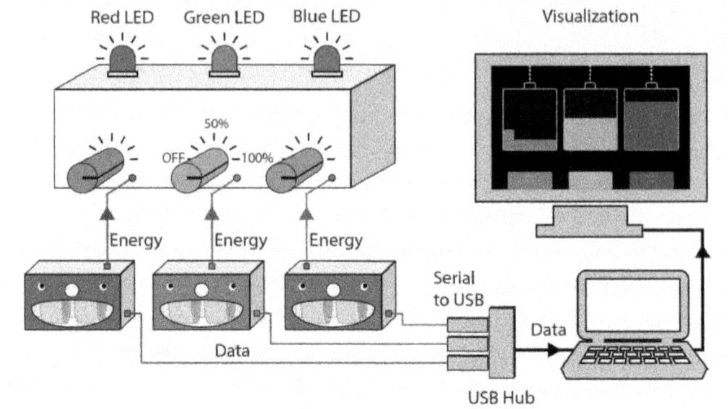


**Figure 5. EnergyBugs system diagram.**

### *Lamp*

RGB color mixing invites children to experiment with consuming the harvested energy at different rates.

The RGB LED's color-mixing system utilizes a 555 oscillator to convert the analog values from the potentiometer to Pulse Width Modulation (PWM) signals, which enables the LED's brightness to change smoothly and uniformly. Bugs can be plugged with a DC power cable into a 1.35mm power jack on the Lamp. After a Bug has been plugged in, a DC converter steps up input voltage from the Bug's 0.6 Farah super capacitors to 3.3 volts, which allows the lamp to work in full voltage input range. The RGB LEDs are housed in a large diffuser (Figure 3).

## Pilot Study with first EnergyBugs prototype

We conducted a pilot study to test our interaction design and the robustness of our system. Our pilot studies took place at two different summer camps in the San Francisco Bay Area. A total of 16 children ages 6-13 participated in the pilot studies (8 children [ages 6-13] at camp A at a public program and another 8 children [ages 6-11] at camp B at a private school). Both groups participated in the pilot study during their regular summer camp hours. The children played in groups of 2-3. In the first 5 minutes, researchers explained the system to the children. In the beginning of the session, the EnergyBugs were connected to the Lamp and display so that researchers could demonstrate how EnergyBugs harvest the energy in real time. After the children explored EnergyBugs for a few minutes, they were then told that their Bugs could be wireless and that their Bugs would still "remember" how much energy had been generated. The children were invited to play as long as they wished.

### *Interaction with the Bugs: Energy Harvesting*

The children spent an equal amount of time working with the Bugs in the wireless mode and the wired mode in front of the Lamp. In wired mode the children could monitor their energy harvesting progress in real time. The children saw each other's progress side by side.

Though we carefully avoided describing the activity as a "game," the side-by-side display of their real time energy production often resulted in the children competing against each other. Upon seeing one's energy level exceeding another's, children exclaimed, "In your face!", "I beat you!", etc. The children also wanted to fill the battery with their energy "all the way up." Some children told their friends, "Whoever gets to the top first is the winner!" Without being told what to do with EnergyBugs, the children defined their own activities, set goals, and challenged each other to competitions.

The children shook the Bugs vigorously, but also experimented with different types of shaking (e.g., fast, slow, strong, soft, different angles, etc.). The tactile feedback of the unit (physically feeling the weight of the heavy magnet move from one side to another) and the sound of the magnet hitting the piezo disks each time, provided acoustic and kinetic feedback.

The children moved around the room with the Bugs first, trying out different moves, positions, and even dances. As soon as the children found out that the Bugs could be unplugged, they wanted to go outside the study room and run around with the Bugs. While in wireless mode, the older children (age 8 and up) worked with the Bugs in a variety of manners. Some of the older children attached the wristband to their legs allowing them to move faster or try different types of movements with their body. The older children also tried different combinations of shaking relative to their body movements. For example, one 10 year old told us "It works better if I shake it this way while I'm running around."

**Figure 6. Children working with EnergyBugs.**

Many children were curious about how the technologies inside the bug worked. The transparent case allowed children to see the mechanisms inside (e.g., the magnet moving inside the coil and the accompanying electronics), prompting many children to ask researchers questions about the technology inside. Many children told us that they liked that the Bug's "heartbeat," indicated the unit was working even during the time it was unplugged.

*Interaction with the Lamp: Energy Consumption*

At the beginning of each session, we showed the children how the Lamp worked, but did not tell them how they should play with the lamp. The children figured out on their own that they could control multiple LEDs at varied brightness simultaneously, and as a result, they could create different colors. We purposely did not tell the children that they had to use up their harvested energy. We also did not tell them that if they ran out of the energy they had to collect more. The children decided independently when they should collect more energy or when they should use their energy. In going through the cycles of harvesting energy and using their energy, the children in all age groups developed a personal attachment to "their" energy. Quite often they were protective of their own energy and unwilling to share it with other students. For example, upon seeing another child trying to use one's energy, a child yelled, "It's *mine*!" and another, "Don't you dare touch mine!" Yet creating different colors other than red, green, and blue meant that they had to share some of their energy and collaborate. Seeing colors other than their own was sometimes sufficient motivation for children to share their energy with others, and rewarded them with the outcome, e.g., "Wow, I like that purple!" For the children, the trial often seemed like a balancing act. They worked hard to get their own energy, but had to negotiate and collaborate with other children for more interesting effects.

*The Mattering of Microgenerated Energies*

The word choice of the children when describing EnergyBugs revealed a sense of care and ownership for the energy created. For example, upon seeing a lamp accidentally left on, children quickly informed each other, "You are *wasting* your energy!" By pointing at the lamp and its display showing decreased energy, some children said, "It's *eating* my energy!" When another child had accidentally turned on their energy, a few children even said, "You wasted *my* energy! I *worked very hard* for that!" The children also showed a sense of accomplishment towards their work and felt protective about the energy as a reflection of their hard work. One child yelled at another child, "Don't touch it! It's *my history*!"

The kind of care the children showed towards their energy and the vocabulary they used in talking about energy were similar to what Pierce and Paulos found in their studies with "Energy Mementos," where energy *mattered* to people because *"they made it themselves"* [24,25].

The quantities of energy children obtained from EnergyBugs were tiny compared to what they could get from a regular battery or wall plug. So why did the energy "matter" and "hold significance" to the children? One explanation is the engagement with human-powered microgeneration: if one has to work hard for energy and get so little energy in return, one may increase one's sense of care and appreciation towards energy.

Another explanation stems from the way EnergyBugs made energy tangible and personal: because individual children were able to hold onto and claim it their own, they cared for it. This required further investigation, and motivated our second study.

## SECOND STUDY

The goal of our second study was to investigate whether or not the type of children's behaviors observed in our first study, i.e., curiosity, care, and empathy towards energy, were due to microgeneration in the EnergyBugs system. In order to empirically study this, we conducted the second study where we manipulated the presence and absence of microgeneration between two groups.

*Age Appropriateness*

In our pilot study we observed that children in a wide age range enjoyed working with our system. However, the children under age 9 seemed too young to grasp the concept that EnergyBugs were producing energy, and not just accumulating points in the battery display. According to the current California State Board of Education Science Content Standards [3], by grade four, children should "know the role of electromagnets in the construction of electric motors, electric generators, and simple devices, such as doorbells and earphones." Therefore, we decided to work with fourth graders in an elementary school in our second study.

### Methods

*Participants*

Eighteen children ages 9-10 participated in the study. All children (12 girls and 6 boys) were enrolled in a fourth grade classroom in a private elementary school. The children were randomly assigned to two groups, using a system that resulted in consistent gender distribution so that each group consisted of 2 girls and 1 boy.

*Materials and Procedure*

We designed a between-subject study wherein the experimental group played with the EnergyBugs and the second group played with a "plug-in" version of EnergyBugs. The "plug-in" Bug was designed to appear exactly like the EnergyBug, but acted like a rechargeable battery. It could be directly plugged into the wall and fully charged within 2 minutes (the nose LED would light up after 2 minutes to indicate the charge status). We concluded that this was an appropriate condition to compare, as many current wireless devices work this way (people do not usually physically exert themselves for energy). Our primary goal was to vary the presence or absence of human-powered microgeneration between the two groups. Otherwise, both groups had the same activity of using their energy to light up the Lamp and mix colors. The difference was that the EnergyBugs group had to work physically hard to acquire the energy while the plug-in group did not.

Prior to the activities, all 18 children received a 20-minute lesson from their usual classroom teacher about different types of energy and energy harvesting techniques such as solar, wind, and water by using everyday examples (e.g., solar powered calculators, water mills, etc.). This lesson provided context for the subsequent activities of both the EnergyBugs (EB) group and the plug-in (PI) group.

Immediately after the 20-minute lesson, all children were asked to fill out a survey about energy. The survey was designed jointly by the research team and the fourth grade teacher (4th author) with reference to the Science Framework for California Public Schools [3]. The questions were designed to probe the children's attitudes towards energy use as well as their curiosity for energy, and were open-ended (rather than yes/no) to elicit maximum input from children. After the survey, the children worked in groups of three with either EnergyBugs or "plug-in" version of EnergyBugs for 30 minutes. The two groups, EB and the PI group, were isolated from each other. After the 30-minute intervention, we repeated the same survey so that we could observe whether or not the intervention influenced the children's attitude towards energy. We ended each of the 6 groups' sessions with a semi-structured interview about their experience working with EnergyBugs. To ensure that the interviews were consistent, we used a script comprised of three questions: "How do you like EnergyBugs?" "What do you not like about EnergyBugs?" and "Outside of school, how might you use EnergyBugs?" During the study, researchers carefully monitored word choice to avoid influencing the children's vocabulary. All the sessions were video recorded so that we could transcribe the children's dialogue and analyze their physical interaction with the system.

### Results

Both the EB and the PI groups spent equal amounts of time engaging with their respective systems. Both groups began in the school's computer lab, and they were free to move around both inside and outside the room. Yet, there were clear differences between the two groups in their physical activity levels during the 30 minutes. As predicted from the pilot study, as soon as the EB group members found out that they could unplug their Bugs, they wanted to go outside and run around. Similar to the pilot testing, the EB groups spent a third to half of their time running around outside.

EnergyBugs being a wearable device seemed to encourage different types of engagements. Physically, the EB group members explored many different ways they were able to generate energy. At the end of each session, the EB group members were breathing hard and covered with sweat.

In contrast, all three PI groups remained inside the computer lab, even though they were free to go anywhere they wanted. They found wall outlets inside the computer lab. They seemed content using them and did not appear to see any point in moving outside the lab. In contrast to the EB groups, the PI groups spent their time patiently waiting for their plug-in Bugs to be ready.

Because of these anticipated activity level differences, we were concerned that the PI group would not enjoy their devices as much as the EB group. However, all three PI groups wanted to continue playing with their Bugs even after the allotted 30 minutes. In the post-study interview, we heard similar reports from children in both PI and EB groups indicated that their activity was "Awesome!", "Cool!", and "Really fun!"

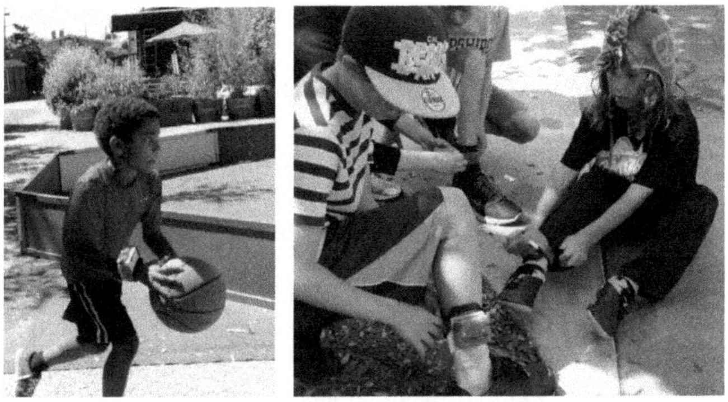

**Figure 7. A child practices basketball while a Bug is attached on his wrist (left). Children attaching Bugs on their legs prior to running (right).**

*Vocabulary for Energy: Mattering of Human-Powered Microgenerated Energies*

From our pilot study, we anticipated that the energy would matter to the children in the EB groups because they personally harvested it from their own physical efforts. But how about the PI groups who did not physically work as hard (relative to the EB groups) to generate their own energy via human microgeneration? Using transcripts, we analyzed how children in each group described energy. We used Pierce and Paulos' framework of "materializing energy" [24], treating energy as a tangible manipulable "thing" that can be 1) *shared*, 2) *activated*, 3) *kept*, and 4) *collected*. For both groups, we tallied the occurrences of keywords within these four categories. Table 1 summarizes the number of occurrences in each group.

The language the children used in both the PI and the EB groups were more similar than we had predicted. The children in both the PI and the EB groups felt strong ownership over their energy. When their classmates tried to use their energy without asking, the children clearly indicated it was unwelcome by yelling, "No!" or "That's mine!" and sometimes physically thrashing their hands. Yet, children in both groups eventually managed to "borrow" others' energy by asking before touching their dimmers.

Children in both the EB and the PI groups used a similar vocabulary for describing how their energy was being used. The occurrence of words such as "wasting," "losing," "going fast," and "emptying" was similar across groups. Both EB and PI groups therefore, in interaction with EnergyBugs system, seemed to perceive and describe energy *use* as a somewhat negative event. Using energy was an event of energy retreating (going negative) as opposed to an event of activation (powering the Lamp). This was interesting because the EnergyBugs visualization, in both the EB and PI groups, showed the Lamp being activated by their energy. We believe the Lamp's numerical indication of energy level going up and down in real time elicited this interpretation.

| | Plug-in Group | EnergyBugs Group |
|---|---|---|
| **Sharing** energy (distributing) | "It's **mine**!" (7)<br>"Could you give me **permission** (to use the energy)?" (3)<br>"Don't even think about it!" (2) | "It's **mine**!" (8)<br>"Can I **borrow** yours?" (5)<br>"**Don't touch**!" (3) |
| **Activating** energy (using/consuming) | "You're **wasting** your energy" (5)<br>"**Using up** all my energy!" (4)<br>"You **lose** it (energy)…" (3)<br>"It **goes away** real fast when it's at 100% (brightness)" (3) | "You've just **wasted** energy!" (4)<br>"I'm **using up** my energy" (5)<br>"I'm **losing** my energy" (4)<br>"**Going away** very fast!" (3) |
| **Keeping** energy (storing/ maintaining) | "I'm **saving** my energy" (5)<br>"**It's at** …" (6)<br>"I'm **going to save** my energy so that when I go back…" (3) | "I'm **saving** my energy" (6)<br>"Mine **is at** 3 and yours is…" (5)<br>"I'm going to **keep** mine at …" (4) |
| **Collecting** energy (generating/ producing) | "Woo! All **done**!" [looking at the charge indicator] (9)<br>"Mine **isn't (done)**" (8)<br>"Let me go **unplug** mine" (5)<br>"Going to **charge** mine" (3) | "**Worked** so hard for this!" (8)<br>"Mine is **growing**!" (8)<br>"OMG you **have so much**!" (7)<br>"**How** do you get so much?" (6)<br>"I'm **making** energy!" (6)<br>"I'm **shaking** it really hard!" (5)<br>"My hard work paid off finally!" (1) |

**Table 1. Occurrences of keywords summarized for the Plug-in group and the EnergyBugs group.**

Both EB and PI groups indicated their wish to save or sustain their energy at certain level (e.g., "I'm *saving* my energy!" "I'm keeping mine at 3.5!"). When they saw their energy level went down, they wanted to fill it up again. Both groups noticed that different levels of brightness produced different energy burn rates. Both groups hesitated equally before using up their energy all at once. Rather, they wanted to carefully control how their energy was being used. Dimmer controls with immediate feedback seemed to invite explicit monitoring of the Bugs' energy level. Both groups also monitored and talked about numerical energy levels relative to their peers, e.g., "I'm at 1.4 and you are at 1.5."

A primary difference between the groups was the manner in which EnergyBugs group members discussed the process of their energy making. The EB group often mentioned physically working hard (e.g., "I'm working so hard!" "I'm sweating!"), and acknowledged others' accomplishments (e.g., "Wow, you've got so much!"). The EB group members also asked each other about techniques for collecting energy (e.g., "How are you getting so much energy?") and showed each other their physical movements. Physical and acoustic rhythm of children's shaking seemed to influence each other. When one of the children sped up their shaking, other children tried to catch up with the faster pace. While they were shaking their Bugs, the EB group children also spontaneously asked researchers questions such as "Can I use this in my room?" "Can I charge an iPad with this?" and sometimes responded to their own questions such as, "Wow, I would have to work very long time for that!"

For the PI group, talk around the energy collecting process was minimal and typically took the form of an announcement of the beginning and/or end of the charging ("I'm going to charge again"). During the 2-minute charging times, they were either quiet or talked amongst themselves about topics unrelated to EnergyBugs (e.g. homework, other friends).

In summary, from the children's language use, energy seemed to *matter* to both groups equally when it comes to *sharing*, *activating*, and *keeping* energy. Both groups interpreted *ownership* of their energy and its use in similar ways. However, microgeneration did engage children in more explicit discussions around energy *collecting* and *making* process and led them to ask more questions about energy production and real-world energy use.

### *Concern for energy use*

Did children's interaction with EnergyBugs influence their attitude towards energy use in general? This question in the pre- and post-test survey aimed to evaluate such general attitudes:

Pretend someone named Micky turned the heat way up in the building on a Friday in the winter. Micky went home and realized that he had forgotten to turn down the heat. He knew that a lot of energy would be used keeping the building very warm all weekend. But he was having a great time playing with his friends and didn't want to go back to school and turn the heat down. Please write a one-sentence note to Micky.

We compared the children's answers before and after the intervention. In the pre-test survey, all children in both groups wrote text indicating that Micky should go back and turn the heat off. This pattern suggests that all of the children in our study were already energy conscious to some degree prior to their exposure to EnergyBugs. In the post-test survey, all children's responses remained the same. They wrote the similar text indicating Micky to go back and turn the heat off. Across groups, their answers did not change before and after the intervention. What was different between the PI and EG groups, however, was that the EB group expanded their answers in the post-test survey. In the EB groups, 4 of the 9 children provided additional reasons for Micky (e.g. "to save *more* energy," "very hard to make energy") in contrast to 1 out of 9 in the PI group.

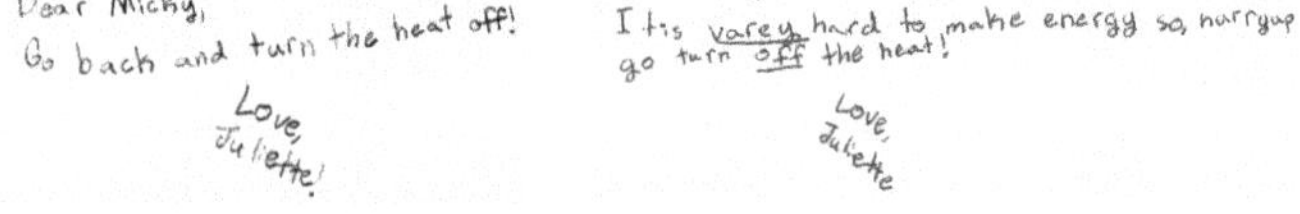


**Figure 8. One child's answer before (left) and after (right) the intervention.**

### *Asking Questions Differently and More Lessons*

We were interested in finding out whether the interaction with EnergyBugs led to increased curiosity towards energy and how things work with energy. In the survey, we asked how much the children wanted to learn about energy:

How many more lessons about energy do you hope we do this year? (0 - 10)

We compared the children's answer before and after the intervention. The average score for both groups were initially similar (average score of 4.1 for the EB group and 4.5 for the PI group). The EB group members, after the intervention, indicated that they would like to have more lessons about energy significantly more than the PI group; $t(16)=2.55$, $p=0.021$. According to our post-test interview, both EB and PI groups equally enjoyed their activities with respective version of EnergyBugs. Then why did the EB group want to have more lessons than the PI group? How the children responded to the following questions in the survey seems to explain this:

An energy expert may come and would want to know what the class would like to learn more about and what the class is wondering. Please write a question for the experts.

We compared what children wrote before and after the intervention. Before the intervention, children from both groups asked about the origin of energy (e.g., "Where does energy come from?"), how is energy made (e.g., "How … ?"), and specific technical questions (e.g., "Can you use solar panel to power an iPod?"). After the intervention, 6 out of 9 children in the EB groups asked different questions (e.g., "Can you *see* electricity? When and who invented electricity?" "How (does) 'moving a lot' make energy?" "How do you (PG&E) make *so much* energy?"). In contrast, 8 out of 9 children in the PI groups repeated exactly the same responses they made previously in the post-test.

Similarly, we asked the following question in the survey:

Our electricity company ("PG&E") has two big coal-burning electricity plants that have to be closed down because they are old. PG&E won't be able to generate enough electricity for all their customers after the two plants are shut down. Please write a suggestion for PG&E.

Before the intervention, about a third of the children in both groups wrote, "I don't know" (4 children in EB group and 3 children in PI). The children in both groups responded that either the plants should be fixed (e.g., "Fix the plants") or resort to other technologies (e.g., "Buy solar panels"). After the intervention, 6 out of 9 children in the EB group changed their response (e.g., "Sell people things they can make their own energy!" [emphasis inserted by the child], "… find out what's wrong!" "… find *other ways* to *create* electricity"). In contrast, as with the previous questions, 8 out of 9 children in the PI group repeated exactly the same responses they made previously in the post-test.

The children's answers to the open-ended questions in the survey suggest that the experience of human-power microgeneration seemed to encourage children to ask questions regarding energy more actively or from a different perspective than they had before.

## Discussion

The results of our study revealed that human-powered microgeneration activities can enhance and increase curiosity in children, can prompt them to more actively ask questions about energy harvesting and energy in general, and can lead children to want to participate in subsequent lessons about energy. Compared to the PI group, the children working with EnergyBugs directly experienced how energy could be harvested through physical activity. Such exposure to novel experiences seemed to engage children to consider why things work the way they work, or question things they may not usually question (e.g., "Can you *see* electricity?" or how would "so much energy" be created by an energy company?). Therefore, microgeneration seems to be an effective way to encourage children's curiosity and learning about forms of energy and their production.

The results of our studies also revealed that all children working with EnergyBugs, whether they physically exerted themselves to generate the energy or not, *cared* for their energy. The way energy *mattered* to the children (i.e., how they related to energy personally by protecting their own energy, and how conscious they were in using their harvested energy) did not seem directly influenced by the experience of human-powered microgeneration.

One possible explanation is that, in a way, both the EB and the PI groups *worked* for their energy. The EB group worked physically harder, but the PI group children also worked for their energy by patiently waiting for their Bugs to be charged each time they wanted energy. The feeling of "*I* made this" seemed to be the same for both groups, even though *how* they made it was different across the two conditions.

Another possible explanation is the representation the EnergyBugs system used to make energy visible and tangible for children. Both EB and PI groups were able to *hold* a physical representation that stood for energy in their hand, connect the Bug to the Lamp and physically control how their energy was used. This made it visible to children, and gave them a concrete way to talk about, play with, and have a personal relationship with energy. One may compare a scenario of a child playing with a regular battery: The child connects a battery to a toy train and the train moves. The battery is a tangible object the child can hold in her hand, but the object does not typically allow her to see the content (quantity of energy) nor allow her to control how the energy flows into the battery and out to the toy. Therefore, the EnergyBug's design to turn energy into a manipulable and tangible form, inviting children to play with and relate to, was a successful way to engage children.

Through our iterative evaluation of EnergyBugs with children, we were able to tease out some important aspects of human-powered microgeneration and how it might influence the way children interact with and think about energy. It is difficult to separate the actual microgeneration production process from the representations we designed for that process, and to study how they are perceived by children and people in general. Both the product and process of microgeneration need a perceivable representation so that people can relate to it with their bodies. We have increased appreciation for energy through the experience of microgeneration, but is it because the energy is manifested in such a small and unexpected way? Or is it because it is difficult to generate electrical energy by using human body? What does it mean to feel like one "worked for" the energy? Even though we have some answers, our research opens up follow-up questions about human-powered microgeneration that will be relevant for future HCI research that deals with energy.

## LIMITATIONS & FUTURE WORK

We are currently making a number of improvements to the system. For example, our next iteration is capable of powering up other devices including commercial mobile devices.

We also are preparing to conduct a study where children will be invited to play with EnergyBugs while we observe their activities in a longer time frame, over multiple days and even weeks. More specifically, we are interested in analyzing children's activities over time relative to the quantity of energy. In addition, our evaluation of what children actually learned about energy harvesting technology was limited to the pre- and post-test surveys. We are currently working with elementary school teachers to design more targeted science lessons involving energy harvesting mechanisms inside the Bugs.

Finally, we note that EnergyBugs encouraged physical movements from children voluntarily in different manners (running, dancing, etc.), at a variety of indoor and outdoor locations. While it was not the focus of the current research, future design research might combine physical exercise and science learning, as childhood obesity continues to be a problem in the United States. Systems such as EnergyBugs could simultaneously encourage physical exercise and engaging children in relevant scientific topics. EnergyBugs could be a technology that encourages physical exercise while engaging children in relevant scientific topics.

## CONCLUSION

Energy can seem like an abstract and distant concept to both children and adults. In contrast to informing children what energy is and how energy is used in the typical fashion, we took a constructionist approach of engaging children directly in the energy harvesting process—not through simulation, but through the production of tiny, yet usable energy from the motion of their bodies.

Two studies of EnergyBugs with 34 elementary school children revealed that such microgeneration through bodily movements invites children to discuss their energy making process more explicitly, and to more actively ask questions about energy from new perspectives. Emotional attachment to one's energy however, came from the EnergyBug's design to materialize energy in a way children can directly interact with, not whether producing the energy required physical labor. This highlights the important role interface design can play in making abstract concepts concrete and personal for children.

## ACKNOWLEDGMENTS

We thank all the children and their parents who have participated in our study at Park Day School, Camp 510, and Emeryville Recreation Center. Our special thanks go to Deqing Sun for his boundless support. We thank Yoon Jeong, James Pierce, Eric Paulos, Laura Devendorf,

Elizabeth Goodman, Brian Carver, and Stefan Marti for their help and invaluable discussions.

## REFERENCES


1. Backlund, S. et al. 2006. Static! The aesthetics of energy in everyday things. Proc. of DRSIC.
2. Badshah, A., Gupta, S., Cohn, G., Villar, N., Hodges, S., Patel, S.N. Interactive Generator: A self-powered haptic feedback device. Proc. CHI '11.
3. California State Board of Education. http://www.cde.ca.gov/be/st/ss/
4. Darby, S. 2001. Making it obvious: Designing feedback into energy consumption. In Proc. CEEHA. Springer.
5. Darby, S. 2006. The effectiveness of feedback on energy consumption. A review for DEFRA.
6. Desjardins, A. & Wakkary, R. How children represent sustainability in the home. In Proceedings IDC'11.
7. Disalvo, C., Sengers, P., Brynjarsdottir, H. 2010. Mapping the landscape of sustainable hci. In CHI'10.
8. Dourish, P. HCI and environmental sustainability: the politics of design and the design of politics. Proc. DIS '10.
9. Erickson, T., Li, M., Kim, Y., Deshpande, A., Sahu, S., Chao, T., Sukaviriya, P., & Naphade, M. The dubuque electricity portal: evaluation of a city-scale residential electricity consumption feedback system. In CHI '13.
10. Fenix International. http://fenixintl.com
11. Fitzpatrick, G. & Smith, G. 2009. Technology-enabled feedback on domestic energy consumption: Articulating a set of design concerns. IEEE Pervas. Comput. 8, 37–44.
12. Foster, D., Lawson, S., Wardman, J., Blythe, M. & Linehan, C. 2012. "Watts in it for me?": design implications for implementing effective energy interventions in organisations. In Proceedings CHI '12.
13. Gaver, W., Bowers, J., Boehner, K., Boucher, A., Cameron, D., Hauenstein, M., Jarvis, N., Pennington, S. 2013. Indoor weather stations: investigating a ludic approach to environmental HCI through batch prototyping. CHI '13.
14. Goodman, E. 2009. Three environmental discourses in human-computer interaction. In CHI '09 EA.
15. Grufberg & Jonsson. Sciensations: making sense of science by designing with sensors. IDC'12
16. Håkansson, M. and Sengers, P. 2013. Beyond being green: simple living families and ICT. In Proceedings of CHI '13.
17. Johansson, C., Ahmet, Z., Tholander, J., Aleo, F. Weather Gods and Fruit Kids - Embodying Abstract Concepts Using Tactile Feedback and Whole Body Interaction. CSCL2011.
18. Johnson, L., Broms, L. & Katzeff, C. 2010. Watt-Lite:Energy Statistics Made Tangible. DIS '10.
19. Kymissis, J., Kendall, C., Paradiso, J., Gershenfeld, N. 1998; IEEE Conference on Wearable Computing.
20. Mankoff, J., Matthews, D., Fussell, S. R., Johnson, M. 2007. Leveraging social networks to motivate individuals to reduce their ecological footprints. In HICSS'07.
21. Neustaedter, C., Bartram, L. & Mah, A. 2013. Everyday activities and energy consumption: how families understand the relationship. In Proceedings of CHI '13.
22. Papert, S. (1980). Mindstorms: Children, Computers, and Powerful Ideas. New York: Basic Books.
23. Piaget, J. (1972). The Principles of Genetic Epistemology. New York: Basic Books.
24. Pierce, J. and Eric Paulos. 2010. Materializing energy. In Proceedings of DIS'10.
25. Pierce, J. and Eric Paulos. 2012. Designing everyday technologies with human-power and interactive microgeneration. In Proceedings of DIS '12.
26. Raffle, H., Parkes, A., Ishii, H. Topobo: a constructive assembly system with kinetic memory. Proc. CHI '04.
27. ReRev. http://rerev.com
28. Resnick, M., Martin, F., Berg, R., Borovoy, R., Colella, V., Kramer, K., Silverman, B. 1998. Digital manipulatives: new toys to think with. In Proceedings of the CHI '98.
29. Schwartz, T., Denef, S., Stevens, G., Ramirez, L., & Wulf, V. Cultivating energy literacy: results from a longitudinal living lab study of a home energy management system. In Proceedings of CHI '13.
30. Shenck, N. & Joseph A. Paradiso. "Energy Scavenging with Shoe-Mounted Piezoelectrics," IEEE Micro, Vol. 21, No. 3, May-June 2001, pp. 30-42.
31. SolePower. http://solepowertech.com
32. Villar, N. & Hodges, S. 2010. The Peppermill: A Human-Powered User Interface Device. Proc. TEI'10.
33. Wyche, S.P. and Murphy, L.L. (2013). "Powering the Cellphone Revolution: Findings from Mobile Phone Charging Trials in Off-Grid Kenya," Proc. of CHI'13
34. Zhang, Z., Shrubsole, P., & Janse, M. 2010. Learning Environmental Factors through Playful Interaction. IDC.
35. Zuckerman, O., Arida, S., Resnick, M. 2005. Extending tangible interfaces for education: digital montessori-inspired manipulatives. In Proceedings of the CHI '05.

# OJAS - Open Source Bi-Directional Inductive Power Link

**Jussi Mikkonen**
Aalto ARTS
PL 11000, FI-00076 AALTO
jussi.mikkonen@aalto.fi

**Ramyah Gowrishankar**
Aalto ARTS
PL 11000, FI-00076 AALTO
ramyah.gowrishankar@aalto.fi

**Miia Oksanen**
Aalto ARTS
PL 11000, FI-00076 AALTO
miia.oksanen@aalto.fi

**Harri Raittinen**
iCraft Oy
Åkerlundinkatu 3B
FI-33100 Tampere
harri.raittinen@icraft.fi

**Arto Kolinummi**
iCraft Oy
Åkerlundinkatu 3B
FI-33100 Tampere
arto.kolinummi@icraft.fi

**ABSTRACT**
We present the design, development and evaluation of a bi-directional inductive power transfer circuit for prototyping purposes in the watt-range. Our device does not require any configuration and is intended for the development of wearable and tangible systems. Our approach allows a bi-directional power flow without any change in the circuit, such that the same circuit can be used for charging and discharging a battery. The contribution of this work is an enabling technology for researchers and practitioners in the fields of Wearable Electronics, Ubiquitous Computing and Human-Computer Interaction interested in exploring new interactions powered by watt-range inductive links. It enables smaller battery sizes, and therefore lighter devices, as the power can be distributed in a way that has not been feasible before. We discuss the motivations, technical details and the workshop evaluating our inductive approach.

**Author Keywords**
Wearable electronics; bi-directional inductive power; smart garments; prototyping.

**ACM Classification Keywords**
H.5.m. Information interfaces and presentation (e.g., HCI): Miscellaneous.

**INTRODUCTION**
Definition of 'wearable' has been explored by several, but ideally summarized by Starner [20] as something not requiring conscious attention and being a natural extension of the user, "similar to riding a bicycle". It is usually reserved for devices worn, or otherwise not requiring the user to actively hold it, such as a shirt or a glove. Wearable technology is still a relatively new field that has gained more research momentum in the last twenty years, even though the first project was built already in the early sixties [23].


*CHI 2014*, April 26 - May 01 2014, Toronto, ON, Canada
Copyright 2014 ACM 978-1-4503-2473-1/14/04...$15.00.
http://dx.doi.org/10.1145/2556288.2557041

When it comes to supplying energy, inductive power might be well suited for wearable applications. As Waffenschmidt and Staring [26] note, inductive power transfer is feasible only on short ranges, due to high losses of efficiency at longer ranges. Even though the power can be stored to the clothing structure, so that the garment itself could act as an energy storage [2], it still has to be collected there, either by harvesting or by transferring it from outside the garment. What does this mean for the user, then?

We have identified the one critical problem in wearables to be in cabling, especially in powering the wearables. Although there have been many good ideas on how to solve this, such as wireless charging using coat hangers by Iso-Ketola et al. [9], and battery powered backpack by Deyle et al. [7], the problem still exists: there is no simple way to charge and discharge power using the same link. In effect, these solutions are charged using one method and then prepared to be discharged using another. This suggests that there is a need for the power to be wirelessly charged, discharged or distributed.

The idea of the bi-directional power is not a new one, and charger solutions exist already in the watt-range. One such example is a patent application by Schuessler [19], describing a generic setup with a complex control mechanism. Even though the patent application does not provide any details or specifics, the basic idea of selectively charging and discharging a battery through a coil is presented.

With such a link, the whole wearable and its contained circuitry can be water-proofed, and still be able to power associated devices and other wearables, without the need for taking it apart to charge the battery. Without having to attach physical cables, the use situations could be made simpler. Wireless power helps us get closer to the origins of ubiquitous computing, although our focus is with power [27].

The circuit was developed for easy prototyping of wireless applications. Our way of teaching industrial and interaction design is very prototype-centric. The students create and test working prototypes, which have proper background research with related concepts behind them, following the idea of Koskinen et al. [11][12]. As a base for their prototypes, the students often use ready-made boards, such as Arduino Lilypad [5] and algorithm generation tools designed for visual thinkers such as Flowcards [15]. Since we wish our students to focus on the actual interaction and use situations, we see electronics and programming as tools, something that should be as simple to use as a screwdriver. The focus of the work should not be on the tools, which set the requirement for usability to a rather high priority. In most cases, there is no need to know how parts of the circuit or a prototype work, in order to be usable for designing interactions. If the students ask, we encourage them to find out more.

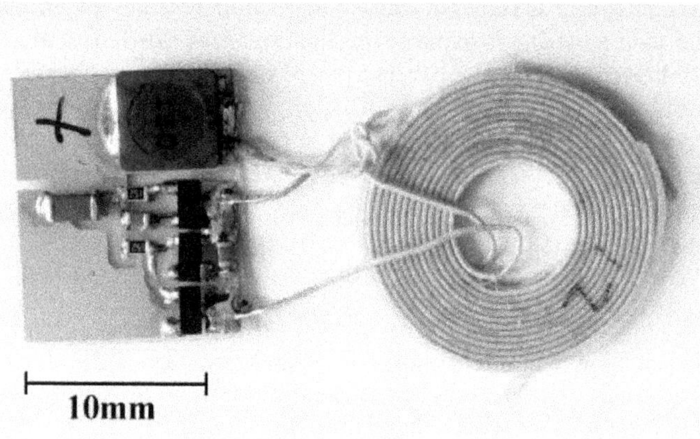


**Figure 1. Bi-directional inductive link, OJAS**

With these considerations in mind, we developed an inductive voltage balancer, shown in Figure 1. Our circuit allows charging and distributing of power, and operates as a bi-directional wireless inductive link. It can act as a transmitter or receiver without any necessary configuration, and is practically 'just sew it in': it is designed to be wired with either a sewing- or embroidery-machine. In order to transmit the power, we used Litz-wire coils as an air-gap transformer. The printed circuit boards and the coils are flexible and can be easily attached to soft surfaces with embroidery. While intended for wearable applications, it might also benefit other fields, such as tangible bits [8]. The circuit is within the size specifications suggested in work on 3D-printed fabrics [16], and has only nine components and a coil. The overall surface area is roughly two square centimeters, excluding the coil. Two identical circuits are required for transferring power, and the direction of the current can be interchanged 'on the fly'.

We present the design, development and some use cases with 'OJAS', a bi-directional embroiderable inductive voltage balancer. We chose the name OJAS, a Sanskrit word for vigor, because it fittingly describes this potent power source. Our intent is to release the circuit as open source hardware, so that everyone could benefit from it. In this paper we explore the motivations, suggestions and examples for its use. We describe the theory of operation and implementation in detail. The paper also contains results from a workshop, as well as an example of a prototype designed around the OJAS system. Finally, we discuss feedback, limitations and intended impact.

## RELATED WORK

In addition to the generic patent mentioned earlier, there are bi-directional chargers commercially available in the range of 5W and 40W, although there is not much information available about them [28], and we were not able to find papers regarding their usage. In their paper on steady state analysis of a bi-directional inductive power transfer, Thrimawithana et al. [24] focus on high-power applications. Their work seems to hint that the majority of the bi-directional inductive research is on vehicle-to-grid, or grid-to-vehicle power transfer, with power in the range of kilowatts.

There are several papers available regarding the typical directed inductive link. There has also been published work that explores links capable of exchanging data in two directions, while the power still only goes toward the end-device, such as in the implantable bio-medical link by Arshad et al. [1].

The ease of maintenance and management of smart garments has been explored in the paper by Toney et al. [25], introducing conductive charging using hangers. The advantage is that the galvanic connection is relatively straightforward to implement, but somewhat more difficult to maintain, due to physical wear on the contacts. A similar idea was explored earlier by Iso-Ketola et al [9], where the charging was inductive. The paper also explored the washability of smart garments, which is a necessity for its long-term use. Both these examples utilize a conveniently practical coat hanger charging method. Toney also points out, that the connection between the coat hanger and the bar where it rests must be properly designed.

Deyle et al. [7] have examined some basic ideas for using inductive power transfer, including RFID-tags and toothbrushes, and even mentioning Tesla's groundbreaking work. They developed a backpack for easy charging of devices that contains a separately chargeable battery, and a circuitry for inductive power transfer with a low bandwidth data transfer. There is no cable between the backpack and the endpoint device, thus providing ease-of-use and cable-free, design simplicity. The backpack pocket can be used to charge endpoint devices of USB-power level, "pocket-to-endpoint", and there is potential means for harvesting power from human actuation, such as piezoelectric generators.

Since our aim is to provide something for the people who build prototypes, we searched for kits and DIY-instructions from the Internet. The closest that we could find to a commercial kit was from Adafruit, published in June 2013 [29], and one circuit for hobbyists at Instructables [30]. The Adafruit circuit seems to be a surplus batch from a toy manufacturer and not intended for prototyping; it is also quite inefficient. The latter one is more related in principle to ours and with diligent manufacturing could be very useful. The employment of a linear regulator at the output strips the circuit of any efficiency, and as such, the circuit is slightly too large to be used directly with garments. It remains, however, a good example of higher power implementation of an inductive power transmitter for prototyping purposes.

The above-considered sources demonstrate a variety of ideas for how one could wirelessly charge a device and how to charge a wearable or a smart garment. However, all of them are isolated or missing key factors in usability. Conductive connections need protection from moisture. On the other hand, inductive charging provides the possibility for the protection from moisture, but so far the battery used to wirelessly charge other devices cannot itself be wirelessly charged. OJAS provides a solution. Figure 2 shows the use case: in the upper picture, the battery is charged while powered from USB, and in the lower picture it is taking power out of the battery to supply to the device.

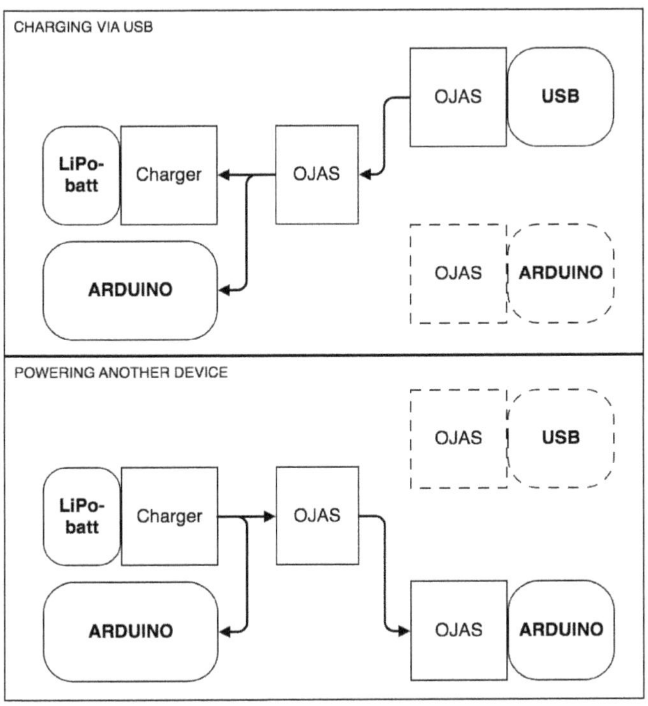


**Figure 2. Block diagram of using OJAS**

#### Wearable uses

To our knowledge, there have been very few applications applying wireless bi-directional power transfer with mobile or wearable devices. Therefore we will take a look at works that could benefit from using such a device in their use or user interface.

Since our circuit was developed to be used in wearables and eTextiles, some example applications we considered were from that domain. Kukkia and Vilkas [3] introduced a set of dresses with kinetic decoration. Both dresses had an effect made with Nitinol-wire. In Kukkia-dresses, flower petals moved, and in Vilkas', a bit more functional effect was achieved that raised the hemline. The petal moving takes roughly 3.8W, which is not much for an effect that is triggered only once before it has to be manually reset, though in continuous use it would be rather battery-demanding. This first version was already reached with an early prototype circuit, suggesting new interaction possibilities. For example, the user could power the effect via a rechargeable handbag, only touching the dress briefly for activation. Thus, the dress could contain less electronics, with most of the electronics hidden for example, inside-seams and coated, in order to be washable.

Berzowska has also explored energy transfer by creating constellation dresses and leeches [4]. The constellation dresses have LEDs, which light up only when the user gets energy from another person wearing a similar dress. The connection is galvanic, and uses magnets to easily connect the power pads. The leeches work with a similar approach: they steal power from another dress, then releasing the stolen power by lighting LEDs. As the LED power consumption is minimal, our wireless circuit could be easily used to first charge the battery, and then to supply power, maintaining the original ideas, but in a wireless manner. In practice, LEDs would also be somewhat safer, as there would not be a need for open electric contacts and the batteries could be charged using the same link.

Reach, Jacobs and Worbin [10] explored the use of thermochromic inks, electroluminescent wires and other materials for social interaction in garments and accessories, such as a handbag. One of the examples is the 'Reach Out' hat, which can acquire a decoration from another hat near it using thermochromic inks for the effect. In the article, the power source's location needed for the exchange is unclear, but the system could easily be made functional with the use of bi-directional inductive power. One could charge a hat wirelessly, and then later supply the power for someone else, powering the change effect. This kind of power-exchange should be explored further since it would be relatively easy to prototype a system that e.g., borrows the power needed for a decorative change.

As an example of a medical system, Tanaka et al. [21] have developed a small measurement system that measures heart rate, acceleration and related variables. The system can be continuously worn and has a relatively small footprint. It has an independent battery lasting roughly 2h, but could be easily powered or charged using inductive power. Continuous ECG measurements could be made more convenient for patients if the system could be left on the skin for a longer duration, such as a full day, with the battery recharging inductively simply by sitting on a chair or through a jacket needed to be worn once in a while. For the medical industry, the development of lightweight wearables with a small battery size would be interesting.

The reading glove introduced by Tanenbaum et al. could be further developed with the use of the circuit [22]. The glove itself is used to read RFID-tags from objects and helps the user construct a story while physically examining the objects in their hands. The energy required by the reading glove setup appears to be well within the limits of our described circuit. Our circuit could be used in a number of ways, by placing wireless links on both the glove and the objects and even to the table. The glove could be wirelessly charged during use and it could transfer the power to the objects that are being picked up, allowing for much broader interactions while reducing their weight. Additionally, the glove itself could be made lightweight, by replacing the battery with a circuit. This however, would require the power to be fed from the objects.

## OJAS - CIRCUIT DESCRIPTION

The power transfer link consists of a power transmitter and receiver. In our case, the transmitter and receiver are identical, so that their role is interchangeable and power can be transmitted in both directions. Power is transferred through an air core transformer that consists of two coils of approximately 20mm in diameter and 1mm thick.

The coil La+Lb forms the transformer primary or secondary depending on whether the circuit is operating as transmitter or receiver. When the transmitter and receiver coils are brought in close proximity to each other, an air core transformer is formed and power can be transmitted through this transformer. The relative supply voltages of the two circuits determine the power flow direction. The circuit with the higher supply voltage operates as transmitter and the other one as receiver. By increasing the receiver supply voltage, the roles can be interchanged and the receiver starts to operate as transmitter.

### Operation as power transmitter

The center tapped coil La+Lb and C1 form a parallel resonant circuit. Sinusoidal current is circulating in this resonant circuit and sinusoidal voltages can be measured across C1 and La+Lb. The sinusoidal resonant current also produces a magnetic field around the air-cored coil La+Lb. If the receiver coil is placed in close vicinity to the transmitter coil, this magnetic field also goes through the receiver coil, inducing sinusoidal voltage and current to the receiving resonant circuit.

The transformer is driven with a simple modified current fed Royer type oscillator [18], the schematic of which is shown in Figure 3, right side. As a receiver, the same circuit operates as a synchronous rectifier and transforms the received AC power to DC.

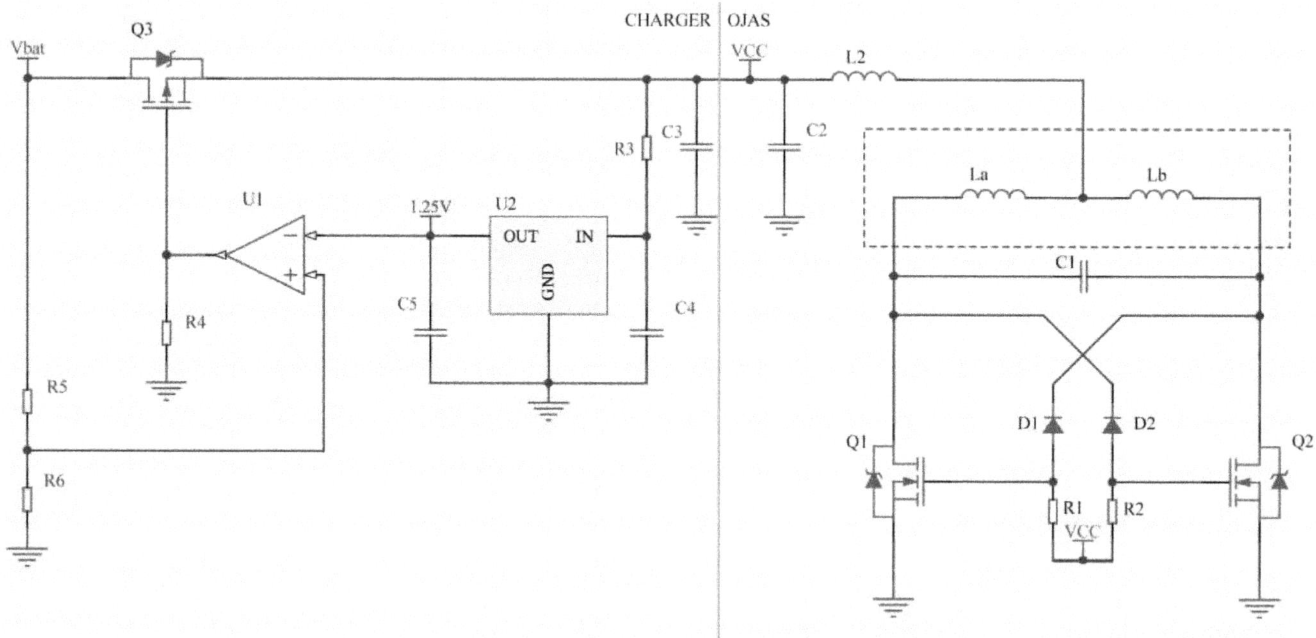


**Figure 3. Schematics of OJAS and a charger**

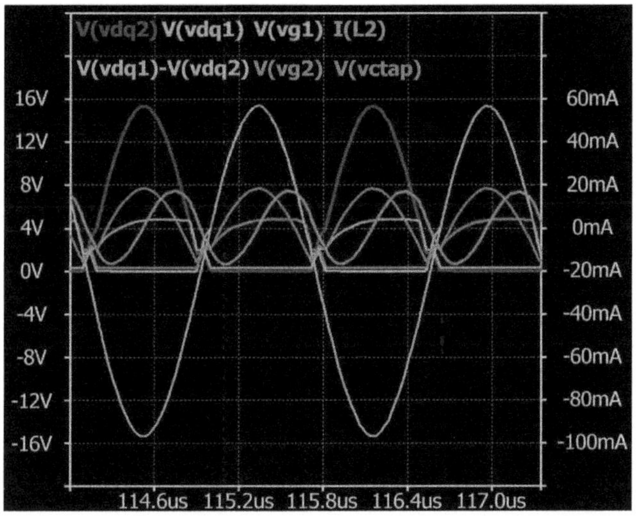


**Figure 4. Operating waveforms of the OJAS circuit**

The operating waveforms are shown in Figure 4. The resonant circuit is fed by the two cross-connected transistors Q1 and Q2, which conduct alternately. For example, when Q1 is conducting its drain, voltage is close to zero, and the gate voltage of Q2 is also forced close to zero through the conducting diode D2. This forces Q2 to remain off. When the resonant circuit voltage reaches the transistor threshold voltage, Q1 starts to switch off and Q2 turns on, simultaneously drawing the Q1 gate voltage to zero through the diode D1. Alternatively, the circuitry formed with Q1, Q2, D1, D2 and R1, R2, can be seen as cross-coupled inverters, which form an SR flip-flop. The resonant circuit voltage then forces this latch to change state.

Inductor L2 acts as an approximation for constant current source and allows the oscillator to draw current from the Vcc, while the La+Lb center tap voltage follows the resonant circuit's sinusoidal voltage. Ideally, the inductance of this coil should be significantly larger than the resonant circuit inductance. As can be seen in Figure 3, the resonant circuit voltage (VdQ1-VdQ2) is sinusoidal, although the drain voltage waveforms are slightly distorted due to the FET Miller-capacitance charging. The image also shows the drain (V(vdq1), V(vdq2)) and gate voltages (V(vg1), V(vg2) ), the center tap voltage (V(vctap)) and the current through L2 (I(L2)). It should also be noted, that when the receiver circuit is brought close to the transmitter, the magnetic coupling between the circuits changes the oscillation frequency considerably.

### Operation as a power receiver

In the receiver the magnetic flux that goes through the coil La+Lb induces sinusoidal voltage and current to the resonant circuit. As the resonant circuit's voltage polarity changes, the Q1, Q2 MOSFETs are alternately switched on and off exactly as in the case of the transmitter. In this case, however, the MOSFETs operate as a synchronous rectifier, rectifying the resonant circuit voltage. The voltage is further filtered through the low pass filter formed by L2 and C2.

If the connection point of R1 and R2, normally connected to the Vcc, is grounded, the MOSFETs can no longer conduct and the synchronous rectification action is disabled. The body diodes of the MOSFETs still conduct alternately and the circuit operates as a normal, full-wave rectifier.

### Operation of the charger

The charging circuit can be seen at the left side of Figure 2. Operational amplifier U1 and voltage reference U2 are powered from the VCC. If the Vbat is greater than the VCC, the current flows through Q3 towards the OJAS, supplying power to it. If the VCC is greater than the Vbat, the operational amplifier U1 keeps Q3 open until the Vbat reaches 4.1V. The Vbat is measured using a voltage divider created with R5, R6, and compared against 1.25V reference voltage from U2.

### Components used

Q1, Q2 = PMV185XN from NXP. Selected MOSFET should have small gate capacitance, low gate threshold voltage (1-2V) and sufficient maximum drain voltage (min. 30V for 5V operation).

Q3 = FDN304P P-MOSFET from Fairchild, controlling the charging current.

D1, D2 = BAS70-07. Low capacitance Schottky diodes with sufficiently high reverse voltage withstand, in dual-diode casing in order to reduce component count.

R1, R2 = 1.5kOhms. Smaller resistance increases the idle current, larger value increases FET switching time and losses under load. Optimum value depends on MOSFET gate capacitance and selected operation frequency.

R3 = 10k, low-pass filter for reference input

R4 = 22k, pull-down for Q3 gate

R5 = 27k, R6 = 11.8k, voltage divider feedback to op-amp, sets the charge cut-off-voltage to 4.1V

U1 = OPA171AIDB, op-amp for controlling Q3

U2 = REF3312 low-power voltage reference

C1 = 5.6nF NP0 25V min. Determines the operation frequency. Must be of low loss type (NP0, polypropylene) with sufficient maximum voltage.

La-Lb = 2 x 2,5uH, 10uH end-to-end (series connected) inductance. Bifilarly wound spiral coil with 30 x 0.05mm Litz wire. The two coils are connected in series so that a center tapped coil is obtained. Coil diameter approximately 20mm, thickness 1mm.

L2 = 22uH. Constant current feed inductor. In ideal case much larger than La-Lb.

C2 = 10uF X7R 6.3V-10V. Filter capacitor for VCC. In our circuit, it is augmented with an additional 100nF X7R.

C3, C4, C5 = 1uF bypass capacitors for VCC and the reference

### Measurements

In these measurements the free oscillating frequency is 700kHz, and the component values are as explained above. Idle current of the device was measured at three different input voltages, as shown in Table 1. Power transfer efficiency with some load resistances and output ripple are shown in Table 2. In these measurements the coils were placed on top of each other as close as possible, and the input voltage was kept at 5V.

| Supply voltage | Idle Current |
|---|---|
| 5V | 11.5mA |
| 4V | 9.2mA |
| 3V | 6.8mA |

**Table 1. Idle-currents**

| Rload [ohm] | Vin [V] | Iin [mA] | Vout [V] | efficiency [%] | ripple [mVp-p] |
|---|---|---|---|---|---|
| 23.3 | 5 | 190 | 4.25 | 82 | 20 |
| 23.3 | 4 | 153 | 3.39 | 81 | 18 |
| 23.3 | 3 | 111 | 2.44 | 77 | 17 |
| 11.4 | 5 | 339 | 3.80 | 75 | 22 |
| 11.4 | 4 | 269 | 3.00 | 73 | 20 |
| 11.4 | 3 | 191 | 2.13 | 70 | 19 |
| 47.1 | 5 | 110 | 4.57 | 81 | 18 |
| 47.1 | 4 | 88 | 3.65 | 80 | 17 |
| 47.1 | 3 | 65 | 2.68 | 78 | 17 |

**Table 2. Efficiency and ripple measured at different voltages**

In order to determine the maximum transmitted power, the input voltage for the transmitting circuit was set to 5V. After the distance was set, the receiving resistance was adjusted to find out the maximum power. This does not necessarily mean that the voltage would be of good quality, nor would it be optimal as an output voltage.

For an efficient, long-distance transfer, the transmitter and the receiver must be accurately tuned to the same frequency. Results are listed in a Table 3, and plotted in Figure 5, showing the effects of distance.

| Distance [mm] | Receiver voltage [V] | Load [ohm] | Power received [W] |
|---|---|---|---|
| 0 | 2,5 | 3,2 | 1,95 |
| 1 | 4,3 | 11,6 | 1,59 |
| 2 | 4,3 | 13,6 | 1,36 |
| 3 | 4,4 | 21 | 0,92 |
| 5 | 4,4 | 30 | 0,65 |
| 7 | 4,4 | 48 | 0,40 |
| 10 | 4,8 | 100 | 0,23 |
| 15 | 4,7 | 290 | 0,08 |
| 20 | 4,3 | 785 | 0,02 |

**Table 3. The power transfer at different distances**

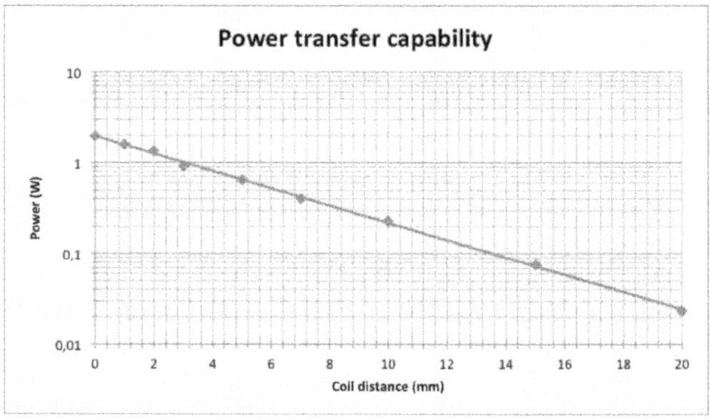


**Figure 5. The plotted transfer at different distances**

### Embroiderability

For embroidery, we tested two different substrate materials. The tests were based on the work by Linz et al. [14], exploring the use of embroidery to attach flexible circuit boards to textile substrates. We tested a commonly-available, thin, flexible circuit board, and a slightly stiffer board, used for laminating multilayer printed circuit boards. With future applications in mind, we chose thin, flexible circuit boards based on the potential to create two-sided pads with commercial processes, even though the current version of OJAS has been designed to be one-sided. The embroiderable pads were sized to be roughly 25mm^2, in order to work with the commercial embroidery machines, which require a smaller clearance around the pad than standard domestic sewing machines.

## POWERING A MEASURING SYSTEM

In order to evaluate the usage of OJAS for powering more voltage-sensitive systems, we constructed a sensor measurement circuit using an Arduino FIO and a temperature-humidity sensor unit. A common method for measuring a physical variable is to use a sensor in an integrated chip. Integrated sensor modules are commonly available, and we used SHT11-module from Sparkfun. In addition, Arduino FIO was chosen as the prototyping board, as there is a well-established knowledge base for attaching sensors and transmitting data with commonly-available libraries.

Three different alternatives for powering the Arduino were tested for comparison. In the first option, we attached the OJAS directly to the 3V3 line, bypassing the built-in voltage regulator. This required feeding the power through another OJAS, connected directly to a 3.7V LiPo-battery. In order to have a typical use situation with OJAS, we transmitted the measured data to a computer using Series 1 XBEE-modules.

In the second option we used 3.3V FTDI-USB serial adapter to directly power the Arduino, in addition to transmitting the data. Our third option was to supply the power from a LiPo-battery attached to the FIO battery connector, and transmit the data using XBEE. In all cases, the only additional component was a 47uF electrolytic capacitor, connected between 3V3 and GND pins.

As we did not have a steady environment for measuring humidity and temperature, we let the device rest on a lab table and recorded the values. The values were similar, behaving consistently in an open environment. The changes caused by the environment were greater than any noise we could detect from the data. Because of this, we measured the noise in the supply voltage and looked for anomalies.

When powered through the USB, the noise amplitude was roughly 18mV, although there were spikes every 25us with the amplitude of roughly 60mV. When powered using OJAS, the noise amplitude is roughly 21mV, except when the XBEE circuit transmits the data. There is a spike of 160mV, with a duration of 4ms, immediately after data has been sent to the XBEE-module. The same spike can be seen when the Arduino is powered using USB with the XBEE-module connected. Powering the Arduino from a battery does not produce the same spike, and the noise amplitude was well under 20mV.

## PROTOTYPING WITH OJAS: JACKET FOR FIRST GRADERS

In order to get a concrete example of a system that could utilize OJAS, we created a jacket for first graders. As a safety feature, in addition to commonly-worn reflectors, the jacket lights up when the child is walking to and from school. The lights on the jacket are powered wirelessly using OJAS, with a battery placed inside the child's backpack. We assume that the child, when leaving the home or school, would be wearing the backpack and thus the power connection is easily established when the backpack is worn over the jacket, and otherwise remains switched off. Figure 6 shows the final jacket and the backpack.

We bought and modified an off-the-shelf, water-resistant jacket and backpack. In our choices for module location, we took into consideration user comfort and safety as well as OJAS functionality and protection. Further, a number of design features were incorporated. Both the jacket and backpack were chosen for their simplicity of construction, making them easy to take apart and modify. We chose to place the OJAS on the coat back, just below the collar because this part of the garment does not move or bend as much as other parts. This placement worked with the test-determined maximum thickness of fabrics that can adequatly be between the modules: 15mm.

The LEDs were placed on the highly-visible upper part of the arm near the shoulders. The LEDs were attached to pieces of bias tape, connected in parallel with the conductive yarn.

**Figure 6. Backpack supplying power to the lights of a child's jacket.**

The backpack can supply power to the jacket, and be charged without having to take the battery out. The placement in the backpack was also convenient for charging since it can be hung. Of course, one needs to have the OJAS unit that supplies the charging power where the backpack is hung while not being used.

By using the same link for both actions, without any additional steps in the normal usage, the moisture protected backpack and the jacket can add safety during normal use.

## WORKSHOP

Soon after the jacket was built, we held a small half-day workshop on the use of OJAS with seven expert users at Universität der Künste, Berlin. The goal of the workshop was to get feedback on the usefulness and ease of use in prototyping, as well as get some initial concepts on how it could be developed. Before introducing the technology to larger audiences, especially before arranging workshops with users unfamiliar with eTextiles or wearable electronics, we wanted to estimate how it would be received with educated participants. As one of our goals is to start disseminating the knowledge at different levels of educational institutions, from primary schools to universities, we needed to be sure it is suited for it. We already had a good level of reference coming from the workshops by Kuznetsov et al. [13] and Perner-Wilson et al. [17].

The workshop was divided into three parts, starting with a brief lecture on OJAM's capabilities and instructions for use. The second part was spent creating concepts, and finally, a hands-on part for creating quick prototypes. The workshop began with an introduction to the technology, followed by a brief demonstration and a discussion on first impressions. The participants were positively taken and had questions, such as, is the size of the coils fixed, and what would happen if the coils are misaligned. Of greatest concern were the functional distance and the alignment accuracy. For the craft-oriented participants, the circuit layout was a big question. Before the actual hands-on act part started, participants were already interested to know if the circuit board and the coil could be separated for longer distances, and raised the importance of developing the possibility to use a sewing machine. Further, participants discussed the important possibility of changing the shape of the coil, for instance, oval buttons or square cuff links.

After some initial individual thinking, the concepts were sketched in groups. We chose to disregard finesse in the implementation, and facilitate interactions that better focused on the core properties [6]. The developed concepts were mostly concerning using OJAS in garments, including drawing power from public transport and then using it at home. Another concept was an integrated reading light on a chair that would be powered only when the person sat in the chair. A quick test was done, with the user carrying a rechargeable battery in their pocket and OJAS tucked inside their belt loop at the back of the pants. When the user sat on a chair, it supplied power to the reading light, as shown in Figure 7.

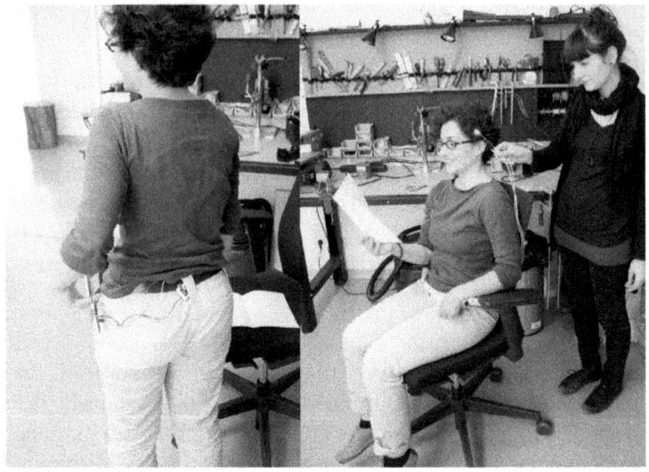

**Figure 7. OJAS with a battery attached to belt loop (L), powering a reading light just by sitting (R)**

This generated a lot of discussion about powering only what one needs and collecting power where easily available. In the case of a tram, it was suggested that for a small increase in the ticket price, travelers could also draw some power. Some of the concepts from the workshop are shown in Figure 8, including a reading light (the same tested in Figure 6) for seats in a bus.

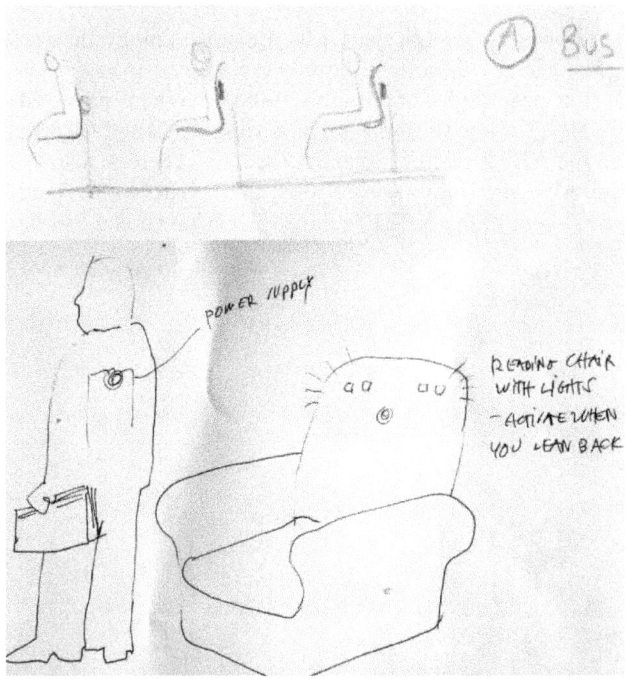


**Figure 8. Workshop concepts, charging in a bus and powering the reading chair lights**

The idea of exchanging power with surrounding systems was seen as interesting, as was using it as a way to spread power between garments. Quoting: *"If the system could be used for power distribution, it would be really good."* Two of the participants then tested how the devices could be used as a power -distribution network, with several OJAS and high-power LED connected in parallel. If any component would be fed with power, then the others would be distributing the power. One participant was very pleased with the possibilities OJAS suggested: *"Because this is normally what bothers me, I work with eTextiles, that you either have a big battery or, you want to have a contact like, a patch that you turn on, that you have to construct it in a way that is insulated and that you don't short circuit things. This would be an easy way of doing it, adding the power component."*

The circuit also sparked very fundamental ideas. As one of the participants connected the circuit to a small vibration motor, and used two-sided tape to attach it to her fingernail, she gained the ability to detect the resonant fields' useful boundaries. This simple tool could be used for finding a good placement for the circuits in garments.

## ANALYSIS

The circuit itself performs well, although the components are quite critical. For example, C1 must be NP0 or better. We tried replacing it with cheaper X7R, with the result of idle current being roughly five times larger. The capacity of the transferred power is suitable for a wide variety of applications, and by sacrificing the idle current, can be increased. In our case, we focused on achieving a small idle current. The efficiency is also quite good, due to resonant operation and the synchronous rectification while receiving. As the circuit does not have an active regulator, varying the load does have a direct effect to the output voltage. Another issue is the coil, which currently is hand-made. On a positive note, it is easier to prototype different sizes, as we are not tied to any single manufacturer.

During the creation of the jacket, and at the workshop, one of the first issues encountered was the size of the coil. We chose a small size because the OJAS can then be hidden inside buttons, belt buckles and other soft areas of clothing, such as shoulder pads and seams. The motivation is to 3D-print a casing for it and use it as a part of a quick snap connector. The biggest problem comes from maintaining the alignment of the corresponding locations where the garments of different layers are able to move with respect to each other, such as pant legs and socks.

Another issue stemming from the coil size is the usable distance. Larger coil size determines a larger usable distance, and therefore, transmitted power. In general, the OJAS units worked well, but the alignment area was really small and sometimes needed to be adjusted when worn to get sufficient alignment. The good thing is the possibility to connect to a larger power capacity, as that is more beneficial from the wearability point of view, that is, to separate power from the rest of circuit. A heavier power source can be carried in a bag or backpack and can be in more fixed places while the rest of the circuit can be more subtle and portable.

## CONCLUSIONS

We have shown a simple solution for prototyping bi-directional inductive power in the watt-range. OJAS is most powerful in the bi-directional use, such as when charging a battery, and then discharging it through the same link. It could be used to create a whole variety of practical “simple-to-power” effects, bypassing the need for a user interface by directly controlling the effects. This would allow natural interactions, where the user does not have to perform actions through a specific user interface. One such effect could be achieved with thermochromic inks as decorations, which are activated only when wanted, while keeping the garment simple and without a complex user interface.

The possibility to transmit power back and forth between garments, accessories or objects gives numerous new possibilities for sharing, charging and especially, in distributing power. Some locations were seen as promising for transferring the power between e.g. the shirt and a jacket, or shirt and a chair, but were not explored thoroughly. As this technology is still new, there needs to be further research on the possibilities and the locations for the bi-directional power.

The usability of the operating frequency for detecting another circuit is also interesting. It is possible to measure the frequency of the circuit using a microcontroller, and deduce if there are other coils in close proximity. In combination of shutting down the circuit, this could be used to create more complex applications, such as greater intelligent power distribution.

The coil size could be explored further, with sizes up to a circumference of a person. This way the power might be transmitted between all garments even during very heavy movement. Regardless of that, using OJAS with the garments will remain true to the definition of a wearable: the user would have to mind about the garment only when dressing and undressing, allowing it to be just a natural extension to the user.

## ACKNOWLEDGEMENTS

The project was funded from EIT-ICT Connected Textiles program. We would like to warmly thank Katharina Bredies, whose considerable efforts have made the whole project possible. Our gratitude for supplying expert users goes to the staff at UdK Design Research Lab. We would also like to thank Sari Kujala for her help during the writing.

## REFERENCES

1. Arshad, A., Khan, S., Alam, A.H.M.Z. and Tasnim, R. Investigation of inductive coupling approach for non-

contact bidirectional transfer of power and signal, *In Proc. ICCCE* (2012), 570-573.

2. Bao, L., Li, X. Towards Textile Energy Storage from Cotton T-Shirts. *Advanced Materials*, (2012) 3246–3252.
3. Berzowska J. and Coelho M. Kukkia and Vilkas: kinetic electronic garments. In *Proc. ISWC,* (2005), 82–85.
4. Berzowska, J. Constellation Dresses and the Leeches: Questions of Power for Electronic Garments. *In Anonymous International Foundation of Fashion Technology Institutes Conference*, 2007.
5. Buechley, L., Eisenberg, M., Catchen, J., and Crockett, A. The LilyPad Arduino: using computational textiles to investigate engagement, aesthetics, and diversity in computer science education. In *Proc. CHI 2008*. ACM Press (2008).
6. Buxton, B. *Sketching User Experiences: Getting the Design Right and the Right Design: Getting the Design Right and the Right Design*. Morgan Kaufmann, 2007.
7. Deyle, T. and Reynolds, M. PowerPACK: A wireless power distribution system for wearable devices, In *Proc. ISWC*, 2008.
8. Ishii, H. and Ullmer, B. Tangible bits: Towards seamless interfaces between people, bits, and atoms. In *Proc. CHI.* ACM Press, (1997), 234–241.
9. Iso-Ketola P., Karinsalo T., Myry M., Hahto L., Karhu H., Malmivaara M. and Vanhala J. A Mobile Device as User Interface for Wearable Applications. In *Proc. PERMID*, 2005.
10. Margot J., and Worbin L. Reach: dynamic textile patterns for communication and social expression. *In Extended Abstracts CHI.* (2005), 1493-1496.
11. Koskinen, I., Mikkonen, J., Ahde, P., Eckoldt, K., Helgason, T., Hänninen, R., Jiang, J., Niskanen, T. and Schultz B. Hacking a Car: Re-Embodying the Design Classroom. *In Proc. NORDES*, 2009.
12. Koskinen I., Zimmerman J., Binder T., Redstrom J. and Wensveen S. *Design research through practice: from the lab, field, and showroom*. Waltham, MA: Morgan Kaufmann/Elsevier, 2011.
13. Kuznetsov, S., Trutoiu, L., Kute, C., Howley, I., Paulos, E., and Siewiorek, D. Breaking boundaries: strategies for mentoring through textile computing workshops. In *Proc. CHI 2011*, ACM Press (2011).
14. Linz T., Kallmayer, C., Aschenbrenner, R. and Reichl, H. Embroidering electrical interconnects with conductive yarn for the integration of flexible electronic modules into fabric, In *Proc. ISWC*, (2005), 86-89.
15. Mikkonen J. Flowcards - a communication tool, In *Proc. DRS*, (2012), 1215-1229.
16. Mikkonen, J., Kivioja, S., Suonsilta, H., Myllymäki, R. and Vanhakartano, S. Printed Material as Fabric, *In Proc. NORDES*, 2013.
17. Perner-Wilson, H., Buechley, L. and Satomi, M. Handcrafting textile interfaces from a kit-of-no-parts. In *Proc. TEI*, 2011.
18. Royer, G. H., A switching transistor D-C to A-C converter having an output frequency proportional to the D-C input voltage, *American Institute of Electrical Engineers, Part I: Communication and Electronics, Transactions of the*, (1955), 322-326.
19. Schuessler, J. E., Bi-directional wireless charger, US Patent 20120229071. (2012)
20. Starner T. The challenges of wearable computing: Part 1, *IEEE Micro*, (2001), 44–52.
21. Tanaka, T., Sonoda, K., Okochi, S., Chan, A., Nii, M., Kanda, K., Fujita, T., Higuchi, K. and Maenaka, K. Wearable Health Monitoring System and Its Applications, In *Proc. ICETET*, (2011), 143-146.
22. Tanenbaum, K., Tanenbaum, J., Antle, A., Bizzocchi, J., el-Nasr, M. and Hatala, M. Experiencing the reading glove. In *Proc. TEI*, 2011.
23. Thorp E.O. The Invention of the First. Wearable Computer. In *Proc. ISWC*, IEEE CS Press (1998).
24. Thrimawithana, D.J., Madawala, U.K. and Neath, M. A steady-state analysis of bi-directional inductive power transfer systems, In *Proc. ICIT*, (2013), 1618-1623.
25. Toney, A.P., Thomas, B.H. and Marais, W. Managing Smart Garments, In *Proc. ISWC*, (2006), 91-94.
26. Waffenschmidt, E. and Staring, T. Limitation of inductive power transfer for consumer applications, In *Proc. EPE,* (2009), 1-10.
27. Weiser, M. The Computer for the 21st Century. *Scientific American*, (1991), 94-104.
28. 5W Bi-directional wireless charging solution, http://www.idealez.com/80520355/product-detail/en_US/70714, Cited 20th Dec. 2013
29. Inductive charging set, http://www.adafruit.com/products/1407, Cited 9th Sept. 2013.
30. Wireless Power Charger!, http://www.instructables.com/id/Wireless-Ipod-Charger/, Cited 9th Sept. 2013.

# Using Asymmetric Cores to Reduce Power Consumption for Interactive Devices with Bi-stable Displays

**Jaeyeon Kihm** **François Guimbretière** **Julia Karl** **Rajit Manohar**
Cornell University
Ithaca, NY 14850
jk2443@cornell.edu francois@cs.cornell.edu julia@csl.cornell.edu rajit@csl.cornell.edu

## ABSTRACT
Low power "helper" cores have been increasingly included on application processors to accomplish low intensity tasks such as music playing and motion sensing with minimum energy consumption. Recently, Guimbretière et al. [1] demonstrated that such helper cores could also be used to execute simple user interface tasks. We revisit this approach by implementing a similar system on an off-the-shelf application processor (TI OMAP4). Our study shows that in the case of high event rate interactions (pen inking and virtual keyboard), significant battery life gains (×1.7 and ×2.3 respectively) can be achieved with the helper core executing the interface. Having the helper core only dispatch input events incurs a 18% penalty relative to the maximum savings rate, but allows for simplified deployment since it merely requires a change in toolkit infrastructure.

### Author Keywords
Energy efficiency, User interface system, Asymmetric architecture, Pen interaction, Bi-stable display

### ACM Classification Keywords
H5.2 [Information interfaces and presentation]: User Interfaces. - Graphical user interfaces.

## INTRODUCTION
The power efficiency of everyday information appliances such as general-purpose slates or specialized ebook readers has made striking progress in recent years. Most of this progress can be traced back to improvements in the underlying hardware such as the use of dynamic voltage and frequency scaling to optimize power management, the use of solid state disks, and in some cases, the use of bi-stable displays which consume power only while refreshing pixels. Redesigning the interface can further reduce power consumption [3, 5, 6]. Recently, Guimbretière et al. [1] introduced a new solution for devices using bi-stable displays which does not require visual changes to the interface. They observed that common reading tasks, such as turning a page or annotating, can be performed using a slow, yet highly efficient micro-controller without having the main processors involved (akin to playing music in the background). Using a custom design board combining an application processor (TI OMAP3) and a microcontroller driving a bi-stable e-ink display, they demonstrated a possible increase of battery life by a factor of 1.7 for reading and 3.2 for writing.

To further explore the potential of using an asymmetric dual-core to run the user interface, we re-implemented Guimbretiere et al.'s approach [1] on an off-the-shelf application processor, the TI OMAP 4460, featuring two high-performance ARM Cortex-A9 (A9) cores and two low power ARM Cortex-M3 (M3) cores. Since the TI OMAP 4460 has a shared memory system for all cores, we streamlined the inter-processor communications and assigned a shared memory for the whole interface description tree in order for all cores to access it directly.

Using our prototype, we conducted an experiment comparing four main settings: 1) the traditional single application processor, 2) the single application processor but the display driver is only switched on when it is needed; 3) the M3 only dispatches user inputs and an application processor executes callbacks, and 4) the M3 dispatches inputs and executes callbacks. All four settings offer similar end-user experiences, and our results confirm the benefits of using low power cores for high event rate user interactions such as inking (×1.7 in battery life) or a virtual keyboard (×2.3). In low event rate interactions such as reading, the benefit is much smaller and driven by display driver management savings. For high event rate interactions, the M3 dispatch-only setting is 18% less efficient than the M3 dispatch and execute setting, but had the advantage of being easier to deploy requiring no recompiling of current applications for new architecture.

## RELATED WORK
Several previous systems have studied overall interface design for optimized power consumption. Vallerio [5] demonstrated that by reformatting the interface layout to optimize pointing performance or by introducing auto-completion mechanisms, one can increase user speed and thus reduce energy requirements for short interactions. Zhong and Jha [6] utilized a secondary display (i.e. the display of a watch) and voice recognition to reduce the overall energy consumption of the primary display for interaction. These solutions are not well suited for interactions such as


*CHI 2014,* April 26 - May 01 2014, Toronto, ON, Canada
Copyright 2014 ACM 978-1-4503-2473-1/14/04Ⓢ$15.00.
http://dx.doi.org/10.1145/2556288.2557135

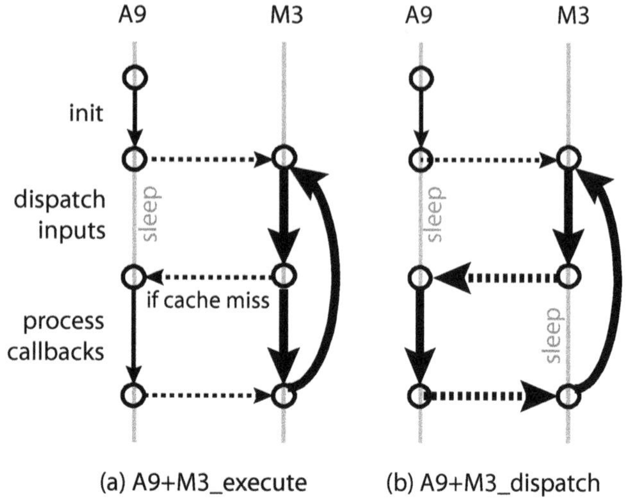


**Figure 1. Asymmetric dual-core system. (a) The M3 is used for dispatch and callbacks, and (b) for dispatch only. The stroke width represents the execution frequency.**

reading or note-taking since the display needs to stay on for prolonged periods of time. Harter et al. [3], in turn, studied how users react to the visual redesign of an interface to leverage the fact that in an OLED display, "off" pixels have a low energy signature.

More recently, Guimbretiere et al. [1] studied the possible impact of bi-stable displays on the energy signature of interfaces. Bi-stable displays only consume power while being updated, but then maintain an image with little or no power. While the first generation of bi-stable displays offered a low refresh rate, the most recent systems, such as the Mirasol display by Qualcomm, are video capable. Noticing that many interactions such as page turning and annotations require little computational power, Guimbretiere et al. proposed an architecture combining an application processor with a micro-controller. During high demand tasks, the application processor runs as usual, but when the demand is reduced, the application processor shuts off and the micro-controller handles user interactions. Using custom hardware, they demonstrated improvements varying from 1.7 to 3.2 in energy demand without requiring a significant redesign of the interface.

In this paper, we revisit Guimbretiere et al.'s approach by demonstrating its implementation on commodity asymmetric multi-core hardware (OMPA4) and comparing two possible policies for the use of the power efficient core. We empirically evaluate energy savings for different tasks related to reading and note-taking. As asymmetric multi-core designs (e.g., the ARM big.LITTLE architecture) are becoming the norm, it is important to systematically explore their energy-savings potential.

## LOW POWER USER INTERFACE FRAMEWORK

The system design proposed by Guimbretiere et al. [1] introduced a trade-off between power management and communication bandwidth to combine two asymmetric processors. Their custom board design allowed for a complete shut-off of the Linux processor including memory and peripherals to maximize energy savings. At the same time, the design offered only limited bandwidth between the two processors making it difficult to share the interface state between them.

We re-implemented this system on a commodity chip, the TI OMAP4. The OMAP4 is a typical application processor including two high performance ARM Cortex-A9 cores (running at up to 1.2 Ghz) and two energy efficient ARM Cortex-M3 helper cores (running at up to 384 Mhz) as well as interfaces modules to manage memory, displays, cameras, networks, USB, etc. The A9 core and the M3 core are running at very different efficiency points. Thus, preventing the A9 from processing small tasks such as dispatching user events will result in energy savings. Since both cores share memory access, this configuration offers a greater bandwidth between cores but might come at the cost of a higher power signature than the configuration used by Guimbretiere et al. [1] because some subsystems always stay on.

### Role of the low core processor

Considering the OMAP4 architecture, the logical extension of Guimbretiere et al.'s design would utilize the low power M3 not only to execute event dispatches but also the corresponding callbacks, thus minimizing the use of the high power A9. In that setting, the main system first initializes an application by loading a user interface tree and caching image data on the shared memory region. Then it sends a message to the M3 to initiate user interactions. The A9 can now safely fall asleep and the M3 will execute interface events upon user inputs until the use of the A9 is required. When this happens, the M3 will issue a remote-procedure call to perform the required computation such as updating a page cache (Figure 1a).

This approach promises to be very energy efficient, but, as in Guimbretiere et al.'s solution, it requires developers to review the application code to identify which part of the code should be run on the M3 and which part must be run on the A9. Developers must then re-structure the code to manage transitions between the two architectures. Depending on the compiler support, this could be done by inserting pragma, using specific system libraries embedding the remote procedure call, or introducing explicit remote procedure calls. Most likely the latter approach (and the most labor intensive) will provide better results, but in all cases the executable must be recompiled.

#### *The dispatch only approach*

To address this problem, we considered a new setting in which the M3 role is limited to dispatching events along the interface tree to identify a proper callback. This callback is then executed by the A9 (Figure 1b). The dispatch process can be very inefficient on the A9 when the full OS is active to process simple callbacks because many events do not lead to a callback. For example, in a pen-based interaction, the system will generate hover events, but often an application does not assign callbacks for them. Although one could dynamically filter the input stream, the use of a low power dispatch offers more control to the current program. In this configuration, developers do not need to know about the use of the M3. Thus, legacy applications can be run with little or no modifications depending on the linking strategy.

### Implementation

We use a Pandaboard ES embedding a TI OMAP 4460. A Wacom sensor or a keyboard is connected through a serial port accessible to both cores. Ubuntu Linux with Kernel 3.7 (with power management) runs on Cortex-A9 with all the unnecessary system modules disabled. SYS/BIOS 6.32 runs on Cortex-M3. RPMsg, an inter-processor communication driver, is used to call remote procedures.

## EVALUATION

The main focus of our evaluation was to better understand overall energy efficiency of power management policies for information appliances using bi-stable displays. We considered four reference configurations:

**A9_single:** The reference single-core system. The OMAP4 display subsystem is always on, but the display is activated only when it should be refreshed. This represents the simplest implementation.

**A9+display_control**: The same configuration as A9_single, but we control the OMAP4 display subsystem to leverage the bi-stable display.

**A9+M3_execute:** The M3 dispatches events and executes callbacks. The A9 sleeps except when it is strictly required. The display sub-system runs on demand.

**A9+M3_dispatch:** The M3 dispatches events, and the A9 executes the corresponding callbacks using remote procedure calls. The display sub-system runs on demand.

Acknowledging that results may be task dependent, we considered two task domains - reading and note-taking - as important aspects of reading activities. With respect to note-taking, we considered 3 different approaches spanning a range of computing requirements: inking, a virtual keyboard using a pen, and a standard keyboard.

### Energy Measurements

The main dependent variable for our experiment was the energy consumed to perform a given task in each setting. We measured energy consumption by replacing filter beads with 1% resistors of known values. Wacom power was measured by a separate shunt to the Wacom controller. These real-time measurements were sampled by a National Instruments USB-6251, controlled by a custom designed LabView application. One of the key features of bi-stable displays is that the application does not have to drive the display when it is not in use, thus further increasing power savings. Since appropriate bi-stable displays are not yet available, we cannot switch off the display controller while users interact with the system. To obtain accurate data, we therefore captured accurate interaction logs and then replayed them in a same system configuration with display controls. While all data were sampled in real-time, bi-stable display power consumption was estimated by referring Mirasol power data [2]. With the exception of the data for the A9_single, the analyses reflect the data captured during replays.

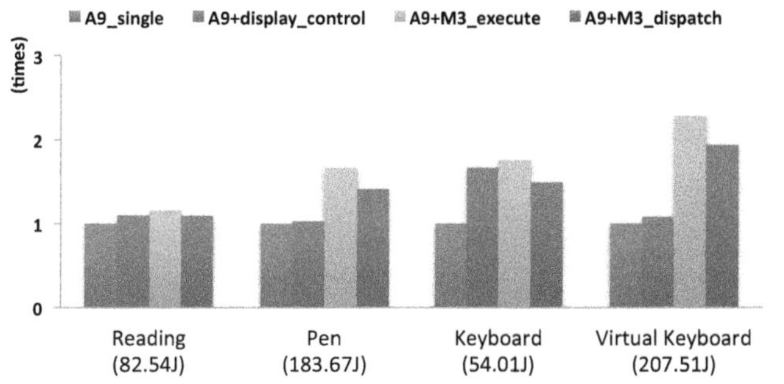


**Figure 2. Battery life extension for different tasks. Numbers in parenthesis show the energy consumption for A9_single.**

### Protocol

The experimental procedure consisted of demonstrating a task, having users try out the interface, and finally having users complete the designated tasks. All participants completed four tasks in all configurations excluding A9+display _control which was simulated using A9_single data. We assigned different datasets to each technique using a Latin Square to address order effects, and different documents in each condition to limit learning effects. For the reading task, participants read four pages (188 ± 8 characters on each page), and for the note-taking task, they typed or wrote down a short text (61 ± 6 characters) at their own pace. We recruited 9 participants with prior experience on mobile devices. They received $10 for a 1.5-hour session.

## RESULTS

We use the Greenhouse-Geisser correction to address deviations from sphericity and the Bonferroni correction for all pairwise comparisons. Reading and annotation tasks are analyzed separately. For the **reading task**, a one-way repeated measure ANOVA on total energy consumption shows a main effect for technique, ($F(3,24) = 27.29$, $p < .001$, partial $\eta^2 = .773$). Pairwise comparisons show a significant difference between A9_single and all other conditions ($p < .005$), but no other significant differences. This suggests that the modest savings (×1.10 - 1.15) are primarily driven by the direct control of the display.

With respect to the **note-taking tasks**, a two-way repeated measures (task×condition) ANOVA on total energy consumption shows main effects of task ($F(2, 16) = 105.3$, $p < .001$, partial $\eta^2 = .929$) and condition ($F(1.065, 8.517) = 195.8$, $p < .001$, partial $\eta^2 = .961$) qualified by a strong interaction ($F(1.590, 12.724) = 98.514$, $p < .001$, partial $\eta^2 = .925$). We therefore report a task-by-task analysis.

The **keyboard entry task** shows a pattern similar to the reading task. A one-way repeated measures ANOVA shows a main effect of technique ($F(1.207,9.658) = 109.97$, $p < .001$, partial $\eta^2 = .932$). Pairwise comparisons show a significant difference between A9_single and all other conditions ($p < .001$). Further, A9+M3_execute offers a significant increase in battery life (×1.76) over display-control

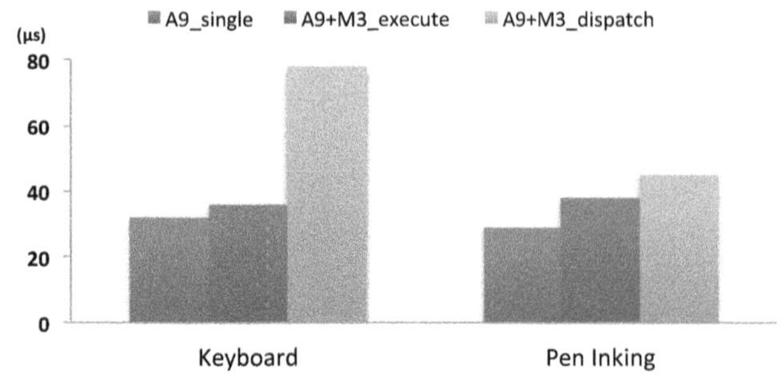


**Figure 3. Average frame buffer update latency**

(×1.67) and the simpler A9+M3_dispatch (×1.49). The overhead caused by the remote procedure calls in the A9+M3_dispatch might explain these results.

With respect to the **virtual keyboard**, a one-way repeated measures ANOVA shows a main effect for technique ($F(1.013, 8.107) = 143.5$, $p < .001$, partial $\eta^2 = .947$). Pairwise comparisons show that all pairs are significantly different ($p < .001$), with A9+M3_execute offering the best battery life improvement (×2.29), followed by A9+M3_dispatch (×1.93) and display control (×1.08). The **inking task** follows a very similar pattern ($F(1.243, 9.943) = 187.3$, $p < .001$, partial $\eta^2 = .959$). All pairwise comparisons are significantly different ($p < .001$), with A9+M3_execute offering the best battery life improvement (×1.66), followed by A9+M3_dispatch (×1.41), and display-control (×1.03).

### Task time and latency

Our results show that there is no statistical difference between task times (all ps > .05). The reading task took 224s for A9_single, 221s for A9+M3_execute and 225s for A9+M3_dispatch. The inking task took 148s, 144s, and 148s respectively, the virtual keyboard took 222s, 220s, and 223s respectively, and the keyboard task took 83s in all three configurations. With respect to the **latency**, we measured the time from user inputs to display update for keyboard and writing interactions by replaying user traces. We show the results in Figure 3. While the differences between settings are statistically significant ($p < .001$) for both keyboard and pen writing tasks, the differences between A9_single and A9+M3_exe-cute are small. The A9+M3_dispatch configuration is slower, probably due to the message passing mechanism. In all cases, the values are very small and not likely to impact user experience.

## DISCUSSION

Our results suggest that extending Guimbretiere et al.'s [1] approach to off-the-shelf commodity hardware can realize significant energy savings although savings rates are more modest than those seen for custom hardware. This may be explained by the fact that the present system uses a Linux kernel, which is already implementing an effective power management scheme. For **low event rate tasks** (reading and keyboard text entry), battery life improvement is primarily driven by more efficient control of the display, and whereas full use of the M3 offers small additional improvements (about 5%), the M3 dispatch-only is counterproductive in such tasks because of the extended use of remote procedures. For **high event rate tasks** (writing and virtual keyboards), in contrast, efficient display control only offers small benefits (×1.05), but the full use of the M3 brings significant improvements in battery life (×1.6 - 2.3). If the M3 is only used for dispatch, energy savings in high event rate tasks are about 18% lower, but still substantial.

Our findings imply that by simply using the low power core to dispatch pen events in interactive frameworks, designers can realize significant system-wide power savings. This might be even more important in the near future as designers can leverage high refresh displays to reduce interaction latency [4]. Our results suggest that techniques such as Space-filling Thumbnails can take advantage of this approach, and allow for the creation of a highly efficient digital document review system. We believe that interactions such as Marking Menu, which require limited feedback from expert users will also benefit from this design.

## CONCLUSION AND FUTURE WORK

In this paper, we extended Guimbretière et al.'s [1] approach to a commodity processor (TI OMAP4) and demonstrated that, in high event rate applications, it provides significant energy savings (up to ×2.3). Somewhat more modest savings (about 18% less) could be achieved by having the small core (M3) only dispatch the input events, but this solution is simpler to deploy. We plan to build a toolkit to take full advantage of our system on current mobile architectures before conducting more extensive evaluations.

## ACKNOWLEDGMENTS

This work was supported by NSF (ISS-0916217 and CCF-1065307). We thank Ohad Ben-Cohen, Omar Ramirez, and Robert Nelson for their contributions on development.

## REFERENCES

1. Guimbretiére, F., Liu, S., Wang, H., and Manohar, R. An asymmetric dual-processor architecture for low-power information appliances. *ACM Transactions on Embedded Computing Systems* (in press).
2. Gusev, E. Mems Growing Mainstream; Mirasol Display Technology. 2011. http://asdn.net/ngc2011/presentations/gusev.pdf.
3. Harter, T. and Vroegindeweij, S. Energy-aware user interfaces: an evaluation of user acceptance. *In proc. of SIGCHI 2004*, (2004), 199–206.
4. Jota, R., Ng, A., Dietz, P., and Wigdor, D. How fast is fast enough?: a study of the effects of latency in direct-touch pointing tasks. *In proc. of the SIGCHI 2013*, (2013), 2291–2300.
5. Vallerio, K.S., Zhong, L., and Jha, N.K. Energy-efficient graphical user interface design. *Mobile Computing, IEEE Transactions on 5*, 7 (2006), 846–859.
6. Zhong, L. and Jha, N.K. Energy efficiency of handheld computer interfaces: limits, characterization and practice. *Proceedings of MobiSys 2005*, ACM (2005), 247–260.

# Consumed Endurance: A Metric to Quantify Arm Fatigue of Mid-Air Interactions

**Juan David Hincapié-Ramos, Xiang Guo, Paymahn Moghadasian, Pourang Irani**
University of Manitoba
Winnipeg, MB, Canada
{hincapjd, umguo62, umpaymah, irani}@cc.umanitoba.ca

## ABSTRACT
Mid-air interactions are prone to fatigue and lead to a feeling of heaviness in the upper limbs, a condition casually termed as the gorilla-arm effect. Designers have often associated limitations of their mid-air interactions with arm fatigue, but do not possess a quantitative method to assess and therefore mitigate it. In this paper we propose a novel metric, *Consumed Endurance* (CE), derived from the biomechanical structure of the upper arm and aimed at characterizing the gorilla-arm effect. We present a method to capture CE in a non-intrusive manner using an off-the-shelf camera-based skeleton tracking system, and demonstrate that CE correlates strongly with the Borg CR10 scale of perceived exertion. We show how designers can use CE as a complementary metric for evaluating existing and designing novel mid-air interactions, including tasks with repetitive input such as mid-air text-entry. Finally, we propose a series of guidelines for the design of fatigue-efficient mid-air interfaces.

### Author Keywords
Gorilla-arm, mid-air interactions, mid-air text-entry, endurance, consumed endurance, SEATO mid-air keyboard.

### ACM Classification Keywords
H.5.2. Information interfaces and presentation (e.g., HCI): Evaluation/Methodology.

## INTRODUCTION
The proliferation of low-cost gestural tracking systems has warranted the investigation of mid-air interaction as a new class of natural user interface (NUI) [20, 19]. This style of interaction has shown particular value in sterile medical rooms [7, 25], in educational settings [12], and in gaming environments [22]. Nonetheless, users engaged with mid-air input often report fatigue and a feeling of heaviness in the arm [9, 20], a condition coined as the gorilla-arm effect [9]. Gorilla-arm was first reported with the introduction of touch-screens, and was one reason for the early dismissal of such systems [1, 2]. Ignoring this factor in the design of mid-air interactions can also lead to the demise of this form of NUI.


*CHI 2014*, April 26 - May 01 2014, Toronto, ON, Canada
Copyright 2014 ACM 978-1-4503-2473-1/14/04...$15.00.
http://dx.doi.org/10.1145/2556288.2557130

Current approaches to assess arm fatigue include obtrusive measurements of bodily variables (heart-rate [30], oxygen level [16] or EMG [28, 32]) or the collection of subjective assessments (Borg [8], NASA-TLX [21] or Likert ratings). However, these methods have limited practical value for evaluating mid-air interactions as they require specialized equipment or have high variance. We propose a method for quantitatively characterizing the gorilla-arm effect based on the concept of endurance (Figure 1 and equation 1) [29, 17]. Endurance is the amount of time a muscle can maintain a given contraction level before needing rest. Using a skeleton-tracking system we capture users' arm motions and compute endurance for the shoulder muscles. *Consumed Endurance* (CE), our novel metric, is the ratio of the interaction time and the computed endurance time.

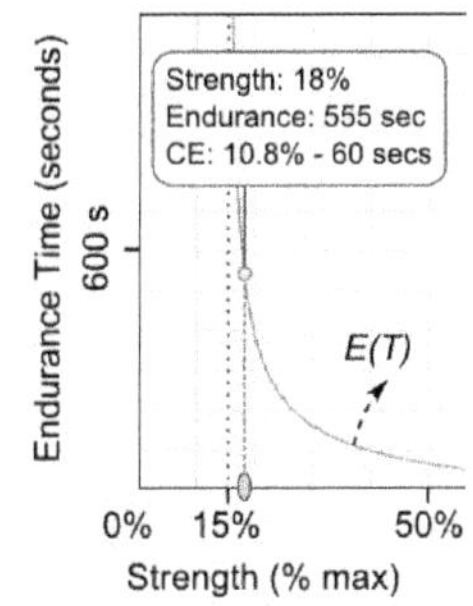


**Figure 1. Endurance metrics for the mid-air interactions include Arm Strength, Endurance and Consumed Endurance (CE).**

We validate CE against fatigue ratings as obtained using the Borg CR10 scale of perceived exertion. Further, we demonstrate CE's value as a complementary metric for evaluating mid-air interactions. For mid-air pointing and selection on a 2D plane, we used CE to identify the most suitable interaction parameters, such as arm extension, plane location and plane size. For example, users consumed the least amount of endurance when the arm was bent and operating on the interaction plane located midway between the shoulder and the waist. *Dwell* selections have the lowest CE for single hand interactions. We also demonstrate the value of using CE to inform the design of an endurance-efficient text-entry layout, SEATO (Figure 7-left). Users entering text with SEATO had lower CE than with QWERTY without compromising text-entry speed. Finally, we describe how our results inform the design of mid-air menus and other interactive systems. CE and other fatigue-related metrics are publicly available in a software toolkit (http://hci.cs.umanitoba.ca/projects-and-research/details/ce).

Our contributions include: 1) CE, a metric for characterizing shoulder fatigue or gorilla-arm effects resulting from mid-air interactions; 2) the use of CE to inform the choice of various mid-air interaction parameters; 3) an endurance-efficient mid-air text-entry layout, SEATO; and 4) guidelines for designing endurance-efficient mid-air interactions.

## RELATED WORK

This section gives a summary of the existing qualitative and quantitative tools for assessing muscular fatigue.

### Qualitative Assessment of Fatigue

Qualitative methods for assessing arm fatigue include Likert-scale questions [9], the NASA Task Load Index (NASA-TLX) [21] and the Borg RPE and CR10 scales [8]. Likert-scales reduce the users' subjective ratings to whether or not they experienced fatigue in an interaction. The NASA-TLX questionnaire captures workload along categories such as Physical Demand and Effort [21], rated on a 20-point scale. However, as pointed by Bustamante and Spain, the TLX lacks "scalar invariance, thereby biasing the estimation of mean scores and making the examination of mean differences misleading" [10]. Subjectivity is further reinforced as each participant can weigh the various TLX categories differently. The Borg CR10 scale [8] is tailored to physical exertion. It maps numeric ratings to carefully chosen verbal cues and provides scalar invariance.

While qualitative assessments provide a coarse estimation of fatigue, a finer characterization is required, particularly for repetitive tasks. Subjective assessments cannot give an account of the small yet significant differences, and are prone to confounding variables such as the participant's fitness, comfort level or general state of mind. Complementing such methods with objective metrics of fatigue can provide a more holistic handle over gorilla-arm effects.

### Objective Assessment of Fatigue

Fields such as the sports sciences, ergonomics and physiology have long studied the relationship between muscular exertion and fatigue. Their methods range from external measurements such as monitoring muscle swelling [5], muscle oxygenation [16], heart rate (mentioned in [6]), and blood flow and pressure [30]; to invasive techniques such as measuring the intra-arterial levels of lactate and potassium [30]. Morris et al. [26] show a strong relationship between different fatigue-related factors obtained externally (rate of force exertion and relaxation) and those captured invasively (lactate, oxygen level), indicating that the former are highly reliable measures of fatigue. However, these approaches require specialized equipment (such as EMG and NIRS devices, dynamometers or exoskeletons) or are invasive, limiting how users engage with mid-air systems, and thus impractical for the design of interactive systems. Unlike previous approaches [5, 16, 30, 4], our method provides an objective and non-invasive metric of shoulder fatigue, calculated using a low-cost gestural tracking system.

## FATIGUE IN MID-AIR INTERACTIONS

Gorilla-arm is a manifestation of fatigue in the arm muscles. Fatigue is defined as the ability to maintain a given muscular contraction level [17] and depends on the amount of blood flow, and thus oxygen, that reaches the muscle cells. A contracted muscle hardens arteries and restricts blood flow. With low levels of oxygen muscle cells switch their energy source from aerobic to glycolytic metabolism. Given the limited amounts of stored glucose, the muscle cells can produce energy and maintain the contraction only for a short period of time. Fatigue occurs when this energy is used up.

A well accepted result in human physiology is Rohmert's study of the impact of fatigue on endurance: the maximum amount of time that a muscle can maintain a contraction level before needing rest [29]. Figure 1 illustrates Rohmert's formulation of endurance *E(F)* as a function of the value of force applied (F) in relation to the maximum force ($F_{max}$) of the muscle (see equation 1). An important observation is that equation 1 is asymptotic at 15% of the maximum force, meaning that forces exerted below that level could be sustained for long time periods. The presence of fatigue in mid-air interactions [9, 20] suggests that current interaction techniques require arm forces above the 15% mark.

$$E(F) = \frac{1236.5}{\left(\frac{F}{F_{max}} * 100 - 15\right)^{0.618}} - 72.5 \qquad (1)$$

We derive metrics based on this mathematical formulation of endurance to study and guide the design of mid-air interact-tions. A higher endurance time for an interaction implies that it triggers lower amounts of fatigue in users and thus allows for longer engagements with a system. Ultimately, this should foster a broader adoption of such technologies.

## CHARACTERIZING SHOULDER ENDURANCE

This section details a non-intrusive method for determining endurance for mid-air interactions. Although multiple body parts are involved in mid-air arm interactions we focus on the shoulder joint as it largely dominates the forces required for moving the arm. Measuring endurance using Rohmert's formulation requires capturing the two variables in equation 1: the maximum force of the shoulder ($F_{max}$), and the force acting on the shoulder at a given time (F). For the first variable, we rely on values of maximum force as determined previously by others [31, 14]. For the second variable, we use a biomechanical model of the arm where it is represented as a compound rotational system encompassing the upper arm, the forearm and the hand, and with its pivot on the shoulder joint (see Figure 2-left). This compound system can be simplified as a single-part system where all forces are applied at the arm's center of mass (CoM) (see Figure 2-right).

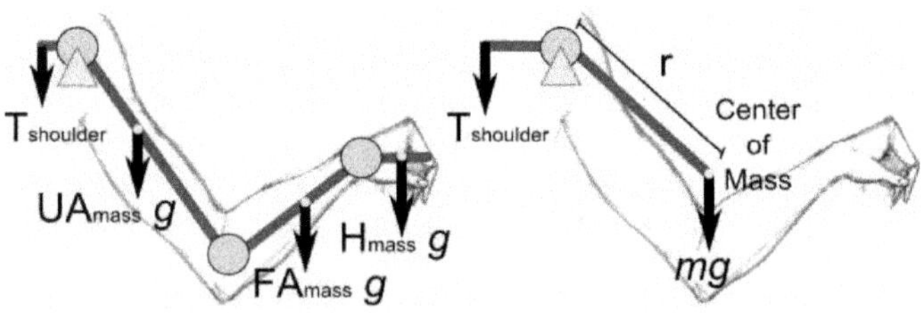


**Figure 2. Left: The primary forces acting on the arm. Right: The forces aggregated at the CoM.**

Rohmert's formulation assumes that $F$ and $F_{max}$ are comparable, that is, they are applied at the same distance from the shoulder joint. However, given that $F_{max}$ is determined at the elbow [31] and $F$ at the CoM, these two forces are not comparable. A solution is to express all forces in terms of torque. Appendix A shows the relationship between $\frac{\|\vec{F}\|}{F_{max}}$ and $\frac{\|\vec{T}\|}{T_{max}}$; and therefore endurance in terms of torque is:

$$E(T_{shoulder}) = \frac{1236.5}{\left(\frac{T_{shoulder}}{T_{max}} * 100 - 15\right)^{0.618}} - 72.5 \quad (2)$$

Equation 3 formalizes the sum of torques ($\sum \vec{T}$) acting on the system at a given time. The first torque pulls the arm downwards and is due to the interaction of gravity ($g$) and the mass of the arm ($m$) at the CoM (distance $r$ from the shoulder joint). The second torque is provided by the shoulder muscles and it compensates for the effects of gravity and moves the arm. The final torque is due to the arm's inertia and its angular acceleration ($I\alpha$), and represents the tendency of the arm to maintain its rotational movement once in motion.

$$\sum \vec{T} = \vec{r} \times m\vec{g} + \vec{T}_{shoulder} + \vec{I\alpha} \quad (3)$$

When the arm is static the $\sum \vec{T}$ and $\vec{I}\alpha$ components are equal to zero, and therefore $\|\vec{T}_{shoulder}\| = \|\vec{r} \times m\vec{g}\|$. That is, the shoulder has to match the gravity torque. Conversely, when the arm is in rotation the resulting $\sum \vec{T}$ and $\vec{I\alpha}$ are not equal to zero. The next section shows how to calculate $\vec{T}_{shoulder}$.

### Measuring Torque at the Shoulder Joint

By following the process described in Appendix B, a skeleton tracking system can compute the CoM location $r$ at time $t$. Tracking the CoM allows us to determine its velocity and acceleration. Knowing the arm mass it is possible to determine the force acting at the CoM:

$$\overrightarrow{force}_{motion,t} = \overrightarrow{acceleration}_t * m \quad (4)$$

Thus, the total torque of the system can be expressed as[1]:

$$\sum \vec{T}_t = \vec{r} \times \overrightarrow{force}_{motion,t} \quad (5)$$

Equaling equations 3 and 5, we can derive the actual torque exerted by the shoulder muscles at time $t$:

$$\|\vec{T}_{shoulder,t}\| = \|\vec{r} \times \overrightarrow{force}_{motion,t} - (\vec{r} \times m\vec{g} + I_t \vec{\propto}_t)\| \quad (6)$$

The final term in equation 6, $I_t \vec{\propto}_t$, represents the tendency of a rotating body to continue its rotational movement. Angular acceleration ($\vec{\propto}$) at time $t$ can be calculated as $\vec{\propto}_t = \frac{acceleration_t}{\|\vec{r}\|}$. See Appendix C for a detailed account on how to calculate the moment of inertia ($I$) of a moving arm.

### Maximum Torque of the Shoulder

Tan et al. studied the force output range at different joints in the body [31], and established the maximum controllable force of the shoulder applied at the elbow to be 87.2 $N$ for females and 101.6 $N$ for males. In a similar study, Edmunds et al. found that such maximum force varies slightly according to the movement direction (x,y,z), with an approximate 100 $N$ as the most common value [14]. We use Tan et al.'s maximum force to get the maximum torque $T_{max}$ of the shoulder muscles; based on their experimental set-up, we remove the effect of the arm weight from the max torque.

### Endurance Metrics

Based on the above, we can calculate the following metrics:

- Strength (S): The ratio between the average torque applied in the interaction and the maximum torque. This metric corresponds to the $\frac{\|\vec{T}_{shoulder}\|}{T_{max}} * 100$ term of equation 5.
- Endurance (E): The time, in seconds, the participant could sustain such interaction before needing to rest the arm.
- Consumed Endurance (CE): The ratio of the interaction time and the computed endurance time (see equation 7). We interpret CE as the percentage of the energy used or as the amount of fatigue.

$$CE(T, TotalTime) = \frac{TotalTime}{E(T)} * 100 \quad (7)$$

## ENDURANCE METRICS IMPLEMENTATION

We used Microsoft's .NET to implement the CE equations. We used the Microsoft Kinect, an off-the-shelf human skeleton tracking system, to capture the arm joints needed. We applied a noise reduction filter averaging the last 10 skeleton frames. The system operates at approximately 32 frames/sec, which is sufficient to support the small delta ($\partial t$) assumption made for equation 5. We used the 50$^{th}$ percentile male or female values[2] for weight, length, center of mass, and inertia of the upper arm, lower arm, and hand (a standard approach [18]) as compiled by Freivalds [17]. Using these values and the captured skeleton, our system determines the arm's CoM and normalizes it to the 50th percentile (we use the skeleton's upper arm's length as a frame of reference). The system calculates all metrics from the normalized CoM.

## VALIDATING THE CONSUMED ENDURANCE METRIC

In this section, we assess the validity of CE as a measure of fatigue by 1) comparing CE measurements to Borg CR10 ratings [8] and 2) analyzing the effects of gender-specific constants. The Borg CR10 scale provides a ratio-scale measure of physical exertion which values are matched to verbal anchors. Borg CR10 values range from 0 to 10, where 0 corresponds to "Nothing At All" and 10 to "Very Very Hard (Maximal)". Electromyograms (EMG) measure muscle cell activations and is the bases for several objective metrics (see [32]). Studies have shown that Borg CR10 ratings and EMG-based metrics for shoulder muscles strongly correlate and therefore either method can be used to assess shoulder fatigue [28, 32]. More importantly, they showed that Borg CR10 can be more reliable than EMG metrics. At low levels of physical exertion (such as the ones in optimized mid-air gestures) EMG metrics are not valid fatigue indicators [27]. Also, EMG metrics have lower repeatability than Borg CR10 [13] and their validity is task-dependent [15].

We asked 16 participants (8 female) to hold their dominant arm at different angles from the vertical axis (90°, 60°, 30°,

[1] The cross product in equation 5 indicates that only the forces tangential to the rotation axis are relevant for the torque. When ($\partial t \rightarrow 0$), then $\overrightarrow{force}_{motion,t} \rightarrow \overrightarrow{force}_{tangential,t}$.

[2] An alternative method measures the length of a volunteer's upper limbs and uses this data to retrieve the average corresponding weights based on data provided by the Visible Human Project [3].

and at rest, controlled within ±2 degrees) and for different periods of time (15, 30, 45 and 60 seconds). We used a Latin-square design on *angle* with *time* and *gender* as random factors. We captured 3 trials per condition per participant for a total of 16×16×3 = 768 CE measurements. Participants rated each condition (3 trials) for a total of 16×16 = 256 Borg CR10 ratings. Figure 3 shows the overall results.

We used linear regression analysis and the Mixed Factors ANOVA test with *angle* and *time* as within-subject factors and *gender* as a between-subjects factor. We used Bonferroni correction for post-hoc tests. Linear regression analysis between CE and Borg CR10 ratings (see Figure 3-bottom) revealed a significant correlation ($F_1 = 1902.722$, $p < 0.001$) with $R^2 = 0.716$. For the ANOVA, normality tests showed a normal distribution for all conditions ($p < 0.001$). Results showed a main effect in *angle* for CE ($F_{3,42} = 8543.719$, $p < 0.001$) and Borg CR10 ($F_{3,42} = 89.806$, $p < 0.001$); a main effect in *time* for CE ($F_{3,42} = 23323.431$, $p < 0.001$) and Borg CR10 ($F_{3,42} = 68.460$, $p < 0.001$); and no main effect in *gender* for CE ($F_{1,14} = 0.951$, $p = 0.346$) and Borg CR10 ($F_{1,14} = 2.379$, $p = 0.145$). Results showed interaction effects for *angle* × *time* in CE ($F_{9,126} = 4874.636$, $p < 0.001$) and Borg CR10 ($F_{9,126} = 10.301$, $p < 0.05$). Post-hoc analysis of *angle* and *time* showed significant differences between all conditions for both CE and Borg CR10.

Our results show that CE and Borg CR10 ratings present a "very strong to perfect association" (R = 0.846) where the value of CE is used to predict 72% of the variability of Borg CR10 ratings ($R^2 = 0.716$). The remaining 28% can be explained by differences in fitness level of the participants and the subjective nature of the Borg CR10 scale (affected by factors such as tiredness, comfort, and general state of mind). Moreover, CE and Borg CR10 ratings are equally capable of yielding significant differences for changes in *angle* and *time* (main effects on both factors). Furthermore, results show that CE is gender neutral, suggesting that the different sets of constants for arm metrics (weights, lengths, and max force) do not affect CE. In other words, given Borg CR10's correlation to objective measurements of fatigue (such as EMG), these results show that CE is a valid objective fatigue metric for the shoulder muscles.

## CONSUMED ENDURANCE AS AN ANALYTICAL TOOL

We first demonstrate the use of our model to evaluate different mid-air interaction factors. In the first experiment we investigate the effects of different plane locations and arm extensions on CE. In the second experiment we study the effects of plane size and selection method on CE.

### Experiment 1: Plane Location and Arm Extension

*Methods*

*Apparatus* – The system ran on a Windows 7 PC connected to a 4×2.3 meters projector screen with a resolution of 1366× 768 pixels (1 pixel = 3 mm) and a Microsoft Kinect. The Kinect was in front of the screen and 1 meter above the floor; participants stood 3.3 meters from the screen. We used the same set-up for all experiments.

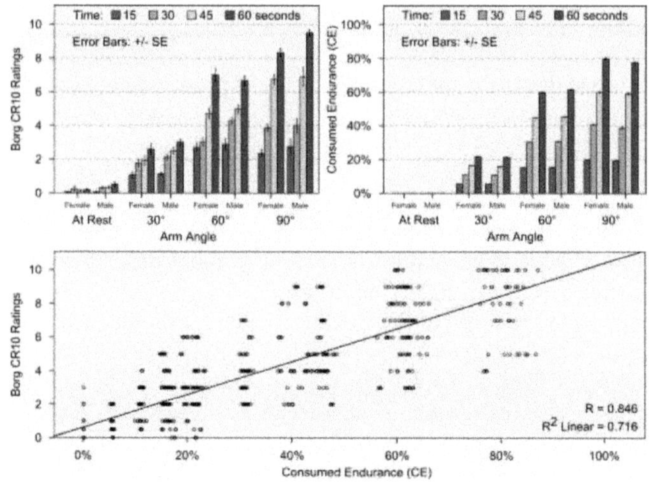


**Figure 3. Top – Both CE and Borg CR10 present a main effect for *angle* and *time* but not for *gender*. Bottom – Linear correlation between Borg CR10 and CE show a strong correlation (R = 0.846) where CE predicts 72% of the variability in Borg CR10 ratings ($R^2 = 0.716$).**

*Subjects* – 12 participants (3 female) volunteered, ages 18-40 (mean 26), right handed. All participants had previous experience (mean: 0.6 years) with mid-air interaction systems (Wii, Kinect, etc.) and were familiar with mid-air selection.

*Task* – Participants had to select 20 fixed targets (one after the other) in a square 2D plane (35 cm sides) by moving the cursor (small red circle) with their right arm from the current position to the target. Participants were asked to select using a mouse button held in the left hand. We relegated selection to a mouse to avoid any overhead. All targets were solid squares organized in a 6x6 matrix (black border, white background). Upon selection, the target was highlighted in red, and the next target turned blue. The task finished when the participant selected the 20 targets in the order presented. The 20 targets were randomly distributed across all positions and no position was repeated. A landing error was marked when the user left the target before selecting it. This measure describes the level of control a user has over the cursor, i.e., how precise the movements are.

*Design* – Independent variables were *plane location* and *arm extension* (see Figure 4). We used a 2x2 within-subject design to compare CE in each condition. We considered two 2D plane locations relative to the body (all planes aligned to the right side of the shoulder):

- *Shoulder*: is a vertical plane with the vertical center at the shoulder joint.
- *Center*: is a vertical plane with the vertical center located halfway between the shoulder and the waist.

We considered two arm extensions: Extended and Bent. The system detects the arm as extended when the hand is at least

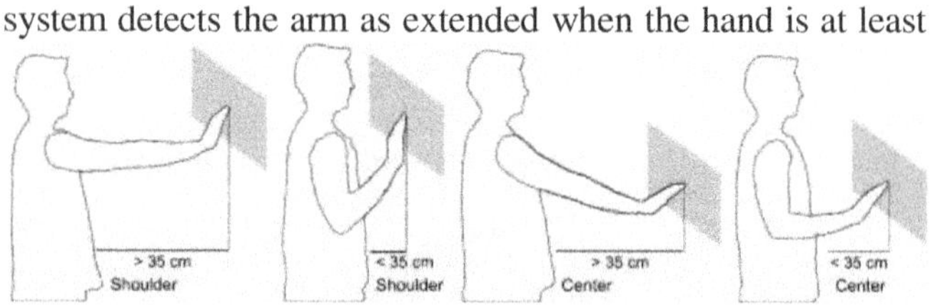


**Figure 4. Two location planes (shoulder, center) with two arm configurations (extended, bent)**

35 cm away from the body, and as bent when the hand is 35 cm or closer to the body plane. The system ignores the arm (removes the cursor from the screen) when it is under or beyond these limits, forcing the participant to stretch out or bend it as necessary. We settled on these measures after iterative pilot testing.

Participants were trained with each condition after the experimenter demonstrated the task. With a total of 2×2 = 4 conditions and 4 trials per condition, we registered 2×2×4 = 16 trials per participant, or 192 trials in total (each trial consisted of 20 selections). Participants had a mandatory 3 minute break between conditions. All participants completed the experiment in one session lasting approximately 30 minutes. The trials were counter-balanced using a Latin-square on plane location and arm extension.

*Measures* –We collected values for CE, completion time, and landing error rate. Participants filled a Borg CR10 rate scale questionnaire after each condition.

### Results

None of the dependent variables comply with the ANOVA assumptions (normality and equal variances) and therefore we applied the Aligned Rank Transform for nonparametric factorial analysis [33] with a Bonferroni correction for pairwise comparisons. Figure 5 presents the results.

*Consumed Endurance (CE)* – Results showed a main effect of *plane location* ($F_{1,11}$ = 102.249, $p < 0.001$) and *arm extension* ($F_{1,11}$ = 86.959, $p < 0.001$). There were not significant interaction effects for *plane location* × *arm extension* (p = 0.637). CE was lowest in the center plane location with an average of 27.23% (standard deviation or std = 15.33) and the bent arm extension at 23.44% (std = 13.45).

*Borg CR10* – Results showed main effects of *plane location* ($F_{1,11}$ = 7.111, $p < 0.05$) and *arm extension* ($F_{1,11}$ = 21.082, $p < .001$). There were no significant interaction effects for *plane location* × *arm extension* (p = 0.134). Borg CR10 was lowest on the center plane location at 3.00 (std = 1.87) and the bent arm extension at 2.75 (std = 1.51).

*Completion Time* – Results did not show a main effect of *plane location* (p = .092) or *arm extension* (p = .223). There were no significant interaction effects for *plane location* × *arm extension* (p = .893). Average completion time was 45 seconds (std = 13.81).

*Landing Error Rate* – Results did not show a main effect of *arm extension* (p = .619) or *plane location* (p = .357). There were no significant interaction effects for *plane location* × *arm extension* (p = .220). Average landing error was 0.93 (std = 2.22).

### Discussion

We first observe that both CE and Borg CR10 yield similar main and interaction effects, highlighting CE's capacity to reveal the same fatigue effects as Borg CR10. On the other hand, differences in completion times and error rates are not significant. This is an important observation because it suggests that differences in fatigue emerge even when other measurements are flat. Therefore, completion time and

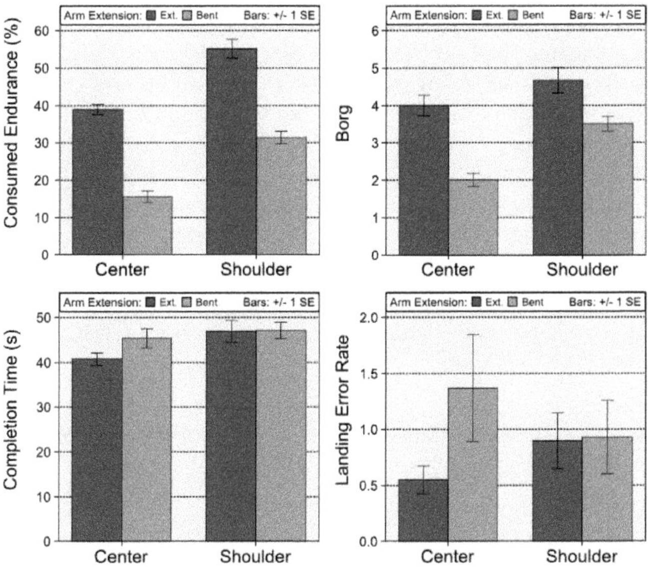


**Figure 5. Consumed Endurance, Borg CR10 ratings, completion time and landing error rate for experiment one.**

landing error rate were limited in determining the optimal combination of *plane location* and *arm extension* for mid-air input, given our conditions. With equivalent accuracy to Borg CR10, a system can calculate CE unobtrusively and in real-time by simply tracking arm movements.

Interactions in the shoulder plane consume more endurance as the arm is higher up from its resting position. Similarly, interactions with arm extended also consumed more endurance as the center-of-mass is further extended from the body, thus requiring a higher torque. Interactions with the bent arm consumed the least endurance, the lowest being in the center plane at 15.55%. We select the center + bent condition as the optimal area for interaction and use it in the next experiments which evaluate CE for other factors.

## Experiment 2 - Plane Size and Selection Method

The goal of this experiment is to examine the effect of larger arm movements and different selection methods on CE.

### Methods

*Subjects* – 12 participants (4 female), ages 18-40 (mean 22.3), volunteered. All participants were right handed and half had no experience with in air interactions.

*Task & Design* – The experimental task was the same as in experiment one. The independent variables were *plane size*, and *selection method*. We used a 2x4 within-subject design. We tested two plane sizes: 35x35 cm and 25x25 cm. Selection method indicates the mechanism by which participants select a target. We designed four methods:

- *Click*: as in experiment one; participants click a mouse held in their left hand.
- *Swipe*: is a quick horizontal arm movement to both sides at min 50 cm/sec and for a movement of at least 15 cm.
- *Dwell*: participants highlight a target for 1.5 seconds (threshold determined through iterative pilot testing).
- *Second Hand*: participants move the left arm 20cms away from its resting position (i.e., from the hips).

The experimenter demonstrated each selection method and participants had an initial training with each condition, testing each selection method until they had control over it. The experiment had a total of 2×4 = 8 conditions and each condition had 3 trials, yielding 2×4×3 = 24 trials per participant, or 288 trials in total. All participants completed the experiment within approximately 45 minutes. The trials were counter-balanced with a Latin-square approach on selection method and plane size appeared in a random order.

*Measures* –We collected values for CE, completion time, and landing error rate. Participants filled in a Borg CR10 scale after each condition.

### Results

We used the same statistical tests as in experiment one (ART ANOVA). Figure 6 shows an overview of the results.

*Consumed Endurance (CE)* – Results showed a main effect of *selection method* ($F_{3,33}$ = 19.612, p < 0.001) and *plane size* ($F_{1,11}$ = 16.165, p = 0.002). There were no significant interaction effects for *plane size* × *selection method* (p = 0.323). Post-hoc pair-wise comparisons on *selection method* yielded significant (p < 0.04) differences between all pairs except between dwell and swipe, and dwell and second hand. In general, CE was lowest for click at 8.18% (std = 9.06) and the small plane at 10.80% (std = 12.00).

*Borg CR10* – Results showed a main effect of *selection method* ($F_{3,33}$ = 8.425, p < 0.001) but not for *plane size* (p = 0.837). Results did not show interaction effects for *plane size* × *selection method* (p = 0.586). Post-hoc analysis on *selection method* yielded significant differences for all pairs (p < 0.04) except second hand and dwell. In general, Borg CR10 was lowest for click at 1.188 (std = 0.845).

*Completion Time* – Results showed main effects of *selection method* ($F_{3,33}$ = 58.076, p < 0.001) and *plane size* ($F_{1,11}$ = 5.143, p = 0.044). Analysis also revealed interactions effects for *plane size* × *selection method* ($F_{3,33}$ = 3.167, p = 0.037). Post-hoc analysis on *selection method* revealed significant differences (p < 0.017) between all pairs. Click was the fastest selection method at 40.76 seconds (std = 10.62). The larger plane had a lower mean completion time of 54.52 seconds (std = 17.92).

*Landing Error Rate* – Results showed a main effect of *plane size* and *selection method* (all p<0.003) on error rate with $F_{1,11}$ = 17.112 and $F_{3,33}$ = 22.167 respectively. There were no interaction effects between *plane size* and *selection method* (p = 0.131). Post-hoc pair-wise analysis showed a significant difference between swipe and all other selection methods (all p<0.001). Error rate was lowest for dwell at 0.66 (std = 0.59) and the big plane at 0.83 (std = 0.86).

### Discussion

This experiment highlights the capacity of CE for uncovering differences where subjective ratings cannot. A larger plane requires stretching and lifting the arm which clearly results in increased effort. CE reveals a significant difference between plane sizes which Borg CR10 hides due to the high variance and small size of the sample.

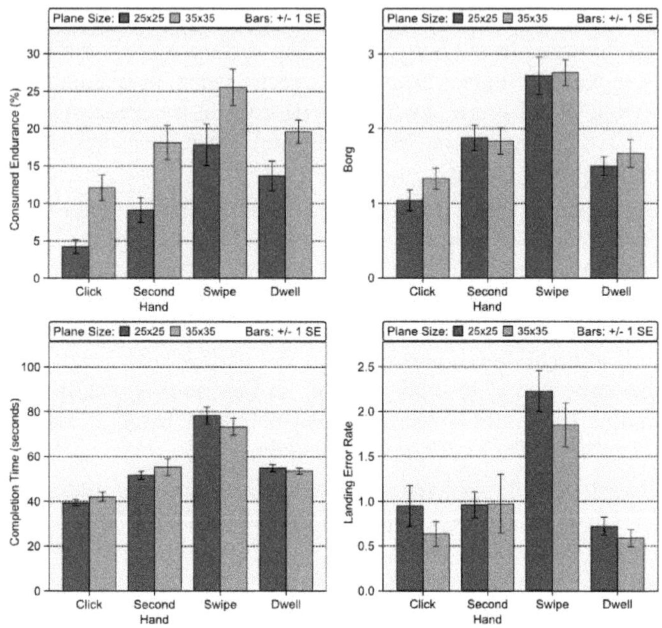


**Figure 6. Consumed Endurance, Borg CR10, completion time and error rate for experiment two.**

Selection methods which do not require movement of the selecting hand perform best across all metrics. Swipe, which performs worst, sees its CE increased due to the greater amount of movement it requires due to the gesture design and to tracking errors. Tracking errors, more noticeable in the small plane, are due to problems of distinguishing the arm from the body and to follow the hand back (such as in swipe). This results in poorly controlled gestures which miss the target, leading to repetition, and therefore higher completion time and CE. A better tracking technology would increase the controllability of the gesture, reducing the need to correct and flattening error rates and their effect on CE.

The best plane in terms of CE is the small plane. However, the best performance in terms of completion time and landing error rate is the big plane. A designer may have to choose the larger plane to reduce errors which could quickly lead to fatigue and a bad user experience. As expected, Click outperforms all other selection methods in terms of CE and therefore it should be used when possible, else Dwell and Second Hand use similarly little CE.

## ENDURANCE AS A DESIGN PARAMETER

The previous experiments demonstrate the use of CE as a tool to assess various design alternatives. In this section we use another endurance-related metric, *strength* (defined earlier), as a design parameter for a mid-air text-entry system. We choose text-entry because it is a common task and one that involves repetition. From our previous experiments we know that: (a) interactions consumed the least endurance when they occur on the center plane with a bent arm; (b) a 25x25 cm plane size consumes lower CE; and (c) for single hand situations dwell selections are recommended.

In this section we propose a new text-entry layout optimized for such a set of interaction parameters (see Figure 7). We collected data from 4 participants (all male) who held the cursor at each position of the 6x6 grid for 10 seconds (center

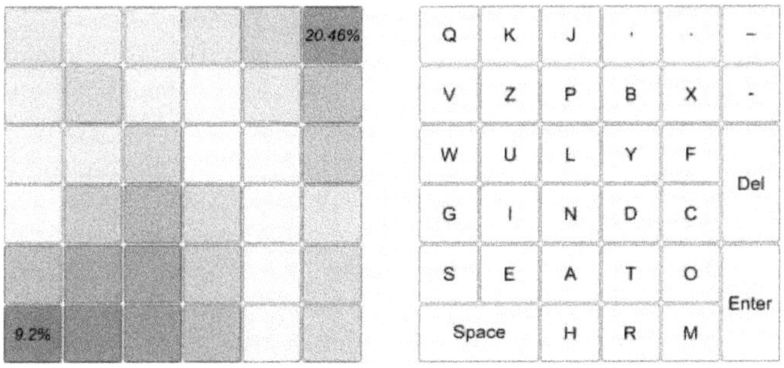


**Figure 7. Left: Heat-map of strength. Cells in blue require the least strength and those in red require the most. Right: SEATO key layout based on character probability in the English language and strength.**

plane, arm bent, 25x25 cm plane size). We recorded arm *strength* ($\frac{\|\vec{T}_{shoulder}\|}{T_{max}} * 100$) for each cell because, unlike endurance and CE, it is not affected by the asymptote of equation 2 and thus reveals differences even when the physical effort is low. Figure 7-left shows the resulting heat-map for strength throughout the grid: on average. The cell on the lower-left corner requires 9.2% of the maximum strength, while the cell on the upper-right corner required 20.46%. All bluish cells in Figure 7-left are below the 15% threshold. Figure 7-right shows the resulting SEATO text-entry layout for mid-air interactions. We obtained the SEATO layout by mapping the cells with the lowest strength demands to the characters with the highest probability in the English language, ideally resulting in a less physically demanding interaction than with other text-entry layouts like QWERTY.

### Experiment 3 - Text Entry Layout

In this experiment we compare the SEATO and QWERTY layouts in terms of CE, text-entry speed and error rate.

#### Methods

*Subjects* – 12 participants (5 female), ages 18-40 (mean 24), volunteered. All participants were right handed and all but three had previous experience with mid-air interactions.

*Task* – Participants had to type a sentence that was shown on the screen. For typing a character participants had to move the cursor to the cell with the character and use the dwell gesture for selection. We selected a list of 53 sentences between 19 and 23 characters long from MacKenzie et al.'s set [24]. When the wrong character was selected the system would not allow any more typing until the wrong character is deleted by selecting the DEL key; this is counted as an entry error. The task finishes when the correct phrase is typed in and the participant selects the ENTER key.

*Design* – The independent variable is layout: SEATO and QWERTY. We used a within-subjects design to compare CE between layouts. Participants had an initial training with the SEATO layout and with the mechanics of selecting a letter. Participants were trained by typing sample sentences with both layouts, terminating a phrase with the ENTER key. There were 2 conditions, and each condition had a total of 4 blocks and 3 trials per block, yielding 2×4×3 = 24 trials per participant, or 288 trials in total.

*Measures* – We measured CE, words per minute (WPM), and error rate. Users filled a Borg CR10 scale after each block.

#### Results

We used the same analysis tools as for experiments one and two. Figure 8 shows an overview of the results.

*Consumed Endurance (CE)* – Results showed a main effect for *layout* ($F_{1,11}$ = 51.332, p < 0.001) and *block* ($F_{3,33}$ = 14.285, p < 0.001). Results did not show significant interaction effects (p = 0.174). Post-hoc analysis showed a significant difference between the first and second block (p = 0.003). SEATO had a lower average CE compared to QWERTY at 6.43% (std = 11.08).

*Borg CR10* – Results did not show a main effect of *layout* (p = 0.258) or *block* (p = 0.257). Interactions effects were also not significant (p = 0.300).

*Words Per Minute* – Results showed no main effect of *layout* on words-per-minute (WPM) (p = 0.124), but a main effect for *block* on WPM ($F_{3,33}$ = 6.120, p=0.002). Results showed no *layout* × *block* interaction effect (p = 0.581). Post-hoc analysis revealed significant differences between the first and third (p < 0.02) and last (p = 0.003) blocks. The last block had the highest WPM at 4.55 (std = 1.26).

*Typing Error* – Results showed a main effect of *layout* ($F_{1,11}$ = 15.868, p = 0.002) and *block* ($F_{3,33}$ = 8.572, p < 0.001), but no interaction effects (p = 0.378). Post-hoc analysis revealed the first block to be significantly different from all other blocks (p < 0.022). The last block had the lowest mean error rate at 0.05 (sd = 0.07) and the Qwerty layout had a lower mean error rate at 0.06 (sd = 0.1).

#### Discussion

Our data shows that layout has an effect on CE, with our proposed SEATO layout consuming significantly less endurance than QWERTY (a quarter), at no cost in terms of words-per-minute and only slightly higher error rate. Moreover, results show no significant difference in the Borg CR10 rankings, outlining the added value of our metric for situations where differences do not surface with subjective ratings. Finally, the similar typing speed we observed reinforces the notion that designers could also look at other factors beyond interaction time for making interface choices.

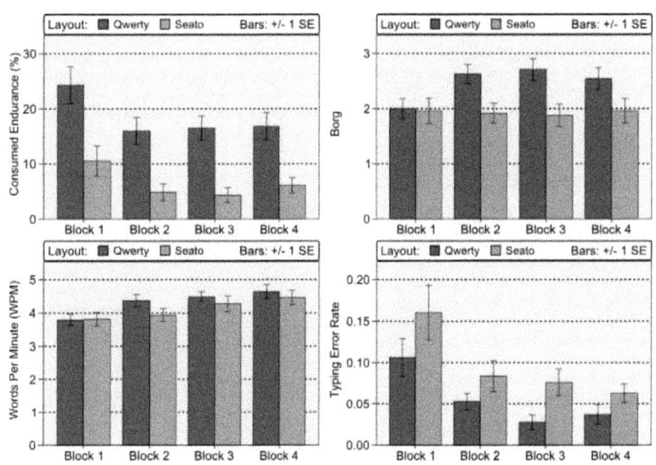


**Figure 8. Consumed Endurance, Borg CR10, words per minute and error rate for experiment three.**

## GENERAL DISCUSSION

We discuss our findings in light of mid-air interactions.

### Applications of endurance-based metrics

Our results demonstrate the value of adopting CE as a complementary guide for evaluating the impact of mid-air input parameters like plane size or selection mechanisms on fatigue. In a similar vein, CE can be used to evaluate alternative sets of mid-air gestures for controlling an interactive system (as in Barclay et al. [6]).

Aside from designing endurance-efficient text-entry layouts, our metrics can be used in the design of mid-air menus, document navigation controls and arm gestures. Based on the heat-map shown in Figure 7-left, when selecting a menu with a pointer, the most frequently used menu items should be in the lower left corner (or lower right if interacting with the left arm): buttons on the top or the right side of the interaction plane should be avoided (Figure 9-middle). Similarly, navigation controls, if used frequently, should appear in those regions marked in blue in Figure 7 (see image in color).

Our results also suggest that when possible mid-air gestural interactions should consider relative movements rather than absolute ones that have fixed positions in the air (Figure 9-right). In this manner, gestures could take place in regions of least effort. For example, gesturing the letter 'B' could take place by allowing users to start the gesture by moving the arm from its rest position without having to lift it up to an absolute start position of engagement.

Finally, to control for arm position (bent or extended) in our experiments, our application did not allow the user to operate outside a certain distance region. While we do not advise enforcing such restrictions in mid-air interactions, application designers could include guidelines to users, in the form of a quick image or video clip, to reduce fatigue during use.

While we demonstrated the use of our metric to minimize CE, other applications may choose to increase it or adjust it dynamically. For example, mid-air gaming applications could introduce CE for better control over game balancing. Dynamic game-balancing is possible by gradually shifting the need for selecting or interacting with different positions within the interaction plane or by requiring the user to use different arm positions (switching between extended and bent). This could have direct benefits in virtual therapy applications where movements can become increasingly demanding as the patient's upper limb functions improve, or conversely if the patient's progress is slow.

To support the different explorations and usages of CE, researchers and designers of mid-air interfaces can download our implementation here http://hci.cs.umanitoba.ca/projects-and-research/details/ce.

### Our findings complement existing guidelines

Our results, obtained with a view on reducing fatigue, empirically confirm and further complement human interface guidelines proposed by some manufacturers of gestural tracking systems (for details see: www.microsoft.com/en-us/kinectforwindows/develop/learn.aspx). Such guidelines mainly provide designers with parameters for optimal tracking efficiency. For example, the Kinect guidelines suggest using Dwell to avoid inadvertent selections (page 55, in above document) and recommend that gestural systems allow seamless hand switching or provide alternative gesture sets to reduce fatigue (page 22). Our results further provide specific insight on how such alternative gesture sets should be designed to reduce effort, such as for text-entry.

### Our findings in light of previous results

Our results justify the fatigue-related findings of prior work. Harrison et al.'s participants preferred a position with "elbows tucked in, hands held front, and palms up" [20]. In light of our results that position seems natural as it closely resembles the center bent arm position. Similarly Boring et al.'s participants who did not move their whole arms and relied on tilt reported less fatigue [9]. This result also seems natural as the arm was not fully extended and thus all of its mass did not have to be moved by the shoulder muscles. Finally, our results can explain why Cockburn et al.'s ray-casting technique was ranked the least physically demanding [11], as the upper-arm was held in a resting position.

Our results can also be used to re-consider existing interactions. For example, Li et al.'s VirtualShelves introduce mobile interactions across the horizontal and vertical axis in front of the user [23]. As these movements require full arm extension their CE is high. An endurance-efficient alternative can use only movements of the forearm, with the upper arm in rest position, i.e. with bent elbow. Similarly, Cockburn et al.'s 2D plane technique can improve in terms of CE by fixing their interaction plane at the center plane location, i.e. between the hip and shoulders, and by reducing the size of the plane to one where less arm extension is needed.

### Lessons learned

We take away these lessons from our initial exploration:

- The center + bent arm position for selections on a 2D plane is the least tiring of all positions we tested.
- The regions at the bottom of the interaction plane improve CE. Interacting in the lowest possible region should be dictated by the tracking system's accuracy.
- In the center bent arm position a bigger plane can be used to reduce tracking-induced errors.
- A clicking device for selection minimizes fatigue. When only one arm is available, the *dwell* method is best.

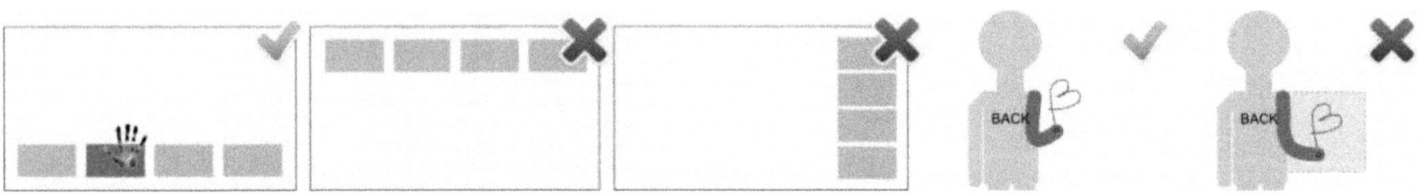


**Figure 9. Design implications of consumed endurance. Left, menu items should be located in the bottom of the UI. Right, for some applications, such as free gesturing, designers may consider relative input which is possible anywhere in the interaction plane instead of a fixed location.**

- Time-based metrics are incomplete indicators of fatigue.
- Strength can be used to inform the design of endurance-efficient interactions techniques.
- The SEATO layout supports endurance-efficient mid-air text-entry, without compromising efficiency.

## LIMITATIONS

Our CE implementation for Microsoft Kinect presents two main limitations. First, it requires line of sight to the user's complete body in order to form a complete skeleton. Second, the skeleton measurements become noisy due to difficulties differentiating between the user's arm and body (especially when the arm is close to the body). These difficulties can be avoided in future versions of the sensors (higher resolution, improved tracking) or using alternative tracking systems.

In future work, we will extend our model to capture other arm-segments and use individual body metrics (length and mass). Moreover, while this paper shows a strong correlation between CE and Borg CR10 during simple mid-air arm movements; further research is needed into highly dynamic settings and the effects of experience and accumulated fatigue. Finally, as advances in the fields of sport sciences and ergonomics refine the notion of muscle fatigue in an objective manner, the definition and validity of CE should also be revisited against such objective metric.

## CONCLUSIONS

In this paper we introduce *consumed endurance*; a metric to characterize shoulder fatigue in mid-air interactions. CE only requires the tracking system used to interact with the NUI itself, and thus it is a real-time, objective, non-invasive and non-obtrusive approach to assess gorilla-arm. Through an initial study, we showed CE's validity as a metric of fatigue and its gender neutrality. Using CE, researchers do not need to ask participants about their perceived physical effort due to the strong correlation between CE and the Borg CR10 scale.

We showed how CE can be used as an evaluation tool for selecting suitable mid-air interaction parameters. We focused our exploration on item selection in a 2D plane and investigated the suitable variables for *plane location*, *arm extension*, *plane size* and *selection method*. Our results show that the combination of plane location and arm extension with the least endurance demands (i.e., creating the least fatigue) is at the vertical center of the body, on the side of the moving arm, and with a bent posture. Finally, selections by the dwell method are most appropriate when only one hand is available. Our results along with a related metric, *strength*, guided the design of the SEATO text-entry layout for mid-air interactions. Results show that SEATO is on par with QWERTY in terms of words per minute and typing error rate, and consumes only a quarter of endurance.

## APPENDIX A – FORCE AND TORQUE CALCULATIONS

From the definition of torque ($\vec{T}$) we know that $\vec{T} = \vec{F} d sin\theta$. Where $d$ is the distance from the shoulder joint to where the force is applied, $\theta$ is the angle between the force vector and the axis, and $F$ is the measured force at distance $d$. Given that all forces are tangential to the distance vector, we know that $sin\theta = 1$. Therefore, the equivalent $F_{max}$ at the CoM at distance r ($F_{max,r}$) is:

$$F_{max} d_{elbow} = F_{max,r} r \quad \rightarrow \quad F_{max,r} = \frac{F_{max} d_{elbow}}{r} \tag{8}$$

The $\frac{F}{F_{max}}$ ratio at the CoM can be expressed as:

$$\frac{\|\vec{F_r}\|}{F_{max,r}} = \frac{\|\vec{F_r}\|}{\frac{F_{max} d_{elbow}}{r}} = \frac{\|\vec{F_r}\| r}{F_{max} d_{elbow}} = \frac{\|\vec{T}\|}{T_{max}} \tag{9}$$

## APPENDIX B - ARM CENTER OF MASS CALCULATION

The CoM of a two segment body is located along the vector linking the CoMs of each segment, at a distance from the first segment's CoM equal to the ratio between the second segment's mass and the combined masses of both segments. Figure 10 shows the arm as a three segments body composed of upper arm (ShEb), forearm (EbWr), and hand (WrHa). Applying the process described above for a two segment body, and using the values presented by Freivalds [17], we calculate the CoM of the forearm + hand combination as:

$$D = B + \frac{WrHa_{mass}}{EbWr_{mass} + WrHa_{mass}} \overrightarrow{BC} \tag{10}$$

Then, we apply a similar process for the CoM of the upper arm + (forearm + hand) combination as:

$$CoM = A + \frac{EbWr_{mass} + WrHa_{mass}}{Arm_{mass}} \overrightarrow{AD} \tag{11}$$

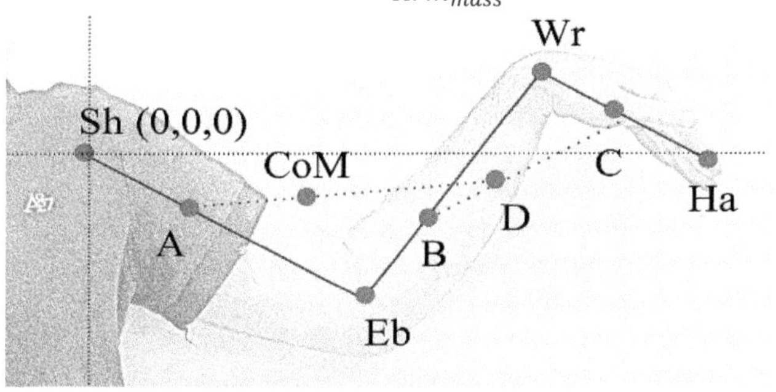


**Figure 10. Arm segments involved in calculating its CoM.**

## APPENDIX C - ARM INERTIA CALCULATION

The inertia of a multi-segment body like the arm ($\overrightarrow{I_{arm}}$) is a vector of magnitude equal to the sum of each segment's inertia, and in the direction (unit vector = $U_{\overrightarrow{I_{arm}}}$) of the cross product of the movement of its CoM:

$$\overrightarrow{I_{arm}} = U_{\overrightarrow{I_{arm}}} * \|\overrightarrow{I_{arm}}\| \tag{12}$$

Where the unit vector of the direction ($U_{\overrightarrow{I_{arm}}}$) is equal to:

$$U_{\overrightarrow{I_{arm}}} = \frac{\overrightarrow{ShCoM_{prev}} \times \overrightarrow{CoM_{prev}CoM}}{\|\overrightarrow{ShCoM_{prev}} \times \overrightarrow{CoM_{prev}CoM}\|} \tag{13}$$

And the magnitude ($\|\overrightarrow{I_{arm}}\|$) is equal to:

$$\|\overrightarrow{I_{arm}}\| = \|\overrightarrow{I_{upper}}\| + \|\overrightarrow{I_{fore}}\| + \|\overrightarrow{I_{hand}}\| = 0.0201 \tag{14}$$

## REFERENCES


1. Gesture recognition. http://en.wikipedia.org/wiki/Gesture_recognition.
2. Gorilla arm. www.computer-dictionaryonline.org/index.asp?q=gorilla+arm.
3. Visible human project. www.nlm.nih.gov/research/visible/visible_human.html.
4. Bachynskyi, M., Oulasvirta, A., Palmas, G., and Weinkauf, T. 2013. Biomechanical simulation in the analysis of aimed movements. In CHI '13 EA. ACM.
5. Bakke, M., Thomsen, C., Vilmann, A., Soneda, K., Farella, M., and Miller, E. 1996. Ultra sonographic assessment of the swelling of the human masseter muscle after static and dynamic activity. Archives of Oral Biology 41, 2, 133 – 140.
6. Barclay, K., Wei, D., Lutteroth, C., and Sheehan, R. 2011. A quantitative quality model for gesture based user interfaces. In Proc. OZCHI '11, ACM, 31–39.
7. Bigdelou, A., Schwarz, L., and Navab, N. 2012. An adaptive solution for intra-operative gesture-based human-machine interaction. In Proc. IUI '12, ACM.
8. Borg, G. 1998. Borg's Perceived Exertion and Pain Scales. Human Kinetics.
9. Boring, S., Jurmu, M., and Butz, A. 2009. Scroll, tilt or move it: using mobile phones to continuously control pointers on large public displays. In Proc. OZCHI '09. ACM.
10. Bustamante, E.A., and Spain, R.D. 2008. Measurement invariance of the Nasa TLX. In Proc. of the Human Factors and Ergonomics Society Annual Meeting 52, 19.
11. Cockburn, A., Quinn, P., Gutwin, C., Ramos, G., and Looser, J. 2011. Air pointing: Design and evaluation of spatial target acquisition with and without visual feedback. Int. J. Hum.-Comput. Stud. 69, 6, 401–414.
12. Cuccurullo, S., Francese, R., Murad, S., Passero, I., and Tucci, M. 2012. A gestural approach to presentation exploiting motion capture metaphors. In Proc. AVI '12, ACM.
13. Dedering, Å., Gnospelius, Å., and Elfving, B. 2010. Reliability of measurements of endurance time, electromyographic fatigue and recovery, and associations to activity limitations, in patients with lumbar disc herniation. Physiotherapy Research International, 15(4), 189-198.
14. Edmunds, T., Gentner, R., d'Avella, A., and Pai, D. 2012. Feasible wrench space and its estimation for isometric haptic interaction. In Proc. HAPTICS '12. IEEE.
15. Elfving, B. and Dedering, Å. 2007. Task dependency in back muscle fatigue – Correlations between two test methods. Clinical Biomechanics, 22(1), 28-33.
16. Ferguson, S.A., W. Gary, A., Le, P., Rose, J.D. and Marras, W.S. 2011. Shoulder Muscle Oxygenation During Repetitive Tasks. Human Factors and Ergonomics Society Annual Meeting 55,1, 1039-1041.
17. Freivalds, A. 2004. Biomechanics of the Upper Limbs: Mechanics, Modeling, and Musculoskeletal Injuries. 1 ED. CRC Press.
18. Garner, B.A., and Pandy, M.G. 2001. Musculoskeletal model of the upper limb based on the visible human male dataset. Computer Methods in Biomechanics and Biomedical Engineering 4, 2, 93–126.
19. Garzotto, F., and Valoriani, M. 2012. Don't touch the oven: motion-based touchless interaction with household appliances. Proc. AVI'12, ACM.
20. Harrison, C., Ramamurthy, S., and Hudson, S.E. 2012. On-body interaction: armed and dangerous. In Proc. TEI'12, ACM.
21. Hart, S.G., and Stavenland, L.E. 1998. Development of NASA-TLX (Task Load Index): Results of empirical and theoretical research. Human Mental Workload, P. A. Hancock and N. Meshkati, Eds. 139-183.
22. Huang, M.-C., Chen, E., Xu, W., and Sarrafzadeh, M. 2011. Gaming for upper extremities rehabilitation. In Proc. WH '11, ACM.
23. Li, F.C.Y., Dearman, D., and Truong, K. N. 2009. Virtual shelves: interactions with orientation aware devices. In Proc. UIST '09, ACM.
24. MacKenzie, I.S., and Soukoreff, R.W. 2003. Phrase sets for evaluating text entry techniques. In CHI EA '03, ACM.
25. Mentis, H. M., O'Hara, K., Sellen, A., and Trivedi, R. 2012. Interaction proxemics and image use in neurosurgery. In Proc. CHI '12, ACM.
26. Morris, M. G., Dawes, H., Howells, K., Scott, O. M., and Cramp, M. 2008. Relationships between muscle fatigue characteristics and markers of endurance performance. Sports Science and Medicine 7, 431-436.
27. Öberg, T., Sandsjö, L., and Kadefords, R. 1994. Subjective and objective evaluation of shoulder muscle fatigue. Ergonomics, 37(8), 1323-1333.
28. Peres, S.C., Nguyen, V., Kortum, P.T., Akladios, M., Wood, S.B., and Muddimer, A. 2009. Software ergonomics: relating subjective and objective measures. In CHI EA '09, ACM.
29. Rohmert, W. 1960. Ermittlung von erholungspausen fr statische arbeit des menschen. European Journal of Applied Physiology and Occupational Physiology 18. 123–164.
30. Sjgaard, G., Savard, G., and Juel, C. 1988. Muscle blood flow during isometric activity and its relation to muscle fatigue. European Journal of Applied Physiology and Occupational Physiology 57, 327–335.
31. Tan, H., Radcliffe, J., Ga, B.N., Tan, H.Z., Eberman, B., Srinivasan, M.A., and Cheng, B. 1994. Human factors for the design of force-reflecting haptic interfaces. Dynamic Systems and Control, 55(1), 353-359.
32. Troiano, A., Naddeo, F., Sosso, E., Camarota, G., Merletti, R., and Mesin, L. 2008. Assessment of force and fatigue in isometric contractions of the upper trapezius muscle by surface EMG signal and perceived exertion scale. Gait & Posture, 28(2), 179-186.
33. Wobbrock, J.O., Findlater, L., Gergle, D., and Higgins, J.J. 2011. The aligned rank transform for nonparametric factorial analyses using only ANOVA procedures. In Proc. CHI '11. ACM, 143-146.

# Vulture: A Mid-Air Word-Gesture Keyboard

**Anders Markussen** amark@diku.dk
**Mikkel Rønne Jakobsen** mikkelrj@diku.dk
**Kasper Hornbæk** kash@diku.dk
Department of Computer Science, University of Copenhagen
Njalsgade 128, Building 24, 5th floor, 2300 Copenhagen, Denmark

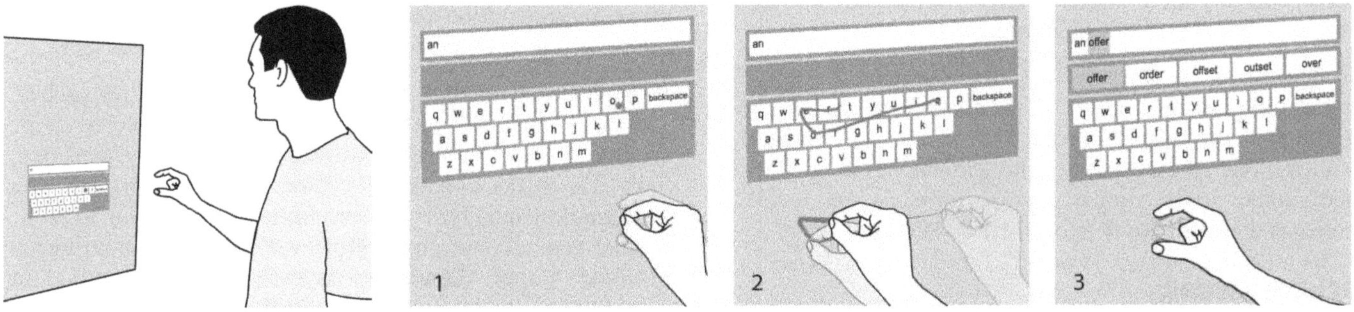


**Figure 1. Text entry using word-gestures in mid-air: By moving the hand, the user places the cursor over the first letter of the word and (1) makes a pinch gesture with thumb and index finger, (2) then traces the word in the air—the trace is shown on the screen. (3) Upon releasing the pinch, the five words that best match the gesture are proposed; the top match is pre-selected.**

## ABSTRACT

Word-gesture keyboards enable fast text entry by letting users draw the shape of a word on the input surface. Such keyboards have been used extensively for touch devices, but not in mid-air, even though their fluent gestural input seems well suited for this modality. We present Vulture, a word-gesture keyboard for mid-air operation. Vulture adapts touch based word-gesture algorithms to work in mid-air, projects users' movement onto the display, and uses pinch as a word delimiter. A first 10-session study suggests text-entry rates of 20.6 Words Per Minute (WPM) and finds hand-movement speed to be the primary predictor of WPM. A second study shows that with training on a few phrases, participants do 28.1 WPM, 59% of the text-entry rate of direct touch input. Participants' recall of trained gestures in mid-air was low, suggesting that visual feedback is important but also limits performance. Based on data from the studies, we discuss improvements to Vulture and some alternative designs for mid-air text entry.

## Author Keywords

Word-gesture keyboard; shape writing; text entry; mid-air interaction; in-air interaction; freehand interaction.


*CHI 2014,* April 26 - May 01 2014, Toronto, ON, Canada
Copyright 2014 ACM 978-1-4503-2473-1/14/04···$15.00.
http://dx.doi.org/10.1145/2556288.2556964

## ACM Classification Keywords

I.3.6 Methodology and Techniques: Interaction techniques

## INTRODUCTION

Mid-air interaction is an emerging input modality for large displays [20], mobile phones [9], augmented reality [23], and desktop computers [29]. Facilitated by improved tracking equipment, mid-air techniques cover many types of interaction. For instance, mid-air pointing enables selection and manipulation of objects (e.g., [2, 6, 10, 28, 30]). Writing text in mid-air, however, has received less attention. Text entry is an important activity and supporting it in mid-air would be beneficial for a number of scenarios such as work in sterile conditions (e.g., operating theatres), in augmented reality (e.g., with Google Glass), and when writing on public displays. It has been shown that people can write in mid-air with devices such as game controllers and dedicated gloves [21], but also using their hands [12, 18]. However, text-entry rates for mid-air interaction are low, around 13 [18] to 18.9 WPM [27]; the latter rate was obtained with tactile feedback on errors and no character production on errors. Furthermore, most techniques support only single-character text entry (e.g., [18, 21, 27]). So mid-air text entry is still relatively slow and better techniques should be developed to make mid-air text entry practical. Hence, we study if speed can be improved by moving from selection-based text entry to gestural input.

Word-gesture keyboards (WGK) (e.g., SlideIT, Swype and ShapeWriter) have gained popularity (e.g., a WGK is now shipped as standard on Android devices) and perform well on touch screens [11, 36, 37]. The key idea of WGKs is that the user enters a word by drawing the pattern formed by its letters on the input surface rather than by typing the letters. When implemented with the QWERTY layout,

WGKs allow users to benefit from previous experience. Furthermore, WGKs provide a fluent way of writing words as gestures while also supporting simple tapping input.

The present paper suggests that WGKs may be beneficial to mid-air text entry. However, transferring WGK to mid-air is hard: what are the delimiters of words, what is the equivalent of tapping and releasing in mid-air, and will the prediction algorithms for WGKs, developed for direct surface input [13], work in mid-air?

In the rest of the paper we describe a system, Vulture, for doing mid-air text entry that answers some of these questions. We also describe two formative studies of Vulture: one study estimates the text-entry rate of Vulture and another study compares the performance and recall of gestures with Vulture to a touch-based WGK.

## RELATED WORK

To our knowledge, the potential of WGKs in mid-air have not before been evaluated, but the literature offers relevant research on in-air gestures [31], freehand gestures [30], and mid-air interaction [20, 27]. This walkthrough of related work focuses on mid-air pointing, mid-air text entry, and WGKs, as these directly relate to the focus of this paper.

### Mid-air Pointing

Much research on mid-air interaction concerns pointing [2, 6, 10, 28, 30]. Mid-air pointing is generally done through variations of ray casting that differ in speed, error rate, and fatigue. Generally, ray-casting techniques are fast for coarse movements, but provide limited precision due to for instance hand tremor. Furthermore, ray-casting techniques are generally distance-dependent [27], meaning that precision degrades as the user moves away from the display. One way to minimize distance-dependence is to project movement orthogonally onto the display as done by Markussen et al. [18]. Orthogonal projection limits the user's reach, but maintain a constant control-display ratio across distances.

### Mid-air text entry

Earlier work on text entry in mid-air takes two main forms. In *selection-based techniques*, users make series of movements and selections to produce individual characters. Shoemaker et al. [27] used a Nintendo Wiimote for mid-air interaction, and proposed three selection-based text-entry methods using a 3D cube layout of letters, a circular layout, and a regular QWERTY layout. The QWERTY-based keyboard was preferred and fastest with 18.9 WPM. Contrary to more recent text-entry studies, Shoemaker et al. used a restricted text-entry setup that provided tactile feedback on errors and no character production on errors. Markussen et al. [18] adapted three text-entry methods to selection-based mid-air text entry. A mean text-entry rate of 13.2 WPM was observed for a QWERTY-based text-entry method that used orthogonal projection of the hand position onto the display.

In *gesture-based techniques*, users produce gestures that are interpreted as letters. Ni et al. [21] created AirStroke, a Graffiti based text-entry method that was evaluated with word completion (11.0 WPM) and without (6.5 WPM). Kristensson et al. [12] showed that continuous recognition of gestures within a defined input zone in front of the user is possible using the Graffiti alphabet [5]. The system was implemented using a Kinect. The focus of the paper was on gesture recognition rather than on text-entry rate, and the paper reported no performance measure relating to speed.

Two alternatives to these approaches have been researched. Mid-air handwriting recognition has been explored using various sensors and camera-based recognition systems (e.g. [1, 25, 26]). Experiments have primarily focused on recognition quality, with recognition rates of up to 97%, rather than text-entry rate. However, regular hand-writing is limited to approximately 15 WPM [7]. We expect mid-air handwriting to be subject to similar limitations. Another alternative for mid-air text entry is sign language for which conversational speeds of 175 – 225 WPM have been reported [19]. However, sign language recognition is challenging and learning sign language requires more training than most users are willing to invest.

### Word-Gesture Keyboards (WGKs)

WGKs, originally referred to as shape writing keyboards, were introduced by Zhai and Kristensson [11, 13, 35, 36, 37]. Instead of typing a word, the user draws its shape (the line connecting the letters in the word) on top of a visual representation of the keyboard. The method was designed for stylus input and has later proven useful for touch-based text entry. On mobile devices, WGKs have gained enough success to become a standard part of many soft keyboards. Studies have shown that novice users of WGKs write 25 WPM after 35 minutes of practice and 46.5 WPM for single well-practiced phrases [11].

An important part of implementing a WGK is to develop efficient and effective shape recognition algorithms. Previous studies of WGKs give few details on the algorithms behind the recognition of word gestures, possibly due to the commercialization of WGKs for mobile phones. To our knowledge, $SHARK^2$ [11, 13] provides the most detailed descriptions of a WGK implementation.

$SHARK^2$ bases its recognition on two recognition channels: A shape channel and a location channel. The channels estimate the probability of a given shape being a word from the vocabulary. The shape channel normalizes the drawn shape to a specific location and size, and estimates how well it matches the shape of each word in the vocabulary. The normalization has the disadvantage that a relatively large number of ambiguous shapes occur in a normal English vocabulary. The location channel helps minimize these ambiguities by distinguishing similar shapes by their different locations. Ultimately, the probabilities from the two channels are integrated into one probability measure.

We are unaware of work trying to adapt WGKs to mid-air; the next section outlines the main challenges in doing so.

## VULTURE: A MID-AIR WORD-GESTURE KEYBOARD

Below we describe how interaction with Vulture works, the design choices made, and how the word-gesture recognition in Vulture is implemented.

### Writing with Vulture

The operation of Vulture is illustrated in Figure 1. The system works by tracking the user's hand and fingers. To enable input using both elbow and wrist movement, the hand's position, orientation, and an initial calibration of the user's pinch is used to estimate the position where pinches are expected to occur. This position controls a cursor, represented as a dot. The interaction was originally based on orthogonal projection, but a control-display (CD) ratio was applied to support interactions from a distance while maintaining a readable user interface. The user writes a word by placing the cursor in the first letter of the word, making a pinch gesture (with the index finger and the thumb), then tracing the letters of the word, and finally releasing the pinch. While the user is not writing, the cursor is red. Upon pinching the cursor turns green and the cursor's movement is traced over the keyboard. After completing a word-gesture, the five words that best match the gesture are shown in the list of suggestions; more than five was expected to provide little improvement [14]. The user can continue writing and implicitly confirm that the highlighted word was a *match* or the user can *select* a word from the list of suggestions. Also, the user can *undo* the suggested word in the text input field by selecting backspace or *delete* previously typed words by multiple selections of backspace. The four basic interactions—*match, select, undo,* and *delete*—will be used extensively in later parts of the paper.

### Designing a Mid-Air WGK

Previous WGKs have been designed for use on touch- or stylus-enabled surfaces. Bringing WGKs away from the surface and into mid-air implies three major considerations.

#### *Separating words*

Surface-based WGKs benefit from an implicit delimiter, in that a gesture begins when the finger or stylus is put on the surface, and ends when it is lifted away from the surface. This implicit delimiter is not available in mid-air. We consider four options: (1) Implement a WGK that requires no delimiter, requiring auto segmentation of input in order to identify words similar to what has been done for unistroke gestures [12]; (2) incorporate delimiters into the shape that is written (e.g., pig-tails [33] or crossing a certain part of the keyboard to end a word); (3) use some of the extra degrees of freedom available in mid-air (e.g., depth) to indicate word separation; or (4) use recognizable hand gestures that can serve as word delimiters (e.g., pinching while gesturing).

All four options could potentially provide good results, but the first two require recognition algorithms significantly different from existing WGK implementations; they could be topics for future research if WGKs shows to be useful in mid-air. We tested (3) and (4) with users and found the last option to be liked the most. We therefore settled on pinching as a word delimiter in Vulture.

#### *Separation of motor space and display space*

One advantage of surface-based WGKs is the direct coupling of input and output space, which gives users direct feedback on interaction as it occurs. A mid-air WGK offers no such direct coupling. Designing the mapping of input and output space for mid-air interaction opens up a complex design space. We prototyped different mappings of the input and output space (e.g., providing a slanted or horizontal input plane to minimize user fatigue). However, users found it hard to adapt to these mappings. To minimize effects of separation, we therefore chose a planar input space parallel to the display.

#### *Size of motor space*

The size of the motor space that users are interacting within can potentially impact performance. However, a priori prediction of the optimal size is hard. Even with advanced biomechanical simulations, the interplay between recognition algorithms and biomechanics is highly complex. To add further complexity, the optimal size is expected to vary among users and to evolve over time. We informally tested different sizes of motor space to identify a size that allowed for fast movements while maintaining the user's ability to draw shapes of sufficient quality. We ended up mapping the boundaries of the keyboard to a rectangle of approximately 20 × 5.5 cm.

### Word-Gesture Recognition

Vulture is based on the same integration of shape and location channels as SHARK[2]. Below, we describe the specific implementation of Vulture.

Initially, each word in the dictionary is processed into a template for comparison. The optimal shape, calculated as the line connecting the key center of each of the letters in the word, is resampled to a fixed number of equidistant points. We found 50 samples to perform well. Furthermore, a normalized shape is calculated based on the resampled shape and the shape channel calculation described below.

Before processing a drawn shape, the shape is resampled to the same number of equidistant points as the dictionary templates. To minimize the number of ambiguities and to reduce processing time, the vocabulary is pruned by considering only words with an optimal starting position less than 1 key-width and ending position less than 2 key-widths away from the evaluated shape's start and end point.

We iteratively developed and refined the implementation of the shape and location channels based on user feedback from informal evaluations. Below we describe the implementation found to perform the best.

*Shape channel*

The resampled shape is translated to the origin and normalized to make it location and size invariant. Normalization is done by scaling the shape to a square in the same way as in the $1 recognizer [34].

The distance function that produces the output of the shape channel is identical to the one used in SHARK[2]: The output of the shape channel is the average spatial distance between corresponding equidistant points in the compared shapes.

*Location channel*

The location channel score $x_L$ is calculated as follows:

$$x_L = \sum_{i=1}^{N} \alpha(i)\delta(i)$$
$$\delta = \max(\|u_i - t_i\| - r, 0)$$

where $\alpha(i), i \in (1, N), \sum_{i=1}^{N} \alpha(i) = 1$ are the sample weights, $u$ is the unknown shape that are being compared to the template word $t$, and $r$ is a radius that is used to reward individual samples.

The location channel has two primary features. First, each sample index has an associated alpha weight. This is used to modify the weight of the individual samples so that some samples can receive higher weight. Second, the pairwise distances between corresponding samples are calculated. If the sample distance is less than a half key-width ( $r$ ), the sample distance is set to zero. This has the effect that slightly more words are considered good candidates by the location channel, and increases the shape channel's discriminatory power in cases of location similarities. The sample distances are weighed using the alpha weights and summed to provide the location channel score.

Participants in a pilot study felt more precise in the starting location of the word than in the rest of the word. We collected data showing that the first sample of the trace fell within the desired key 95 % of the time, whereas the last sample of the trace was only within the desired key 80 % of the time. Hence, we decided to assign extra weight to the first sample using the following weighing function:

$$\alpha(i) = \begin{cases} 0.1, i = 1 \\ \frac{0.9}{N-1}, otherwise \end{cases}$$

*Single key words*

Due to the scaling function of the shape channel, single key input becomes a challenge. Very short shapes drawn in an attempt to produce single characters are rescaled and the shape channel promotes longer words with similar shapes.

To avoid this behavior, shapes of lengths less than 0.4 key width are truncated to contain only the starting point before resampling, effectively cancelling the unwanted effect of the shape channel scaling.

**STUDY 1: THE POTENTIAL OF A WGK IN MID-AIR**

This study was designed to provide us with: (1) estimates of the potential text-entry performance of mid-air WGKs, both users' initial performance and improvement over time, (2) text-entry data for tuning the parameters of Vulture, and (3) data for analyzing the errors that users make.

**Study Design**

Participants completed 10 sessions of text entry using Vulture. During each session, participants transcribed 4 blocks of 10 phrases sampled randomly (no phrases occurred twice in a session) from the MacKenzie and Soukoreff corpus [16]. This resulted in a total of 6 participants × 10 sessions × 4 blocks × 10 phrases = 2400 transcribed phrases.

**Study Setup**

The study was conducted on a 2.8 × 1.2 m large high-resolution display, one use case of mid-air text entry, with 7680 × 3240 pixels (see Figure 2). We used an OptiTrack motion-capture system, providing 100 frames per second of tracking information. Although expensive, the system ensures reliable results and minimizes the effects of tracking noise. Furthermore, as low-cost tracking systems are currently improving rapidly, using the OptiTrack system could also improve comparability with future research. To minimize the effects of participants' hand tremor, we smoothed the input using the 1€ filter [4].

Participants stood 1.5 m from the display while using Vulture. To make the keyboard easy to read, the window containing the keyboard was 40 × 11 cm. The difference in keyboard size in motor space and display space results in a CD ratio of 1:2.

For the study, Vulture matched shapes against a dictionary of 10,246 words. This number was based on the assumption that an average English speaker has a vocabulary of approximately 10,000 words [22]; it is also similar to that of the initial design criteria for SHARK[2]. The dictionary was constructed from the British National Corpus (ftp://ftp.itri.bton.ac.uk/) by taking words with a frequency greater than or equal to 600 and that contain only alphabetic characters. To support word-gesture based transcription of

**Figure 2: The study used a large high-resolution display and users wore a glove with reflective markers in order to track the position of their hand and fingers.**

the MacKenzie–Soukoreff corpus [16], words missing from the corpus were added to the dictionary.

To enable analysis, all tracking data were logged along with details on text entry including the four basic interactions described earlier, the word gestures produced, the presented and transcribed phrases, and timing data.

### Participants

We recruited 6 paid volunteers (1 male), 5 right-handed, Participant ages ranged from 21 to 53 ($M$ = 29.3). Participants' previous experiences with WGKs were between 1 and 3 ($M$ = 1.3) on a seven-point scale from "1 - No experience" to "7 - Expert". Their written English skills were between 3 and 6 ($M$ = 4.5) on a seven-point scale from "1 - No English skills" to "7 - Native".

### Procedure

Before text entry began, the system was calibrated. During calibration, participants defined the hand position that mapped to the center of the keyboard by placing their elbows to their sides and the writing arm bent to 90 degrees. Hand movement relative to this posture was mapped to cursor movement on the keyboard. This posture was preferred by pilot participants.

In each of the 10 sessions, participants were allowed some time to (re)-familiarize themselves with the operation of Vulture before starting to write. On average, participants wrote 1.8 phrases at the beginning of each session.

Participants were instructed to write the phrases "as quickly and accurately as possible - as if typing e-mail to a colleague". Between each block of 10 phrases, users were allowed a break of up to three minutes. To complete a phrase, participants clicked a "Phrase done" button shown below the keyboard. Before continuing to the next phrase, participants were shown a window with their mean text-entry rate and the rate of the previous phrase.

After each session, participants were interviewed about their impression of Vulture, the recognition quality, and any technical issues they had experienced. On average, each session lasted approximately 30 minutes.

### Dependent Measures

On the phrase level, we analyze text-entry rate and error rates; on the word-gesture level we analyze correctness and distance measures.

*Text-entry rate* is measured in Words Per Minute (WPM), as in [3], with this formula

$$WPM = \frac{|T|}{S} \times 60 \times \frac{1}{5}$$

where $|T|$ is the length of the transcribed string, S is time in seconds. We use $|T|$ instead of $|T-1|$ since the time to produce the first character is included when timing word gestures [17].

*Error rate* is based on Minimum Word Distance (MWD). MWD is calculated in same way as the Minimum String Distance (MSD) [15], but on a per-word level rather than on a per-character level. Hence, MWD describes the minimum number of word-substitutions, -insertions, and -deletions needed to make strings identical. MWD error rate is calculated in the same way as MSD error rate, but on a per-word level:

$$MWD\ error\ rate = \frac{MWD(P,T)}{\overline{S_P}} \times 100\%$$

where $P$ and $T$ are the sets of words in the presented and transcribed strings, and $\overline{S_P}$ is the mean size of the optimal alignments calculated on a per-word level rather than a per-character level. MWD error rates will generally be higher than MSD error rates, because whole words are classified as wrong if they contain one or more erroneous characters.

*Correctness* of a single word gesture was determined by comparing it to the users' intended word. As long as the current words in the transcribed string match the beginning of the presented string, we consider the next word in the presented string to be intended. When the strings do not match (e.g., due to errors earlier in the string), we classify the users' intention manually based on a visualization of the drawn shape on top of a keyboard, the currently transcribed words, and the presented string: We did this manually both because deletion makes this classification non-trivial and so as to learn from the errors users made.

*Distance measures* are reported as centimeters of movement in the input plane.

### Results

#### *Text-Entry Rate*

Figure 3 shows the mean text-entry rate per participant over sessions. Participants reached a mean text-entry rate of 20.6 WPM ($SD$ = 7.3) in the last session, which is 75% faster than the first session ($M$ = 11.8 WPM). The development of text-entry rates in Figure 3 indicates that participants could improve further with more practice. As expected, a repeated measures analysis of variance (RM-ANOVA) on WPM with session as factor revealed a main effect, $F(9, 45) = 17.593$, $p < .001$. We also found participants' movement speed to consistently increase over sessions (70% from first session to last session) as users were familiarized with Vulture. An RM-ANOVA on movement speed with session as factor showed a main effect, $F(9,45) = 12.916$, $p < .001$, providing a potential explanation of the increased performance over time.

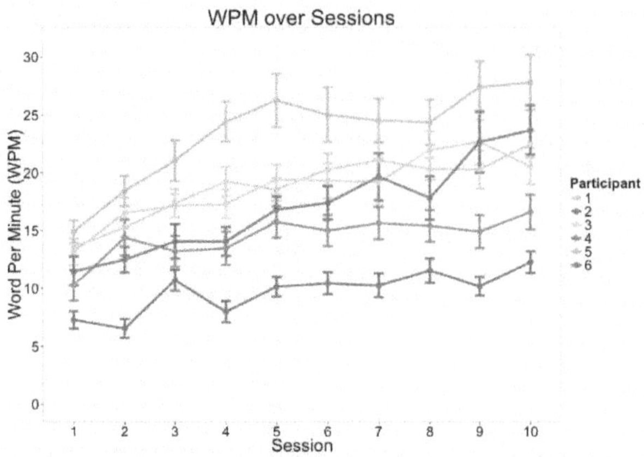


**Figure 3: Text-entry rates in Words Per Minute (WPM) over sessions with error bars showing 95% confidence intervals.**

Figure 3 also suggests large performance differences among participants. This is related to differences in movement speed: the mean movement speed of the fastest participant was 155% higher than that of the slowest.

### *Errors*

The mean MWD error rate was 4% ($SD$ = 9.3). An RM-ANOVA with session as factor did not reveal a main effect, $F(9, 45) = .699$, $p = .707$. Of the 2400 transcribed phrases, 1941 phrases (80.9%) contained no transcription errors and for 1330 (55%) of those no corrections were made. Surprisingly, the highest MWD error rate ($M$ = 8%) was found for the participant with the lowest text-entry rate, indicating that acceptance of errors in the transcribed string may not be the primary factor for higher text-entry rates.

### *Interaction with Vulture*

Next, we look in more detail on how users interacted with Vulture. Table 1 shows an overview of users' actions. The table reports median durations and distances so as to reduce the influence of outliers. The most frequent action was *match*, writing a word gesture and implicitly confirming the default suggestion (73%). In 9.7% of the word-affecting actions the user had to *select* another word than the default. Performing a *select* is generally done either because of word ambiguities (words with the same optimal shape) or due to the shape being close, but not close enough to make the intended word a *match*. In 8.1% of the actions, users had to *undo* the gesture they had produced, presumably because the intended word was not among the alternatives. In 9% of the actions, users had to *delete* a previously confirmed word to fix errors earlier in the transcribed string.

Table 1 also shows the correctness of word production compared to the users' intended word. It is seen that 3,070 of the 16,356 (19%) produced word-gestures are either *undone* or *deleted*, suggesting that a relatively large amount of time is spent correcting errors.

For the *match* class, 18% of the words were incorrect, whereas for the *select* class only 3% were incorrect. For the matches, participants seem to have produced some unintentional word-gestures, resulting in unintentionally confirmed words. This typically occurred when participants did only small finger movements when pinching. We identified 966 of the 2,022 incorrect gestures with a duration of less than 100ms (48%) that we deemed as unintentional.

For correct words, the gesture time is larger for *matched* than for *selected* words. This can in part be explained by increased precision in participants' gestures as expressed by the mean sample distance and gesture start/end distance in Table 1.

The low duration and length of word gestures that are *undone* have two potential explanations: (1) some of the very short word-gestures caused by the pinch implementation will have to be undone; (2) participants were often observed to realize an error and abandon their word-gesture early, possibly resulting in a lower median gesture duration and length than other classes of action.

The median accuracy measures for correct words are generally relatively precise taking into account the actual motor space key-width of 1.8 cm. We see this as an indication that participants continue to be visually bound rather than starting to rely on recalled shapes as suggested by Kristensson and Zhai [13]. The study design does not allow us to conclude if participants are visually bound, but the indication is supported by our own experiences from the development process, where we continually felt bound by visual feedback rather than typing based on gesture recall.

| Class (% of total) | Correct | N | Gesture Duration (s) | Selection- / Backspace-Click Duration (s) | Mean Sample Distance (cm) | Gesture Start Distance (cm) | Gesture End Distance (cm) | Gesture Length (cm) | Gesture Speed (cm/s) |
|---|---|---|---|---|---|---|---|---|---|
| Match (73.2%) | Yes | 11130 | 2.28 | | 0.54 | 0.36 | 0.36 | 18.93 | 8.13 |
| | No | 2022 | 0.135 | | 3.32 | 0.78 | 3.40 | 0.00 | 0.00 |
| Select (9.7%) | Yes | 1689 | 1.9 | 1.82 | 0.77 | 0.37 | 0.41 | 16.94 | 8.99 |
| | No | 57 | 1.63 | 1.9 | 1.44 | 0.43 | 0.77 | 19.20 | 9.20 |
| Undo (8.1%) | | 1458 | 1.28 | 1.86 | 2.84 | 0.71 | 1.89 | 8.91 | 6.60 |
| Delete (9.0%) | | 1612 | | 0.18 | | | | | |

**Table 1: The word-affecting actions done with Vulture ($N$ = 17,968). Mean Sample Distance is the mean distance between the individual samples of the resampled input shape and the resampled optimal shape of the intended word. Gesture Start/End Distance is the distance from the start/end point of the input gesture to the start/end point of the shape of the intended word.**

### Improving Vulture

We did two improvements to Vulture based on the results. First, we modified the pinch implementation so as to reduce the number of unintended word-gestures.

Second, the interaction data provided by the study allowed us to adjust the parameters of the recognition algorithm. Optimization of a WGK based on SHARK$^2$ is a non-trivial task due to the interactions between the different channels [11]. Hence, the optimizations did not aim to find a globally optimal set of parameters. Instead they were done by running the recorded word-gestures through permutations of parameters, aiming to bring as many word-gestures as possible into the *match* and *select* categories. We ended up using a set of parameters that resulted in approximately 5% more of the total gestures being *matched*.

## STUDY 2: TOUCH AND GESTURE RECALL

The results from Study 1 show that WGKs can improve text entry in mid-air. However, there is a discrepancy compared to the text-entry rates of 25 WPMs that have been reported for touch-based WGKs after just 40 minutes of practice [36]. In order to directly compare the performance of WGKs in mid-air and touch, we conducted a second study. In particular, we were interested in understanding how the separation of motor space and display space impacts performance. Also, while we saw an increase in performance over time in Study 1, we were unable to tell whether users become faster because they learn the shapes of familiar words and shift from visually-guided tracing of words [36]. Thus, we examine how well users recall word gestures.

### Study Setup

For the mid-air interaction, the same apparatus was used as in Study 1. Touch on the large display was detected with diffused surface illumination. Input from six cameras was analyzed using Community Core Vision and multiplexed to form input for tracking touch points.

The touch WGK used the same algorithm and parameters as the mid-air WGK. However, the touch keyboard was scaled and relocated to the size of the motor space of the mid-air keyboard (20 x 5.5 cm), making it comparable to the size of the keyboard on a landscape oriented 10.1-inch tablet.

### Study Design

The study used a between-subjects design with input modality as the independent variable: One group of participants used Vulture, the other group used the same WGK implementation with touch interaction. A between-subjects design was used to avoid knowledge transfer and other interference between touch and mid-air conditions.

Each session consisted of two parts. First, participants repeatedly transcribed three phrases from the MacKenzie and Soukoreff corpus [16]. To select the phrases for transcription, the mean WPM for each phrase was calculated for the last session of study 1. The three phrases selected were those with the WPM closest to the mean WPM of that session ("destruction of the rain forest", "an offer you cannot refuse", "dolphins leap high out of the water").

The second part tested the participants' ability to recall word-gestures. Participants had to produce each of the 15 unique word gestures that comprised the transcribed phrases. They had no visible keyboard on the display, and no cursor. A blank rectangle marked the previous location of the keyboard.

### Participants

We recruited 12 paid volunteers (5 male), all right-handed. None of them had participated in Study 1. The participants were randomly assigned each of the two conditions (six participants each). Participant ages ranged from 18 to 31 years ($M$ = 24.4). Participants' previous experiences with WGKs were rated between 1 and 4 ($M$ = 1.8) and their written English skills were between 5 and 7 ($M$ = 5.6); scales as in Study 1.

### Procedure

Before starting the actual text entry, participants were allowed to familiarize themselves with the operation of the keyboard. We encouraged participants to experiment with doing fast movements during training.

After training, participants transcribed 9 blocks of 6 phrases (2 repetitions of each phrase per block in randomized order), resulting in a total of 648 transcribed phrases. Participants were allowed to rest between blocks. Text entry is completed as unrestricted text entry, allowing users to delete and correct previously entered text. Participants were instructed to perform the text entry tasks as in Study 1.

After transcribing all the phrases, participants were asked to produce each of the 15 unique words in the phrases. For this part, only the word that the users were to produce and the keyboard frame (that is, without any keys) was shown. Participants received no feedback on touch or mid-air tracking. Participants had to produce gestures based only on their memory of the word gestures as well as the location and size of the input space. Participants were asked to produce each word twice. The words were shown in randomized order.

### Results

#### *Text-Entry Rate*

Figure 4 shows text-entry rates for the two methods over the blocks of the study. An RM-ANOVA with method as between-subjects factor found touch to be significantly faster than mid-air, $F(1, 10) = 10.681$, $p < .05$. On the last block, touch text entry ($M$ = 47.5 WPM) was 69% faster than mid-air text entry ($M$ = 28.1 WPM). Compared to the first study, the initial text-entry rates are much higher. This suggests either that the optimizations of the recognition

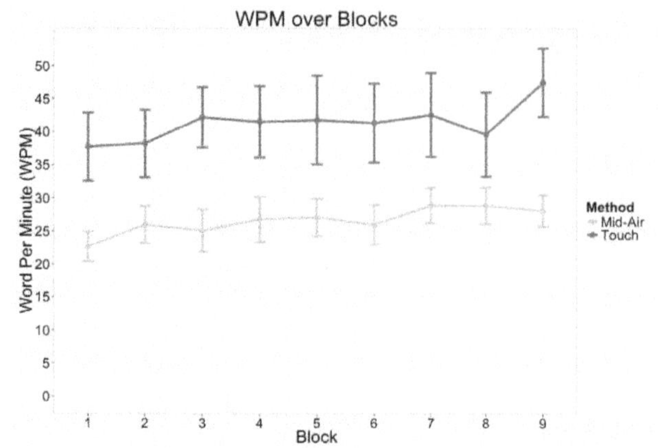


**Figure 4: Text entry rates in words per minute (WPM) over blocks with error bars showing 95% confidence intervals.**

algorithms have had an effect or that the instruction to try fast movements during training boosted the initial performance. The reason is most likely a combination of both. Touch is 26% faster on the last block than on the first. Mid-air is 24% faster.

### Errors

An RM-ANOVA with method as between-subjects factor found that the MWD error rate for touch ($M$ = 3.7%, $SD$ = 8.1) and mid-air ($M$ = 1.7%, $SD$ = 5.7) was not significantly different, $F(1, 10) = 2.648, p = .135$.

### Interaction With Vulture

Table 2 categorizes participants' behavior into the same 4 classes as in Study 1 and shows that touch and mid-air have similar behavior compared to Study 1, but with a slightly higher percentage of *matched* words for mid-air. It is worth noting that the improved *match* percentage is similar to the ~5% effect of the WGK optimization.

Study 1 found gesture speed to be the most important factor affecting text-entry rate. Touch gesture speed ($M$ = 21.44, $SD$ = 13.83) in study 2 is 74% faster than mid-air ($M$ = 12.36, $SD$ = 4.89). Comparing this to the 69% difference in text-entry rate supports that gesture speed is a good indicator for text-entry rate.

### Recall

We analyzed participants' recall with regards to the location, size, shape of gestures, and gesture speed. As expected, participants were more accurate in recalling the location and size of gestures with touch input than in mid-air because they could point directly to the keyboard frame on the display. This can be seen from Table 3, which shows data for word gestures produced in the text entry part of the experiment (the first two rows) compared to participants' recall of the word gestures (the last two rows). We note two important findings: (a) Gesture start distance averaged about 1 key-width for touch compared to more than 5 key-widths for mid-air; and (b) participants made twice as long recall gestures as they did in the text-entry part for mid-air

| Method | *Match* | *Select* | *Undo* | *Delete* |
|---|---|---|---|---|
| Mid-air | 78.4% | 8.6% | 7.9% | 5.1% |
| Touch | 72.7% | 9.4% | 10.2% | 7.7% |

**Table 2: Distribution of Study 2 interaction classes across mid-air and touch interaction.**

input, whereas recall gestures and text-entry gestures were comparable in length for touch input.

In order to assess participants' ability to recall the shape of word-gestures, we ran the recalled gestures and the text-entry gestures through Vulture's shape channel (note that we used only the shape-channel in order to normalize for location offsets). Table 3 also shows how the intended word would be ranked if only the shape channel was used (the very high rankings indicate that the shape channel alone is very poor). The ranks for the recalled gestures are more than double that of the text-entry gestures, indicating that the participants' ability to recall the shapes of gestures was low. Moreover, participants seem to recall gestures worse for mid-air (rank 808.7) compared to touch (rank 696.3). As for participants' ability to redo shapes from memory, several participants stated that they recalled gestures by imagining the keyboard layout in front of them, thus making them bound by an imagined keyboard rather than relying on remembered movement patterns.

Touch and mid-air show very similar movement speed in the recall conditions, whereas participants' movements are much slower for mid-air during text entry. This suggests that visibility of the keyboard slows participants only for mid-air input.

## DISCUSSION

We have suggested that WGKs may be beneficial to mid-air text entry. The issues in designing Vulture, a WGK that works in mid-air, have been described and two studies aiming to characterize its performance have been run. Next we try to answer some remaining questions about WGKs.

### Do WGKs in mid-air work?

Study 1 showed text entry rates of 20 WPM; Study 2 showed 28 WPM using a small phrase set. Earlier studies of mid-air text entry have found 13.2 [18] to 18.9 WPM [27]. Thus, the studies indicate that Vulture provide text-entry rates that surpass earlier work.

Study 2 showed that Vulture worked comparably to touch in some aspects: an equal number of errors were made, the types of actions made were similar, and the gestures produced were comparable. However, participants were much slower at making gestures in mid-air than for touch; text-entry rates, therefore, were also about 60% lower. Due to the increased complexity of performing mid-air text entry compared to touch-based text entry, we did not expect mid-air text entry to compete with touch input. This hypothesis was confirmed by our studies.

Zhai and Kristensson theorize that the use of WGKs "automatically shifts from the ease end (visual tracing) to

| Method | N | Shape channel rank (lower is better) | Gesture Start Distance (cm) | Gesture Length (cm) | Gesture Speed (cm/s) |
|---|---|---|---|---|---|
| Mid-air (feedback) | 2119 | 315.9 (*SD*=1385.6) | 0.80 (*SD*=1.75) | 20.20 (*SD*=12.70) | 12.36 (*SD*=4.89) |
| Touch (feedback) | 2265 | 333.0 (*SD*=1385.0) | 0.83 (*SD*=1.61) | 18.68 (*SD*=11.81) | 21.44 (*SD*=13.83) |
| Mid-air (recall) | 180 | 808.7 (*SD*=1735.1) | 9.79 (*SD*=5.36) | 41.56 (*SD*=21.06) | 23.70 (*SD*=12.31) |
| Touch (recall) | 180 | 696.3 (*SD*=1582.7) | 1.75 (*SD*=1.44) | 20.43 (*SD*=9.22) | 21.21 (*SD*=9.29) |

**Table 3: Word-gesture statistic for text entry and recall. Shape channel rank is the location of the intended word in a list of dictionary words sorted ascending by the shape channel score of the dictionary words.**

the efficient end (recall gesturing)". Participants in the present studies did not seem to shift from visual tracing. In contrast, they seemed to depend on visual feedback even after substantial training (Study 1) and after practicing the same words repeatedly (Study 2).

### Why are mid-air WGKs slower?

Figuring out why Vulture was slower than touch seems to be key to improving it. We see three potential explanations. First, the input plane and the display plane are decoupled in mid-air text entry. Users must therefore mentally couple their gestures in motor space to the keyboard and feedback on the display; the principle of stimulus-response compatibility [24] suggests that difficult.

Second, users of Vulture seem to rely heavily on visual feedback; this has been shown problematic in other studies of text entry [32]. Data suggest that mid-air users have slower movement speed than touch users, but that they start and end equally precisely; across both studies, they seem to have emphasized accuracy over speed. This observation is supported by the increased movement speed for the mid-air recall condition.

Third, users of Vulture must explicitly delimit words by pinching, while touch provides implicit delimiting of words. Several participants said that pinching was natural in that it resembled gripping a pen. However, pinching adds to the complexity of text entry in mid-air compared to touch input.

### How can mid-air WGKs be improved?

A first potential improvement of Vulture would be to pace users, with the aim of increasing their gesture speed. Ideas for doing so include diminishing visual feedback based on speed or diminishing visual feedback over the course of a gesture (strong initially, then gradually removing feedback).

A parameter of the design of Vulture that could be varied is the size of the motor space. In particular, reducing the size of the users' gestures might increase their speed and decrease accuracy.

The results on gesture recall from Study 2 indicate that text entry with no visual feedback does not seem promising. The idea proposed in Imaginary Interfaces [8] of using the non-dominant hand to provide an explicit reference point might make recall of location better. This explicit point of reference could potentially provide the location context needed to support text entry with limited visual feedback.

Word gestures seem to work well in mid-air, because they remove some of the need to repeatedly select characters, which makes other mid-air text-entry techniques tedious to use (e.g., [18]). Other techniques for predictive text entry may be beneficial to mid-air. One such technique is to add a language model to the gesture recognition engine: this would allow users to make less precise and thus faster gestures for producing the intended word.

## CONCLUSION

Word-gesture keyboards (WGKs) allow efficient text entry by tracing of words instead of typing individual letters. WGKs are widely used on touch-based devices. This paper demonstrates how WGKs can be adapted for use also in mid-air. Empirical results from two studies show clear usability benefits compared to existing mid-air text-entry methods. Several issues in designing for mid-air interaction have been discussed. A key issue is that input space and output space are separated, which seems to make interaction more mentally demanding: Participants' gesture movements in mid-air text entry were slower, but with the same accuracy as in touch-based text entry. Based on the empirical results we discussed ideas for improving mid-air WGKs and raised key questions for future research.

## ACKNOWLEDGEMENTS

This work has been supported in part by the Danish Council for Strategic Research, grant 10-092316.

## REFERENCES

1. Amma, C., Georgi, M., and Schultz, T., Airwriting: Hands-Free Mobile Text Input by Spotting and Continuous Recognition of 3d-Space Handwriting with Inertial Sensors. In *Proc. ISWC*, (2012), 52-59.
2. Banerjee, A., Burstyn, J., Girouard, A., and Vertegaal, R., MultiPoint: Comparing laser and manual pointing as remote input in large display interactions. *Int. J. Hum.-Comput. Stud. 70*, 10 (2012), 690-702.
3. Bi, X., Chelba, C., Ouyang, T., Partridge, K., and Zhai, S., Bimanual gesture keyboard. In *Proc. UIST*, ACM (2012), 137-146.
4. Casiez, G., Roussel, N., and Vogel, D., 1 € filter: a simple speed-based low-pass filter for noisy input in interactive systems. In *Proc. CHI*, ACM (2012), 2527-2530.
5. Castellucci, S.J. and MacKenzie, I.S., Graffiti vs. unistrokes: an empirical comparison. In *Proc. CHI*, ACM (2008), 305-308.

6. Cockburn, A., Quinn, P., Gutwin, C., Ramos, G., and Looser, J., Air pointing: Design and evaluation of spatial target acquisition with and without visual feedback. *Int. J. Hum.-Comput. Stud. 69*, 6 (2011), 401-414.
7. Devoe, D.B., Alternatives to Handprinting in the Manual Entry of Data. *IEEE Transactions on Human Factors in Electronics HFE-8*, 1 (1967), 21-32.
8. Gustafson, S., Bierwirth, D., and Baudisch, P., Imaginary interfaces: spatial interaction with empty hands and without visual feedback. In *Proc. UIST*, ACM (2010), 3-12.
9. Jones, B., Sodhi, R., Forsyth, D., Bailey, B., and Maciocci, G., Around device interaction for multiscale navigation. In *Proc. MobileHCI*, ACM (2012), 83-92.
10. Jota, R., Nacenta, M.A., Jorge, J.A., Carpendale, S., and Greenberg, S., A comparison of ray pointing techniques for very large displays. In *Proc. GI*, Canadian Information Processing Society (2010), 269-276.
11. Kristensson, P.O., 2007. *Discrete and Continuous Shape Writing for Text Entry and Control*, Doctoral dissertation, Linköping University, Sweden.
12. Kristensson, P.O., Nicholson, T., and Quigley, A., Continuous recognition of one-handed and two-handed gestures using 3D full-body motion tracking sensors. In *Proc. IUI*, ACM (2012), 89-92.
13. Kristensson, P.O. and Zhai, S., SHARK2: a large vocabulary shorthand writing system for pen-based computers. In *Proc. UIST*, ACM (2004), 43-52.
14. MacKenzie, I.S., Chen, J., and Oniszczak, A., Unipad: single stroke text entry with language-based acceleration. In *Proc. NordiCHI*, ACM (2006), 78-85.
15. MacKenzie, I.S. and Soukoreff, R.W., A character-level error analysis technique for evaluating text entry methods. In *Proc. NordiCHI*, ACM (2002), 243-246.
16. MacKenzie, I.S. and Soukoreff, R.W., Phrase sets for evaluating text entry techniques. In *Proc. CHI*, ACM (2003), 754-755.
17. MacKenzie, I.S. and Tanaka-Ishii, K., *Text entry systems : mobility, accessibility, universality*. Boston : Morgan Kaufmann, Amsterdam, 2007.
18. Markussen, A., Jakobsen, M., and Hornbæk, K., Selection-Based Mid-Air Text Entry on Large Displays. In *Proc. INTERACT*, Springer Berlin Heidelberg (2013), 401-418.
19. McGuire, R.M., Hernandez-Rebollar, J., Starner, T., Henderson, V., Brashear, H., and Ross, D.S., Towards a one-way American sign language translator. In *Proc. AFGR*, (2004), 620-625.
20. Nancel, M., Wagner, J., Pietriga, E., Chapuis, O., and Mackay, W., Mid-air pan-and-zoom on wall-sized displays. In *Proc. CHI*, ACM (2011), 177-186.
21. Ni, T., Bowman, D.A., and North, C., AirStroke: bringing unistroke text entry to freehand gesture interfaces. In *Proc. CHI*, ACM (2011), 2473-2476.
22. *Oddities in words, pictures and figures*. Reader's Digest, London, 1975.
23. Piumsomboon, T., Clark, A., Billinghurst, M., and Cockburn, A., 2013. User-Defined Gestures for Augmented Reality. In *INTERACT*, P. Kotzé, G. Marsden, G. Lindgaard, J. Wesson and M. Winckler Eds. Springer Berlin Heidelberg, 282-299.
24. Proctor, R.W. and Vu, K.P.L., *Stimulus-Response Compatibility Principles: Data, Theory, and Application*. Taylor & Francis, 2006.
25. Schick, A., Morlock, D., Amma, C., Schultz, T., and Stiefelhagen, R., Vision-based handwriting recognition for unrestricted text input in mid-air. In *Proc. ICMI*, ACM (2012), 217-220.
26. Shengli, Z., Zhuxin, D., Li, W.J., and Chung Ping, K., Hand-written character recognition using MEMS motion sensing technology. In *Proc. AIM*, (2008), 1418-1423.
27. Shoemaker, G., Findlater, L., Dawson, J.Q., and Kellogg, B.S., Mid-air text input techniques for very large wall displays. In *Proc. GI*, Canadian Information Processing Society (2009), 231-238.
28. Shoemaker, G., Tang, A., and Booth, K.S., Shadow reaching: a new perspective on interaction for large displays. In *Proc. UIST*, ACM (2007), 53-56.
29. Sutton, J., Air painting with Corel Painter Freestyle and the leap motion controller: a revolutionary new way to paint! In *Proc. ACM SIGGRAPH Studio Talks*, ACM (2013), 1-1.
30. Vogel, D. and Balakrishnan, R., Distant freehand pointing and clicking on very large, high resolution displays. In *Proc. UIST*, ACM (2005), 33-42.
31. Wigdor, D. and Wixon, D., *Brave NUI World: Designing Natural User Interfaces for Touch and Gesture*. Morgan Kaufmann Publishers Inc., 2011.
32. Witt, H., Lawo, M., and Drugge, M., Visual feedback and different frames of reference: the impact on gesture interaction techniques for wearable computing. In *Proc. MobileHCI*, ACM (2008), 293-300.
33. Wobbrock, J.O., Myers, B.A., and Chau, D.H., In-stroke word completion. In *Proc. UIST*, ACM (2006), 333-336.
34. Wobbrock, J.O., Wilson, A.D., and Li, Y., Gestures without libraries, toolkits or training: a $1 recognizer for user interface prototypes. In *Proc. UIST*, ACM (2007), 159-168.
35. Zhai, S. and Kristensson, P.O., Shorthand writing on stylus keyboard. In *Proc. CHI*, ACM (2003), 97-104.
36. Zhai, S. and Kristensson, P.O., The word-gesture keyboard: reimagining keyboard interaction. *Commun. ACM 55*, 9 (2012), 91-101.
37. Zhai, S., Kristensson, P.O., Gong, P., Greiner, M., Peng, S.A., Liu, L.M., and Dunnigan, A., Shapewriter on the iphone: from the laboratory to the real world. In *Proc. CHI*, ACM (2009), 2667-2670.

# Understanding Finger Input Above Desktop Devices

**Chat Wacharamanotham** **Kashyap Todi** **Marty Pye** **Jan Borchers**
RWTH Aachen University
52062 Aachen, Germany
{chat, borchers}@cs.rwth-aachen.de, {kashyap.todi, marty.pye}@rwth-aachen.de

## ABSTRACT
Using the space above desktop input devices adds a rich new input channel to desktop interaction. Input in this elevated layer has been previously used to modify the granularity of a 2D slider, navigate layers of a 3D body scan above a multitouch table and access vertically stacked menus. However, designing these interactions is challenging because the lack of haptic and direct visual feedback easily leads to input errors. For bare finger input, the user's fingers needs to reliably enter and stay inside the interactive layer, and engagement techniques such as midair clicking have to be disambiguated from leaving the layer. These issues have been addressed for interactions in which users operate other devices in midair, but there is little guidance for the design of bare finger input in this space.

In this paper, we present the results of two user studies that inform the design of finger input above desktop devices. Our studies show that 2 cm is the minimum thickness of the above-surface volume that users can reliably remain within. We found that when accessing midair layers, users do not automatically move to the same height. To address this, we introduce a technique that dynamically determines the height at which the layer is placed, depending on the velocity profile of the user's initial finger movement into midair. Finally, we propose a technique that reliably distinguishes clicking from homing movements, based on the user's hand shape. We structure the presentation of our findings using Buxton's three-state input model, adding additional states and transitions for above-surface interactions.

## Author Keywords
Finger input; midair; near-surface; height; thickness

## ACM Classification Keywords
H.5.2. Information Interfaces and Presentation (e.g. HCI): User Interfaces

## INTRODUCTION
Sensing midair input in horizontal near-surface space has been used to augment keyboards, mice, and touchscreens. The horizontal near-surface space provides better ergonomics than vertical midair space because users can rest their arms or elbows on the desk surface. Additionally, users can quickly switch to existing desktop devices for already-efficient tasks, e.g., using the keyboard for typing. To facilitate this switching between midair and desk-based devices, we focus on midair near-surface input with bare fingers.


*CHI 2014*, April 26–May 1, 2014, Toronto, Ontario, Canada.

ACM 978-1-4503-2473-1/14/04..$15.00.
http://dx.doi.org/10.1145/2556288.2557151

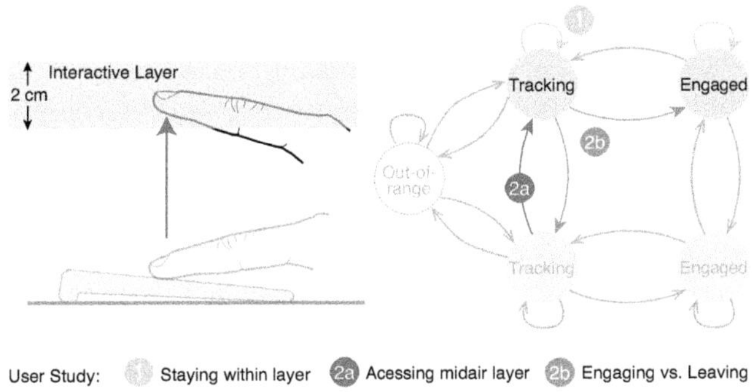


Figure 1: Interacting within an above-surface layer. We applied Buxton's three state model to explain the relevance of the user studies for such interactions.

Designing interactions for the near-surface space is difficult because the lack of haptic and direct visual feedback leads to input errors. Physiological tremor can cause the finger height to be unstable. Previous work partitioned the space into multiple interaction layers and determined appropriate layer thickness for using a stylus in midair. However, the movement behaviour of free hands differs from that of holding a stylus.

Another problem of midair input is distinguishing the intention of finger use. A finger in the near-surface volume may be intended for different kinds of interactions, such as tracking a cursor or activating an object, akin to clicking with the mouse. Alternatively, the presence of the finger in the volume may be unintentional while homing towards physical devices on the desk. We show that these states can be reliably classified, and brought into compliance with Buxton's three-state reference model for input [2].

This paper thus makes the following contributions:

- We determine an appropriate thickness for near-surface interaction layers through an empirical study.
- Based on an analysis of users' finger velocity during near-surface input, we propose a method to dynamically place the layer, which prevents over- and undershoots upon entering the volume.

- We present a near-surface "engagement" technique (clicking) that minimizes inadvertent layer changes and unintended engagements upon leaving the near-surface space.

In the following section, we describe the challenges of designing an interaction technique in the near-surface volume, using Buxton's model.

## INTERACTION MODEL

Buxton's three-state model can be applied to near-surface interaction (Fig. 1). Ideally, an input technique would allow three states, "out of range", "tracking" and "engaged", and the transitions between them. As we will see in the following paragraphs, certain characteristics of the midair volume make this hard to achieve.

First of all, we need to disambiguate the midair volume above the desk surface from desk-bound devices. This means that users should be able to switch between desk-bound devices and midair at will (Fig. 1 transition 2a). Therefore, the volume needs to be placed at a certain *height* above the surface. This height is defined as the orthogonal distance from the desk surface to the bottom of the volume, and requires careful consideration. A volume that is positioned too high leads to more exertion and makes the interaction more overt, whereas a volume that is placed too low can lead to ambiguous interaction with desk-bound devices. One method to avoid ambiguous interaction would be to use a toggle button or a quasimode, where the user holds down a designated key, thus "enabling" the midair space for interaction. However, these switches add an additional step, which can introduce mode errors. A press-and-hold mode would forbid bimanual input. Having a static starting height for the volume could cause the user to not move high enough (undershoot) when homing into the volume. In order to optimize for all these factors, we propose a dynamic solution for accessing the volume, derived from the movement behaviour of the human hand into midair space.

Once the user has reached the midair volume, he needs to be able to remain in this volume (Fig. 1 transition 1). This means that the volume needs to have a minimum *thickness*. Thickness is defined as the distance from the bottom of the layer to the top of the layer, and also needs careful consideration. On the one hand, a thin volume is more susceptible to drifting, which can cause erroneous, unintended input. The user is required to carefully stay within the layer, which slows down their interaction and may lead to frustration. On the other hand, a thick volume, increases the distance the user has to move the hand when clutching out of the interaction area. This leads to slower input, fatigue and again, potential user frustration. Applications that use multiple layers for different semantics of interaction will have fewer possible layers, as the range of the human hand is limited. Increasing the thickness of the total volume requires tracking hardware that covers a larger area, and at the same time is more prone to catch unintended hand movement as an input signal. If we knew the minimum thickness in which a user can reliably remain without visual feedback, we would not be dependent on that visual feedback, which can clutter the screen and increase cognitive load. Therefore, we conducted a study in order to determine the smallest possible layer thickness that still allows the user to reliably interact with it.

Assuming access to the midair-layer has been achieved, and the user is able to stay comfortably within it, what remains is an *engagement method* that allows entering the engaged state, similar to depressing a mouse button (Fig. 1 transition 2b). Such an engagement method should be an explicit action to reduce the likelihood of accidental engagement. The engagement method should allow each hand to be in the engaged state separately, enabling bimanual input if necessary. It should occupy a minimal amount of fingers, so that ideally, multiple fingers could maintain the engaged state separately, comparable to multitouch interaction. Therefore, we study the characteristics of the human hand's movement in midair space and derive a suitable engagement technique.

In the next section, we review the literature of midair interactions in order to draw lessons relevant to the design considerations of height, thickness and engagement method.

## RELATED WORK

The third dimension, added through the near-surface space, has previously been exploited for input techniques. Marquardt et al. investigated continuing touch input when the hand is raised above the surface to reduce content occlusion [10]. Hilliges et al. tracked the shadow of the hands when hovering over the surface of a tabletop to use it as a proxy to interact with objects [5]. The height of the hand can also be used as a parameter for a transfer function which can be additionally applied to the 2D input, e.g., modifying the granularity of a slider on a touchscreen [10]. Yu et al. used midair layers parallel to a trackpad to select different C/D-ratios [22]. Near-surface space can provide an additional layer of information associated with the two dimensional input. This additional layer has, for example, been used for a stylus over the tabletop [17], or for magic lenses [16]. Subramanian visualized the information on the existing device (tabletop), whereas Spindler visualized it directly in the midair layer using a projection on the magic lens. The additional dimension above the keyboard can also be used purely for control, decoupled from any horizontal movement. For example, Benko visualized the output directly on the hand, so that the user could navigate through a stack of menus vertically [20].

Previous work has discovered the need for a suitable thickness when placing multiple layers in near-surface space, and recommendations exist. Spindler et al. studied how accurately people are able to maintain a paper lens in a specific layer with two hands while hovering, and while performing a horizontal search task [15]. They found that the minimum layer thickness for hovering is 1 cm, while the minimum thickness for horizontal movement is about 4 cm. Subramanian investigated different layer thicknesses for stylus interaction with arm support on the desk in an informal study and recommended 4 cm [17]. A follow-up with a formal steering study in 1D, 2D and 3D showed that 2 cm sufficed to minimize movement time [8]. However, only movement along one axis was investigated, and continuous height feedback of the stylus within the layer was provided.

Although free finger interaction seems to require a similar layer setup as previous work, the finger movement differs from the aforementioned techniques in some crucial aspects, therefore jeopardizing the applicability of their guidelines. While a minimum 4 cm thickness may apply for the bimanual usage of magic lenses while standing at tabletops [15], this thickness may not apply in a seated position, where only one hand is used. Although it is plausible that the thickness acquired by Kattinakere et al. [8] would apply to free finger movement, this assumption cannot be made, as a finger moves along a different trajectory than a stylus. The movement path of a finger is more curved than that of a stylus, making the path longer, and therefore more prone to drifts [4].

Additionally to the inherent differences of free finger interaction, several other factors differ from previous work. While Spindler's setup increases the stability of the object by spreading the load over two hands [16], the stability is potentially reduced by the user having to hold the object in midair without allowing arms to be rested. The continuous visual feedback provided in Kattinakere's study allows closed-loop adjustment of the height, potentially resulting in a more precise movement [8].

Another important factor of near-surface input is the engagement technique, analogous to clicking. Existing engagement techniques that have been proposed for midair input allow at most one input state per hand, and can be classified as follows. First, a hardware button can be used. This can be either on a separate device, e.g., Mysliwiec used one hand to point, the other to press a clicking-key [12], or be on the pointing device, e.g., Subramanian used a button on the stylus for clicking [17]. Second, the movement can be used to change state, like crossing in and out of targets (horizontal movement), or crossing midair layers (vertical movement) [17]. Finally, hand-shape gestures can be used to decouple the movement from the engagement. Wilson used a pinching gesture of index finger and thumb to click [19]. In order to improve the stability of the tracked cursor, Kato and Yanagihara tracked the knuckle position instead of the finger tip, making the pinching engagement independent from the movement [7]. Vogel used the striking of the thumb on the index finger to detect a click [18]. This was improved by Banerjee et al. to striking the middle finger instead of index finger to enhance stability of the cursor movement [1]. Perhaps the most intuitive of all engagement techniques is to emulate tapping by using the same finger motion in the air [18]. This was ranked best by users because of the familiarity with mouse clicking [3]. Pyryeskin et al. performed a gesture elicitation for above multitouch-surface selection. Air-tapping ("push with a finger") was the second most frequent gesture (26.6%), slightly less frequent than grabbing (35.2%), which occupies the whole hand [14]. Our paper takes a closer look at this index finger tapping, and addresses the shift of the finger that can cause erroneous input.

Before tackling the challenges of layer access and engagement, we will determine the required layer thickness for maintaining the tracking state in the next section.

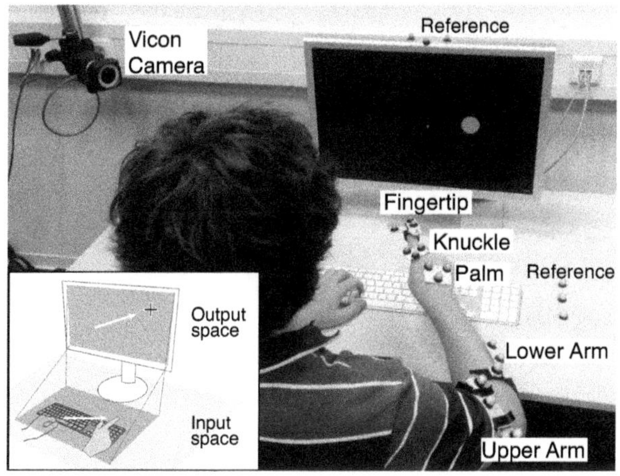


Figure 2: The physical setup of the user studies. Reflective markers were attached to the participants to record data for various sections of the right arm. Indirect mapping was used to prevent effect of hand occlusion.

## STUDY 1: THICKNESS OF ABOVE-SURFACE LAYERS

In layered mid-air interactions, having thin layers allows for a large number of such layers within a given interaction volume. However, we need to take into consideration the ergonomics of the human arm and hand. Factors like hand tremor and drifting, and lack of haptic feedback in the near-surface space, make it difficult for users to maintain their hands at a constant level. This makes thinner layers harder for users to stay inside. This study aims to determine a suitable thickness of such near-surface layers while the finger remains in the tracking state (Fig. 1 transition 1).

### Apparatus

The position of the users' index fingertip was used as input to the application, to control a screen cursor. To obtain accurate positional coordinates, we used a Vicon motion-capture system to track passive infrared-reflective markers, which provided three-dimensional data with sub-millimeter accuracy at 100 Hz. Markers were attached to the user's finger with lightweight patches (<8g each). Before the test, users flexed their fingers to ensure that the patches did not inhibit their movements. In addition, we recorded the position of the user's index fingertip, wrist and elbow for analysis purposes (Fig. 2). The position of knuckle and palm was only recorded in the second study. The experiment tasks were displayed on an Apple Cinema Display (49.5 cm $\times$ 30.5 cm; 1920 $\times$ 1200 pixels). To prevent the influence of hand occlusion, the user's finger was mapped from the orthogonal projection onto the desk surface, to the vertical screen. The participants sat in front of a desk, approximately 50 cm away from the screen, on an adjustable chair with armrests. The height of the chair was adjusted by each user according to preference.

### Participants

Eight right-handed volunteers (two female) of computer science background were recruited (mean age of 24). Participants did not exhibit any known hand disabilities (severe tremor, etc.). Any visual impairments were noted down prior

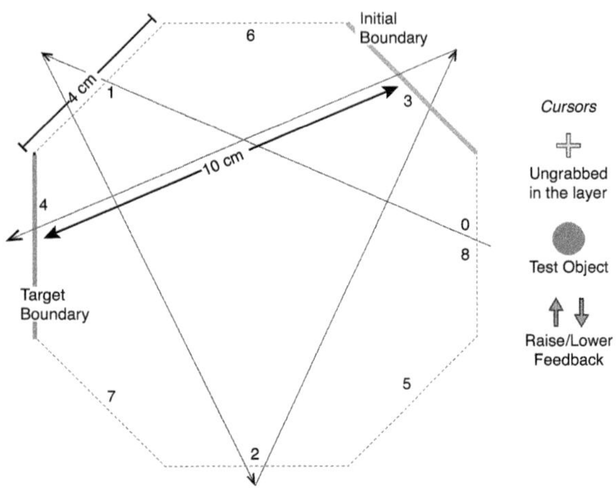


Figure 3: The steering tasks performed by the users. The cursor was used to grab a test object, and drag it from the initial to the target boundary. Different cursors provided feedback about the z-direction in which the finger needed to be moved to re-enter the layer.

to the test and it was confirmed that they had been corrected. All participants had a computer science background.

### Task

The task users performed involved finger steering within a near-surface layer, similar to Kattinakere et al.'s [8]. Users controlled an on-screen cursor with their index finger to drag the object from an initial boundary across a target boundary (Fig. 3). After crossing each boundary, the next target boundary was shifted anti-clockwise. When the cursor enters the object, the object was automatically grabbed (no engaging gesture required). When the finger exited the layer, the object was released. Users could only pick the object back up again by readjusting their finger height.

Whenever the finger was outside the near-surface layer, the cursor changed to an arrow indicating whether the finger was too high or too low. Therefore, during the movement within the layer, the users needed to rely on proprioception to maintain the height of the finger.

To ensure constant initial velocity of hand movement, a short pause was programmed after crossing each goal. Since arm movements vary depending on the direction, the eight boundaries were evenly distributed, in order to make sure that the results were applicable to 2D movements in general.

### Design

A within-subjects design was used for the user study. The independent variables used were the *Thickness*, *SurfaceSupport*, and *MovementDistance*. The different layer thickness values used were 1, 2, 3 and 4 cm. The two hand support configurations tested were (1) the users rested the wrist on the desk surface, and (2) the wrist had no support. Two types of movement sizes were used *SmallMovement* (1 cm) and *LargeMovement* (10 cm).

- *DriftCount*: Less drifts indicate that the user can reliably maintain the finger in the layer. This is the main measurement for determining optimal thickness. However, less drifts may results from the fact that the user carefully moves the finger during the test.
- *ManipulationTime*: Time taken for dragging the object from the initial boundary to the final boundary. This is measured only when the finger is within the given thickness and the object has been grabbed. This time excludes instances where the finger drifts outside the layer, causing the object to be released. Lower cursor manipulation time results from faster movement within the layer. This indicates that the user is more confident in moving the object in the layer.

In summary, the experimental design was: 8 participants × 4 *Thickness* × 2 *SurfaceSupport* × 2 *MovementDistance* × 8 boundaries × 3 repetitions = 3072 total trials.

### Data analysis

In order to make each row of the data represent the performance across all movement directions, we averaged the *ManipulationTime* across all movement directions in the same repetition. *DriftCount* was also summed across movement directions.

We used mixed-effect model analysis of variance (henceforth "ANOVA") in which *Thickness*, *MovementDistance*, and *SurfaceSupport* are fixed effects and *UserID* is a random effect. We used Tukey HSD for post-hoc tests (henceforth "post-hoc test"). For all significant interaction effects, we performed the post-hoc tests for both main and interaction effects. The statistically significant results in the following section have the agreement of post-hoc tests up to the highest degree of significant interaction effects.

As expected, both *DriftCount* and *ManipulationTime* are not normally distributed. Appropriate transformations were applied before ANOVA and post-hoc tests. Neither Poisson nor Gamma-Poisson distribution fitted the *DriftCount*; therefore, it is aligned-rank transformed [21]. The *ManipulationTime* fits log-normal distributions, so we applied a $y = log(x)$ transformation.

Due to the lack of normality, descriptive statistics (mean, median, and 95% confidence interval) derived directly from the data may not be an accurate representation, e.g., means of *ManipulationTime* are pulled higher by a long tail of the log-normal distribution. The resolution of the statistics could be too low, e.g., the median of many *DriftCount* conditions are 1 regardless of their distributions. Also, simple inverse-transforms of CIs may produce the interval that excludes the sample mean. Therefore, to provide useful estimates, we calculated the descriptive statistics by ordinary non-parametric bootstrapping (10,000 replicates). CIs were calculated with the bias-corrected and accelerated method (BCa).

We used the original scales for the charts and the descriptive statistics. Error bars denote 95% confidence intervals.

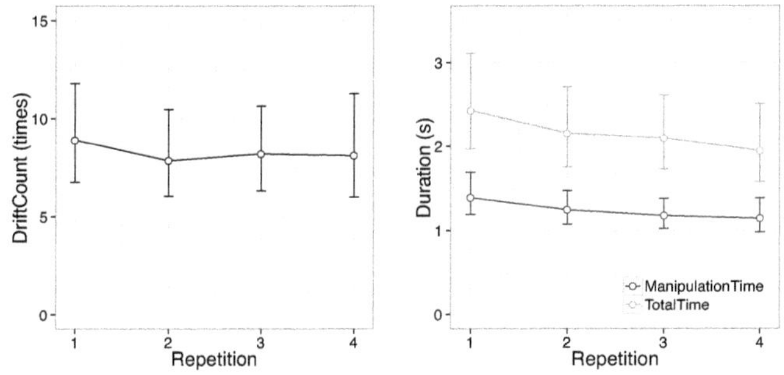


Figure 4: User's performance in the first repetition differs from the others, indicating the learning effect. The learning curve stabilizes after the first repetition.

Table 1: The significant main- and interaction effects to the both *DriftCount* and *ManipulationTime*.

| | df | | F | p |
|---|---|---|---|---|
| **DriftCount** | | | | |
| Thickness | 3 | 329 | 79.534 | <.0001 |
| Height | 1 | 329 | 171.09 | <.0001 |
| MovementSize | 1 | 329 | 162.01 | <.0001 |
| Thickness * Height | 3 | 329 | 60.57 | <.0001 |
| MovementSize * Thickness | 3 | 329 | 53.87 | <.0001 |
| MovementSize * Height | 1 | 329 | 110.95 | <.0001 |
| MovementSize * Thickness * Height | 3 | 329 | 28.88 | <.0001 |
| **ManipulationTime** | | | | |
| Thickness | 3 | 329 | 41.68 | <.0001 |
| Height | 1 | 329 | 330.38 | <.0001 |
| MovementSize | 1 | 329 | 215.10 | <.0001 |
| Thickness * Height | 3 | 329 | 11.35 | <.0001 |
| MovementSize * Thickness | 3 | 329 | 20.59 | <.0001 |
| MovementSize * Height | 1 | 329 | 29.10 | <.0001 |

### Results and Discussion

#### Learning Effect

As expected, we found a statistically significant learning effect of repetitions on *ManipulationTime* ($F_{3,441} = 4.91, p = .0023$). The post-hoc test indicated that only the first repetition stood out from the rest (16% slower in *ManipulationTime*, Fig. 4). The faster movements suggest that the users were rapidly gaining confidence after one repetition whereas the drifts occurred independently of the users' confidence ($F_{3,441} = 1.12, p = .3394$). The interaction effects between repetitions and other independent variables were not statistically significant. To rule out the influence of users' confidence, we excluded the first repetition from the following analysis (resulting in 384 data rows).

#### Layer Thickness Analysis

The ANOVA results are shown in Table 1. As expected, we found significant main effects of *Thickness*, *SurfaceSupport*, and *MovementDistance* on both dependent variables. Due to significant interaction effects, we will take a closer look at each condition to determine suitable thickness.

*Movement with surface support*

When the hand was supported by the desk surface, post-hoc tests found no statistically significant differences in *DriftCount* and *ManipulationTime* among the 2, 3, and 4 cm thicknesses. The users drifted more in the 1 cm layer ($M$ = 6.50 times) than in the others (4.46 times). This difference was independent of the movement sizes (Fig. 5). The users also moved 29% slower in the 1 cm layer than the others. Post-hoc comparison in the *SmallMovement* condition, which is the easiest condition, highlighted the worsened performance of the 1 cm compared to the 2 cm layer. When users achieved comparable *DriftCount*, the post-hoc test indicated that the *ManipulationTime* is significantly slower. In summary, when surface support is available, the near-surface layer can be as thin as 2 cm without worsening the user's performance.

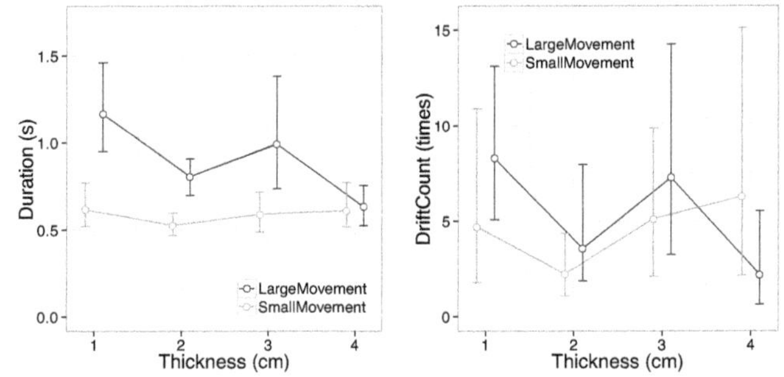


Figure 5: Drift occurrences and manipulation time for hand-on-desk conditions. Post-hoc tests shows that the 2 cm thickness yields similar performance to thicker layers.

In contrast to [8], our visual feedback only indicates whether the finger is in the layer, too high, or too low. The similar result of the 2 cm thickness suggests that maintaining a finger in these conditions may not require continuous visual feedback of the finger height with respect to the layer.

*Movement without surface support*

When the hand and arm are not supported by the desk surface, the effect of *Thickness* was different between *SmallMovement* and *LargeMovement*.

*SmallMovement*: Post-hoc tests found no statistically significant differences in *DriftCount* and *ManipulationTime* among the 2, 3, and 4 cm thicknesses. Fig. 6 shows that drifts in the 1 cm thickness ($M_{1cm}$ = 10.79 times) triples those of the others ($M_{2,3,4cm}$ = 3.25 times). Longer *ManipulationTime* in the 1cm layer ($M_{1cm}$ = 1.17 s vs. $M_{2,3,4cm}$ = 0.95 s) suggests that users moved with significantly less confidence for this thickness.

Although the 2 cm result is similar to the hand-on-surface condition, the *SmallMovement* in midair is only comparable to the *LargeMovement* with surface support ($M_{DriftCount}$ = 4.33 times and $M_{ManipulationTime}$ = 0.81 s). *SmallMovement* with surface support in the 2 cm thickness is slightly better than both ($M_{DriftCount}$ = 2.25 and $M_{ManipulationTime}$ = 0.53).

*LargeMovement*: Post-hoc tests found no statistically significant difference in *DriftCount* between the 3 cm and 4 cm thickness ($M_{3cm}$ = 9.58 times, $M_{4cm}$ = 4.15 times, Fig. 7). However, users were faster in the 4 cm ($M_{3cm}$ = 1.91 s, $M_{4cm}$ = 1.10 s). The 4 cm thickness in midair also performed simi-

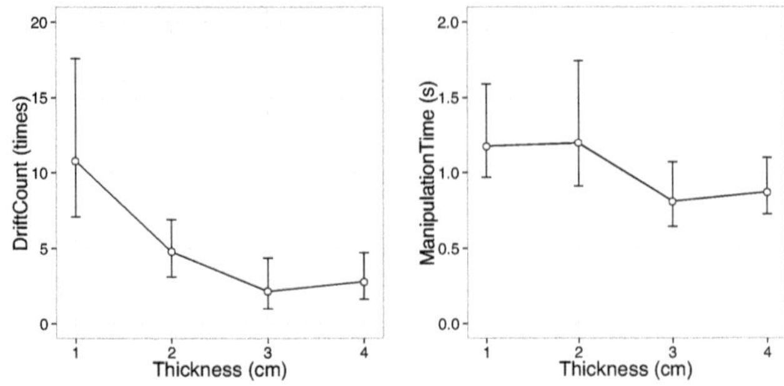


Figure 6: Drift count and manipulation time for *SmallMovement* in midair. The 2 cm thickness yields similar performance to thicker layers, similarly to the hand-on-surface condition.

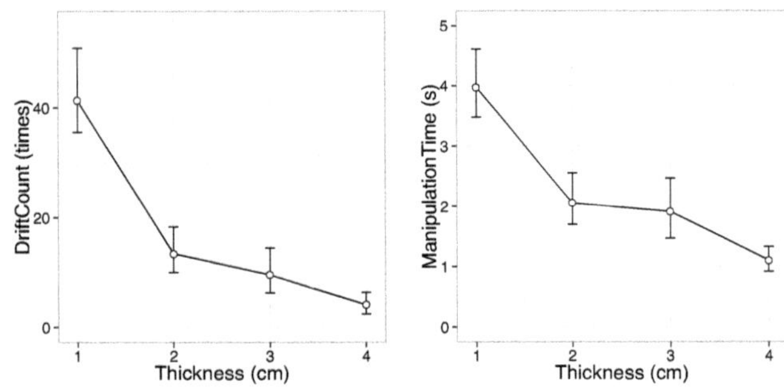


Figure 7: Drift occurrences and manipulation time for *LargeMovement* in midair. Although users drift by comparable amounts in the 3 cm and 4 cm layers, they were significantly faster in the 4 cm layer.

larly to the 2, 3, and 4 cm thickness on the surface ($M_{DriftCount}$ = 4.45 times, $M_{ManipulationTime}$ = 0.69 s). Therefore, it is possible to compensate the lack of surface support by increasing the thickness to 4 cm.

Will layers thicker than 4 cm be better? We repeated the study for 4 cm, 5 cm, 6 cm, and 7 cm thickness for large movements in midair. The test was done with a different group of participants (average age 25.84 years, 2 female). The increased thickness did not significantly improve *DriftCount*, $F_{3,77} = 0.27, p = .76$. However, the thicker layer allowed users to move more freely, therefore, significantly reducing the *ManipulationTime*, $F_{3,77} = 6.97, p = .0003$. However, each of the 1 cm thicknesses reduced the *ManipulationTime* by only 0.1s. This improvement is much smaller than the 0.8 s improvement from 3 cm to 4 cm.

In summary, for finger movement in the near-surface space without the arm touching the surface, we recommend 2 cm thickness for short movements (1 cm) and 4 cm thickness for long movements (10 cm).

## STUDY 2: ELICITING USER'S MOTION DURING ACCESSING, ENGAGING, AND LEAVING THE MIDAIR LAYER

This elicitation study aims to determine how the user's finger moves when homing into a midair layer, and how the characteristics differ from those of moving the cursor. Also, we wish to investigate how the hand parts behave during engagement (clicking and dragging). Some characteristics of the motion may be consistent enough for real-time detection of engagement gestures.

### Apparatus

We refer to the Apparatus section of the first study. In addition to the positions of fingertip, wrist and elbow, we recorded the positions of the major knuckle and the opisthenar.

### Participants

Ten unpaid right-handed participants (three female), without any known hand disabilities (severe tremor, etc.), with a mean age of 25 were recruited for the study. Any visual impairments were noted down prior to the test and it was confirmed that they had been corrected. All but two of the participants had a computer science background.

### Task

Users performed a two-dimensional point-and-write task, similar to Ortega and Nigay for AirMouse [13]. They alternated between typing and pointing, controlling an on-screen cursor with their right index finger. A trial consisted of first typing some text, and then pressing enter with the right hand. After that, the user had to raise their hand into midair and point to the target, which they then clicked by tapping their index finger down and back up again, thus clicking the target. They then had to drag the target by pressing the index finger down and moving it to the next goal, while keeping the index finger down. Once the goal had been reached, they had to release the target by bringing their index finger back up into a normal pointing state. Once the target had been released, a new text field appeared, and the user homed back down to the keyboard in order to start typing again, and repeat the cycle.

No engagement or midair-access recognition algorithm was used in this study, so as not to taint the user's data by a specific algorithm. Instead, a Wizard-of-Oz technique was used to trigger the state of the application based on the user's finger motion. The user's finger was mapped with a 1:1 absolute mapping.

Pilot studies showed that the users' performance in term of overall duration was stable during the second to fourth repetition. Therefore, the test was conducted with 4 repetitions, with the first repetition marked as a training run. In summary, this resulted in 10 participants $\times$ 16 tasks $\times$ 4 repetitions = 640 total trials.

### Results and Discussion

The results and discussion are divided into two parts. We begin by discussing the layer height, followed by a discussion about distinguishing between homing and engagement.

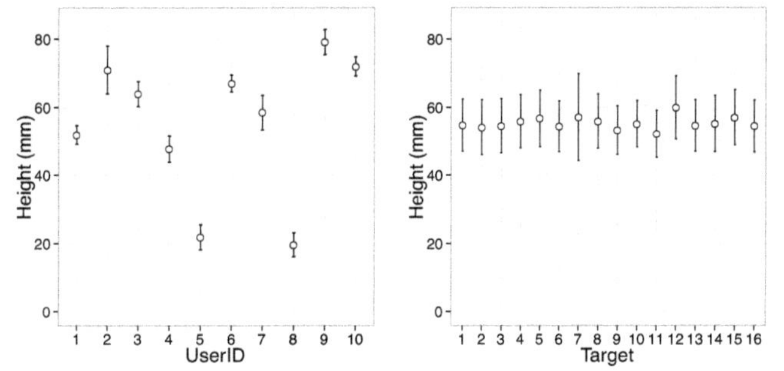


Figure 8: The initial homing stroke height greatly varies across users, whereas it is consistent across target locations. (User 5, 9, and 10 were female.)

### *Layer Height*

After having removed 13 erroneous trials from the data, a mixed-model analysis of variance with the user as a random effect resulted in no significant effect of repetition and target number. This implies that no learning effect was to be observed within the four repetitions. A three-way analysis of variance showed a significant effect of the user ($F_{9,617} = 102, p < .0001$). Levene's test indicated unequal variances ($F_{9,617} = 1.93, p = .0452$) across users (Fig. 8).

The substantial variation among users suggests that an initial static height would require practice, as different users prefer different heights. There are two possible solutions to deal with this user preference. The initial layer height could be either personalized or dynamically calculated for every homing stroke. The effectiveness of the personalization method would depend on whether individual users stably home to the same height, with little deviation. The effectiveness of the dynamic method would require some characteristic measure, which could be used to reliably calculate the height every time. Next, we analyze the data for hints whether personalization or dynamic calculation is more suitable.

In order to judge whether personalization of the layer height would be a suitable technique, we analyzed the average standard deviation of individual users, and found it to be 1.5 cm. Even with the highly conservative estimation that users will reliably home the finger with a maximal deviation of 1.5 cm, the fluctuation exceeds more than half of the 2 cm layer thickness learned from the first study. Therefore, having a personalized static height is unlikely to result in a satisfactory user experience. Instead, determining the initial height dynamically for every homing stroke seems to be more suitable.

It remains to be analyzed which parameter is a suitable measure to determine the initial layer height. A strong correlation of the overall velocity to both the horizontal (Pearson's $r(627)$ = .93, $p < .0001$) and vertical peak velocity ($r(627)$ = .74, $p =< .0001$) indicates that users move in both the horizontal and vertical direction while raising the finger. Therefore, using the motion vector alone would not suffice to detect the moving-to-midair gesture. However, a non-significant correlation between the horizontal and vertical valley velocity ($r(627)$ = .06, $p = .13$) suggests that once the user stops raising his finger, the movement in horizontal direction does not necessarily stop. Therefore, the vertical finger velocity is a good candidate for detecting lifting-to-midair.

Table 2: The significant main effect of participants, suggesting the potential to personalize the initial height.

| | *df* | | *F* | *p* |
|---|---|---|---|---|
| Vz (Peak-Valley) | | | | |
| UserID | 9 | 9 | 2.27 | .0167 |
| RepetitionNo | 3 | 554.2 | 0.45 | .7189 |
| TargetNo | 15 | 554.2 | 0.51 | .9367 |
| RepetitionNo * TargetNo | 45 | 554.2 | 0.48 | .9983 |
| Vz (Peak) | | | | |
| UserID | 9 | 9 | 2.58 | .0063 |
| RepetitionNo | 3 | 554.2 | 0.50 | .6804 |
| TargetNo | 15 | 554.2 | 0.49 | .9472 |
| RepetitionNo * TargetNo | 45 | 554.2 | 0.50 | .9975 |
| Vz (Valley) | | | | |
| UserID | 9 | 9 | 10.03 | <.0001 |
| RepetitionNo | 3 | 554.2 | 2.28 | .0785 |
| TargetNo | 15 | 554.2 | 1.05 | .3986 |
| RepetitionNo * TargetNo | 45 | 554.2 | 0.98 | .5030 |

Further mixed-model ANOVA of the vertical peak velocity, valley velocity and the difference between both revealed no significant main effect of repetition and target number. Three-way ANOVA revealed a significant main effect of the user for all variables (Table 2). This suggests the possibility of personalizing the velocity threshold for transition to the layer by detecting either the peak velocity or velocity difference. Analysis showed radical difference between the magnitude of the valley velocity ($M$ = 5.13 cm/s, $SD$ = 1.79 cm/s) and the peak velocity ($M$ = 138.37 cm/s, $SD$ = 41 cm/s). Therefore, it is possible to use a cut-off by velocity method to detect the transition to the midair layer. Based on the empirical rule, a threshold of 21.25 cm/s is suitable.

### *Distinguishing Engagement Gesture from Leaving Midair*

We manually filtered erroneous movement (e.g., starting to drag without clicking) in the first test repetition for each user based on the 3D coordinate of the fingertip. In total, we have reliable data from 157 clicks, 153 Mouse-downs, and 148 Mouse-ups. For this analysis, the data is classifed into the following movement phases:

- *Pre-depressing*: The movement between the click and the height (during the cursor wait). We used all points in this phase before the user initialized the high velocity to depress.

- *DragDepressing*: The high velocity downward stroke followed by a large movement amplitude along the planar direction. All the points within this movement phase with the overall velocity greater than above the 97.5% quantile (200 cm/s) are used.

- *ClickDepressing*: The high velocity downward stroke followed by the upward stroke during the phase that the user is assigned to click in midair. We used the same velocity criteria as in *DragDepressing*.

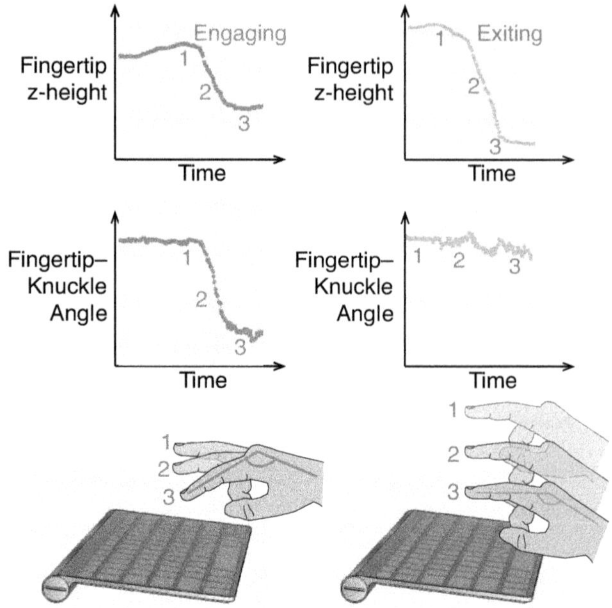


Figure 9: During engagement gesture (left), users flex their finger, causing the knuckle angle to change over time. During exiting movements (right), users did not change their knuckle angle. This difference in the movement profile can be used to identify the user's intention.

- *Pre-leaving*: This is the point after the user lifts the finger from the dragging movement. It is manually annotated during the study.
- *Leaving*: The stroke after Pre-leaving point, but before the user reaches the keyboard. Again, we use all data points with velocity greater than 200 cm/s.

We considered positional and velocity features of the fingertip, knuckle and hand in order to help distinguish the engagement gesture by tapping from the leaving action, e.g., homing the hand back to the keyboard for typing.

As expected, we found that knuckle angles (Fig. 9) are significantly different between *Pre-depressing* and *DragDepressing* ($t_{87} = 5.87, p < .0001$) along the movement direction. However, the differences of the knuckle angle in *Pre-leaving* and *Leaving* are not statistically significant ($t_{157} = -.1632, p = .1047$). This suggests that the change in the knuckle angle could be used to distinguish the engagement from the leaving gesture. Additionally, the difference of the knuckle angles between *ClickDepressing* and *DragDepressing* is also not statistically significant, ($t_{87} = 1.88, p = .0639$). This indicates that the knuckle angle can be used reliably, regardless of the duration that the finger dwells in the engaged state.

These results indicate that the angle between the fingertip, knuckle and palm do not significantly change when the users leaves midair space to the desktop devices. This feature allows us to distinguish the engagement from the leaving midair action.

### Limitation

Our study used a keyboard as a representation of desk-based devices. Prehension research indicates that grip forms only after 75% of the movement [6]. While this suggests that our finding should generalize to device of different shapes, the influence of the affordance of each desktop device during leaving the midair space warrants further studies. Sensing the shape of the desktop devices may allow more accurate classification of the engagement gesture from the leaving midair action.

The small number of participants biased towards male may influence the results. However, we did not find statistically significant effect of gender or lower arm length. We surmised that the difference across users were greater (Fig. 8).

## DYNAMIC ENTRY HEIGHT

Analysing these three different behaviour patterns of users, while switching from on-surface to near-surface interactions, has helped us in devising an algorithm which does the following:

1. Intention detection: We can estimate whether the user wishes to either simply start near-surface interactions, browse through the stack of mid-air layers, or if the movement is unintentional, and the user wishes to perform other activities.
2. Layer Positioning: In the case of the user wishing to start near-surface interactions, we can intelligently position the first interaction layer dynamically. In the scenario where users browse through a stack of layers, the layers are positioned statically.

The algorithm is formulated in Fig. 10. For the velocity threshold $v_{min}$, we recommend the result from Study 2 (21.25 cm/s). From iteratively tuning the parameter, we found that 0.1 s is a suitable minimum duration $d_{min}$. Figure 11 illustrates the stages of this algorithm.

We performed 10-fold cross-validation of the algorithm with the data from Study 2. The results show 95.16% accuracy with stable $v_{min}$ thresholds among iterations ($M$=19.41 cm/s, $SD$=3.46).

### Bimanual Hand Usage

While using dynamic layer positioning, special care needs to be taken while designing for bimanual interactions. The implementation of the technique can vary depending on the usage scenarios:

*Symmetric Hand Movements:* When the application involves bimanual interactions, where both hands need to be coordinated, the positioning of the layers should be the same for both hands. Hence, to determine the exact placement of the layer, using dynamic positioning, the point of entry of the first hand into the interaction volume is considered, and the layer position is fixed with reference to this point.

*Asymmetric Hand Movements:* When the application involves asymmetric bimanual interactions, each hand has its own reference frame. In such a case, it is possible to position the near-surface layer independently for each hand. Hence,

```
The DynamicHeight function is called to determine the height of the interactive
layer while the finger is out of the interactive layer.

Constants:
h1: default height of the lowest layer.
t: layer thickness
vmin: minimum velocity for a fast intended stroke.
dmin: minimum duration in for a slow intentional stroke.

Variables:
C: current frame number
Z[0, C]: array of buffered z-coordinates
V[0, C]: array of buffered z-velocities
Z and V are cleared everytime the finger leaves the tracking range

Helpers:
FireEvent(i) fires above-surface interaction event using data at frame i
FindPeak(M) returns the index of the highest peak in array M
FindValley(M) returns the index of the lowest valley in array M

DynamicHeight(C, Z, V):
P = FindMax(V[0, C])
if (P == INVALID)
    return INVALID
if V[P] > vmin                          (Detects fast strokes)
    L = FindValley(V[P, C])
    if (L != INVALID)
        for j from P to C               (Fire events retrospectively)
            FireEvent(j)
        return Z[P] – (t / 2)
else if C > dmin                        (Detects slow strokes)
    FireEvent(C)
    return h1
else
    return INVALID
```

Figure 10: Dynamic entry height algorithm

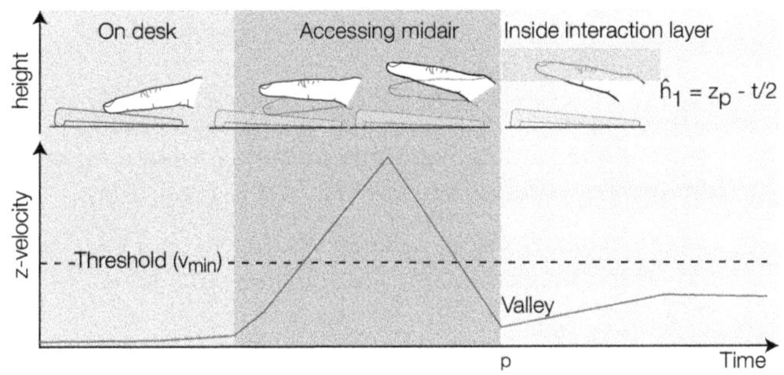


Figure 11: User's action while accessing a midair layer and the corresponding velocity profile. Dynamic height ($\hat{h}_1$) of the layer is set at the velocity valley, at time *p*.

the two hands can work in different interaction spaces, and this can avoid the occurrence of collisions.

## IMPLICATIONS

The understanding of elementary operations presented in our paper (entering, staying, engaging, and leaving) is a basis for further above-surface interaction designs. We summarize these implications to the previously discussed interaction model.

*Switching in and out of above-surface interaction without explicit switch or gestures:* Using our dynamic height algorithm and leaving/engaging classification criteria could lead to more fluent switching between above-surface and destop device input.

*Enabling above-surface interaction without continous height feedback:* Using the recommended layer thicknesses reduces the need of visual feedback for the relative position of the fingertip to the surface. This reduces accidental layer switching and reduces users' cognitive load in close-loop maintenance of finger height.

*Natural engagement with air-tapping:* Tracking knuckle angle allows air-tapping as above-surface engagement technique without being ambigous to the leaving motion.

These implication could be applied to previous works.

*Example 1:* Hover Paint [14] lets users lift their finger above a tabletop to select brush size (z) and color (x,y). It could benefit from our work in 3 ways: (a) It uses a quick upward flick to activate the brush UI. However, such sudden movements can lead to fatigue. Our dynamic height algorithm would allow for a less tiring activation: the user can move their finger up more naturally, and our algorithm establishes the interaction layer dynamically and reliably based on this initial movement. (b) Hover Paint could also improve the stability of its brush size setting while picking a color by using a minimum layer thickness that does not trigger size changes. We provide the suitable thickness of this layer. (c) Finally, Hover Paint does not allow canceling a selection, and when users confirm their settings by flicking down, the Hover Paint video actually shows that they accidentally start painting. Air-tapping would have avoided this, and the knuckle-angle method we contribute could distinguish moving down (to cancel) from air-tapping (to confirm).

*Example 2:* SpaceTop [9] lets users interact with a virtual 3D world behind a transparent screen in midair above a keyboard. To avoid hitting virtual objects while typing, objects are placed into a layer whose height and thickness are fixed, and which is substantially high, preventing users from resting the hand on the surface. However, with extended use, this height leads to fatigue. We provide the findings to place SpaceTop's object layer closer to the surface, establish its height dynamically, and use the right layer thickness for interaction. Our knuckle-angle technique could also be applied to detect when users air-tap to activate vs. when they leave the midair area.

## CONCLUSION AND FUTURE WORK

In our studies, we wished to determine the parameters necessary for enabling three-state input in the near-surface space. Our results show that 2 cm is the minimum thickness necessary for maintaining the tracking state. Furthermore, we found that users do not automatically use a consistent height for accessing the midair volume. Therefore, we designed a dynamic algorithm that reliably detects access to the midair volume, based on the empirical data gathered from our second user study. Motions of the human hand when engaging the midair layer are consistent enough to differentiate between engagement and homing to the desk device. We therefore proposed an engagement technique that reliably detects engagement of the midair layer, based on the empirical data from our second study.

Clearly, our approach has some limitations. The above results are applicable when the user interacts with the midair layer in the middle of the desk surface. Other placements of the midair volume are possible, e.g., above the mouse to the right hand side of the user. The movement in this area uses different joint angles, therefore, the result we propose in this paper may have limited generalizability. For example, the thickness recommendations for maintaining the tracking state may not apply when the arm is almost fully outstretched to the far right.

As a next step, we will design and evaluate an interaction technique that uses bare finger input in near-surface space, containing our methods for midair access and engagement. Furthermore, we will investigate whether our techniques hold for multiple stacks of midair layers, and whether our techniques for layer engagement are not only able to differentiate between engagement and homing to the keyboard, but also between engagement and accessing higher and lower layers.

Further future work could involve investigating slanted layers, e.g., caused by a keyboard that is slanted for ergonomic reasons, and how they influence performance. However, the performance influence should be during layer access, which is already compensated by our dynamic height algorithm. The thickness should not be affected. Whether the keyboard frame is used as a frame of reference during orientation will be interesting to investigate. Also, there is research that uses a slanted touchscreen as a digital sketching board [11]. Investigating the effect of orientation will be useful to such applications.

## ACKNOWLEDGMENTS

This work was funded in part by the German B-IT Foundation. We thank Thorsten Karrer for his valuable feedback, Philipp Wacker and Ignacio Avellino for their helps in the user studies.

## REFERENCES

1. A. Banerjee, J. Burstyn, A. Girouard, and R. Vertegaal. Pointable: an in-air pointing technique to manipulate out-of-reach targets on tabletops. In *ITS '11*, 11–20. 2011.
2. W. Buxton. A three-state model of graphical input. In *INTERACT '90*, 449–456. 1990.
3. F. Camp, A. Schick, and R. Stiefelhagen. How to click in mid-air. In *Distributed, Ambient, and Pervasive Interactions*, volume 8028 of *LCNS*, 78–86. 2013.
4. M. Desmurget, M. Jordan, C. Prablanc, and M. Jeannerod. Constrained and unconstrained movements involve different control strategies. *J NEUROPHYSIOL*, 77(3):1644–1650, 1997.
5. O. Hilliges, S. Izadi, A. D. Wilson, S. Hodges, A. Garcia-Mendoza, and A. Butz. Interactions in the air: adding further depth to interactive tabletops. In *UIST '09*, 139–148. 2009.
6. M. Jeannerod. The timing of natural prehension movements. *J MOTOR BEHAV*, 16(3):235, 1984.
7. H. Kato and H. Yanagihara. Pacman ui: vision-based finger detection for positioning and clicking manipulations. In *MobileHCI '13*, 464–467. 2013.
8. R. S. Kattinakere, T. Grossman, and S. Subramanian. Modeling steering within above-the-surface interaction layers. In *CHI '07*, 317–326. 2007.
9. J. Lee, A. Olwal, H. Ishii, and C. Boulanger. SpaceTop: integrating 2D and spatial 3D interactions in a see-through desktop environment. In *CHI '13*, 189–192. 2013.
10. N. Marquardt, R. Jota, S. Greenberg, and J. Jorge. The continuous interaction space: Interaction techniques unifying touch and gesture on and above a digital surface. In *INTERACT '11*, 461–476. 2011.
11. C. Mueller-Tomfelde, A. Wessels, and C. Schremmer. Tilted tabletops: In between horizontal and vertical workspaces. In *Wksp on Horizontal Interactive Human Computer Systems, TABLETOP '08*, 49–56. 2008.
12. T. Mysliwiec. Fingermouse: A freehand computer pointing interface. In *Int'l Conference on Automatic Face and Gesture Recognition*, 372–377. 1994.
13. M. Ortega and L. Nigay. Airmouse: Finger gesture for 2d and 3d interaction. In *INTERACT '09*, 214–227. 2009.
14. D. Pyryeskin, M. Hancock, and J. Hoey. Comparing Elicited Gestures to Designer-created Gestures for Selection Above a Multitouch Surface. In *ITS '12*, 1–10. 2012.
15. M. Spindler, M. Martsch, and R. Dachselt. Going beyond the surface: studying multi-layer interaction above the tabletop. In *CHI '12*, 1277–1286. 2012.
16. M. Spindler, S. Stellmach, and R. Dachselt. Paperlens: advanced magic lens interaction above the tabletop. In *ITS '09*, 69–76. 2009.
17. S. Subramanian, D. Aliakseyeu, and A. Lucero. Multi-layer interaction for digital tables. In *UIST '06*, 269–272. 2006.
18. D. Vogel and R. Balakrishnan. Distant freehand pointing and clicking on very large, high resolution displays. In *UIST '05*, 33–42. 2005.
19. A. D. Wilson. Robust computer vision-based detection of pinching for one and two-handed gesture input. In *UIST '06*, 255–258. 2006.
20. A. D. Wilson and H. Benko. Combining multiple depth cameras and projectors for interactions on, above and between surfaces. In *UIST '10*, 273–282. 2010.
21. J. O. Wobbrock, L. Findlater, D. Gergle, and J. J. Higgins. The aligned rank transform for nonparametric factorial analyses using only anova procedures. In *CHI '11*, 143–146. 2011.
22. C. Yu, X. Tan, Y. Shi, and Y. Shi. Air finger: enabling multi-scale navigation by finger height above the surface. In *UbiComp '11*, 495–496. 2011.

# Exploring the Usefulness of Finger-Based 3D Gesture Menu Selection

**Arun Kulshreshth**
Department of EECS
University of Central Florida
4000 Central Florida Blvd
Orlando, FL 32816, USA
arunkul@knights.ucf.edu

**Joseph J. LaViola Jr.**
Department of EECS
University of Central Florida
4000 Central Florida Blvd
Orlando FL 32816, USA
jjl@eecs.ucf.edu

## ABSTRACT
Counting using one's fingers is a potentially intuitive way to enumerate a list of items and lends itself naturally to gesture-based menu systems. In this paper, we present the results of the first comprehensive study on Finger-Count menus to investigate its usefulness as a viable option for 3D menu selection tasks. Our study compares 3D gesture-based finger counting (Finger Count menus) with two gesture-based menu selection techniques (Hand-n-Hold, Thumbs-Up), derived from existing motion-controlled video game menu selection strategies, as well as 3D Marking menus. We examined selection time, selection accuracy and user preference for all techniques. We also examined the impact of different spatial layouts for menu items and different menu depths. Our results indicate that Finger-Count menus are significantly faster than the other menu techniques we tested and are the most liked by participants. Additionally, we found that while Finger-Count menus and 3D Marking menus have similar selection accuracy, Finger-Count menus are almost twice as fast compared to 3D Marking menus.

## Author Keywords
Menu Selection; Finger-Count menu; Hand-n-Hold Menu; Thumbs-Up Menu; 3D Marking Menu; Depth Camera; Gesture Recognition; Selection; 3D Interaction; User Study; Video Games.

## ACM Classification Keywords
H.5.2 User Interfaces: Graphical user interfaces (GUI), input devices and strategies, interaction styles; H.5.m Information Interfaces and Presentation (e.g. HCI): Miscellaneous.

## General Terms
Design, Experimentation, Measurement, Performance, Human Factors.


*CHI 2014*, April 26–May 1, 2014, Toronto, Ontario, Canada.

http://dx.doi.org/10.1145/2556288.2557122

**Figure 1. Finger-based menu selection**

## INTRODUCTION
Menu systems are an integral component of any video game and can significantly impact user experience. Due to the availability of various unobtrusive motion sensing devices (e.g., Microsoft Kinect, Leap Motion, Creative Interactive Gesture Camera), many gesture based menu systems [4, 7, 10, 24] have been explored both in academia and commercially in recent years. However, these menu selection methods are often slow (taking about 3-5 seconds) to perform and can suffer from accuracy problems making them less desirable compared to traditional keyboard-mouse or button based menu systems. Since response time and ease of use of a menu system can significantly affect user experience in applications (such as video games), it is essential that they be fast, efficient, and not be a burden on the user while setting up and during play.

People often use fingers to count or enumerate a list of items. In the past, such finger-counting strategies have been investigated for interaction with multi-touch surfaces [3] and distant displays [4]. However, a gestural input system based on finger count gestures (e.g., holding up two fingers) also holds the potential to be a natural and intuitive approach for menu selection in gesture- and motion-based games (see Figure 1). We posit that using one's fingers for menu selection offers several distinct advantages. First, finger count gestures are easily understood (assuming appropriate menu design) and are fast to perform. Second, users do not need to move the cursor to different locations on the screen since finger count gestures are not dependent on the layout of menu items. Third, since no cursor movement is needed with finger count menus, possible errors in menu item selection with motion controlled devices are also minimized.

Based on these suppositions, we explored the utility of finger count gestures in two user evaluations. First, we compared a finger count based menu selection approach (Finger-Count menu) against two other gestural menu selection techniques (Hand-n-Hold and Thumbs-Up menu) adapted from existing motion controlled video games. We examined both menu depth and different menu layouts. Second, we compared the Finger-Count menu with 3D marking menus (adapted from Marking menus proposed by Zhao et al. [26] ). In this evaluation, both menu selection strategies also had an expert selection mode (where users can select menu items without the menu appearing on screen). In both experiments, we examined selection time, accuracy, and user preference.

## RELATED WORK

As mentioned in the introduction, menu systems based on finger counting are not a new technique. Finger-Count menus were first proposed for multi-touch surfaces [3]. They were later adapted for distant displays [4], using the Kinect as the gestural input device. However, the algorithm presented by [4] is too slow (average selection time of 8.5 seconds) to be used in realistic scenarios. Additionally, the technique was limited to a circular layout and required both hands & multiple gestures to select an item. We have improved the selection time of this technique by simplifying it to use a single gesture for selection and by using a faster finger recognition algorithm (adapted from the Intel Perceptual Computing SDK), resulting in an average selection time that is more suitable for our user evaluations and practical use.

Vision-based hand and finger recognition algorithms have been explored by many researchers. The Kinect is a popular choice as input device for some of these algorithms [17, 22, 23]. Jennings et al. [13] used multiple cameras for finger tracking. Kölsch et al. [15] proposed a robust hand detection algorithm based on a single camera but their technique requires a classifier to be trained prior to gesture recognition. Trigo et al. [25] proposed an algorithm for detecting finger tips based on template matching. All these techniques are mostly focused on algorithm design and not on investigating interesting interaction mechanisms based on finger gestures.

Marking menus proposed by Kurtenbach [18] are gesture based menus where the menu items are arranged in a circle and selection is performed by drawing a mark from the center of the menu towards the desired item. Marking menus support two modes: novice and expert. In novice mode, the user selects a menu item from a circular menu displayed on a screen. In expert mode, the menu is not displayed, forcing a user to trace a continuous sequence of marks from memory, which is then recognized by the system. FlowMenus by Guimbretiere and Winograd [11] are also based on the Marking menu. FlowMenus let users make a sequence of selections without moving the pen away from the touch surface but no user evaluations were done as part of this work. Zhao et al. [26] proposed multi-stroke Marking menus with improved accuracy where a user performs a sequence of simple marks instead of a single complex trail. Recently, Marking menus have also been adapted for menu selection in 3D gestural environments [21] . We based our implementation of 3D Marking menus on multi-stroke Marking menus [26] because of its higher selection accuracy.

Researchers have also explored selection performance of several layouts for menu items on screen. Callahan et al. [6] showed that menu items in a circular layout can reduce selection time compared to a linear layout in a 2D plane. A similar result was obtained by Komerska and Ware [16] for their haptic menu system designed for Fishtank VR. Chertoff et al. [7] designed a Nintendo Wiimote based menu system and found pie menus to be faster than linear lists. The results of all these studies are in line with Fitts's law [9], as pie layouts provide a smaller average distance to menu items.

Several menu techniques have been proposed for virtual environments. TULIP [5] menus assign a menu item to each finger of a pinch glove and selection is made by pinching a finger with the thumb. Ni et al. [24] developed the rapMenu which is based on hand gestures and requires a pinch glove. To select an item using the rapMenu, the user rotates his wrist to highlight a group of four menu items and then a finger is pinched with the thumb. Spin menus [10] arrange items on a portion of a circle and enabled selection by rotating the wrist in a horizontal plane. Their system used a workbench from BARCO and an Intersense IS900 Tracker with a wand as an interaction device. Ring menus [19] also arrange items in a circle and attached a tracking device to the user's hand. To select an item, users would rotate their hand and move the desired item into a selection bucket. Body centered menus [20] assign menu items to parts of a user's body (head not included). These menus do not support hierarchical menu items and due to limited mapping locations on body, the number of menu items is also limited. All these techniques use expensive hardware and are not feasible options for consumer oriented products. For our experiments, we used the Creative Interactive Gesture Camera (readily available for $150) for gesture input. However, it should be noted that the techniques examined in this paper can be implemented using any input device that can recognize hands and fingers. To best of our knowledge, this work is the first to systematically explore the usefulness of finger-based menu selection, especially with relevance to menu item layout and hierarchy, given prior Finger-Count menu selection approaches were not fast enough for thorough user testing.

## MENU SELECTION TECHNIQUES

This section describes the Hand-n-Hold menu, Thumbs-Up menu, Finger-Count menu, and 3D Marking menu. All these techniques were implemented using a finger/hand recognition algorithm adapted from the fingertip/hand detection algorithm included in the Intel's Perceptual Computing SDK [1]. The main properties of these menu techniques are summarized in Table 1. The Creative Interactive Gesture Camera operates at an input frequency of 30 frames per second. We delineate the beginning and end of a selection event by utilizing a frame window of 15 frames to help with segmentation. Thus, each technique requires the user to maintain the selection pose for 0.5 seconds.

| | Hand-n-Hold | Thumbs-Up | Finger-Count | 3D Marking |
|---|---|---|---|---|
| **Gestures** | Static | Dynamic | Static | Dynamic |
| **Cursor Movement Required?** | Yes | Yes | No | Yes |
| **Expert Mode Supported?** | No | No | Yes | Yes |
| **Selection time dependent on Layout?** | Yes | Yes | No | Yes |

**Table 1. Properties of menu techniques**

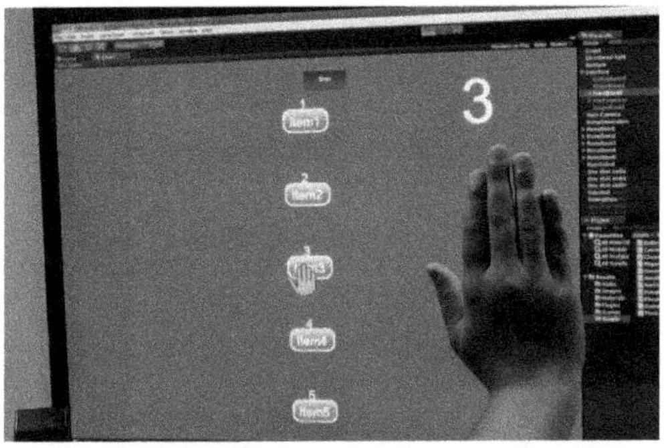


**Figure 2. Hand-n-Hold menu with vertical layout.**

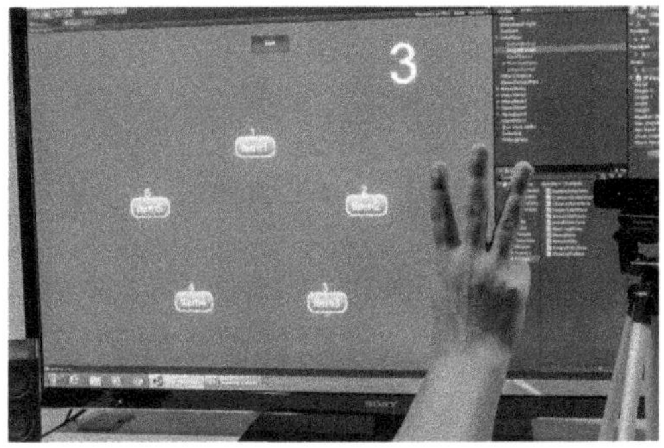


**Figure 4. Finger-Count menu with circular layout.**

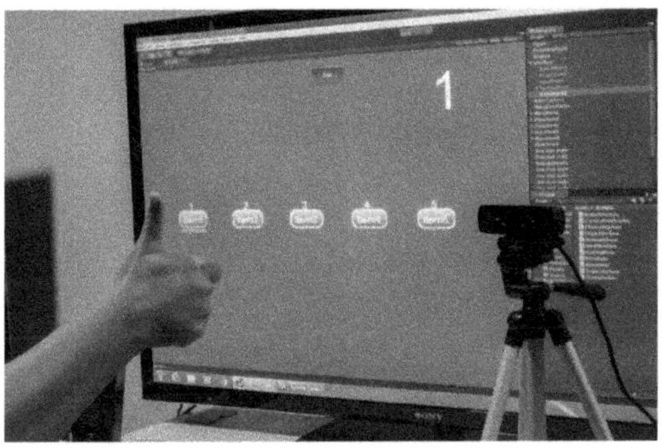


**Figure 3. Thumbs-Up menu with horizontal layout.**

### Hand-n-Hold Menu

In this technique, users control a cursor by moving their hand in the air (see Figure 2). The position of the cursor on screen is directly related to the 2D position of their hand in a virtual plane. A menu item is selected by holding the cursor over the desired item for a short duration (about one second). If the menu item has a sub-menu then the sub-menu appears in place (replacing the current menu items). The sub-menu items are selected in the same manner as the main menu. This technique requires visual feedback and supports any layout (horizontal, vertical, and circular were implemented) of items. As a pointer based technique, the efficiency of this menu technique is dependent in part on how the items are arranged on screen.

### Thumbs-Up Menu

A user holds her fist in front of the input device (see Figure 3). The user then has to move her fist either horizontally, vertically or radially in a virtual plane, depending on the layout, to highlight an item corresponding to their fist position and then give a thumbs up gesture to confirm the selection. Sub-menus appear in place and the selection strategy is the same for sub-menus. Visual feedback is also required for this technique. We chose to use the fist for pointing at menu items because it is extremely easy to transition into the Thumbs-Up gesture from the pointing stance. This technique is similar to Hand-n-Hold in that both require the user to point to an item and then confirm the selection. Hand-n-Hold implements an implicit confirmation mechanism based on a timeout while Thumbs-Up requires explicit confirmation from a user. Like Hand-n-Hold, this technique is layout dependent, and consequently, its efficiency also depends in part on the spatial arrangement of menu items. It is important to note that while we chose to use a fist for pointing at menu items, theoretically, any hand posture can be used for this purpose, followed by any other gesture for confirmation.

### Finger-Count Menu

All the menu items are numbered and the user has to extend a corresponding number of fingers to select a given item (see Figure 4). Items can be arranged in any layout and sub-menus appear in place. We tested three different layouts: horizontal, vertical and circular for this technique. Eyes-free selection is supported since visual feedback is not needed as long as the user knows the corresponding number of the desired item. In novice mode, the menu appears on screen with a number displayed next to each item and the user has to extend a corresponding number of fingers to select an item. In expert mode, the menu does not appear but the selection strategy is the same as novice mode. Expert mode supports a series of finger gestures (extending the appropriate number of fingers) to get to an item under a sub-menu.

This techniques supports using both hands simultaneously, so we can have up to 10 items on screen at a time. In case there are more items, we can label the last item as "Next" indicating that there are more items. If the user selects "Next" then more items appear on screen in place of the original menu. We can extend this idea to include any number of items. Similarly, the last item under a sub-menu can be labeled as "Back." The user can select "Back" to reduce the menu depth and see the parent menu in place.

### 3D Marking Menu

Our 3D Marking menu design is based on the multistroke Marking menu [26] because of its higher selection accuracy. The 3D Marking menu gestures are easy to learn and menu item locations can be remembered easily due to spatial memory [3]. In this technique, the user performs a series of simple gestures instead of a compound stroke. Menu items are always presented to the user in a circular layout. To select an item, the user positions her fist in the center of the menu and moves it towards the desired item, followed by a thumbs up gesture to finalize the selection. Sub-menus appear in place and the selection strategy is the same as the main menu. In novice mode, the menu appears on screen and a single selection is made at a time. In expert mode, the menu is not shown and the user has to perform the required gestures to select an item from memory.

## USER EVALUATIONS

We conducted two experiments to evaluate the usefulness of Finger-Count menus. Our first experiment focused on comparing Finger-Count menus with Hand-n-Hold and Thumbs-Up menu selection techniques. We also conducted a second experiment to compare Finger-Count menus with 3D Marking menus. We chose to conduct two experiments because 3D Marking menus support only circular layouts and were very different from Hand-n-Hold and Thumbs-Up. In our pilot tests with two participants, we found the Finger-Count menu to be the fastest technique, therefore we chose to compare only Finger-Count menus with 3D Marking menus. We chose a within-subjects design for our experiments in order to be able to measure and compare user perceptions of the menu selection techniques on a variety of quantitative and qualitative metrics. All menu items were labeled with numbers in our experiments. The setup and participants were the same for both experiments. Participants completed both experiments in order (experiment 1 followed by experiment 2) in a single session. We had the following hypotheses about the chosen menu selection techniques:

**Hypothesis 1 (H1)** : Finger-Count menus are faster than the other menu techniques.

**Hypothesis 2 (H2)** : Finger-Count menus have higher selection accuracy than the other menu techniques.

**Hypothesis 3 (H3)** : People will prefer to use Finger-Count Menus than the other techniques.

### Subjects and Apparatus

We recruited 36 participants (31 males and 5 females ranging in age from 18 to 33) from the University of Central Florida, of which two were left handed. The experiment duration ranged from 50 to 70 minutes and all participants were paid $10 for their time.

The experiment setup, shown in Figure 5, consisted of a 55" Sony HDTV and the Creative Interactive Gesture Camera (a readily available and affordable depth sensing camera)

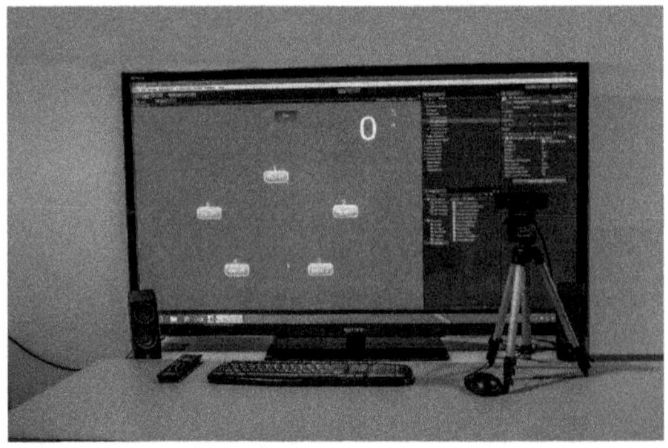

**Figure 5. The Experimental Setup.**

mounted on a mini tripod. We used the Unity3D game engine [2] and Intel Perceptual Computing Software Development Kit (PCSDK) [1] for implementing all four menu techniques. Participants were seated about 3 feet away from the display and the camera was placed about 1.5 feet away from the participant, in order to ensure that the participant's hand was completely visible to the camera. The position of the camera was changed either to the left or right of the participant, while maintaining the distance from the participant, based on dexterity (left handed or right handed) in order to enable optimal viewing of the menu items on screen.

### Procedure

The experiment began with the participant seated in front of the TV and the moderator seated to the side. Participants were given a consent form that explained the experiment procedure. They were then given a pre-questionnaire which collected general information about the participant (age, sex, dexterity, etc.). Participants then completed both experiments in order. At the beginning of each experiment, the moderator explained the selection techniques and allowed the user to practice each technique for as long as necessary. Details of experiment tasks are provided in the respective sub-sections of the experiments.

We recorded selection time and accuracy of all the techniques presented in both experiments. For both experiments, selection time was measured as the time from when a random number appeared on screen to the time the corresponding item was selected. Selection accuracy of a technique was measured as the percentage of correct selections out of total selections made for that technique. After each experiment, the participant filled out a post-questionnaire (see Table 2) with questions about their experiences with the techniques they tried.

### Experiment 1: Hand-n-Hold, Thumbs-Up, and Finger-Count Menu Comparison

The first experiment compared Hand-n-Hold, Thumbs-Up, and Finger-Count menus. All these techniques support horizontal, vertical and circular layouts. Hand-n-Hold and Thumbs-Up only support single handed interactions. As a result, we chose to use a one handed variation of the Finger-Count menu in order to remove a potential confounding variable. Moreover, Hand-n-Hold menu and Thumbs-Up menu

| Post Experiment Questions | |
|---|---|
| Q1 | To what extent did you like this menu selection technique? |
| Q2 | How mentally demanding was this technique? |
| Q3 | To what extent your arm was tired when using this technique? |
| Q4 | Did you feel hurried or rushed when using this technique? |
| Q5 | How successfully you were able to choose the items you were asked to select? |
| Q6 | Did you feel that you were trying your best? |
| Q7 | To what extent you felt frustrated using this technique? |
| Q8 | To what extent did you feel that this technique was hard to use? |
| Q9 | Which layout of menu items would you prefer for this technique? Horizontal, vertical, circular or all equally? |

**Table 2. Post-Questionnaire. Participants responded to question 1-8 on a 7 point Likert scale. Question 9 was a multiple choice question.**

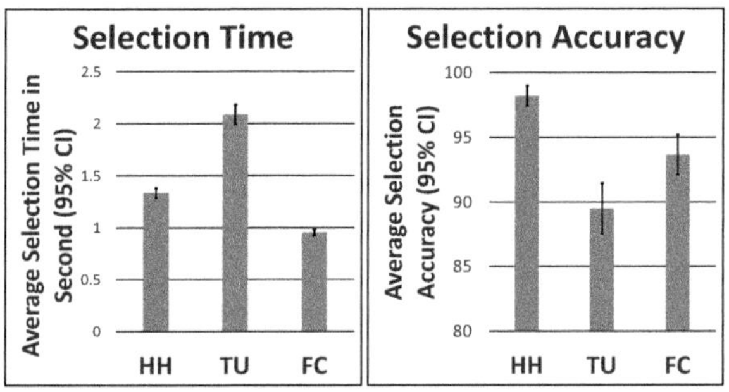


**Figure 6. Average selection time and accuracy of each technique where HH is Hand-n-Hold, TU is Thumbs-Up and FC is Finger-Count menu.**

do not support expert mode so we did not have any expert mode as part of this experiment.

### *Experiment Design*

This within-subjects experiment had 3 independent variables: technique (Hand-n-Hold, Thumbs-Up, and Finger-Count), layout (horizontal, vertical and circular) and menu depth (0 and 1). In total we had $3 \times 3 \times 2 = 18$ conditions and for each condition the user conducted 10 trials which makes a total of 180 selections per participant as part of this experiment. Our dependent variables were average menu selection time and selection accuracy, where the average is taken over the 10 trials for that condition.

Each condition was presented to the user in random order based on a Latin square design [8]. For each condition, users were asked to select 10 randomly generated items displayed on screen one item at a time. After completing the experiment, users filled a post-questionnaire (see Table 2) with the same set of questions for each technique and then ranked the techniques based on ease of use, arm fatigue, efficiency, and overall best.

### *Quantitative Results*

We used repeated-measures 3-factor ANOVA per dependent variable. We did a post-hoc analysis using pairwise sample t-tests. We used Holm's sequential Bonferroni adjustment to correct for type I errors [12] and the Shapiro-Wilk test to make sure the data was parametric.

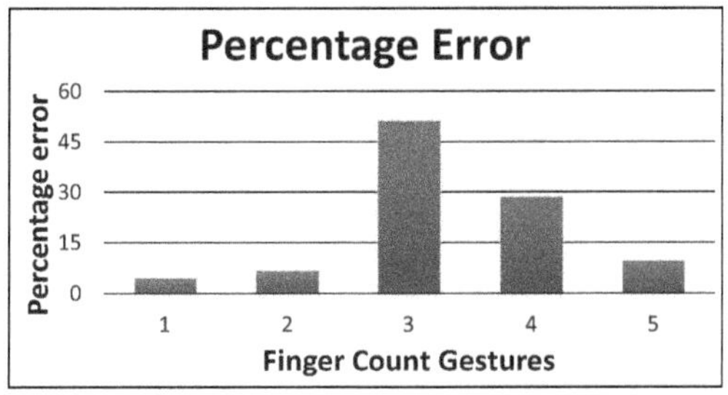


**Figure 7. Error percentage (out of 6.81% errors) of individual gestures for Finger-Count menu. Most of the errors were due gesture 3.**

Mean selection time and selection accuracy for each technique is shown in Figure 6. We found significant differences in mean selection time ($F_{2,34} = 363.657, p < 0.005$) and selection accuracy ($F_{2,34} = 45.758, p < 0.005$) between the menu techniques. The Finger-Count menu was faster than Hand-n-Hold ($t_{35} = -21.505, p < 0.005$) and Hand-n-Hold was faster than Thumbs-Up ($t_{35} = -21.433, p < 0.005$). Hand-n-Hold was more accurate than the Finger-Count menu ($t_{35} = -5.586, p < 0.005$), which in turn was more accurate than Thumbs-Up ($t_{35} = 4.488, p < 0.005$).

The Finger-Count menu was the only technique that uses different gestures (different number of fingers extended) for different numbered items. Therefore, we also analyzed the individual gesture error percentage (see Figure 7) and found an overall error rate of 6.81%, with 51.09% of the errors attributed to the gesture for number 3 (three fingers extended) and 28.46% due to the gesture for number 4 (four finger extended).

Menu depth did not have any significant effect on selection time ($F_{1,35} = 1.340, p = 0.255$). Depth showed significant effect on accuracy ($F_{1,35} = 0.258, p < 0.05$) but post-hoc analysis did not find any significant differences.

We also found that the layout of menu items significantly affects the mean selection time of all techniques ($F_{2,34} = 9.384, p < 0.005$). However, there was no significant effect of item layout on mean selection accuracy ($F_{2,34} = 2.651, p = 0.135$). Horizontal layouts were faster than vertical layouts ($t_{35} = -3.095, p < 0.005$) and circular layouts ($t_{35} = -4.243, p < 0.005$). There was no significant difference in average selection time between vertical layout and circular layout.

We also analyzed each technique separately to study the effects of layout (see Figure 8 and 9). The results are as follows:

**Hand-n-Hold Menu** Layout had significant effect only on accuracy ($F_{2,34} = 5.548, p < 0.05$). A post-hoc analysis revealed that the circular layout was significantly more accurate than the horizontal layout ($t_{35} = -3.366, p < 0.005$).

**Thumbs-Up Menu** Layout had significant effect on time ($F_{2,34} = 20.563, p < 0.005$) and accuracy ($F_{2,34} = 7.776, p < 0.005$). The horizontal layout was significantly faster than the vertical ($t_{35} = -4.075, p < 0.005$) and the

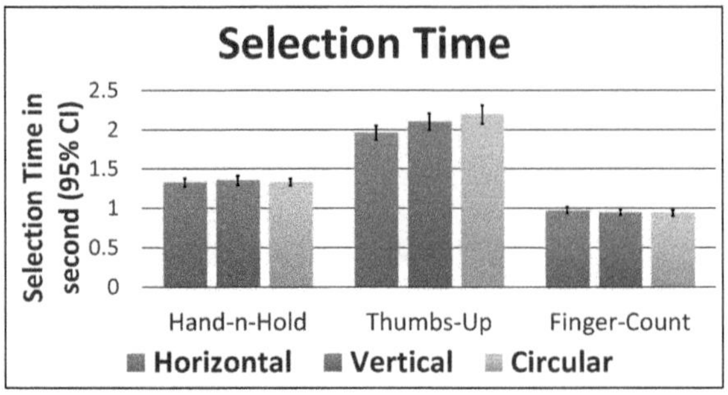


**Figure 8. Average selection time of each menu technique for different layouts. The Hand-n-Hold and Finger-Count menus did not have any significant changes in selection time with layout.**

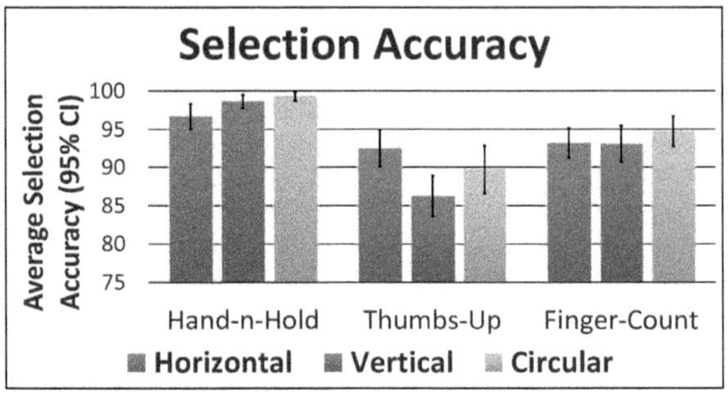


**Figure 9. Average selection accuracy for each layout.**

circular layout ($t_{35} = -5.831, p < 0.005$). The horizontal layout was significantly more accurate than the vertical layout ($t_{35} = 3.668, p < 0.005$).

**Finger-Count Menu** As expected, layout had no effect on selection time and accuracy of the Finger-Count menu.

*Qualitative Results*

Based on the post-questionnaire data, 22 people preferred the circular layout for the Hand-n-Hold menu, 21 preferred the horizontal layout for the Thumbs-Up menu, and 32 people thought that all layouts were equivalent for the Finger-Count menu (see Figure 10). The Finger-Count menu was ranked as the overall best technique and the Thumbs-Up menu as the worst technique. The Finger-Count menu was also ranked as best (see Figure 11) in terms of ease of use, efficiency and arm fatigue (less fatigue is better).

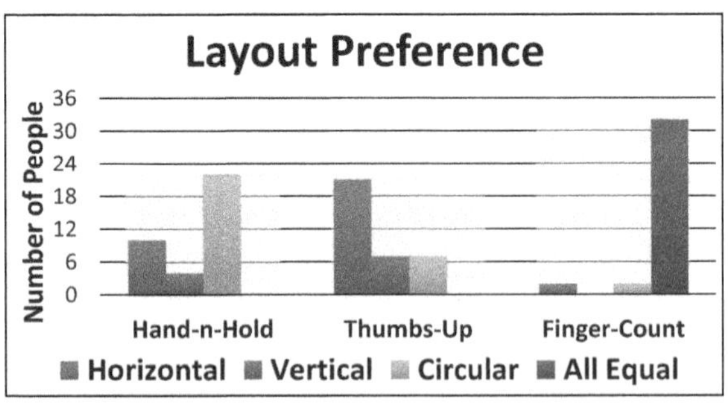


**Figure 10. Layout preference for each technique. Finger-Count menus are layout independent.**

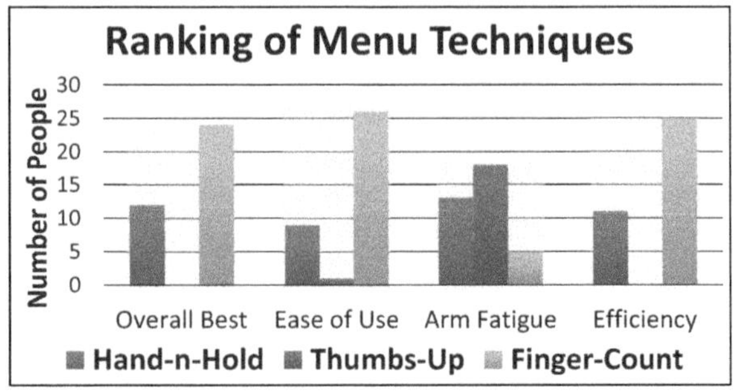


**Figure 11. Ranking of techniques based on overall best, ease of use, arm fatigue, and efficiency. Finger-Count menu was ranked as the best technique by majority of participants.**

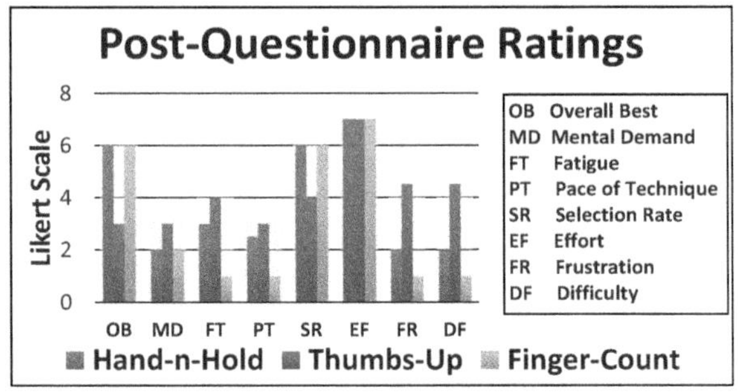


**Figure 12. Median ratings for post-questionnaire questions for each technique.**

To analyze the Likert scale data, we used Friedman's test and then a post-hoc analysis was done using Wilcoxon signed rank tests. These results are displayed in Table 3. Median rating for post-questionnaire questions 1 to 8 is summarized in Figure 12. From the results we an see that:

- People liked Hand-n-Hold and Finger-Count more compared to Thumbs-Up.
- Finger-Count and Hand-n-Hold are mentally less demanding than Thumbs-Up.
- Finger-Count causes less arm fatigue compared to Hand-n-Hold and Thumbs-Up.
- For Thumbs-Up, more people thought they were not able to select items they were asked to select than Hand-n-Hold and Finger-Count.
- Frustration level was higher for Thumbs-Up than Hand-n-Hold and Finger-Count.
- People thought that Thumbs-Up was significantly harder to use than Hand-n-Hold and Finger-Count.

### Experiment 2: Compare Finger-Count Menu with 3D Marking Menu

This experiment focused on comparing the Finger-Count menu with a 3D Marking menu. 3D Marking menus support only a circular layout, so we restricted the Finger-Count menu to a circular layout for a fair comparison. Menu depth for this experiment was set to one in order to the keep the same environment for both novice and expert mode. As 3D Marking

| Question | Friedman's test | HH vs TU | HH vs FC | TU vs FC |
|---|---|---|---|---|
| Q1 | $\chi^2(2) = 41.603, p < 0.0005$ | $Z = -4.389, p < 0.005$ | $Z = -1.649, p = 0.099$ | $Z = -4.907, p < 0.005$ |
| Q2 | $\chi^2(2) = 19.855, p < 0.0005$ | $Z = -3.809, p < 0.005$ | $Z = -1.029, p = 0.304$ | $Z = -3.151, p < 0.005$ |
| Q3 | $\chi^2(2) = 35.138, p < 0.0005$ | $Z = -1.524, p = 0.128$ | $Z = -3.780, p < 0.005$ | $Z = -4.386, p < 0.005$ |
| Q4 | $\chi^2(2) = 17.196, p < 0.0005$ | $Z = -2.656, p < 0.010$ | $Z = -1.837, p = 0.066$ | $Z = -3.197, p < 0.005$ |
| Q5 | $\chi^2(2) = 35.613, p < 0.0005$ | $Z = -4.459, p < 0.005$ | $Z = -0.996, p = 0.334$ | $Z = -3.972, p < 0.005$ |
| Q6 | $\chi^2(2) = 3.250, p = 0.197$ | $Z = -0.000, p = 1.000$ | $Z = -1.076, p = 0.282$ | $Z = -0.964, p = 0.335$ |
| Q7 | $\chi^2(2) = 41.407, p < 0.0005$ | $Z = -4.778, p < 0.005$ | $Z = -0.574, p <= 0.566$ | $Z = -4.330, p < 0.005$ |
| Q8 | $\chi^2(2) = 41.333, p < 0.0005$ | $Z = -4.890, p < 0.005$ | $Z = -0.330, p = 0.742$ | $Z = -4.523, p < 0.005$ |

**Table 3. Results of Friedman's test and post-hoc analysis for Likert scale data of Experiment 1. (HH : Hand-n-Hold, TU: Thumbs-Up and FC: Finger-Count)**

menus also only support interaction using a single hand, we again restricted the Finger-Count menu to use a single hand, resulting in a maximum of 5 items per menu.

### *Experimental Design*

Our second within-subjects experiment had two independent variables: technique (Finger-Count and 3D Marking menu) and user mode (novice and expert). There were a total of $2 \times 2 = 4$ conditions with 10 trials for each making it a total of 40 selections per participant. Our dependent variables were average menu selection time and average selection accuracy, where the average is taken over 10 trials for that condition. Each condition was presented to the user in a random order based on a Latin square design [8]. In novice mode, users were asked to select 10 randomly generated items. In expert mode, a sequence of two numbers were generated for each trial and users were asked to pick the corresponding items in order. After completing the experiment, users filled out a post-questionnaire (only questions 1 to 8 of Table 2) with the same set of questions for each technique.

### *Quantitative Results*

A repeated-measures 2-factor ANOVA was used per dependent variable. We did a post-hoc analysis using pairwise sample t-tests. We used Holm's sequential Bonferroni adjustment to correct for type I errors [12] and the Shapiro-Wilk test to make sure the data was parametric. Table 4 shows the results of repeated measures two-factor ANOVA analysis. The Finger-Count menu was significantly faster (see Figure 13) than the 3D Marking menu in both novice mode ($t_{35} = 11.868, p < 0.0005$) and expert mode ($t_{35} = 10.942, p < 0.0005$). In novice mode, the average selection time was 0.933 seconds ($\sigma = 0.098$) for the Finger-Count menu and 2.09 seconds ($\sigma = 0.643$) for the 3D Marking menu. In expert mode, selection time was 2.307 seconds ($\sigma = 0.223$) for the Finger-Count menu and 4.024 seconds ($\sigma = 1.067$ ) for the 3D Marking menu. Overall, there was no significant difference in selection accuracy between the menu techniques (see Figure 13). Novice mode had significantly higher selection accuracy than expert mode ($t_{35} = 3.448, p < 0.005$). Average selection accuracy was 96.25% ($\sigma = 5.123$) for novice mode and 91.25% ($\sigma = 9.131$) for expert mode.

### *Qualitative Results*

The qualitative data was analyzed separately for novice and expert modes. To analyze the Likert scale data, we used Wilcoxon signed rank tests. Median ratings for post-questionnaire questions 1 to 8 are summarized in Figure 14.

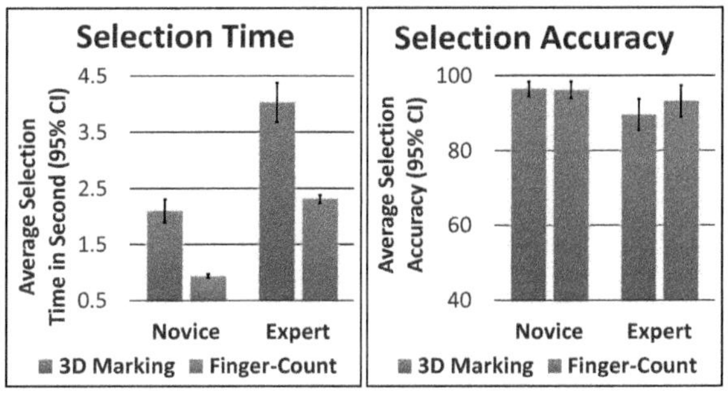


**Figure 13. Selection time and accuracy by technique and mode.**

In novice mode (see Figure 14), people liked the Finger-Count menu significantly more than the 3D Marking menu ($Z = -4.059, p < 0.0005$). The 3D Marking menu is significantly more mentally demanding than the Finger-Count menu ($Z = -3.272, p < 0.005$). The 3D Marking menu also lead to significantly more arm fatigue than the Finger-Count menu ($Z = -3.383, p < 0.005$). People thought that using the Finger-Count menu let them select items with significantly higher accuracy than the 3D Marking menu ($Z = -3.106, p < 0.005$). People also felt significantly less frustrated with the Finger-Count menu than the 3D Marking menu ($Z = -3.778, p < 0.0005$). Finally, the 3D Marking menu was significantly harder to use than the Finger-Count menu ($Z = -3.357, p < 0.005$).

Statistics for expert mode were similar to novice mode (see Figure 14). In expert mode, people liked the Finger-Count menu significantly more than the 3D Marking menu ($Z = -4.335, p < 0.0005$). The 3D Marking menu is significantly more mentally demanding than the Finger-Count menu ($Z = -4.196, p < 0.005$). 3D Marking menu usage also lead to significantly more arm fatigue than the Finger-Count menu ($Z = -4.115, p < 0.0005$). People thought that when using Finger-Count menus they were able to select items with significantly higher accuracy than with the 3D Marking menu ($Z = -3.751, p < 0.005$). People felt significantly less frustrated with the Finger-Count menu ($Z = -3.348, p < 0.005$). Finally, the 3D Marking menu was significantly harder to use than the Finger-Count menu ($Z = -4.307, p < 0.0005$).

## DISCUSSION

Our experiments indicate that Finger-Count menus let participants select items significantly faster than either Hand-n-

| Source | Selection Time | Accuracy |
|---|---|---|
| Technique | $F_{1,35} = 145.774, p < 0.0005$ | $F_{1,35} = 0.864, p = 0.359$ |
| Mode | $F_{1,35} = 751.146, p < 0.0005$ | $F_{1,35} = 11.887, p < 0.005$ |
| Technique×Mode | $F_{1,35} = 26.831, p < 0.0005$ | $F_{1,35} = 1.755, p = 0.194$ |

**Table 4. Repeated measure 2-factor ANOVA analysis for comparing the 3D Marking menu with the Finger-Count menu. There was significant difference in selection time based on menu technique as well as mode. Accuracy was significantly different between the user modes.**

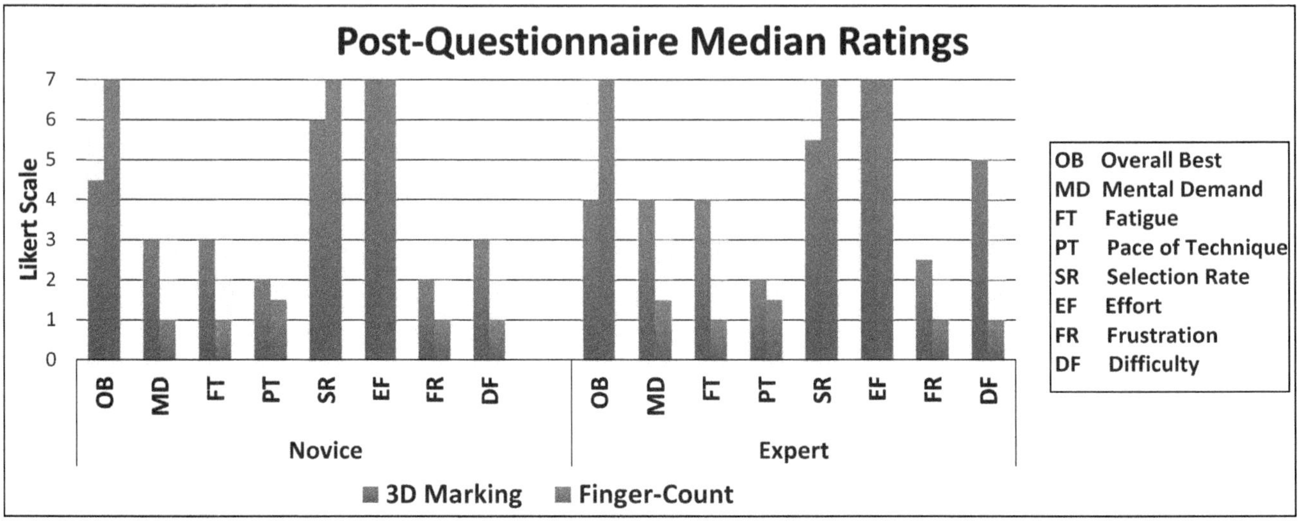


**Figure 14. Median ratings for post-questionnaire questions for each technique.**

Hold, Thumbs-Up or 3D Marking menus. This is primarily because Finger-Count menus do not require the user to move their hand in accordance with the position of items on screen, resulting in a constant selection time for all items. For Hand-n-Hold menus, the second-fastest technique, the user has to continuously move his hand to select an item, increasing the selection time. Thumbs-Up not only requires a user to move his hand for selecting a menu item, but to also give a thumb's up gesture to finalize the selection. 3D Marking menus have similar hand motion characteristics as Thumbs-Up, as both techniques require hand motion and then an explicit thumbs-up gesture to finalize item selection. This additional motion and a gesture takes significantly more time than simply extending one's fingers.

We found that Hand-n-Hold was the most accurate out of all selection techniques tested because it involves controlling a pointer with one's hand with implicit finalization, making it less error prone than recognizing extended fingers or the thumb's up gesture. Even though Hand-n-Hold is the most accurate technique, we found that users preferred Finger-Count menus more because of its faster selection time and its natural interaction metaphor. In the future, we foresee better selection accuracy for Finger-Count menus due to the availability of better gestural input devices and recognition algorithms.

Our analysis of menu item layout presents an interesting picture. Finger-Count menus have a constant selection time and are not at all affected by the layout of menu items. For Hand-n-Hold, item layout did not have any effect on selection time but circular layouts resulted in higher selection accuracy than horizontal and vertical layouts, probably due to the similar spacing of menu items, resulting in a similar amount of movement. When using Hand-n-Hold with horizontal and vertical layouts, participants occasionally tended to accidentally bump into wrong items while moving the pointer to a desired item, resulting in a wrong selection. But with circular layouts, they could keep the pointer inside the circle and reach all menu items at the periphery without accidentally selecting other items. For Thumbs-Up, we found that horizontal layouts resulted in faster selection and increased selection accuracy. We believe this is primarily because a person's arm has a more natural and relaxed posture when moved horizontally. In the case of vertical and circular layouts, participants often oriented their hand in such a way that their thumb was not pointing upwards making it difficult for the gesture recognizer to identify it as a thumb's up gesture. This orientation decreased the mean selection accuracy in these layouts for Thumbs-Up.

For Finger-Count menus, three fingers can present a possibly difficult combination for detection because users in our experiments tended to keep the middle finger and ring finger close enough to be detected as a single finger. However, detecting the number four proved easier because participants automatically provided sufficient spacing to alleviate confusion in the recognizer. This issue can also be remedied by using both hands simultaneously (e.g., index finger in one hand and index & middle finger in the other hand to indicate a 3 gesture). Our implementation of Finger-Count menus support using both hands simultaneously. But since the other techniques in our study were single handed only, we restricted Finger-Count menus to use single hand interaction for a fair comparison.

Our subjective responses indicate that Finger-Count menus were the most preferred and most efficient, had the least arm fatigue, and was the least frustrating technique. This seems promising for future games and applications with short range gestural input. Participants were impressed by the selection time of the Finger-Count menus. The second most preferred technique was Hand-n-Hold because of its ease of use and high accuracy. People are used to controlling a pointer using a mouse and this technique seems familiar to them. People did not like Thumbs-Up because of high error rate. Participants thought that 3D Marking menus are more mentally demanding than the Finger-Count menu. This is because for Finger-Count menus, the user does not have to worry about the location of items on screen. This fact is much more noticeable in expert mode where the menu does not appear on screen. For 3D Marking menus, people need to memorize the location of items with respect to the center to be able to perform a radial mark to select the desired item. Finger-Count menus were rated as less frustrating and most liked technique than the 3D Marking menu.

Based on the results of our experiments, we were able to accept H1, H3 and were unable to accept H2. Consequently, we believe that Finger-Count menus have the potential to be used as a menu system in future 3D gesture controlled applications and video games. Finger-Count menus have a very low response time making users spend a minimal amount of time interacting with menus. All the Finger-Count gestures are intuitive and easy to remember. Both casual and expert gamers could use this technique with a limited learning curve. Once players get used to the menu system, they can transition to expert mode and can change game setting (e.g., change appearance of game character, selecting a weapon from inventory, switching camera position in racing games, etc.) with no interference from menu items on screen. It could also be a good idea to mix traditional mouse based menus with Finger-Count menus. Mouse pointer menus could be used to select game settings at the beginning of a game and Finger-Count menus for changing in-game settings while playing. For example, in a gesture controlled car racing game, a user can set display resolution, select a track and car using traditional menus. While racing, he can switch between first person view to third person view using Finger-Count menus. Similarly, a user could select weapons from an inventory for a First Person Shooter (FPS) games using Finger-Count menus. Finger-count menus could be combined with other hand gestures to increase the number of possible gestures thereby increasing the number of possible motion controlled tasks in video games.

There are a few factors that could have affected our results. When comparing layouts for a given technique, items were equally spaced for a given layout but the item spacing was not the same across the three layouts. It could have a minor effect on our results but we still believe that horizontal layout would be slightly faster than vertical layout for hand based interaction because a person's arm has more natural and relaxed posture when moved horizontally. The shape of the menu items could also have had some influence on how well users perform in an horizontal or vertical layout. Ideally, a circular menu item would be more balanced across all dimensions but we don't find such menu items in video games. Hence, circular menu items were not considered to simulate real world menu items. Our study design could also have had an influence on our results. The two experiments were performed in order, experiment 1 and then experiment 2 but conditions in each experiment were randomized. This could have some effect on our results but we believe that people would have still preferred Finger-count menus over 3D Marking menus (in experiment 2) due to its ease of use and fast response time. Moreover, we did not consider studying learning effects because all the gestures performed were easy to learn requiring very little time to train the users.

Finger-Count menus do have some limitations. Hand physiology also plays an important role. Some people found it difficult to keep their fingers separated. One of the participants had arthritis in one hand. It was difficult for him to keep enough separation between the fingers to be counted as separate fingers by the recognizer. But the Finger-Count menu worked fine for him when he used his other hand. We think that it could also be a problematic for some old age people because of the weakening of intrinsic hand muscles with age [14]. Thus, such an interface could be a challenge for people with arthritis or any form of ailment preventing them from keeping their fingers separated for the gesture recognizer.

## CONCLUSION AND FUTURE WORK

We presented an in-depth exploration comparing Finger-Count menus with Hand-n-Hold, Thumbs-Up, and 3D Marking menus using different layouts and modes (novice and expert). Our results show that Finger-Count menus are a viable option for 3D menu selection tasks with fast response times and high accuracy and could be well suited for gesture controlled applications such as games. In terms of horizontal, vertical and circular layouts, selection time and selection accuracy of Finger-Count menus did not change with layout. However, the circular layout had higher selection accuracy for Hand-n-Hold menus while the horizontal layout was faster and more accurate for Thumbs-Up menus. A significantly higher number of participants ranked Finger-Count menus as their favorite technique and the second best technique was the Hand-n-Hold menu. In the future, it will be interesting to see how well Finger-Count menus perform in real application environments. We would also like to see the performance of Finger-Count menus in the context of 3D environments where menu item selection is in 3D space.

## ACKNOWLEDGMENTS

This work is supported in part by NSF CAREER award IIS-0845921 and NSF awards IIS-0856045 and CCF-1012056. We would also like to thank Salman Cheema & the other members of ISUE lab for their support and the anonymous reviewers for their useful comments and feedback.

## REFERENCES

1. Intel perceptual computing SDK. `http://software.intel.com/en-us/vcsource/tools/perceptual-computing-sdk`.
2. Unity3D. `http://unity3d.com/`, 2013.

3. Bailly, G., Lecolinet, E., and Guiard, Y. Finger-count & radial-stroke shortcuts: 2 techniques for augmenting linear menus on multi-touch surfaces. In *Proceedings of the SIGCHI Conference on Human Factors in Computing Systems*, ACM (2010), 591–594.
4. Bailly, G., Walter, R., Müller, J., Ning, T., and Lecolinet, E. Comparing free hand menu techniques for distant displays using linear, marking and finger-count menus. In *Human-Computer Interaction INTERACT 2011*, vol. 6947 of *LNCS*. Springer Berlin Heidelberg, 2011, 248–262.
5. Bowman, D., and Wingrave, C. Design and evaluation of menu systems for immersive virtual environments. In *Virtual Reality, 2001. Proceedings. IEEE* (March 2001), 149 –156.
6. Callahan, J., Hopkins, D., Weiser, M., and Shneiderman, B. An empirical comparison of pie vs. linear menus. In *Proceedings of the SIGCHI Conference on Human Factors in Computing Systems*, CHI '88, ACM (New York, NY, USA, 1988), 95–100.
7. Chertoff, D. B., Byers, R. W., and LaViola, Jr., J. J. An exploration of menu techniques using a 3D game input device. In *Proceedings of the 4th International Conference on Foundations of Digital Games*, FDG '09, ACM (New York, NY, USA, 2009), 256–262.
8. Fisher, R. A. *The design of experiments*. Oxford, England: Oliver & Boyd, 1935.
9. Fitts, P. The information capacity of the human motor system in controlling the amplitude of movement. *Journal of Experimental Psychology 47*, 6 (Sep 1954), 381–391.
10. Gerber, D., and Bechmann, D. The spin menu: A menu system for virtual environments. In *Proceedings of the 2005 IEEE Conference 2005 on Virtual Reality*, VR '05, IEEE Computer Society (Washington, DC, USA, 2005), 271–272.
11. Guimbretiére, F., and Winograd, T. Flowmenu: combining command, text, and data entry. In *Proceedings of the 13th annual ACM symposium on User interface software and technology*, UIST '00, ACM (New York, NY, USA, 2000), 213–216.
12. Holm, S. A simple sequentially rejective multiple test procedure. *Scandinavian Journal of Statistics 6*, 2 (1979), 65–70.
13. Jennings, C. Robust finger tracking with multiple cameras. In *Recognition, Analysis, and Tracking of Faces and Gestures in Real-Time Systems, 1999. Proceedings. International Workshop on* (1999), 152 –160.
14. Kapur, S., Zatsiorsky, V. M., and Latash, M. L. Age-related changes in the control of finger force vectors. *Journal of Applied Physiology 109*, 6 (2010), 1827–1841.
15. Kölsch, M., and Turk, M. Robust hand detection. In *Proceedings of the Sixth IEEE international conference on Automatic face and gesture recognition*, IEEE Computer Society (2004), 614–619.
16. Komerska, R., and Ware, C. A study of haptic linear and pie menus in a 3d fish tank vr environment. In *Haptic Interfaces for Virtual Environment and Teleoperator Systems, 2004. HAPTICS '04. Proceedings. 12th International Symposium on* (March 2004), 224 – 231.
17. Kulshreshth, A., Zorn, C., and LaViola, J. Real-time markerless kinect based finger tracking and hand gesture recognition for HCI. In *Proceedings of the IEEE Symposium on 3D User Interfaces* (March 2013), 187–188.
18. Kurtenbach, G. *The design and evaluation of marking menus*. PhD thesis, University of Toronto, Ontario, Canada, 1993.
19. Liang, J., and Green, M. JDCAD: A highly interactive 3D modeling system. *Computers & graphics 18*, 4 (1994), 499–506.
20. Mine, M. R., Brooks Jr, F. P., and Sequin, C. H. Moving objects in space: exploiting proprioception in virtual-environment interaction. In *SIGGRAPH*, ACM (1997), 19–26.
21. Ren, G., and O'Neill, E. 3D marking menu selection with freehand gestures. In *IEEE Symposium on 3D User Interfaces (3DUI)*, IEEE (2012), 61–68.
22. Ren, Z., Yuan, J., and Zhang, Z. Robust hand gesture recognition based on finger-earth mover's distance with a commodity depth camera. In *Proceedings of the 19th ACM international conference on Multimedia*, MM '11, ACM (New York, NY, USA, 2011), 1093–1096.
23. Ryan, D. J. Finger and gesture recognition with microsoft kinect. Master's thesis, University of Stavanger, Norway, 2012.
24. Tao, N., McMahan, R., and Bowman, D. Tech-note: rapmenu: Remote menu selection using freehand gestural input. In *Proceedings of the IEEE Symposium on 3D User Interfaces* (March 2008), 55–58.
25. Trigo, T., and Pellegrino, S. An analysis of features for hand-gesture classification. In *17th International Conference on Systems, Signals and Image Processing (IWSSIP 2010)* (2010), 412–415.
26. Zhao, S., and Balakrishnan, R. Simple vs. compound mark hierarchical marking menus. In *Proceedings of the 17th annual ACM symposium on User interface software and technology*, ACM (2004), 33–42.

# In the Blink of an Eye: Investigating Latency Perception during Stylus Interaction

**Albert Ng[1], Michelle Annett[2,3], Paul Dietz[2], Anoop Gupta[2], and Walter F. Bischof[3]**

[1]Microsoft Applied Sciences Group
Redmond, WA, USA
v-albeng@microsoft.com

[2]Microsoft Research
Redmond, WA, USA
{paul.dietz, anoop}@microsoft.com

[3]University of Alberta
Edmonton, AB, Canada
{mkannett, wfb}@ualberta.ca

## ABSTRACT

While pen computing has become increasingly more popular, device responsiveness, or latency, still plagues such interaction. Although there have been advances in digitizer technology over the last few years, commercial end-to-end latencies are unfortunately similar to those found with touchscreens, i.e., 65 - 120 milliseconds. We report on a prototype stylus-enabled device, the High Performance Stylus System (HPSS), designed to display latencies as low as one millisecond while users ink or perform dragging tasks.

To understand the role of latency while inking with a stylus, psychophysical just-noticeable difference experiments were conducted using the HPSS. While participants performed dragging and scribbling tasks, very low levels of latency could be discriminated, i.e., ~1 versus 2 milliseconds while dragging and ~7 versus 40 milliseconds while scribbling. The HPSS and our experimentation have provided further motivation for the implementation of latency saving measures in pen-based hardware and software systems.

### Author Keywords

Latency; stylus; pen; pen computing; perception; psychophysics

### ACM Classification Keywords

B.4.2 **[Input / Output Devices]**; H.5.2 **[User Interfaces]**: Input devices and strategies; H.1.2. **[User/Machine Systems]:** Human factors.

## INTRODUCTION

Recently, there has been an explosion of stylus-enabled devices available on the market. Styli harness fine motor control to offer increased precision and accuracy compared to a finger [17, 20, 32]. This precision enables users to perform inking tasks such as note taking and sketching with ease. Unlike the mouse and keyboard, styli afford direct interaction with content, which enables users to diagram, work out equations, sketch, create calligraphy, annotate, or sign their name in a more natural and fluid manner than with a mouse or keyboard [5]. When coupled with touch, styli also afford natural bimanual interaction, supporting the transfer of behaviors and interaction techniques found with traditional pen and paper [10, 15, 16].

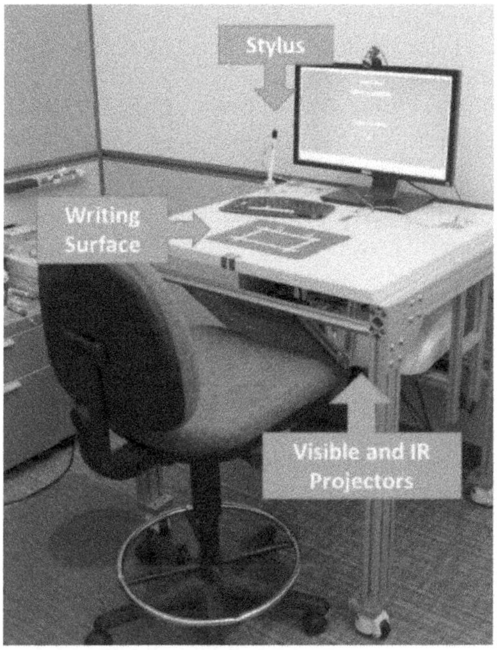


**Figure 1. The High Performance Stylus System (HPSS) and experimental setup used for our latency perception studies.**

The stylus experience on today's devices is unfortunately far from optimal. One of the foremost grievances regarding stylus-enabled devices involves the responsiveness, or latency, encountered while inking [28]. If digital ink does not appear directly under the stylus nib, users complain that their writing is illegible and their drawings are messy because strokes and letters are disconnected. To accommodate poor latency, users often slow their movements to allow their device to 'catch up'. Others divert their attention away from the screen, thereby sacrificing legibility and precision. If a child is learning to write using a stylus, for example, illegible ink and behavioral accommodations are unacceptable.

Regardless of the technology used to detect the stylus, the end-to-end latency on most commercial tablets is between 65 and 120 milliseconds [25]. This is significantly different from pen and paper, where latency is essentially zero as ink instantly flows from the nib onto the page. Latencies are much higher on digital devices because input information and feedback travels through a complex pipeline composed of input sampling from the digitizer, the filtering and reporting of samples to the operating system, the processing samples by the operating system, the reporting and processing of events by an application, and the updating of the display [15]. Each step in this pipeline adds to the lag or delays that users perceive.

Reducing the issues caused by latency will require advances in both hardware and software. As it is unlikely that stylus-enabled devices will ever achieve true zero latency, an achievable goal is to minimize latency such that users have the illusion, or perceive that a device is more responsive than it truly is [27]. To users, the *perceived latency* would thus seem identical to true zero latency.

Although touch and stylus interaction are both direct, there is reason to believe that the minimum perceivable latency would differ. Since a stylus nib occludes much less of the screen than a fingertip, it is likely that less occlusion, i.e., stylus-based interaction, enhances the ability to detect latency. The natural loci of attention and eye gaze required for stylus-based and finger-based tasks may also affect the perception of latency. Perception will likely differ while selecting or moving objects with the finger, where attention is focused on the visual feedback, compared to inking tasks where attention is often elsewhere. Stylus inking tasks may differ from dragging tasks, as a user may focus on the trailing ink as opposed to the stylus nib. While the level of perceivable latency has been explored using direct touch-based interaction [11, 25], the minimum perceivable latency for stylus-based interaction is currently unknown.

This work presents three main contributions. The first is the design and implementation of the High Performance Stylus System (HPSS; Figure 1). The HPSS is a stylus-enabled device capable of variable end-to-end latency from latencies found on devices today, down to a minimum possible latency of one millisecond for dragging tasks and seven milliseconds for inking tasks. Using such a system, we investigated users' perception of latency while performing a number of stylus-based tasks. The results constitute the second contribution - the identification of the minimum latency perceivable while performing stylus-based activities. The ability to test a range of delays, many of which are not achievable in the near future, provided a wealth of information and understanding regarding latency perception. The last contribution is thus an understanding of how latency is perceived and a discussion how lower latencies can be achieved with future the touch and stylus systems.

## RELATED WORK

Although latency has been a complaint for years, very little work has assessed its influence on the user. Research on latency outside virtual reality and video games has focused on direct-touch input. Work by Anderson, Doherty and Ganapthy used two touchscreen devices to determine the effects of touch latencies between of 80 to 780 milliseconds during everyday tasks such as reading, photo browsing, and web browsing [3]. They found that delays of less than 580 milliseconds were acceptable to users. In work by Ng and colleagues, a low latency touch device assessed the latency perception while performing a dragging task [25]. The device consisted of an opaque touch sensor interfaced with a TI Discovery 4100 DLP development kit [8]. The kit's FPGA performed all of the processing and directly controlled a DMD at very high frame rates, allowing a baseline latency of one millisecond. It was found that users were unable to perceive latencies below six milliseconds (range 2 - 11 milliseconds). In follow up work by Jota et al., the influence of latency, target location, and width of the target was examined [11]. Performance was found to decrease as target width decreased, latency increased, and target distance increased. The just-noticeable difference while perceiving the 'land-on' portion of the dragging event was found to be 64 milliseconds. These varying results suggest that task may have a great effect on the perception of latency. The device used in this prior work was unfortunately not suitable for a stylus because the sensor resolution was suited for larger input modalities such as fingers and no disambiguation between the hand and a stylus was possible. We thus developed a new low latency prototype specifically targeted towards stylus input.

Although much further work can be done within the touch domain, this work focuses on exploring latency perception while using a stylus. Just as with direct-touch input, few have assessed stylus latency, largely due to technical limitations within digitizers and tablets. In early work with a light pen system, Miller estimated that 100 milliseconds of delay would be acceptable to users while drawing slow deliberate strokes [23]. Unfortunately, few details are available regarding the derivation of this estimate. In recent work, Henzen and colleagues developed a low latency electronic ink display for drawing and animation applications [13, 14]. The display had a minimum latency of 40 milliseconds and exhibited zero parallax. The setup was a prototype and did not undergo experimental evaluation with participants. Unlike Henzen et al.'s work, our system was capable of displaying latencies as low as one millisecond (~1.4).

## HIGH PERFORMANCE STYLUS SYSTEM

Many factors in addition to latency, such as resolution and parallax, influence the stylus experience. As these factors are often confounded, the goal of the High Performance Stylus System was to build a system as close to ideal for as many parameters as possible. As latency has been shown to be perceptible down to single digit levels [25], a minimum latency of about one millisecond was targeted. As display and sensing resolution directly influence the aesthetics of the visual response, a resolution of at least 200 dpi was desired. Additionally, parallax error due to separation of the stylus from the display posed a great source of frustration for users [30], so we ensured that the stylus could actuate directly on the display with no parallax.

Guided by these requirements, the HPSS utilized two projectors, a fiber optic stylus, and a first-surface mirror for rear-projection (Figure 2). A rear-projected display, with the diffuser applied directly to the writing surface, allowed the stylus to actuate directly on the display with no parallax. An optical sensing system was used for the stylus, with another rear-projector displaying IR patterns on the diffuser. The IR patterns were detected by the stylus and later decoded to obtain the current stylus location. High resolution was achieved using HD projectors with short throw distances and low latency was achieved via hardware acceleration, as opposed to software approaches.

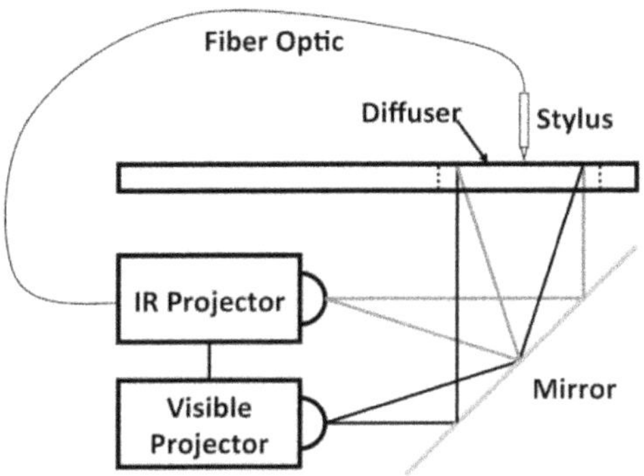


**Figure 2. The system setup wherein one projector displayed IR gray-code patterns, a second displayed visible images, and an optically-based stylus detected gray-code patterns.**

Given the system design, there were thus three engineering challenges to overcome, i.e. sensing, display, and processing, with each requiring a custom solution to achieve the intended level of performance.

## Sensing

None of the commercial or research stylus sensing systems available met the latency, resolution, and parallax requirements that were desired. Although camera-based solutions have worked in the past (i.e., a high-speed imager views the screen from behind, and the pen emits an infrared light [16]), finding a high-speed, high-resolution camera with a low latency interface proved to be very challenging. While the sensing system used in Ng et al.'s low latency work was sufficiently fast, it was unfortunately optimized for input the size of the finger [24, 25]. Additionally, it had an opaque surface, making it unsuitable given our needs. We were thus forced to design our own sensing system utilizing fiber optics and structured IR light.

### *IR Projector*

A Texas Instruments Discovery 4100 DLP projector development kit was used for the IR pattern projector [8]. The DLP projector used a Digital Micromirror Device (DMD), consisting of an array of micromirrors with one mirror per pixel. Each mirror had two orientations - an "on" orientation that directed light from a light source out through the lens, and an "off" orientation that directed the light away from the lens. The mirrors had response times on the order of microseconds, thus allowing for binary frame rates of tens of kHz. Typically, the DMD is multiplexed and duty-cycle-modulated to obtain color and grayscale images.

The Discovery 4100 platform provided a custom interface to a 1920x1080 DMD controlled by an FPGA. This allowed the DMD to be driven at 17,636 binary fps, using the global reset mode by omitting color and grayscale capabilities [8]. Global reset mode updated the DMD mirrors simultaneously after the pixel data has been loaded, as opposed to block reset modes, which incrementally updated portions of the DMD and hid the mirror update and settling times. While block reset modes achieve frame rates as high as 23,148 fps, the use of global reset mode avoided position-dependent latency. At 17,636 fps, with 24 frames required per sample, a sample rate of ~735 Hz was achieved, resulting in an input sampling latency of approximately one millisecond (~1.4).

The DMD was mated to an Optoma HD80 DLP projector that had its light source removed. As a sufficiently bright, non-varying, IR light source was required for the projector, an OSRAM SFH4740 20W, 850nm IR LED array was placed inside the projector's optical integrating tube. A custom heat sink coupled the light source to a commercial liquid cooling system.

### *Infrared Gray-code Structured Light*

Lee et al.'s gray-code structured light technique was used to determine the location of the stylus [18, 19]. A 1920 x 1080 IR pattern was rear-projected onto the diffuse writing surface, measuring 148 x 91 millimeters with a resolution of 323 pixels per inch. Gray-codes were sent in the X and Y dimensions (Figure 3). To encode every pixel on the screen uniquely, $\log_2 Xdim$ and $\log_2 Ydim$ images were required. Two constant images were also included for synchronization purposes. Thus, the use of 24 images ensured that there was a unique sequence of flashes at each pixel. The codes were inverted on every other frame so that the average intensity was constant for all pixels. This allowed the sensor circuitry to obtain an accurate threshold to distinguish between light and dark pixels.

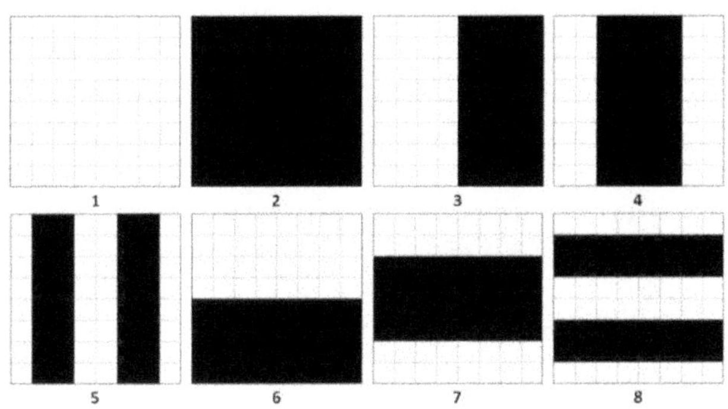


**Figure 3. Gray-code patterns for an example 8x8 pixel area. The patterns include two synchronization patterns (1-2), $\log_2 Xdim$ patterns for the X coordinate (3-5), and $\log_2 Ydim$ patterns for the Y coordinate (6-8).**

Using gray-codes, the encodings of two adjacent pixels differ by one bit. This property guarantees that samples between pixels will be recovered correctly. In addition, sampling errors due to fast stylus motions are minimized. While in motion, the stylus may change pixel position mid-read. Any bit boundaries that are crossed may thus be incorrectly sensed. This property guarantees that crossing a single bit boundary will generate at most a one least significant bit error. This error generalizes such that crossing bit boundaries at any given level generates a worst-case error of that bit level, independent of location. Given our high sample rate and the limitations of the human motor system, the distance that can be covered on one frame is quite small, resulting in benign errors. A simple binary encoding would not exhibit these behaviors.

### *Fiber Optic Stylus*

As the DMD was not designed for IR efficiency, very sensitive circuitry was required to detect the IR gray-code patterns. To ensure that the stylus was thin and light, an optical fiber transmitted the received light patterns to a Hamamatsu Avalanche Photodetector, Model C5460-01 [1]. The received signal was then amplified, filtered, and quantized into a bit stream. To prevent interference from the visible light projector, an IR-blocking filter with 850 nm cutoff was used.

**Figure 4. The fiber optic-based stylus used in the experiments.**

As users vary greatly in the way they hold a stylus, it was important that the stylus could be robustly actuated at a variety of angles. We thus went through many iterations of the stylus design, finally settling on one that used a one-millimeter flexible fiber optic cable. The cable was bundled within a stylus constructed from PVC tubing, a cap, and a hollowed out laser pointer (Figure 4). The fiber optic cable was placed inside the laser pointer casing, and the casing was nested inside the PVC tubing. Attached to the end of the laser pointer casing was a momentary switch. Whenever the stylus was pressed or removed from the screen, the laser pointer (de)pressed the switch against the cap, switching the ink on or off. This simple construction allowed participants to write with the stylus at any angle comfortable to them.

As the fiber optic cable was very thin, the nib of the stylus was 3D printed from UV cured ABS plastic and a one-millimeter hole was drilled in the tip. The diameter of the nib's tip was 1.2 millimeters. The resulting stylus was 187 millimeters long, had a 13-millimeter barrel diameter, and weighed 19 grams, which is close in weight and size to a typical Wacom stylus.

### *Limitations and Considerations*

The precision of the stylus is dependent upon the width of the optical hole in the stylus nib. Ideally, the stylus nib would be the width of one pixel. However, a one-pixel wide hole received too little light for the optical circuitry to detect, so the width was increased to one millimeter. Due to the gray-code scheme, this results in spatial jitter of about one millimeter. As jitter has been shown to decrease performance in direct pointing tasks [26], it is important to consider its effect within our system. The reduction of jitter involves filtering the samples over a certain window, thereby increasing the latency. In typical devices, increasing the filter window size would drastically increase the latency. However, due to our extremely high sample rate, we can filter over larger windows while only adding a few milliseconds of latency.

Jitter may interfere with one's perception of latency, especially at latencies as low as we explored. However, this jitter is actually constant spatial jitter that is exhibited regardless of the latency. Even with random jitter, higher latencies still yield higher gap distances between a moving stylus and the visual response on average. We thus explored the perception of latency in spite of this jitter. The exploration of jitter and the understanding of its effects at low latencies are left for future work.

## Display

Similar to the IR pattern projector, another Texas Instruments Discovery 4100 projector development kit was used to display visible images. The visible projector refreshed at the maximum 23,148 binary fps using a block reset mode [8], with a pixel resolution of 1920 x 1080. This setup was similar to that used previously in the High Performance Touch System by Ng et al. [24, 25].

As the sensing system used infrared light, we needed a light source that was limited to the visible range. Thus, the DMD was mated to the optics of another Optoma HD80 projector, wherein the metal halide light source was replaced with a commercial white LED lighting unit.

## Processing

In a commercial system, there is typically a CPU running a non-real-time operating system and associated applications, contributing greatly to the latency pipeline. Sensor control, display control, and stylus sample processing for the HPSS were performed by FPGAs, thereby removing the 'software latency' from the system. Each of the Discovery 4100 kits contained an onboard Xilinx Virtex 5 FPGA. The IR projector FPGA was responsible for providing stylus sample coordinates to the visible projector FPGA, while the visible projector FPGA rendered to the display and communicated with a PC for parameter control.

### *IR Projector FPGA Processing*

The IR projector FPGA processing included five general blocks (Figure 5). A pixel generator cycled through the 24 1920 x 1080 gray-code patterns at 17,636 fps and communicated with the DMD controller to render to the DMD. These patterns were computed on a per pixel basis on the fly, without the use of an image buffer. The pattern was inverted with each scan, simplifying the design of the IR receiver by maintaining a constant average intensity level, independent of position.

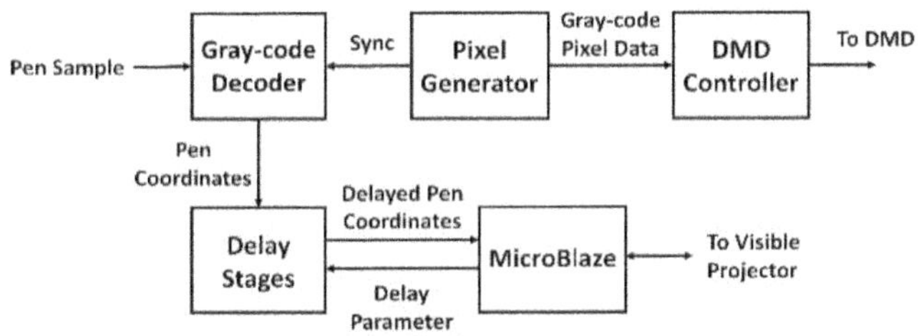


**Figure 5. Block diagram of the processing performed on the IR pattern projector's FPGA.**

A gray-code decoder received and decoded the pen sample bit stream from the stylus circuitry. The gray-code decoder sent the pen sample coordinates to a 100-stage variable delay buffer that introduced artificial latency into the pipeline, with a granularity of 100, 50 MHz clock periods, or 2 microseconds. This 100-stage buffer allowed for the introduction of up to 100 pen sample periods (approximately 140 milliseconds) of latency without losing any samples.

A Xilinx MicroBlaze soft processor controlled the variable delay, received the pen sample coordinates, and sent the coordinates over a high-speed serial link to the visible projector FPGA. Additionally, the MicroBlaze accepted commands from the visible projector FPGA to set the delay.

*Visible Projector FPGA Processing*

The processing performed in the visible projector FPGA was organized into four blocks (Figure 6). A MicroBlaze soft processor received pen sample coordinates from the IR projector FPGA, ran simple applications, and rendered images to the frame buffer. The soft processor also communicated with a host PC over serial to allow for the selection of applications and the controlling of various parameters such as latency.

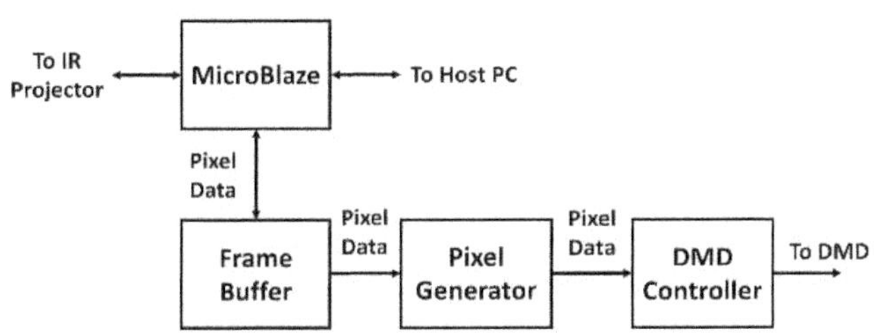


**Figure 6. Block diagram of the processing performed on the visible projector's FPGA.**

Calibration was necessary to map the coordinates from the IR and visible pattern projectors. A linear mapping between the two projection planes using five coordinate pairs was used to compute a sufficiently accurate mapping. The mapping was applied by the MicroBlaze.

The frame buffer was synthesized in the on-chip BRAM blocks. The Virtex 5 only had enough BRAM for a 1280 x 800 image, so the active area was limited to a portion of the full image. The DMD Controller continuously read out frames at 23,148 fps to render to the DMD.

### Applications

Two applications were implemented on the MicroBlaze, a box dragging application and an inking application. Both applications received input coordinates through an interrupt event handler. On each frame of the box dragging application, a box was drawn at the sensed location. The minimum latency of the box dragging application was approximately one millisecond (~1.4), with latency being due to the sensing mechanism and rendering latency.

Within the inking application, the unfiltered ink trail was not smooth due to the jitter described previously, so a moving average filter with a window size of 10 filtered each coordinate and the Bresenham method [6] drew a line to the previous coordinate. Since the ink thickness was no more than a few pixels wide, the latency introduced while rendering was negligible. Due to the 10-frame filter window, the minimum latency of the inking application was five frames, or approximately seven milliseconds.

To minimize latency, rather than double buffering and redrawing the entire frame, the application simply modified the pixels in the frame buffer that changed between frames. Because the images were drawn so quickly, no tearing of the image was apparent, even without the double buffers.

### Latency Verification

Accurately measuring the end-to-end latency of such a high performance device is a great challenge. Recently, Berard and Blanch proposed statistical methods to measure the distribution of latencies in the face of high variability in common touch devices [4]. As our system was developed to tightly control latency by design, such methods were not required. All processing and controls were in the form of a clock-cycle granular FPGA design and primitive MicroBlaze RISC processor software that was measurable with timer registers. By design, there was no significant variable latency in the system. The baseline latency was limited by the sample rate of the stylus, which was approximately one millisecond (~1.4) per sample. Image rendering on the MicroBlaze was below 0.1 milliseconds, with the latency from the remainder of the FPGA logic being negligible. The artificially introduced latency was accurately settable in two microsecond increments.

A high-speed camera was also used for further verification [25]. From the camera footage, the gap distance and stylus velocity of a stroke were used to compute the estimated latency. This approach allowed us to verify the accuracy of our designed latencies to within several milliseconds. The high-performance time-driven design, combined with the high-speed camera footage, provided us with sufficient evidence that the system was performing as intended.

## USER STUDY

As little is known about the perception of latency while inking or using a stylus, three psychophysics experiments were conducted. Each was designed to determine the lowest latency detectable using a task hypothesized to increase latency perception, i.e., dragging and scribbling. Such tasks ensured ecological validity and comparability to prior work.

### Participants

Sixteen naïve individuals (4 female) participated in the study (M = 33, range 24-52 years). All participants were right handed and had normal or corrected-to-normal vision. Participants had varying levels of exposure to tablets and styli, from complete novices to others who worked with stylus-enabled devices each day. Each participant was provided a $10 honorarium for the 30-minute experiment.

### Tasks

Three tasks were used to determine the lowest latency participants could perceive: *large box dragging*, *small box dragging*, and *scribbling*.

In the *large box dragging* task, participants placed their stylus on the left hand side of the screen underneath the left arrow, dragged the stylus laterally to the right hand side underneath the right arrow, and then dragged the stylus back underneath the left arrow (Figure 7). While doing this, a 20 millimeter x 20 millimeter white box was continually centered at the location of the nib. To maintain consistency with prior work, the same box dimensions were used [25]. We also verbally encouraged participants to maintain the same dragging speed throughout all trials.

**Figure 7. During box dragging, a box appeared around the stylus and participants dragged the stylus from the left to right and back to the left. The orange arrows have been added to indicate the direction of stylus movement.**

As the size of the nib was much smaller than the finger, a variation of the box dragging task, *small box dragging,* was also conducted. By closely matching the size of the box to the dimensions of the nib, it should have been much easier for participants to notice if the nib fell outside the box or was not in the center, and hence enhance their ability to perceive latency. To compute the appropriate box dimensions for this condition, we determined the finger-to-box ratio used by Ng et al. using the average width of the index finger at the proximal interphalangeal joint, i.e. 16 millimeters [9], and the large box dimensions of 20 x 20 millimeters. Using this ratio and the size of our nib, a 6.25 x 6.25 millimeter box was appropriate for this condition.

In the *scribbling* task, participants drew a curvilinear line, or scribble, starting in the upper left corner and moving towards the lower right corner (Figure 8). To encourage the same motor motions, participants were instructed not to touch the edge of the interactive area with their scribble nor draw a shallow, wavy line. Feedback was provided in the form of a 1-pixel thick on-screen ink trace. Similar to the dragging tasks, participants were verbally encouraged to maintain the same speed throughout all trials.

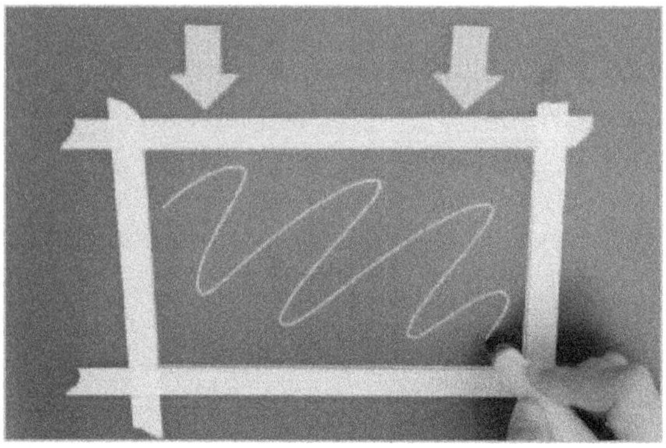

**Figure 8. In the scribbling task, participants were instructed to move the stylus from the upper left down to the lower right.**

### Methodology

Similar to Ng et al. and Jota et al., a psychophysical just-noticeable difference methodology governed the latencies presented to participants and ultimately converged at the minimum perceivable latency [11, 25]. JND paradigms are used to determine perceivable latency because they assume that the converged latency threshold is the result of participants being unable to discriminate between the baseline and all latencies below the converged threshold. We thus assume that participants would not perceive such latency on an actual device because they were unable to discriminate it from the minimum baseline latency.

The baseline latency while dragging was one millisecond and seven milliseconds while scribbling. The testing latency was refined using the Parameter Estimation by Sequential Testing (PEST) adaptive technique [28] because it allowed for maximal efficiency, whilst maintaining comparability to legacy JND methodologies such as staircase methods used in prior work. Such efficiency allowed for maximal engagement and minimal fatigue, which given the repetitive nature of the motor movements required was necessary.

With PEST, the choice of the testing latency was dictated by the history of a participant's prior responses at the given stimulus level. PEST determined the step size using the Wald sequential likelihood-ratio test [31]. For comparability to Ng et al. and Jota et al.'s work, the initial testing latency was 65 milliseconds, the step size was 8 milliseconds, and an expected probability of 75% was used. Our experiment terminated using the Minimal Overshoot and Undershoot Sequential Estimation (MOUSE) technique [21]: once the step size reached one millisecond, the experiment concluded. The JND was the last testing latency participants experienced before the experiment terminated.

### Equipment and Apparatus

During the experiment, a C# and WPF program running on an HP Z400 Workstation automatically determined the appropriate latency values to send to the HPSS (over serial) using the PEST algorithm. The program also recorded all participant responses and the final JND values obtained for post-analysis. A Dell 21" monitor provided feedback about the current task and trial condition.

### Procedure

During the recruitment process, participants were naive to the purpose of the experiment. This removed any bias or experience they may have had towards latency from pen or touch-enabled systems or video games. At the start of each experiment, participants sat in an adjustable drafting chair in front of the High Performance Stylus System. Latency was explained to participants, and participants were informed that we were measuring the minimum latency they could perceive while performing a number of tasks.

Each trial was composed of two conditions. In the first condition, participants completed the task using one latency, either the baseline or target. Participants then pressed the space bar to go to the next condition where they completed the task again using the other latency value. Once finished, participants again pressed the space bar. A tone played and participants then indicated "which condition had less delay" using the A or B keys. Once PEST had converged at their JND level, participants had a break and the next task began. The presentation order was counterbalanced using a Latin square design.

Although forcing participants to attend to latency intentionally primes them, the use of subjective questions, such as "Which condition did you like more" would have allowed for too much interpretation of what could be focused on or attended to by participants, confounding our results.

## RESULTS

As the baseline latencies for the dragging and scribbling tasks were different (i.e., one millisecond versus seven milliseconds), the two tasks could not be statistically compared. As such, two separate analyses were conducted.

Even though the baseline latencies for the dragging tasks were the same, the resulting JND threshold values were not normally distributed (Figure 9, Figure 10). A Wilcoxon signed-rank test compared the two box sizes and revealed that participants were able to discriminate between lower latencies when the smaller box (*Mdn* = 2 milliseconds, range 2 - 16 milliseconds) instead of the larger box (*Mdn* = 6 milliseconds, range 2 - 7 milliseconds) appeared around the nib, $z = -2.769$, $p < 0.01$, $d = 1.03$. Users were able to perceive minute differences caused by latency, similar to results found prior by Ng et al. [25]. The different threshold values suggest that the dimensions of visual feedback in reference to the physical input likely play a role in the perception of latency. Dimensions that complement the relation between the physical reference and digital feedback provide better visual cues and assist in latency perception.

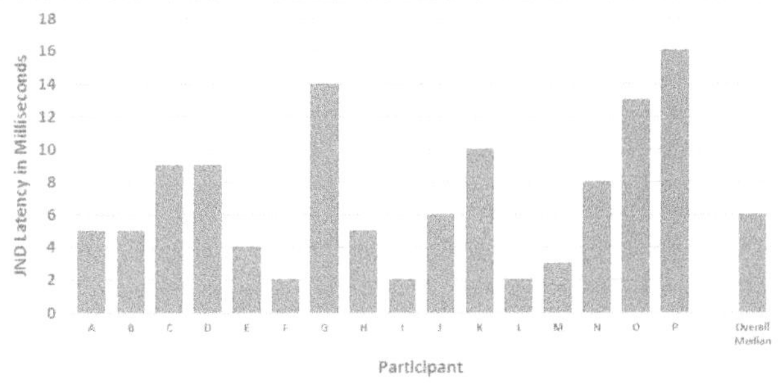


**Figure 9. Minimum latency perceived by participants while dragging the large box. Results ranged from 2 to 16 milliseconds, with a median latency of 6 milliseconds.**

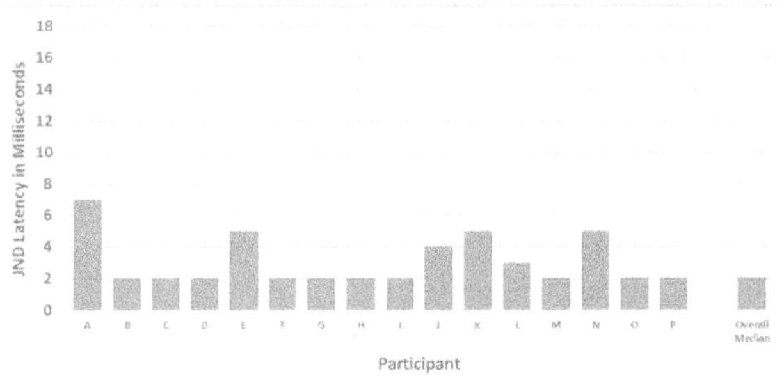


**Figure 10. Minimum latency perceived by participants while dragging the small box. Results ranged from 2 to 7 milliseconds, with a median latency of 2 milliseconds.**

The results from the scribbling task demonstrated that participants were able to discriminate between the 7-millisecond baseline latency and a median of 40 milliseconds (Figure 11; range 10 - 70 milliseconds). Although not directly comparable to the dragging tasks, such results suggest that task demands may play a role in the perception of latency. The higher perceived latency found while scribbling compared to dragging are likely due to the different visual feedback available, the strategies used to determine latency, or the cognitive loading encountered while scribbling versus dragging the box.

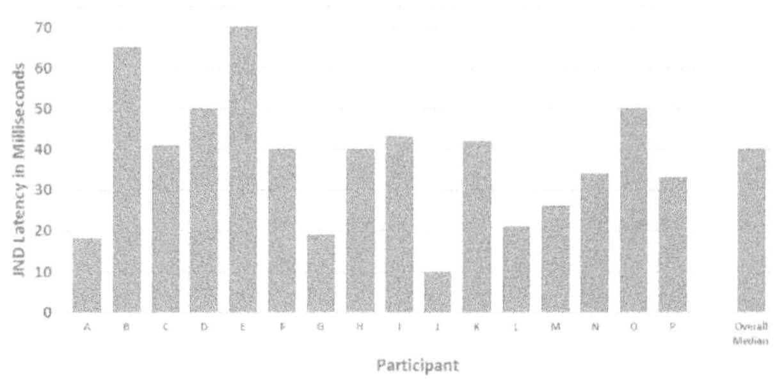


**Figure 11. Minimum latency perceived by participants while performing the scribbling task. Results ranged from 10 to 70 milliseconds with a median latency of 40 milliseconds.**

## DISCUSSION

The results found with the dragging and scribbling tasks provide valuable information about the basic visual process and the ability of participants to detect and notice latency. Given the latencies possible on devices today, i.e. 65 - 120 milliseconds, these results additionally provide support for decreasing latency along all levels of the pipeline.

### Understanding the Perception of Latency

Users appear to detect latency by attending to the visual disparity between a visual reference, which may move, and corresponding feedback available from the display. The perceptibility of this disparity appears to depend on a number of factors. The size and type of feedback presented likely influenced participant's comparisons. With the scribbling task, a small, persistent line was visible, whereas with the dragging tasks, a large box was visible. As there was minimal occlusion from the stylus nib, it is likely that participants had an easier time viewing feedback as the box(es) activated a larger area within the foveal or parafoveal region. In the original latency experiments by Ng et al., the finger occluded a larger area of the visual feedback than our stylus nib, so this may explain why our participants found it easier to detect latency, especially when the dimensions of the physical input were appropriately scaled to the feedback. When considering Jota et al.'s tapping task, it is likely that the haptic feedback generated by touching the screen was integrated with the visual feedback from the display to make latency judgments. The combination and synchronization of feedback from other modalities likely decreases the perception of latency, hence the higher thresholds found by Jota et al. Further work is thus needed to truly understand the role of feedback in the perception of latency.

As participants were free to use whatever method necessary to make their latency judgments, it is also possible that the location of focus and subsequent visual cues available influenced perception. When asked how comparisons were made, participants reported different focus loci for the dragging versus scribbling tasks. While dragging, participants reported fixating on the box's edges to determine if the nib was inside, outside, or in the center of the box, likely similar to what occurred in the prior touch work by Ng et al. As there was high contrast on the screen, and little occlusion from the nib, such a determination was easier with the stylus than with touch. The smaller the box, the easier it was to make this judgment. While scribbling, the location of focus was not always on the nib. Some participants reported focusing on the ink, others on the pen or hand, some continually switched between the ink and the pen, while others held a bird's eye view of the whole screen. Such strategies changed the location of the nib and ink on the eye as well as the distance between them. While varied, such attentional patterns made different visual cues available to participants and fall in line with those found in the eye tracking literature [2, 7, 12, 22].

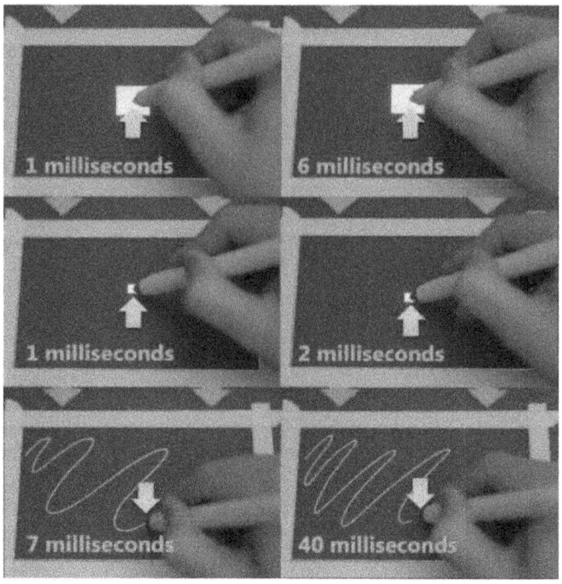


**Figure 12. Demonstration of the latencies perceivable by participants, with the yellow arrow indicating the current nib location. From top: The nib was on the right side of the box during the large box dragging task, the nib was slightly off center during the small box dragging task, and there was a visible gap between the nib and ink while scribbling. The images were recorded using a high speed camera at 480 fps.**

Cognitive load and attention required to complete a specific task may also influence latency perception. The tapping and dragging tasks used in this and prior work with touch had low levels of cognitive difficulty and did not divert much attention from the latency judgments being made. Repeatedly drawing the same pattern on the screen and trying to maintain its shape and length (scribbling), on the other hand, is more cognitively challenging and attention diverting because participants had to focus on maintaining the same shape and speed of stroke on each trial. Although our scribbling task is a rudimentary form of inking, it is likely that tasks with even more cognitive and attentional demands such as taking notes, solving mathematical equations, or sketching a portrait, will divert more cognitive resources away from latency perception and likely decrease latency perception even more. This, of course, requires further investigation. Based on our initial results, it may be reasonable to target latencies closer to 40 milliseconds for stylus-based experiences, instead of the 10 milliseconds recommended prior for touch-based tasks.

While our results provide many insights into the perception of latency, they are not without their limitations. Approximately 63% of participants could discern between one and two milliseconds of delay. When asked if they were guessing or confident in their comparisons, most indicated that they could still discriminate between the two conditions, but it was difficult to do so. There was a very small difference in the location of the box for one versus two milliseconds, compared to one versus six milliseconds (Figure 12). As the human eye can discern motion or deviations in spatial patterns separated by one arc minute ($1/60^{th}$ of a degree), if the HPSS could display latencies of finer fidelity, e.g., 1.5, 1.6, etc. or the baseline latency could be lowered below one millisecond, it is likely that most participants would be able to discriminate between latencies smaller than one millisecond while performing dragging tasks.

The results demonstrate the minimum latency users can detect, but under conditions where users were explicitly primed to look for latency and do not have attentional competition. In situations where explicit cueing is not available, the minimum noticeable latency will likely be higher. Although the results suggest that developers and device manufacturers have much further work before latency is no longer a complaint from users, they should be considered carefully.

### Improvements Necessary for Low Latency in the Future

The High Performance Stylus System was not intended to be a commercially viable technology. Rather, it was a system through which extremely low latency stylus interaction could be experienced and evaluated. Bringing such experiences to future commercial systems will involve substantial development and innovation across *all* sensing, processing, and display subsystems.

The latency of the HPSS was primarily limited by the sensing mechanism. Twenty-four frames were required for the full 1920 x 1080 sensing area, resulting in a sampling latency of approximately one millisecond. To increase the sample rate and reduce the latency, one could take advantage of the fact that a stylus will not move very far between samples, especially at such high sample rates. Instead of scanning the full frame every sample, the system can sample only a small region of interest about the last sample point, at much higher rates. This technique can raise the sample rate by several factors.

The HPSS hardware was successful in producing extremely low latencies due to the extremely high sampling rates across the sensing, display, and processing subsystems. The current systems of today run nowhere near as fast as the HPSS. Often, the sampling frequencies of the stylus digitizers are low (~100 Hz), display frame rates are low (60 Hz or possible 120 Hz if stereo is supported), and applications typically run at 30 Hz, resulting in high latencies within each subsystem. In addition, unlike current commercial systems, the subsystems of the HPSS were synchronized. Upon sampling the pen location, all processing and display updates were performed within one frame, resulting in only one frame of latency. In current systems, subsystems are pipelined for simpler composability, resulting in several frames of latency. Across all of these subsystems, innovations and improvements in the update rate and synchronization processes are required before users can experience true low-latency when using commercial devices.

The Accelerated Touch toolkit has been proposed previously as a method to decrease perceived latency [25]. By combining high performance and current generation hardware, one can render both low and high latency feedback and visualizations. Ng et al. hypothesized that the combination of two such 'layers' of visual information could be used to mitigate many of the issues and complaints about latency. While certainly possible today, such an approach does however require the augmentation of existing hardware with a low latency system.

Outside of high performance hardware approaches, there are a number of software-based pen-specific enhancements that can be implemented today. The use of pen location and stroke prediction algorithms can not only increase the smoothness and beautification of strokes, but can also be used to pre-render strokes before they occur and then adapt them after the stylus has reached or surpasses a given point. The current application context and knowledge about hand postures or grip could also be useful in sampling sub-regions of the input sensor and redrawing targeted sub-regions of the display. Vogel's hand occlusion model [29], for example, could be implemented within an inking application to define the region of interest. As the location of the stylus reveals much about the intentionality of current and future interaction, harnessing it within applications should help decrease the latency perceived by users and ultimately improve the stylus experience both today and in the future.

## CONCLUSION

In this work, we explored the perception of latency using a prototype stylus-based system, the High Performance Stylus System. The HPSS was composed of two high-speed DLP projectors and a fiber optic stylus and enabled participants to experience latencies as low as approximately one millisecond while dragging objects and seven milliseconds while inking. Such low latencies were made possible by performing all sensing and processing on FPGAs, thereby removing the latency typically introduced by the operating system and application layers.

Through experimentation, we determined that users can perceived latencies at substantially lower levels than those possible on devices today, i.e., 2 milliseconds while dragging a box and 40 milliseconds while scribbling. Our results corroborate with prior work and suggest that the perception of latency is influenced by the visual feedback available, location of focus, and the cognitive demands of the task. Future experimentation of these factors, in addition to hardware-based factors such as parallax and resolution, should broaden our understanding of latency and its role in the stylus experience.

## ACKNOWLEDGEMENTS

We express our sincerest gratitude to Microsoft's Applied Sciences Group and Microsoft Research's Hardware Lab for their assistance in designing and assembling the High Performance Stylus System. We also thank Chris O'Dowd, Patrick Therien, Ken Hinckley, and Ed Burress for their assistance with the HPSS's stylus.

## REFERENCES


1. APD module C5460-01 | Hamamatsu. https://www.hamamatsu.com/jp/en/product/alpha/A/4162/C5460-01/index.html. Accessed December 2013.
2. Alamargot, D., Chesnet, D., Dansac, C., and Ros, C. Eye and Pen: A New Device for Studying Reading During Writing. *Behavior Research Methods*, 2006, 38(2), pp. 287 - 299.
3. Anderson, G., Doherty, R., and Ganapathy, S. User Perception of Touch Screen Latency. *Design, User Experience, and Usability Part 1*, 2011, pp. 195 - 202.
4. Bérard, F. and Blanch, R. Two Touch System Latency Estimators: High Accuracy and Low Overhead. In *Proc. of ITS,* 2013, pp. 241 - 250.
5. Brandl, P., Forlines, C., Wigdor, D., Haller, M., and Shen, C. Combining and Measuring the Benefits of Bimanual Pen and Direct-Touch Interaction on Horizontal Interfaces. In *Proc. of Advanced Visual Interfaces*, 2008, pp. 154 - 161.
6. Bresenham, J.E. Algorithm for Computer Control of a Digital Plotter. *IBM Systems Journal*, 1965, 4, pp. 25 - 30.
7. Calgi, R.C., Coraggio, P., Napoletano, P., Schwartz, O., Ferraro, M., and Boccignone, G. Visuomotor Characterization of Eye Movements in a Drawing Task. *Vision Research*, 2009, 49(8), pp. 810 - 818.
8. DLP Discovery 4100 Development Kit. http://www.ti.com/lit/er/dlpu008a/dlpu008a.pdf. Accessed December 2013.
9. Dreyfuss, H. and Tilley, A. *The Measure of Man & Woman*. 2002, John Wiley & Sons, Inc., New York.
10. Guiard, Y. Asymmetric Transfer of Labor in Human Skilled Bimanual Action: The Kinematic Chain as a Model. *Journal of Motor Behavior*, 1987, 19, pp. 486 - 517.
11. Jota, R., Ng, A., Dietz, P., and Wigdor, D. How Fast Is Fast Enough? A Study of the Effects of Latency in Direct-Touch Point Tasks. In *Proc. of CHI,* 2013, pp. 2291 - 2300.
12. Gowen, E. and Miall, R.C. Eye-tracking Interactions in Tracing and Drawing tasks. *Human Movement Science*, 2006, 25, pp. 568 - 585.
13. Henzen, A., Ailenci, N., Di Fiore, F., Van Reeth, F., and Patterson, J. Sketching with a Low-Latency Electronic Ink Drawing Tablet. In *Proc. of Graphite,* 2005, pp. 51 - 60.
14. Henzen, A., Ailenci, N., Di Fiore, F., Van Reeth, F., Vansichem, G., Zehner, R.W., and Amundson, K. An Electronic Ink Low Latency Drawing Tablet. In *SID International Symposium Digest of Technical Papers,* 2004, 35(1), pp. 1070 - 1073.
15. Hinckley, K. and Wigdor, D. Input Technologies and Techniques. *The Human Computer Interaction Handbook: Fundamentals, Evolving Technologies and Emerging Applications*, 2002.
16. Hinckley, K., Yatani, K., Pahud, M., Coddington, N., Rodenhouse, J., Wilson, A., Benko, H., and Buxton, B. Pen + Touch = New Tools. In *Proc. of UIST*, 2010, pp. 27 - 36.
17. Holzinger, A., Holler, M., Schedlbauer, M., and Urlesberger, B. An Investigation of Finger versus Stylus Input in Medical Scenarios. In *Proc. of Information Technology Interfaces*, 2008, pp. 433 - 438.
18. Lee, J.C., Dietz, P., Maynes-Aminzade, D., Raskar, R., and Hudson S. Automatic Projector Calibration with Embedded Light Sensors. In *Proc. of UIST*, 2004, pp. 123 - 126.
19. Lee, J.C., Hudson, S.E., Summet, J.W., and Dietz, P. Moveable Interactive Projected Displays Using Projector Based Tracking. In *Proc. of UIST*, 2005, pp. 63 - 74.
20. Mackenzie, I.S., Sellen, A., and Buxton, B. A Comparison of Input Devices in Elemental Pointing and Dragging Tasks. In *Proc. of Computer Human Interaction*, 1991, pp. 161 - 166
21. McMillian, N.A. and Creelman, D.C. *Detection Theory: a User's Guide*. 1991, Cambridge University Press, Cambridge.
22. Miall, R.C., Imamizu, H., and Miyauchi, S. Activation of the Cerebellum in Co-Ordinated Eye and Hand Tracking Movements: An fMRI Study. *Experimental Brain Research*, 2000, 135, pp. 22 - 33.
23. Miller, R.B. Response Time in Man-Computer Conversational Transactions. *Fall Joint Computer Conference*, 1968, pp. 267 - 277.
24. Ng, A. and Dietz, P. The Need for Speed in Touch Systems. In *SID International Symposium Digest of Technical Papers,* 2013, 44(1), pp. 547 - 550.
25. Ng, A., Lepinski, J., Wigdor, D., Sanders, S., and Dietz, P. Designing for Low-Latency Direct-Touch Input. In *Proc. of User Interfaces and Software Technologies* 2012, pp. 453 - 462.
26. Pavlovych, A. and Stuerzlinger, W. The Tradeoff between Spatial Jitter and Latency in Pointing Tasks. *ACM SEICS*, 2009, pp. 187 - 196.
27. Seow, S. *Designing and Engineering Time: The Psychology of Time Perception in Software*. 2008, Pearson Education, Boston.
28. Taylor, M.M. and Creelman, C.D. PEST: Efficient Estimates on Probability Functions. *Journal of the Acoustical Society of America*, 1967, 41, pp. 782 - 787.
29. Vogel, D. *Direct Pen Input and Hand Occlusion*. PhD Thesis, University of Toronto, 2010.
30. Vogel, D. and Balakrishnan, R. Direct Pen Interaction with a Conventional Graphic User Interface. *Human Computer Interaction*, 2010, 25, pp. 324 - 388.
31. Wald, A. *Sequential Analysis*. 1947, John Wiley & Sons, Inc. New York.
32. Zabramski, S. Careless Touch: A Comparative Evaluation if Mouse, Pen, and Touch Input in Shape Tracing Task. In *Proc. of the Australian Computer-Human Interaction Conference*, 2011, pp. 329 - 332.

# Pinch-Drag-Flick vs. Spatial Input: Rethinking Zoom & Pan on Mobile Displays

Martin Spindler
User Interface & Software Engineering Group
University of Magdeburg, Germany
martin.spindler@acm.org

Martin Schuessler
Quality and Usability Lab
Telekom Innovation Laboratories
TU Berlin, Germany
schuesslerm@acm.org

Marcel Martsch
Dep. of Vocational Education & Human Resources Development
University of Magdeburg, Germany
marcel.martsch@ovgu.de

Raimund Dachselt
Interactive Media Lab
Technische Universität Dresden
01062 Dresden, Germany
dachselt@acm.org

## ABSTRACT
The multi-touch-based pinch to zoom, drag and flick to pan metaphor has gained wide popularity on mobile displays, where it is the paradigm of choice for navigating 2D documents. But is finger-based navigation really the gold standard? In this paper, we present a comprehensive user study with 40 participants, in which we systematically compare the Pinch-Drag-Flick approach with a technique that relies on spatial manipulation, such as lifting a display up/down to zoom. While we solely considered known techniques, we put considerable effort in implementing both input strategies on popular consumer hardware (iPhone, iPad). Our results show that spatial manipulation can significantly outperform traditional Pinch-Drag-Flick. Given the carefully optimized prototypes, we are confident to have found strong arguments that future generations of mobile devices could rely much more on spatial interaction principles.

## Author Keywords
Spatial Input; Spatially Aware Displays; Mobile Displays; Multi-Touch Input; User Study

## ACM Classification Keywords
H.5.2. Information interfaces and presentation: User Interfaces – *input devices and strategies*.

## INTRODUCTION
The exploration of large 2D information spaces, such as maps, pictures and web documents, is a very common task carried out on mobile displays by millions of users every day. Due to the rather small screen size of the devices, this often involves heavy usage of zoom and pan, usually performed using multi-finger gestures. In this context, the Pinch-Drag-Flick paradigm has proven to be one of the most (commercially) successful gesture sets: pinch to zoom, drag and flick to pan. While these gestures are considered to be easy to learn and perform, there are inherent problems with the approach: fingers occlude virtual items on the screen [29]; virtual travel distances per gesture are short [16]; pinch gestures are difficult to execute if one hand is occupied; and elderly or disabled persons may not possess sufficiently fine motor skills to perform gestures accurately. Besides that, ambiguities of gestures may trigger unintended actions, such as the accidental selection of items, or may require users to explicitly switch between edit and navigation mode, which in turn may induce disorientation [17]. These shortcomings motivated the development of navigation techniques that, for example, employ different finger gestures [2] or extend the interaction to the side [23] or the back of devices [29]. Although such approaches soften some of the issues of Pinch-Drag-Flick, the underlying input strategy still remains surface-constrained and thus continues to rely mostly on fine finger motor skills.

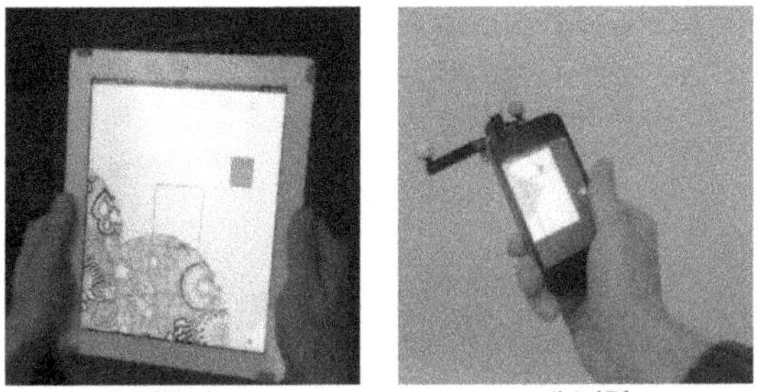
(a) iPad (b) iPhone

**Figure 1: We augmented an iPad and iPhone with IR reflective markers for the support of spatial tracking.**

In this paper, we study a radically different approach that is based on an alternative input channel: the spatial position and orientation of mobile displays (see Figure 1). Well-known examples of such spatially aware displays are the Chameleon [7] and the Peephole Displays [30]. In contrast to the metaphor of grabbing a document, they build upon the concept of Magic Lenses [1] and thus use the metaphor of moving a viewport (the display) over a virtual information world. For this purpose, distinct motion patterns are mapped to specific navigation tasks, e.g., horizontal movements may change the viewport center (panning), whereas lifting a display up/down may control the zoom factor. As this requires users to move a display through the physical space surrounding them, the motor space is increased considerably (large 3D volume vs. small 2D screen) and a different set of motor skills is addressed (arms vs. fingers).

We see this difference in motor control as a significant opportunity that may help overcome the problems of con-


ACM 978-1-4503-2473-1/14/04...$15.00.
http://dx.doi.org/10.1145/2556288.2557028

ventional touch-based navigation – not as a superior form of interaction, but as a complimentary one. This implies many advantages including the addition of a more natural way of interaction by addressing principles of spatial manipulation, the support of longer travel distances per gesture, a reduction of item occlusions on the screen, and less mode switches, e.g., by assigning spatial input to navigation and touch input to selection. For these reasons, we consider spatially aware displays an important research topic that has the potential of changing the way we interact with mobile displays – with 2D document navigation being only one possible use case.

Surprisingly little practical work has been done on systematically studying how both navigation approaches perform against each other on mobile displays. Previous attempts either addressed different setups, e.g., involving a wall [15, 20], occupied both hands for spatial input [11], or did not succeed in finding hard evidence in favor of the spatial approach [10, 19] – a gap that we fill with our work. In this paper, we contribute a comprehensive user study with 40 participants that we conducted using state-of-the-art mobile displays (iPhone 4, iPad 3). We found overwhelming proof that spatial input-based navigation does – if designed and implemented properly – outperform Pinch-Drag-Flick for 2D document navigation. We believe that this is due to our design decisions, e.g., regarding the importance of an easy to use clutch and the role of a high quality prototype.

The remainder of this paper is organized as follows. First, we review related work and discuss key design decisions. We then outline the scope of the study and present the method, results, and discussion. This is followed by design recommendations for future generations of mobile displays as well as conclusions and an outlook on future work.

## RELATED WORK

Pinch-Drag-Flick-is a well understood and established technique. We will therefore restrict our review of related work to spatial input-based interaction and its evaluation.

One of the first spatially aware mobile displays is the Chameleon presented by Fitzmaurice [7]. Inspired by the notion of see-through interfaces [1], it serves as a "peephole in hand" providing access to a virtual world that can be explored by moving the device around. This concept was later adapted to arm-mounted displays, e.g., the Boom Chameleon [27], or to a tabletop environment, e.g., PaperLens [25]. These systems add further aspects to the overall interaction equation, e.g., the opportunities of multi-display environments or additional input modalities, such as digital pens. While we studied the specifics of mobile displays, we believe that our findings are transferable to such setups.

Evaluating specific spatially aware display systems has been the goal of some research projects. Oh and Hua tested various aspect ratios and sizes of spatially aware peepholes [18]. They concluded that the aspect ratio of a display plays a more important role for smaller screens than for larger ones and that screen sizes are more dominant in impacting the user performance. Spindler et al. [24] tested the specifics of multi-layer interaction above a horizontal reference surface. Two recent projects compared touch- and spatial-based 2D document navigation on handheld devices that share some similarities with our work, yet are based on completely different setups: Kaufmann & Ahlström [15] projected the workspace onto a wall with a Pico projector and Rädle et al. [20] combined a tablet with a wall-sized display. Both projects found advantages of the spatial techniques – particularly in terms of recall performances, which was not our focus. Jones et al. [11] investigated free hand around device input for 2D navigation on a handheld display. They are one of the first to show that spatial input can be as good as touch. In some respects, our spatial technique is a simplified variant of their "1 button simultaneous" condition, as our clutch works differently and our technique does not require a second hand for pointing in mid-air (we use relative device positions instead). These are two likely reasons for why fatigue (guerilla arm effect) was only a negligible problem in our study, as opposed to Jones et al. who let their participants rest every 3 to 5min.

To our knowledge, there is only one previous work that bears considerable resemblance to our work: the Lens Chameleon [19] by Pahud et al., who were driven by similar motivations. They also conducted a series of experiments to compare spatial-based navigation with standard Pinch-Drag-Flick. In contrast to our work, their implementation of spatial-based navigation was significantly slower than Pinch-Drag-Flick. This may be attributed to our design decisions: no use of clutching and a lack of state-of-the-art technology (e.g., cable-bounded device).

## DESIGN RATIONALE

While the interaction design specifics for Pinch-Drag-Flick are straightforward (it is the default on most devices), spatial-based navigation is a more complex case. We will now discuss a few design decisions that we made in the process of building the prototype for the spatial technique.

### Mapping the Physical to the Virtual World

One key question is how to properly map the physical space to the Space-Scale-Diagram [8]. In pre-tests, we tried various mappings and finally decided on a dynamic mapping that uses the current orientation of the display as the new reference plane for future interpretations of motions. This means that zooming is mapped to movements along the normal of the display (local Z-axis), whereas motions within the display's XY-plane define panning. Our experiences show that the dynamic mapping supports body-centric usage even better than a spherical mapping [7], which was also recently confirmed in [19]. In addition, it has the benefit of working independently of the user's position, thus simplifying the interaction design and spatial tracking.

### Clutching and Relative Mode

As opposed to [19], where clutching was considered to be of minor relevance (it had performed slightly slower in a pre-test), we argue that mobile devices are moved most of the time without any intention to interact. We therefore think that spatial input should be inactive by default, only to be *enabled on purpose* for a brief moment of interaction – by activating a clutch. With a clutch, the nature of spatial navigation can be changed from absolute to relative mode. We believe that this is a very important and necessary step to support mobile usage. In relative mode, the "volumetric" 2D document (represented by a pyramid Space-Scale-Diagram) travels along with the device like a bubble surrounding it. This enables users to put away the phone, e.g., into the pocket, and to resume navigation later on with the last visited position.

While we fiercely advocate the use of *tactile* clutches (see the discussion in section "A Built-in Tactile Clutch"), we decided on using a touch-based clutch for the user study. This choice was primarily motivated by practical reasons: Existing volume buttons are known to be unsuitable for this purpose [11] and it proved to be challenging to build an adequate alternative in the given time. In our prototype, users can activate the clutch by touching the screen with one or more fingers, e.g., close to the screen bezel in order to prevent occlusion of items in focus. Likewise, removing the finger(s) deactivates the clutch. We believe to have found a close enough approximation of tactile clutches, as this enables users to quickly access the clutch without spending much mental effort on locating it. Hence, we expect that our findings will also apply to the latter case.

### Zoom Direction

At first sight, the choice of the proper zoom direction may appear trivial: "If you observe how users react when they can't see something, they always bring the device closer to their eyes" as one of our reviewers wrote. Having implemented both variants, we conducted an informal pre-test with 5 users. All of them preferred the opposite zoom direction, i.e., zoom out when the display gets closer to the user. A look into the literature [19, 30] confirmed this finding. Apparently, the inverted zoom direction would not match the peephole-in-hand metaphor that most users are familiar with (and thus expect), e.g., from using a magnifying glass or looking through a camera. Hence, we decided to conduct the study with the "zoom-out-when-getting-closer" option (the participants could not change this setting).

### Zoom Mapping

We tested several mappings and chose one that multiplies each movement along the device normal (Z-axis) by the current zoom factor, thus exponentially speeding up the zoom if the zoom level is getting larger, and vice versa.

### Zoom Center

In an early version of the prototype users could dynamically reposition the zoom center via the touch point on the screen (touch-based clutch). We later turned this option down and decided to leave the zoom center in the middle of the screen (out of the user's control) for the following three reasons: First, touching the screen violates the idea of a tactile clutch. Second, it added further complexity as users were forced to keep holding the finger at a particular position on the screen. Third, it caused occlusion of items in focus.

### Pan Boundaries

Special care must be taken for handling document boundaries, e.g., to prevent users from traveling into the void [30]. For Drag-Flick-based panning, this may be accomplished by stopping pan motions at the document boundaries (often accompanied by some sense of physicality, e.g., bouncing). For spatial input, we adjusted the boundaries to guarantee that users can align even the document corners to the zoom center (the middle of the screen) as illustrated in Figure 2c.

## GOALS AND SCOPE OF THE STUDY

For the reasons discussed above, the main focus of this work is on designing, conducting and evaluating a user study that systematically investigates and compares the two navigation techniques (touch, spatial) on state-of-the-art mobile displays. In particular, we pursued two major goals:

**G1** *Efficiency:* We aimed at comparing how fast users perform common navigation tasks with the techniques.

**G2** *User satisfaction:* We aimed at investigating how users relate to different usability aspects of the techniques.

### Factors of Influence

We considered the following major factors in our study:

*Navigation Technique* – Our primary attention was, of course, on the two navigation techniques (*touch*, *spatial*).

*Target Visibility* – Zoom and pan are used in diverse application contexts with a variety of intentions that have an influence on the visibility of target items. In our study, we considered *on-screen targets*, i.e., items that are (partially) visible on the display and *off-screen targets,* i.e., items that are not initially visible on the display, e.g., a distant node in a node-link diagram.

*Display Size* – The screen size is another key factor that can influence the cognitive performance of users [21] and thus the time required for completing navigation tasks [4, 12]. We focused on the two predominant classes of mobile display: *phones* and *tablets*. These do not only differ in screen size, but also in weight, device size, pixel resolution and density that may also affect the navigation performance.

*Gender* – Previous studies [5, 6] show that women and men differ in their cognitive strategies when performing navigation tasks. In order to compensate for such effects, it is vital to properly incorporate the gender into the study design.

### Scope of the Study

Sufficient ecological validity was very important to us. While we believe to have taken into account the most essential factors, there are further variables that may additionally affect the navigation performance. Examples for this are: sitting/standing/walking usage, public/private usage (e.g., shyness and social habits), touch vs. haptic clutches, the mapping from physical to virtual space, and the use of

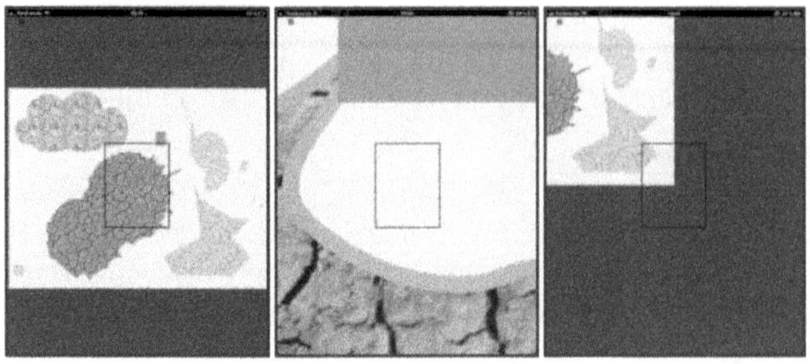

(a) Entire scene (b) Maximum zoom (c) Pan boundaries

**Figure 2: The abstract scenario used in the user study (screenshots taken from iPad prototype).**

more complex scenarios that involve frequent mode switches (e.g., navigation vs. annotation mode). For practical reasons, we limited our investigations to a user standing in the middle of a free space in an office-like lab (private environment) performing simple navigation-only tasks on a mobile display with a touch-based clutch. We decided to focus on technologically affine users of both genders with advanced multi-touch experiences. This decision was motivated twofold. First, we wanted our baseline (touch) to score very well. Second, we expect that sooner or later the majority of people will acquire similar skills as mobile displays become more widespread.

## METHOD

### Participants

Forty unpaid students of different departments at the local university participated in the study. Genders were evenly distributed (20 male, 20 female). The average age was 23 years (M = 23.48, SD = 2.27) ranging from 19 to 33 years. All participants (normal eyesight, no colorblindness) were daily users of smart phones or tablets and thus considered themselves as experienced with such devices. This implies that they were confident in performing Pinch-Drag-Flick-based navigation, which we verified in a pre-test.

### Study Design

We designed a controlled lab experiment with four independent variables. Our main focus was on the *navigation technique* (touch, spatial), which was the primary independent variable. *Display size* (phone, tablet), *target visibility* (on-screen, off-screen), and *gender* (female, male) were the secondary independent variables. We conducted the user study as a mixed-model design. For *display size* and *gender*, we used an in-between subjects design, i.e., participants were either assigned to work with a phone or a tablet (by balancing out the gender). For *navigation technique* and *target visibility*, we chose a within-subjects design (repeated measures), i.e., each participant performed both techniques exactly once (counter-balanced) using the same task sequence. We used the same task sequence for all users.

### Apparatus & Implementation

The experiment was conducted in a quiet lab environment (see Figure 3c). We used popular devices that users were familiar with: iPhone 4 (640×960 pixels @ 51×74mm$^2$) and

(a) Tolerance zone (b) Task succeeded (c) During the study

**Figure 3: Screenshots of the prototype (a, b) as a participant is performing the navigation tasks (c).**

iPad 3 (1536×2048 pixels @ 148×198mm$^2$). This ensured the touch technique to be a strong baseline condition, as these devices provide a high standard of Pinch-Drag-Flick navigation out of the box.

*Spatial Tracking:* We opted for an optical tracking based on 12 infrared (IR) cameras (Optitrack FLEX:V100R2). This provided precise spatial device positions and orientations at 100Hz with an error of less than 1mm within the tracking volume. Its projected area on the floor was about 3×3m$^2$. A designated server (running Tracking Tools 2.2) streamed the spatial raw data over a local Wi-Fi network in a standardized form (VRPN). This included time stamps, device IDs, and 4×4 transformation matrices describing the spatial position and orientation in six degrees of freedom (6DoF).

*Marker Design:* We glued 6 IR-reflective stickers to the iPad's display bezel (see Figure 1a). Only 3 of them needed to be visible at a given time, enabling users to hold it freely in their hands without accidentally interrupting the tracking. Due to the smaller device size, this was not practicable on the iPhone. Here, we built a small, lightweight plastic frame (± 8cm×8cm×3cm$^3$, 30g) with 4 IR-reflective balls that we plugged into the iPhone's headphone output (see Figure 1b). This guaranteed a robust tracking and ensured enough flexibility for operating the phone with one or both hands.

*App Development:* We implemented the prototype in Objective C using iOS 6.0 (XCode 4.5). We integrated the touch and spatial technique within a single universal app that runs on both devices. A major problem was the limited RAM of the devices – a problem others [2] faced, too. We solved this by combining several strategies: A zoom pyramid consisting of three layers containing different resolution of the scene, with the most detailed one being built up of tiles that are loaded on demand.

### Scenario and Task Design

In order to minimize side effects caused by prior knowledge of data, we used an abstract 2D scene for both conditions (touch, spatial). The scene provided visual context to avoid disorientation (Desert Fog) [14]. For this purpose, the scene background featured a thin grid and several distinctively colored and textured shapes (see Figure 2a). The scene had a fixed resolution of 4734 × 3683 pixels (approx. 46×36cm$^2$

in physical space). We used a maximum zoom factor of 5 (see Figure 2b), which translates to approx. $230\times178cm^2$.

In the scene, participants completed a pre-defined sequence of 128 navigation tasks using one of the two devices held in portrait mode. They had to match a red rectangular search target with a black reference frame in the middle of the screen ($4\times5cm^2$, see Figure 2). Only one target was visible at a time. If a search target came close to the reference frame, it automatically snapped in and the task was done (Figure 3a illustrates the snapping tolerance). Then, the rectangle turned green and a progress bar was shown (see Figure 3b). After 2 seconds, the next target appeared in the scene. The use of red search targets above a green-bluish background was motivated by the feature integration theory [26], as it reduces the cognitive load (pop-out effect).

### Composition of the Task Sequence

To test the user performances depending on the navigation intent (pan/zoom/combined × target visibility), we designed a single sequence of 128 navigation tasks. We wanted this sequence to contain a well-balanced combination of pure and mixed pan/zoom tasks with both on- and off-screen targets. To achieve this, we defined a set of basic composition rules (see Figure 4). We chose *5 zoom factors* (0.5x 0.7x, 1.43x, 2.0x, and no zoom) that we joined with *12 pan directions* (2 × each of the 4 major display sides + 1 × each of the 4 diagonals). To address *target visibility*, we placed the navigation targets either within (on-screen) or outside the display (off-screen). At the beginning of a task, on-screen targets appeared fully visible on the tablet, yet only partially on the phone (due to its smaller screen estate). We used these rules in a script that produced a sequence of 120 navigation tasks (2 *target visibilities* × 5 *zoom factors* × 12 *pan direction)* in a random order. The script also created small randomized local positional offsets. As all tasks of the sequence involved panning, we added 8 extra zoom-only tasks, i.e., 2 × (0.5x, 0.7x, 1.43x, 2.0x). Hence, we obtained a total number of **128 navigation tasks**.

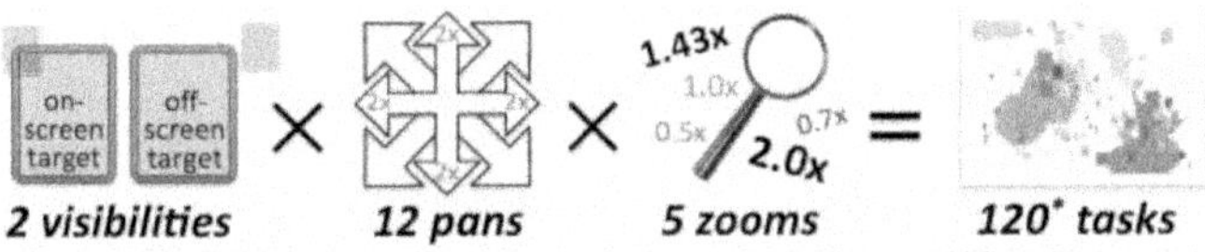


*There were 8 additional zoom-only tasks, i.e., user performed **128 tasks** in total.

**Figure 4: Basic composition rules for the task sequence**

### Procedure

Participants completed the study within 50 to 70 minutes. Before conducting the experiment, we had collected basic demographic information about potential participants via an online form. This included the personal experience with touch screens to sort out applicants with insufficient multi-touch skills. We grouped suitable candidates so that exactly half of the women and men worked with an iPhone or iPad.

*(1) Introduction Part*

After briefly verifying the personal data of the participant, we explained the goals and procedure of the study by reading out aloud from a sheet of paper. This also included the specific request to complete the tasks as quickly as possible.

*(2) Main Part*

The main part of the study consisted of three phases that were executed in two runs, once for the touch condition and once for the spatial condition (in counter-balanced order).

*Trial Phase:* Depending on the group, the participant either started with the touch or spatial technique that we explained and demonstrated using the iPhone or iPad prototype. This also included a brief explanation of the underlying interaction metaphor, e.g., the possibility of clutching (in addition to the standard press-and-hold activation). We then invited the participant to perform a few exercise trials using an example dataset, until he or she felt confident with the technique. In most cases, this took no longer than 5min, even for the spatial condition.

*Interaction Phase:* In both conditions, participants were asked to walk to the center of the interaction space, marked with a cross on the floor. We enforced a standing usage. Participants were free to move within an area of $2\times2m^2$.

*Assessment Phase:* After completing the tasks, we asked the participant to sit down and to fill out a questionnaire. We then conducted a brief interview, where we encouraged the participant to provide additional feedback in form of free comments. Before commencing with the second condition, participants were allowed to remain seated and to rest as long as they wanted (this did not take longer than 7min).

## RESULTS

In this section, we present the results of the study, including a detailed analysis of performance and self-report data.

### Statistical Methodology

We analysed the data using *three-way repeated measurement ANOVAs*. For all ANOVAs, the in-between factors were *display size* (phone, tablet) and *gender* (male, female).

The repeated-measures factor depended on the analyzed data type. We either used the *navigation technique* (spatial, touch), the *target visibility* (on-screen, off-screen), or their *combination* (spatial on-screen, spatial off-screen, touch on-screen, touch off-screen). All $p$-values were Greenhouse-Geisser corrected. The alpha level for tests of statistical significance was set to $\alpha = .05$. When effects were significant, we reported Bonferroni adjusted $p$-values for post hoc comparisons ($t$-test, two-tailed). For descriptive data, we provided mean values (M) and standard deviations (SD).

### Collected Performance Data

For spatial input, the collected raw performance data consists of the spatial position and orientation (6DOF) of the devices over time with a sampling rate of 30 Hz as well as the start/end time of each clutch-cycle. For touch input, we logged relevant events provided by the iOS-framework, e.g., the gesture type, on-screen positions, and start/end times. We also recorded the start and end time of each task.

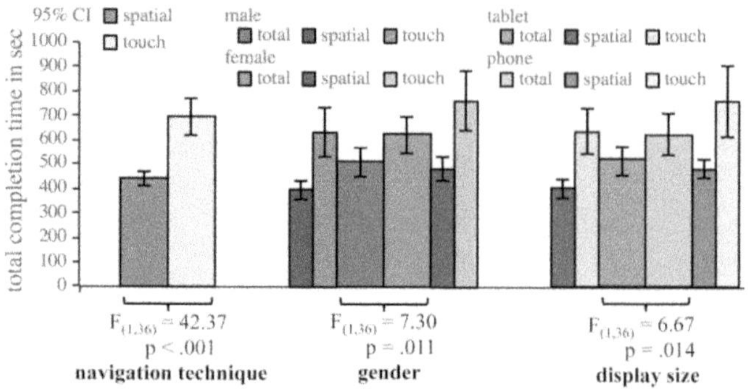


**Figure 5: Total completion times broken down by navigation technique, gender, and display size. Error bars denote standard deviations (95% CI).**

## Completion Times

We used the times that participants spent on completing the tasks as a *measure of performance*. We considered two variants: The *total completion time* is the overall time that participants needed to finish all 128 navigation tasks with either the touch or the spatial condition. In contrast, the *task completion time* is the average time that participants spent on finding on-screen and off-screen targets, respectively. All times are in seconds.

### *Total Completion Times*

The key results concerning total completion times are summarized in Figure 5. We found a main effect of the *navigation technique*, i.e., participants completed the tasks significantly faster with the spatial condition (M = 445.55, SD = 94.96) than with the touch condition (M = 701.15, SD = 259.38). There was also a main effect of the *display size*, i.e., participants worked significantly faster with the tablet (M = 522.46, SD = 121.06) than with the phone (M = 626.93, SD = 168.22), independent of the navigation technique. Beyond that, we found a main effect of *gender*, i.e., males (M = 517.28, SD = 128.90) were significantly faster than female participants (M = 626.62, SD = 158.72).

### *Task Completion Times*

Our analysis confirmed a main effect of *target visibility* (see Figure 6, left). Post-hoc comparisons show that participants reached on-screen targets significantly faster (see Figure 6, middle) with the spatial (M = 2.04, SD = .42) than with the touch condition (M = 3.38, SD = 1.36). The same applies to off-screen targets (see Figure 6, right), where a direct comparison shows that the spatial technique (M = 5.25, SD = 1.25) is faster than touch (M = 8.16, SD = 3.09).

The analysis revealed an interaction effect between *target visibility* and *display size* ($F_{(3,109)} = 4.21$, p = .038). While the display size had only little influence on the completion time for on-screen targets (see Figure 6, middle), participants reached off-screen targets significantly faster with the tablet than with the phone (see Figure 6, right). The relative performance gain on the tablet was only marginally higher for touch (22.67%) than for spatial input (18.77%).

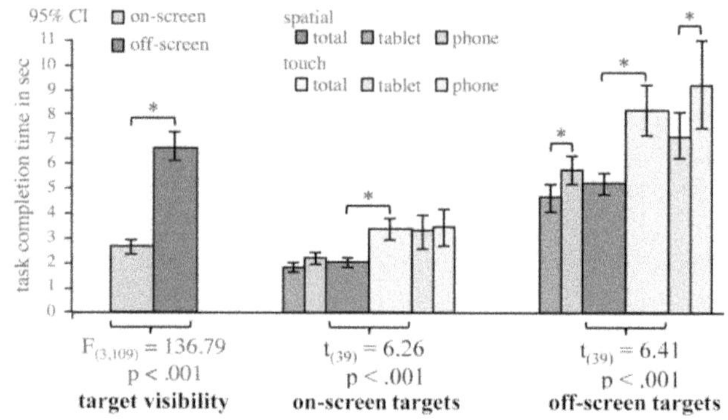


**Figure 6: Average task completion times (gender-neutral). Error bars denote standard deviations (95% CI).**

We found a main effect of *gender* ($F_{(1,36)} = 7.45$, p = .01) and *display size* ($F_{(1,36)} = 7.27$, p = .011). This means that independent of the *target visibility*, males were faster than females and tasks were completed in less time on the tablet than on the phone.

## Number of Discrete Actions

We investigated how many discrete actions were initiated for on-screen and off-screen target tasks. We did this by counting the number of clutches (spatial condition) and individual touch gestures (touch condition). We used these numbers as a *measure of handicap*. The rationale behind this is that starting a new action interrupts the navigation and thus negatively affects the overall performance. For example, executing three drag gestures in a row requires the user to lift the finger from the screen two times more if compared to just performing a single continuous drag. The same applies to the spatial condition, where releasing the clutch, e.g., to move the display to a more conformable position, briefly pauses the actual navigation.

### *Number of Clutches (Spatial Condition)*

We found a main effect of *target visibility* (Figure 8, left). Significantly fewer couplings were performed for on-screen (M = 1.18, SD = .36) than for off-screen targets (M = 2.26, SD = 1.41). There was no effect of *display size* or *gender*.

### *Number of Touch Gestures (Touch Condition)*

There was a main effect of *target visibility* (see Figure 8, right), i.e., on-screen targets were reached with significantly less touch gestures (M = 3.93, SD = 1.09) than off-screen targets (M = 10.2, SD = 3.89). We also found an interaction effect between *target visibility* and *display size* ($F_{(1,36)}$ = 17.00, p < .001). For on-screen targets, the number of touch gestures did not vary much between devices. For off-screen targets, in contrast, participants spent four gestures more on the phone (M = 12.01, SD = 4.15) than on the tablet (M = 8.47, SD = 2.74) on average.

## Utilized Motor Space (Spatial Condition Only)

The motor space of the spatial technique, i.e., the physical room surrounding the user, is considerably larger than a touch screen. We were interested in how much of the motor space was actually utilized by participants during the spatial condition and whether there were differences between on-

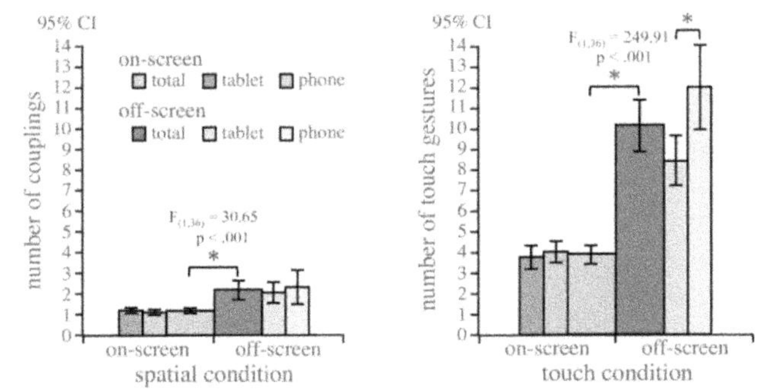


**Figure 8: Number of discrete actions (gender neutral). Error bars denote standard deviations (95% CI).**

screen and off-screen target tasks. For this purpose, we extracted the 3D bounding box of the physical space that participants used while solving the tasks (i.e., with activated clutch). This was done for each of the 120 tasks (i.e., except zoom-only tasks). We then computed an average bounding box for on-screen and off-screen targets, respectively. We analysed both bounding boxes in terms of the maximum extent along each of the three principle axes (X, Y, Z). We can show that the amount of used motor space significantly depends on the target visibility (see Table 1).

| Axis | On-screen targets | | Off-screen targets | | $F_{(1,36)}$ | p |
|---|---|---|---|---|---|---|
| | M in mm | SD | M in mm | SD | | |
| X | 57.78 | 43.81 | 237.17 | 102.70 | 116.66 | < .001 |
| Y | 49.95 | 16.06 | 176.61 | 65.17 | 121.61 | < .001 |
| Z | 78.00 | 35.75 | 298.69 | 69.15 | 290.41 | < .001 |

**Table 1: Size of the utilized motor space for the spatial condition. Mean values (M) and standard deviation (SD) are provided for the physical extent along the main axes.**

### User Feedback & Observations

*Usability Ratings:* We compiled a questionnaire with 36 items using a 7-point Likert scale ranging from 1 ("strongly disagree") to 7 ("strongly agree"). These items addressed generic usability aspects [22] as well as specific issues regarding the tested techniques, in particular the perceived influence of zooming and horizontal/vertical panning on the overall performance. To ensure a high degree of validity, we used 3 to 6 items per usability issue (reverse-worded). Both techniques were generally assessed very positively without significant differences, except for *ease of use*, *efficiency to use*, *user experience*, and *zooming* that were rated in favor of the spatial condition (see Figure 7).

*Free Comments:* Participants gave us very positive feedback about the spatial technique. Some (N = 5) were even a little surprised that completing the 128 tasks with the touch technique *"felt somehow more difficult than with the other one [spatial]"*. One user said that she *"could almost 'see' the map behind and beside the iPad, making it easier to decide where to move the device to next"*.

*Fatigue:* All participants completed the tasks without a break. After each condition, participants were asked to choose from a list, which part(s) of their body felt tired.

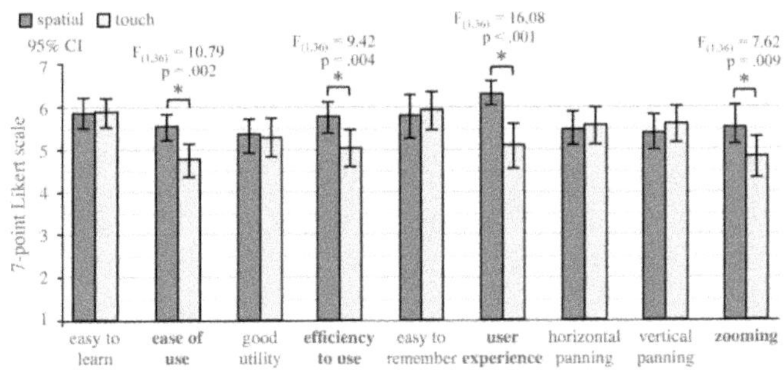


**Figure 7: Usability ratings from the questionnaires. Error bars denote standard deviations (95% CI).**

Table 2 summarizes the results that reflect the frequency of fatigue among participants, but not its intensity. Both techniques caused fatigue in the shoulders and the upper arms. The touch technique was more demanding for the fingers, the neck and the forearm, whereas spatial input affected the back and the upper arm more frequently. To our surprise, 10 participants did not experience fatigue for spatial input, yet there were only 4 for the touch condition.

| | Spatial | Touch |
|---|---|---|
| None | 10 | 4 |
| Shoulders | 10 | 10 |
| Back | 6 | 4 |
| Forearms | 3 | 9 |
| Upper arms | 7 | 6 |
| Fingers | 4 | 12 |
| Wrists | 2 | 9 |
| Neck | 5 | 13 |
| Elbows | 1 | 3 |

**Table 2: Occurrences of fatigue as reported by users**

## DISCUSSION

Not a single participant completed the 128 navigation tasks faster with the touch than with the spatial condition, even though all of them were multi-touch-experienced and used the spatial technique for the first time. When performing the tasks, several (N = 7) participants already expressed that they liked the spatial technique, even though we had not asked for that yet. While we had predicted a decent performance for the spatial approach, it *outperformed Pinch-Drag-Flick by 36.5%* (M ≈ 445s vs. M ≈ 701s) on overall average – a finding that we had not expected in such clarity.

*Influence of Display Size*

Independent of the technique, participants benefited most from a larger display for off-screen targets (see Figure 6, right). There are two reasons for that. First, search tasks typically start by zooming out for overview. This phase is usually shorter on devices with a larger screen, because search targets appear earlier on the display. Second, users see more information on a larger display allowing them to come to navigation decisions earlier, e.g., see [9]. We observed that most participants used the phone with one hand, while the tablet was usually taken into both hands.

*Influence of Gender*

On average, males completed the tasks 17% faster than females, independent of the navigation technique, target visibility, and display size. Hence, the spatial technique is not suitable for compensating gender effects.

*Use of Clutching for Repositioning the Device*

By design, all participants had to use the clutch in order to activate spatial input. Hence, the minimum number of clutches per task was one. Apart from that, clutching could also be used to move the device to a more convenient position, e.g., closer to the body. In the data, a clutch number larger than one reflects this. For on-screen targets, participants rarely used the clutch for this purpose (M = 1.18). For off-screen targets, however, where the size of the motor space was utilized much more, we counted one or two extra clutches for most participants (M = 2.26). Only the minority of participants (N = 8) did not make use of the technique. Instead, they stretched out their arms farther or did an extra footstep forward. When asked why, common reasons included convenience issues, avoidance of slowing down, or being oblivious of the possibility.

*Learning Speed & Other Groups of the Population*

All participants learnt how to use the spatial technique very quickly. The majority (N = 31) needed less than 5 minutes for that. Supported by the steep learning curve of the young, healthy and technological-affine users, we expect our findings can be transferred to other groups of the population. One example for this are elderly people or persons having difficulties in precisely controlling their fingers, e.g., due to age-related motor impairment, Gout, or Osteoarthritis. We believe that these groups may particularly benefit from the different motor skills that are relevant for spatial input.

**Explaining the Effects**

Based on our observations and data analysis, we identified two key factors that we believe are the main reasons for why the spatial navigation technique performed so well.

*Motor Space*

One key benefit of the spatial navigation technique is the size of its motor space. If we consider the space between hip and chest as the preferable interaction zone, then this space is more than one order of magnitude larger than the average mobile touch screen. This is an important advantage in terms of physical resolution and accuracy. By performing only one continuous gesture, it allows users to cover very long distances within the document – by maintaining a high level of precision at the same time. For touch gestures, travel/zoom distances are considerably smaller per gesture [16], thus forcing users to perform multiple gestures to achieve the same result.

We found clear evidence supporting these claims. Users performed many touch gestures for both on-screen ($M \approx 4$) and off-screen target tasks ($M \approx 10$). In contrast, clutching was used only marginally in the spatial condition ($M < 2.3$). Here, participants clearly benefited from the larger motor space that they used more extensively for off-screen targets if compared to on-screen targets (see Table 1).

*Motor Skills*

Both navigation techniques target different parts of the human muscle system and thus demand different motor skills. The Pinch-Drag-Flick approach primarily addresses fine motor skills of the fingers, usually involving a high physical pointing accuracy within a small (screen) area. In our study, we repeatedly witnessed participants having difficulties with the pinch gesture. As a consequence, many participants found it easier to lift a display up/down for zooming, which is reflected by the user ratings for zooming, as depicted in Figure 7. Apart from that, touch input also requires a high visual attention, e.g., due to little tactile/haptic feedback. In contrast, spatial navigation explicitly supports proprioception, i.e., the sense of relative positions of neighboring body parts. We believe that such kinesthetic cues can reduce the demand of visual attention. As hinted in [7, 28], such cues can also enable users to associate important regions in the document with specific physical positions around their body, making it easier for them to quickly travel within the document. Another important benefit of spatial navigation is simultaneous zooming & panning, which is naturally supported by moving a display diagonally through the space-scale diagram [10, 19]. Participants made use of this very frequently in the study.

**Limitations**

As standard deviations of completion times indicate, most participants were similarly fast with the spatial technique, but showed diverse performance times for Pinch-Drag-Flick – even though they had prior experiences with the latter technique. One possible reason for this might be that participants were motivated more to succeed in the spatial technique, because it was new to them. Yet, we believe the high performance variations for touch can also be attributed to issues with the touch condition: First, displays were prone to get soiled by a thin film of sweat and grease after working on them for some time. As this affected the touch recognition, we carefully cleaned the displays each time before a participant started to work with them. Second, while holding the device, the (ball of the) thumb of participants occasionally came in contact with the display, thus accidentally interfering with the detection of other touch gestures. Third, we witnessed a few female participants (N = 4) who had problems, caused by their fingernails. Although the nails were not unusually long, these women struggled with a less reliable touch recognition. Many participants reported that they had experienced similar problems before, e.g., when working with their personal phone. Hence, we conclude that these issues do not weaken our findings, but rather reflect the condition of the world outside the lab.

**Suggestions on Improving Spatial Navigation**

In retrospect, the use of a dynamic spatial mapping based on local device orientations has proven to be a good choice. However, our observations indicate that there is room for improvement. In interviews, several participants (N = 5) asked for a finer mapping, allowing them to move the device less by still covering the same virtual distance in the document. We propose to provide a user setting for this, though it may be worth investigating suitable thresholds that might depend, for example, on the display size. To further improve on that, some participants proposed to adjust the travel speed within the document depending on how fast they were moving the device in physical space.

## FUTURE GENERATIONS OF MOBILE DISPLAYS

Current mobile displays are lacking a few technical qualities that hinder a broader success of spatial-based navigation in the mass market. We identified two areas that future generations of mobile devices should address:

### Device-Intrinsic Spatial Tracking

One major technical challenge is the support of reliable 6DoF spatial tracking for real mobile usage, where requirements different from those in the lab apply: First, the workspace is not stationary anymore. Therefore, external sensors are unavailable and light conditions are likely to vary considerably. Second, spatial tracking should be relative to users, so they can walk without affecting the interaction (body-centric tracking). Third, the algorithm should be energy efficient to ensure long working times.

Prior to conducting the study, we experimented with alternative sensing approaches that use the built-in sensors of mobile displays, e.g., gyroscopes [15]. Accelerometers are energy efficient and offer low-latency feedback, though cannot detect positional changes of the user (e.g., when walking) and also are prone to induce error drifting. Alternatively, Hansen et al. [10] suggested the tracking of facial landmarks by the front camera for zooming, thus facilitating body-centric tracking. However, this limits the interaction to 3DoF and does not work when the user's face is not within the camera's field of view. To overcome these shortcomings, sensor fusion [13] combines gyroscopic data with face tracking. Yet, this approach still suffers from potential inaccuracies and technical pitfalls, so we found a proper implementation to be too time-consuming. It is also questionable, whether this or similar approaches are already advanced enough in terms of fidelity, spatial range and energy consumption. Nonetheless, we believe that integrating such capabilities into future generations of mobile displays is the one major technical challenge that needs to be solved before spatial interaction becomes more widespread.

### A Built-in Tactile Clutch

In our prototype, we used touch input for the de/activation of spatial input, which was primarily due to the lack of alternatives. While this worked generally well in our study (e.g., due to its limited scope), we do not consider touch-based clutches as our preferred solution. There are several reasons for that. First, touching the screen with a finger occludes parts of the viewport. Second, mixing on-screen touch input with spatial input is contrary to the philosophy of hybrid input paradigms, where different input channels should work independently from each other. Third, the clutch must be easily detectable preferably by non-visual cues so users can keep their visual attention on the document. Fourth, users should be provided with eyes-free feedback regarding the current state of a clutch. This is to provide precise control on when and how long the clutch is activated. These requirements may appear trivial, but their influence on the user performance and satisfaction should not be underestimated, e.g., see [11]. This is also supported by our observations and interviews with participants.

Hence, we propose to equip future generations of mobile devices with a clutch that provides some form of tactile feedback. This may be a simple physical button, though it should be larger than the tiny volume controls usually found on mobile phones. Ideally, the clutch would be readily usable independent of the current orientation of the display, for example, by squeezing the display bezel [3].

## CONCLUSION AND FUTURE WORK

In this paper, we presented a comprehensive user study that systematically compares the efficiency and user satisfaction of two contrarian input strategies for 2D document navigation on mobile displays: the predominant touch-based Pinch-Drag-Flick approach with a spatial-input-based approach that utilizes positional changes of a mobile display in the physical space surrounding a user. The results surpassed our expectations in various ways. On average, participants were more than 35% faster with the spatial approach, even though all of them were conversant with Pinch-Drag-Flick and used the spatial technique for the first time. This finding was further supported by the questionnaires, where participants rated the spatial approach at least as good as or even better than the touch-based counterpart. To the best of our knowledge, we are the first who provide such clear evidence in favor of spatial input. This was only possible by building high quality prototypes that make use of state-of-the-art mobile devices. Considering the popularity of Pinch-Drag-Flick, our findings could be of interest for future interaction designs of mobile devices – as a complimentary method of interaction, yet not as a complete replacement. Because there are also limitations: social protocols may limit its application, users may perform differently when sitting, and users may prefer to put a display on a desk for certain tasks. However, given the additional advantages of a supplemental input channel, we hope that our findings will help mobile computing embrace spatial interaction principles much more than before.

For future work, we plan to address the technical challenges and design recommendations that we discussed in the previous section, in particular device-intrinsic spatial tracking via sensor fusion and tactile clutches. With this technology, we will then continue our investigations by testing how in-the-wild usage (e.g., when walking) affects performances as well as the accuracy and recall [20]. Beyond that, we intend on studying compound tasks [19] that involve additional tasks, such as selection or annotations, and thus may particularly benefit from combining touch with spatial input.

## ACKNOWLEDGEMENTS

We would like to thank all the participants who generously shared their time for the study. We are also grateful to the anonymous reviewers for their valuable comments and suggestions to improve the quality of the paper.

## REFERENCES


1. Bier, E.A., Stone, M.C., Pier, K., Buxton, B., and DeRose, T.D. Toolglass and Magic Lenses: The See-Through Interface. In *Proc. SIGGRAPH 1993*, ACM (1993), 445–446.
2. Boring, S., Ledo, D., Chen, X., Marquardt, N., Tang, A., and Greenberg, S. The fat thumb: using the thumb's contact size for single-handed mobile interaction. In *Proc. MobileHCI 2012*, ACM (2012), 207–208.
3. Burstyn, J., Banerjee, A., and Vertegaal, R. FlexView: An evaluation of depth navigation on deformable mobile devices. In *Proc. TEI 2013*, ACM (2013), 193–200.
4. Chae, M. and Kim, J. Do size and structure matter to mobile users? An empirical study of the effects of screen size, information structure, and task complexity on user activities with standard web phones. *Behaviour and Information Technology 23*, 3 (2004), 165–181.
5. Cutmore, T., Hine, T., Maberly, K., Langford, N., and Hawgood, G. Cognitive and gender factors influencing navigation in a virtual environment. *Int. Journal of Human Computer Studies 53*, 2 (2000), 223–249.
6. Dabbs, J., Chang, E., Strong, R., and Milun, R. Spatial ability, navigation strategy, and geographic knowledge among men and women. *Evolution and Human Behavior 19*, 2 (1998), 89–98.
7. Fitzmaurice, G.W., Zhai, S., and Chignell, M. Virtual reality for palmtop computers. *ACM Trans. Inf. Syst. 11*, 3 (1993), 197–218.
8. Furnas, G.W. and Bederson, B.B. Space-Scale Diagrams: Understanding Multiscale Interfaces, In *Proc. CHI 1995*, ACM (1995), 234–241.
9. Gutwin, C. and Fedak, C. Interacting with big interfaces on small screens: a comparison of fisheye, zoom, and panning techniques. In *Proc. Graphics Interface 2004*, Canad. H.-C. Comm. Society (2004), 145–152.
10. Hansen, T.R., Eriksson, E., and Lykke-Olesen, A. Mixed interaction space - Expanding the interaction space with mobile devices. In *Proc. HCI 2006*. Springer London (2006), 365–380.
11. Jones, B., Sodhi, R., Forsyth, D., Bailey, B., and Maciocci, G. Around device interaction for multiscale navigation. In *Proc. MobileHCI 2012*. ACM (2012), 83–92.
12. Jones, M., Marsden, G., Mohd-Nasir, N., Boone, K., Buchanan, G. Improving web interaction on small displays. *Computer Networks 31*, 16 (1999), 1129–1137.
13. Joshi, N., Kar, A., and Cohen, M. Looking at you: fused gyro and face tracking for viewing large imagery on mobile devices. In *Proc. CHI*, ACM (2012), 2211–2220.
14. Jul, S. and Furnas, G.W. Critical zones in desert fog: aids to multiscale navigation. In *Proc. UIST 1998*, ACM (1998), 97–106.
15. Kaufmann, B. and Ahlström, D. Studying spatial memory and map navigation performance on projector phones with peephole interaction. In *Proc. CHI 2013*. ACM (2013), 3173-3176.
16. Malacria, S., Lecolinet, E., and Guiard, Y. Clutch-free panning and integrated pan-zoom control on touch-sensitive surfaces: the cyclostar approach. In *Proc. CHI 2010*, ACM (2010), 2615–2624.
17. Norman, D. The Design of Everyday Things. Basic Books, 2002.
18. Oh, J. and Hua, H. User Evaluations on Form Factors of Tangible Magic Lenses. In *Proc. ISMAR 2006*, ACM (2006), 23–32.
19. Pahud. M., Hinckley, K., Iqbal, S., Sellen, A., and Buxton, B. Toward compound navigation tasks on mobiles via spatial manipulation. In *Proc. Mobile HCI 2013*. ACM (2013), 113–122.
20. Rädle, R., Jetter, H.-C., Butscher, S., and Reiterer, H. The effect of egocentric body movements on users' navigation performance and spatial memory in zoomable user interfaces. In *Proc. ITS 2013*. ACM (2013), 23–32.
21. Reeves, B., Lang, A., Kim, E.Y., and Tatar, D. The effects of screen size and message content on attention and arousal. *Media Psychology 1*, 1 (1999), 49–67.
22. Rogers, Y., Sharp, H., and Preece, J. Interaction Design: Beyond Human-Computer Interaction. John Wiley & Sons, 1st edition, 2002.
23. Spelmezan, D., Appert, C., Chapuis, O., and Pietriga, E. Side Pressure for Bidirectional Navigation on Small Devices. In *Proc. MobileHCI*, ACM (2013), 113–122.
24. Spindler, M., Martsch, M., Dachselt, R. Going Beyond the Surface: Studying Multi-Layer Interaction Above the Tabletop. In *Proc. CHI*, ACM (2012), 1277–1286.
25. Spindler, M., Stellmach, S., and Dachselt, R. Advanced Magic Lens Interaction above the Tabletop. In *Proc. ITS 2009*, ACM (2009), 77–84.
26. Treisman, A., Gelade, G. A Feature Integration Theory of Attention. *Cogn. Psychology 12*, 1 (1980), 97–136.
27. Tsang, M., Fitzmaurice, G., Kurtenbach, G., Khan, A., and Buxton, B. Boom Chameleon: Simultaneous Capture of 3D Viewpoint, Voice and Gesture Annotations on a Spatially-aware Display. In *Proc. UIST 2002*, ACM (2002), 111–120.
28. Ullmer, B., Ishii, H., and Jacob, R. Token + constraint systems for tangible interaction with digital information. *ACM Trans. C. - H. Interaction 12*, 1 (2005), 81–118.
29. Wigdor, D., Forlines, C., Baudisch, P., Barnwell, J., and Shen, C. Lucid touch: a see-through mobile device. In *Proc. UIST* 2007, ACM (2007), 269–278.
30. Yee, K. Peephole Displays: Pen Interaction on Spatially Aware Handheld Computers. In *Proc. CHI 2003*, ACM (2003), 1–8.

# InkAnchor: Enhancing Informal Ink-Based Note Taking on Touchscreen Mobile Phones

**Yi Ren** [1] **Yang Li** [2] **Edward Lank** [1]

[1] Cheriton School of Computer Science
University of Waterloo
Waterloo, ON, Canada N2L 3G1
{y45ren, lank}@uwaterloo.ca

[2] Google Research
1600 Amphitheatre Parkway
Mountain View, CA 94043
yangli@acm.org

## ABSTRACT

Although touchscreen mobile phones are widely used for recording informal text notes (e.g., grocery lists, reminders and directions), the lack of efficient mechanisms for combining informal graphical content with text is a persistent challenge. In this paper, we present InkAnchor, a digital ink editor that allows users to easily create ink-based notes by finger drawing and writing on a mobile phone touchscreen. InkAnchor incorporates flexible anchoring, focus-plus-context input, content chunking, and lightweight editing mechanisms to support the capture of informal notes and annotations. We describe the design and evaluation of InkAnchor through a series of user studies, which revealed that the integrated support enabled by InkAnchor is a significant improvement over current mobile note taking applications on a range of mobile note-taking tasks.

### Author Keywords

Multi-touch; digital ink; note-taking; multi-scale sketching, drawing; mobile interaction.

### ACM Classification Keywords

H.5.2 [Use Interfaces]: Input devices and strategies, Interaction style. I.3.6 [Methodology and Techniques]: Interaction techniques.

## INTRODUCTION

It is common for people to capture small, but often critical, pieces of information in their daily lives, such as ideas, reminders or driving directions [6, 9, 18]. Although physical paper such as Post-Its remains a favorite medium for this kind of note taking, more and more people are using digital tools such as email or text editors [6]. We foresee the trend becoming even more pronounced with the rapid adoption of touchscreen mobile phones [2, 4], which are often more accessible than pen and paper.


*CHI 2014*, April 26 - May 01 2014, Toronto, ON, Canada

ACM 978-1-4503-2473-1/14/04...$15.00
http://dx.doi.org/10.1145/2556288.2557302.

**Figure 1: A store design director sketched on a photo to illustrate a light valance for a new restaurant.**

An important challenge with existing mobile note-taking tools is the lack of efficient methods for note entry [6, 18]. Many smartphone apps for informal note-taking (e.g. Evernote [11], Keep [14], ColorNote [8]) assume a text-only format for informal notes, and, while touch keypads and technologies such as handwriting and speech recognition have made steady progress, low-level interaction details like tapping on correct keys or verifying text input still distract users. In contrast, extensive work has shown that hand-drawn ink, without recognition, is often preferred for note taking, e.g., [16, 22, 23, 28]. Using ink allows arbitrary content, such as diagrams and symbols, and offers a close analogy to the paper-based approach. Because mobile notes are consumed mostly by the note takers themselves, the informal look of ink is often less of an issue [16]. As we interviewed end-users who drew and sketched on multi-touch phones, it became clear that the capture of informal ink-based notes was a common but poorly supported task on multi-touch smartphones. One of our participants, a site coordinator (civil engineer) who frequently sketched on his smartphone at construction sites, stated:

*I would rather draw with my fingers on the dusted windshield of my car than draw with [on] the phone. [P8]*

Figure 1 is an example of an ink-based annotation of a photograph shared with us by a commercial store designer who discussed his note-taking practices. While sharing this smartphone sketch, the store designer also said:

*To be honest, I don't really sketch on my phone anymore. I bought the Samsung Note 10.1 specifically to make my sketching easier and more accurate. [P17]*

Obviously purchasing a specialized device such as a phablet (a phone with 5- to 6.9-inch screen and an active stylus [21]) or a tablet that better supports sketching is one option for users who wish or need to sketch on electronic devices in mobile contexts. However, another option to resolve this problem, which we intend to explore, is to enhance the sketching experience sufficiently on small-screen smartphones so that people are not left with the need to purchase more specialized devices. Essentially, we seek to understand how best to design an effective, multi-touch sketching experience for mobile phones.

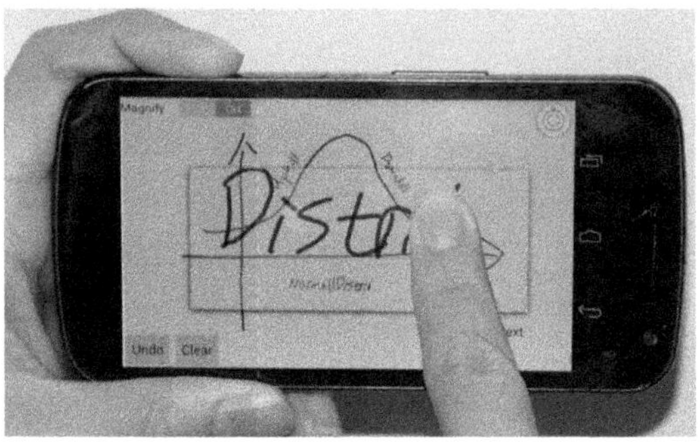

**Figure 2: InkAnchor allows users to easily create ink-based notes on a touchscreen mobile phone.**

Our discussions of sketching with our participants and our experience designing system variants for ink-based multi-touch sketching resulted in InkAnchor, an ink editor for creating finger-drawn ink-based notes on a touchscreen mobile phone (see Figure 2). InkAnchor addresses two major problems. The first issue is interaction space. In contrast to pens and tablets, which prior work focused on [1, 12, 28], the small form factor of mobile phones and the occlusion caused by finger-based touch input provide a limited effective space for interaction. Touch-based input also has low precision because of the large contact area of the finger on a touchscreen (the "fat finger" problem [5]). InkAnchor allows users to alter the scale and precision of strokes by supporting separate modes for screen-sized drawings and text-sized stroking. Second, many ink notes (e.g., Figure 1) incorporate a significant number of text strokes, which must be entered efficiently. InkAnchor supports word-grouping based on user-pauses to auto-advance and flow text, allowing the rapid entry and flexible editing of hand-drawn letters and words.

As the design of InkAnchor evolved from a series of exploratory user studies, it represents the culmination of feedback from a number of end-users. To assess the overall design of the application, we present the results of a first-use study (c.f. ButterflyNet [29]) to highlight the effectiveness of the individual features and of the overall system. Based on the results of this first-use study, we argue that the inter-related set of features in InkAnchor are important components of any multi-touch mobile phone drawing application.

The remainder of this paper is organized as follows. We first review related work in informal note-taking. Next, we present the results of a survey that we conducted to understand existing mobile note-taking practices. We then describe the design of the InkAnchor system, by first giving an overview of the system and then elaborating on the design process of each major feature of the tool. Finally, we present two evaluations of InkAnchor and discuss our findings of its benefits for informal note taking.

## RELATED WORK

There has been much previous work on note-taking practices [1, 6, 18, 23, 29]. In particular, recent studies [6, 18] investigated note-taking in informal situations, such as creating a reminder or capturing a phone number. The design of InkAnchor was built on prior work as well as our own investigation through an online survey.

A significant body of work in note-taking tools is focused on activities such as active reading [12, 15, 20] or classroom note taking [10, 15]. Lin et al. [18] argue that informal note taking is often more lightweight and spontaneous. In addition, much of the above past research has focused primarily on stylus-based ink editing on a larger surface, such as a tablet, rather than on multi-touch note taking.

Mobile phone applications (*apps*) that support some form of ink-based note taking for mobile phones exist. TreadMill Ink [24] addressed the limited writing space on touchscreen mobile phones by automatically scrolling a designated writing area, but requires the written ink to be recognized as characters to be added into a text editor. Recognition limits ink formatting to flowed ascii text and constrains what a user can write to what the recognizer supports. As a result, a mathematical expression or a simple sketched map cannot be entered. In addition, recognition errors can distract the user from taking notes. DIZI [1] and Note Taker [26] are focus+context note-taking apps. DIZI [1] allows a user to zoom into a specified region of a document and then write in the magnified window on a pen-based tablet device. Similarly, Note Taker [26] employs focus+context but adds more dedicated support for writing text and shifting the zoom focus. While focus+context is useful for drawing (see, e.g. Lank and Phan [17]), text entry benefits from high-level structuring of ink (chunks, lines, and blocks) to support formatting (e.g., wrapping) and editing (e.g., selection, insertion and deletion). Researchers have designed algorithms to automatically group ink strokes and infer layouts [20, 22, 23, 25], but these have rarely been incorporated into commercial smartphone apps due to the problem of recognition errors that accompany automatic reasoning in informal note-taking.

Past research has, however, informed the design of InkAnchor. We use horizontal projection of strokes in a chunk to determine the chunk's baseline and flow layout to manage the layout of ink groups. Both of these techniques have appeared in the research literature. Moran et al. [20] used horizontal projection on a large electronic whiteboard, albeit for a different use: to infer line grouping. aha! InkWriter [19], a tablet pc application, treats ink objects as text and uses flow layout to reflow ink. While both of the above systems provide inspiration for components of our system, they do not address the particular challenges of sketching on finger-based, touchscreen mobile phones.

Finally, a large body of work has focused on integrating virtual paper into computers so as to leverage the convenience of paper and the processing power of a computer [12, 19]. InkAnchor complements prior work, by focusing on everyday informal note-taking situations that use only multi-touch input.

## EXISTING PRACTICES OF MOBILE NOTE TAKING

The practice of informal note taking has been extensively studied [6, 18]. Building on prior knowledge, we conducted an online survey to refresh our understanding and capture any potential changes caused by the rapid evolution of the mobile user experience. The survey covered topics such as the situations in which users take informal notes, the type of content they capture, what tools they use, and the difficulties in note-taking practice. We sent the survey to a mailing list in an IT company that included software engineers and users in non-technical departments such as human resources and marketing. We received a response from 138 people (a 9% response rate).

Overall, we found results similar to those identified by a previous study [6]. Informal note taking is equally distributed between at-work and on-the-go situations. When people are on the go, they often have their mobile phones with them. Among the problems that our survey participants constantly cited was how cumbersome it was to enter notes, which is consistent with the findings of a previous study [6]. We also found that the primary use of notes was targeted for note creators themselves (e.g., as a reminder or temporary storage), implying that the informal look of ink strokes should not be a major concern.

Beyond our informal survey, many of the participants that we worked with over the course of our iterative design studies and during our first use evaluation of InkAnchor had used their smartphones to capture ink drawings. For these participants, the challenge of mixing large-scale strokes with more precise lines and with text strokes was particularly acute. Participants need to adjust zoom level to support text entry. In the rest of this section, we focus on the findings that heavily influenced our design of InkAnchor.

### *Text Is the Dominant Form of Informal Notes*

To support efficient note entry, we need to first understand what types of content were in our participants' notes. In our survey, 99% of the participants (137 out of 138) responded that their notes involved typed text, while only 43% of the participants used drawings (which could include text content as well). This finding confirmed the result from the previous study [6], in which 96% of the collected note samples contained text, while only 7% had drawings. This result informed us that our application should support the editing of text content but not exclude drawings.

### *Ink Input Requires Drawing at Multiple Scales*

In prior work, a typical approach for ink editing on touchscreen phones is to apply focus+context to a drawing canvas [17, 26]. In this approach, a specific area of the drawing canvas is zoomed large enough so that the users can comfortably write with a finger. At the same time, the surrounding ink on the canvas remains visible. The zoom focus, a rectangular region, has to be moved before the users can write in another area of the canvas. The strokes drawn with the finger are scaled down on the basis of zoom focus size relative to the entire screen.

These focus+context note-taking tools employed various ways for moving the zoom focus, e.g., by panning with two fingers [26] or switching to the panning mode [17]. Users could also dismiss the existing zoom focus and select another area of the canvas to zoom (e.g., [1]). In particular, Note Taker, a commercial iPhone application [26], employs a semi-automatic approach to shift the zoom focus by providing several hint areas on the screen for users to shift the zoom focus either horizontally (similar to a space) or vertically to the next line (similar to an enter). This design is specifically tailored for entering text in a horizontal, line-based layout. It does not support arbitrary orientations. As well, ink is unstructured, making editing challenging.

## CREATING INK-BASED NOTES WITH INKANCHOR

Based on our understanding of existing mobile note-taking practices, we created InkAnchor, a tool for mobile users to easily enter and edit an ink-based note on a finger touchscreen. We here give an overview of how a user would use this tool.

In InkAnchor, users can add multiple ink *blocks*, each at a different size, position, and orientation on the canvas (see Figure 3d). An ink block can have a single *line* or multiple lines, and each line may consist of a sequence of text strokes clustered into groups of characters, *chunks*, that nominally represent words. Semantically, an ink block can be a paragraph, a bulleted line, a chart legend, or any information fragment that is meaningful to the users, and a chunk is a primitive object that consists of a group of strokes that can be manipulated as a whole.

As we mentioned earlier, one challenge when writing on a mobile phone touchscreen is limited space for users to write as much as they want. For example, writing a single word such as "Renew" with a finger would use up the entire screen (see Figure 3c). To address this issue, we anchor raw, finger-drawn strokes into a scaled-down, well-arranged form. An anchor is shown when the editor is started (see

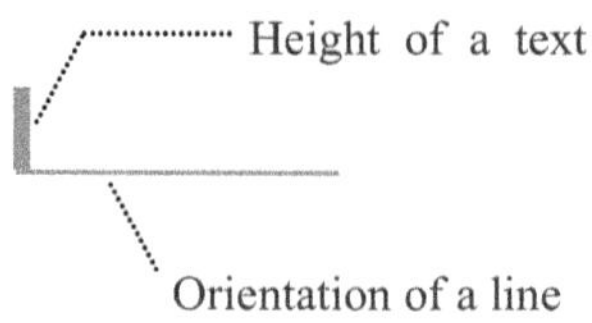


**Figure 3a: The anchor defines height, position, and orientation of the ink block.**

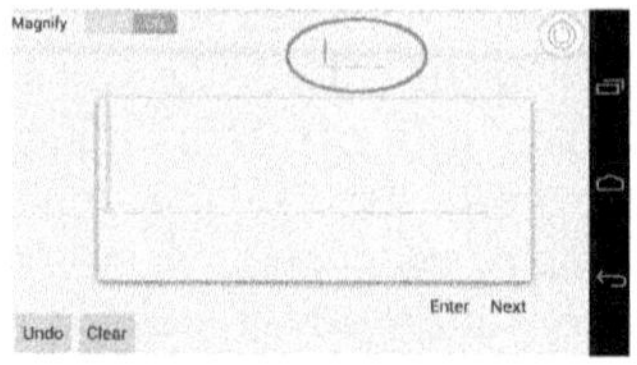

**Figure 3b: InkAnchor launches with the anchor (circled in the figure) and a rectangular magnifying lens.**

**Figure 3c: Users can write on the lens, and the ink is scaled down and shown on the background in real time.**

**Figure 3d: InkAnchor detects and avoids collisions of ink blocks.**

Figure 3a, 3b). Similar to the cursor in a text editor, which specifies where the next typed character will occur, the anchor indicates where the next ink strokes will be added.

The anchor also defines how the strokes will be geometrically transformed. Users can write anywhere on a virtual magnifying lens, and the strokes of their handwriting are transformed and organized into a line-based flow layout according to the anchor's size, position, and orientation (see Figure 3d). While the users write, the touch trace is displayed at the original scale and the transformed ink is shown on the background in real time (see Figure 3c).

Users will pause when they finish a semantic unit (e.g., a word) or they reach the edge of the touchscreen. After a timeout (650ms in our design), the anchor advances to the end of their current input, thus repositioning automatically to allow the user to continue writing. When the line reaches the boundary of the canvas or collides with another existing block, it automatically wraps and left-aligns with the start of the previous "line", leaving an interval between the two "lines". For example, the block "A new Insurance is needed" in Figure 3d automatically wrapped at the chunk "new" and "is", when it collided with the block "Renew the Insurance by Sept. 18". Consequently, users can keep writing without having to pay attention to how the strokes are organized.

Users can directly start a new ink block anywhere on the canvas by a long finger press at the target position on the touchscreen. Once the system detects a long press, a vibration feedback is given as a notification, and InkAnchor is in the adjustment stage. The anchor jumps to the finger's position, following the finger's movement until the users exit the adjustment stage by lifting their finger. In addition, since the user's finger can occlude the anchor, a big cross centered at the anchor is shown in the adjustment stage. The lines of the cross coincide with the short bar and the line of the anchor (see Figure 4). With the cross, users can easily see where the anchor is positioned before dropping it.

Users can also change the anchor's orientation in the adjustment stage (see Figure 4). While the users rotate the mobile phone, the anchor and the cross remain horizontal relative to the ground. After users exit the adjustment stage, the orientation of the anchor is fixed.

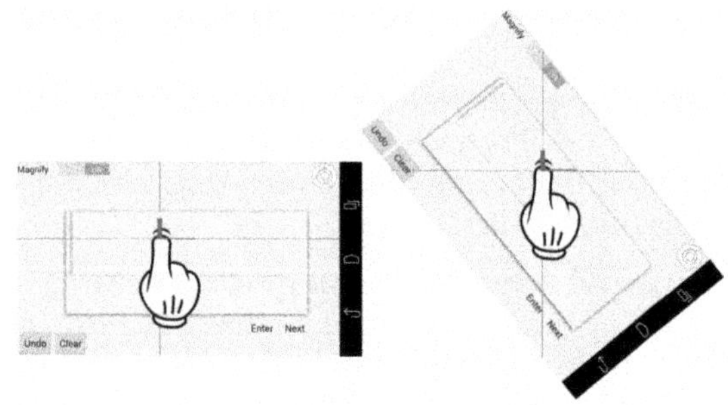

**Figure 4: Users reposition the anchor by holding. Users change the orientation by rotating the physical device. The red cross allows the users to adjust the cursor when the finger occludes the anchor.**

## DESIGNING AND TUNING INKANCHOR

Informed by our survey of note-taking practices, and specifically by the importance of text in ink note-taking, InkAnchor incorporates four features to support ink entry on touchscreens: focus+context views, text anchoring, free-form orientation, and auto-delimiting of text. There are many different ways that these features can be realized in an application, so we conducted a series of four design studies to refine the design of these features in InkAnchor.

Our design studies used thinkalouds to assess participants' perspectives on how well InkAnchor supported a set of simple tasks. The tasks in our design studies included asking the participants to write some basic text, to draw a simple node-link diagram, or to draw a graph and annotate the graph. We provided participants with exemplars of the tasks, but also allowed participants to specify their own content and to play with the InkAnchor interface. Finally, we walked through individual features being explored in the design study with each participant and collected their thoughts on how the features could be improved.

A total of seven participants participated in our design studies. Because our design studies incorporated an aspect of participatory design, we considered it important that participants be skilled users of touchscreens. As a result, our participants were all chosen from technical disciplines within our university community, and all were owners of touchscreen smartphones. While scheduling constraints did not permit all participants to participate in all design studies, at least four participants participated in each design study, and all participants participated in at least two design studies.

### Focus+Context

As we have discussed in Related Work, focus+context benefits note taking on small screen devices. However, sketches and text often require input at different scales, which implies that focus+context should be switched off when users want to sketch instead of entering text. While researchers have explored methods for automatically classifying ink strokes into text and drawings [25], automatic segmentation remains challenging, particularly for real-time situations in which there is often insufficient information for inference. Therefore, we decided to allow users to activate focus+context in InkAnchor manually.

As depicted in our screenshots, we incorporate a “Magnify” mode to support multi-scale drawing, which can be enabled or disabled by the user. While a mode switch seems somewhat inelegant, in our design studies, we observed that users would draw in a large scale, then spend significant time drawing text, then revert to large scale drawing briefly, then return to text for another block of time. Essentially, our mode-based approach mimics the behavior of our participants, where text entry was segmented in time from large-scale drawing.

To reduce mode errors, we experimented with various visualizations to highlight the fact that the system is in the anchor mode, including grayed background and flashing cursor. With no clear preference, we chose a glass lens in our design of InkAnchor (see Figure 3b, 3c).

### Text Anchoring

To facilitate text input, we developed text anchoring as a novel way of moving the zoom focus, where users' handwritten ink is scaled down automatically to a specific size at a specific position. We explored a variety of techniques for users to easily understand the effects of ink scaling. Perhaps the most important feature added through our design studies, to support accuracy of inking, was real-time scaling of ink content. The immediacy of the visual feedback allowed users to intuitively adjust size and position to produce a more accurate drawing.

Even with real-time scaling, screen occlusion and misjudgments of participants still caused problems accurately scaling ink. We experimented extensively with baseline detection techniques. Combining baseline analysis with the height of the anchor can determine both the scaling factor and the translation for the vertical alignment in a line (see Figure 5). However, two facts impair the worth of baseline detection. First, there is no perfect way to find the baseline of an English word without handwriting recognition. Second, since we take the real-time visual feedback of ink editing as an important part of our design, we need to decide the absolute position of the transformed ink as soon as the user starts writing. As a result, we are not able to wait for the users to finish writing an ink *chunk* to calculate the baseline or to dynamically scale. Some other feedback mechanism to allow users to adjust the scale is needed.

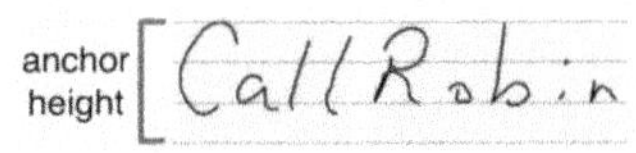


**Figure 5: InkAnchor fits a chunk into a three-row template.**

When children begin learning to write, they are asked to write on notebooks with guidelines that allow them to judge the size and the relative position of ascending and descending characters. We experimented with 3 different variants of these guidelines as shown in Figure 6. Participants in our study, however, disliked the 4-line guideline common in school notebooks. While either the anchor mapping (Figure 6a) or the two-line variant (Figure 6b) was acceptable, for simplicity we chose the anchor variant of Figure 6a as our final design.

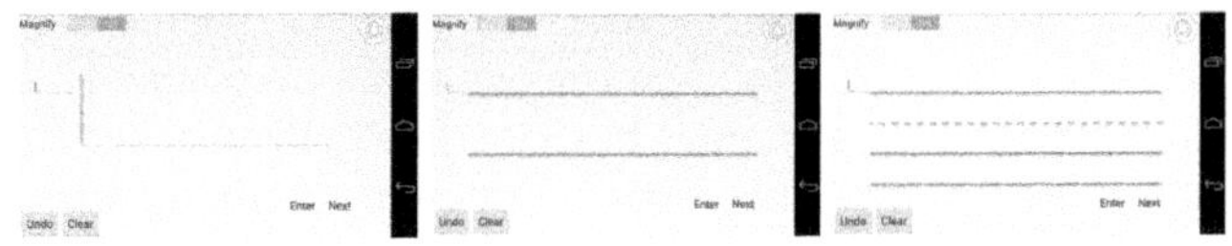

**Figure 6: (a) A larger anchor mapped to the anchor on the background; (b) 2-line guideline; (c) 4-line guideline.**

In our preliminary design, to change the size of the scaled-down strokes or the height of a line, users could adjust the anchor height via a long press on the anchor. However, we observed that our participants typically used a long press followed by a drag to adjust the anchor's position, rather than teleporting the anchor for repositioning as we expected.

Interestingly, in studying the re-sizing of ink, it became obvious to us that re-sizing was not a frequent operation. If the system provided a good default scaling for ink based on screen size and resolution, participants would leave this default unchanged. If they wished to create larger or smaller text, for example a title or a superscript, participants would simply adjust the size of their input strokes. This behavior seems analogous to what is observed when people draw on a whiteboard or a sheet of paper: There is an expected viewing distance for any given medium, and writing is frequently scaled to that expected viewing distance. Figure 6 depicts our default scaling for the hardware we used in our studies (Samsung Galaxy Nexus phones). This scaling was tuned via several initial sessions, and, once set, new participants saw no need to adjust the default scaling of ink.

As a result, we replaced ink resizing via long-press on the anchor by radio options (small, medium, large) in a settings menu. Long-press on the anchor would then allow participants to drag the anchor around the screen, and a long press at any other location on the screen would cause the anchor to teleport to that location.

### Auto-Delineation of Chunks

We provide two kinds of delimiters to chunk ink in InkAnchor. The first is an auto-delimiter, which chunks handwritten ink automatically after a certain period of time and advances the anchor for subsequent input, i.e. repositioning the anchor to the right edge of the ink chunk that was created via the timeout. We ran a user study in order to find an optimal timeout for the auto-delimiter. Participants were asked to accomplish several basic tasks with different timeouts (420ms, 650ms and 1000ms) and we selected 650ms as the timeout in our final design. Users can also manually advance the anchor and chunk ink by clicking the "Next" button or the "Enter" button at the bottom right of the magnifying lens. Specifically, the "Enter" button also functions like the "Enter" key on the keyboard, which advances the anchor to the start of the next line.

This timeout was the most controversial feature in our design. Participants in our design studies began by disliking the feature. As we could easily disable auto-advance, we experimented frequently with manual advance or with longer timeouts. However, in every case, as participants became more comfortable with the interface they would typically want the auto-advance/timeout re-enabled to support the entry of longer blocks of text. If, instead, we simply left it enabled at the beginning of the studies, participants seemed to quickly acclimatize to the timeout. As a result, auto-advance with timeouts is a useful feature as users become familiar with the tool, and our timeout worked well as participants became comfortable with the specific timeout setting.

### Free-Form Oriented Ink Layouts

Flexible layouting of ink content is essential for creating rich ink-based notes. We designed and experimented with methods for users to easily arrange their ink content via a touchscreen mobile device.

#### *Global and Inner-Block Ink Layouts*

Physical paper offers direct, easy content entry–we can write anywhere on paper with an arbitrary orientation and size. In contrast, all the text in a text editor is constrained to a horizontal flow layout, which offers an efficient way to maintain the layout of sequential text-based content while it is being edited, such as deleting a word from a sentence. One of the constraints of many ink-based note-taking apps is the assumption that a text editor's horizontal flow layout would work best in any situation. This assumes that notes are solely comprised of text. As we found in our survey, despite the prevalence of text, many users occasionally (or frequently) wish to combine text with drawings or use text to annotate other content such as photographic images.

To combine advantages of both physical paper and electronic text editing, we incorporate two distinct layout strategies at different levels of ink structuring (see Figure 3-d). For the global, inter-block layout, InkAnchor employs an absolute layout as a physical paper does. A block can appear anywhere on the canvas and at various orientations. For the local, inner-block layout, InkAnchor employs a flow layout, as in a text editor. Stroke chunks in a block are laid out sequentially and wrapped automatically when the block grows to the boundary of the canvas or runs into other blocks. We selected this design to mediate between the benefits of horizontal flow layout and the flexible positioning paper provides.

#### *Determining Anchor Orientation via Accelerations*

In contrast to the horizontal layout of a text editor, users frequently write text along an arbitrary orientation as on physical paper, such as while annotating the vertical axis of a graph in a mathematical document or labeling a road in a hand-drawn map (see Figures 2 and 7). As a result, InkAnchor must be able to detect the intended orientation of users so as to determine how ink strokes should be geometrically transformed.

There are two options for changing the orientation of ink on a smartphone. A user can either manipulate the anchor as a widget by rotating it, or a user can rotate the device to change the orientation of the ink. When asked how best to rotate the anchor, all of our participants wished to simply twist a single finger on the display. While it may be possible to monitor the shape of a finger on the display and detect when the finger is turning [27], variations in the size of participants' fingers, the contact force, and the fidelity of the multi-touch sensors on different smartphones all affect the ability to recognize single-touch finger rotations in a generic way. The alternative, multi-touch rotations (e.g. two-finger rotation), have the disadvantages of ergonomic failures [13], were not intuitive for our study participants, and were inefficient on small screen devices due to the limited size of the display (i.e. it is sometimes difficult to precisely rotate two fingers without contacting the boundary of the sensor).

As a result, we designed InkAnchor to capture the user's intended orientation by detecting the mobile phone's physical orientation. In other words, no matter how the phone is rotated, InkAnchor keeps the anchor's orientation horizontal relative to gravity using accelerometer data. Our approach for detecting screen orientation is similar to that used by existing mobile devices such as Android phones [3]. The basic idea is first to extract the acceleration caused by gravity from readings of the phone's 3D accelerometer using the 1€ Filter [7] and then to analyze the distribution of gravity along the device's three axes.

This technique works when the user is in a normal upright posture, such as sitting or standing. When gravity is distributed along only the z-axis, e.g., when the phone lies flat on a table, it is not feasible to determine the device's orientation by using acceleration alone. We tried to resolve this defect by combining the data from the geomagnetic field sensor. However, since the geomagnetic field sensor is not sufficiently accurate, we abandoned this idea and do not detect changes in orientation when the phone is resting on a horizontal surface. In testing the feature, we found that this constraint was acceptable. Participants adjusted quickly to the need to hold the phone in their hands to rotate. In fact, creating drawings with the phone flat on a horizontal surface was much more awkward than with the phone held in one hand and angled toward a participant's face.

We also found that orientations that are horizontal or vertical should be advantaged over arbitrary angles.

InkAnchor stabilizes anchor orientation by snapping to the horizontal and the vertical orientation when a user is within ten degrees (0.175 radians) of horizontal or vertical. Ten degrees worked well as a balance between stabilizing to horizontal and vertical while still permitting arbitrary orientations that were off-axis. As an alternative, a snap-and-go technique might work well for all orientations, but, in practice it seemed unnecessary as participants simply angled their input while drawing to support small deviations from horizontal or vertical.

## COMPARING WITH EXISTING TECHNIQUES

To test the efficiency of InkAnchor, we conducted a small scale user study contrasting InkAnchor (Anchor condition) with two existing techniques. The first technique was a focus+Context view found in Note Taker, Figure 7, where a small zoomed window is shown in the background and full screen input is scaled to that window (Zoom condition). The second technique was typing text on a soft keyboard on the multi-touch mobile phone (Type condition). The goal of our evaluation was not to prove that InkAnchor was faster, but instead to ensure that it was not significantly worse at basic text or text-plus-drawing note taking tasks.

We asked six participants to draw six different diagrams, specifically an email contact (name plus email address), a reminder, an address, a grocery shopping list with nine items, a simple graph of data with axes labels and three annotations, and a simple map of driving directions showing three streets with names. The first four diagrams were created using all three techniques. The remaining two, the graph and map task were only performed using the Zoom and Anchor, as they included drawing. For text notes, participants were told that they did not need to pay attention to capitalization or punctuation. They were also asked not to be influenced by the layout used in the instructions. However, for the chart and the map, we asked participants to enter them exactly as shown on the instruction sheet, in terms of the position and orientation of textual labels. Both the graph and map task required participants to switch between the writing and direct drawing modes. Technique was fully counterbalanced across participants; drawings were performed in the order listed above, essentially from simplest (shortest average time) to most complex (longest average time).

Based on this study, we found InkAnchor had similar overall time performance to both Focus+Context drawing and typing on the set of tasks in the experiment. However, we observe potential advantages of using InkAnchor for complex note taking tasks as shown by the chart and map tasks in Figure 8.

## A FIRST-USE EVALUATION OF INKANCHOR

The comparative study shows the overall performance of InkAnchor. However, as an integrated solution to note taking, we are more interested in how each of the features

**Figure 7: The zoom condition is based on a focus+context-based drawing canvas.**

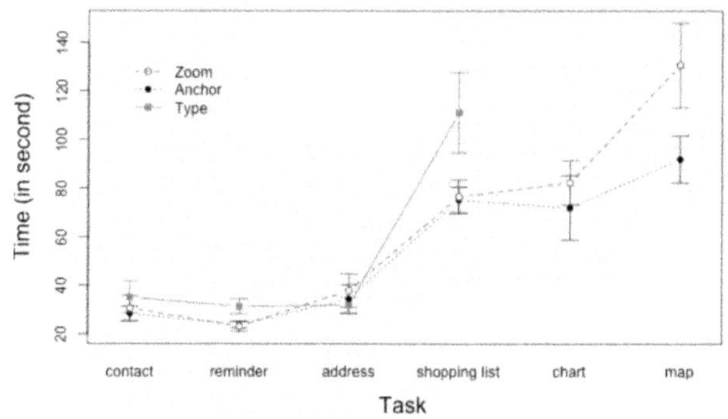


**Figure 8: The time performance of three different techniques on six note-taking tasks.**

in InkAnchor contributes to the application. As a result, we conducted a first-use study [29], focusing on prospective users' ability to perform a series of diagram entry tasks. We specifically screened for participants who had experience with multi-touch sketching, with a preference for multi-touch sketching on smartphones. Our goal was to first assess their past experiences with multi-touch sketching, to have them perform sketching tasks using InkAnchor, and to then evaluate the individual features of InkAnchor and the overall utility of the InkAnchor application.

Participants were recruited from within our university community, but included both students and professionals. The constraint that participants had some experience with multi-touch sketching seemed in the end to restrict our participant pool to more technical disciplines. However, we felt that the need for preconceived impressions of multi-touch sketching was particularly important for a first-use study of a novel sketching app.

Fifteen participants completed our study (thirteen male; two female). Nine of the participants had experience sketching on smartphones, three on multi-touch tablets, and one on both. The remaining two participants had extensive sketching experience, and responded to the call for participants because of an interest in multi-touch sketching. We chose to include them in our first-use evaluation because of their extensive background in sketching, albeit on tablets with an active stylus (e.g. Microsoft Surface, Samsung Galaxy Note).

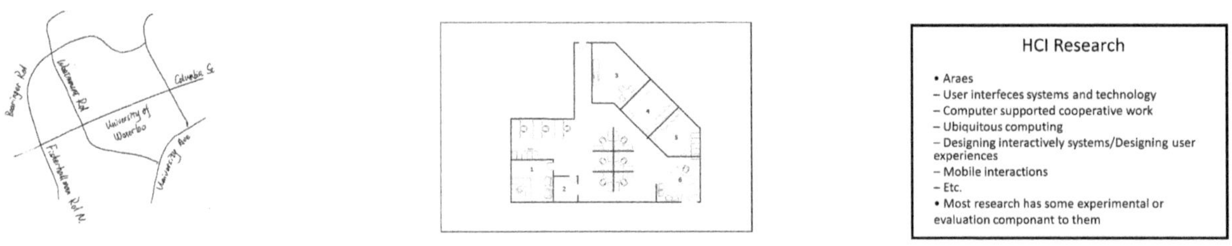


Figure 9: The experimental tasks.

Sessions lasted for one hour, and participants received a $10 gift certificate to a local café as a token of appreciation. Each session began with a semi-structured interview that explored participants' impressions of multi-touch sketching apps and the overall experience of sketching via multi-touch. We also discussed sketches participants had created using multi-touch, if available. Next, we provided a brief description of the InkAnchor program and asked participants to complete three tasks using InkAnchor (see Figure 9): a map drawing task, a labeling task, and an annotation task. Finally, an interview and questionnaire were used to assess overall impressions of InkAnchor's features.

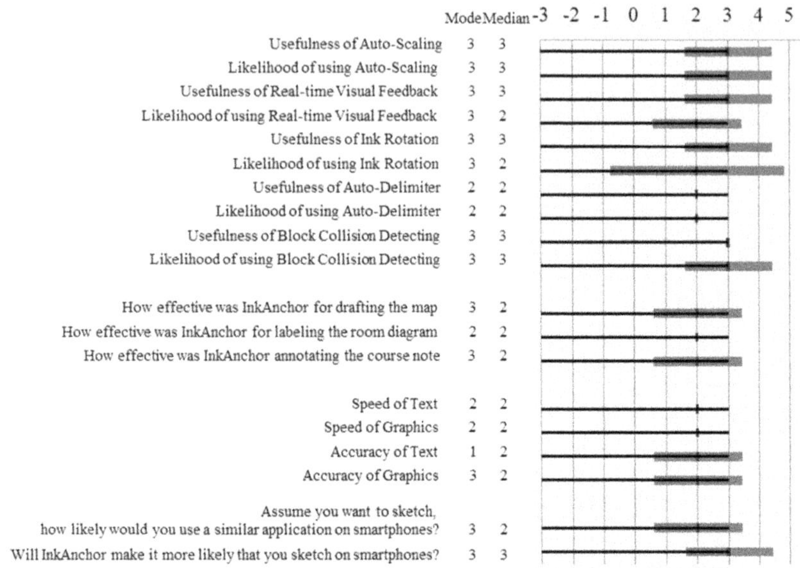


**Figure 10: Each question was graded on a -3 (not useful/highly unlikely) to +3 (extremely useful/extremely likely) scale. The bars show the 95% confidence interval of the median.**

## Experimental Tasks

### *Map Sketching*

The map sketching task mimics the creation of an informal ink note that contains both drawings and text. Sketching informal maps or diagrams was a common task among participants in our iterative design studies. Participants were asked to draw a simple sketch map of our locale with InkAnchor, as shown in Figure 9a. We included street names that were particularly long (e.g. "Anonymized") to determine participants reactions to words that required movement of the anchor to complete the word so we could gauge participants' perspective on entering longer words: Would they notice the need to only enter half of the word at a time before advancing the anchor? Would auto-advance cause any particular problems? Would they adjust their behavior by writing smaller? Would they short-circuit the timeout?

### *Room diagram labeling*

Our room labeling task mimics the photo annotation task shown in Figure 1. Participants were shown a room diagram with a list of room names. The background of InkAnchor was replaced by a picture of the room diagram and we asked participants to label each room with the corresponding name in a list (Figure 9b). Participants were asked to fit each word into the corresponding blank space, which is very limited in size.

### *Text Editing and Annotation*

Many of the participants mentioned that sketching would be useful as a tool to annotate other text content, for example during active reading, proof reading, or note taking in a course or classroom environment. As a result, we designed a simple annotation task, shown in Figure 9c, to simulate editing a text document or annotating other text content using InkAnchor. We gave participants a PowerPoint slide image with 3 typos to correct and 1 definition to annotate. We gave no specific directions on how to correct the typos or how to incorporate the definition into the slide.

## Experimental Results

In this section, we highlight several outcomes of the user study. We analyze InkAnchor's key features and examine participants' overall impressions of the system.

### *Evaluation of the Key Features*

InkAnchor combines four key features to support informal sketching: real-time feedback, auto-scaling, ink rotation, and auto-delimiter via timeout. While these features were derived from our iterative design studies, the purpose of this first-use study is to evaluate how participants, all of whom had some experience with multi-touch sketching, would

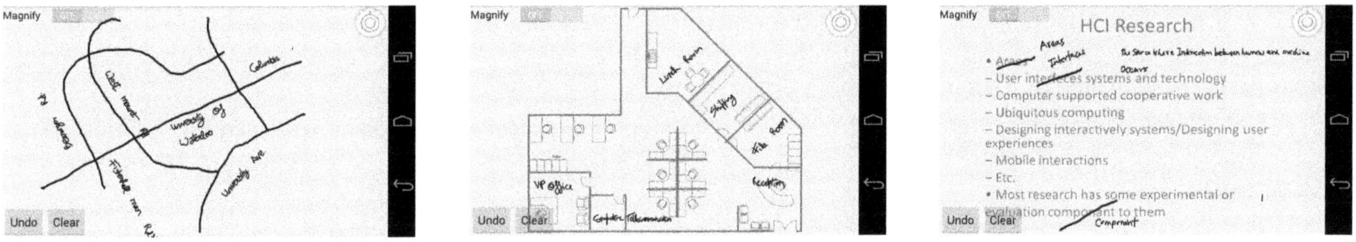


**Figure 11: Sketches drawn by three different participants in our study.**

react to each of these features, given that their use in combination is unique to InkAnchor.

Figure 10 summarizes the quantitative results from our questionnaire, and Figure 11 shows notes from one of the participants. Each question is graded on a -3 to +3 scale. We depict median values and 95% confidence intervals for the median. You may note that confidence intervals extend significantly beyond +3 in many cases. This is an artifact of extremely high median and mode values for InkAnchor's features. In particular, real-time visualization, auto-scaling, ink rotation and block collision/word wrapping were all considered highly useful, with median and mode values of +3 for usefulness. Even our timeout auto-delimiter had median and mode values of +2, indicating the value of the linked feature set in InkAnchor.

In our observation of participants, we noted that the behavior of ink rotation was the one feature that was not self-revealing for our participants. One participant used both a finger rotation and a device rotation when re-orienting ink, and noted:

*Yeah, I'm not quite sure what kind of tech you are using for rotation; maybe it's multi-touch, or the gravity, so I tried to use both of them to make it work. [P1]*

Participants pointed out that rotating a finger instead of the device would be more intuitive, similar to our early finding.

*Just the rotation, I'm not sure which direction I'm actually writing. I think if you can, instead of rotating the phone, maybe rotate your two fingers to address the text alignment. It may be better. [P2]*

With the exception of P1, other participants eventually realized that accelerometers were controlling rotation, and then had few problems with ink rotation in our system. Ink rotation worked particularly well when users were cradling the phone (as opposed to setting it on a desk). However, because it is more comfortable for users to draw while holding the phone, this did not seem to impede usability.

The other feature that caused some difficulty for our participants was the auto-delimiter timeout of 650ms. Despite our tuning efforts, participants universally complained about quick timeout early in their evaluation, and argued for a longer time-out.

*So the pause time is a bit is too short. When I'm writing "Fisher Hallman", the first words I wrote was "Fisher", and I'm considering how much space I need to write the "Hallman", but I automatically wrapped it up [the system auto-advanced]. [P2]*

However, participants adjusted to the time-out, and were able to comfortably enter longer strings of text efficiently by the time the experiment ended.

*Yeah, I like it. It's professional. If I want to move to the next word, it helps a lot. I think it's professional... But for me, I think it's ideal. The time is perfect. I like it. [P3]*

From our observations of participants habituating to the timeout, it might be useful to explore gradually tightening the timeout during first use, perhaps beginning with a timeout of approximately 1.5s and shortening it over the first ten or twelve timeouts down to our current 650ms. Tightening the timeout might allow participants to perform better initially, but it might also cause problems for participants as they need to continue to adjust to an ever-shorter timeout during initial use. Given the speed with which participants adapted to the current timeout, it is questionable whether a looser initial timeout is necessary.

Beyond individual features, we also explored the utility of InkAnchor for the experimental tasks of map drawing, labeling, and annotation. Figure 11 depicts output from one of our participants. Our participants rated InkAnchor very high for each of the representative tasks: Median and mode scores were either 2 or 3, and 95% confidence intervals were all positive. We also asked participants about the perceived speed and accuracy of InkAnchor for text and graphics, with equally positive feedback.

### *Overall Assessment of InkAnchor*

Initially, most of the participants had a negative feeling about sketching on touchscreen phones. Our civil engineer participant quoted in the introduction was not alone in his desire to avoid multi-touch sketching. Other participants from P4, a graduate student in computer science, to P2, a graduate student in engineering, all expressed similar sentiments:

*I think, hmm, I think a mouse gives more control to a certain extent, I'm pretty good at mouse. I'm not quite used to this, you know, drawing with your finger things. [P4]*

*On a smartphone, sometimes I feel like my fingers are blocking my vision, so I can't really see what I'm drawing on the graph, as my finger blocks most of the things on the screen. ... [P2]*

However, at the end of the study, participants held positive attitudes towards sketching with InkAnchor. Thirteen of our sixteen participants expressed a desire or a strong desire to use the app, and one of our participants requested a download link for the app from the Android Market.

## CONCLUSION

We present the design of InkAnchor, a multi-touch tool for informal note-taking for mobile phones. InkAnchor offers a unique combination of a set of features, including text anchoring, focus+context input, free-form layouts and auto-delineation of ink groups. We derived the design of InkAnchor through an iterative design process that involved testing and revising each aspect of InkAnchor repeatedly with a group of user participants. InkAnchor provides the integrated support to allow flexible entry of rich ink-based notes that consist of larger drawings and detailed text annotations. We evaluated InkAnchor via two user studies and reported the initial user response to InkAnchor.

## ACKNOWLEDGEMENTS

We thank the participants in our studies. Funding for this research was provided by Google Research, the Natural Science and Engineering Research Council of Canada (NSERC), and by NCE-GRAND.

## REFERENCES

1. Agrawala, M. and Shilman, M. DIZI: A Digital Ink Zooming Interface for Document Annotation. In *INTERACT'05*. 69–79.
2. Android. http://www.android.com/.
3. Android. SensorEvent. http://developer.android.com/reference/android/hardware/SensorEvent.html.
4. Apple. iPhone. http://www.apple.com/iphone/.
5. Baudisch, P., and Christian, H. My new PC is a mobile phone. XRDS: Crossroads, The ACM Magazine for Students 16.4 (2010), 36-41.
6. Bernstein, M., Van Kleek, M., Karger, D., and Schraefel, M.C. Information scraps: How and why information eludes our personal information management tools. In *Journal TOIS (2008)*, 24:1–24:46.
7. Casiez, G., Roussel, N., and Vogel, D. 1€ Filter: A Simple Speed-based Low-pass Filter for Noisy Input in Interactive Systems. In *CHI'12*, 2527–2530.
8. ColorNote. https://play.google.com/store/apps/details?id=com.socialnmobile.dictapps.notepad.color.note
9. Dai, L., Sears, A., and Goldman, R. Shifting the focus from accuracy to recallability: A study of informal note-taking on mobile information technologies. In *TOCHI 2009*. 16, 1 (2009), 4:1–4:46.
10. Davis, R.C., Landay, J.A., Chen, V., et al. NotePals: lightweight note sharing by the group, for the group. In *CHI'99*, 338–345.
11. Evernote. http://www.evernote.com/.
12. Hinckley, K., Zhao, S., Sarin, R., et al. In Situ Search for Active Note Taking. 2008. http://patentscope.wipo.int/search/en/WO2008124658.
13. Hoggan, E., Williamson, J., Oulasvirta, A., Nacenta, M., Kristensson, P.O., and Lehtiö, A. Multi-touch rotation gestures: performance and ergonomics. In *CHI'13*, 3047–3050.
14. Keep. https://play.google.com/store/apps/details?id=com.google.android.keep
15. Kam, M., Wang, J., Iles, A., et al. Livenotes: a system for cooperative and augmented note-taking in lectures. In *CHI'05*, 531–540.
16. Kienzle, W. and Hinckley, K. Writing handwritten messages on a small touchscreen. In *MobileHCI'13*, ACM (2013), 179–182.
17. Lank, E. and Phan, S. Focus+Context sketching on a pocket PC. In *CHI '04*, 1275–1278.
18. Lin, M., Lutters, W.G., and Kim, T.S. Understanding the micronote lifecycle: improving mobile support for informal note taking. In *CHI'04*, 687–694.
19. Microsoft, aha! InkWriter Handbook. 1993: Mountain View, CA.
20. Moran, T.P., Chiu, P., van Melle, W., and Kurtenbach, G. Implicit structure for pen-based systems within a freeform interaction paradigm. In *CHI*'95, 487–494.
21. Newman, Jared, Phablets Are a Niche, Not a Fad, Time, April 02, 2013.
22. Pedersen, E.R., McCall, K., Moran, T.P., and Halasz, F.G. Tivoli: an electronic whiteboard for informal workgroup meetings. In *INTERACT'93*, 391–398.
23. Saund, E., Fleet, D., Larner, D., and Mahoney, J. Perceptually-supported image editing of text and graphics. In *UIST'03*, pp. 183–192.
24. Seni, G. Treadmill ink - enabling continuous pen input on small devices. In *IWFHR'02*, 215–220
25. Shilman, M Discerning Structure from Freeform Sketches. In *EECS 2003*, 60–65 vol.1.
26. SoftwareGarden. Note Taker. http://itunes.apple.com/us/app/notetaker/ id342284707?mt=8.
27. Wang, F., et al. Detecting and leveraging finger orientation for interaction with direct-touch surfaces. In *UIST*'09, 23-32.
28. Wilcox, L.D., Schilit, B.N., and Sawhney, N. Dynomite: a dynamically organized ink and audio notebook. In *CHI*'97, 186–193.
29. Yeh, R., Liao, C., Klemmer, S., et al. ButterflyNet: a mobile capture and access system for field biology research. In *CHI*'06, 571–580.

# Perception of Ultrasonic Haptic Feedback on the Hand: Localisation and Apparent Motion

**Graham Wilson[1], Tom Carter[2], Sriram Subramanian[2] & Stephen Brewster[1]**

[1]Glasgow Interactive Systems Group
School of Computing Science
University of Glasgow, UK
{first.last}@glasgow.ac.uk

[2]Department of Computer Science
University of Bristol, UK
{t.carter, sriram.subramanian}@bristol.ac.uk

## ABSTRACT
Ultrasonic haptic feedback is a promising means of providing tactile sensations in mid-air without encumbering the user with an actuator. However, controlled and rigorous HCI research is needed to understand the basic characteristics of perception of this new feedback medium, and so how best to utilise ultrasonic haptics in an interface. This paper describes two experiments conducted into two fundamental aspects of ultrasonic haptic perception: 1) localisation of a static point and 2) the perception of motion. Understanding these would provide insight into 1) the spatial resolution of an ultrasonic interface and 2) what forms of feedback give the most convincing illusion of movement. Results show an average localisation error of 8.5mm, with higher error along the longitudinal axis. Convincing sensations of motion were produced when travelling longer distances, using longer stimulus durations and stimulating multiple points along the trajectory. Guidelines for feedback design are given.

### Author Keywords
Ultrasound; haptic feedback; perception; localisation.

### ACM Classification Keywords
H.5.2. User Interface – Haptic IO.

## INTRODUCTION
Ultrasonic haptic feedback involves the creation of focused air pressure waves from an array of ultrasound transducers. These are reflected off the skin to create tactile sensations without being in direct contact with an actuator [15, 22, 25]. It is potentially useful for gestural interfaces, such as those that utilise body position [27], hand movements [10] or finger gestures [7, 17] for input, as these interfaces suffer from a lack of tactile feedback [7, 8, 10, 17]. The technique is relatively new compared to other forms of tactile feedback, such as vibration motors or pin-arrays. Consequently, there has been less controlled and rigorous research into the perception of ultrasonic haptic feedback, which is vital if it is to be used in HCI. We help to address this by identifying the factors that influence the perception of two fundamental aspects of tactile feedback: localisation and motion across the hand. Research on ultrasonic haptics has tested the detection or differentiation of one [13, 22] or multiple points of feedback [1, 2], the two-point visual-tactile threshold [28] and presented interaction prototypes with limited user studies [9, 11]. Research is needed on what spatial or temporal parameters influence localisation and perception of motion. This paper presents two lab experiments. The first tested localisation of static feedback on the hand to determine spatial resolution for ultrasonic haptics. The second tested the perception of motion across two axes on the hand, to identify which characteristics of feedback (distance, duration, number of stimulated positions and movement direction) elicit convincing sensations of motion.

A limitation of existing ultrasonic haptic devices is that they are relatively large and fixed in place, so feedback can only be presented from one global location and in one orientation (directly facing the array). This limits the usable interaction space for gestural interfaces that could otherwise track users throughout open space and in a variety of orientations. Smaller arrays could be embedded in a range of devices, such as mobile phones/tablets, laptops, desktop phones or kiosks. They could also be carried by a user, who would be freed from the restrictive space above a static array. A wearable ultrasound array mounted on the wrist, facing the palm, would give feedback regardless of hand position or orientation. This could be especially useful in gestural interfaces as the hands and fingers are free to move, form gestures or hold objects, and feedback can be generated dynamically and aimed precisely on the hands.

While there are many advantages, there would be challenges in designing such a wearable device. Firstly, the device would need to be small, reducing the number of transducers that can be used to produce feedback. This will result in lower feedback intensity and limit the system to produce only a single point of stimulation at a time. Secondly, in some previous research on perception of ultrasound feedback, the users have been free to move their hands over the array to actively investigate the feedback [11, 13]. A wrist-mounted array could provide feedback to specific points but the hand would be static relative to this feedback. Therefore, perception of feedback may be reduced.

To examine the efficacy of a small mobile or embedded array for feedback, our experiments utilised an 8 x 8 array


*CHI 2014*, April 26–May 1, 2014, Toronto, Ontario, Canada.

ACM 978-1-4503-2473-1/14/04...$15.00.
http://dx.doi.org/10.1145/2556288.2557033

of transducers held in place a small distance from the hand. The paper begins by discussing the research related to ultrasonic haptic feedback and the perception of localisation and motion using physical stimuli. The two experiments are then described and the results are discussed in relation to guidelines for use in HCI.

## BACKGROUND RESEARCH

Ultrasonic haptic feedback is based on the principle of acoustic radiation pressure, where a phased array of ultrasonic transducers creates a beam focused at a point in 3D space. The narrow focus of the beam is determined by the wavelength of the ultrasound (e.g., 8.6mm at 40kHz) and the ultrasound is modulated with a lower frequency, such as 200Hz, so as to be perceivable by mechanoreceptors in the skin [16]. When a focal point is reflected off the skin, the force produced creates a localised tactile sensation akin to "air", "breeze" or "wind" [13, 22]. Focal points can be produced at high spatial resolution and moved rapidly in the space above the array. The applications of this novel form of haptic feedback in HCI have been steadily increasing. It has the advantage of providing tactile feedback in mid-air, without the user holding a device or having one attached.

Traditionally, ultrasound arrays are placed on a flat surface such as a desk [15, 25], or suspended above a surface on a mount [9, 14], at a set orientation facing one direction. Feedback can be used to generate objects or surfaces that the user can feel and investigate by moving his/her hand through the space. Ultrasonic haptics has been investigated as a means of transmitting handwriting [12] and, in conjunction with projection, touchable virtual objects [14]. Hoshi [11] combined a Kinect sensor with two arrays, facing out towards the user and placed either side of a display to produce a touchable gestural interaction surface in mid-air. Alternative configurations include attaching an array to the back of a mobile device to provide media-relevant feedback for TV [1] and using acoustically transparent displays to provide feedback above interactive surfaces [2].

Researchers have begun to study the perception of ultrasonic haptics. During a controlled study, Yoshino *et al.* [28] presented a visible dot and a focal point to the hand of the user. They estimated the two-point visual-tactile threshold (VTT: minimum distance required for perceptual co-location) as ~10mm, by asking if the two stimuli were in the same location. From informal experiments, Hoshi [13] suggested that users could accurately identify the direction of longitudinal movement of a focal point on the hand, could orient the hand to the location of a focal point and judge the pattern of focal point movement. Alexander *et al.* [1] found that users could identify the number of present focal points (between 0 and 4) with 87.3% accuracy during active investigation. Hasegawa *et al.* [9] tested identification of four discrete stimulation patterns presented to a static hand and found accuracy of ~55-90%. Carter *et al.* [2] presented users with two focal points and examined the effects of physical distance and modulation frequency on the perceptual distinction of the two points. Two points of the same frequency only became reliably distinct at 5cm separation, while using different frequencies decreased the distance to 3cm, although performance improved over time.

There are important limitations to consider. There has been little systematic research on identifying the underlying characteristics that influence the perception of, for example, location or movement of ultrasound feedback. Some initial informal testing has been done on the perception of one-dimensional movement and position of focal points [13][28] or the number of present focal points [1]. Yoshino *et al.* [28] only estimated the VTT as they did not measure where the focal point was perceived to be, nor how far away it was from the visible dot. Therefore, their results do not inform on the accuracy of absolute localisation. Carter *et al.* [2] identified the influences of physical separation and modulation frequency on the perception of focal points. Nothing is known about what influences the perception of direction, movement or position of feedback and so research is needed to understand the components of perception to enable the design of effective and useable tactile sensations for the user interface.

### Tactile Perception on the Hand

As we are interested in testing the perception of location and motion of ultrasonic feedback across the hand, it is necessary to understand how the hand perceives tactile signals and what features of physical stimulation influence localisation and motion perception. Pacinian corpuscles (PC), the rapidly adapting mechanoreceptors that are sensitive to vibration and ultrasonic haptic stimulation [22], are most densely populated in the fingertips and less dense in the fingers and palm [16]. Due to the lower force of the small ultrasound array, the more superficial, rapidly adapting mechanoreceptor (RA I; Meissner) may also be stimulated. These have greater population density than PC at the fingertip and are more densely populated in the fingers than the palm [16]. The density of mechanoreceptors is likely responsible for higher tactile acuity, measured by the two-point threshold, in the fingertips followed by the fingers and the palm [16]. Therefore, perception of feedback may differ between the fingers and the palm, which is highly relevant for the design of effective ultrasound feedback.

Research on the localisation of a single point of stimulation on the fingers has found that participants only reached 50-60% accuracy in identifying the specific point of stimulation [23], even after several days of training. This study stimulated one of 42 points on the fingers using a Von Frey hair (0.1g force), with 3 points equally spaced horizontally along each phalanx. Of the incorrect localisations (mislocalisations), 19.5% were localised within the same phalanx, 16.9% were within the same finger but 63.6% were mislocalised to another finger entirely (mostly an adjacent digit). Therefore, stimulation may be difficult to localise even within the same finger. Research looking at localisation on the palm found that participants regularly mislocalised points towards the thumb and the wrist (i.e., they often felt closer to the thumb or wrist than they were), possibly due to "anchoring" landmarks in an ambiguous space [3].

### Apparent Motion

Research has shown that stimulating a small number of physically distal positions on the skin can produce the illusory sensation of motion between those points (called "apparent motion" (AM)). The most famous example is that of the "cutaneous rabbit" [5], where 5 'taps' from a stimulator at each of 3 positions spaced 10cm apart on the forearm felt like taps equally spaced along the whole forearm. Therefore, it is possible that sensations of motion could be created using individual ultrasonic focal points that are activated in specific patterns. Kirman [18, 19] looked at the quality of AM across the fingers using two 0.63mm bronze rods. He was interested in isolating the stimulation characteristics that result in "good movement", defined as "impressive and continuous movement from one stimulating point to the other". The characteristics included distance (between the points of stimulation), the duration each point was presented for and the interstimulus onset interval (ISOI): the time between the first and second point being presented. Within the range of 5 to 50mm, physical separation of the two stimuli had no effect on good movement and neither did the location of stimulation (finger vs. forearm) [18].

Overall, the quality of movement improved as stimulus point duration increased from 1 to 200ms, with particularly good movement coming from only 100ms and 200ms durations [18]. However, point duration and ISOI interact in the production of good movement. The optimal ISOI (for good movement) increases as the stimulus duration increases and the range of ISOI that can produce good movement also increases. Therefore, as longer stimuli are used, a wider range of activation timings can produce the illusion of movement. For example, for 100ms stimuli, ISOI of 70-110ms are suitable and, for 200ms stimuli, ISOI of 110-200ms are suitable. Kirman [19] also found that increasing the number of stimulating points from two to eight greatly increased the quality of movement, particularly for durations of 100ms.

In summary, 1) shorter stimulus durations lead to poor movement, 2) sequential stimuli of greater than 50ms should produce good movement and 3) increasing the number of stimulating points improves movement, so it appears that it is the number of stimulated points that is more influential than the space between them. Although ultrasound arrays are capable of "continuous" motion, due to high spatial resolution, we would argue that continuous movement is a perceptual factor and not a technical one, as AM studies show that continuous movement/stimulation along the skin is not necessary. This is important for the design of ultrasound feedback, as a single focal point is sufficient for creating convincing motion. Also, AM is desirable due to the reduced computation and power requirements, particularly for a wearable device scenario. Pre-computing fewer focal points and refreshing the output at a slower speed mean the system can be built with cheaper, smaller, less power-consuming hardware. Identifying the minimum activity that produces continuous sensation helps to build the most efficient system. Using AM also makes it easier to move very quickly across larger distances.

## USE CASE: GESTURAL INTERFACES

Providing tactile feedback in vision-based gestural interfaces is a challenge, as the user may not be wearing or touching anything. The use of external cameras leaves the user unencumbered by sensors but limited in interaction space due to the field of view of the camera. Cameras worn on the body result in a less practical and more complex setup but provide an interaction space on the move. Actuators worn on the body may be limited to locations physically separated from the point of interaction, such as actuators on the arm [20]. Instrumented gloves can provide richer tactile feedback but may be limited in the number of available actuators, can be complex and costly to setup [4] and may get in the way of the hands. Like ultrasonic haptics, AIREAL [24] can provide tactile feedback in mid-air using air vortices without user instrumentation. Feedback could be directed quickly and accurately within 1m distance to an 8.5cm diameter target. This is precise enough to target a whole hand, but finer details are not possible with this device. Ultrasonic haptic feedback can produce focal points only ~1cm wide, allowing for much finer details as well as the creation of two-dimensional shapes/patterns. They could also be made small enough to be worn on the body.

A wrist-mounted array could provide feedback directly across the whole hand, targeted to specific parts depending on the interaction and gesture performed. Projected displays on the hand [8] could be made physical by stimulating both the projected hand and the pointing finger. The spatial boundaries and content of "imaginary interfaces" [7] in mid-air could be provided to aid in precise gesture orienting and pointing. And, because the device is worn on the person, interaction can occur anywhere in space. A benefit of placing a gestural interaction device on the wrist is that it leaves the hands free to perform input movements. Digits [17] can create gestural interfaces anywhere and at any orientation. The input method moves with the hands and, by adding a wrist-mounted ultrasound array, tactile feedback could also move with them. There are potential issues with the use of a wrist-mounted array, however. Having an attached device could affect fatigue and interfere in interactions with objects or devices. Array size/weight could be minimised by using smaller, more efficient components. The array would be positioned ~10cm from the palm, so objects can still be held and the fingers are free to gesture.

Due to the lack of controlled perceptual research into ultrasonic haptics and the challenges in producing feedback from a small array, the focus of the research in this paper was to use a small array to establish the perceptual characteristics of two fundamental features of tactile feedback: the localisation of a point of feedback and the perception of movement. The results can be generalised to form the foundation for studies on large arrays, as well as starting to test the feasibility of a wrist-mounted array.

## ULTRAHAPTICS SYSTEM

Our Ultrahaptics system is a scaled down version of Carter *et al.*'s [2]. It features an 8 x 8 array of muRata MA40S4S ultrasound transducers, which have a diameter of 10mm. The array was driven by a single Ultrahaptics driver board with two XMOS L1-128 processors providing synchronised output. To create a focal point, each transducer is driven with a specific phase delay and amplitude. These values are computed with the waveform algorithm described in [2]. Even with a small array, achieving a run time fast enough for real time applications requires the computing power of a high-end desktop PC. This does not align with the prospect of a wearable system. We therefore pre-computed the phase delays and amplitudes for a large set of focal points, which were then stored in a lookup table on the driver board. A lightweight UART protocol was then used to communicate with the system and move it into a pre-defined state.

Due to the nature of phased array focusing, focal points closer to the centre of the array will exert a greater force. For our array, a focal point produced 20mm to the right of the centre, 100mm above the array, was 91.5% the force of one produced 100mm above the centre. A focal point offset from the centre by 20mm along both X- and Y-axes was 83.7% the force. During our evaluations, no focal point was produced closer to the edge of the array.

**Figure 1: 8 x 8 ultrasound array (left). Experimental setup (right) with participant hand in position under the array.**

## EXPERIMENTAL SETUP

This paper describes two experiments carried out to test 1) the localisation of ultrasonic haptic feedback and 2) the perception of movement across the hand, in order to identify the factors that influence perception. This section describes the shared aspects of the experimental setup.

Both experiments took place at a desk in a usability lab. The ultrasound array was held face down towards the desk, as seen in Figure 1. The focal points were generated at a distance of 10cm, so the height of the array was set to 10cm from the palm surface. The participant sat at the desk with the non-dominant hand placed directly underneath the array, with the palm facing up. The hand rested on a cloth for comfort. Research suggests there is no significant difference in tactile sensitivity between the dominant and non-dominant hand [26], so the dominant hand was used to control the mouse for making responses. The configuration was very similar to that used by Yoshino *et al.* [28] and was chosen to ensure the hand remained stationary relative to the array. It was imperative that the hand remained in the same fixed position for each condition, as the feedback was presented in fixed positions relative to the array, rather than relative to the hand. Three rigid walls were stuck to the desk surrounding the north, east and west sides of the area beneath the array to keep the hand in place.

The hand was placed under the array so that the join between the proximal phalanx of the middle and ring fingers was directly under the centre of the array. An adhesive ring (paper ring reinforcer) was put on the cloth in this position to indicate where to place the hand and the experimenter ensured the positions matched. This location was considered a central position on the hand, and the position would allow for comparison of sensitivity of the fingers vs. the palm [16]. The drop in focal point force away from the centre would affect both areas equally. The participant was instructed to maintain the hand in a flat position with the fingers together, as in Figure 1. The experimenter monitored the hand position and shape throughout the experiment to ensure they remained correct. Because of the size of the array, low-intensity side lobes (secondary focal points) could be produced within close proximity to the array and, depending on participant hand size, could be felt at the base of the palm. To mask these potentially confusing distractor signals, a folded cloth was placed over the base of the palm and wrist. The software controlling the ultrasound array and the experiment were run on a desktop PC, connected to a monitor and mouse to provide output and input. Headphones were worn, and white noise was played, to mask any sound from the ultrasound array and remove any extraneous aids as to the presence or form of feedback.

### Participants

Fourteen participants took part (8 male, 6 female), aged from 18 to 39 (mean = 25.5, std = 6.27) and were paid £6 for participation in both experiments (localisation and movement). All were right-handed by chance. Participants completed the two experiments in a counterbalanced order, which took approximately 60 minutes in total.

## EXPERIMENT 1: POINT LOCALISATION

This study tested how precisely participants could localise a single, brief focal point presented to the hand when both the array and hand are static, and so give an indication of the spatial resolution useful for feedback. No research has yet conducted this type of study on ultrasonic haptic feedback, as research on localisation [13] or identifying the number/presence of focal points [1, 2] have allowed for active movement of the hand in front of the array. As mentioned, although we use a similar design to Yoshino *et al.* [28], their research did not measure or report on localisation accuracy, only whether the visual and tactile stimuli were perceived as co-located. Our experiment stimulated 25 *positions* in an equally spaced 5 x 5cm grid centred on the centre of the array (see Figure 2). Each position was spaced 1cm from the vertically and horizontally adjacent positions. Two stimulus *durations* were compared (100 and 1000ms), to judge if duration impacted perception.

The experimental design is a variation on research studying tactile localisation on the hand using physical stimuli such as Von Frey hairs [3, 23]. In these studies, individual stimuli are applied to specific locations on the hand and the participants report a) if they felt a stimulus and, if they did, b) where it was felt. To record where stimuli were felt, other research has used generic outlines of the hand printed on paper [23] or have marked on the participant's own hand [3]. This method was not suitable for our study, as the position of feedback is relative to the array, not to fixed positions on the hand (e.g. a fingertip) and hand size varies. Instead, a digital photograph was taken of the participant's hand and was presented on the monitor. Participants used the mouse to click the location on the hand image where the stimulus was felt. An adjustable arm held a camera facing down towards the desk. The participant rested the non-dominant hand on a cloth underneath the camera. This gave a view directly downwards showing the whole hand.

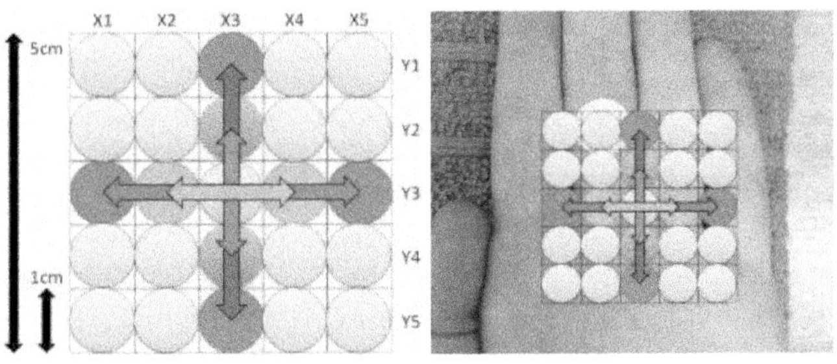


**Figure 2: 5 x 5 focal point grid, also showing apparent motion start and end points (left); overlaid on hand at scale (right).**

The centre point in the array was known to be at the join between the proximal phalanx of the middle and ring finger, and the position clicked on the hand was known from the image, but because of differences in hand size, the relative scale was not known. Therefore, another adhesive ring was stuck to the pad on the proximal phalanx of the middle finger before the image was taken. The diameter of the ring was 1.4cm and so provided a scale for each image/hand. Dividing the number of pixels in the ring's diameter by 1.4 gave the number of pixels per centimetre. The intended position (in mm) of each focal point in the grid could therefore be calculated from the centre point at the join between the middle and ring finger. The position of each perceived (clicked) location on the hand image was converted to mm and its distance to the intended position gave the localisation accuracy measure. Only the adhesive ring was shown in the image, with no guides as to feedback positions.

### *Procedure & Variables*

The experiment was divided into two halves by *duration* and participants completed them both in a counterbalanced order. This was also fully balanced across the experimental ordering (localisation and movement). After the experiment had been explained to the participant, the adhesive ring was placed on the middle finger and the image was taken of the hand. The image was then transferred to the experimental software while the participant removed the ring from the finger. The headphones were put on before the hand was positioned beneath the centre of the array and the cover cloth was put in place to mask any side lobes.

During each *duration* condition, a focal point was produced at each of the 25 stimulus *positions* from the 5 x 5 grid twice in a random order. After an initial gap of ten seconds at the start of the condition, a random focal point was presented for the set *duration* before stopping. Immediately, a dialogue box appeared on the monitor asking if the stimulus had been felt. Clicking "Yes" would bring up the hand image for the participant to indicate where it was felt. A black circle, centred on the clicked position, was drawn on screen to show the perceived position and the participant could correct the position, moving the circle, by clicking elsewhere. Clicking "Submit" recorded the responses. Clicking "No" required no further input. The responses were logged and another stimulus was presented after a gap of three seconds. This repeated until all 50 stimuli had been presented.

The Independent Variables for the study were: *Duration* (100ms & 1000ms), *X-position* (5 columns in the 5cm x 5cm grid, from left-to-right) and *Y-position* (5 rows in the grid, from top-to-bottom). The Dependent Variables were: *Detection* (if the stimulus was detected) and *Localisation* (where it was felt: distance, in mm, from actual location).

## Results

### *Stimulus Detection*

Overall there was a mean stimulus detection rate of 98.9%. A 2 x 5 x 5 (*duration* x *x-position* x *y-position*) repeated measures ANOVA was carried out on the percentage of detected stimuli. A significant effect of *x-position* was found ($F_{(4,108)} = 3.809$, $p < 0.01$), however, no *post hoc* Bonferroni pairwise comparisons reached statistical significance. Mean detection rates for each *x-position* were 97.9%, 97.9%, 100%, 100% and 98.9% for columns 1 to 5, respectively. There was no main effect of *duration*, with mean detection rates of 98.4% for 100ms and 99.4% for 1000ms, nor for *y-position*, with means of 97.9%, 99.6%, 99.3%, 98.9% and 98.9% for rows 1 to 5, respectively.

There was a significant *duration* * *x-position* interaction ($F_{(4,108)} = 3.566$, $p < 0.01$). At 1000ms, *x-position* 1 had 97.1% detection rate while all other positions had 100%. In contrast, at 100ms, *x-positions* 1, 2 and 5 had <100% accuracy. There was also a significant *x-position* * *y-position* interaction ($F_{(16, 432)} = 2.801$, $p < 0.001$). In general, top-left grid positions had lower detection rates more often.

### *Localisation*

The data were analysed in terms of absolute localisation error (distance from intended location along x- and y- axes) and the distributions of perceived points relative to the intended locations. To analyse absolute error, the x- and y-axis distance of each perceived location (in mm) from the intended x- and y- position was calculated and a 2 x 5 x 5 x 2 (*duration* x *x-position* x *y-position* x *axis*) repeated measures ANOVA was carried out. The average localisation error was 8.5mm (std = 6.84mm). There was a significant effect of *duration* ($F_{(1,24)} = 19.798$, $p < 0.001$), with the short duration having a larger mean localisation error of 9.2mm, compared to 7.9mm for 1000ms. There was also a significant effect of *x-position* ($F_{(4,96)} = 5.086$, $p < 0.01$): Bonferroni-adjusted comparisons showed that column 1 (mean = 10mm) had higher error than columns 2 and 3 (both 7.8mm). The mean error for columns 4 and 5 were 8.4mm and 8.5mm, respectively. There was no effect of *y-position*, with mean error of 8.6mm, 8.6mm, 7.7mm, 9.0mm and 8.7mm for rows 1 to 5, respectively. Several interaction effects were also found (see Table 1).

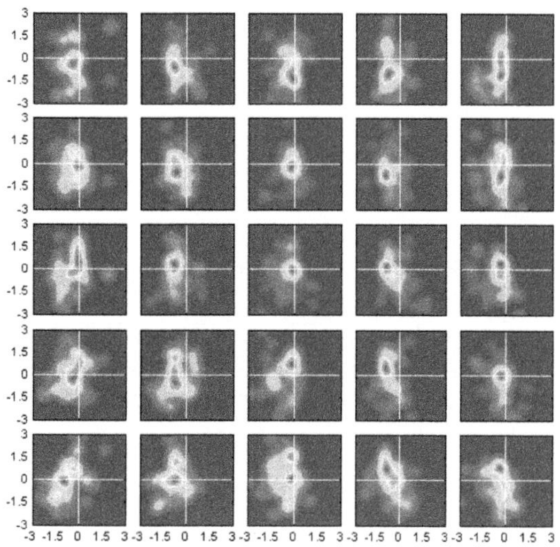


**Figure 3: Heat map of perceived stimulus locations relative to intended locations (crosshairs) in the 5 x 5 grid, averaged across both durations. Density increases from blue to red.**

Figure 3 shows the distributions of perceived stimulus locations around the intended locations in the 5 x 5 grid. Each plot has a scale of -3 to 3 cm along both axes. As targets were spaced only 1cm apart, overlapping of points into adjacent distributions would occur and so the plots for each target are separated for clarity. What is clear from the distributions is the significant difference in localisation error (see Table 1, "Axis") along the y-axis (10mm) compared to the x-axis (7mm), illustrated in the elongated heat patterns.

## EXPERIMENT 2: APPARENT MOTION

This study followed a similar design to research on apparent motion using pin arrays [5, 18, 19] and sequentially activated vibration motors [21]. The focus of previous research has been to identify the influence of various stimulus characteristics, such as distance, ISOI or the number of stimulators on the "quality" of apparent motion. In these studies, no continuous motion is present but the illusion of motion can be triggered by the activation of spatially distributed stimulators across the skin. Some studies used pin arrays, which are capable of presenting multiple pins simultaneously. Because of the size of our ultrasound array, only one focal point of sufficient force can be produced at one time, so it was necessary to adjust the experimental design.

As only a single focal point can be presented, we could not vary ISOI as widely as previous research, which often involved overlapping pin presentations when the ISOI was shorter than the duration of a single point. Therefore, ISOI was ignored as a variable in this study, and set equal to the duration of each focal point, resulting in sequential presentation of focal points. Previous research suggests that sequential presentation of pins results in good apparent motion at the 100ms and 200ms durations used here [18]. As in previous research, each stimulus consisted of at least a start and an end point, located a given distance apart [18, 19] (see Figure 2). Four stimulus characteristics were varied in the study: *distance* (the gap between the inside edges of the start/end points), *direction* (the relative direction the focal points moved across the hand), *number of points* (the number of focal points presented between the start/end points) and point *duration* (the time each focal point was presented for). It is unclear whether physical distance influences perception of motion [18, 19] and so it was included. As hand size varies, two distances were compared which would be small enough to fit within a small hand: 1cm and 3cm.

Although full two-dimensional movement is possible with the array, we limited this initial study to perception of the four cardinal directions: up, down, left and right. Figure 2 shows the start and end points along each dimension and direction, with the short arrows indicating 1cm movement, and the long arrows 3cm movement. Perception of *direction* depends partly on the number of stimulators used and the rapidity of stimulus presentation [21]. Research has also shown that these factors influence the perception and quality judgments of apparent motion [18, 19]. Only a single focal point could be produced from the array and so the number of stimulators here relates to the *number of points* in space the focal point is positioned at between the end points. We used *two points* (only the two start/end points) or *every point* (each point in the grid between the start/end points). Finally, four *durations* were used to compare to previous research [18]: 50, 100, 200 and 300ms. Therefore, a *two-point* stimulus consisted of: 1) a focal point is presented at the start position for the duration (e.g., 100ms), 2) the focal point is stopped, 3) immediately the second focal point is presented at the end point for the set duration.

Participants were instructed that the focus of the study was on sensations of "continuous movement" [18, 19]. If they perceived that the sensation met this criterion then they were asked to rate the movement as one of three categories, labelled "A", "B" and "C". "A" was defined as "movement was impressive and continuous"; "B" was "movement was present but unimpressive"; and "C" was "movement was very partial or ambiguous", from Kirman [18, 19].

*Procedure & Variables*

As in the Localisation experiment, participants first put headphones on to mask any noise before positioning their hand under the centre of the array. The experiment was divided into two blocks of the same stimuli and all participants took part in both blocks. In each block there were 2 *distances*, 4 *directions*, 2 *numbers of points* and 4 *durations* giving a total of 64 stimuli per block: each stimulus was presented once in a random order. For each stimulus, the same pattern was presented twice, to aid perception, with a gap of 1.5 seconds between repetitions. A gap of five seconds separated stimulus presentations. Once the stimulus has been given, a dialogue box appeared on screen asking "Did you feel movement?". Clicking "Yes" presented a second dialogue box with two sets of radio buttons to indicate the perceived *direction* and *quality* of movement. The first contained four labelled *direction* buttons along with an arrow illustrating the direction. The second contained three buttons, labelled with the categories of movement quality: A, B and C (including the relevant descriptions). Clicking "No" was recorded as a lack of continuous movement.

The Independent Variables were: *Distance* (1cm and 3cm), *Direction* (up, down, left and right), *Number of Points* (2 and all) and *Duration* (50, 100, 200 and 300ms). The Dependent Variables were: *Movement Perception* (whether continuous movement was perceived), *Perceived Direction* (up, down, left, right) and *Movement Quality* (A, B or C). Analysis of the apparent motion data was only done on trials where continuous movement was perceived, and included the perceived quality and direction of movement.

## Results

*Movement Perception*

The overall percentage of trials that resulted in "continuous movement" was 62.9%. The data were analysed using a 2 x 4 x 2 x 4 (*distance* x *direction* x *number of points* x *duration*) repeated measures ANOVA. The details of the ANOVA can be seen in Table 1. There were main effects of *distance*, *number of points* (*"num points"*) and *duration*, as well as several interaction effects. The short *distance* of 1cm produced significantly fewer reports of movement (mean = 57.8%) than 3cm (mean = 68.0%). Using only two *points* produced significantly fewer reports (49.6%) than using all intervening *points* (76.2%). Finally, the number of movement reports increased as the *duration* of each *point* increased: 50ms was significantly lower (mean = 27.2%) than 100ms (61.8%), 200ms (79.2%) and 300ms (83.3%). 100ms was also significantly lower than 200ms and 300ms. There was no effect of *direction* (means of 58.9%, 65.4%, 64.3% and 62.9% for up, down, left and right, respectively).

*Movement Quality*

As 62.9% of trials resulted in perceived continuous movement, the same number had a movement quality value, leading to an uneven number of trials for each condition. Therefore, the data were normalised into the percentage of all trials in each condition that produced ratings of "A", "B" and "C". For analysis, the three ratings were converted into percentage scores of movement quality, so that *A =100%*, *B = 67%* and *C = 33%*, in a similar manner to Kirman [18, 19]. Due to a low number of data points for some stimuli (e.g., 1cm + down + 2 points + 50ms) data were collapsed and variables were analysed separately using non-parametric analyses: Friedman's for comparing more than two levels and Wilcoxon for pairwise comparisons (using Bonferroni adjusted p-values for *post hoc* tests).

| **Point Localisation** | | | | **Movement Perception** | | | |
|---|---|---|---|---|---|---|---|
| **Effect/ Interaction** | *df* | *MS* | *F-value* | **Effect/ Interaction** | *df* | *MS* | *F-value* |
| Duration (A) | 1, 24 | 10.80 | 19.80 ‡ | Distance (E) | 1, 27 | 4.62 | 18.52 ‡ |
| xPos (B) | 4, 96 | 6.41 | 5.09 † | Direction (F) | 3, 81 | 0.36 | 1.32 |
| yPos (C) | 4, 96 | 1.68 | 1.74 | Num Points (G) | 1, 27 | 31.88 | 113.11 ‡ |
| Axis (D) | 1, 24 | 54.64 | 39.00 ‡ | Duration (H) | 3, 81 | 48.01 | 99.04 ‡ |
| AxB | 4, 96 | 2.21 | 5.22 † | ExF | 3, 81 | 0.97 | 7.22 ‡ |
| AxC | 4, 96 | 1.32 | 2.19 | ExG | 1, 27 | 9.58 | 85.25 ‡ |
| AxD | 1, 24 | 0.93 | 3.15 | ExH | 3, 81 | 2.40 | 18.80 ‡ |
| BxC | 16, 384 | 1.65 | 2.19 * | FxG | 3, 81 | 0.30 | 1.87 |
| BxD | 4, 96 | 3.97 | 4.81 † | FxH | 9, 243 | 0.39 | 3.27 † |
| CxD | 4, 96 | 2.21 | 2.40 | GxH | 3, 81 | 1.07 | 7.57 ‡ |
| AxBxC | 16, 384 | 0.41 | 1.21 | ExFxG | 3, 81 | 0.11 | 0.98 |
| AxBxD | 4, 96 | 1.81 | 4.42 † | ExFxH | 9, 243 | 0.39 | 2.30 * |
| AxCxD | 4, 96 | 0.88 | 2.80 * | ExGxH | 9, 243 | 0.07 | 0.57 |
| BxCxD | 16, 384 | 0.36 | 0.62 | FxGxH | 3, 81 | 1.04 | 9.43 ‡ |
| AxBxCxD | 16, 384 | 0.30 | 1.20 | ExFxGxH | 9, 243 | 0.17 | 1.51 |

**Table 1: ANOVA results for point localisation (left) & movement perception (right), including main effects (A-F) and interactions (e.g., AxB). Significance indicated by: *, † and ‡ (≤ 0.05, ≤ 0.01 and ≤ 0.001, respectively).**

The overall mean quality rating was 73.15%, between "B" and "A". There was a significant main effect of *distance* (Wilcoxon $Z = 5.346$, $p < 0.001$), as 1cm movements had lower quality (mean = 68.3%) than 3cm movements (78.7%). Using two *points* resulted in significantly lower quality movement (65.4%) than using all *points* (79.4%; $Z = 7.06$, $p < 0.001$). Movement quality was also significantly affected by *duration* ($\chi^2$ (3) = 34.429, $p < 0.001$): *post hoc* Wilcoxon tests showed 50ms (mean = 63.2%) producing lower quality than 100ms (66.2%), 200ms (77.7%) and 300ms (79.9%) and 100ms producing lower quality movement than 200ms and 300ms. There was no effect of *direction*, with mean quality values of 72.8%, 71.8%, 74.9% and 76.7% for up, down, left and right.

*Direction Identification*

Direction identification was measured in terms of the percentage of correct responses. Like the movement quality data, only those trials where movement was perceived had an associated *direction*. Data were normalised, collapsed and analysed in the same manner as movement quality. The percentage values relate to the proportion of trials in that condition that produced continuous movement. A Wilcoxon test showed a significant effect of *distance* on direction accuracy ($Z = 5.620$, $p < 0.001$), with the 1cm *distance* resulting in lower accuracy (mean = 82.0%) than 3cm (93.6%). A Friedman test found a significant effect of *direction* ($\chi^2$ (3) = 23.389, $p < 0.001$). *Post hoc* Wilcoxon tests showed that the up *direction* was identified significantly less well (mean = 79.9%) than all other directions:

92.0%, 91.3% and 89.0% for down, right and left, respectively. There was no effect of *num points*, with means of 87.3% and 89.6% for two *points* and all *points*, respectively. There was also no effect of *duration* (87.7%, 87.7%, 86.9% and 90.2% for 50ms, 100ms, 200ms and 300ms).

## DISCUSSION AND DESIGN GUIDELINES

### Point Localisation

*Detection:* 98.9% of all stimuli were detected and there was no main effect of stimulus duration, so even rapid low-force ultrasound feedback is reliably detectable on the hand. However, *where* the feedback was presented had an impact on detection rates. The x-position had a significant effect, but no comparisons between positions reached significance, so it is difficult to draw strong conclusions. In general, positions towards both the left and right extremes had lower detection rates, but the real world differences were very small (98-99%, instead of 100%). While duration had no effect by itself, the slightly lower detection rate at the extremes was slightly increased when using only the short stimuli. There was no effect of y-position but x- and y-position interacted, as it appears that positions towards the top-left of the 5 x 5 grid were more likely to have <100% detection. Of the six positions that had <100% detection, five were along the extreme sides of the grid. A technical limitation of ultrasound arrays is that focal points around the extreme edges have lower force than those near the centre (see above). While this appears to have had a small influence on detection rates, the uneven patterns of lower detection rates around the edges suggests differences in tactile sensitivity are also present.

*Localisation:* The average localisation error was 8.5mm (std = 6.8mm). This is comparable to the figure Hoshi [13] found (mean of 8.9mm, std of 7.4mm) when using active investigation (users could move their hands), suggesting that active investigation may not influence localisation. It is slightly lower than the estimated 10-13mm two-point visual-tactile threshold [28] during passive feedback reception. While duration had no effect on detection, it had a significant effect on localisation, with 1000ms stimuli being localised 1.3mm more accurately than the shorter stimuli, on average. Therefore, longer stimuli appear to be easier to localise. The slightly higher sensitivity for central regions mentioned for detection is also highlighted in the localisation error, with duration and position also interacting strongly. X-position again had a significant effect, as localisation of points at the extreme left (column 1) were significantly less accurate than points in columns 2 and 3, with the effect stronger at 1000ms, compared to 100ms. The force output of the array drops equally regardless of direction, so the uniquely poorer localisation along the far left again indicates that there are other influences at work, such as lower tactile sensitivity. X-position and y-position interacted: positions in the top-left and bottom-left corners suffered higher localisation error. However, there was no significant effect of y-position, which might suggest that the fingers and palm were comparably sensitive.

Localisation for a given point was significantly worse along the y-axis than the x-axis by as much as 3mm (43%), on average. Therefore, localisation of static ultrasound on the hand along the longitudinal axis (long axis of body) is considerably worse than along the transverse axis (across the body). Previous research on tactile acuity has found that judgements along the longitudinal axis have a smaller Weber function than judgements along the transverse axis (suggesting poorer acuity), but not significantly so [6]. The error axis interacted with both x-position and y-position individually, but in different ways. In general, as x-position increases (moves from left to right on the grid) x-axis error increases and y-axis error stays flat. As y-position increases (moves from top to bottom on the grid) y-axis error increases and x-axis error stays fairly flat.

An exception to these trends is higher error along both axes, but particularly along the y-axis, in the far left column (x-position 1). The bottom-left corner is more error-prone than other areas. Y-axis error increases the further down the hand, and the bottom-left corner is the closest area to the thumb, as all participants were right-handed (left hand was stimulated). Research has shown that static stimuli are often mislocalised towards the thumb, particularly those closer to it [3]. The distributions in Figure 3 also appear to show this bias towards the thumb (towards the left).

### Apparent Motion

*Movement Perception:* 62.9% of all stimuli were reported as producing a sensation of "continuous movement", although this number ranged from 12.5% up to 91.5%, depending on the combination of variables. Increasing the distance between the start and end points increased the sensation of continuous movement, which is in contrast to the results from previous research [18], possibly due to the larger and less defined focal point we used compared to the small diameter rods used in other research. Carter *et al.* [2] found that focal points of the same modulated frequency needed to be 5cm apart to be perceptually distinct, so when the points are too close, they may feel like one entity. In accordance with other research [5, 18, 19, 21], the number of stimulating points had a large effect on movement perception. 76.2% of trials stimulating all points resulted in continuous sensations, compared to only 49.6% when using only the two start and end points. The negative impact of using only two points was exacerbated when travelling the longer distance or using shorter durations, as movement reports decreased from 1cm to 3cm and from 300ms to 50ms. These results support the assertion that the number of stimulators (or intervening points) is more important for the illusion of movement than the distance between them.

The effect of duration was also marked. Movement perceptions increased significantly as the duration increased from 50ms to 200ms, with no difference above 200ms. Research using rigid stimuli found similar trends, as longer durations produced good movement more reliably [18]. Only 27.2% of 50ms trials felt continuous, compared to 83.3% of 300ms trials. It seems that there is no extra benefit in increasing the duration beyond 200ms. However, the interaction between distance and duration suggests fast movement (50-100ms) should be across larger distances, and slow movement (200-300ms) should be across shorter distances. There was no effect of direction on movement perception but, as is described below, it strongly interacted with other variables.

Overall, there was a pattern that transverse movement was more often felt as continuous, and that the benefits of duration and number of points had a stronger impact on longitudinal movement. Longitudinal movement was more convincing when using the larger distance, while transverse movement was less affected. This could be because transverse movement crosses multiple fingers, making the change in location more apparent, while longitudinal movement only moves within the same digit. The borderline significant interaction between distance, direction and duration showed that upwards movements suffered the most from the small distance and short duration, but therefore benefited the most by increasing those. It is unclear why this might be. The results also suggest that transverse movement needs shorter distances and durations of 100ms+ for good movement, while longitudinal movement needs longer distances and longer durations (200ms+).

*Movement Quality:* The overall quality of movement was high, at 73.1%, although this is lower than movement quality using pins/rods [18, 19]. Therefore, ultrasound feedback from a small, static source using only a small number of focal points can reliably produce good sensations of movement. Like movement perception, longer distances, larger number of points and longer durations led to better movement quality, however, there was no extra benefit of increasing duration past 200ms, echoing previous research [18, 19]. In contrast, this previous research suggested physical distance had no effect on movement quality across similar distances to those used in our experiment, so our less defined focal points may require more distance to be distinct [2]. Direction did not significantly affect quality.

*Direction Accuracy:* Overall, participants were able to identify the direction of movement well, at ~88%. The longer distance led to significantly better accuracy (93.6%, compared to 82.0%), so direction is easier to judge when the start and end points are further from each other. There was no effect of either number of points or duration, suggesting that these factors are more important for producing a convincing sensation of movement, rather than the direction of that movement. Movement upwards was significantly less well identified than all other directions. It is unclear why movement up the fingers from the palm would be worse than movement towards the palm from the fingers. When moving down, perhaps the more sensitive fingers give a clearer starting point and the more vague sensation on the palm is sufficient to determine direction. When moving up, given a more vague starting position, attention may be preoccupied during the clearer sensation on the fingers. Hoshi [13] found that users were able to identify the direction of longitudinal movement at 100% accuracy, but he used a larger array (384 transducers), a larger distance (4cm gap between end points) and it is unclear which parts of the hand were stimulated.

### Design Guidelines

Based on our results, we propose guidelines for the design of ultrasonic haptic feedback in HCI. Due to the functional similarities, the guidelines here can also be applied to larger ultrasonic arrays. The influence of each feedback characteristic is explained in relation to localisation and the creation of motion, as are general interaction guidelines: spatial resolution and the feasibility of a wrist-mounted array.

*Distance:* The use of larger distances improves the sensation and quality of movement. However, if using fewer points of stimulation, it is best to use shorter distances and longer durations to improve movement. If using more points, use longer distances and moderate-to-long durations.

*Number of Points:* Increasing the number of intervening stimuli improves the sensation and quality of movement.

*Duration:* Rapid stimuli (100ms) are reliably detectable, but longer durations improve perception and localisation. Longer stimuli also improve the perception and quality of movement. If fast movement (50-100ms per point) is needed it should be across larger distances, while slower movement (200-300ms) should be across shorter distances.

*Location/Direction:* Sensitivity and localisation are better nearer the centre of the hand (near the metacarpophalangeal joints), and particularly bad towards the thumb. Localisation is worse, and movement is generally less clear, along the longitudinal axis, and longer distances are needed for good movement. Transverse movement benefits from shorter distances and longer durations.

*Spatial Resolution:* Localisation error was 8.5mm on average, with a standard deviation of 6.8mm. As error along the y-axis was 3mm worse than x-axis, this suggests that focal points can be reliably localised at a spatial resolution of one point (i.e., one pixel) per 1.5 x 2cm. This could give a display of 5 x 7 pixels across a hand area of 7.5 x 14cm.

*Virtual object size:* A virtual object would need to be at least $2cm^2$, otherwise users may not be able to accurately resolve its spatial location or movement, especially if movement is small, potentially leading to inaccurate interaction or a perceptual mismatch, if using visual feedback.

*Wrist-Mounted Array:* Part of our motivation was to examine the efficacy of a small mobile or embedded array for feedback, particularly during gestural interaction. The results from our experiments indicate that a wrist-mounted ultrasonic haptic array could provide as effective and salient feedback as larger static arrays [13]. 99% of static stimuli were detected and the majority of non-static stimuli produced sensations of continuous movement at a high quality, even when using a small, low force array and passive feedback reception. There are issues to consider, however, such as the influence of array angle relative to the hand on perception of focal points, or the impact of user and array movement, such as when gesturing.

## CONCLUSIONS

This paper reported two experiments that identified some of the underlying perceptual characteristics of location and movement of ultrasound feedback on the hand. By using a small array we also investigated the feasibility of a wrist-mounted array for gestural interaction. The results showed that users could localise a static point of ultrasound feedback within 8.5mm across 25cm$^2$ of the hand. Using only a single focal point, a range of feedback characteristics can provide a convincing sensation of continuous motion, but using larger distances, longer stimulus durations and stimulating more intervening points maximises movement perception. Due to the functional similarities, our results and guidelines can also be used in the design of feedback produced by larger ultrasonic feedback arrays. Passive feedback from a small array can provide as effective feedback as active investigation over large arrays, suggesting a wrist-mounted array for gestural interaction is feasible.

## ACKNOWLEDGEMENTS

This research was funded by EPSRC grant EP/J005312/1. Thanks also go to Euan Freeman and Mark McGill.

## REFERENCES

1. Alexander, J., Marshall, M. & Subramanian, S. Adding haptic feedback to mobile TV. *Proc. CHI 2011 Ext. Abs.*, pp 1975-1980.
2. Carter, T., Seah, S., Long, B., Drinkwater, B. & Subramanian, S. UltraHaptics: Multi-Point Mid-Air Haptic Feedback for Touch Surfaces. *Proc. UIST 2013*, pp 505-514.
3. Culver, C. Errors in Tactile Localization. *The American Journal of Psychology*, 1970. 83(3), pp 420-427.
4. Dipietro, L. & Sabatini, A. A Survey of Glove-Based Systems and Their Applications. *Transactions on System, Man and Cybernetics*, 2008. 38(4), pp 461-482.
5. Geldard, F. & Sherrick, C. The cutaneous "rabbit": a perceptual illusion. *Science*, 1972. 178, pp 178-179.
6. Green, B. The perception of distance and location for dual tactile pressures. *Perception & Psychophysics*, 1982. 31(4), pp 315-323.
7. Gustafson, S., Bierwirth, D. & Baudisch, P. Imaginary Interfaces: Spatial Interaction with Empty Hands and without Visual Feedback. *Proc. UIST 2010*, pp 3-12.
8. Harrison, C., Benko, H. & Wilson, A. OmniTouch: Wearable Multitouch Interaction Everywhere. *Proc. UIST 2011*, pp 441-450.
9. Hasegawa, K. & Shinoda, H. Aerial Display of Vibrotactile Sensation with High Spatial-Temporal Resolution Using Large-Aperture Airborne Ultrasound Phased Array. *Proc. World Haptics 2013*, pp 31-36.
10. Hilliges, O., Kim, D., Izadi, S., Weiss, M. & Wilson, A. Holodesk: Direct 3D interactions with a situated see-through display. *Proc. CHI 2012*, pp 2421-2430.
11. Hoshi, T. Development of Aerial-Input and Aerial-Tactile-Feedback System. *Proc. World Haptics 2011*, pp 569-573.
12. Hoshi, T. Handwriting Transmission System Using Noncontact Tactile Display. *Proc. WorldHaptics 2012*, pp 399-401.
13. Hoshi, T., Takahashi, M., Iwamoto, T. & Shinoda, H. Noncontact tactile display based on radiation pressure of airborne ultrasound. *Transactions on Haptics*, 2010. 3(3), pp 155-165.
14. Hoshi, T., Takahashi, M., Nakatsuma, K. & Shinoda, H. Touchable holography. *Proc. SIGGRAPH 2009*.
15. Iwamoto, T., Tatezono, M. & Shinoda, H. Non-contact method for producing tactile sensation using airborne ultrasound. *Proc. EuroHaptics 2008*, pp 504-513.
16. Johansson, R. & Vallbo, A.B. Tactile sensory coding in the glabrous skin of the human hand. *Trends in Neurosciences*, 1983, pp 27-32.
17. Kim, D., Hilliges, O., Izadi, S., Butler, A., Chen, J., Oikonomidis, I. & Olivier, P. Digits: Freehand 3D Interactions Anywhere Using a Wrist-Worn Gloveless Sensor. *Proc. UIST 2012*, pp 167-176.
18. Kirman, J. Tactile Apparent Movement: The effects of interstimulus onset interval and stimulus duration. *Perception & Psychophysics*, 1974. 15(1), pp 1-6.
19. Kirman, J. Tactile Apparent Movement: The Effects of Number of Stimulators. *Journal of Experimental Psychology*, 1974. 103(6), pp 1175-1180.
20. Lee, S., Li, B. & Starner, T. AirTouch: Synchronizing in-air hand gesture and on-body tactile feedback to augment mobile gesture interaction. *Proc. ISWC 2011*, pp 3-10.
21. Niwa, M., Lindeman, R., Itoh, Y. & Kishino, F. Determining appropriate parameters to elicit linear and circular apparent motion using vibrotactile cues. *Proc. World Haptics 2009*, pp 75-78.
22. Obrist, M., Seah, S. & Subramanian, S. Talking About Tactile Experiences. *Proc. CHI 2013*, pp 1659-1668.
23. Schweizer, R., Maier, M., Braun, C. & Birbaumer, N. Distribution of mislocalizations of tactile stimuli on the fingers of the human hand. *Somatosensory & Motor Research*, 2000. 17(4), pp 309-316.
24. Sodhi, R., Poupyrev, I., Glisson, M. & Israr, A. AIREAL: Interactive Tactile Experiences in Free Air. *Transactions on Graphics*, 2013. 32(4), Article 134.
25. Takahashi, M. & Shinoda, H. Large aperture Airborne Ultrasound Tactile Display using distributed array units. *Proc. SICE 2010*, pp 359-362.
26. Vega-Bermudez, F. & Johnson, K. Differences in spatial acuity between digits. *Neurology*, 2001. 56, pp 1389-1391.
27. Wilson, A. & Benko, H. Combining multiple depth cameras and projectors for interactions on, above and between surfaces. *Proc. UIST 2010*, pp 273-282.
28. Yoshino, K., Hasegawa, K. & Shinoda, H. Measuring Visio-Tactile threshold for Visio-Tactile Projector. *Proc. SICE 2012*, pp 1996-2000.

# Understanding Quantified-Selfers' Practices in Collecting and Exploring Personal Data

**Eun Kyoung Choe[1], Nicole B. Lee[2], Bongshin Lee[2], Wanda Pratt[1], Julie A. Kientz[1]**

[1]University of Washington
{eunky, wpratt, jkientz}@uw.edu

[2]Microsoft Corporation
{nilee, bongshin}@microsoft.com

## ABSTRACT

Researchers have studied how people use self-tracking technologies and discovered a long list of barriers including lack of time and motivation as well as difficulty in data integration and interpretation. Despite the barriers, an increasing number of *Quantified-Selfers* diligently track many kinds of data about themselves, and some of them share their best practices and mistakes through Meetup talks, blogging, and conferences. In this work, we aim to gain insights from these "extreme users," who have used existing technologies and built their own workarounds to overcome different barriers. We conducted a qualitative and quantitative analysis of 52 video recordings of Quantified Self Meetup talks to understand what they did, how they did it, and what they learned. We highlight several common pitfalls to self-tracking, including tracking too many things, not tracking triggers and context, and insufficient scientific rigor. We identify future research efforts that could help make progress toward addressing these pitfalls. We also discuss how our findings can have broad implications in designing and developing self-tracking technologies.

### Author Keywords

Quantified Self; self-monitoring; self-tracking; health; personal informatics; personal analytics; self-experimentation.

### ACM Classification Keywords

H.5.2. Information interfaces and presentation (e.g., HCI): User-centered design; J.3. Life and medical sciences: Health.

## INTRODUCTION

Although many people do not routinely track personal data, *Quantified-Selfers* (Q-Selfers) are notable exceptions who diligently track many kinds of data about themselves. They are a diverse group of life hackers, data analysts, computer scientists, early adopters, health enthusiasts, productivity gurus, and patients. Believing in the notion of "self-knowledge through numbers," Wired Magazine editors Gary Wolf and Kevin Kelly created a blog called quantifiedself.com in 2007, which has become the repository for people to share self-tracking practices. At the core of Quantified Self (QS) are the frequent, in-person grassroots Meetups (meetings) where participants share their best practices, experiences, and mistakes.

On the academic side, human-computer interaction researchers and designers have developed and studied many self-tracking technologies in the domain of health and wellness [13,27]. Similar to the QS movement, the field of Personal Informatics (or Personal Analytics) adopts the approach that through knowledge of one's data, it becomes possible to reflect on one's activities, make self-discoveries, and use that knowledge to make changes. Although researchers acknowledged the value of self-tracking technologies (e.g., [2,4,19,20,23]), they also discovered a long list of barriers toward the adoption of self-tracking technologies. These barriers included lack of time, insufficient motivation, unsuitable visualization and analytics tools, poor skills for analyzing data, and fragmented data scattered across multiple platforms [17].

In light of the barriers they face, Q-Selfers offer us a useful perspective from which to re-examine the current design of self-tracking technologies and ways to improve them. Q-Selfers encompass a broad spectrum of people ranging from those who use pen and paper to those who build their own tracking applications. Because they can be categorized as a somewhat *extreme user group*, their stories, including the successful ones, might not be generalizable or applicable to the broader population. However, as other researchers point out [29], the perspective of those who represent "extremes" gives us distinct insights because they have used existing technologies and spent numerous hours building their own workarounds when faced with problems.

We had many questions about this particular group. What motivates Q-Selfers to keep tracking data, despite numerous barriers? What tools do they use to collect and explore data? What insights do they gain from tracking? What are the outcomes of tracking? What challenges do they face and how do they overcome these? We explored these questions through a qualitative and quantitative analysis of 52 video recordings of QS Meetup talks stored on the QS blog [25]. Each talk illustrates a distinctive self-tracking approach that



*CHI 2014,* April 26 – May 01 2014, Toronto, ON, Canada

ACM 978-1-4503-2473-1/14/04$15.00.
http://dx.doi.org/10.1145/2556288.2557372

could benefit human-computer interaction, health informatics, and information visualization researchers whose work is within the domain of self-tracking and personal analytics.

In what follows, we present the results from our study on Q-Selfers' practices of collecting and exploring their personal data. We begin by providing background on self-monitoring and the rise of Quantified Self movement. Next, we explain our study methods, dataset, and profiles of Q-Selfers. We then detail themes that arise from our qualitative and quantitative analysis as we answer the Three Prime Questions posed to the QS Meetup speakers—(1) what they did, (2) how they did it, and (3) what they learned. While addressing these questions, we highlight several common pitfalls Q-Selfers experience. These pitfalls include tracking too many things, not tracking triggers and context, and lacking scientific rigor. Q-Selfers offer workarounds in addressing some of these issues, but the questions of how to easily explore data and how to bring scientific rigor to the Quantified-Self movement remain open and require further research. We identify future research efforts that could help make progress toward addressing these issues.

## RELATED WORK

In this section, we provide some background on self-monitoring, the rise of Quantified Self movement, and scholarly and business endeavors in this space.

### Self-Monitoring (or Self-Tracking)

Although using technology to monitor one's own behavior is a relatively new concept, self-monitoring (or self-tracking)—the process of recording one's own behaviors, thoughts, and feelings—is an area of research within behavioral psychology, which dates back to 1970 [14]. Self-monitoring has been traditionally employed in clinical and research settings to serve an *assessment* function as well as a part of *treatment* function within behavior therapy [15]. The role of clinicians was important in self-monitoring—they used self-monitoring for all stages of assessment, such as diagnosis, target behavior selection for treatment, functional assessment, and treatment monitoring.

More recently, self-monitoring has been widely embodied in the design of sensing and monitoring applications because of its effectiveness on increased awareness and behavior change. Sensors have become smaller and better integrated with mobile devices, making it easy for people to track numerous types of data. Recognizing the power of self-monitoring in promoting health behavior change, researchers and designers often incorporate automated sensing or manual tracking feature in designing self-monitoring technology. Within the health domain, researchers and companies designed technology for tracking physical fitness (e.g., [4,6,9,16,19,22]), sleep (e.g., [6,11,16,31]), diet [20], smoking [1], and stress [21]. In addition, the Mobile Health Mashups system shows significant correlations across sensor data from multiple sources such as exercise, weight, food, sleep, and mood [2].

Tracking a health indicator or symptom has become popular among the general public. In a nation-wide survey on peoples' health tracking practice, researchers showed that seven in ten U.S. adults track a health indicator for themselves or for a loved one [7]. However, among those who track one or more health indicators, only 21% use some form of technology for tracking while 49% keep track of progress "in their head" and 34% track data on paper [7]. In the same survey, researchers found that people with chronic conditions are significantly more likely to track a health indicator or symptom. Mobile phones have become a promising platform for patients to do health tracking because of their ability to support journaling, text messaging, and automated sensing [13]. Through qualitative inquiry of cancer patients' symptom tracking technology use, Patel and colleagues revealed how patient-led information capture and management could help patients feel psychosocial comfort, be prepared for the attending rounds, and improve symptom communication with clinicians [23].

### Quantified Self and Personal Analytics

Quantified Self (QS) refers to the name of a community as well as the practice of self-tracking. The prevalence of low cost monitoring sensors accelerated the rise of the Quantified Self movement [25]. Initially started in the Silicon Valley area among technology enthusiasts, QS has become a community of people practicing self-monitoring and building self-monitoring technology. QS as a community promotes sharing of individual self-tracking practices through Meetups, blogging, and annual conferences. As of January 2014, QS is an active, international community, with Meetups held in 106 cities in 36 countries. They have held an annual conference since 2011. Identifying health tracking as a promising area for growth, toolmakers of self-monitoring devices and software attend Meetups to promote their products and sponsor the annual QS conference.

QS goes by other terms, such as personal analytics [28] and personal informatics [17]. These all refer to a class of systems or practices that help people collect and reflect on personal information. Stephen Wolfram, a creator of software Mathematica and of Wolfram Alpha (a knowledge engine) as well as an avid self-tracker himself, coined the term personal analytics and now applies analytical techniques to people's personal data [30]. His company recently deployed Personal Analytics for Facebook, which automatically analyzes and generates a report on personal relationship and other behaviors on the site.

Li and colleagues coined the term personal informatics, proposed a stage-based model of personal informatics systems composed of five stages (preparation, collection, integration, reflection, and action), and identified barriers people have in each of the stages [17]. In a follow-up paper, they explored how ubiquitous computing technologies could properly support the *self-reflection* stage [18]. Although we share similar goals to understand self-trackers' practice, our work differs in three regards. First, we attempt to learn self-tracking practices from the extreme user group—Quantified-Selfers who volunteered to give a talk in front of other Q-Selfers and share success and even failure stories. Second, we detail how Q-Selfers *explore* data, which encompasses both data analysis and visualization. To better understand how Q-Selfers explored data, we analyzed how they gained insights and what visualizations they created. Lastly, we created profiles of Q-Selfers to characterize their backgrounds and motivations for tracking. In conducting our study, we strived to learn Q-Selfers' common pitfalls and their workarounds to avoid those pitfalls.

## THREE PRIME QUESTIONS AND STUDY METHOD

At the QS Meetups, people talk about their firsthand experiences with self-tracking methods and tools using a "Show & Tell" format. Talks on scientific theories, demos of tools and apps, and philosophical speculation are discouraged unless they are grounded in actual attempts at self-tracking and self-experimentation. The uniqueness of the QS Show & Tell comes from the fact that they follow the specific guideline, provided beforehand, to organize the talk to answer the Three Prime Questions:

- What did you do?
- How did you do it?
- What did you learn?

The consistent structure of the talks makes them a valuable dataset. In answering *what they did*, speakers talk about initial problems and motivations to do self-tracking and track items. In answering *how they did it*, they talk about tools and methods they used and the visualizations they created from personal data. In answering *what they learned*, they talk about insights gained and the outcomes of their tracking. The talks are usually 5 to10-minute-long followed by a question and answer period. The talks, including the Q&A, are often video-recorded and uploaded to the quantifiedself.com blog by Meetup organizers for sharing.

### Dataset

As of April 8, 2013, 205 video posts had been uploaded to the QS blog since 2008. Of those, we analyzed 83 recent video posts, those uploaded since January 2012, to examine the most up-to-date landscape of QS practice (Figure 1).

Not all of the posts fit within our area of interest for this study. For example, despite the three prime questions guideline, some speakers presented a new tool that they developed without describing their actual self-tracking practice. Others presented academic research on other people's data. Some videos failed to capture the speakers' visual aids (i.e., slides) so it was difficult to understand the specific context. Thus, video posts had to meet the following two inclusion criteria in order to be added to our dataset: (1) the speaker should present their own QS practices; and (2) video posts should include personal data visualizations of some kind (e.g., table, graph) created with the speaker's own data. Of the 83 videos we reviewed, 52 videos met the inclusion criteria. The average length of these videos was

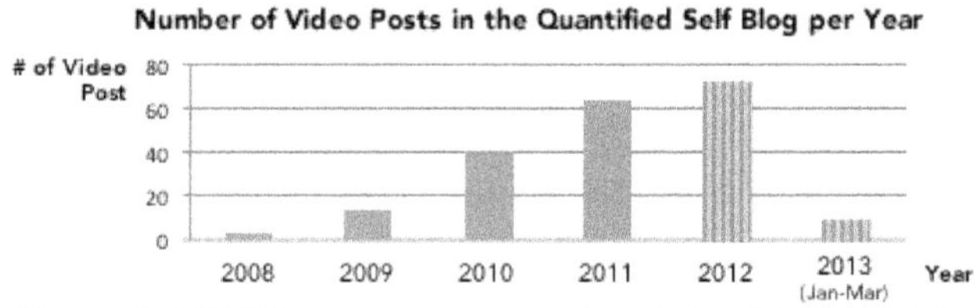


**Figure 1. QS Video posts per year. Our dataset is colored in orange with vertical stripes.**

15 minutes, 53 seconds (including Q&A). We transcribed this entire corpus of videos to aid with analysis.

The speakers of QS Meetup talks were a self-selected group of people who volunteered to give a talk, and might not accurately represent the whole community of Q-Selfers, not to mention the general public. We suspect that they are more extreme in terms of technical ability and experience with self-tracking than typical Q-Selfers. We also note that not all the QS Show & Tell videos are recorded and uploaded to the QS blog.

### Analysis Techniques

We employed a variety of techniques to analyze our dataset. First, with an aim to understand and characterize Q-Selfers, we created a profile for each speaker by systematically capturing the following information: location, gender, job description, health condition, types of data collected, self-tracking duration, data collection tool, data exploration tool, type of tool (user-generated vs. commercial), and data sharing aspects. Given that we had to rely on the information speakers disclosed during the talk, some information is missing for some speakers. Second, we conducted an affinity analysis [3] as a group (Figure 2). After several passes, the video transcripts were broken into approximately 400 quotes, each of which contained one main idea. We inductively organized these into categories to identify key themes. We drew several bottom-up themes regarding people's motivations for self-tracking, self-tracking methods and tools, insights gained, outcomes of tracking, and common pitfalls of self-tracking. Lastly, we captured 188 screenshots (and the slides when available) that included personal data visualizations. We analyzed the screenshots by categorizing the visualization type.

**Figure 2. Affinity analysis of the video transcript quotes.**

## PROFILES OF THE QUANTIFIED-SELFERS

Here we provide the profiles of Q-Selfers based on qualitative and quantitative coding analysis.

*Location.* Seventeen (33%) video posts were recorded from San Francisco / Mountain View / Silicon Valley area. This location is where the QS movement first started and still remains very active. Nine (17%) video posts were from Seattle followed by seven (13%) videos from London and New York respectively. Other locations included Toronto (6%), Pittsburgh (4%), Singapore (4%), Washington DC (4%), Boston (2%), San Diego (2%), and Portland (2%).

*Gender.* Forty-one (79%) speakers were male, while only 11 (21%) were female. Pew Research reports that in the general population, men and women are equally likely to report tracking their weight, diet, or exercise routine [7].

*Health Condition.* Eighteen (35%) reported having some health conditions, such as sleep disorders, diabetes, panic attacks, cancer, obesity, or allergies. For them, their health conditions highly influenced what they tracked because they wanted to maintain a certain condition, find triggers, identify a medication's effect, or achieve some health goal.

*Job Description.* Twenty-one (40%) speakers were working at a startup. Eighteen (37%) speakers described themselves as a software engineer or programmer. Seven (13%) were working in data analytics and four (8%) were electrical engineers. Other job titles included creative director, psychologist, designer, product manager, graduate student, operations analyst, professor, and professional athlete.

*Tracking Duration.* The average duration of tracking was 25 months, where the obtained range was 5 days–20 years (*SD* = 44.0 months, *Median* = 8 months).

## WHAT DID YOU DO?

We organize our findings based on the Three Prime Questions. We begin by answering the first question—"what did you do?" We here describe the types of data Q-Selfers tracked and the motivations behind tracking. We also identify common pitfalls regarding data collection phase and Q-Selfers' approaches to alleviate some of the pitfalls.

**Figure 3. Number of people tracking a certain item.**

### Items Tracked

Activity (40% of Q-Selfers), food (31%), weight (29%), sleep (25%), and mood (13%) were the most popular items Q-Selfers reported tracking. In contrast to our results, bank statements, email history, and credit card bills were the top 3 items people reported in Li et al. [17]. This is possibly because Q-Selfers did not consider readily available data "self-tracking," or if they did, they did not report on it during the Meetup talks. On average, Q-Selfers track 2.92 items (*SD* = 2.41) where the obtained range was 1–11. In all, they reported 57 unique items. The long-tail shape of Figure 3 indicates that Q-Selfers have diverse interests. Other items they reported tracking include cognitive performance, blood glucose, location, heart rate, symptoms, knowledge, stress, body fat, productivity, snoring, movies, posture, medicine, skin condition, home energy usage, clothes, and public transit usage. Some people track multiple items simultaneously with the intention of identifying correlations among the factors, while others track one or two items at a time but apply the self-tracking practice on several topics over time as their interests change.

### Motivations to Practice Self-Tracking

We classified Q-Selfers' motivations to track into three main categories: (1) to improve health, (2) to improve other aspects of life, and (3) to find new life experiences. In Table 1, we break down these categories further and include tracking examples for each of the categories. Thirty-five (67%) speakers tracked one or more health-related items with an aim to improve aspects of health. Considering the number of people who had a health condition (35%), improving health was a prevalent motivation regardless of the presence of a health condition. Furthermore, they had very

| Motivations | Sub-categories | Tracking example |
|---|---|---|
| To improve health | To cure or manage a condition | Track blood glucose to hit the target range [P37] |
| | To achieve a goal | Track weight to get back to the ideal weight of 135 pounds [P39] |
| | To find triggers | Log triggers that cause atrial fibrillation [P55] |
| | To answer a specific question | Track niacin intake dosage and sleep to identify how much niacin to take for treating symptoms [P76] |
| | To identify relationships | Track exercise, weight, muscle mass, and body fat to see the relationships among the factors [P31] |
| | To execute a treatment plan | Log food, exercise, and panic as a recovery plan for panic attack [P35] |
| | To make better health decisions | Record ideas of things that thought were healthy and unhealthy to make better decisions [P18] |
| | To find balance | Log sleep, exercise, and time to get back from erratic lifestyle [P23, P42, P54] |
| To improve other aspects of life | To maximize work performance | Track time to know the current use of time and ways to be more efficient [P43, P63] |
| | To be mindful | Take a self-portrait shot everyday for 365 days to capture each day's state of mind [P26] |
| To find new life experiences | To satisfy curiosity and have fun | Log the frequency of "puns" to see how often these puns happened and what triggered them [P12] |
| | To explore new things | Track every street walked in Manhattan to explore as much of the city as possible [P34] |
| | To learn something interesting | Track heart rate for as long as possible and see what can be learned from it [P62] |

**Table 1. Quantified-Selfers' tracking motivations and examples for each category.**

specific health-related goals—such as finding triggers for an allergy, finding out how exercise affects body mass and weight, finding the right drug dosage, or executing a treatment plan for treating panic attacks—rather than merely "to become healthy" or "to change health behaviors." Some people in this group claimed that they "treated" or "cured" a disease through self-tracking. For those who experienced positive outcomes from self-tracking, QS was an *approach* to better life, not just a data collection method.

Another group of Q-Selfers was interested in improving other aspects of life—predominantly work efficiency and cognitive performance. They used self-tracking to measure their current use of time (with time tracking apps or calendar logging), cognitive performance (by taking an online cognitive test), or time spent on a computer (with productivity tracking software). People in this group—who were either software engineers or students—wanted to find ways to "optimize" their work and life and "maximize" learning.

The last category consists of those who wanted to have new life experiences through self-tracking. They often had no specific goals in mind when starting to track, but quickly discovered interesting patterns from data that led to data collection becoming habitual. For example, P62, who did not have a heart condition, collected heart rate data for 24 hours a day for over a year. He streamed his heart rate data to various channels online, which were updated every 30 minutes. He learned how his body responds to various routines and stressful events, which in return influenced his decision-making (e.g., avoiding heavy meals because his heart rate would go up 20%). The technical ability of people in this group combined with their creativity allowed them to explore new life experiences through self-tracking.

### Common Pitfall 1: Tracking Too Many Things

Q-Selfers described that they were often too ambitious at first and tried to track too many things, as P61 remarked: "*I can honestly say that I've made the classic newbie self-tracking mistake which is that I track everything*." Tracking too many things often led to either stop tracking entirely due to *tracking fatigue* or failure to do data analysis due to too much data in different formats.

Q-Selfers offered some suggestions on how to alleviate tracking fatigue. First, they suggested automating the tracking and data uploading if possible. P39 had been tracking her weight, food, and exercise for 6 years using several different tracking methods, such as manual entry with an Excel spreadsheet, pen and paper, Google docs, and most recently, automatically through a WiFi-scale. Her definition of successful tracking was to capture many data points for a long period of time. The use of a WiFi-scale, which automatically uploads data to a website, allowed her the longest and the most regular data acquisition (compared to other methods). Second, if automating is not possible, Q-Selfers suggested making tracking very simple and easy to do by (1) lowering data granularity (e.g., "*If you can't automate your tracking, make your tracking binary*" [P51]) or (2) making manual capture very easy. P35 built a manual counter app whose main design goal was to reduce user burden in capturing his panic symptoms and triggers: "*...recording is a one-tap process—have a drink at the bar, tap alcohol, go on a run, tap to start, tap to stop, simple*." At the expense of data granularity, they were able to lower the user burden associated with capturing, thereby capturing more data points overall. Lastly, Q-Selfers suggested making tracking a *rewarding experience*. P11 drew an interesting analogy to explain what tracking means to her: "*...when I was pretty young, I was really susceptible to being awarded Gold Stars, it makes me want to do the thing I've been awarded Gold Star for more. So the process of tracking was like awarding myself the Gold Star... So what I learned was track what you want to do more*." P11 explained that focusing on the positives makes the tracking experience rewarding and less of a burden.

### Common Pitfall 2: Not Tracking Triggers and Context

People who were new to QS made a common mistake of focusing too much on tracking symptoms or outcome measures but failing to capture the important triggers or context. This failure resulted in not having enough clues on how to improve outcome measures. P9 described, "*...I've been trying all this biometric tracking trying to be more consistent in my health than have more healthy habits. But the whole time, not just my health habits, but even my tracking habits were completely reliant on my emotional state. So here I was trying to track all these symptoms, and I was completely ignoring the cause*." After a few months of trial and error, P9 modified her tracking routine from capturing biomedical data to capturing negative emotion and the biometric data surrounding it. Likewise, P3—a student who diligently tracked every activity—was able to alter his initial question after a few months of tracking. He initially wanted to know *where his time was going* as specifically as possible. He kept track of time and planned everything ahead using a calendar. However, after tracking for four months, he realized he needed to step back from the day-to-day events and ask a different question: "*how to balance my life?*" It is difficult to know exactly what to track or what questions to ask in the beginning. In fact, the initial tracking phase helped Q-Selfers redefine what to track or what questions to ask. Q-Selfers thus endeavored to step back from time-to-time and reflect on whether they are tracking the right thing for the right reason. This finding is in line with Li et al.'s report on the transitions between the Maintenance phase and the Discovery phase during self-reflection [18].

## HOW DID YOU DO IT?

In this section, we address the second prime question, "*how did you do it?*" We examine tools for data collection and exploration, reasons for building custom tools, and visualizations Q-Selfers created. We also describe the notion of *self-experimentation*, a prevalent practice among Q-Selfers to get concrete answers to their questions.

### Data Collection and Exploration Tools

Q-Selfers reported using a variety of tools for self-tracking, which we categorize into *Data Collection Tools* and *Data Exploration Tools* (see Table 2). Data exploration tools include data analysis and visualization tools. On average, Q-Selfers used 2.1 data collection tools ($SD = 1.08$) and 1.4 data exploration tools ($SD = 0.63$).

*Data Collection Tools.* Commercial hardware, such as a health monitoring device (e.g., Fitbit, ZEO, WIFI-scale, heart rate monitor), was the most popular tool (56%) followed by spreadsheets, such as Excel or Google Docs (40%). Eleven (21%) built custom software such as a snoring app, mood/stress tracking app, activity/location tracking app, or productivity tracking software. Ten (19%) used commercial software, such as standalone mobile apps for tracking sleep, productivity, or food. Two speakers reported building custom hardware, such as wearable sensors for tracking posture and smiles.

*Data Exploration Tools.* The most popular data exploration tool was a spreadsheet (e.g., Excel, Google spreadsheet) for running simple statistics and creating graphs (44%). Eighteen (35%) built custom software that required some programming such as using open-source JavaScript libraries to create a website or mobile apps with data visualization features. Fourteen (27%) relied on a commercial website (e.g., Fitbit, ZEO, Quantified Mind) where visualizations are auto-generated once data is manually entered or uploaded from commercial hardware. Six (12%) used commercial software that often interconnected with commercial hardware to aid with analytics and data storage (e.g., software that comes with blood glucose monitor). Only two speakers used statistical software, such as R. None mentioned using commercial data exploration software (e.g., Tableau).

In all, thirty (58%) used only commercial tools, twelve (23%) used only user-generated (custom) tools, and ten (19%) used a mix of commercial and user-generated tools for collecting and exploring data. Our analysis shows that not many tools support the whole spectrum of QS from data collection to data exploration. We also found that many Q-Selfers built custom tools, especially for data exploration purposes. Both findings indicate issues with data portability, regarding people having to export and import data from a tracking tool to an exploration tool. To further exacerbate the situation, some companies (e.g., Fitbit) charge fees for people to export their data, which makes it hard to combine data from different sources.

| Data Collection Tool | % (#) |
|---|---|
| commercial hardware | 56% (29) |
| spreadsheet | 40% (21) |
| custom software | 21% (11) |
| pen and paper | 21% (11) |
| commercial software | 19% (10) |
| commercial website | 10% (5) |
| camera | 6% (3) |
| open-source platform | 6% (3) |
| custom hardware | 4% (2) |
| other | 10% (5) |

| Data Exploration Tool | % (#) |
|---|---|
| spreadsheet | 44% (23) |
| custom software | 35% (18) |
| commercial website | 27% (14) |
| commercial software | 12% (6) |
| open-source platform | 8% (4) |
| statistical software | 4% (2) |
| pen and paper | 2% (1) |

**Table 2. Types of data collection tools and data exploration tools and usage frequency.**

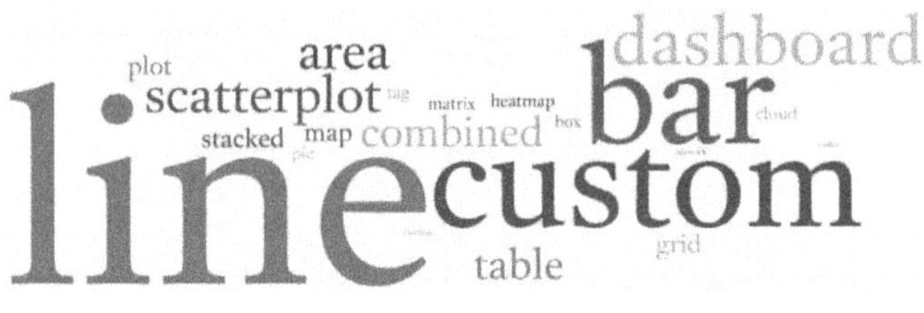


**Figure 4. Tag cloud showing the usage frequency of visualization types. Line chart, bar chart, and custom visualizations were the top 3 most commonly used ones.**

### Visualization Types

Visualizations were the key means to gain insights from data. To analyze how Q-Selfers explored data, we captured 188 screenshots composed of 243 charts and types of graphical feedback. From these, we analyzed visualization types and frequency of usage. We identified 21 unique visualization types, which are shown in Figure 4 (word size reflects the frequency of usage).

Line charts were by far the most frequently used, followed by bar charts and custom visualizations such as an infographic-style website, calendar (Figure 5-a), physical light (Figure 5-b), map and photo grid on timeline (Figure 5-c), and a combined visualization composed of line charts, stacked bar charts, and tables (Figure 5-d). Figure 5-a is an example of "*appropriation*" where iCal, a personal calendar application, was used for tracking and visualization purposes. Figure 5-b was a rare example of real-time feedback—the blue lights blink whenever wearable EEG sensors detect smiling. Figure 5-c and Figure 5-d were highly customized and complex timeline visualizations, which helped creators understand how they spent time online and offline (Figure 5-c) and how to optimize performance (Figure 5-d).

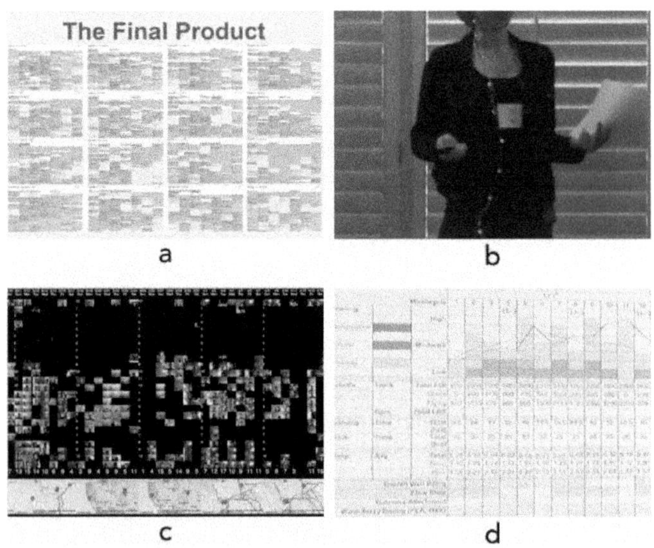


**Figure 5. Examples of custom visualizations.**

### Reasons for Building Custom Tools

Although numerous commercial self-tracking tools are available, many Q-Selfers built their own tools. We identified common reasons for building custom tools. First, few commercial tools support the two key features that Q-Selfers prefer—(1) being able to track and explore data using a *single tool*, and (2) being able to perform *self-experimentation*. When Q-Selfers had the technical ability, they built a custom tool to meet their needs. For example, P15 had a snoring problem. He first looked for existing snoring apps, but they did not have the features he wanted. He envisioned an app that could do both snore tracking and analysis. He also wanted to test if certain things (e.g., snoring remedies, drug, alcohol) affected his snoring. Not finding what he wanted, he built an app called SnoreLab, which he released to a commercial app store. Second, Q-Selfers built a new tool when they wanted to do centralized tracking as P23 remarked, "*I found myself using Nike Plus for my exercise, my Foursquare for social check-ins and several different apps just for tracking my time. When I finally said, 'You know what? I'm fed up with this. I want to make my own tool that allows me to do this in a more cohesive manner.'*" Third, many Q-Selfers built custom websites for data presentation, which was typically done with publicly available visualization APIs such as d3 [5] and the Google Charts API [8]. Lastly, some Q-Selfers built a custom tool simply because no existing tool supported their needs. One example is software developed by P70 who tracked her inventory of clothes that would help her coordinating clothes and simplify her wardrobe.

### Self-Experimentation

Q-Selfers wanted to draw definitive conclusions from their QS practice—such as identifying correlation (e.g., sleep and cognitive performance are not correlated) or even causation (e.g., weight tracking causes weight loss). To accomplish this goal, they needed to first generate hypotheses to test. Testing ideas came from careful observations of previous behavioral patterns (e.g., P39 strongly suspected a beer allergy), other speakers' Show & Tell talks (e.g., P33 was inspired by another Q-Selfer who tested whether eating butter increases cognitive performance), or individual needs (e.g., P76 wanted to find the right medication dosage).

Q-Selfers often described the process of seeking answers as *self-experimentation*. When used in an academic context, self-experimentation means participating in one's own experiments when recruiting other participants is not feasible. However, in QS, the goal of self-experimentation is *not* to find generalizable knowledge, but to find meaningful self-knowledge that matters to individuals. P33 emphasized, "*I discovered the importance of testing for myself because what works for some people does not work for me.*"

### Common Pitfall 3: Lack of Scientific Rigor

Q-Selfers conducted a wide variety of self-experimentations without having a control condition. A typical personal experiment resembles the experiment that P69 conducted—he observed patterns between his allergic reactions and spending on beer, so he suspected that beer might have caused his allergy: "*So ignoring the doctor, who said I was fine, I decided to do one final experiment. We had colleagues going away, and it was a very happy day, I drank lots of beers. By the following Sunday and the following Monday I was in the worst form that I had ever been, and I decided that was enough for me. This must be the trigger.*" P69 did not control for other confounding factors, which threatens the internal validity of his finding. However, as long as Q-Selfers were happy with the outcomes of tracking, most of them did not seem to care about the lack of scientific rigor, as it is not the main goal of QS.

Although a minority, some Q-Selfers attempted to design more rigorous personal experiments. We identified three approaches that could possibly increase internal validity—(1) having a control condition, (2) triangulating with other methods, and (3) using the experience sampling method. We note that the terms we used in this paper such as "internal validity" and "triangulation" are our interpretation of the behavior, not the language used by the Q-Selfers.

Some Q-Selfers conducted self-experimentation with a control condition to reduce biases. As a doctor and researcher, P55 was well aware of skepticism his colleagues had about QS. He said, "*When I talk about these things, I feel like I'm talking by myself because most of all in medicine, and in science, they're going to roll their eyes. It's like science is being done in your garage, but I really think that there's some real potential.*" Then he explained how he conducted a within-subjects design to identify what triggers his atrial fibrillation by comparing what he did right before the onset of the disease (hazard period) to the usual routine (control period). Then he calculated an Odds Ratio—a measure of association between an exposure and an outcome—and identified risk factors for his atrial fibrillation such as caffeine, air flight stress, more than 1 glass of wine, and public speaking in the previous 2 hours of the onset of the disease.

*Triangulation*—using two or more different methods to measure the same phenomenon—was commonly used to facilitate data validation through cross verification from multiple sources. P28 said, "*... if I compare my Zeo data to my Fitbit data I really only wake up when I flip over in bed, so it's actually very accurate for me.*" However, P7 came up with a disturbing finding: "*I discovered that my glucose meters aren't that good. So, comparing the measurements from these two different meters, I only came out with R-squared of 0.46, which I would have hoped for a lot better agreement between the two meters.*"

Some Q-Selfers employed the *experience sampling method* (ESM). P59 used an app called 'The Mappiness' to track his stress level. He configured the app to prompt him at random times during the day. The number of prompts was also configurable. He acknowledged that ESM produces the gold standard of experience measurement.

Nevertheless, critics abound. Although some biases might be reduced from some of these attempts, critics claim that *experimenters* might be biased to produce the result they expect to see [26]. By definition, QS is designed and conducted by the experimenter, and thus, the issue regarding experimenter's bias remains open.

## WHAT DID YOU LEARN?

The way Q-Selfers reported their learning was twofold. First, they reported insights gained from their data exploration. Second, they reported desirable and undesirable outcomes in a broader tracking context. After we report on these two types of learning, we discuss the key hurdle in gaining insights, which is data interpretation.

### Gained Insights

Q-Selfers often summarized their findings by reporting *descriptive statistics*. For example, after tracking the usage of tabs in a web browser, P4 learned that in a two-month period he opened or closed 32,000 tabs, which averages to about 500 a day. This finding led him to think about his next project: extending his code to track every time he switches tabs as a proxy for how much attention he is giving to something. *Comparison measures* were common descriptive statistical methods that helped Q-Selfers quickly gain insights. When both control and intervention conditions were in place, they typically reported differences in means or Odds ratio. However, they could still compare within themselves without the explicit control condition by categorizing data points in several bins after data collection was complete and then comparing differences across the bins. One example is how P78 reported his sleep data—he compared sleep efficiency and time to fall asleep across restless nights and restful nights. Q-Selfers also compared themselves against the general population with similar demographics if they had access to the population data. P70, a Canadian engineer who tracked work time, learned that she worked more hours than average for Canadian workers.

Q-Selfers with a statistical background reported statistical test results. *Correlation* was the most commonly reported statistical test. For example, P18 learned that "*high idea days were correlated with conferences, sedentary events, Internet usages, high calories, and very little working out*," which he found problematic. People were surprised when they found low correlation between things that they thought were highly associated: "*So far, I had pretty much no correlation, so it's really interesting to think about how I have found no correlations between even the most meaningful things in my life and how I rate the day*" [P17]. Q-Selfers with no statistical background still reported perceived correlation in layperson's language: "*When my symptoms were good or when my body felt good, I happened to be in a good mood. When my symptoms were bad or my body felt bad, the mood or my mental state was bad*" [P61].

Stepping back from the data, Q-Selfers articulated high-level, qualitative take-away points. For example, P11 learned that "*the biggest contributors to my daily happiness are the small things*," and P26 learned "*how tragic it is that we all age*" after taking self-portrait shots every day for a year. Some of them took an interpretive approach and declared that, "*it's not all about the numbers*" [P23]. After 6 months of tracking GPS data, P23 emphasized, "*Numbers are very important, but I think we can aspire for something higher, and I think it also is about the perspective that it allows you to gain.*" The general agreement was that important things are found from long-term tracking although people are easily influenced by a day-to-day activity or single data point. The challenge, however, was to find meaningful measures that reflect long-term trends and to keep preserving the initial motivation to tracking even when the latest data point conveys discouraging information.

### Tracking Outcomes

Q-Selfers discussed various outcomes of self-tracking, most of which were desirable outcomes such that tracking helped them achieve their initial goals. Many people improved their health and created healthy habits, such as eating healthy, losing weight, and being physically active. Others identified triggers of symptoms and managed to avoid them. P35 realized that driving and drinking coffee were triggers for his panic attacks, and eliminated coffee altogether from his diet, which resulted in a decrease in frequency and severity of the attacks. On the contrary, P8 found a disease that he had not known before, which was ironically a positive outcome for him. P8 initially got into QS to improve his body and get back into shape, but he later discovered that he had Crohn's disease by noticing anomalies from the stool tests he ordered online and his genetic test data. Another positive outcome was the increased awareness of oneself and of the surrounding environment. Being mindful of these things helped people see themselves in a new way such that they were able to understand where ideas came from and how the ideas evolved [P1] or how to create a suitable learning environment for maximizing performance [P41]. Lastly, Q-Selfers reported a positive *reactivity effect* (i.e., change in frequency of the behavior often occurred in the desirable direction) in tracking emotion [P9] and posture [P53]. "*I realized that just by tracking my emotions, I was completely changing them*," said P9, who was able to stabilize her emotional state and prevent herself from experiencing negative emotions.

A few Q-Selfers experienced undesirable outcomes, such as frustration, tracking fatigue, or relapse. Being aware of and confronting negative emotions through tracking caused frustration. "*Because I'm aware of it, it makes it even worse because now I can tell that I'm more anxious than I should be. Before, I was oblivious of being anxious*," said P54, who tracked anxiety and stress. Tracking fatigue was another common outcome of tracking, especially for intensive trackers. After one month of intense tracking on public transit usage, P77 learned many surprising and unexpected findings—such as average commuting time, total cost of using the bus, cost per hour of travel time, and cost per mile. He would not have learned this had he not been tracking, but he said, "*By the end of it, I was really sick of doing it. I just got really fatigued.*" However, as the result of a month-long tracking, P77 decided to buy a bike instead of taking the bus because taking the bus was more costly and time-consuming than he had expected. Stopping tracking was not harmful in this case. In fact, P77 used his findings to make a good decision. However, P35, who thought that his panic disorder was under control, stopped tracking and consequently started having panic attacks again. To deal with the relapse and to sustain his commitment to tracking, he built a custom tool to lower the user burden of capturing and looked for a recovery partner for accountability.

### Open Challenge: Difficulty in Data Interpretation

Data interpretation was a key hurdle for many Q-Selfers. "*It's not that we lack the information, we're virtually drowning in it. The obstacle is that we don't have the proper tools to interpret the significance of our data,*" said P61, a personal trainer who used to track 11 different things and cross-referenced them with sleep, mood, energy level and acuity. However, after he could not figure out how to extract meaningful information from the 2 years of data, he simplified his tracking strategy to track only two variables. We observed many people who simplified their tracking strategy after their first failed attempt because there was no easy way to analyze and interpret data. Visualizations were helpful in gaining insights, but again, the learning curve for data manipulation (i.e., data cleanup and formatting) and identifying and creating the most appropriate visualization for a given data type was very steep. Helping the general public effectively explore and easily understand their data using visualizations is an active research area for the Information Visualization research community.

## IMPLICATIONS FOR SELF-TRACKING TOOL DESIGN

We have identified Q-Selfers' common pitfalls and workarounds when they practice self-tracking. Better self-tracking tool designs could help any potential tracker avoid some of the pitfalls. Here we identify future research efforts that could help address these problems. We discuss how our findings can have broad implications in designing and developing self-tracking technologies.

### Provide Early Feedback to Help Identify What to Track

In deciding what to track, Q-Selfers encountered two common pitfalls—tracking too many things, which might cause tracking fatigue, and not tracking triggers and context, which might undermine attempts to gain insights later. When the tracker's motivation is high, it is not a problem to track many things, especially at the beginning of the tracking practice. Tracking multiple things could help people decide which items to keep and which items to stop tracking. What is important then is the self-tracking tool's ability to automate data analysis, provide early feedback on the relationships between different factors, and to suggest eliminating variables that do not seem to correlate with anything. Q-Selfers usually put off data exploration (e.g., running correlations, visualizing data) until later because often, the process involved tedious tasks such as cleaning up data, formatting, and running statistical tests, which could be dramatically reduced by largely automating the process [10]. We envision a self-tracking tool extracting meaningful information, initiating early check-ins, providing real-time visual/textual feedback, and showing comparisons across conditions or correlations among significant factors that can be easily understood.

### Support Self-Experimentation by Design

Q-Selfers conducted self-experimentation while compromising scientific rigor. Although innate limitations of self-experimentation (e.g., the experimenter's bias) are hard to avoid, we could help people conduct more rigorous self-experimentation by integrating the single-case research design format [12] into the self-tracking technology design. The three requirements for single-case research design include continuous assessment, baseline assessment, and variability in data [12]. Automated sensing allows easy, unobtrusive, and repeated capturing of a behavior, which could facilitate continuous assessment of the target behavior. Moreover, self-tracking technology could become a platform where people can systematically configure a varying length of baseline and intervention period, tracking frequency, and independent/dependent variables. Quantified-mind [24], a cognitive performance testing website, conveys the similar idea of walking people through setting up self-experimentation. However, cognitive performance is measured by a set of cognitive game scores (hence the fixed dependent variables), which is known to have large practice effects (i.e., repeated testing increases the score).

### Maximize the Benefits of Manual Tracking

Sensing and computer automation have many advantages in collecting personal data in terms of reducing mental workload and increasing data accuracy. However, these advantages do not come for free: this automated data collection could reduce awareness and self-reflection resulting from people's engagement with data collection. Q-Selfers expressed that they feel "intimacy with data" when they track data manually. It appears that people make sense of data not only when they explore data but also when they collect data. In addition, some types of data (e.g., subjective sleep quality and pain), by definition, can only be collected via manual tracking. For these reasons, several Q-Selfers built manual tracking tools that drastically lower the user burden, which helped them easily track data and increase awareness. Pushing this idea further, we envision striking a balance between fully automated sensing and manual self-report that can increase awareness, achieve better accuracy, and decrease mental workload.

### Promote Self-Reflection

Ironically, the name, Quantified Self is misleading in that it makes people think that Q-Selfers' goal is to quantify their behaviors. It is not. Collecting and quantifying data is just one aspect of QS. The ultimate goal is to reflect upon one's data, extract meaningful insights, and make positive changes, which are the hardest part of QS. HCI research on supporting self-reflection on health monitoring data includes helping people create *unstructured, open-ended* diaries and *sharing* them with others in-person [20]. QS Meetup is another example of engaging people—both speakers and the audience—in self-reflection through storytelling. These are good starting points, and we should further examine ways to support self-reflection on personal data with an aim to enhance *positive reactivity effects*.

## CONCLUSION

We analyzed QS Meetup talks and identified that Q-Selfers wanted to improve health, maximize work performance, and find new life experiences through self-tracking. Although many Q-Selfers had positive outcomes from self-tracking, some of them had difficulties throughout the process, such as tracking too many things which led to tracking fatigue, not tracking triggers and context which led to not gaining insights, and lacking scientific rigor which led to inconclusive results. Our goal was to gain insights from Q-Selfers for designing better self-tracking tools in general. Experienced trackers' workarounds might help people avoid some of the pitfalls, but better designs could promote broad adoption of self-tracking technologies by fundamentally boosting their benefits. Specific areas for future research include exploring ways to provide early feedback, to support designing rigorous self-experimentation, to leverage the benefits of—while easing the burden of—manual tracking, and to promote self-reflection. Once a motivated tracker meets a well-designed self-tracking tool, exciting possibilities will arise for gaining insights for health, wellness, and other aspects of life.

## ACKNOWLEDGMENTS

We thank Daniel Epstein, Tamara Denning, and A.J. Brush for their feedback. This work was in part supported by Intel Science and Technology Center for Pervasive Computing.

## REFERENCES

1. Ali, A.A., Hossain, S.M., Hovsepian, K., Rahman, M.M., Plarre, K., & Kumar, S. mPuff: automated detection of cigarette smoking puffs from respiration measurements. *IPSN '12*, (2012), 269–80.
2. Bentley, F. et al. Health Mashups: Presenting statistical patterns between wellbeing data and context in natural language to promote behavior change. *ToCHI*, (2013).
3. Beyer, H. & Holtzblatt, K. *Contextual Design: Defining Customer-Centered Systems*. Morgan Kaufmann (1998).
4. Consolvo, S. et al. Activity sensing in the wild: a field trial of Ubifit garden. *CHI '08*, (2008), 1797–806.
5. d3. d3js.org.
6. Fitbit. http://www.fitbit.com.
7. Fox, S., & Duggan, M. Tracking for health. *Pew Internet & American Life Project*, January 28, 2013. http://pewinternet.org/Reports/2013/Tracking-for-Health.aspx, accessed on September 17, 2013.
8. Google Charts. https://developers.google.com/chart.
9. Jawbone UpBand. https://jawbone.com/up.
10. Kandel, S., Paepcke, A., Hellerstein, J., & Heer, J. Wrangler: Interactive visual specification of data transformation scripts. *CHI '11*, (2011), 3363–72.
11. Kay, M. et al. Lullaby: a capture & access system for understanding the sleep environment. *UbiComp '12*, (2012), 226–34.
12. Kazdin, A.E. *Single-case research designs: Methods for clinical and applied settings*. Oxford University Press (2011).
13. Klasnja, P., & Pratt, W. Healthcare in the pocket: Mapping the space of mobile-phone health interventions. *J Biomed Inform 1* (2012), 184–98.
14. Kopp, J. Self-monitoring: A literature review of research and practice. *Social Work Research & Abstracts 24, 4*, Oxford University Press (1988), 8–20.
15. Korotitsch, W.J., & Nelson-Gray, R.O. An overview of self-monitoring research in assessment and treatment. *Psychological Assessment 11(4)* (1999), 415–25.
16. larklife. http://lark.com/products/larklife/experience.
17. Li, I., Dey, A., & Forlizzi, J. A stage-based model of personal informatics systems. *CHI '10*, (2010), 557–66.
18. Li, I., Dey, A., & Forlizzi, J. Understanding my data, myself: supporting self-reflection with Ubicomp technologies. *UbiComp '11*, (2011), 405–14.
19. Lin, J.J., Mamykina, L., Lindtner, S., Delajoux, G., Strub, H. Fish'n'Steps: encouraging physical activity with an interactive computer game. *UbiComp '06*, (2006), 261–78.
20. Mamykina, L., Mynatt, E., Davidson, P., Greenblatt, D. MAHI: investigation of social scaffolding for reflective thinking in diabetes management. *CHI '08*, (2008), 477–86.
21. Morris, M., & Guilak, F. Mobile heart health: project highlight. *Pervasive Computing 8(2)* (2009), 57–61.
22. Nike Fuelband. http://www.nike.com/cdp/fuelband.
23. Patel, R.A., Klasnja, P., Hartzler, A., Unruh, K.T., & Pratt, W. Probing the benefits of real-time tracking during cancer care. *AMIA '12 Fall Symposium*, (2012).
24. Quantified Mind. http://www.quantified-mind.com.
25. Quantified Self. http://quantifiedself.com.
26. Rosenthal, R. *Experimenter effects in behavioral research*. Appleton-Century-Crofts (1966).
27. Swan, M. Emerging patient-driven health care models: an examination of health social networks, consumer personalized medicine and quantified self-tracking. *Int J Environ Res Public Health 6(2)* (2009), 492–525.
28. Technology Review. http://www.technologyreview.com/news/514356/stephen-wolfram-on-personal-analytics.
29. Troshynski, E., Lee, C., & Dourish, P. Accountabilities of presence: reframing location-based systems. *CHI '08*, (2008), 487–96.
30. Wolfram. http://www.wolfram.com.
31. Zeo. http://myzeo.com.

# BodyDiagrams: Improving Communication of Pain Symptoms through Drawing

**Amy Jang**
Computer Science Dept.
Stanford University
Stanford, CA 94305 USA
insunj@cs.stanford.edu

**Diana MacLean**
Computer Science Dept.
Stanford University
Stanford, CA 94305 USA
malcdi@stanford.edu

**Jeffrey Heer**
Computer Science & Engineering Dept.
University of Washington
Seattle, WA 98195-2350
jheer@uw.edu

## ABSTRACT
Thousands of people use the Internet to discuss pain symptoms. While communication between patients and physicians involves both verbal and physical interactions, online discussions of symptoms typically comprise text only. We present BodyDiagrams, an online interface for expressing symptoms via drawings and text. BodyDiagrams augment textual descriptions with pain diagrams drawn over a reference body and annotated with severity and temporal metadata. The resulting diagrams can easily be shared to solicit feedback and advice. We also conduct a two-phase user study to assess BodyDiagrams' communicative efficacy. In the first phase, users describe pain symptoms using BodyDiagrams and a text-only interface; in the second phase, medical professionals evaluate these descriptions. We find that patients are significantly more confident that their BodyDiagrams will be correctly interpreted, while medical professionals rated BodyDiagrams as significantly more informative than text descriptions. Both groups indicated a preference for using diagrams to communicate physical symptoms in the future.

### Author Keywords
Health; pain diagrams; symptom communication; drawing.

### ACM Classification Keywords
H.5.2 Information Interfaces and Presentation: UI

## INTRODUCTION
Millions of people use the Internet as a source of medical information. A 2013 Pew Survey on "Health Online" reports that one third of American adults use the Internet as a diagnostic tool [7]. While most users tend to read information contributed by others, thousands also initiate discussions around personal health conditions. A typical format is for a user to compose a textual description of her condition, and then post it on a forum such as MedHelp (`www.medhelp.org`) or PatientsLikeMe (`www.patientslikeme.org`) in an effort to garner feedback. Although people discuss a wide range of medical conditions online, here we focus on what we call *physically-oriented conditions* (POCs): conditions in which physical attributes of symptoms such as location and severity are a differentiating factor in diagnosis or treatment. Examples of POCs include chronic pain, digestive health conditions and musculoskeletal problems.

Text is often an ineffective communication medium for POCs. Consider the following example from MedHelp.com:

> *"hi iv had this awfull sharp nervey pain in the middle of my back which shoots round to my ribs on the left side..."*

Here the poster is describing back pain. However, the precise location of where the pain starts in the back and how it shoots to the rib is vague. As a result, respondents had a wide range of interpretations for this symptom, and the user had to clarify (again with text) the precise physical location of the pain. Even when users include highly detailed information on symptom location, the resulting description can be confusing:

> *"the pain is at the right side of my right knee, its situated near the fibula, not indicating that my bone is the one hurting, the pain is distinctive as it only hurts in a manner or form of a thread, the pain doesn't take up all of the right part of my knee, its just a thread shape pain that seems to extend from the femur down to the fibula."*

Reading this description, the reader must translate the poster's words into locations on her body to interpret and respond to the information. The overhead entailed in this parsing process might not only damage the reader's interpretation of the condition, but also affect the type and quality of response given.

In addition to being a poor expression of physical location, text can impose other shortcomings: users may have an insufficient vocabulary for describing symptoms, or poor writing skills. Moreover, a single symptom can be described in several ways without using shared terminology. This last issue may complicate searches for related posts.

In contrast, drawing provides a natural way of directly indicating physical locations. Indeed pain diagrams, such as the ones used in Figure 1, are commonly used in medical practice. In addition to location, symptom properties such as severity or depth also lend themselves to a visual encoding.

We offer two primary research contributions. First, we present *BodyDiagrams*, an online interface for expressing


*CHI 2014*, April 26–May 1, 2014, Toronto, Ontario, Canada.

http://dx.doi.org/10.1145/2556288.2557223

symptoms via drawing and text. BodyDiagrams is based on insights distilled from multiple rounds of design iteration, and synthesizes the benefits of text (flexibility, high resolution) with those of drawing (precise location and directness). With BodyDiagrams, users can visually encode symptom attributes such as severity, frequency and temporal sequence. BodyDiagrams is available at `www.mybodydiagram.com`.

Second, we conduct a two-phase user study with both patients and medical professionals in which we assess the efficacy of BodyDiagrams as a communication medium compared to plain text. Patients regard their BodyDiagrams descriptions as significantly more interpretable, while medical professionals regard BodyDiagrams as significantly more complete and relevant. We also find ordering effects in description content and quality. Our results help validate our design decisions and provide insights for future deployments, including use of an iterative description process to further improve medical communication.

## RELATED WORK

In everyday medical practice, pain questionnaires with diagrams are sometimes used as self-report tools for patients to communicate with their doctors [12]. In these questionnaires, users select a characteristic word, location, severity and time information to describe their pain.

Researchers have conducted studies on the utility of pain diagrams as screening or diagnostic tools. Results vary, and may depend on the condition being screened for. Jamieson et al. [9] studied whether experts could distinguish between healthy individuals with pain and individuals suffering from chronic pain using only pain diagrams. They found that experts performed only slightly better than random, while a decision model based on the area covered by the drawings achieved 70% accuracy. Fortin et al. [6] achieved no false positives in using pain drawings to screen for sacroiliac joint dysfunction; they were not able to measure false negatives.

Other literature uses pain diagrams to discover and define regions of referred pain cased by joint inflammation. Dreyfuss et al. [4] extracted consistent pain referral patterns from subjects whose thoracic zygapophyseal joints were stimulated via intra-articular injection. A similar but separate study by Dreyfuss et al. [3] found consistent referral patterns stemming from lateral atlanto-axial inflammation, while atlanto-occipital inflammation resulted in varying referral patterns. The authors conclude that pain drawings might be useful for differential diagnosis.

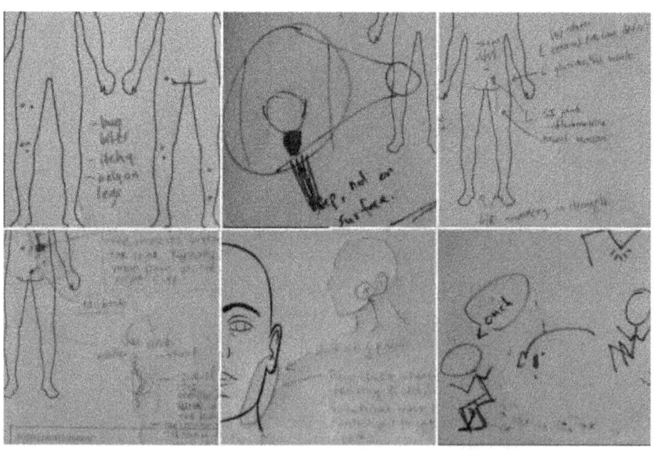

Figure 1: Sample hand-drawn diagrams from our pilot study, drawn on a traditional pen-and-paper pain diagram.

Ghinea et al. [8] propose a GIS-based system for digitizing hand-drawn back pain diagrams, motivated by the desire to search for symptoms on particular bodily regions. However, their system includes no interface for direct user input. Felix et al. [5] conducted a study to determine whether computerized pain drawings by patients undergoing spinal surgery could be used to automatically evaluate recovery. Their preliminary studies supported the feasibility of this approach. Spyridonis and Ghinea [17] found that patients with spinal cord injuries found 3D diagrams a more expressive medium for describing their pain symptoms than 2D diagrams.

In the HCI research space, several tools have been developed to aid physician interpretation of clinical histories, the most notable being the LifeLines project [14, 15] and Bui's TimeLine [2]. Both projects integrate HCI principles to visualize patient records for medical professionals. However, they are designed as browsing tools rather than communication aids.

Finally, several visual pain trackers are available as downloadable apps or as online services on sites like MedHelp [11] and Partners Against Pain [13]. WedMD's visual symptom checker allows users to explore symptoms by clicking affected body parts on a model [18]. However, these tools are limited in expressivity, and are designed either for self-tracking or dispensing information rather than communication. To our knowledge, Body Diagrams is the first tool developed through researching user needs in this space, and is unique in its synthesis of visual symptom expression with traditional textual communication.

## DESIGNING BODYDIAGRAMS

Our overarching goal in developing BodyDiagrams was to improve digital communication of physically-oriented conditions by leveraging natural visual relationships between symptoms and their attributes. To this end, we anchored our process around two design goals:

*Support natural symptom-drawing patterns.* To facilitate intuitive authoring of POC descriptions, we wanted BodyDiagrams to support drawing and annotation patterns expressed by users drawing symptoms with pen and paper.

*Enhance interpretability through a synthesis of increased content and compact representation.* To support accurate interpretation of physical symptom descriptions, we sought to incorporate more relevant content and represent it visually.

In this section we discuss our design process, summarizing our pilot study [10] and describing our iterative testing via Amazon's Mechanical Turk, and present a set of resulting design insights. We then present the BodyDiagrams interface design.

Table 1: Drawing patterns observed in our paper pilot study.

| Pattern | Example | Notes |
|---|---|---|
| color |  | rarely utilized; most participants used only one color even when describing a range of symptoms. |
| precise marks | 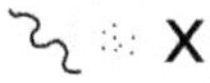 | indicates precise symptom location |
| regions |  | indicates general location of symptom |
| text | captions | describe drawn marks |
| arrows |  | link text annotations to drawn marks |
| zoom | call outs with more detail | users drew scaled versions of body parts for higher resolution |
| views | side-view, cross-section | users drew body parts in different perspectives |
| reference marks | vertebrae, knee cap | users drew body parts as reference "anchors" for the relative location of their symptoms |

Table 2: BodyDiagrams encodings for symptom attributes.

| Attribute | Severity | Frequency | Location |
|---|---|---|---|
| Control |  |  | 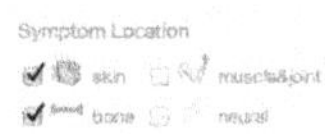 |
| Examples | 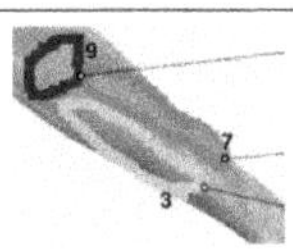 | 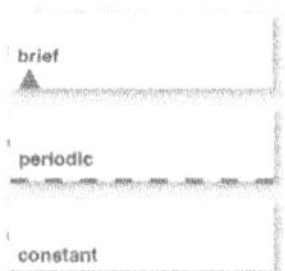 |  |

## Pilot Study

To better understand how people conceptualize and communicate symptoms, we first conducted a pen-and-paper pilot study. Our pilot study comprised 8 participants (4 female, 4 male, most early 20's) recruited through an open email call at our university. We provided participants with a paper body diagram template and several colored pens. We prompted them to "describe a physical symptom [she/he] experienced recently". We interviewed each participant upon completion. Each session took about 45 minutes, and participants received a $10 Amazon Gift Card.

Figure 1 shows a selection of pilot study diagrams. We observed several commonalities (summarized in Table 1) as well as procedural patterns, which we discuss below.

*Users draw accurately.* Both location and shape of drawn marks is intentional and accurate. Users often physically referred to their own body (by touching the area in question) before drawing thè corresponding mark on paper.

*Users draw, link, describe, and repeat.* When recording a symptom, users would first draw it (sometimes utilizing multiple lines or marks), then create a reference line from the mark to white space, and finally describe the symptom in text. Then, they would move on to draw then next symptom. This procedural pattern was uniform across participants.

*Users draw the most severe symptom first.* Though most users' symptoms had chronological structure, users drew the most severe symptom first and then "filled in" secondary symptoms, regardless of chronological order.

*Users tend not to iterate, but iteration provides better results.* Only one user drew a "draft" description before drawing a final one. He noted that while the first drawing contained the relevant information, the second one called out important details and was superior. Other users commented that categorizing symptoms without drafting them first was difficult.

### Iterative Design Process

Based on our pilot study observations, we developed a prototype BodyDiagrams interface. We then followed an iterative design process including evaluations with Amazon's Mechanical Turk (MTurk). Over four major interface revisions, we recruited 10-12 MTurk workers (Turkers), gave them a synthesized pain description, and asked them to replicate it using BodyDiagrams. Turkers then completed a post-task survey and were paid $1.00. By fixing the input condition, we were able to observe the effect of new features on the BodyDiagrams descriptions and compare them across iterations.

### Design Considerations

Over the course of iterative design, we distilled a set of key design insights for effective visual communication of symptoms. We summarize these below, highlighting supporting observations from our design process.

**DC1:** *Implement both freehand and regional drawing tools.* As drawing accurately with a mouse is difficult, our initial designs favored a purely shape or palette-based annotation approach. In our pilot study, however, users utilized regional marks in concert with free-form marks. The latter were used primarily when the precision of a symptom's location or shape was key to the description. This behavior was sustained in our online MTurk studies.

**DC2:** *Support the draw, link, describe, repeat cycle.* This cycle (described in our pilot study observations) embodies a natural procedural framework for how users develop visual symptom descriptions. Transitioning through the cycle's stages should be frictionless so as to allow the user to focus her attention on her description. In earlier versions of BodyDiagrams, which supported this process poorly, users reported higher levels of frustration. In later versions, Turkers utilized this feature seamlessly, without prior tutelage.

**DC3:** *Group consecutive marks into a single symptom.* It may take several marks to describe one symptom (e.g., a rash or a series of bug bites). We observed that users drew these compound symptoms consecutively before moving to annotate them. A natural way to extract compound symptoms and follow **DC2** is to automatically group consecutive marks.

**DC4:** *Structure symptom description input to capture inherent attributes.* Formal pain questionnaires, such as the McGill questionnaire [12], often ask patients to describe specific attributes of their pain symptoms. These include severity (typically scored on a horizontal, 1-10 scale [12]), descriptive characteristics (e.g., flickering, burning, radiating), location,

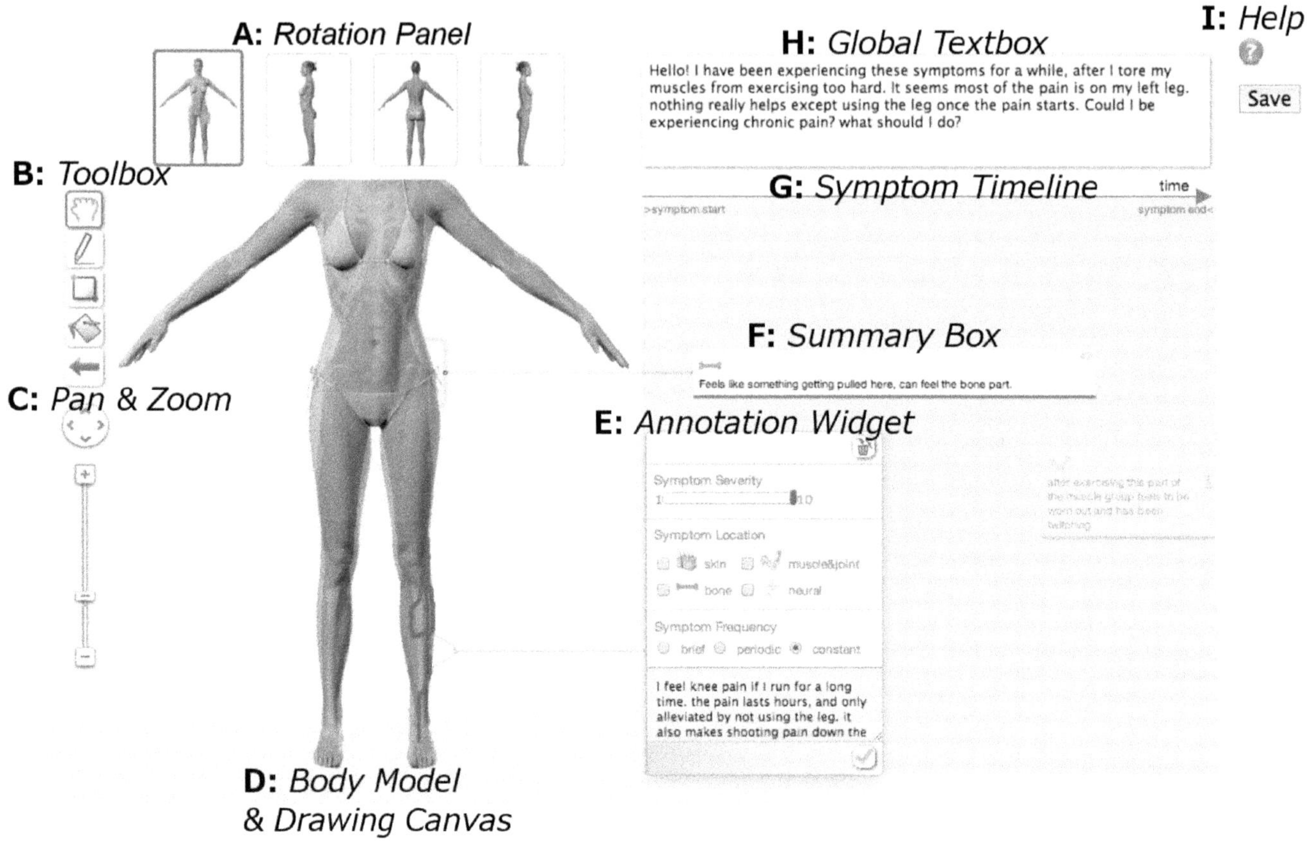


Figure 2: The BodyDiagrams interface, showing a user's description from Experiment 1.

depth and frequency. Table 2 illustrates how we mapped these features onto visual encodings in the annotation box. This was well received by participants: in comparison with their responses from prior iterations, Turkers reported that they felt their BodyDiagrams were a more complete, expressive, and useful complement to the prompt text. Structuring these attributes also resulted in a decrease in the quantity of text used to describe marks (194.5 vs. 226 characters on average).

**DC5:** *Represent symptoms chronologically.* In our pilot study we observed that users listed symptoms out of chronological order, starting with the most severe symptom. However, in all our studies, users still indicated chronological relationships between symptoms, sometimes explicitly labeling their annotations with numbers.

**DC6:** *Use a realistic body diagram.* In our pilot study we noticed that cartoonish diagrams are both difficult to identify with and also lack important physical detail. This led users to draw in reference lines (one user drew all the vertebrae in his back) as contextual anchors. To facilitate grounding and reference-finding, we introduced two accurate 3D body models (one male, one female) about halfway through our design process. The new diagrams were received positively. Average frustration decreased, and Turkers reported feeling comfortable with the model. One user commented, *"I really liked the model, it was easy to see the bones and the muscles"*.

**DC7:** *Encourage users to contribute difficult-to-draw information.* Some important information, such as medical history, medications and dosages, do not lend themselves to drawing. In early versions of BodyDiagrams, we noticed that Turkers omitted these details or shoehorned them into drawing annotations due to the lack of anywhere else to put them.

**DC8:** *Support detailed zooming.* Pilot study users vocalized frustration at not being able to zoom into the diagram, noting that describing symptoms present on small bodily regions, such as a finger, is difficult. Some frustrated users even drew zoomed-in versions of their own.

## THE BODYDIAGRAMS INTERFACE

Figure 3 shows a screenshot of BodyDiagrams being used by a patient to describe exercise-related muscle strain. We discuss key features (annotated with letters *A-I*) and how they instantiate our design considerations.

*A) Rotation Panel:* Clicking on a thumbnail rotates the main model. Drawings from each view are summarized on each respective panel, preserving context across view switches.

*B) Toolbox:* The toolbox provides a variety of mechanisms for authoring BodyDiagrams descriptions: undo, drag, pen (freehand) drawing, region drawing, and region fill. Supporting freehand drawing allows users to denote regions and shapes with accuracy when necessary **(DC1)**.

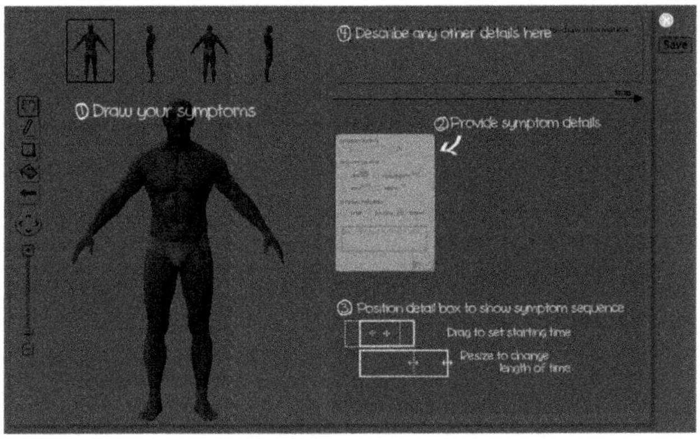


(a) Tutorial overlay.

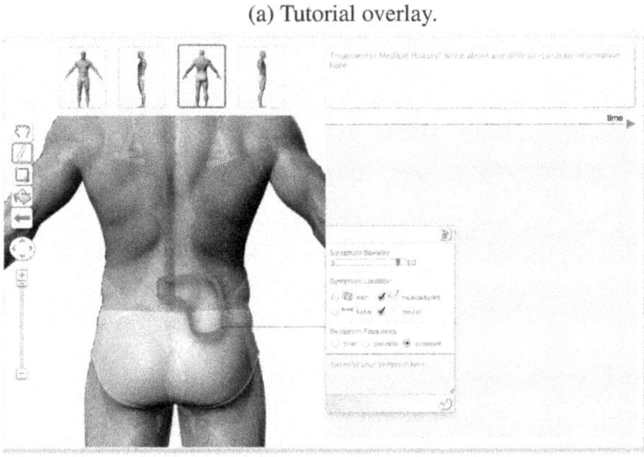


(b) Back pain drawn using pen.

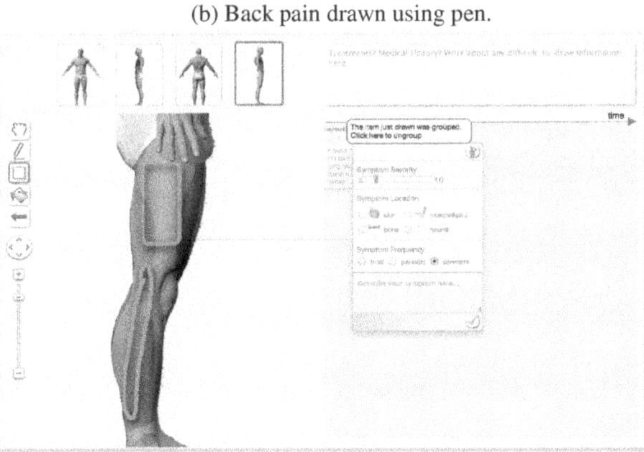


(c) Grouped leg pain drawings.

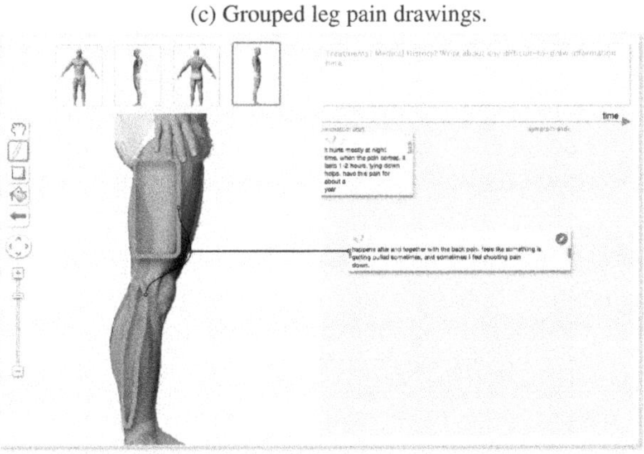


(d) Changing the duration and starting time.

Figure 3: Pain annotations using BodyDiagrams.

*C) Pan and Zoom:* Users can pan the model to a region of interest, and zoom to a desired level of detail **(DC8)**.

*D) Body Model / Drawing Canvas:* Users draw on the model using a mouse or trackpad. We created an anatomically accurate model using images from materials for medical students. The model includes both internal and external bodily reference points for drawing **(DC6)**.

*E) Annotation Widget:* This widget pops up after a mark is drawn, offering the user a place to input structured symptom metadata **(DC4)**. If the user draws multiple marks before entering data into the widget, these marks are grouped into a single symptom **(DC3)**. Upon clicking Save, the annotation is summarized in the summary box (F). This interaction process supports iterative authoring of symptom descriptions **(DC2)**.

*F) Summary Box:* A summarized representation of prior annotations. Clicking on this box opens it for editing.

*G) Symptom Timeline:* Horizontal positioning of symptom summaries on the timeline denotes symptom sequence and duration; vertical positioning matches, as closely as possible, the vertical position of the summary's corresponding drawn mark. Users can drag symptom summaries left or right to indicate their relative starting time, and resize them horizontally to indicate their duration, supporting chronological ordering of symptoms regardless of the order in which they were drawn **(DC5)**. In the figure shown, the user has indicated that he experiences knee pain which starts before and ends after a muscle spasm on her left leg.

*H) Global Textbox:* Allows users to provide additional information that may be difficult to draw, such as medical histories and medications used **(DC7)**.

*I) Help:* Clicking on the help icon overlays a tutorial.

BodyDiagrams is a web application built using Ruby on Rails. The annotation UI is written in JavaScript using D3 [1], with graphics rendered using SVG. A server tracks each session state and persists user data.

### User Scenario

We illustrate a sample use of BodyDiagrams through a hypothetical user Mark, who is a composite drawn from real examples. Mark has been experiencing severe back pain and occasional muscle strain in his legs. He is wondering whether these are related, and whether there is anything he can do to alleviate his symptoms.

Upon opening BodyDiagrams and selecting the model gender, Mark sees an overlay tutorial indicating how to get started with the tool (Figure 3a). After reading through it, he clicks on the *close* button in the right hand corner, and the overlay disappears. Mark starts with his most severe symptom: his back pain. He switches to the posterior view of the model using the rotation panel. Mark touches his back to confirm that the pain occurs precisely between his tailbone and L4. He zooms into the model: the higher resolution allows Mark to precisely locate the regions of interest on the model, because he can see the model's skeletal structure lightly expressed beneath the skin.

Mark's pain radiates to the right, and so he uses the pen tool to draw an asymmetric region where it hurts the most (Figure 3b). As soon as he finishes the drawing, the annotation widget pops up in the symptom timeline panel. It is connected via a reference line to his drawing. He fills in additional details about his back pain, clicks save, and sees a summary of his annotation on the timeline.

Next, Mark wants to express his leg pain. As he navigates to the right profile view, the reference lines for his pain symptom fade, and the summary box indicates which view the symptom mark appears on. This time he uses the region tool to define a general area in the upper thigh. He wants to indicate shooting pain down his leg, so with the annotation widget open, he defines another region in the calves area. He now sees that the two drawings are grouped as one symptom; the UI prompts him to ungroup if he wishes (Figure 3c). He wants them to be grouped, and so he proceeds to add details in the annotation widget.

Having described both of his symptoms, Mark recalls that he experiences the leg pain only after the back pain starts. The back pain often continues for hours, but the leg pain lasts longer. He drags the summary boxes to indicate their relative start time on the timeline (Figure 3d), and resizes them to indicate their duration. Satisfied, Mark finally uses the general text box to describe the remaining relevant information about his condition and to ask for feedback.

## EXPERIMENT 1: PATIENTS

In our first experiment, we sought to evaluate BodyDiagrams' efficacy as an authoring tool for patients trying to describe physical symptoms online. Based on our design process observations, we developed the following hypotheses:

*H1 (Recall):* Patients will produce more comprehensive condition descriptions using BodyDiagrams than with text only.

*H2 (Resolution):* Patients will describe symptoms in finer detail using BodyDiagrams than with text only.

*H3 (Effectiveness):* Patients will have higher confidence in their BodyDiagrams descriptions being correctly interpreted by readers than their text only descriptions.

*H4 (Preference):* Patients will express a preference to use BodyDiagrams to describe physical conditions in the future.

### Participants

We recruited 21 participants (7 male, 14 female) via an open email call at our university, asking them to sign up for the study only if they had experienced physically-oriented symptoms which they might seek advice about on an online health forum. To encourage sufficiently complex conditions, we gave musculoskeletal and digestive system disorders as example conditions, and sprained ankles and bug bites as non-examples. We informed participants that the study would take place entirely online, be anonymous, and that their contribution would be shared with medical professionals. Subjects received a $20 gift card for participation.

### Methods

The experiment followed a within-subjects design with interface presentation order randomized. Upon beginning the study participants were presented with the following prompt:

> *Please recall a set of physical symptoms that you have recently experienced. Imagine that you want to solicit feedback from people who have experienced a similar condition. On the next page, please describe your symptoms - and any related information - with the hypothetical goal of sharing this description with an online community in order to get feedback.*

After reading the prompt, subjects used either the BodyDiagrams or text-only interface. After completing their pain description, subjects were given the same prompt and asked to describe their symptoms again using the alternative interface. Finally, they completed a survey. Throughout the study and recruitment phases, we referred to the interfaces as "text-only" and "drawing+text" in order to avoid branding effects.

#### *Quantifying information and detail overlap*

To quantify *information overlap* between BodyDiagrams and plain text descriptions, we read through each BodyDiagram and identified any piece of information (symptom, medical history item, etc.) that was missing from the corresponding text description, and vice versa. For example, if a user mentioned taking Tylenol in their text description, but there was no mention of Tylenol in their BodyDiagram, we counted this as an additional piece of information in the text description.

We repeated this process for *detail asymmetry*, considering only shared information between the descriptions (so as not to double-count information overlap). For example, if both descriptions mentioned stomach pain, but only the BodyDiagrams description mentioned the pain duration, we counted this an an extra detail in the BodyDiagrams description. We disregarded the *quality* of detail in this analysis. For example, if both descriptions mentioned the physical location of a symptom, we did not credit BodyDiagrams with extra detail simply because it renders such details in higher resolution.

### Results

Three users described conditions that were not physically-oriented, leaving 18 participants (6 male, 12 female). Unless otherwise noted, all survey responses were on a 5-point Likert scale (1=Strongly Disagree, 5=Strongly Agree), with significance determined by Wilcoxon signed-rank tests (test statistic in tables denoted $V$) with paired samples, or Wilcoxon rank-sum tests otherwise (test statistic in tables denoted $W$).

#### *BodyDiagrams rated as more likely to be correctly interpreted*

Users were significantly more confident that readers will correctly interpret both their individual symptoms as well as their overall condition using their BodyDiagrams description (Table 3). Ordering effects are not significant in this result.

#### *Each description comprises some exclusive information*

As shown in Table 4, both description types comprise, on average, one piece of information not mentioned in their counterpart description. While information quantity differences were not significant, we noticed that medical histories and treatments are more often included in text descriptions, while symptoms are more often included in BodyDiagrams.

### *BodyDiagrams descriptions are more detailed*

On average, BodyDiagrams descriptions contain 0.9 more detailed facts than their plain text counterparts (Table 4), a statistically significant difference. Despite this, in self-report data users were neutral about which description was more detailed (mean=3.2, median=3.0, sd=1.0 on a 5-point Likert scale where 1=PT and 5=BD). Segmenting users into those who prefer BodyDiagrams (rating $\geq 4$, 9/18 subjects) shows no significant preference ($p = 0.5$, one-tailed binomial test).

### *BodyDiagrams take more time and contain less text*

Description length (in characters) and time to completion are shown in Table 7. We replaced one outlying value (1,347 seconds in the text condition) with the group mean; we believe the subject temporarily abandoned the task. On average, users took about 100 seconds longer using BodyDiagrams, and wrote about 110 fewer characters.

### *Second descriptions are rated more complete and relevant*

Table 7 shows users' estimates of information asymmetry in each description. While the difference is not significant for either interface, comparison of results by interface presentation order shows a significant effect: users report that their second description contains more information than their first.

Users also reported agreement on whether each description contains all the relevant information about their condition, as shown in Table 8. Again, there is no significant difference between interfaces, but a significant ordering effect is present.

### *Users prefer BodyDiagrams descriptions*

Users expressed a preference for using the drawing+text interface in the future (mean=3.8, median=4.0, sd=0.9). Segmenting users into those who prefer BodyDiagrams (rating $\geq$ 4, 13/18 subjects) and others, we find a significant preference for BodyDiagrams ($p < 0.05$, one-tailed binomial test).

### *Qualitative User Feedback*

In commenting on the strengths and weaknesses of each interface, reported advantages of text include its expressiveness, flexibility, familiarity, and the fact that it can pressure users to be precise. Cited advantages of BodyDiagrams include the ability to pinpoint or highlight regions of concern (*"in my opinion, the drawing+text interface has a clear advantage over the text-only interface because sometimes it is hard to describe and locate a specific part/point of human body."*), that it provides a template for symptom details (*"It helped me think about each distinct symptom, the timing of the symptoms, and about measuring those symptoms in ways I wouldn't have otherwise."*), and that it facilitates comparisons (*"It is easier to compare my pain to others by looking at a picture instead of having to read everyone's comments"*).

However, some users did not feel that the benefits of text were fully integrated into BodyDiagrams. As one user said, *"If we could combine the two, I would vastly prefer that. I also would like a way to aggregate all the data and information so that I can compare data points between at least 3 people to gain a better understanding of my physical symptoms and what I can do to relieve the pain."* Another stated, *"I think it will be really useful to have the drawing interface in addition to the text interface, so long as the information is not lost due to the 'easiness' of providing the drawings."*

Table 3: Agreement with "I am confident readers will correctly interpret my individual symptoms/overall condition"

| | Descr. | Mean | SD | Median | IQR | V | P-value |
|---|---|---|---|---|---|---|---|
| individual symptoms | BD | **4.1** | 0.7 | 4 | 0.5 | 12 | < 0.01 |
| | PT | 3.5 | 0.8 | 4 | 1.0 | | |
| overall condition | BD | **3.9** | 0.9 | 4 | 1.5 | 10 | < 0.05 |
| | PT | 3.5 | 0.8 | 4 | 1.0 | | |

Table 4: Extra information content (number of facts) and extra detail (number of more detailed facts) in BodyDiagrams (BD) and plain text (PT) descriptions.

| | Descr. | Mean | SD | Median | IQR | V | P-value |
|---|---|---|---|---|---|---|---|
| content | BD | 1.3 | 1.6 | 1.0 | 2.0 | 43.5 | n.s. |
| | PT | 1.1 | 1.4 | 1.0 | 2.0 | | |
| detail | BD | **0.9** | 1.4 | 0.0 | 1.0 | 48 | < 0.05 |
| | PT | 0.2 | 0.4 | 0.0 | 0.0 | | |

Table 5: User responses to the question "In which interface were your symptom descriptions more detailed?" On the response scale, 1 = plain text, 5 = BodyDiagrams.

| Order | Mean | SD | Median | IQR | W | P-value |
|---|---|---|---|---|---|---|
| BD first | 3.0 | 0.7 | 3.0 | 0.0 | 65 | < 0.05 |
| PT first | **3.6** | 1.2 | 4.0 | 0.0 | | |

Table 6: Response time (sec) and response length (chars) for BodyDiagrams (BD) and plain text (PT) descriptions.

| | Descr. | Mean | SD | Median | IQR | V | P-value |
|---|---|---|---|---|---|---|---|
| Time | BD | 276.4 | 177.2 | 278.0 | 194.5 | 146 | < 0.05 |
| | PT | **177.3** | 155.9 | 150.5 | 142.2 | | |
| Length | BD | **163.4** | 115.0 | 141.0 | 123.5 | 25.5 | < 0.05 |
| | PT | 289.7 | 179.8 | 229.0 | 231.5 | | |

Table 7: User responses to the question "There was information in my *A* description that was not in my *B* description."

| *A* Desc. | *B* Desc. | Mean | SD | Median | IQR | V | P-value |
|---|---|---|---|---|---|---|---|
| BD | PT | 3.5 | 1.2 | 4.0 | 1.5 | 18 | n.s. |
| PT | BD | 3.3 | 1.3 | 3.0 | 2.0 | | |
| first | second | 3.1 | 1.2 | 3.0 | 2.0 | 37 | < 0.05 |
| second | first | **3.6** | 1.3 | 4.0 | 2.0 | | |

Table 8: User responses to the question "My $x$ description contained all the relevant information about my condition."

| $x$ Description | Mean | SD | Median | IQR | V | P-value |
|---|---|---|---|---|---|---|
| BD | 3.5 | 1.0 | 4.0 | 1.0 | 27.5 | n.s. |
| PT | 3.5 | 1.0 | 4.0 | 1.5 | | |
| first | 3.3 | 1.0 | 4.0 | 2.0 | 10.5 | < 0.05 |
| second | **3.7** | 0.9 | 4.0 | 1.0 | | |

### Discussion

*H1 (Recall): Patients will produce more comprehensive descriptions of their condition using BodyDiagrams than with text only.* We indeed find that users provide more details when using BodyDiagrams—roughly one piece of information per condition. Our results also indicate an ordering effect, as users perceive improvements in their description after refining it. This finding agrees with our pilot study observation that *iteration provides better results*. As users include different types of information in each interface, it may be helpful to cue users to include information they are likely to omit.

*H2 (Resolution): Patients will describe symptoms in finer detail using BodyDiagrams than with text only.* Users included significantly more detail in their BodyDiagrams than in plain text descriptions (Table 4). However, differences in users' opinions regarding detail were not significant. We attribute the increase in detail to BodyDiagrams prompting users to record attributes like location, severity and frequency.

*H3 (Effectiveness): Patients will have higher confidence in their BodyDiagrams descriptions being correctly interpreted by readers than their text only descriptions.* Users are significantly more confident in the interpretability of their BodyDiagrams (Table 3) than their text only descriptions.

*H4 (Preference): Users will prefer to use BodyDiagrams for describing physically-oriented conditions.* In addition to commenting positively on BodyDiagrams, users significantly preferred to use a drawing + text based interface in the future for communicating physically-oriented conditions.

### EXPERIMENT 2: MEDICAL PROFESSIONALS

In our second experiment, we evaluated BodyDiagrams for communicating patients' descriptions to medical professionals online. We posed the following hypotheses:

*H5 (Interpretation):* Professionals will have a clearer understanding of conditions described with BodyDiagrams than conditions described with plain text.

*H6 (Confidence):* Professionals will feel more confident in their advice given in response to BodyDiagram descriptions than to plain text descriptions.

*H7 (Content):* The information content of professionals' responses to BodyDiagram descriptions will be higher than that given in response to plain text descriptions.

### Participants

We recruited 10 medical professionals (5 licensed doctors, 3 registered nurses, 1 community pharmacist and 1 4th-year med student) through oDesk (`www.odesk.com`). We screened subjects for frequent patient interaction experience and English skills. Subjects were paid $5 for each assessment.

### Methods

Although a direct comparison between BodyDiagrams and plain text descriptions was desirable for this experiment, a within-subjects design presented several difficulties. Foremost was the problem of information transfer: regardless of the order in which experts read corresponding text descriptions and BodyDiagrams, they would have strictly more information about the patient's condition upon reading the second description. We were concerned that this would impede subjects' ability to compare the interfaces objectively. Alternatively, we might have presented experts with non-corresponding BodyDiagram and plain text descriptions. In this case, however, we were concerned that subjects would not have a clear basis for comparison.

We instead used a between-subjects design with interface as the independent variable. Each professional evaluated several patient descriptions using only one of the interfaces (BodyDiagrams or text). 18 BodyDiagrams and 18 text descriptions from Phase 1 were each evaluated by 2 medical professionals. Upon starting an assessment, participants were shown a patient's description and asked to *"respond with advice [they] would give this patient"* in an adjacent text box. After each assessment, participants completed a post-task survey.

Table 9: Response to the question "I felt that this description was missing information relevant to the user's condition."

| Description | Mean | SD | Median | IQR | $\chi^2(2)$ | P-value |
|---|---|---|---|---|---|---|
| BD | **2.40** | 1.30 | 2 | 1.50 | 12.25 | $< 0.001$ |
| PT | 3.40 | 1.10 | 4 | 0.70 | | |

Table 10: Responses to "I felt that this description contained information that was not relevant to the user's condition."

| Description | Mean | SD | Median | IQR | $\chi^2(2)$ | P-value |
|---|---|---|---|---|---|---|
| BD | **1.60** | 0.50 | 2 | 0.00 | 4.57 | $< 0.05$ |
| PT | 2.00 | 0.80 | 2 | 0.00 | | |

### Results

Survey responses were on a 5-point Likert scale (1=Strongly Disagree, 5=Strongly Agree). To account for non-normal responses and patient variability, we analyzed responses using a non-parametric Friedman rank sum test, in which plain text vs. BodyDiagrams was the condition and patients the block.

#### *BodyDiagrams rated as more focused than plain text*

Tables 9 and 10 show subjects' ratings of completeness and relevance of the descriptions that they evaluated. Subjects evaluating plain text descriptions felt significantly more strongly that their descriptions were both lacking relevant information and contained extraneous information.

#### *Subjects are confident in their advice, regardless of interface*

We asked subjects to report their confidence in overall diagram interpretation, individual symptom interpretation, diagnosis given, correctness of advice given, and helpfulness of advice given. Differences between interface conditions were not significant. Scores were uniformly high, suggesting that medical professionals are highly confident in their interpretations and contributions regardless of presentation interface.

#### *No time or length effects*

Both subject groups reported reading the description twice on average before responding, and referring back to the description about twice while writing. Differences in response time are not significant (mean = 1857 seconds (PT) vs. 1181 (BD), median = 1135 vs. 1054, $\chi_1^2 = 0.9$, $p = 0.34$); neither are differences in response length (mean = 591 characters (PT) vs. 999 (BD), median = 749 vs. 457, $\chi_1^2 = 2$, $p = 0.16$).

### Response Content

We analyzed the content of medical professionals' responses in order to get a sense of typical response components. Overall, subjects gave detailed responses in which they typically discussed possible causes of the symptoms, and presented potential diagnoses, both often conditional on an aspect of the user's health omitted from the description (e.g., smoking history). In addition, they often gave suggestions for alleviating symptoms and advice on whether to seek proper medical attention. Finally, medical professionals often utilized repair dialogue to indicate missing description components. Repair dialog is characterized by both direct questions such as "how many hours do you work?" and indirect comments such as "if you have been sick recently then ...", implying that inclusion of such information would have been helpful.

To measure content difference between conditions, we manually coded the number of questions (mean = 1.0 (PT) vs. 0.8 (BD), median = 0 vs. 0, $\chi_1^2 = 0.06$, $p = 0.81$), pieces of repair dialogue (mean = 1.7 (PT) vs. 1.5 (BD), median = 2 vs. 0, $\chi_1^2 = 0.0$, $p = 1.0$) and suggestions given (mean = 4 (PT) vs. 3.6 (BD), median = 3 vs. 3, $\chi_1^2 = 0.25$, $p = 0.62$) for each response. None of these differences are significant.

### Qualitative Feedback

We asked medical professionals who had evaluated BodyDiagrams descriptions to submit free-form feedback. All participants responded positively. One user wrote: *"[BodyDiagrams] clearly points out the effected site of patient so because of this, diagnosis becomes very clear. Now the diagramatic description helps a lot because the risk of misunderstood medical conditions is minimized."* Another indicated that she felt more empathy towards the patients, as *"[BodyDiagrams helps you to easily imagine your patient..."*. Furthermore, users said that BodyDiagrams provide more detailed descriptions: *"The image + description concept is great as it gives medical professionals more detailed knowledge about the patient's condition."* Finally, one user compared BodyDiagrams to text directly, saying *"I think, it is far better than [a] text description. The way of showing the pain area and symptom timeline was most useful to me."*

Suggestions for improvement included incorporating a general patient information box for data like age, BMI, and weight, as well as incorporating existing assessment tools such as the PQRST (Provocation Quality Region and radiation Severity Time) [16] method for pain assessment.

### Discussion

*H5 (Interpretation): Professionals will have a clearer understanding of conditions described with BodyDiagrams.* While confidence in interpretation is no different between interfaces, qualitative feedback from professionals supports the claim that BodyDiagrams aids condition interpretation. These comments specifically mention the ease of identifying symptoms' physical locations and the symptom timeline view as helpful. In addition, subjects rated BodyDiagrams descriptions as significantly more complete and relevant (Tables 9 and 10).

*H6 (Confidence): Professionals will feel more confident in their advice for conditions described using BodyDiagrams.* We found that professionals have high confidence in their advice regardless of presentation interface. One possible explanation is that subjects were reluctant to admit uncertainty. Another is that the interface does not affect confidence of response, because experts account for uncertainty in the advice that they give. In either case, these results underscore the importance of patients creating complete and accurate descriptions of their conditions.

*H7 (Content): The information content will be higher in professionals' responses to BodyDiagrams descriptions.* We found no differences in content between professionals' evaluations of BodyDiagrams and those of plain text descriptions.

## DISCUSSION AND FUTURE WORK

Our results demonstrate BodyDiagrams' perceived efficacy as a communication tool from the perspective of both patients (Experiment 1) and medical professionals (Experiment 2). In this section, we revisit our original design goals and discuss how these results relate to our design considerations.

*Support natural symptom-drawing patterns.* The ease with which patients expressed their symptoms using BodyDiagrams suggests that supporting freehand drawing (**DC1**) and structuring input flow via the draw-link-describe-repeat pattern (**DC2**) enhances BodyDiagram's ease of use. Moreover, the introduction of grouping multiple consecutive marks into single symptoms (**DC3**) triggered a notable decline in users' frustration levels with the tool. However, supporting natural drawing behaviors does not necessarily entail mimicking their precise pen-and-paper mechanisms. Our symptom timeline (based on **DC5**), for example, leverages affordances of a digital interface (easy repositioning and resizing) to render chronology in a manner that would be difficult to draw on paper. Similarly, after incorporating a realistic diagram (**DC6**) users stopped spending time drawing in reference lines on the diagram. To this end, we propose that natural drawing behaviors be used as guidelines, but that implementations of symptom-drawing interfaces should extend interactions beyond those available using pen-and-paper.

*Enhance interpretability through a synthesis of increased content and compact representation.* Medical professionals rated BodyDiagrams descriptions are more informative and relevant than their textual counterparts. BodyDiagrams naturally capture physical content and context that is difficult to record and interpret via text. In addition, acquiring inherent symptom attributes via structured input boxes (**DC4**) helps to standardize symptom descriptions and capture information that might otherwise have been omitted. However, there is a tradeoff between structuring data collection and maintaining expressiveness. While we felt that symptom input was only lightly structured (and included a free-form text field), one participant didn't like the symptom depth categories; another *"wanted there to be an 'inner' area, vs. skin/joint/muscle,* *for [her] symptoms (abdominal pain).*" Moreover, while we anticipated that users would write difficult-to-draw information in the general text box (based on **DC7**), in our opinion this feature was underutilized. Prior to a large-scale deployment of BodyDiagrams, additional thought should be given to structuring and standardizing information on the one hand, and maintaining flexibility on the other. Nonetheless, our experiments find that BodyDiagrams lead to more detailed patient descriptions that are rated more informative by medical professionals, suggesting that BodyDiagrams achieves a productive balance of compactness and descriptiveness.

### *Limitations and Future Work*

High priorities for future work include better synthesizing text input into BodyDiagrams (despite the inclusion of the general text box, users still noted that the diagram distracted them from entering other information), incorporating more realistic and racially-neutral body models, and the introduction of iterative symptom description into the interface workflow. While our results showed general user preference for BodyDiagrams, differences in content quantity and quality point to strong ordering effects: second descriptions are almost always better. To this end, we propose that facilitating easy symptom "drafting" prior to final authoring would result in significantly better descriptions. Moreover, we are eager to evaluate BodyDiagrams in a collaborative environment, with back-and-forth communications between readers and patients.

We also plan to deploy BodyDiagrams on mobile devices that support drawing via touch input. Drawing with a mouse can be difficult; we believe that touch may provide a better input modality. Finally, BodyDiagrams can be used for visual indexing of symptoms, enabling effective aggregation and search over common pain patterns.

## ACKNOWLEDGMENTS

We thank the subjects who volunteered to participate in our experiments, and the Division of Clinical Anatomy at Stanford University for providing 3D body models. This research was supported by Sloan Foundation Fellowship.

## REFERENCES

1. Bostock, M., Ogievetsky, V., and Heer, J. D3: Data-Driven Documents. *IEEE Trans. on Visualization and Computer Graphics 17*, 12 (2011), 2301–2309.
2. Bui, A. A., Aberle, D. R., and Kangarloo, H. Timeline: visualizing integrated patient records. *IEEE Trans. on Information Tech. in Biomedicine 11*, 4 (2007), 462–473.
3. Dreyfuss, P., Michaelsen, M., Fletcher, D., et al. Atlanto-occipital and lateral atlanto-axial joint pain patterns. *SPINE 19*, 10 (1994), 1125.
4. Dreyfuss, P., Tibiletti, C., Dreyer, S., et al. Thoracic zygapophyseal joint pain patterns. a study in normal volunteers. *SPINE 19*, 7 (1994), 807.
5. Felix, E., Galoian, K., Aarons, C., Brown, M., Kearing, S., and Heiss, U. Utility of quantitative computerized pain drawings in a sample of spinal stenosis patients. *Pain Medicine 11*, 3 (2010), 382–389.
6. Fortin, J., Aprill, C., Ponthieux, B., Pier, J., et al. Sacroiliac joint: pain referral maps upon applying a new injection/arthrography technique. Part II: Clinical evaluation. *SPINE 19*, 13 (1994), 1483.
7. Fox, S., and Duggan, M. *Health Online*. Pew Internet & American Life Project, 2013. [Online; accessed 2-April-2013].
8. Ghinea, G., Gill, D., Frank, A., and De Souza, L. Using geographical information systems for management of back-pain data. *Management in Medicine 16*, 2/3 (2002), 219–237.
9. Jamison, R., Fanciullo, G., and Baird, J. Usefulness of pain drawings in identifying real or imagined pain: accuracy of pain professionals, nonprofessionals, and a decision model. *Pain 5*, 9 (2004), 476–482.
10. Jang, A., MacLean, D., and Heer, J. Designing a prototype interface for visual communication of pain. In *Ext. Abstracts CHI 2013*, ACM (2013), 427–432.
11. MedHelp. MedHelp Pain Tracker. `http://www.medhelp.org/land/pain-tracker`. [Online; accessed 10-December-2012].
12. Melzack, R. The McGill Pain Questionnaire: major properties and scoring methods. *Pain 1*, 3 (1975), 277–299.
13. Pain, P. A. Partners Against Pain: Tracking Solutions. `http://www.partnersagainstpain.com/tracking-pain/management.aspx`. [Online; accessed 10-December-2012].
14. Plaisant, C., Milash, B., Rose, A., Widoff, S., and Shneiderman, B. Lifelines: visualizing personal histories. In *Proc. CHI 1996*, ACM (1996), 221–227.
15. Plaisant, C., Mushlin, R., Snyder, A., Li, J., Heller, D., and Shneiderman, B. Lifelines: using visualization to enhance navigation and analysis of patient records. In *Proc. AMIA Symposium* (1998), 76.
16. Powell, R. A., Downing, J., Ddungu, H., and Mwangi-Powell, F. N. Pain history and pain assessment. In *Guide to Pain Management in Low-Resource Settings*, IASP (2010), 67–68.
17. Spyridonis, F., and Ghinea, G. 2D vs. 3D pain visualization: User preferences in a spinal cord injury cohort. *Design, User Experience, and Usability. Theory, Methods, Tools and Practice* (2011), 315–322.
18. WebMD. WebMD Symptom Tracker. `http://symptoms.webmd.com/symptomchecker`. [Online; accessed 10-January-2013].

# Personal Tracking as Lived Informatics

**John Rooksby, Mattias Rost, Alistair Morrison, Matthew Chalmers**
School of Computing Science,
University of Glasgow, UK.
{john.rooksby, mattias.rost, alistair.morrison, matthew.chalmers}@glasgow.ac.uk

## ABSTRACT
This paper characterises the use of activity trackers as 'lived informatics'. This characterisation is contrasted with other discussions of personal informatics and the quantified self. The paper reports an interview study with activity tracker users. The study found: people do not logically organise, but interweave various activity trackers, sometimes with ostensibly the same functionality; that tracking is often social and collaborative rather than personal; that there are different styles of tracking, including goal driven tracking and documentary tracking; and that tracking information is often used and interpreted with reference to daily or short term goals and decision making. We suggest there will be difficulties in personal informatics if we ignore the way that personal tracking is enmeshed with everyday life and people's outlook on their future.

### Author Keywords
Activity Tracking; Data; Qualitative methods

### ACM Classification Keywords
H.5.m. Information interfaces and presentation (e.g., HCI): Miscellaneous.

## INTRODUCTION
Over the past few years there has been a proliferation of mobile apps and consumer devices for tracking personal information, particularly those related to health and wellbeing (for example diet, weight, sleep, walking and exercise). Many apps can be downloaded for free or at low cost. Some physical devices (such as pedometers) cost trivial amounts (see [19]). Yet there is also a market for premium devices (see [11] for a discussion of the FitBit). Mobile phone manufacturers including Apple and Motorola have also begun to make specific provisions for activity tracking by, for example, incorporating always-on accelerometers into their latest high-end mobile devices. The advent of smart watches, smart glasses and other forms of wearable computing in the consumer domain is also likely to bring further innovation and proliferation in this area. Personal tracking is, however, not new. People have long been able to track and manage activities using diaries and/or personal computers. Tracking can in fact be traced back to at least Roman times (where trackers were used not as personal devices but for measuring the mobility of soldiers). However, with the popularity of smartphones and digital devices with built in accelerometers and location services, the area of personal tracking appears to be one of great investment and growth.

Previous research in this area has predominantly focused on individual, researcher-supplied technologies. From a health research perspective, a tracker is either an instrument with which to measure activity, or an intervention to be applied across a cohort of people. Standard devices are used, and often treated as invisible lenses on activity (e.g. [19, 21]). In health research, consumer trackers are usually used, whereas evaluation in HCI is usually of a novel prototype (e.g. [13, 10]). In HCI the devices themselves are not treated invisibly but, as with health research, evaluation is predominantly of an individual technology and oriented to intervention. There is some research looking at integration of technologies, notably Bentley et al.'s [2] work on health mashups for behaviour change. Yet even here the researchers selected what the study participants should use. The *agency* of the people using such technologies is too often denied; Maitland et al.'s [12] study of weight loss and Mamykina et al.'s [14] study of diabetes management are rare exceptions. They point out that people choose, use, interweave and abandon various technologies in their own, lived efforts to improve their health. They found people were not changing their behaviour because of a technology, but were using technology because they wanted to change.

What people decide to track using consumer products, what trackers they decide to use, and how they use them over days, weeks, months and potentially lifetimes remains understudied. Studying individual, researcher supplied technology is somewhat at odds with the literature around personal informatics, which suggests that people can and should track various aspects of their lives. It is also somewhat at odds with what we already know about smartphone use. Barkhuus et al. [1] have pointed out that



*CHI 2014,* April 26 - May 01 2014, Toronto, ON, Canada. Copyright is held by the owner/author(s). Publication rights licensed to ACM.
ACM 978-1-4503-2473-1/14/04 $15.00
http://dx.doi.org/10.1145/2556288.2557039

the smartphone is not an information appliance but a "seamful" device that people artfully work with and around. We know for example that people do not just use one messaging service, social network site, or Web browser, but combine, work across and work between them. It seems unlikely then that people will choose one activity tracker and stick with it indefinitely. We also know that people find some surprising uses for technology. In this paper, therefore, we address what people are making of personal trackers for themselves. In the following section we discuss personal informatics. We then report findings from interviews with 22 people. In the final section we characterise personal tracking as 'lived informatics', a view that emphasises the practical, prospective and felt aspects of personal tracking for health and wellbeing.

## PERSONAL INFORMATICS

The areas of personal informatics and the quantified self concern the collection and use of personal data, often from trackers and life-loggers. The rhetoric in these areas is to "*live by numbers*" (see e.g. [22]), to quantify and then optimize areas of one's life. When, for example, does one sleep well, and what is it that affects sleep? Is one's weight going up, and if so, is there data that can be used to tell why? It is clear from Quantified Self (quantifiedself.com) online forums, and the annual reports published by Nick Felton (feltron.com) that such ideas can be put into practice. But are such people early adopters, leading the way for the rest of us? Or is mainstream tracking something different?

Li et al.'s staged model of personal informatics systems [9] is often cited as a key representation for this area. This model was designed to offer "*a comprehensive list of problems that users experience*". This model holds five stages: 1) at the *preparation* stage, people need to determine what information they will record and how to record it; 2) at the *collection* stage people do the data gathering; 3) at the *integration* stage people should prepare, combine and transform data; 4) at the *reflection* stage people can think about, explore and interact with the information; and finally 5) at the *action* stage people can "*choose what they are going to do with their newfound understanding of themselves*".

Li et al.'s model is technology–centric. The problems that users experience are technical problems to be resolved firstly by selecting the correct technology. Only once the technologies are in place, and the datasets transformed and integrated, can things like reflection and action take place. While we do not deny that it would be useful to have a rational and systematic set of tools for collecting data, we have known since Simon [20] that it is problematic to assume that people will postpone action until they have rationally determined "*newfound understanding*". We find Li et al.'s vision reminiscent of the idea in health informatics and information systems that computerization can and should set the rational underpinning for (a consequently rationalized) human action. Pollock and William's [18] history of enterprise systems, and Berg's [3] analysis of decision support in healthcare both show such rationalisation is rarely achieved.

### Personal Informatics for Health and Wellbeing

In the research reported in this paper, our central concern has been for personal trackers associated with health and wellbeing. A number of approaches can be taken to tracking in this domain. Accelerometers are often used to measure movement and are typically incorporated into devices like pedometers and sleep trackers. Location–based tracking is also heavily used, particularly for tracking exercise such as running and cycling, in which people cover geographic areas. Such sensor–based systems can collect information without the user needing to actively engage with them. Many pedometers are designed to be always on, with the users only having to remember to wear them. Other trackers require active engagement. Food and medication trackers, for example, require users to enter details manually. This can be cumbersome and many of the more successful trackers in this area seek to make logging easier through, for example, support for barcode scanning. Some trackers are beginning to shift from requiring active tracking to support for passive tracking. Smart scales, for example, wirelessly transmit information to a computer. Smart watches (e.g. Garmins) are able to monitor one's pulse.

Personal informatics encompasses health and wellbeing, but goes far beyond it. For example, personal informatics covers personal finance, personal communications, life photography, travel information, diary keeping and so on. Sometimes wider personal informatics tools find application for health and wellbeing. However, we must be clear: this paper focuses only on a fraction of the personal informatics domain (and related domains such as life-logging).

## THE STUDY

Following Maitland et al. [12], and Barkhuus et al. [1], qualitative, exploratory methods have been used in this study. Posters were placed in coffee shops, a bookshop, and a university building in a city in Scotland. The posters advertised for 1) people that used a pedometer or activity tracker, 2) people that had used pedometers or activity trackers in the past, 3) people that would like to borrow and use a pedometer or activity tracker.

### Method

The research process involved an initial unstructured interview, and then follow-up contact approximately one month later. Initial interviews were conducted with 23 people, and 22 agreed to follow-up contact. Nineteen follow-ups involved one or more further interviews, and often email contact as well. Three follow-ups were done solely by using email (two interviewees had left the UK, and the other was suffering from health problems). One interview was conducted using a video conferencing tool.

This paper reports on the 22 people we had extended contact with. That we were using unstructured methods does not mean that we just let participants talk. Questions of clarification were an essential part of the study. In particular we found that participants would often demonstrate features of apps that they did not use. The social features of apps almost became a running joke during the study. People would often say that the app connected to social networks such as Facebook, but when directly asked if they use that feature they invariably said "*no*". The initial interviews lasted from 20 to 90 minutes, with most lasting about 45 minutes. The follow up interviews lasted 10 to 50 minutes. The length of the interview was contingent upon how much a person had to say and how many different activity trackers that person was using. Interviewees were either lent a tracker or were paid ten UK pounds.

The interviews were transcribed and thematically analysed. There is a long running debate in qualitative research as to whether themes should emerge purely from the transcribed data, or can emerge with reference to researchers' experiences and reading beyond the study. Our work is in the latter camp; it has been undertaken while research and development has progressed on several activity-tracker projects, and was motivated and shaped by that fact (indeed it was inspired by our recognition that we knew little about how trackers other than our own were used).

A methodological dilemma we faced was that the study was designed on a false assumption. It was initially assumed that participants would either be people that used a tracker or would be people interested in trying out a tracker. As it transpired, people that used activity trackers were also interested in trying new ones out. In this situation, we conducted the first interview before lending a tracker. As we will discuss, we often found that people did not use our equipment to replace existing trackers, but to interweave with the trackers they already had. The data presented in this paper does not concern trackers lent to people, except in two cases where we discuss the use of a pedometer we lent to a nurse (P21), and to a cricket player (P20).

### Participant Overview

We report on interviews with twenty two participants. Twelve participants were male and ten were female. Eleven were in their twenties, eight in their thirties and three in their forties. Ten were UK nationals, others came from North and South America, Europe, China and India. Eleven participants were full time students (six postgraduate and five undergraduate). Three worked in administrative roles, three worked in financial services, one was a nurse, and one person was unemployed. The three others worked in the software industry. All participants were able bodied. Seven participants were serious runners, two were training for marathons, and one for a cross-country race. One was a serious cyclist. Six others were regular sports players. Eight participants did not regularly exercise other than walk. Several participants were obese, and one had had weight-loss surgery. Many participants, overweight or not, were concerned about weight. All but the two youngest female participants were dieting (one of whom told us in the second interview that she might begin dieting as her father had suggested she lose weight). One male, and the male partner of another participant wanted to gain weight.

Four people in the study were lent an activity tracker having never (or barely) used one before. The other 18 participants had used at least one tracker, and the majority were using several tracking and logging technologies. P12 was the most extreme, using or trying eight trackers at the time of the first interview. She had a long history of tracking, driven by a life-long desire to lose weight.

Reasons for participation in the study were mixed. Some participants were clearly gadget lovers, some very interested in borrowing a new device, and others wanted to talk about the devices they were using. Several participants were clearly struggling emotionally with their body image and seemed to value having someone to talk to. Two students were open about doing the study for the money. There was a self-selection issue in this study. Notably, a disproportionate number of interviewees (four) had run or were training for marathons. All participants were clearly socially mobile, relatively affluent, educated and were numerate. Several, in particular the financial traders and the software developers, were clearly adept in statistics and data analysis. This is not a typical cohort to evaluate health technology with, and does not represent any general population. Rather we suggest the participants, in their unique ways, provide good cases for considering the idea of personal informatics.

## FINDINGS

The interviewees were using diverse tracking technologies. The technologies in use by each interviewee at each interview are represented in Table 1. Most people used more than one tracker and many were accessing information from the same tracker in more than one way. The kinds of technology in use included:

- *Physical devices*. We found eleven participants were using a dedicated, physical device for the purpose of tracking. Popular devices included Garmins (used for running), and wrist worn trackers such as the Jawbone UP.
- *Apps*. Thirteen participants were using tracking apps on their smartphones. Some physical devices are integrated with a smartphone app. Other apps do a standalone data collection. A calorie tracker called My Fitness Pal was popular.
- *Exergames*. Two participants were using games consoles to log information. One had been using the Wii Fit for four years to log his and his partner's weight. Another played exergames using an Xbox Kinect.

| | 1 | 2 | 3 | 4 | 5 | 6 | 7 | 8 | 9 | 10 | 11 |
|---|---|---|---|---|---|---|---|---|---|---|---|
| Nike Fuelband | | | | | · / X | | | · / X | | | |
| Nike+ | | | | | ■ / ■ | | | ■ / ■ | | | |
| Nike Sportsband | | | | | | | | | | ■ / ■ | |
| Garmin | | | | ■ / ■ | | | | · / ■ | | | |
| FitBit Zip/One | · / ■X | | | · / X | | · / X | | | | | |
| Fitbit Flex | | | | | | | | | | | |
| Jawbone UP | | ■ / · | · / X | | | | | | ■ / ■ | | |
| Fit Bug | | | | | | | | | | | |
| Basic Pedometer | | | | | | | | | | | ■ / · |
| Striiv | | | | | | | | | | | |
| Moves | ■ / · | | | | | | | | | | |
| Endomondo | | | | | | | | | | | |
| Map My Run | | | | ■ / · | | | ■ / ■ | | | | |
| Run Keeper | | | | | | | | | | | |
| Daily Mile | | | | | | | | | | | |
| Sleep Cycle | | | | | | | | | | | |
| Map My Ride | | | | | | | | | | | |
| Strava | | | | | | | | | | | |
| My Trax | | | | | | ■ / · | | | | | |
| Pedometer App | | | ■ / · | | | | | | | | |
| My Fitness Pal | | ■ / · | | ■ / ■ | | | | | | | |
| Other Food App | ■ / · | ■ / · | | | ■ / · | | | | | | |
| Heart monitor | | | | | | | | · / ■ | | | |
| Gym Pact | | | | | | | | | | | |
| Wii Fit / Xbox | | | ■ / · | | | | ■ / ■ | | | | |
| Smart Scales | · / ■ | | | | | | | | | | |
| Period Tracker | | | | ■ / ■ | | | | | | | |
| Alcohol Tracker | | | | | | | ■ / · | | | | |

| | 12 | 13 | 14 | 15 | 16 | 17 | 18 | 19 | 20 | 21 | 22 |
|---|---|---|---|---|---|---|---|---|---|---|---|
| Nike Fuelband | | | | ■ / ■ | | | ■ / ■ | | | | |
| Nike+ | | | | | | | | | | | |
| Nike Sportsband | | | | | | | | | | | |
| Garmin | ■ / ■ | | | | | | | | | | |
| FitBit Zip/One | | | | | | | | | | · / X | · / X |
| Fitbit Flex | ■ / ■ | · / ■ | | | | | | | | | |
| Jawbone UP | | | ■ / ■ | | | ■ / ■ | | | | | |
| Fit Bug | | | ■ / ■ | | | | | | | | |
| Basic Pedometer | | | | | | | | · / X | · / X | | |
| Striiv | ■ / · | ■ / ■ | | | | | | | | | |
| Moves | | | | | | | | | | | |
| Endomondo | | | ■ / ■ | | | | | | | | |
| Map My Run | | | | | | | | | | | |
| Run Keeper | ■ / · | | | | | ■ / ■ | | | | | |
| Daily Mile | ■ / · | | | | | | | | | | |
| Sleep Cycle | ■ / · | ■ / · | | | | | | | | | |
| Map My Ride | | | | | ■ / · | | | | | | |
| Strava | | | | | · / ■ | ■ / · | | | | | |
| My Trax | | | | | ■ / · | | | | | | |
| Pedometer App | | | | | | | | | | | |
| My Fitness Pal | ■ / ■ | ■ / ■ | ■ / ■ | | | · / ■ | | | | | |
| Other Food App | | | | | | | | | | | |
| Heart monitor | | | | | | | | | | | |
| Gym Pact | ■ / ■ | ■ / ■ | | | | | | | | | |
| Wii Fit / Xbox | | | | | | | | | | | |
| Smart Scales | | | | | | ■ / ■ | | | | | |
| Period Tracker | | | | | | | | | | | |
| Alcohol Tracker | | | | | | ■ / · | | | | | |

**Table 1: Trackers in use at the first (left column) and second interview (right column) for each of the 22 participants. An "X" denotes a tracker lent to a participant. Table does not include trackers used by participants in the past.**

- *Web apps*. Several devices and apps enabled participants to examine data on the Web.

Other means of tracking were also discussed. One participant described using written charts to keep a record of her weightlifting. Others referred to having kept written records in the past, or to having used spreadsheets. One participant regularly blogged about her activity. We found people were tracking a range of activities:

- *Walking*. Many participants were using or had used pedometers to track their walking. For some participants it would be occasional 'big' walks or hikes. For others, an always-on pedometer was used to gain a sense of steps over a day.
- *Physical exercise*. Thirteen participants were tracking vigorous physical activity, including running, cycling and swimming. The most common of these by far was running. These activities were usually specifically scheduled and conducted as physical exercise, for example no one would track running for a bus or moving a sofa at home, but would track the runs they did or weights they lifted for exercise and training (although sometimes running or cycling would be a means of commuting to work).
- *Food and Drink*. Most participants tracked, or at some point had tracked, their intake of food and drink. Some study participants said they had done this over the long term, but most seemed to have dipped in and out of tracking. Participants did this if they were interested in losing or maintaining weight. Two males also tracked their alcohol consumption.
- *Weight and Size*. Participants that were managing their weight would also regularly weigh and sometimes measure themselves. Three participants used 'smart' scales or a Wii Fit. Others entered their details into apps.
- *Sleep*. Six participants tracked their sleep, including how long they slept, and their patterns of deep and light sleep. One participant (P9) had bought a Jawbone UP specifically to deal with a sleep problem.
- *Nothing*. One participant (P18) was not tracking anything. Her Nike Fuelband was "*a pretty watch*".

This is not an exhaustive list. One participant discussed tracking her menstrual cycle (the interviewer was male and it is possible other participants did not reveal this). One (P17) had written diary entries every day for three years, was an avid user of a reminder app and Evernote Food. He also used Foursquare as a means to record which cafés and bars he liked (Cramer et al. [4] discuss this kind of appropriation of Foursquare). P17 was attempting to track as many aspects of his life as possible, although it was clear to him that it was impossible to track everything:

"*My girlfriend gets annoyed with me for all these things. ... You know if we're in bed [my Jawbone UP] is comfortable for me, but it may not be comfortable for her. ... If we're in a restaurant ... she's like, you're allowed thirty seconds and then put [the iPhone] away, cos its rude. She understands some of those things, but I think if I was in a restaurant like writing down all the things I had, that takes time and it would annoy me as well.*" *(P17)*

That participant was alone in wanting to track as much as possible. Other people were modest and selective about tracking. For example, while at least ten people went to the gym, only two kept records of gym visits. When it came to individual activities (such as walking or running) some people wanted to track as much of that activity as possible. For many, walking was something to be tracked in its entirety. Every step counted for some participants, meaning for example that smartphone apps were insufficient as a tracker "*would be left in my bag a lot of the time."(*P1*)* For others, some steps were more important than others. One person (P14) differentiated between "*normal*" and "*active burn*" walking, seeing the latter as most worthy of tracking. Two participants were interested in tracking only their long walks or hikes, and not their day-to-day movement. For one person, everyday walking was specifically something not to be tracked because "*It is not proper exercise*" (P7). Tracking is often, we see here, selective.

### *Temporalities of Tracking*

One of the problems with establishing what trackers people use is that these technologies can be used in a number of ways. What counts as use? Certainly, some trackers were being used day in and day out, but others seemed to be used irregularly. For example P16 used a tracker only for some cycle rides. Food trackers also seemed to be used in bouts. While several participants tracked their eating and drinking, some were doing this for everything they ate, and others went through short periods of tracking. P4, a long-term user of My Fitness Pal, explained "*You get in the habit... If it doesn't matter enough to you then you wouldn't use it.*" This opinion is perhaps harsh, especially given that P4 was relatively slim and that the participant struggling most with obesity also struggled with food logging.

Very few people in the study had been using the trackers discussed in the first interview for more than a few months. Less than half of the participants had used an app or device for more than a year, although most had a long history of tracking. Table 1 represents two 'snapshots' of what trackers the participants were using. It is not a nuanced picture, but good enough to characterise that people can and do mix and change trackers. Our study participants did not select trackers along purely functional lines. For many, particularly the users of Nike products, branding was very important. Several participants were committed to this brand. Users of several of the physical devices reported their pleasure at having purchased it through an Apple Store. Physical trackers are also exchanged as gifts. P11 had received a tracker for her birthday, and P10 had bought a tracker on her birthday as a gift to herself. Two others (P3 and P4) said the new FitBit Flex was "*on my birthday list*". A few systematically went through apps in online app stores trying out various products. Many went on the recommendations of friends and relatives, and many read media articles and reviews. Participants did not stick with the same tracker indefinitely but were switching between them. Reasons for uptake and switching included the uptake of a new activity, or a new technology being released. We encountered several examples of switching being occasioned by switching phone (for example, when switching from an iPhone to a Windows phone; P1 was forced to move away from the Moves activity tracker). For P16, switching from one Android device to another provided an occasion to switch from MyTrax to Map My Ride. Loss and breakage also occurred.

The physicality of trackers was often important. Wrist worn trackers were being chosen partly because people were worried about losing or forgetting devices kept in pockets. Runners would sometimes prefer wrist worn trackers because they are less bulky, and although they are expensive they are less valuable than a phone (two reported damaging a phone when running). Some liked the conspicuousness of wrist worn trackers: "*I've chosen lime green!*" (P2). Whereas others preferred to be more discreet "*I clip it to my underpants, who's gonna know*?" (P4). Physicality then, including the physicality of a smartphone, is an important consideration in tracking.

## Five Styles of Personal Tracking

Trackers can be used in various ways. We have noticed several (overlapping) styles in which trackers can be used: directive tracking, documentary tracking, diagnostic tracking, collecting rewards, and fetishised tracking.

### *Directive Tracking*

Much tracking was goal driven. Many participants aimed to either lose or maintain weight, and would set a goal or limit (typically a calorie burn and intake) with reference to this. Many other participants were following a training program and therefore were striving to adhere to the goals set out by that program. Sometimes the goal would come directly via the tracker itself; most pedometers for example suggest appropriate goals. However, goals would often also come for external sources. A 10,000 steps a day goal was reported by several participants (and attributed to various sources, although the true origin seems to be in a Japanese marketing campaign [21]). The participants that were in training, particularly the marathon runners, were using trackers alongside a training programme. In one case this programme came from a book a friend had told the participant about, and in another case from the "My Asics" website. Even though many trackers did not necessitate a goal, some participants found themselves wanting to set one. For example P7 found he "*might as well*" start following a 10k training plan given he liked Map My Run.

### *Documentary Tracking*

Another common style of use of trackers can be characterized as documentary tracking. In this case, the participants were interested in documenting their activities rather than changing them. Sometimes this was out of interest, for example P21 carried a pedometer with her during her working day and would discuss step count and calorie burn with the other nurses at break time.

*"So they'd be like, how many steps did we walk? We were kind of using it like a collective. We all discussed it and we'd be like, oh that's shit, heh heh. It's only that many calories for all we've been doing ... But we lost interest ... it was the same day in, day out." (P21)*

Some seemed to be using trackers in this way because they were aggrieved by the amount of activity they were doing and somehow wanted to underline their effort. For example P6 had previously worked in a shop and used a pedometer app one day in order to show how far he was walking "*quite a considerable distance ... without leaving a building!*" P20 on the other hand seemed convinced he ran around more than other fielders in his cricket team and the pedometer was used to underscore his effort (if not make a comparison). In these instances both participants were using pedometers to tell stories about themselves.

Several others were doing documentary tracking to work out information about their routine activities. For example once some people had a sense of how many steps it was to work, or what speeds they were doing on a regular cycle ride, then it was no longer necessary to record them. An example given by someone who only occasionally used a tracker was:

*"I was visiting my parents and used MyTracks. And even though I'm really familiar with that area because I grew up there, I didn't really know the mileages between different places. And over time I got to know if I did a certain circuit it would be a certain number of km..., it would be 60 or 70 km and that's all I needed to know. And also it would give me an idea of how long that was going to take me, so that I could plan my day." (P16)*

There were also examples of people using food and drink trackers to document pleasurable experiences, and couples using trackers on special walks. Documentary tracking was not usually a long-term endeavour. Little tracking was being done for the sake of building up a stock of data about life. Sleep tracking was perhaps the only area where logs were being accrued in isolation from specific goals. Participants P15 and P16 had been using a sleep tracker seemingly just to keep an eye on things, and P1 also seemed to like the confirmation that she was sleeping:

*"my sleep pattern is averaging 7 hours a night deep sleep .., I know I sleep well ... I suppose I really value sleep. It's so so important."* (P1)

To some extent, all participants would do some sort of documentary tracking. For some, this could then be transformed into goal driven tracking, but for others documentary tracking is a form of data collection necessary only on occasion.

### *Diagnostic Tracking*

A form of tracking mentioned by two interviewees can be characterized as diagnostic tracking. This form of tracking is looking for a link between one thing and another. P3 spent some time logging medication and diet in an attempt to find out why he was having stomach problems. P9 had purchased a Jawbone UP specifically because he wanted to know why he was tired in the mornings even after getting what he saw as an adequate length of sleep. Diagnostic tracking was done over a period of time but did not need to carry on indefinitely, just until the person was satisfied that they have an answer. P3 felt he was able to use trackers to show that his stomach problem resulted from combining medication with particular foods. For P9, it seemed just the very fact that he was tracking had come to help him get better sleep. The ability to diagnose and perhaps avoid a serious illness by analysing data is one of the grand ideas in the Quantified Self discourse (e.g. [22]) but we found this was an interest for only a couple of participants and that the realities of diagnostics were rather mundane.

### *Collecting Rewards*

A form of tracking discussed by four people was tracking in order to score points or register achievements. This had some overlap with documentary tracking, for example P16 paid particular attention to a downhill section of his cycle route on which he would attempt to reach as high a speed as possible. This section seemed to be the key reason why he had used a tracker more than just once on this regular route. Two other runners who were following a training plan also liked to "race" other users of the app.

Three participants were tracking in order to claim rewards. One was tracking as a part of his health insurance scheme (this scheme rewarded people for gaining at least 40,000 steps a week), and two were using the app Gym Pact as a way of generating some income (users of the app that fail to reach targets make small payments to users that do). The irony of this for all three was that this points scoring was being done in addition to their own tracking. Similarly, P13 who bought a FitBit pedometer, continued to also use the Striiv pedometer as she was part way into a competition:

*"I ended up getting one of the FitBit things [but am] still using Striiv. Yeah, they had some sort of contest, like you walk 7500 steps per day, for the next two months, then you can win a 500 pound Amazon gift voucher." (P13)*

Some participants were interested in gaining achievements for achievements' sake:

*"Sometimes I want to cheat, I just take it off and do the shaking so the fuel goes up. ... There's a record of how many days you have been consecutively been reaching your goals. You don't want that number to jump back to zero" (P15)*

### *Fetishised Tracking*

Some participants were tracking because of a purer interest in gadgets and technology. P17 was collecting a lot of data seemingly for data's sake. Regarding an online diary he kept, he said: "*when it gets to a few hundred days you can't miss it you know*". Several others, particularly the users of wrist worn trackers, liked the conspicuousness of these devices. Users of the Nike Fuelband in particular saw this as being a "*cool*" (P15) or "*pretty*" (P18) technology.

## Interweaving Personal Trackers

We found that many participants used several trackers (a situation that may be related to the self selection issue noted earlier). Often trackers were being used to track different aspects of life. Sometimes these had clear separation. For example P7 could use his Wii Fit to monitor his weight and Map My Run to monitor running with no problem. Some participants had trackers that had crossover functionality and yet were able to keep these separate. As an example, food logging is supported by several apps, and yet participants had little trouble choosing one with which to do this. Several people liked to use both a pedometer and a running app. For some these could be separated by carrying a pedometer when they were walking and switching to a Garmin or other running technology while they were running. P4 would use the pedometer for her jogs to work, and a Garmin when she was specifically training. Others would just have both a pedometer and running app on at the same time. To have two measures of the same activity would not necessarily be cause for confusion. However, problems crept in where people were integrating data. Integration was usually done using the My Fitness Pal app as a hub. Integration was popular as a means of comparing calories consumed and expended. However this could be problematic:

"*I just always have to remember to just synch one of them to My Fitness Pal, or if it gets confused.*" (P13)

"*The Jawbone Up synchronisation back to My Fitness Pal has been broken for about three weeks. There's a time zone issue, which means that the number of calories that you burn doesn't work, there's a black hole between midnight and 6am. So unfortunately at the time of day when you synch you calories with the Jawbone UP back to My Fitness Pal it cuts off a quarter of the daily activity*" (P14)

Several participants reported using several trackers with ostensibly the same functionality. The example of P13 using both a FitBit and a Striiv pedometer (because she was part way into a competition) was given earlier. P14 was also using two pedometers. He was extremely particular about calculating calorie expenditure and although he generally preferred to use his Jawbone UP he told us:

"*So I've kind of stopped using Endomondo but I'm kind of still using it for what I call my active burn calories.*" *(P14)*

P14 was also using a third pedometer, the FitBug. This was offered to him through his health insurer and could be used to collect points and claim free gifts.

Activity trackers are also increasingly interweaved with an infrastructure. Data from some devices such as the Jawbone and Nike+ sensor cannot be viewed on the device itself but require a computer or phone. Physical devices required charging and often needed to be synched with a smartphone or computer. Smartphone choice affected use and choice of apps. Some infrastructure was shared. P7 said that when he moved in with his partner, he began using his partner's Wii and therefore lost his accrued Wii Fit data.

Interweaving trackers is not a case of rationally organizing them, but working with, through and around them. The situation is reminiscent of what Nardi and O'Day refer to as "*information ecologies*" [16].

## Uses of Tracking Data

Many trackers present not just a single measurement but several. For example, pedometers typically show calories burned, distance travelled, and steps. Nike apps also show a proprietary measure, "fuel". People had different preferences:

"*I just switch off the calories and steps. Because I don't think they're as necessary for me. ... What I need is the Nike Fuel, the number, to motivate me ... it's not very accurate but it makes sense*" *(P15)*

For others, the relevant measure and goals would come from a programme or training plan.

"*The target that Rosemary Conley tells you to do is 10,000 steps a day. Which is about 40 minutes walking. And, if you do ten, at 10,000 steps your metabolism is burning fat.*" (P1)

"*I really want to know the time and distance I've run. Its good that [my Nike Sportsband] has got the pace because on [the My Asics training plan] it gives you a pace you should be running at.*" *(P10)*

Accuracy was something some participants were more concerned with than others. Some participants had clearly gone to lengths to configure devices with correct measurements (such as their stride size) whereas others were happy to guess. Most interviewees realized or accepted that accuracy just was not guaranteed, and found ways to work around this:

"*I did 4 hours 29, but the app was slightly different from what my time was in the Marathon ... I did 27 point 6 miles on the app but the marathon is 26 point 4, but I think the app is using GPS.*" *(P8)*

"*So accuracy is not that good, but it wouldn't bother me ... it's got to be a ballpark of am I moving enough*" *(P1)*

Some were happy to shake their trackers in order to meet goals or unlock badges. Others wanted their steps to be steps: "*I'm slightly concerned ... I do a lot of knitting*" (P2).

### *Temporality of Tracker Data*

The main use of tracker data appeared to be short term, usually on the day that the data was generated. Running data was being used during a run in order to do things like keep to a set pace, and decide what was an appropriate place to turn around so that a run ends at home. Pedometer users were working on daily targets and would refer to that number at points during the day in order to decide whether they needed to do more to meet target.

*"And if I get home at night and I've done 7000 I'll go out and do another 2000. So it's keeping me on that sort of 10,000 track." (P1)*

There was some evidence of short-term comparative analysis of data. For example some pedometer users were interested in reaching their targets on several days in a row. Runners would also compare their runs to their previous 'equivalent' run.

*"Yeah so once I've finished running that's the screen it shows you, and it shows you the routes and everything. I'll then go into the workout screen ... and I'll look at what I've just done, and how long it was as a run, and how long the comparative run was before." (P7)*

The study found very few examples of long-term data sets being valued. Several people clearly had accrued a number of years of data, and several took pride in that fact. However, there was little interest in using tracker data from years, or even weeks ago.

"*Every marathon I've done since I got this, I've got all the training runs in a folder. I don't look at them. But at the time, when you're training for something, [the data is] really important." (P4)*

Most participants did not have a regime for saving data. Many did not seem concerned about transferring data from a device to a computer. Often data transfer would happen only if synching was automated (for example wirelessly or via a charger cable). Many did not seem concerned about losing old data when moving to new services and devices, and one person said he purposefully deleted data because "*I like to keep things rather tidy*" (P16).

## The Sociality of Personal Tracking

As Maitland et al. [12] pointed out, personal tracking is often social. This is not necessarily to say that the nominally social features of trackers are put to use, for example no one in the study published data to Facebook or Twitter; most would only write on Facebook about a major or newsworthy achievement such as the completion of a marathon (Newman et al. [17] discuss people's reluctance to discuss wellbeing information on general social network sites). One person did occasionally write about her activity in a healthy eating group set up by her and two friends, although she used this to announce achievements, for example posting a screenshot when she beat her personal best in Moves. In fact, several participants were scathing of others that do post to Facebook:

*"You always get some people like that who are like 'oh yeah, I had a great run today: five miles.' Ooh! Well done! Nobody ever does that! Five whole miles!" (P6 - sarcastically)*

"*I don't know, I find it kind of egotistical ... it's almost one of those things where you set yourself up for failure" (P10)*

Some apps allow you to 'friend' others within the app itself and to view others' data that way. Most people appeared to be connected to one or two others. P8 reported that she would sometimes play a tag game with one of her in-app friends, but otherwise few people made use of or saw benefit in such social functions. One thing several participants liked however was to compete with other users of an app (usually strangers). Some apps offered routes where runners of cyclists could race each other and post records. The Nike+ website also allowed people to see their performance against the averages for their gender and age group.

Moreover, tracking was often a co-present activity. Tracking was often done among families, friends and co-workers. Walks can be special when undertaken together by couples, and for P7 Map My Walk had been used to document such "special" activities. P3 on the other hand, wanted to have the same pedometer as his wife. They would take them together on walks, and compare information about their commutes. Couples and families could also share scales, P7 described how he would persuade his partner onto the Wii Fit once in a while as he was concerned he was underweight. Not all family relations are convivial. P1 recounted a story in which her son took her FitBit on a long walk in order to smash her own record.

*"I said it's not about walking further than me. It's about your own fitness and everything!"*

Kinship, as Harper [5] has discussed, is played out through technology in complex ways. Others reported using activity trackers among friends and colleagues. The use of a pedometer by nurses on their ward rounds was discussed earlier. P16 described how, when he went running, he and his running partner would share the data from the partner's Garmin.

*"She's a bit fastidious about things like this, so she would have a spreadsheet, and because I was with her, running all the time, regularly at weekends, we were running both at the same speed, same distance, we'd keep an eye on this thing together." (p16)*

There were also examples given by participants where the device was totemic of wellbeing. Colleagues would recommend devices to each other (or sometimes talk behind people's backs about who ought to get one). Colleagues, it seems, would only sometimes show their data to each other—but the very fact of device ownership could signify a shared outlook, and serve as a bond and talking point.

## DISCUSSION: LIVED INFORMATICS

The participants were invited to interview by a poster asking "*Do you use an activity tracker?*" and the interviews began with a vague request along the lines of: "*I'm interested to hear what trackers you use, what you like and dislike, and so on.*" This request was not met with a naming of what apps and devices that person had, or what kinds of thing they wanted to measure, but something more akin to a life story. Often this story concerned weight management, or ever-developing interests in sports and training. Often this story involved family and friends. Often the story extended over years, and followed people who would move countries, form and leave relationships, and start or change careers. Tracking was explained in terms of people's lives, worries, hopes, interests, careers and so on. Something that we were perhaps a little underprepared for was the emotionality of activity tracking. For most people, tracking was directly tied to self-esteem. For some it tied into pride at completing marathons, achieving fantastic speeds on a bicycle and/or raising thousands of pounds for charity. For others the tracker tied into body image problems, to aging, and/or to broken relationships. Often tracking seemed to tie into people's mental health. The situation is reminiscent of McCarthy and Wright's discussion of "technology as experience" [13] and we find ourselves drawn to their call for design to engage with *the felt life*.

There was a range of different people in the study. Not only were their circumstances different, but there were clear differences of interest and personality. Some people identified as being (in the words of P3) "*a stats person*" and liking to see data, charts and other information. Some people were very organized and tidy. Others said they were (in the words of P1) "*not a data person at all*", but made the effort to track and even found they could take pleasure in it. Some reported that they were (in the words of P4) "*into fitness*" whereas others were (in the words of P2) "*not a gym person*". One person was P13 "*into games*" but another P14 "*not a games person*". Each person, in his/her own way, made the activity of tracking his/her own. Although participants regularly referred to personality, it seems unlikely that cognitive models can explain their tracking. Personality was only part of a larger story of body image, family, personal circumstances and so on.

Nobody was just a *user* in this study. Behaviour change, where this was even an issue, was not being done with a tracker, but across multiple technologies over time. Nobody had downloaded an app or bought a device and then decided to lose weight or start running because of it, but rather they were using apps often over short-term periods to support longer-term interests and issues. Sometimes apps and devices would inspire people to walk more, or perhaps follow a training plan. Only one participant was interested in the retrospective use of long-term data. Tracking data is overwhelmingly for use in the short term. In fact, personal tracking might best be understood as prospective rather than retrospective. Tracking is often about where you are heading in life. It is often about trying to lose weight, about training for a marathon and similar goals. People here do not aspire to do dispassionate data analysis about their bodies, but on the contrary, are doing something deeply emotional and often passionately focused on a future. We are reminded of Ingold's notion of "*dwelling*" [7]. When people track their activities (when they *dwell* in data) they are not building a description of their lives, but are *wayfaring* in information. To know ourselves is not to look at the past or even to the present, but to the future. Ingold uses the term 'wayfaring' specifically to suggest that one is not following a set path to one's imagined future but is navigating using a variety of information, cues and intuitions as best one can. Knowing oneself may involve collecting and reflecting on information about oneself but is for the purposes of a life being lived. In Harper's [6] terms, tracking is part of "*a praxis of living*".

Our observations about 'documentary' and 'diagnostic' tracking are a little closer to the vision of personal informatics than our observations of other forms of tracking. Here people seem to want to create a reasonably accurate account of something, but for the sake of understanding routine, keeping a record or finding something out. These forms of tracking are not long term, and can sometimes playfully involve the creation of false data. Building a long term, accurate record was a minority pursuit. Long-term collection may become popular and may prove very valuable, but we emphasise that to track over the short term is not necessarily to give up or fail.

To characterize the situation we have observed we introduce the term 'lived informatics'. With this term we are underscoring our observations, trying to characterize a state of affairs rather than laying out a vision. The term is meant to mean just that people are using information and finding its meaning in their day-to-day lives. Li et al. [8] have previously pointed out that people collect personal data for reasons other than personal informatics, such as reminiscing about the past, aiding memory, and personal information management. But our point is more radical. We are not saying that things are done in addition to personal informatics, but that personal informatics must be done over a range of lived activities. We do not suggest that our work undermines the grand vision of personal informatics. All we do is show it is unrealistic to assume that people can or want to do rational data collection, and act only when data has been validated and thoroughly analysed. From a lived informatics perspective, we suggest:

- Do not expect people to act as rational data scientists. Understand that people will pick and choose trackers, switch over time, and will have times when they track a lot and times when they track just a little. Consider collecting metadata on app use alongside activity data.

- (Re)consider personal tracking as social tracking. Look beyond support for publishing data to social networks, for example to co-present tracking, kinship, friendship, support, competition and play.
- Design for interweaving, not just integration. It is not reasonable to expect that people will have a rational set of trackers each with a clearly defined function. When evaluating a new technology, consider how it might be used alongside others in an information ecology.
- Consider that behaviour change is not just a possible outcome of using an individual technology, but is something that is achieved by people, potentially across various technologies that they interweave.
- Recognise that data can be meaningful in the context it is produced, but may lose meaning when it is removed from that context.
- Evaluation should address more than measuring 'improvements' in activity. Consider, for example, the emotionality, the hope and the fun people may have.
- Attend to the physicality of tracking. This includes the physicality of phones when designing smartphone apps.

We have critiqued personal informatics but must emphasise this is from a perspective that does not address or envisage what might be most effective in terms of public health. We have explored the perspectives of current users of personal trackers, and we seek to open discussion of what people want, do, and experience when using personal trackers.

## REFERENCES


1. Barkhuus, L, Polichar, V. Empowerment through seamfulness: Smartphones in everyday life. *Personal and Ubiquitous Computing* (15)6, 2011: 629-639.
2. Bentley, F., Tollmar, K., Stephenson, P., Levy, L., Jones, B. Robertson, S, Price, E. Catrambone, R., Wilson, J. Health Mashups: Presenting statistical patterns between wellbeing data and context in natural language to promote behavior change. *TOCHI* 20(5):30, 2013.
3. Berg, M. *Rationalising of Medical Work: Decision Support Techniques and Medical Practices*. MIT Press, 1997.
4. Cramer, H., Rost, M., and Holmquist L. E. Performing a Check-in: Emerging Practices, Norms and 'Conflicts' in Location-Sharing Using Foursquare. *Proc MobileHCI 2011*.
5. Harper, R. *Texture: Human Expression in the Age of Communications Overload*. MIT Press, 2010.
6. Harper, R., Bird, C., Zimmermann, T. Murphy, B. Dwelling in Software: Aspects of the Felt-Life of Engineers in Large Software Projects. *Proc ECSCW* 2013:163-180.
7. Ingold, T. Being Alive: Essays on Movement, Knowledge and Description. *Routledge*, 2011.
8. Li, I., Dey, A. & Forlizzi, J. Understanding My Data Myself: Supporting Self-Reflection with Ubicomp Technologies. *Proc UbiComp* 2011.
9. Li, I., Dey, A., & Forlizzi, J. A Stage Based Model of Personal Informatics Systems. *Proc CHI* 2010: 557-566.
10. Lin, J.J., Mamykina, L., Lindtner, S., Delajoux, G., & Strub, H.B. Fish'n'Steps: Encouraging Physical Activity with an Interactive Computer Game. *Proc Ubicomp 2006*: 261-278.
11. Mackinlay, M.Z. Phases of Accuracy Diagnosis: (In)visibility of System Status in the FitBit. *Intersect: The Stanford Journal of Science, Technology and Society*, 6(2), June 2013.
12. Maitland, J., Chalmers, M. Designing for Peer Involvement in Weight Management. *Proc CHI* 2011: 315-324.
13. Maitland, J., Sherwood, S., Barkhuus, L., Anderson, I., Chalmers, M. and Brown, B., Increasing the Awareness of Moderate Exercise with Pervasive Computing. *Proc PerHealth 2006*.
14. Mamykina, L., Mynatt, E.D., & Kaufman, D.R. Investigating Health Management Practices of Individuals with Diabetes. *Proc CHI* 2006: 927-936.
15. McCarthy, J., Wright, P. *Technology as Experience*. MIT Press. 2004.
16. Nardi, B, O'Day V. *Information Ecologies. Using Technology with Heart*. MIT Press. 1999.
17. Newman, M., Lauterbach, D., Munson, S., Resnick, P., Morris, M. "It's not that I don't have problems, I'm just not putting them on Facebook": Challenges and Opportunities in Using Online Social Networks for Health. *Proc CSCW 2011*: 341-350.
18. Pollock, N., Williams, R. *Software and Organizations. The Biography of the Enterprise-Wide System, or How SAP Conquered the World*. Routledge, 2008.
19. Shaw, R, Fenwick, E., Baker, G., McAdam, C., Fitzsimons, C., & Mutrie, N. 'Pedometers Cost Buttons': The Feasibility of Implementing a Pedometer Based Walking Programme within the Community. *BMC Public Health* 2011, 11:200.
20. Simon H. *Sciences of the Artificial*. MIT Press, 1969.
21. Tudor-Locke, C., Basset, D. How Many Steps/Day are Enough? Preliminary Pedometer Indices for Public Health. *Sports Med* 2004; 34(1):1-8.
22. Wolf, G. Know Thyself: Tracking Every Facet of Life, from Sleep to Mood to Pain, 24/7/365. *Wired*, July 2009: 92-95.

# Towards an Holistic View of the Energy and Environmental Impacts of Domestic Media and IT

**Oliver Bates, Mike Hazas, Adrian Friday, Janine Morley, and Adrian K. Clear**
Lancaster University, UK
{o.bates,m.hazas,a.friday,j.morley,a.clear}@lancaster.ac.uk

## ABSTRACT
To date, research in sustainable HCI has dealt with eco-feedback, usage and recycling of appliances within the home, and longevity of portable electronics such as mobile phones. However, there seems to be less awareness of the energy and greenhouse emissions impacts of domestic consumer electronics and information technology. Such awareness is needed to inform HCI sustainability researchers on how best to prioritise efforts around digital media and IT. Grounded in inventories, interview and plug energy data from 33 undergraduate student participants, our findings provide the context for assessing approaches to reducing the energy and carbon emissions of media and IT in the home. In the paper, we use the findings to discuss and inform more fruitful directions that sustainable HCI research might take, and we quantify how various strategies might have modified the energy and emissions impacts for our participants.

### Author Keywords
Home energy; sustainability; embodied emissions; life cycle assessment.

### ACM Classification Keywords
H.5.2 Information interfaces and presentation (e.g., HCI): Miscellaneous.

## INTRODUCTION
The domestic energy demand of consumer electronics, digital home entertainment and computing devices (which we will call *media and IT* in this paper) is on the rise worldwide [5]. Between 2000 and 2009 IT consumption in the UK more than doubled [17]. These devices comprise about 25% of the total domestic electricity demand [18]. Despite the fact that these devices are individually becoming more efficient, the total energy use of these devices continues to rise [17]. While the HCI and ubicomp communities have considered ways to reduce media and IT's environmental and energy impacts, these have tended to focus on issues such as improved computer power management [4], understanding device attachment [16], or eco-feedback [7]—what is lacking is a broader view of the impacts of media and IT at home, and how these relate to everyday practice.


*CHI 2014*, April 26–May 1, 2014, Toronto, Ontario, Canada.

http://dx.doi.org/10.1145/2556288.2556968

With the growing ownership of media and IT devices, we attempt to answer several more contextual questions, such as: how are all these devices used in everyday life? What are the resource and environmental impacts of these configurations, and how is this related to their implication in practice? What are the links between variation in similar practices, and variation in impacts? With answers to these questions, sustainable HCI might be better equipped to identify and pursue new avenues of research and design.

Based on in-depth studies involving 33 students living in on-campus university accommodation, we explore the media and IT device inventories, the day-to-day practices that they support, their measured direct energy demand, and their approximate embodied greenhouse gas emissions. We put forth three contributions. (1) We quantify the embodied carbon and direct energy of domestic media and IT using participant inventories and energy-use data. To date, studies of domestic technology in sustainable HCI haven't included embodied emissions; we believe the inclusion of these impacts, alongside direct energy, is crucial to better understanding the wider 'sustainability picture'. (2) We link the variation in these impacts to the role that these technology configurations play in supporting our participants' everyday practices. In so doing, we develop and explore the prominence of *constellations* and *connoisseurs*, two concepts which we briefly introduced [2, p. 15–16] in our discussion of domestic energy use. (3) Based on our findings, we discuss the potential impact reductions of specific solutions previously proposed in the HCI literature, and go on to highlight some new implications for design.

## RELATED WORK AND MOTIVATION
The concern with direct and indirect impacts of appliances and devices has been a consideration for some years in HCI. Direct energy impact is a particular sensitivity for those involved in so called 'eco-feedback' technologies, as surveyed by Froehlich et al. [9] and exemplified in recent domestic eco-feedback interventions [8]. While eco-feedback aims to promote understanding and awareness of how energy is spent [7] and encourage energy saving behaviours [8], such technologies have not been found to be particularly effective. Moreover, eco-feedback has been critiqued for casting individuals as 'rational actors', and failing to recognise that energy use is intertwined with everyday practices [23]. In our paper, we concern ourselves with understanding the impacts, and con-

nection between media and IT and everyday practices, in the home.

Energy use related to IT in the home has been studied previously. Chetty et al. found power management strategies on home computers were often underused [4]. Pierce et al. similarly found an unwillingness to power down or 'micromanage' IT devices [20]. Reinforcing Strengers [23], Pierce observes how our everyday interactions with home appliances more broadly, are unconscious or habitual rather than the result of rational decision-making, and proposes a design vocabulary of energy saving behaviours. We consider largely personal media and IT appliances, and while time of use is sometimes a factor in our study, we do not concern ourselves directly with the practices surrounding power management.

Of course, the direct energy demand of media and IT hardware, its peripherals, and supporting infrastructure within the home are only a part of the story. A more complete view of media and IT's impacts should include: the *embodied* greenhouse gas emissions arising from manufacturing and transport of hardware (hereafter *embodied emissions*); the *direct* energy impacts of the devices themselves; and the *indirect* impacts (embodied emissions and direct energy) of the network infrastructure, computation and data storage relied upon, far outside the home.

While there appears to be little quantification of these embodied and indirect impacts in the HCI literature, it is true to say that reducing these impacts have been widely acknowledged: in Blevis's influential paper [3], several Sustainable Interaction Design principles are elucidated, challenging designers to consider the disposal of old technology in the invention of new ones, and exhorting the incorporation of renewal and reuse in design. Wakkary and Tanenbaum build on these principles to show how families appropriate and extend everyday technologies for continued use [25].

The longevity of device use (over which embodied impact is defused) is considered with respect to mobile phones by Huang and Truong [13] in 2007. The style and features of a phone do not spur phone upgrades, so much as end-of-contract and special offers from mobile phone carriers. Hanks et al. covered university students' attitudes toward environmental issues, and their purchasing of mobile phones and computers [12]: respondents showed an openness to refurbishment and contributing to responsible disposal, yet there was a high rate of device replacement across relatively short time periods (especially for phones), a reticence to buy used and refurbished phones and laptops, and an unwillingness to share these devices.

Odom et al. looked more broadly at the reasons people feel attachment to certain possessions, and make efforts to preserve them [16]. He noted relatively little attachment to digital artefacts, and discussing the design of more enduring objects. More recently, Gegenbauer and Huang considered how attachment is a critical factor for influencing the longevity of device ownership, and how appliances that have fallen out of use are far more likely to be kept 'just in case' than disposed of [10]. Kim and Paulos develop a framework for the creative reuse of e-waste based on surveys of personal stockpiling behaviours [14].

In our work we focus on offering a holistic view of the impacts of media and IT appliances for a university student population. We quantify both the direct energy and embodied impacts of these appliances and link these to the everyday practices they support.[1] Our goal is to help sustainability researchers decide where best to apply their efforts by highlighting the stark variations in impact, and relating these to specific configurations of everyday practice and technology.

## METHODS AND DATA GATHERED

In this paper we are focusing on three areas of impact: embodied emissions, direct energy, and indirect impacts. We provide quantitative measures of embodied emissions (in the form of kilograms of carbon dioxide equivalent, abbreviated kg $CO_2e$), and of direct energy (in kilowatt-hours). Despite our detailed study methods, the indirect impacts (e.g. those arising from Internet service, mobile cellular data, and data centres) were not quantifiable. However, we use interview data to qualitatively comment on the frequency and role of these services in our participants' lives, and we make specific suggestions for how indirect impacts might be accounted for in future enquiry.

A mixed-methods approach was used to study media and IT in the homes of student participants living on campus at university. The findings in this paper are based on data collected across three different studies (Table 1). One study was undertaken in March 2011 by Bates et al. [2], and we are utilising the data from twenty-one of their participants.[2] The second study was conducted by Clear et al., and involved four participants during March–April 2012 [6].[3] The third study involved eight participants in November 2012.

The students had private study-bedrooms arranged around a central corridor with shared kitchen. Their devices (Table 2) occasionally were shared, however these weren't communal or "common-use" devices.

For the participants across all three studies, device and appliance inventories were taken on an initial visit to their room. Plugwise socket-monitors were used to capture the fine-grain energy consumption data for a total of 191 devices over several weeks from each study. Semi-structured interviews were

[1]While we acknowledge disposal or recycling of a product is an important component in its overall footprint, we neglect it for the purposes of this paper. Recycling and disposal methods are highly dependent on locality, and for IT, the greenhouse emissions impacts are relatively low compared to manufacturing, transportation, and usage (typically less than 5%).

[2]Bates et al. report on 'entertainment and IT' using a subset of the data [2, pp. 112-5]. It is important to note that their characterisation was relatively brief and primarily qualitative; they only quantified the direct laptop/desktop energy for nine of their participants. By contrast, this paper leverages the per-socket sensor data for twenty-one participants from that study, and twelve more from later studies, to bring out new, insightful details of both direct energy variation, and embodied emissions.

[3]Clear et al. wrote about thermal comfort in the lives of the participants; the per-socket energy data and the interviews on media and IT have not been previously reported.

| Study | Study Period | Participants | Interviewed Participants | Total Devices |
|---|---|---|---|---|
| 1 | March 2011 - April 2011 | 21 | 11 | 127 |
| 2 | March 2012 - April 2012 | 4 | 4 | 21 |
| 3 | November 2012 | 8 | 8 | 43 |
| Total | - | 33 | 23 | 191 |

**Table 1. Summary of the media and IT studies**

used to help understand the role of media and IT devices in the day-to-day lives of our participants. The interviews were fully transcribed and coded. In our discussion below, we refer to each of the 33 participants using pseudonyms. Per-socket energy consumption data in the latter two studies has been limited to a representative 20-day window during term time, to be comparable with the first study.

### Limitations and assumptions

We acknowledge that students' media and IT practices are not necessarily generalisable (e.g. accessing a VLE). However, students are a specific and sizeable demographic: 7% of the UK population, and 15% of the US. Similar IT related practices are described in 14 Danish homes by Røpke et al. [21]. Compared to other areas of practice (e.g. laundry, home heating, cooking), there may be more parallels between the IT of students, and other parts of the population. Regardless, we should stress that our goal is not generalisability *per se*, but rather to richly characterise *variations* in practice, technology and impact.

Since the lifetimes of our participants' devices were not known (the devices all remained in use during the study), we show the approximate embodied carbon (e.g. Figures 1 or 2) that would have arisen from the manufacture and transportation of a single device of that type. And while as a long term goal we aim to include cloud and content distribution networks (CDNs) in our impact analysis, we are unable to cover this in detail in this paper. Indirect (cloud and CDN) impacts are problematic to measure, as they depend on traffic, network path, data centre location and power source. However, to give a feel for how these contribute, we do give examples of what some of the relative impacts might be, based on our qualitative data.

## INVENTORIES

Across all 33 participant rooms, there were a total of 191 devices and appliances (Table 2). There were 50 appliances that did not explicitly support media and IT related services (e.g. hair dryers, hair straighteners, coffee machines, kettles, alarm clocks, fans, and a toothbrush charger). While we list these in the table for completeness, we focus our analysis on the remaining 138 media and IT devices.

All 33 participants had computers: 29 had just a laptop; 1 had just a desktop; and 3 had both. 16 of the participants had one or more computer monitors or peripherals (e.g. powered speakers, external hard disk drives (HDDs), and printers). 8 participants had TVs, all of which were connected to at least one other device (e.g. DVD player, video game console). The number of media and IT devices and appliances in each room

| Participant | Constellations | Non constellation media and IT devices | Other Devices | No. Devices | Total Constellations |
|---|---|---|---|---|---|
| Zoe | - | Laptop | - | 2 | - |
| Ellie | - | Laptop | Kettle | 3 | - |
| Thomas | - | Laptop | Alarm Clock | 3 | - |
| Aaron | - | Laptop | Alarm Clock | 3 | - |
| Wendy | - | Laptop | Hair Dryer | 3 | - |
| Jess | - | Laptop | Hair Straighteners | 3 | - |
| James | - | Laptop | Lamp | 3 | - |
| Jill | - | Notebook -> Laptop | Lamp | 4 | - |
| Donna | - | Laptop | Hair Straighteners, Lamp | 4 | - |
| Luke | - | Laptop | Lamp, Guitar Amp | 4 | - |
| Leah | {TV, Nintendo Wii} | Laptop | - | 4 | 1 |
| Miranda | - | Laptop | Hair Dryer, Hair Straighteners | 4 | - |
| Vincent | {Laptop, Laptop Fan} | Camera | - | 4 | 1 |
| Nathan | {Laptop,Speakers,Printer} | - | Toothbrush | 5 | 1 |
| Kevin | {TV, Xbox 360} | Laptop | Alarm Clock | 5 | 1 |
| Polly | - | Laptop | Lamp, Iron, Hair Dryer | 5 | - |
| Omar | {TV, Xbox 360}, {Laptop,Speakers} | - | - | 5 | 2 |
| Stan | {Desktop, Monitor} | TV | Hair Dryer | 5 | 1 |
| Darren | {Laptop,Speakers} | Camera | Lamp | 5 | 1 |
| Callum | {Laptop, Monitor, Tube Amp} | - | Coffee Machine, Hair Dryer | 6 | 1 |
| Emily | {Laptop, Printer} | - | Lamp, Kettle, Iron | 6 | 1 |
| Jack | {Laptop, Speakers} | - | Guitar Amp, Lamp, Fan | 6 | 1 |
| Natasha | - | Laptop, Record Player, Camera | Hair Dryer, Hair Straighteners | 6 | - |
| Rachel | {Laptop, Printer} | iPod Dock | Hair Dryer, Hair Straighteners, Lamp | 7 | 2 |
| Nadia | {Laptop, Printer} | iPod Dock | Hair Dryer, Alarm Clock, Hair Straighteners | 7 | 1 |
| Chloe | {TV, DVD Player}, {Laptop, Printer} | - | Fan, Alarm Clock | 7 | 2 |
| Kate | {TV, Xbox 360}, {Laptop, Printer} | Stereo, MP3 Player | - | 7 | 2 |
| Stephanie | {TV, Portable HDD} | Laptop | Lamp, Hair Dryer, Hair Straighteners, Toothbrush | 8 | 1 |
| Feng | {TV, Playstation 3}, {Laptop, Speakers} | iPod | Hair Straighteners, Lamp | 8 | 2 |
| Ian | {Laptop, Speakers}, {Laptop, Screen, Speakers}, {Xbox 360, Screen, Speakers} | iPod | Hair Straighteners, Alarm Clock | 8 | 3 |
| Henry | {Desktop, Monitor (2), Router, External HDD (2), Audio Receiver}, {Xbox, Monitor, Audio Receiver} | Laptop | - | 10 | 2 |
| Gary | {Audio Receiver, EQ, CD Player}, {Desktop, Monitor (2), Audio Receiver, Router, NAS}, {Xbox, Monitor, Audio Receiver} | Laptop | Guitar Amp (2) | 13 | 3 |
| Matt | {Laptop, Monitor, Stereo (2), Router, Airport Express}, {TV, IPTV, Stereo (2), Xbox 360, Mac Mini Server, Bluray player}, {Mac Mini Server, USB hub, HDD (2), Router, Airport Express} | - | Coffee Machine, Guitar Amp | 18 | 3 |

**Table 2. Overview of the inventories and constellations for the 33 participants, sorted by increasing number of devices. Mobile and smart phones have been left out as all users owned one, except Gary who owned 2.**

ranged from just a few (e.g. Zoe, Ellie and Thomas) to 18 (Matt). Where applicable, brackets in Table 2 shows how the devices were connected as groupings, or what we call *constellations*.

### Constellations

We observed people using multiple interrelated devices to perform a task, requiring them to be left on so that a task can be performed without interruption. This is nicely exemplified by Henry, who told us "*I suppose it's not really my computer I use as much but my stereo. I use that a lot, which is connected to my computer*". We consider a constellation to be active when two or more connected or associated devices are consuming electricity at the same time, often working in concert to support the same practice. Constellations are potentially complex, since media and IT devices have a variety of different ways of being connected, both physically or over a wireless network.

From the data collected and analysed we have found that constellations are a crucial entity in understanding media and IT impacts, for three reasons: (1) they are commonplace (there are 30 constellations owned by 20 participants); (2) they are involved in supporting many areas of media and IT practice; and (3) their composition is strongly linked to their emboded emissions and patterns of direct energy consumption.

### Embodied Emissions

The field of life cycle analysis (LCA) deals with estimating the embodied emissions that arise from the production and delivery of a certain product or service. Because of the complex and layered nature of materials extraction, processing, manufacturing and transport, it is widely acknowledged that there will be inaccuracies in the overall emissions estimates, particularly for sophisticated products such as media and IT devices. Malmodin et al. [15] surveys previous studies on IT carbon estimations and highlights how a lack of transparency in the surrounding processes of raw-material extraction and manufacturing in LCA leaves a lot of room for error. An in-depth survey of carbon accounting for media and IT devices by Anders et al. shows that typical errors in LCA literature are on the order of about 50%, even for similar products [1].

Despite the relative levels of inaccuracy, it can be informative to (1) compare the embodied emissions of different types of media and IT device, particularly where those devices can be used to deliver similar services; and (2) compare a particular device's embodied emissions, to the carbon that arises due to that device's direct electricity consumption.

Teehan and Kandlikar [24] highlight a lack of LCA performed on newer IT devices. Their results show that there has been a 50–60% decrease in carbon equivalent produced between pre-2004 products and post-2009 products, and that this is due to use of fewer materials. By combining their own mass data and using the 'ecoinvent' database, Teehan et al. show that there is a linear relationship between mass and embodied emissions created in the manufacturing phases of three pre-2004 and eleven post-2009 manufactured devices.

Our embodied emissions figures (see Table 3) use the coefficient reported by Teehan et al. of 27 kg $CO_2e$ per kg of product [24, p. 4002], supplemented by data from Apple whitepapers[4]. Due to their use of ecoinvent, Teehan et al.'s impact coefficients are lower than those of Apple and those reported in the survey by Anders et al. [1]—our embodied impact estimates thus represent *a lower bound* on these impacts, and the actual impacts could be higher.

Figure 1 shows how the estimated embodied emissions are distributed across the inventories of our participants, grouped by device type. All but one participant had a laptop, and these account for about 40% of the total embodied emissions. Displays (monitors and TVs) are the next largest, accounting for 32% of the total embodied emissions.

Before we go on to discuss the impacts, we will give a brief snapshot of media and IT with these participants.

| | Embodied emissions (kg CO2e) | Mass (kg) | Source |
|---|---|---|---|
| Smart Phone | 8 | - | Teehan et al. |
| Desktop | 180 | - | |
| Laptop | 200 | - | |
| Monitor | 190 | - | |
| Mac Mini Server | 180 | - | Apple Tech Report |
| TV | 405 | 15 | Calculated using 27 kg CO2e per kg of mass. (Teehan et al.) |
| Computer Peripheral | 8.1 | 0.3 | |
| Games Console | 94.5 | 3.5 | |
| Router/Switch | 6.75 | 0.25 | |
| DVD/Blu-ray Player | 67.5 | 2.5 | |
| CD/Record Player Separate | 135 | 5 | |
| Audio Receiver (Inc. Speakers) | 405 | 15 | |
| Computer Speakers/Dock | 62.1 | 2.3 | |
| Printer | 81 | 3 | |
| Camera | 8.1 | 0.3 | |
| MP3 Player | 5.4 | 0.2 | |

**Table 3. Embodied emissions for media and IT devices that were included in our participants' inventories.**

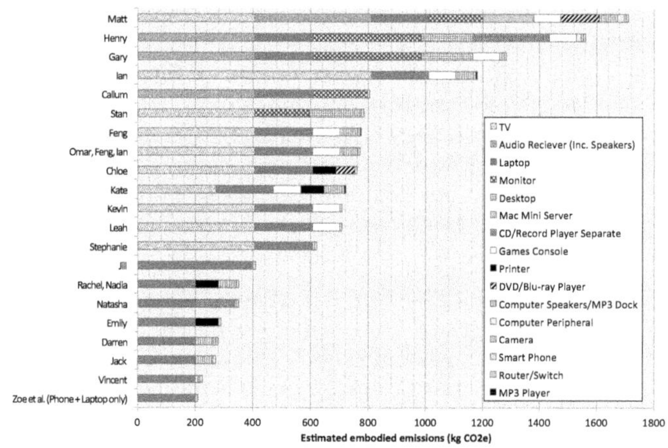


**Figure 1. The breakdown of embodied emissions across the 33 inventories.**

## MEDIA AND IT PRACTICES

Unsurprisingly, we see that media and IT devices feature heavily in the day-to-day activities of our participants. These devices were used for a wide variety of tasks which can broadly be categorised as work, education, entertainment and communication. In this section, we describe some of the more prominent activities in detail. The term 'practice' in this paper is used to describe an activity, or set of actions carried out by our participants.

### IT devices

The principal IT devices that we saw were smart phones, and computers, each supporting a variety of practices. In general, we found that desktop and laptop computers were used for similar tasks, and that these tasks were multiple and simultaneous, often related to different practices. For example, instant messaging and email are used to support communication, both personal and work-related, which is often intertwined with work-related tasks such as reading documents for coursework, and essay writing. According to our participants,

[4]`http://www.apple.com/uk/environment/reports/`, accessed February 19, 2014.

applications switch in and out of participants' focus as different practices come into play, and interrupt one another. The portability that is characteristic to laptop computers leads to a further blurring of the lines between practices [21].

In general, we found acute awareness of the extent of laptop use. All participants noted using their laptops almost every day, and many participants reported having them on most of the time whilst awake. Our participants used IT for many of the things one might expect: reading blogs or news, browsing, and online shopping. Below, we provide a brief summary of the IT and media practices that featured in the interviews as particularly meaningful to our participants, or were manifest by their specific ways of playing and working.

### IT Practices

Social networking and communication practices become difficult to separate from other activities when carried out on IT devices, largely because they are achieved through social media tools like Facebook and Twitter, and instant messengers that support asynchronous communications. In these cases, parties may respond in-between other tasks or even when they are next online. Communication can take place synchronously if all parties are focused on the task, as is generally the case with voice or video chat. For example, Ellie describes her chatting: "*I like Skype my family on the weekends and I Skype my boyfriend, at night usually*". Our participants reported regularly intertwining social networking with work, often as a means of procrastination.

Our participants regularly used their computers for studying and other university work. This usually consisted of using word processors, course-specific software, and the virtual learning environment (VLE) for access to course materials. Some participants stored the documents on their laptops in categorised folders, filling in notes on them during lectures; others kept the VLE open on their laptops for easy access to course content; and some of our participants printed them for revision and use in lectures. Henry used his desktop computer for running and monitoring a test-bed for an outside professional project he was working on.

### Media Practices

We found variation in the ways that our participants consumed digital media (e.g. listening to music, watching TV). Quite often, participants reported watching movies and TV on their laptops, using video-on-demand services; from DVD; or downloaded from the Internet. However, three participants mostly watched movies and TV on televisions. Chloe did this using a DVD player, Kate through her Xbox 360, whereas Stephanie would download content to a USB hard drive and watch it on her TV because it had a bigger screen than her laptop. Ian, Donna and Henry mentioned that group film and TV nights would happen occasionally. The hosts of "film nights" tended to be the participants with larger displays or TVs.

Almost all participants reported listening to music. Some had dedicated MP3 players for this. Others used their laptops or mobile phones. In some instances, participants listened to music with multiple devices, using external powered speakers in their rooms into which they could plug their laptops or MP3 players. Darren would bring his laptop and speakers to the kitchen so that his friends could take turns playing songs that they liked. Gary and Natasha had specific media devices for audio playback (CD Player, and record player respectively). Gary and Natasha, reported that audio was often listened to in the background, for instance, whilst studying or getting ready to go about their day.

Nine of our participants owned games consoles. These were either connected to televisions or computer monitors. Henry and Jill did not own consoles, but gamed on their laptops. We saw variation in the extent of use across participants (between 0 and 5 hours per day), and University schedules also affected this. Jill notes how "*Usually in the evening I game before I go to bed,*" whereas Henry recalled how his gaming habits had changed as he became busier with coursework. As Jill notes, gaming is an activity that is often not overlapped with other tasks: "*While I'm gaming I can't do anything else ... because it takes up the screen.*" Group game nights—in a similar vein to group film nights—happened, although less often.

## CONFIGURATIONS AND IMPACTS

To give a broader view of impacts of media and IT we discuss the embodied emission impacts of our participants' devices, and then characterise the relationship between the embodied emissions and direct energy consumption. From here, we move onto constellations, focusing on how hub devices are relied upon, and what this means for the direct impact of a constellation. Following this, we examine how connoisseurs of media and IT configure their constellations, along with how this increases direct energy impacts. We conclude with a discussion of the kinds of practices that our participants took part in that lead to indirect impacts, and how Internet-connectedness affects both direct and indirect impacts.

#### *Large embodied emissions, even larger direct energy*

In Figure 2 we can see a comparison of estimated embodied emissions footprint alongside the estimated direct carbon emissions over the course of a year. This figure illustrates two things; 1) devices and constellations with larger embodied emissions tend to have greater direct emissions, and 2) the largest quantities of direct emissions are due to large constellations.

**For small mobile devices** (such as smartphones and tablets), **the direct emissions is vanishingly small compared to the embodied emissions.** Laptops, assuming they have a lifetime of several years, can have comparable direct and embodied emissions, depending on the laptop's daily durations-of-use. But it is important to note that even for the largest, power-hungry constellations on for the majority of the day (as was the case with Henry), the yearly direct emissions still only reached half of the embodied emissions. Thus, while direct energy can be justifiable as a target for reduction through methods such as eco-feedback [23], the embodied emissions should never be underestimated.

#### *Similar practices, different impacts*

A constellation becomes subsumed into more practices with the connection of additional IT devices, increasing the impact of a given practice. For example, connection of a laptop to a

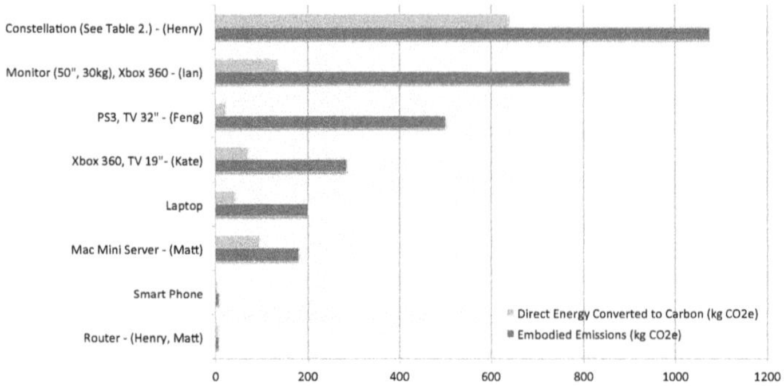


**Figure 2. Seven examples of the embodied emissions alongside direct emissions. Embodied emissions values are estimated using the values in Table 3. We based our yearly direct emissions estimate on the 20-day energy we observed in the study, and are calculated using the DEFRA 2010 conversion factor, adjusted to include Scope 3 emissions: 0.60 kg $CO_2$e/kWh.**

display, now enables the use of the display to support practices that would have previously been conducted just using the laptop. Eighteen of our participants had peripherals (e.g. displays, speakers, printers, seen in table 2) for use with their computers. We found that connected devices roughly mimic the time-use patterns of the hub device they are connected to. Small, basic constellations were the lowest contributors (Jack, Ellie, Rachel), for example: a laptop and a couple of peripherals (e.g. printer, speakers). Inventories containing a larger number of media and IT devices (Matt, Henry) contributed between 3.8 and 41.1 times the amount of daily energy when compared to the small constellations (figure 3). If our participants changed their media and IT practices and only used laptops, the total embodied emissions would have been reduced by roughly 55%.

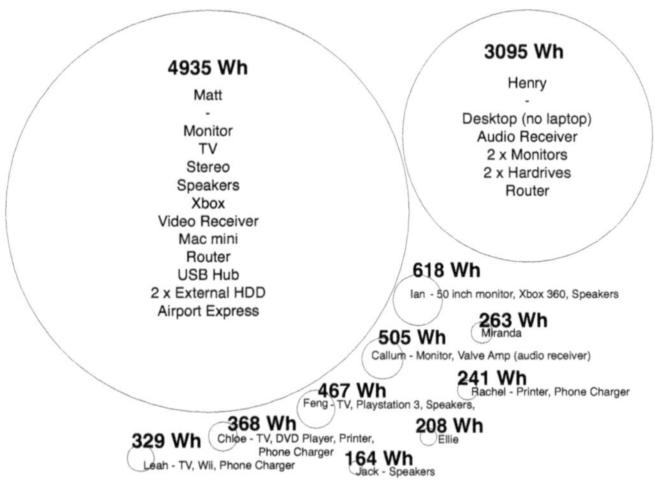


**Figure 3. The average daily consumption of 11 participants' devices, demonstrating the variation in inventory and direct energy consumption. Laptops and mobile phones are not listed, as all participants had one of each.**

Constellations are interesting in that they are often comprised of a number of not particularly energy intensive devices, yet acting in concert they together consume a significant amount simultaneously (e.g. Nathan's laptop, speakers and printer, or Callum's laptop, monitor and valve amp). A participant might put one device in a constellation to sleep (the laptop), but others (valve amp) might well carry on consuming energy.

### Hub devices

Constellations are often configured or set up around a central, hub or basis device, e.g. peripherals connected to a laptop, games console connected to a TV. Among the 31 constellations, we found that laptops were the hub device in 14 of the constellations, desktops in 3 and TVs as the hub in 9 instances. There are 3 occasions where monitors are used instead of TVs; this requires yet another device in the media constellation (e.g. amplifier or powered speakers) so that audio can be provided. It is hard to know when a well-peripheralised hub device is going to be called upon, making low power modes particularly difficult to automate (e.g. knowing when Henry's external HDDs, or Matt's server is needed, figure 4). As a result, we observed hub devices in large constellations powered for all or most of the day (16 – 24 h.).

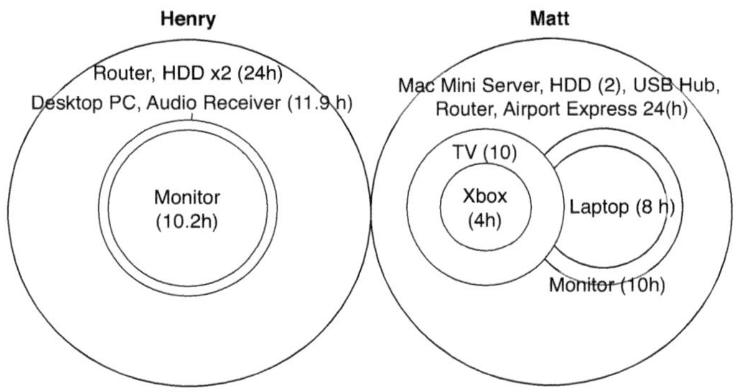


**Figure 4. The median daily use-time of Henry's and Matt's constellations. Henry's constellation had a router and 2 external HDDs as always-on, the monitor on average was in sleep (or off) for 2 hours of the desktop's consumption. Matt's always-on infrastructure included a router, Airport Express, Mac Mini Server, 2 external HDDs and a USB hub. There was cross-over of the laptop, and TV constellations, but the laptop and Xbox both relied upon access to the server..**

### Connoisseurs

The most complex constellations were observed to be owned *by connoisseurs*. We have previously defined media and IT connoisseurs as individuals who "spend more time gaming, working with IT, and watching TV and movies typically with linked complexes of specialised devices" [2]. We elaborate futher on the concept here, and relate it to variations in impacts. Whereas constellations are sometimes configured to support additional practices of the individual, connoisseurs promote meaningful experiences in practice, by for example, adding speakers to a laptop so that the perceived quality of audio is higher.

Evidence of media and IT connoisseurship was observed across 8 of our participants. Four participants (Matt, Callum, Gary, Henry) all had specialised devices for audio playback. Matt used a HI-FI plugged into additional powered speakers for audio. Callum had a tube amp for better appreciation of music and Gary had stereo separates including an amplifier, equaliser, and CD player. Henry also had an amplifier and stereo speakers that were connected to his PC and Xbox. Four other participants had constellations with large TVs specifically for a better visual experience when playing video games (Ian, Feng, Omar, and Kate). Ian had a 50" screen for playing video games with his Xbox, and watching movies.

Among our participants there were two (Henry and Matt) who have constellations that contribute about 42% of the overall media and IT direct energy across all participants. As well as this high direct energy impact their constellations contribute 16.5% of the total embodied emissions. Their constellations contain always-on infrastructure, with one or two constellations layered on top of one another (Figure 4). These connoisseurs have always-on requirements as well as a more customised selection of media and IT devices (e.g. custom desktop computer, dual monitors, IPTV receiver, wireless router, and dedicated audio set ups). This shows that connoisseurship in one area of practice may inadvertently affect impacts of other practices (i.e. the attitude that Henry and Matt have towards quality of experience leads them to own specific devices, and therefore perform similar practices in more energy intensive ways). The connoisseurs not only own constellations (complexes) of devices, they in fact own more constellations, and more specialised devices within those constellations.

Moreover, **media and IT connoisseurs strive for a high quality of service or experience**, choosing to change or upgrade their constellations when circumstance and enthusiasm allow. Henry gives us an account of the upgrades that he performed on his constellation:

> "*Yeah, a lot. A lot different things. In my first year I had er (.) erm I bought my computer, a desktop computer and a single monitor and some cheap speakers, 15–20 quid speakers. And then, and then in my first year I bought a second monitor and some slightly better speakers and I upgraded some of my computer. Er then I bought an external hard drive. Then I my second year I bought a network switch, then some slightly better speakers, I've upgraded the speakers as I've gone, erm, and a better second monitor. ... Then I my third year I brought back even better speakers [laughs]*".

### Indirect Impacts
Through analysis of interview data we are able to make observations concerning the practices that contribute to impacts outside of the home (e.g. reliance on Internet based video streaming services, accessing lecture notes through VLE, audible notifications on mobile devices that occurred during interviews).

#### *Frequency of access and total data amount*
Internet connectedness is a salient attribute of a majority of practices supported by media and IT devices. The streaming of media, social networking, mobile and laptop notifications, video gaming and education (VLE usage) illustrates that our participants relied heavily on the connectedness of their devices, even without explicitly mentioning being 'connected'.

All 23 interviewed participants used the Internet to access course materials (e.g. assignments, lecture slides) for studying. 22 relied on streaming websites or other Internet-based services for TV watching. Callum "*downloaded off the Internet rather than live TV*", whilst Ellie mentioned a shared access (with another participant) to a service that allowed her to download TV shows that she watched regularly. Aaron used the Internet to "research" new music, and to download music to fill his iPod.

It is possible to roughly estimate the indirect energy impacts of practices involving Internet-based services by drawing on impact estimates from current scholarly articles, such as those derived by Schien et al. [22]. For example, Ellie's streaming of two hours of TV per day might have added 50% to her typical daily direct energy impact; while Darren's frequent social networking might have incurred an additional 10% to his direct energy impact.

Still, there are some practices that don't require network access. Chloe for example exclusively relied on her TV and DVD player for media content. Other 'un-networked practices' include single player video games (purchased on optical storage), and word processing for an assignment.

Connectedness and the opportunities that 'being connected' provides, seems to **increase direct energy consumption**, because connectedness leads to more frequent, and longer durations of use of media and IT devices. For example, Miranda's laptop provided her with the opportunity to stream video-on-demand content whilst getting ready for a night out. Chloe likes to have her laptop running whilst watching video on her TV so she can see any new messages on Facebook. Jill likes to watch TV on her laptop whilst waking up and eating breakfast, and then has Facebook in the background while she works. These examples of opportunistic connections (video-on-demand whilst getting ready) and maintaining connection (Facebook chat in the background) show us that having a connection allows Internet enabled media and IT activities to become part of practices not strictly reliant on media and IT (e.g. getting ready to go out, eating breakfast).

## IMPLICATIONS FOR DESIGN
In this section, we start by discussing how previous HCI sustainability research might have shifted our participants' media and IT impacts. We then outline additional areas for consideration and suggest how new strategies might decrease the impact of media and IT. Our impact analysis of previous work are summarised Table 4.

### Power management
As Chetty et al. suggested, laptop and desktop power management software should be modified to support easy configuration and short, reliable computer wake-up [4]; and also that this should be easy to accomplish across wired and wireless networks particularly for media and file servers where instant access has come to be expected (Matt). Based on our observations on durations of daily active use, versus when computers were idling, this could lead to a direct energy reduction of up to 2.5%, where the vast majority of these savings is made with Matt's always-on server.

Device constellations present particular challenges for power management. Direct energy impacts of constellations can

| | Scope of effect indicated by our study | | |
|---|---|---|---|
| Strategy for change | No. Participants | Direct energy | Embodied carbon |
| Longer use and more re-use of mobile phones and small portables [Hanks et al. 2008, Huang et al. 2008] | 33 | | 2% |
| Software/hardware designs to double expected IT lifetimes [Odom et al. 2009, Pierce and Paulos 2011] | 33 | | 18% |
| Improve power management interfaces/response times [Chetty et al 2009] | 1 | 2.5% | |
| Replace desktops with laptops or low-energy servers | 3 | 9.3% | 16% |
| Replace large constellations with laptops | 2 | 40% | |
| Feedback for engaged connoisseurs [Costanza et al. 2012] | 2 | 7% | |

**Table 4. The scope of effect when modifying home media and IT's impact. This table shows the possible reduction in impacts as suggested by existing literature. The reduction is computed only for the participants it would affect. Improving power management applies to Matt. Replacing desktops applies to Henry, Gary and Matt. Replacing large constellations, and feedback for engaged connoisseurs applies to Henry and Matt.**

be high: the number of devices in these set-ups, and their role in multiple practices, makes user-initiated power management particularly problematic. For example, Matt relied on an always-on server to back up his laptop; a connected TV for video playback; and a connected stereo for TV audio and music. Reductions in direct energy through power management (contesting Chetty et al. [4]) are complex to automate, since devices can belong to more than one constellation. Power management strategies that respect constellations might aim to capture their context of use—the practices that they are supporting at a given point in time—e.g. sensing the power being drawn by individual devices, and/or sensing media and IT activities using software on smart phones, PCs, etc. The interpreted context could be used to ensure that only the required components of the constellation are powered up.

Streaming digital media presents a further challenge, since there is an inherent need for local infrastructure to enable on-demand services (e.g. wireless routers, cable modems); but also the not insignificant impact of the Internet and cloud service infrastructures that enable such services—which are equally (over-)provisioned for spontaneous use [11]. And yet, we note our participants' use of what could be regarded as legacy devices (e.g. media players, offline media), suggesting there is still a role for enjoying such things. Certainly, we would advocate that local storage and playback of content should be enabled as a default behaviour, even in network-enabled devices, potentially lowering their indirect impact.

### Longevity and attachment

Another area of intense interest has been in the extension of IT device lifetimes as explored by Hanks et al. [12], with mobile phones being highlighted as notoriously short-life by Huang et al. [13]. Authors have envisioned longer lifetimes through: longevity in OS/app support [3]; or passing on the devices to others who would have otherwise bought a new phone [13]. For our participants this might lead to a small improvement (2% of embodied emissions). Replacing a laptop every four years is roughly six times as damaging as replacing a smartphone every year; so perhaps laptop, not phone, longevity is a more fruitful focus for HCI?

Odom et al. and Pierce et al. have extended this concept more broadly to consider lifetimes of all media and IT devices [16, 19]: if the devices seen in our studies were kept for twice as long (doubling their lifetime), this would reduce the embodied emissions by 18%. This is particularly significant for the connoisseurs that we saw in our study. Practices of connoisseurship usually entail frequent upgrading and replacing of devices with, typically relatively high embodied emissions, like televisions and games consoles. These inventories account for a disproportionately large share of the overall embodied emissions, supporting previous research on the need for better device longevity and attachment [10]. And the sharp variations in embodied emissions of different configurations (e.g. fig. 2), suggests the importance of carefully considering the particular devices and profiles of use, of design for longevity and sustainability.

But, depending on the usage and intensity of device configurations, longevity may not always be the most effective goal. For energy-intensive configurations with high use-time (e.g. Henry's in fig. 2), it might be more effective to replace a high-consumption constellation of devices sooner with more efficient alternatives, such as a laptop plus an Internet-enabled TV, or a single multi-function device such as an all-in-one PC. In a number of cases, a desktop or laptop was used to stream media and play back on an external display. An Internet-enabled or peripheral-enabled television might have saved 2.7% of the direct energy across all participants. Among 9 of our participants, we saw constellations of a TV combined with a games console and/or DVD player—this hints at some potential for integration of displays, games consoles, and media playback. Across all participants this might have resulted in an embodied emissions reduction of 5%, as well as likely direct energy savings.

There are also drawbacks to the degree of integration. All-in-one PCs tend to be replaced wholesale, since they tend not to be upgradeable in a modular way—for example, with a traditional desktop PC one might replace just the graphics card, or buy a new desktop but carry on using an older display. And particularly for connoisseurs, there is important meaning and satisfaction in acquiring used or new objects with enhanced functionality or aesthetics, and finding innovative ways to incorporate these into existing constellations.

The sharing of high-end (and usually high-impact) constellations, such as with group movie and game nights (Ian), or watching TV together (Donna), amortises the impact of these configurations to a certain extent, and clearly has additional meanings and significance for our participants. There are opportunities for designers to encourage shared use of media and IT devices in certain contexts, and even to think of more profound shifts from individual towards communal media and IT facilities, similar to those for laundry and cooking in co-housing communities.

We observed laptops and desktops implicated in very similar sets of practices: doing coursework, chatting with friends and family, social networking, reading the news, watching TV and listening to music. Laptops are designed to be mobile, so typically have lower impact attributes of fewer raw materials (less embodied emissions than desktops) and much lower power consumption as was evidenced in our energy data. Thus, at the point where a desktop might be upgraded or replaced, it can make sense to procure a laptop instead; across our particular participants, this might have saved 9.3% direct energy and 16% embodied emissions, even though it applies to just the three participants with desktops (Matt, Gary, and Henry).

### Designing for connoisseurs

While appliance energy consumption typically has little relevance to peoples' everyday experience [20] and the effects of eco-feedback can be quite limited [23], there is also evidence that those interested in sustainable living or home automation engage well with and act upon information about appliance consumption [7, 26]. Our connoisseurs might be just such people; despite the high consumption overall of his devices, Henry made clear efforts to power down the constellation when he was away, and to turn off the corridor lights at night. If informed about the sources of direct consumption, Henry might have acted further to reduce it. Supposing Henry and Matt were to actively power down during idle times, this may have reduced the total direct energy impacts by up to 7%. But, being so invested in the nuanced properties of their devices, connoisseurs might also be interested and engaged with information about the total energy required by large constellations. Replacing their constellations with laptops (even high-end or gamer-tailored models) would have reduced the direct energy impacts by up to 40%.

## CONCLUSION

Our UK undergraduate participants living in on-campus accommodation provide a highly situated, socially-specific view of media and IT in everyday life, and are not necessarily representative of other populations. However, we would stress that across these 33 participants, the 138 media and IT devices observed had highly varying levels of time-use, size, customisation, perceived qualities of service provision, and roles in practice. Our qualitative and quantitative 20-day snapshot of the variations in technology, practice and greenhouse gas emissions provides a new, informative basis for HCI researchers and practitioners to understand the range and nature of variations that exist with media and IT; and the fruitful (lower impact) directions to take future design, intervention and holistic impact enquiry.

Specifically, our more holistic account of the impacts (Figure 2) showed that the yearly carbon emissions arising from IT's direct energy are a *small fraction* of the emissions arising from manufacturing and transport (typically less than 20%). The important exceptions to this were the large constellations exhibiting long mains-powered durations, and/or had many of their interconnected devices powered up simultaneously (Figure 3). Compared to the total impacts of home media and IT across our studies, personal and wearable devices such as phones and tablets have very small embodied emissions (2%), and a vanishingly small direct energy demand (Figures 2 and 3).

Despite the fact that we observed remarkably similar sets of IT-supported practices among all 33 participants, we found that these were tied to very different sets of impacts. In our study, these large variations could in a few cases be attributed to specific hardware differences in similar devices: laptops which are easy to put to sleep, versus ones with faulty batteries. But for the most part, impact variation arose from *vastly different* capabilities and qualities in service provision: watching TV, surfing and writing essays on a laptop; versus the same practices carried out using a desktop connected to two monitors. The larger, more complex constellations had tended to be set up primarily for a specific purpose, such as gaming or listening to favourable reproductions of the latest music. However, the desktop PCs at the hubs of these customised constellations made them multi-purpose, resulting in exceptional durations of energy demand (Figure 4) temporally stretching well beyond the practices they were configured to support. As a result, connoisseurship presided over a share of about one-third of the total media and IT impacts in our study: 42% of the direct impacts, and 16.5% of the embodied emissions.

Media and IT connoisseurs can be challenging to sustainably design for: they have uniquely demanding, specific, and continually evolving expectations. The devices they pursue tend to have nuanced qualities in service provision (e.g. Henry and his audiophile speakers), and connoisseurs reconfigure constellations and apply upgrades, as they evolve in their role as enthusiast practitioners. However, connoisseurs present important opportunities for sustainability. They might adopt highly specialised, lower-demand devices much earlier than others. And, echoing prior empirical findings [7, 26], our connoisseurs tended to show more engagement and sympathy towards monitoring and managing resources; they might respond well to eco-feedback and act as local experts to help others do the same.

Our holistic framing has exposed some important avenues for future exploration in sustainable HCI. In particular, the impacts of the cloud's supporting infrastructure (large-scale networks and data centres) are not particularly well-understood, yet those impacts are strongly implicated in the always-on communication, information, and entertainment our participants had come to expect and rely upon across their devices. Frequency, bandwidth and durations of access to different cloud services need to be monitored and analysed, to understand how precisely these are called upon to support everyday life.

In our future work, we will be using analysis of home network data alongside associated carbon foot-printing of Internet based services (impacts of geographical location on the energy footprint of digital media [22]) to explore to what extent we can begin associating indirect carbon contributions with particular devices and practices, further filling in the holistic view of media and IT impacts.

## ACKNOWLEDGEMENTS

This work was funded by the UK Research Councils (refs. EP/G008523/1 & EP/I00033X/1), and the Facilities Division and the Faculty of Science and Technology at Lancaster University. This work was supported by a PhD CASE studentship funded by the EPSRC and Microsoft Research. We would like to thank Mike Berners-Lee, Darren Axe, Candace Davies and John Mills for their ongoing cooperation in enabling our studies in student residences. We are grateful to Carolynne Lord for her significant contributions. Finally, we are grateful to our reviewers for their insightful comments and giving us the opportunity to improve this work for publication.

## REFERENCES


1. Andrae, A. S., and Andersen, O. Life cycle assessments of consumer electronics — are they consistent? *Journal of Life Cycle Assessment 15* (2010).
2. Bates, O., Clear, A. K., Friday, A., Hazas, M., and Morley, J. Accounting for energy-reliant services within everyday life at home. In *Proc. of Pervasive* (June 2012).
3. Blevis, E. Sustainable interaction design: invention & disposal, renewal & reuse. In *Proc. of CHI*, ACM (New York, NY, USA, 2007), 503–512.
4. Chetty, M., Brush, A. B., Meyers, B. R., and Johns, P. It's not easy being green: understanding home computer power management. In *Proc. of CHI* (2009).
5. Chetty, M., Tran, D., and Grinter, R. E. Getting to green: understanding resource consumption in the home. In *Proc. of UbiComp* (2008).
6. Clear, A. K., Morley, J., Hazas, M., Friday, A., and Bates, O. Understanding adaptive thermal comfort: new directions for UbiComp. In *Proc. of UbiComp* (2013), 113–122.
7. Costanza, E., Ramchurn, S. D., and Jennings, N. R. Understanding domestic energy consumption through interactive visualisation: a field study. In *Proc. of UbiComp* (2012).
8. Erickson, T., Li, M., Kim, Y., Deshpande, A., Sahu, S., Chao, T., Sukaviriya, P., and Naphade, M. The dubuque electricity portal: Evaluation of a city-scale residential electricity consumption feedback system. In *Proc. of CHI* (2013).
9. Froehlich, J., Findlater, L., and Landay, J. The design of eco-feedback technology. In *Proc. of CHI* (2010).
10. Gegenbauer, S., and Huang, E. M. Inspiring the design of longer-lived electronics through an understanding of personal attachment. In *Proc. of DIS* (2012).
11. Glanz, J. Power, pollution and the Internet. *The New York Times* (22 September 2012).
12. Hanks, K., Odom, W., Roedl, D., and Blevis, E. Sustainable millennials: attitudes towards sustainability and the material effects of interactive technologies. In *Proc. of CHI* (2008).
13. Huang, E. M., and Truong, K. N. Breaking the disposable technology paradigm: opportunities for sustainable interaction design for mobile phones. In *Proc. of CHI* (2008).
14. Kim, S., and Paulos, E. Practices in the creative reuse of e-waste. In *Proc. of CHI* (2011).
15. Malmodin, J., Moberg, Å., Lundén, D., Finnveden, G., and Lövehagen, N. Greenhouse gas emissions and operational electricity use in the ICT and entertainment & media sectors. *Journal of Industrial Ecology 14* (2010).
16. Odom, W., Pierce, J., Stolterman, E., and Blevis, E. Understanding why we preserve some things and discard others in the context of interaction design. In *Proc. of CHI* (2009).
17. Owen, P. The elephant in the living room. Tech. rep., UK Energy Saving Trust, 2011.
18. Owen, P. Powering the nation: Household electricity using habits revealed. Tech. rep., UK Energy Saving Trust, DECC, and Defra, 2012.
19. Pierce, J., and Paulos, E. Second-hand interactions: investigating reacquisition and dispossession practices around domestic objects. In *Proc. of CHI* (2011).
20. Pierce, J., Schiano, D. J., and Paulos, E. Home, habits, and energy: Examining domestic interactions and energy consumption. In *Proc. of CHI* (2010).
21. Røpke, I., and Christensen, T. H. Energy impacts of ICT – insights from an everyday life perspective. *Telematics and Informatics 29*, 4 (2012).
22. Schien, D., Shabajee, P., Wood, S. G., and Preist, C. A model for green design of online news media services. In *Proc. of WWW* (2013).
23. Strengers, Y. A. Designing eco-feedback systems for everyday life. In *Proc. of CHI* (2011), 2135–2144.
24. Teehan, P., and Kandlikar, M. Comparing embodied greenhouse gas emissions of modern computing and electronics products. *Environmental Science & Technology 47*, 9 (2013).
25. Wakkary, R., and Tanenbaum, K. A sustainable identity: The creativity of an everyday designer. In *Proc. of CHI* (2009).
26. Woodruff, A., Hasbrouck, J., and Augustin, S. A bright green perspective on sustainable choices. In *Proc. of CHI* (2008).

# Beyond Ethnography: Engagement and Reciprocity as Foundations for Design Research Out Here

**Margot Brereton, Paul Roe, Ronald Schroeter**
Electrical Engineering and Computer Science,
Queensland University of Technology
2 George St, Brisbane, QLD 4000, Australia
[m.brereton, p.roe, r.schroeter]@qut.edu.au

**Anita Lee Hong**
Oodgeroo Unit,
Queensland University of Technology
2 George St, Brisbane, QLD 4000, Australia
anita.leehong@qut.edu.au

## ABSTRACT
This paper explores an emerging paradigm for HCI design research based primarily upon engagement, reciprocity and doing. Much HCI research begins with an investigatory and analytic ethnographic approach before translating to design. Design may come much later in the process and may never benefit the community that is researched. However in many settings it is difficult for researchers to access the privileged ethnographer position of observer and investigator. Moreover rapid ethnographic research often does not seem the best or most appropriate course of action.

We draw upon a project working with a remote Australian Aboriginal community to illustrate an alternative approach found in Indigenous research, where the notion of reciprocity is first and foremost. We argue that this can lead to sustainable designs, valid research and profound innovation.

### Author Keywords
ICT4D; Postcolonial HCI; Participatory Action Research

### ACM Classification Keywords
H.5. Information interfaces and presentation (e.g., HCI): H.5.3 Group and Organization Interfaces

## BEYOND ETHNOGRAPHY
We acknowledge the Australian Aboriginal peoples and in particular the Anindilyakwa people of Groote Eylandt, who inspire and educate us in their tradition of reciprocity.

Design in remote and economically poor settings has become of increasing interest to researchers in Computer Human Interaction. Traditionally in these settings the method of choice has been ethnography, an approach derived from anthropology. Ethnography involves field study to understand a culture, and usually involves living and being accepted into a culture to understand and articulate it. It may involve observation, note-taking, interviews, photography etc., which are synthesized into an ethnographic analysis. Anthropology aims to understand cultures, but not to change them. Design, as a discipline that aims to intervene to change for the better, has come up with forms of "rapid ethnography" e.g. [13] that are quicker than those traditionally used in anthropology to more quickly come to understandings that can inform design.

While the purpose of ethnography is often mistaken by designers as a form of data collection [1], ethnography is a powerful means to "open up the play of possibilities for design". Indeed the contribution that ethnography can make is to "enable designers to question the assumptions embedded in the conventional problem-solution design framework" [1]. Dourish also identified that ethnography does not necessarily produce "Implications for Design" [10].

Ethnography has been used very effectively in ICT4D projects, particularly when combined with forms of Action Research to create "a more holistic picture" of local environments and to integrate this understanding into ICT project design, ongoing evaluation and monitoring in a continual cycle of research and project development [6, 21].

However as Holcombe [11] identifies, the "ethnographic method can provide the researcher with a false sense of his or her own knowing and expertise and, indeed, with arrogance". Furthermore, ethnography began as an enterprise funded by and in the service of colonial administrators who were interested in managing others, the so-called native peoples of the colonies, providing both the workforce for and sources of resistance to imperialist enterprises [19]. As a result of the history of ethnographic research, many in Aboriginal communities are wary of being investigated [8]. Rapid forms of ethnography found in design research, run a particular risk of taking without giving back to communities and rushing to quick and possibly ill-conceived design approaches.

Indigenous people world-wide have often been researched with little thought given to culturally appropriate methods of engagement, what will happen to the resulting knowledge, who really benefits from the research and how the community will benefit from the engagement. As a result, an ethnographic first approach may be hard to justify



*CHI 2014,* April 26 - May 01 2014, Toronto, ON, Canada
Copyright 2014 ACM 978-1-4503-2473-1/14/04...$15.00.
http://dx.doi.org/10.1145/2556288.2557374

in these communities. Bessarab and Ng'andu [4] call for culturally appropriate engagement processes with Aboriginal groups and individuals as being essential for valid research outcomes such as the ten-step model of engagement proposed by Ranzijn et al [15], that begins with self-reflection on one's own assumptions, understanding the culture and history and establishing cultural supervision through to determining how to obtain feedback on the effectiveness of the engagement.

Winschiers et al [26] identify the tendency in research with other cultures to unwittingly adopt a compensatory approach by considering differences as "deficiencies" to be remedied. They argue for deeper engagement as a way to counter the undue influence of external logics.

Suchman [20] has long argued that we should see design as an "entry into the networks of relations that make technical systems possible". Taylor [22] echoes this calling for imagining computer systems that enrich and are founded upon local emergent practices [12]. But Suchman cautions that sustainable innovations are dependent upon substantial investments of time and resources in infrastructure: the range of social relations that develop only with time, and the human labor needed to put the material arrangements in place and keep them going. She questions the assumption that knowledge in the form of a product can be handed off, arguing instead the need for mutual learning and partial translations [19].

Thus, design informed by rapid ethnography struggles with:

- The difficulty of gaining access to do ethnography itself.
- The implied power relations between the knowledge gatherer and those studied.
- The problem that ethnographic investigation may not serve well to inform design anyway.
- The difficulty of developing useful designs from the resulting ethnographic knowledge, given that much of what makes a design sustainable are the relationships and learnings that take place over time.
- The third person perspective, wherein people are designed for but do not develop the skills or have technologies to design for themselves.
- The nature of the relationship with a local community and their derived design aspirations. It potentially results in 'fishing', with engagement and design a distant second.

We propose that HCI and design research considers an alternative to ethnographically inspired design. The approach is based upon engagement and reciprocity first! Such approaches are already evident in the work of existing Indigenous researchers and those working with Indigenous communities [5,17,24]. Maori Indigenous scholar Tuhiwai Smith notes that "research requires critical sensitivity and reciprocity of spirit by a researcher" [23]. Aboriginal Australians, George and Steffenson designed their Traditional Knowledge Revival Pathway system on the principal of reciprocity [18]. Aboriginal researcher Peter Radoll notes "time spent fixing people's cars is valuable in nurturing trust in Aboriginal communities jaded by being objects in non-indigenous designers' temporary, research-focused attention. This direct and tangible reciprocity is a customary conduit" [7].

Before proceeding, it is worth framing the approach in relation to Participatory Design (PD) and Co-Design [16]. PD has always been concerned with power relations. It is an ethical and pragmatic stance that commits the designer to engage from the outset with those people affected by a design outcome. PD explicitly attends to designs not being neutral but creating power and agency for particular people, whereas many variants of "user-centered design" seek participation and information from "users" without further consideration of them. PD relies on partnership with participants in which participants bring essential knowledge of their own context and culture while designers bring technical and design facilitation skills creating opportunities for mutual learning and development. However, in the context of a remote and discrete Aboriginal community, participatory methods must be considerably revised to ensure successful engagement. As Winschiers found in Namibia, common PD methods such as workshops and brainstorming were incompatible with the socio-cultural habits of Namibian participants [25].

## THE CONTEXT OF REMOTE ABORIGINAL AUSTRALIA

The Groote Eylandt Archipelago is a unique and diverse environment, and is the homeland of the Warnindilyakwa people (Anindilyakwa) who are its traditional owners. The history of Groote Eylandt has seen dramatic changes and injustices in the social and cultural landscape of the island in a relatively short time since the arrival of missionaries, and a mine [9]. The cumulative effects of long-term disengagement between governments and the communities on Groote Eylandt has led to poor socio-economic outcomes [3,9]. However, the Warnindilyakwa endeavor to "combine a traditional lifestyle with the comforts of the 21st century" [2].

The Anindilyakwa Land Council (ALC) is a progressive council that has initiated approaches across the spectrum to reconnect and re-engage the people of Groote. Fundamental to these initiatives is communication and connection, which has led the ALC to seek new ways of using technology to support communication and connection within and outside the island. Our research team is engaged in a collaborative project with the ALC to design "digital noticeboards" to support communication in the local community and externally. The design of digital noticeboards so that they are useful and sustainable is a considerable challenge and necessitates understanding local aspirations, communication practices and indeed what form and kinds of technologies make sense.

## ENGAGEMENT AND RECIPROCITY FIRST

Given the difficulty of undertaking ethnographic research or traditional PD, our approach prioritizes engagement, reciprocity and sustainability. Reciprocity is core to Aboriginal culture [14] and the idea of mutual and cooperative exchange. Previously we have emphasized the importance of building relationships across cultures through the Aboriginal cultural practice of "yarning" [4] to facilitate in-depth discussions in a relaxed and open manner. This is done without any form of recording device as a mark of respect and may take place in different settings, e.g. walking or driving; often the relevance of particular discussions only becomes apparent after the fact. Questions may be posed, but are not answered until much later, after community deliberation, not during a workshop.

We have also emphasized time spent together in practical activities. We were first engaged in work on Groote to address the environmental threat of cane toad invasion, a pest species in Australia. This led to the deployment of environmental sensors in collaboration with the local Indigenous Ranger groups. Such practical projects involve time spent together engaged in activities on country. This provides time for talking, noticing each other's different ways, and helping each other out. The digital noticeboard project was first conceived in this context: on country, yarning and with local designs, and importantly was initiated by the community rather than the researchers.

We have undertaken dialogue with Elders to seek suggestions and advice about the noticeboard and to propose ideas. Dialogue and activities have also taken place with the Linguistics Centre staff, the Indigenous Land and Sea Rangers, the School principals and other groups on the Island. We have always started by talking with people and helping them first and doing so with many different groups. This engagement has helped define us within the community and resulted in reciprocation.

Many of the activities undertaken have involved learning about devices, fixing and configuring computers and iPads. It is amazing the insights you gain into technology use and failure from fixing and configuring computers for others! All sorts of technology and design issues become apparent through helping with the seemingly most mundane of issues, like creating a user account. The ALC were keen to reduce their high travel costs, so we helped install and configure Skype on their computers, thereby reducing their travel costs and benefitting the research project with greater engagement through video conferencing. In addition to visiting the community, we host members of the community in our city and university: reciprocity again.

Initially where to start was a vexed issue: a radically different culture, a remote island (expensive and time consuming to visit) and the evident past failures of other researchers was off-putting: everything could go wrong. Yet the answer was simple: start with existing indigenous designs, engage with people and help people with existing technology (reciprocity). Remote communities are understandably wary of visitors offering solutions. At worst a large Aboriginal industry preys on unsuspecting communities. At best external consultants must be flown in to provide expensive advice. But reciprocity, in word, deed and spirit, builds mutual trust, engagement and benefit.

**Figure 1: Kids at the local festival exploring the noticeboard**

It became clear through meetings and time together that a first noticeboard design should build on an existing community poster representing the Indigenous Protected Area around the island and the Ayakwa newsletter. This became an important aspect of our design process. We presented digital Noticeboard prototypes to Elders to seek their permission, before trialing them at the local Festival. This quickly revealed that 'publicly' available community content was inaccessible to the Elders due to lack of computers, internet access and technical literacy. So given the elders love of watching DVD's of their people, we produced a DVD for them comprising all the community content and noticeboard media. Continual engagement with Elders is vital in a community like the Warnindilyakwa. Our project is still at an early stage but next steps are to engage the community in studying their technology use, and developing school based traineeships for local youth to learn about IT and to participate in noticeboard design.

## DISCUSSION

To Aboriginal people in remote Australia the development and kudos of a new paper may not matter, (though in some communities authorship beyond acknowledgement may be an important part of reciprocity). What is important is that engagement is mutually beneficial and discussed. Why conduct HCI projects here at all? Are they sustainable?

First, if engagement involves researchers and locals helping out with technologies and sharing knowledge about language and country, then mutual learning is occurring. The Warnindilyakwa do appropriate existing technologies, such as iPads. But external expertise can support and enhance local design efforts, where kits and appropriation fall short of their aspirations. By working together, building upon locally used and available technologies, designs can fit within cultural practices and locals can maintain and extend them.

Second, local designs and innovations form the interesting exemplars from which new theories arise. Theories are not born in armchairs. Local designs can be read and understood for their contextual details to assess how they arose and how they might transfer and mutate to a different context; just as the local example of Facebook from a Harvard college dorm formed a new design that seeded new theories of social media. This grounded approach can potentially yield new apps, theories and design strategies, which benefit those on the outside as well as locals. There is great potential to learn from the Warnindilyakwa about design in a highly collective and reciprocity driven culture, where everyone knows and is related to each other. Facebook was derived from an American College Culture and employs a highly transactional and individualistic notion of sharing. The world might have been and can be otherwise by learning from other places.

We conclude that the process of engagement, learning and reciprocity is primary for valid research, and that this approach may usefully apply to design in any local context and culture, not only remote and Aboriginal communities.

## ACKNOWLEDGMENTS

We thank the communities that we work with, the reviewers for helpful comments and the Australian Research Council for Linkage Grant LP120200329

## REFERENCES

1. Anderson, R. J. "Representations and requirements: The value of ethnography in system design." *Human-computer interaction* 9.3 (1994): 151-182.
2. Anindilyakwa Land Council Annual Report 2007-2008 http://www.anindilyakwa.com.au
3. Anindilyakwa Land Council, New Ownership, New Responsibilities, 2009 - Review of Education in the Groote Eylandt and Bickerton Island Region.
4. Bessarab, D. and and Ng'andu, B. (2010). Yarning About Yarning as a Legitimate Method in Indigenous Research. International Journal of Critical Indigenous Studies, 2010, Volume 3, Number 1, 2010.
5. Bidwell, N., & Hardy, D. Dilemmas in situating participation in rural ways of saying. *Proc.OzCHI 2009*
6. Bidwell, N., et al. "Walking and the social life of solar charging in rural Africa." *Transactions on Computer-Human Interaction* (2013).
7. Bidwell, N., Radoll, P. and Turner, J. (2007) Redisplacement by Design, *Interactions* ACM
8. Brands, J. and Gooda, M. (2006). Putting the Users of Research in the Driver's Seat: The CRC for Aboriginal Health's new approach to research development. Australian Aboriginal Studies, 2006, No. 2, pp. 27-35.
9. Brasche, I 2008, Cultural resilience and social wellbeing: A case for research on Groote Eylandt. Australian Aboriginal Studies Journal. Issue 2 Pp93-98
10. Dourish, P. "Implications for design." *Proc. CHI 2006* ACM, 2006.
11. Holcombe, S. "The arrogance of ethnography: Managing anthropological research knowledge." *Australian Aboriginal Studies* 2 (2010): 23.
12. Iran, L., et al. "Postcolonial computing: a lens on design and development." *Proc.CHI.* ACM, 2010.
13. Milen, D. R. "Rapid ethnography: time deepening strategies for HCI field research." *Proc. 3rd conference on Designing Interactive Systems,* ACM, 2000.
14. Pearson, N. 2007, 'Reciprocity resurrected', Opinion *The Australian*, May 12, 2007.
15. Ranzijn, R., McConnochie, K. R. and Nolan, W. (2010). Psychology and indigenous Australians: foundations of cultural competence. Palgrave Macmillan, Vic.
16. Simonsen, J, and Robertson, T eds. *Int.Handbook of Participatory Design*. Routledge, 2012.
17. Sinanan, J. "Social tools and social capital: reading mobile phone usage in rural indigenous communities." *Proc. OzCHI 2008* ACM, 2008.
18. Standley, P-M, Bidwell, N.J. George Snr, T., Steffensen V. and Gothe J. (2009) Connecting Communities and the Environment through Media. Media Journal of Community, Citizen's & 3rd Sector Media & Com. 5.
19. Suchman, L. A. "Practice-based design of information systems: Notes from the hyperdeveloped world." *The information society* 18.2 (2002): 139-144.
20. Suchman, L. "Located accountabilities in technology production." *Scandinavian Journal of Information Systems* 14.2 (2002): 91-106.
21. Tacchi, J., Slater, D. and Lewis, P. "Evaluating community based media initiatives: an ethnographic action research approach." *Information Technology for Development Conference*. Vol. 18. 2003.
22. Taylor, A. S. "Out there." *Proc.CHI2011* ACM, 2011.
23. Tuhiwai Smith, L. *Decolonizing methodologies: Research and indigenous peoples*. Zed books, 1999. (pp. 145-152). ACM.
24. Verran, H., Christie, M., Arbins-King, B., van Weeren, T., Yunupingu, W., "Designing Digital Knowledge Management Tools with Aboriginal Australians" Digital Creativity 2007 Vol 18, No3, pp129-142
25. Winschiers, H. (2006, January). The Challenges of Participatory Design in an Intercultural Context: Designing for Usability in Namibia. In *PDC* (pp. 73-76
26. Winschiers-Theophilus, H., *et al.* Being Participated - A community Approach. Proc. PDC 2010 ACM

# Visualization of Personal History for Video Navigation

**Abir Al-Hajri, Gregor Miller, Matthew Fong, and Sidney Fels**
Human Communication Technologies Laboratory, University of British Columbia, Vancouver, BC, Canada
{abira, gregor, mfong, ssfels}@ece.ubc.ca

**Figure 1. Our prototype history-based interface called the *Video History System* (VHS) aids navigation through the management of a user's personal viewing history. Playback of video is controlled with familiar tools such as play/pause, seek and filmstrip (*left*) - the VHS records each part of the video viewed by the user. The history is then visualized in one of two ways: as Video Tiles (*centre*) or as a Video Timeline (*right*).**[1]

## ABSTRACT
We present an investigation of two different visualizations of video history: *Video Timeline* and *Video Tiles*. *Video Timeline* extends the commonly employed list-based visualization for navigation history by applying size to indicate heuristics and occupying the full screen with a two-sided timeline. *Video Tiles* visualizes history items in a grid-based layout by following pre-defined templates based on items' heuristics and ordering, utilizing screen space more effectively at the expense of a clearer temporal location. The visualizations are compared against the state-of-the-art method (a filmstrip-based visualization), with ten participants tasked with sharing their previously-seen affective intervals. Our study shows that our visualizations are perceived as intuitive and both outperform and are strongly preferred to the current method. Based on these results, *Video Timeline* and *Video Tiles* provide an effective addition to video viewers to help manage the growing quantity of video. They provide users with insight into their navigation patterns, allowing them to quickly find previously-seen intervals, leading to efficient clip sharing, simpler authoring and video summarization.

## Author Keywords
Video; Navigation; History; Visualization

## ACM Classification Keywords
H.5.2. Information Interfaces and Presentation: User Interfaces; H.1.2. Models and Principles: User/Machine Systems


*CHI'14*, April 26–May 1, 2014, Toronto, Canada.

ACM 978-1-4503-2473-1/14/04$15.00.
http://dx.doi.org/10.1145/2556288.2557106

## INTRODUCTION
Watching videos is a major online activity, accounting for a large proportion of time spent online: according to comScore[2], 187 million people in the U.S.A. watched more than 48 billion online videos in July 2013. 100 hours of video are uploaded to YouTube™every minute, over 6 billion hours of video are viewed a month and 68% of people who watch online videos share them with friends[3]. 500 years of YouTube video are watched every day on Facebook, and over 700 YouTube videos are shared on Twitter every minute[3]. Given the volume of available video, new interfaces are required to help manage and manipulate video spaces. Existing interfaces and services have not addressed problems managing previously seen video, and using this data allows for novel and improved applications. We present an investigation into two visualizations of personal video navigation history, to determine how users behave when given a history and if they feel is beneficial to the state-of-the-art methods.

Video navigation histories are a simple archive that a person can use to easily find a previously viewed video interval. They may navigate to the exact location within the original video simply by clicking on the references within their history. This provides the user with a record for historical navigation and removes much of the burden of relying on memory. This history offers users multiple applications such as video chaptering, monitoring their own navigation behaviour, re-watching clips, saving clips that can then be used for sharing, videos summarization, or highlights creation. However, finding previously viewed content in a navigation history is

[1] **Video and screenshots licenced under Creative Commons Attribution 3.0, © 2006 - 2012, Blender Foundation**
[2] `www.comscore.com/Insights/Press_Releases/2013/8/comScore_Releases_July_2013_U.S._Online_Video_Rankings`
[3] `www.youtube.com/t/press_statistics`

often a difficult task due to the design, organization, and volume of information to visualize. This issue has received significant attention within the context of web browsing histories, but little attention has been paid to video navigation history. Aside from the commonly employed list-based representation of the visited videos in a reverse chronological order (e.g. YouTube, Netflix), to our knowledge, our previous work [1] was the first that provided a detailed visualization of a single video navigation history. Thus, the goal of this research is to extend the work for multiple-video history by testing different design layouts that support user-centred management of history, and evaluate the benefits this brings.

The benefits of a navigation history come from two user behaviours. First, users do not always watch a video straight through, but may skip parts (they view only intervals within the video) - this is one of the uses of the seek mechanism, for example. (Even if users watch all videos without interruption, our interface effectively presents a recently viewed videos list, much like YouTube currently does.) Second, an emerging behaviour is that users re-watch parts of the video, allowing visualizations to present additional information such as view count or provide estimates of the location of affective intervals within the video. The fact that re-watching behaviour is becoming more common is not so obvious or intuitive; however, it has been shown that users re-watch segments of video as part of the contemporary browsing and navigation experience, for re-experiencing and enjoying favourite parts or to discover subtle details which were previously missed such as with instructional videos [17]. Studies have also shown that videos containing certain emotional triggers, such as comedy or personal attachment, cause repetitive watching [22, 18]. Thus, a personal navigation history may improve the user experience for these use cases.

To illustrate this behaviour and how a visualization for a video history can be utilized, a usage scenario is presented below.

*As a university student, Nick watches a lot of course lectures along with other online videos. As he watches a video, he frequently jumps around the video trying to understand the content or to find answers to specific questions. These jumps (seeks) on the video are captured on his history which is available to him at anytime. This allows him to favourite the intervals he thinks are important to note, delete the clips that are not worth keeping, or just browse his history to recap the lectures.*

*For his university courses, he sometimes goes back to a specific lecture to find answers for his assignments. He could either use his history if he has seen the clip that contains the information, or if he has time he could navigate the video again. If he decides to look at his history trying to find the answer, he could easily look for the lecture title or thumbnail from his history. Accessing the details of that lecture would give him a full history of how he consumed that video and all the portions he watched. The viewing history of the lectures would be full of unnecessary segments if he had not cleaned or managed his history. However, using the provided filters he could find the parts or segments that he has watched multiple times as well as the marked 'favourite' ones. Moreover, if he remembers roughly where the intended information is located within the video timeline, then he can sort the events based on their temporal location within the video. The intended clip can then be easily viewed, saved or shared by clicking on the corresponding thumbnail.*

To offer such accessibility described in the above scenario, we propose two visualizations of a detailed multiple-video navigation history: *Video Tiles* and *Video Timeline*. These are both part of our Video History System (VHS) framework, and utilize the same underlying representation. A user study which compares the history visualizations to an interface without access to a detailed history is presented; results demonstrate that searching for and sharing personal affective intervals using the proposed visualizations is faster and preferred by participants.

## RELATED WORK

The human visual system can perceive graphical information such as pictures, videos and charts in parallel, however, text can only be perceived sequentially [7], since the human brain processes visual input earlier than textual input [19]. Nadeem *et al.* showed that the use of visual aids in history mechanisms is more effective than the use of only textual data [16], thus having a visualization of the video navigation history can help extensively when searching for information. Nadeem *et al.* also demonstrated that the use of history mechanisms may have a significant effect on user satisfaction and performance when revisiting previously viewed content. These findings reveal that it is important to develop and enhance history visualization mechanisms. However, since there is little work on historical video navigation, we are going to explore this from the perspective of web browsing history.

In most web browsers, history is represented as a list of the visited web pages' titles sorted by date, popularity or aggregated by some time period. The history menu opens in a new window where pages are visualized as titles or with thumbnail images. Researchers have tried various visualizations to simplify searching within the history, which can be divided into three categories: timeline-based, graph-based and 3D.

In the timeline-based visualization, history consists of a linear scrollable list of thumbnails, which appear in reverse chronological order: the most recently visited page is at the top of the list, and clicking on any of these thumbnails (or icons) redirects the user to the corresponding web page. Most web browsers, YouTube, Netflix, Hodgkinson [8] and Girgensohn *et al.* [6] use this visualization to represent the history of user's visited content as shown in Figure 2(a), where clicking on one of the thumbnails navigates to the corresponding content. Li *et al.* [11] and Hupp *et al.* [9] used this approach for their detailed histories with the addition of a list of coloured icons next to each thumbnail describing the user's performed actions. However, this visualization faces problems when multiple tabs or multiple browsers are opened at the same time. Vartiainen *et al.* [20] developed the Rolling History for mobile devices where they proposed four directions of navigation control: instead of having one reel of thumbnails, they used two - horizontal and vertical, shown in Figure 2(b). All opened browsers are in the vertical reel;

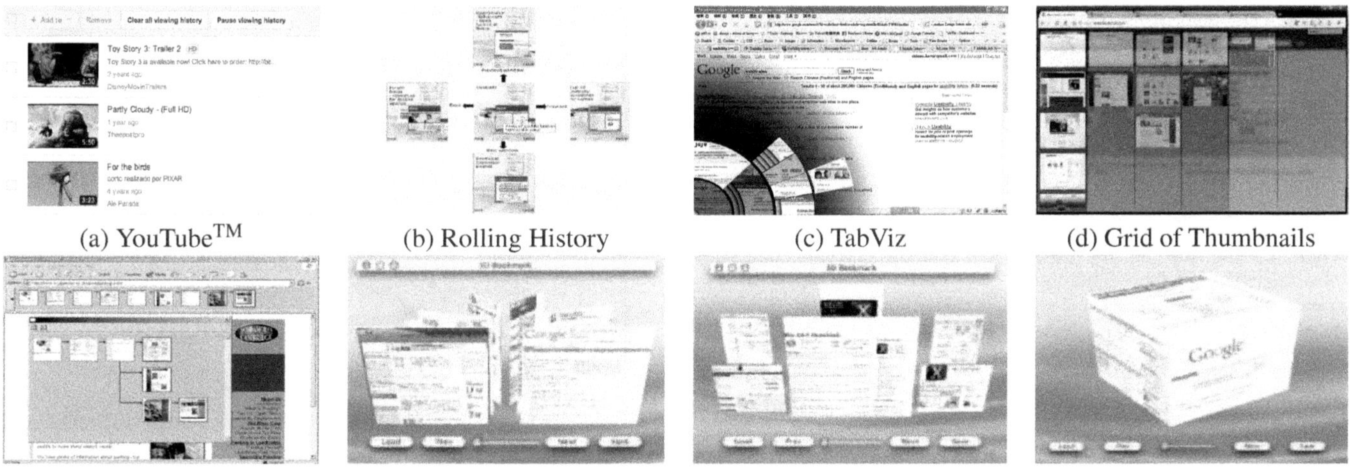

(a) YouTube™ (b) Rolling History (c) TabViz (d) Grid of Thumbnails

(e) Tree (Directed Graph) (f)WebBook (g) Circle (h) Cube

**Figure 2. Previous work on video or web histories can be divided into three categories of visualization: (1) Timeline based: *YouTube*'s history consisted of a list of thumbnails ordered chronologically; *Rolling History* [20] used four directions of navigation control to cover the history of multiple tabs or browsers opened at the same time; *TabViz*[4] employed a fan-shaped hierarchical visualization to show the history of multiple tabs; *Grid of thumbnails* [10] displayed the history of each tab in a vertical column of the grid; (2) Graph-based: *Tree* or directed graph [14] visualized each visited page as a node and links as the edges between nodes; (3) 3D visualization: *WebBook* [21] represented each web page as a traditional book page; *Circle* mode [21] placed thumbnails of the visited web pages at the circumference of a circle; *Cube* mode [21] placed thumbnails of pages on the faces of a cube.**

the currently active browser appears in the middle, and its history is visualized in the horizontal reel. Blankenship *et al.* proposed TabViz[4], which uses a fan-shaped browser tab visualization where concurrent active tabs are represented in a radial hierarchical structure, visualizing the parent of each opened tab (Figure 2(c)). Khaksari proposed a Grid as another solution for multiple tabs opened at the same time [10]. The Grid consists of a number of labeled tabs, where each tab corresponds to the relevant tab in the browser. Each vertical column of thumbnails is mapped to the history of corresponding tabs in the background (shown in Figure 2(d)). According to the article this visualization reduces cognitive workload, increases enjoyability and reduces user frustration.

Milic-Frayling *et al.* [14] deduced that high effectiveness during search requires users to have a mental map of both the hierarchical structure and the access sequence of web pages. Using the timeline-based visualization, back-tracking or visiting new content from the currently viewed history item would affect the structure of the history, creating confusion and affecting the searching task. This can be solved using a 2D graph-based visualization where the history is presented as a horizontal tree (e.g. [14, 15]). A new branch is generated from the parent node whenever a user back-traces and visits a new page, as shown in Figure 2(e). Mayer [12] used a directed graph where each visited page is a node and the edge between them is the link. Pages that are visited multiple times are visualized using a single node to avoid repetition. Mayer used the size of the node to represent the time spent on the corresponding web page.

The final category is the use of 3D visualizations for browsing history. Frecon *et al.* [5] developed WEBPATH, which visualizes the graph of the user's browsing history using a 3D representation. Each visited page is a cube labeled with the page title on top and the surface of the cube shows an extracted image from the HTML description of the page. Users have control over which image can be used to represent the page. This visualization has not been evaluated to check its usability and performance. Card *et al.* proposed WebBook [2], which used a book metaphor to aggregate web pages in virtual 3D books. A web page is represented as a traditional page in a WebBook as shown in Figure 2(f). However, in terms of search speed, this design might not perform well due to the need for flipping or visiting most of the pages that precede the desired page. Yamaguchi *et al.* also proposed two other visualizations: a circle mode and a cube mode as shown in Figure 2 (g) and (h) respectively. In a circle layout, the thumbnails of web pages are placed around the circumference of a circle while in the cube layout thumbnails are put on the surfaces of cube. However, it is not clear how scalable the cube is, since the surface area is limited.

None of the approaches proposed to date have been evaluated or used to visualize a detailed video navigation history aside from our recent work [1]. Research within video history (e.g. [6, 15] and YouTube) used the aforementioned approaches only to visualize the previously watched videos but not how these videos were navigated (i.e. intervals). However, Al-Hajri *et al.* [1] visualized a single video history as a list of interactive segments, whereas, in this paper we are looking at multiple-videos navigation history. In this research, we suggest and evaluate two other visualizations for a detailed video navigation history and investigate which layout improves search efficiency and user preference.

### VIDEO HISTORY SYSTEM (VHS)

The goal of this work is to provide users with intuitive access and management of their personal video viewing history. This requires an interface that can capture and visualize the detailed navigation history of the videos viewed by a user. To

[4] `http://tabviz.org/`

**Figure 3. The video library provides a grid of videos from which users may select the one they would like to view. Each video is represented as a thumbnail containing a small video preview; clicking on any video will begin playback in the main player. As part of our interface, we consider this analogous to the results of a search, or as a set of suggested content.**

be able to test our proposed visualizations, we need an interface to be quite functional to support realistic video watching experiences comparable to commercial systems so that the visualizations are integrated with the same fidelity. Thus, due to the lack of such interfaces we developed a prototype viewer, we called Video History System (VHS), for evaluating history visualizations. In this section we give a detailed description of this interface, how the history is captured, the different visualizations designed for the history, and the scalability of the visualizations.

### History Record Representation Structure

The principle goal of our interface is to provide efficient access to previously viewed videos, and in particular, the intervals viewed within those videos. We accomplish this by applying our approach, described in [1], where a continuous video history is recorded for the user as they consume video. Using the video navigation interface described below, navigation-level events are captured by recording high-level user actions such as seek, play, pause, and changing video. Each time a user watches a video segment, a new entry is added to the history record. It records the video segment using a unique ID for each video along with the segment start and end time. An accumulated view count for every instant of time in all viewed videos is calculated from the intersection of all viewed intervals for each video. This provides the user with a better understanding of the importance of each interval based on their viewing frequencies. This can be used later to facilitate fast navigation and search.

### Video Navigation Interface

The interface is based on three modes: the *video library*, the *viewer* and the *history*. Users can easily switch between modes using the navigation controller. To choose a video, users can either use the video library shown in Figure 3 or they can load a video from disk. Once users select a video to view, the interface transitions to the viewer.

The viewer represents the core component of the interface, allowing users to watch video while their history is captured. The viewer's video player (similar to YouTube, QuickTime, etc.), shown in Figure 4, contains: play/pause via a button (bottom left) or by clicking directly on the video; seek via playhead (white circle) or mouse click on the timeline (red/grey bar); a current playhead time label (white text, bottom right). The viewer also contains a filmstrip, shown under

**Figure 4. Video playback is performed and controlled within the viewer. The video player occupies the majority of the space; the video can be played/paused using the dedicated button below the player (on the left) or by clicking on the video itself; seeking is controlled via the white circle playhead or simply by clicking/dragging on the red/gray video timeline. The filmstrip below the player provides real-time previews based on the cursor position, allowing faster navigation of the current video.**

the player, which consists of a fixed number of thumbnails sampled from the video. The entire video is divided into $n$ equal length intervals ($n = 6$ for our interface), where each interval is represented by a single video segment visualized by the starting frame of that interval. We applied this design since thumbnails are an accepted form of preview in nearly all digital video retrieval interfaces. Moreover, the filmstrip metaphor is commonly used to present content of video as a navigation device, and is considered effective on desktop systems [3], while also providing a quick summary. As such, we chose to employ the filmstrip metaphor to aid video navigation within the viewer. The filmstrip supports level-of-detail manipulation via zooming using mouse wheel gestures with the cursor over the target segment.

Each video segment, shown in Figure 5, can be individually searched (via seek) and played to minimize the time needed to search for a specific event. Moving the cursor over the lower portion of the segment pops up a high-resolution visualization of the interval's timeline which can be used to seek within the video interval using mouse motion as a cue. The seek point is communicated by a yellow line and the thumbnail image updates to reflect the current seek position. To play the interval in the main player, users can drag the seek location in the segment to the white square (with an arrow) at the top right corner.

Every time a user seeks or plays a different video/segment within the main player, a new record is added to their history. The user can switch to the history shown in Figure 6 by clicking on the 'History' button: each record is visualized as a video segment with a size indicating how often that interval was viewed. Previous work applied varying colour intensities to indicate the importance of each segment [13]. We used size since we are representing intervals using thumbnails where colour discrimination would be confused with the thumbnail content and would be difficult to differentiate for some videos.

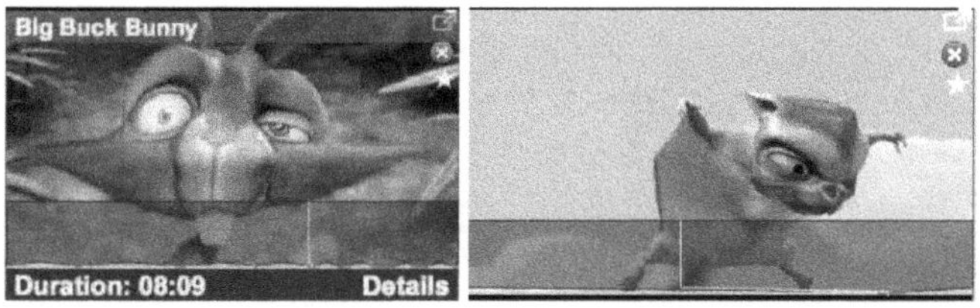


**Figure 5. The user's history is visualized as a set of small video segments. An *intra-video segment* (left) is used to visualize an aggregated history of a single video as one thumbnail, where the union of its segments are visualized in the thumbnail timeline (red/gray bar) and the combined segment has a single seek bar. The *single video segment* (right) represents a single interval from the history, and is the furthest possible zoom level.**

Segment size is determined based on a weight factor which is derived from how often the segment has been viewed as well as its duration. For our study we used a weight factor of 75% of the peak view count plus 25% of the duration in minutes (normalized duration is not used to ensure short segments are not biased to a larger size). We define three different sizes for segments within our interface based on this weight factor: small, medium and large. Thumbnail sizes are proportional to each other such that they fit the tile template patterns; for our interface, we use $320 \times 180$ (large), $210 \times 118$ (medium) and $100 \times 56$ (small), measured in pixels on a one-to-one PPI display.

The history visualizations contain an inter-video history, which shows the different videos the user viewed, with all intervals watched within a single video aggregated into an *intra-video segment* (Figure 5, left). The union of the viewed intervals of a single video is easily visualized in the timeline of the video segment representing the accessed video in the history. To access the detailed history of a specific video, the user can click on the 'Details' link, which opens a detailed history of the selected video only. The detailed history has a similar structure to the history mode with the exception of the removal of the Details info for the detailed history video segment as shown in Figure 5 (right).

## History Visualization Designs

The main goal of this paper is to provide users with a history management tool via an effective visualization. Based on a review of the literature, existing interfaces and services, we made various design decisions to create a visualization of the complete history of a user's video navigation. Since the list (Figure 2(a)) and grid (Figure 2(d)) layouts are the most commonly used visualization for browsing history, we decided to apply these layouts within our interface due to their familiarity with users and their applicability to video visualizations. We intend to investigate how users would employ these layouts for video history and how they could accomplish their tasks compared to the previous design.

From our pilot study (described in the evaluation section) investigating the time taken to search for events, users with a detailed history and our history visualizations performed faster than when compared to without a history, but these results were not significant. However, users' comments indicated a strong liking (6.3 on a 7-point Likert scale) for the interface and commented that they enjoyed it. User feedback

**Figure 6. Each history visualization (presented in the History mode) displays the user's navigation history, and provides top-level access to all previously viewed videos from which the user may zoom into any history entry for more detail. The history can be filtered by date, sorted by time or popularity, and the type of visualization used can be chosen. The thumbnails' size is based on the view count within each video.**

inspired us to extend the list and grid interfaces by utilizing the size of thumbnails for heuristics (in both) and expanding the list to occupy a full screen (by using two lists). Our refinement ended with two novel visualizations: Video Timeline and Video Tiles, as described below. These visualizations were tested to evaluate their performance when performing a search task, while also measuring user satisfaction.

### *Video Timeline*

This visualization of video history was an extension to the familiar list visualization, with the exception of having two columns of variable-sized thumbnails instead of just one. It is designed to display a significant number of thumbnails within a small area, while also maintaining an explicit order, by dividing them into two columns along the user's vertical timeline.

For users to relate these thumbnails to their occurrence in time, they are attached to the user's vertical timeline, where the attachment location indicates their order with respect to the other thumbnails in the history, as illustrated in Figure 7 (left). By default the thumbnails are in reverse chronological order (based on user time), however this order can be changed to interval start time (*Time*, only available in detailed history), recently viewed (*Recent*), and viewing weight (*Most*) by using the corresponding radio buttons shown at the top right of the Figure. The interface also supports filtering the user's history based on favourite segments and/or intervals that have been watched twice or more (these features are available in both visualizations).

### *Video Tiles*

This history visualization was designed to take advantage of the entire screen space, using an implicit ordering. This design is essentially a grid layout of thumbnails, which is commonly used for web browsing history with the exception of having varied sizes for the thumbnails in our design. Moreover, in our design the grid represents a detailed video history where each grid cell corresponds to an interval within a video. Using this design allows us to display more thumb-

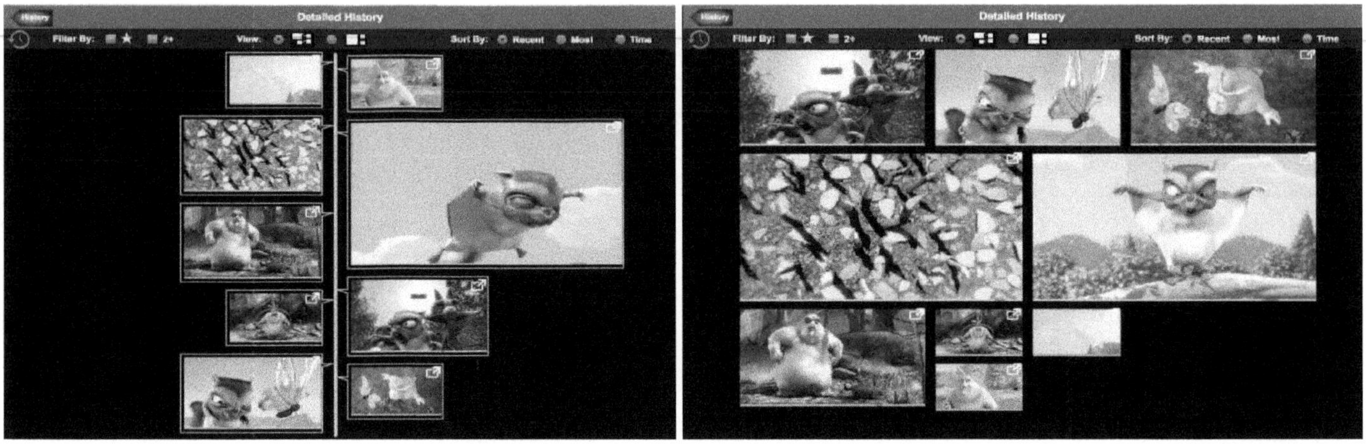


**Figure 7. We propose and investigate two history visualization designs: *Timeline* (left) attaches history segments to a user's vertical navigation timeline using two columns; *Tiles* (right) displays history segments based on template patterns following Algorithm 1, based on their view count and chosen order. Both use VHS-based heuristics to choose the size of thumbnails and offer level-of-detail control via "zooming" into individual segments.**

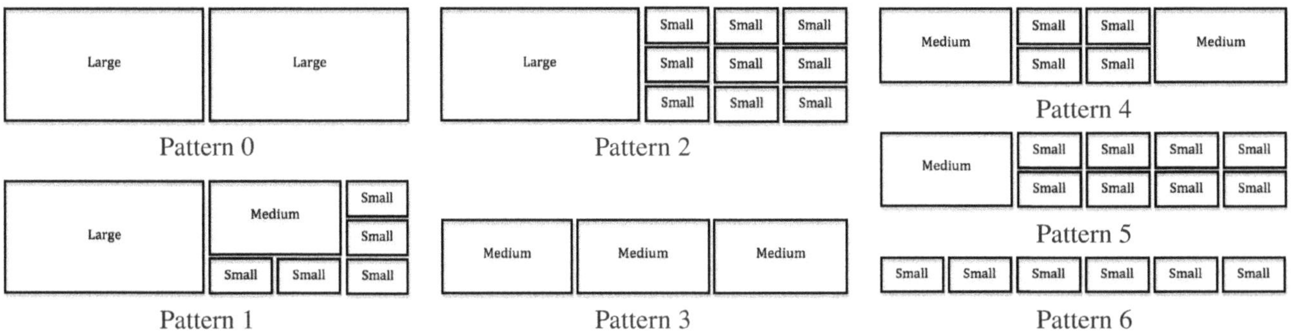


**Figure 8. Template patterns are used for the Video Tiles visualization, to provide a clean set of thumbnails with an implicit order (top-to-bottom, left-to-right, based on a single pattern). Patterns 1, 2, 4, and 5 have alternatives where either the entire pattern is reflected or just the portion containing medium and small tiles: Pattern 1 has 8; Pattern 2 has 4; Pattern 4 has 6; Pattern 5 has 5. These are applied using Algorithm 1.**

nails at once with less scrolling needed when searching for video segments.

In our design shown in Figure 7 (right) we used seven different templates (Figure 8), where the order of the segments and their sizes determines the template to be used and the location of segments within these templates. The template is selected based on the conditions explained in Algorithm 1. Within each template, thumbnails are displayed top-to-bottom and then left-to-right based on their order within history.

### Visualization Scalability

As users view hundreds of videos and interact with them, their history will continue to grow. Clearly our visualizations must scale with the data being recorded. In our visualization, the length of a video does not have an effect on the visualization when it is viewed passively (i.e. no user interaction) where it is represented by one video segment. However, the number of interactions or seek actions a user performs with any length of a video and the number of videos viewed determines the size of the history. One way to address scalability issues is to keep the size of the visualized history down, by choosing some policy to limit the number of segments visualized on screen at any one time. This leads to the need for features and interaction techniques to be able to bring the other history segments into view.

Web browsers visualize a user's browsing history by date. For instance, Google Chrome uses a fixed number of data entries to be visualized per page starting from the last visited URL arranged by date with the option of viewing previous history using the 'Older' link. When 'Older' is activated, three other options are provided: 'Newest', 'Newer', and 'Older'. Some of these web browsers provide users with filters that can be applied when viewing their browsing history, for example, by date, name, most frequently visited, and most recently visited. In our visualization for the inter-video history, we follow this approach by limiting the number of visualized items at any time and provide access to the older history items, as shown in Figure 6. For the detailed history visualization, we group close segments in history together as a stack of thumbnails when the number of elements exceeds the limit, as shown in Figure 9. Using the mouse wheel on these stacks, we can zoom in and out, which reveals a new visualization of only that zoomed stack. The front thumbnail of the stack is represented by a seekable and playable video segment while the other thumbnails in the stack are representative images. Our visualization also supports filtering by most frequently viewed, most recently viewed, starting timestamp, favourite intervals, and intervals viewed more than once.

**Algorithm 1** Pattern selection: every possible pattern is compared against the current set of thumbnails to find a match.

$P \leftarrow$ {Pattern 0, Pattern $1_0$, Pattern $1_1$,..., Pattern 6}
Retrieve ordered set of thumbnail sizes $S = \{S_1, S_2, \ldots, S_n\}$
$index \leftarrow 1$; $pattern \leftarrow nil$
**repeat**
  **for each** $p \in P$ **do**
    $S_p = \{S_{index}, \ldots, S_{index+size(p)-1}\} \subset S$
    **if** $S_p = p$ **then**
      $pattern \leftarrow p$; **break**
    **end if**
  **end for**
  **if** *pattern* **then**
    Apply *pattern*
    $index \leftarrow index +$ size(*pattern*)
  **else**
    Re-order the thumbnails to fit one of the patterns
  **end if**
**until** $index > n$

## EVALUATION

A user study was performed to evaluate the different visualization layouts for navigation of video history. Our aim was to investigate which visualization layout would be most efficient when finding previously watched segments within videos, which one would make history navigation easier, and which layout users prefer. Thus, we designed comparative studies where the participants were asked to freely watch a set of videos and then find and share their liked segments from their personal history with two different visualization layouts. We also tested whether these history visualizations performed better than without detailed history where users simply find a video from a grid of previously seen videos (Figure 3) and then search for intervals using the video's filmstrip (similar to what they would have in an online video website such as YouTube).

### Design

Three different visualization layouts were tested. In the pilot test: List, Grid and Filmstrip were investigated, while in the actual study: Video Tiles, Video Timeline, and Filmstrip were experimented. The layout order was alternated between subjects to eliminate the mode order effect. Each participant used the three visualizations to find 7 different clips using each layout. For each clip, participants had to find the corresponding video first using either inter-video history (Figure 6) when one of the proposed visualizations was experimented, or the videos library (Figure 3) when Filmstrip was tested. After finding the video, participants searched for the questioned clip using the provided layout.

Each participant freely watched a set of 5 different short videos of length between 3 and 5 minutes (sourced from YouTube, chosen based on total number of views). They had the option to edit their navigation history by hiding the intervals they did not want to keep using button in the corresponding video widget or favouriting the intervals they liked using button. They were instructed to keep at least 7 segments in the history of each video to be able to start the tasks. Each participant performed 21 search tasks (3 layouts $\times$ 7 segments per mode). The participants were asked to find the segments as quickly as possible. For each task, the completion time, the number of previews, and the number of scrolling events were recorded. The completion time was measured once the participant clicked on the Find button until the moment the researcher advanced the task for the participants based on the submitted segments. The navigation heuristics were also recorded during the viewing phase. The participants were asked to rank the different visualization modes based on their speed, easiness and preference,(1=best, 3=worst). The experiment lasted approximately one hour per participant.

Figure 9. A thumbnail stack is used when the number of segments to be visualized exceeds the limit - this addresses scalability of the history visualization. The user may zoom into or out of the stack via a mouse wheel gesture to obtain control over the presented level-of-detail.

### Pilot Test

The pilot study was conducted with 5 participants where each subject tried 3 modes to find their previously-seen affective segments. It was carried out to determine user feedback and also, to test the history visualization and the experimental design. In this pilot, two history visualizations, which were chosen due to their familiarity by users viewing videos online and their applicability to what we are trying to visualize, were tested against the Filmstrip. These visualizations are as follows.

#### *List*

The List visualization simply displays the history segments on one vertical strip as shown on the left of Figure 10, where these segments are organized on a reversed chronological order having the last viewed segment at the top of the list. This layout is our previous visualization [1] with the exception of having varied sizes for the thumbnails.

#### *Grid*

History segments in this visualization are organized into $n \times m$ grid of thumbnails as demonstrated on the right of Figure 10, where they are ordered left to right and then top to bottom. The recently viewed segment appears at the most top left corner while the first viewed segment appears at the most bottom right thumbnail. The order of the thumbnails is changeable based on the user preference using the sort options. In this visualization all thumbnails are displayed using a fixed size (medium size), which does not take the viewing weight into account. The fixed size of the thumbnails allowed this visualization to display more thumbnails at a time

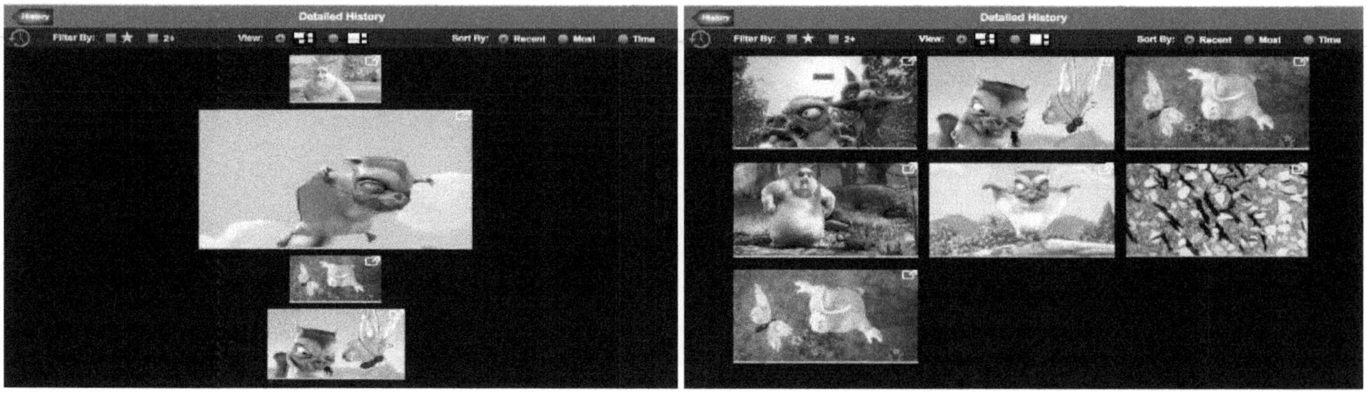


**Figure 10. The piloted video history visualization designs: List (on the left ) where history segments are displayed on one vertical scroll-able column, Grid (on the right) where history segments are visualized on an $n \times m$ matrix going from left to right top to bottom.**

compared to the other visualization. Thus, less scrolling and searching time are needed for a certain segment.

### Results and Lessons Learned from Pilot Test

The pilot study showed positive results on the features of the interface which encouraged us to continue running the experiment. Most participants commented that they enjoyed their time using the interface and they can imagine seeing its features applied, especially in social networking websites. For the finding task, each participant was able to complete 9 search tasks in less than 40 seconds per segment. Search using the video Filmstrip (no detailed history available) took more time than when having history using the different visualizations. This indicates that having access to the user's personal navigation history leverage finding previously seen interested parts within videos.

Participants ranked Grid as the most liked visualization, then List, and Filmstrip ranked as the least liked mode. However, for the fastest mode they ranked Grid as the fastest, then Filmstrip, while List came last. Some participants mentioned that the List layout needed more scrolling which made them think they were slower than the Filmstrip. However, they liked having different sizes for the thumbnails to indicate how an interval was consumed. This made some participants favour the List visualization over the Grid which is worth investigation.

Based on these pilot results and users feedback, we extended the two visualization layouts as explained in the *History Visualization Designs* section to utilize different sizes for the Grid layout and including more thumbnails into the List design. To evaluate the new proposed visualization, we run the same experiment but with the new visualizations: Video Timeline and Video Tiles. Moreover, to illustrate the differences between methods, more subjects were recruited for the experiment and more tasks were performed per method. In this experiment, we hypothesized that users would perform better when history is available in terms of time needed to find their previously-seen favourite segments, and that less navigation would be required. In terms of the visualization layouts, we anticipated that the Video Tiles layout would outperform Video Timeline layout for time and scrolling needed since more thumbnails can be viewed at once. However, in terms of seeking or navigation events used, we expected no difference since they both have the same thumbnail representations. For modes preference, we predicted that it would highly depend on participants familiarity with List and Grid layouts.

### Participants

Ten paid volunteers, 6 female and 4 male, participated in the experiment (different from those in the pilot). Participants ranged in ages from 19 to 35. Each participant worked on the task individually. All participants were experienced computer users and have normal or corrected to normal vision. Seven participants watch online videos on a daily basis and the other three watch videos 3-5 times a week. Five of the participants watch 1-3 videos on average per day, while three watch 3-5 videos per day and two watch more than 10 videos per day.

### Results and Discussions

The study showed strongly positive results for the interface. Each participant was able to complete all 21 search tasks in less than one minute per segment. A one-way, within-subjects ANOVA test analysis was carried out to examine the significance of the results in terms of the average completion time per segment, average number of previews and average number of scrolling events. The results are shown in Table 1. A post-hoc analysis showed that the filmstrip had significantly more previews and took more time than the other two modes, as we hypothesized. This can be explained by the fact that when searching using personal history, participants had a defined context and mental map of their segments [14]. Moreover, when analyzing the participants' navigation history, we found that participants created 11 history segments on average per video. This means that when using history, they had to search for their segment among 11 different thumbnails, whereas when using the video's filmstrip they had only 6 different segments. Despite this, they performed even better when using history as illustrated by the results confirming that detailed history helped them completing the task.

For the history visualization layouts, Video Timeline method was not significantly different from Video Tiles method in both the average number of previews and the completion time. The non-significant results of the completion time might be due to the confusion caused by the flow of the Video

| | Video Timeline | | Video Tiles | | Filmstrip | | |
|---|---|---|---|---|---|---|---|
| | Mean | SD | Mean | SD | Mean | SD | F-test |
| Completion Time | 17.76 | 5.28 | 17.88 | 4.91 | 24.31 | 10.42 | 23.01* |
| No. of Previews | 25.11 | 28.24 | 23.41 | 21.03 | 35.53 | 27.56 | 5.03* |
| No. of Scrolls | 6.64 | 7.74 | 1.54 | 3.96 | - | - | 28.72* |

**Table 1. Usage comparisons for the three methods, using the F-test for equality of means. The results demonstrate that history-based search for personal affective intervals is more efficient than search using Filmstrip and the video library. Notes: SD is Standard Deviation; Completion time is measured in seconds; $*p < 0.01$.**

Tiles mode as discussed below. However, a significant effect was observed on the number of scrolling events, where Video Tiles had significantly less scrolling events than the Video Timeline. This proves the second part of our hypothesis and the third hypothesis. The more history segments (thumbnails) displayed by the visualization at one view (i.e. less interaction to view more thumbnails), the less scroll events occurred and less time was needed for searching. This was anticipated since all the sizes makes the thumbnails content recognizable and easily identified among other thumbnails. The results for the Video Tiles visualization support this conclusion where less scrolling events occurred in comparison to the Video Timeline visualization. Nevertheless, as the history grows, it becomes almost impossible to view all the segments at once without the need for scrolling when different thumbnail sizes are used. If the scrolling event is disabled following [4], then thumbnails size will shrink as the history builds up making the thumbnails difficult to identify. As is known with visualization scalability of any system there is a trade off between size and scrolling or zooming needs.

When participants were asked to rank the different modes for preference, ease and speed, they ranked Video Timeline as the most liked, easiest and fastest visualization, then Filmstrip, and Video Tiles ranked as the least liked mode. However, the quantitative results for the Filmstrip and Video Tiles modes contradict with the participants ranking for speed, where Filmstrip became last quantitatively and second qualitatively. Some participants mentioned that the flow of the thumbnails in Video Tiles mode created some confusion which they thought it made their performance worse which as we can see is not true. Participants pointed out that the vertical timeline indication used in the Video Timeline mode helped them easily visualize the relationship between the thumbnails. Moreover, some participants indicated that since they are familiar with this layout, it was easier for them to recognize the sequence of the thumbnails and understand the flow. This aligned with what we predicted in our last hypothesis. Thus, more exposure time to the Video Tiles visualization might also help in understanding its representation and flow.

In terms of ease and usefulness of the interface components and features, the average ranking across all components and features was 5.82 out of 7. All features were ranked above 5 except for two items: the easiness of finding previously seen segments using the Video Tiles visualization ($M = 4.7$), and using the zoom in/out functionality ($M = 4.3$). The low ranking for the ease of finding previously seen segments using the Video Tiles visualization was due to the confusion of understanding the layout and the thumbnails sequence as participants commented. For the zoom in/out functionality, some participants pointed out that it was a bit confusing where a small mouse-wheel gesture triggered multiple zoom-in events, causing some frustration. This could also explain the low usage of this feature while performing the tasks where only 2 participants used it when searching for events. The problem with this feature can be resolved by reducing the sensitivity of the mouse wheel. Participants appreciated having this functionality which helped them to get a more detailed view of the Filmstrip segments.

In this study we went with a personalized history approach to get better insight on how this would work in direct real world scenarios. The results and the participants' valuable comments motivate us to present our interface to a larger community. Thus, we plan to design a field study where these visualizations can be investigated on a large scale. By deploying the interface on the internet we can gather more data that would help recommend new features for a video navigation interface.

## CONCLUSIONS AND FUTURE WORK

We have presented two new methods, Video Timeline and Video Tiles, to visualize and navigate a video space using a personal video history. These methods could be integrated easily in a video viewer together or individually as demonstrated in our Video History System (VHS). These visualizations are based on observations of web browsing visualizations and the increasingly temporal nature of video navigation. We performed a comparative study based on a use case of fast searching and sharing, and found significant results in favour of the Video Timeline method. The visualizations were positively perceived and showed significantly faster times for finding previously seen parts when history is used. We conclude that visualizing history is a valuable addition to any video navigation interface and the visualizations we have designed are effective and useful.

We intend to investigate different tasks and procedures that can be used to evaluate the video navigation history within a field study. Through the field study, we will further explore the different visualization approaches (e.g. 3D visualizations) and interactions required when using multiple-video navigation history in a less controlled setting to further refine the utility of our approach. Based on our observations from the study and the results in this work, we are encouraged to perform future empirical studies within social website and educational contexts to investigate how this could change the way users consume and navigate video.

## REFERENCES


1. Al-Hajri, A., Miller, G., Fels, S., and Fong, M. Video navigation with a personal viewing history. In *Human-Computer Interaction – INTERACT 2013*, vol. 8119 of *Lecture Notes in Computer Science*. Springer Berlin Heidelberg, 2013, 352–369.
2. Card, S. K., Robertson, G. G., and York, W. The webbook and the web forager: an information workspace for the world-wide web. In *Proceedings of the SIGCHI Conference on Human Factors in Computing Systems*, CHI '96, ACM (New York, NY, USA, 1996), 111–ff.
3. Christel, M., and Moraveji, N. Finding the right shots: assessing usability and performance of a digital video library interface. In *Proceedings of the 12th annual ACM international conference on Multimedia*, MULTIMEDIA '04, ACM (New York, NY, USA, 2004), 732–739.
4. Cockburn, A., Gutwin, C., and Alexander, J. Faster document navigation with space-filling thumbnails. In *Proceedings of the SIGCHI Conference on Human Factors in Computing Systems*, CHI '06, ACM (New York, NY, USA, 2006), 1–10.
5. Frecon, E., and Smith, G. Webpath-a three dimensional web history. In *Information Visualization, 1998. Proceedings. IEEE Symposium on* (oct 1998), 3 –10, 148.
6. Girgensohn, A., Wilcox, L., Shipman, F., and Bly, S. Designing affordances for the navigation of detail-on-demand hypervideo. In *Proceedings of the working conference on Advanced visual interfaces*, AVI '04, ACM (New York, NY, USA, 2004), 290–297.
7. Hendee, W. R., and Wells, P. N. T., Eds. *The Perception of Visual Information*. Springer New York, 1997.
8. Hodgkinson, G. *Visually Representative Web History Browser*. PhD thesis, Massey University, Wellington, may 2007.
9. Hupp, D., and Miller, R. C. Smart bookmarks: automatic retroactive macro recording on the web. In *Proceedings of the 20th annual ACM symposium on User interface software and technology*, UIST '07, ACM (New York, NY, USA, 2007), 81–90.
10. Khaksari, G. H. Direct manipulation of web browsing history. *International Journal of Computer Science and Information Technology 3*, 5 (October 2011), 185–192.
11. Li, I., Nichols, J., Lau, T., Drews, C., and Cypher, A. Here's what i did: sharing and reusing web activity with actionshot. In *Proceedings of the 28th international conference on Human factors in computing systems*, CHI '10, ACM (New York, NY, USA, 2010), 723–732.
12. Mayer, M. *Visualizing Web Sessions: Improving Web Browser History by a Better Understanding of Web Page Revisitation and a New Session- and Task-Based, Visual Web History Approach*. PhD thesis, Universitt Hamburg, 2007.
13. Mertens, R., Farzan, R., and Brusilovsky, P. Social navigation in web lectures. In *Proceedings of the seventeenth conference on Hypertext and hypermedia*, HYPERTEXT '06, ACM (New York, NY, USA, 2006), 41–44.
14. Milic-Frayling, N., Sommerer, R., and Rodden, K. Webscout: support for revisitation of web pages within a navigation session. In *Web Intelligence, 2003. WI 2003. Proceedings. IEEE/WIC International Conference on* (oct. 2003), 689 – 693.
15. Miller, G., Fels, S., Finke, M., Motz, W., Eagleston, W., and Eagleston, C. Minidiver: A novel mobile media playback interface for rich video content on an iphonetm. In *Proceedings of the 8th International Conference on Entertainment Computing*, ICEC '09, Springer-Verlag (Berlin, Heidelberg, 2009), 98–109.
16. Nadeem, T., and Killam, B. A study of three browser history mechanisms for web navigation. In *Information Visualisation, 2001. Proceedings. Fifth International Conference on* (2001), 13–21.
17. Russell, C. A., and Levy, S. J. The temporal and focal dynamics of volitional reconsumption: A phenomenological investigation of repeated hedonic experiences. *Journal of Consumer Research 39*, 2 (August 2012), 341–359.
18. Syeda-Mahmood, T., and Ponceleon, D. Learning video browsing behavior and its application in the generation of video previews. In *Proceedings of the ninth ACM international conference on Multimedia*, MULTIMEDIA '01, ACM (New York, NY, USA, 2001), 119–128.
19. Teelink, S., and Erbacher, R. F. Improving the computer forensic analysis process through visualization. *Commun. ACM 49*, 2 (Feb. 2006), 71–75.
20. Vartiainen, E., Roto, V., and Kaasalainen, J. Graphical history list with multi-window support on a mobile web browser. In *Internet and Web Applications and Services, 2008. ICIW '08. Third International Conference on* (june 2008), 121 –129.
21. Yamaguchi, T., Hattori, H., Ito, T., and Shintani, T. On a web browsing support system with 3d visualization. In *Proceedings of the 13th international World Wide Web conference on Alternate track papers & posters*, WWW Alt. '04, ACM (New York, NY, USA, 2004), 316–317.
22. Yu, B., Ma, W.-Y., Nahrstedt, K., and Zhang, H.-J. Video summarization based on user log enhanced link analysis. In *Proceedings of the eleventh ACM international conference on Multimedia*, MULTIMEDIA '03, ACM (New York, NY, USA, 2003), 382–391.

# WaaZam! Supporting Creative Play at a Distance in Customized Video Environments

**Seth Hunter[1], Pattie Maes[1], Anthony Tang[2], Kori Inkpen[3], Sue Hessey[4]**

[1]MIT Media Lab
Cambridge, MA, USA
{hunters, pattie}
@media.mit.edu

[2]CS Department
University of
Calgary, CAN
tonyt@ucalgary.ca

[3]Microsoft Research
Redmond,
Washington, USA
kori@microsoft.com

[4]BT Research
and Innovation
Ipswich, UK
sue.hessey@bt.com

## ABSTRACT
We present the design, and evaluation of *WaaZam,* a video mediated communication system designed to support creative play in customized environments. Users can interact together in virtual environments composed of digital assets layered in 3D space. The goal of the project is to support creative play and increase social engagement during video sessions of geographically separated families. We try to understand the value of customization for individual families with children ages 6-12. We present interviews with creativity experts, a pilot study and a formal evaluation of families playing together in four conditions: separate windows, merged windows, digital play sets, and customized digital environments. We found that playing in the same video space enables new activities and increases social engagement for families. Customization allows families to modify scenes for their needs and support more creative play activities that embody the imagination of the child.

## Author Keywords
Video mediated communication; customized video environments; composited video; family play; remote play; shared experiences at a distance; play at a distance.

## ACM Classification Keywords
H.5.3. Information interfaces and presentation: Group and Organization Interfaces: Synchronous interaction.

## INTRODUCTION
Our networks of families, colleagues and friends are progressively more geographically separated [28]. Conventional video conferencing technologies provide a live window between remote spaces but do not typically support users who want to design and interact in a shared video space. Although possible with current technologies, there are very few communication platforms that facilitate creative interaction at a distance. The benefits of creative telepresence systems for families are under-explored in the research literature, particularly in the context of customizing environments. In this work we were motivated by the question: "How can we empower children to build and share worlds with us even when we are apart?"

**Figure 1: A conceptual diagram of the setup: remote participants are together in the same virtual play space.**

The problem we are addressing is that in conventional video communication systems many young children have trouble staying in the field of view of the camera and often become impatient and distracted without an activity [2]. Conventional video mediated communication (VMC) systems (like Skype) do not have tools available for families imagine activities and do them together in a shared virtual space (Figure 2). Prior research [7] has demonstrated potential applications of composited video spaces but no one has implemented a system to allow families to build and play in their own video environments together.

**Figure 2. A girl plays in a scene she designed with her mother.**

Our answer to this problem and primary research contribution is the design and evaluation of a unique networked play application (Figure 1) called *WaaZam*, which supports customization and creative play at a distance. Customization is possible via the "scene-maker",


*CHI 2014,* April 26–May 1, 2014, Toronto, Ontario, Canada.

ACM 978-1-4503-2473-1/14/04..$15.00.
http://dx.doi.org/10.1145/2556288.2557382

an environment that allows users to capture physical objects, search for digital assets, remove backgrounds and arrange the elements in 3D play-space. Playing together at distance is enabled by the "scene-player", a rendering engine that allows users to interact together, transform their video images and incorporate objects into play sessions.

To contextualize our approach we present findings from interviews with creativity experts, a pilot study and a formal evaluation of the system with children and adult relatives. In the study we use the *WaaZam* system to examine differences between families playing together in separate and merged spaces, realistic and imaginary environments, and customized digital environments. Our results include quantitative data on activities, mutual engagement and play types across conditions and interviews of adults and children. We discuss key insights from our observations, video coded sessions, and interviews of participants.

We are excited to share the results of this work because of the potential improvements to the design of systems for separated and extended family that live far away from child relatives. The design insights and research findings may also interest researchers developing applications in other VMC domains such as language learning, co-broadcasting and social gameplay.

## BACKGROUND AND RELATED WORK

Our approach is informed by theoretical and psychological theories of play and creativity. Our system builds on research systems that enable shared VMC experiences in the workplace, gallery, theatre and the family room.

### Play and Creativity

Psychologists [11] describe play as spontaneous, self-initiated activities that are relatively risk free and not always goal oriented. Time spent in self-organized, social play is critical to children's social and cognitive development [25]. Sociocultural theorists discuss the importance of play in childhood development as the most significant activity of the early childhood years. [36]. An essential characteristic of play is pretending and imagination in which roles and rules govern the symbolic use of representation [25]. Some scientists consider pretend-play and narrative play to be a key component of innovation and creativity [3].

Our focus on creative customization in the scene-maker is informed by constructionist theories of play, creativity and learning. Developed by Papert [26], constructionism builds on Piaget's [27] ideas that children build knowledge through experience and creative actions they find personally meaningful. Learning theorists [8] argue for designing experiences that are imbued with individual purpose.

### Shared Space Collaboration Systems

*WaaZam* builds on prior work on remote collaboration spaces in the workplace, gallery, theatre, and home. VMC systems in the workplace have been shown to enhance communication and build trust in organizations [12]. *VideoWindow* [9] was one of the first shared video portals. *VideoDraw* [34] and *Clearboard* [13] unified remote spaces for real-time drawing in a video sketchbook. *Colla-Board* [23] and *VideoArms* [33] extended this work to whiteboards and horizontal displays. The *Reflexion* [7] project used background subtraction techniques to composite viewers on the same screen while they were watching media content together. *MirageTable* [4] and *KeckCaves* [37] combine views from 3d sensors to create the illusion of in the same virtual space together while manipulating data.

*VideoPlace* [17] was the first art installation that includes a mirror-like representation of viewers in a virtual space. Other artists [32, 19] have extended this approach in the gallery. Roy Ascott coined the term "telematic arts" to describe artists like Paul Sermon who build systems for distributed creativity. *Telematic Dreaming*, *Telematic Vision*, and *All the Worlds a Screen* [31] connected live performance spaces between remote locations. *HyperMirror* [21] projected remote users on the same screen to facilitate cultural exchanges in geographically separated classrooms.

Several projects have been developed in collaboration with the authors. *InReach* [35] explores how users can "reach in" and manipulate 3D data at a distance. *OneSpace* [18] demonstrates that being together in the same virtual space encourages active forms of free play, where children are creatively engaged with their play partners. *Waazam* contributes to this research by adding a creative studio and a rendering engine so users can build and interact together in worlds they construct. We introduce gestural transformation, object tracking, effects and recording to help users to inhabit worlds they imagine together and share their experiences with others.

### Video Mediated Systems for Families

According to a Pew Internet survey [28] there has been a steady increase in the adoption of VMC technologies by families living in the US in the last ten years. Of the 74% of Americans in the study with access to the Internet, 24% reported using video calls with family. VMC systems have been shown to be particularly beneficial to families. Using body language, gestures, and facial expressions helps children convey emotion and reduces confusion [20] during VMC sessions. Common ground theory suggests that video communication increases mutual awareness [5] and enables more synchronous activities [5, 1, 14].

Yarosh et al. [42] studied free play at a distance in multiple configurations and found that children's model of the other persons view was vague or incorrect at times. They also found that interacting with toys in conventional VMC systems was awkward because it was difficult for children to manage visibility. They suggest combining local and remote views into a shared view to resolve these problems.

The Illumishare [15] and ShareTable [40] projects subsequently found that combining spaces makes for more natural and seamless interactions.

Several researchers have used a collaboration space to support family activities. The Family Portals [14] and TA2 [43] projects designed shared spaces for drawing and interacting with board games. Nokia Research has several projects that support shared experiences through mobile storytelling [29], putting the child in the story [30], and scaffolding VMC sessions with activity prompts [10].

Research on role of technology to support divorced families [1,41] shows that many families express dissatisfaction with the limits of audio communication and instead sought ways to maintain contact through shared activities and routines but found little technological support to do so while separated. In our user study we try to address this problem by examining shared activities [14, 24], engagement [1], and play types [42] common to separated families. We contribute insights and methods to support creative play in customized VMC environments with this demographic in mind.

## DESIGN AND IMPLIMENTATION

This section outlines our design approach, unique feature set and the software implementation.

### Design Approach

At the beginning of the project we outlined guidelines that motivated our design approach based on prior work:

1. *Support fantasy play: Can I do impossible things?* Children's imaginations are not limited by empirical knowledge. They love superpowers and magic. Fantasy is about enacting the impossible because it is exciting! But it's also a critical part of the child's development. Imagination precedes rule based play, the ability to think divergently, and can assist in helping children imagine the perspective of others [25].

2. *Enable transformation: Can I become something new?* Sherry Turkle [26] depicts online environments as liminal spaces that are both real and fictional; not quite a mirror of the child but reflecting aspects of themselves. Transformation is imbued with surprise and delight because it allows children to experiment with their identities.

3. *Support shared experiences: Can I interact with others?* As bandwidth and hardware capacities increase, synchronous remote systems will support new types of embodied presence. A community of researchers [24] is working to connect families by supporting active, social and creative play in the same virtual space.

4. *Add customization tools: Can I make my own?* We are interested in designing open-ended environments that can embody the imagination of children. By focusing on creative expression we hope to encourage a culture of participation and learning that extends beyond gameplay.

### Design Features

*WaaZam* is a networked video system that allows people to play together in a creative environment that they create and share with others. We refer to the play environment as the scene-player and the creative studio as the scene-maker to describe the feature sets and user experience.

#### *Play Environment*

The *WaaZam* system is composed of a networked PC, a Kinect depth camera, and a HD TV (Figure 1). Video, audio, user and scene data is streamed directly between clients via a peer-to-peer protocol (Figure 7).

**Figure 3. Puppet mode, everywhere mode, transformation in everywhere mode, and ghost mode (clockwise from top left).**

The software supports conventional videoconferencing (I see your space and you see mine), a merged "magic mirror" mode (you can appear in my space or I can appear in your space), and constructed fictional environments (where we can be together in digital sets). Users can use gestures or the mouse to transform their video image in the environment. This allows users to step behind objects, hide from each other, and inhabit environment at different scales.

**Figure 4. The gestural menu used to select a scene.**

The WaaZam environment has several rendering modes (Figure 3). *Puppet mode* tracks the objects in users' hands and only shows the objects on the screen. *Everywhere mode* tracks the user and supports scaling, transformation, and layering in the depth space. *Ghost mode* allows users to experiment with blending their bodies together and appearing and disappearing at a fixed depth boundary.

Users can select scenes during a networked session with others via a gestural menu (Figure 4). The menu is designed to allow users to switch between scenes and rendering modes (puppet, ghost, or everywhere) during a play session. Users can also choose to record videos from the gestural menu. This feature is designed to allow users to share short videos of play episodes with friends and family.

*Scene-Maker User Interface*

The scene-maker is composed of an asset menu, a layout canvas, asset management windows, and scene management windows (Figure 5a).

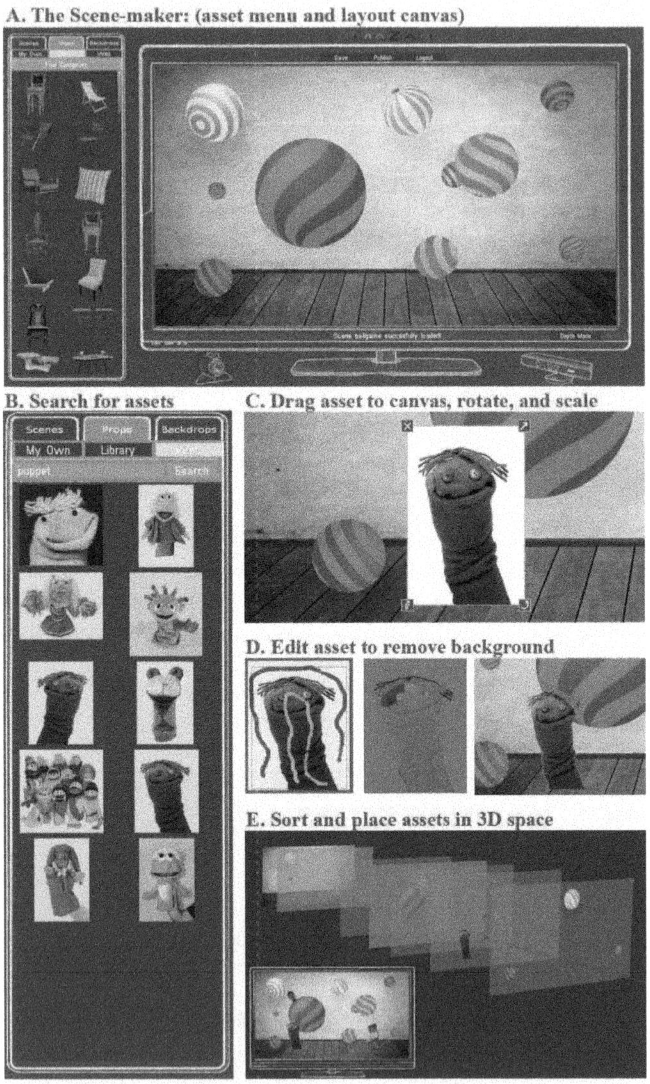


Figure 5. The scene-maker user interface elements.

Users create a library of assets by either capturing physical objects with a web camera or by searching (Figure 5b) for assets by a keyword. Sets are composed of background wallpapers and foreground props (images, animated sprites, or movies) that are placed in the space relative to the position of a user. Individual assets are dragged onto the canvas and can be scaled, rotated and translated via buttons on the corner of the asset (Figure 5c).

A GUI implementation of a segmentation algorithm (Figure 5d) is included to assist with background subtraction and create the illusion of a seamless space. A visualization of an orthographic 3D view (Figure 5e) is provided to allow users to drag elements along a depth axis and select a position in space. The sets are sharable with other users of the WaaZam software through the web syncing function that is activated when users click the "publish" button.

**Software Overview**

WaaZam was implemented in C++ using openFrameworks libraries for OSX.

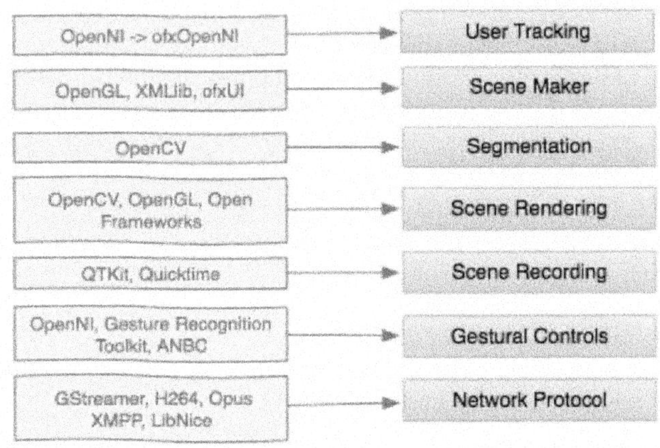


**Figure 6. Software dependencies in the WaaZam application.**

A high level view of the open source library dependencies is shown in Figure 6 for interested application developers. Further information is available at *WaaZam.com*.

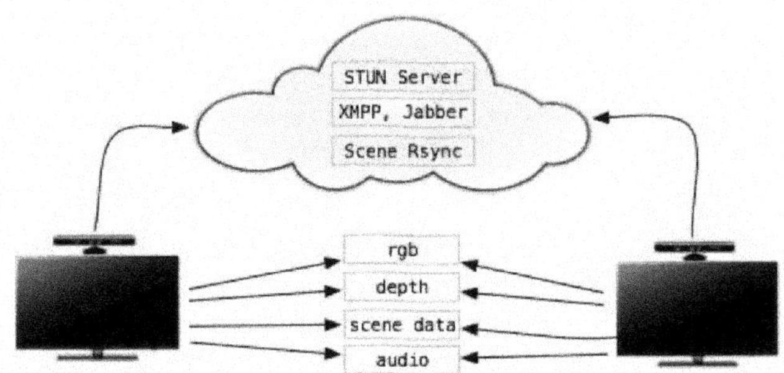


**Figure 7. A simplified view of the network protocol**

Details regarding the network implementation in Figure 7 can be found online with simplified examples in the OFStreamer [39] toolkit, which we posted for other developers. The protocol utilizes GStreamer libraries and NAT Traversal techniques to synchronize audio, video, depth, and metadata between peer-to-peer clients.

## USER EVALUATIONS

This section describes our pilot studies and the design of a comprehensive user study to examine research questions, our system design, and the experiences of adult/child pairs.

### Pilot Studies

There are many possible application domains for composite VMC systems. To determine the feature set in our system and to understand how to support creative play we demoed frequently during development and conducted pilot studies with families, educators and creativity experts. We chose family play based on the engagement levels of participants and needs reported by the families in our pilot study.

#### *Creativity Experts*

We invited one professional puppeteer, two improvisation actors and two graphic designers to visit our lab on separate occasions. Each of the experts used the system with a remote participant and was interviewed regarding suggestions for improvement, scaffolding the interaction and desired features.

The experts suggested focusing on application scenarios that require coordination between participants because activities like co-broadcasting, improvised skits and live animation were the most social and creative. They wanted more control to determine the content in the system, how participants are rendered, and more creative ways to incorporate objects and props. We subsequently added gestural controls, the scene maker, new render modes, puppet tracking and recording. The experts also made many suggestions that are included in the future work section.

#### *Laboratory Pilot*

When the initial play features were completed, we invited 12 participants from 5 families with children between the ages of 4-14 to our lab and observed their behaviors, activities, play types, attention, and engagement. We asked participants to play together for 20 minutes in premade scenes developed based on the recommendations of creativity experts. We monitored sessions and recorded videos to code behaviors and summarize activities after the study. We also interviewed the parents and children to gain a basic understanding of their experiences, debug our system, and identify a target demographic.

Based on our observations and interviews of parents and children we noted some fundamental insights:

- Using real objects increased engagement because it introduced a shared activity that involved object play.
- Children ages 6-11 were the most engaged and get the "what I see is what you see" mirror metaphor.
- Backgrounds that suggested activities such as dancing and play-acting tended to increase engagement.
- Activities differed between genders. Girls tended to do more social role-playing games and activities such as dancing or yoga. Boys tended to engage in body play, play fighting and fantasy role-playing.
- Groups of three competed for the camera view and were not as cooperative as one-on-one groups.

Some general trends can be seen in the data from our informal observations. Participants were very engaged in pretend play and bodily movement was higher when they were in the same virtual space. Coordination between participants, visibility and attention suffered at times when the background scene did not suggest an activity. The child participants had many suggestions for content and activities and indicated that they had strong preferences about what the environment should look like.

### Formal Study Design

Following the pilot studies and creativity recommendations, we developed the scene-maker, added gestural navigation, improved tracking, and added recording capabilities to our system. We also consulted with researchers who have done prior work on VMC systems for families to design a comprehensive study to examine the effects of different configurations on play behavior.

#### *Research Questions*

We designed the structure of our study to correlate our findings with prior research [42, 24] and examine the features of the scene-player (fantastic sets) and the scene-maker (personalization) separately. The resulting research questions can be divided into three areas:

1. *Separate vs. merged spaces:* Does being together in the same virtual space enable families to have shared experiences not available in conventional VMC systems? If so, what are the activities that repeat across participants?

2. *Fantastic vs. realistic sets:* How do play patterns, activities and behaviors of participants differ in imaginary sets? What types of set designs promote shared activities for families?

3. *Customizing environments:* Does allowing participants to create their own play environments add additional depth, richness and meaningfulness to the play experience? Do our customization tools serve the needs of individual families?

#### *Study Procedure*

We recruited 12 adult/child pairs and informed them that we were studying family connectedness and needed their assistance finding fun activities to do during video play sessions. We scheduled two 90-minute sessions (Figure 8) two weeks apart to allow families to accommodate to the novelty, learn the features, and reflect on scene designs.

Session 1 was focused on getting to know the participants, assessing play across three conditions, and introducing the scene-maker. Session 2 was focused on customization with assets from their lives, addressing novelty factors by extending playtime, and interviewing the participants.

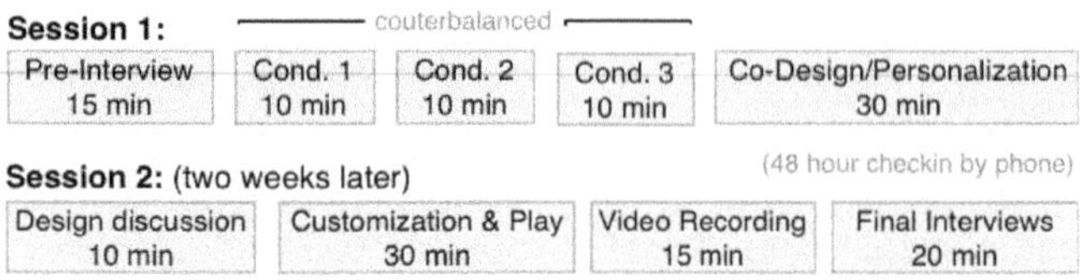


**Figure 8. A timeline of the study procedure.**

In session one we interviewed adults and children individually to determine their technology experience, frequency of VMC use, existing play patterns, personal interests, and rating of connectedness to their playmate. Participants were brought to separate spaces with physical props in the room such as puppets and toys. They were asked to find the most fun thing to do in three counterbalanced 10-minute sessions (Figure 10). The session conditions were: Skype (conventional VMC configuration), magic mirror (participants are composited into one window with the background of one of the participants), and digital sets (fictional background sets with layers designed by artists).

This was followed by a co-design session where groups discussed ideas for a new scene, used the scene-maker tools with the facilitator, and played in one of the sets they made. After the first session we gave each group a thumb drive to archive images and movies between sessions.

In the second session the participants used the scene-maker to design a few more sets with physical and digital assets they brought from home. We asked them to play in these customized sets and record a short video. We concluded the sessions by conducting post-interviews of the parent and child regarding their experiences and suggestions for future use cases.

### Study Participants

We selected groups based on the child's age and the number of days the adults and children are away from each other each month in order to focus on geographically separated families.

| Group | Adult A/S | Child A/S | Same home | D. away p/m | Use VMC | Use phone |
|---|---|---|---|---|---|---|
| 1 | 43/f | 10/m | no | 8 | some | often |
| 2 | 42/f | 8/m | yes | 2 | some | often |
| 3 | 36/f | 10/f | yes | 0 | none | none |
| 4 | 70/f | 8/f | no | 20 | some | some |
| 5 | 43/f | 10/f | yes | 0 | none | some |
| 6 | 38/m | 8/f | no | 10 | often | often |
| 7 | 38/m | 7/f | yes | 0 | none | some |
| 8 | 43/f | 12/m | no | 15 | often | often |
| 9 | 47/m | 12/f | yes | 1 | none | some |
| 10 | 48/m | 11/m | no | 2 | none | none |
| 11 | 49/m | 6/m | no | 15 | some | often |
| 12 | 45/m | 8/f | yes | 18 | often | often |

**Figure 9. Pairs: age, sex, days away per month, and VMC use.**

Figure 9 shows the age of the adults and children, if they live in the same home, the number of days they are separated each month, and the group familiarity with video communication technologies. We selected seven groups who have a real need to connect due to travel, divorce, or work related geographical separation. Six of the groups were familiar with VMC technologies and use them occasionally. Nine of the groups were parent/child relationships and there were two grandparents and one aunt. Many participants stated that they responded to the study to learn about ways to connect with the child when they were apart.

### Video Coding Criteria

During play sessions we recorded video of the screen and each of the physical play spaces. We coded videos using the following metrics:

*Type of Play:* The National Institute for Play [22] identifies patterns that constitute elements of play. We coded for body play, object play, social play, pretend play, and narrative play. We used a binary coding technique to determine if a play type occurred in a 15 second interval.

*Adult/Child Play Engagement:* We examine play mutuality using the Piaget/Parten Scale [31], which rates levels of play engagement on a scale of 1 to 5 in intermittent states progressing from solitary play to parallel play to associative/cooperative play activities.

*Adult-Child Mutuality*: The Adult-Child Rating Scales [6] developed by Crawley and Spiker (1983) were coded for each play episode. They are rated from 1 to 5 in two sections: child measures of play maturity, social initiative, and object initiative and adult guidance ratings of directiveness, elaborativeness, and sensitivity.

*Behavioral Characteristics of Participants*: We marked if a pair smiled, laughed, or made a non-word exclamation like "ahhh" every 15 seconds. We also noted if the attention of the child and adult were on themselves, the other person, the mutual activity, the virtual space, or the physical space.

To ensure the reliability of our coding criteria, two researchers outlined a procedure and coded the first group together, discussing engagement, attention, and play types for each 15-second interval. Then they coded a second group separately and computed a Kappa scores between .6 and .8 for each metric. Each of the videos was coded twice once for episodic characteristics (activities and adult-child mutuality) and again in 15 second intervals (play types, behavioral signals like smiles, engagement, and attention).

## Results

We present our observations, the results of the coded videos across four conditions (Figure 10), a summary of the most common activities and qualitative feedback from participants on customization and desired usage scenarios.

### Observations During the Study

In Skype mode show and tell and object play were the most common activities. Engagement was loosely correlated with children that had high social initiative and adults who were directive and sensitive.

In the second condition participants exclaimed in surprise when they first saw each other in the same space. In mirror mode, body play, mock fighting and tickling, playing with the camera, and object play commonly followed. Participants focused more on each other in mirror mode.

**Figure 10. The four study conditions (from top left clockwise): skype, mirror, customized and digital.**

In digital mode participants explored and inhabited the environment as families might in a new playground. The most popular scenes had lots of layers or suggested an activity. Common activities in digital mode included exploring layers, hide and seek, shrinking to the scale of the scene content, pretending to inhabit the virtual spaces.

**Figure 11: Example customized scenes: flying with harry potter, meeting Obama, eating together, and a dance party.**

During customization families had more intentional activities and specific preferences. In the second session groups were less focused on novelty and more interested in enacting ideas the child had expressed. Most groups would make a scene, try it, and then return to make small modifications. Groups with more supportive parents seemed to have higher engagement in both sessions. Adults and children reported that the customization tools allowed them to make the scenes they imagined but they wanted more interactive features like driving a car and costuming.

In customization mode the behavior of groups was highly individualized (Figure 11). Some groups were interested in creating familiar spaces while others were attracted to more fantastic backgrounds such as a movie set. Other groups created backgrounds for physical activities like dancing or swimming. Please see the video figure for specific examples of individual group play activities.

*Summary of Activities*

Of the top ten activities in our study, eight were collaborative activities with a component of pretend play. Parents reported their favorite highlights as body play (8), hide and seek (4), exploring an environment with the child (3), playing with puppets together (3), and creating sets (3).

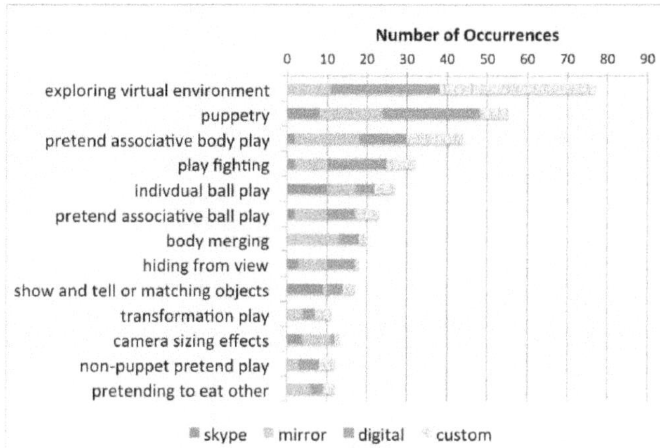


**Figure 12. Top activities across conditions in the study.**

Children reported their favorite activities as customization (7), being in the environment (4) being in scenes they made (4), transformation (3), hide and seek (2), being with the parent (2), and playing with glitches (1). The total numbers of occurrences of top activities are shown in Figure 12.

*Engagement and Types of Play*

Figure 13 shows the subjective ratings from interviews with participants rating engagement and connectedness across conditions.

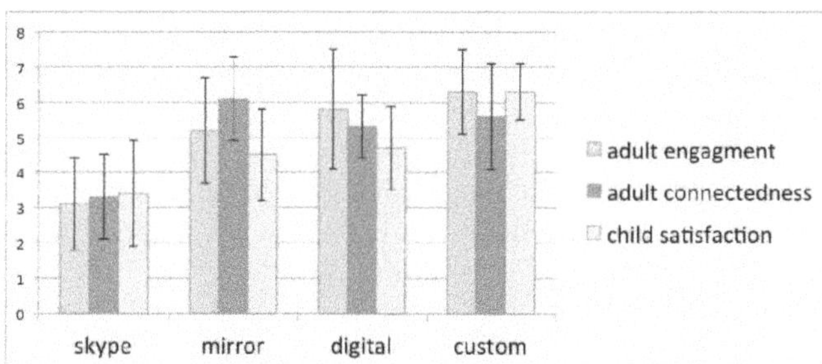


**Figure 13. Adult and child ratings of the four conditions.**

Overall the findings indicate an increase in engagement in the custom condition and low engagement in the Skype condition. Children gave customization the highest rating. Adults felt more engaged and connected in merged configurations (mirror, digital, and customization) than in Skype. Adults reported that the mirror condition was the most viscerally fun because body play felt more intimate. They reported enjoying digital scenes but felt less connected when they were not engaging in a shared activity.

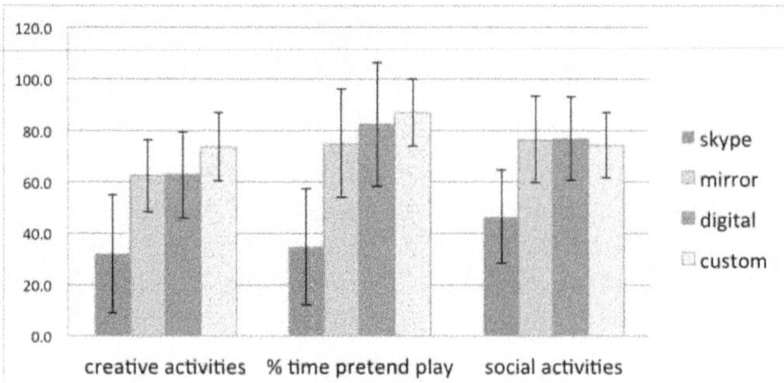


**Figure 14. Creative activities, pretend play, and social play.**

Figure 14 shows common types of activities grouped across conditions. Social activities and pretend play were 28-46% higher across all three merged configurations than in Skype. Being together in the same space appears to be the most important factor to supporting more creative and social activities.

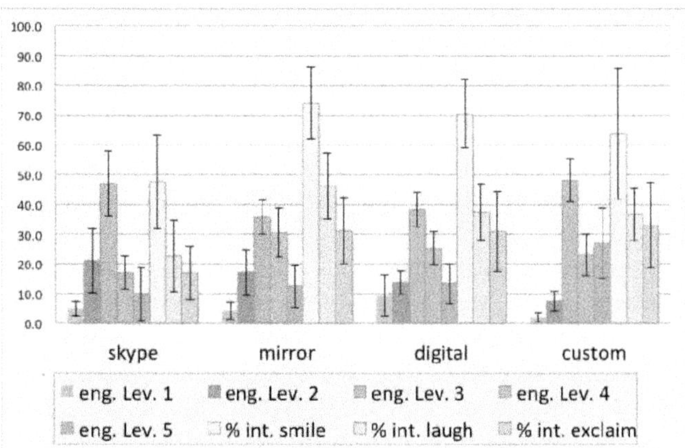


**Figure 15. Engagement levels on a Piaget/Parten scale of 1-5 and intervals with smiles, laughs and non-word exclamations.**

Although play is subjective and unique to each group, the observed data from the videos reflects key observations from the interviews. Overall engagement was low in Skype and differences in behavior between mirror, digital, and customization were more nuanced. Groups had more frequent engagement at the level of 5 in custom mode (Figure 15), but spent more time smiling and laughing in mirror mode because they were more directly engaged with each other's bodies. The standard deviations resulted from differences in play styles. For example, groups that engaged in pretend play in digital and mirror conditions were more likely to have higher engagement in the custom condition. Please refer to the video figure to relate these findings to specific examples of group play for each condition.

*Customization Feedback*

Between digital and customization conditions families shifted from adapting to the environment to directing activities. Customized scenes expressed more about the personalities, memories, desires and needs of families. The scene-maker was challenging for the 6 and 7 year olds but was much easier for the three 8 year olds who had some technology experience. Most of the children thought customization was fun because they could do anything they wanted and the content related to their interests. Regarding remixing scenes, many preferred to have direct ownership:

*"I like modifying other peoples sets but since mine are better I could make my own with their backgrounds"*

Most parents reported they were inclined to support the child during the scene making process. They also reported that customization allowed them to adapt the environment to specific needs. One grandparent and her granddaughter brought pictures from recent trip together. They made a scene with a lake and pretended to go swimming together. The grandmother said she enjoyed playing because:

*"I could do things that are not possible for me in reality. For example, I am not a very active person anymore but I could run up the walls with her or swim with her."*

One mother saw customization as a way of enacting her son's ideas with him. Her son had drawings of an imaginary trip to Paris where he said they visited a café and climbed the Eiffel tower together:

*"What was interesting for us is that we can act out his ideas and then I can help him develop them into something that we can do together in his worlds."*

Having a supportive partner is a key component of customization. One grandparent was not very sensitive and directed activities frequently. The child said that playing in scenes was more fun than creating them because she had to design the scene for herself and her grandmother's preferences.

*Usage Scenarios*

All of the adult participants said they would use the system as an alternative to conventional VMC systems. Many parents said they would start in mirror mode so they could be with the child in their home and catch up on their day and proceed to a digital mode when they wanted to play together. Parents suggested activities like inviting children into travel pictures while on a trip, eating together in their home kitchen, and reading a bedtime story in a picture book. Children said they wanted do things like flying a plane, going to a foreign country, playing with toys, making movies, playing with each other, and making new scenes.

One third of the groups had a real need for the system because the adults are separated from the children more than two days a week (because the parents are divorced). As a result, they expressed interest in a home installation of *WaaZam*. These families were the most emotive during the post-interviews and had the most suggestions about how they would use the system. For example one father really missed his daughter and wanted to try enacting familiar scenarios. His daughter had similar ideas about what they would do together saying:

*"I would have a sushi picnic with my dad, show him my cat, have him tell me a story at bedtime, play with toys, and make different backgrounds to show him where I've been"*

In contrast another child said that he felt closer to his dad on the phone than in our system because he can tell him whether he had a good day or a bad day. *WaaZam* may help these families have fun together by supporting video play but it might be best to use in tandem with media that provides privacy for children to establish an emotional connection with the adult.

## DISCUSSION

As use of VMC systems in the home increases [28] and researchers focus on developing shared video spaces for families [24] we hope the following insights can serve as design guidelines that encourage the development of more creative systems which empower families to build worlds that serve their individual needs.

Regarding the initial research questions, like other researchers [18, 42] we found that being in the same space increased play engagement and made more shared activities possible. Our analysis of activities indicates that social, body, and pretend play are more prevalent in when participants are in the same space.

Engagement was higher in the mirror condition but pretend play and coordinated activities increase in the digital condition. Using the analogy of *WaaZam* as a playground provides a context for understanding the behavior of participants and the value of scenes that suggest active, social and creative activities. Customization is important to children because they develop feelings of ownership and are able to enact their ideas and share them with the adult participant.

Our findings can be summarized as the following key insights:

1. Being together in the same virtual space enables new activities, tends to increase play engagement, and increases the diversity of play types.

2. Support shared activities by: using suggestive scenes, adding interactivity, and providing customization tools.

3. Digital scenes are like going to the playground and customization is like designing your own playground.

4. Personalization appears to foster feelings of ownership, and can increase the richness and depth of play activities.

5. Playing in customized scenes fosters creativity and communication by allowing children to enact their ideas.

6. Families play in many different ways. Provide support for active, social and creative play scenarios.

## CONCLUSION

In this paper, we presented the design and evaluation of the *WaaZam* system, which is uniquely focused on helping families build and play together at a distance in customized VMC environments. The system places remote users in the same virtual space and includes support for object play, body merging, transformation, and gestural interaction. The scene-maker allows users to author, share, remix and record content in customized environments.

In our future work plan to improve the platform by adding contact management, increasing interactivity, letting users map effects to specific props, adding parental controls, and scaffolding storytelling activities. We also plan to do a study of our system in the home. The use of the system in everyday life (including the effects it may have on existing behaviors and choices of communication) will need to be tested in longitudinal studies to understand the implications of our approach long term. Although we were able to reduce some of the effects of novelty by having extended play sessions in the second session, we don't know how families would use the system over the course of many months. Our hope is that providing customization features will encourage long-term use because participants take ownership of the environment.

Central to our aspirations is the question: How can we empower children to build and share worlds *with us* even when we are apart? We found that when adults and children are together in the same video space it enables more creative play activities and tends to increase feelings of connectedness and engagement. But what was truly satisfying about this research was watching children customize environments in creative ways that were personally meaningful to them. Seymour Papert said: "Computers serve us best when they allow everything to change". Papert's work empowered children to construct their own understanding of systems by building worlds. We believe that when we are separated, children should be able to design new and delightful experiences that build their imaginations and strengthen our relationships with them.


## ACKNOWLEDGEMENTS

We would like to thank Mitch Resnick, Mike Bove, Edith Ackerman, Stephen Quaterno, Anette Von Kapri, Jason Moran, Noura Howell, Arturo Castro, John Bowler, Jonathan Trevino, Kevin Wong, and Arjun Narayanana.


## REFERENCES


1. Ames, M. G., Go, J., Kaye, J., and Spasojevic, M., "Making Love in the Network Closet: The Benefits and Work of Family Videochat," CSCW, 2010.
2. Ballagas, R., Kaye, J. J., Ames, M., Go, J., and Raffle, H., "Family communication: phone conversations with children," in Proc. of IDC, pp. 321–324, ACM, 2009.
3. Bekoff, M and Byers J.,(Ed.s) (1998) Animal Play: Brown, S. Play as an Organizing Principle, p. 243-259
4. Benko, H., Jota, R., and Wilson, A.D. MirageTable: freehand interaction on a projected augmented reality desktop. In Proc. of ACM SIGCHI, 2012, 199-208.
5. Clark, H. H., & Brennan, S. E. (1991). Grounding in communication. Perspectives on social shared cognition. Washington, DC: American Psychological Association.

6. Crawley, S. B., and Spiker, D. (1983) Mother child interactions, Child Development, 54, 1312-1323
7. Cullinan, C. and Agamanolis, S. Reflexion: a responsive virtual mirror. Conference Companion, UIST 2002, (2002).
8. Dewey, J. (1938). Experience and education. New York: Collier Books.
9. Fish, R. Kraut, R and Chalfonte, B. 1990. The VideoWindow system in informal communication. (CSCW '90). ACM, New York, NY, USA, 1-11.
10. Follmer, S., Raffle, H., Go, J., Ballagas, R., and Ishii, H., "Video play: playful interactions in video conferencing for long-distance families with young children," in Proc. of IDC, pp. 49– 58, 2010.
11. Garvey, C. Play. Cambridge, Mass.: Harvard University Press, 1977
12. Isaacs, E.A. and Tang, J.C. (1993). What video can and can't do for collaboration. Multimedia, ACM, N.Y.
13. Ishii, H. and Miyake, N., "Toward an open shared workspace: computer and video fusion approach of TeamWorkStation," Commun. ACM, pp. 37–50, 1991.
14. Judge, T. K. and Neustaedter, C., "Sharing conversation and sharing life: video conferencing in the home," in Proc. of CHI, ACM, 2010.
15. Junuzovic S., Inkpen K., Blank, T and Gupta, A "IllumiShare: Sharing Any Surface", in CHI 2012, ACM, May 2012
16. Kirk, D. S., Sellen, A., and Cao, X., "Home video communication: mediating 'closeness'," in Proc. of CSCW, pp. 135–144, ACM, 2010.
17. Krueger, Myron: Artificial Reality, Addison-Westly, 1991
18. Ledo, D., Aseniero, B.A. Greenberg S. Boring, S. and Tang, A (2103) OneSpace: Shared Depth-Corrected Video Interaction. In Proc. ACM CHI 2013 April 27-May 3. A CHI Work in Progress.
19. Levin, Golan, Messa di Voce, 2003 http://www.flong.com
20. Mehrabian, A. (1972). Nonverbal communication. Chicago: Aldine-Atherton.
21. Morikawa, O. and Maesako. T 1998. HyperMirror: toward pleasant-to-use video mediated communication system. (CSCW '98). ACM, New York, NY, USA
22. National Institute for Play: http://www.nifplay.org/
23. Nescher, T., & Kunz, A. (2011). An interactive whiteboard for immersive telecollaboration. The Visual Computer: International Journal of Computer Graphics - Special Issue on Cyberworlds 2010 , 27 (4), 311-320.
24. Neustaedter, Oduor, Venolia, Judge. 2012. Moving beyond talking heads to shared experiences: the future of personal video communication. CSCW, New York, NY, USA, 327-330.
25. Nikolopolou, A. (1993): Play, cognitive development, and the social world: Piaget, Vygotsky, and beyond. Human Development 36:1–23.
26. Papert, S. (1980). Mindstorms: Children, Computers, and Powerful Ideas.
27. Piaget, Jean The construction of reality in the child (New York: Basic Books, 1954)
28. Rainie, L. and Zickuhr, K., "Video calling and video chat," in Pew Internet & American Life Project, http://pewinternet.org/Reports/2010 , 2010.
29. Raffle, H., Ballagas, R.,"Family Story Play: Reading with Young Children (and Elmo) Over a Distance," in Proc. of CHI, ACM, 2010.
30. Raffle, H., Revelle, G., Mori, K., Ballagas, R. "StoryVisit : Family Video Chat and Connected E-Books," in Proc. of CHI 2011.
31. Sermon, Paul, Telematic Artworks: http://www.paulsermon.org/
32. Snibbe, Scott: Deep Walls, 2002: http://www.snibbe.com/projects/
33. Tang, A., Neustaedter, C., & Greenberg, S. (2007). VideoArms: Embodiments for Mixed Presence Groupware. In People and Computers XX
34. Tang, J. C. and Minneman, S. L., "Videodraw: a video interface for collaborative drawing," ACM Trans. Inf. Syst., vol. 9, no. 2, pp. 170–184, 1991.
35. Von Kapri, A, Wong, K, Hunter, S, Gillian, Maes, P "InReach: Manipulating 3D Objects Remotely Using your Body" (CHI 2013), Workshop paper.
36. Vygotsky, L.S. (1977): Play and its role in the mental development of the child. New York, Basic Books.
37. W.M. Keck Center for Active Visualization in the Earth Sciences. KeckCAVES. Retrieved April 20, 2013
38. Watson, Theo: Knee Deep, 2009: http://www.theowatson.com/
39. *WaaZam* network protocol: https://github.com/arturoc/ofxGstRTP
40. Yarosh, S., Cuzzort, S., Muller, H., and Abowd, G. D., "Developing a media space for remote synchronous parent-child interaction," in Proc. of IDC, 2009.
41. Yarosh, S., Chew, D., Abowd, G. "Supporting parent-child communication in divorced families. Journal of Human Computing Studies, 2009, 192-203
42. Yarosh, S., Inkpen, K., and Brush, A., "Video playdate: toward free play across distance," in Proc. of CHI, (Atlanta, GA), pp. 1251–1260, ACM, 2010.
43. Zsombori, et al. 2011. Automatic generation of video narratives from shared UGC. (HT '11)

# LACES: Live Authoring through Compositing and Editing of Streaming Video

**Dustin Freeman, Stephanie Santosa, Fanny Chevalier, Ravin Balakrishnan, Karan Singh**

Department of Computer Science, University of Toronto
{dustin,ssantosa,fanny,ravin,karan}@dgp.toronto.edu

### ABSTRACT

Video authoring activity typically consists of three phases: planning (pre-production), capture (production) and processing (post-production). The status quo is that these phases occur separately, with the latter two having a significant amount of "slack time", where the camera operator is watching the scene unfold during capture, and the editor is re-watching and navigating through recorded footage during post-production. While this process is well suited to creating polished or professional video, video clips produced by casual video makers as seen in online forums could benefit from some editing without the overhead of current authoring tools. We introduce LACES, a tablet-based system enabling simple video manipulations in the midst of filming. Seamless in-situ integration of video capture and manipulation forms a novel workflow, allowing for greater spontaneity and exploration in video creation.

### Author Keywords

Video editing; video production; compositing.

### ACM Classification Keywords

H.5.2 [Information Interfaces and Presentation]: User Interfaces – Graphical user interfaces.

### INTRODUCTION

Ever since consumer camcorders were introduced to the mass market, video has become a powerful way of capturing and sharing personal experiences. The current pervasiveness of recording devices and social media sites such as YouTube and Facebook has further increased casual video creation and distribution. However, unlike still photography, for which there are reasonable tools for quick, convenient editing, video manipulation typically requires a tedious and cumbersome offline process with tools that are often too complex or unsuited for casual video. This mismatch between the ease at which video can be captured and the difficulty of making edits is evident in the rawness of much of the videos posted in online forums today.


*CHI 2014*, April 26 - May 01 2014, Toronto, ON, Canada
ACM 978-1-4503-2473-1/14/04...$15.00.
http://dx.doi.org/10.1145/2556288.2557304

Whether documenting an event, performing surveillance, or recording takes for a scene of a film, the ratio of captured video to useful content is always high. During editing, a great deal of off-line time is devoted to sorting through the corpus of video content to recall, analyze and make cuts. On the other hand, there is often a fair amount of downtime for the camera operator during capture while passively watching the scene unfold. We refer to these two periods of low user activity as "slack time", and explore how overlapping production with pre- and post-production can make video authoring a more spontaneous and less time-consuming experience. Applying this strategy, we propose the seamless integration of video capture and manipulation operations into the same phase of a fluid workflow to make the authoring of videos more spontaneous and accessible.

We start with a few motivating scenarios of modern casual video production which we feel are under-served by current techniques, and we follow with a related work review. We next examine limitations and issues in the traditional video production workflow, and discuss how the live workflow with LACES addresses these shortcomings, as well as the associated new challenges and opportunities it introduces. We then describe the LACES system and present several use cases brought forth by users in an informal evaluation.

### MOTIVATING SCENARIOS

Below are three scenarios where we feel traditional video tools are lacking. These examples target casual video makers collecting footage to be post-processed off-line. This footage can have a range of uses from reviewing and extracting information to producing video creations, which extend beyond short single-clip segments. We aim to demonstrate that the realization of such scenarios should be possible with low overhead.

#### Scenario 1. Curating Content

Isa is a parkour artist visiting Toronto. At High Park, she encounters another parkour group with a unique style. Isa has a social media following, and wants to upload a highlights compilation of their stunts from her phone. She starts recording the group and collects a series of clips, each focusing on different members as they make numerous attempts at each trick. Even after catching a good stunt, Isa continues recording through breaks and failed attempts to avoid missing anything. She ends up with half an hour of footage which she will review and patch together offline.

**Scenario 2. Annotating Content**
Jane is a primatologist; Taz is her assistant. They are examining how chimpanzees grasp objects while completing puzzles. Jane is standing behind a camera, and Taz sits across from a chimpanzee. Taz presents the puzzles to the chimpanzee, and helps prompt them when they get stuck or distracted. Jane's goal is to get the timestamp of the beginning and end of each grasping activity, for further analysis by herself as well as others. This is difficult to do precisely – she writes down the timestamp that she thinks is nearest to the start of a grasping activity. She will have to review the video later to refine these timestamps.

**Scenario 3. Coordinating Content**
Jill and Pradeep are high school students working on a film. The film will have a shot of Jill, dressed as a gorilla, climbing Toronto's CN Tower. Pradeep goes out and films the tower from an arbitrary vantage point on a windy day. Later, they film Jill making climbing motions in a studio. These two videos get passed to an editor, Cheryl, and while compositing, she finds it too hard to line up Jill's motions with the tower. She also points out that it would be nice to have a shot of Jill grabbing the top of the tower from just the right angle. Pradeep is sent out to film the tower from a different angle, and Jill records a few more takes, hoping that Cheryl can make it work in editing.

In the above scenarios, we see opportunities to improve workflows by integrating video capture and post-processing. This would provide a means for on-the-fly adjustments and spontaneity in the video making process.

## RELATED WORK

This section reviews related work in manipulation techniques aiming at improving video authoring, as well as video tools designed for live usage.

### Video Authoring

A key component of video authoring lies in the diverse manipulations of raw footage, such as browsing, cutting, assembling and compositing input segments to create a refined output clip. Goldman [10] and Borgo [6] both provide comprehensive reviews of the space. In particular, the latter divides the space into *video manipulation*, the browsing, editing and compositing of video segments, and *video visualization,* the visual representation of the segments. We are primarily interested in ad hoc video authoring, and therefore manipulation techniques that are quick and easy to perform in the midst of capturing, as well as visualizations that facilitate understanding or further decision-making about the video at a glance.

### Video Navigation

A large body of research has explored video navigation. Scrubbing provides a real-time update of the current frame of the video as the user moves the slider along the timeline [19, 22]. ZoomSlider [13] and PVSlider [26] explore different dynamics of playback sliders for finer control while scrubbing. Victor demonstrates a comic strip view of the video that may be scratched [38]. We later describe how we apply scratching within our live context. Several projects have explored video navigation through direct manipulation, where the user directly drags objects in the video rather than relying on the timeline [8, 10, 17].

Another approach to facilitate browsing exploits visual cues for video content. Most common are thumbnail visualizations, which provide an overview of the entire video stream [14], or summaries, where duplicate content has automatically been discarded [20, 36]. Enhanced timelines, which augment the seeking bar to make it content-aware, have also been explored to aid quick retrieval of content of interest [1, 25]. Videotater [7] and Swifter [23] are two examples of seamless combination of interaction and visualization, displaying near-context thumbnails during navigation.

All of the above navigation techniques have the common goal of facilitating quick access to segments of interest through enhanced interaction or visualizations that spare the user from passively watching the entire stream at normal speed. While they have primarily been designed for offline manipulation, similar approaches are suitable in the context of live manipulation.

### Video Manipulation: Editing

We refer to video editing as the act of cutting and joining pieces of one or more sources together *in time* to make one edited movie [24].

Effectively collecting video segments of interest is made difficult by the current crude nature of the play/pause status of cameras—they can either be recording, or not. Vine [39] allows for a more fluid time control, where the video only records when the user is touching their finger on the screen, functioning as a quasimode [27]. In the status quo and with Vine, the captured videos are immutable in that recording applications usually do not support editing, which is therefore performed off-line.

Several techniques support fully automated video editing based on content analysis of the footage, such as the sound track [5, 31, 33], or by leveraging meta-data captured during recording, such as geographical location [35]. All of these works reinforce the idea that video editing is usually tedious and painstaking, especially when performed separately from and long after the actual capturing. Fully automating the editing process eliminates this problem but is lacking in flexibility and control.

In contrast to prior work, we propose a seamless integration of manual editing capabilities with video capture, enabling quick cutting and slicing of segments of footage on set, in the midst of recording the scene.

### Video Manipulation: Compositing

In contrast to editing, video compositing refers to the assembling of video segments together in *space* to make one composite video, mainly by combining different areas of each source frame [24].

Live compositing has been addressed for still photographs, with projects such as Group Shot [21], that allow the combination of several pictures of the same scene by rubbing to remove parts of the photo that are undesired. In a similar vein, Cinemagram [9] allows users to create hybrid photo and video, instilling dynamics to still images, similar in the spirit of Cliplets [16], but more instantaneous.

Live compositing of several video inputs, however, remains an open problem. Some works have explored compositing the present and the near-past together, where a person can directly compose themselves with their own shadow, played with a few seconds delay [32]. Similar systems include Dancing with myself [3], DELEM [15] and Social Comic [18]. These approaches involve specific settings, including a video projector or a green screen, and are limited to a single, pre-determined compositing style. We propose to extend such approaches to any video stream, by supporting simple yet rich compositing capabilities of the live stream with recently recorded videos, while providing instant feedback of the result.

### Live Video Authoring

Progress in digital technologies has yielded a new form of movie pre-production: virtual production enables filmmakers to interactively visualize and explore digital scenes using CGI pre-visualizations [2]. Such techniques afford a visually dynamic, non-linear workflow, blurring the barriers between planning, capturing and editing. We bear similar motivation to this process, but with live streaming video.

In the realm of live manipulation of videos, video jockey (or VJ) interfaces have captured researcher and artist attention [11, 12, 34]. However, these interfaces only allow for live editing of pre-recorded video segments, and do not support compositing operations. In contrast, systems for live broadcasting as traditionally used by television networks do support live capture and editing, but these are typically targeted to professionals and require extensive training, planning and human coordination. Dedicated camera operators and editors are typically working together in such cases, whereas we propose interactions that a single casual operator can perform.

Vaucelle and Ishii [37] demonstrate a video storytelling interface for children, where several toys have attached cameras. Video recording is toggled by physical gestures. The authors delineate separate video-making activities of rehearsing, recording, and playback. Ryokai et al. explored instantaneous re-use of captured video for artistic purposes in I/O Brush [28, 29]. A physical brush records images of real-world texture, and allows users to "paint" these textures onto a special canvas. These are targeted for production of abstract artworks and do not support video authoring in the traditional way.

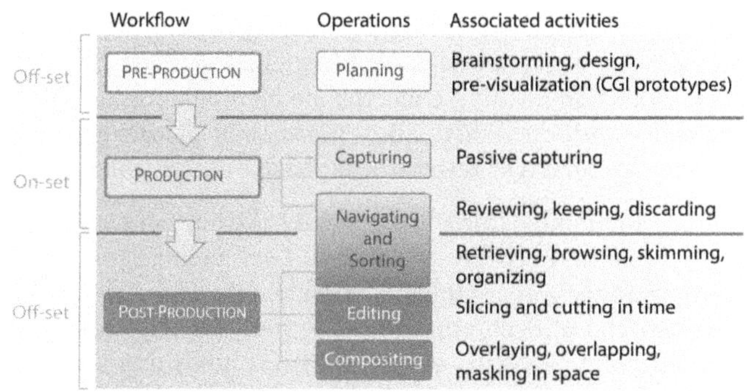


**Figure 1. Traditional workflow**

## TRADITIONAL VIDEO PRODUCTION WORKFLOW

We first describe the traditional video production workflow and discuss the issues and challenges associated with it. We provide a broad workflow description here, encompassing both casual and professional video creation. We identify several limitations, and thus opportunities for exploration. In the subsequent section, we will introduce our proposed workflow within this unexplored space.

The traditional workflow for video production, shown in Figure 1, consists of 3 stages: pre-production, production, and post-production [2, 24]. Pre- and post-production typically take place separately and with different tools, enforcing a linear, forwards-only process and leaving little opportunities for back-and-forth iteration between the different stages.

**Pre-production** concerns the planning of the video. In professional environments, it includes activities such as brainstorming, designing, and pre-visualizing. The outcomes can be storyboards and scripts, to be used for the controlled, planned capturing of the video segments. In the context of casual or spontaneous usage, planning is not as thorough as in professional filming. An example of this is illustrated in Scenario 3 above, where desired shots are roughly planned out prior to execution.

**Production** concerns capturing the raw files, which are either informed by planning, as in Scenario 3 or ad hoc recording of live moments, as in Scenario 1. User interaction during capture is mainly passive, where the sole task of the operator simply is to observe the video as it is being shot. If a specific shot is needed, there may be many takes of a single scene before an adequate one is captured, possibly involving re-watching for verification

**Post-production** concerns manipulation of the raw files to generate ready-to-share movies. As with planning, this stage may be bypassed completely for casual users that consider the raw camera data the final product. The level of interaction can then range from minimal clip alteration to extensive, professional production. Actions during this stage include navigation, editing, and compositing.

Video navigation is performed to review footage and locate key moments, in support of editing and compositing. We refer to video editing as manipulating video segments *tem-*

*porally*. This involves slicing and removal of clips to isolate segments of interest, and assembling clips together. In contrast, video compositing concerns the manipulation of video segments *spatially*, where all or portions of the image from one clip are mixed or layered with those of other clips.

Editing and compositing are typically off-line processes, in both casual and professional cases. Tool support for video editing can vary in complexity from simple trimming of the start and end of each clip to joining multiple clips together with different transition effects. Video compositing tends to be an advanced practice, and tools supporting such actions are not generally targeted towards casual users. However, as shown in all three motivating scenarios, there can be a wide range of situations which require off-line processing.

### Limitations and Opportunities

There are several limitations we perceive with the current workflow that highlight problem areas we seek to address in the design of our workflow.

*Slack Time:* In the traditional workflow, we observe that both production and post-production have "slack time"—periods of low-intensity user activity. Overlapping operations from production and post-production stages allows slack time during capture to be used more efficiently for performing editing and compositing. This makes video authoring a more spontaneous, flexible, and less time-consuming experience. For example, we see in Scenario 1 that there is opportunity for Isa to cut out footage of failed stunts while the group is not doing anything of interest.

*Precision Timing:* Desired editing operations are often reactive to precise events in video. For example, a user may want to add a bookmark to a clip when an exciting event occurs, but would not know to do this until the event has passed. Jane from Scenario 2 needs to review footage in order to achieve precision in event time markers. In another case, an interesting event may start before the user is able to turn the camera on—the operator intending to be parsimonious about recording to avoid having to sort through excess video content later.

*Workflow Phase Separation:* Since the toolsets for each phase of the traditional workflow are separate, a clear choice must be made when transitioning from one phase to another. In Scenario 3 for example, all footage must be captured on site first, and an off-line compositing process follows elsewhere. Since going back to shoot more footage when you have moved on to the post-production phase can be frustrating and costly [24], the ability to visualize raw video with some rough editing and compositing effects would be beneficial.

*Coordination:* In the final outcome of a traditional workflow, several different clips may contribute to a scene, whether alternating in time or composited together as with the CN tower scene in Scenario 3. While large production studios can afford to use multiple cameras, with one camera a scene must be recorded twice, inevitably with different timing due to real-world variation. The changes in timing must be later fixed by an editor.

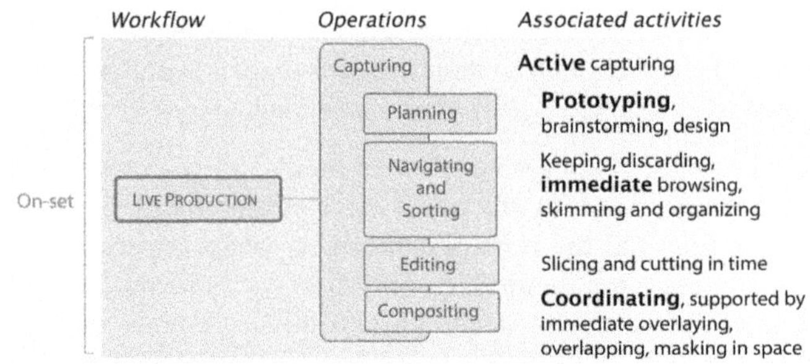


**Figure 2. Our proposed live authoring workflow**

## LACES: A FLUID WORKFLOW

We propose a workflow which blurs the boundaries of the traditional phases of video production, by allowing the co-located, simultaneous and seamless operation of planning, capturing, navigating, and manipulating in the same, fluid, flexible workflow (Figure 2). Our fundamental question is: How can a user interact with a live video stream? The live workflow we propose addresses many issues we find with traditional tools. We will now present the new challenges it presents, as well as design goals for a system supporting it.

### Challenges in working with a live stream

Performing manipulation on a live stream while new video content is coming in presents several challenges.

*Conflicting operations:* Capturing and manipulating the same video are interfering operations *a priori*, and traditional video manipulation tools have expected video to be immutably stored in a file. While manipulating requires freeform temporal navigation, capturing will continually extend the file of interest—the meaning of "present time" will be constantly changing.

*Catching up:* Bezerianos et al. [4] discuss the difficulty of interacting with changing content, and techniques to "catch up" when the user did not observe a visual change. Silva et al. [30] present the Hold and Speed Up technique so users may apply annotations to the current frame of a live video. For a user to be able to edit while also paying attention to capture, the system must allow these two activities to share focus effectively—neither one can consume the full attention of the user.

*No preview mode:* While the saved video output from the system could conceivably be sent through a traditional post-production workflow, for the purposes of our exploration, the output is live. This means that there will be decreased opportunity to fine-tune a manipulation before it is applied to the live video. However, we see this as a trade-off: the traditional workflow applies video manipulations separate and off-line, whereas our workflow aims to apply these manipulations at the time of filming.

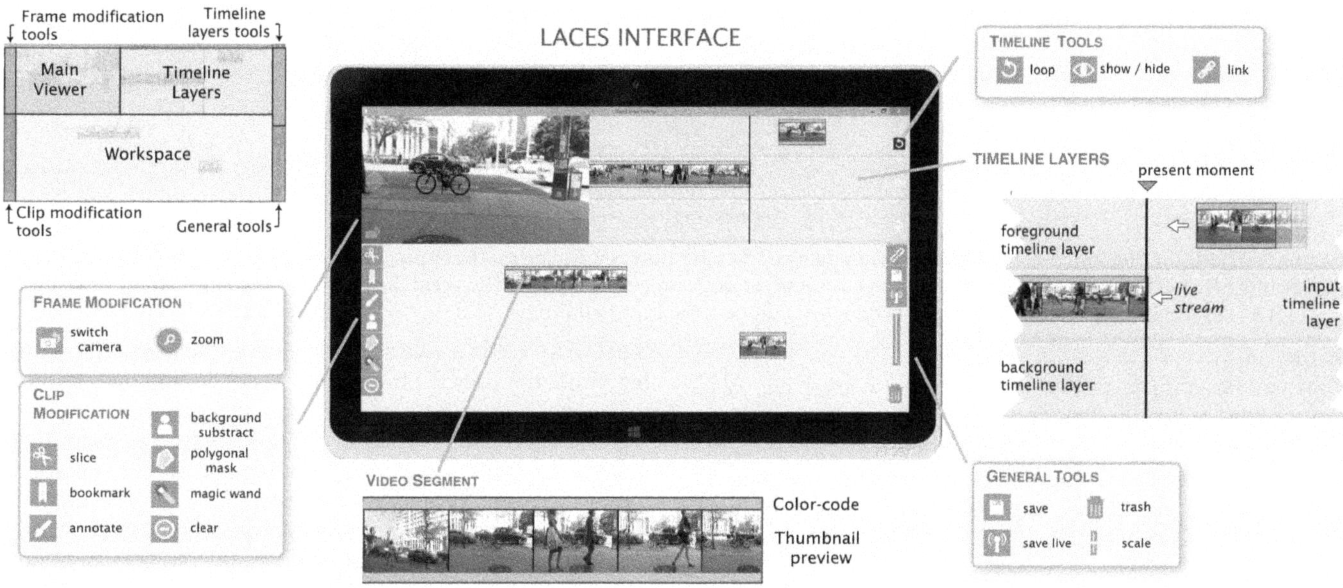


**Figure 3. The LACES user interface, comprising the interactive main viewer (top left panel), timeline layers (top right) and workspace (bottom). Clip modifications can be performed through bi-manual interaction on the layers and side toolbar**

## THE LACES SYSTEM

We implemented LACES, a live video editing and compositing system supporting our fluid, live workflow (Figure 3). The interface contains three main interactive components: the *main viewer*, displaying the current video frame, the *timeline layers*, a stack of timelines featuring the captured live stream and additional layers for compositing, and the *workspace*, a library area where the user can save and arrange assorted video clips. We provide a set of tool palettes on both sides of the interface, for easy access while holding the tablet with two hands [40].

### Overview

LACES is characterized by the continuous recording of the input video from the tablet. As the user launches the application, the recording of the live stream automatically starts. As time progresses, the associated movie strip progressively builds up in the *input timeline layer* (Figure 4). Videos clips on LACES timelines move right to left. In the middle of the timelines is a black vertical marker indicating the "present". The main viewer shows the real-time view of the camera. When passively capturing, the user can use LACES as a traditional recording device.

**Figure 4. Capturing the live stream as seen in LACES. The main viewer (top picture) shows the real-time view of the camera. The recorded clip is visualized as a comic strip, progressively building up as time passes**

At any moment, the user can interact with the live stream and assorted clips in the workspace. Video clips can be dragged to and from the workspace or the timeline layers. There are 3 timeline layers, ordered from top-to-bottom as *foreground, input,* and *background* (see Figure 3). The foreground and background timeline layers start empty, while the system continually adds new frames from the camera to a clip on the input timeline layer.

Video can be sliced at the input and dragged to the workspace or to other layers, in which case the viewer outputs the blended view of all clips including the input overlapping at the present marker. The real-time input stream can be blended with other camera footage, displaced it into the past, or even hidden from view to place focus on a prerecorded video clip in one of the other layers.

LACES provides several features to users, with interactions that can be performed while capturing: clip control, frame editing, clip transform control, layer control and saving.

### Clip Control

#### *Slicing and Bookmarking*

A typical feature of video editing is the chunking of video into clips that may be sliced and arranged into sequence. We provide *slice* and *bookmark* buttons. The slice button separates the current clip into two clips on either side of the slice, and the bookmark button adds a marker to that frame within the clip. By default, if the user presses the slice or bookmark button, the corresponding operation is applied to the current real-time frame in the input layer clip—cutting it into two segments, or placing a frame mark for future reference. Slices are colored to provide additional visual cues for recall and organization.

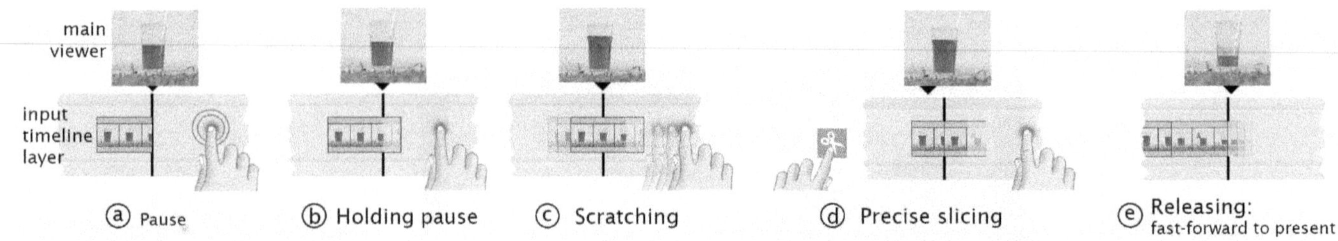


**Figure 5. Manipulating clips on the input timeline layer. The user places a finger on the input timeline layer, which freezes the current frame (a); portions of the clip the user has not seen yet are shaded yellow (b). She scratches the clip into the past (c) then slices it at the desired frame (d). When she releases her finger, the input clip plays back to the present at an accelerated rate**

*Sorting*

Clips can be dragged from the input to the workspace. We think of the input timeline layer as a queue of clips to be sorted. If not dealt with by dragging to the workspace, they move off the timeline to the left. However, removing a clip from the input closes the gap between its neighbouring clips, so all clips may eventually be retrieved.

*Re-using*

Clips can be dragged from the workspace, or even directly from the input timeline layer, to the foreground or background layer. The display of several clips underneath the present time marker is, by default, an alpha blend in the viewer. The meaning of foreground or background only comes into play with different blending styles, which we will discuss later. We support snapping when the ends or bookmarks of clips are dragged near those of other clips.

*Navigating*

Inspired by "scratching" as it appears in disc jockey (DJ) performance, the user can move both the background and foreground timeline layers left or right using their finger. If the user simply holds their finger still on a layer, it stops that layer from playing forwards and freezes it on a specific frame (Figure 5a-b). We refer to scratching as moving the medium while the play marker stays fixed, as in our interface or with a vinyl record and a needle. The term "scrubbing" is used when a user moves a player marker while the medium remains fixed, such as with most digital video player interfaces. This is a subtle but important difference—especially if multiple media are playing and one marker indicates the present-time position in all of them, as with our interface.

To support the typical video editing activities of slicing and bookmarking described earlier during capture, but it is very difficult to anticipate the correct time to slice or bookmark a live video stream until after the key event has gone past. To this end, we support *scratching the input.*

To apply a slice or bookmark operation to a specific time in the recent past, the user places their finger on the input layer. By holding it still, the viewer's display will be frozen at the exact time the user began the scratch. The user can scratch the input layer right to left to tune the exact timing of the desired slice or bookmark, and then press the desired operation's button to apply it to the frame underneath the present time marker.

Since LACES is a live interface, the camera is still recording while the user is performing this operation. We provide a visualization of how new, unviewed video builds up during this operation (Figure 5b). When the user releases their hold on the input timeline layer at the end of any operations they want to perform, the input layer plays at an accelerated rate to catch up to the real time display of video (Figure 5e). The high-speed play is a useful alternative to a sudden transition to real time, giving the user a summary of the video they missed while focusing on their editing operation [4]. The user can slice or bookmark previously-recorded clips using a similar technique, with the operation button applying to whatever layer the user is currently touching, or to the input if none are currently touched. We find it possible to perform this bimanual operation without an obvious disruption in the filmed video [10].

When a user drags a clip from the workspace to a layer, it is possible to lose that clip when it progresses off the timeline. Thus, references each clip are maintained the workspace. Excess clips can be removed from the workspace by dragging them to the *recycle bin*. Frames in each clip are visualized as a comic strip, with a default frequency of one frame every three seconds. With longer clips, this scale can get cumbersome, so a scale slider is provided to increase the amount of time each displayed frame represents.

Examining our first two motivating scenarios, these simple clip controls would allow Isa to cut discard uninteresting parts and, during such times, recombine shots of cool stunts, which she can add bookmarks for, into a final highlights reel. Similarly, Jane would be able to review footage during capture by scrubbing back to determine precise timestamps corresponding the chimp grasping activites, eliminating the need to review all footage offline.

## Frame Editing

Here we discuss options to control the input coming from the camera. First, note that we have a *camera flip* button that controls whether we use the tablet's back or front camera. Other frame edit controls are applied to frames as they come in from the input: *ink annotations*, and a variety of methods for creating. Annotations persist on the frame they are drawn over and on subsequent frames. *Masking operations* are also supported. The results from multiple different masks are merged into a final mask. If a clip has a mask and is blended with another layer, the mask replaces the default alpha blend with a direct pixel overwrite.

To perform *background subtraction*, the user must ensure the camera's scene will be stable and clear of any foreground objects. As the user taps the button, LACES captures a background frame and immediately begins masking out the background from any foreground. We used a basic hue-based discriminant on a Gaussian-blurred image, followed by an erosion and dilation pass. While this occasionally worked sufficiently in a carefully prepared environment, it did not in real world examples.

To create a user-defined *polygonal mask*, the user taps the polygonal mask button, and then sketches the mask outline directly on the main viewer. All pixels not belonging to the mask are hidden. This is useful to grab specific portion of a video that is not likely to move significantly.

The *magic wand* removes all pixels that closely match a given hue. To do this, the user taps the magic wand button and then taps a location on the viewer. The hue in a small region around the tap is averaged, and subsequent pixels that closely match that hue are masked out. This worked well with solid colors. In contrast to the user-defined polygonal mask, this suits objects that will change shape significantly, such as moving limbs and hands.

Multiple masks can be combined—for instance, a magic wand to remove all elements in the frame with a certain colour, and then a user-define polygonal mask to remove the remainder. All annotations and masks can be removed from subsequent frames using the *clear* button.

### Clip Transform Control

We provide traditional *panning and zooming* capabilities. This is particularly useful when we have multiple video clips playing simultaneously, and want to create a spatial relationship between them for compositing.

Pan and zoom operations are performed directly on the viewer. Similar to the slice and bookmark operations, pan and zoom transformations are applied to the input timeline layer by default, or any currently scratched timeline layer. These operations are keyed to the frame they are performed on, allowing the user to "act out" a pan and zoom sequence as they scratch through a video clip, and then replay the transformations at regular speed as many times as desired.

The user applies a pan by dragging their finger in either dimension on the viewer. While zoom is typically performed with two fingers on touch interfaces, in most of our scenarios the user is holding the interface with both hands and can only operate it with their thumbs [40]. Thus, we provide a zoom handle on the left side of the viewer. Pulling this handle upwards or downwards increases or decreases the zoom of the current video clip. A tap on the handle resets the pan and zoom.

### Layer Control

Each timeline layer can hold a collection of clips. In the input layer, incoming frames will always be added to the last clip. We provide a few simple layer controls.

The foreground and background layers have a *loop* toggle button. When the button is activated and the present marker reaches the end of a clip on that timeline layer, the timeline layer will shift back to the start of that clip.

The input timeline layer has a *hide* toggle button. The user can use this to view previously-recorded video on the foreground or background layers, without it blending with the input layer. Input is still recorded even if it is hidden.

We provide a layer *link* toggle button. By default, scratching any layer moves it independently of the other layers. When the layer link button is activated, a scratch on any of the layers scratches all layers together, preserve intra-layer timing relationships.

In Scenario 3, Frame Editing, Clip Transforms and Layer control as described above could be used to isolate Jill as she performs her climbing motions, scale her as required while filming the CN tower, and layer her climbing clip over this background footage.

### Saving

We provide two modes to save the resulting video: *saving out*, and *live saving*. Saving out renders all video clips on the timeline, similar to a traditional nonlinear video editor. Live saving records the stream as seen on the viewer. In contrast to saving out, this preserves any live performance components, such as scratching back and forth.

### Device and Platform Information

We implemented LACES on a Microsoft Surface Pro tablet, which provides high performance and memory capacity in a tablet that could be comfortably held in two hands, or one for short periods of time. For video processing, we use Emgu, a C# wrapper of OpenCV. We capture frames from the camera at 30 fps with 424x240 resolution.

## INFORMAL EVALUATION

Designing a suitable evaluation was difficult - we could either assess quality of video outcomes from traditional versus LACES workflows, or we could perform a usability study of specific areas of the system (i.e. simultaneous scratching and cutting). The former is difficult, as our motivation for LACES was to enable editing where it did not occur before, and the latter would miss evaluation of the concept of capturing and editing in one interface.

We gave the LACES system to 4 people to use in a self-determined manner for extended periods (2 hours to several days each) in their own environments. Our goal was to observe their use cases and creations without imposing specific use scenarios on them, and to observe whether the interaction techniques we presented would be effective in fostering creativity in opening up new options for expression with video.

We found that our informal evaluation participants invented many interesting uses. One collected all clips from a comedy show of a performer laughing, intending to create a long track of her continually laughing. Another prototyped a two-view guitar lesson one could imagine broadcasted on social media. Another notable use case we observed is tracing; tracing is typically done over a still image, and if done over a moving image with a longer duration, it is called rotoscoping. However, our participant noted that tracing over a short, looping clip of a few seconds could lead to sketches that capture the movement sequence.

Participants also saw value of LACES as an improvement over traditional video capture—one referred to it as "*organized taping*" and noted that *"[what] I hate most about [video capture] is getting rid of the chaff because at the end of taping I have all this video I have to go through.*"

## DISCUSSION

We have presented an instance of a fluid video workflow that seamlessly integrates video authoring tasks usually performed at separate phases with different tools. We discuss the performance of this relative to our motivating scenarios, the challenges we identified in working with a live stream, and the potential for issues with cognitive load.

Our scenarios motivated a tool that enabled in-situ *Curating*, *Annotating* and *Coordinating* of video content. The LACES workspace, being adjacent to the live timeline layers, affords collecting and arranging video clips without having them disappear, and without committing them to a location on the timeline. LACES' compositing on multiple layers supports coordinating.

The input timeline layer clip was effective in providing access to live footage. One of the subjects described the movement as "*initially stressful*", but relaxed after recognizing he could collect clips in the workspace instead of having to use them immediately. In terms of the anticipated design challenges of *conflicting operations* and *catching up*, we have addressed these with scratching and accelerated playback. For the design challenge of *no output preview*, the lack of an additional viewer to preview changes is a trade-off to maintaining focus on the live action.

There is potential for the cognitive load of performing capture and editing together to be overwhelming if the user is required to divide focus on both operations at once. LACES accounts for this by providing flexibility in the timing of editing. Interactions such as scratching input and workspace clip pooling allows for editing to be performed when appropriate. We found users naturally edited during slack time–moments of low interest, during or immediately following capture: ideal opportunities where low cognitive load can be capitalized on to perform quick edits.

## USE CASES

We present a few use cases, some developed by users in our informal evaluation, to illustrate the design principles and features in this interface, starting with the simple case of collecting interesting sub-clips for later use during capture, and building to complex compositing scenarios. Our accompanying video demonstrates some of these use cases, as well as other interesting examples.

### Editing during Capture

Karim turns on music at home and his two children start dancing to it enthusiastically. He wants to film this to share with friends. Traditionally, he would take out his smartphone and record the entire moment. This results in a large video file, tens of minutes long. Karim could edit this video down to key moments, but this is very time consuming, as after transferring it to his computer he will need to re-watch it to retrieve the interesting segments. If he shares the entire unedited video, it can be boring to watch and cumbersome to upload. Karim needs to be always recording video, but have an ability to mark key moments, and remove uninteresting sections. This ability to edit while recording is what our interface is designed to support.

Karim holds the tablet running LACES with both hands and films his children. He is able to see the live view in the viewer, but he can also see a comic strip view of previous frames. As the music changes in style, Karim can press the slice button to segment the input video into separate clips for each style. He drags these to the workspace and arranges them based on the different styles of music.

At one point, Karim turns to talk to his wife, and shortly after, both of his children sit down to take a break. Karim notices his children stopped dancing and wants to discard this part of the video. He scratches the input timeline layer back to the beginning of the break and slices it, and then scratches to the end of the break and slices again. He drags the sliced clip containing the break from the input timeline layer to the recycle bin. As the input video quickly plays back the live events that occurred while he was editing, he sees that one of his children jumps in a funny way. He scratches the input again to this exact point and sets a bookmark—this would be a good still to send in an email.

### Storytelling With Props

Derek is a big fan of the Star Wars movies. His favourite sequence is the floating air speeders navigating through the forest moon Endor in *Star Wars VI*. This was filmed by compositing a green-screen scene on vehicle models in a studio with footage of a camera moving through a forest.

Derek takes a tablet with LACES and films a "flying" view by walking through wooded area in his local park. He slices and drags the scene clip to the workspace. He then drags the forest clip to the background layer, which now is blended with the live view of the tablet's rear camera. He takes out the speeder toy he brought and puts it in front of the rear camera (Figure 6).

He then moves it around so it appears to be steering to avoid trees. Since the forest clip was filmed at a walking pace, he scratches the layer to increase the playback speed, making the flight appear much faster. As Derek is moving

**Figure 6. Storytelling with props, mimicking a speeder run from Star Wars VI. Demonstrates blending a live and recently-recorded video. The user scratches the previously-recorded video so it runs at a higher speed.**

the speeder toy around live, blended with the forest clip, the movement of the speeder toy is itself being recorded. He can slice this clip and overlay it on the live view for yet another walkthrough of the forest. The ability to keep one source of a compositing constant while adjusting the other is very compelling as a prototyping tool.

### Overlaying Faces

With a user-sketched polygonal mask, a user can overlay parts of their face on other objects or people in fun and interesting ways. This is seen in popular online videos as *The Annoying Orange* or the Quebecois *Têtes à claques*.

When Flint is at a fruit market and comes across a stall of oranges, he is reminded of the funny Annoying Orange videos, and is inspired to use LACES to put his face on an orange. He starts off by using the front camera and makes a few funny faces in anticipation of placing them on a fruit.

Flint presses the polygonal mask button and draws a mask carefully around the boundaries of his eyes and mouth. Once finished, everything outside the mask is blacked out, and he only sees his eyes and mouth. He makes funny faces for a few seconds, looking left and right and wiggling his tongue. He needs to capture a good section of his performance to use as an overlay on the fruit, so he scratches the input layer to the start of his performance, slices it, then scratches it to the end and slices it again. He drags the face-making video clip onto the workspace, then removes the polygonal mask from the input.

Flint presses the "flip camera" button so the viewer shows the stall of oranges in front of him. Flint drags the face-making clip from the workspace to the foreground layer. He presses the loop button on the foreground layer so that this short clip will loop continuously. The masked part of his funny faces clip is overlaid on to the live view. However, it is not aligned with any fruit in particular, so Flint uses pan and zoom controls to align it spatially. Flint holds his finger on the foreground layer to indicate operations will be applied to it. First, he uses the zoom handle to scale his face down so it will fit inside a fruit. Next, he pans his face so it appears on a fruit by direct dragging on the viewer.

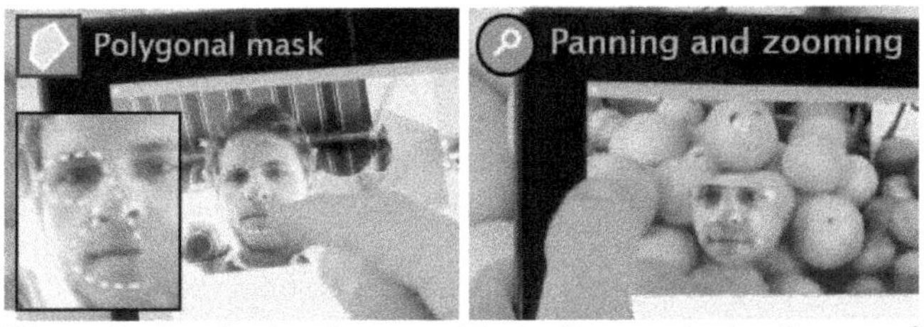


**Figure 7. Overlaying face on objects. Demonstrates the use of a user-defined polygonal mask.**

### Fighting with Yourself

Patrick and his friend Felicity want to play a game where Patrick fights a video version of himself. They find a large wall with a uniform pink colour and Patrick stands in front of it. While Felicity films Patrick, she selects the magic wand and taps a pink part on the wall in the viewer. This masks out any pink pixels in subsequent frames.

Patrick turns to the side and makes a punch, pauses, and then makes a kick. Felicity uses our input scratching technique to isolate this clip form the input layer, and drags it to the workspace then clears the wand. The clip of Patrick now consists of a first part where he punches, a brief neutral rest in the middle, and a second part where he kicks.

Next, Felicity turns the tablet around, reversing the camera at the same time so Patrick can see himself. She drags the punch and kick clip to the foreground layer and holds it so the middle of the clip, where Patrick is neutral, straddles the present-time marker. This freezes Patrick's previous video in time. Real-time Patrick takes up a position opposite his pre-recorded self. Felicity can choose to play a punch or a kick by scratching the video in one direction or the other - forwards to play the punch section, or backwards to play the kick section, always returning to the middle (Figure 8).

**Figure 8. Self-fighting scenario: From a neutral frame in the centre, scratching right and back produces a kick; scratching left and back produces punch.**

### CONCLUSION AND FUTURE WORK

We have presented LACES, a system that combines video capture, editing and compositing to make video production more accessible to everyone. We have presented techniques to perform operations on live, moving media, methods for compositing live action with recently-recorded video, and several compelling use cases for LACES. We believe that that ability to operate on and annotate live, incoming data is important, whether video or not, as it closes the gap between capture and usage of media for any application.

While we have presented several short video authoring use cases, we have not explored scenarios of extended video activities, such as using the tool to help document a live event or produce a finished film, both of which expect a traditional video file as output. Our interactions can be extended for such cases, and we leave this to future work, and limit our exploration of live video manipulation to a smaller scale here.

## REFERENCES


1. Alexander, J., Cockburn, A., Fitchett, S., Gutwin, C., and Greenberg, S. (2009). Revisiting read wear: analysis, design, and evaluation of footprints scrollbar. *ACM CHI*. 1665-1674.
2. Autodesk (2009). *The new art of virtual moviemaking*. Whitepaper.
3. Bartneck, C., Funk, M., and ten Bhömer, M. (2009) Dancing with myself: the interactive visual canon platform. *ACM CHI EA*. 3501-3502.
4. Bezerianos, A., Dragicevic, R., and Balakrishnan, R. (2006) Mnemonic rendering: an image-based approach for exposing hidden changes in dynamic displays. *ACM UIST*. 159-168.
5. Boiman, O., et al. Magisto. http://www.magisto.com/
6. Borgo, R., Chen, M., Daubney, B., Grundy, E., Heidemann, G., Höferlin, B., Höferlin, M., Leitte, H., Weiskopf, D., and Xie, X. (2012) State of the Art Report on Video-Based Graphics and Video Visualization. *Comp. Graph. Forum*. 31(8):2450-2477.
7. Diakopoulos, N. and Essa, I. (2006) Videotater: an approach for pen-based digital video segmentation and tagging. *ACM UIST*. 221-224.
8. Dragicevic, P., Ramos, G., Bibliowitcz, J., Nowrouzezahrai, D., Balakrishnan, R., and Singh, K. (2008) Video browsing by direct manipulation. *ACM CHI*. 237-246
9. Factyle. Cinemagram. http://cinemagr.am
10. Goldman, D., Curless, B., Salesin, D., and Seitz, S. (2006) Schematic storyboarding for video visualization and editing. *ACM Trans. Graph*. 25(3):862–871.
11. Hook, J., Green, D., and Olivier, P. (2009) A short film about vjs: using documentary film to engage performers in design. *ACM CHI EA*. 3491-3492.
12. Hook, J. and Olivier, P. (2010) Waves: multi-touch vj interface. *ACM ITS*. 305-305.
13. Hürst, W. (2006). Interactive Audio-Visual Video Browsing. *ACM MM*. 675-678.
14. Hürst, W. and Darzentas, D. (2012). Quantity versus quality: The role of layout and interaction complexity in thumbnail-based video retrieval interfaces. *ICMR*. 45.
15. Jimenez, G., Sanmartín, F., and Mazza, E. (2005) "DELEM - Delayed Mirror". *ACM ACE*. 196-199.
16. Joshi, N, Mehta, S., Drucker, S., Stollnitz, E., Hoppe, H., Uyttendaele, M., and Cohen, M. (2012) Cliplets: juxtaposing still and dynamic imagery. *ACM UIST*. 251.
17. Karrer, T., Wittenhagen, M., and Borchers, J. (2012) Draglocks: handling temporal ambiguities in direct manipulation video navigation. *ACM CHI*. 623-626.
18. Lapides, P, Sharlin, E, and Sousa, M.C. (2011) Social comics: a casual authoring game. *BCS-HCI*. 259-268.
19. Li, F.C., Gupta, A., Sanocki, E., He, L., and Rui, Y. (2000) Browsing digital video. *ACM CHI*. 169-176.
20. Ma, Y., Lu, L., Zhang, H., Li, M. (2002) A User Attention Model for Video Summarization. *ACM MULTIMEDIA*. 533-542.
21. Macadamia Apps. Group shot. www.groupshot.com/
22. Matjeka, J., Grossman, T. and Fitzmaurice, G. (2012) Swift: Reducing the effects of latency in online video scrubbing. *ACM CHI*. 637-646.
23. Matjeka, J., Grossman, T. and Fitzmaurice, G. (2013) Swifter: Improved Online Video Scrubbing. *ACM CHI*. 1159-1168.
24. Okun, J. A., and Zwerman, S. (Eds.). (2010). The VES handbook of visual effects: industry standard VFX practices and procedures. Taylor & Francis US.
25. Pongnumkul, S., Wang, J., Ramos, G., and Cohen, M. (2010) Content-aware dynamic timeline for video browsing. *ACM UIST*. 139-142.
26. Ramos, G. and Balakrishnan, R. (2003) Fluid interaction techniques for the control and annotation of digital video. *ACM UIST*. 105-114.
27. Raskin, J. (2000). *The humane interface: new directions for designing interactive systems*. Addison-Wesley Pro.
28. Ryokai, K., Marti, S., and Ishii, H. (2004) I/O brush: drawing with everyday objects as ink. *ACM CHI*. 303.
29. Ryokai, K., Marti, S., and Ishii, H. (2005) Designing the world as your palette. *ACM CHI*. 1037-1049.
30. Silva, J., Cabral, D., Fernandes, C. and Correia, N. (2012) Real-time annotation of video objects on tablet computers. *ACM MUM*. Article 19.
31. Shrestha, P, de With, P., Weda, H., Barbieri, M., and Aarts, E. (2010) Automatic mashup generation from multiple-camera concert recordings. *ACM MULTIMEDIA*. 541-550.
32. Snibbe, S. (2003) Body, screen and shadow. *San Francisco Media Arts Council (SMAC) Journal*.
33. Sumner, J. Vyclone. http://vyclone.com
34. Taylor, S., Izadi, S., Kirk, D., Harper, R., and Garcia-Mendoza, A. (2009) Turning the tables: an interactive surface for vjing. *ACM CHI*. 1251-1254.
35. Tompkin, J., Kim, K.I., Kautz, J., and Theobalt, C. (2012) Videoscapes: exploring sparse, unstructured video collections. *ACM Trans. Graph*. 31(4):68:1–68:12
36. Truong, B.T. and Venkatesh, S. (2007) Video abstraction: A systematic review and classification. *ACM Trans, Multimedia Comp, Appl.*, 3(1). Article 3.
37. Vaucelle, C. and Ishii, H. (2009) Play-it-by-eye! Collect movies and improvise perspectives with tangible video objects. *AIEDAM*. 23:305-316.
38. Victor, Bret. Inventing on Principle. Talk, 2012. URL: http://worrydream.com/#!/InventingOnPrinciple
39. Vine Labs. Vine. http://vine.co/
40. Wagner, J., Huot, S. and Mackay, W. (2012) BiTouch and BiPad: Designing Bimanual Interaction for Handheld Tablets. *ACM CHI*. 2317-232

# ThumbReels: Query-Sensitive Web Video Previews Based on Temporal, Crowdsourced, Semantic Tagging

**Barnaby Craggs**
HighWire DTC
Lancaster University, UK
b.craggs@lancaster.ac.uk

**Myles Kilgallon Scott**
HighWire DTC
Lancaster University, UK
m.kilgallonscott@lancaster.ac.uk

**Jason Alexander**
SCC
Lancaster University, UK
j.alexander@lancaster.ac.uk

## ABSTRACT
During online search, the user's expectations often differ from those of the author. This is known as the 'intention gap' and is particularly problematic when searching for and discriminating between online video content. An author uses description and meta-data tags to label their content, but often cannot predict alternate interpretations or appropriations of their work. To address this intention gap, we present ThumbReels, a concept for query-sensitive video previews generated from crowdsourced, temporally defined semantic tagging. Further, we supply an open-source tool that supports on-the-fly temporal tagging of videos, whose output can be used for later search queries. A first user study validates the tool and concept. We then present a second study that shows participants found ThumbReels to better represent search terms than contemporary preview techniques.

### Author Keywords
ThumbReels; video; thumbnails; crowdsourcing; video summarisation; video surrogates; metadata

### ACM Classification Keywords
H.5.m. Information Interfaces and Presentation (e.g. HCI): Miscellaneous

## INTRODUCTION
Thumbnail previews are surrogate objects used by Video-Sharing Websites (VSWs) to provide users with concise representations of content. Video generated over half of all IP traffic in 2012; Cisco predict this will account for 80-90% of global consumer traffic by 2017[1]—underlining the importance of techniques that allow users to discover and discrimintate relevant content.

VSWs, in response to user-defined queries, typically return search results as a populated list of surrogate objects, composed of a thumbnail and author defined metadata such as a title and description. Problems with discovery and discrimination arise when the returned surrogate objects do

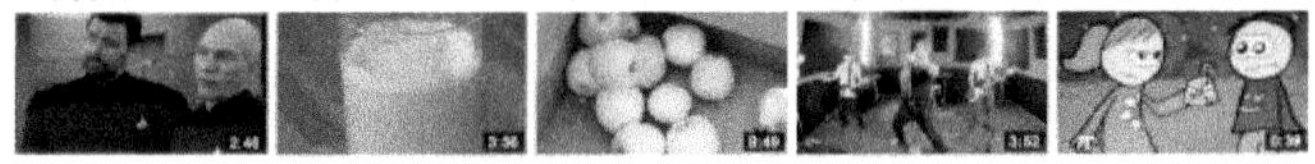


**Figure 1. Top five results for the query "apple juice" on `youtube.com`.**

not accurately represent the content of the video, creating an 'intention gap' [6]; a discrepancy between the information sought by the user and the actual content of the video. For example, of the top five YouTube search results for the term "apple juice" (see Figure 1) only one returns a contextually relevant thumbnail (result 2). Only by watching the video can the user know the actual content; undermining the purpose of the surrogate objects in providing a mechanism for discrimination.

To address this problem, we created ThumbReels. The ThumbReel concept involves two steps. First, viewers (as a crowd) temporally tag videos whilst watching them—these tags are stored on the search server. Second, when a search query is issued, the tag data, along with traditional meta-data is used to create a result list. A ThumbReel is then generated for each result. ThumbReel frames are extracted from points on the video timeline where the crowd's tags match the query terms. These are then animated to create a query-sensitive preview of the video.

We validate the ThumbReel concept in two steps. First, we crowdsource the tagging of three videos using our open-source tool. Second, we evaluate the generated ThumbReels against traditional preview mechanisms. This paper therefore contributes: (1) The ThumbReel concept, (2) An open-source tool for crowdsourcing temporal video tags, with accompanying proof of operation, and (3) An evaluation of ThumbReels; highlighting a significant proportion of participants found ThumbReels to better represent search terms in comparison to contemporary preview techniques.

## RELATED WORK
The process of producing surrogate objects to represent previews of video content is widely studied. Christel [1] highlights that surrogates "quickly and accurately ... focus attention on the relevant material" and defines three key types of traditional surrogate objects for video content [2]. Poster frames are contemporary thumbnails and filmstrips are animations of multiple poster frames extracted at set intervals from the video. Most VSWs present static thumbnails, however adult websites commonly use filmstrips to preview content. There is no standardised approach to creating such

[1] `http://newsroom.cisco.com/release/1197391/`


*CHI'14*, April 26 - May 01 2014, Toronto, ON, Canada

ACM 978-1-4503-2473-1/14/04...$15.00.

filmstrips, with variance in the number of extracted frames and the portions of the video from where they are drawn. Skims are genre specific surrogates; a temporal video-edit, closely resembling movie trailers, where key moments are used to promote a movie. Again, skims are not commonplace online.

### 'Intention Gaps'

When seeking online videos, users engage a search engine with the intention of discovering specific content using query terms rather than explicitly stating their intent [5]. When authors provide video content and meta-data (as titles, descriptions and tags) their intent is to gain an audience. Allowing the author to curate thumbnails returned in a search may present an 'intention gap': a discrepancy between the intended information sought by the user and the perceived intention by the content author [6]. While the observed intention gap may purely be due to the author mistakenly choosing the wrong thumbnail, or indeed that only one thumbnail is available for the whole content, it is well known that the affordance of author curated surrogates can invite deliberate misrepresentation or intentional abuse, such as the meme of "Rick-Rolling."

Previous work has shown that users would discover relevant content more rapidly when thumbnails are dependent on context (query-sensitive) and that these are preferable to thumbnails chosen by the video authors [2, 6]. Despite this, none of the popular VSWs appear to return query-sensitive thumbnails when populating search results, employing algorithmic or author-curated thumbnails instead.

### Video Metadata

Video content on VSWs contains both surface and semantic features, the latter including metadata such as the title and description. There are additional semantic metadata schemes for captioning, subtitles and categorisation; but "these elements are not constrained to any framework or ontology, making automated interpretation difficult" [8]. Whilst researchers have applied "considerable effort" into making video content on the Web more accessible, it still remains opaque on websites [8]. The lack of semantic information (in metadata tags) creates problems related to synonymy and polysemy and can reduce the efficiency of content search [7]. Given the use of semantic query terms when searching for content, the need for better metadata about the actual video content is critical to discoverability.

### Crowdsourcing Video Tags

Enriching semantic data algorithmically is problematic. Image processing solutions can identify pixel-arrangements to a great degree of accuracy, however they are unable to tell us whether a picture is beautiful or whether an instruction is useful. Crowdsourcing has successfully enriched the semantic metadata of video [8] by asking users to describe the content through tagging. Estellés and Guevara [3] suggest that people will volunteer their support in return for personal esteem or wellbeing.

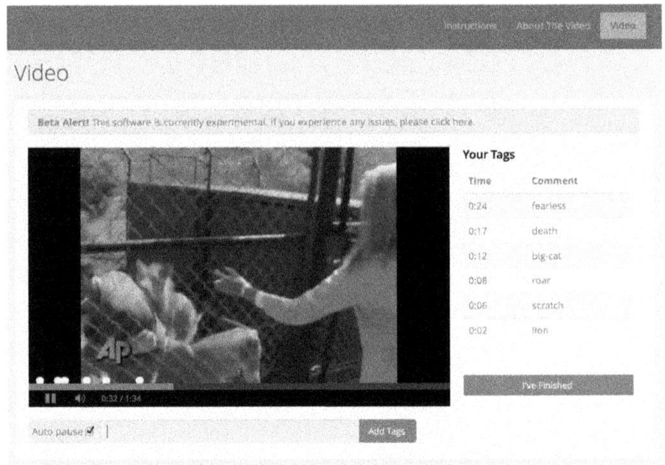


**Figure 2. Crowdsourcing video tagging tool.**

## THUMBREELS

ThumbReels address the 'intention gap' by providing a crowdsourced set of semantic temporal tags for the video content. These tags (as metadata) can be used to create a preview that is tailored to a user's query terms when searching for content. To create a ThumbReel we need be able to both gather tags about a video and to generate a preview.

### Crowdsourced Video Tagging Tool

To source tags we created a Web based tool using HTML and Javascript and hosted this as a Web page on publicly accessible servers (see Figure 2). The tool enables a viewer to watch a video and describe what is happening, using keywords. When they start to type, the video is paused and the tag along with timestamp of the current frame is recorded. Throughout the process the viewer can see a list of their previous tags along with respective timestamps; the tags of other viewers are hidden so as to not distract or influence. We have made this tool open-source and is available for download from: `http://thumbreels.com`.

### Creating a ThumbReel

ThumbReels consist of frames that are extracted from points on the video timeline where a search term matches previous viewer's tags. These frames are then animated to create a query-sensitive preview of the video. With no previously formalised method for constructing ThumbReels, we derived a specification by analysing and replicating the frame rates, sizes, and inter-frame delays used in filmstrips. Further, observations suggest that users primarily search for videos using semantic query terms [9] and so we only use these in our preview generation. We break ThumbReel creation into two steps: (1) Tag Processing and, (2) Preview Generation.

#### *Tag Processing*

The user-generated temporal tags need processing before they are suitable for search and preview generation. The process we followed was: (1) Split compound and comma-separated tags into separate keywords, (2) Card-sort keywords to remove erroneous data, (3) Lemmatise keywords, (4) Remove non-semantically categorised keywords, and (5) Plot a matrix of unique lemma, sorted by frequency, indicating

| Video | YouTube ID | First Term | Second Term |
|---|---|---|---|
| V1 | fAZpWctgZrY | "Water" ($f = 15$) | "Cannon" ($f = 7$) |
| V2 | kjWBgA81LM | "Lion" ($f = 23$) | "Man" ($f = 10$) |
| V3 | U82Xc0Oedmw | "Apple" ($f = 25$) | "Juice" ($f = 19$) |

**Table 1. Selected YouTube videos & search terms. ($f$ = tag frequency)**

| | V1 | V2 | V3 | ALL |
|---|---|---|---|---|
| No. Participants | 28 | 36 | 31 | 95 |
| Sort Correlation | 89% | 83% | 85% | 86% |
| Separated Tags | 211 | 238 | 455 | 904 |
| Discards | 6 | 5 | 4 | 15 |
| Total Tags | 205 | 233 | 451 | 889 |
| Unique Tags | 95 | 109 | 186 | |
| Uniques as % | 46% | 47% | 41% | |

**Table 2. Descriptive tagging statistics.**

chronological timestamps. This matrix identifies potential frame extraction points and is used to compile a ThumbReel.

### *Generating a Preview*

Tag processing would typically happen 'offline' from the user query, while preview generation would occur 'on-the-fly' so ThumbReels could best match the user's search terms. This process consists of: (1) Extracting a single frame from each point on the video timeline where the query term matches the crowdsourced tags stored in the matrix generated above, (2) Selecting 10 evenly distributed frames from this extracted frameset in chronological order, (3) Compile these frames into an animation using an inter-frame delay of 500 ms (for our user studies we generated animated GIFs).

## THUMBREEL EVALUATION

To evaluate the ThumbReel concept, we conducted two user evaluations. The first aimed to assess the effectiveness of gathering temporal, semantic video tags. The second aimed to compare the ThumbReel visualisation against traditional preview techniques. For both evaluations we used three short raw news footage videos. These were selected to require only a small time commitment from participants given the average YouTube video is approximately 5 minutes. The videos we used are listed in Table 1.

### Tag Sourcing

Anonymous participants were recruited by invitation using social networks. This attracted 95 participants who were directed to the tool. Participants were offered the ability to tag, using keywords, one or all of three of the videos.

The participants created a total of 904 tags on the three videos. The crowdsourced tags were manually processed independently by the two primary investigators. Interpretation disagreements were negotiated where possible; providing an 86% correlation of the 889 usable tags, after erroneous responses were removed (N = 15). Those tags not agreed upon (N = 124) were used as provided by participants. A summary of the collected tags is presented in Table 2. Lemmatisation was performed using NorthWestern University's MorphAdorner[2]. A meta-analysis of the was tags was conducted to leave only those categorised as semantic (N = 724).

[2] http://morphadorner.northwestern.edu/

Overall, the crowd-sourced gathering of temporal tags was deemed successful. Participants created a large number of tags which (as discussed below) were suitable to generate ThumbReels. While real-world deployment is necessary to understand true crowd dynamics, this study shows promise for this within-video tagging technique.

### Comparing Preview Representations

The second evaluation compared ThumbReels against traditional previews to find which better addressed the intention gap by more closely representing query search terms. To do this, we ran an online user evaluation, again with anonymous, self-selecting respondents.

### *Video Surrogates*

For each of the test videos, we selected a pair of tags from the top ten most frequent. This pair: (1) Represented a reasonable set of query terms when searching for the test video, and (2) Yielded search results that did not return the test video on YouTube. The chosen terms are shown in Table 1.

Three preview surrogates were produced for each video, with following formats: (1) A copy of the static thumbnail from YouTube, (2) A filmstrip by extracting 10 equally spaced frames from the total length of each video, animated at 500 ms intervals, and (3) A ThumbReel constructed using the chosen query terms and the method described above.

### *Procedure*

Task group one (TG1) compared thumbnails with filmstrips; task group two (TG2) compared filmstrips with ThumbReels. Each task group consisted of three preview comparisons, six in total. Respondents were assigned to groups with a formula that balanced responses across tasks and allowed completion of up to six tasks. In each task the participant was asked to observe a pair of surrogates matching the query terms and to state whether the second was 'worse', 'the same', or 'better' than the first. The respondent was also asked to supply a qualitative statement elaborating the reason(s) for this rating.

### *Analysis & Results*

As this was a repeated-measures design with non-trivial within-subject correlations across comparison tasks, Generalised Estimating Equations (GEEs) allowed valid statistical inference. We collapsed the 'worse' and 'the same' responses into a single 'not better' category and estimated, for each task group separately, the GEE model of the resulting binary dependent variable using a logit link function.

*Task Group 1:* Across all three tasks, 81% of responses rated the filmstrip as being the better representation of the query terms than the thumbnail displayed by YouTube (see Table 3). Across-task working correlation matrix entries were high: $\rho_{12} = \rho_{21} = 0.490$, $\rho_{13} = \rho_{31} = 0.998$, $\rho_{23} = \rho_{32} = 0.507$. Exp($\beta$) is the estimated odds of the 'better than' response, which would take the value of 1 if the probability of a 'better than' response were equal to a 'not better than' response (i.e. if both probabilities were equal to 0.5). However, the GEE model's two-sided Wald tests strongly rejected the null hypothesis of $H_0$: Exp($\beta$)=1 across all three TG1 tasks.

| Task | 'Better than' | $n$ | Exp($\beta$) | $p$-value |
|---|---|---|---|---|
| Task Group 1 (TG1) | | | | |
| V1 | 21 (84%) | 25 | 4.528 | 0.001 |
| V2 | 19 (79%) | 24 | 3.435 | 0.008 |
| V3 | 19 (79%) | 24 | 4.398 | 0.001 |
| Task Group 2 (TG2) | | | | |
| V1 | 18 (75%) | 24 | 2.674 | 0.028 |
| V2 | 11 (46%) | 24 | 0.759 | 0.507 |
| V3 | 21 (81%) | 26 | 4.427 | 0.003 |

**Table 3. ThumbReel evaluation results.**

*Task Group 2:* Across all three tasks, 68% of responses rated the ThumbReel as being the better representation of the query terms than the filmstrip (see Table 3). Across-task working correlation matrix entries are moderate: $\rho_{12}=\rho_{21}=0.066$, $\rho_{13}=\rho_{31}=0.346$, $\rho_{23}=\rho_{32}=0.274$. The GEE model's two-sided Wald tests strongly rejected the null hypothesis of $H_0$: Exp($\beta$)=1 for V1 and V3, but not for V2.

*Overall:* This study showed that participants found ThumbReels to better represent query serch terms than FilmStrips, which were in turn where better than thumbnails. Whilst it did not test 'real world' searching, it does provide positive support for the ThumbReels surrogate concept.

## DISCUSSION

*Scalability*: Given time, and as the number of tags naturally increases, it may become difficult to identify distinct clusters of a specific tag within a video. One solution is to apply a weighting to clusters of tags, so that these become the primary area for frame extraction. This results in the discarding of lesser-clustered tags until they reach a determined level of significance as the tag distribution stabilises [4]. A stabilised tag distribution would also help to mitigate the risk that malicious users will join the crowd and corrupt the work of other volunteers.

*Generalisability*: Inviting participants to the study via social networking websites, has both a selection bias (given that we have targeted a particular group) and a self-selection bias (given that the study is voluntary). We acknowledge there may be an element of video selection bias present and future work is required to examine whether the preference for ThumbReels can be generalised to videos of different genre, varying length, across different demographics, and different varieties of VSWs.

The use of thumbnail surrogates is not exclusive to VSWs. Thumbnails are used online by a wide variety of digital content providers, with video and crowdsourced images for product descriptions prevalent amongst online retailers. These retailers increasingly rely on customer-sourced content to provide thumbnail previews for their expanding catalogues of products. This presents an alternative use case for ThumbReels by returning previews, images or video frames that are contextually relevant.

## CONCLUSION

In this paper we introduced ThumbReels, a new type of surrogate for video content that helps bridge the 'intention gap'. ThumbReels are an animated preview, constructed of frames taken from a full video, marked by a crowdsourced tagging process and matched with query terms. We provided an open-source tool for end-user temporal tagging of videos. Two user studies evaluated the effectiveness of crowd-sourcing temporal video tagging (with good success) and participant perception of ThumbReels in representing query search terms (showing a significant improvement over other contemporary techniques for the test videos).

Planned future work includes algorithmically creating ThumbReels based on natural-language interpretation of crowd-sourced tags and further evolution to using query-sensitive (video) skims. Work is also planned to test the viability of dynamic creation versus cached ThumbReels.

## ACKNOWLEDGEMENTS

We wish to thank Kim Kaivanto for his invaluable help with statistical evaluation and Curtis Kennington for help with the creation of the software tools used in this study. This research was supported by HighWire, a post-disciplinary Doctoral Training Centre at Lancaster University funded by the RCUK Digital Economy Programme through the EPSRC (Grant Reference EP/G037582/1).

## REFERENCES

1. Christel, M. G. Evaluation and user studies with respect to video summarization and browsing. *Multimedia Content Analysis, Management, and Retrieval* (Jan. 2006), 60730M–60730M–15.
2. Christel, M. G., Winkler, D. B., and Taylor, C. R. Improving Access to a Digital Video Library. In *Proc. Interact 1997*, Chapman & Hall, Ltd (1997).
3. Estellés-Arolas, E., and Gonzalez-Ladron-de Guevara, F. Towards an integrated crowdsourcing definition. *Journal of Information Science 38*, 2 (Apr. 2012), 189–200.
4. Halpin, H., Robu, V., and Shepherd, H. The complex dynamics of collaborative tagging. *Proc Int. Conf. on World Wide Web* (2007), 211–220.
5. Haubold, A., and Natsev, A. Web-based information content and its application to concept-based video retrieval. In *Proc. Content-based Image and Video Retrieval*, ACM Press (2008).
6. Liu, C., Huang, Q., and Jiang, S. Query sensitive dynamic web video thumbnail generation. In *18th IEEE International Conference on Image Processing (ICIP)* (2011), 2449–2452.
7. Marchetti, A., Tesconi, M., and Ronzano, F. Semkey: A semantic collaborative tagging system. *Workshop on Tagging and Metadata for Social Information Organization at WWW* (2007), 8–12.
8. Steiner, T., Verborgh, R., Van de Walle, R., Hausenblas, M., and Vallés, J. G. Crowdsourcing event detection in YouTube video. *Proc. Detection, Representation, and Exploitation of Events in the Semantic Web* (2011), 58–67.
9. Yamamoto, D., Masuda, T., Ohira, S., and Nagao, K. Video Scene Annotation Based on Web Social Activities. *IEEE Multimedia 15*, 3 (2008), 22–32.

# Panopticon as an eLearning Support Search Tool

**James Nicholson, Mark Huber[+], Dan Jackson, Patrick Olivier**
Culture Lab, School of Computing Science
Newcastle University, United Kingdom
{first.lastname}@newcastle.ac.uk
[+]Mark.Huber@student.uni-siegen.de

## ABSTRACT
We present an evaluation of Panopticon, a video surrogate system, as an online eLearning support search tool for finding information within video lectures. A comparison was made with a standard video player (YouTube) in two scenarios with two classes of users: revision students and independent learners. Results showed that users of Panopticon were significantly faster at finding information within the lecture videos than users of the YouTube player. It was also found that videos predominantly featuring a talking lecturer took longest to navigate, presenting design implications for lectures to be uploaded to open eLearning platforms.

## Author Keywords
Video browsing; eLearning;

## ACM Classification Keywords
H.5.2 User Interfaces: Evaluation/methodology.

## INTRODUCTION & RELATED WORK
Learning using online materials and guides – or eLearning – has become increasingly popular to enhance distributed and local learning (e.g. [6,7]). eLearning in a local context can refer to the availability of course slides, videos and other materials in an online portal to supplement live lectures. On the other hand, in a distributed context it usually refers to Massively Open Online Courses (MOOCs) which have seen a recent rise in popularity due to their global availability and flexible learning times.

Lecture videos are an important component in both eLearning contexts and vary widely to support a range of learning habits – from 11 hours for a university-level MOOC [1] to 44 hours for a typical university course. In addition to the primary consumption of the video material, the videos are provided as refreshers during revision periods [3]. In a local situation, students are known to take fewer notes during lectures when they know the video will be available at a later date [2], suggesting the need for a usable facility to search such content.


*CHI 2014*, April 26 - May 01, 2014, Toronto, ON, Canada.

http://dx.doi.org/10.1145/2556288.2557082.

Furthermore, little thought has been given to independent learners who may access the freely-available lectures in order to complement their existing courses or to further their own knowledge [8]. *iTunes U* and *YouTube Education* allow users to freely view lecture videos covering a wide range of subjects, and users who view videos from these platforms have a need to search the content, for example to find sample problems or to revisit information that they found difficult to understand [4].

Existing player interfaces for iTunes U – QuickTime Player – and YouTube Education – Adobe Flash based player – equip the user with basic controls like as pause, play, fast-forward and rewind. YouTube also presents temporal context in the form of thumbnails of adjacent frames. However, the random access approach provided by these interfaces is not well suited to searching for specific content.

Panopticon was originally conceived as a video surrogate system and has been shown to help users in finding points of interest in certain videos faster than other player interfaces including YouTube [5]. The system displays a tiling of video thumbnails for a complete film and does not exclude any frames. The animated tiles scroll from left to right as the video plays, thus removing the distracting effects of static thumbnails that reset regularly. Users can mouse over the tiles to reveal an enlarged presentation of the tile and its corresponding audio (see Figure 2 for example interface). In principle this should make Panopticon an effective search tool for lecture videos, but the composition of the videos may play a role, e.g. [5].

With this in mind we evaluated Panopticon's suitability for searching lecture videos by comparing it to the YouTube player with three classes of lecture videos (mean length: 30 minutes; standard deviation: 2 minutes 45 seconds) obtained from the *HEC Paris* iTunes U portal. The first video predominantly featured a talking lecturer with minimal focus on the PowerPoint slides (Talk), the second video focused predominantly on PowerPoint slides (Slides) and the final video featured interactive content such as videos in addition to PowerPoint slides (Interactive). The videos were tested in two scenarios: a student using the lecture video from a course they are enrolled in for revision and an independent learner looking to further their knowledge on a subject.

The next section describes the design and materials of the user studies and the details of each individual study along with its results. The final section discusses the implications of the findings and presents design guidelines for uploading lecture videos to eLearning platforms.

## USER STUDIES

The two studies shared the same two factors: interface (YouTube, Panopticon) and class of video (talk, slides, interactive). The variable under investigation was the time taken to correctly find all the points of interest in each video (seconds).

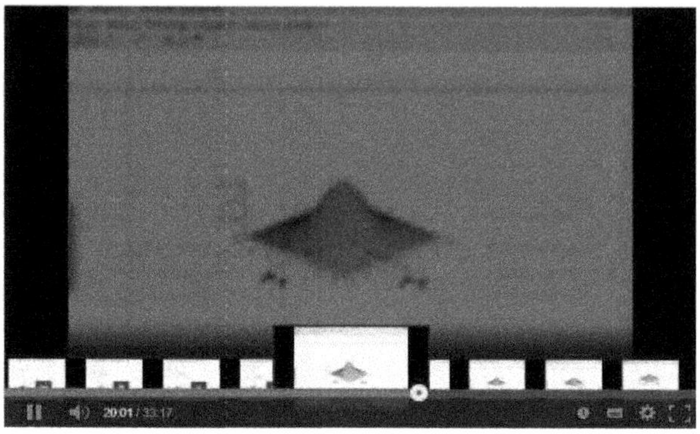

**Figure 1: YouTube Interface (with localised context)**

The YouTube player (see Figure 1) presents an improvement over QuickTime Player – the default video application for iTunes U content – by providing the user with localised context when scrubbing. The context on screen only covers approximately 10 seconds of a 30 minute video. Panopticon (see Figure 2) was initially conceived as a video surrogate system that presented a complete overview of the whole video without missing out any frames. As such, every frame is viewed in its original context.

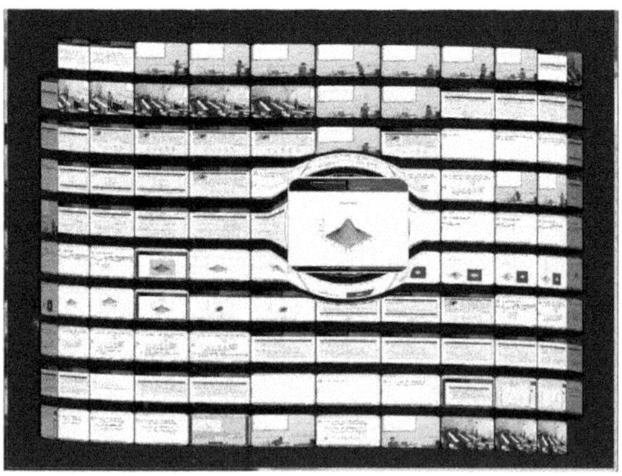

**Figure 2: Panopticon Interface (with viewing window, centre)**

Three questions accompanied each video which covered three styles of search for each lecture: visual search where the answer was present on the on-screen material, verbal search where the answer was delivered verbally but cued with on-screen material, and problem search where participants had to find the answer to a question posed by the lecturer. These three mechanisms were chosen to cover a range of possible behaviours that viewers may want to perform.

Study 1 looked at participants who had previously seen the video and were looking to answer the three questions posed by the researcher. Study 2 looked at participants who had not seen the video before but were looking to answer the same three questions. As such, Study 1 simulated revision students while Study 2 simulated independent learners.

### Study 1: Revision Students

A 3x2 independent design was used with the factors under investigation being the video player (Panopticon, YouTube) and lecture type (Talk, Slides, and Interactive).

#### *Participants*

24 participants from the local population (mean age: 25 years, SD: 7.3 years) were recruited to take part in the study. Participants were recruited in person by the researchers and no financial reward was given. They were required to have used a video hosting website (e.g. YouTube) at least once.

#### *Procedure*

Participants were randomly assigned to one lecture type and a video player. They were required to carry out the search tasks (i.e. the study) in isolation, but were allowed to watch the videos in a group.

Once participants had been briefed, and informed consent collected, they were shown one of the lecture videos (approximately 30 minutes in length) on a laptop screen. Participants were asked to be quiet and pay attention to the material as they would be quizzed on it later. The experimenter supervised participants throughout the duration of the video.

Once the video was finished, participants were individually introduced to their randomly-selected system. This process consisted of participants using a practice video ('Big Buck Bunny') to answer practice questions to familiarise themselves with the different functionalities of their system.

Following the practice, participants were given the first question both orally and on a tablet device and were asked to answer the question verbally. Once participants had correctly answered the initial question, they were asked another question. Once the second question had been answered, the third and final question was asked.

#### *Results*

A 2-way independent ANOVA was carried out on the data with system and lecture as the independent factors and time (seconds) as the dependent variable.

A main effect of system was found ($F(1,18)=4.408$, $p=.05$) where participants using Panopticon (38.03 seconds) were significantly faster than those using YouTube (51.17 seconds).

| | Interactive | Slides | Talk | **Total** |
|---|---|---|---|---|
| Panopticon | 16.87 (3.98) | 25.75 (5.31) | 71.47 (16.22) | **38.03 (8.50)** |
| YouTube | 39.50 (2.88) | 40.87 (8.94) | 73.13 (32.14) | **51.17 (14.65)** |
| **Total** | **28.19 (3.43)** | **33.31 (7.13)** | **72.30 (24.18)** | |

**Table 1: Means (and standard deviations) for completion times in seconds for revision students.**

A main effect of video was present (F(2,18)=19.707, p<.001) where the Talk lecture (72.30 seconds) took significantly longer to complete when compared to both the Interactive lecture (28.19 seconds; p<.001) and the Slide lecture (33.31 seconds; p<.001). No interaction effect was found.

### Study 2: Independent Learners

A 3x2 mixed design was used with the factors under investigation being the video player (Panopticon, YouTube) – independent – and lecture type (Talk, Slides, and Interactive) – repeated.

#### *Participants*

16 different participants from the local population (mean age: 24 years, SD: 4.9 years) were recruited to take part in the study. The same recruitment procedure and inclusion criterion was used as for the first study.

#### *Procedure*

A similar procedure to Study 1 was used. The main differences were that participants were evaluated on all three videos (order counterbalanced) and they did not watch the videos prior to commencing the main task.

#### *Results*

A 2-way mixed ANOVA was carried out on the data with system as the independent factor and lecture as the repeated factor and time (seconds) as the dependent variable.

| | Interactive | Slides | Talk | **Total** |
|---|---|---|---|---|
| Panopticon | 151.24 (106.28) | 194.51 (125.00) | 714.13 (393.74) | **353.29 (208.34)** |
| YouTube | 452.63 (67.34) | 439.48 (159.49) | 582.88 (245.90) | **491.66 (157.58)** |
| **Total** | **301.94 (86.81)** | **317 (142.25)** | **648.51 (319.82)** | |

**Table 2: Means (and standard deviations) for completion times in seconds for independent learners.**

A main effect of system was found (F(1,14)=5.124, p<.05) where participants using Panopticon (353.29 seconds) were significantly faster than those using YouTube (491.66 seconds).

A main effect of video was present (F(2,13)=7.608, p<.010) where the Talk lecture (648.51 seconds) took longer to complete when compared to both the Interactive lecture (301.94 seconds; p<.005) and the Slide lecture (317 seconds; p<.010). No interaction effect was found.

## DISCUSSION

The effectiveness of searching lecture videos using two video interfaces – Panopticon and YouTube was investigated. Searching was evaluated in two studies of distinct scenarios: revision students using a lecture video and independent learners using the lecture video to clarify topics. In accordance with previous studies, Panopticon was significantly more effective than YouTube for finding specific information in lecture videos for both scenarios. Additionally, the type of lecture video played a role in the ease of finding information. Participants searching the Talk lecture video fared the worst (slowest) in both scenarios, while no difference was found between highly interactive and slide-based lectures. These findings present some important implications for the design and editing of video lectures as well as for the tools that are available to users for online courses.

### Implications

The advantage that users of Panopticon had over YouTube users means that students could save a significant amount of time when using this interface for searching within lecture videos. While the advantage was observed for both revision students and independent learners, the latter are set to benefit the most from using Panopticon: they on average saved upwards of two minutes while revision students on average saved just over 13 seconds.

While Panopticon was effective for searching videos, the practicality of using the interface for watching the video in its entirety or to obtain its gist are up for debate. QuickTime Player, for example, is a good option for watching the videos from start to finish with its minimalistic interface and basic controls. Meanwhile, a short text summary of the video written by the lecturer would probably be preferable for gist comprehension rather than skimming through the video. In other words, we do not propose that Panopticon should be the sole video player for lecture videos, but rather that it should be an optional search tool for students.

With regards to designing video lectures, the study has shown that talk-only lectures – or lectures with minimal focus on visual aids – are not optimal for students in need of searching for information. Our Talk lecture did include slides in its original live form, but the main focus of the recording was the speaker. Therefore, it is recommended that videos destined for eLearning platforms heavily feature slides in the edited final video. Work by [4] found that the presence of a lecturer on screen during a video lecture improved the students' enjoyment of the video, but not the retention of the material. As such, they also recommend that slides feature heavily in lecture videos.

No time difference was found between the Slides video and the Interactive video, suggesting that the presence of a visual aid is more important than the type. This supports our other finding that a video with little focus on slides leads to longer search times. While it is not expected that this finding will influence the design of the live lectures themselves, it does mean that lecturers should focus the video recording on the visual aids to support independent learners and their own students for revision.

### Limitations & Future Work

There are a couple of limitations with this study that should be considered. Firstly, the subject matter covered in the videos was different for all three videos – marketing, statistics, and education. They were all chosen from the same institute – HEC Paris – to minimise the impact of confounds such as video quality (e.g. encoding) and participants' previous exposure to the videos. The questions for each video covered the same aspects – visual search, problem search, and oral search – but it is possible that participants may have been more familiar with one topic and that could have played a part in their performance. However, we believe that any effects of participants' previous knowledge would have been minimal given the questions were video-specific rather than subject-specific meaning they could not be answered based on subject knowledge alone.

This plays into the second limitation: participants in the revision condition had not attended the live lectures. An evaluation using these types of students would yield a more accurate result for revision students where they have more knowledge of the material and less knowledge of the editing of the video.

We note that errors were not measured directly in our design, but they were measured indirectly in that the overall time taken to complete the task took into consideration any mistakes made by participants – i.e. they could only move on once they had answered the question correctly. While we believe this measurement evaluates an important aspect of the search tools, we acknowledge that other measures should be considered for evaluating the usability of the systems, including error rates and qualitative measures.

As another future step, it may prove beneficial to refine the Panopticon application to allow more seamless multitasking. In its current state, Panopticon operates in a full screen window mode that easily allows users to take notes on paper, but may prove inconvenient for note-taking on the same machine.

In order to make it easier to find the desired section of the video, a feature could be implemented where keywords are displayed near or around a selected frame. The keywords should reflect the content or the spoken word of the selected scene. With this the user would be able to simply hover over the single frames to get an overview of its content. It might be even possible to see where a specific topic starts and ends.

## CONCLUSION

Panopticon was evaluated as an online eLearning support search tool for finding information within video lectures. We found that users of the interface could find information in lecture videos significantly faster than users of the YouTube player. We also found that participants took significantly longer finding information in the video that did not predominantly feature visual aids. We therefore recommend that recordings of lectures destined for eLearning platforms should principally focus on the slides rather than the lecturer to support both local students and independent learners.

## ACKNOWLEDGEMENTS

Part of this research was funded by the EPSRC Digital Economy theme Social Inclusion through the Digital Economy Research Hub (EP/G066019/1).

## REFERENCES

1. Belanger, Y. and Thornton, J. *Bioelectricity: a quantitative approach.* 2013.
2. Brotherton, J.A. and Abowd, G.D. Lessons Learned From eClass : Assessing Automated Capture and Access in the Classroom. *11*, 2 (2004), 121–155.
3. Copley, J. Audio and video podcasts of lectures for campus-based students: production and evaluation of student use. *Innovations in Education and Teaching International 44*, 4 (2007), 387–399.
4. Dey, E.L., Burn, H.E., and Gerdes, D. Bringing the Classroom to the Web: Effects of Using New Technologies to Capture and Deliver Lectures. *Research in Higher Education 50*, 4 (2009), 377–393.
5. Jackson, D., Nicholson, J., Stoeckigt, G., Wrobel, R., Thieme, A., and Olivier, P. Panopticon: A Parallel Video Overview System. *In Proc. of UIST 2013*, (2013), 123-130.
6. Machun, P.A., Trau, C., Zaid, N., Wang, M., and Ng, J. MOOCs: Is There an App for That? Expanding Mobilegogy through an Analysis of MOOCS and iTunes University. *In Proc. of WI-IAT 2012*, IEEE (2012), 321–325.
7. Pappano, L. The Year of the MOOC. *New York Times*, 2012, ED26.
8. Young, J.R. YouTube professors: Scholars as online video stars. *Chronicle of Higher Education 54*, 2008, 14–17.

# Searching for Analogical Ideas with Crowds

**Lixiu Yu, Aniket Kittur, Robert E. Kraut**
Carnegie Mellon University
5000 Forbes Avenue, Pittsburgh, PA 15213
{lixiuyu, nkittur, robert.kraut}@cs.cmu.edu

## ABSTRACT

Seeking solutions from one domain to solve problems in another is an effective process of innovation. This process of *analogy searching* is difficult for both humans and machines. In this paper, we present a novel approach for representing a problem in terms of its abstract structure, and then allowing people to use this structural representation to find analogies. We propose a crowdsourcing process that helps people navigate a large dataset to find analogies. Through two experiments, we show the benefits of using abstract structural representations to search for ideas that are analogous to a source problem, and that these analogies result in better solutions than alternative approaches. This work provides a useful method for finding analogies, and can streamline innovation for both novices and professional designers.

### Author Keywords

Analogy searching; schema; crowdsourcing; creativity

### ACM Classification Keywords

H.5.3. Group and Organization Interfaces

## INTRODUCTION

The emergence of large online idea repositories has the potential to radically improve design practice by increasing designers' access to ideas relevant to the problems they are trying to solve. There now exist an enormous selection of ideas that embody design patterns that could spark creative ideas. For example, InnoCentive (innocentive.com) contains more than 40,000 business, social, policy, scientific, and technical problems and solutions in various domains, hundreds of new product ideas are submitted to Quirky (quirky.com) every day by a pool of nearly 500,000 inventors, and OpenIDEO has collected hundreds of solutions for a variety of social problems since 2010 (openideo.com).


*CHI 2014*, April 26 - May 01 2014, Toronto, ON, Canada

http://dx.doi.org/10.1145/2556288.2557378

Online idea repositories could provide a treasure trove of useful solutions to problems that are analogous to the original idea but in different domains. For example, a method for extracting a lost cork from a wine bottle might be adapted to save a baby stuck in the birth canal [33]. Analogy can be a highly effective tool for increasing innovation in domains ranging from scientific discovery to creative problem-solving to product development. Scientific and technological breakthroughs are often the result of taking a solution from a source domain and transferring it to a target domain [14]. Numerous psychological studies have shown that analogy transfer improves creative problem-solving [17,18]. Similarly, both empirical observation and experimental studies in product development find a positive relationship between the extent of analogical transfer and the originality of the product concept [8]. However, being able to harness the power of these idea repositories depends on designers' ability to find, recognize, and use analogies.

Searching for analogous ideas across domains is challenging for a number of reasons. Ideas that are analogous may share the same deep relational structure but be very different in terms of surface attributes [16]. For example, Chrysippus in the second century B.C. made an important analogy that sound waves behaved like water waves, despite the many different surface features between the two [22]. Some far analogies may eschew physical similarities altogether, such as Luria's analogy between bacterial mutation and a slot machine [22]. Thus a key challenge in finding analogous ideas is the need to look for sets of structural relations between objects, rather than attributes of those objects [13]. For example, a love triangle is defined by the set of relations between three people rather than the characteristics of the individuals composing it [22]. Unfortunately, online idea databases are typically represented by object attributes (such as domain, material, manufacturing method, etc.), which may not be useful for and indeed might actually impede search based on relational structure.

Recognizing the similarity in relational structures between two entities remains a challenging computational problem. In order to find analogies in text computer scientists have developed a variety of natural language techniques including using words, parts of speech or other language-feature-based vector representations of objects in order to calculate similarity measures or associations between object pairs [see 30]. Such approaches are challenged when there is little textual similarity between analogs, as when the source and target domains are very different, and when those analogs are more complex than linguistic metaphors, involving multiple-relation mappings between two problems. Another approach to finding analogies has been to use the structural similarity of sentences or texts, such as using coupled clustering for detecting structural correspondence of text [3, 34]. However, these approaches typically require rich data sets with clear substructures, whereas most description of problems or ideas in existing online databases are short, sparse, and lack consistent structure. In addition, these approaches all rely upon on textual descriptions and fail when ideas are described in other modalities (for example, images or videos).

Finding analogies can be challenging for people as well. Memory retrieval is highly sensitive to surface similarity, favoring near, within-domain analogs that share object attributes over far, structurally similar analogs that share object relations [15, 16, 17, 24]. Analogical processing also incurs a heavy cognitive load, taxing working memory when even a few relations are required to be processed at once [19]. Thus searching through datasets with hundreds or thousands of ideas for structurally similar ones may be a daunting prospect.

In summary, the need to search for underlying structure rather than object attributes creates a major challenge for analogical search. Such relations are difficult for machines to find and recognize, and can even be challenging for people to retrieve unaided. In this paper, we propose and evaluate an approach for using crowds to find analogies by searching for a structural representation of a problem (i.e., a schema). We demonstrate that this procedure leads to people finding more deep structural analogies than having them search with other instructions, and that the ideas they find are more useful for solving the original problem and other related problems. Finally we discuss the implications of these results for systems aiming to increase innovation.

## EXPERIMENTS

Analogy-based search requires going beyond surface features to search for common underlying structure between problems. One approach that has been shown to promote the recognition of analogies is to induce schemas and use them as the basis for retrieval [6, 7, 13, 17, 21, 22, 28]. A schema refers to a structured mental representation consisting of entities and the relations between them. For example, a schema for a love triangle involves three entities each of whom loves and is loved by different entities. However, inducing schemas and recognizing when they are applicable is difficult even in carefully controlled laboratory conditions with small numbers of potential analogs to choose from [13,18]. Unlike cognitive science experiments where participants are given both a problem and a solution that are perfect matches to a target problem [15, 16, 17, 18, 29], we are interested in open-ended real world problems where participants must search for examples themselves, and where most matches are messy and incomplete.

To address this problem we propose taking advantage of recent developments in crowdsourcing. Web technologies now enable us to assemble hundreds of thousands of people across the globe to process large amounts of data [1,5]. Provided with the right structure, many individuals could search simultaneously, allowing the crowd to navigate large datasets. However, realizing this possibility will require the development of processes and structures enabling novice crowd workers to search for ideas based on analogical structure rather than surface features, and to do so in large, uncontrolled idea repositories where descriptions are sparse and inconsistent.

In the experiments below, we test the viability of using a crowd to search in a large, real-world dataset for ideas that are analogically similar to a given source problem. Specifically, we ask participants to find ideas that may be relevant to a source problem in the online idea repository of Quirky.com, which has thousands of community-submitted ideas. We examine whether giving people schemas (Experiment 1) increases their ability to find ideas analogous to the source problems, and whether the analogical ideas they find result in better solutions to the source problem and related problems than alternative methods (Experiment 2).

## EXPERIMENT 1: SEARCHING FOR ANALOGIES

Experiment 1 aimed to test whether providing the schema for a source problem increases the likelihood of finding analogically similar ideas in an idea repository, and whether using these ideas improves solution quality. By analogically similar, we mean ideas that share the same underlying abstract structure as the source problem but may have different surface features. For example, the top left row of Table 6 shows an idea (Ventu) that shares a similar underlying structure to the top right row (Jar problem): both aim to solve the problem of reaching hard-to-access parts of an object by making part of the object removable.

We conducted the experiment in the context of product innovation, specifically using an online idea repository from Quirky, a crowdsourced product development website in which people submit and vet product ideas, with Quirky manufacturing and selling the top ideas. Quirky's idea repository contains thousands of products and is publicly accessible. Product ideas are described with names, text, images and sometimes videos. These characteristics make the website particularly suitable as real-world dataset for people to look for analogs to solve given problems.

| Problem description |
|---|
| **Dough problem:** When you knead dough, the dough gets stuck in between your fingers. This makes it difficult to clean your hands, and you also lose a lot of the dough in the process. The problem is to get dough off your hands easily. |
| **Cat problem:** Cats often come in the house bringing in lots of junk like leaves, burr, even lint on their fur -- and it gets all over the house. People often have to use a cat brush to get this debris off the cat. This is unpleasant and time-consuming. The problem is how to get debris off cats easily. |
| **Bathroom problem:** Many people like to read in their bathroom. But when they sit down, stand up, or move, books or Kindles get dropped often. They either get dirty or damaged. |
| **Strap problem:** Purse straps or backpack straps keep slipping off your shoulder, especially when you walk or run. It is very annoying that you have to constantly push the straps on your shoulder or hold them with your hands. The problem is how to keep the straps on your shoulder. |
| **Cup problem:** Cups or glasses can easily fall and coffee, juice, wine, or water spills. This happens often on dinner tables, nightstands, and office desks. When the liquid spills, it can ruin important files, phones, and even laptops. The problem is to prevent cups or glasses falling and spilling. |

Table 1. Experiment 1: the problems used in the experiment

We created two sets of source problems (the five problems shown in Table 1) which we believed would have analogous ideas in Quirky's product repository. For example, one problem consisted of removing dough from someone's hands after kneading. Another instantiation of the same fundamental problem was removing debris from a cat's fur. Both these problems share the abstract problem schema of "detaching one object from another". We created three more problems that shared the problem schema of "keeping an unstable object in place" (see the Bathroom, Strap, and Cup problems in Table 1).

The experiment consisted of two phases: first, finding potential ideas in Quirky that might be useful for solving the source problem, and second, generating a solution to the source problem. Our experimental manipulation centered on the way in which people searched for ideas in Quirky: specifically, whether they used an abstract schema in their search process, or one of two other control conditions described in detail below.

### Participants

In all experiments, subjects were recruited by posting tasks to Amazon Mechanical Turk [25], a crowdsourcing marketplace. In total 183 workers participated in the experiment. Fifty-seven percent were women, and 96% were native English speakers. Their average age was 31, and the ages ranged from 18 to 70.

### Design and Procedure

After accepting the task, participants were randomly assigned to one of four conditions:

*1. Use Schemas.* Participants were given a source problem and a schema (referred to as a *pattern* for participants to avoid introducing unfamiliar terminology) for that problem. We operationalize a specific type of schema in this context of this paper as an idea schema, consisting of a *problem* an idea aims to solve (e.g., preventing something fragile from breaking) and a *mechanism* for doing so (e.g., using a flexible cord to secure it to a stable object). Importantly, the description of a problem and the mechanism of its solutions abstracts away surface details to focus on the underlying structure.

For example, some participants saw the Cup problem in Table 1 and its schema "keeping an unstable object in place". Schemas were selected from a sample generated by participants in a previous study [35] that were rated highly by multiple judges. Prior to this step, participants engaged in a short training phase in which they generated a schema for a sample problem and received feedback on what a good schema looked like.

We then asked participants to find a product idea from Quirky that would be useful for solving the problem and also fit the schema they were given. Specifically they were told: *"To solve the above problem, you can use the pattern to find similar problems which are already solved. For example, in what other situations do people need to hold an unstable object in place? Now please use this pattern to search problems which also share this pattern in the website shown below."*

After they found an analogous idea, they were asked to generate a solution for the problem. In this and all other conditions, participants were told that their solutions would be evaluated in terms of their *practicality* (the idea can be designed and produced easily), *usefulness* (the solution solves the problem effectively) and *novelty* (the idea hasn't been thought of by others).

*2. Use Features.* As discussed previously, retrieval of analogies is highly biased by surface features [16]. Furthermore, many ideas are represented in online idea repositories in terms of an object's features. We designed this control condition to test whether providing features as an intermediate representation would help participants to search for useful and relevant ideas. This also serves to control for the amount of information provided to participants in comparison to the *Use Schemas* condition.

Participants were given a source problem and a list of features relevant to the problem. These features were generated by a separate group of twenty participants who were asked to list features of the source problem. Features mentioned by more than half of the twenty participants were included in the list. For example, the common features for the Dough problem were "dough", "fingers", "sticky", and "difficult to clean".

We then asked participants to look for useful ideas using some of the features. Specifically they were told: *"To solve the above problem, you can use these features to find similar problems which are already solved. For example, what*

| A far analogy | A near analogy | A non-analogy |
|---|---|---|
|  |  | 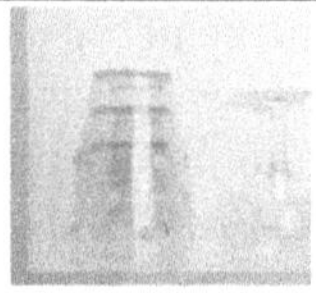 |
| Wing span: It is a bike rack that is capable of holding more cargo without the risk of having them topple over. It is very similar to how a scissor operates. These bars can be positioned in any orientation and locked in place to accommodate a wide variety of gear, large or small. | Tether: Washing your wine glasses can be risky business, especially when you are using your dishwasher. Save your stemware with Tether, a flexible plastic rod that stabilizes your stemware as it goes through the cycle. | Totem is a stackable cup for use in your bathroom or kitchen. Each cup has three bumps around the top circumference to keep them slightly separated when stacked so air can flow around the entire surface and dry them faster than normal stacked cups. |

Table 2. Experiment 1: Ideas found for the Cup problem.

*features are critical to solving this problem and might be shared by other problems? Now please use these features to search for problems which also share some of these features in the website shown below."* After they found an idea, they were told to generate a solution for the problem using the same procedure as in the *Use Schemas condition.*

3. *Find Inspiration.* While the Use Features condition attempted to control for the amount of information and processing participants would engage in during the search process, in real life people do not have a structured process for searching for examples. In this condition participants were simply asked to find an idea for inspiration but given no further constraints. Specifically they were told: "*To solve the above problem, you might be able to get inspiration from other ideas on the following website.*" After they found an idea, they were asked to generate a solution for the problem using the same procedure as the *Use Schemas condition.*

4. *Solve Problems.* We also created a baseline condition in which people were asked to solve the problems without any intermediate steps or pointer to the Quirky repository.

### Rating analogical similarity and solution quality

We were interested in evaluating two outcome variables: the analogical similarity of the ideas people found in Quirky, and the quality of their solutions to the source problems. To evaluate the ideas people found, two judges blind to the condition rated each product idea independently as to whether it was a valid analog to the source problem. One judge was the first author of this paper and the second judge was an undergraduate student. After the first round, the judges achieved inter-rater reliabilities of .75 as calculated by the Intraclass Correlation Coefficient (ICC) [10]. The judges then resolved any discrepancies by discussion.

We also examined the similarity of the analogies to the given problem, in order to judge whether an analog was a far or near analogy [11]. If an analogy shared surface similarities with the description of the problem, it was classified as a near analog. Otherwise, it was coded as a far analog. For example, for the Cup problem, if an analog had features such as "desk," "cup," or "glass," it was coded as a near analog. Two raters judged all the analogs independently. After the first round, the inter-rater reliability was .92 as measured by the ICC. Remaining discrepancies were resolved by discussion. Table 2 shows three examples of ideas found for the Cup problem.

We next rated the quality of the solutions, using criteria from prior research that argues that good creative ideas need to be both novel and practical [9]. We considered a product novel if it was not obvious and was different from existing products on the market[1]. We operationalized practicality in terms of *usefulness* to the user of the product and the *practicality* of manufacturing it today. For example, a teleportation device might be both novel and useful, but is infeasible to manufacture.

Two judges, who were blind to the experimental condition, rated each product idea on three 7-point Likert scales of novelty, usefulness, and practicality. One judge was the first author, and the second judge was an undergraduate student. For training, the judges independently rated a subset of 20 solutions and discussed these ratings to reach agreement on the dimensions. They then independently rated the full set of ideas. The judges achieved high interrater reliabilities of .86, .77 and .84 for usefulness, novelty, and practicality, as calculated by the ICC. They then discussed ratings with discrepancies of more than two points. The final quality of the ideas was computed as the geometric mean of the three dimensions in order to weight against ideas that were low on any given dimension [12].

### Results and Analysis

Sixteen participants whose answers failed to provide a solution to the problem were excluded from the analysis (7 from the *Find Inspiration* condition, 6 from *Use Features,* and 3 from *Use Schemas*). Table 3 shows percentages of examples participants found that were analogs to the problem, the percentage that were far analogs, and the means and standard deviations of the solutions' ratings they generated.

We first looked at the number of analogs found by experimental condition. We used logistic regression analysis to

[1] Raters judged novelty based on their experience rather than a market survey or patent because we wanted to assess an idea's relative novelty compared to products that most people would know about, rather than using the patent office's standard that the idea was unique in historical time [31, p.169].

| Condition | Percentage with analogs | SD | Percentage with far analogs | SD | Mean Quality | SD | Freq. |
|---|---|---|---|---|---|---|---|
| 1. Use schemas | .74 | .44 | .86 | .35 | 4.00 | 1.72 | 47 |
| 2. Use features | .48 | .50 | .30 | .46 | 3.78 | 1.56 | 52 |
| 3. Find inspiration | .44 | .50 | .29 | .47 | 3.69 | 1.50 | 34 |
| 4. Solve problems | NA | NA | NA | NA | 2.96 | 1.63 | 34 |
| Total | .56 | .49 | .48 | .43 | 3.66 | 1.63 | 167 |

Table 3. Experiment 1: the percentage of analogies, the percentage of far analogies among the analogies, and the quality of the solutions in all conditions

compare the *Use Schemas*, *Use Features* and *Find Inspiration* conditions to predict whether or not participants found an analog for the problem. We controlled for participants' education level and time spent on the task. In addition, we also included the problem used in the experiment as a random variable. We found that the number of valid analogs found in the *Use Schemas* condition was significantly higher than in the *Use Features* condition ($b = 1.22$, $z = 2.65$, $p < .01$) and the *Find Inspiration* condition ($b = 1.78$, $z = 3.17$, $p < .01$). The difference between the *Use Features* and *Find Inspiration* conditions was not significant ($b = .49$, $z = .95$, $p = .34$).

These results indicate that people are more likely to return product ideas analogous to a problem they were trying to solve when given the problem schema than when given features describing the problem or simply looking for inspiring examples. We next looked at whether using schemas led people to find more ideas that were far analogs (i.e., in other domains and not sharing surface features with the source problem). Participants found more far analogs as a percentage of all analogs in the *Use Schemas* condition compared to the *Use Features* condition ($b = 3.53$, $z = 3.73$, $p < .001$) and the *Find Inspiration* condition ($b = 4.20$, $z = 3.45$, $p < .001$). Again, no significant difference was found between the *Use Features* and *Find Inspiration* conditions ($b = 1.16$, $z = 1.00$, $p = .32$). Together these results provide evidence that people are more likely to find valid analogical matches using schemas, and furthermore are more likely to find far analogies in different domains that do not share surface features with the problem.

We next examined the quality of the solutions to find out whether people generated better solutions after finding product ideas using schemas. We first compared all the conditions to the baseline *Solve Problems* condition, in which participants were asked to solve the problem but given no further instructions. The results showed that the solutions generated in the *Find Inspiration*, *Use Features*, and *Use Schemas* conditions were all of higher quality than ones from the *Solve Problems* condition ($b_{Use\ Schemas} = 1.23$, $t(80) = 3.46$, $p < .001$; $b_{Use\ Features} = 1.03$, $t(85) = 2.93$, $p < .01$; $b_{Find\ Inspiration} = .79$, $t(67) = 2.21$, $p < .05$; all tests corrected for multiple comparisons). This confirms previous research showing that finding useful ideas can help people solve problems better than trying to solve them alone. However, contrary to our initial hypothesis, the *Find Inspiration*, *Use Features*, and *Use Schemas* conditions did not differ from each other.

**Understanding the Searching Process**

In order to understand the process by which schema-based analogy searching was more effective than feature- or inspiration-based searching, we invited seven participants across conditions (two for feature-based searching, two for inspiration-based searching, and three for schema-based searching) into a laboratory study, asking them to think aloud during their search process.

We found that people used similar search processes in both the *Find Inspiration* and *Use Features* conditions. They often used the search bar of the website to look for terms related to the specific objects of the problems. For example, for the Dough problem, they searched for "dough", "fingers", etc. When they were not using the search bar, they went to the relevant product category, such as "kitchen," to look for useful ideas. For example, one participant clicked the kitchen category and said, "*I am looking for products related to dough or flour or finger cleaning, and they should be in this category.*" These observations are consistent with the theories in prior literature. The literature indicates that retrieval of analogs by people is extremely sensitive to the degree of semantic overlap between the source analog that provides retrieval cues and the target analog to be found in memory [32]. This leads to a higher chance that people will find non-analogs or analogs that share surface similarity.

By contrast, when people were looking for useful ideas using schemas, they seldom used the search bar of the website. They browsed product ideas by quickly examining their images and names, and tried to find the ones fitting the schema for the given problem. For example, one participant was instructed to solve the Cup problem, and he looked through many products and then said "*that is not about stabilization...I guess I need to think deeper about each of these ideas to see if there is actually any related.*" As he continued to browse product ideas, he said, "*I am looking for products holding something in place. Yeah, this seems like... it is trying to hold things together, stabilize it...so I am not sure it will work with the cup but it does hold it in place which fits the pattern in general.*" These observations provide some process level suggestions about how using schemas led people to pay less attention to the domains and surface features. Instead, they focused on the structural aspects of the given problem, leading them to find more far analogs.

## EXPERIMENT 2: SOLVE PROBLEMS WITH ANALOGS

The results from Experiment 1 suggested that people are more likely to find analogs and especially far analogs for source problems with the help of problems' schemas. However, the analogs did not seem helpful in solving the problems better than ideas found using features or for inspiration. In further investigation we identified several potential reasons for this.

First, in Experiment 1 participants only searched for a single product idea. However, previous research has shown that having multiple examples is highly beneficial to schema induction and creative problem solving [18]. Furthermore, because we were providing participants with only a problem schema, the search space was relatively unconstrained. That is, there can be many potential ideas with an analogous problem to the source problem in the Quirky dataset that do not provide a good solution to the source problem. For example, an idea for scraping ice off a car windshield presents an analogous problem to the Dough problem: they both aim to detach one object from another object. However, the Dough problem has different constraints: hands are more delicate than windshields, and might not be well served by using the blades involved in scraping ice. Presenting multiple ideas to a participant may increase the chance of finding one or more useful solutions for the source problem.

Second, we noticed in Experiment 1 that there were often no clear connections between the ideas people found in Quirky and the solutions they proposed. One explanation for this, as identified in prior literature, is that spontaneously noticing and transferring analogies is difficult [17]. We thus reminded participants to utilize the given product ideas in Experiment 2, and encouraged them to do so by having them explicitly cite any ideas they used in their solution.

Third, even though we asked participants to generate their own solutions, they may have copied existing products they had used or seen. This may also account for the disconnect between the ideas participants found and their proposed solutions. To address this we asked people to generate multiple solutions for a given problem, under the assumption that even if they had seen one instance of an existing matching product they would still have to generate more. This also enables us to test whether people could generate more good solutions using product ideas found with schemas, providing a more sensitive measure than a single binary outcome.

We focused on the Dough and Cup problems, and selected three samples of the product ideas found by the participants from different conditions in Experiment 1 (samples of six product ideas for the Dough problem and samples of five product ideas for the Cup problem). These samples had different characteristics. The samples of schema-based ideas ended up with having 85% analogs. By contrast, 85% of the sampled ideas found with features or inspiration were not analogs and shared surface features with the source problems.

In addition to testing the usefulness of the ideas in solving the source problems, we were also interested in their usefulness in solving new analogical problems to the source problems. The schema-based ideas might have higher transferability because most of them were analogies and didn't share surface features with the Dough and Cup problems. Consequently they might be equally helpful in solving new problems analogous to the Dough and Cup problems. In contrast, the usefulness of the product ideas found with features or through inspiration might be more limited. These ideas might be more useful for the Dough and Cup domains than for new domains with similar problems. To test this we created an analogous problem for each of the Dough and Cup problems: the Jar and the Airplane problem, which we called far-transfer problems, shown in Table 4.

Experiment 2 was also designed with another purpose. One of our goals is to build a crowd analogy searching process: when people have problems, being able to assemble a crowd to search for analogs for these problems and in turn use these analogs to solve their problems. Thus we wanted to test whether one set of people could find analogs, and another set use those analogs to solve problems.

### Participants

In total 228 workers participated in the experiment. Fifty-one percent of participants were women, and 95% were native English speakers. Their average age was 31, and the ages ranged from 19 to 59.

### Design and procedure

After accepting the task participants were randomly assigned to one of three conditions. In all conditions participants were given a sample of ideas (six ideas for the Dough and Jar problems, and five ideas for the Cup and Airplane problems) collected from Experiment 1 and asked to generate multiple solutions to a source problem as well as an

| **Problems description (far-transfer problems)** |
|---|
| **Airplane problem:** Baggage placed in the overhead storage of airplanes or other traveling vehicles is sometimes shuffled during the traveling. It is very dangerous if they suddenly fall out of storage when people open the door of the overhead storage. The problem is to prevent baggage falling and hurting people. |
| **Jar problem:** It bothers people when they try to scrape the last bits of peanut butter, honey, jam, etc. from a jar. These leftovers hide in various hard-to-reach corners. People often lose their patience and a lot of peanut butter, honey or jam is wasted. The problem is to extract jarred food product easily even if there is relatively little left. |

Table 4. Experiment 2: The far-transfer problems used in the experiment: the Airplane problem was analogous to the Cup problem, and the Jar problem was analogous to the Dough problem.

analogous far-transfer problem. The only difference between conditions was the source of the set of ideas provided: whether they were collected using schemas, features, or for inspiration (resulting in *Schema-based ideas*, *Feature-based ideas*, and *Inspiration-based ideas* conditions, respectively). Checkboxes for each idea were provided to encourage participants to use and attribute the given ideas in their solutions. Specific instructions for each problem read: "*Below are some selected product ideas that may help you come up with solutions.*" After reading the ideas, they were told: "*Please generate three different solutions for solving the problem. For each solution, please check any ideas that influenced or inspired it from the examples given above.*"

### Rating

Solutions scores were calculated the same way as in Experiment 1, using two judges blind to the condition. After the first round, the judges achieved inter-rater reliabilities, .76, .74, and .57 for usefulness, novelty and practicality respectively, calculated as the ICC. They then discussed any ratings with discrepancies of more than two points. Their averaged resulting ratings were used for the analysis.

### Results and analysis

Thirty-seven participants' answers were excluded from the analysis (12 from *Schema-based ideas* condition, 17 from *Feature-based ideas* condition and 8 from *Inspiration-based ideas* condition) because no solutions to the given problems were provided. The means and standard deviations of the remaining ideas are shown in Table 5.

We first examined whether ideas found based on schemas inspired better solutions to the source problem than ideas found in the other conditions. We conducted a regression analysis predicting solution quality based on conditions, with education and time spent on task as control variables, and source problem as a random variable. Results indicated that the *Schema-based ideas* condition resulted in significantly higher-rated solutions than both the *Feature-based ideas* condition ($b = .80$, $t(198) = 6.23$, $p < .001$) and *Inspiration-based ideas* condition ($b = .91$, $t(200) = 6.72$, $p < .001$) and no significant difference was found between the *Feature-based ideas* and *Inspiration-based ideas* conditions ($b = .06$, $t(183) = .40$, $p = .69$).

| Condition | Mean | SD | Freq. |
|---|---|---|---|
| 1. Use schema-based ideas | 3.40 | 1.48 | 207 |
| 3.1 Source problems | 3.40 | 1.46 | 108 |
| 3.2 Far-transfer problems | 3.41 | 1.51 | 99 |
| 2. Use feature-based ideas | 2.54 | 1.28 | 174 |
| 2.1 Source problems | 2.31 | 1.16 | 91 |
| 2.2 Far-transfer problems | 2.78 | 1.38 | 83 |
| 3. Use inspiration-based ideas | 2.51 | 1.25 | 180 |
| 3.1 Source problems | 2.28 | 1.04 | 93 |
| 3.2 Far-transfer problems | 2.76 | 1.40 | 87 |
| Total | 2.85 | 1.41 | 561 |

Freq. is the number of ideas.

Table 5. Experiment 2: effects of base-ideas on the quality of solutions

We next examined the usefulness of the found ideas in solving the analogous far-transfer problems, which shared similar structure to the source problems but were in different domains (e.g., bags falling in an airplane vs. cups falling off a table). Here we found the same basic pattern as for the source problems: the *Schema-based ideas* condition generated significantly better solutions than the *Feature-based ideas* condition ($b = .63$, $t(181) = 2.93$, $p < .01$) and the *Inspiration-based ideas* condition ($b = .65$, $t(185) = 3.06$, $p < .01$). Again, there was no significant difference between the *Feature-based ideas* and *Inspiration-based ideas* conditions ($b = .02$, $t(169) = .09$, $p = .92$).

These main effects for far-transfer problems mirror those for the source problems. However, there was a significant interaction between condition and problem type (source problem vs. far-transfer problem). As shown in Figure 1, while the *Schema-based ideas* condition did equally well on source and far-transfer problems, the two control conditions (*Feature-* and *Inspiration-based ideas*) actually did better on the far-transfer problems than the source problem ($b_{\text{Feature-based ideas}} = .44$, $t(173) = 2.12$, $p < .05$; $b_{\text{Inspiration-based ideas}} = .49$, $t(179) = 2.42$, $p < .05$).

On the surface, this is a particularly counterintuitive finding. Why would the *Feature-* and *Inspiration-based* conditions do worse solving the problem for which the ideas were specifically targeted than a structurally similar problem in a different domain? One possible explanation is that the match in surface similarity between the found ideas and source problem might overly fixate participants on those ideas that are in the same domain but do not have useful structural similarities. Switching to a different domain would release participants from the fixation and enable them to make better use of the structurally similar analogs in the found ideas.

This explanation suggests that a critical factor in solution success is whether the idea that influences a solution is one that shares surface similarity or structural similarity to the

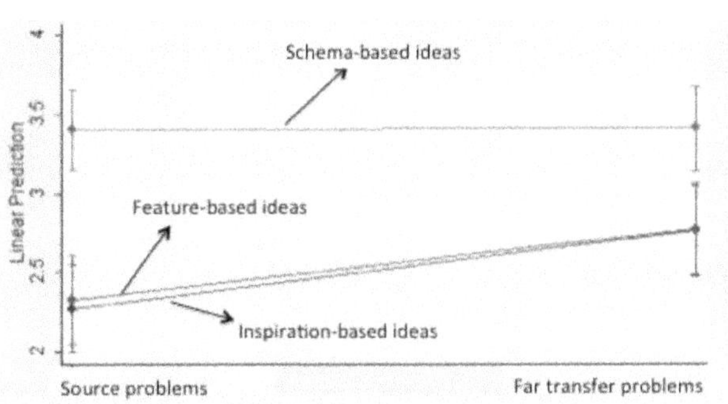


Figure 1. Predictive margins of the interaction between the type of problems and the base-ideas with 95% CIs.

problem being solved. For example, Table 6 shows two ideas that were marked as influencing solutions and their respective solutions. In this case the analogical idea – which shared structural similarity to the Jar problem – resulted in a highly rated solution, while the non-analogy – which shared surface similarity to the Cup problem – resulted in a poorly rated solution. To test this hypothesis explicitly we ran a mediation analysis examining whether the type of idea participants marked as influencing their solution (i.e., analog vs. non-analog, where non-analogs typically shared surface similarity with the problem but not structural similarity) accounted for the quality of the solution.

Specifically, utilizing the method of Baron and Kenny [2], the mediator function was examined with regression equations. The quality (the outcome variable) was regressed on the type of problems (the predictor variable), and was found to be significant ($b$ = .48, $p$ < .01). The relationship between the type of problems (the predictor) and the types of inspiring ideas (the mediator variable) was also significant ($b$ = 1.24, $p$ < .001); as was between the type of problems and the quality, ($b$ = .37, p < .01). Multiple regression of quality (the outcome variable) on both the types of the inspiring ideas (the predictor) and the type of problems (the mediator) resulted in the effect from the type of problems (the predictor variable) becoming non-significant ($b$ = .28, $p$ = .18). We found the same results for the *Feature-based ideas* condition. The quality was regressed on the types of problems, and was found to be significant ($b$ = .47, $p$ < .01). The relationship between the type of problems and the types of inspiring ideas was also significant ($b$ = 1.71, $p$ < .001); as was between the type of problems and the quality ($b$ = .98, $p$ < .001). Multiple regression of the quality on both the predictor and the mediator resulted in the effect from the types of the type of problems becoming non-significant ($b$ = .33, $p$ = .09). These results suggest that the type of idea that influenced a participants' solution completely mediated the causal relationship between the type of problem (source vs. far-transfer) and solution quality.

In other words, solution quality was higher when an idea was influenced by an analog that shared structural but not surface similarity. For far-transfer problems in which there was little or no surface similarity with the found ideas, participants could focus on structurally similar analogs. When ideas with high surface similarity to the source problem existed, these ideas may have prevented people from noticing and using analogies. For example, a product idea about designing a rolling pin containing flour was found by people in both *Feature-* and *Inspiration-based ideas* conditions. Many people in Experiment 2 generated solutions based on this product idea, and these solutions were different variations of the rolling pin idea. None of these ideas solved the Dough problem.

However, even though far-transfer problems in the *Feature-* and *Inspiration-based ideas* conditions benefited more from the analogical ideas, their solutions were still not as good as the ones inspired by schema-based ideas. This suggests that providing additional structurally similar analogs (as was the case in the *Schema-based ideas* condition) is particularly advantageous, perhaps providing people with additional useful potential solutions for transfer.

Another important implication of Experiment 2 is that the analogs found in Experiment 1 were found helpful, even though Experiment 2 involved a different set of participants. This suggests that the process of searching for analogies can be effectively decomposed and distributed to crowds.

## CONCLUSION AND DISCUSSION

In this paper we investigated the feasibility of searching for analogical ideas with the crowd in a live dataset of thousands of ideas at Quirky.com. We proposed a novel approach for improving analogical search by using the abstract schema of the source problem, and demonstrated the effectiveness of our approach through two experiments. Experiment 1 showed that using schemas could assist in finding more analogies, and, in particular, finding more far analogies that did not share surface features with the source problem. Experiment 2 showed that analogical ideas found by previous participants could be used by participants to generate better solutions for the source problems, and were also useful for solving structurally similar problems in oth-

| | Inspiring ideas | | Solutions |
|---|---|---|---|
| Analogy |  | Ventu: Prep, strain, serve, and store, all in one elegant solution. That's Ventu, a serving bowl that also allows you to strain excess moisture from fruit, salads, pasta, and more. Just remove the base to easily switch between straining and serving functions, and save yourself from washing more dirty dishes | The Jar problem: The Ventu inspired this idea by having the twist-off bottom to serve different purposes. It is hard to reach the bottom of a container with a spoon, knife, or other utensil. However, if the bottom would come off, it would make the hard to reach parts more easily accessible. |
| Non-analogy |  | Totem is a stackable cup for use in your bathroom or kitchen. Each cup has three bumps around the top circumference to keep them slightly separated when stacked so air can flow around the entire surface and dry them faster than normal stacked cups. | The Cup problem: Pour a little bit of liquid in each of the totem glasses and stack them on top of each other. Due to the heaviness of the totem glass, the glasses will not fall and water/juice might not spill |

Table 6. Experiment 2: two inspiring ideas and the inspired solutions. The first solution was scored 6.50, and the second solution was scored 1.27.

er domains.

These findings extend previous literature in analogical reasoning by scaling from small-scale laboratory studies using contrived analogical problems to explore how analogies might be identified from large, real-world datasets and used to solve problems [17, 18]. They also have important practical implications for search. While semantic web and other technologies (e.g., faceted search) aim to improve search by generating higher-level classes, developing a process for generating abstractions that accurately captures the essential structure of a product idea has been a significant challenge. While there have been some approaches to doing so (e.g., patent search tools) such tools have still had trouble identifying generalizable patterns and schemas, instead focusing on either inferences over surface features or a limited mechanism vocabulary that can be difficult to apply to a wide arrange of products [20, 26]. In this paper, we demonstrate a promising approach showing that even novice crowd workers can find deep analogies given an appropriate process.

### Limitations and Future Work

One limitation of the present study is that in all experiments, we showed people good schemas, which described the relational structures appropriately. This raises the question: how can we enable crowds to come up with good schemas by themselves? A schema should abstract away surface details to focus on the underlying structure. The particular process by which humans do so remains an open research question [13, 23]. Thus while defining the right level of schema is indeed challenging and surface features in some contexts can be structural features in others [5], our key finding is that participants were able to generate what they considered more abstract, structural features and those features resulted in better solutions than the originating representation. Formalizing the abstraction process is a profitable area for follow-up work.

In the experiments, participants were asked to search analogies in a website containing thousands of product ideas. However, in scaling up to repositories with millions of products (e.g., patents) or sparser analogs, browsing may not be sufficient. Instead, some kind of search component may be needed. In a follow up during the laboratory experiment, we asked people in the schema condition to explicitly use the search bar to see how compatible the schema-based approach would be with search. We found that participants searched for the complete schema or the keywords of the schema and their synonyms. Because most product ideas are not described in terms of their relational structures on the website we provided, they could not easily find the ideas they wanted by searching for such terms. Thus augmenting products or search processes with relational structures may be a profitable avenue for further research.

What domains benefit from this approach? Currently, we tested this approach in the field of consumer product design. Ideas were shown in images and simple descriptions. It is an open question whether the crowd can also generate and apply schemas in other domains involving more complex problems.

### Towards a Future of Crowd-powered Analogy Searching

Our research provides a first step towards a future of crowd searching of analogies that is more efficient and effective than existing approaches. Today, most crowd inventors have little knowledge of, and few strategies for, seeking existing solutions to help with their own problems. With the growing number of publicly available idea repositories, it will be increasingly important and valuable to make connections between ideas and problems. Rather than relying on intuitions or surface features to find useful and relevant ideas, we suggest that problem schemas could be the future glue that ties multiple problems or multiple idea repositories together and makes them useful to each other. Such schema-based searching could help connect people who have specific problems with those who may have relevant solutions in other domains. Although much more research is needed on how to distribute the searching to the crowd and how to structure them in search within or across idea repositories to make such a future possible, the present research provides one step towards harnessing the crowd to find analogies. We envision a future crowd-powered analogy searching system to aid problem-solving which can benefit both novices and professional designers.

## ACKNOWLEDGMENTS

This work was supported by NSF grants IIS-1149797, IIS-1217559, OCI-0943148, IIS-0968484, IIS-1111124, Bosch, Google, and Microsoft, and Carnegie Mellon's Center for the Future of Work.

## REFERENCES

1. Von Ahn, L. and Dabbish, L. Labeling images with a computer game. *In Proc. CHI2004*, 319–326.
2. Baron, R.M. and Kenny, D.A. The moderator–mediator variable distinction in social psychological research: Conceptual, strategic, and statistical considerations. *Journal of personality and social psychology 51*, 6 (1986), 1173.
3. Bollegala, D.T., Matsuo, Y., and Ishizuka, M. Measuring the similarity between implicit semantic relations from the web. In *Procs of the 18th international conference on World wide web*, (2009), 651–660.
4. Chi, M.T., Feltovich, P.J., and Glaser, R. Categorization and representation of physics problems by experts and novices. *Cognitive science* 5, 2 (1981), 121–152.
5. Chilton, L., Little, G., Edge, D., Weld, D.S., and Landay, J.A. Cascade: Crowdsourcing Taxonomy Creation. In *Proc. CHI* 2013.
6. Clement, C.A. Effect of structural embedding on analogical transfer: Manifest versus latent analogs. *The American journal of psychology, (1994), 1–38.*
7. Clement, C.A., Mawby, R., and Giles, D.E. The effects of manifest relational similarity on analog retrieval.

*Journal of Memory and Language* 33, 3 (1994), 396–420.

8. Dahl, D.W. and Moreau, P. The influence and value of analogical thinking during new product ideation. *Journal of Marketing Research*, (2002), 47–60.
9. Finke, R.A., Ward, T.B., and Smith, S.M. Creative cognition: Theory, research, and applications. MIT press Cambridge, MA, 1992.
10. Fisher, R., *Statistical methods for research workers.* Oliver and Boyd, 1954.
11. Fu, K., Chan, J., Cagan, J., Kotovsky, K., Schunn, C., and Wood, K. The Meaning of "Near" and "Far": The Impact of Structuring Design Databases and the Effect of Distance of Analogy on Design Output. *Journal of Mechanical Design 135*, (2013), 021007.
12. Galton, F. The geometric mean, in vital and social statistics. In *Proc RSL 29*, (1879), 365–367.
13. Gentner, D. Structure-mapping: A theoretical framework for analogy. *Cognitive Science* 7, (1983), 155–170.
14. Gentner, D., S. Brem, R. Ferguson, P. Wolff, A. B. Markaman, K. and Forbus. *Analogy and creativity in the works of Johannes Kepler.* T. N. Ward, S. M. Smith, J. Vaid, eds. Creative Thought. Amer. Psych. Association, Washington, DC, (1997). 403–460.
15. Gentner, D. and Landers, R. Analogical reminding: A good match is hard to find. *Proceedings of the international conference on systems, man and cybernetics*, (1985), 607–613.
16. Gentner, D., Rattermann, M.J., and Forbus, K.D. The roles of similarity in transfer: Separating retrievability from inferential soundness. *Cognitive psychology 25*, 4 (1993), 524–575.
17. Gick, M.L. and Holyoak, K.J. Analogical problem solving. *Cognitive psychology* 12, 3 (1980), 306–355.
18. Gick, M.L. and Holyoak, K.J. Schema induction and analogical transfer. Cognitive psychology 15, (1983), 1–38.
19. Halford, G. S., Baker, R., McCredden, J. E and Bain, J. D. How many variables can humans process? *Psychological Science* 16(1), 2005, 70-76.
20. Hirtz, J., Stone, R.B., McAdams, D.A., Szykman, S., and Wood, K.L. A functional basis for engineering design: reconciling and evolving previous efforts. Research in engineering Design 13, 2 (2002), 65–82.
21. Holyoak, K.J. and Koh, K. Surface and structural similarity in analogical transfer. Memory & Cognition 15, 4 (1987), 332–340.
22. Holyoak, K. J., & Thagard, P. *Mental leaps: Analogy in creative thought.* Cambridge, MA: MIT Press, 1995.
23. Hummel, J.E. and Holyoak, K.J. Distributed representations of structure: A theory of analogical access and mapping. Psychological Review 104, 3 (1997), 427.
24. Keane, M. On retrieving analogues when solving problems. *The Quarterly Journal of Experimental Psychology* 39(1), 1987, 29-41.
25. Kittur, A., Chi, E.H., and Suh, B. Crowdsourcing user studies with Mechanical Turk. *Proceedings of the SIGCHI conference on human factors in computing systems*, (2008), 453–456.
26. Kumar, R., Satyanarayan, A., Torres, C., Lim, M., Ahmad, Klemmer, S.R., and Talton, J. O., Webzeitgeist: Design mining the web. *CHI'13.*
27. Lakhani, K.R. and Panetta, J.A. The principles of distributed innovation. *Innovations* 2, 3 (2007), 97–112.
28. Linsey, J., Laux, J., Clauss, E., Wood, K.L., and Markman, A. Increasing innovation: A trilogy of experiments towards a design-by-analogy method. Proceedings of the ASME 2007 International Design Engineering Technical Conferences & Computers and Information in Engineering Conference, (2007).
29. Linsey, J., Wood, K.L., and Markman, A.B. Increasing innovation: presentation and evaluation of the wordtree design-by-analogy method. Proceedings of the ASME IDETC Design Theory and Methodology Conference, (2008).
30. Shutova, E. Models of metaphor in NLP. Proceedings of the 48th annual meeting of the association for computational linguistics, (2010), 688–697.
31. Sternberg, R.J. Handbook of creativity. Cambridge University Press, 1998.
32. Thagard, P., Holyoak, K.J., Nelson, G., and Gochfeld, D. Analog retrieval by constraint satisfaction. *Artificial* Intelligence 46, 3 (1990), 259–310.
33. The New York Times, http://www.nytimes.com/2013/11/14/health/new-tool-to-ease-difficult-births-a-plastic bag.html
34. Turney, P.D. Similarity of semantic relations. *Computational Linguistics* 32, 3 (2006), 379–416.
35. Yu, L., Kittur, A., and Kraut, R. Distributed analogical idea generation: inventing with crowds. In *Proc. CHI 2014.*
36. Yu, L. and Nickerson, J.V. Cooks or cobblers? Crowd creativity through combination. In *Proc. CHI 2011*, 1393–1402.

# skWiki: A Multimedia Sketching System for Collaborative Creativity

Zhenpeng Zhao,[1] Sriram Karthik Badam,[1] Senthil Chandrasegaran,[2] Deok Gun Park,[1]
Niklas Elmqvist,[1] Lorraine Kisselburgh,[3] and Karthik Ramani[1,2]
[1]School of Electrical & Computer Engineering, [2]School of Mechanical Engineering, and [3]Brian Lamb School of Communication
Purdue University, West Lafayette, IN 47907, USA
{zhaoz, sbadam, senthil, park573, elm, lorraine, ramani}@purdue.edu

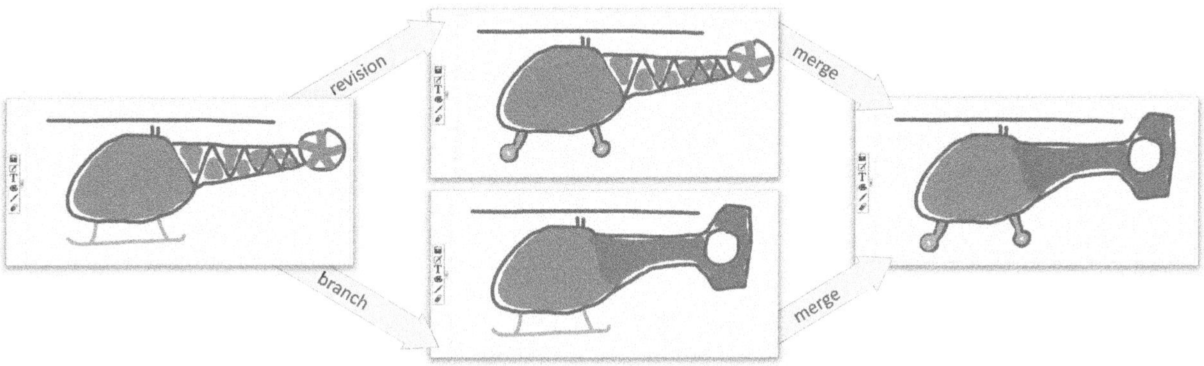


**Figure 1. Two parallel paths of concept sketches of a toy helicopter in skWiki. skWiki supports multiple co-existing revision histories for the same multimedia object. This is possible using *paths*, which track state changes over time and users so that the complete operation history is preserved.**

## ABSTRACT
We present skWiki, a web application framework for collaborative creativity in digital multimedia projects, including text, hand-drawn sketches, and photographs. skWiki overcomes common drawbacks of existing wiki software by providing a rich viewer/editor architecture for all media types that is integrated into the web browser itself, thus avoiding dependence on client-side editors. Instead of files, skWiki uses the concept of paths as trajectories of persistent state over time. This model has intrinsic support for collaborative editing, including cloning, branching, and merging paths edited by multiple contributors. We demonstrate skWiki's utility using a qualitative, sketching-based user study.

## ACM Classification Keywords
H.5.3 Information Interfaces and Presentation: Group and Organization Interfaces—*Web-based interaction*

## Author Keywords
Collaborative editing; creativity; wikis; sketching.


*CHI'14*, April 26–May 1, 2014, Toronto, Canada.

http://dx.doi.org/10.1145/2556288.2557394

## INTRODUCTION
While more of a design philosophy than a technology in its own right, the Web 2.0 revolution has turned the traditional content creation model on its head. Instead of a few highly institutionalized creators distributing content to a mass audience, these new technologies are empowering users themselves to become creators, distributors, and marketers of digital content in vast collaborative enterprises on the Internet.

So far, computer support for such large-scale distributed collaboration has mostly centered on *convergent processes*: processes where the outcome is a single artifact, concept, or idea; where the role of the computer is to mediate communication, arbitrate conflicts, and consolidate information. However, intellectual pursuits are often a combination of *convergent* (or analytical) processes and *divergent* (or creative) processes [22]. For example, during early design for a new line of toys, the goal is to generate as many and as diverse ideas as possible rather than to prematurely fixate on a particular one. Most computer-supported collaboration tools, be they for socially constructed knowledge bases such as Wikipedia, collaborative text editors such as Google Docs, or product lifecycle management (PLM) systems such as Enovia, are designed for analytical and convergent processes, but have little provisions for divergent ones.

Inspired by source code management (SCM) systems [24] such as Git or SVN, where *branching*—creating a divergent version of a project, directory, or a single file—is a natural operation in any project, we adopt the concept of *paths* as persistent state over time owned by a particular user. A document or file represented as a path is thus stored as the ordered (and timestamped) sequence of document-specific operations that created and modified it. For example, a digital photograph is the sum of all its changes, such as importing pixels from a digital camera, adding a Gaussian blur filter, and finally changing the image data to grayscale. Furthermore, because paths also track ownership, the concept intrinsically supports divergent collaborative editing: modifying someone else's entity simply branches its path and creates a new list of changes since the original state. Convergent processes are also supported: merging two paths means accepting all or some of the changes into the merged path.

To validate the path concept, we present SKWIKI (pronounced Squeaky), a web-based collaborative content editing framework that implements the path model for divergent creative digital media processes. skWiki supports multiple multimedia path types beyond the marked-up text traditionally supported by Wiki software. Each such multimedia type, implemented as a plugin in the skWiki framework, comes with separate viewers and editors. *Viewers* are used to render the content that users see in their web browser when visiting a skWiki page. *Editors*, on the other hand, provide basic editing operations for each entity type inside the browser itself. This eliminates the dependency on offline client-side media editors—e.g., Photoshop, Visio, and CorelDRAW—and provides a unified editor interface inside the user's own web browser. Our skWiki prototype currently supports rich text, free-hand sketches, and photographs.

Beyond these viewers and editors, one of the main components of skWiki is the *path viewer*: a visual management interface for viewing and navigating in the evolving graph structure formed by the media paths in the system. The path viewer visually represents how these paths are created, modified, deleted (although deletion is not persistent in the path model), branched, and merged. Most of these path operations are transparent from the user's point of view. For example, the path viewer allows a user to view and edit a path—their own or someone else's—at any time, thereby creating a new branch from that point. Similarly, changes to a media entity are automatically saved and committed to the skWiki system. Because of this automatic support for both collaboration and revision control, we posit that skWiki can be adopted by virtually any audience involved in digital content creation, including both product, industrial or web designers as well as engineers, researchers, and creative artists.

## RELATED WORK

In today's highly networked and increasingly complex world, most intellectual endeavors are collaborative in nature [2]. Many digital media projects today are built by a wide range of contributors distributed across the Internet. Wikipedia is a prime example, with more than 24 million articles in 285 different languages that is maintained by more than 100,000 active contributors working together. This form of collaborative editing of digital media is now gaining acceptance in a broad set of domains. In this section, we describe the prior art in wikis, creative design, version control, and collaborative editing.

### Wikis for Collaboration

Ward Cunningham developed the first Wiki in 1995, calling it "the simplest online database that could possibly work" [17]. Wikis quickly caught on as a means for collaboratively creating, vetting, and maintaining online documents, its application made famous by Wikipedia. Wagner [34], emphasizes its versatility in providing a repository and a means for many-to-many collaboration by incorporating aspects of various communication tools such as email, chat, and multimedia applications, with a temporal database for history support. Traditional wiki systems such as MediaWiki, TWiki, and Confluence, enable such collaborative editing via a web browser, and support rollback, external links, and heterogeneous content such as code, documents, images, and rich text content. The use of wikis for content creation and not just content storage was extended to software development as well [17], especially for project management, where project documentation and discussion can be placed in context with project content. The use of traditional wikis is further extended by semantic wikis that capture and identify metadata in wikis using RDF and OWL frameworks, such as IkeWiki [28], SeMedia Wiki [3], and PlatypusWiki [32].

Recent work on wikis are starting to extend the traditional wiki history model for text. Sabel's work [26] on version history of a wiki page considers an adoption coefficient that is defined by the structural similarity between two versions of a text document, and uses it to arrange versions of a wiki page into a weighted tree. Similarly, Priedhorsky and Terveen [21] discuss implementation challenges and solutions for maintaining a single global state and history for non-textual objects using the Cyclopath geowiki as an example. They propose solutions for some of the challenges inherent with maintaining multiple object types, such as a ordering revisions, global state and undo, and access control.

### Collaboration in Design

Design is often defined as an ill-defined problem whose solution is obtained through creative exploration alternated with pruning of the design space [22]. This alternating of the creative or *divergent processes* and the analytical or *convergent processes* has been studied extensively, resulting in now-commonplace creative methods such as brainstorming [20], brainwriting [25], and collaborative sketching [29]. While technology has long been used in an attempt to scaffold creativity, part of the challenge in this endeavor lies in the nature of creativity itself. Torrance [33, p. 47] describes creativity as "the process of sensing difficulties, problems, gaps in information, missing elements, something askew; making guesses and formulating hypotheses about these deficiencies; evaluating and testing these guesses and hypotheses; possibly revising and retesting them; and finally communicating the results." This continuous inspiration, guesswork, and evaluation results in a stream of ideas, only some of which are developed further.

Early work in collaborative creative support for design was in the form of multi-user drawing support [14, 19, 31] for collaboration between geographically distributed participants. The i-LAND environment [30] was pioneering in its use of (now) ubiquitous technology such as display walls and tabletops along with conventional computers in support of creativity. Recent work in this area includes IdeaVis [7], TEAM STORM [10], and GAMBIT [27].

Greene [8] lists support for exploration and experimentation, collaboration, iteration, and domain-specific action as essential for applications intended to support creativity. Hilliges et al. [13] also recommend an interface that allows actions to be carried out both individually and collaboratively.

### Version Control and Collaborative Editing

Version control systems manage content change and maintain a history of its evolution, and are commonplace in the software industry. The Source Code Control System (SCCS) was one of the earliest source code management systems developed in the early 70s to store, update, and retrieve all versions of code [24]. Currently popular SCM systems include CVS, Subversion, and Git. More recent developments record and visualize developer activity at interaction level to enhance program history representations [23, 35].

While these version control systems were primarily created for software engineering, most can be used for any text file, and, to some extent, binary files as well. Furthermore, while not strictly classified as version control, systems such as Chronicle [9]—which clusters, probes, and visualizes a document's workflow history—and MeshFlow [6]—which visualizes, clusters, annotates, and filters the history of operations on polygonal meshes—are significant contributions towards managing history on binary files.

Collaborative editing is essentially a version control system integrated with the editor itself, and has a rich history in the CSCW field [1]. Social code-hosting repositories such as GitHub have been studied to gain insight into the influences of activity volume, commit histories, community interest, and personal interest of contributors [5]. A modern collaborative editor such as Google Docs allows multiple users to work on a document by propagating all edits in real time, thus alleviating the explicit need to commit/save versions of the document to a server. This means that the only way to "branch out" (diverge) at a given time is to make an explicit copy of the document. Google Docs maintains a history of edits to the document ordered by timestamps.

Recovering editing operations for binary data is more difficult than for text, posing another challenge for collaborative editing of digital media. To address this, Chen et al. [4] propose a version control system for image editing that integrates with the image manipulation program itself to capture the drawing commands that transformed the image. This work is perhaps the most related to skWiki, but differs in several important ways: (1) skWiki is a collaborative system designed for more than a single user; (2) we support revision control of multiple media types beyond photographs, including text and sketches; and (3) our system is entirely web-based and requires no dedicated client-side software.

## SUPPORTING DIGITAL CREATIVITY

Our goal with the skWiki project is to support digital creativity in collaborative, potentially distributed, teams. Here we explore the design space for this research topic.

### Requirements

Based on the literature and our collaborations with professional designers, we formulate the following requirements for a software framework to support digital creativity:

R1 **Mobility:** A basic goal is that the platform should be designed for mobile devices so that the designer can bring skWiki to any design session "anywhere, anytime;"

R2 **Collaboration:** Virtually all realistic design endeavors involve more than one participant working together in teams [2], often distributed in time and/or space [1];

R3 **Revision history:** Effective collaborative content creation requires support for branching, editing, and merging different versions of the media entities being manipulated;

R4 **Transparency:** Complexities of collaboration and revision histories should be hidden from non-expert users;

R5 **Rich media:** Even simple digital media projects today often incorporate a wide range of media types, such as rich text, photographs, audio, video, and illustrations; and

R6 **Divergent/creative work:** We want to support creative work where the focus is on creating multiple, separate, and diverse content, often drawing on other collaborators.

We found no existing software framework that fully supported all of these requirements. For this reason, we decided to create our own software framework for collaborative creativity called SKWIKI, which is described in the next section. In designing skWiki, we also felt that there was need for a new theoretical model that would capture these requirements on a storage level. Drawing from work on semantic-level revision control of images by Chen et al. [4], we propose the idea of *paths* for digital media. This is reviewed next.

### The Paths Model

We define a *path* as a tuple $\langle I, O, R, L \rangle$ consisting of a unique entity identifier $I$, an owner $O$, a reference to a parent revision $R$ (possibly empty), and an ordered and timestamped list $L$ of *state transformation operations* that, when taken together, recreates the current state of the entity. One way to think of a path is thus as persistent state over time, i.e., all of the different versions of a particular file from the time it was created. However, this view is somewhat misleading since paths are *not* snapshots, or even deltas, at different times, but rather the actual operations that yielded those states.

Abstractly speaking, a *state transformation operation* is a function $f_T : \mathbb{S} \rightarrow \mathbb{S}$ for revision number $T$ (a serial number starting from 0) that takes an entity state $s_{T-1} \in \mathbb{S}$ from the previous revision number and produces a transformed state $s_T \in \mathbb{S}$. A revision $R$ for a particular path is thus a pair $\langle I, T \rangle$ comprising a path identifier and the revision number referred to in its operation list. Recreating the state for any revision number $T$ thus becomes a function composition series

$$s_T = f_T \circ f_{T-1} \circ f_{T-2} \circ \ldots \circ f_0(\emptyset).$$

The benefit of representing paths in this way is that it avoids storing entire snapshots of the entity at every time step. In fact, in many cases, using a sequence of operations will also result in a more economic representation even than storing binary deltas of an entity's state. For example, whereas a file diff would have to replicate the entire image data if a photograph is inverted, a path just stores the invert operation.

Similar to files in a traditional file system, there are several fundamental operations defined for paths:

**Create:** A new path is created by allocating a unique entity identifier, assigning the owner reference, and initializing the operations list to $\emptyset$. Paths are tied to owners; the owner reference is an immutable part of the path tuple.

**Render:** Rendering an entity is similar to recreating its entire state up to a certain revision number $T$ (it is also possible to map a specified time to a revision number using the time stamp associated with each operation). This is performed using the function composition above. Rendering a branched path (i.e., one with a non-null parent revision $R$, see below) will first recursively render the parent revision $R$ before rendering the child path.

**Modify:** Changing a path is equivalent to adding one or more transformation operations to the operations list in the path. All operations are timestamped and have a revision number, which is a monotonically increasing serial number (starting from 0). Note that only the owner of a path can modify it; others would first have to branch it.

**Delete:** Paths cannot be deleted. However, a null operation ($f(s) = \emptyset$) can be added to the end of the operations list, which effectively renders the path's state empty. Prior versions of a deleted path can always be rendered up to the penultimate revision number to recover deleted state.

**Branch:** Paths cannot be copied, but can be branched. Branching a path creates a new path with a unique identifier, appropriate owner reference, and a parent revision $R$ that specifies the original path and revision number. The operations list $L$ for the branched path will initially be empty, but rendering it will recursively render its parents.

**Merge:** A path $p_A$ can be merged with another path $p_B$ by selectively appending one or several operations from $p_A$ into $p_B$. Both paths are preserved by this operation, and the net effect is simply that $p_B$ is modified. For a merge operation to make sense, however, the paths should be related, e.g., one of them being an ancestor of the other.

Note that operations can never be removed from the operation list in a path; a change can only be undoed either by (a) branching from a previous state, or by (b) appending the inverse operation to the end of the operations list. This is because branching for paths relies on parent revisions to never disappear, which would otherwise cause inconsistencies.

## Implementing Paths

Actually realizing the theoretical paths model above requires overcoming several implementation challenges. Representation is perhaps central amongst them: the optimal way to implement paths using current technology is to use a database management system (DBMS) that stores individual paths in one table, and all of the operations in another using the path identifier as a primary key and including the revision serial number. Users should be represented in another table that can be used to track path ownership and access permissions. Below we review additional challenges in implementing paths and our recommendations for how to tackle them.

### Transformation Operations

Representing the actual transformation operations is a major challenge. Because operations are specific to different types of data, this consideration is dependent on the document formats that the paths implementation supports. The best solution may be to store source code in a *domain-specific language* (DSL) [18] for each document format. A particular paths implementation may have to support several DSLs, one for each document format supported. Also, care must be taken to not mix incompatible DSL operations in one path.

The database representation for an operation thus becomes a table consisting of a path reference, a revision number (a serial number unique to each path), a time stamp, and an operation string. For example, an operation string for a bitmap image DSL might have the form `crop(100, 100, 1024, 768)` to crop an image to 1024×768 dimensions starting at position (100, 100), whereas one for text might be `insert("d", 10)` to insert the character "d" in position 10 in the current state. If the database inputs are cleaned appropriately, it might even be possible to execute these operation strings using direct evaluation (i.e., with the `eval()` function for a DSL built in JavaScript).

### Operation Chunking

To minimize the number of operations for each path, a practical solution might be adopt the *chunking* approach used in graphical histories [12, 16] to group together related operations. For example, a sequence of character insertions that together spell the word "design" might be more economically represented as a single insertion of the whole word. Similarly, a list of movements of a graphical object could be replaced by a single translation for the resulting vector.

The disadvantage of operation chunking is that the time stamp for each chunked event is replaced by a single one, making it impossible to branch from the constituent events. However, such fine branch granularity is generally not necessary for practical path implementations.

### Path Caching

The paths model takes a somewhat extreme view of state as the sum of all operations performed on an entity. For this reason, rendering a path may sometimes be a lengthy operation, particularly if the path has undergone many revisions or if individual operations are time-consuming. For example, certain image filters (edge detection, motion blur, image distortions) may take up several seconds to complete. In such situations, it is not practical to render a path from scratch. Instead, we use *path caching* to speed up the process.

Formally speaking, a *path cache* is the complete rendered state $s_T$ for a path up to revision number $T$. Rendering any paths at revision numbers $T+N$ now simply reduces to performing the abbreviated function composition

$$s_{T+N} = f_{T+N} \circ f_{T+N-1} \circ f_{T+N-2} \circ \ldots \circ f_{T+1}(s_T).$$

In practice, this means that when rendering a revision number $T$, the render operation first fetches the cached path with the most recent revision number $T' \leq T$. These cached versions should be saved under unique file names in an internal directory and tracked using a cache table in the database. Caching itself should be transparently performed, for example whenever rendering a path, or when encountering a particularly time-consuming operation (or sequence of operations). By the same token, a practical implementation should probably incorporate a path cleaning mechanism that periodically removes cached versions (from both cache table and directory) whenever they have not been accessed recently.

### *Transparent Path Operations*

The paths model may appear complex, but most of its complexity can be hidden from the point of view of the end user. In fact, to achieve most benefit from the concept, a practical implementation should most likely make all of the path operations transparent to the user. For example, a paths implementation needs no explicit "save" functionality, but will instead automatically commit all modifications (using the modify command). Similarly, rendering (particularly in the presence of any path caching), deleting, and branching paths should also not expose the above details to the end user.

Perhaps the only path operation that cannot be entirely transparent is the merge, which requires that the user explicitly selects the operations to merge from a source path into a destination path. At the same time, it might be possible to encapsulate this operation in a form of copy-and-paste that most users are already familiar with, or to use a smart merge.

### *Path Navigation*

In a normal file system, a file explorer is sufficient to navigate and manage files and directories. In a paths implementation, however, it is not only necessary to be able to navigate the path structure (which may or may not incorporate the traditional hierarchical structure of classic file systems), but also to navigate the revisions of each path. In other words, a practical paths implementation needs a *path explorer*.

Several considerations factor into creating an effective path explorer. One visual representation of a path is to display the list of operations, suitably chunked into semantic units. However, this may result in a representation that is unfamiliar to users who are accustomed to traditional file systems. An alternative representation may use rendered snapshots (as thumbnail images or summaries, for example) of the path at various time intervals. Such a representation would even be amenable to semantic zooming, where zooming in would reveal a different visual representation with more detail, and zooming out would afford a broad overview of the path's evolution. Furthermore, it might be advantageous to use this visual snapshot representation to highlight changes from one snapshot to the next using a suitable visualization.

Several additional operations are needed in a practical path explorer. For example, the visualization should visualize branching to show how different paths build on other paths, as well as different users and their individual paths. The interface should also contain mechanisms for searching for paths by name, time, or owner, as well as bookmarking, filtering, and tagging paths. Such an interface would not only aid creative collaboration, but would also provide a framework for determining contributions, ownership, and influences of ideas, especially in early stages of design.

## THE SKWIKI SYSTEM

Based on our exploration of the design space of digital creativity support, we developed a web-based collaborative editing framework for multimedia documents called SKWIKI. skWiki is based on a web service architecture (Figure 2) with server-side components to manage persistence using a practical paths implementation, and any number of users participating in the collaboration using only a web browser. The framework supports digital media projects consisting of multiple media types, such as text, hand-drawn sketches, vectorized illustrations, and digital photographs. skWiki clients can run on standard computers, mobile phones, and tablets with popular operating systems such as Android, iOS, and WebOS. The framework is built to allow extensions with additional media types as plugins.

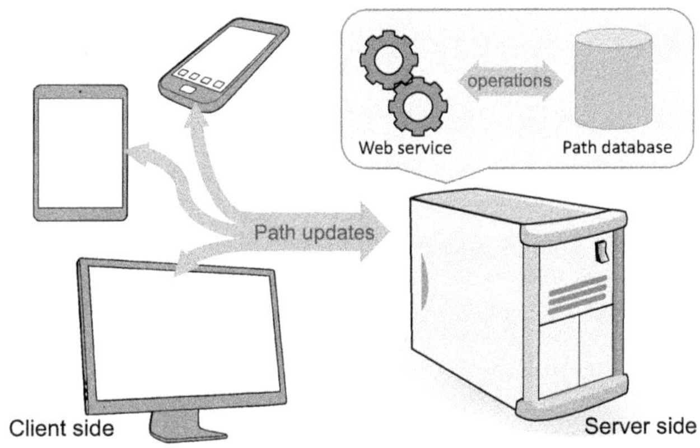


**Figure 2. skWiki system architecture. The client maintains workspace and local paths storage, whereas the server is the main paths repository.**

skWiki was designed primarily to support *divergent creative processes*, i.e., early design, brainstorming, conceptual art, ideation, and design alternatives. We will now explain the implementation of the paths model in skWiki, and how its practical features support collaborative creativity.

- **Transformation Operations:** Because skWiki is a controlled deployment of the paths model (as opposed to, say, implementing it for an entire operating system), we bound the operation set to the domain-specific languages used to create and modify the state. Our implementation currently supports four DSLs: bitmaps (for digital photographs), rich text (in HTML format), drawings (including free-hand sketching and vector drawing), and layouts (hierarchical and spatial arrangements of entities on a page).

  Note that some operations in the above table include object identifiers as arguments to name newly created objects. Object identifiers are used by other operations, such as `removeShape()`, to refer to specific objects, and they must be explicitly named so that the operations list is a complete representation of the state of a path.

- **Operation Chunking:** Our current implementation performs only a minimum of operation chunking; for example, sequences of character insertions or deletions are chunked into strings, and long series of lines captured from a user sketching are chunked into polylines. However, similar to caching, chunking is a largely independent mechanism that can be progressively improved to be more aggressive without affecting overall skWiki functionality.

- **Path Caching:** The current implementation of skWiki uses no explicit path caching. We found that none of our DSL operations were particularly time-consuming to perform, and thus render each path completely from their creation. Furthermore, since browser-based web applications have very limited support for local storage, we wanted to avoid large network transfers of cached state. However, a practical skWiki implementation in the future should certainly provide an appropriate level of caching.
- **Transparent Operations:** All path operations in the skWiki implementation are transparent from the viewpoint of the user, including branching, undoing, and deleting paths. In our informal evaluation, we found that normal users still prefer access to standard operations such as "save" and did not fully understand the new conceptual model underlying skWiki. For this purpose, we provided an "add bookmark" button to replace the traditional "save." This is a transitional remedy until the paths concept becomes more familiar to our end users.
- **Path Navigation:** We implemented a traditional graph viewer, similar to those used in source code management systems, to explore and manage paths. We currently use bookmarked revisions to guide which important states to visualize in the path viewer. This also supports the users' mental model that their bookmarked revisions are the main units of the history. Of course, the path implementation allows the user to also drill into any revision between bookmarked ones whenever necessary.
- **Viewers and Editors:** A *Viewer* is an interpreter for a domain-specific language that is capable of decoding a sequence of transformation operations implemented in a DSL and recreating the corresponding digital content. Similarly, an *Editor* is a command generator that can generate new DSL operations in response to user interaction. Viewers and Editors in skWiki are thus plugins tied to a specific media type. Both Viewers and Editors are part of the same user interface. Viewers get allocated a content space for its associated path. Content spaces may also have an associated Editor that will partner with the Viewer to allow path modifications. The Editor will also provide a DSL-specific toolbar (Figure 3) to support editing.

### Interactions

The skWiki client is a JavaScript web application that runs entirely in the user's own browser, regardless of operating system, hardware platform, and with no special software dependencies. Figure 3 shows an annotated screenshot of the main skWiki interface, which includes the editing toolbar and the path explorer. In addition to the tree-based path explorer, we also provide a gallery-based path explorer where entities are represented by thumbnails of their latest revision, but can be traversed in time using the mouse wheel.

### Implementation Notes

The skWiki front-end web application is implemented in Java using the Google Web Toolkit (GWT). GWT compiles Java code into JavaScript, which runs in virtually any web browser as a rich internet application (RIA). This enables building web applications without requiring expertise in browser quirks, JavaScript, and AJAX requests.

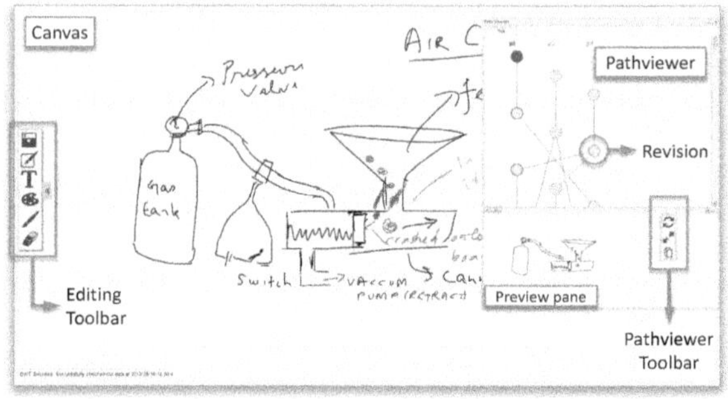


**Figure 3. The skWiki browser-based user interface showing the editing toolbar and the path viewer for a sketch entity.**

The skWiki server is implemented as a Java Servlet hosted in an Apache Tomcat servlet container. The server also runs a PostgreSQL database for storing all paths and DSL information. The client talks to the server using GWT-RPC (Remote Procedure Call). When the skWiki servlet receives a request, it fetches information from the database and performs the required operations. It then sends a reply to the skWiki client, which updates its own state in response. This architecture makes client-side editing into a real-time and synchronous process, whereas network-intensive or computationally expensive operations such as searching, rendering, and sorting remain asynchronously performed on the server.

## USER STUDY

Our goal with skWiki is to support digital creativity in collaborative teams, both co-located as well as distributed. To evaluate our prototype, we performed a study of co-located teams on a creative task. Since free-form creativity not only takes training but is also difficult to quantify, we used a form of controlled brainstorming called C-sketch [29]. C-sketch is a sketch-oriented adaptation of the more generic method of 6-3-5 brainwriting [25], contextualized in a design environment. In the C-sketch method, designers first spend 6-10 minutes sketching out an idea, and then pass it on to the next person. Each designer then spends the next 6-10 minutes working on editing or extending the design idea given by their teammate. This process continues for 2-3 iterations, at the end of which all designs sketched initially have undergone iterative development by at least 3 people. The C-sketch workflow is shown in the left part of Figure 4.

### Experimental Conditions

One of the main drawbacks of methods such as C-sketch is that some promising ideas can be lost in the series of iterative edits. Additionally, at the end of the session, there are only as many ideas as there are designers, with intermediate—and potentially promising—ideas being "lost". We hypothesized that the history support afforded by skWiki, along with the option to branch out and create multiple versions of the same sketch, will provide designers with more potential sources of inspiration and development for the design problem at hand.

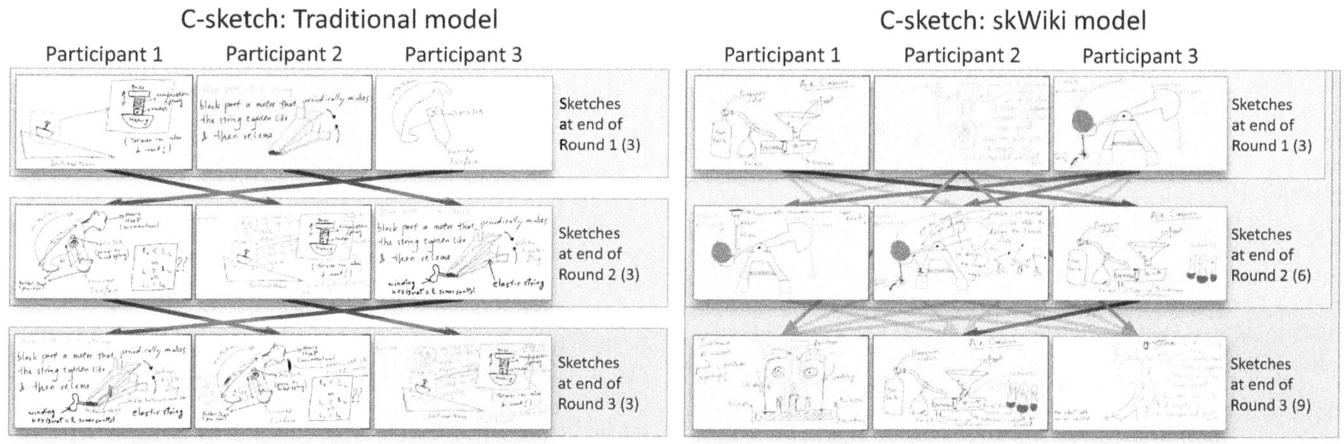


**Figure 4. Schematic diagram of the two processes used in the user study: traditional (left) versus the skWiki version of C-sketch (right). Each column shows sketches made or modified by each participant (team of three). The grey arrows show the paths of the traditional C-sketch method, and colored arrows show a departure from the model enabled by skWiki. Potential paths are shown as translucent arrows, while actual paths taken are shown with solid arrows. The traditional C-sketch model emulates the pen-paper paradigm, with no duplication, and no saved states for the sketches. Thus, there are only three concepts available at the end of this session, with all intermediate concepts lost. The skWiki model allows duplication and multiple copies at each round (shown as aquamarine arrows), as well as for branching from earlier states (shown as orange arrows). The team thus has more choices at the end of each round, and nine concepts at the end of the session.**

In order to study the effects of the affordances offered by skWiki, we involved each team in two different conditions:

- **Traditional:** The team used a traditional three-round C-sketch workflow as described above, with only sketch movement (no copying) between participants, and with only the latest sketch version available for each round.
- **Full skWiki:** Here the team used the same three-round method as above, with two main differences: (1) at the beginning of the second and third rounds, they could choose any sketch to work on except the sketch they had created in the previous round, and (2) when selecting a final design (end of round 3), they could choose sketches from rounds earlier than the immediately preceding one.

While the C-sketch method typically involves sketching on paper. our intent was not to compare paper vs. digital media. We thus used skWiki for both versions: a version without branching and history "rollback" for the C-sketch condition, and a version with both these features for the full skWiki condition. The aquamarine and orange arrows in Figure 4 show the branching and rollback operations respectively.

### Participants

We recruited 4 teams of 3 paid participants each (11 mechanical engineering graduate students and 1 post-doctoral researcher, all male). Participants were aged between 21 and 33 years. 10 participants were comfortable with sketching, and 5 considered themselves proficient. 4 participants had prior knowledge of the C-sketch method. Participants were randomly assigned to teams based on available time slots.

### Apparatus

All participants used Microsoft Surface Pro tablets, equipped with the Surface Pen for sketching and annotations. Both conditions used different versions of the skWiki interface, running on the Google Chrome browser. For the traditional C-sketch condition, the skWiki interface was provided with curbed features based on the C-sketch method, such as adopting a sketch and editing it, with no copy or history support. The skWiki C-sketch condition also required a level of feature curbing: history support was minimized to what was available at the end of each round, but not to a stage between them. These constraints helped control the experiment conditions, in addition to allowing the participants to concentrate on the method rather than spend their time on learning and remembering commands.

### Tasks

The teams were assigned two tasks, one for each condition: (1) design a toy catapult with an innovative launching mechanism, and (2) design a new kind of somersaulting toy. The order of conditions and tasks were varied among the team to balance out learning effects as well as testing bias.

Each task was split into three rounds of 6 minutes each. In the first round, participants were asked to sketch one idea each for the toy, and annotate it so that their team could understand the idea without additional explanation. No verbal communication between team members was allowed during the three sketch rounds. In the second and third rounds, each participant was asked to develop or edit the sketch of another participant, without completely erasing it. In the case of the traditional C-sketch method, participants were asked to circulate their sketches clockwise to their adjacent teammate. For the full skWiki condition, participants could choose any of their teammates' sketches from any stage, but not their own. This restriction was imposed to prevent participants from continuously working on their own idea for the duration of the session. At the end of the session, participants were asked to spend 5 minutes to discuss and select the most promising concept from the set of available concepts.

### Data Collection

Participants were asked to respond to questions pertaining to the usefulness and ease of the methods on a Likert scale.

A log of participant choices in rounds two and three in the skWiki condition was also recorded to identify cases of departure from the traditional method afforded due to the branching (creating copies) and history support (choosing a sketch from the first round during the third). Finally, each team's selection of the "most promising idea", and its corresponding round, was noted.

## RESULTS AND DISCUSSION

The branching operations performed by participants in each team for both the traditional C-sketch and the full skWiki conditions are shown in Figure 5. Below we discuss how features that are unique to skWiki were used by the teams.

### Cloning and History Rollback

The C-sketch flow of design follows a linear sharing model through a "passing the paper around" paradigm prescribed by the method that the participants were required to follow. For the skWiki method, participant activity shows instances of multiple copies of a sketch in every round, for every single team. Of these instances, three teams branched out (cloned) from earlier versions of their team members' sketches, made possible through the "history rollback" support. Three out of four teams selected their final design from the last set of iterations, shown by the "starred" nodes in Figure 5. However, it is noteworthy that one team selected a design from their second round, which would have been lost had it not been for the history rollback support.

Participant responses to survey questions support the usefulness of the branching and history rollback afforded by skWiki: of the 12 participants, 11 preferred the full skWiki model of C-sketch. Reasons cited for the preference ranged from the ability to choose a more promising idea, the availability of a larger variety of ideas to choose from, and the ability to see more popular or "growing ideas", as one participant put it. Participants also cited the ease of collaboration as another reason for preferring skWiki. The one participant who preferred the traditional C-sketch model of sharing cited his reason as the full skWiki system allowing the designer to stick to a limited set of designs if he so chooses, as opposed to C-sketch, which ensured that everyone worked on everyone else's designs. However, all 12 participants reported that they found the option to select ideas useful.

### Path Viewer with Preview

Recall that the traditional C-sketch path viewer for the user study was configured to show only the latest sketches of all the users at any point of time, while for the skWiki model it showed the revisions of all users that were uploaded at the end of each 6-minute session. The post-survey responses suggest that a majority of the users (average of 75%) found it easy to decide on a version to download for the next round during full skWiki model even though more versions are shown than in the traditional C-sketch. For the full skWiki sharing model, we anticipated a decrease in the ease of browsing and choosing ideas in later rounds owing to an increase in the number of ideas to choose from. Participant responses, however, were mixed: 7 out of 12 participants mentioned that it was easy for them to choose an idea to work on in the second round, while 1 participant reported finding it difficult. 4 participants were undecided. Surprisingly, the number of participants who found it easy to choose ideas increased for the third round to 9 participants, while 3 participants found it difficult. Interestingly, this increase was accompanied by a mix of transitions: all participants who found it difficult to choose in the previous round found it easier to choose in the last round, whereas 3 participants who found choosing in the second round easy, had the opposite experience in the third round. The increase in participant ease could be explained by a greater familiarity with their team member's designs by the third round, assuming changes are clear in the thumbnail view. A more complex design change, however would entail checking out the sketch and examining it closely, a process that becomes more tedious the more choice one has. This is echoed by the participants: some suggested using larger previews, or larger thumbnails with the facility to flip through them easily.

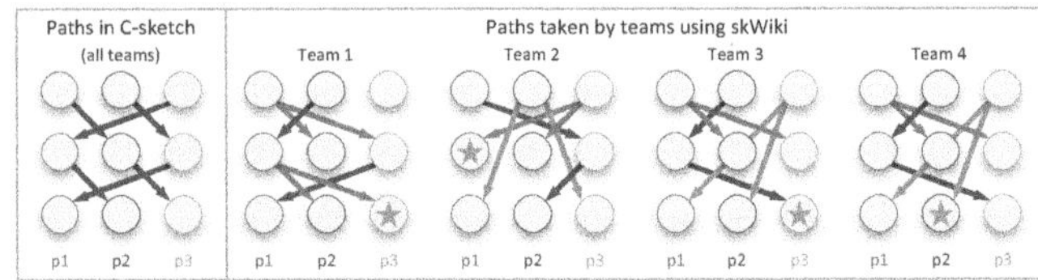


**Figure 5. Comparison between paths taken in the C-sketch model (left) and skWiki (right) in the user study. Each gray node represents a sketch by a participant (labeled as p1, p2, p3) at the end of every round. Standard "passing on a sketch" operations are shown as gray arrows, branching to create multiple copies is aquamarine, and branching from history is orange. Stars indicate a sketch was selected as the best design.**

From a methodology point of view, it is premature, based on this study alone, to conclude that more choice for the designer is better. In fact, allowing the designer, especially a design engineer, to freely choose a design could lead to fixation, as engineers tend to favor previously encountered designs or designs they developed themselves [15]. However, the purpose of skWiki is not to merely provide choice, but to preserve every stage of work as well as to allow for potential branching (cloning) of ideas at every such stage. In the context of the C-sketch method, Shah et al. state saturation—participants feeling "that they could no longer contribute to the idea generation process" [29, p. 191]—as one of the issues of their method. With skWiki, this saturation can be delayed since each designer can have the opportunity to work on every other designer's *initial* design, without incremental additions or modifications of features done by other designers, thus geometrically increasing the number of potential iterations. Additionally, designers can return to the problem days later and pick up where they left off, owing to the persistence of every state of their design on the server. Finally, as seen with Team 2 in Figure 5, skWiki preserves promising ideas that would otherwise be lost to further iterations.

## DESIGN IMPLICATIONS

A user of the Web 2.0 generation is not only a consumer of digital content, but a creator, distributor, and marketer as well. However, most current content creation tools are geared towards convergent processes which strive to create a single article, a unified data table, or a common illustration agreed upon by all. In this work, we have tackled a diametrically opposite approach—a collaborative creativity framework for divergent processes: many design alternatives, multiple iterations, and competing yet comfortably coexisting versions. However, in traversing this path (no pun intended), we had to make several design decisions that affected the final skWiki implementation presented in this paper.

Our skWiki implementation uses the paths concept to support effortless collaborative creating, sharing, and merging for multimedia. A key component for managing these meandering paths is the path explorer, which not only tracks paths in space but also in time and across multiple users. However, a visual path explorer of this type will inevitably encounter presentation difficulties as the number of revisions and users grows. For example, our current explorer implementation uses a node-link representation that would not scale to more than a few hundred revisions and users. Because of this, applying it on a large scale in a system such as Wikipedia would simply not be feasible. More work is required here not only in visual summaries and alternate representations, but also in methods for filtering, navigating, and searching within paths and between users in the path explorer.

Scale also affects more than the mere interface layer of the system. One weakness of the paths model is that it could lead to a profliferation (if not explosion) of concurrent paths, with much of the data being redundant and replicated. Even deleted files would remain in storage forever, effectively making it impossible to ever "clean up" a hard disk or storage system. On the other hand, a paths model with appropriately designed DSL operations can also be significantly more economical than an equivalent file system. For one thing, storing an operation is often less space-consuming than storing its effect; one example is inverting a raster image. Second, the branch operation in the paths model, which corresponds to a copy in a traditional file system, is extremely lightweight: an empty branch simply contains a few bytes to store the new path identifier and track the parent path and revision number. Nevertheless, we recognize that the paths model described here is not a general replacement for a traditional file system by any measure. We simply found it well suited to our overall design rationale.

One potential weakness of the paths model is the merge operation, which is somewhat difficult to characterize to the user. It is partly a copy operation, because it replicates one or more transformation operations from a source path to a destination path. Also, it is typically performed on paths that are somehow related, for example, having a common ancestor. In our current implementation, merging two paths is operationally equivalent to branching a new child from one of the two paths followed by applying one or more latest operations of the other. However, merging is an even more powerful concept, which for example can allow identical operations to affect a large set of paths based on the operation sequence. More work is needed to explore the potential of the merge operation in future versions of skWiki. Further, the current version of skWiki does not incorporate consensus: a final idea or set of ideas that are selected by a team. In our model, all ideas exist simultaneously, and final ideas are not explicitly shortlisted or tagged for future reference. We plan to explore the use of collaborative tagging [11] to allow for tag-based selection and filtering in the paths.

One of the most closely related existing projects for skWiki is Google Docs, which supports much of the same functionality for collaborative multimedia authoring while retaining a revision history. However, compared to skWiki, Google Docs lacks many of our visualization mechanisms as well as multi-user revision tracking. It is also designed for a convergent workflow. For a group of brainstorming toy designers, one alternative be to use a single Google Docs document where each designer works on separate pages while routinely referring to each other's work. However, branching from another designer's work is not a native operation in Docs, and requires replicating that work first before editing.

Finally, it is worth comparing skWiki to wikis, which the system at least shares some common ancestry with. For one thing, wikis are notoriously difficult to use with anything other than textual content. Images are not first-class objects in a typical wiki software, and must be edited using offline desktop applications. Part of the goal for skWiki is to provide a multimedia authoring environment that is not dependent on offline desktop applications, at least not for the most common operations. However, the differences go a lot further than this: a traditional wiki and skWiki represent two radically different designs. Whereas a wiki has one copy of each document and will always show its latest version, skWiki is based on the very concept of multiple and concurrent versions of a document across time, space, and users.

## CONCLUSION AND FUTURE WORK

We have presented skWiki, a web-based content authoring framework for creative processes that implements an abstract paths model in favor of a traditional file system. Paths represent entity state over time, and consists of the operations that were performed to create and modify an entity rather than snapshots or diffs. This model is particularly powerful for multi-user collaborative settings where the aim is to brainstorm and generate many design alternatives for a particular theme. The skWiki system is a practical paths implementation and allows users to collaborative work on multimedia documents consisting of images, vectors, sketches, layouts, and rich text. To validate the work, we conducted a qualitative user study involving four teams of three engineering students using the tool for designing children's toys.

This work is merely one contribution to a dialogue of how to support the new content authoring model where users themselves are involved in all stages of the process. We expect this dialogue to continue well into the future. Our own future research directions include supporting additional media types, improving the fluidity of the interface where it entirely replaces desktop applications, and further exploring the paths model presented here to its full potential.

## ACKNOWLEDGMENTS

This work is partly supported by the U.S. National Science Foundation on grants IIS-1227639, IIS-1249229, and IIS-1253863, as well as the Donald W. Feddersen Chaired Professorship and the Purdue School of Mechanical Engineering. Any opinions, findings, and conclusions or recommendations expressed in this material are those of the authors and do not necessarily reflect the views of the sponsors.

## REFERENCES


1. Baecker, R. M. *Readings in Groupware and Computer-Supported Cooperative Work*. Morgan Kaufmann Publishers, San Francisco, 1993.
2. Bruffee, K. A. Collaborative learning and the conversation of mankind. *College English*, 46(7):635–652, 1984.
3. Buffa, M., Erétéo, G., and Gandon, F. A wiki on the semantic web. In *Emerging Technologies for Semantic Web Environments: Techniques, Methods and Applications*, 115–137, 2008.
4. Chen, H.-T., Wei, L.-Y., and Chang, C.-F. Nonlinear revision control for images. *ACM Transactions on Graphics*, 30(4):105:1–105:10, 2011.
5. Dabbish, L., Stuart, C., Tsay, J., and Herbsleb, J. Social coding in GitHub: transparency and collaboration in an open software repository. In *Proc. ACM Computer Supported Cooperative Work*, 1277–1286, 2012.
6. Denning, J. D., Kerr, W. B., and Pellacini, F. MeshFlow: interactive visualization of mesh construction sequences. *ACM Transactions on Graphics*, 30(4):66:1–66:8, 2011.
7. Geyer, F., Budzinski, J., and Reiterer, H. IdeaVis: a hybrid workspace and interactive visualization for paper-based collaborative sketching sessions. In *Proceedings of the Nordic Conference on Human-Computer Interaction*, 331–340, 2012.
8. Greene, S. L. Characteristics of applications that support creativity. *CACM*, 45(10):100–104, 2002.
9. Grossman, T., Matejka, J., and Fitzmaurice, G. Chronicle: capture, exploration, and playback of document workflow histories. In *Proc. ACM User Interface Software & Technology*, 143–152, 2010.
10. Hailpern, J., Hinterbichler, E., Leppert, C., Cook, D., and Bailey, B. P. TEAM STORM: demonstrating an interaction model for working with multiple ideas during creative group work. In *Proceedings of the ACM Conference on Creativity & Cognition*, 193–202, 2007.
11. Halpin, H., Robu, V., and Shepherd, H. The complex dynamics of collaborative tagging. In *Proc. ACM Conference on the World Wide Web*, 211–220, 2007.
12. Heer, J., Mackinlay, J. D., Stolte, C., and Agrawala, M. Graphical histories for visualization: Supporting analysis, communication, and evaluation. *IEEE Transactions on Visualization and Computer Graphics*, 14(6):1189–1196, 2008.
13. Hilliges, O., Terrenghi, L., Boring, S., Kim, D., Richter, H., and Butz, A. Designing for collaborative creative problem solving. In *Proceedings of the ACM Conference on Creativity & Cognition*, 137–146, 2007.
14. Ishii, H., and Kobayashi, M. ClearBoard: a seamless medium for shared drawing and conversation with eye contact. In *Proceedings of the ACM Conference on Human Factors in Computing Systems*, 525–532, 1992.
15. Jansson, D. G., and Smith, S. M. Design fixation. *Design Studies*, 12(1):3–11, 1991.
16. Kurlander, D., and Feiner, S. Editable graphical histories. In *Proceedings IEEE Workshop on Visual Language*, 127–134, 1988.
17. Louridas, P. Using wikis in software development. *IEEE Software*, 23(2):88–91, 2006.
18. Mernik, M., Heering, J., and Sloane, A. M. When and how to develop domain-specific languages. *ACM Computing Surveys*, 37(4):316–344, Dec. 2005.
19. Minneman, S. L., and Bly, S. A. Managing a trois: A study of a multi-user drawing tool in distributed design work. In *Proceedings of the ACM Conference on Human Factors in Computing Systems*, 217–224, 1991.
20. Osborn, A. *Applied imagination; principles and procedures of creative problem-solving*. Scribner, 1963.
21. Priedhorsky, R., and Terveen, L. Wiki grows up: arbitrary data models, access control, and beyond. In *Proceedings of the International Symposium on Wikis and Open Collaboration*, 63–71, 2011.
22. Rittel, H., and Webber, M. Dilemmas in a general theory of planning. *Policy Sciences*, 4(2):155–169, 1973.
23. Robbes, R., and Lanza, M. A change-based approach to software evolution. *Electronic Notes in Theoretical Computer Science*, 166:93–109, 2007.
24. Rochkind, M. J. The source code control system. *IEEE Trans. in Software Engineering*, 1(4):364–370, 1975.
25. Rohrbach, B. Creative nach regeln: Methode 635, eine neue technik zum lösen von problemen. *Absatzwirtschaft*, 12(19):73–75, 1969.
26. Sabel, M. Structuring wiki revision history. In *Proceedings of WikiSym*, 125–130, 2007.
27. Sangiorgi, U. B., Beuvens, F., and Vanderdonckt, J. User interface design by collaborative sketching. In *Proceedings of the ACM Conference on Designing Interactive Systems*, 378–387, 2012.
28. Schaffert, S. IkeWiki: A semantic wiki for collaborative knowledge management. In *Proceedings of the IEEE International Workshop on Enabling Technologies*, 388–396, 2006.
29. Shah, J. J., Vargas-Hernandez, N., Summers, J. D., and Kulkarni, S. Collaborative sketching (c-sketch)–an idea generation technique for engineering design. *Creative Behavior*, 35(3):168–198, 2001.
30. Streitz, N., Geissler, J., Holmer, T., Konomi, S., Müller-Tomfelde, C., Reischl, W., Rexroth, P., Seitz, P., and Steinmetz, R. i-LAND: An interactive landscape for creativity and innovation. In *Proc. ACM Conf. on Human Factors in Computing Systems*, 120–127, 1999.
31. Tang, J. C., and Minneman, S. L. VideoDraw: a video interface for collaborative drawing. *ACM Transactions on Information Systems*, 9(2):170–184, 1991.
32. Tazzoli, R., Castagna, P., and Campanini, S. E. Towards a semantic wiki wiki web. *Demo at ISWC*, 2004.
33. Torrance, E. P. The nature of creativity as manifest in its testing. In *The Nature of Creativity: Contemporary Psychological Perspectives*. Cambridge Univ. Pr., 1988.
34. Wagner, C. Breaking the knowledge acquisition bottleneck through conversational knowledge management. *Information Resources Management Journal*, 19(1):70–83, 2006.
35. Yoon, Y., Myers, B. A., and Koo, S. Visualization of fine-grained code change history. In *Proceedings of the IEEE Symposium on Visual Languages and Human-Centric Computing*, 2013.

# Distributed Analogical Idea Generation: Inventing with Crowds

**Lixiu Yu, Aniket Kittur, Robert E. Kraut**
Carnegie Mellon University
5000 Forbes Avenue, Pittsburgh, PA 15213
{lixiuyu, nkittur, robert.kraut}@cs.cmu.edu

## ABSTRACT
Harnessing crowds can be a powerful mechanism for increasing innovation. However, current approaches to crowd innovation rely on large numbers of contributors generating ideas independently in an unstructured way. We introduce a new approach called *distributed analogical idea generation*, which aims to make idea generation more effective and less reliant on chance. Drawing from the literature in cognitive science on analogy and schema induction, our approach decomposes the creative process in a structured way amenable to using crowds. In three experiments we show that distributed analogical idea generation leads to better ideas than example-based approaches, and investigate the conditions under which crowds generate good schemas and ideas. Our results have implications for improving creativity and building systems for distributed crowd innovation.

### Author Keywords
Crowdsourcing; schema; innovation; creativity; analogy

### ACM Classification Keywords
H.5.3. Group and Organization Interfaces

## INTRODUCTION
Innovation is becoming increasingly driven by crowds. Many companies are turning to crowds to provide solutions to a given problem: Innocentive (innocentive.com) posts research challenges for its crowd of scientists and inventors to solve, 99Designs (99designs.com) uses the crowd to generate a variety of graphic designs, and Threadless (threadless.com) manufactures t-shirts from crowd-submitted designs. Other firms, like Quirky (quirky.com), ask the crowd to identify interesting problems as well as solutions to them.

However, crowd innovation can also fail or produce poor quality ideas. For example, Quirky has developed and manufactured 340 distinct products from ideas generated using a crowdsourcing paradigm, but these products have been culled from hundreds of thousands of contributed ideas. Such numbers are indicative of current crowd innovation approaches, which rely on large numbers of individuals or small teams working independently, under the assumption that each has a small chance of contributing a valuable idea or solution. In such an environment enough people may produce a few good ideas, but the process is highly dependent on chance, and results in many ideas that provide little value to the company and many members of the crowd who do not gain any monetary benefits. Improving the effectiveness of crowd idea generation could thus have significant benefits to both companies and crowds.


*CHI 2014,* April 26 - May 01 2014, Toronto, ON, Canada
Copyright 2014 ACM 978-1-4503-2473-1/14/04...$15.00.
http://dx.doi.org/10.1145/2556288.2557371

Researchers have investigated ways to boost the quality of the idea generation process. Research in multiple domains shows that creativity is often built on existing work [e.g., 14], and an established technique is to use multiple previous examples to inspire new ideas [3]. However, while prior examples may help an inventor generate new ideas, they may also stifle creativity [27].

One promising approach to these challenges may be found in studies of analogy in discovery and innovation. Analogy is a powerful and prevalent mechanism for leveraging prior knowledge into new insights [11]. Scientific and technological breakthroughs rarely occur in a vacuum, and are often the result of taking a solution from a source domain and transferring it to a target domain [10, 15]. Studies of creative problem solving show that recognizing similarity in structure between problems and then applying the common structure is an effective way of solving problems [12].

However, previous work in analogy has focused on well-defined problems and well-specified target and source domains [10, 11], and even in these constrained domains problem solvers have tremendous difficulty spontaneously identifying an idea's structure and transferring it to another domain [12]. Furthermore, such approaches still rely on a single inventor or small team to engage in the entire creative process from identifying analogies to generating solutions for the problems.

In this paper we present a novel approach to generating innovative ideas through directed analogical transfer that results in more creative ideas than the common approach of using multiple examples. Furthermore, our approach provides a structured way to decompose the creative idea generation process into multiple steps so that it is amenable to using multiple groups of people. By breaking the analogical transfer process up into discrete stages we can recruit different individuals in different phases as well as select and prune ideas. Through a series of studies we show that distributed analogical idea generation leads to better ideas than example-based approaches, and investigate the conditions under which crowds generate good schemas and ideas.

## RELATED WORK

### Crowd Innovation

Many attempts to crowdsource creative work and idea generation have used online contests, in which an open call is made and a small number of submissions are chosen as winners [24]. Contests generally aim to collect contributions from many contributors, relying on large numbers of submissions to surface at least one quality product. A number of approaches have been proposed to improve the efficiency of the contest approach. For example, some contests encourage submitters to provide feedback to each other [31] or to collaborate in small teams [16]. Our work differs from these because it does not require direct interaction between inventors, which can introduce challenges in coordination, incentives and scaling [21].

### Examples and Creativity

One established technique in design practice is leveraging examples of prior work [3]. At IDEO, arguably the most influential design firm in the world, product designers store samples of past products and reuse them when there is valuable connection with current problems [14]. Studies on crowd creativity have found that providing and combining multiple examples can increase the quality of new ideas [33], and combining novel features of examples is especially useful [34]. Presenting examples early and multiple times can be especially effective improved creative work [23].

However, studies have also found that examples can lead to unintentional conformity effects, constraining the generation of creative ideas [27]. For example, a recent study on online design contests found that showing designers high quality design examples caused them to produce designs that were more homogeneous and less distinctive [22]. Perhaps because of the tension between the use of examples to inspire creativity and its tendency to constrain it, there are neither consistent findings about the examples' effects on the quality of new ideas nor a consensus about how to use examples to improve creativity. Whether presenting examples leads to a positive effect is contingent on many factors, such as the number, variety, features, and timing of presented examples. Furthermore, selecting the right examples is a challenge: with so many examples available, inventors could be easily overwhelmed.

### Design Patterns

A concept that is related to our current work is that of *design patterns:* standard solutions to common problems that can be used in many different situations [2]. Design patterns have been used in domains including architecture, software engineering, and website design [30]. However, a challenge with design patterns is that it is often difficult to induce them: in architecture and software design, experts develop the design patterns. More scalable computational methods to induce patterns (e.g., [29]) have been largely limited to highly structured domains such as structured websites. Our work aims to support the induction and application of patterns by the crowd, increasing the scalability and generality of the idea generation process.

## DISTRIBUTED ANALOGICAL IDEA GENERATION

Many innovative solutions and discoveries occur when people take an idea from one domain and apply it to another domain, a process known as *analogical transfer*. A canonical example used in numerous studies of analogical transfer is the problem of a doctor who wants to destroy a tumor with X-rays but not harm the surrounding tissue [12]. A solution to the problem is to use a divide and converge strategy: divide the x-ray into multiple small beams converging on the tumor. People are more likely to solve this problem if they first see how an analogous problem was solved (e.g., a general who conquers a castle by dividing his army into small groups and having them attack from different directions). By generating a high-level structure or *schema* of the problem and its solution, people can then use that schema to solve other problems that are structurally similar to the original problem, even if they are in different domains and have very different surface features [10, 17, 18, 20].

While a potentially powerful mechanism for innovation, researchers have found analogical transfer difficult to robustly induce. There are a number of essential steps to successful analogical transfer, any of which can cause it to fail. One core challenge is getting people to generate appropriate schemas. A schema refers to a structured mental representation consisting of entities and the relations between them[1]. To induce a schema people must generate a representation of a problem abstracted from the surface features of the source example (i.e., inducing *divide and converge* from the general/castle example) [12]. Even if an appropriate schema has been generated, another challenge has been getting people to notice that the schema is relevant and could be applied to the target domain (i.e., recognizing that *divide and converge* could solve the X-ray problem) [12].

As a result of these challenges, research on analogical transfer in cognitive science and design has focused on solving well-defined problems and using analogies from well-specified target and source domains given to participants [12, 17, 6, 25]. Unfortunately, these constraints have important limitations when applied to creative idea generation and invention, where problems are often not well-defined, target domains are not given, and where the goal may be to find a new problem, a new solution or a new domain – or potentially all three. For example, take the case where an

[1] For example, a schema for a love triangle involves three entities each of whom loves and is loved by different entities.

inventor wants to develop a new idea for a product. Unlike the analogy example described above, the inventor does not have a defined target problem or even a defined target domain; indeed, the goal is to create something novel that has not been previously imagined.

How can we develop a robust, repeatable, distributed process that can promote analogical transfer for creative idea generation? A key development is that inventors now have access to repositories of thousands of proposed ideas. Many of these ideas may share the same schema – for example, Table 1 shows three ideas from Quirky.com that share the same high-level stability schema: stabilizing something by attaching it to a more stable object. The presence of diverse, real-world embodiments of schemas in the form of proposed ideas enables us to introduce a more general framing of the analogical transfer process that supports crowd invention:

Step 1: Choose two products as examples. In this case the inventor chooses Props and Tether, shown in Table 1.

Step 2: Induce a common analogical schema from these examples. Here the inventor may induce a *stability* schema: stabilizing a mobile object by connecting it to a more stationary object. This schema provides a representation of both ideas at a more abstract level that is not specific to the source domain or surface features of the examples.

Step 3: Identify other domains where the schema could be applicable. The inventor may think of domains where things are unstable, such as bumpy bus rides, airplane turbulence, earthquakes or people with Parkinson's disease.

Step 4: Applying the schema to the target domain to generate a new product. For example, applying the *stability* schema to the bus ride domain might result in the Eclipse idea shown in Table 1, which stabilizes a person's head by connecting it via a strap to their seat.

We call this process *distributed analogical idea generation* (illustrated in Figure 1). This process has a number of attributes that makes it especially appropriate for crowdsourcing creative tasks, in which the four steps just described can be distributed among different groups. In contrast to most design contests or online brainstorming, it exploits the wisdom of the crowds for multiple subtasks, including selecting relevant examples, identifying common schemas and generating domains, problems, and solutions. This decomposition helps crowd members know what to do by providing a structured process. It supports contributions in small units of effort by decomposing the creative process into smaller steps. Because it does not require direct interaction among crowd members, it minimizes coordination costs and scales well. And because the crowd can generate multiple possibilities at each step, the process may be directed by selectively retaining intermediate products with the most potential.

In the following three experiments we empirically investigate the value of distributed analogical idea generation and the conditions under which it is most effective. As there are

| The stability schema: Stabilize a mobile object by using an attachment device to connect it to a more stable object. | |
|---|---|
|  | Props: This headphone keeper is designed to keep your earbuds tethered to you, making them easily accessible when you want to return to your musical oasis. Worn around the neck, Props extends like arms to your earbuds, keeping them in place and in the vicinity of your ears. |
| 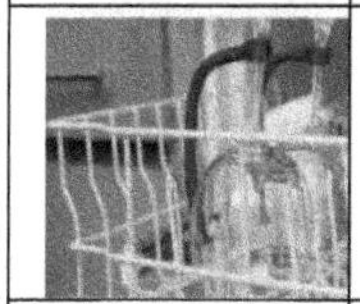 | Tether: Washing your wine glasses can be risky business, especially when you are using your dishwasher. Save your stemware with Tether, a flexible plastic rod that stabilizes your stemware as it goes through the cycle. |
|  | Eclipse: Eclipse is a plush, padded eye mask designed to keep you comfortable while you travel. The mask comes with a webbing strap which can be wrapped around a headrest, and velcros to the back of the eye mask to keep your head from bobbing while sleeping. |

**Table 1. Examples and the shared schema.**

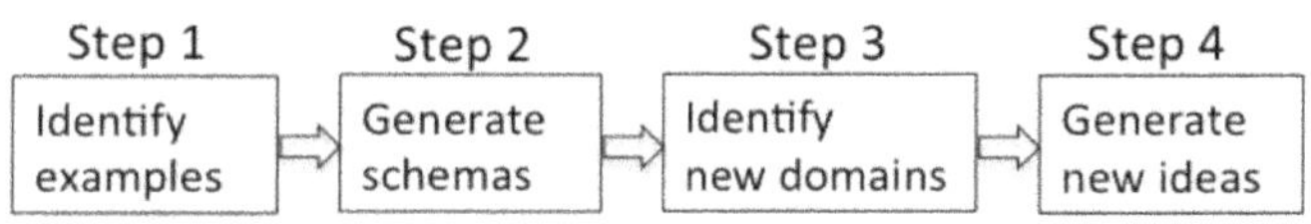


**Figure 1: The distributed analogical idea generation.**

a number of challenges at each step that could derail the process, we order the presentation of experiments working backwards from the desired final state. Thus in Experiment 1 we investigate whether given an analogical schema participants generate better ideas than if not given such a schema (i.e., Steps 3 & 4). We describe this experiment first as it tests our core hypothesis. In Experiment 2 we then examine the conditions under which participants are able to generate good schemas (Steps 1 & 2). Finally in Experiment 3 we demonstrate how the full process can be accomplished in a distributed manner by using different participants for different steps.

## EXPERIMENTS

### Experiment 1: Generating Ideas from Analogical Schemas

In this experiment we aim to test whether the crowd generates better ideas from analogical schemas than from examples. We operationalize a specific type of schema in the context of this paper as an idea schema, consisting of a *problem* an idea aims to solve (e.g., preventing something fragile from breaking) and a *mechanism* for doing so (e.g., using a flexible cord to secure it to a stable object). Importantly, a schema abstracts away surface details to focus on the underlying structure [10, 12].

One important factor governing the effectiveness of a schema is likely to be how concrete versus abstract is its representation. Abstract schemas may help people avoid fixating on specific features, promoting far transfer to diverse domains and solutions. However, abstract schemas may be difficult for people to use if they are at too high a level to usefully constrain the possible domains and solutions for an idea. Although there have been conflicting views regarding the role of examples and schemas in analogical transfer, abstract schemas alone seem to be difficult to communicate if they are not grounded in specific examples [26]. However, these examples may lead to greater fixation on details that may be detrimental [27]. For example, problem solvers may become fixated on details like the Velcro or plastic rods used to attach one object to another, constraining their creativity.

To examine the effects of abstract versus concrete representation of schemas, we created two ways of presenting schemas: as abstract schemas alone (*Use schemas*) and as abstract schemas illustrated with concrete examples (*Use schemas and see examples*). We compared these to two control conditions in which participants brainstorm product ideas after merely seeing examples (*See examples*) or being encouraged to use these examples as the basis of their product ideas (*Use examples*).

### Participants

In this and all experiments, participants were recruited by posting tasks to Amazon Mechanical Turk [19]. Overall 209 workers participated in Experiment 1. Forty-seven percent of participants were women, and 90% were native English speakers. Their average age was 31 and ranged from 19 to 69.

| | |
|---|---|
| The stability schema: Stabilize a mobile object by using an attachment device to connect it to a more stable object. | |
|  | Eclipse: Eclipse is a plush, padded eye mask designed to keep you comfortable while you travel. The mask comes with a webbing strap which can be wrapped around a headrest, and velcros to the back of the eye mask to keep your head from bobbing while sleeping. |
| The separation schema: Detach one object from another by using comb-like mechanisms. | |
|  | Broom Groomer: it is a step-on dustpan with added functionality that makes sweeping easier. Rubber "teeth" on the back of the dustpan let you quickly and easily comb out dust bunnies from your broom's bristles, while a smooth rubber "lip" on the front keeps the dustpan flush with the floor so nothing slips through the cracks. |
| The space schema: Create space and organize things by raising the work surface and creating storage. | |
|  | Spacebar: The Space Bar is a desk accessory that minimizes clutter while providing additional USB ports for your computer. After a long day of work, simply slide your keyboard into the designated space below the shelf and store your office miscellany-keys, digital camera, etc.-up top. |

**Table 2. Experiment 1: Examples and schemas.**

### Design and Procedure

After they accepted the task, participants were randomly assigned to one of the four conditions and asked to generate a product idea. In all conditions, participants were told that their ideas would be evaluated in terms of *practicality* (the product can be designed and produced easily), *usefulness* (the product solves an important problem) and *novelty* (the product hadn't been thought of by others). The conditions were:

*1. See examples.* Participants brainstormed a new product idea after seeing the three examples shown in Table 2. They were not explicitly required to use any of the examples as the inspiration for their product idea.

*2. Use examples.* Participants were first asked to read the three examples in Table 2 as well as summaries describing their novel properties. We created these summaries to control for processing and engagement differences involved in the *Use schema and see examples* condition (the third condition). Because participants in the latter condition were asked to read both the examples and the schemas, they may have been more likely to engage in deeper cognitive processing than the naturalistic *See examples* condition. To avoid this engagement difference, which might affect the final results, we asked people to read both the examples and their summaries. Specifically they were told,

*"Product ideas have different features, which are special properties of the products to attract consumers. The above product ideas have their own features that make them different from their similar products. For example,*

*Eclipse: A mask that not only keeps the light out, but stabilizes your head by using a strap so it doesn't bob around during travel.*

*Broom groomer: It makes sweeping easier just by adding rubber "teeth"."*

*Space bar: It minimizes clutter while providing additional USB ports for your computer.*

Participants were asked to generate one new product idea based on the given examples.

*3. Use schemas and see examples.* Participants were asked to read the three examples shown in Table 2 along with experimenter-generated schemas for each (referred to as 'design rules' in the instructions). These schemas are also shown in Table 2 above the description of each example. Participants were then asked to generate a new product idea by using one of the schemas.

They were told, *"Now please generate a new product idea by using one of the design rules."*

*4. Use schemas.* Participants only saw the three schemas shown in Table 2 without seeing the examples. They were asked to generate a new product idea by using one of the schemas.

### Rating idea quality

As rating the creativity of ideas is by nature a subjective judgment, we base our outcome measures on prior research that argues that creative ideas need to be both novel and practical [7]. We considered a product novel if it was not obvious and was different from existing products on the market[2]. We operationalized practicality in terms of *usefulness* to the user of the product and the *practicality* of manufacturing it today. For example, a teleportation device might be both novel and useful, but is infeasible to manufacture.

Two judges blind to the experimental condition rated each product idea on three 7-point Likert scales of novelty, usefulness, and practicality. One judge was the first author, and the second judge was an oDesk worker with skills in product development and marketing. After several rounds of training and discussion, the judges achieved high inter-rater reliabilities of .90, .86 and .88 for practicality, usefulness, and novelty respectively, calculated as the Intraclass Correlation Coefficient (ICC) [8]. The final quality of the ideas was computed as the geometric mean of the three dimensions to weight against ideas that were low on any given dimension [9].

Below we present an example of a highly-rated idea generated from the *separation* schema (to detach one object from another by using comb-like mechanisms). This idea was rated high in novelty, usefulness, and practicality.

*The problem when kneading dough is that the dough gets stuck in between your fingers. This makes it difficult to clean your hands, and you also lose a lot of the dough in the process. The solution is a device that has a space for each of your fingers. It will come in three sizes so that you can pick the size that best suits the size of your fingers. You run your fingers through the device and the extra dough is removed. The surface of the finger-comb does not allow the dough to stick to it, and thus is easily removed and cleaned. The extra dough can be added to the kneaded dough to [eliminate] waste and speed up clean-up time.*

### Analysis and Results

The means and standard errors of the ratings for the ideas are shown in Figure 2. We were interested in the quality of ideas produced by different idea generation processes. Among the four conditions, two conditions were analogy-based (*Use schema and see examples* and *Use schema*), and two conditions were example-based (*See examples* and *Use examples*). To determine whether analogy-based idea generation led to better ideas than example-based idea generation we ran a regression analysis with the dependent variable the quality of the ideas, with a planned contrast between the analogy- and example-based conditions. The results showed that analogy-based idea generation resulted in significantly better ideas than the example-based conditions, $b = .32$, $t(208) = 3.34$, $p < .001$; $d = .47$.

[2] Raters judged novelty based on their experience rather than a market survey or patent because we wanted to assess an idea's relative novelty compared to products that most people would know about, rather than using the patent office's standard that the idea was unique in historical time [28, p.169].

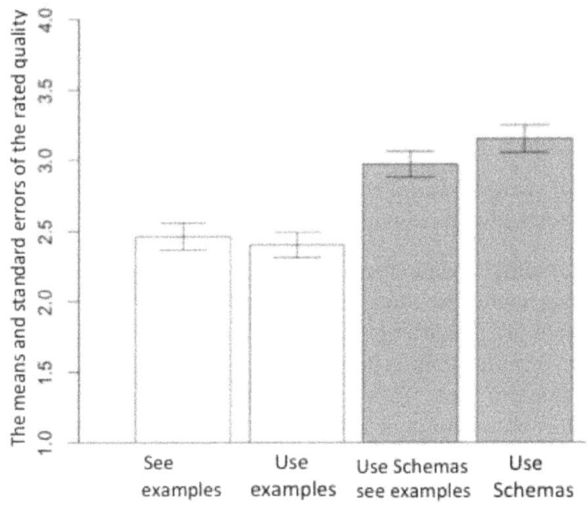


**Figure 2. Experiment 1: the quality of the ideas**

We further examined the question of whether analogy-based idea generation would be helped or hindered by showing concrete examples along with the analogical schema. However, we found no significant difference between the *Use schemas* and *Use schemas and see examples* conditions, $b=.12$, $t(113)=.94$, $p=.35$. Thus the benefits of using analogical schemas appear to be robust to whether they are shown grounded in concrete examples.

Although prior research has suggested that combining schema and examples improves analogical problem solving [28], our task was different from typical analogical transfer in that we asked people to generate completely new ideas by finding both problems and solutions. In this context it is possible that adding examples to schemas might produce two conflicting effects: fixating people on surface features, while helping them better understand the schemas. These two forces might counteract each other's influence on quality. Further research is needed to understand the conditions under which these results may hold.

### Experiment 2: Generating Schemas from Examples

After demonstrating that schemas can improve idea generation, we turn to the question of how to help people generate good analogical schemas. Even though previous research shows that good schemas are critical to analogical transfer, getting people to induce them has been remarkably challenging [13]. Researchers have asked participants to summarize analogous problems, provide a verbal statement of the underlying principle or generate a diagrammatic representation, all with limited success [12, 13]. The most effective method for schema induction appears to involve having participants explicitly map multiple problems sharing a schema onto each other [12]. When people find correspondences between these instances, they are more likely to create good schemas that focus on deep relations rather than surface features. Based on these findings, we predicted that

| | |
|---|---|
|  | Pivot Power: a creative outlet with adjustable outlets. It has a flexible form that bends into circular, semi-circular, and zig-zag shapes to fit around furniture and in tight spaces. Every plug fits into every outlet. |

**Table 3. The contrasting example used in Experiment 2.**

having people induce schemas from multiple examples would help them produce useful schemas.

Additionally, prior research has found that adding contrasting examples can enhance the quality of generated schemas [13]. Showing a contrasting example that does not share an underlying schema could help highlight similarities between the ideas that do share the schema and therefore result in better schema induction.

### *Participants*

Overall 145 workers participated in Experiment 2: 53% percent were women, and 91% were native English speakers. Their average age was 33 and ranged from 19 to 66.

### *Design and Procedure*

All participants in this experiment were exposed to a training session, similar across experimental conditions, where they were asked to generate a schema for the *Broom Groomer* product idea from Table 2. We then showed them a correct schema generated by the experimenters for the example (the *separation* schema in Table 2). Participants were informed that a good schema should meet the following criteria:

"*It specifies a purpose (e.g., detaches things); it specifies a mechanism (e.g., uses comb-like features); it shouldn't be too vague (e.g. "make things easy" is too vague); it shouldn't have too many details (e.g., the details of the given idea, such as the color or the dustpan, should not be included).*"

After training, participants were shown one or more examples from a fixed set of ideas (depending on condition) and asked to generate a single schema that applied to one or more examples. Specifically, the instructions stated:

"*A schema refers to the underlying structure of an idea. It is a description or template for how to solve a problem that can be used in many different situations. Can you find a schema that applies to one or more of the above product ideas?*"

Participants were randomly assigned to one of four conditions. In the *one example, two examples,* and *three examples* conditions, participants respectively saw a random set of one, two or three of the examples from Table 1, all of which share the *stability schema* (though the schema was not provided to them). Additionally, a *contrasting example* condition was used in which participants saw two random examples sharing the stability schema and one product idea ("Pivot Power") that did not share the *stability* schema or any other schema from the examples in Table 3. Thus the *contrasting example* condition had the same total number of examples as the *three examples* condition, and the same number of analogous examples as the *two examples* condition.

### *Rating schema quality*

In order to rate participants' schemas, we developed a rubric for what makes a high quality schema based on previous literature on schema induction and transfer [12] and adapting it to the domain of creative idea generation and product development. We operationalize a good schema as capturing the essential problem and mechanism from examples without including specific example details (e.g., "Detach one object from another by using comb-like mechanisms"). Schemas could be scored poorly for multiple reasons: they could be too general to describe the essence of the idea because they do not describe the problem or mechanism (e.g., "Make sweeping easier" does not include a mechanism); or they could be too specific because they include features from specific examples (e.g., "Add a rubber comb to a dustpan"). Two raters blind to the condition rated participants' schemas using this rubric on a 7-point Likert scale. Schemas from three participants were removed because they ignored or misunderstood the instructions. After several rounds of training and discussion, the judges achieved high inter-rater reliability of .93. The reported results are based upon the averaged scores of the two raters.

### *Analysis and Results*

Table 4 shows the means and standard deviations of all conditions. We first tested the effects of the number of examples on the quality of the generated schemas. We ran a regression analysis with the quality of the schemas as the dependent variable. We performed two contrast coding: a linear contrast testing whether schemas improved with an increasing number of examples, and a curvilinear contrast testing for diminishing returns of the number of examples. The results revealed that the linear relationship between *One example*, *Two examples* and *Three examples* was significant, $b = .72$, $t(113) = 3.69$, $p < .001$ and the curvilinear relationship was not, $b = .12$, $t(113) = .95$, $p = .35$. These results suggest that adding analogous examples facilitates schema generation, and that adding additional analogous examples beyond the first continue to improve the resulting schemas.

We next examined the effects of adding a contrasting example on the quality of the generated schemas. Two conditions had been included to test this: *Three examples* and *Contrasting examples*. The *Three examples* condition had a third similar example and *Contrasting examples* had a third contrasting example. A regression analysis comparing *Three examples*, *Two examples* against *Contrasting examples* conditions showed that the difference between *Three examples*

| Condition | Mean | SD | Freq. |
|---|---|---|---|
| 1. One example | 2.09 | 1.82 | 45 |
| 2. Two examples | 3.16 | 1.68 | 31 |
| 3. Three examples | 3.53 | 1.78 | 38 |
| 4. Contrasting examples | 2.68 | 1.68 | 28 |
| Total | 2.86 | 1.74 | 142 |

**Table 4. Experiment 2: Effects of example number and type on schema quality.**

and *Contrasting examples* was significant, $b = .85$, $t(65) = 1.94$, $p < .05$, and the difference between *Two examples* and *Contrasting examples* was not significant, $b=.48$, $t(58) = 1.06$, $p = .29$. These results suggest that adding a contrasting example is not as useful as adding another analogous example. One explanation for this may be that while Gick and Paterson [13] found benefits for adding contrasting examples, their contrasting examples had dimensions in common and could be aligned with the analogous examples. Our contrasting examples on the other hand were very different from the analogous examples, and thus may not have been useful for drawing participants' attention to schema-relevant aspects of the examples.

### Experiment 3: Distributed Analogical Idea Generation

In Experiments 1 and 2 we established the building blocks of the distributed analogical idea generation process. We have shown that participants were able to generate better ideas using experimenter-generated schemas than using examples (Experiment 1), and also identified conditions under which participants can generate good schemas themselves (Experiment 2). We now close the loop by examining whether the schemas generated by participants in Experiment 2 also lead to better ideas than using examples. In doing so we aim to answer two questions: first, whether the quality of the schema generated in Experiment 2 affects the quality of the resulting ideas; and second, whether the process can be run end-to-end in a distributed way; that is, using different individuals at different stages.

There are a number of potential advantages to having a distributed idea generation process. Breaking the task into stages enables multiple people to engage in the process iteratively, potentially benefiting from the diversity of their ideas and backgrounds. It reduces the participation costs of the task, opening it up to those who may be less committed or have less expertise. It also enables quality control to take place between stages. For example, once people generate schemas, those schemas can be evaluated and only the good ones used in the idea generation step. In theory, having multiple stages could also allow for flexible control and direction of the ideation process, as the examples, schemas, domains, and ideas could be selectively pruned at each stage to focus on areas of interest to the process creator.

In Experiment 3 we selected some of the good and poor schemas produced in Experiment 2 as input and asked new participants to generate ideas based on them. We compared the quality of the ideas to those produced after seeing good or poor schemas to those produced after seeing examples (using the procedures from the *See examples* condition in Experiment 1).

#### Participants

Overall 121 workers participated in the experiment: 47% were women, and 95% were native English speakers. Their average age was 28, and ranged from 19 to 48.

#### Design and Procedure

Participants were asked to generate a new idea after seeing a product idea (*See an example*), or generate a new idea using a schema, after seeing the schema and the product idea it was based on (the experimental conditions). Participants were either presented with a bad schemas (*Use a bad schema & see its example*) or good schema (*Use a good schema & see its example*). These schemas were randomly selected from the schemas generated by the crowd in Experiment 2. There were nine bad schemas (schemas rated 3 or lower on the 7-point quality scale), and nine good schemas (schemas rated 5 or higher). Examples of good and bad schemas are shown in Table 5. The product ideas these schemas were based on were the ideas shown in Table 1, one of which randomly showed up in the experiment.

#### Rating product quality

We used the procedure from Experiment 2 in which two raters blind to the experimental condition rated each product idea. The inter-rater reliabilities were .91, .80 and .81 for practicality, usefulness, and novelty respectively.

#### Analysis and Results

The means and standard errors of the ideas are shown in Figure 3. We tested hypotheses using a regression analysis with *quality* as the dependent variable, conditions as the independent variable, and education level and language as control variables. Results showed that ideas in *Use a good schema & see its example condition* were significantly better than those in *See an example*, $b = .78$, $t(76) = 2.64$, $p < .01$, as well as better than those in *Use a bad schema & see its example*, $b = .65$, $t(80) = 2.21$, $p < .05$. On the other hand, quality in the *Use a bad schema & see its example* and *See an example* were not significantly different, $b = .13$, $t(83) = .48$, $p = .64$. These results suggest that participants were more likely to generate good ideas using good schemas than seeing examples or using bad schemas. Table 5 shows

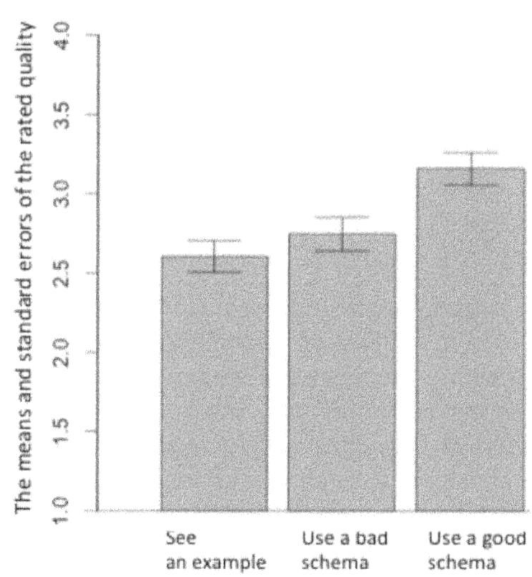


**Figure 3. Experiment 3: the quality of the ideas**

| | |
|---|---|
| Good schemas | *Schema 1: The idea aims to attach from one unstable object to another stable object to keep the unstable object from moving.*<br>Idea 1 (scored 4.40): Photographers can easily lose lens caps when shooting, especially if they're shooting in a crowded venue, such as a sporting event, or if they're shooting in nature. "Lens Cap Leaves" doubles as a lens hood and a lens cap. Imagine that the lens hood for a lens, rather than be one solid piece, is made up of interlocking leaves, like a vegetable steamer (here's an amazon link to what I'm talking about: http://www.amazon.com/Trudeau-Stainless-Steel-Vegetable-Steamer/dp/B00062B0K6). When you're done shooting, these leaves close up to seal the end of the lens, forming a cap that's permanently attached to the end of the lens. This will not only give the lens a permanently mounted lens hood, but will also give the lens a permanently mounted lens cap. |
| | *Schema 2: Use an object to stabilize another object. It keeps it from moving around.*<br>Idea 2 (scored 4.56): My cat is very messy with her food and water. She is constantly knocking her bowls around, wasting food and water, creating a mess, and attracting ants and other critters. The bowls need to be held in place.<br>A rubber base, specifically tailored to the size of common pet food bowls. The mechanism involves gripping tightly around the bowl, so as to not spill food and water in the base, as well as gripping to the floor, using a suction-cup system that leaves no trace, to ensure the bowls will be held in place. |
| Bad schemas | *Schema 3: The idea refers to something being secured to your head.*<br>Idea 3 (scored 1.00): Too much light and sound during sleep time. Put on the eye and ear cover to get better sleep during the day. |
| | *Schema 4: The idea aims to grab and hold.*<br>Idea 4 (scored 1.50): You are out protecting your hood with your gang of brothers and its late at night. You sit down for a quick rest, leaning up against the concrete wall. There is no way to get comfort in that position. What will you do? Now introducing the Power Nap Hoodie. You just raise your hood over your head and lean back. The extra fabric within creates a cushion between you and the wall. |
| Examples | Idea 5 (scored 2.00): Have you ever lost your ear buds or found them lying on a counter or table with a bunch of knots in them? This product attaches your waist strap or a belt loop of your pants. It is retractable ear buds. Never get knots or tangles in your ear buds again. |

**Table 5. Experiment 3: Examples of schemas and ideas. Scores range from 7 (best) to 1 (worst).**

examples of ideas produced in different conditions.

In summary, Experiment 3 shows that participants using good schemas generated by others were more likely to generate good ideas than those who just saw examples. However, bad schemas did not have this effect. These findings further support the idea that distributed analogical idea generation is more effective than example-based idea generation. Importantly, together with Experiment 2, they demonstrate the viability of a crowdsourced, distributed analogy idea generation process, with one group generating schemas from examples and a second group generating ideas using the first group's schemas.

## DISCUSSION

We introduced a novel approach for idea generation that leverages analogy to produce ideas better than those generated by just providing examples by spurring creativity in a structured way. We demonstrated the effectiveness of this approach through three experiments. Experiment 1 showed that people generate better product ideas when given good analogical schemas (in this case, experimenter-generated) than when given examples. Experiments 2 and 3 demonstrated that the crowd could generate useful schemas from examples, and that these crowd-generated schemas could be used by others to generate better product ideas than the examples that formed the basis of the schemas.

While the current work provides encouraging support for the value of using analogical transfer in creative ideation, it provides only one step towards understanding the cognitive processes involved in applying schemas in generating new ideas. Understanding exactly what makes a good vs. poor schema remains an important area for future research. For example, schemas containing both a purpose and a mechanism might provide people with "hammers" for searching for problems in different domains and therefore facilitate the searching process. If this is true, a good schema must have a good abstract purpose and a solution mechanism to assist this searching and mapping process. A bad schema, which doesn't meet such requirements (e.g., being too abstract without purpose or mechanism or being too concrete with many details of the examples), might fail to facilitate such a process. For example, in Table 5, Idea 3 and Idea 4 were generated using a very concrete schema and a very abstract schema, respectively. Idea 3 is overly similar to the given example and Idea 4 is not relevant to Schema 4 at all.

Why were schemas more effective than examples? Previous findings in analogy transfer model schema induction as a one-to-one mapping process of abstracting correspondences and eliminating differences [12]. This is consistent with our hypothesis that schemas abstract out surface features and thus might avoid fixation and conformity effects. For example, the "retractable ear buds" idea generated by a participant (Idea 5 in Table 5) is highly similar to one of the examples we provided, suggesting fixation at work. However, unlike studies on analogical transfer, the participants in our experiment did not have an analogous target problem to solve. Instead, they needed to search for a target domain, identify a candidate problem in that domain, and transfer the original schema to that problem in order to generate an idea. Given the challenges that previous research in analogical transfer have identified in promoting transfer even when the source and target problems have been hand-selected and perfectly alignable, we find it somewhat remarkable that crowds of untrained novices can accomplish this process consistently and show robust benefits.

One explanation for our success is that we are using realistic problems our participants could easily understand. Prior research has shown that people can accomplish complex abstract reasoning in familiar domains they would otherwise be unable to; for example, the notoriously challenging Wason selection task (testing if people understand the rule "if p then q") can be correctly solved if framed in a familiar domain (e.g., "if one is to drink alcohol, one must be over eighteen") [4]. If true, this would suggest that the crowd used for a given task should be familiar enough with the domain that they can induce the correct schemas for it. However, an interesting question is whether a small expert crowd (or the requester) might be able to generate a good schema and then use a larger, less expert crowd to generate ideas using the schema. Such an approach would maximize for expertise for inducing good schemas and maximize for diversity and scale for idea generation.

One question that merits further investigation is how to select appropriate examples (Step 1). In the present work we manually selected analogous and non-analogous examples in order to experimentally test the value of the approach. Promisingly, we did find it easy to find multiple analogous examples even among the relatively small selection of Quirky's existing products. However, scaling this process to the thousands of ideas that have been submitted to Quirky, let alone the millions of products in the U.S. patent database, is a formidable prospect. Some encouraging research shows that people are able to find examples based on deep analogical similarity even in Quirky's large product submission database [32]. Other crowdsourcing studies have shown the power of human workflows for classifying large datasets on deep structural features [e.g., 5, 1]. Such workflow designs, especially if combined with computational methods [29], might be a promising way to find ideas sharing common schemas. However, given our results that even given one example some participants could still generate good schemas, we believe our results can be useful even today for improving crowd idea generation.

### Further Distributing Idea Generation

One significant advantage of schema-mediated idea generation is that it can be decomposed into subtasks, which can be further assigned to different individuals. As shown in our experiments, it is possible to implement the process with different crowds: one set of people for schema generation and another for idea generation. This process may be able to be broken down into even more sub-steps. For example, generating an idea from a schema involves multiple substeps which we combined into a single task: generating a target domain in which the schema may be applicable (e.g., "what are some domains in which objects need to be stabilized"), mapping the schema to that domain (e.g., "what are some possible objects in the new domain that map to elements of the *stability* schema"), and generating a solution (e.g., "this configuration of objects solves the problem in this domain using the *stability* schema"). One might implement these steps with different crowds and thereby benefit from their diversity.

Decomposability also allows for greater direction and management of the creative process. Each stage produces an output that is input to the next stage, meaning that the process can be restarted at any point to gather more options (e.g., schemas, domains, ideas). Quality control could be built into each stage, culling poor quality ideas before they propagate. Alternatively, if a requester is interested in a particular direction for ideas, schemas and domains that are of less interest could be pruned in order to focus attention on areas of greater relevance.

### System design

These results from these experiments could inform the design of systems for crowd innovation. For example, an easy way to implement such an idea could be through a two-stage contest in crowdsourced innovation websites such as Quirky in which the crowd is asked to generate schemas and then the best schemas are chosen as the basis to generate ideas. Long term, one promising advantage of abstracting schemas from examples is that schemas could be aggregated and searched over. For example, the Props, Tether, and Eclipse examples in Figure 1 all share the *stability* schema. If such schemas were stored along with the examples then inventors could search for ideas based on schemas rather than being limited to keywords or surface attributes, finding potential solutions that could be transferred to their target domain. There are already many ideas on the Internet that could comprise the basis for such a schema-mediated search engine: Quirky alone has over 300,000 contributed ideas. Such a system could also increase the value of the many ideas that are not selected in design or ideation contests, making them potentially useful for sparking other ideas. Understanding how to represent schemas at the right level of abstraction and how to search for them remains an important issue for future research.

### Limitations and Future Work

As with any initial study, there are many interesting questions left for future work. The participants in all our experiments were recruited from Mechanical Turk workers who are used to performing simple micro-tasks. One area for profitable future research is investigating whether this process will still be effective for experienced inventors or even teams of experts. On the one hand, it might be even more effective, because real inventors or experts could generate better schemas, domains, and ideas. On the other hand, they might be already using schemas in their process, limiting the additional gains.

### Towards a Future of Improved Crowd Innovation

Today, most crowd inventors have little knowledge of, and few strategies for, effective innovation. Current crowd innovation sites typically reward only a tiny fraction of those contributing ideas, with the vast majority's contributions providing no benefits. With the growing number of publicly available idea repositories, it will be increasingly important and valuable to make existing ideas more useful for spurring new ideas. Such efforts might also help to address incentive issues: instead of only one idea which wins a contest being rewarded, imagine if unselected ideas that spur future ideas could be rewarded based on the success of the spurred ideas. Although more research is needed on how to abstract, represent, search across and integrate schemas to make such a future possible, the present research provides one step towards harnessing the power of crowd through analogy. We envision a future of interconnected crowd idea generation in which ideas and schemas build on and inspire each other, leading to a cycle of continuously accelerating innovation.

## ACKNOWLEDGMENTS
This work was supported by NSF grants IIS-1149797, IIS-1217559, OCI-0943148, IIS-0968484, IIS-1111124, Bosch, Google, and Microsoft, and Carnegie Mellon's Center for the Future of Work.

## REFERENCES
1. Andre P., Kittur, A., and Dow, S. P. 2014. Crowd synthesis: Extracting categories and clusters from complex data. In *Proc. CSCW*, ACM.
2. Alexander, C., Ishikawa, S., and Silverstein, M. A., *Pattern Language: Towns, Buildings, Construction.* Oxford University Press, 1977.
3. Buxton, B. *Sketching User Experiences: Getting the Design Right and the Right Design.* Morgan Kaufmann, 2010.
4. Cheng, P.W. and Holyoak, K.J. Pragmatic reasoning schemas. *Cognitive psychology* 17, 4 (1985), 391–416.
5. Chilton, L., Little, G., Edge, D., Weld, D.S., and Landay, J.A. Cascade: Crowdsourcing Taxonomy Creation. In *Proc. CHI* 2013.
6. Clement, C.A. Effect of structural embedding on analogical transfer: Manifest versus latent analogs. *The American journal of psychology*, (1994), 1–38.
7. Finke, R.A., Ward, T.B., and Smith, S.M. *Creative cognition: Theory, research, and applications.* MIT press Cambridge, MA, 1992.
8. Fisher, R., *Statistical methods for research workers.* Oliver and Boyd, 1954.
9. Galton, F. The geometric mean, in vital and social statistics. In *Proc RSL 29*, (1879), 365–367.
10. Gentner, D. Structure-mapping: A theoretical framework for analogy. *Cognitive Science* 7, (1983), 155–170.
11. Gentner, D., S. Brem, R. Ferguson, P. Wolff, A. B. Markaman, K. and Forbus. *Analogy and creativity in the works of Johannes Kepler.* T. N. Ward, S. M. Smith, J. Vaid, eds. Creative Thought. Amer. Psych. Association, Washington, DC, (1997). 403–460.
12. Gick, M.L. and Holyoak, K.J. Schema induction and analogical transfer. *Cognitive psychology 15*, (1983), 1–38.
13. Gick, M.L. and Paterson, K. Do contrasting examples facilitate schema acquisition and analogical transfer? *Canadian Journal of Psychology* 46, 4 (1992), 539.
14. Hargadon, A.B. Brokering knowledge: Linking learning and innovation. *Research in Organizational behavior* 24, (2002), 41–85.
15. Hesse, Mary B., *The Structure of Scientific Inference.* Macmillan, London, 1974.
16. Hutter, K., Hautz, J., Füller, J., Mueller, J., and Matzler, K. The Tension between Competition and Collaboration in Community-Based Design Contests. *Creativity and Innovation Management* 20, 1 (2011), 3–21.
17. Hummel, J. E. and Holyoak K. J., Distributed representations of structure: a theory of analogical access and mapping. *Psychological Review* 104, (1997), 427–66
18. Hummel, J. E. and Holyoak, K. J., A symbolic-connectionist theory of relational inference and generalization. *Psychological Review* 110, (2003), 220–264.
19. Kittur, A., Chi, E.H., and Suh, B. Crowdsourcing user studies with Mechanical Turk. In *Proc. CHI'*2008, 453–456.
20. Kittur, A., Holyoak, K. J. and Hummel, J. E. Using idea observers in higher-order human category learning. In *Proc. CogSci, 2006.*
21. Kittur, A.,Kraut, R. E. 2008. Harnessing the Wisdom of Crowds in Wikipedia: Quality Through Coordination. CSCW 2008. ACM.
22. Koh, T.K. *Essays on Technology-Enabled Platforms.* PhD Dissertation, Carnegie Mellon University, 2012.
23. Kulkarni, C., Dow, S.P., and Klemmer, S.R. Early and Repeated Exposure to Examples Improves Creative Work. In *Proc.* CogSci, 2012.
24. Lakhani, K.R. and Panetta, J.A. The principles of distributed innovation. *Innovations* 2, 3 (2007), 97–112.
25. Linsey, J., Laux, J., Clauss, E., Wood, K.L., and Markman, A. Increasing innovation: A trilogy of experiments towards a design-by-analogy method. Proceedings of the ASME 2007.
26. Reeves, L. and Weisberg, R.W. The role of content and abstract information in analogical transfer. *Psychological Bulletin 115*, 3 (1994), 381.
27. Smith, S.M., Ward, T.B., and Schumacher, J.S. Constraining effects of examples in a creative generation task. *Memory & Cognition* 21, 6 (1993), 837–845.
28. Sternberg, R.J. *Handbook of creativity.* Cambridge University Press, 1998.
29. Talton, J., Yang, L., Kumar, R., Lim, M., Goodman, N., and Mech, R. Learning design patterns with Bayesian grammar induction. In *Proc. UIST*, 2012, 63–74
30. Wolfgang, P., *Design patterns for object-oriented software development.* Addison-Wesley Publishing, England, 1995.
31. Yang, Y., Chen, P. Y., and Pavlou, P. Open innovation: An empirical study of online contests. In *Proc. ICIS* 2009.
32. Yu, L., Kittur, A., and Kraut, R. Searching for analogical ideas with crowds. *CHI'14.*
33. Yu, L. and Nickerson, J.V. Cooks or cobblers? Crowd creativity through combination. In *Proc. CHI 2011*, 1393–1402.
34. Yu, L. and Sakamoto, Y. Feature selection in crowd creativity. In *Foundations of Augmented Cognition. Directing the Future of Adaptive Systems.* Springer, 2011, 383–392.

# Frenzy: Collaborative Data Organization for Creating Conference Sessions

Lydia B. Chilton[1] Juho Kim[2] Paul André[3] Felicia Cordeiro[1] James A. Landay[1]
Daniel S. Weld[1] Steven P. Dow[3] Robert C. Miller[2] Haoqi Zhang[2,4]

[1]University of Washington
Seattle, WA
{hmslydia, felicia0, landay, weld}@cs.uw.edu

[2]MIT CSAIL
Cambridge, MA,
{juhokim, rcm}@mit.edu

[3]HCI Institute, CMU
Pittsburgh, PA
{pandre, spdow}@cs.cmu.edu

[4]Northwestern University
Evanston, IL
hq@northwestern.edu

## ABSTRACT

Organizing conference sessions around themes improves the experience for attendees. However, the session creation process can be difficult and time-consuming due to the amount of expertise and effort required to consider alternative paper groupings. We present a collaborative web application called *Frenzy* to draw on the efforts and knowledge of an entire program committee. Frenzy comprises (a) interfaces to support large numbers of experts working collectively to create sessions, and (b) a two-stage process that decomposes the session-creation problem into meta-data elicitation and global constraint satisfaction. Meta-data elicitation involves a large group of experts working simultaneously, while global constraint satisfaction involves a smaller group that uses the meta-data to form sessions.

We evaluated Frenzy with 48 people during a deployment at the CSCW 2014 program committee meeting. The session making process was much faster than the traditional process, taking 88 minutes instead of a full day. We found that meta-data elicitation was useful for session creation. Moreover, the sessions created by Frenzy were the basis of the CSCW 2014 schedule.

### Author Keywords

Crowdsourcing; groupware; communitysourcing

### ACM Classification Keywords

H.5.m. Information interfaces and presentation (e.g., HCI): User Interfaces – Graphical user interfaces.

## INTRODUCTION

When planning an academic conference, organizers group papers into thematic sessions so that attendees can see related talks in the same time-block. However, constructing and arranging conference sessions can be a challenge, especially for a small group of organizers. First, organizers often need to consider a large number of accepted papers from multiple sub-disciplines. Knowledge about these papers is typically distributed within the community. Second, accepted papers can be grouped in multiple ways (e.g., by topic, by problem domain, by method of study), so maintaining a global outlook of how and why papers fit together is often non-trivial. Third, sessions must satisfy two hard constraints: each paper must be assigned to exactly one session and every session should be the same length. This implies that even coherent paper groupings may be infeasible if they contain too many or too few papers, and that clever alternative groupings may be required to avoid stray papers or incomplete sessions. Since creating a session affects what other sessions can be created, the process of coming up with coherent sessions that satisfy global scheduling constraints requires effective coordination.

To manage this process, many conference-organizing committees use printouts of the accepted paper abstracts. Through informal observations and interviews with organizers of two large conferences, we learned that a small group of dedicated organizers typically spend a day or two in person creating sessions by printing abstracts on cards, then tangibly arranging cards in piles, and trading cards between piles, until the piles roughly form session-sized groups. After all this, the information on the cards is manually entered into a computer.

This time-consuming process has several shortcomings. First, the one-to-one correspondence of a paper to a physical card limits the number of people that can work on grouping a paper at one time. Second, connections between papers are often made organically as an organizer walks around the room to collect related cards. This can lead to sessions with odd papers mixed in. Third, the time constraints and difficulty of navigating through piles of cards makes it difficult to consider parallel alternatives for grouping papers. Organizers often feel "locked in" with these initially created sessions, because any modification requires them to add to or break apart another session. Further, to account for stray papers, organizers often leave the meeting


*CHI 2014*, April 26–May 1, 2014, Toronto, Ontario, Canada.

ACM 978-1-4503-2473-1/14/04...$15.00.
http://dx.doi.org/10.1145/2556288.2557375

with thematic sessions that contain too many or too few papers, leaving additional work for refining the schedule.

We introduce *Frenzy*, an alternative approach for creating sessions that draws on the distributed knowledge of the entire program committee. First, Frenzy breaks the task of session making into two sub-problems: *meta-data elicitation* and *global constraint satisfaction*. During meta-data elicitation user can see all the accepted papers, search them by text, and add two types of meta-data: they can add suggested categories for a paper and they can indicate that they like a suggestion category and think it has "high session making potential" by clicking a "+1" button. This stage allows us to use many experts in parallel to contribute their intuitions about likely sessions. This stage can be done during the breaks of the program committee meeting, or after the wrap-up meeting. The next stage is global constraint satisfaction which uses a smaller group of volunteers who are co-located and can communicate easily with one another to use the suggested categories and "+1" votes to solve the global constraint of assigning all papers to exactly one session that has 3 or 4 papers.

To enable both stages we introduce a web application called Frenzy that facilitates parallel collaboration among large and small crowds. Frenzy uses some familiar concepts from social media such as Twitters' "feed" and Facebook's "tagging' and Google Plus' "+1" button to help view and add meta-data to papers. It also has standard features such as search and autocomplete. Frenzy allows parallel collaboration by providing each user with their own view of the data which they can search without affecting other users, but which propagates all their meta-data to other users immediately to eliminate redundant meta-data and give an active sense of collaboration.

We evaluate Frenzy by deploying the tool to the CSCW 2014 Program Committee, at which 48 committee members contributed to Frenzy. The session-creation meeting took 88 minutes compared to the traditional process, which often takes all day.

This paper makes the following contributions:

1. We introduce Frenzy, a collaborative web interface for constrained data organization that uses **goal completion with actionable feedback** to alert users of what needs work, while providing them freedom to choose their task.
2. We address the challenge of using groups at different scales to collectively satisfy constraints and achieve a cohesive global structure by **decomposing the problem of creating sessions into two sub-problems**: meta-data elicitation and constraint satisfaction.
3. **We evaluate Frenzy by deploying it to a conference program committee over two days**. We show that providing actionable feedback allowed users to pursue their own strategies for completing the goals. We show that the meta-data elicited was useful for session creation. Moreover, the meta-data collected from Frenzy was more useful that the legacy paper categories used by that conference.

The paper proceeds as follows. We first describe related work in crowdsourcing and groupware. Next, we discuss the design motivation for Frenzy and describe the system and its implementation. We chronicle the deployment of Frenzy to the CSCW 2014 Program Committee (PC) with data analysis and interviews. The sessions created by Frenzy were the basis of the CSCW 2014 schedule.

## RELATED WORK

Frenzy is a collaborative tool that builds on results from groupware, crowdsourcing, communitysourcing and design.

Groupware has a long history in HCI and has proven to be unexpectedly challenging. In analyzing several expensive failures of groupware systems, Grudin [9] observes that developing for groups is more difficult than developing for individuals and he supplies eight challenges of developing groupware systems. His insights on social processes are at the core of Frenzy's design.

The existing solution for creating conference sessions is a social process. There are people in a room reading over accepted papers, accumulating knowledge of some of the papers, and talking to people with other knowledge hoping to form connections between papers and dealing with conflicts and failures as they arise. As Grudin describes, social process are often guided by personalities, tradition and convention. Computers don't have access to this knowledge and thus our challenge is to provide support to the process without seeking to replace these behaviors. Grudin also points out that especially for social systems, there is often a big difference between our description of how the system work and how the system actually works. Social systems have many exceptions to the rule, unforeseeable errors and aspects of personality that we don't know how to account for. The challenge for Frenzy is to remain flexible and not impose rigid structures that will fall apart as exception and errors naturally arise.

Crowdsourcing takes a different approach to collaboration than groupware. Crowdsourcing – particularly microtask based crowdsourcing – avoids many of the social complications of groupware by replacing the current social process with its own workflows. Crowdsourced workflows [3,12,13,16] stitch together the results of microtasks which workers perform in isolation. A benefit of workflows is that computers understand and can optimize them [7]. However, the downside is that they can be perceived by users as inflexible and not enabling true collaboration, which might not matter on platforms such as Mechanical Turk, but does matter when the users are in a community with shared goals and knowledge which can be leveraged. Frenzy was influenced by the notion of workflows. Instead of having a detailed microtask-based workflow, it simply has two stages, each one with freedom as to what data the users want to see and what contributions they want to make.

Microtasks have the benefits that users know what to do, they know that it will take only a few minutes, and they don't have to worry about the big picture. These factors tend to make contribution more attractive and more easily parallelizable. Successfully breaking a problem into microtasks is challenging, but there are common microtasks have emerged in several crowdsoucing systems. Voting is a common microtask used in [14, 16, 20]. Soliciting tags, categories, or labels has been used in the ESP Game [1] and many other systems [4,6,8]. Frenzy builds on the idea of microtasks by allowing users to make contributions as simple as tagging and voting, but integrating these contributions into an interface that is open and collaborative rather than combining them in a workflow.

Frenzy addresses the challenge of facilitating collaboration: How do you create a single artifact, such as a conference program, out of many diverse opinions? Most crowdsourcing systems avoid this challenge by picking problems that parallelize well, such as labeling images. However, a few crowdsourcing systems do output a single artifact. Often machine learning or other statistical techniques are used to create artifacts such as transcribed text [15], a clustering of data [2, 8, 20] or a taxonomy [6].

A departure from the statistical approach is a crowdsourcing trip-planning tool called Mobi [21]. Trip-planning is a constraint satisfaction problem, and Mobi solves it by presenting a no-workflow interface where users can choose their own contribution from a list of "to do" items. Frenzy builds on ideas in Mobi by introducing a platform for parallel work, a two-stage workflow, and by generalizing the notion of "to-do" items into "actionable feedback," where the feedback can be changed based on the stage of the system and what goals need the contributors need to focus on.

Another general approach which is introduced in the design literature is "flare and focus" also called "divergence and convergence" [5]. This is a technique used in ideation processes such as brainstorming where many ideas are solicited in the "flare" stage and then a few of them are chosen to be deepened in the "focus" stage. This was the inspiration for Frenzy's two-stage collaboration process.

Frenzy is part of a growing literature on communitysourcing [10] and conference planning [2, 11, 19]. Frenzy builds on a previous conference scheduling research tool called Cobi [11] which allows the conference organizers to schedule sessions at times that abide by constraints such as "no author can have his papers scheduled for presentation at the same time." Cobi starts with a preliminary set of unscheduled papers based on paper sessions grouping. It allows the organizers to select times for each session, and possible swap papers in between session to avoid conflictions. Frenzy is a tool that helps create the initial sessions and affinity data if papers need to be swapped.

## SYSTEM DESCRIPTION

The Frenzy interface (Figure 1) consists of four sections: the *query bar*, *results feed*, *results hyperbar*, and goals with *actionable feedback*.

The *query bar* is a good place for users to start exploring Frenzy by performing a text search over papers. A paper matches the query text if the paper's title, author list, author affiliations, or abstract contains that text. Text search helps users narrow the list of papers by broad terms such as "Crowdsourcing", and also helps retrieve particular papers by an author or from a keyword in the title. Users can also see all the papers by clicking the "Show all papers" button.

The results of the query are displayed in the *results feed* which shows a vertical list of *data cards* (Figure 2) for each of the papers returned by the query. A *data card* displays the papers information (title, authors, and abstract) on the left side and the user-generated *meta-data box* on the right. The meta-data box contains a list of categories suggested for the paper, as well as a count of how many people have added a "+1" vote to the category, indicating that they think they category has high session potential. If the users are in the constraint satisfaction stage of Frenzy, there is also a text box to enter a session name. Users may add their own meta-data by adding a category, adding their own "+1" vote, adding or editing the session name (if applicable) or removing a category from the paper. We call this area the results feed because it draws some similarity to the social media concept of a feed of updating information. The interface draws visual connections to the Twitter interface, which is familiar to most of our users.

When the results feed is updated by a query, Frenzy also update the *results hyperbar*. The results hyperbar displays feedback about the query that was performed – how many results are returned, and a statement of the query. It also returns additional filters which the user can apply to their query. For example, if the user searches for "Crowdsourcing" the results hyperbar will say "26 papers in 'Crowdsourcing'" and will list up to 5 categories the user can filter by, such as 'paid crowdsourcing.' If the user clicks these additional filter categories, the results will update to have "5 Results for papers in 'Crowdsourcing' and 'paid crowdsourcing.'" These additional filters make it easy to drill down into large categories.

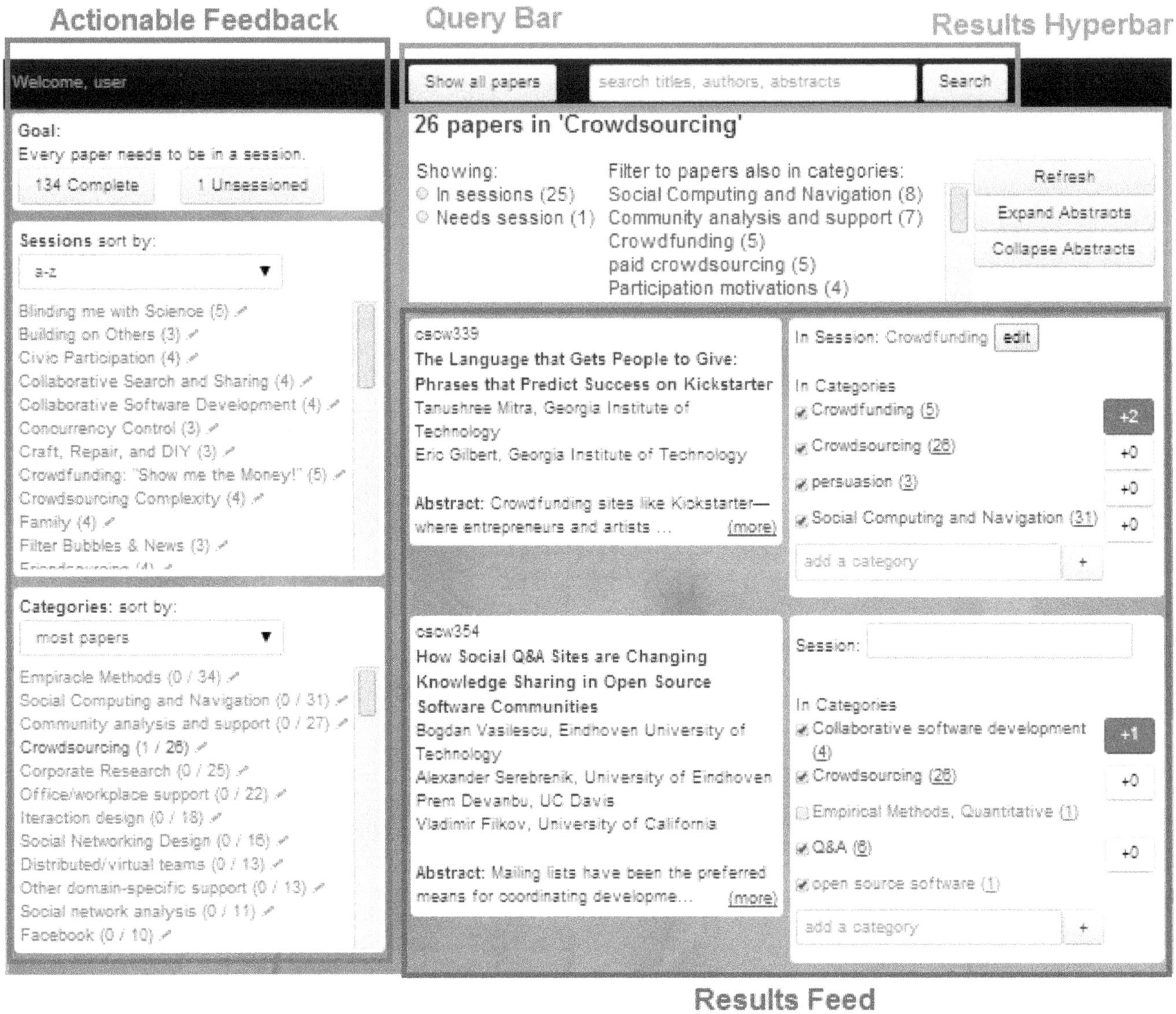


**Figure 1. Frenzy interface, highlighting 4 sections: actionable feedback, query bar, results hyperbar, and results feed.**

The left panel of Frenzy displays the *actionable feedback*. In both stages of Frenzy (meta-data elicitation and constraint satisfaction) there are two goals for users to achieve as a group. For example, in the meta-data elicitation stage one of the goals is: "Every category must have at least two papers in it (No singleton categories.)" Instead of instructing users how to achieve this goal, Frenzy provides two types of feedback on progress towards that goal that users can easily take action on (hence the name actionable feedback.) One type of actionable feedback for this goal is the list of categories, with the number of papers in that category in parenthesis. Any categories with only one paper are displayed in red text, indicating a problem. Users can then click on that category to see what paper is in it, and either remove the paper from it (thus deleting the category), or add more papers to the category. An additional type of actionable feedback is the number of papers that meet the goal and the number that do not. By clicking the number of papers that do not meet the goal, users generate a query that returns papers that need work. This provides an easy and direct way to find papers in need of contribution.

Frenzy is a web app implemented in node.js and Bootstrap. Each user logs in and then sees the Frenzy interface. When users query the system, their query is private to them. However, all meta-data generated is propagated to other users within 5 seconds. If a user adds a category to the paper, that category will appear in other users' data cards, and in the actionable feedback pane, the number of papers in that category will update, as well as the number of completed goals, if applicable.

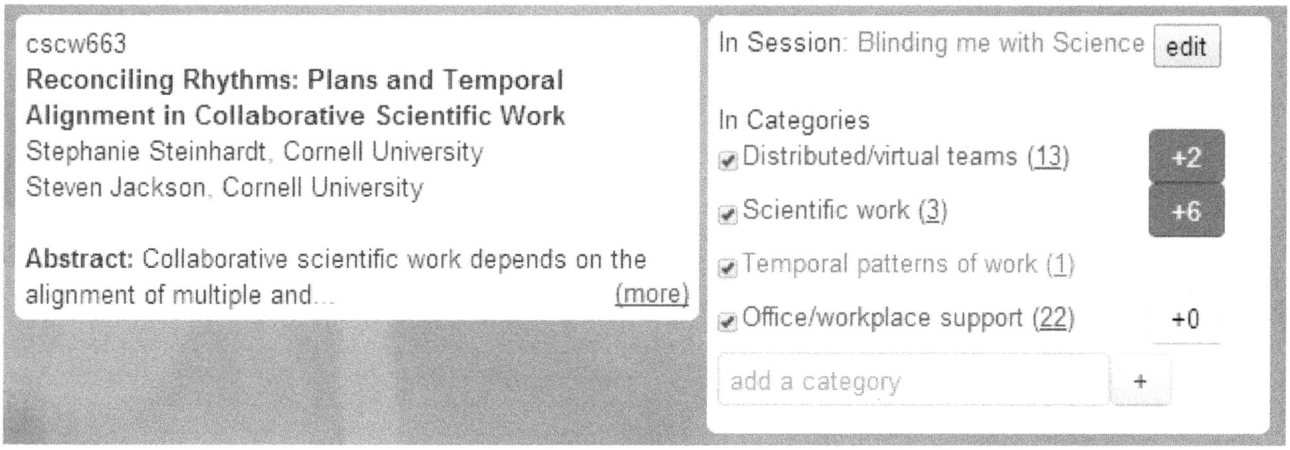


**Figure 2. The data card for paper cscw663. The left side is paper details and the right side is the meta-data box.**

To make Frenzy a flexible microtask platform, our design has three goals:

1. Enable lightweight contributions.
2. Allow users to access all the data and tasks.
3. Promote completion of goals with actionable feedback tailored to user groups and stages of problem solving.

We next describe how the Frenzy interface supports these design goals.

**Design Goal 1: Enable Lightweight Contributions**

In order to encourage as much participation as possible even in only short periods of free time, all contributions to Frenzy are small tasks that a user can complete in a under a minute. Users can choose their contributions and move easily between tasks. This allows users to make contributions that best fit their availability and expertise.

All user contributions are made using the meta-data boxes associated with each meta-data card. There are four ways a user can make contributions on each meta-data card:

*Add a category.* If a user can think of a new category the paper fits into, they are encouraged to add it. Autocomplete in the "add a category" textbox helps users reuse categories that are already in Frenzy. Additionally, categories with only one paper appear in red to indicate that they are singletons.

*Remove an existing category.* In order to remove a paper from a category, the user simply unchecks the category. Unchecked categories become less visually salient by turning grey, and their upvote button disappears. Category names remain visible and can be checked again to reassign a paper to a category.

*Upvote a category.* We expect every paper to be assigned to multiple categories. Categories may represent different aspects of a paper, such as its topic (e.g., education, question answering, games, health) or contribution type (e.g., study, system) Categories may also vary in their levels of granularity or quality. Up-voting a category indicates that the category has high potential of becoming a session. Typically this means the category is small (3-8 papers) rather than being overly broad such as "Empirical methods" which has over half the papers in it.

*Create/update/delete session names.* Users can place a paper in a session by entering a session name in the meta-data box. Session assignments can be deleted or edited at will. To distinguish sessions from categories, Frenzy only allows each paper to be placed in a single session at any given time. This feature is only turned on during the constraint satisfaction stage.

Giving users more control and freedom also comes with potential disadvantages. First, users have to navigate the set of tasks and take the time to figure out how they will contribute. Second, seeing current work could potentially bias the results of future work. While some of these issues are mitigated by the actionable feedback presented to users, they also represent some inherent tradeoffs of having no fixed microtask workflow.

**Design Goal 2: Give users access to all data and tasks**

Lightweight contributions are convenient, but are only useful if users can find a place to contribute. Fixed workflows present users with a designated place to work, but we rejected the idea of using workflows in Frenzy because we wanted users to make contributions based on their expertise. Nobody knows a user's expertise as well as the user does, thus our solution to enabling contributions was to offer access to all papers and tasks through domain-specific search features. Because papers are attached to tasks to be done on those papers, users can search for papers that fit their expertise as a way for searching for tasks to be done that match their expertise. Frenzy supports text search over the titles, authors, affiliations and abstracts of the papers. Frenzy enables category-based searches in the actionable feedback panel, and the results hyperbar allows search results to be further filtered by relevant categories.

A benefit of this search-based solution to giving access to tasks is that it supports the existing discussion-based social process rather than replacing it. Users can discuss papers and then search for them, see their details and add meta-data that may results from that conversation. Search provides the user control and freedom [17] that communities want to feel in their collaborative efforts.

### Design Goal 3: Promote completion of goals with actionable feedback

Showing hundreds of items gives users the control and freedom that they want, but can also be overwhelming. Frenzy provides actionable feedback to allow users to quickly find places to work that need their attention and which they are knowledgeable about.

In order to effectively coordinate work between a large group of users providing meta-data and a small group of users making sessions, we associate with each sub-problem its own set of goals, based on which to present feedback.

In the case of meta-data elicitation, we set two goals:

MDE1. Every category must have at least two papers in it (No singleton categories)

MDE2. Every paper needs to be in a least one category with +1 for session-making potential

In the case of session constraint satisfaction to assign all papers to session, we set these two goals:

SCS1. Every paper needs to be in a session

SCS2. Every session must have more than 2 papers.

Associated with every goal is visible feedback. For example, the MDE2 goal is displayed at the top of the actionable feedback panel with two buttons, one saying "100 Items Complete" and the other saying "35 items need work." This feedback is actionable because the user can click on the button and filter the results to only the items that need work, or that are already completed. For the MDE1 goal, Frenzy highlights any singleton categories in red. When the user clicks on the red category name and sees which paper it contains, they can either remove the singleton category from it (which deletes the category from the system because it then will have no papers in it), or find other papers for the category.

It is important to note that Frenzy does not assign tasks to users. The affordance in the actionable feedback is a shortcut for a search that nudges users towards finding a subset of the data to attend to. Once users find a place to work, there are many strategies for meeting the goals. A user may find that they need to add categories to a particular item, or remove them from another, or merge two categories, or split large categories into multiple smaller categories. Results from the psychology literature indicate that setting goals is an effective management style that gives people freedom in how they choose to achieve a goal [18].

## DEPLOYMENT

We partnered with the chairs of the CSCW 2014 Program Committee (PC) and deployed Frenzy for the initial session creation process. The traditional process involves 10-15 PC members meeting face-to-face after all the paper decisions have been made with the accepted papers' information printed on cards that they organize into piles which then become sessions. This process has two drawbacks: 1) it can only involves a limited number of people, and therefore fails to leverage the expertise of all the members of the communities, and 2) The amount of exploration is limited by that fact that there is only one copy of each paper that must be assigned to exactly one pile at any particular time. This process tends to take the better part of a day.

Traditionally, session making can only start after all the paper decisions are final because the problem has constraints that don't make sense to solve until the data is complete. In contrast, Frenzy breaks down the problem into two stages: meta-data elicitation (referred to hereafter as MDE Frenzy) and session constraint satisfaction where the session-making is finalized (referred to hereafter as SCS Frenzy). MDE Frenzy and SCS Frenzy use the same Frenzy platform, but with minor adjustments to the actionable feedback portion of the user interface. In MDE Frenzy, the goals are MDE1 and MDE2 (see previous section) and the actionable feedback focuses on categories. In SCS Frenzy, the goals are SCS1 and SCS2 and there is actionable feedback for both categories and sessions. All the meta-data gathered in MDE Frenzy appears in SCS Frenzy.

The CSCW PC received over 500 submissions. Of those, approximately 100 were fast-tracked for likely acceptance and approximately 100 were slated for discussion. We loaded the ~100 fast-tracked papers into Frenzy before the meeting started, and as the committee made decisions about individual papers, they were manually added to the Frenzy interface. This way, Frenzy always contained a current view of the accepted papers.

CSCW has a set of 32 *legacy categories* for papers such as "Entertainment/games" and "Social Network Site Design and Use." The authors of the paper selected multiple of these categories that apply to their paper. We imported this pre-existing meta-data into Frenzy as categories. As a result, all papers had at least two categories at the start of Frenzy.

### Meta-Data Elicitation (MDE) Frenzy

The PC meeting had 63 attendees, 43of whom participate in meta-data elicitation for Frenzy. At PC meetings, there are several times when certain members must step out of the room and into the hallway due to conflicts with the authors of the paper being discussed. We used this free time by setting up Frenzy on a computer with a large monitor in the hallway. Thus, PC members could browse the accepted papers and enter meta-data during free time. Since PC members tend not to take their laptops with them into the hallway, this was the only computer available, and often multiple people gathered around the screen and discussed the papers and meta-data together. PC members also used the interface during breaks from the meeting and from their own laptops inside the meeting. After all the paper decisions were complete, the PC members engaged in a 5-minute session dedicated to entering meta-data in Frenzy.

### Session Constraint Satisfaction (SCS) Frenzy

After the PC meeting ended, nine volunteers including the PC chairs moved to a smaller location to create a preliminary set of sessions for the conference. Sessions needed to have between 3-5 papers in them, ideally four. The number did not need to be exactly four since sessions were likely to change when refining the schedule, e.g., if presenters have conflicts. The goal was to have initial sessions to work from, and the actionable feedback encouraged sessions to have at least 3 papers.

The group started with the meta-data collected from the all the PC members, including 330 category entries made and 236 category upvotes.

## DATA ANALYSIS

During the two days of Frenzy deployment, we logged all user actions: sign-ins, sign-outs, queries, and data entries. We observed people using the system and conducted interviews with the SCS Frenzy participants. We now analyze this data to evaluate Frenzy. We show that the overall goal of session making was achieved in record time and successfully incorporated the view of a large group of experts. We show that the design of breaking the problem into two subproblems was effective by showing that the meta-data collected in MDE Frenzy was used extensively in SCS Frenzy. We show that goals with actionable feedback in both MDE Frenzy and SCS Frenzy provided the users the control and freedom to define their own strategies for successfully achieving their goals.

### Achieving overall goals

Frenzy saw substantial usage over the 2-day deployment. A total of 48 participants contributed over 10.28 hours of usage. In that time, 2,365 queries were issued and 1,088 meta-data contributions were made. Over 250 contributions were made during the 5-minute period where all PC members were asked to spend 5-minutes simultaneously using Frenzy. This demonstrates the capacity of Frenzy to allow simultaneous contributions from a large group of users.

During SCS Frenzy usage, the 9 volunteers to complete the sessions achieved the goal of assigning every paper to a session and having every session have 3-5 papers in 88 minutes.

### Breaking Session-Making into 2 Sub-problems

Frenzy breaks session-making into 2 sub-problems: MDE Frenzy and SCS Frenzy. We evaluate this design by testing whether the meta-data from MDE Frenzy was useful for making sessions in SCS Frenzy. The usefulness of category meta-data was tested by looking at how many of the papers ended up in a session that matched one of the categories give for it. The usefulness of upvote meta-data was tested using a logistic regression to model the effect of upvoted categories on session creation. We defined a category as "matching" a session if one or more important keywords were shared between the category name and the session name.

#### *How useful was category meta-data?*

In total, 93 of 135 papers (68.9%) had a category that matched a session. The categories on those 93 papers could have come from two sources: the 32 predefined categories assigned by the PC or the 63 non-singleton categories contributed by users of MDE Frenzy. Although both are helpful in making sessions, only categories contributed by users of MDE Frenzy can be claimed as a benefit of asking users to add meta-data. Of the 93 papers with matching sessions, 40 of the matches came from predefined categories and 53 came from user contributions. MDE Frenzy more than doubled the number of useful categories.

#### *How useful was upvote meta-data?*

MDE Frenzy generated 99 non-singleton categories. After constraint satisfaction, there were 34 sessions, of which 25 matched categories. We want to know if the +1 voting for categories helped to determine which of the categories would be turned into sessions. To test if +1 voting provides a useful signal that a category will match a session, we run a logistic regression predicting the probability that a category will match a session (*prMatchesSession*). The dependent variable is an indicator of whether that category was the most +1 upvoted category for at least one paper (*wasMostUpvoted*).

$$prMatchesSession \sim a + b * wasMostUpvoted$$

| Coeff. | Estimate | Std. Error | Pr(>\|z\|) |
|---|---|---|---|
| a | -2.0794 | 0.4330 | 1.57e-06 |
| b | 1.7658 | 0.5278 | 0.000821 |

**Table 1. A logistic regression predicting whether the probability a category matches a session is dependent on whether that category was the most upvoted category at least once.**

Table 1 shows the coefficient estimates. A chi-squared test shows coefficent $b$ is statistically significant (p = 0.0082). The interpretation of this logistic regression model is that for a category where *wasMostUpvoted* = 0, the predicted probability that it will match a session is 0.12. In contrast, for a category that was the most upvoted category for at least one paper (*wasMostUpvoted* =1), the predicted probability is 0.42. Thus, if a category is ever the most upvoted category for a paper, it has high session-making potential, which confirms the usefulness of upvote meta-data to session-making.

### Goals and Actionable Feedback in MDE Frenzy

The main mechanism that drives workers to make progress in Frenzy is having goals with actionable feedback. This helps users find a subset of the data on which to work in order to achieve the goals. Because we do not know what actual items are best to give to each worker and we do not know what tasks to give them (adding labels vs. removing labels vs. placing items into sessions), we provide an interface that grants users control and freedom (Design Goal 2) that allows them to find their own strategies for contributing towards the goal (Design Goal 3). In our deployment of MDE Frenzy we found 3 strategies for contribution:

*Browse and Edit*

Users often came to Frenzy because they were curious to browse the list of accepted papers and to see how the conference was shaping up. As they browsed, the meta-data box was clearly visible, and often they made a contribution. For example, by browsing the system, a PC member who was not an expert in education added the category "MOOCs." Another user noticed several papers about teens, adolescents or children and added the category "youth" based on several key word searches for "children," "teens," and "adolescents". The categories "email", "facebook" and "twitter" were added by users who noticed the terms pop up, searched for them to see if they were themes in the program, and then added the categories.

*Check for Patterns within One's Area of Expertise*

The papers already had good category labels given by the authors from a checklist provided by the conference organizers. Thus workers could enter Frenzy, select their subfield of expertise and look over the existing meta-data. For example, a crowdsourcing expert selected the "Crowdsourcing" category, which had 26 papers. He looked over the list and found that a few of them had something in common. He added the category "Crowdfunding" to five of the items. These five papers were ultimately grouped together in a session called "Crowdfunding: Show me the money!"

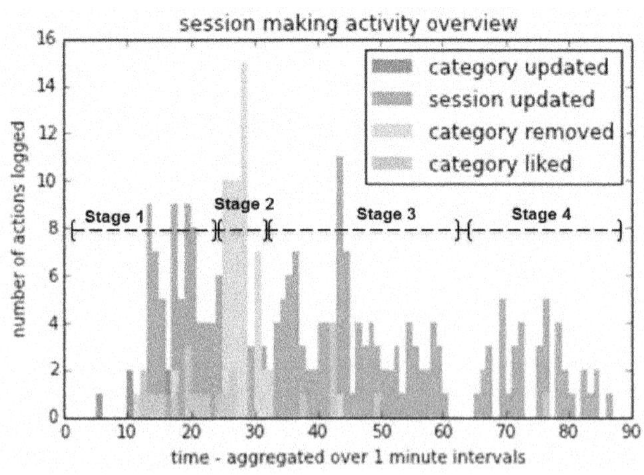


**Figure 3. Data entry activity during SCS Frenzy. Data entries are broken into 4 types and stacked on the graph: category updates, session updates, category removal, and category upvotes.**

Similarly, a social media expert searched for "Social Networking Site Design and Use" which had 16 papers and created the category "Politics/Social Media" which had 4 items. These four items were ultimately grouped in session called "Social Media & Politics."

*Direct contribution*

As PC members were actively discussing papers in the meeting, they would occasionally see connections or patterns during the meeting then want to come out to the hallway to enter them into the system. For example, during the PC meeting discussions, one PC member realized two papers were accepted about social media and depression ("Social Structure and Depression in TrevorSpace" and "Characterizing and Predicting Postpartum Depression from Facebook Data"). At the next opportunity, they used Frenzy to do a text search for "depression" and added "Depression" as a category to both papers.

### Goals and Actionable Feedback in SCS Frenzy

As shown earlier, the session making goals were completed in record time and SCS Frenzy made heavy use of metadata collected in MDE Frenzy. Figure 3 shows data entry activity averaged over 1-minute intervals. Types of data entry and color codes and stacked. From this graph and the interviews conducted with the users, we identify four distinct stages of the session making process: additional dataentry, removing clutter, session making, and lastly session negotiation.

*Stage 1: Additional data entry and low hanging fruit*

Figure 3 shows that during the first 28 minutes, more categories were added and more upvotes were contributed. In addition, some of the more obvious sessions were created, such as turning the 4 papers in the category "Crowdsourcing" into a session called "Crowdsourcing: Show me the money!" We call such sessions made directly from categories low hanging fruit. During this period, volunteers largely worked alone without communicating to one another. One volunteer stated:

> I started with stuff I knew… I have a pretty good sense if a paper belongs there or not.

*Stage 2: Removing Clutter*

Figure 3 shows that from minutes 24-32, many categories were removed. A large number of the more obvious sessions had been created but now the low hanging fruit was gone. The volunteers pointed out a number of categories that were created for fun such as "Pacific Northwest Pride" "What's Niki doing now?" They felt these were cluttering the data and making it hard to find meaningful meta-data, and so they had them removed. One volunteer commented:

> I tried to remove some of the joke labels because they were starting to clutter up the user interface.

*Stage 3: Session making with discussion*
Figure 3 shows that from minutes 32 to 62, more sessions were created. In contrast to the beginning of the process where volunteers with taking low hanging fruit and not communicating, there was lots of communication both to coordinate efforts and to get reassurance from others. Our volunteers said:

> A couple of times I would try to make a session, but confirm verbally I was making that session [so] that they didn't have to do it.

> People would be working on their stuff, then somebody would speak up and say. Where could this paper possibly go?

*Stage 4: Session Negotiation*
Figure 3 shows that from minutes 60 to 88, category addition slowed with many gaps in time where no sessions were updated. During this period, there was a lot of discussion about how to resolve the most difficult remaining constraints. Discussion dominated data entry, and the discussion resembled a negotiation with volunteers making proposals of switches and coming up with creative ways of reconfiguring existing sessions. For example, they took the 7 papers in "Q and A", found an additional paper on social networks and then split "Q and A" into two categories, "Q and A" and "Friendsourcing" which focused on using Facebook and Twitter friends for information needs. This creative problem solving is characteristic of the session negotiation stage.

### User feedback
Our interviews revealed a consensus that Frenzy was an improvement over past experience with paper-based conference session-making:

> It was definitely much less painful to create those initial sessions, [but that] it was more fun to do it with a social tool... it was nice to do it in a group, to have a few other people in the room … especially when we ran into tricky ones, helpful to talk it over.

There was also consensus that face-to-face aspects of the collaboration during SCS Frenzy were still vitally important to the process:

> I wouldn't want to do this remotely, having everyone there was important, awareness of what other people were doing, touching certain papers, or thinking about sessions.

In particular, the social interactions in the room were essential for resolving some of the session making problems:

> Sometimes people would go in different directions and make simultaneous edits. We had to stop and negotiate a little.

## DISCUSSION
While Frenzy is a special purpose tool for creating conference sessions, it solves a more general problem: collaborative data organization. There are three techniques Frenzy uses that are critical to enabling the collaborative process within the community.

*Technique 1: Flare and focus*
As discussed in the related work section, flare and focus is an approach to ideation introduced in the design literature. Frenzy's two-stage process borrows from this idea: metadata elicitation, wherein users generate categories and contribute +1 votes is similar to the flare stage, and constraint satisfaction, where the main focus is eliminating options and focusing on the best of the generated options. The flare stage is what allows Frenzy to use a large crowd of collaborators in parallel without worrying about how the constraints will be solved and the focus stage is where the constraints are solved.

One important detail of Frenzy's flare and focus process is that there is such a thing as too much flare. Between the flare stage and the focus stage, it is necessary to get rid of clutter created in the flare stage – categories clearly too large or too small, joke categories. Eliminating clutter is crucial to a successful focus phase.

*Technique 2: +1 Voting*
Voting is a common crowdsourcing technique. +1 Voting is slightly different from true voting because users don't necessarily have all the options set before them when they cast their +1 vote. +1 voting is an analog of voting which is not limited by the synchronization barrier: you don't need to control the workflow of microtasks to ensure that voting is only done after all the options are listed.

A subtle point about +1 voting is that if you want to include pre-existing categories, you need to have a mechanism like +1 voting in order to set reasonable goals for the users. Without pre-existing categories, a simple goal such as "every paper must have at least one category" will suffice. However, if there are pre-existing categories, that simple goal may already be satisfied. Changing the goal to say "every paper must have at least one category with a +1 vote" the means the users will look at every paper, even if it has already been categorized.

*Technique 3: Social interaction*
Frenzy uses design patterns from crowdsourcing such as tagging and voting microtasks. However, microtasks alone, even in a platform that affords a great deal of user control and freedom, are not enough to solve the problem of session making. Face-to-face communication is crucial for solving many small but important issues: resolving conflicts, coming up with new terms that will be acceptable to the community, and arriving at a consensus that the process is complete and the results, while not perfect, are satisfactory. One of the major lessons Grudin [9] derives from the failures of groupware systems is that social processes have subtle inner workings that we do not always understand, are difficult for computers to have access to and reason about, but are essential to the process. Thus we should not seek to replace the existing social process with a rigid workflow, but to add lightweight microtasks on top of the current process.

Frenzy is a hybrid approach which can take advantage of the lightweight and efficiently parallelized contributions of microtasks and still incorporate the inspiration and social cues that drive consensus which transpires from face-to-face communication. Our general observation is that microtasks do not have to be distributed to strangers in rigid workflows, they can be made social and can enhance face-to-face interaction rather than aim to replace it.

## FUTURE WORK

The area of biggest potential improvement in Frenzy is to speed up Stage 3 of Constraint Satisfaction: Session Making with Discussion. Frenzy could be extended to offer machine learning based analysis to suggest paper groupings to decrease the amount of time spent searching for connections after the low-hanging fruit has been taken.

There is also the potential to extend the techniques for collaborative data organization to other domains. One area that has shown early promise is collaborative creation of photo albums. For example, guests of a wedding could all be invited to upload photos they took, browse, categorize and add +1 votes and collectively output an album using each photo at most once, and not more than 200 photos.

## CONCLUSION

In this paper we present Frenzy, a tool for collaborative data organization applied to the complex task of conference session making. Frenzy enables groups of experts to simultaneously contribute by breaking the problem into two sub-problems: meta-data elicitation and session constraint satisfaction. Frenzy gives users control and freedom in identifying their own strategies for accomplishing set goals. Actionable feedback promotes meeting goals and steers users toward useful work.

In our deployment of Frenzy at the CSCW 2014 PC meeting, we evaluated the actionable feedback features by identifying three strategies used to satisfy the goals. We showed the benefit of breaking the problem into two sub-problems by showing that the meta-data collected in MDE Frenzy helped form more sessions that the categories created by the PC before the PC meeting. Moreover, the sessions created by Frenzy were the basis of the CSCW 2014 schedule.

## ACKNOWLEDGEMENTS

This work is supported by Quanta Computer as part of the Qmulus project, the Ford-MIT Alliance, NSF awards SOCS-1111124 and SOCS-1208382, the WRF / TJ Cable Professorship, ONR grant N00014-12-1-0211, and NFS Grant IIS 1016713 and IIS-1110965. Juho Kim is partly supported by the Samsung Fellowship. Lydia thanks Kristi Gable, Katlyn Edwards, and Janelle Van Hofwegen.

## REFERENCES

1. von Ahn, L., Dabbish, L. Labeling Images with a Computer Game. CHI 2004.
2. Andre, P., et al. Community Clustering: leveraging an academic crowd to form coherent conference session. HCOMP 2013.
3. Bernstein, M., et al.. Soylent: a word processor with a crowd inside.UIST 2010.
4. Bigham, J. P., et al.. VizWiz: nearly real-time answers to visual questions. UIST 2010.
5. Buxton, B. 2007. *Sketching User Experiences: Getting the Design Right and the Right Design*. Morgan Kaufmann Publishers Inc., San Francisco, CA, USA.
6. Chilton, L. B., Little, G., Edge, D., Weld, D., and Landay, J. Cascade: crowdsourcing taxonomy creation. CHI 2013.
7. Dai, P., Mausam, Weld, D.S. Decision-Theoretic Control of Crowd-Sourced Workflows. AAAI 2010.
8. Gomes, R., Welinder, P., Krause, A., and Perona, P. 2011. Crowd- clustering. In NIPS '11 (2011).
9. Grudin, J. 1994. Groupware and social dynamics: eight challenges for developers.*Commun. ACM* 37, 1 (January 1994)
10. Heimerl, K., Gawalt, B., Chen, K., Parikh, T., and Hartmann, B. CommunitySourcing: engaging local crowds to perform expert work via physical kiosks. CHI 2012.
11. Kim, J., et al. Cobi: A Community-Informed Conference Scheduling Tool. UIST 2013.
12. Kittur, A., Smus, B., Khamkar, S., Kraut, R. E. CrowdForge: Crowdsourcing complex work. UIST 2011.
13. Kulkarni, A., Can, M., Hartmann, B. Collaboratively crowdsourcing workflows with turkomatic. CSCW 2012.
14. Lasecki, W.S., et al. 2013. Chorus: a crowd-powered conversational assistant. UIST 2013.
15. Lasecki, W., Miller, C., Sadilek, A., Abumoussa, A., Borrello, D., Kushalnagar, R., and Bigham, J..Real-time captioning by groups of non-experts. UIST 2012.
16. Little, G., Chilton, L. B., Goldman, M., Miller, R. C. TurKit: human computation algorithms on mechanical turk. UIST'10.
17. Norman, D.A. 2002. *The Design of Everyday Things*. Basic Books, Inc., New York, NY, USA.
18. Pink, D.H. Drive: The surprising truth about what motivates us. Penguin (2011).
19. Sampson, S.E. Practical implications of preference-based conference scheduling. Production and Operations Management 13, 3 (2004), 205–215.
20. Tamuz, O., Liu, C., Belongie, S., Shamir, O., and Kalai, A. Adaptively learning the crowd kernel. In ICML 2011.
21. Zhang, H., Law, E., Miller, R. C., Gajos, K. Z., Parkes, D. C., and Horvitz, E. Human computation tasks with global constraints. CHI 2012.

# End-Users Publishing Structured Information on the Web: An Observational Study of What, Why, and How

**Edward Benson**
MIT CSAIL
32 Vassar St., Cambridge, Massachusetts
eob@csail.mit.edu

**David R. Karger**
MIT CSAIL
32 Vassar St., Cambridge, Massachusetts
karger@mit.edu

## ABSTRACT
End-users are accustomed to filtering and browsing styled collections of data on professional web sites, but they have few ways to create and publish such information architectures for themselves. This paper presents a full-lifecycle analysis of the Exhibit framework—an end-user tool which provides such functionality—to understand the needs, capabilities, and practices of this class of users. We include interviews, as well as analysis of over 1,800 visualizations and 200,000 web interactions with these visualizations. Our analysis reveals important findings about this user population which generalize to the task of providing better end-user structured content publication tools.

## Author Keywords
Web design; Web content editing; Information architectures; Faceted browsing

## ACM Classification Keywords
H.5.4. Information Interfaces and Presentation: Hypertext/Hypermedia - User Issues

## INTRODUCTION
Structured data access and navigation is pervasive on the web. Whenever we visit Epicurious.com to find a recipe, browse Amazon to make a purchase, or visit Facebook to look at photos, we are presented with a collection of objects (recipes, products, photos) that are uniformly rendered based on their structure. We can sort these items based on various properties, filter them using faceted browsing, and often visualize them using different templates offered. The structure of this data makes it easier for us to understand it and find what we seek.

At present, the tools for creating such structure-based web pages remain directed almost entirely at highly trained database engineers and web developers who use SQL databases, custom code, and powerful templating engines. Ordinarily-skilled authors are largely relegated to posting unstructured text on blogs and wikis, or to giving their data to companies like Epicurious and Facebook which provide rich browsing interfaces as long as you fit their schema.

During the "Web 2.0" era, a flurry of research anticipated the idea that, given better tools for structured data, end-users would become prolific data publishers, just as they were prolific hypertext publishers on the early web. But many of the technologies that resulted—like microformats, semantic wikis [23], and RDFa [12]—were not widely adopted into the standard end-user toolset. Given the power and value that structured data sites provide professional developers, it is natural to ask why they have not been adopted by end-users. Was the anticipation of data publishing premature or even incorrect? Do these authors lack the technical skills—or the need—for such publication methods?

This paper studies the use of a web-based data publishing framework called Exhibit, which offers a balance between novice accessibility and power-user extensibility. Introduced in 2008, Exhibit allows anyone to publish an interactive structured data visualization by posting a spreadsheet (describing the data) and a single HTML document (describing the presentation and interaction) to any web site. Exhibit extends HTML with tags such as `<map>`, `<list>`, `<facet>`, and `<template>` that turn into interactive data elements. Over 1,800 Exhibit have been created in the wild.

Our study examines Exhibit using a mixed-method approach at four levels of detail. We interview 12 authors of some of the most popular exhibits. We analyze statistics about the design choices and data used by the full set of 1,800 Exhibits in use in the wild. We take the 100 most used Exhibits according to access logs and further examine and taxonomize them. Finally, we assess logged activity of 200,000 web-interactions by Exhibit site visitors. We also provide our dataset and a design gallery of the Exhibits at `csail.mit.edu/haystack/exhibit-study`.

We conducted this study with three goals in mind. First, we validate that there is a community of authors who seek to publish interactive data visualizations and whose needs are not met by the tools available to them. Our interviews explore what these needs are. Second, we seek to understand whether Exhibit's authoring model, which we call the **star model** for reasons explained in the following section, meets the needs of this community. The star model is a constrained way of exposing and integrating components from data visualization and navigation frameworks. Prior work hypothesized that this programming model supports the needs of a


ACM 978-1-4503-2473-1/14/04..$15.00.
http://dx.doi.org/10.1145/2556288/2557036

wide spectrum of expertise levels in a manner that facilitates code reuse and rapid construction [14]. Studying real-world use of this model provides design guidelines that can be applied to other visualization frameworks. Finally, we seek to synthesize the habits of this community of long tail data publishers and understand how their creations are published and received by web viewers.

We organize our findings by method, which can present a challenge in tying together takeaways which gather support across methods, so we highlight primary ones here and return for a summary at the end of the paper:

- The star model appears to be meeting the needs of a variety of use-cases, from simple to complex, and has provided a platform for many to learn to program along the way.
- Authoring non-tabular data (e.g., multi-valued tables and graphs) is the norm, but authors are "abusing" tabular editors (like spreadsheets) to do so. These authors have no problems with complex data models, but struggle with the text syntaxes we ask them to use to describe these models.
- Authors will choose unnecessarily complex and labor intensive solutions over equivalent simple ones if the copyable design examples address the complicated case.
- Authors are often dependent on, but "boxed in" and limited by, Content Management Systems, and need ways to take control over the entire web page and the structure of the data managed.
- Authors who think their readers want data interaction are **right**: the data browsing features authors create get used, and the kind of browsing widgets offered impacts the way readers browse.

## RELATED WORK

This work aims to make contributions in the vein of other studies about the creation and management of web content. Voida's work with "homebrew databases" identified key challenges for small organizations tasked with managing their own data [22]. Landay's study of design workflow provides an understanding of how web interfaces are created from scratch [20]. Klemmer and others provide additional information about the practice of borrowing and tweaking the designs of others [11, 19, 13]. Our work has parallels to all three: we seek to describe the common practices of authors who create "homebrew" data-backed web pages and identify their needs so that toolbuilders can better serve this community[1].

In-field evaluation of data visualization toolkits has been relatively sparse. Neither Exhibit nor more numerically-focused libraries such as Protovis [4, 6] and D3 [5] have been the subject of follow-up studies which track their usage patterns in the community. Protovis, for example, instead applies a Cognitive Dimensions of Notation analysis and provides reactions to the framework [4, 6], and D3 [5] focuses on performance and developer reactions. This paper provides important insights about how such tools are actually used in the wild, and by end-users rather than programmers.

### Exhibit and the Star Model

Exhibit is a Javascript web framework that enables end-users to author (not program) faceted interactive visualizations like the ones shown in Figure 1, just as they author HTML documents. While number-centric visualizations, such as scatter plots, are possible, the framework is heavily targeted at browsing collections of structured items. Authors create visualizations (called "Exhibits") by writing a simple HTML-based configuration and then linking to data the same way they would link to a CSS file. Many data types are supported: CSV, JSON, MS Excel, BibTeX, and the Google Spreadsheets API.

Exhibit implements an interaction design that we call the **star model** and seek to validate as a useful pattern for enabling end-user data display creation. In this model, a global collection of data items serves as the center of the star, and declaratively specified UI widgets exist as the spokes—the points of the star—that either display, filter, or modify this collection. These widgets are connected only implicitly to the global collection at the center, and they are otherwise completely independent of each other. Unlike D3 or Storytelling Alice [17, 10] everything is specified declaratively, though authors can create their own plugins easily. And unlike D3, Alice, and Yahoo Pipes! [15], there is no notion of dataflow, significantly simplifying construction, copying, and pasting, and reuse. This also means this model lacks the power that raw SQL queries or programming languages afford, but our interviews and usage analysis show this extra power is not necessary for many users. The independence between spokes and implied connection to the data in the center further simplifies identifying and copying individual fragments of a visualization as well.

The star model results in visualization configurations that can easily be scraped and analyzed programmaticaly, unlike procedural frameworks. An Exhibit configuration has three main components that we analyze. The first is one or more **views**—maps, timelines, tables, lists, or scatter plots—that can be shown modally or stacked together. The second is zero or more **facets** and text search widgets. Facets are UI widgets that display the range of some field of data, providing an affordance for viewers to filter that data to only a subset of that range. For example, in a course catalog, a viewer might choose to view only courses from the Computer Science department. Finally, the Exhibit configuration contains **lenses**, small HTML templates that describe styling for items in the dataset.

The star model is not an alternative to frameworks like D3, but a set of constraints that result in a component packaging system that can be layered on top of such systems. With this packaging system, authors do not worry about data flow or widget implementation; they simply say "put this widget here, with these options." We hypothesize that this model strikes a balance between simplicity and power that satisfies the needs of a wide range of authors, and thus deserves wider consideration. We validate this hypothesis in our author interviews.

[1] We consider this a separate group than professional-focused information management tools like Greenstone and Kepler [25, 1]

Figure 1: Nine example Exhibits from our dataset and the resulting design gallery.

## DATASET

We curated three data sets for the use in this paper:

**VIZ1800 Dataset.** We generated a list of 1,897 Exhibits by examining the Apache server logs on the machine that hosts the Exhibit Javascript library. This dataset contains the complete set of assets used to create each visualization: the dataset, the HTML page surrounding the visualization, and the visualization configuration (views, facets, and lenses).

**TOP100 Dataset.** For analyses in the paper that required human coding, we used the subset of the data corresponding to the top 100 most visited exhibits according the Apache logs for a period of months in 2012. Our interview subjects were among the authors of Exhibits in this dataset.

**USAGE Dataset.** Several Exhibit authors we contacted agreed to use a special version of Exhibit with anonymous analytic hooks that recorded usage events such as facet operations, text searches, and view selection (e.g., switching from a Map to a Timeline). In total, we collected 266,747 distinct user events for 32,978 distinct IP addresses (hashed for anonymity) across 57 distinct Exhibits.

## AUTHORS

We interviewed twelve authors to better understand how and why people use Exhibit. The interviewees responded to a request for participation sent out to the authors of the TOP100 dataset. They ranged from school administrators and teachers to business owners and urban planners. Interviews were semi-structured, consisting of a standard set of prompts about visualization creation and maintenance, with follow-up questions based on the answers received. Though this study is centered upon Exhibit, we attempt to make constructive observations that generalize to other tools.

### Skills and Expertise

None of the authors we interviewed were formally trained or employed in web development. Author 1's description is representative of the group at large: "I'm fairly comfortable with HTML. I've been doing HTML stuff for a long time. CSS is doable, but I don't feel as comfortable. I don't do too many fancy things, I guess." Subtle misuse of words from the technical perspective (such as describing HTML editing as "adding brackets") was common in over half the participants, indicating that most of this population is self taught.

Five of the participants had prior experience with data visualization. Two used tools such as Tableau regularly, two were very familiar with cartography, and one runs a consumer product website. Three-fourths also had prior experience editing HTML. Three self-described themselves as having become advocates of structured data publishing, and described transitioning into local "gardeners," to apply Gantt and Nardi's *Gardeners and Gurus* metaphor [9]. In addition to creating visualizations themselves, they educated and provided support to their respective communities.

### Intent

Four common themes were present when authors were asked why they chose to use Exhibit to visualize their data:

**(1) Data navigation.** Eight of the interviewees mentioned wanting some way to let people navigate through the information they were publishing. For some, it was the primary reason they said they chose the framework. As an example, Author 3 saw the ability to dynamically filter and explore datasets as a competitive business advantage, both for customer-facing pages and his employees' own internal use. Author 11 and Author 9 both created their visualizations as a way to help themselves and coworkers interactively filter through sizable library catalogues that they managed for their departments.

**(2) High-level data understanding.** All of the authors who used maps or timelines, and some who did not, mentioned wanting to provide an understanding of their data in a different light than only text allowed. "I wanted to draw students' attention to different categories of information," Author 10, a professor, describes, "so having a marriage of these two visualizations [a map and a timeline] seemed very appealing to me." Author 2, also an educator, created curations of prior work for new projects. At first, "there were other people working on the project that said, 'Ah, this is great,' because they could have a quick look at all the different papers." Later, he discovered that the information displayed on facets themselves were a useful indicator of aggregate trends in his data (e.g., publications over time, or by school), not just a way to filter information.

**(3) A programming-free way to publish data.** Some interviewees were not thinking of themselves as data publishers, but rather just looking for a way to create a web page with information from some other source. Author 7 wanted to put an Excel spreadsheet of employee information into an HTML table. She had copied the Exhibit configuration from another department's web page and simply changed the data link. Unknowing that Exhibit provides faceted browsing and text search, she showed off the new employee-page they had recently paid a PHP developer to create that added facets to the employee directory, commenting that she wished "Exhibit was capable of doing all this stuff [faceted browsing]" so that they wouldn't have needed a custom system.

**(4) Frustration with traditional web development.** Tech savvy interviewees also commented about their desire for respite from the complexity of web development. Author 3's company had gone through a custom PHP-based product catalogue ("that was particularly clumsy"), storefront management software ("didn't work so well"), and Google's enterprise search solutions ("didn't really work well either"), before choosing Exhibit because it provide a product catalogue with "fast, cross-referencable information" without any need to set up multiple web pages or maintain complex software.

These motivations affirm the initial needs Exhibit sought to target: navigating and visualizing sets of data without requiring programming. They also provide evidence that Exhibit's "star model" of programming provides a "pay-as-you-go" complexity that meets the needs of both novices (point 3 above) and experts (point 4). These users replaced, rather than complimented, their traditional techniques — exporting to HTML for (3), and SaaS/bespoken systems for (4).

### Data Creation

All of the authors we spoke to authored data in a GUI-based tool, such as FileMaker Pro, Excel, or Google Spreadsheets. Even though Exhibit supports Excel as a data source, Excel-based authors reported converting their data to JSON for publication. After this initial export, some would later update the data in JSON format rather than its source format.

While a few authors described switching to JSON as an authoring format as they became more familiar with it, the majority had negative opinions about JSON's usability, citing it as one of the larger challenges of the visualization process. "I taught a course where we built [Exhibits] from JSON files, instead of Google Spreadsheets...and students unfamiliar with programming just found it too tedious and too difficult to chase after every missed comma and every unequal bracket...it defeated too many of them...quite a few just sort of threw up their hands in defeat," says Author 10. Author 3 has similar experience: "With JSON one of my concerns is not the coding but the missing brackets, and I've since found applications that help me find when I've got a missing bracket or an extra comma or something, but that gets to be an issue." As does Author 1: "that was the part that was less intuitive to me, setting up the JSON file."

These conversations suggest that the problem is one of syntax and tooling, not understanding. These authors (and their students) are capable of organizing and thinking about structured data, but not skilled in the practice and tools of structured text editing that programmers take for granted. Editors that support syntax highlighting and bracket matching are largely unknown outside the technical community.

### Trial and Error Editing

Despite the lack of formal training, these authors were able to accomplish an impressive array of visualizations, using HTML and sometimes CSS and Javascript. The majority referenced a trial-and-error development style in which they would iteratively experiment with modifications to their code and check the results, often without firm knowledge of how to accomplish their goal.

During one interview, an author whose HTML skills were among the most basic of the group opened the Chrome debugging console to demonstrate experimenting with different CSS styles. Quick feedback is a good substitute for *a priori* knowledge, as this author had discovered. And a common request by interviewees was to be able to edit visualizations in the browser and save them somehow, as a way to shorten this feedback loop. This theme has broader implications for web development, suggesting benefits to making the web browser capable of replacing a separate program for editing and saving web documents.

### Copy, Paste, and Tweak Workflow

Armed with a basic knowledge of web syntax and semantics, but a lack of formal knowledge, *examples* from which to draw become incredibly important. Nearly all of the authors reported creating visualizations by coping and then modifying an existing visualization. This is concordant with previous findings about the both the practice and utility of copying and modifying code and design examples to create new artifacts [19, 11, 13].

Author 8, a repeat user of Exhibit, describes his process as "basically taking an existing file, reusing that, editing it as need be, and then also...unless it's a real time crunch, I'm trying to learn more...add more features or add more components whether that's improved design on the CSS side or trying to do more with the data file." Author 3 describes his creation experience: "I remember back. I was on that wiki a lot...The reason that the exhibits ended up being something I was able to use was that there were some examples, and God I just wished there were more. It was one of the things I remember very clearly, going through and seeing how everybody did things. Examples were invaluable." Author 7's visualizations were copied and pasted from another department's website within her company without any modification: only the data link was changed.

After hearing what an important role design examples played in the authoring process, we decided to repurpose our visualization dataset as a design gallery. Users of the gallery can browse through Exhibits found on the web based on what features of the framework they use (we can programatically extract this). The screenshots in Figure 1 were selected from the visualizations curated in this gallery[2].

### Publication

The struggle to integrate non-text forms of expression into Content Management Systems (CMSs) was a common theme. Author 1, whose office mandates that all web content be published through a CMS, reported that after she created the Exhibit as HTML, "I wasn't able to publish the Exhibit myself. I had to go to the technology people and ask them put

[2]Available at `simile-widgets.org/exhibit/gallery`

it up." Author 7 remarks about posting a new web page online, "I had to get help from a PHP developer. I'm not a PHP developer...to get help from an expert who knows PHP was a big plus." Author 10 states, "I have a love hate relationship with Content Management Systems...[they] very often have overhead that I don't want to mess with."

The crux of this problem seems to be that CMSs provide authors a very narrow canvas on which to draw: a contiguous rectangular region in the middle of the web page, with no easy access to side gutters or the HEAD element. Side gutters are important for design reasons—they are the canonical place for navigation—but the CMS generally does not permit page authors to modify them. And access to the HEAD element is sometimes necessary to include CSS and Javascript. Accessing either of these requires that the user become not only a system administrator, but also a programmer, editing low-level theme files. And authors who did this often made mistakes: our scrape of the web revealed several sites in which a theme file had been mis-configured to include Exhibit's Javascript and CSS on every page, regardless of whether there was a visualization.

Despite the challenges of using external Javascript frameworks alongside a CMS, Author 5, who worked for a newspaper, believes that this is a better way to extend CMS functionality than native CMS plugins. "Media organizations can't work with something new unless that something was explicitly designed to work with [the CMS] they already have. There is an obvious workaround that every single modern CMS will allow you to embed custom Javascript into the published page." Javascript libraries, from his perspective, are the one truly platform independent way to extend web publishing systems. To avoid the problems we observed in our interviews, Javascript library authors should ensure their libraries can be included from within the authoring view of a CMS.

## THE DATA AUTHORS PUBLISH

This section looks at what kinds of data people visualize and how they create and publish that data to the web. We use both the TOP100 and the VIZ1800 dataset to understand the domain, scale, model, and format of data authored by the Exhibit community. Taken together with the interviews, the two chief conclusions supported by this section are: (1) authors understand complex data models, but are stymied by lack of support for them in mainstream editors (like spreadsheets), and (2) authors sers will choose unnecessarily complex and labor intensive data solutions over equivalent simple ones if the copyable design examples address the complicated case.

### The scale and topic of hand-crafted visualizations

Put in spreadsheet terms, the average visualization created with Exhibit is 14 columns wide and 142 rows tall (with medians 12 and 67, respectively). The distribution of sizes is shown in Figure 2. The two are shown as a pair of histograms instead of a scatter plot because there is little correlation between schema size and item count ($r = 0.16$).

We visited each site in our TOP100 dataset and performed three rounds of open coding to characterize the topic about

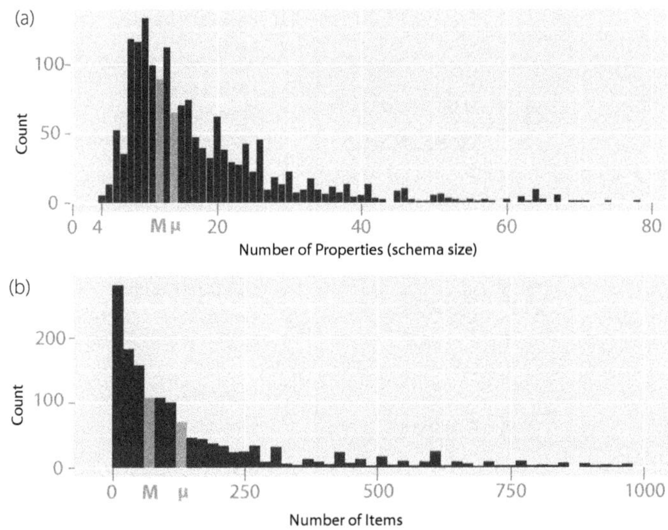


Figure 2: **(a)** The average dataset used with Exhibit has a schema of 14 properties (median 12). This figure and calculation omits two outliers with more than 200 properties. **(b)** The average Exhibit has 142 distinct items (median 67). This graph and calculation is performed after clipping datasets greater than 1000, which hand-sampling shows are more likely to be generated by a dynamic database query.

which the data was created. This process resulted in the two-level breakdown of topics shown in Figure 3. As seen in the diagram, nearly half of the visualization in this dataset were devoted to the topic we called Information Resources, which consisted of abstract facts about the world (such a faceted list of chemical compounds) as well as references to other pieces of information (such as a list of research publications).

Interestingly, only ten of the twenty-three visualizations in the Events cluster made use of Exhibit's timeline visualization, despite "Events" being inherently temporal in nature. The other thirteen used only faceted text-based tables and lists could have easily been created with plain HTML except for the faceted data navigation. This supports the common refrain in interviews and prior work [16] that data *navigation*—rather than visualization—is more important for some authors. HTML alone does not suffice this need, as it provides only the ability to create tables and lists, but not to sort, facet, or filter them.

### (Ab)using Spreadsheets to author non-Tabular Data

A *data model* is an abstract set of rules that dictates how data can be structured. A spreadsheet, for example, uses a *tabular* model which represents a list of items (rows), each with the same set of scalar properties (columns). *Multi-valued tables* are like tables, but allow table cells to contain multiple values (e.g., a list of countries). And a *graph* represents a collection of nodes with relationships drawn between them. These abstract models have different breadths of expressiveness:

$$\text{Tables} \subset \text{M-V Tables} \subset \text{Acyc. Graphs} \subset \text{Cyclic Graphs}$$

Tools (and specialized languages) for authoring data are typically targeted at a particular type of abstract data model, such

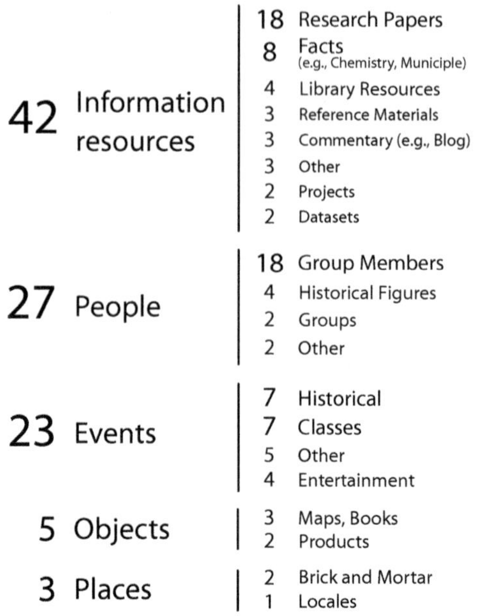


Figure 3: Item types visualized in the hundred most popular Exhibits in our dataset. Types were and sub-types were refined using a three-round open coding process.

as spreadsheets (and CSV) for tabular data. But it is often possible to author data of any model using any tool as long as the writer and reader agree upon the rules to marshal and de-marshal it. Someone might author a multi-valued table inside a spreadsheet by placing comma-separated lists of items inside cells, for example, or they may author graphical data by agreeing upon the columns SUBJECT, PREDICATE, and OBJECT to record the graph.

We programatically analyzed each dataset in the VIZ1800 collection to determine what what underlying data model it used. To our surprise, less than half (41%) of the data sets were strictly tabular. 32% were multi-valued tables, 21% were acyclic graphs, and 6% were cyclic graphs.

Spreadsheets are the overwhelmingly predominant data authoring tool for end-users, and Exhibit authors are no different: all but one interviewee reported having authored their data in a spreadsheet application. Assuming the population of the VIZ1800 dataset continues this trend, this breakdown of data model is alarming: most people author non-tabular data, but they are stuck using table-centric tools to do so.

While Exhibit provides workarounds for encoding nontabular data inside a tabular model (semicolon-separated lists for multi-valued tables and reference-able node IDs for graphs), spreadsheet UIs are not designed to provide any particular assistance for this kind of data. Spreadsheets do not allow authors to navigate or process lists encoded as semicolon-separated strings, for instance, and they force them into narrow cell layouts designed for numbers. Figure 4 shows that mismatches like this create enough friction to drive some graphical data authors to text formats (JSON) instead. A chi-squared test shows the distribution of publishing medium (JSON, RDF, or Google Spreadsheets) is significantly different for graphical data authors ($p < 2.2 \times 10^{-16}, df = 2$). Recall from our interviews that JSON was not a pleasant format among these authors, but they are driven to it by the lack of good graphical data support in spreadsheets.

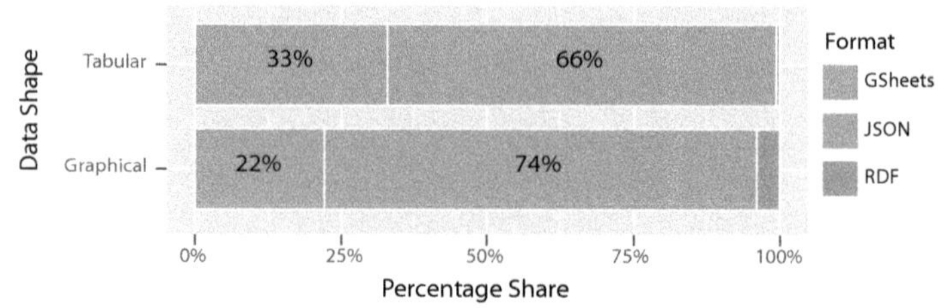


Figure 4: Distribution of data authoring format used conditioned on the shape of data being authored.

This is a quantified gap between the observed habits of data authoring end-users and the tools the community has provided them. Either there has been a failure of industry to understand the sophistication of end-user data modeling, or a failure to properly integrate and educate authors about options available to them. The Related Worksheets line of work provides a promising way to enhance existing spreadsheet UIs to accommodate multi-valued tables and hierarchical data [3]. A similar way to enable better graphical data editing within spreadsheets would also be welcomed by the community.

### "Linked Data" is actually used

Why not just encourage authors to stick to strictly tabular data, which tools like Excel already expertly support? One reason is the ability of the graphical data model to "link" entities together based on their relationships. For example, a list of Bob's grandchildren may be expressed as `Bob.children.children`. This is a powerful expressive capability not possible with the tabular model, and our data shows that authors are taking advantage of this power.

We measured the number of relationship "hops" used in Exhibit configurations in the VIZ1800 dataset. Tabular data is fixed at 1 hop, e.g., BOB.BIRTHDAY, whereas graphical data can contain more than one. A T-Test ($p < 3.2 \times 10^{-6}, df = 591$) shows that visualizations backed by graphical data have configurations that utilize more relationship hops than non-graphical data. In other words, authors who use more flexible data models are also visualizing more complex relationships in their data. Supporting graphical data editing in spreadsheets would therefore directly support end-user visualization needs, not just spurious data editing habits.

### Authors follow examples, not self interest

Another phenomenon we observed was that authors will choose between alternative approaches to a problem based on the availability of design examples rather than personal utility. This validates Weiss' study of API selection in mashups [24]. In our case, the result can be seen in the format authors selected to publish their data.

Exhibit accepts data in a number of formats, including Excel, Google Spreadsheets, CSV, and JSON. Table 1 shows that JSON dominates over the others, and Google Spreadsheets is the clear alternative. CSV is remarkably scarce given that it

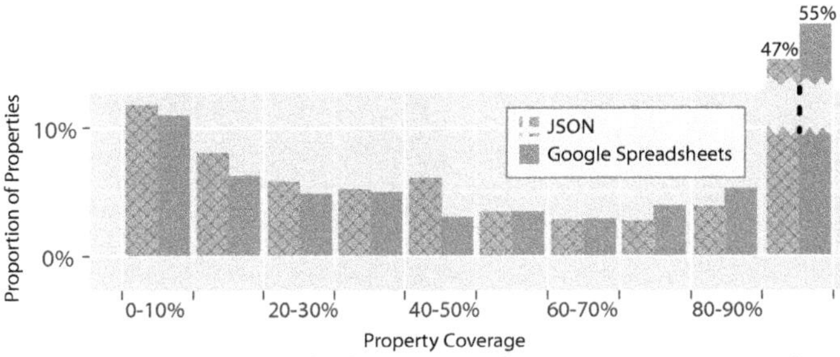


Figure 5: Normalized histogram of property coverage for properties of JSON datasets versus Google Spreadsheet dataset. JSON data is more likely to contain low-coverage properties, while Google Spreadsheets are more likely to contain high-coverage properties.

| Data Format | Count | Percent |
|---|---|---|
| JSON | 1246 | 69% |
| Google Spreadsheets | 580 | 32% |
| Bibtex | 38 | 2% |
| RDF | 25 | 1.4% |
| MS Excel | 2 | 0.12% |
| Freebase | 1 | 0.06% |
| CSV | 1 | 0.06% |

Table 1: Data formats used by Exhibit authors, the total count of visualizations using each type, and the percentage of visualizations using each type. Note that because some visualizations incorporate data from multiples sources of different types, this table adds up to more then 100%.

is the standard text serialization of spreadsheets, and Excel is virtually absent as well. Are Exhibit authors simply more comfortable with JSON and Google Spreadsheets?

If the interview population is representative of the VIZ1800 population, then a different explanation is more likely. Our interviewees reported authoring data in spreadsheets and then converting it to JSON for publication. When asked why they took this unnecessary last step (publishing the Excel file to the web would have sufficed), they cited following the examples they found online. Our *post hoc* review of the Exhibit wiki confirmed that virtually all the design examples used JSON and the documentation tended to focus on JSON and Google Spreadsheets. The easier paths to publication were less documented, and as a result virtually unused.

### Self-describing data formats are used more flexibly

Separate from the topic of data model is that of data format—the rules which govern the way data is written down. Data formats can largely be divided into schema-based (such as CSV and Spreadsheets) and self-describing (such as XML, JSON, and RDF). Schema-based formats are more compact: they list the structure of the data once, like the header row of a CSV file, and it remains implied for the rest of the file. Self-describing formats are more verbose: they always specify the structure of the data in full, so that a fragment can be understood independent of its file.

One of the primary advantages claimed of self-describing formats is that they permit adding "one-off" properties that are relevant to only a small set of items. Adding a PETNAME

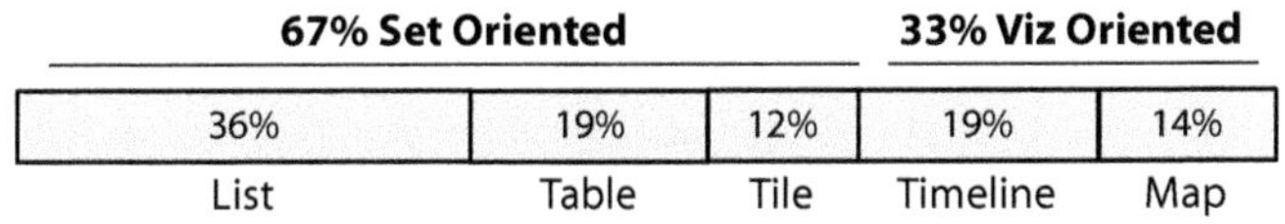


Figure 6: View types used in single-view exhibits.

column on behalf of just a single customer in a spreadsheet might result in thousands of empty cells on the other rows, but with a self-describing format, this change would only affect the one customer record who actually used the property.

These kinds of "one-off" properties are an inevitability in many real-world scenarios. We can measure them by looking at a statistic called *property coverage*: the number of items with a property divided by the total number of items in the dataset. A coverage of 1 means every item has the property, and a coverage of 0.1 means that only 10% do.

Figure 5 shows the distribution of property coverage of visualizations backed by JSON (self-describing) and Google Spreadsheets (schema-based) in the VIS1800 dataset. JSON-based data is more likely to have low coverage (> 50%) properties, and Google Spreadsheet-based data is more likely to have high-coverage (> 70%) properties. This shows that authors are in fact using self-describing formats differently than schema-based ones in exactly the manner that the abstract argument for self-describing formats would suggest.

## VISUALIZATIONS

This section examines how authors designed their visualizations. Recall that Exhibit visualizations are divided into three primary components: views, such as a map, timeline, or table; facets, which provide searching and filtering functionality; and lenses, which are miniature web templates for data items. These three components are woven into the rest of the web page with HTML.

Exhibits can have multiple views, displayed either modally or side-by-side. The mean view count is 1.4 and the median is one. 70% of Exhibits have one view, and 20% have two. The highest view count observed is 6. Exhibit visualizations have a mean of 3.1 facets and a median of 3. The most facets of any Exhibit in our dataset is 26. Only 17.5% of all Exhibit have no facets at all, which means that the vast majority of Exhibit authors both understand the concept of faceted navigation and consider the ability to filter sets of data a useful enough feature to include in their visualization.

This section uses the VIZ1800 dataset to find three results. First, we identify three distinct data publishing needs: navigation, visualization, and "just plain publishing". We show correlation between heavy use of a component and the complexity with which it is used. The most important and final result is that Exhibit authors tend to publish visualizations separately from text articles and need CMSs to allow them to take over the entire web page.

### Navigation, Visualization, and Just Plain Publishing

The motivation of the Exhibit paper hypothesized that there were communities of authors who wanted to (1) *provide navigation through* and (2) *visualize the relationships between*

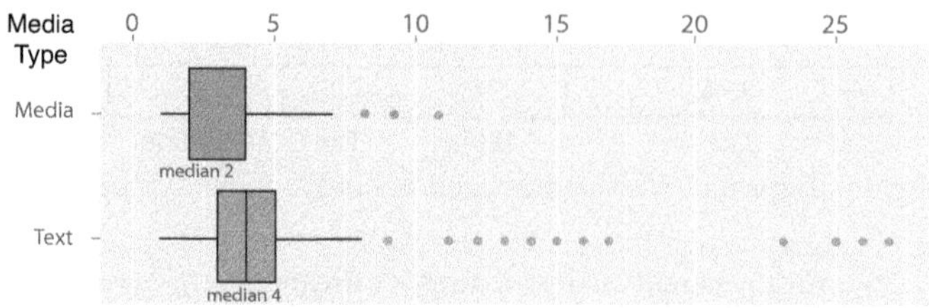


Figure 7: Of Exhibits that have only one view, text-only views have significantly more facets than rich-media views.

sets of items, but they were unable to do so because they lacked the proper tools. This claim was left unevaluated, and in this section we use data from the past eight years of Exhibit use in the wild to supplement our user interviews in demonstrating that this community, and these two needs do exist. We further show a third use evidenced in the data and interviews: using visualization frameworks as an on-ramp to web publishing for individuals not familiar with HTML.

To show this, we simplify the dataset by filtering it to only those Exhibits with a single view, 70% of all Exhibits total. This represents the set of visualizations with a focused purpose (i.e., just showing a map, or just showing a table), the breakdown of which is shown in Figure 6. 80% of these single-view Exhibits have facets.

Maps and timelines make up 33% of these Exhibits, which we claim are primarily used to visualize the relationship between data. Text-only Exhibits (lists, tables, and tiles) make up the other 67% of this collection. These Exhibits could have easily been reproduced in HTML alone *except for* Exhibit's faceting, sorting, and searching functionality. This extra functionality must have been the reason these authors spent time learning and deploying Exhibit on their site, demonstrating that data navigation is at least as important as visualization among Exhibit's user population.

By examining the distribution of facets for these two groups we can strengthen this distinction. We can infer that if an author's goal is to provide data navigation, she will have an incentive to provide more facets than if her goal was visualization of the relationship between items. Figure 7 shows a boxplot of facet count for the groups. Sure enough, text-only Exhibits (lists, tables, and tiles) contain significantly more facets than media-based Exhibits ($t(n = 1005) = -7.75, p < 2.2 \times 10^{-14}$).

Use of Exhibit as an on-ramp to HTML publishing is evidenced by the existence of text-based Exhibits with no facets at all. These tables or lists could easily have been ordinary HTML, but copying and modifying an example Exhibit configuration, which provides separation between the HTML design and data storage, must have been easier for these users than authoring the data as HTML. Author 7, who used Exhibit to publish a solitary HTML table, falls into this group.

### Those who author more, author more complexly

Do big data sets beget complex visualizations? Exhibit certainly permits complicated visualizations: the most views we observed stacked into a single Exhibit were 6 tables and 3 timelines, and the most facets we observed in a single Exhibit

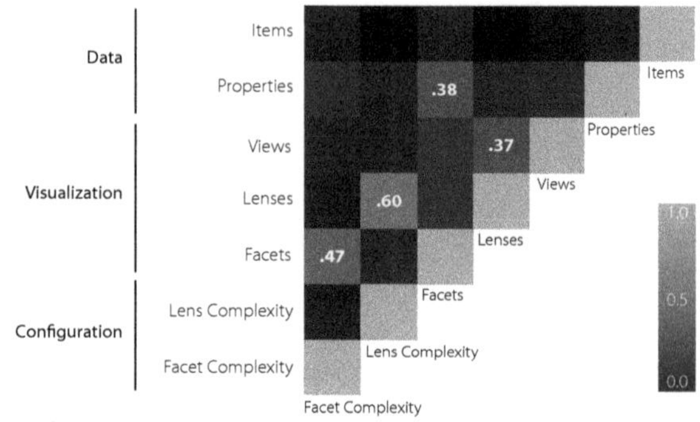


Figure 8: Correlation matrix between several data, visualization, and configuration-centric attributes. Notable is the lack of any strong correlation between aspects of the data and the properties of the visualizations created for that data.

was 28! But, as Figure 8 shows, the cross correlation between several attributes related to data, visualization, and configuration complexity is weak. Big datasets do not necessarily mean big visualizations.

The strongest relationship observed was between lenses (HTML templates used to style an item) and the complexity of configuration expressions within those lenses ($r = 0.6$), indicating that people who override the default design styles of a visualization more often are also likely to be modifying them more heavily. A similar, but weaker relationship was found for facets and facet expression complexity ($r = 0.47$).

### Page Layout

The most important observation in this section is about page layout and what visualization authors need from their CMS software (recall that the CMS publishing experience was a point of complaint in interviews). Here we ask two questions about visualization design to help guide CMS improvements for the visualization community:

- How do authors lay out visualization components?
- How do authors integrate visualizations with the text content on their sites?

To answer this first question, we coded the layout patterns of Exhibits found in the TOP100 dataset. The results are shown in Figure 9, with the view area depicted in white and the facet/search ares depicted in red. The results show that left and right sides of a visualization are overwhelmingly the preferred places for navigational elements. Over 80% of all facets we coded were placed to the side of a visualization, and over 50% of visualizations used the sides exclusively.

CMS software typically constrains authoring to a center column of text flanked on the sides by one or two columns reserved for automated content (links, navigation, etc). But access to this center column alone does not provide authors the required width to display both a visualization and filtering widgets to manipulate the visualization. To support the visualization community, it is therefore important that CMS makers either allow authors to override the side columns with custom, page-specific content, or to take over the page entirely, stripping it of the CMS-provided UI chrome.

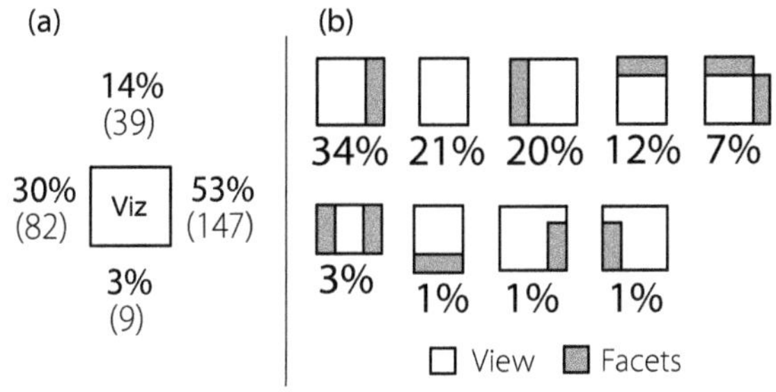


Figure 9: **(a)** Raw counts of facet location in the TOP100 Dataset. Most facets occur to the side of the visualization. **(b)** Counts of global visualization layout in TOP100 Dataset. Over half utilize a two-column format.

To examine how authors integrate visualizations with text content on their sites, we programatically analyzed the HTML structure of the pages which contain each visualization in the VIZ1800 dataset. For each page, we recorded two statistics: the total amount of text on the page in characters and the size of the largest single text node (e.g., what was the longest paragraph (<p>) element?). We also recorded these statistics for several well known websites. We then interpreted these measurements with the following heuristic: if a visualization is embedded in an article as supplementary information, we should expect the text statistics of the web page to appear like other pages known to contain articles. If the visualization stands alone, on a page by it self, we should expect much less text than on an article-containing page.

Figure 10 shows a scatterplot of the data. The horizontal axis is the amount of total text on each page, and the vertical axis is the largest block of text. Web pages containing Exhibits are shown in black, and reference points are shown in red: the 2014 CHI CFP, the front page of Slashdot.org and Reddit.com, and randomly selected articles from the New York Times, Washington Post, and Chronicle of Higher Education.

These results show that Exhibit visualizations are overwhelmingly published as stand-alone content that occupies its own page, not supplementary figures woven into articles. 85% of the points are strictly bound by the point representing the New York Times article, itself the smallest of our reference points. The remaining reference points are at the extremes of the collection. The line visible at $y = x$ represents web pages that contain only a single unit of text outside the visualization.

CMS builders can use this information by prioritizing support for page-centric visualizations over interactive features embedded in prose. It may be that we simply have not yet developed the journalistic culture of mixing the two forms yet, though recent publications like the Snowfall feature by the New York Times [7] and several interactive web adaptations of papers from Berkeley's AMP lab [18, 2] show that there is high payoff when text and interactivity are integrated well.

## BROWSING BEHAVIOR OF EXHIBIT SITE VISITORS

We tracked the behavior of 33 thousand distinct site visitors accessing 57 different Exhibits whose authors agreed to participate in our study. We limited our analysis to only the first 30 minutes of interaction for each IP address, the session timeout suggested by prior work [8]. While we do not have the space for a detailed discussion, we preview here a few observations about browsing behavior:

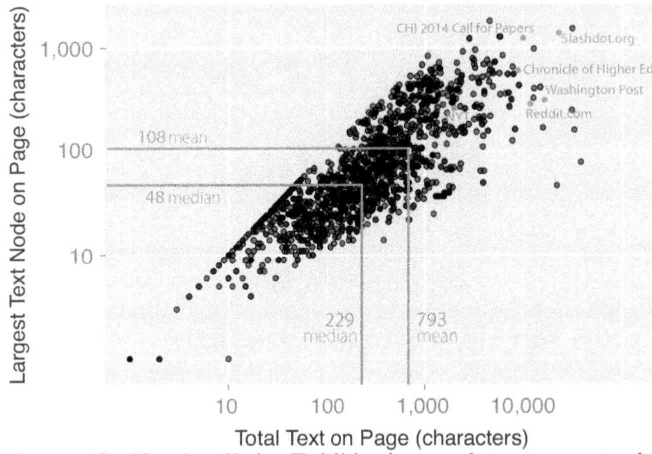


Figure 10: Nearly all the Exhibits in our dataset are stand-alone visualizations, not inline supplements to an article. Reference points (red) of articles on the web contain far more text (horizontal axis) and far larger paragraphs (vertical axis) than the pages in our dataset.

**If possible, visitors favor interaction.** 93% of visitors who could interact with an Exhibit visualization did. Interaction was either switching between multiple views or filtering the data in some way. The duration of interaction nicely fits an inverse exponential curve with respect to time, validating prior results in faceted browsing systems [21].

**Visitors browse in contract-and-expand cycles.** Browsing behavior follows a pattern of contracting the displayed dataset (via text search or facet filtering) and then expanding the dataset—a clear indication of browsing rather than searching for a particular item. The number of contraction-expansion cycles follows an inverse exponential curve, depicted in Figure 11. The average contraction phase consists of 1.7 filter actions (stddev 0.8) and the average expansion phase is 1.2 filter actions (stddev 0.8).

**Design choice affects browsing habits.** The maximum filtering achieved by viewers is significantly different when visualization authors provide just text search, just facets, or both. For facet-only visualizations 41% of viewers filter the dataset to under 5% of its initial dataset size. That number is 84% for text-search only visualizations and 94% if both filtering mechanisms are available.

One advantage of the **star model** for visualization construction is that its constrained processing model (data at the center, filters and views on the spokes) and declarative invocation allow easy collection and processing of usage statistics across wildly different visualizations: actions such as filtering, searching, aggregating, and switching views are invariant to widget implementation details. We plan to follow up on these initial results with a more complete study of *in situ* visualization browsing behavior.

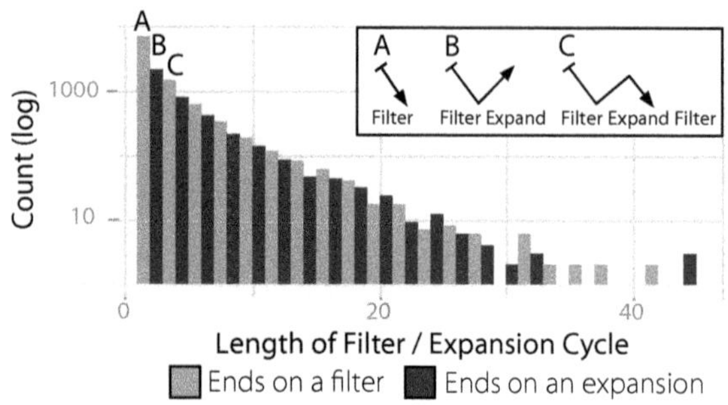


Figure 11: Histogram of the length of contraction-expansion cycles when visitors filter and unfilter data.

## CONCLUSION AND TAKEAWAYS

This work provided a mixed-method, full lifecycle analysis of set-based information visualization on the web using the Exhibit framework. Among our chief takeaways are:

- A wide range of users find that the star programming model is both simple enough (novices could use it) and powerful enough (professionals prefer it to alternatives) to meet their needs. We recommend visualization framework authors consider exposing functionality in this style.
- End-user data modeling habits are more sophisticated than their authoring tools. Most Exhibit users author supratabular data, but spreadsheets lack native support for it, so they often (unhappily) turn to text formats as a result. We recommend that spreadsheet makers consider adding support for data models more complex than a simple table.
- Exhibit authors follow the design examples available to them, even if it results in unnecessary labor. Good documentation remains a critical but undersupplied resource, and copy-able design examples are particularly important.
- Visualization and data interface authors have layout needs that exceed the options CMSs provide, and they struggle with their CMSs as a result. Toolkit builders should ensure their Javascript can be loaded from the `<body>` of a page, and CMS builders should enable user control of either the full page (discarding the theme) or the sidebar gutters (which are typically reserved space).
- The star model offers bright possibility for studying how web readers interact with data. Its constraints allow for a wide variety of interfaces, but provide a standardized data bus that enables unified behavior tracking across varied end-user creations.

We additionally provide an interview-based sketch of the motivations and practices of the Exhibit community and a dataset and design gallery of the visualizations this community has created. This community has sophisticated intentions for their data but often no formal training in computer science. The star programming model Exhibit utilizes has enabled them to translate these intentions into working interfaces, and in many cases has provided an environment within which to learn to build more complex displays.

## ACKNOWLEDGMENTS

This research was funded in part by the ISTC for Big Data.

## REFERENCES

1. Altinas, I., Berkley, C., Jaegar, E., Jones, M., Ludaescher, B., and Mock, S. Kepler: An extensible system for design and execution of scientific workflows. In *Proc. Future of Grid Data Environments, Global Grid Forum* (2004).
2. Bailis, P., Venkataraman, S., Franklin, M. J., Hellerstein, J. M., and Stoica, I. Probabilistically bounded staleness for practical partial quorums. In *Proc. VLDB* (2012).
3. Bakke, E., Karger, D. R., and Miller, R. C. A spreadsheet-based user interface for managing plural relationships in structured data. In *Proc. CHI* (2011).
4. Bostock, M., and Heer, J. A graphical toolkit for visualization. In *IEEE Trans Vis and Comp Graphics* (2009).
5. Bostock, M., Ogievetsky, V., and Heer, J. D3: Data driven documents. In *IEEE Trans Vis and Comp Graphics* (2011).
6. Bostock, Michael and Heer, Jeffrey. Declarative language design for interactive visualization. In *IEEE Trans Vis and Comp Graphics* (2010).
7. Branch, J. Snow fall: The avalanche at tunnel creek. In *The New York Times* (2013).
8. Cooley, R and Mobasher, B. and Srivastava, J. "Data Preparation for Mining World Wide Web Browsing Patterns. *Journal of Knowledge and Information System* (1999).
9. Gantt, M., and Nardi, B. A. Gardeners and gurus: Patterns of cooperation among cad users. In *Proc. CHI* (1992).
10. Gross, P., Herstand, M., Hodges, J., and Kelleher, C. A code reuse interface for non-programmer middle school students. In *Proc. IUI* (2010).
11. Hartmann, B., Doorley, S., and Klemmer, S. R. Understanding opportunistic design. In *IEEE Pervasive Computing* (2008).
12. Herman, I., Adida, B., Sporny, M., and Birbeck, M. Rdfa 1.1 primer: Rich structured data markup for web documents. In *W3C Working Group Note* (2013).
13. Herring, S. R., Chang, C.-C., Krantzler, J., and Bailey, B. P. Getting inspired! understanding how and why examples are used in creative design practice. In *Proc. CHI* (2009).
14. Huynh, D. F., Karger, D. R., and Miller, R. C. Exhibit: Lightweight structured data publishing. In *Proc. WWW* (2007).
15. Jones, M. C., and Churchill, E. F. Conversations in developer communities: A preliminary analysis of the yahoo! pipes community. In *Proc. C&T* (2009).
16. Karger, D. Standards opportunities around data-bearing web pages. In *Proc. HCIR* (2012).
17. Kelleher, C., Pausch, R., and Kiesler, S. Storytelling alice motivates middle school girls to learn computer programming. In *Proc. CHI* (2007).
18. Kraska, T., Pang, G., Franklin, M. J., Madden, S., and Feketey, A. Mdcc: Multi-data center consistency. In *Proc. Eurosys* (2013).
19. Lee, B., Srivastava, S., Kuar, R., Brafman, R., and Klemmer, S. R. Designing with interactive example galleries. In *Proc. CHI* (2010).
20. Newman, M., and Landay, J. Sitemaps, storyboards, and specifications: a sketch of web site design practice. In *Proc. DIS* (2000).
21. Niu, X., and Hemminger, B. Beyond text querying and ranking list: How people are searching through faceted catalogs in two library environments. In *Proc. ASIS&T* (2010).
22. Voida, A., Harmon, E., and Al-Ani, B. Homebrew databases: Complexities of everyday information management in nonprofit organizations. In *Proc. CHI* (2011).
23. Völkel, M., Krötzsch, M., Vrandecic, D., Haller, H., and Studer, R. Semantic wikipedia. In *Proc. WWW* (2006).
24. Weiss, M., and Sari, S. Evolution of the mashup ecosystem by copying. In *International Workshop on Web APIs and Services Mashups* (2010).
25. Witten, I. H., Bainbridge, D., and Boddie, S. J. Greenstone open source digital library software. In *D-Lib Magazine* (2001).

# Designing Usable Web Forms – Empirical Evaluation of Web Form Improvement Guidelines

**Mirjam Seckler[1], Silvia Heinz[1], Javier A. Bargas-Avila[2], Klaus Opwis[1], Alexandre N. Tuch[1 3]**

[1]Department of Psychology
University of Basel, CH
{forename.surname}@unibas.ch

[2]Google / YouTube User
Experience Research, Zurich, CH
javier.bargas@me.com

[3]Dept. of Computer Science
University of Copenhagen, DK
a.tuch@unibas.ch

## ABSTRACT

This study reports a controlled eye tracking experiment (N = 65) that shows the combined effectiveness of 20 guidelines to improve interactive online forms when applied to forms found on real company websites. Results indicate that improved web forms lead to faster completion times, fewer form submission trials, and fewer eye movements. Data from subjective questionnaires and interviews further show increased user satisfaction. Overall, our findings highlight the importance for web designers to improve their web forms using UX guidelines.

### Author Keywords

Web Forms; Form Guidelines; Form Evaluation; Internet; World Wide Web; Form Interaction

### ACM Classification Keywords

H.3.4 Systems and Software: Performance evaluation; H.5.2 User Interfaces: Evaluation/methodology; H.5.2 User Interfaces: Interaction styles

## INTRODUCTION

Technological development of the Internet has changed its appearance and functionality drastically in the last 15 years. Powerful and flexible technologies have added varying levels of interactivity to the World Wide Web. Despite this evolution, web forms – which offer rather limited and unilateral ways of interaction [14] – remain one of the core interaction elements between users and website owners [29]. These forms are used for registration, subscription services, customer feedback, checkout, to initiate transactions between users and companies, or as data input forms to search or share information [31]. Web forms stand between users and website owners and can therefore be regarded as gatekeepers. Due to this gatekeeper role, any kind of problems and obstacles that users experience during form filling can lead to increased drop-out rates and data loss. Accordingly, website developers should pay special attention to improving their forms and making them as usable as possible.


*CHI 2014,* April 26 - May 01 2014, Toronto, ON, Canada
Copyright 2014 ACM 978-1-4503-2473-1/14/04...$15.00.
http://dx.doi.org/10.1145/2556288.2557265

In recent years, an increasing number of publications have looked at a broad range of aspects surrounding web form interaction to help developers improve their forms. These studies shed light on selected aspects of web form interaction, but rarely research the form filling process using holistic approaches. Therefore, various authors have gathered together the different sources of knowledge in this field and compiled them as checklists [17] or guidelines [7, 18, 21]. Bargas-Avila and colleagues, for instance, present 20 rules that aim at improving form content, layout, input types, error handling and submission [7]. Currently there is no empirical study that applies these guidelines in a holistic approach to web forms and shows whether there are effects on efficiency, effectiveness and user satisfaction.

It is this gap that we aim to close with the present study. The main research goal is to conduct an empirical experiment to understand whether improving web forms using current guidelines leads to a significant improvement of total user experience. For this we selected a sample of existing web forms from popular news websites, and improved them according to the 20 guidelines presented in Bargas-Avila et al. [7]. In a controlled lab experiment we let participants use original and improved forms, while we measured efficiency, effectiveness and user satisfaction.

This work contributes to the field of HCI in three ways:
(1) The findings of this paper are empirically tested guidelines that can be used by practitioners.
(2) Thanks to the applied multi-method approach, we were able to better understand the impact of the individual guidelines on different aspects of user experience.
(3) Finally, our study shows that there is a difference between how experts estimate the relevance of the individual guidelines for user experience and how these guidelines actually affect the users' experience.

## RELATED WORK

An online form contains different elements that provide form filling options to users: for instance text fields, radio-buttons, drop-down menus or checkboxes. Online forms are used when user input is required (e.g. registration forms, message boards, login dialogues).

The usability of such forms can vary vastly. Small variations in form design can lead to an increase or decrease of interaction speed, errors and/or user satisfaction. It was shown, for instance, that the placement of error messages impacts efficiency, effectiveness and satisfaction. Locations near the erroneous input field lead to better performance than error messages at the top and the bottom of the form – placements that have been shown to be the most wide spread in the Internet [29].

Due to the importance of form usability, there is a growing body of research and guidelines published on how to make online forms more usable. These include topics such as error message improvement [2, 5, 29], error prevention [6, 26], improvement of various form interaction elements [3, 4, 10, 11], improvement for different devices [27], or accessibility improvement [23]. Some publications present empirical data, whereas others are based on best practices of experts in the fields of Human-Computer Interaction and User Experience [18, 19, 31].

There are extensive reviews on form guidelines research such as publications from Nielsen [24], Jarrett and Gaffney [19], and Wroblewsky [31]. One review that focuses particularly on guidelines that are based on published empirical research is provided by Bargas-Avila et al. [7]. Based on their review, the authors derive a set of 20 practical guidelines that can be used to develop usable web forms or improve the usability of existing web forms (see

| Web Form Design Guidelines |
|---|
| *Form content* |
| 1. Let people provide answers in a format that they are familiar with from common situations and keep questions in an intuitive sequence. |
| 2. If the answer is unambiguous, allow answers in any format. |
| 3. Keep the form as short and simple as possible and do not ask for unnecessary input. |
| 4. (a) If possible and reasonable, separate required from optional fields and (b) use color and asterisks to mark required fields. |
| *Form layout* |
| 5. To enable people to fill in a form as quickly as possible, place the labels above the corresponding input fields. |
| 6. Do not separate a form into more than one column and only ask one question per row. |
| 7. Match the size of the input fields to the expected length of the answer. |
| *Input types* |
| 8. Use checkboxes, radio buttons or drop-down menus to restrict the number of options and for entries that can easily be mistyped. Also use them if it is not clear to users in advance what kind of answer is expected from them. |
| 9. Use checkboxes instead of list boxes for multiple selection items. |
| 10. For up to four options, use radio buttons; when more than four options are required, use a drop-down menu to save screen real estate. |
| 11. Order options in an intuitive sequence (e.g., weekdays in the sequence Monday, Tuesday, etc.). If no meaningful sequence is possible, order them alphabetically. |
| 12. (a) For date entries use a drop-down menu when it is crucial to avoid format errors. Use only one input field and place (b) the format requirements with symbols (MM, YYYY) left or inside the text box to achieve faster completion time. |
| *Error handling* |
| 13. If answers are required in a specific format, state this in advance, communicating the imposed rule (format specification) without an additional example. |
| 14. Error messages should be polite and explain to the user in familiar language that a mistake has occurred. Eventually the error message should apologize for the mistake and it should clearly describe what the mistake is and how it can be corrected. |
| 15. After an error occurred, never clear the already completed fields. |
| 16. Always show error messages after the form has been filled and sent. Show them all together embedded in the form. |
| 17. Error messages must be noticeable at a glance, using color, icons and text to highlight the problem area and must be written in a familiar language, explaining what the error is and how it can be corrected. |
| *Form submission* |
| 18. Disable the submit button as soon as it has been clicked to avoid multiple submissions. |
| 19. After the form has been sent, show a confirmation site, which expresses thanks for the submission and states what will happen next. Send a similar confirmation by e-mail. |
| 20. Do not provide reset buttons, as they can be clicked by accident. If used anyway, make them visually distinctive from submit buttons and place them left-aligned with the cancel button on the right of the submit button. |

**Table 1. 20 guidelines for usable web form design (from Bargas-Avila et al. [7]).**

Table 1). The overall application of these guidelines is meant to improve the form's usability, shorten completion times, prevent errors, and enhance overall user satisfaction [7]. To the authors' best knowledge, there has been no empirical evidence that the usage of these guidelines accomplishes the established claims. Therefore a carefully designed experiment was conducted to answer this question.

## METHOD

### Study Design

In order to investigate as to how forms can be improved by the application of the guidelines compiled by Bargas-Avila et al. [7], we conducted an eye tracking lab study, where participants had to fill in either original or improved versions of three online forms taken from real company websites (between-subject design). Usability was measured by means of objective data such as task completion time, type of errors, effectiveness of corrections as well as eye tracking data (number of fixations, total fixation duration and total time of saccades), but also by subjective ratings on satisfaction, usability, cognitive load and by short interviews about quality of experience.

### Participants

Participants were recruited from an internal database, containing people interested in attending studies. In total 65 participants (42 female) took part in the study. Thirty-two were assigned to the original form and 33 to the improved form condition (see below). The mean age of the participants was 27.5 years ($SD$ = 9.7; range = 18-67) and all indicated to be experienced Internet users ($M$ = 5.4, $SD$ = 0.9 with 1 = "no experience"; 7 = "expert"). Participants received about 20$ or course credits as compensation.

Independent sample t-tests showed no significant differences between the two experimental groups regarding age, level of education, computer knowledge, web knowledge, online shopping knowledge and Internet usage. A chi-square test indicated that there are also no significant differences regarding gender distribution.

### Selection and Improvement of Web Forms

By screening www.ranking.com for high traffic websites we ensured getting realistic and commonly used web forms to demonstrate that the 20 guidelines work not only for an average website with a form or even for poorly designed forms but also for frequently used ones. We focused on top ranked German-language newspapers and magazines that provide an online registration form (N = 23). We chose high traffic news websites because they often include web forms with the most common input fields (login, password and postal address) and are of decent overall length. Subsequently, we evaluated these forms with the 20 design guidelines provided by Bargas-Avila et al. [7]. Moreover,

| Nr. | Guideline | Expert Rating $M$ (range) | Violated by* |
|---|---|---|---|
| 15 | Never clear the already completed fields. | 5.00 (5-5) | - |
| 11 | Order options in an intuitive sequence. | 4.71 (3-5) | Spiegel (1) |
| 19 | Provide a confirmation site. | 4.64 (4-5) | - |
| 14 | Texting of error messages: (...) | 4.57 (3-5) | Suedd (2) |
| 16 | Show all error messages after sending the form. | 4.29 (3-5) | Spiegel (2), Suedd (2) |
| 20 | Do not provide reset buttons. | 4.14 (1-5) | NZZ (2) |
| 13 | State a specific format in advance. | 4.14 (3-5) | Spiegel (1), NZZ (2), Suedd (1) |
| 18 | Disable the submit button as soon as it has been clicked. | 4.07 (2-5) | Spiegel (2), NZZ (2), Suedd (2) |
| 4a | Separate required from optional fields. | 4.07 (2-5) | NZZ (2) |
| 9 | Use checkboxes instead of list boxes (...) | 3.86 (2-5) | - |
| 8 | Use checkboxes, radio buttons or drop-down (...) | 3.86 (2-5) | - |
| 3 | Do not ask for unnecessary input. | 3.86 (1-5) | Spiegel (1), Suedd (1) |
| 1 | Let people provide answers in a familiar format. | 3.79 (2-5) | - |
| 12a | Date entries (...) | 3.57 (2-5) | Suedd (1) |
| 17 | Show error messages in red at the right side. | 3.57 (2-5) | Spiegel (2), NZZ (2), Suedd (2) |
| 2 | If the answer is unambiguous (...) | 3.50 (2-5) | - |
| 6 | (...) only ask for one input per column. | 3.36 (1-5) | Spiegel (2), Suedd (2) |
| 7 | Match the size of the input fields (...) | 3.29 (2-5) | NZZ (2), Suedd (2) |
| 12b | (...) the year field shoud be twice as long (...) | 2.79 (1-5) | Suedd (2) |
| 5 | (...) place the lables above the input field | 2.71 (1-5) | NZZ (2) |
| 10 | Use of radio buttons and drop-down menu: (...) | 2.36 (1-4) | Spiegel (2), NZZ (2), Suedd (2) |
| 4b | Use color to mark required fields. | 2.21 (1-4) | Spiegel (2), NZZ (2), Suedd (2) |

*Note: (1) partial violated, (2) fully violated

**Table 2. Expert ratings and guideline violations for each form.**

we screened the literature to update this guideline set. As result, we refined guideline 17 [29].

Two raters independently rated for each form whether a guideline was fully, partially or not violated (Cohen's kappa = 0.70). Additionally, 14 HCI experts rated independently each of the 20 guidelines on how serious the consequences of a violation would be for potential users (from 1 = not serious to 5 = serious; Cronbach's $\alpha$ = .90). See Table 2 for these expert ratings.

Based on these two ratings we ranked the forms from good to bad and selected three of different quality: One of rather

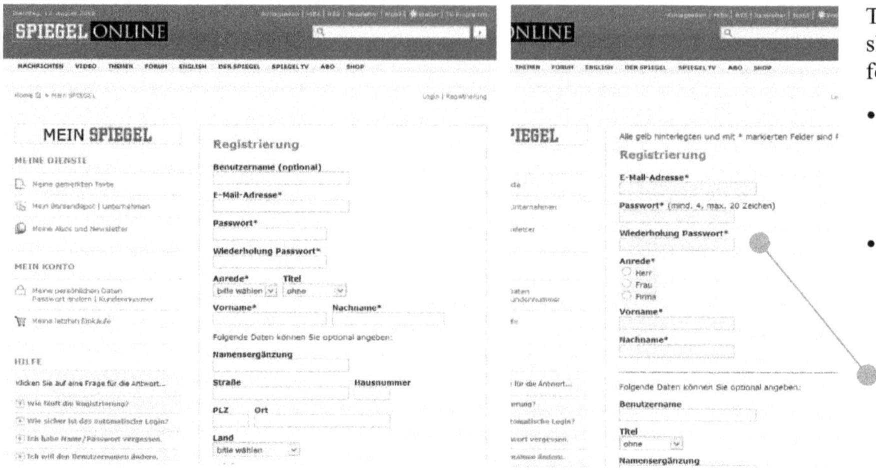


This example (password and repeat password) shows two fields improved through the following two guidelines:

- Guideline 4: If possible and reasonable, separate required from optional fields and use color and asterisk to mark required fields.
- Guideline 13: If answers are required in a specific format, state this in advance communicating the imposed rule (format specification) without an additional example.

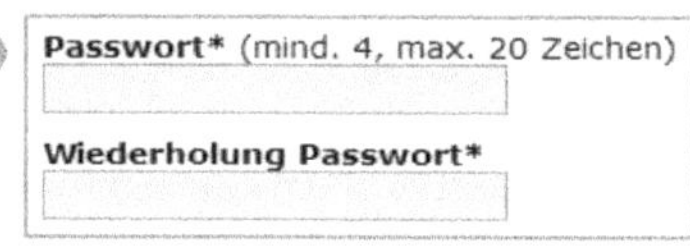


**Figure 1. Copy of the original Spiegel™ form (left), improved form (middle), improvement example (right)**

good quality (Spiegel.de; ranked #11), one of medium quality (nzz.ch; #13) and one of rather poor quality (sueddeutsche.de; #18). Nonetheless, the pool of websites in our ranking is based on top traffic websites – we expect that our three web forms represent rather high quality examples. In total, the NZZ and the Spiegel form violated 9 guidelines each, while the Sueddeutsche form violated 12. See Table 2 for guideline violations for each form.

We refrained from selecting any form from the top third (rank 1 to 8), since these forms had only minor violations and hence showed little to no potential for improvement. By means of reverse engineering of the structure, function and operation, we built a copy of the original form and an improved version according to the 20 guidelines (see Figure 1 for an example). We refrained from applying guideline 3 ("Keep the form as short and simple as possible and do not ask for unnecessary input") in this study, as this would have required in-depth knowledge of the companies' business strategies and goals.

### Measurements

Usability was assessed by means of user performance and subjective ratings. User performance included: time efficiency (task completion time, number of fixations, total fixation duration and total time of saccades) and effectiveness of corrections (number of trials to submit a form, error types). Furthermore, we used the KLM Form Analyzer Tool [20] to compare the different form versions. Eye tracking data were collected with a SMI RED eye tracker using Experiment Center 3.2.17 software, sampling rate = 60 Hz, data analysis using BeGaze 3.2.28.

We used the following subjective ratings: The NASA Task Load Index (TLX) for mental workload [15], the System Usability Scale (SUS) [8] and After Scenario Questionnaire (ASQ) [22] for perceived usability in general, and the Form Usability Scale (FUS) [1] for perceived form usability. Moreover, we conducted a post-test interview consisting of two questions: (1) "What did you like about the form?" and (2) "What did you perceive as annoying about the form?".

As the FUS is not a published questionnaire yet, this is a short introduction. The FUS is a validated questionnaire for measuring the usability of online forms [1]. It consists of 9 items each to be rated on a Likert scale ranging from 1 (strongly disagree) to 6 (strongly agree). The total FUS score is obtained by computing the mean of all items. Items: (1) I perceived the length of the form to be appropriate. (2) I was able to fill in the form quickly. (3) I perceived the order of the questions in the form as logical. (4) Mandatory fields were clearly visible in the form. (5) I always knew which information was expected of me. (6) I knew at every input which rules I had to stick to (e.g. possible answer length, password requirements). (7) In the event of a problem, I was instructed by an error message how to solve the problem. (8) The purpose and use of the form was clear. (9) In general I am satisfied with the form.

### Procedure

At the beginning, participants had to fill in a practice trial form. The quality of this form was medium (rank #14; Computerbase.de). Afterwards, participants were randomly assigned to one of the experimental conditions (original vs. improved). Participants were then sent to a landing page with general information about the selected newspapers and a link to the registration form. They were told to follow that link and to register. After successful completion of the form, participants rated the form with a set of questionnaires. This procedure was repeated for each online form. At the end participants were interviewed on how they experienced the interaction with the forms. The study investigator asked first for positive (what was pleasing) experiences and the participants could answer for as long as they wanted. Then they were asked for negative experiences (what was annoying).

## RESULTS

For all statistical tests an alpha level of .05 was used. Moreover, all data were checked to ensure that they met the requirements for the statistical tests. All time metrics had to be log-transformed to achieve normal distribution.

### User Performance

*Number of form submission*

As expected, users performed better with the improved version of the forms. In all three forms they needed fewer trials to successfully submit the form: Suddeutsche ($\chi^2$ = 11.20, $p$ < .001), NZZ ($\chi^2$ = 12.93, $p$ < .001), and Spiegel ($\chi^2$ = 3.29, $p$ = .035). See Table 3 for corresponding data.

| Form | Trials | Original | Improved |
|---|---|---|---|
| Sueddeutsche | 1 | 10 | 24 |
| | ≥ 2 | 22 | 9 |
| NZZ | 1 | 9 | 24 |
| | ≥ 2 | 23 | 9 |
| Spiegel | 1 | 22 | 28 |
| | ≥ 2 | 11 | 4 |

**Table 3. Number of trials until form was successfully submitted.**

*Initial errors*

Descriptive data showed that errors due to missing format rules specifications were frequent for the NZZ form (see Table 4). Chi-square tests showed that this error type was significantly more prevalent for the original condition than all other error types for NZZ ($\chi2$ = 7.17, $p$ = .007). For the two other forms, no significant differences between the different error types and conditions were found.

| Error types | Original | Improved |
|---|---|---|
| Missing specification | 17 | 2 |
| Field left blank | 1 | 1 |
| Captcha wrong | 0 | 2 |
| Mistyping | 1 | 4 |
| Error combination | 4 | 0 |

**Table 4. Initial errors for the NZZ form.**

*Consecutive errors*

Significant differences for errors made after the form has been validated once (consecutive errors, see Bargas-Avila et al. [5]) were found for the two conditions of Sueddeutsche, $p$ = .033 (Fisher's exact test). Descriptive data showed that in the original condition participants often ignored the error messages and resubmitted the form without corrections (see Table 5). No significant differences between error types were found for the two other forms.

| Error types | Original | Improved |
|---|---|---|
| No corrections | 14 | 0 |
| No input | 0 | 1 |

**Table 5. Consecutive errors for the Sueddeutsche form.**

*Task completion time*

As a consequence of the number of submissions, improved versions of all forms also performed better regarding task completion time than their original counterpart (see Table 6). An independent sample t-test showed significant differences for NZZ (t(63) = 4.39, $p$ < .001, Cohen's $d$ = 1.00) and for Sueddeutsche (t(63)= 3.91, $p$ < .001, Cohen's $d$ = .93). No significant effect was found for Spiegel (t(63)= 1.23, $p$ < .111, Cohen's $d$ = .38).

| Form | Condition | N | M (SD) | Time improvement |
|---|---|---|---|---|
| Suedd. | original | 32 | 113 (36) | |
| | improved | 33 | 85 (25) | - 25% |
| NZZ | original | 32 | 105 (46) | |
| | improved | 33 | 70 (20) | - 33% |
| Spiegel | original | 32 | 104 (66) | |
| | improved | 33 | 85 (30) | - 18% |

Note: Reported values are not log-transformed; statistical tests are based on log-transformed data.

**Table 6. Average task completion time in seconds.**

To further compare task completion times of the two form conditions, we checked the two forms with the Keystroke Level Model (KLM) [9]. We used the KLM Form Analyzer Tool from Karousos et al. [20] with the default settings except for running the analysis with the option "average typist". For all improved forms the KLM predicted time was lower than for the original forms (see Table 7). Nonetheless, participants in our study needed more time than predicted by the KLM analyzer.

| Form | KLM predicted time (sec) | | Improvement |
|---|---|---|---|
| | original | improved | |
| Suedd. | 68 | 52 | -23% |
| NZZ | 53 | 49 | -8% |
| Spiegel | 91 | 84 | -7% |

**Table 7. KLM form analyzer predicted time.**

*Eye Tracking*

The eye tracking data were analyzed using non-parametric Mann-Whitney $U$ tests, as data were not normally distributed. The data shown in Table 8 support results found with the user performance data. Participants assigned to the improved form condition were able to fill in the form more efficiently and needed significantly fewer fixations for the first view time (load until first submission) for Sueddeutsche and NZZ, but not for the Spiegel form: Sueddeutsche (Z = 2.57, $p$ < .005, $r$ = .322), NZZ (Z = 4.10, $p$ < .001, $r$ = .525), Spiegel (Z = 1.50, $p$ = .067, $r$ = .192). The total amount of time participants spent fixating a form before the first submission was shorter in the improved condition, indicating that they needed less time to process the information on screen. Total fixation duration was significantly shorter for Sueddeutsche ($Z$ = 1.71, $p$ = .044, $r$ = .214) and NZZ ($Z$ = 3.29, $p$ < .001, $r$ = .421). No significance difference could be shown for Spiegel ($Z$ = 0.59, $p$ = .277, $r$ = .076).

| Form | Number of fixations *M (SD)* | Fixation duration in sec *M (SD)* | Saccades total time in sec *M (SD)* |
|---|---|---|---|
| Suedd. orig. (N=31) | 157 (54) | 62 (23) | 7 (6) |
| Suedd. improv. (N=33) | 126 (41) | 53 (18) | 4 (3) |
| NZZ orig. (N=30) | 155 (70) | 62 (28) | 9 (9) |
| NZZ improv. (N=31) | 96 (37) | 41 (15) | 4 (3) |
| Spiegel orig. (N=30) | 146 (70) | 58 (34) | 6 (4) |
| Spiegel improv. (N=31) | 121 (43) | 50 (20) | 5 (4) |

**Table 8. Eye tracking measures for the original and the improved condition by form.**

Analyzing the total time of saccades shows that participants in the original form of the Sueddeutsche ($Z$ = 2.20, $p$ = .014, $r$ = .275) and the NZZ form ($Z$ = 3.88, $p$ < .001, $r$ = .497) spent more time searching for information. For the Spiegel form no significant differences could be shown ($Z$ = 1.18, $p$ = .119, $r$ = .151). Figures 2 and 3 visualize scan paths of participants in the original and the improved condition (duration 38 seconds). The participants filling in the improved form show a much straightforward scan path without unnecessary fixations whereas the side-by-side layout with left-aligned labels of the original form provoked longer saccades and more fixations for participants to orient themselves.

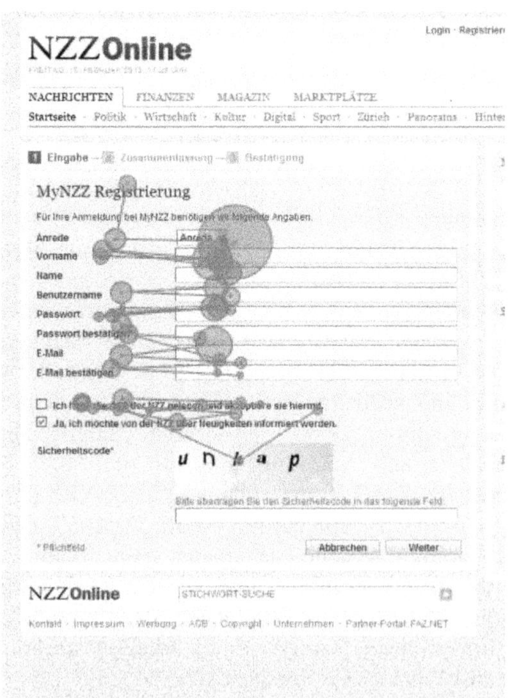


**Figure 2. Sample extract of a scanpath in the original version of the NZZ™ form.**

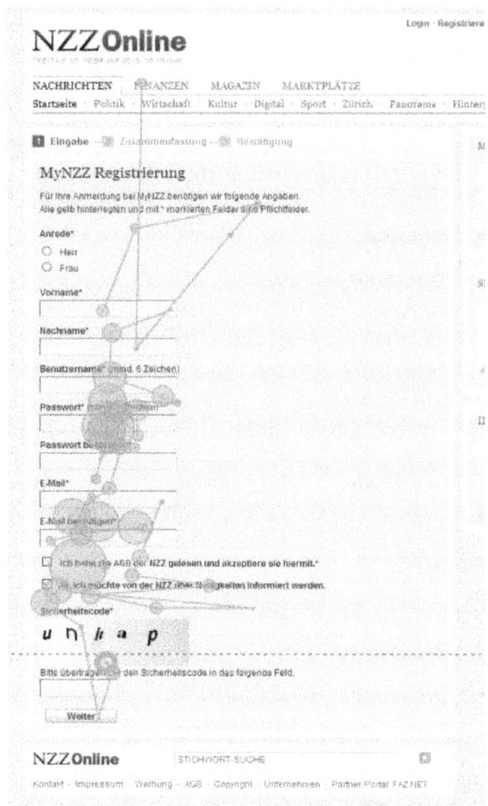


**Figure 3. Sample extract of a scanpath in the improved version of the NZZ™ form.**

*Subjective Ratings*

As not all data follow normal distribution, we applied the non-parametric Mann-Whitney $U$ test to investigate the differences between the improved and the original versions of the forms. Overall, the improved forms received better ratings than their original counter parts. Participants perceived the improved versions as more usable (ASQ, $Z$ = 2.29, $p$ = .011; FUS, $Z$ = 2.71, $p$ < .001; SUS, $Z$ = 2.89, $p$ < .001), as less demanding (NASA-TLX, $Z$ = 1.85, $p$ = .032) and were more satisfied with them (i.e., FUS item 9), $Z$ = 1.99, $p$ = .024). However, when analyzing the three different forms separately, differences emerge. As shown in Table 9, only the NZZ form received significantly better ratings on all scales. The Sueddeutsche form, in contrast, only shows higher ASQ ratings. For the Spiegel form none of the comparisons turn out significant. Nevertheless, one should notice that all comparisons between the original and improved versions of the forms show a tendency towards the expected direction.

*Effects on single items of the FUS*

The original versions of the three forms have different usability issues. Therefore we analyzed the forms separately on single item level of the FUS, which is a questionnaire designed to measure form usability. Figure 4 shows that applying the guidelines on the Sueddeutsche form leads to improvements regarding the user's ability to fill in the form

| Scale | Form | Original (n=32) | | Improved (n=32) | | Z | $r^1$ | Improvement |
|---|---|---|---|---|---|---|---|---|
| | | M | SD | M | SD | | | |
| ASQ | Suedd. | 5.03 | 1.24 | 5.71 | 1.18 | 2.48 | **.31** | 10% |
| | NZZ | 5.40 | 1.46 | 6.35 | 0.70 | 3.00 | **.38** | 14% |
| | Spiegel | 5.79 | 1.56 | 5.93 | 1.03 | 0.60 | .07 | 2% |
| FUS | Suedd. | 4.60 | 0.87 | 4.83 | 0.62 | 0.77 | **.10** | 6% |
| | NZZ | 4.75 | 0.81 | 5.49 | 0.44 | 3.84 | **.48** | 14% |
| | Spiegel | 5.17 | 0.73 | 5.32 | 0.70 | 0.94 | .12 | 5% |
| SUS | Suedd. | 3.86 | 0.78 | 4.13 | 0.50 | 0.88 | .11 | 5% |
| | NZZ | 4.14 | 0.70 | 4.71 | 0.35 | 3.80 | **.47** | 11% |
| | Spiegel | 4.17 | 0.74 | 4.36 | 0.71 | 1.39 | .17 | 4% |
| NasaTLX* | Suedd. | 22.11 | 15.12 | 17.11 | 12.74 | 1.61 | .20 | -5% |
| | NZZ | 18.98 | 14.40 | 12.29 | 8.29 | 2.21 | **.28** | -7% |
| | Spiegel | 18.49 | 15.56 | 16.25 | 13.67 | 0.40 | .05 | -2% |
| Satisfaction (last FUS item) | Suedd. | 4.50 | 1.11 | 4.56 | 1.05 | 0.12 | .01 | 6% |
| | NZZ | 4.72 | 1.37 | 5.47 | 0.88 | 2.57 | **.32** | 16% |
| | Spiegel | 4.84 | 1.11 | 5.06 | 1.13 | 0.98 | .12 | 8% |

*Note.* *Lower values show lower workload. Values in bold are significant at the .05 level (one-tailed test), [1]effect size $r$ Mann-Whitney U test ($r \geq .10$ = small, $r \geq .30$ = medium, $r \geq .50$ = large [12]).

**Table 9. Descriptive statistics for questionnaire scales.**

quickly ($r$ = .23) and the user's perception of the helpfulness of error messages ($r$ = .56). The NZZ form shows improvements on five items: "I was able to fill in the form quickly" ($r$ = .38), "Mandatory fields were clearly visible in the form" ($r$ = .34), "I always knew which information was expected" ($r$ = .46), "I knew at every input which rules I had to stick to" ($r$ = .64), and "In the event of a problem I was instructed by an error message how to solve the problem" ($r$ = .41). Finally, the improved version of the Spiegel form shows higher ratings only on the item "I knew at every input which rules I had to stick to" ($r$ = .49).

### *Effects on single items of the NASA-TLX*

As the NASA-TLX measures workload in a rather broad sense, it might be that its overall score is not able to capture the subtle differences in design between the original and improved versions. Therefore we conducted an analysis on single item level of the NASA-TLX. Results show that the improved version of both, the Sueddeutsche and the NZZ form, is perceived as being significantly less frustrating ($r$ = .23, resp. $r$ = .37) and users feel more successful in performing the task with it ($r$ = .34, resp. $r$ = .36). There are no effects on workload with the Spiegel form.

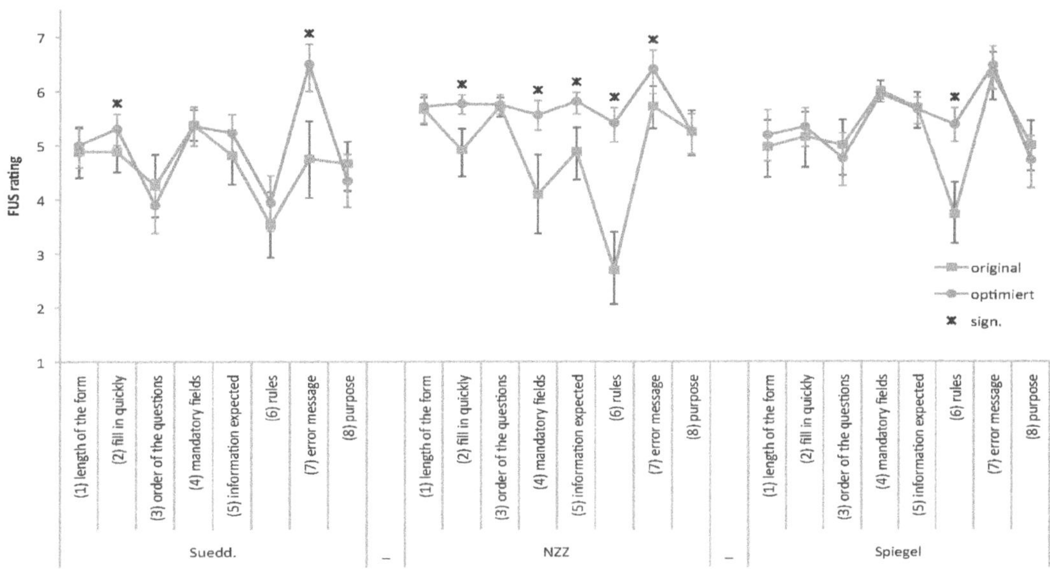


**Figure 4. Single item analysis of all FUS questions for original and improved versions.**

### Interview data

*Most frequently mentioned issues*

All interview data were analyzed by grouping similar issues for positive and negative comments

- Example of a positive comment: *"I think the form is clear, I immediately knew what I had to fill in and where. And I got an error message telling me how to do it right."*
- Example of a negative comment: *"It was annoying not to know the rules for the username and password first but only learn about them in the second step."*

We further made subgroups for each form and version. In a first step, we counted the number of issues per group showing that the most mentioned issues over all original forms were missing format specifications, insufficient identification of required and optional fields and that there were too many fields overall. Positive comments regarding the original forms were about easy and fast filling, clear identification of required and optional fields, and well-structured and clearly arranged forms. The most frequently reported negative aspects over all improved forms were: unappealing design of the whole site, too many fields, and the cumbersome Captcha fields. The positive comments concerned easy and fast filling in, clear identification of required and optional fields, and the logical sequence of the fields. See Table 10 for details.

*Differences between the two versions in issues mentioned*

As the most mentioned issues differ between the original and original versions, we analyzed the comments by means of chi-square tests. Participants assigned to the original form condition mentioned significantly more often missing format specifications ($\chi2$ = 7.74, $p$ = .003) and insufficient identification of required and optional fields ($\chi2$ = 4.93, $p$ = .013) than participants assigned to the improved form versions. Detailed analysis considering the three different forms separately shows that these results are mainly due to the differences between the two versions of the NZZ form (missing format specifications: $\chi2$ = 13.54, $p$ < .001 and insufficient identification of required and optional fields: *Fisher's p* = .002).

Unexpectedly, participants assigned to the improved forms mentioned significantly more often not liking the design of the whole site (as the forms were totally on the left and on the right were advertisements), $\chi2$ = 7.74, $p$ = .005 instead of expressing negative comments about the forms themselves. Detailed analysis considering the three different forms separately shows that these results are due to differences between the two versions of the Sueddeutsche, $\chi2$ = 5.85, $p$ = .016. No significant differences were found for the other most frequently mentioned issues.

### DISCUSSION

This study showed that by applying the 20 web form improvement guidelines, all three web forms showed improvements in regard to user performance and subjective ratings. Eye tracking data revealed furthermore that the original forms needed more fixations, longer total fixation duration and longer total saccade duration than the improved forms.

Our findings highlight the importance for web designers to apply web form guidelines. A closer look at the form submission trials shows that there is great potential for increasing the number of successful first-trial submissions by applying the guidelines. Thereby website owners can minimize the risk that users leave their site as a consequence of unsuccessful form submissions. Especially guideline 13 (addressing missing format specifications) and guideline 17 (addressing the location and design of error messages) had a remarkable effect on submission trials. This finding is in line with previous research on form guidelines [4, 29].

Furthermore, data for task completion times show an improvement between 18% and 33%. These values are even better than predicted by the Keystroke Level Model Analyzer Tool from Karousos et al. [20] that predicts improvements between 7% and 23%. Eye tracking data also indicate that participants could fill in the improved forms more efficiently as they needed fewer fixations and saccades [13, 16]. This indicates that participants needed

| | Original | | | Improved | | |
|---|---|---|---|---|---|---|
| Positive comments | Suedd. | NZZ | Spiegel | Suedd. | NZZ | Spiegel |
| easy and fast filling in | 14 | 17 | 10 | 12 | 16 | 12 |
| well-structured and clearly arranged | 3 | 7 | 7 | 5 | 7 | 7 |
| clear identification of required and optional fields | 5 | 1 | 13 | 3 | 9 | 14 |
| logical sequence of the fields | 1 | 5 | 5 | 6 | 10 | 4 |
| Negative comments | | | | | | |
| missing format specifications | 5 | 15 | 2 | 4 | 2 | 2 |
| insufficient identification of required and optional fields | 1 | 10 | 2 | 2 | 0 | 1 |
| too many fields | 6 | 1 | 6 | 4 | 1 | 6 |
| design of the whole site | 3 | 0 | 5 | 11 | 5 | 6 |
| Captcha | 4 | 8 | 0 | 4 | 5 | 0 |

**Table 10. Number of positive and negative comments for original and improved versions.**

less time looking for specific information during form filling in the improved versions and further supports the performance data. This result is comparable to findings of former usability studies on forms [25].

Subjective ratings showed improvement of up to 16%. Items with a relation to guideline 17 (error messages, see [2, 5, 29]) and guideline 13 (format specification, [4]) showed frequent significant improvements. Finally, interview comments showed that the two conditions differed also regarding subjective feedback. While participants assigned to the original form condition mentioned significantly more often missing format specifications and insufficient identification of required and optional fields, participants assigned to the improved form condition more often criticize the layout of the whole site and not issues about the form itself. Therefore, it can be concluded that from the users' point of view, guideline 13, (addressing missing format specifications) and guideline 4 (highlighting the importance of clear identification of required and optional fields), are the most important. These findings support results of former usability studies on form guidelines [4, 26, 30].

Furthermore, our study shows that the ratings of experts and users differ remarkably. While participants assigned to the original form condition mentioned most often missing format specifications and insufficient identification of required and optional fields, experts rated these two aspects as only moderately important (as seventh and ninth out of 20, respectively). Furthermore, although Spiegel and Sueddeutsche violate two of the five most important expert-rated guidelines (see Table 2), these two forms often performed better than the NZZ form.

To sum up, the effort to improve web forms is relatively small compared to the impact on usability, as shown by our study results.

## LIMITATIONS AND FURTHER RESEARCH

There are two important limitations regarding this study. First, the study took place in a lab and therefore controlled aspects that may arise when people fill in forms in real world situations. Distracting context factors were reduced to a minimum and participants concentrated on filling in forms and did not work in parallel on other tasks. Furthermore, the study focuses on newspaper online registration forms. Further research is needed to explore whether the findings from this study can be replicated with other type of forms (e.g. longer forms with more than one page or other use cases such as web shops, social networks or e-gov forms). Moreover, it would be interesting to study the implications outside the lab and perform extended A/B testings. Additionally, from an economic standpoint it would be important to know how the guidelines influence not only usability aspects, but also conversion rates. Another emerging topic that will be relevant for the future will be guidelines tailored for mobile applications.

## CONCLUSION

This study demonstrates how form improvement guidelines can help improve the usability of web forms. In contrast to former research that focused on the evaluation of single aspects, the present study uses a holistic approach. In a controlled lab experiment we were able to show the combined effectiveness of 20 guidelines on real web forms. The forms used were taken from real websites and therefore reveal that web forms are often implemented in suboptimal ways that lead to lower transaction speed and customer satisfaction. In the worst case, users may not be able to complete the transaction at all. Our results show that even forms on high traffic websites can benefit from an improvement. Furthermore, we showed the advantages of a multi-method approach to evaluate guidelines. We hope this paper animates other researchers to empirically validate existing or new guidelines.

## ACKNOWLEDGMENTS

Note that preliminary data on this study has been presented as "Work-in-progress" at CHI 2013 [28]. In comparison to this publication, we expand these data by investigating more participants and extending our analysis of user performance data (error analysis, eye tracking data, Keystroke Level Model comparison) and of questionnaire data and interviews. Moreover, we compare the ratings from experts and the study data of our participants and discuss the importance of single guidelines.

Alexandre N. Tuch was supported by the Swiss National Science Foundation under fellowship number PBBSP1 144196. Further, the authors would like to thank Lars Frasseck for the technical implementation and the usability experts and all participants for their valuable contribution to this study.

## REFERENCES

1. Aeberhard, A. (2011). FUS - Form Usability Scale. Development of a Usability Measuring Tool for Online Forms. Unpublished master's thesis. University of Basel, Switzerland.
2. Al-Saleh, M., Al-Wabil, A., Al-Attas, E., Al-Abdulkarim, A., Chaurasia, M., Alfaifi, R. (2012). Inline immediate feedback in arabic web forms: An eye tracking study of transactional tasks. In *Proc. IIT 2012*, 333-338.
3. Bargas-Avila, J. A., Brenzikofer, O., Tuch, A. N., Roth, S. P., & Opwis, K. (2011a). Working towards usable forms on the World Wide Web: Optimizing date entry input fields. *Advances in Human Computer Interaction*, Article ID 202701.
4. Bargas-Avila, J. A., Brenzikofer, O., Tuch, A. N., Roth, S. P., & Opwis, K. (2011b). Working towards usable forms on the World Wide Web: Optimizing multiple selection interface elements. *Advances in Human Computer Interaction,* Article ID 347171.

5. Bargas-Avila, J.A., Oberholzer, G., Schmutz, P., de Vito, M. & Opwis, K. (2007). Usable Error Message Presentation in the World Wide Web: Don't Show Errors Right Away. *Interacting with Computers*, 19, 330-341.
6. Bargas-Avila, J. A., Orsini, S., Piosczyk, H., Urwyler, D., & Opwis, K. (2010a). Enhancing online forms: Use format specifications for fields with format restrictions to help respondents, *Interacting with Computers,* 23(1), 33-39.
7. Bargas-Avila, J. A, Brenzikofer, O., Roth, S., Tuch, A. N., Orsini, S., & Opwis, K. (2010b). Simple but Crucial User Interfaces in the World Wide Web: Introducing 20 Guidelines for Usable Web Form Design. In: R. Matrai (Ed.), *User Interfaces*, 1-10. InTech.
8. Brooke, J. (1996). SUS: A Quick and Dirty Usability Scale. In: P. W. Jordan, B. Thomas, B. A. Weerdmeester & I. L. McClelland (Eds.), *Usability Evaluation in Industry* (pp. 189-194). London: Taylor & Francis.
9. Card, S. K., Moran, T. P., & Newell, A. (Eds.) (1983). *The psychology of human computer interaction.* Routledge.
10. Christian, L., Dillman, D., & Smyth, J. (2007). Helping respondents get it right the first time: the influence of words, symbols, and graphics in web surveys. *Public Opinion Quarterly*, 71(1), 113 - 125.
11. Couper, M., Tourangeau, R., Conrad, F., & Crawford, S. (2004). What they see is what we get: response options for web surveys. *Social Science Computer Review,* 22(1), 111 – 127.
12. Field, A. (2009). Non-parametric tests. In Discovering statistics using SPSS (third edition., pp. 539-583). London: SAGE.
13. Duchowski, A. T. (2007). *Eye tracking methodology: Theory and practice* (Vol. 373). Springer.
14. Harms, J. (2013). Research Goals for Evolving the 'Form' User Interface Metaphor towards more Interactivity. *Lecture Notes in Computer Science*, 7946, 819-822.
15. Hart, S., & Staveland, L. (1988). Development of NASA-TLX (Task Load Index): Results of empirical and theoretical research. P. A. Hancock & N. Meshkati (Eds.). *Human mental workload* (pp. 139-183). Amsterdam: Elsevier Science.
16. Holmqvist, K., Nyström, M., Andersson, R., Dewhurst, R., Jarodzka, H., & Van de Weijer, J. (2011). *Eye tracking: A comprehensive guide to methods and measures.* Oxford University Press.
17. Idrus, Z., Razak, N. H. A., Talib, N. H. A., & Tajuddin, T. (2010). Using Three Layer Model (TLM) in web form design: WeFDeC checklist development. *Computer Engineering and Applications (ICCEA)*, 385-389.
18. James, J., Beaumont, A., Stephens, J., Ullman, C. (2002). Usable Forms for the Web. Glasshaus, Krefeld.
19. Jarrett, C. & Ganey, G. (2008). Forms that work: Designing web forms for usability. Morgan Kaufmann.
20. Karousos, N., Katsanos, C., Tselios, N., & Xenos, M. (2013). Effortless tool-based evaluation of web form filling tasks using keystroke level model and fitts law. In *CHI'13 Extended Abstracts on Human Factors in Computing Systems*, 1851-1856. ACM.
21. Koyani, S. (2006). Research-based web design & usability guidelines. US General Services Administration, Washington.
22. Lewis, J. R. (1991). Psychometric evaluation of an after-scenario questionnaire for computer usability studies: The ASQ. *SIGCHI Bulletin*, 23(1), 78-81.
23. Money, A. G., Fernando, S., Elliman, T., & Lines, L. (2010). A trial protocol for evaluating assistive online forms for older adults. *Proc. ECIS*, Paper 90.
24. Nielsen, J. (2005). Sixty Guidelines From 1986 Revisited. <http://www.nngroup.com/articles/ sixty-guidelines-from-1986-revisited/>
25. Nielsen, J., & Pernice, K. (2010). *Eyetracking web usability*. New Riders.
26. Pauwels, S. L., Hübscher, C., Leuthold, S., Bargas-Avila, J. A. & Opwis, K. (2009). Error prevention in online forms: Use color instead of asterisks to mark required fields. *Interacting with Computers,* 21(4), 257-262.
27. Rukzio, E., Hamard, J., Noda, C., & De Luca, A. (2006). Visualization of Uncertainty in Context Aware Mobile Applications. In *Proc. MobileHCI'06*, 247-250.
28. Seckler, M., Heinz, S., Bargas-Avila, J.A., Opwis, K., & Tuch, A.N. (2013). Empirical evaluation of 20 web form optimization guidelines. In *Proc. CHI '13*, 1893-1898.
29. Seckler, M., Tuch, A. N., Opwis, K., & Bargas-Avila, J. A. (2012). User-friendly Locations of Error Messages in Web Forms: Put them on the right side of the erroneous input field. *Interacting with Computers*, 24(3), 107-118.
30. Tullis, T., Pons, A., 1997. Designating required vs. optional input fields. In: Conference on Human Factors in Computing Systems. ACM New York, NY, USA, pp. 259–26
31. Wroblewski, L. (2008). *Web Form Design: Filling in the Blanks.* Rosenfeld Media.

# Choice Overload in Search Engine Use?

**Pawitra Chiravirakul**
Department of Computer Science,
University of Bath
Bath BA2 7AY, UK
p.chiravirakul@bath.ac.uk

**Stephen J. Payne**
Department of Computer Science,
University of Bath
Bath BA2 7AY, UK
s.j.payne@bath.ac.uk

## ABSTRACT
Search engines typically return so many results that choosing from the list might be predicted to suffer from the effects of "choice overload". Preliminary work has reported just such an effect [12]. In this paper a series of three experiments was conducted to investigate the choice overload effect in search engine use. Participants were given search tasks and presented with either six or twenty-four returns to choose from. The results revealed that the choice behaviour was strongly influenced by the ranking of returns, and that choice satisfaction was affected by the number of options and the decision time. The main results, from the third experiment, showed that large sets of options yielded a positive effect on participants' satisfaction when they made a decision without time limit. When time was more strongly constrained, choices from small sets led to relatively higher satisfaction. Our studies show how user satisfaction with found information can be affected by processing strategies that are influenced by search engine design features.

### Author Keywords
Choice satisfaction; search engines; decision behaviour.

### ACM Classification Keywords
H.5.m. Information interfaces and presentation (e.g., HCI): Miscellaneous.

## INTRODUCTION
Users of current web search engines are typically presented with a large number of returns after each query, ordered according to some obscure algorithm that makes it likely, to some extent, that valuable hits will appear early in the list. The length of the list means that users must choose returns to open and inspect without consideration of most of the alternatives.

As noted by Oulasvirta, Hukkinen & Schwartz [12], this situation may lead to "choice overload", i.e. negative psychological effects of being asked to choose from a large set of options (e.g. [1, 4, 9]), a phenomenon that has seen a great deal of empirical research, and some uneven conclusions since the classic work of Iyengar & Lepper [7], and the influential monograph by Schwartz [17].

Iyengar & Lepper's [7] first experiment involved food shopping. Either six different jams or twenty-four different jams were presented to buyers in an upscale retail outlet. After tasting, each buyer was given a discount coupon that could be used when buying a jam. These coupons were more used by those who tasted a chosen jam from a small set than those who had sampled from a large set.

In their second experiment [7] students were asked to choose an essay topic from either six topics or thirty topics and to write a two-page essay for additional course credit. The percentage of students who completed their essay and the quality of those essays were both higher for the students given the smaller set of options.

The final experiment [7] required participants to sample a chocolate that was chosen for them or was their own choice. Participants who could choose were presented with either six flavours or thirty flavours of chocolate. Having made the choice and eaten the chocolate, participants were then offered two options for payment, five dollars in cash or chocolates worth five dollars. Participants who had chosen from only six flavours were more likely to choose chocolates as compensation. Furthermore, participants who chose from the large set reported that the selection process was difficult and frustrating. Although at first the large number of options seemed attractive and enjoyable to consider, these participants felt regret and dissatisfaction with the final choice.

Such negative consequences of too many options have been called "The paradox of choice" [17], because in so many situations consumers and policy makers assume or report that more available choices is a Good Thing. Indeed, the empirical evidence concerning the choice overload effect is itself somewhat paradoxical, with as many studies reporting positive effects of large choice sets as those, since Iyengar & Lepper [7] that have been consistent with their findings. Scheibehenne, Greifeneder & Todd [16] reported a meta-analysis of fifty experiments in which number of alternatives was the major independent variable, combining the effect-size of measures such as unwillingness to choose or satisfaction with final choice. They found a mean effect size close to zero, and failed to identify any sufficient conditions for the choice overload effect.


*CHI 2014*, April 26 - May 01, 2014, Toronto, ON, Canada.

ttp://dx.doi.org/10.1145/2556288.2557149

One example of a positive effect of choice-set size was reported by Oppewal & Koelemeijer [11]. In their study, a set of either five or twelve flower photographs was sent to a florist's regular customers. The results demonstrated that more options had a positive effect, regardless of similarity of items and whether the options already contained a preferred item.

In many ways this study seems similar to [7], so the opposite finding illustrates the difficulty reported by Scheibhenne et al [15] in identifying important causal factors for choice overload effects. Perhaps one issue in the Oppewal & Koelemeijer [11] study is that neither set of options is "large enough" to create an overload effect, but finding an empirical basis for pinning down "large enough" is not yet possible.

It is a little easier to suggest *necessary* conditions for choice overload: in particular the non-familiarity of options seems necessary, because otherwise the decision-maker can fall back on simple recognition and preference judgments [15, 16] that make the size of the choice set less salient.

Returning to information foraging using a search engine, it seems clear that these necessary conditions for a choice overload effect are met – at least in many situations, especially novel searches, the returned choices will be unfamiliar to the searcher, and the choice set is often large by any standards.

However, some typical search engine design features may work against choice overload. First, as mentioned above the fact that the choice set is ordered (however unreliably relative to the searcher's needs) is a factor that may well affect the decision maker's response. If users are very confident that the ordering is a reliable guide to value, then the length of the list may seem irrelevant, and the tendency to select items from early in the list may mean that the list of options appears de facto small and manageable. This argument is supported by evidence that Google users typically select from very early in the list of returned pages [13] and further, by studies that show that judged relevance of documents decreases down lists of more than fifteen documents, even if the documents are in fact randomly ordered [6, 14].

Further, in many designs, the long list of returns is broken into separate pages, so that the length of the list is arguably less salient. Studies have shown that paginated lists lead to better performance and memory than uninterrupted, scrollable lists [2].

We conclude that on the basis of the existing empirical data it is not possible to predict, with any confidence, whether search engines will produce choice overload. For further guidance, we must look at explanations of the choice overload effect, and at the single published study of choice overload that we have found, which models a search engine scenario.

Three broad explanations have been put forward for choice overload. To simplify, we will couch these explanations in terms of a single effect – lower satisfaction with a chosen alternative when the set from which the alternative was chosen was larger rather than smaller. (We believe the arguments can readily be adapted to other dependent measures, such as motivation to consume.)

The first explanation, we will call process-product leakage. A large set of items to choose from is likely to make the process of choosing more problematic in several ways. Most obviously, if one assumes that time is constrained, it will mean less consideration must be given to each item (no consideration at all of some items in many cases of search engine use). More subtly, a bigger set of options makes it more likely that some items are hard to contrast (e.g. a second-best is likely to be closer in perceived quality to a best). If the decision process is difficult, the final choice may be viewed as unsatisfactory because the process that led to it is unsatisfactory in some way (and even if an experimental participant is responding to a question about their satisfaction with a consumed item, it seems plausible that their response may be less specific than the question's wording [15]).

The process-product leakage explanation predicts that decision time will be a moderator of choice overload effects, as has been proposed by Haynes [5]. Participants were asked to choose a prize to be entered in a drawing from a set of prize descriptions; either three prize descriptions or ten prize descriptions were presented. The result showed that under the time pressure participants felt the decision was difficult and reported less satisfaction, especially with a large set of options.

The second, related, explanation for choice overload is regret, i.e. regret about not consuming the un-chosen items [17]. The argument is that the more items rejected, the more likely that the decision-maker regrets doing without some of those items, i.e., a counterfactual, if-only, response negatively impacts the post-hoc evaluation of the chosen item.

Finally, the effect of choice-set size may be on expectations. If a choice set is larger, the decision maker may expect a better outcome, and this expectation works to set a standard against which post-choice comparisons are made. This explanation is in keeping with data that suggests participants have an a priori (pre-choice) more favourable reaction to large sets of alternatives (e.g. [7], experiment 3).

Intuitively, all three of these psychological processes seem plausible in the case of choosing information sources from the set of query returns by a search engine. On this basis, it seems reasonable to predict that choice overload is potentially an important issue for search engine design.

Oulasvirta, Hukkinen & Schwartz [12] conducted an experiment to investigate this prediction, using paper-based materials to model aspects of a typical search engine scenario. Because aspects of their study were an important guide to the design of our own studies, we will report them in some detail.

Participants were given three kinds of "realistic" search tasks: Simple facts, such as "Find out which country is located at the highest altitude"; Problems, with open-ended answers, such as "What determines the cost of railway tickets in Europe?"; and Preferences, such as "Find your favourite novelist's homepage". For each search task a participant was provided with a printed page containing a query for that task and a set of results. Half of these pages were taken from Google, used Google formatting conventions, half used an invented search engine, with different terminology and layout but the same content. The main independent variable was the number of snippets returned, either 6 or 24. Independent variables were manipulated within-subjects. Participants had to select a single snippet from the returned set, within 30 seconds, and then (without consulting the actual web page) rate their satisfaction with the choice and their confidence that they had made the "correct" choice.

There were no significant differences between search engines, but a significant choice-overload effect, with participants reporting greater satisfaction and confidence when they chose from only 6 snippets. Post hoc analysis suggested that this effect was limited to simple fact and problem task types.

Several features of Oulasvirta et al's study limit the generalisation of the conclusions to real search engine use. Obviously, paper presentation is an approximate model in several ways, e.g., not allowing users to specify their own queries or to view any of the found web pages, both of which seem likely to be critical determinants of satisfaction in real scenarios. Further, limiting the judgments to snippets rather than the linked-to pages seems to us to make process-product leakage a very salient determinant of satisfaction. When no end product is actually experienced, what else can a satisfaction judgment rely on except process, or else the snippet information itself, the very basis of the choice. Furthermore, the time limit of 30 seconds seems quite severe, amounting to 1.25 seconds per item in the 24-item condition. Again, this seems likely to engender dissatisfaction with process. This account is supported by participants' report that when they chose from the six-option list they thought more carefully about their decision.

With these issues in mind, we sought to develop Oulasvirta et al's work with online experiments that more closely model real search-engine use, and which allow participants to choose and consult web pages from the sets of snippets their search returned before rating their satisfaction with those web pages.

## EXPERIMENT 1: NUMBER OF OPTIONS AND ITERATION

### Method

*Design*

In this experiment participants performed real-time Google searching, specifying their own search terms and choosing a web page to view before making any judgments. Only the Problem task type was used. Two separate sets of 10 questions were developed and utilised, but after preliminary analysis the question set was not treated as an independent variable in the main analyses. (Example problems are given in various method sections below, the full set is available from the authors.)

This experiment manipulated the number of options returned by Google: six options in a smaller set size condition (on a single Search Engine Results Page (SERP)) and twenty-four options in a large set size condition (on four SERPs, reached by pressing a page number button at the bottom of each page). Individual search terms were created by participants themselves. Half the participants were allowed to iterate or change their search terms after inspecting the returns whereas for the other half of the participants a web page had to be selected after the first search. Both independent variables were manipulated between subjects, giving a 2 (set-size: 6 vs. 24) x 2 (iterate vs. no-iterate) between-subjects design.

For each of 10 questions in their question set, participants were required to search for information using Google then choose a single web page from the SERPs. After each web page was chosen participants inspected the page and then rated their satisfaction with that page, their trust in its reliability and their judgment of the relevance of the web page for the current task.

*Participants*

Thirty-two participants were students and academic staff from University of Bath, aged between 23 and 45, with the average age of 29.9. All participants reported commonly using Google in their everyday life. Participants were told that the quality of selected websites would be evaluated in order to allocate a cash prize. After finishing the experiment, each participant was given a box of chocolates as a compensation for the participation.

*Materials*

HCI Browser [3], an open-source extension to Mozilla Firefox 3, was modified to collect data and to guide participants through tasks. All interactions were logged. Google was used by participants to complete each task: SERPs were altered using Google's API.

After each task was completed participants rated their selected website. All ratings were done on 10-point Likert scales. Additionally, there was a single open-ended question inviting a brief typed answer, giving a questioning protocol as follows:

- How satisfied are you with your selected page?
- Why? (open-ended question – not analysed in this paper)
- To what extent was the information provided by the website relevant to your task?
- To what extent do you trust the information provided by the website?

After the set of 10 search tasks was completed, a final questionnaire asked participants about the strategy they used to choose web pages (an open-ended question), overall satisfaction for their selected web pages and overall satisfaction for the list of options that the search engine returned (10-point Likert scales).

*Procedure*

Participants completed the experiment individually in a laboratory. The experiment was divided into a training session and an experimental session. On arrival at the laboratory, participants were introduced to the HCI Browser interface and instructed that their general task would be to search for web pages that provided valuable information for a series of separate questions or tasks. Then participants completed one sample task in the training session ("Why did ancient Egyptians mummify their dead?"), with the experimenter available to offer guidance as required. After each participant confirmed that they understood the general task and the user interface, the experimental session started. Each task question was presented at the top of the browser window and persisted during the search and the subsequent ratings. No time limit was specified.

### Results

After preliminary comparisons showing no difference on any dependent measure, the distinction between question group A versus B was not considered. The analyses reported below are 2x2, Set Size x Iteration between-subjects ANOVAs.

*Position of Selected Web pages*

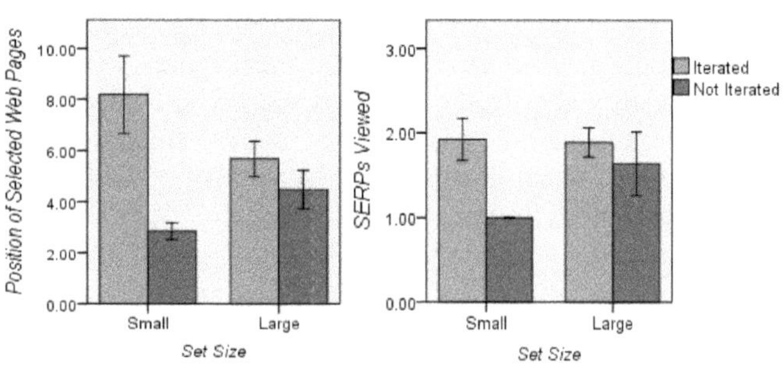


**Figure 1: Mean position of selected web pages (left), and number of SERPs viewed before selecting (right). Error bars show standard errors. In the Iterated condition we accumulated the selected position and the SERPs viewed across iterations, e.g., choosing the second snippet after one iteration in the small set size would yield a Position of 8 and SERPs Viewed of 2.**

Figure 1 (left) shows the mean ordinal position of selected web pages. Most of the selected web pages were chosen from near the top of the result lists in both the small set and the large set of options. Indeed there was no significant effect of Set Size on the ordinal position ($F(1,28)=0.2$, $p=.64$). However, participants who could iterate quite often changed their search term (see right hand panel, the mean of c. 2 SERPs viewed in the small Set Size means a mean of one iteration, i.e., two search-terms used). A simple main effect within the iteration condition showed a significant difference in selected web page positions between the small set size and the large set size ($F(1,28)=12.3$, $p=.002$, $\eta^2_p=.31$).

Figure 1 (right) shows the mean number of SERPs that participants viewed (out of a maximum of 4 separate SERPs for 24 items) before selecting a web page. Participants who were in the large set size condition only sometimes viewed beyond the first screen, and indeed there was no significant effect on the number of SERPs viewed across set size conditions ($F(1,28)=1.5$, $p=.22$). The number of SERPs that participants viewed was also updated by iteration, of course. The number of SERPs viewed between iteration and non-iteration condition were significantly different. ($F(1,28)=5.9$, $p=.021$, $\eta^2_p=.18$). Participants in the small set condition were more likely to iterate ($M=1.92$, $SD=.69$) than were participants in the large set condition ($M=1.26$, $SD=.36$). Independent t-test (among the 16 participants who could iterate) established this effect as significant: $t(14)=2.37$, $p=.038$.

*Performance Time*

Neither of the independent variables had a significant effect on time to select or view a web page, nor was there an interaction effect. The overall mean time to select a web page was 126 seconds; the overall mean time to view a web page before rating it was 34 seconds.

*Rating of selected web pages*

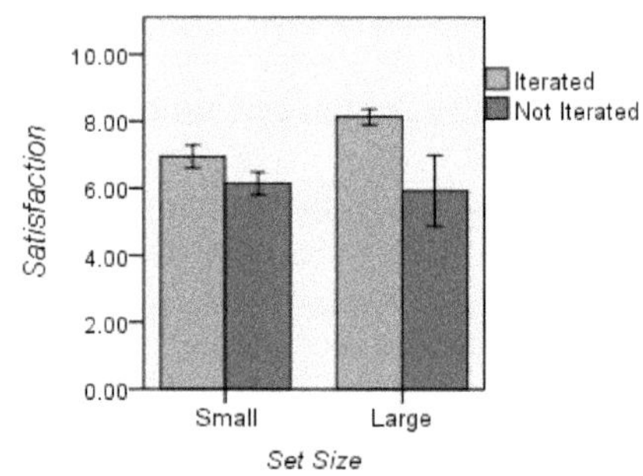


**Figure 2: Mean satisfaction with selected web pages. Error bars show standard errors.**

Figure 2 displays the participants' mean satisfaction with their chosen websites according to experimental condition. Participants given the large set size were more satisfied with their selected web pages but this effect failed to reach significance ($F(1,28)=3.9$, $p=.056$, $\eta^2_p=.12$). Participants who could iterate their search terms were reliably more satisfied with their selected web pages ($F(1,28)=9.9$, $p=.004$, $\eta^2_p=.26$). There was no significant interaction between Set Size and Iteration ($F(1,28)<1$).

No significant effects were found for Trust judgments (Trust was significantly correlated with Satisfaction, $r$=.68, $p$<.001). Relevance judgments behaved very similarly to Satisfaction judgments, and these judgments were very strongly correlated with each other ($r$=.83, $p$<.001). The only significant effect was a main effect of Iteration on judgments of relevance, ($F(1,28)=4.3$, $p$=.046, $\eta^2_p=.14$). All other main effects and interactions failed to reach significance, all $F$s close to 1.

*Overall rating of selected web pages*
Participants were asked to rate their overall satisfaction for selected web pages and for lists of options returned at the end of the experiment and presumably reflecting memory for the overall experience across 10 tasks. Participants were marginally more satisfied with the selected web pages in the large set condition than were participants in the small set condition ($F(1,28)=3.8$, $p$=.059, $\eta^2_p=.12$). In addition participants who could iterate their search term were reliably more satisfied with their selected web pages ($F(1,28)=7.9$, $p$=.009, $\eta^2_p=.22$). The interaction effect between Set Size and Iteration condition was not significant ($F(1,28)<1$). There was no effect of Set Size on overall satisfaction with the lists of options returned ($F(1,28)=2.1$, $p$=.155).

### Discussion

This experiment found no evidence for a choice overload effect. Indeed, the effect of Set Size on satisfaction was in the opposite direction, although failed to reach significance. This result contrasts with the findings from Oulasvirta et al [12], despite the overlap in task context and the identical set sizes in the two experiments. We believe that some of the issues reviewed above may explain the contrast. First, Oulasvirta et al asked participants to report satisfaction with a chosen snippet without actually consulting the web page to which the snippet related. This, it seems to us, makes it even more likely that satisfaction judgments will be judgments of process (because snippets contain far less information and therefore are less differentiated than are full web pages). Second, Oulasvirta et al imposed a very strict time limit, which again, as argued above, is likely to make for an unsatisfactory decision process in the case of large sets: participants in the large set condition in their experiment were allowed just over 1 second per snippet to make their choice. Third, our large sets were paginated, whereas Oulasvirta et al presented them as a single list. Pagination makes the size of the set less salient and more manageable.

The other very important difference in our experimental method was that participants constructed their own search terms, and half the participants were allowed to iterate over search terms if dissatisfied with the initial set of returns.

It is unsurprising that there was a main effect of Iteration on satisfaction judgments. This shows that participants were able to judge the quality of web pages from the snippets and were able to improve their search terms if initial results were disappointing. Participants who received a small set of options iterated more than did those who received a large set of options, which suggests that the small option set was more likely to be judged as unsatisfactory, adding additional support to the conclusion that, in this experiment, larger sets of returned snippets were judged more satisfactory than smaller sets.

It is striking that most participants in the large option set condition usually selected a web page from the first page, often without bothering to iterate their search terms or browse options on later result pages. This is consistent with the finding from [13], which showed that users' choice of a particular web page was mostly based on its position on the result list. It is also consistent with our suggestion above that the size of the returned set was not psychologically salient (although of course this suggestion cannot explain the advantage we observed for the large set).

## EXPERIMENT 2: NUMBER OF OPTIONS AND RANKING

### Method

*Design*
The second experiment was designed to further investigate the role of ordering of the choice set. Participants' expectation about the ranking algorithm was manipulated as a within-subjects independent variable. Participants were informed that one of three processes was used to rank the returns of a search (although in fact, in all cases the Google ranking was preserved, as explained to participants during post-experiment debriefing):

- Expert ranking: Participants were informed that the web pages linked to in the returns-list had been ranked by an expert in the appropriate topic area, according to how well they answer the question.
- Novice ranking: Participants were informed that the web pages had been ranked according to how well they answer the question, but by someone with no particular knowledge of the fields.
- Random ranking: The order of the list of links had been randomised.

To make this manipulation plausible we constrained the design of the study so that pre-specified search terms were used and indicated to participants (in this respect, this second study moves closer to the study by Oulasvirta et al [12]). Search terms were abbreviated versions of the problem specification. For example, when the task question was "What determines the cost of living in the UK?" the search term was "cost of living in UK". Consequently, there was no iterated search in this experiment.

Three separate question sets were used (four questions per set). Participants received all three question sets, with each question set being associated with a particular ranking type. Ranking types were assigned to question sets, and ordered so that each ranking type was associated with each question set and appeared in each ordinal position equally across participants.

For each of 12 tasks, participants were required to select a single web page that provided valuable information from the list of search results. After each web page was selected participants consulted the web page and then rated their satisfaction for the selected web page, their trust in its content, the relevance of the page for the task, and their familiarity with the task question. This last question was added as a check that one of the main necessary factors for choice overload was not compromised by participants' prior experience.

One final change to the procedure was a minor redesign to the user interface, so that the page numbers of search returns beyond the first page in the large set was more salient (the page number was increased in size and each returns page was additionally labelled with "This page is the <Nth> page of 4."

*Participants*
Twenty-four participants from University of Bath were recruited via online ad and posters on notice boards. No participant had taken part in Experiment 1. The participants aged between 19 and 39, with an average of 27.9. Each participant was paid five pounds in cash for participation. Participants were instructed that the quality of the selected web pages would be evaluated in order to allocate the prizes. Three cash prizes were used as a motivation in searching for high quality web pages.

*Materials*
The HCI browser, as used in Experiment 1, was modified, as above, to make the size of larger sets more salient. A single question about familiarity was added to the 10-point Likert ratings requested after each web page was selected, i.e., "To what extent is the task question familiar to you".

*Procedure*
The procedure was unchanged from Experiment 1 except as required by the changes to the Experimental Design. Three types of ranking algorithm were described to participants in written instructions and questions were answered by the experimenter. During the main part of the experiment, participants were informed by a screen message about the type of ranking used for each task: the browser window displayed the task question, the search term and the ranking type at the top of the window. This information persisted during the search task and the subsequent ratings.

**Results**
The main analyses reported below are 2x3, Set Size (6 vs. 24) x Ranking Type (expert vs. novice vs. random) mixed ANOVAs.

*Position of Selected Web pages*
Figure 3 (left) shows the mean ordinal position of selected web pages. The results indicate that participants selected web pages from further down the list when they were provided with the large set of options. The main effect of Set Size on the ordinal position of selected web pages was significant ($F(1,22)=11.2$, $p=.003$, $\eta^2_p=.34$). In the Random ranking condition, the selected web pages were located considerably further down the search result list. The main effect of Ranking Type was significant ($F(2,21)=4.9$, $p=.018$, $\eta^2_p=.32$). Further, the interaction effect between Ranking Type and Set Size was significant ($F(2,21)=4.1$, $p=.031$, $\eta^2_p=.28$).

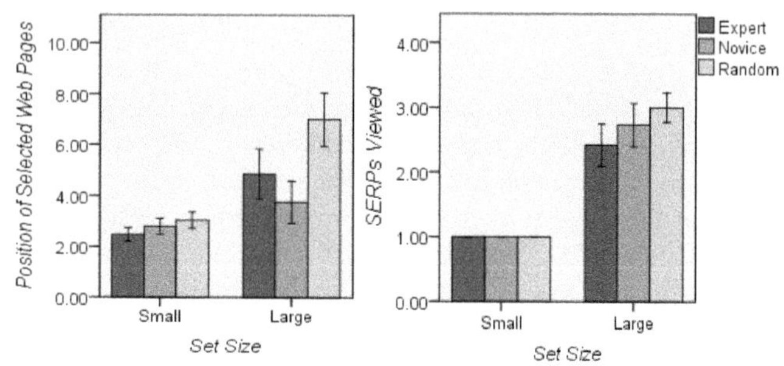


**Figure 3: Position of selected web pages (left), and number of SERPs viewed before selecting (right). Error bars show standard errors.**

Although it remains true that in the large set condition the majority of the selected web pages were located in the first SERP (Figure 3, left), participants mostly checked the search results provided in at least one other SERP before selecting the web page (Figure 3, right). According to a one-sample t-test, the number of SERPs viewed in the large Set Size is significantly greater than 1 ($t(11)=6.4$, $p<.001$). The main effect of Ranking Type on the number of SERPs viewed in the large-set condition was not significant ($F(2,22)=2.98$, $p=.07$).

*Performance Time*
Neither of the independent variables had a significant effect on time to select or view a web page, nor was there an interaction effect. The overall mean time to select a web page was 67 seconds; the overall mean time to view a web page before rating it was 35 seconds.

*Rating of selected web pages*

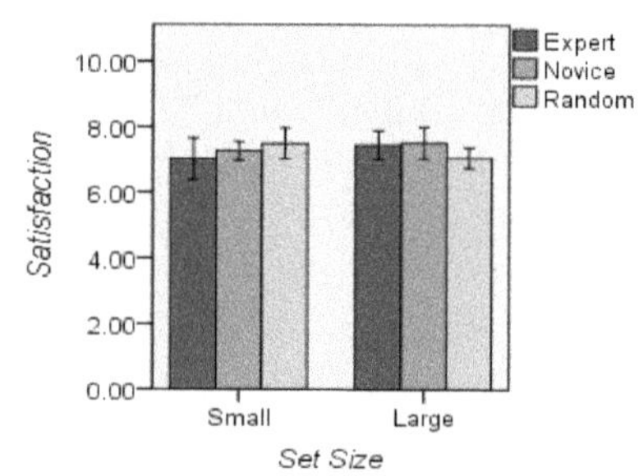


**Figure 4: Mean satisfaction with selected web pages. Error bars show standard errors.**

Figure 4 shows participants' rated satisfaction with chosen web pages. There was no significant main effect of Ranking Type or Set Size and no interaction effect (all $F$s < 1).

Similarly, there were no main effects or interactions on judgments of Trust, Relevance, and Familiarity, all *F*s close to 1. Trust was significantly correlated with Satisfaction ($r$=.52, $p$<.001). Relevance judgment was even more strongly correlated with Satisfaction (r=.87, $p$<.001). Familiarity judgments averaged around 5, suggesting that participants were not over-familiar with the choices they were asked to make. The correlation between Familiarity and Satisfaction was not significant ($r$=.19).

*Overall Rating of selected web pages*

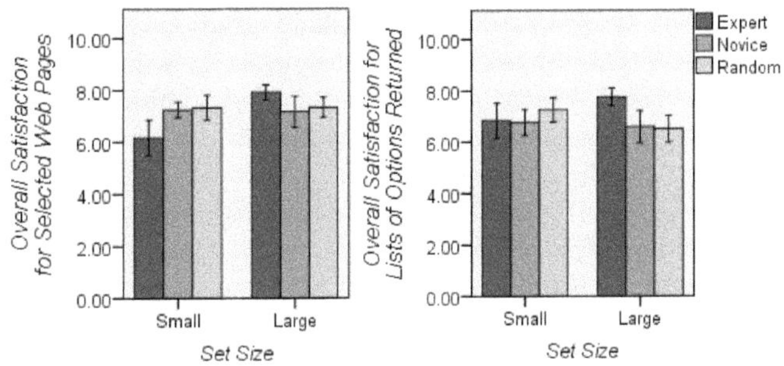


**Figure 5: Overall satisfaction with selected web pages (left), Overall satisfaction with lists of options returned by search engine (right). Error bars show standard errors.**

Figure 5 shows participants' satisfaction ratings at the end of each task-block (i.e. after each ranking type). There was no significant main effect of Ranking Type or of Set Size, but the interaction effect was reliable ($F(2,21)$=3.9, $p$=.036, $\eta^2_p$=.27).

The interaction effect between Ranking Type and Set Size on overall satisfaction for lists of options returned by search engine was not significant ($F(2,21)$=1.98, $p$=.16). Neither Ranking Type nor Set Size yielded the main effect on overall satisfaction for lists of options returned (*F*s close to 1). Participants did not perceive any difference between the overall result lists from different ranking algorithms.

## Discussion

Participants' selection behaviour confirms that they are influenced by what they believe to be true about the ranking of returns. Participants do not typically simply accept the Expert ranking (in that condition, the average rank of the chosen website is 2 in the small set and about 4 in the large set). Nevertheless, participants choose form further down the set of returns when they believe the ranking is by a novice or random, and when more returns are available (i.e., the Set Size is large).

As in Experiment 1, there is no hint of a choice overload effect in the satisfaction ratings of chosen web pages. This is true even when participants believe the ranking of returns is random, showing that participants' belief that the rank ordering is helpful is not necessary to explain the relatively positive reaction to large set sizes. (That the rank ordering IS typically helpful may still be important in this respect.) Participants in the Random, large Set-Size condition certainly process the size of the set (often inspecting all four SERPs and choosing on average the web page ranked seventh), but this does not lead to significantly less satisfaction. As it happens, of course, these participants are still choosing early items more than late items, and this in itself may mitigate any negative effects of the large set.

This experiment does not replicate the marginal satisfaction advantage of large set size reported in Experiment 1, except when overall ratings of chosen web pages in a task block are considered, in the Expert ranking condition (see Figure 5).

One important difference that remains between our first two experiments and the typical choice overload experiment, and especially Oulasvirta et al [12], is that our participants were not given any time constraints. We have suggested that such constraints may be operational in choice overload contexts, because they lead to dissatisfaction with choice process and this "leaks" into judgments of chosen items. The third experiment explores this issue as well as seeking further evidence concerning the importance of the ranking of returns on participants' search behaviour and subjective judgments.

## EXPERIMENT 3: NUMBER OF OPTIONS, RANKING AND TIME PRESSURE

### Method

*Design*

Time limitation was manipulated in this experiment. Participants were given either 45 seconds or 90 seconds to finish each task.

To further study the effect of ranking, participants were provided with search results ordered by one of the two ranking algorithms, explained as follows.

- Google ranking: All the web pages that are linked to in the returns-list have been ranked by Google.
- Random ranking: The order of the list of links has been randomised.

In the Google ranking condition, SERPs were generated by Google. Broken links were eliminated from the lists to reduce noise in the experiment. In the Random ranking condition, the search results in SERPs were those from Google-ordered list. However, the order of those search results was in fact random (a single random order was used for each task/set-size).

As in Experiments 1 and 2 a between-subjects independent variable was the Set Size of a result list returned by the search engine, which was either 6 items (on a single SERP) or 24 items (on four separate SERPs, each reached by pressing a page number button at the bottom of each SERP).

There were 16 tasks in total, which were divided into four blocks (four tasks per block). Each block had a different combination of Ranking and Time Limit. Half the participants performed the two Google blocks before the two Random blocks, whereas for the other half this was reversed. Similarly, half the participants performed the 90s block before the 45s block for each Ranking, whereas for the other half this was reversed.

After each web page was selected participants consulted the web page and then rated their satisfaction for the selected web page, their trust in its reliability, the relevance of the web page for the task, and their confidence that their selected web page was the best in the search result list (10-point Likert Scales).

The use of a confidence rating is novel in this Experiment. It seemed to us that it might tap satisfaction with the decision making process, e.g., confidence would be low if only poor consideration of alternatives was possible. The additional question was "How confident are you that your selected website is the best in the set you choose from?"

After each single session was completed, a questionnaire asked participants about the strategy they used to choose web pages (an open-ended question), overall satisfaction for their selected pages and overall satisfaction for the list of pages that the search engine returned (10-point Likert scales).

### *Participants*

Twenty-four participants were students and staff from University of Bath, who were recruited via online advertisement and posters on notice boards. No participant had taken part in the earlier studies. The participants were aged between 21 and 41, with an average of 29.7. All participants use a search engine in their everyday life. They were given five pounds in cash as compensation for their time. Participants were motivated to search for a good quality web page in order to compete for two cash prizes of 30 pounds.

### *Materials*

The version of the HCI browser used in Experiment 2 was altered only by the addition of a digital clock in the top right-hand corner, counting down the time remaining for each task.

### *Procedure*

The procedure was unchanged from Experiments 1 and 2 except as required by the changes to the Experimental Design. Participants had two training tasks to complete, so as to experience both time conditions. The questions for the training were "Why did ancient Egyptians mummify their dead?" and "How does economics affect our daily life?" with time limit of 45 seconds and 90 seconds respectively. Pre-specified search terms, which were abbreviated versions of the problem specification, were used and indicated to participants. For example, when the task question was "Why is meditation sometimes recommended for managing stress?" the search term was "meditation for managing stress".

The browser window displayed a task question, a search term, a ranking type and a timer at the top of the window. This information persisted during the search task and the subsequent ratings. During each task a beep sounded and a visual sign appeared if and when ten seconds remained.

## Results

The main analyses reported below are 2x2x2, Set Size (6 vs. 24) x Ranking Type (Google vs. Random) x Time Limit (45s vs. 90s) mixed ANOVAs.

### *Position of Selected Web pages*

Figure 6 (left) shows the mean ordinal position of selected web pages. There were significant main effects of Set Size ($F(1,22)= 20.3$, $p=.000$, $\eta^2_p=.48$), Ranking Type ($F(1,22)= 13.5$, $p=.001$, $\eta^2_p=.38$), and Time Limit ($F(1,22)=5.14$, $p=.034$, $\eta^2_p=.19$). The interaction effect between Time Limit and Set Size on the position of the selected web pages was significant ($F(1,22)=6.7$, $p=.017$, $\eta^2_p=.23$). The interaction effect between Ranking Type and Set Size on the position of selected web pages was also significant ($F(1,22)=12.9$, $p=.002$, $\eta^2_p=.37$). Participants in the large set condition selected web pages from further down the list than did participants in the small set condition, especially when they selected from the Random-ordered SERPs and when they had 90 seconds available to make their selection.

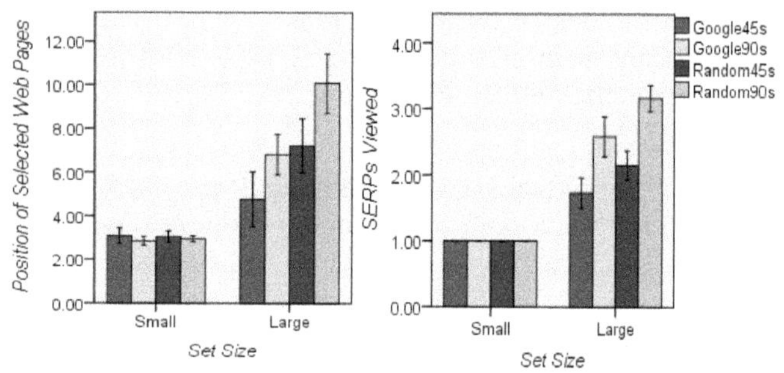


**Figure 6: Position of selected web pages (left), and number of SERPs viewed before selecting (right). Error bars show standard errors.**

According to a one-sample t-test, the number of SERPs viewed in the large set is significantly greater than 1 ($t(11)=12.76$, $p<.001$). The ANOVAs revealed that the main effects of the independent variables on the number of SERPs viewed in the large-set condition were significant, Ranking Type ($F(1,22)=6.77$, $p=.025$, $\eta^2_p=.38$), and Time Limit ($F(1,22)=25.34$, $p<.001$, $\eta^2_p=.68$). There was no significant interaction effect between Ranking Type and Time Limit ($F<1$). Participants in the large set condition browsed through more SERPs when they had to select a web page from the Random-ordered list. With the time limit of 90 seconds, participants in the large set browsed significantly more SERPs more than they did when they had 45 seconds to select a web page.

### *Rating of selected web pages*

Figure 7, left, shows judged satisfaction with chosen web pages in each cell of the experiment. The main effect of

Ranking Type on the participants' mean satisfaction was significant ($F(1,22)=6.31$, $p=.02$, $\eta^2_p=.22$). Participants were more satisfied with pages from Google-ordered lists than from Random-ordered lists. There was no significant main effect of either Time Limit or Set Size on the participants' mean satisfaction ($F(1,22)=.75$, $p=.39$ and $F(1,22)=.05$, $p=.81$ respectively). However, the interaction effect between Time Limit and Set Size was significant ($F(1,22)=5.13$, $p=.034$, $\eta^2_p=.19$). In both the Google and the Random conditions, satisfaction in small set sizes relative to large set sizes increases as time pressure increases.

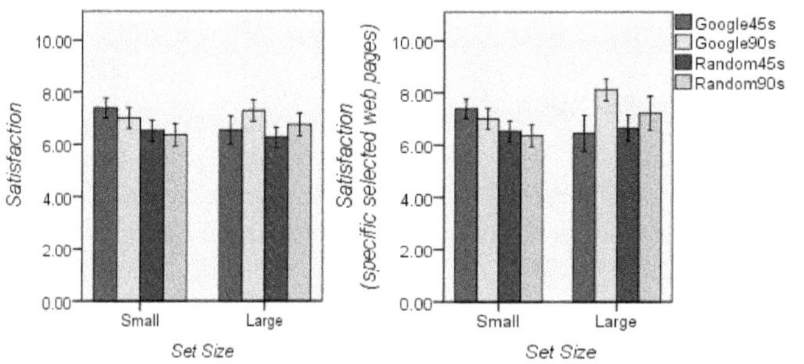


**Figure 7: Mean satisfaction with selected web pages (left), mean satisfaction with selected web pages that are present in the small set (right). Error bars show standard errors.**

The data were pruned so that only chosen web pages that are present in the small set are considered in all cells of the experiment (otherwise, reduced satisfaction in selections from the large set could be a peculiarity of the actual web pages that were chosen). Every participant contributed at least one such judgment in all large set conditions (Figure 7, right). There was now no significant main effect of Ranking Type on the participants' mean satisfaction ($F(1,20)=3.42$, $p=.079$). Nevertheless, importantly, the significant interaction effect between Set Size and Time Limit on participants' mean satisfaction ($F(1,20)=10.04$, $p=.005$, $\eta^2_p=.33$) was maintained.

Ranking Type, Time Limit and Set Size did not have significant effects on Trust judgments. There was no significant interaction effect, all *F*s close to 1 (Trust was significantly correlated with Satisfaction $r=.60$, $p<.001$). Relevance judgments was strongly correlated to Satisfaction ($r=.78$, $p<.001$). The main effect of Ranking Type on Relevance was significant ($F(1,22)=6.18$, $p=.021$, $\eta^2_p=.22$). Participants thought that their selected web pages in Google-ordered lists were more relevant to the task questions than their selected web pages in Random-ordered lists. There was no main effect of Time Limit or Set Size and no interaction effect on Relevance (all $F$s<1).

There was no significant main effect or interaction effect on Confidence judgments, all *F*s close to 1. However Confidence was significantly correlated with Satisfaction ($r=0.86$, $p<.001$). This indicated that if the participant was satisfied with the selected option he/she was more likely to be confident that the selected option was the best in the set that available.

*Overall Rating of selected web pages*

A main effect of Ranking Type on overall satisfaction for selected pages was significant ($F(1,22)=11.42$, $p=.003$, $\eta^2_p=.34$). In both large and small set sizes, participants were significantly more satisfied with their selected web pages from Google-ordered lists more than from Random-ordered lists. However, the main effect of Set Size was not reliable ($F(1,22)=.032$, $p=.86$). There was no significant interaction effect.

A main effect of Ranking Type on overall satisfaction for lists of options returned by the search engine was significant ($F(1,22)=23.38$, $p<.000$, $\eta^2_p=.52$). Participants were satisfied with the result lists ranked by Google more than Random lists. There was no significant main effect of Set Size or interaction effect. (both $F$s<1)

## Discussion

This experiment suggests a crucial role for time pressure in determining the effect of set size on satisfaction with the results of a choice process. When time is more strongly constrained, choices from small sets led to relatively more satisfaction.

The main effect of Ranking Type on participants' satisfaction was significant, yet its interactions with other independent variables were insignificant. Participants were more satisfied with the selected web pages from Google-ordered lists than from Random-ordered lists regardless of time pressure or the number of options provided. This may simply be because better web pages were selected, enabled by Google's ranking.

## GENERAL DISCUSSION

In contrast with [12], there is no suggestion from our studies that choice overload will typically affect satisfaction with web pages found through keyword search. This is not just a matter of failure to replicate through null effects – in most conditions of our studies, the tendency was for larger numbers of returns to be associated with better subjective outcomes, although this tendency was only marginally reliable for judgements of individual web pages in Experiment 1 and for overall satisfaction in Experiment 2.

We had predicted that the ordering of search engine returns would mitigate choice overload effects. We confirmed that ordering does indeed affect selection processes. When participants believed the results had been ordered by Experts they were more likely to choose a web page from earlier in the list, compared to a Novice ranking or Random ordering – even when the order of items was the same. Similarly, participants chose earlier items from Google-ranked lists than from randomly ordered lists (Expt. 3). These ordering effects confirm and extend previous work which has shown that Google users typically select from the first page of returns [13] and that order of a document set affects judgments of relevance [14]. However, these effects of ordering do not seem to affect Choice Overload – the effects of set size on subjective judgments did not interact with beliefs about order, or actual order of search returns.

Instead, we have found evidence that time pressure is an important determinant of choice overload. In Experiment 3, the relative satisfaction with web pages chosen from larger versus smaller sets interacted significantly with the time available to choose.

Our findings challenge search engine design to be sensitive to time pressure. Of course the way time pressure affects users' needs and satisfaction is likely to vary across search contexts, how important it is to find excellent rather than good-enough sources, etc. One important limit of our studies is that participants were asked to choose single web pages. In many contexts multiple information sources will be sought, and in that case we suspect that search results should be diversified; search results from different domain categories could be presented early on the result list, possibly in hierarchical structure. Indeed such a design illustrates one way in which search interfaces could be sensitive to time pressure: users could consider in turn each specific category where the number of options is considerably fewer than the entire result list [see also 12]. On the other hand, with less time pressure, a user could browse across categories to explore and make comparisons between options.

The role of time pressure is also important for theoretical reasons, because it supports the "process-product leakage" account of choice overload, rather than regret or expectation-setting. Our studies confirm that interface design can affect process and strategy in such a way that user satisfaction with retrieved information is affected.

## ACKNOWLEDGMENTS

We thank all the volunteers, and all publications support and staff, who wrote and provided helpful comments on previous versions of this document.

## REFERENCES

1. Arunachalam, B., Henneberry, S. R., Lusk, J. L., & Norwood, F. B. An empirical investigation into the excessive-choice effect. *American journal of agricultural economics, 91* (2009), 810-825.
2. Bernard, M., Baker, R., & Fernandez, M. Paging vs. scrolling: Looking for the best way to present search results. *Usability News, 4* (2002).
3. Capra, R. HCI browser: A tool for studying web search behavior. *Proceedings of the American Society for Information Science and Technology, 47* (2001), 1-2.
4. Fasolo, B., McClelland, G. H., & Todd, P. M. Escaping the tyranny of choice: When fewer attributes make choice easier. *Marketing Theory, 7* (2007), 13-26.
5. Haynes, G. A. Testing the boundaries of the choice overload phenomenon: The effect of number of options and time pressure on decision difficulty and satisfaction. *Psychology & Marketing, 26* (2009), 204-212.
6. Huang, M. H., & Wang, H. Y. The influence of document presentation order and number of documents judged on users' judgments of relevance. *Journal of the American Society for Information Science and Technology, 55* (2004), 970-979.
7. Iyengar, S. S., & Lepper, M. R. When choice is demotivating: Can one desire too much of a good thing?. *Journal of personality and social psychology, 79* (2000), 995-1006.
8. Iyengar, S. S., Wells, R. E., & Schwartz, B. Doing Better but Feeling Worse Looking for the "Best" Job Undermines Satisfaction. *Psychological Science, 17* (2006), 143-150.
9. Loewenstein, G. Is more choice always better?. *Social Security Brief, 7* (1999), 1-8.
10. Lorigo, L., Haridasan, M., Brynjarsdóttir, H., Xia, L., Joachims, T., Gay, G., Granka, L., Pellacini, F., & Pan, B. Eye tracking and online search: Lessons learned and challenges ahead. *Journal of the American Society for Information Science and Technology, 59* (2008), 1041-1052.
11. Oppewal, H., & Koelemeijer, K. More choice is better: Effects of assortment size and composition on assortment evaluation. *International Journal of Research in Marketing, 22* (2005), 45-60.
12. Oulasvirta, A., Hukkinen, J. P., & Schwartz, B. When more is less: the paradox of choice in search engine use. *Proc. SIGIR 2009.* ACM Press (2009), 516-523.
13. Pan, B., Hembrooke, H., Joachims, T., Lorigo, L., Gay, G., & Granka, L. In Google we trust: Users' decisions on rank, position, and relevance. *Journal of Computer-Mediated Communication, 12* (2007), 801-823.
14. Purgalis, Parker, L. M., & Johnson, R. E. Does order of presentation affect users' judgment of documents?. *Journal of the American Society for Information Science, 41* (1990), 493-494.
15. Scheibehenne, B., Greifeneder, R., & Todd, P. M. What moderates the too-much-choice effect?. *Psychology & Marketing, 26* (2009), 229-253.
16. Scheibehenne, B., Greifeneder, R., & Todd, P. M. Can There Ever Be Too Many Options? A Meta-Analytic Review of Choice Overload. *Journal of Consumer Research, 37* (2010), 409-425.
17. Schwartz, B. The paradox of choice: Why less is more. *New York: Ecco* (2004).

# Coming in from the Margins: Amateur Musicians in the Online Age

**Michaela Hoare, Steve Benford**
Mixed Reality Laboratory
University of Nottingham
{psxmh3, pszsdb}@nottingham.ac.uk

**Rachel Jones**
Instrata Ltd
Cambridge, CB1 1EG
racheljones@instrata.co.uk

**Natasa Milic-Frayling**
Microsoft Research Ltd
Cambridge, CB1 2FB
natasamf@microsoft.com

## ABSTRACT
HCI is increasingly interested in amateurism, but the wider literature suggests that the amateur is a complex and distinctive phenomenon. An interview study reveals the nature of the amateur in the digital age. Even though operating non-professionally at a micro-scale, amateur musicians employ a plethora of online services to sustain local fanbases, reach out to new fans, collaborate internationally, and actively promote both digital and material products. Our findings lead to recommendations for event-oriented promotion tools; community-oriented analytics; tangible and embedded products; and limited-edition digital experiences. We conclude that HCI needs to recognise the amateur as an important class of user, one who is serious about their leisure, and who is also distinct from the professional as from the novice and hobbyist.

### Author Keywords
Amateur; music; distribution; promotion; sharing; DIY; social media; craft; tangible; community.

### ACM Classification Keywords
H.5.m. Information Interfaces and Presentation (e.g., HCI)

## INTRODUCTION

> "Amateurs of today, in all fields, to the extent they can be said to be guided by professional standards and share the same spirit of satisfaction are the marginal men of leisure. They are neither dabblers who approach the activity with little commitment or seriousness, nor professionals who make a living of that activity and spend a major portion of their waking hours doing so —for whom it is an occupation."
>
> (Robert Stebbins defining the 'modern amateur' in 1977, before the public Internet [32])

Digital technologies have been transforming creative practice in nearly every field, in music, video, animation, art, performance and writing. While this transformation may have begun with the technologies of production, it has since spread to those of distribution as the Internet brings new ways of engaging audiences. Nowhere is this truer than for music, which has seen an explosion in digital distribution channels. While much attention has been focused on the music industry and its struggle to find new business models in a world of free music sharing [4, 22], it has also, perhaps more quietly, been transforming the world of the amateur musician, opening up new ways of distributing music, in the same way that the affordable digital home studios of the 1980s enabled its production.

This is the focus of our paper—how online distribution and promotion is transforming the world of the amateur and especially of the amateur musician. This is an important focus as there are many millions of passionate amateur musicians worldwide. Moreover, Leadbeater and Miller argue that engaging in amateur activities benefits people through an enhanced sense of identity, achievement, satisfaction, wellbeing and resilience, and benefits society through enhanced social capital, innovation and participation [19]. HCI is also increasingly interested in what might be broadly thought of as amateur practice, from the everyday creativity involved in curating digital media [7, 13, 26, 30, 36] to recent engagements with DIY communities [17, 22, 31, 34, 35].

In spite of its growing interest, we shall argue that HCI currently lacks a sufficiently nuanced view of the serious nature of amateur practice and of the distinctive challenges that amateurs face online. We aim to make three contributions to this understanding. First, we review the wider literature on amateurs from sociology and cultural studies alongside the growing literature to be found in HCI. Next, we present an in-depth study of how one particular amateur community of musicians is using online distribution channels and social media to promote their music, revealing how they wrestle with a complex ecology of online services and how they are torn between addressing small audiences of known fans with handcrafted experiences and trying to reach out to new fans around the world. Finally, we draw together the literature and findings from our case study, reflecting more broadly on the distinctive nature of the amateur in the online age and articulating new challenges to be addressed by future HCI research if our field is to properly address the needs of the many millions of amateurs worldwide.

## DEFINING THE AMATEUR

We begin by reviewing key literature from sociology and cultural studies from 1970s onwards in order to establish a more refined view of what it means to be an amateur and then consider HCI's growing engagement with everyday creativity and amateurism.

### The 'modern amateur'

We opened this paper with a quote from Robert Stebbins [32]. Writing in 1977, he identified the phenomenon of the modern amateur as having emerged in response to the increasing professionalization of many activities, which in its turn had emerged from the activities of 'gentleman amateurs' a century ago. He drew on examples from music and sport to show that this modern amateur was skilled, dedicated and passionate, and also markedly different from professionals on the one hand and from hobbyists, players, dabblers, dilettantes and novices on the other. He cited Huizinga's seminal work on the nature of play [14] to explain this critical distinction. Whereas Huizinga argues that play "lacks necessity, obligation and utility and is produced with a disinterestedness that sets it apart from ordinary real-life", Stebbins notes that necessity, obligation, seriousness and commitment are precisely the key qualities of the modern amateur.

Stebbins provides two definitions of the modern amateur. The first is macro-sociological, as a part of a triad of relationships that form his Professional-Amateur-Public system. Amateurs exhibit complex relationships to professionals, learning from them, supporting them, and (as a supremely knowledgeable audience) 'keeping them straight' [28]. Amateurs also have complex relationships to publics, providing them with opportunities to experience performances when professionals are not available, and shaping the wider language of discussion and critique. Stebbins notes progressions between these categories, with novices becoming amateurs, who may then become professionals, and where some professionals subsequently return to being amateurs on retirement.

Stebbins' second definition is psycho-sociological, identifying five key attitudes that differentiate amateurs from professionals. He argues that amateurs may lack the *confidence* of professionals, doubting their own abilities. They may not show the same *perseverance* in the face of major obstacles such as criticism or injury. Amateurs may not show the same level of *continuation commitment,* meaning they are not financially and contractually bound up with their practice to the point where they cannot walk away. They may not show the same *preparedness*, perhaps arriving tired or even late for a performance after work. Finally, comes *self-conception*; at the end of the day amateurs and professionals describe themselves as such.

### The 'Pro-Am'

More recent discussions of amateurism have reflected on societal changes since 1977, and especially the impact of the Internet. In discussing the rise of the 'new amateurs' Prior draws attention to a "less aristocratic breed of amateur" who is seriously engaged, technologically literate and who works to professional standards but often without the same infrastructural support [29]. In a lengthy report for the Demos think-tank intended to inform UK government policy, Leadbeater and Miller chart the emergence and importance of what they call they 'Pro-Am' in many walks of life, from garden design, rock climbing and astronomy to open-source programing [19]. They argue that Pro-Ams comprise pre-professionals, semi-professionals and post-professionals and position these along a spectrum between fully-fledged professionals and traditional amateurs.

### Remix culture and DIY

While amateurs may have previously lacked the infrastructural support enjoyed by professionals, this may now be changing due to the spread of Internet distribution channels and social media [18]. Billions of people routinely share blogs, photos and videos, and create further content by commenting, collating, curating and mashing them up. Lessig has labeled this transformation as the emergence of 'Remix' culture, passionately arguing that this represents a return to a form of amateur creativity that was widely enjoyed before the mass productisation of the media in the $20^{th}$ century [21]. Related to this is the emergence of 'DIY' culture in which people are able to craft products that were previously industrially produced and increasingly manage their distribution directly. DIY is a broad cultural phenomenon that cuts across a wide variety of creative activities, including music, where professionals are adopting DIY techniques to market their music directly and engage with fans in new ways [3], and where independent musicians and amateurs are also contributing to a thriving DIY music scene [33].

### The amateur in HCI

HCI is far from ignorant of the possibilities for everyday creativity that arise from this Remix culture. Indeed, our literature is replete with studies of the everyday creativity involved in capturing, collecting and sharing digital photographs [12, 26], videos [30] and music [7, 13, 36] and how this enables people to express their identities and sustain communities [6]. There is also a large body of work on new interfaces to enable non-experts to engage in creative activities, for example in learning to play [5] and conduct [20] music.

HCI's interest in everyday creativity has also explicitly addressed more serious amateurs. Linley *et al* studied how amateur musicians and photographers, among others, archive their personal digital materials [23]. Benford and colleagues studied how Irish musicians use social media to build a repertoire in preparation for playing in traditional sessions [3], while Ahmed *et al* have reported on the extensive work of DJs in preparing for, promoting and performing at gigs [1].

Also relevant is HCI's engagement with DIY culture, exploring how people seek out craft knowledge on the

Internet [35], the creative practices of DIY hackers [31], and how hacker and maker communities' knowledge may be democratizing the process design [34]. This engagement with DIY practice is often grounded in a desire to support 'amateurism'. For example, Beuchley and Esisenberg integrate electronics into fabric so as to support hobbyists, garage tinkerers, and other "amateurs'' in engaging with e-textiles [8] while Kuznetsov and Paulos conclude a survey of over 2600 individuals from 6 different DIY communities with the suggestion that hobbyists and enthusiasts who critique and learn from each others' work constitute a type of "expert amateur" [17].

This extensive body of work reveals HCI's growing interest in what might broadly be conceived of as amateurism, from the everyday creativity involved in curating photos, videos and music, to the practices of particular amateur communities, to DIY hobbyists, tinkerers and expert amateurs. And yet, the literature from sociology and cultural studies suggests that the amateur may be a more particular phenomenon than this, one that is distinct from the hobbyist, novice or tinkerer as much as from the professional. This suggests to us that HCI requires a more nuanced and detailed appreciation of the character of the amateur as a firm foundation for future research in this area. This in turn, has motivated our study of the online activities of amateur musicians.

## METHODOLOGY

We chose to focus our study on amateur musicians for two reasons. First, music is an extremely popular form of amateur practice. Second, this is a practice where digital technologies (production and distribution) are already widespread and are having a profound impact across the board from the mainstream commercial industry [22] to independents and amateurs [29]. Music therefore provides an ideal case in which we might expect to observe the relatively mature use of online technologies by amateurs and understand how it shapes their practice.

### Participants

We conducted qualitative semi-structured interviews with 14 amateur musicians in order to gain an understanding of their practices, including the use of online service. We adopted an open-ended approach to interviewing so as to 'enter in an empathic way, the lived experiences of our participants' [25].

Following a period of sounding out the local music scene by searching online and attending gigs, we homed in on a well-established and active community of musicians associated with the local 'DIY' music scene in our city. Individual participants were selected through snowball sampling using social networks and personal contacts. We screened potential participants to select individuals who were currently practicing music part-time, had been doing so for longer than a year, and who were self-promoting and sharing or selling their own music products online through a personal webpage or site and using at least two social media services. The resulting group shown below (Table 1) comprised 14 adults, 13 male and 1 female (P12), ranging in age from 23 to 55.

| Participant | Employment | Musical practice |
|---|---|---|
| P1 | Own business | Songwriter, guitarist in a band |
| P2 | Events manager | Solo guitarist, songwriter |
| P3 | Teacher | Solo guitarist, songwriter |
| P4 | IT director | Guitarist in a band |
| P5 | Unemployed | Guitarist/songwriter in a band |
| P6 | IT contractor | Guitarist/songwriter in a band |
| P7 | Consultant | Solo guitarist, songwriter |
| P8 | Engineer | Songwriter, guitarist in a band |
| P9 | Full-time student | Solo guitarist, songwriter |
| P10 | Teacher | Solo guitarist, songwriter |
| P11 | Full-time student | Guitarist in a band |
| P12 | Full-time student | Solo pianist, songwriter |
| P13 | Website manager | Solo guitarist/pianist |
| P14 | Bio-informatician | Guitarist/songwriter in a band |

**Table 1: Participants in the study**

### Interviews

In-depth semi-structured interviews were conducted in participants' homes or local cafes they chose. Conducting the majority of the interviews in participants' homes not only assured a comfortable interview experience but also prompted discussions and further exploration of the balancing of work, home and music practice, allowing participants to demonstrate the processes of managing these separate everyday activities on their computers and work spaces. Prior to each interview, participants were informed that the study purpose was to discover aspects of their digital activities that might inform ideas for designing future services. We also sought consent to examine their public activities online, including histories of Facebook postings and tweets. The interviews ranged from 60 minutes to 180 minutes in duration, allowing each of the respondents to give rich and detailed narratives. Each interview was audio recorded.

The semi-structured format used open-ended questions and encouraged the interviewee to lead the discussion as far as possible, beginning with general questions such as "tell me about your musical practice" before addressing the key themes of self-producing work, managing an online identity, promotion and staying in touch with fans. Throughout the interview, the participants were encouraged to support their answers by presenting and demonstrating their websites, tools and use of file storage.

### Data Analysis

Interviews were transcribed and analyzed using an inductive, iterative and grounded approach in order to identify key themes. We built a more comprehensive picture of participants' online activities by supplementing interview data with the analysis of online activities. Specifically, we gathered histories of public Facebook postings and tweets related to the participants' music accounts. Analysis and visualization of this data reveal the services they used and provide a more detail account of patterns of activity that they had reported to us.

## FINDINGS

Our findings paint a picture of the engaging activities and the complex online life of the contemporary amateur musician. They depict what it means to be amateurs in the digital age; how they distribute their music; and how intensive the work of online promotion is.

### Being an Amateur Musician

As Table 1 shows, all participants are musicians, singing and playing instruments, either solo or in bands, and composing, performing and recording music.

#### *Being amateur*

Our interviews reveal key characteristics that define our interviewees to be *amateur* musicians. First, they balance their music practice with full-time jobs or study. Second, none are making a significant income from their music, although some gain sufficient return from ticket, music and merchandise sales to sustain their musical practice. As P3 said, *"I'm not trying to make it a primary source of income, it's just something that I'm trying to do and trying to get it to the point where it's self-sufficient but it has to fit in around my family life and my work."* Third, they describe themselves as being distinct from professionals, using terms such as 'hobby', 'semi-professional' or 'independent', for example: *"It's a hobby. I'm not looking to, you know, get anything out from it apart from the enjoyment of writing songs... getting things where it sounds like something I'd like to listen to."* (P1). Nevertheless, five participants did express ambitions to "go professional" and articulated plans to leave their full-time careers and concentrate on composing and performing music. Fourth, and importantly, all were very serious and passionate about their music, devoting extensive time to composing, performing (usually locally but sometimes further afield), recording and promoting. As we shall see from the analysis, they also exhibited a serious attitude towards the quality and value of their music.

#### *Being part of a community*

A striking feature of the interviews was the extent to which our participants felt as being part of a supportive community of like-minded amateurs. They routinely listened to each other's music, played at common venues, attended each other's gigs and promoted one another. P7 reflected on the essential value of reciprocity to this community: *"Yes, it's, kind of, a reciprocal thing, as well, so when I have posted up stuff ... I, kind of, give him an acknowledgement and put a link there through to his own Bandcamp so people can go and check out his stuff...it's just acknowledging that some... this guy has given his time and his skills to us as a favour or for the pleasure."*

This shared sense of a supportive community and identity may merit the development of more community-oriented tools. A sense of community extends to a sense of shared identity around a 'DIY' ethos of making, distributing and promoting one's own music independently of the mainstream. They routinely tagged their websites and postings with the phrases such as 'DIY', 'underground', 'alternative' and 'unsigned'. Interestingly, this ethos transcended musical genres, with participants' music encompassing Psych-pop (P1, P9), folk (P2, P3, P7, P10), Blues (P4), Indie (P5, P6), Power-pop (P8), Psych-rock (P13), Indie-rock (P11), Pop (P12) and Indie-pop (P14).

#### *Beyond the local*

For much of the time, our community operated locally and at a micro-scale, sharing local venues and typically playing to audiences of tens of people. However, our interviews revealed wider connections too. We saw an example of networking with a similar community in a city 100 miles away to arrange for a musician to visit to play a gig. We also uncovered examples of international collaborations made possible by the Internet. P3 described how file-sharing has enabled him to collaborate with a musician based in Amarillo, Texas, performing a guitar duet on a track on his latest album: *"He's just kind of got in touch with a few guitarists that he likes and that entirely happened on Facebook"*. Participants revealed how this is largely a celebrated and welcomed addition to amateur music practice, stimulating and enabling new forms of creativity. P7 reflected on how he had been able to form a collective of artists who collaborated remotely to produce an album entirely online: *"...someone from London, third one, someone in the States, you know, each of whom, who are very, very different styles or genres...Yes, it's all entirely through file-sharing..."*.

### Distributing Music

Having introduced our participants, we now consider the various ways in which they were distributing their music.

#### *The tensions in digital distribution*

Our musicians made use of mainstream distribution channels including iTunes Amazon, CD Baby and Spotify to sell digital downloads or physical CDs. However, this was not without tensions. In reflecting on Spotify's delivery of micro-payments for downloading individual tracks, participants were skeptical as to whether there were benefits for the amateur. First, there was a concern that the financial benefits of this approach only accrue at a large scale, well beyond their micro-audiences. There were also concerns that fans might listen less seriously: "*people [who] might have bought the album will basically just stream it a couple of times and that's it.*" (P14). Thus, although amateurs, our musicians saw sufficient value in their music and did not want to simply give it away. Rather, many enabled the *free* download of *some* music, typically through their websites or Soundcloud, as a tactic to drive conventional sales as P9 explained: *"[Tracks are] on there purely for people to hear and maybe like it, buy it, buy the physical LP"*.

There were also musical concerns with digital distribution, most notably in having to divide up an album that had been conceived of as being a whole into parts as P13 noted: *"My only problem with Bandcamp is if you do an album where you join up all the songs, when it plays back on here they cut them up and there's big gaps"*. P5 adopted an interesting strategy, releasing an entire EP as a single free download before then making separate tracks available for sale: *"So people can listen to it and share it [for free on Soundcloud] and then a couple of weeks later I think I arranged it to be bought on the Internet and on Spotify as separate tracks*". He noted that this also enabled him to get preliminary feedback on a release, a sentiment shared by P7: *"I wait for a new record to get a formal release before I put it up on Bandcamp but I will use the Soundcloud to preview stuff."*

### *Material and handcrafted distribution*

Despite new opportunities to distribute their music digitally, many interviewees also produced limited edition vinyl pressings or one off artworks to emphasize the uniqueness and value of their music.

**Figure 1: P7's handcrafted wooden cassette box.**

At one extreme, P9 had chosen to release his latest album solely on vinyl without a download. Despite putting his music on streaming services, P6 discussed how important it was to provide fans with a more unique and tangible format of their music that allowed them to identify with the band and its retro image: *"I listen to Spotify all the time, but it's nice to own something..."* He chose to release his album on a floppy disk alongside a digital download code, and this turned out to be a sell-out product on his website. P7 had also released his latest album on vinyl and, like P6, had created a series of handcrafted artifacts in the form of cassette tapes and a small booklet packaged in handmade wooden boxes. Reflecting on the time and effort involved in creating these products, P7 stated that, *"...its, kind of, beautifully designed covers and, you know, luxurious inserts and, you know, coloured vinyl and, you know, all sorts of stuff that's a ridiculous amount of work to actually do. But it just makes for a beautiful artifact."*

The material nature of these artifacts enabled musicians to express quirky identities in a way that is difficult with more anonymous digital downloads. In particular, vinyl, material and handcrafted artifacts invoked a nostalgic 'retro' aesthetic that was intended to appeal to the more serious gig goer and collector. P7, for example, reported selling his *"very collectible"* vinyl LP in specialist shops. The apparent value that is attributed to tangible and handcrafted artifacts resonates with HCI's extensive research into tangible and embedded interfaces, and this may offer richer ways of strengthening the link between digital tracks and material products as we discuss below.

## Online Promotion

Beyond distributing their music online, our musicians also made extensive use of the Internet to promote their work.

### *A complex ecology of services*

Interviewees reported using many online services. To obtain a clearer picture, we created an aggregate visualisation of all website and service URLs ever mentioned in their promotional Facebook postings or tweets (Figure 2). This reveals a complex ecology of services spanning social media (Twitter, Facebook, YouTube, Instagram, Vimeo), dedicated music services (Bandcamp, Reverbnation, Soundcloud, Mixcloud), commercial music distribution channels (iTunes, Spotify) online ticketing sites (WeGotTickets), national radio (BBC) and press (DailyMail), but mixed in with smaller local services including 3 local venues, 2 local radio stations and 2 specialist review sites.

### *Honing an identity*

Participants were keen to show us their websites, which they had often designed themselves from scratch, stressing how they had freedom to create their own digital identities. However, despite the restrictive options for self-expression and design, they recognized the value of social media in reaching new fans. As P11 noted: *"It's seems like you get more of an audience like when you do it through the Internet, people who have the same kind of interests ...'cause like say someone likes a poster [online] you've got then their mates are going to see it then their mates are usually into the same kind of music."*

He also noted the importance of networking with other musicians: "it's easier to kind of get your name out there and book shows in other places. Not through like promoters or through venues but through musicians." The reach of social media was balanced by concerns about becoming "lost in the noise" (P13) and a lack of creative control. As P14 noted: "We mostly use the website for kind of bigger news... usually a website does have more of the... identity of the band because of the way it looks and you don't want to kind of, like, overload with data" and "not just, like, endless conversations or something like that, which is what Facebook is good at, I guess.

Participants talked about the necessity of maintaining, as P8 explained, a *"coherent kind of image"* and a consistent voice across services, although this could be an arduous task as we discuss below.

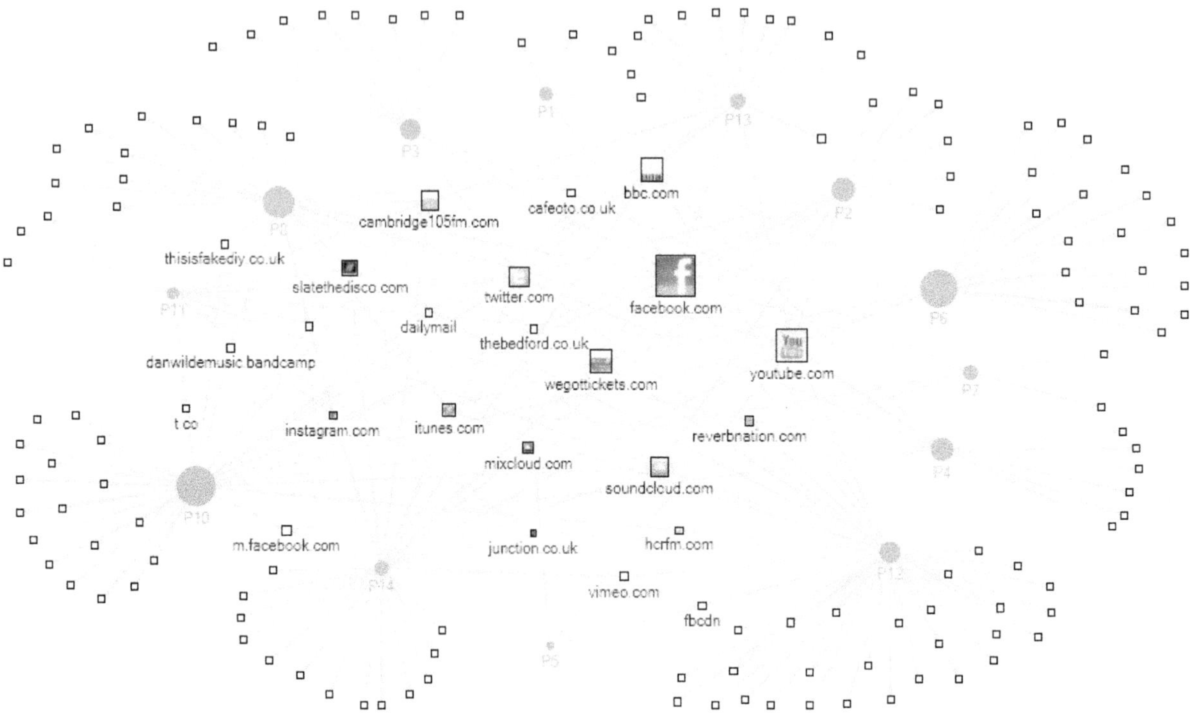


**Figure 2: Ecology of services used by participants. Participants are round nodes, services are square nodes. Links show which participants link to which services. Node size shows how actively they link. Plotted in NodeXL (Harel-Koren layout).**

*Really knowing your audience*

Our musicians were operating online at a relatively small scale: hundreds of followers were typical, with a thousand regarded as an achievement: *"...a thousand followers it was quite a big thing for me"* (P2). In spite of this, they bemoaned the lack of visibility of exactly who is listening to a track or album in its entirety, reading a post or watching a video. They were particularly skeptical about the validity of the analytics presented by current services, viewing statistics as inevitably skewed by spam bots: *"So it's, like, if it says, this has been hit 100 times, what can I really do about that?"* (P6).

In contrast, P12 revealed how she had handcrafted a physical archive by writing fans' comments onto paper and attaching them to her piano as a source of inspiration when composing (Figure 3): *"Some comments I just scribble down on a piece of paper, keep it on top of my piano in case people are, like, you should write a song about this or with these chords or something, so yes...I just stick them with Blu-Tack on my piano, comments and stuff... I've grown to know that people like to hear different things."*

*Scheduling online promotion*

While participants recognized the necessity to *"keep everything up to date"* (P6), they were generally sporadic in their promotional activities, timing them around gigs and releases and fitting them in with work and family. Promotion often followed a tried and tested pattern with different tactics being used for Facebook and Twitter, as well as knowing the times of the day when their posts would get the most attention: *"I will share the event on the band's Facebook page which will say 'we are playing this event'. I think then probably a week before I put a post on the band's page and I usually share it with my personal page saying we're playing a gig and then a couple of days before the gig do a reminder and then the day of the gig another reminder. Probably even the afternoon of the gig. Catch people's attention."* (P8). The content of promotional messages included announcing the release of tracks and videos, forthcoming gigs, pointing to radio broadcasts and external reviews, and also promoting other musicians. Our participants' distinctive approaches to

**Figure 3: P12 attaches fans comments on her piano.**

scheduling their promotional activities points towards the development of more event-oriented tools that aim to support this key promotion strategy as we discuss later.

*The etiquette of online promotion*

Promotion was governed by a sense of etiquette. When dealing with small audiences, many of whom are other musicians, friends or family, it is important to walk a line between self-promotion and the risk, as P3 puts it, of being seen as a *"rabid self-promoter"*. P10 viewed this as about striking a balance: *"you don't want to annoy people [or give the impression that] it's about making money or that I am pushing the hard-sell"*. Similarly, P3 stated that he avoids a *"me, me, me"* approach to posts and has found sharing information in a *"not directly promotional"* way a more successful method of online self-promotion.

*The hard work of online promotion*

In spite of being sporadic, online promotion was time consuming: *"You have an artist that's a singer, songwriter, graphic designer, manager, promoter and doing everything so it's quite difficult to make time for everything and prioritize as well."* (P2). Importantly, it was also not creative: *"I find it very time consuming and not aesthetically rewarding or pleasurable in any way"* (P7) and *"I could have spent that three hours writing a new tune."* (P7). P11 revealed how it was difficult to maintain an identity across services: *''Keeping up to date on every single site we've been on is quite difficult."* However, automatically syncing posts was undesirable due to a loss of control: *"I don't want any automatic things; I want to be able to decide every decision myself, rather than having a computer do it."* (P5).

Reflecting on these findings, tools to support musicians' online promotion could be further developed, easing the burden of both timed and sporadic promotion without the artist losing a sense of creativity and control.

*Keeping up with the latest developments*

Finally, this hard work extended to keeping up with new developments as the ecology of services is in constant flux, with services coming and going and audiences migrating. Not only must an amateur musician learn new services, but they then face a serious legacy problem of moving content that they carefully crafted in one service into a new one and of knowing what to do with the old one. As P13 put it: *"the more I think no one knows what to do because it's ever-changing."*

Comments from several interviewees suggest that the move away from MySpace several years ago had been a seismic moment when the problems of transition became apparent: *"I remember the day it changed....they just made it completely counterintuitive. Everyone migrated away to Facebook"* (P3). While new services beguile with the potential to reach new audiences they also present the serious challenge of needing to refresh knowledge and migrate content.

## DISCUSSION

Our findings shed light on the complex online lives of one particular amateur community; how they are serious about their music, how they employ digital but also material practices to distribute this music to small fan bases, locally and internationally, and how they wrestle with diverse online services to promote themselves. We now consider the wider implications of our findings and propose generalisations from these that necessitate the need for further research, both in terms of the particular challenges that confront amateur musicians but also with regard to HCI's broader conception of amatuers.

### Operating at a Micro-scale in a Global World

An evident tension that runs throughout our findings concerns operating at a micro-scale in a global world. On the one hand we see a local community of musicians who play live to tens of people and for whom a thousand likes online is an impressive achievement. On the other, we see them eager to sell their music online through mainstream services, reach new fans and audiences, and even enjoy international collaborations. This tension between addressing small, personally known, and often local audiences, and being excited by reaching out to new fans around the world is reflected in the complex mix of services they use, spanning the social and commercial and also the local and global. While these services bring new opportunities for DIY promotion and international collaboration, they also involve considerable non-creative work and raise other challenges as we now discuss.

*Maintaining an identity across multiple services*

It is difficult to maintain an individual identity across different services and not become "lost in the noise". Not only is each different in terms of content, layout, purpose and interface, but there is a general lack of artistic control that limits the ability to craft a suitably quirky image. Even if this can be achieved, there is always the risk that a valued layout will change under your feet or that your audience will migrate onto some new platform. This problem of maintaining digital material across multiple services is not a new one. Linley *et al* studied attitudes towards online personal material among creative people, including amateur musicians, identifying five different types of collections (high value, curated online, emergent through use, for consumption in the moment, and personal pages and profiles) associated with different archiving strategies. While our musicians may potentially engage with all of these categories, our findings on the importance of carefully scheduling promotional activities lead us to suggest an alternative strategy.

*Recommendation 1: Event-oriented promotion tools.* Amateurs may benefit from more 'event oriented' promotional tools that enable them to create packages of material in advance of a gig or album release, define a schedule to manage their release, make it easier to edit them into different external media with a suitable voice in each, and possibly also archive them after the event (along with reviews, videos, comments and other feedback). We suggest that a more event-oriented approach that cuts across services, if suitably lightweight and controllable, might reduce the burden of online promotion and make it easier to archive valuable collections for future reuse.

*Harvesting fine-grained feedback*

The wider challenge of micro-scale operation in a global world is also reflected in gathering feedback. Our findings show that amateur musicians are keen to gather feedback from distributing their work online, but that this is difficult with current analytics. While numbers of views, downloads, sales and likes may give a useful picture at large scale, they lack the detail required to build a picture of how the work is received at a smaller scale and how to maintain personal relationships with a micro fanbase. Moreover, it is difficult to harvest analytics from across many services or to maintain a long–term and ongoing view of a particular event such as an album launch.

*Recommendation 2: Community-oriented analytics.* We propose that amateurs require distinctive analytic tools that lie somewhere between the personal feedback offered by social media and the large-scale analytics of professional marketing. The community-focused outlook of our musicians suggests the development of more community-oriented analytics that might help musicians inspect and learn about others promotional networks (at least as revealed through publicly available information) alongside their own, and to more easily discover lynchpin members of the community, key promotional sites, venues and also emerging new services. Such tools might be based upon more interactive versions of Figure 2, in which different notes could be dynamically interrogated or placed at the center of a network visualisation.

We note that, as our sample includes a significant number of soloists, our study has not touched upon the likely impact of 'band politics' (e.g., bands splitting up) on the online promotion and networking activities of amateur music communities. We also recognise that our study provides a micro-scale observation of closely connected musicians. Future research could perhaps further explore the interactions between musicians collaborating and networking remotely as part of a wider amateur network.

### Handcrafted Limited-edition Experiences

An especially striking finding is that, while our musicians are distributing their music digitally online, many of them are strongly drawn to more material forms of distribution from vinyl to personally handcrafted physical artefacts. When working at a micro-scale, every product sold is essentially part of a limited edition and so it becomes both possible and desirable to handcraft them. Handcrafting limited edition physical packaging adds value to their music that digital services such as Spotify may threaten to remove. It may also help establish a deeply personal connection with individual fans, and also encourage them to talk about the products or display them in prominent ways (P7's handcrafted wooden box will not easily sit among the CD collection on the shelf). This observation mirrors previous studies in HCI that have pointed to the continued value of physical forms such as vinyl and CDs in everyday music collections [7] and to the value of vinyl to DJs, both for its sound quality and its rarity [1]. However, while distinctive physical packaging, including limited editions, can be utilised by all manner of musicians, including professionals, the strategy of *individually handcrafting* these resonates most strongly with those working at a micro-scale, i.e., amateurs. This observation leads us to three further recommendations.

*Recommendation 3: Exploit tangible & embedded interaction.* Developments in tangible and embedded computing may enable amateur musicians to better associate digital tracks with handcrafted physical artefacts. Previous research has addressed tangible interfaces for both playing [16] and consuming music [11], as well as for integrating electronics in material craft practices [8]. We recommend that amateur musicians would be good candidates to take up such developments.

*Recommendation 4: harvest feedback through handcrafted musical products.* If handcrafting physical artifacts helps create a personal relationship with individual fans, might these then become channels for harvesting fine-grained feedback in return as discussed above? Future research might explore how to embed mechanisms for gathering feedback and communicating back to musicians into handcrafted musical products.

*Recommendation 5: Enable limited-edition and handcrafted digital listening experiences.* We also recommend exploring the alternative approach of how to add limited-edition value to the *purely digital* distribution of music. How might amateur musicians transform the act of downloading a digital track into being a handcrafted and deeply personal listening experience? Here we envision exploring more "performative" approaches to digital distribution, for example associating tracks with specific locations, times, instructions and modes of listening, distributing previews that can only be listened to once before being passed on, and other ways of delivering one-off listening experiences.

## COMING IN FROM THE MARGINS

We finish by broadening our perspective to reflect more generally on the emergence of the amateur from the margins and its implications for HCI and Remix culture.

### Highlighting the Amateur in HCI

Amateurs appear to be becoming less marginal in HCI as researchers exploring everyday creativity and DIY culture engage with amateur practice of various kinds. We therefore propose that it is time to bring the amateur fully into focus and to clearly articulate their distinctive nature. This means, recognizing—as the wider literature suggests—that amateurs are not professionals, but nor are they novices, hobbyists, dabblers or players. Our amateur musicians are certainly not beginners or novices undertaking casual creative practices. Rather they are expert composers and musicians who dedicate extensive time to their craft, including using online services. We believe that the evident seriousness of amateur practice holds an important lesson for HCI. Recently, our field has drawn heavily on Huizinga [14] to motivate explorations of ludic technologies [10] and playful interactions [27]. While play is certainly important and fully deserving of our attention, we should be careful not to confuse it with the seriousness of amateurism. Equally, our focus on DIY culture might encompass a wide variety of practitioners, from independent professionals who are pursuing DIY methods to DIY hobbyists. While amateurs may naturally be attracted to DIY, we should be careful to recognise that they may have distinctive needs.

Why do such apparently fine distinctions matter? In short, our study has shown that amateurs face particular challenges that arise from the seriousness of their activity as they work hard to stay in touch with their audience and promote themselves online. If professionals are served by commercial distribution channels, and everyday creatives by social media, then amateurs may fall uncomfortably between the two as they try to bridge both worlds. In short, serious amateurs face distinctive and important challenges that HCI must recognize and strive to address.

### The Amateur of the Digital Age

Finally, how does our study speak to notions of the amateur from sociology and cultural studies? Our amateur musicians who are distributing and promoting their work online in 2013 exhibit many of the characteristics of Stebbins' Modern Amateur and Leadbeater and Miller's Pro-Am. They are indeed skilled, passionate, knowledgeable and innovative. While not professional they may derive sufficient financial reward to sustain their music. Some of them may be 'pro-ams' with plans to turn professional. However, there are ways in which they differ, and here we return one more time to Stebbins' two definitions as these provide perhaps the most systematic attempts to define the amateur to date.

In terms of the Professional-Amateur-Publics system of relationships, our amateurs now avail themselves of the same distribution and promotional channels as professionals as well as many of the same production technologies. In turn, independent professionals (e.g., micro-independent labels) are adopting DIY techniques to sustain careers outside of the commercial mainstream [33] and established professionals are also experimenting with using social media to establish more direct and personal connections to fans [2, 28]. Thus, online services would appear to be complicating, perhaps even blurring, what were once relatively clear distinctions. They may also be affecting amateur's attitudes, especially their confidence which was one of the key attitudinal differences highlighted by Stebbins. Not only are our amateurs apparently confident in their music, but, through their association with DIY, are also confident in their values and approach. A good example is their confident skepticism towards commercial services, such as Spotify, that they devalue *their* music. If underground music has always set itself apart from the mainstream, there is the possibility that the Internet is enabling amateurs to more confidently 'mix it up' with the mainstream while proclaiming their difference.

## CONCLUSION

For Stebbins, writing in 1977, modern amateurs were 'the marginal men [and women] of leisure'. For us, writing over thirty years later, they would appear to be very much emerging from the margins, into the mainstream of Remix culture and consequently into the mainstream of HCI. By studying the activities and attitudes of amateur musicians as they navigate rich ecologies of online services, we hope to have revealed something of the complexities of their world; how the Internet affords tremendous opportunities for engaging local fan bases, while also reaching new audiences, and even collaborating internationally, but also how it introduces new challenges in terms of maintaining distinct identities, gathering appropriate feedback and coping with the work involved. Strikingly, we have also uncovered distinctive material practices involving the production of limited edition and handcrafted artefacts that add value to their music and engage individual fans in powerful ways. We suggest that there is much for HCI to learn here. We make specific recommendations for event-oriented promotion tools; community-oriented analytics; tangible and embedded products; and also limited-edition digital experiences. More generally, however, is the need to recognise and support the amateur for what he or she is – a dedicated individual, passionate about their art and serious in pursuit of leisure. Just as the amateur takes their art seriously, so we should take them seriously.

## ACKNOWLEDGEMENTS

We thank our study participants and also Evan Frayling for his work on visualisation of online data. We gratefully acknowledge support from the EPSRC through the Horizon Doctoral Training Centre EP/G037574/1, Dream Fellowship EP/J005215/1, and Platform Grant EP/FO3038X/1.

## REFERENCES

1. Ahmed, A., Benford, S., Crabtree, C. Digging in the crates: an ethnographic study of DJs' work. *Proc. CHI 2012,* ACM Press (2012), 1805-1814.
2. Baym, N. Fans or friends?: Seeing social media audiences as musicians do, *Participations: Journal of Audience and Reception Studies,* 9, 2 (2012), 286-316.
3. Benford, S., Tolmie, P., Ahmed A, Crabtree, A., Rodden, T. Supporting traditional music-making: designing for situated discretion, *CSCW '12* (2012), 127-136.

4. Beer, D. Making friends with Jarvis Cocker: Music culture in the context of Web 2.0. *Cultural Sociology*, 2, 2 (2008), 222-241.
5. Blaine, T., Fels, S. Collaborative Musical Interfaces for Novices, *Journal of New Music Research*, 32, 4 (2003), 411–428.
6. Bogdan, C. Bowers, J. Tuning In: Challenging Design for Communities through a Field Study of Radio Amateurs. *Communities and Technologies 2007*, Springer London (2007), 439-461.
7. Brown, B., Sellen, A., Geelhoed, E. Music Sharing as a Computer Supported Collaborative Application, *ECSCW* (2001), 179-198.
8. Buechley, L., Eisenberg, M. Fabric PCBs, Electronic Sequins, and Socket Buttons: Techniques for E-textile Craft, *Personal and Ubiquitous Computing*, 13,2 (2009), 133-150.
9. Cunningham, S., Nichols, D.M. Exploring Social Music Behavior: An Investigation of Music Selection at Parties, *ISMIR '09* (2009), 747-75.
10. Gaver, W.W. Designing for Homo Ludens, *I3 Magazine*, No. 12, June 2002.
11. Graham, J., Hull, J. Icandy: a tangible user interface for itunes, *CHI EA '08*, (2008), 2343-2348.
12. Grinter, R. Words about images: Coordinating community in amateur photography. *Computer Supported Cooperative Work (CSCW)* 14,2 (2005), 161-188.
13. Håkansson, M., Rost, M., Holmquist, L.E. Gifts from Friends and Strangers: A Study of Mobile Music Sharing, *ECSCW '07*, (2007), 311-331.
14. Huizinga, J. *Homo Ludens: A Study of the Play-Element in Culture*, Boston: The Beacon Press, 1955.
15. Jones, S. Music and the Internet, *Popular Music Journal*, 19, 2 (2000), 217-230.
16. Jorda, S., Geiger, G., Alonso, M., Kaltenbrunner, M. The reacTable: Exploring the Synergy Between Live Music Performance and Tabletop Tangible Interfaces, *TEI '07* (2009), 139–146.
17. Kuznetsov, S., Paulos, E. Rise of the Expert Amateur: DIY Projects, Communities and Cultures, *NordiCHI '10* (2010), 295-304.
18. Lanier, J. *Who Owns the Future?* Simon and Schuster, London, 2013.
19. Leadbeater, C., Miller, P., *The Pro-Am Revolution: How enthusiasts are changing our economy and society*, Demos, 2004.
20. Lee, E., Marrin Nakra, T., Borchers, J. You're the conductor: a realistic interactive conducting system for children, *NIME '04* (2004), 68-73.
21. Lessig, L. *Remix: Making Art and Commerce Thrive in the Hybrid Economy*, Penguin, London, 2010.
22. Leyshon, A., Webb, P., et al, On the reproduction of the musical economy after the Internet, *Media Culture & Society*, 27, 2 (2005), 177-209.
23. Linley, S., Marshall, C., Banks, R., Sellen, A., Regan, T. Rethinking the Web as Personal Archive, *WWW '13*, (2013), 749-760.
24. Loi, D., Roibas, A. DIY i-TV producers: emerging nomadic communities, *International Journal of Web Based Communities*, 3, 4 (2007), 416-426.
25. McLeod, J. *Doing Counselling Research*, Sage, 1994.
26. Miller, A., Edwards. K. Give and take: a study of consumer photo-sharing culture and practice, *CHI '07*, (2007), 347-356.
27. Morrison, A., Viller, S., Mitchell, P. Building sensitising terms to understand free-play in open-ended interactive art environments, *CHI '11*, (2011), 2335-2344.
28. Ploderer, B,. Howard, S., Thomas, P. "Collaboration on social network sites: amateurs, professionals and celebrities." *Computer Supported Cooperative Work (CSCW), 19, 5.* (2010), 419-455.
29. Prior N. Rise of the New Amateurs: Popular Music, Digital Technology and the fate of Cultural Production, In Hall, J., Grindstaff, L., Lo, M. (Eds.) *Handbook of Cultural Sociology*. London: Routledge, 2010, 398-407.
30. Roibas, AC., Sala, R. Beyond Mobile TV: Understanding how mobile interactive systems enable users to become digital producers, *HCI'07*, (2007), 801-810.
31. Rosner, D.K., Bean, J. Learning from IKEA Hacking: "I'm Not One to Decoupage a Tabletop and Call It a Day", *CHI '09*, (2009) 419-422,
32. Stebbins, R.A. The Amateur: Two Sociological Definitions, *Pacific Sociological Review*, 20, 4 (1977), 582-606.
33. Strachan, R. Micro-independent record labels in the UK-Discourse, DIY cultural production and the music industry, *European Journal of Cultural Studies*, 10, 2 (2007), 245-265.
34. Tanenbaum, J.G, Williams, A.M, Desjardins, A., Tanenbaum, K. Democratizing technology: pleasure, utility and expressiveness in DIY and maker practice, *CHI'13*, (2013), 2603-2612.
35. Torrey, C., Churchill, E., McDonald, D. Learning How: The Search for Craft Knowledge on the Internet, *CHI '09*, (2009), 1371-138.
36. Voida, A., Grinter, R.E., Ducheneaut, N., Edwards, W.K., Newman, M.W. Listening In: Practices Surrounding iTunes Music Sharing, *CHI '05*, (2005), 191-200.

# Watching the Footwork: Second-Screen Interaction at a Dance and Music Performance

**Louise Barkhuus**
Stockholm University
Forum 100, 16440
Kista, Sweden
barkhuus@dsv.su.se

**Arvid Engström**
Mobile Life @ Stockholm University
Forum 100, 16440
Kista, Sweden
arvide@mobilelifecentre.org

**Goranka Zoric**
ABB Corporate Research
Forskagränd 7, 72178
Västerås, Sweden
goranka.zoric@se.abb.com

## ABSTRACT
Interactive mobile technologies have become part of audience experiences of live performances in terms of both general media sharing and specific (sometimes official) extra content. At the same time, high bandwidth affords streaming of live events to mobile devices. We take advantage of these technologies in our high resolution, panoramic image video stream and study a scenario of audience members viewing the very same live event they are watching on a tablet. The video stream on the tablet is navigational and enables audience members to pan and zoom in the real-time video feed. We studied audience interaction and impressions in three performances of a dance and music show and found distinct uses of the second-screen video stream. We emphasize that despite initial reluctance, the observed utilization of the technology opened up for new potential practices. Our study shows how working with perceived conflict in technology can still open up design space for interactive technologies.

### Author Keywords
Interactive television, second-screen interaction, mobile entertainment.

### ACM Classification Keywords
H.5.1. Information interfaces and presentation (e.g., HCI): Multimedia Information Systems: video.

## INTRODUCTION
New interactive technologies provide intriguing possibilities for augmenting live music and theater performances. Opportunities are plentiful, and several strands of productions and research address, for example, social content for audience interaction [2, 14, 18], technology-facilitated experiences [6, 26] and interactive drama [29]. Today, spectators at live events increasingly use mobile technology to capture, share and interact with content; clips of theater performances are being recorded and shared online, and the personal background of a particular sports player is looked up online after she scores a goal. This increased use of mobile technology has been viewed as a distraction — but also as enhancing the live experience with new creative and social possibilities [33]. As devices and mobile networks become more powerful, the amount of content available to spectators will only increase, both in terms of venue- and performance-specific content, and as open interaction between audience members through other channels. This poses a challenge for technology and performance design in terms of developing services and interaction tools that add to the live experience rather than divert attention away from it.

From the perspective of recording and broadcasting live events, high bandwidth and more powerful computing devices have recently made possible real-time streaming of live performances to personal and mobile devices. Technology prototypes focus particularly on the spectator as "being their own director" in that the video stream can be selectively watched using several video feeds [19, 27]. Such an opportunity presents many possible scenarios in terms of personalized viewing of live events and complimentary viewing of an event. Yet, these live events are being broadcast to devices *outside* the sphere of the live event and are often tested with recorded content in laboratory conditions. In this paper we explore the novel scenario of users having access to the live stream in a high resolution, panoramic format, with the possibility to pan and zoom within the video stream, *as they are watching* the live performance. In essence we are extending the concept of "second-screen" interaction to include a stream of the live performance for close-up and navigational viewing. The "second-screen" is then a second image source in the hands of the spectator, complementing the view of the live event rather than a television screen.

In this study we take advantage of a state-of-the-art recording studio setup to capture and broadcast a live dance and music performance to explore how audience members use and interact with an optional screen. We observed the audience as well as the interaction on the tablets at three performances and interviewed a select set of audience members immediately after the performance to gain insights into their motivations and impressions of the experience. Our analysis focuses on audience members'


*CHI 2014,* April 26 - May 01 2014, Toronto, ON, Canada.

subjective experiences and their actual interactions with the live video feed.

The results of our inquiries and observations inform detailed descriptions of possible applications of secondary screens. We emphasize how this technology can be advantageous despite initial skepticism, but also how the audience members' added sense of control kept them focused on the performance. Our study contributes a further understanding of how streaming technologies can be used at live performance events, but also, more broadly, how deploying non-obvious functionality in real situations allows the researcher or designer to uncover new possibilities for interactive technologies.

## RELATED LITERATURE

Several strands of research are relevant to our setup and study. Although we are focusing on a live event, most existing interactive media systems have been studied or tested as part of watching television or prerecorded content. Similarly, second-screen interaction has mainly been explored in a large-screen context rather than within live event situations, which is why most related literature is related to interactive television technologies.

### Interacting with Video Content

Many systems are developed to provide viewers with a live video streamed event with the option to choose their own viewpoint and angle. Olsen et al., for example, describe an interactive TV sports event broadcast where an application prototype gives viewers the option to choose the view and to control replays [25]; experiments with the prototype showed that sport viewers made use of functions such as changing between cameras and "moving in time" rather than passively watching the broadcast. In contrast, Patrikakis et al. pointed to users' potential annoyance when receiving continuous annotations and recommendations for channel switching in a similar interactive video stream [27]. Many different types of interactions have been addressed in terms of video, but the spread of tablet computers and their established interaction paradigm (of pinching to zoom and moving the picture to pan) has made them a modern intuitive way to interact with image media on touch screens. Yet, few video browsers are capable of this type of interaction within video content. Some prototypes have been designed to facilitate, for example, scrolling visually through a video on a tablet [17] or using gestures to browse videos on smart phones [15]. Other researchers have developed direct manipulations techniques with objects in video [20] and simple zoom and pan interaction [36].

### Second-Screen Technology and Interaction

Although interaction with other objects during television watching is perhaps as old as the television itself, the distinct behavior of dual screen use, actively using another device or technology, is only as new as portable technology. Most research into dual attention of media technologies — so-called *second-screen interaction* — is recent, and made possible through the emergence of smart phones and tablets. Courtouis and D'heer, for example, surveyed 260 tablet owners in terms of tablets' ability as second-screen media for television watching and concluded that there is an untapped potential since a majority of the respondents reported combining a range of media technologies in actual use [9]. The same authors conducted a qualitative study of media technology use in the home and point out that the television is as often used as secondary to computers and tablets as vice versa [11]. Another approach to second-screen companions to television or video content is a customized information feed related to the television content. One example is FanFeeds, a social media application that provides social, contextualized information about television content. The authors report how FanFeed enabled socializing around television shows, even when time-shifted, due to the flexible availability of the commentary content [4, 5].

When taking the second screen out of the living room and into live events, literature focus particularly on sporting experiences where the screen facilitates extra information (e.g. about the players), essentially attempting to augment the event with technology-enabled content [23].

### Mediated Live Events

Live events, and live performance in particular, is often described as having inherent qualities of authenticity that can only be experienced in the moment and that are lost when that event is mediated, e.g through television [1]. The idea that mediating technologies is somehow detrimental to the "essence" of a live performance has recently returned to the public discourse, with performers and artists banning the use of camera phones at concerts. More positive accounts identify the characteristics of mediated "liveness" as being immediacy, intimacy, anticipation, participation and engagement, among others [13, 31, 34]. Dayan and Katz go so far as to say that a mediated live event is in better focus and that a home audience sees more of the event, because the performance is combined with an interpretation or narrative structure [10]. In research, live mediation is also closely tied to the concept of presence, as seen in a range of application areas from video conferencing, media spaces and virtual reality to iTV. Lombard et. al. [22] identify similar characteristics of presence, including immersion, realism and social richness. HCI research has proposed numerous means for engaging with live performances in new ways using mobile media technology [12, 21, 35]. However, in both research and commercial products, there has been a natural focus on mediating events to remote audiences or participants. With the concept of viewing a mediated live event *while attending*, some of the values of mediation, e.g. conveying a sense of immediacy and intimacy, are less relevant to an audience that is present and able to see the actual event as it unfolds. Instead, the potential value of a second video image in the event context itself speaks to characteristics of engagement, participation and a visually enriched live experience [10, 13, 22].

**Figure 1: Panorama view of the performance**

## PERFORMANCE AND TECHNOLOGY

The live event studied was a dance and music performance, serving as the center of a larger showcase of technologies for broadcasting ultra high definition (UHD) panoramic television from live events [30]. The performance was 22 minutes long and included two dancers, two singers and five musicians (see figure 1). It was the inaugural show by a modern composer, and performers were a mix of professionals and performing arts students. The dancers were at the center of the performance, moving around using the whole stage but regularly returning to the center. The two singers moved only occasionally from their positions on either side of the stage. The musicians were fixed in position apart from a midway intermezzo where all performers moved around and interacted physically with one another in a carefully choreographed fashion. At the end of the show, all performers left the stage (and the studio), leaving just one of the singers performing the final part a cappella. The audience members' fixed seated perspective meant that each performer was likely to, at one point or another, be outside the view of one or more individual audience members. The show was recorded and broadcast real-time to tablets where users could navigate the video stream by zooming and panning. See figure 2 for view of tablets with different views.

**Figure 2: The view of the nine tablets with individual streams**

## SYSTEM ARCHITECTURE

The panoramic, ultra high resolution video is captured by an omnidirectional camera (see figure 3). This camera consists of five individual cameras whose images are stitched in real time to form a panoramic scene covering 180 degrees at 5K x 2K resolution. The system transmitting the image, with support for interactive navigation, is a fully implemented end-to-end broadcast system comprising a complex chain of stitching, scripting and delivery engines, control nodes and relays connected by 20Gbps Infiniband lines and 10Gbps-Ethernet. For practical reasons, the architecture presented here is simplified, and focuses on the interchange of interactive commands and rendered video between the tablet end user clients and their access point to the larger system, the Rendering Proxy.

**Figure 3: The omnidirectional camera**

The Rendering Proxy [24] (see Figure 4) receives the entire panoramic image in the form of 64 high-resolution segments or "tiles". The Rendering Proxy then recreates the image and performs GPU-based rendering of the panorama for each of the end-user clients. The image is encoded using low-latency H.264 encoding and transmitted over TCP/IP. The Tablet Client supports real-time interactive navigation in the panoramic video by means of pan, tilt (swipe) and zoom (pinch) gestures. The video served to these terminals is processed in parallel Streamer instances on a single desktop machine, equipped with a single AMD GPU card. Each Streamer client in the Rendering Proxy listens to interactive commands form their respective tablet device over a TCP port, and operates an OpenGL virtual camera according to the received navigation gestures.

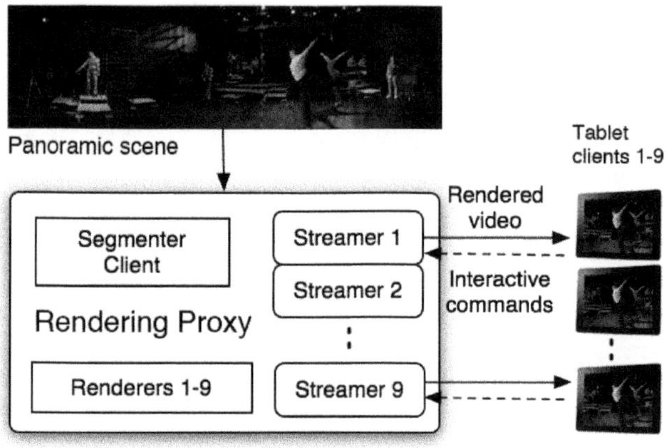


**Figure 4: Rendering Proxy and Tablet Clients**

In the instance of the system used in this study, nine end-user clients running on tablets were supported, with an end-to-end delay (from the camera to each tablet) of 2 to 3 seconds, due to the massive amount of data to be ingested by the video delivery system (around 3Gbps before compression). The round-trip delay between the rendering proxy and a tablet was well below a second, leading to a sufficiently responsive handling of the user interactions (zooming and panning). Note that these latency values are very low compared to many live IP-based video delivery systems. As an example, HTTP-based delivery on the web, typically leads to 10 seconds (or more) of end-to-end delay. For more details on the Rendering Proxy used in this study and the underlying optimizations for panoramic video delivery, we refer the reader to [24, 28].

## METHOD

We wanted to explore audience members' experience and interaction with the real time navigational video stream during the live performance. Although the streaming system was not developed for this specific use, but was provided here as part of a larger technology showcase, we found the opportunity to investigate this initially contrary setup intriguing. Streaming high-definition real-time video might be technically impressive, but our question was how the audience would actually use this navigational video stream in a real setting.

The event we leveraged to study the tablet interaction was performed in total six times; three rehearsals and three regular performances with invited outside viewers. Due to technical limitations, material from audience interaction was recorded from just three performances: one rehearsal and two regular performances. For each performance we collected two video recordings for analysis: One of the audience watching the show while interacting with the tablets, and one with all the actual tablet interaction in a split-screen view (see figure 2 for a composite of the tablets). For the three performances altogether 16 audience members were using tablets.

### Interviews

Thirteen audience members were interviewed after the performances about their experiences (three of the 16 audience members using tablets did not have time or declined to be interviewed after the show). We asked questions in relation to how the secondary video content influenced their experience and what they used it for while watching the performance. Participants were not affiliated with the project but all had a relation to the performance or the location of the showcase, either being relatives of the performers, employees of the local media industry or people affiliated with the university where the performance took place, such as students and teachers. Eight of the participants reported they had a personal interest in dance and music; for example, two of interviewees were dance students and two were professional musicians and music teachers. The interviewees were between 25 and 60 years old with a median age of 32 (seven people were 30 and under and five people were 45 and over). Five were female and the remaining eight were male. Pseudonyms have been used to protect anonymity. Interviews were semi-structured and lasted between ten and 20 minutes. They were recorded and transcribed right after the showcase day.

### Analysis

The overall analysis was based primarily on interviews with audience members. Analysis of video recordings complement these, and were used to uncover viewing and interaction patterns beyond participants' self-reports, though not at the level of a transcribed interaction analysis.

The video content was analyzed by noting each time an audience member looked down at the tablet, when they interacted with the content, and if they zoomed or panned. This was made possible through a synchronized composite screen of the two camera feeds: one of the audience from the side (the audience sat in a soft semi-circle) and one of the screen with each of the tablet feeds running (see figure 5). Thus we could see exactly what the audience members did on each tablet. This enabled quantitative analysis of interaction instances in addition to qualitative analysis.

Before coding the composite video feed it was time-stamped with 0 as the start of the performance. Owing to the setup, audience members' faces were occasionally obscured behind other people or because someone walked in front of our camera. Whereas a laboratory setup (e.g. using eye tracking equipment) can measure gaze and interaction in more detail, maintaining a natural environment was more valuable for the purposes of this study. The coding was done in a coarse-grained manner, with short glances down defined as one second and with blocks of time describing zooming and panning, but without detailing the precise targets. The coding was done individually by one author, with another one spot-checking key moments in the videos.

**Figure 5: Composite of the video recordings for analysis of observations**

The interviews were transcribed and analyzed through qualitative methods using constant comparison to draw out themes and categories. We also compared the audience member's expressed interactions with actual interactions recorded through the two video streams. This allowed us to interpret the audience members' own view of what 'little interaction' or 'a lot of interaction' meant.

Interviewees were informed that we were not directly involved in the development of this technology and that we wanted their honest and critical opinion. However, as previous research has pointed out, there will always be a participant bias, and this small set of interviews evidenced this overly positive response [7], possibly due to participants' initial impression of the technology.

## AUDIENCE EXPERIENCES WITH TABLET INTERACTION

The responses to the concept and technology of the zoomable second screen were mixed. Several participants were dismissive, saying that it did not work with a live performance like the one they were attending, mainly owing to its modest size given that several activities going on at the stage at the time. If anything, they felt it would work with a smaller-scale performance in a more intimate setting, or in a larger performance such as a rock concert. Rebecca expressed: "I didn't see a big advantage to using a device to look at [the performance] while I was also at the event, just because I didn't think that it could do as good a job as my eye, just following what I wanted to watch without thinking about it". Yet other participants were more positive, highlighting what they felt the second screen was good for: "I wanted to see the 180 degrees so I could watch everything at once, which you can't do when you just turn your head side to side. So that was really good" [Sally]. Three audience members admitted that they had been hesitant and skeptical at first but enjoyed the actual experience. One explains: "To be totally honest, at first I thought it's not going to be that useful because if anything it's going to distract from the actual performance from being there but I found that you can actually interact in a way that you couldn't otherwise." [Malcolm]

While we did not expect everyone to embrace the second-screen interaction with equal enthusiasm, it was interesting to us that some of the participants were initially highly critical of the concept of having another device while experiencing a live show. This might be a factor of the nature of the particular show chosen, as it was a performance designed for intensive viewing, as opposed to, for example, team sports events, but it might also reflect skepticism borne of inexperience at being presented with a parallel media stream: Why would I want to look at a video of the same performance that I am attending? Several participants expressed this view, or said that they had at least wondered about that before the show. Interestingly, however, almost all users found creative ways to use the extra media stream, often due to the stream being just slightly different from what the viewer could see as real-life audience of the performance. We now review three distinct uses that audience members explored.

### Viewing Strategies

We found three distinct ways in which users took advantage of the navigational video feed: to get around obstacles and see viewing angles they were otherwise not able to, to look at something related to a special interest of theirs, and to go back in time.

#### *Viewing Inaccessible Parts of the Performance*

Five of the 13 participants specifically explained that they used the second screen during the performance to view parts of the scene that were not visible from their viewpoint in the audience. This included views that were obstructed (e.g. by the camera) or views that were at a very different angle than the audience member's own. Gautier for example said: "I looked at the two ladies that were singing [...], because they were really at the extreme of the landscapes. So it was very interesting to see the [dancer] that I couldn't see with the tablet. [...] I saw a completely different viewpoint". Rebecca also expressed how she used the tablet to see inaccessible parts: "I had quite a good view of the center of the drummer [...], and when the dancers are in the middle, but not of the far right. I couldn't really see sort of that side, I used the tablet to look at it". Ben tied his low expectations but surprisingly positive experience to the fact that he could view these inaccessible parts of the scene: "[First] I was thinking, if I'm in a live performance, I wouldn't be using a tablet. I'd be enjoying the live performance. Then, where I was sitting in the back row, and the camera and the other equipment in the way, so, actually, yeah, it was quite interesting to see what was going on beyond".

The fact that several participants, independently of each other, reported that they found a useful way of 'seeing around' the obstacles, illustrates a commonly encountered challenge in live performances such as theater and concerts: for most spectators, there are occasional blind spots due to infrastructure such as columns, angle of viewing and, in filmed live experiences, cameras. Although attendees may not consider this before a performance — or perhaps even consciously after if they have had an overall positive experience — when they are actually experiencing the performance, these obstacles become real and the tablet video feed becomes an easy method of seeing the otherwise hidden object of interest.

#### *Special Interest*

Another way audience members used the secondary screen was to pursue their personal interests. Four participants were performing artists themselves, two dancers and two musicians. Three of these people reported that they used the tablet to zoom in and follow their 'special interest' person. Rachel, who recently finished her bachelor degree in dance as performing art, was particularly interested in the moves of the female dancer. She was able to look at the details of the body moving with the music through the secondary screen: "I try to [...] get all the movement in without ... you can lose really nice moments while trying to move about, so I try to keep [the tablet view] quite open like that in dance pieces". She did not zoom all the way in on the dancer but kept 'an open view' so she could follow her closely on the screen as well as in her view of the stage. Both our observations of her in the audience and her media stream confirmed this claim.

Stephen, on the other hand, who was a musician himself, was not as enthusiastic about the technology because he worried it would take away from the experience. He did zoom in on the musicians in the beginning though but then addressed most of his attention to the live performance. He mused around the technology's potential: "[this tool ...] would be quite cool, because you could have that advantage. Let's say it was a regular gig and an arena gig, [...] being a musician as well, you have your own things that you might want to look at, so it would be good in that situation. [...] [Y]ou do occasionally get the situation where something's happening that might quite interest you".

The special-interest viewing pattern was particularly facilitated by the video zoom function, in that it enabled close-ups of the performers. This highlights the advantages of being able to pan and zoom rather than just streaming a produced video of the performance to second screens.

#### *Automated Rewind Through Time Delay*

Due to network latency the tablet feed had a fixed delay of 2-3 seconds during the performances. Most participants were able to abstract from this but for some, it was a deal breaker. Most participants were fully aware of the technology's prototype stage and reassured us that this did not color their opinion much since they knew it would be 'fixed' in a real implementation. However, this does highlight a serious problem with many state-of-the-art systems consisting of new components: It takes a lot of work to have a fully working prototype, and often small aspects of infrastructure affect the quality in unpredictable ways. At earlier technical testing we had not experienced this delay; it was a surprise at final rehearsals where all the technologies came together. It is important to note that with a system as sophisticated as this, there might always be a 'missing piece' from a fully and flawlessly working system.

What we witnessed though was an ability on the part of a few of the audience members to turn this bug into a feature. Two audience members reported specifically that they used the tablet to see parts of the performance that they had missed two seconds before. Rachel, for example, would quickly shift her view down to the tablet if she saw an interesting piece of footwork, in order to see it in detail again. Sarah was also a dancer and explains: "... if I saw something I liked, because of the latency on it, I could go back and have a look and like see things... [...] Like if someone would ... If one of the dancers did a move I quite liked [I thought] 'Oh, I'll go and have a look at that again'".

This is a good example of technology appropriation, where users find an alternative way of using a technology, a way that fits the needs at hand better [4]. In essence, audience members were turning a disadvantage into an advantage and this case points to the value of having more than one temporality. These three viewing strategies led to the experience of control that can emerge from having an interactive second-screen stream.

### Obtaining a Sense of Control and Active Production

The audience members who were most positive towards the concept of an interactive secondary video stream reported that they enjoyed the control that the tablet interaction provided to them. "I thought it was really good fun because then I get to chose how I view it", was one common comment. Others also found it difficult to follow the elements of the show, particularly the dancers who moved faster than the audience members could sometimes pan: "The end space would jump a bit [...] when I was zooming in or out, which made it hard to follow if I was trying to follow the dancers, [...] They suddenly went out of shot because they're quite unpredictable. I couldn't follow them very easily just because I didn't feel I had complete control over it". The control of the view on the tablet was not necessarily the same as control over where to look at the stage. To counteract the lack of performer predictability, some audience members kept a wide view on the tablet.

While this increased control over how and what parts of the performance to see worked well for some audience members, others expressed a 'lazy' preference for having directors creating the view for them: "If I were watching it on Screen, I would prefer to have a directed view from a director in a traditional television coverage where the camera focuses on what's of interest" [Ben]. This opinion echoes a common criticism of interactive television: that viewers most often want to lean back while watching a show and interact only occasionally with the content. On the other hand, control over the view enabled the different viewing strategies described above, in essence creating the experience. It is important not to interpret what participants say they would prefer as actual design guidelines.

### Being in the performance

One characteristic of experiencing live performances is the experience of presence in terms of being part of a live event. This sense of presence and immersion in the show contributes to the popularity of live performances and is the difference in perception from, for example, televised shows. Some audience members rightly expected the secondary screen interaction to take away from this experience of presence but several participants had additional insights. Malcolm explained: "[...] even if you are the most interesting performers, at some point your eyes are going to wander around and lose concentration for a few minutes. That lack of concentration was then passed on to the tablet". Admitting that it is not always possible to focus a hundred percent on the show without his attention drifting, this participant used the secondary screen to retain focus on at least the same content, if not the live part of it. Another participants felt it was okay to follow the live performance and the tablet screen at the same time. It was not easy to follow singers, dancers and the band simultaneously anyway, so the tablet provided an extra viewpoint that could be utilized for the overall experience. Other research using eye-tracking equipment for determining focus between television screen and a secondary screen (tablet) also showed that 5-10 % of the time, the participants were in fact looking away from both screens, meaning their attention drifted from the interactive content [16].

## OBSERVATIONS OF TABLET INTERACTION

Where possible, we scrutinized the observational videos to confirm the interaction practices reported by the interviewees. This made clear, for example, that Rachel specifically followed the dancers but also kept her view fairly wide (as she explained), and we were able to determine that a craned neck followed by a glance down at the tablet was an attempt to view an otherwise obscured angle.

Our observational analysis of interaction also illustrated specific unarticulated uses. One common behavior was to use the tablet to pan around quite a bit during the first 3-5 minutes of the show. Then, as the audience member became familiar with the zoom and pan options, they used it less but still regularly throughout the show. One participant, Stephen, on the other hand, only interacted with the tablet in the beginning, then put it aside and watched the show normally. Others kept sporadically glancing down briefly at the screen, even without interacting with the content.

All in all, out of the 22 minute performance, audience members interacted between four and six-and-a-half minutes with the tablets, meaning looking down at them and/or panning or zooming. The average was five minutes and 24 seconds. We found that users mostly used the panning function, with about one third of the instances of panning also including zooming. At the most, one instance per person per show was an activity of zooming *without* panning, illustrating how the object of interest was most often not in the center of view. The panning sessions[1] were between one second and almost two minutes with averages for each audience member ranging between six and 18 seconds. The overall average of panning sessions was ten seconds. Considering the total length of active interaction during the performance, audience members panned and/or zoomed for four minutes and 41 seconds on average. They would obviously be looking down while panning or zooming, but they also often just glanced down at the screen without interacting: on average 24 times with glances lasting between less than a second and 32 seconds.

All in all the audience members were using the tablets in a fairly predictable way and to a level compatible with still taking part in the live performance. The main difference between audience members was not how much they panned and zoomed but how often they glanced down at the tablet without touching it; this corresponds well with the diverse expressions of the system's appropriateness we found in the interviews.

The ratio of panning to zooming that we observed underscores and adds to our observational findings regarding two primary viewing behaviors. Panning was dominant in both finding better viewing angles and locating points of interest, and was more intuitive as an interaction technique. Zooming was valuable for added detail, but focusing on a point of interest was observably more difficult for viewers and involved the risk of losing the overview. Still, the frequent use of combined pan-zooms, actions (moving quickly between the two), a fairly complex navigation technique, indicates that both these navigation modes for "content interaction" [see e.g. 20, 36] on tablet devices are feasible and familiar enough to be used with confidence by participants without prior training in this particular interface.

From these observations we infer that the initial, more intense interaction is due to familiarizing oneself with the interface and to its novelty value. The following more mixed attention, although likely affected by the trial situation, suggests a more realistic range of use patterns.

---

[1] A panning session is defined as the time between the audience member looking down and starting to pan until they looked up again. Their fingers were not necessarily touching the tablet the whole time, but as with all interaction with touch screens, fingers would be lifted, paused, and sometimes taken to the side.

Importantly, the interface supported these different levels of engagement equally well.

## DISCUSSION

Introducing mobile media technology into a live event setting is not uncontroversial, and may even seem to be at odds with the live experience the spectators seek. Yet, the way mobile devices have entered and changed this space is unmistakable. In particular, the use of camera-phones for taking pictures and filming at events has been both hugely popular and hotly debated. As an alternative to trying to reverse this development, we see an opportunity for designers and developers to produce interactive media technology that enhances experiences rather than disrupting them. The tablet system presented in this study contains a novel set of features that allow spectators to interactively navigate an ultra high resolution panoramic video of the event they are attending in real time as the event is unfolding.

Several participants in this study were initially skeptical when presented with a second screen for viewing and interacting with the live performance content. As described in the analysis their skepticism largely had to do with whether the video on the screen would give them anything they would not otherwise get from the performance itself, or just be a distraction. After trying out the application, a few remained dubious, stating that they did not see themselves using an additional live video device, no matter the functionalities offered. Still, the majority of participants, skeptics and enthusiasts alike, discovered specific ways of using the live video panorama that complemented their experience of viewing the live event. The following section draws on these behaviors to propose situations where an interactive second-screen application could enhance the live event experience and features to explore further in design.

### Advantages of Second-Screen Video Stream

There are several situations and manners in which such live video stream is useful, as evidenced from our observations and audience inquiries; we here explore four core advantages:

Firstly, the fact that most spectators do not have ideal viewing positions in the audience implies an obvious advantage of being able to choose a better viewpoint. Any performance or show that is televised will have both equipment and personnel between the audience and the stage, and even traditional theater experiences have seats with limited view due to columns and other building infrastructure. Premium seats still have one set vantage point, while the actors might be positioned in a different side of the stage. The camera used for the second-screen stream will typically be placed at the best position available since its view is presented to the larger (sometimes remote) audience.

Second, and related, the viewing angle in our system is 180 degrees, which provides a more detailed view to the audience. Our participants noticed the extra viewing angles compared to their own view, where a focused 180-degree view required turning their head. Taking advantage of the panoramic possibilities in video content can provide a condensed overview over the activities on stage and inform spectators where the attention should be directed.

A third valuable use of a secondary screen is apparent when considering larger events. Although our event was a small studio-based show with only nine performers, a larger audience would have placed some spectators even further from the stage, with consequences for detailed watching. Large-scale performances such as stadium concerts potentially benefit from viewers being able to zoom in and find detailed parts, illustrated by the now-common placing of large screens on the side of the stage. These large screens most often show a directed video stream of the performer with additional camera angles and occasional replays, which was one of the specific preferences from a few of our interviewees. Yet, it is not clear if the stated preference for a directed stream came from an established standard of practice or an actual lived preference.

Fourth and finally, even at engaging live events, there are times when spectators' eyes wander or the spectator needs a visual break. At these times, a second screen may provide variation, and actually make event attendees *more* engaged with the performance at points when they otherwise would turn away from the event. As we described, many of the audience members were observed looking down at the tables on multiple occasions throughout the performance, often for just a few seconds, without interacting with the stream.

These findings are relevant to a current interest in HCI research in providing tools for participation and content creation at live events [18, 21, 32]. Where this prior work has proposed means of creating, sharing and saving content to be viewed afterwards, our work presents an alternative route that provides the visitor with additional content to engage with in the moment. Combining the two approaches by adding basic broadcasting and recording functions would allow visitors to share and save their experiences as memorabilia.

### Broader Lessons for Design

From the experiences with a panoramic, navigational stream of a live event, we now broaden our findings and examine implications for interactive media technology at live events. We found, despite our initial doubts, that this type of technology has the potential to enhance the live experience rather than detract from it.

On a broader level we found that flaws or 'seams' [8] in the technology worked to our advantage and illustrated a potential use: the "replay" functionality caused by the video delay, although not intentional, was in some cases valued. It became clear that the secondary screen video stream would benefit from just such a function. This does not need to be a replay in the production sense (manually produced), but simply the ability to play back material, for example a fixed number of seconds back. A full rewind functionality might not be necessary but a simple way of moving a couple of seconds back in time, then forward to synchronous time again, might be valuable for some spectators.

Secondly, audience members' sense of control in terms of attention is a relevant issue to consider. A live performance is often a more focused experience than a televised (even if live) show and attention is more likely to be on the performance for a higher proportion of the time. But even so, attention occasionally diverges, particularly to other media devices and perhaps other audience members. As we pointed out, the system afforded a feeling of control, and the second screen not only provided them with a place to turn, but also content that was still part of the performance. In addition, this illustrates the room for media sharing in terms of both 'in the moment' and after the event. Instead of having the spectators record the event themselves, such a secondary stream will have the benefit of being readily available for sharing through mobile devices.

Finally, we want to highlight that it is important to work *with* the conflict in technology adoption and appropriation, extracting potential practices from real-life situations, rather than avoiding interactive technology deployment because of assumptions that it will not add much. The FascinatE high-resolution panoramic video system was not designed *just* to support a second-screen stream, but for many other purposes, such as automatized editing and directing of a large live event and to record a panoramic scale video of a live event. The possibilities for streaming this content live to tablets came later in the development process, and let us examine this a real-life situation. This provided us with a unique opportunity to see how potential users approach such a tool.

## CONCLUSION

We have described how audience members interact with a secondary navigational video stream of a live event while being present at the event itself. Despite audience members' initial skepticism, our observations and inquiries uncovered and elucidated several unique uses. Many participants were themselves surprised to find the second video stream appropriate and not necessarily in the way of their real-life experience of the performance. Our study showed that audience members were able to keep control over their viewing experiences through the second-screen video feed while maintaining a presence in the live performance.

## ACKNOWLEDGMENTS

We thank all the audience members for taking the time to talk to us after the show. We also especially thank our project partners at ALU (Bell Labs Multimedia Technologies Domain, Alcatel-Lucent Bell NV, Antwerp, Belgium) for providing the prototype for tablet interaction.

This research was conducted as part of the FascinatE project, which received funding from the European Union's Seventh Framework Programme (FP7/2007-2013) under grant agreement no. 248138.

## REFERENCES

1. Auslander, P. *Liveness: Performance in a networked culture*, 2nd ed. New York, US, Rutledge, 2008.
2. Barkhuus, L. and Jørgensen, T.. Engaging the crowd: studies of audience-performer interaction. *Ext. Abstracts CHI 2008*, ACM Press (2008), 2925-2930.
3. Barkhuus, L., and Polichar, V. E. Empowerment through seamfulness: smart phones in everyday life. *Personal and Ubiquitous Computing* 15 (6), 2011, 629-639.
4. Basapur, S., Harboe, G., Mandalia, H., Novak, A., Vuong, V. and Metcalf, C. Field trial of a dual device user experience for iTV. In *Proc. EuroITV 2011*, ACM Press (2011), 127-136.
5. Basapur, S., Mandalia, H., Chaysinh, S., Lee, Y., Venkitaraman, N. and Metcalf, C. 2012. FANFEEDS: evaluation of socially generated information feed on second screen as a TV show companion. In *Proc. EuroITV 2012*. ACM Press (2012), 87-96.
6. Bedwell, B., Schnädelbach, H., Benford, S., Rodden, T., and Koleva, B. In Support of City Exploration. In *Proc. CHI 2009*. ACM Press (2009), 1171-1180.
7. Brown, B., Reeves, S. and Sherwood, S. Into the wild: challenges and opportunities for field trial methods. In *Proc. CHI 2011*, ACM Press (2011), 1657-1666.
8. Chalmers, M. and Galani, A. Seamful interweaving: heterogeneity in the theory and design of interactive systems. In *Proc. DIS 2004*, ACM Press (2004), 243-252.
9. Courtois, C. and D'heer, E. Second screen applications and tablet users: constellation, awareness, experience, and interest. In *Proc.* EuroITV 2012, ACM Press (2012), 153-156.
10. Dayan, D. and Katz, E. *Media events: the live broadcasting of history*. Harvard University Press, 1992.
11. D'heer, E., Courtois, C. and Paulussen, S. Everyday life in (front of) the screen: the consumption of multiple screen technologies in the living room context. In *Proc. EuroITV 2012*, ACM Press (2012), 195-198.
12. De Sá, M., Shamma, D. A., Churchill, E. Live Mobile Collaboration for Video Production Design, Guidelines, and Requirements. *Personal Ubiquitous Computing, Special issue on Video Interaction*, 2013, 1-15.
13. Engström, A. and Perry, M. 2011. 'Liveness' in live TV: production, experience and future design. *Ext. Abstracts CHI 2011,* ACM Press (2011).
14. Esbjörnsson, M., Brown, B., Juhlin, O., Normark, D., Östergren, M. and Laurier. E. Watching the cars go

round and round: designing for active spectating. In *Proc. CHI 2006*, ACM Press (2006) , 1221-1224.

15. Ganhör, R. ProPane: fast and precise video browsing on mobile phones. In *Proc MUM 2012*, ACM Press (2012), article 20, 8 pages.

16. Holmes, M. E., Josephson, S. and Carney, R. E. Visual Attention to Television Programs With a Second-Screen Application. In *Proc ETRA 2012*, ACM Press, (2012), 397-400.

17. Hudelist, M. A. Schoeffmann, K. and Boeszoermenyi, L. Mobile video browsing with a 3D filmstrip. In *Proc. ICMR 2013*, ACM Press (2013), 299-300.

18. Jacucci, G. Oulasvirta, A., Ilmonen, T., Evans, T. and Salovaara, A. Comedia: mobile group media for active spectatorship. In *Proc. CHI 2007*, ACM Press (2007), 1273-1282.

19. Jiang, J., Köhler, J., Williams, C.M., Zaletelj, J., Güntner, G., Horstmann, H., Ren, J., Löffler, J. and Weng, Y. Live: An integrated production and feedback system for intelligent and interactive TV broadcasting. *IEEE transactions on broadcasting,* first, 2011.

20. Karrer, T., Weiss, M., Lee, E. and Borchers, J. DRAGON: a direct manipulation interface for frame-accurate in-scene video navigation. In *Proc. CHI 2008,* ACM Press (2008), 247-25.

21. Kennedy, L. and Naaman, M. Less talk, more rock: automated organization of community-contributed collections of concert videos. In *Proc WWW 2009*, ACM Press (2009), 311-320.

22. Lombard, M., Reich, R. D., Grabe, M. E., Bracken, C. C. and Ditton, T. B. Presence and Television. The Role of Screen Size. *Human Communication Research*, 26(1), January 2000, 75-98.

23. Ludvigsen, M. and Veerasawmy. R. Designing technology for active spectator experiences at sporting events. In *Proc. OZCHI 2010*, ACM Press (2010), 96-103.

24. Macq, J.-F., Verzijp, N., Aerts, M., Vandeputte; F. and Six, E. 2011. Demo: Omnidirectional video navigation on a tablet PC using a camera-based orientation tracker. In *Proc. Distributed Smart Cameras (ICDSC 2011), IEEE (*2011) , 1-2.

25. Olsen, D.R., Partridge, B. and Lynn, S. Time warp sports for internet television, *ACM Transactions on Computer-Human Interaction*, 17 (4) December 2010, article no. 16.

26. Oppermann, L., Flintham, M., Reeves, S., Benford, S. Greenhalgh, C., Marshall, J., Adams, Farr, J. R. and Tandavanitj, N.. Lessons from Touring a Location-Based Experience. In *Proc. of Pervasive Computing*, (2011). 232-249.

27. Patrikakis, C., Papaoulakis, N., Papageorgiou, P., Pnevmatikakis, A., Chippendale, P., Nunes, M., Cruz, R., Poslad, S. and Zhenchen, W. Personalized Coverage of Large Athletic Events, *Multimedia, IEEE*, 18 (4), 2012, 18–29.

28. Rondao-Alface, P., Macq, J.-F. and Verzijp, N. Interactive Omnidirectional Video Delivery: A Bandwidth-Effective Approach. In *Bell Labs Technical Journal* 16 (4), 2012, 135-147.

29. Saltz, D. Z. Live Media: Interactive Technology and Theater. *Theatre Topics*, 11(2), September 2001, 107-130.

30. Schreer, O. Thomas, G., Niamut, O. A. Macq, J-F., Kochale, A., Batke, J-M., Ruiz Hidalgo, J. Oldfield, R., Shirley, B. and Thallinger, G. Format-agnostic Approach for Production, Delivery and Rendering of Immersive Media, *NEM Summit 2011, Torino, Italy*, Sept. 27-29, 2011.

31. Thompson, J. *The media and modernity: a social theory of the media.* Cambridge, Polity, 1995.

32. Vihavainen, S., Mate, S., Liikkanen, L and Curcio, I.. Video as memorabilia: user needs for collaborative automatic mobile video production. In *Proc. CHI 2012*, ACM Press (2012), 651-654.

33. Vihavainen, S. Mate, S., Seppälä, L., Cricri, F. and Curcio, I. D. D.. We want more: human-computer collaboration in mobile social video remixing of music concerts. In *Proc. CHI 2011,* ACM Press (2011), 287-296.

34. Wurtzler, S. 1992. She Sang Live, But The Microphone Was Turned Off: The Live, the Recorded and the Subject of Representation. In Altman (Ed.), *Sound Theory Sound Practice*, New York, Routledge, 1992.

35. Yonezawa, T. and Tokuda, H. Enhancing communication and dramatic impact of online live performance with cooperative audience control. In *Proc. of the UbiComp 2012*, ACM Press (2012), 103-112.

36. Zoric G, Engstrom A, Barkhuus L, Önnevall E. 2013. Panoramic video: design challenges and implications for content interaction. In *Proc. EuroITV*, ACM Press (2013),153-162.

# Streaming on Twitch: Fostering Participatory Communities of Play within Live Mixed Media

**William A. Hamilton[1], Oliver Garretson[2], and Andruid Kerne[1]**
Interface Ecology Lab
Dept. of Computer Science and Engineering[1] | Dept. of Sociology[2]
Texas A&M University, College Station, Texas USA
{bill, andruid}@ecologylab.net, olivergarretson@tamu.edu

## ABSTRACT
Previously, video streaming sites were at the fringes of online social media. In the past two years, live streams of video games, on sites such as Twitch.tv, have become very popular. Live streams serve as meeting grounds for player communities. The Twitch streaming medium combines broadcast video with open IRC chat channels. In conjunction with gameplay, viewer participation and community building gain emphasis. Twitch streams range in size and nature, from intimate communities with fifty viewers, to massive broadcasts with tens of thousands. In this paper, we present an ethnographic investigation of the live streaming of video games on Twitch.

We find that Twitch streams act as virtual third places, in which informal communities emerge, socialize, and participate. Over time, stream communities form around shared identities drawn from streams' contents and participants' shared experiences. We describe processes through which stream communities form, the motivations of members, and emergent issues in the medium. Finally, we draw from our findings to derive implications for design of live mixed-media environments to support participatory online communities.

## ACM Classification Keywords
H.5.3 Group and Organization Interfaces: Synchronous Interaction

## Author Keywords
live streaming; Twitch; video games; online communities; third places; ethnography

## INTRODUCTION
We investigate how the popular new medium of live video streaming, i.e., *live streaming*, fosters participation and community. Live-streaming combines high-fidelity computer graphics and video with low-fidelity text-based communication channels to create a unique social medium. Live streaming previously was at the fringes of social media, with a small population producing and consuming content. Around 2009, live streams of people playing games began growing in popularity. Four years later, the video game live streaming scene has exploded. Twitch.tv, or just Twitch, a website solely supporting video game streaming, has over 34 million unique monthly viewers and tens of thousands of streamers. We present an ethnographic investigation of the emergence of communities amidst live streaming on Twitch.


*CHI 2014*, April 26–May 1, 2014, Toronto, Ontario, Canada.

ACM 978-1-4503-2473-1/14/04..$15.00.
http://dx.doi.org/10.1145/2556288.2557048

**Figure 1. Twitch streams enable streamers to broadcast high-fidelity video of gameplay and real-life. Participants simultaneously communicate through streamed media and an associated chat channel (right).**

Live streaming, in its current form, enables public broadcast of live audio and video streams alongside a shared chat channel (Figure 1). In video game live streaming on Twitch, *streamers*, those who broadcast streams, share live video content of their gameplay composited with a video feed of themselves in real life. Viewers of the stream communicate with the streamer and other viewers through chat. Meanwhile, streamers simultaneously engage in game play and communicate via audio and video. Participation in streams is open. All that is required to chat is a free Twitch account.

We found that people engage in live streaming for two reasons: they are drawn to the unique content of a particular stream, and they like being interacted with and participating in that stream's community. Many Twitch streams are what we consider to be *participatory communities*, characterized by openness as well as the means for and encouragement of members to engage in shared activities. The primary activity stream participants engage in is *sociability*, defined by George Simmel as a playful experience of social association characterized by the "sheer pleasure of being together" [23]. Sociability in streams takes the form of humorous banter and light-hearted conversation, alongside play. Core community members engage in key activities: building community by engaging other participants, promoting participation, and moderating chat.

Ray Oldenburg introduces the concept of *third places*, informal public spaces where people engage in sociability to form and maintain communities [19]. We posit that streams function as virtual or online third places. We draw from the concept of third places to discuss the genesis and evolution of stream communities. Stream communities form around a shared identity drawn from the stream's content and the shared experiences of its participants. To analyze stream community identity, we draw from McMillan and Chavis' *sense of community* [18].

We find that dual emphasis on streamed content and accessible participation results from a medium that mixes high-fidelity broadcast with open low-fidelity chat. Beyond fidelity, these various media afford different levels of participation. We use McLuhan's concepts of "hot" (high-fidelity/low-participation) and "cool" (low-fidelity/high-participation) media to analyze how components of live streaming contribute to its overall function as a social medium. By combining hot and cool media, streams enable the sharing of rich ephemeral experiences in tandem with open participation through informal social interaction, the ingredients for a third place.

As the popularity of live streaming has increased in recent years, many streams have become very large, some regularly in excess of 5,000 live participants. However, as streams scale up, information overload renders chat unreadable, and moderation becomes overwhelming. Some large streams continue to grow. However, participants become frustrated with the difficulty of interacting in these streams. We found that for this reason, many choose to participate in smaller streams, which they experience as affording more meaningful interaction.

We begin with a socio-technical description of Twitch streams. Next, we present the methodology of our ethnography. We develop sensitizing concepts from relevant work in sociology and media theory. We discuss findings concerning the motivations of stream participants, the formation of stream communities, forms of participation through streaming media, and emergent issues concerning participation. We discuss our findings, and relate prior work. We draw from our findings to derive implications for design. We articulate the role of mixed live cool and hot media in supporting participatory communities. We develop solutions for scaling participatory communities amid large online audiences. We conclude by considering the potential broader impact of live streaming on other contexts.

## WHAT IS A TWITCH STREAM?

Twitch streams combine live audio/video media and text-based chat channels. Streams belong to *streamers*, Twitch users who upload streaming media to be broadcast. Other Twitch users, known as *viewers*, can then watch the streamed content. Video content on Twitch is primarily of streamers playing various digital games, either by themselves or with friends. Streamers often embed in person webcam video of themselves and others they are playing with on top of their streamed game content to facilitate richer engagement (Figure 1). Streamed content is not always gameplay, many streamers spend significant time interacting with their viewers out of game.

Every Twitch stream has an associated Internet Relay Chat (IRC) channel. Stream pages have an embedded IRC client adjacent to the streaming video (see Figures 1 & 2). Within a stream, interaction between participants is typically as follows: the streamer talks through the stream's broadcast audio, and the viewers then send messages to the streamer and each other in the chat. The streamer will typically try to read the chat and respond to viewers as they play.

We describe several types of viewers to convey the topology of a typical stream community. Every stream has *followers*. By following the stream, these viewers choose to receive email notifications when the stream goes live. Some viewers become *moderators* ("mods"), are given the privileges to perform administrative duties within the stream. Moderators are given a special icon in the chat client to denote their status. They have the power to permanently ban or temporarily timeout viewers. Normally moderators exercise these powers to prevent people from posting abusive messages or links to inappropriate websites. Streamers are moderators and can promote stream viewers to be moderators. As we will see, moderators often perform a variety of other tasks to support the stream community.

Twitch invites some streamers who bring in a certain threshold of views to participate in their "partnership" program. Streamers who enter into this agreement are known as *partners*. Twitch partners earn a share of the ad revenue generated from their streams and can choose when and how ads appear on their stream. The revenue that streamers may earn from ad impressions varies between 2 and 5 USD per 1000 impressions. Along with the money from ads, Twitch partners can offer "subscriptions" to their viewers. *Subscribers*, viewers who purchase stream subscriptions, pay a monthly fee to Twitch, half of which goes to the streamer. Subscribers do not have to watch stream ads. They may also use the stream's special emoticons and are denoted by a icon in chat (see Figure 2). Streamers often offer additional incentives for subscribers in the form of more opportunities to interact with them on stream. With all of these potential revenue sources, more streamers are going full-time, quitting their jobs, and attempting to live the dream of being payed to play video games.

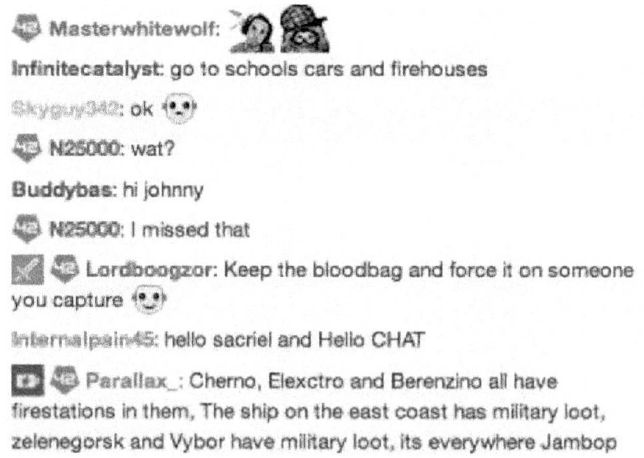


**Figure 2. Every Twitch stream has an embedded chat channel. Twitch uses a custom IRC client with special features for showing stream specific emoticons and denoting stream subscribers and moderators.**

Table 1. Streamers interviewed, ordered by number of followers.

| ID | Followers | Average Viewer Count | Partnered (Y/N) | Gender (M/F) | Frequently Plays |
|---|---|---|---|---|---|
| S1 | 55 | 15 - 30 | N | M | League of Legends, Street Fighter |
| S2 | 378 | 20 - 50 | N | M | World of Warcraft, DayZ |
| S3 | 648 | 10 - 200 | N | M | Ni no Kuni, Surgeon Simulator, Dead Space |
| S4 | 2,673 | 100 - 400 | N | M | League of Legends |
| S5 | 4,199 | 100 - 150 | N | M | League of Legends |
| S6 | 4,654 | 200 - 400 | N | M | DayZ |
| S7 | 8,140 | 50 - 250 | N | M | Oregon Trail, Organ Trail, Punch Out |
| S8 | 13,463 | 400 - 600 | Y | M | Don't Starve, Shovel-Knights, Terraria |
| S9 | 17,245 | 150 - 2000 | Y | M | DayZ, StarCraft 2, EuroTruck Simulator |
| S10 | 24,474 | 150 - 2000 | Y | M | Diablo 3, DayZ, Smite, Neverwinter |
| S11 | 45,206 | 400 - 2000 | Y | F | League of Legends, HearthStone |

## METHODOLOGY

To construct an understanding of streaming practice and communities, we conducted an ethnographic investigation of live streams on Twitch. This study began informally, in early 2010, when we started to become active participants in different streams on JustinTV, Twitch's predecessor. Over nearly four years, we became immersed in the Twitch community, as a whole, and a plethora of particular stream communities. As a result, we have developed deep firsthand knowledge of stream viewer experience, streaming practice, and communities. In addition to our long term involvement, we interviewed 11 Twitch streamers and 4 viewers over the past year.

Initially, we specifically chose to interview streamers, because of the core role they play in streaming communities. Most streamers spend hours everyday not only streaming, but trying to build a stronger understanding of streaming phenomena and interacting with other stream communities. This makes streamers a dense source of inside knowledge and understanding. We later decided to interview 4 viewers who are core members of their respective stream communities: interviewing them helped us better understand individual viewer experiences.

In order to build rapport with the interviewed streamers and viewers, we started to participate in their streams' chats during the weeks prior to recruiting for interviews. By doing this, the researchers became part of each streamer's regular viewership. With some of the streamers interviewed, we already had prior rapport, based on our long term involvement in particular streams. This process also helped familiarize us with each stream's community and enabled us to ask participants focused questions during interviews. Once a level of rapport was reached, we went on to recruit streamers via the private messaging system of Twitch.

Table 2. Viewers interviewed.

| ID | Streams Followed | Watches | Gender (M/F) | Moderator (Y/N) |
|---|---|---|---|---|
| V1 | 52 | S11 | F | Y |
| V2 | 31 | S5 | M | N |
| V3 | 235 | S8, S10 | M | Y |
| V4 | 71 | S8 | F | Y |

In selecting streamers for interviews we used a purposive sampling method: selection was based on characteristics both exhibited by the streamer and the stream's community. Time spent as viewers enabled us to ascertain each stream's atmosphere, chat moderation policy, and community. We sought to interview a gamut of streamers from different game communities, attitudes, and stream sizes. Table 1 summarizes the streamers that we recruited for interviewing. We will refer to the interviewed streamers by the identifiers given in Table 1.

In selecting viewers, we similarly focused on recruiting viewers who were active stream participants. We specifically tried to recruit a number of stream moderators. By recruiting these viewers we were able to interview those who had a strong understanding of their respective communities. Table 2 summarizes the viewers we interviewed.

Participants were interviewed via audio/video chat, with the exception of S1 and S10, who we interviewed in person. The interviews, which typically lasted between 1 to 2 hours, were recorded, and later transcribed. We used a semi-structured interview format, focusing on each streamer's experiences, their stream's community, and their goals. Many of the questions focused on evoking important moments and experiences from the streamer's tenure. After completing the interviews, we continued efforts to be active participants in their streams.

We proceeded to conduct a grounded theory analysis by first transcribing the recorded interviews. Transcripts were then unitized, breaking them up into units of meaning. We then used the constant comparative method to code the unitized interview transcripts into emergent themes and categories [8, 15]. All codes emerged through the coding process, and were iteratively derived to describe observed phenomena. Other data collected from researcher field notes and reflexive journals were also used in the coding process. In total, approximately 1,700 data units were coded in the analysis.

## SENSITIZING CONCEPTS

We develop sensitizing concepts from prior work to frame our investigation of live streaming communities and media. We consider Oldenburg's concept of third places and how they serve as important environments for the formation and maintenance of communities [19]. We discuss McMillan and Chavis's components of community and apply them in conjunction with data to show how communities form around Twitch streams [18]. Finally, we connect McLuhan's concepts of "hot" and "cool" media to analyze the participatory nature of live streaming's constituent media components [17].

### Third Places

Oldenburg establishes the concept of third places as "public places that host the regular, voluntary, informal, and happily anticipated gatherings of individuals beyond the realms of home and work" [19]. Third places serve as alternative locations, for people to come together, form, and maintain communities through informal public social interactions. Oldenburg identifies typical third places, such as cafes, coffee shops, and bars. Later, Rheingold connected a study of virtual communities with Oldenburg's third places [22]. Since then, it has been used to describe the roles of various media in the formation of online communities. These include Bruckman and Resnick's work on MUDs [4] and Ducheneaut et. al's study of massively multiplayer online games [6]. We introduce the some of the characteristics of third places, and use them to show how streams function as such.

*Conversation is the main activity* inside a third place. Participants experience this talk as good, lively, humorous, and colorful. In this way, the third place fosters sociability. Oldenburg discusses how talk in third places is often playful and is situated around games such as gin rummy or dominoes. Conversation becomes continuously driven by play, as participants talk about the players', "slyness, slowness, quickness, meanness, [and] allusions to long-remembered incidents in club history." Indeed, the primary form of participation that occurs in streams is playful discussion in the chat. Discussion is driven by the events occurring in the game being streamed.

Third places have *regulars*, those who frequent the place to enjoy the company of other regulars and newcomers. These people strongly define the place. As Oldenburg explains, "It is the regulars whose mood and manner provide the infectious and contagious style of interaction and whose acceptance of new faces is crucial." Every regular was once a newcomer There are no strict requirements on who can participate. All that is required is a shared understanding that a newcomer is of a "decent sort", capable of carrying on a civil and playful discussion, and that they will likely be seen again. Thus, to become a regular, "One simply keeps reappearing and tries not to be obnoxious" [19]. As we will show, this process of inducting newcomers and the emergence of regulars plays a key role in the formation and growth of stream communities.

### Sense of Community

McMillan and Chavis define sense of community through four components: membership, influence, fulfillment of needs, and emotional connection [18]. We use these as a basis for characterizing stream participants' conceptions of community.

The status of membership is developed through personal investment in the community, yielding feelings of the right to belong and community identity [18]. Membership serves as the primary boundary determining who is in and outside of the community. The primary form this investment takes in stream communities is through members' spending their time and personal energy. Participants often also invest personal skills and money into a stream community.

Influence revolves around two oppositional ideas. Participants are attracted to groups whose activities they can impact [18]. In the case of stream communities, viewers are attracted to streams where they are recognized by the streamer and other participants, and can participate in stream activities, such as gameplay. Communities also evoke a sense of conformity, members naturally adopt shared qualities inherent to the group. In practice, a stream community tends to exhibit a shared social atmosphere instituted by the streamer and regulars.

A core part of members' sense of community is that communal benefits fulfill their needs in some way. This fulfillment takes several forms including emotional rewards such as sociability, the status of membership, and the success of the community. These rewards and their importance to participants is evident in stream communities. Another common reward is the gaining of knowledge and skills available from other community members. In stream communities, this often takes the form of game skill and knowledge, which may be uniquely available from the streamer or their viewers.

Community members develop an emotional connection through shared history and an identification with other members. This shared connection is developed primarily through continued participation: "The more people interact, the more likely they are to become close" [18]. The more positive the experience that members have in the context of the community, the greater their emotional connection to that group. In third places, such as streams, regulars take it upon themselves to engender positive experiences making the community attractive to newcomers, building the community through encouraging participation and open acceptance of new members.

### Hot & Cool Media

McLuhan used fidelity and participation as correlated features for the analysis of forms of media [17]. Telephone, he said, is a *cool medium* of low fidelity and high participation, because so little is given and so much must be filled in by the listener. A photograph and a film are high definition (hot), while a comic is low and cool. Cool media afford participation. Hot media afford spectating.

Live streaming is a hybrid form, conjoining game graphics (high fidelity), live webcam video (medium fidelity), and chat (low fidelity). We found that streaming's hybrid assemblage of synchronized low to high fidelity media components engages people in Twitch. Not surprisingly, participation is most directly afforded by the low fidelity medium of IRC, making streams open and accessible, empowering newcomers. It is through this medium that core community interaction occurs through congenial and playful conversation. At the same time, hot live video, based on relatively common computer graphics and networking, powerfully facilitates sharing rich experiences of play. It gives participants opportunities to engage more deeply. These shared ephemeral experiences afforded by high-fidelity media are the foundation of a stream community's shared history and emotional connection.

## FINDINGS AND DISCUSSION

In the following sections, we present findings on streaming practices and communities. We discuss these findings in light of the sensitizing concepts to clarify the nature of streams as third places and the senses of community shared by their participants. We start by discussing factors that draw viewers to particular streams and how these factors influence stream community identity. We follow this with a discussion of the importance of viewer participation and influence in streams. We then proceed to a discussion of community regulars, addressing their roles in keeping stream communities inviting and promoting stream participation. Finally, we discuss how the streaming medium affords the formation of shared community history, and how it starts to break down in terms of supporting participation as audiences grow larger.

### Identification with Content, Streamer, and Community

When we asked viewers about how they started watching streams, almost invariably they responded that they wanted to learn something about a particular game. Many had similar experiences to V1's:

> I [had] just picked up League, and I wanted to improve. Why don't I just look for a streamer ... I found a bunch. I click on one, and this is pretty much how I joined.

Our own induction into the world of streaming started with wanting to learn to become better StarCraft II players in 2010 [25]. McMillan and Chavis note the importance of learning from other community members. He observes that the chance to benefit from the unique competencies of others is a strong motivating factor in community.

A major theme that emerged through our analysis is that streams develop an atmosphere that reflects the streamer's attitude and values. This projection of the streamer's personality then influences those who stay, because their attitudes and values are shared not only by the streamer, but by the community that emerges. For the viewers we interviewed, a sense of friendliness is an important criterion, because it let them feel comfortable enough to talk and interact with others. Friendliness came up repeatedly throughout the study as important for a healthy stream community. This sense of friendliness was frequently attributed to a streamer's congenial attitude and behavior. Interviewees identified other streamers who exhibit silliness or open anger on their streams. They noted that these qualities tend to draw a similar crowd. Even in these cases, the streamer still generally exhibits a congenial attitude toward their viewers. From a third places perspective, congeniality helps maintain a sense of openness and acceptance.

Several streamers indicated that they notice the reflection of their personality having a beneficial impact on their stream's community. S6 pointed out that this has a quality control effect on the stream; that if the streamer is calm, collected, and respectful, then the stream will attract viewers who are the same. S11 reported that she felt this effect helps her focus her stream and maintain meaningful interactions with her viewers. Female streamers are sometimes targets of sexist behavior. S11 developed strategies for dealing with this in the live streaming medium: "It really depends on the way you carry yourself ... because the attention isn't on me being a girl, its on the game ... if you go to any stream, what they [the streamer] is focused on is what chat will be focused on."

### The Importance of Interaction and Influence

McMillan and Chavis describe how communities serve to fulfill their members' emotional needs [18]. In the case of stream communities, many people watch streams for social interaction with other human beings with whom they identify. In the case of V1, participating in S11's stream is one of her primary means of socializing. She explains:

> I'm studying overseas. I find that there is no one that I can really identify with, and then I go online and there are all of these fucking awesome people, and they all like the same games. So it just comes natural to you.

Similarly, V4 is a stay-at-home mom. Participating in S8's stream gives her a chance to interact with others during the day while she is at home with her kids.

Conversely, many streamers stream because they want to build a community. They want to have a place where they can make friends and hang out. S1, S2, S3, S6, S7, S9, and S11 indicated that an important part of why they stream is because of the associated community and their chance to interact with members. Many see their regular viewers as friends. Their stream is their primary way to bring those friends together and sociably interact with them.

McMillan and Chavis also note that people are drawn to communities in which they can have influence and impact [18]. We observe this sense of attraction in stream communities. Viewers desire to be recognized and interacted with. While all the viewers we interviewed are all very involved in their respective stream communities, it is clear that for less involved viewers, even minimal personal interaction can be rewarding. This is generally understood by streamers. Many make special efforts to recognize every person at least once in their streams. V3, a long time viewer and moderator in many different streams explained that, "There are a lot of people in here that are self conscious, have other certain problems, and just saying hello and being nice to them, you know interacting with them, can really make their day."

Streamers also make concerted efforts to give participants chances to have influence on the stream in ways beyond that possible in chat. A common practice is for streamers to play games with their viewers to give them some time in the spotlight and a chance to stand out. S9 explained, "I think that is a big draw for a lot of people that come to my stream. They want to get a chance to play with the people that they watch." Streamers also create other participatory activities besides direct play for their viewers. For example, we participated in one of S7's streaming sessions, in which he was playing Family Feud, using answers suggested by his viewers.

Polls are frequently conducted on many streams. The streamer will either do a rough poll based on the chat, or create a poll on a site such as strawpoll.me. Polls are often used to decide what the streamer will do at critical points in a game. Polls are also used to make important community decisions. We participated in a poll to determine who should be made a moderator in S7's stream. V1 was similarly made a moderator in S11's stream.

There are many other ways that viewers can participate in streams. One particularly afforded by the streaming medium is the sharing and adoption of fan art created by a stream's viewers. Streamers can easily overlay these digital images over and around the game graphics and webcam video on their stream. For example, S9 has collected approximately 90 different viewer created artworks. He displays a slideshow of all of these periodically during game load screens. In another stream that focuses on tabletop role-playing games, the streamers accept viewer art of their encounters and display it on their stream during their play sessions. This practice is particularly interesting because it provides a direct way for viewers to have a lasting impact on the stream and make it their own.

### Becoming a Regular

Oldenburg describes how at the core of every third place are *regulars*, those people who most frequently visit the place [19]. McMillan and Chavis describes how the more people interact the more they will develop a shared history and are more likely they are to become close [18]. It is the regulars who have invested the most of themselves into the community and who most strongly define its qualities through their participation. By regularly showing up, participants start to build a level of trust and recognition among other regulars, which is hard to develop any other way.

This process of becoming a regular is strongly at play in stream communities. Those viewers who regularly show up, eventually become recognized community members. V1 described this process as it pertained to her becoming a mod and an important part of S11's stream:

> Sometimes people seem to place more eminence [sic] on you, because you are around a lot of the time, and to them you are a crucial element to the entire element of the channel ... according to [anon], I have been a pretty crucial part in helping the community grow. Cause when somebody sees some of their faces all of the time, I mean their names, it kind of helps to give them that sense of familiarity. And that is why we keep coming back.

When asked, streamers often identified regulars as their friends, those with whom they became closest. They felt like these were people that they identified with and could count on to continue as positive parts of their stream's community. When we asked V3 about S10's stream community, which became much smaller during the 9 months between when we interviewed S10 and V3, he indicated that the community was now mostly comprised of regulars. He reported that the community is now, "Stronger with the amount of people that are there because of how well we know each other now ... everybody kinda feels like they are part of it. That is why we show up every day." In stream communities, regular participation is the primary path to membership, through the development of familiarity, recognition, and history with other members.

### Regulars Encouraging Participation and Sociability

During our interviews, we inquired about moderators, because they clearly play an important role in stream communities. What we learned is that most moderators are given the status largely to demarcate them as regulars. This makes them easy to recognize, because they are given a special badge next to their handle in chat. What also became clear is that the role of moderators is not only to keep the discussion in line, but to engage viewers and promote participation and sociability.

This most often involves greeting viewers, answering questions, and trying to connect personally with newcomers. Greeting individual viewers is an activity that can be seen on most streams of a reasonably small size. As discussed before, being greeted is greatly appreciated by many viewers. It is an important part of some stream communities. Question asking and answering occurs constantly on most streams. For V2, having questions answered, his own and other viewers', by the streamer is his favorite part of participating in S5's stream. V1 also indicated that as a moderator, she felt like it was her responsibility to personally connect with viewers. Streamers indicated that the viewers they noticed frequently taking it upon themselves to fill these roles were those that they felt could be trusted to be moderators. Through these roles of community building and promotion of interaction, viewers become core members.

Viewers expect many of these roles to be performed by the streamer. Indeed, many of the streamers we interviewed are happy to perform them. However, they have to split their focus between the game they are playing and engaging with their viewers, which becomes difficult in some games, particularly with large numbers of viewers. Thus, having moderators and other regulars fill these roles helps a stream operate smoothly, and keeps viewers engaged.

According to Oldenburg, a third place's regulars are those "whose mood and manner provide the infectious and contagious style of interaction and whose acceptance of new faces is crucial." Regulars are the lifeblood of stream communities. They take it upon themselves to welcome viewers, whether newcomers or old regulars.

### Shared History through Hot & Cool Media

Stream communities grow and build a shared sense of history through the streaming medium. Both Oldenburg and McMillan note the importance of shared history in the formation of communities [18, 19]. It is a key part of the emotional connection that community members share.

Significant shared experiences in stream communities happen around ephemeral in-game events. We asked participants about favorite moments in the streams they participate in. Many indicated that these moments occur when something unusual happens in the game being played.

> S5: If there is a very exciting moment and I capture some exciting thing that people go crazy about in chat, that is the most rewarding thing.

We note that there are two parts to this kind of experience. The first is witnessing something surprising, the likes of which may never happen again. Seeing something like this live is a compelling feeling, the same kind of feeling that one might experience at a live concert or sporting event. Video games are an interesting context for live streams, because unique

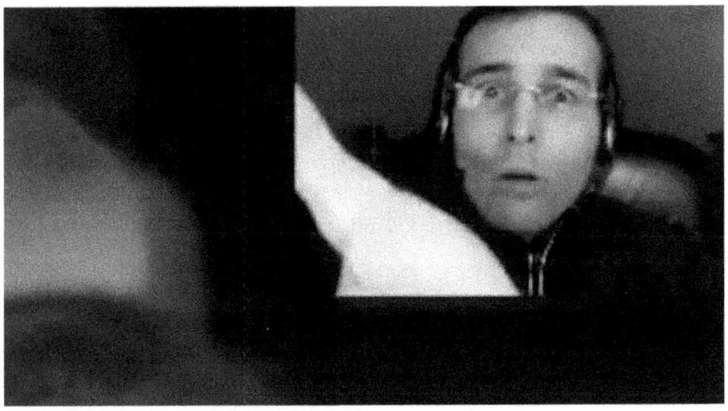

**Figure 3. Twitch viewers expect streamers to use webcams, so they can share their emotional reactions.**

ephemeral events happen relatively frequently, and can be specifically created by a streamer.

However, there is a second part to these experiences, in which the "chat goes crazy." It rapidly fills up with messages like "LOLOLOL" or other humorous phrases and emoticons specific to the game or the stream. For instance, "ヽ༼ຈل͜ຈ༽ﾉ RAISE UR DONGERS ヽ༼ຈل͜ຈ༽ﾉ" is a popular phrase on the streamer Imaqtpie's stream. This feedback lets everyone share in the emotional high of the moment. It reminds everyone that they are part of a unique group of people that saw something special as it happened. Streamers also reported that viewers expected them to have webcams, so that they could share their emotional reactions to these events through facial expressions (Figure 3).

The combination of cool with hot media affords the development of shared histories through intense game experiences, resulting in the formation of a stream community's emotional connection. Hot live video and game graphics enable audiences to observe unique, rich experiences. Cooler webcam video and coolest text chat enable them to contribute to and experience these things *together*, seeing each other's reactions.

### Big Streams and the Breakdown of Participation

We consider streams that draw more than 1,000 viewers to be *massive*. Usually, there are 20 to 60 massive streams live on Twitch. At the time of writing, we sampled a Twitch audience of approximately 440,000 viewers. Roughly, 20% were in streams of less than 1,000 viewers, and 50% were in streams with more than 5,000. The viewers we interviewed watch both massive and smaller streams. In smaller streams, the focus is more on participation, on interacting with other viewers and building community. When watching massive streams, they are there for the unique content available from that streamer. V3 explained this:

> [In] the big streams they are there for the person [the streamer] to be honest. They are not there to talk to a ton of people. They are there for the actual entertainment.

As a stream grows, the chat becomes a source of breakdowns. It transforms from a meaningful medium of discussion into an illegible waterfall of text, scrolling up the page so quickly that it cannot be read. Participants can no longer follow the conversation. At best, they can try to pull out a few comments every so often. When this happens, the one-on-one interaction between stream participants stops.

We note that in streams that are this large, the quality of the chat stream changes to something like the roar of a crowd in a stadium. It is possible to sense an overall feeling of the audience from a few recognized messages and fluctuations in the rate at which they appear. Posting in a chat stream like this is still a form of participation. However, the impact of any one individual is miniscule. Despite not being able to converse meaningfully in these streams, watching these steams is still compelling to some. V2 explained:

> Even if the chat is ... undesirable on the bigger streams, it's still nice to see how sometimes as much as 50k + people go to one place to see one person play.

From a third places perspective, anything that interrupts the flow of conversation is ruinous. Oldenburg cites the use of overly loud music, or the din generated by too many visitors, as ruining the potential of a third place: because it renders healthy conversation impossible [19]. In the same way, overly crowded chat rooms on Twitch streams destroy the potential for communities to form through participation.

When asked how many viewers they could interact with effectively, streamers frequently reported 100-150; some felt they could support up to 500. Past this threshold, they felt personal interaction between them and the viewers breaks down. For various reasons, some streamers want massive streams. Streamers who are full-time rely solely on donations and ad impression revenue for their financial income. This presents a problem, as S10, a full-time streamer reported:

> Honestly, if I could have [only] 150 people in my stream at all times, I would love that. But it's impossible to always have 150 viewers, at least in my position ... because I won't make any money at all.

There are other factors at play. Many streamers seek the fame and notoriety of a large audience. To others, success does not mean having a massive stream. Some focus on building their stream's community for the pleasure of being with those people. S3 and S7 reported that they specifically enjoy their communities, because they interact with their viewers meaningfully. They have been maintaining these communities for years. S3 explained:

> When you get a lot of people in the channel, it will no longer be my channel; it will be a flood of chat. I will no longer be able to keep up and it won't be me, because I won't be able to do what I normally do, and that is give everyone the time to talk. I actually feel guilty when I can't read everyone's chat.

#### *Subscribers Only: Sacrificing Openness for Quality*

An approach that some large streams have adopted is the use of chat mode called subscriber-only. In this mode, only people who pay a 5 USD monthly subscription fee to the stream can type in chat. The conversation is still public. Everyone can still read the chat, but only subscribers can contribute.

A motivation for subscriber-only mode is to cut down on the inherent noise of having thousands of people together in a single chat room. V3, who is a subscriber to several channels that use this interaction mode, explained:

> If there are a ton of viewers in there, that's why a lot of these sub only chats are a lot nicer. Obviously if you don't have a sub you can't talk, but if you do it's a lot nicer. If you want to be a part of that community and you have enough money to do so then you'll be able to do that and it's no big deal. Obviously, it kind of stinks for other people.

We found this point of view intriguing because it reveals the underlying user need for meaningful interaction. Prior to interviewing V3, our impression of subscriber-only mode was that it was used as a reward for subscribers at the expense of those who cannot afford the subscription. However, it became clear that, while this may be a factor, some stream communities are searching for ways to preserve their personal interactions despite the ever-growing sizes of stream audiences.

While the use of subscriber-only mode is a kind of kludge to maintain some of the coolness of the chat medium, it fundamentally undermines accessible participation in stream communities. Many streamers who use subscriber-only mode recognize this dilemma and turn it off occasionally or on a specific day of the week. Inevitably, after the mode is turned off, you will see the chat explode with messages like "FREEDOM!" and "RELEASE THE KRAKEN!". Non-subscribers are elated that they can participate in an open chat.

## RELATED WORK

We discuss two areas of online communities research particularly relevant to our own. First, we address the IRC communication modality and issues of information overload in chat based communities. Second, we review relevant work in online game communities. We compare and contrast them with Twitch streams. Finally, we consider eSports phenomena and how they have coevolved with live streaming.

### IRC Communities and Information Overload

IRC emerged in the late 1980's as a popular form of computer-mediated communication. It remains widely used today. Reid recognized IRC early on as a compelling communication modality that led to the emergence of intimate real-time online communities [21]. IRC's text chat is essentially a building block of the live streaming medium. Participants similarly engage in stream chats, and suffer similar difficulties. However, without game graphics and webcam video, IRC does not afford the same experiences as a live stream. As discussed above, live audio and video help stream communities develop emotional connection by sharing rich experiences of play.

Jones et al. identify information overload as a major problem of IRC [10]. They apply an information-processing constraints model [12] to investigate how IRC, by removing normal limits on communication, puts increased demand on human information-processing capabilities. As the number of posts increases, participants' capacities to digest and understand dialogue becomes overloaded. Thus, the number of messages per participant asymptotically approaches 0 as the number of participants increases. The main observable outcome is an inherent limit on the size of IRC channels. Specifically, they find that IRC can support a maximum of 300 concurrent users, with no more than 40 active posters [10].

We see a similar maximum, of 500 participants, in live streams. How are we to interpret then the emergence of streams with as many as 10 to 50 times this many viewers? While it is apparent that these streams often become more spectacle than conversation, we have seen that the shared experiences afforded by hot video are sufficient to loosely bind the stream audience together beyond the breakdown of meaningful conversation.

### Participation in Online Game Communities

A large body of work explores social interaction and community formation in multi-player online games [1, 20, 7, 6, 16]. We recognize a connection between communities emerging on Twitch, and those found in online games. In many cases, the lines between these communities blur. For instance, in the early months of S10's stream, he created an approximately 500 member Star Wars: The Old Republic guild, primarily comprised of his stream's viewers.

However, there are subtle differences between contexts. In a live stream, participants do share play experiences. However, most viewers are focused on the streamer's experience. They lack agency in the game world. Consistent with Oldenburg's discussion of a magic circle effect in third places [19], streams afford their own special space somewhere outside that of the game's, and still separate from the rest of the world. The integration of webcam video helps participants connect on a more personal level. Stream participants are not acting through in-game characters. They are acting as themselves.

Another difference is accessibility. Soukup identifies accessibility as a sticking point when it comes to treating computer-mediated communications (CMCs) as third places [24]. He argues while many CMCs are open, many are context specific and require specific knowledge and skills to participate. This issue comes up if we consider in-game environments as third places, as Ducheneaut et al. do [6].

Participation in games often requires considerable skill and engagement. In contrast, a viewer can log onto a stream with little to no understanding of the game being played, making it an accepting place for n00bs as well as veteran gamers. That viewer can then choose the level to which he or she participates, whether passively watching for days, or actively chatting daily for months. A stream viewer can come and go as s/he pleases; whereas, an involved player may be obliged to participate for the duration of a gaming session or raid. This may last 30 minutes to several hours. A gamut of levels is important, because it allows participants to seamlessly interweave their involvement with the third place in-between the more pressing demands of their home and work life [19].

Ducheneaut et al. observe that much interaction in Massive Multiplayer Online Role Playing Games addresses development of reputation and performing in front of others [7]. They predicted that "providing more ways for players to play not only for themselves, but 'in front' of others, would build on this trend." Live streaming instantiates this model of performative play, while supporting the formation of communities.

### eSports and Live Streaming

The emergence of eSports, the high-level play and spectating of competitive digital games, has coevolved with the rise of video game live streaming. The phenomena of eSports spectating was explored by Cheung and Huang [5]. They found similarities in spectating traditional and electronic sports. Spectacles of high-level play and information asymmetry in eSports games motivate people to watch. We found that while eSports spectating is a significant live streaming activity, many streams focus not on the highest level of play, but on social engagement and community building.

Kow and Young present a case study of media technologies supporting learning within eSports communities [14]. While they cite the importance of "Internet TV" as a medium, they do not discuss interactive components of live streaming. Kaytoue et al. recently examined Twitch as a platform for live streaming, developing a quantitative analysis of the growth of particular eSports streams [13]. Our research, in contrast, indicates that the formation of participatory communities is at the core of the live streaming experience. Large streams struggle to maintain meaningful social engagement.

## IMPLICATIONS FOR DESIGN

We present implications for the design of streaming media systems to support the formation of participatory communities. We show how mixing cool and hot media supports environments that foster the emergence of communities and serve as third places. We consider solutions to the breakdown of participation in large communities due to information overload.

### Integrate Cool & Hot Media to Form Third Places

While live streams are comprised of streaming video and IRC, both fairly commonplace technologies, the result is more than the sum of its parts. Cool text chat affords accessible participation and a medium through which to converse, the main activity of the third place. Conversely, hot video affords the sharing of rich experiences, driving the conversation and formation of shared history. The broadcast video of live streams is relatively cool in comparison to other video forms. We have shown how by mixing these media, streams function as third places for emergent online communities. Holistically, the live streaming medium is relatively cool, affording ample room for participation when scale is accounted for.

A key aspect of live streaming's mixed-media integration is that core participants can dynamically control the layout and mixture of visual media in a stream's broadcast. This empowers them to compose the media in situated ways to afford rich engagement through participation and shared experiences. Participants compose the presence, size, and layout of cool media components, such as webcams, chat logs, and viewer art, amidst hot game graphics. This compositing of hot and cool components is essential to the live streaming medium. We prescribe further investigation of how dynamic media composition can support participation in live streaming communities.

### Preserve Meaningful Interaction through Subdivision

As we have seen, the scale of streams sometimes grows very large. Large streams initialy draw viewers in with content that is unique and compelling, independent of how many are viewing. As more people start to watch, a stream stands out more. It draws more new viewers. Further, in many streams there is a sense that the community wants to grow. Streamers, moderators, and regulars interact with newcomers to make the stream inviting. Thus, the stream functions as a third place. However, there are no physical constraints, as in a bar or coffee shop, to keep the number of participants manageable. At a certain point, some streams cross a threshold and go viral.

As we have seen, conversation starts to break down as the audience scales. So what is there to do? We recount a decentralizing practice that we noticed within some Twitch streams. Smaller streamers will sometimes stream as they are watching some other major stream. These other streams, are usually huge and have completely unreadable chats. For instance, S11 recently gathered her comparatively small community of 600 to watch and converse about the League of Legends All-Star event, a stream with more than 200,000 viewers. We find this practice compelling because it enables smaller, already formed intimate communities to participate in large-scale events, while maintaining connection and meaningful interaction.

We hypothesize that, by developing mechanisms to subdivide large followings into smaller groups, we can help maintain meaningful participation. We note that Jones and Rafaeli have previously discussed the potential of splitting virtual publics to maintain legible communication [11]. However, they suggested doing this without regard for prevailing social connections within the group. We argue that, given the importance of shared histories in virtual third places, such as streams, segmentation should not be performed blindly. Randomly grouping people without regard for their interests, existing relationships, and participation history will destroy participants' senses of shared identity.

We propose to account for the vitality of community by building a model representing participants' interests, relationships, and histories. This model will inform algorithms that dynamically subdivide an audience into socially viable subgroups. Given the importance of shared histories, such a system needs to prioritize social continuity, as well as spontaneous encounters. One approach is to keep people in touch with their friends, acquaintances, and core community members, while filtering out other communications. This will enable users to maintain relationships and participate, while keeping communication legible. To inform the design of subdivision experiences, we propose drawing conceptual models from physical experiences of small groups in large crowds such as performances, rituals, academic conferences, and political demonstrations.

Given the impact that such subdivision would have on community members' social interactions and relationships, it is important to make such a system intelligible and accountable [3]. Make the model and its impact visible to users. We envision such a tool as mixed-initiative, inferring how to automate the complex subdivision process, while employing dialog to resolve key uncertainties with participants [9]. The system would identify potential social groups and provide mechanisms for dynamically forming them. The system would then clearly present information about identified subgroups to participants, enabling them to make informed decisions about how and when to sub-divide.

Of course, sub-division would not always be needed. It would be used in cases when communication overwhelms a single shared medium. As discussed, having space in which to participate and influence a community is important to members. Sub-dividing so that there is a space for everyone to participate, would be a big step in meeting participants' social needs. We recognize that creating such a system would not be simple. One approach to doing this without denying users' agency is to enable participants to toggle semi-automatic subdivision off and on. Other problems will lie in how to support core members engagement with the whole audience. In any case, user-centered iterative design will be essential.

## CONCLUSION

Oldenburg discusses the importance of third places in society, due to the social benefits they provide to participants [19]. The assemblage of hot and cool media enable streams to provide an open place for people to go socialize, play, and participate in something larger than themselves. The openness and participatory nature of streaming communities played an important role in our own initial interest. Participating in all of the streams throughout the study was rewarding in that it helped fulfill our own need to find a place to kick back, have a laugh, and be part of a community. During the study, we were always welcome in the different stream communities that we participated in. We experienced this as inherently gratifying.

We note that when we first started participating in streams, the largest still possessed only hundreds of viewers. Now that so many streams have grown to massive scales, pressure mounts to find ways to maintain streaming communities' participatory nature. We have proposed that this problem be approached through mixed-initiative subdivision into smaller groups that maintain both the sense of community and level of participation sought by stream community members.

The participation and experiences afforded by the cool and hot components of the streaming medium are integral to the nature of stream communities. The emergence of participatory communities on Twitch shows how the integration of cool and hot media can foster third places that broadly impact a gamut of digitally mediated real time experiences of entertainment and education. Cool + hot streaming media methods have the potential to similarly increase the sense of participation in second screen audience interaction experiences, which are being developed for television shows and sports [2]. Likewise, streaming media can help make MOOC education experiences more organic and participatory, and less factory like.

Streaming on Twitch establishes a new paradigm for online communities in a range of emerging contexts. The growing availability of streaming media capabilities will enable broadening impact. At the same time, Twitch has shown us how participation can break down as streams scale. Modeling social user experiences, and using these models to drive mixed-initiative interfaces has the potential to overcome breakdowns and scale participatory communities.

## REFERENCES


1. Bardzell, J., Nichols, J., Pace, T., and Bardzell, S. Come meet me at ulduar: Progression raiding in world of warcraft. In *Proc. CSCW* (2012), 603–612.
2. Basapur, S., Mandalia, H., Chaysinh, S., Lee, Y., Venkitaraman, N., and Metcalf, C. Fanfeeds: evaluation of socially generated information feed on second screen as a tv show companion. In *Proc. EuroiTV*, EuroiTV '12 (2012), 87–96.
3. Bellotti, V., and Edwards, K. Intelligibility and accountability: human considerations in context-aware systems. *Human–Computer Interaction 16*, 2-4 (2001), 193–212.
4. Bruckman, A., and Resnick, M. The mediamoo project constructionism and professional community. *Convergence: The Intl. J. of Research into New Media Tech. 1*, 1 (1995), 94–109.
5. Cheung, G., and Huang, J. Starcraft from the stands: understanding the game spectator. In *Proc. CHI* (2011).
6. Ducheneaut, N., Moore, R. J., and Nickell, E. Virtual "third places": A case study of sociability in massively multiplayer games. *JCSCW 16*, 1-2 (Apr. 2007), 129–166.
7. Ducheneaut, N., Yee, N., Nickell, E., and Moore, R. J. "alone together?": exploring the social dynamics of massively multiplayer online games. In *Proc. CHI* (2006).
8. Glaser, B. G. The constant comparative method of qualitative analysis. *Social Problems 12*, 4 (1965).
9. Horvitz, E. Principles of mixed-initiative user interfaces. In *Proceedings of the SIGCHI conference on Human factors in computing systems*, ACM (1999), 159–166.
10. Jones, Q., Moldovan, M., Raban, D., and Butler, B. Empirical evidence of information overload constraining chat channel community interactions. In *Proc. CSCW* (2008), 323–332.
11. Jones, Q., and Rafaeli, S. Time to split, virtually:'discourse architecture'and'community building'create vibrant virtual publics. *Electronic Markets 10*, 4 (2000), 214–223.
12. Jones, Q., Ravid, G., and Rafaeli, S. Information overload and the message dynamics of online interaction spaces: A theoretical model and empirical exploration. *Info. Sys. Research 15*, 2 (June 2004), 194–210.
13. Kaytoue, M., Silva, A., Cerf, L., Meira, Jr., W., and Raïssi, C. Watch me playing, i am a professional: a first study on video game live streaming. In *WWW Companion* (2012).
14. Kow, Y. M., and Young, T. Media technologies and learning in the starcraft esport community. In *Proc. CSCW* (2013).
15. Lincoln, Y., and Guba, E. *Naturalistic Inquiry*. Sage focus editions. SAGE Publications, 1985.
16. McEwan, G., Gutwin, C., Mandryk, R. L., and Nacke, L. "i'm just here to play games": social dynamics and sociality in an online game site. In *Proc. CSCW* (2012), 549–558.
17. McLuhan, M. *Understanding media: the extensions of man*. McGraw-Hill, 1964.
18. Mcmillan, D., and Chavis, D. Sense of community: A definition and theory. *Journal of Comm. Psych. 14*, 1 (1986), 6–23.
19. Oldenburg, R. *The great good place: Cafes, coffee shops, bookstores, bars, hair salons, and other hangouts at the heart of a community*. Da Capo Press, 1997.
20. Pearce, C. *Communities of Play: Emergent Cultures in Multiplayer Games and Virtual Worlds*. The MIT Press, 2011.
21. Reid, E. *Electropolis: Communication and Community on Internet Relay Chat*. 1991.
22. Rheingold, H. *The virtual community: Homesteading on the electronic frontier*. Basic Books, 1993.
23. Simmel, G., and Hughes, E. C. The sociology of sociability. *American Journal of Sociology* (1949), 254–261.
24. Soukup, C. Computer-mediated communication as a virtual third place: Building oldenburg's great good places on the world wide web. *New Media & Society 8*, 3 (2006), 421–440.
25. *StarCraft II: Wings of Liberty*. Blizzard Entertainment, 2010.

# Long Tail TV Revisited: From Ordinary Camera Phone Use to Pro-Am Video Production

**Oskar Juhlin, Arvid Engström, Elin Önnevall**
MobileLife @ Stockholm University
[oskar, arvid, elino]@mobilelifecentre.org

## ABSTRACT

Pro-Am live video producers broadcast events on a regular basis. Their continuous content generation can teach us something of what it takes for amateurs, who currently struggle with mastering the video medium, to become proficient producers. We learn from media theory that Pro-Ams are distinguished from professionals in terms of inherent skills and identities, and have therefore focused on these characteristics. Our ethnographic study adds to this research by showing on-going challenges that the former face in their production, i.e. how their learning practices are situated and related to particular settings. Learning and development of skills are done as organizations, rather than as individuals. Furthermore, the recurrent nature of both events and broadcasts appears to be an important condition for establishing the terms needed to carry out a production, and to learn the skills of a producer. This understanding may explain in part why accounts in previous research point to such difficulties in mastering the medium. The findings guide design to better support activities contiguous with the set-up of the production, rather than the broadcast per se.

### Author Keywords

Video, camera phones, ethnography, user-generated content, live video, Pro-Am, learning, organizational theory, media studies, identity, negotiation

### ACM Classification Keywords

H.5.m Information interfaces and presentation (e.g., HCI): Miscellaneous

## INTRODUCTION

The ubiquity of camera phones and consumer-level digital cameras has brought great anticipation in the public discourse of how new video services and new forms of use would emerge and become everyday practice [36]. News coverage has incorporated high profile examples of videos captured by bystanders to illustrate breaking news reports from events around the world [1], as well as more negative discussions of privacy implications of video capture "anytime and anywhere" [29,18].


*CHI 2014*, April 26 - May 01 2014, Toronto, ON, Canada
Copyright 2014 ACM 978-1-4503-2473-1/14/04...$15.00.
http://dx.doi.org/10.1145/2556288.2557315

Anderson´s concept of "Long Tail" TV-content describes the phenomenon of niche content becoming increasingly available and in demand, as the costs for production and distribution fall [4], and content that "...is not available through traditional distribution channels but could nevertheless find and audience" [3]. Apart from old or non-mainstream TV shows getting an extended life cycle, through on-demand programming, he also includes "video that could and would be made if only there were a good way to find an audience for it." [3]. At the time this was written, there were only indications of what this far end of the tail would contain. With time, we now see more distinct categories of video services forming. On the one hand, there is everyday "snapshot" video captured and shared mostly with groups of friends, and on the other hand more niche services for advanced user-generated video production, as seen in commercial development and research. The concept draws on a growing category of amateurs who aspire to meet professional standards in various forms of media production. This emerging category has been labeled Pro-Ams (for Professional-Amateurs) [27], and has been described in contemporary media studies, in terms of their motivations and the varying skills they possess [6,36]. It is the challenges in achieving these skills that will be discussed in this paper.

In HCI research, mobile video has received substantial interest, in work describing the characteristics of mobile video use [25,29,34], investigations of new features and specific use domains for the next generation of user-generated mobile video [16,10,8,13,41]. As a counterweight to the anticipation of Pro-Am video, Lehmuskallio et al., in a key study of everyday mobile video use, point to a slower and much more mundane development [29]. They find that people model their mobile video capture on snapshot photography, rather than imitating professional media and the novel uses proposed in the public discourse.

Adopting mobile video in the more production-oriented sense, beyond snapshot video, is far from trivial. Previous research has identified a number of characteristics that make video production challenging. The need for editing material before presenting it is a burden; the majority of user-created videos are never edited [29,25,43]. Finding relevant content and capturing it in the moment is problematic [22,29]. Visual storytelling in video is challenging and involves skills that until recently were exclusive to the professional domain. Video-specific controls, e.g. beginning and ending a clip smoothly, require more effort than taking a photograph [16,22,29,43]. Filming also requires a focus that may distract from attending an event [16,29]. With live video, these problems are emphasized further, as production decisions become increasingly time critical [22,21].

This paper is built on the premise that: a) a smaller subset of users are candidates for adopting more advanced mobile video production services e.g. those proposed in HCI: b) there are real problems that non-professional adopters of these technologies have to overcome to become video producers. Some of these problems for individual users are described in research, but there is a lack of understanding of how aspiring video producers manage these problems, and develop new skills within existing social settings.

We will here present an ethnographic study of three independent video producers who recurrently produce and broadcast live video from sports events in modern dance, volleyball and football. Rather than viewing ProAm producers as having a set of individually contained characteristics, we will here view them as a transitional category, where aspiring producers are practically working on acquiring the necessary skills. In doing so, we draw on recent theory on learning, to unpack how production skills and being acknowledged as a producer are intimately related and develop over time. Our analysis of Pro-Am video production reveals both members' learning practices and a more social, heterogeneous and situational form of knowledge acquisition. The key contribution can be summarized in two points. First, the skills of aspiring video producers are developed organizationally and individually, both within the production teams and in negotiations with others in the context of the covered event. Second, recurrent production where producers cover a series of events over time seems to be more than a quantitative sign indicating mastery of this medium. Rather, their recurrent production seems to be an important condition for both individual and institutional learning, making the broadcasts possible.

Taken together, this understanding may explain in part why accounts in previous research, of single users struggling with the affordances of the live video, point to such difficulties in mastering the medium. It also points to interesting directions for design, and especially the way learning could be improved by finding new ways beyond copying professional tools to camera phone applications.

## BACKGROUND

Our analysis and is influenced by three strands of research i.e. research on human computer interaction with video; media studies analysis of the mechanisms, including skills and motivation, that drive Pro-Am production, and finally theories on knowledge development in pedagogics.

### User-generated video in HCI

The term "snapshot video", used by Lehmuskallio and Sarvas in their study of early camera phone use [29], accurately anticipated what has grown to be common user behaviours in mobile video. In their study, they find that people model their mobile video capture on snapshot photography, rather than imitating professional media and the novel and high profile uses proposed in the public discourse. Years later, their proposed design implications – simple editing, quick browsing, summarization and restricting the length of shared videos – may seem obvious in the light of available features in today's services. But the services that are now gaining broad adoption (e.g. Instagram Video, Vine and Viddy), clearly prioritize precisely these types of features focusing on sharing with close friends, ease of use and aesthetics over advanced features such as publishing, multicamera collaboration and live broadcasting. In the race the future success story of mobile video, these services have closely modeled themselves on snapshot mobile photography, which is evident from their focus on features such as aesthetically appealing filters, one-click sharing on social networks enabling the type of "distant closeness" Van House observed in photo sharing [38], and tight limits on clip length (6 and 12 seconds for Vine and Instagram, respectively). This supports Lehmuskallio's et al concept of "snapshot video" being the key type of use for a large majority of users, with only a gradual change to more "professional" or "production-oriented" practices.

On the other hand, HCI research has presented convincing cases for such production-oriented uses for a smaller niche of more advanced users such as local producers or enthusiast visitors at live events [16,13,8] and in specific use domains such as emergency rescue [10], and education [41]. The contrast of these proposed technologies to more mundane video sharing practices points to two main directions for user-generated mobile video production; a broader use of "snapshot video", while the more advanced technologies proposed in research realistically will be targeting a smaller subset of the growing masses of camera phone users, closer to the niche producers of "Long Tail TV".

### Media studies on Pro-Ams' skills and motivation

Media theory has taken an interest in the emergent area of Pro-Am production, and especially in understanding the characteristics of the people involved. Knowledge and motivations are seen as something an individual contains, and thus they can be discussed separately. First, Pro-Am producers are seen as carrying a specific set of skills, whereas professional categories have often arisen out of a scarcity of production tools rather than unique skill sets [36]. The wide dissemination of digital production technology has blurred these categories and brought a range of content that does not easily fit the one or the other [12]. At the same time, views on amateur production tend to be skewed towards the notion of users' lack of professional expertise and knowledge. The distinction between them often focuses on possessing skills and being a competent practitioner [23]. Professionals are often seen as possessing exclusive domain knowledge, while amateurs are seen either as inept, or having romantic qualities of authenticity. The successes of early amateur production projects were surprising and difficult for some of their counterparts in the more traditional media business to fully explain. Benkler [6] argues that viewing them as curiosities or transient fads misses the bigger picture, a new mode of production emerging in the margins of the most developed production systems in the world. While people do act for material gain, they are also driven by a diverse range of other motivations. In their work on commons-based peer production, Benkler and Nissenbaum [7] argue that a set of motivations is one of the key characteristics of these new production forms. They are made up by social cues and motivations, rather than monetary compensation or commands, as traditional production is organized. These motivations can be structured in a number of virtues or attributes that participants adhere to, divided into four broad clusters. First, a group of attributes related to autonomy and independence has been a driving force in e.g. the open source programming movement, operating outside of the industry. Second, creativity, productivity and being active in engaging in one's interests make up a key theme. Third, many peer production projects arise from charity and altruism, speaking to participants' desire to contribute to a good cause. Fourth, and thematically related to the third, are social connectedness and a sense of membership. This involves the conception of the self as being part of a community and contributing to a collective effort. The sense of belonging to a community seems to be an overarching motivation, but the other motivations for participation are highly individual, and often change over time [26]. The first two clusters reflect personal aspirations, while the second pair is inherently social in nature. Benkler et al. [7] conclude that social motivations reinforce personal ones; they are rewarding in themselves as well as helping participants be autonomous and develop individual skills. The support for both personal and social motivations, and the fact that participants can join a project with any one of these motivations, are success factors in peer production.

In his work on online culture, Shirky [36] argues that these clusters of motivations – desires for autonomy and creativity, social connectedness and generosity – are intrinsic motivations that people possess in varying combinations, and that people will gravitate to experiences that reward them. The motivations are not new, but the activities associated with them used to be largely private, such things as making home videos, playing in a band, or collecting photographs. The new practices of amateur production in the public sphere can be seen as an extension of these activities with a number of important constraints removed; finding likeminded peers, organizing socially beyond small groups, producing content collaboratively, and distributing content to other people on a large scale.

In sum, the approach taken displays an understanding of this group of media producers as containing a set of characteristics, which they bring into use when creating media. Their specific competence or identity explains the character of the resulting content. At the same time, media theorists also describe Pro-Am production as an evolving entity where the participants learn by doing productions of various sorts. In this perspective, something seems to happen in production, and the sum of the activities would not be reducible to motivations and skills they contained when engaging in an event. What is missing in this research, which we need to understand to discuss the possibilities of amateur video production in particular, are accounts of the challenges that faces Pro-Am in on-going production.

### Theories of learning and identity

A body of literature within pedagogics understands skills and identities as characteristics of individuals [2, 17, 37], similar to the perspective outlined above [7]. Lately, research has emerged that extends this understanding by recognizing features in learning as emergent, also being linked in a complex way to an individual identity, social interaction, situations and institutions.

First, the development of skills is connected to the feeling of being someone. Learning creates an inner dialogue [20] forming a connection between skills and identity. The experience of mastering or understanding something creates personal development as various tools become manageable. Second, learning depends on social agreement including power struggles, which define learning situation "for self and others [2]." A person's own definition of their learning, practice and identity is therefore also dependent on how others interpret them. Murphy and Hall [31] believe that "learning and knowledge can be understood as the relationship between people in a certain activity and learning." Wenger [42] suggests that "knowing / knowledge is shaped by a kind of negotiating with the other." Third, development of skills is a gradual process that is tightly connected to the environment: "…their interaction is characterized by a clear division of labor tied to their positions as teacher and student, or, more specifically, instructor and instructed [30]." Learning by doing is interactionally dependent on the physical setting, as well as how the learning unfolds. Taken together, we can see learning as "a movement deeper into practice, and as a transformation of identity, where identity is understood as evolving forms of competence [30]". Fourth, learning can be understood as done by institutions and organizations [19]. Learning is then understood as being "…undertaken by members of an organization to achieve organizational purposes, takes place in teams or other small groups, is distributed widely throughout the organization and embeds its outcomes in the organization's system, structure and culture [9]." Engeström [15] refers to the learning of an "activity system" where all work within a group, or organization, is formed by rules, cultural artifacts (e.g. meetings and physical artifacts like computers). The organizational approach brings with it a new perspective [19]. Both identities and skills are those of a collection of people that are distributed. In sum, these theories provide an enriched understanding of the challenges facing amateur video producers, when learning is embedded in a context.

## METHOD AND SETTING

Inspired by anthropology, and in line with several ethnographic studies within HCI, we use an ethnographic approach, which allows a focus on interpretation of in-situ interviews and field notes [33,35,39], complemented with audio recordings, to inquire into how production is performed and learned. The method provides accounts of people's practices and their orientations, in environments. Within anthropological ethnography, the main instrument for acquiring data about what people do, as well as their motivations and identities, is the ethnographer per se and the understanding that grows out of spending time with people. The presentation reflects our ambition to discuss a set of situations occurring among several Pro-Am producers. Hence, the need to present several excerpts and three cases. The study draws on three full day observations of volleyball events, two days of observations of football events and two days of observations of dance events. Interviews were made during setup and breaks, and after the broadcasts. The collected data consists of audio files, photos, our own video recordings and field notes. All of the interviews were done with key people within the three organizations, i.e. people who were mainly involved in producing the broadcast. The interviews were recorded and transcribed. The transcriptions were then read several times by the research team and specific topics of particular interest were chosen. The Pro-Ams were selected because they frequently broadcast different local sport events.

**Fig. 1. a-c Pro-Am producers of volleyball match, football match and dance event.**

We searched two websites for live video [5,32] to identify repeated broadcasters, who were then contacted. We recruited three individuals that were in charge of the broadcasts, with varying experience in live video production. The football broadcasts are produced a couple of times a month during the season, and they have been active since 2008. The volleyball producer has broadcast video since the beginning of 2006. Throughout the season, he sometimes broadcasts several times a week. The dance events we studied were broadcast only for the second and third time, but were supervised by persons with extensive experience of the medium.

The studies were made in five different cities in Sweden during the spring of 2011. The volleyball producer is using one main video camera, which he typically mounts high on one of the stands. He also operates this camera for player interviews after the game. A small mixer table is used to combine the video stream, with different audio tracks. A commentator's microphones, headphones and computers are also part of the equipment. The producer of the soccer tournament has two computer screens, of which one shows the broadcast and the other present graphics and updated scores. Most of the technical equipment is placed in the secretariat but they also have a microphone mounted to the fence by the field and a sky lift where the video camera is placed. During the first broadcast occasion, the dance producers have one video camera and one large microphone placed on one of the stands. A computer with the broadcasting information is placed in a commentator booth just beside the equipment. At the second broadcast site the producers are situated close to the floor. All their equipment is at a single table, except for the microphones that are positioned by the dance floor.

## ANALYSIS

In the following, we analyze the ways in which Pro-Ams' continuous learning can be understood both from an individual perspective and from an organizational view. In the first part of the analysis we discuss aspects of learning as individuals; its contingent and situated character as well as the intermingling of learning and identity creation. In the second part we discuss how Pro-Am productions are faced with the challenge of developing as an organization, and in many occasions within an existing institution. This challenge includes socially negotiating the character of the broadcast and negotiating learning opportunities.

### Individual and situated learning

With reference to the following two excerpts, we discuss how a perspective on individuals' learning refers to specific situations, rather than universal skills, and that learning blends into identity making.

#### *Attending to situated instructions*

The individualistic perspective on Pro-Ams' learning, as outlined in media studies, is relevant also when accounting for our producers, such as in the following case when beginners are trained by attending to instructions given by experienced producers. Then and there it is a single person who is acquiring skills from another better-trained individual. Instructions are given by a producer who is simultaneously organizing the event and producing the broadcast. The latter involves handling the equipment and instructing the assigned cameraperson, who could be a parent, a sibling or another community member. In the following excerpt the new cameraperson is a sister to a player, who has volunteered to capture today's game from a sky lift.

**Excerpt 1: Instructing others in the community to broadcast**

| | |
|---|---|
| *01 Producer* | *The sound will not be up there so you can talk and* |
| *02* | *chew gum and whatever you want.* |
| *03 Camera* | *That was what I was most worried about* |

*04 Producer We put the sound [microphone] here.*
*05 Camera Yes:::*
*06 Producer So just to follow the (inaudible). Follow the game*
*07 and if it gets to a shootout. Patrick shows you*
*08 how you can pull up the sky lift basket so you are*
*09 almost straight above us here. Otherwise you*
*10 have the pole in the middle of the picture.You have*
*11 to bring the lift more outward. Are you afraid*
*12 of heights?*
*13 Camera Oh, no.*
*14 Producer It's like an amusement park.*
*15 Associate It will be fine.*
*16 Producer Yes, it's fine.*
*17 I'm happy that you could do this.*

The excerpt demonstrates how the senior organizer instructs the beginner to use visible features in the local setting to get the right camera angle (line 9). The instructions also consider technical features of the sky lift (line 7), something that also has to do with the type of content that will be filmed. The producer is concerned with getting as much as possible of the field in view (line 7) and to move the sky lift "almost straight above us here." The physical environment, that is the pole, is also used to explain what should and should not be included in the picture. Learning from instructions depended on understanding its situated relevance. Lindwall et. al [30] describe how such learning develops through instructions-in-interaction, highlighting in this case both the relationship between the instructor and the amateur and how it is "characterized by both parties being reciprocally attentive and finely tuned towards each other and the developing skill."

The excerpt further demonstrates how the instructions account for the specifics in the situation, such as the need for the producer to attend to the heterogeneous interest of the cameraperson and the event management. First, the instructions are easy going and attentive to the beginner's enjoyment, e.g. mentioning chewing gum (line 2) and likening the production to an amusement park (line 14). The producer motivates the photographer by suggesting that she is in an "amusement park", where the sky lift becomes a tool for her to enjoy herself. This is in line with the concept of "recreational orientation" [16] which accounts for the need to provide for amateurs' attention to their own enjoyment, and for other peoples' demands on them, when enabling user-generated content production as part of their leisure. This attentiveness to the present cameraperson also includes soothing. Another adult tells the photographer (line 15) that everything "will be fine". This consoling of her probably anticipates the photographer's fear of heights, as expressed in line 12. The producer continues assuring her "yes, it's fine", which points to the necessity to account for the experience of the team members. Furthermore, the producer motivates her by referring to how pleased he is that she is willing to make this effort for the community (line 17), which shows his attempt to form a community. In an interview, he describes this motivation in a way that resembles Benkler's et al. [7] account of ProAms' attention to "social connectedness."

Second, the instructions account for the producer's needs to keep the production manageable and simple, in order to make it fit with other event management that requires his attention. The quick instructions and delegation of the tasks to the team can be seen as doing the two tasks of. supporting broadcasts and providing space for event management. The fact that the broadcast producer is focused on the organization of the event as a whole, factors into the instructional situation, and make it a locus for "various forms of dialogical interaction [35]."

In all, the instructions given from an individual to another do not transfer a set of well-bounded knowledge. The learning is intertwined with the situated event itself. Instructions also account for heterogeneous needs and motivations of the individual, broader organizational requirements, and the situated setting at hand.

### *Individual learning by mimicking professionals*

The next excerpt reveals how learning is blended into the producers' identity making. The volleyball producer learns through mimicking professionals, but then mixes acquiring skills with the process of acquiring an identity, which is not always the same thing. In the interview excerpt below, he discusses how he learn to improve his skills:

**Excerpt 2: Getting inspiration from professional production**

*01 Producer ...describes every little flower as a great work of*
*02 art, or whatever you do. Mats Strandberg on*
*03 "Radiosporten" for example, is very good at that.*
*04 He can make a tennis match exciting on the radio.*
*05 And it's like, two players who play back and*
*06 forth. It is so unbelievably exciting just because he*
*07 is so good at commentating.*
*08 Researcher Are you trying to get inspiration from television*
*09 sports and radio sports that exist today?*
*10 Producer Yes, absolutely. Whatever TV sports you are*
*11 watching you look at it in a different way when you*
*12 are doing it yourself. You can't watch a game*
*13 on TV without observing that 'ok, that's how they*
*14 solved that TV-production'. You create ideas of*
*15 your own and so on.*

To become a skilled cameraperson and commentator he watches TV and listens to radio and then copies what the professionals are doing. In his strategy of learning by doing, he strives to develop an expert's eye and the practical skills that come with that perspective, through "embodied apprenticeship [40]." His domain knowledge is a useful reference, but attaining the actual production skills must be done through practice in a broadcast situation.

At the same time, he is also striving to acquire an identity of a professional broadcaster. This is visible in the outfits he wears such as a suit during the play-offs, and specific clothes in colors matching his own channel logotype. His personal car is also marked with the same logotype. In this sense, he displays what Wenger calls "ways of being a person" in a certain context [42] i.e. both the way he presents himself and the way he learns. The way this is done makes it difficult to separate his identity creation, thorough the visual expressions on signs and clothes, from his focused attention to professional broadcasts on TV and radio commenting. His aspiration makes visible how learning is intertwined with developing an identity.

### Organizational learning

In the following we will turn our attention to how learning ProAm production occurs through institutional development. Changes in broadcasting are conceived as occurring in-between people in particular settings. In particular, we discuss a controversy on sound capturing during a dance competition, and a discussion during a volleyball tournament. These cases display various aspects of the value of an organizational perspective in ProAm production such as pointing to necessary "strategies" in which to alter the institutions that affect the end result. Here we point to event adaptation, or visualization of a "professional" identity.

#### *Negotiating production through event adaptation*

We examine a situation where the sound capture needs to be negotiated when a conflict emerges during a dance broadcast. The participants in the discussion are members of the broadcast production crew and the competition's referees. It has come to the former team's attention that the referees want to change the setup of the production system and move some microphones, since the discussions, concerning the dancers' performances, which they considered to be private, were broadcast live. In the following excerpt, the producer (P) and his assistant (PA) discuss what to do with the researcher (R):

**Excerpt 3: Discussion on how to please referees**

| | |
|---|---|
| *01 P:* | *If they see a mic, we'll have to hope they'll keep quiet.* |
| *02 PA:* | *Can't we put up a big sign. (laughs)* |
| *04 P:* | *(inaudible) shows! It's not a hidden microphone.* |
| *05 R:* | *Did they hear anything? Or did they discover...* |
| *06 PA:* | *No, they only heard like by coincidence...On Air. I can* |
| *07* | *write that (laughs) Should I do that? Should I write* |
| *08* | *"On Air?"* |

The topic of the controversy is which part of the event that should be broadcast, and especially who should be audible by the online audience. The location of the microphone becomes a visual and concrete manifestation of that discussion. The producers had placed them close to the dance floor, which is also the area where the referees are standing.

The discussion makes visible that a number of people are involved in making decisions that affect the media broadcast. The producers must make their case in a particular way to be allowed to broadcast from the event. The producers pursue a particular strategy, i.e. they try to negotiate with the referees and solve the problem by letting the microphone stay and by asking the referees to adapt and "keep quiet" (line 1). The producers turn the controversy into a problem of visualization. If they make the broadcast more visible, for example by displaying a sign saying "on air" (line 6), the referees would accept its presence and adapt by not speaking about delicate matters.

The conflict is further handled in between themselves by joking about the event as if the referees were stupid not to understand what the microphone was doing. The humor itself can also be seen as handling the referees' rejection of what the production crew try to achieve; an interesting broadcast including the sound generated by the dancers. That rejection is then handled amongst themselves by not being completely serious in their own role as Pro-Ams. Their answer to the critique of the ways they do the broadcast could be seen as them "playing" the role of producers, rather than attempting to fully have that identity.

In sum, this negotiation makes visible the adaptations that are necessary when doing Pro-Am production. If the referees get it their way, the setup of the system needs to be changed, which affects the sound captured since they need to put the microphone somewhere else. Then the Pro-Am production gets a more marginal position within the event. If the producers get it their way, the microphone stays, but the sound, i.e. what is said in front of it, will be altered. Hence, developing the media and learning how to do a production depends on the acceptance it receives. Second, the identities of the producers are not entirely in their own hands but dependent on what other people think of them.

#### *Defending production by evoking professionalism*

In the following example we discuss how Pro-Ams' learning is embedded into an organizational context, and specifically how the role of professionalism is evoked.

In the excerpt, the person who is responsible for the broadcast discusses the setup of the system with an event organizer. The producer is a former volleyball player and referee, and manages a one-man production company beside his second job as a bus driver. This producer is always trying to make sure that he has an overview spot, which is usually situated on the top of the stands. In this case, the producer (P) has been given an undesirable broadcast location and raises the issue with the event organizer (EO):

**Excerpt 4: Discussing the set up with an event organizer**

| | |
|---|---|
| *01 EO* | *Where do you want to be? Do you want to broadcast* |
| *02* | *without a lot of disturbing noises then there for you.* |
| *03 P:* | *Yes. I think that will be difficult if you want to pan with* |
| *04* | *the camera and stuff.* |
| *05 EO:* | *You can't (stand by) the emergency exit. The firemen will* |
| *06* | *think it's bad. There you have the web-broadcast from* |
| *07* | *Hallands' News and the radio and here's your own.* |

The producer refers to his inability to move the camera around (line 3-4), whereas the event organizer argues that alternative places are either not permitted (line 5-6) or taken by other media producers (line 6-7). At the suggested location he can be by himself. The discussion makes visible the production as negotiated and dependent on its role in a wider organizational context. There are several people who have influence on the broadcast content, e.g. the location of equipment. In the end it depends on broader organization, and the production should be seen as something that should fit into something that is already there as an event before Pro-Am productions.

The following case is similar to the previous excerpt, since it involves a discussion that has consequences for media capture, but it is different since the latter involves an explicit formulation of the identity that is challenged along with the positioning of production equipment. The volleyball producer usually attaches some of his microphones to the referees and team leaders. During the game he can then switch the broadcast sound from his own commentating to the teams' 'technical chat', specifically when there is a break in the game. On this occasion, a team leader refuses to wear a microphone, which seems to make the producer frustrated: He says: "This would never happen if it were [national public service television]".

His comment can be understood in the light of his aspiration to being or becoming a professional (see excerpt 2). Thus, he interprets the conflict as being due to the team leader not recognizing him as a professional.

Pro-Am production is often an endeavor that depends on an organization. The production teams often consist of more than a single person, and the events that are being broadcast are in themselves organized and have existed much longer than the broadcast activity. The broadcaster therefore needs to fit their organization into this social space. This mixing of the new and the old organizational tasks sometimes depends on changes in the latter. The organizer of the event needs to help out, for example by providing space and changing their behavior in front of cameras and microphones. Thus, Pro-Ams depend on learning skills and identities among people who would not describe themselves as video producers.

Furthermore, we see that there are negotiations that involve both learning and identity creation, which takes place in a specific situation. First we have pointed out the way that this situation depends on environmental concerns such as how the system features are located at a specific site. Second, we have pointed at the strategies through which the producers negotiate a broadcast according to their requests. These strategies include either a narrow and visual request for adaptation, or a broader visualization of a "professional" identity. If these claims are not recognized by the broader organization, it will have consequences for learning, identity, and the actual broadcast.

## DISCUSSION

The findings have implications for the HCI community, for media theory, and for future directions of design of technology for Pro-Am video production.

### From contained skills to learning by doing

This ethnographic study revealed how video producers not only bring knowledge into a specific broadcast event, but also learn by doing, using strategies such as instructions by experienced broadcasters and mimicking professionals. This perspective draws attention to the relation between the skills and identity of an individual. First, we saw how the organizer of the football event gave instructions to a novice cameraperson. Importantly, the instructions included statements, which *combined practical advice* on how to turn the camera with *motivations* including the enjoyment in that practice, as well as the value for the rest of the community. The instruction in action was thus designed to combine production advice with motivations. Second, the study also revealed the importance of *mimicking* features of professional broadcasts, such as the way a famous commentator narrates a game. This learning approach was also made visible by both clothing and branding, which were used to form a complementary identity. Thus, in both cases we saw the importance of Pro-Ams' learning in concrete productions, through various strategies, and the way that both skills and identity were linked to each other and co-developed over time. The need to learn by doing production in a situation adds to the challenges previously discussed in HCI; editing [29,25,43], finding and capturing relevant content [22], handling controls [22,29, 43] and combining production with other interests [16, 29].

*Designing tools for individual learning.* In designing production technology, there is a natural focus on guiding the user in the production process, with the aim to achieve a satisfactory end result, i.e. a broadcast or produced video. Based on our findings on the growing class of live video Pro-Am producers, learning and improving skills are key motivations that could be emphasized in design even further. Returning with these findings to HCI, tools and interfaces could be designed to support learning styles, such as mimicking professionals or engaging community members, as well as production skills. The type of learning seen here would be further supported by tools for recording and reflecting upon one's own production process. Using the current study context as an example, this could involve automatically documenting configurations and process steps, e.g. of setups of cameras and microphones, and recording editing decisions to be revisited afterwards.

### From individual development to organizational learning

Our findings expand on current theory's explanations of the Pro-Am phenomenon as consisting primarily of individually held qualities and motivations. In this study we have shown Pro-Am production to sometimes be an organized effort in the sense that it is dependent on *several people*; it is *embedded* into pre-existing organizations; it is *situated in a physical setting* and *socially negotiated.* These general features are true for all broadcast occasions we observed, and would arguably transfer to similar forms of socially situated media production. First, even in the single camera set ups studied here, two of the cases were dependent on several people for their operation. The football production required an instructor, who also did the mixing and broadcasting, as well as a camera operator. The dance broadcast required a producer, an assistant, and an expert advisor. Second, the broadcast production activities must be integrated, or embedded in, the on-going production of the event itself, including its present audience, other media and the rules of the game. Both the Pro-Ams' occasional dependence on several people, and the request to fit with other organized activities, require us to understand production as a collective activity that needs to be negotiated and structured. Third, those activities were *situated* in local environments, with fire escape doors at specific locations and dance floor areas for referees. These contingent characteristics are approached by the members of the organizations, in discussions or negotiations, which involve skills, identities and strategies. For instance, professional identities were at play in acquiring sounds of the referees during the dance contest. In such situations, the characteristics that are negotiated appear then and there, in the situation. Furthermore, the necessary understanding of the identities of the participants is distributed in the organization and part of what is at stake, for example in a conflict. Compared to media studies, and the views presented there on Pro-Am production, this is a different perspective, which highlights negotiations, collaboration and strategies as important in media production.

*Non-disruptive design.* Tools for media production in contexts where the production does not have full professional authority should be designed to be as non-disruptive as possible. They should ideally be quick to set up, and not interfere with the covered activity, in competing for space or for the attention of other participants. Tools derived from professional technology (e.g. consumer video cameras, studio equipment and software suites) are typically designed for performance and not with such considerations in mind. Mobile technology, such as camera phones and microphones connected through wireless networks, has the potential of reducing bulky and space demanding equipment. It also offers mobility outside of fixed activity settings and is less intrusive when capturing media. Another potential lies in designing spaces that are intended for both activities and media capture. Following the model of large sports arenas, where design considerations are made in order to integrate both activities without unnecessary interference, e.g. by integrating some of the infrastructure and tools in the physical space.

These finding are of relevance for established HCI research on media spaces, with its interest in live video and audio communication to provide a sense of "presence" [28,14,11]. Our analysis suggests that we should not only consider the design of the digital systems, but also the design of architecture more broadly. It is not just about broadcasting the activities in the physical context, but also about how the physical context could be designed to support it.

*Design for inter-organizational communication: "social tally lights".* Professional cameras are equipped with a red tally light, which indicates to a cameraperson that they are "on air", an important communication feature in multi-camera broadcasts. Our findings reveal complex institutional arrangements, such as negotiations on where to place microphones, which depend on tense discussions between people at the event as well as on the making of paper notes and signs. These activities might be supported by digital interaction. For example, a mobile device that is similarly placed beside a referee could communicate with surrounding people through its screen. It could then provide extensive information that goes beyond a red tally light. It could present people involved in the negotiations and agreements, and represent the recurrence of the productions. Using screens of mobile devices is perhaps not optimal, but it is a pragmatic solution for a social tally light.

Tools such as live comments and embedded social media functionalities could be further emphasized, and would make up contact points towards communities intended as receivers of the produced content. The fact that one of the studied producers chose to include Facebook on a separate computer in his setup, as an ad-hoc communication channel, highlights the usefulness of social media in the production context. For live media producers, dedicated live chat functionalities could be implemented in the user interface. Location based technology adds to the opportunities for connecting to people locally, e.g. by allowing people in the audience to check in and provide comments on the production, in text or face to face.

### Recurrent production as a design resource in HCI

Broadcasting recurrent events can function as a strategy for organizational development, as well as for the individual practice of learning by doing. The recurrent nature of these broadcasts follows from the fact that the pre-existing organization is set up to handle a number of recurrent games or events. If the producers, and other people that matter for creating both broadcast and the event per se, are successful in reaching agreements on what to capture and when to do it, this becomes a resource for future negotiations. Recurrence is thus not only a contingent circumstance, but also an important condition, that enables producers to establish working conditions for themselves over the course of several productions. The coverage of recurrent events is a type of production that points to the future of live video media, as they provide a resource for continuous organizational learning and identity formation.

Both individual and institutional learning would be supported by targeting recurrent events. Such a strategy could also inform the handling of two previously identified challenges in live video production, i.e. finding and capturing relevant content [22,25] and knowing when to start and stop [22,25,41]. The performative nature of events provides exactly such features; action that makes an effort to stand out from the ordinary, as well as easily identifiable start and end points. This point to the necessity of designing for increased opportunities for aspiring video producers to collaborate with organizers of recurrent events.

### Extending media studies

Ethnography in HCI has historically been used to inform design, and has had a specific inclination towards unpacking the details on on-going everyday interaction. That sort of knowledge interest also has a wider importance. In media theory there has been an extensive discussion on the characteristics of Pro-Am production. The focus has been on the identification of individual skill sets and motivations that would explain the emergence of this type of video media. Accordingly, content producers have been seen as people holding qualities and personality traits of different kinds, and their skills' evolvement over time has been dealt with only implicitly, in terms of for instance the motivation to excel in a particular craft, alongside other motivations. This focus was adequate for describing the broader Pro-Am phenomenon as it emerged. Our ethnographic study adds to media theory's descriptions by providing an understanding of the development of skills as it occurs over time, in real production contexts. We shift the empirical focus to the social practices that precede and generate Pro-Am broadcasts, and add to the theoretical understanding of how they are enabled. Through this empirical focus we also make it possible to inform media studies of recent research in learning studies. The findings add the significance of organizational learning and negotiation between co-located activities to previous descriptions.

Similarly, the Long Tail concept addressed broad tendencies in society, and when it was extended to TV, it only scantly anticipated the developments we now see happening in amateur and Pro-Am production, beside broader trends of mass availability of content for consumption. Revisiting long tail TV means an increased attention to aspects of that concept that have been the least recognized. We already see mass availability of TV content in downloads and on-demand TV, but the expected mass production of new TV content through the democratization of professional means of production is only an emerging promise. We point to the complexities involved in extending the production "tail". It appears that on the production side, growing the Long Tail involves more than developing inexpensive technology for production and distribution. Creating trust, developing knowledge and involving local organizations are also of great importance, as Long Tail TV leaves the traditional broadcast model of one-to-many for a community-based model.

## CONCLUSION

We report on Pro-Am live video production, and contribute to current research through detailed analysis of how skills and identities are developed in practice. Live video has been conceived as a promising next genre of media to be conquered by amateurs using broadly available technology and working to professional standards. At the same time it has been pointed out that users find live broadcasting difficult to master, and they may need to acquire skills over time. In contrast to existing accounts of Pro-Ams, as people holding individual qualities and motivations, we describe how both individuals and the organizations around them develop through on-going and recurrent production activities. Skills and identities are important in this practice but need to be understood in their local context. It is also evident that in order to produce regularly, it is large groups of users or organizations, rather than individuals, that develop new ways of working and relating to each other. When that social context is made visible, a range of challenges stand out, such as negotiating the production's role and setup within a broader organizational setting.

## ACKNOWLEDGEMENTS

The research was made possible by VINNOVA and the Mobile Life Centre, in partnership with Ericsson, Microsoft, Nokia, and IKEA, and by the EU funded project FascinatE (FP7/2007-2013, grant no. 248138).

## REFERENCES

1. Al-Ani, B., Mark, G., Chung, J. et al, The Egyptian blogosphere: a counter-narrative of the revolution. In Proc. CSCW '12. ACM, NY, USA, 17-26.
2. Altheide, A. L.: Identity and the Definition of the Situation In a Mass-Mediated Context. In Symbolic Interaction, Vol. 23, No. 1, p. 1-27 (2000)
3. Anderson, C. (2005) Long Tail TV. Article in five parts on Wired.com, January 10-17 2005. Last viewed 2013-09-16
4. Anderson, C. (2006) The Long Tail: How endless choice is creating unlimited demand. Random House Business Books, London
5. Bambuser http://bambuser.com/ (accessed 2013-01-20)
6. Benkler, Y.: The wealth of networks: How social production transforms markets and freedom. Yale University Press, New Haven (2006).
7. Benkler, Y., Nissenbaum, H.: Commons-based peer production and virtue. Journal of Political Philosophy p. 394-419 (2006)
8. Bentley, F.R., Groble, M. TuVista: Meeting the multimedia needs of mobile sports fans. Proc. ACM MM'09 (Beijing, China, October 19-24), 471-480.(2009)
9. Boreham, N., and Morgan, C.: A sociocultural analysis of organizational learning. In Oxford Review of Education, Vol. 30, No. 3 (2004)

10. Bergstrand, F., Landgren, J. (2011) Visual reporting in time-critical work: Exploring video use in emergency response. Proc. MobileHCI 2011, 415-424.
11. Bly, Harrison, Irwin, Media spaces: Bringing People together in a Video, Audio and Computing Environment, Communications of the ACM, Jan 1993, Vol 36 No 1.
12. Burgess, J., Green, J.: The entrepreneurial Vlogger: Participatory culture beyond the professional-amateur divide. In Snickars, P., Vonderau, P. The Youtube Reader. National Library of Sweden, Stockholm 89-107 (2009)
13. De Sá, M., Shamma, D.A., Churchill, E., Live Mobile Collaboration for Video Production Design, Guidelines, and Requirements. In J. of Personal and Ubiquitous Computing. Springer, London (2013).
14. Dey A. and Guzman de, E. From awareness to connectedness: The design and deployment of presence Displays, In proc. CHI 2006 Montreal, Canada, p 899 – 908
15. Engeström, Y.: Learning by expanding: an activity-theoretical approach to developmental research. Orienta-konsultit, Helsinki (1987)
16. Engström, A., Perry, M., and Juhlin, O.: Amateur Vision and Recreational Orientation: Creating Live Video Together. In Proc. of the SIGCHI conference on Human factors in computing systems (CHI '12). ACM, New York, NY, USA (2012)
17. Erikson, E. H.: Identity: Youth and Crisis. New York: Norton (1968)
18. Gillmor, D. (2010), Mediactive. Published under a Creative Commons A-NC-SA license.
19. Hutchins, E.: Cognition in the Wild. Bradford: MIT Press (1995)
20. Hrastinski, S.: Participating in Synchronous Online Education. PhD. Diss. Dept. of Informatics, Lund University (2007)
21. Juhlin, O., Zoric, G., Engström, A., Reponen, E. (2013) Video interaction: a research agenda. J Personal and Ubiquitous Computing, Springer London, p 1-8
22. Juhlin, O., Engström, A., and Reponen, E.: Mobile Broadcasting: The Whats and Hows of Live Video as a Social Medium. In Proc. MobileHCI 2010, 35-43 (2010)
23. Keen, A.: Cult of the amateur: how today's Internet is killing our culture. Doubleday, New York (2007)
24. Kennedy L. and Naaman M. 2009. Less talk, more rock: automated organization of community-contributed collections of concert videos. In *Proc.* WWW '09. ACM, NY, 311-320.
25. Kirk, D., Sellen, A., Harper, R. & Wood, K. 2007. Understanding Videowork. In proc. CHI'07, San Jose, USA
26. Lampe, C., Wash, R., Velasquez, A., Ozkaya, E.: Motivations to participate in online communities. In Proc CHI '10. ACM, NY, USA, 1927-1936 (2010)
27. Leadbeater, C., Miller, P.: The pro-am revolution: How enthusiasts are changing our economy and society. Demos, London (2004)
28. Lee, Nass C., Designing social presence of social actors in human computer interaction, CHI 2003, Ft Lauderdale Florida USA p 289-296
29. Lehmuskallio, A., Sarvas, R. Snapshot video: everyday photographers taking short video-clips. In Proc. NordiCHI '08. ACM, NY, USA, 257-265.
30. Lindwall, O., and Ekström, A.: Instruction-in-Interaction: The Teaching and Learning of a Manual Skill. In Springer Science+Business Media B.V. (2012)
31. Murphy, P., and Hall, K.: Learning and Practice: Agency and Identities. Sage Publication Inc., London (2008)
32. Qrodo http://qrodo.com/ (accessed 2013-01-20)
33. Rangaswamy, and Cutrell (2012). Anthropology, Development and ICTs: Slums, Youth and the Mobile Internet in Urban India. ICTD'12, ACM, NY, USA, 85-93
34. Reponen, E., Lehikoinen J., and Impiö J.. 2007. Mobile phone video camera in social context. In Proc. *CHI'07* J. A. Jacko (Ed.). Springer-Verlag, Berlin, Heidelberg, 460-469
35. Räsänen and Nyce 2006. A new role for anthropology?: rewriting "context" and "analysis" in HCI research. NordiCHI '06), pp 175-184
36. Shirky, C.: Here comes everybody: the power of organizing without organizations. Penguin Books, New York (2008)
37. Sutherland, L., Howard, S., et al: Professional identity creation: Examining the development of beginning preservice teachers' understanding of their work as teachers. In Teaching and Teacher Education 26 (2010), 455-465 (2009)
38. Van House N.A. 2007. Flickr and public image-sharing: distant closeness and photo exhibition. In Proc. CHI EA '07). ACM, NY, USA, 2717-2722.
39. Wang, T., and Brown, B.: Ethnography of the telephone: changing uses of communication technology in village life. In Proc. MobileHCI (2011)
40. Weddle, A. B., and Hollan, J. D.: Professional Perception and Expert Action: Scaffolding Embodied Practices in Professional Education. In Mind, Culture, and Activity, 17, p. 119-148 (2010)
41. Weilenmann, A., Säljö, R., Engström, A. Mobile video literacy: Negotiating the use of a new visual technology. In J. of Personal and Ubiquitous Computing. Springer, London (2013).
42. Wenger, E.: Communities of Practice: Learning, Meaning, and Identity. Cambridge University Press, Cambridge (1998)
43. Vihavainen, S., Mate S., et al. 2012. Video as memorabilia: user needs for collaborative automatic mobile video production. In Proc. CHI '12. ACM, New York, NY, USA, 651-654.

# Estimating County Health Statistics with Twitter

**Aron Culotta**
Department of Computer Science, Illinois Institute of Technology, Chicago, IL 60616
culotta@cs.iit.edu

## ABSTRACT
Understanding the relationships among environment, behavior, and health is a core concern of public health researchers. While a number of recent studies have investigated the use of social media to track infectious diseases such as influenza, little work has been done to determine if other health concerns can be inferred. In this paper, we present a large-scale study of 27 health-related statistics, including obesity, health insurance coverage, access to healthy foods, and teen birth rates. We perform a linguistic analysis of the Twitter activity in the top 100 most populous counties in the U.S., and find a significant correlation with 6 of the 27 health statistics. When compared to traditional models based on demographic variables alone, we find that augmenting models with Twitter-derived information improves predictive accuracy for 20 of 27 statistics, suggesting that this new methodology can complement existing approaches.

### Author Keywords
social media; public health; natural language processing

### ACM Classification Keywords
H.3.4 H.5.2: H.5.3

## INTRODUCTION
Chronic diseases are the leading cause of death and disability in the U.S. and account for 75% of health care costs.[1] Understanding the interaction among environment, behaviors, and health outcomes is critical to developing informed intervention strategies. In response, the U.S. Centers for Disease Control and Prevention leads multiple community health data collection and intervention efforts such as the Behavioral Risk Factor Surveillance System, the National Health Interview Survey, and the Health Communities Program. A major goal of these initiatives is to identify vulnerable populations in order to better target intervention strategies. While these programs provide tremendous insight, they require considerable time and effort and are often limited in sample size, frequency, or geographic granularity.

[1] `http://www.cdc.gov/chronicdisease/overview`


*CHI 2014*, April 26–May 1, 2014, Toronto, Ontario, Canada.

ACM 978-1-4503-2473-1/14/04..$15.00.
http://dx.doi.org/10.1145/2556288.2557139

In this paper, we investigate the use of social media as a complementary data source to identify at-risk communities. The popularity of websites like Twitter and Facebook continues to grow, making unprecedented amounts of information about attitudes and behaviors publicly available. Given the research in economics [2], socio-linguistics [18], and psychiatry [13] indicating the relationship between language and health, we examine whether linguistic patterns in Twitter correlate with health-related statistics.

For each of the 100 most populous counties in the U.S., we collect 27 health-related statistics from the County Health Rankings & Roadmaps project, including health outcomes, behaviors, socio-economic status, and environmental factors. We also collect over 1.4M user profiles and 4.3M posts from Twitter over a nine month span from the same 100 counties. We then perform a statistical analysis to identify how accurately these health outcomes can be predicted from the Twitter data and which linguistic markers are most predictive of each statistic.

Our experiments[2] investigate four research questions, the answers to which we summarize below:

RQ1. **Predictive accuracy.** Is Twitter activity predictive of county-level health statistics? We find a significant correlation on held-out data for 6 of 27 statistics, including obesity, diabetes, teen births, health insurance coverage, and access to healthy foods.

RQ2. **Representation.** How does the linguistic representation affect accuracy? We find that the LIWC lexicon [24] is more predictive than alternatives, and that normalizing linguistic vectors by the number of users in a county can greatly improve accuracy.

RQ3. **Beyond demographics.** Does Twitter activity provide more information than common demographic covariates? We find that models that augment demographic variables (race, age, gender, income) with linguistic variables (from Twitter) are more accurate than models using demographic variables alone for 20 of the 27 health statistics we consider. For two (limited access to health foods, prevalence of fast foods), the Twitter model in isolation is actually more accurate than the demographic variable model. These results suggest that the two sources of information are complementary.

RQ4. **Identifying linguistic indicators.** What are the linguistic indicators that are most predictive of each outcome? After controlling for five demographic vari-

[2] Code is available: `https://github.com/tapilab/twcounty`.

ables, we identify 33 linguistic categories that are significantly predictive of 6 different health-related statistics. For example, references to religion and certain pronouns ("we", "her") correlate with better socio-emotional support; references to money and inhibition correlate with lower unemployment; and references to family and love correlate with higher rates of teen births.

While this new methodology requires further experimentation, we believe it can aid public health researchers by providing (1) a more nuanced alternative to demographic profiles for identifying at-risk populations; (2) a low-cost method to measure risk across different subpopulations; (3) a process to help formulate new hypotheses about the relationship between environment, behaviors, and health outcomes, which can then be tested in a more controlled setting.

The remainder of the paper is organized as follows: we first review related work, then we describe the data and its collection. We next present our method for representing the linguistic activity of each county and the experimental framework for measuring accuracy and identifying significant linguistic variables. Finally, we present the results and discuss their implications.

## RELATED WORK

We first briefly review related work in the study of language, health, and social media.

### Language and Heath

Language has long been investigated as an indicator of health. For example, Gottschalk [13] performed a content analysis of patients to determine psychological state, such as anxiety, hostility, and alienation. Pennebaker [18] provides an excellent review of research connecting linguistic patterns to demographics, personality, psychology, mental health.

While many studies support the connection between mental health and language, the connection between physical health and language is less well-established. Some studies have reported correlations between "Type A" language and heart diseases[14] and positive emotional language with longevity [7]. Given growing evidence supporting the link between emotional well-being and health [17], estimating psychological health may serve as a predictive surrogate for physical health.

The emerging study of the economics of language has also investigated how language relates to decision-making, which in turn can affect health. For example, in a study of 76 countries, Chen [2] found that certain grammatical properties correlate with higher rates of savings and lower rates of smoking and obesity, concluding that some linguistic constructs may foster future-oriented behavior. Chiswick [3] investigates how language proficiency of immigrants can impact employment and other socio-economic factors.

### Social Media and Health

There is a growing body of work investigating social media to track health concerns such as influenza [20, 5, 22, 30, 27], E. coli [32], alcohol consumption [6], Adderall use [15], insomnia [19] and depression [8]. See Dredze [9] for an overview. Most of these focus on detecting explicit mentions of a symptom of interest (e.g., "Staying home from work today with a sore throat"). In contrast, the present work investigates more nuanced linguistic cues that correlate with the overall health of a population.

Ghosh & Guha [12] identified geo-spatial patterns in specific obesity-related tweets (e.g. "fast food"), using topic models to qualitatively characterize discussions of obesity on Twitter. While some ancillary data is used for comparison (e.g., location of fast food restaurants), no correlation analysis is performed with obesity statistics. Additionally, Paul & Dredze [22] use a topic model to discover obesity-related tweets, finding a .28 correlation with state obesity statistics.

Our methodology is most similar to that of Schwartz et al. [28], who find tweets to be predictive of county-level surveys of life satisfaction. Here, we also use LIWC and PERMA lexicons as features in a regression model of county statistics.

In the context of this related work, the primary contributions of this paper are as follows: (1) we present the first large-scale social media analysis across a diverse set of 27 measures of community health; (2) we provide an empirical comparison of several important methodological decisions, such as linguistic lexicons, vector normalization, and source of linguistic content; (3) we provide a rigorous statistical treatment that identifies linguistic indicators from social media that are significant predictors of health outcomes even after controlling for demographic variables.

## DATA

Here we describe how we collected the health and Twitter data and provide descriptive statistics of their contents.

### County Health Data

Using data from the U.S. Census' State-Based Counties Gazetteer,[3] we collected the top 100 most populous counties in the U.S. along with their geographical coordinates. Each county is assigned a Federal Information Processing Standards (FIPS) code as a unique identifier. The County Health Rankings & Roadmaps,[4] a partnership between the Robert Wood Johnson Foundation and the University of Wisconsin Population Health Institute, aggregates county-level health factors from a wide range of sources, including the Behavioral Risk Factor Surveillance System, American Community Survey, and the National Center for Health Statistics, collected over the past three years.[5] These publicly available data contain county statistics on 30 measures of mortality, morbidity, health behaviors, clinical care, socio-economic factors, and physical environment.

[3] `http://www.census.gov/geo/maps-data/data/docs/gazetteer/Gaz_counties_national.zip`

[4] `http://www.countyhealthrankings.org/`

[5] While the Twitter was collected more recently, most county-level statistics, and particularly their relative differences, are slow to change.

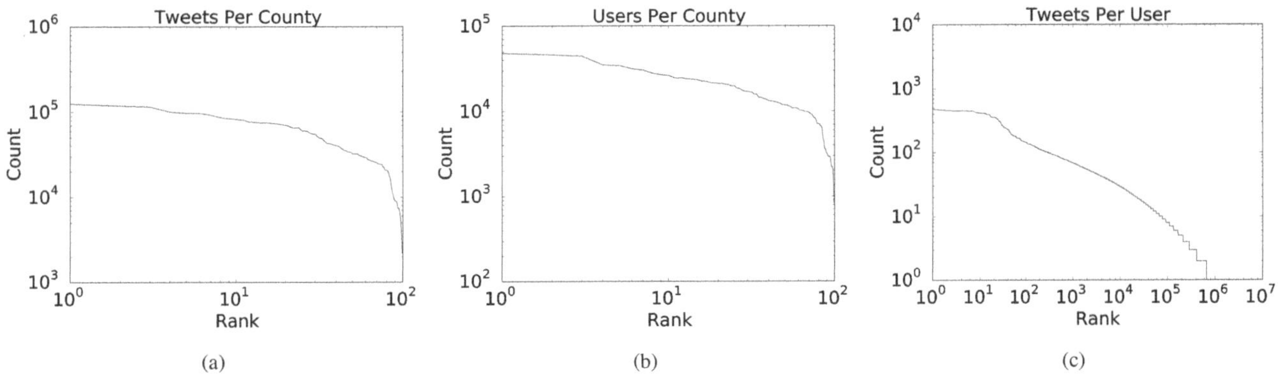


Figure 1: Distributions over the 4.31M tweets, 1.46M users, and 100 counties in the dataset.

For each of the top 100 most populous counties, we collected 27 health statistics (3 were removed because of missing values for some counties). These are listed in Table 3. As space precludes a precise definition of how each statistic was computed, we refer the reader to the County Health Rankings website for more information. We describe some of these in more detail in the Discussion section.

### Twitter Data

We next constructed a set of 100 Twitter queries consisting of one geographical bounding box for each county, approximated by a 50 square mile area centered at the county coordinates obtained from the U.S. Census.[6] We then submitted these queries continuously to Twitter's search API from December 5, 2012 to August 31, 2013 (with intermittent stoppages for technical difficulties). These queries return tweets that have been geolocated, typically tweets issued from a mobile device. This resulted in 4.31M tweets from 1.46M unique users. For each tweet, we retain the tweet content as well as the user description field, a short, user-provided summary (e.g., "motivated law student"). Figure 1 shows distributions of tweets per county, users per county, and tweets per user. While the demographic distributions of Twitter users are thought to skew young and urban [10], it is worth noting that these 1.46M users represent over 1% of the total population of these 100 counties (130M). As expected, Twitter usage varies significantly by county size. On average, we collect 14.5K users per county, with 66 counties containing at least 10K users. Hudson County (part of the New York metropolitan area) has the most with 52K users, Honolulu County the least with 845. The tweets per user graph exhibits a typical long tail — a few users tweet very often, but most tweet infrequently.

We note that this data collection methodology differs from that of Schwartz et al. [28], who collect the 10% "garden hose" sample of the entire Twitter stream, then use heuristics to filter by location using the user's profile information. This can yield more tweets (since only a small percentage of tweets are geocoded), but can introduce additional geolocation noise due to the unreliability of the location field [16].

[6]This introduces a small amount of noise – 957 tweets came from overlapping bounding boxes. This can be eliminated by using the county polygon data from the Census. We thank the anonymous reviewer for this suggestion.

## LINGUISTIC REPRESENTATION

Given a collection of tweets categorized by county, we next must distill them into a set of variables to correlate with the health statistics. Due to the small number of validation points (100 counties) and the large number of potential variables (hundreds of thousands of unique words), rather than considering words as variables, we instead consider word categories. We build on prior work that considers two lexicons:

- **LIWC:** The 2001 Linguistic Inquiry and Word Count lexicon [24] contains 74 categories and 2,300 word patterns (which includes exact matches as well as prefixes like *awake**). Each word pattern may belong to multiple categories (e.g., *Physical, Sleep*). This lexicon was developed over a number of years to identify categories that capture emotional and cognitive cues of interest to health, sociology, and psychology. It has been used in numerous studies [18], including Twitter studies [25, 28, 8].
- **PERMA:** The PERMA lexicon [29] contains 10 categories and 1,522 words. The categories reflect the five dimensions of positive psychology (Positive emotion, Engagement, Relationships, Meaning, Achievement) — each category is either positive or negative. For example, *R+* indicates positive relationships and *P-* indicates negative emotions. Only exact matches are considered, and each word belongs to exactly one category.

We select these lexicons based on their use in prior work [28] and the fact that they were designed to represent categories of relevance to health and personality.

For each county, then, we record the frequency with which each lexical category is used. To do this, we use a simple tokenizer to process each tweet that removes punctuation and then splits by whitespace to return a list of tokens. Additionally, we remove all mentions and URLs. The remaining tokens are matched against the above lexicons, resulting in a vector of category frequencies for each county.

We distinguish between tokens appearing in the tweet text and tokens appearing in the user description, denoted by the prefixes (*d=*) and (*t=*). For example, [*d=Sleep: 2, t=R+: 1*] indicates that two tokens in the description field map to the *Sleep* category and that one token in the tweet text maps to the positive relationship category.

We found that only 70 of the LIWC categories appear in our data, along with all 10 of the PERMA categories, yielding a total of 80 linguistic categories.

For each county, we create a vector of 160 values reflecting the frequency of each category (80 categories each for description and text tokens). Since the magnitude of these values will vary greatly based on the number of tweets collected from each county, we consider several normalization strategies to make the vectors comparable across counties:

- **None:** No normalization used; each vector contains the raw frequency of each category.
- **Log:** We take the natural log of one plus the value (as advocated by Schwartz et al. [28]). This dampens large values.
- **Word:** We divide each value by the sum of all values in that county's frequency vector. This represents the relative prevalence of a category as compared to overall usage in that county.
- **User:** We store the proportion of users from the county who use a word from this category. Note that if one user tweets the same word category many times, this will only increase the numerator by one; the denominator is the total number of users from that county.

## EXPERIMENTS

To address our four research questions from the Introduction, we perform regression to predict each of the 27 health-related statistics using the 180 linguistic variables described above. Given the large number of independent variables (180) relative to the number of validation points (100 counties), we use ridge regression to reduce overfitting.[7]

To estimate generalization accuracy, we use five fold cross-validation — each fold fits the model on 80 counties and predicts on the remaining 20. The splits are created uniformly at random, except that we additionally ensure that counties from the same state do not appear in both the training and test split in one fold. This is to confirm that the model is learning more than simply the state identity of each county.[8]

We report two measures of accuracy:

- **Pearson's $r$:** We collect all the predicted values from the held-out data in each fold (100 counties total) and compute the correlation with the true values; $r \in [-1, 1]$; larger is better.
- **SMAPE:** Symmetric Mean Absolute Percentage Error [11] measures the relative error between the predicted and true value. This is a useful alternative to the more common mean-squared error as it can compare outcome variables that have different ranges. If $y_i$ is the true value and $\hat{y}_i$ is the predicted value, then SMAPE $= \frac{\sum_i |y_i - \hat{y}_i|}{\sum_i y_i + \hat{y}_i}$. For non-negative $y$ values, SMAPE $\in [0, 1]$; smaller is better.

In addition to LIWC and PERMA, some experiments also include five demographic control variables:

- **$<$ 18**: the proportion of people under the age of 18.
- **65 and over**: the proportion of people at least 65 years old.
- **Female:** the proportion of people who are female.
- **Afro-Hispanic:** the proportion of people who are African-American or Hispanic.
- **Med_income:** the log of the median household income.

We select these variables because of they are used in prior Twitter work [28], they are prevalent in governmental data collection for health studies (e.g., the Behavioral Risk Factor Surveillance System), and they have been linked to health outcomes in epidemiological studies [31, 21, 26]. We collect these variables from the County Health Rankings Roadmap data.

## RESULTS

Below, we first briefly summarize the main results, then discuss them in more detail.

### RQ1: Predictive accuracy

Our first research question asks whether Twitter-derived linguistic variables are predictive of a county's health statistics. Columns labeled **T** (Twitter) in Table 3 display the results for our two evaluation metrics across 27 statistics for the model containing all 160 linguistic variables (**LIWC+PERMA**) with **User** normalization (we will revisit these choices in the next section). To compute statistical significance of each correlation value, we use a Bonferroni correction to adjust for multiple comparisons. Additionally, we replace the traditional $p$-value calculation with the Clifford & Richardson correction [4], which computes an effective sample size based on spatial autocorrelation[9], as measured by Moran's I (using the R SpatialPack[10] library.)

We find that for nine statistics the prediction of the linguistic model is significantly correlated with the health statistic. The strongest correlations are for No Insurance (percent of population under the age of 65 without health insurance) ($r = .59$), Vehicle Mortality (motor vehicle crash deaths per 100k) ($r = .52$), Limited Healthy Food (percent of population who live in poverty and are 1 mile from a supermarket in urban areas or 10 miles in rural areas) ($r = .51$), teen birth rate (per 1k females age 15-19) ($r = .50$), Dentist Access (ratio of population to dentists) ($r = .44$), and Obesity (percent of adults that report a BMI $\geq 30$) ($r = .43$).

Figure 2 shows scatter plots of the true and predicted values on held-out data for three of the significantly correlated predictions using the **LIWC+PERMA** model. The largest errors generally appear at extreme values. For example, Hidalgo County in Texas has the highest Teen Birth rate of the 100 counties (8.7%, about 1.5% higher than the next highest

[7] We use the implementation in `scikit-learn` [23] with smoothing parameter $\alpha = 0.1$.

[8] Indeed, we find that splitting at random instead of by state increases the overall average correlation for the LIWC model from .25 to .29.

[9] We thank the anonymous reviewer for this suggestion.

[10] `http://spatialpack.mat.utfsm.cl`

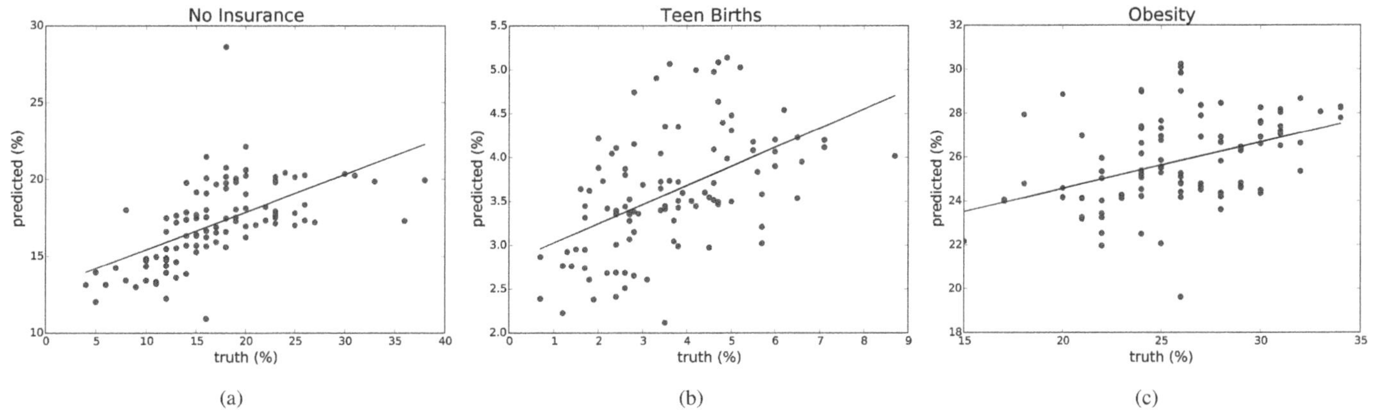


Figure 2: Scatter plots of true versus predicted values on held-out data using the user-normalized LIWC+PERMA model (no demographic variables used) for No Insurance ($r = .59$), Teen Births ($r = .50$), and Obesity rates ($r = .43$).

| Variables | r | SMAPE |
|---|---|---|
| PERMA | -0.07 | 10.45% |
| LIWC | 0.25 | 9.67% |
| LIWC+PERMA | 0.25 | 9.67% |
| Controls | 0.59 | 7.65% |
| Controls+PERMA | 0.60 | 7.57% |
| Controls+LIWC | 0.63 | 7.37% |
| Controls+LIWC+PERMA | 0.63 | 7.37% |

Table 1: Held-out correlation and SMAPE averaged across all 27 output variables using various combinations of input variables. All models use **User** normalization.

county), though the linguistic model predicts only 4%. Similarly, Miami-Dade County in Florida has a high uninsured rate of 36%, while the model predicts only 17%. The outlier in the No Insurance plot (predicted=28.6%, truth=18%) is Pima County, AZ — this may in part be explained by the limited Twitter data from that county (4k users).

### RQ2: Representation

Our second research question asks how the choices of representation and normalization affects accuracy. Table 1 displays the evaluation metrics averaged across all 27 outcomes for all combinations of lexicon choice and inclusion of the demographic control variables. Somewhat surprisingly, the PERMA lexicon does not appear to add much value — this may in part be due to the fact that it only contains 10 categories (versus 74 for LIWC). As it does not hurt performance, we retain it in other experiments — we show below that for certain health statistics it does produce statistically significant predictors. We delay discussion of the demographic control variables until the next section.

Table 2 evaluates the different normalization strategies using the **Controls+LIWC+PERMA** model. It is clear that using no normalization at all leads to poor results. This is not unexpected, since the variables will have very different ranges across different counties. We do find it informative that user normalization outperforms the alternative, more common normalization strategies. For example, Schwartz et al. [28] use **Log** normalization, and many Twitter influenza models use **Word** normalization [30]. We speculate that the superiority of **User** normalization here is mostly due to the inclusion of user description variables, which should only be counted once per user.

| Norm | r | SMAPE |
|---|---|---|
| None | 0.07 | 25.23% |
| Log | 0.47 | 11.34% |
| Word | 0.59 | 7.63% |
| User | 0.63 | 7.37% |

Table 2: Held-out correlation and SMAPE for the Controls+LIWC+PERMA model averaged across all 27 output variables using various normalization strategies.

### RQ3: Beyond demographics

Our third research question asks what if any predictive value these linguistic variables provide beyond that of commonly used demographic covariates. It is possible that the correlations found in the linguistic variables in RQ1 are simply surrogates for demographic variables. Given the strong predictive accuracy of the control variables (c.f., Table 1), it is important to quantify the additional value added by Twitter. Table 1 provides a partial answer to this question — averaged across all 27 health statistics, including linguistic variables leads to an absolute 3% improvement in held-out correlation and a .28% improvement in SMAPE.

Table 3 provides a more detailed answer for each health statistic. By comparing values for **C** and **T+C**, we can see the change in held-out accuracy obtained by including linguistic variables in the model. We see that higher correlation is obtained by including linguistic variables for 19 of the 27 statistics and lower SMAPE is obtained for 20. Performing a Wilcoxon signed-rank test on the SMAPE values, we find three statistics that are significantly more accurately predicted (no socio-emotional support, no insurance, low birth weight) versus one that is significantly less accurately predicted (high school graduation rate). Moreover, for two statistics (Limited Healthy Food, Fast Food) the model using linguistic variables

| | Pearson's r | | | | SMAPE | | | |
|---|---|---|---|---|---|---|---|---|
| **Outcome** | **T** | **C** | **T+C** | **Δ** | **T** | **C** | **T+C** | **Δ** |
| Ambulatory Care | 0.08 | 0.15 | 0.30 | 105% | 9.1% ± 1.8 | 9.1% ± 2.4 | 8.5% ± 2.1 | 7% |
| Limited Healthy Food | 0.51** | 0.31 | 0.48** | 53% | 21.1% ± 4.6 | 26.2% ± 4.0 | 23.4% ± 4.3 | 11%∘ |
| Fast Food | 0.31 | 0.24 | 0.31∘ | 30% | 4.3% ± 1.5 | 4.5% ± 0.9 | 4.4% ± 1.1 | 4% |
| No socio-emotional support | 0.32∘ | 0.59*** | 0.72*** | 22% | 7.0% ± 1.3 | 6.2% ± 1.0 | 5.2% ± 0.8 | 16%* |
| Vehicle Mortality | 0.52 | 0.52* | 0.62∘ | 20% | 12.5% ± 2.5 | 11.8% ± 3.0 | 10.5% ± 1.8 | 10% |
| Unemployment | -0.11 | 0.36* | 0.43*** | 19% | 10.1% ± 1.4 | 9.1% ± 3.5 | 8.9% ± 2.3 | 2% |
| Diabetes | 0.35** | 0.45** | 0.53*** | 17% | 1.4% ± 0.2 | 1.3% ± 0.2 | 1.3% ± 0.1 | 4% |
| No Insurance | 0.59 | 0.70** | 0.80** | 15% | 11.6% ± 1.9 | 10.5% ± 1.6 | 8.4% ± 1.3 | 20%* |
| Low Birth Weight | 0.41*** | 0.68*** | 0.77*** | 13% | 5.8% ± 0.9 | 4.5% ± 0.8 | 3.9% ± 0.8 | 12%* |
| Obesity | 0.43*** | 0.57*** | 0.64*** | 13% | 6.0% ± 1.2 | 4.9% ± 1.2 | 4.7% ± 1.2 | 3% |
| Poor Health | 0.23 | 0.71*** | 0.76*** | 6% | 9.6% ± 1.7 | 6.8% ± 1.4 | 6.5% ± 1.2 | 4% |
| Unhealthy Days | 0.01 | 0.63*** | 0.66*** | 6% | 6.0% ± 0.6 | 4.3% ± 0.3 | 4.3% ± 0.6 | 1% |
| Inactivity | 0.11 | 0.55*** | 0.58*** | 6% | 7.6% ± 1.2 | 6.0% ± 1.0 | 6.0% ± 1.0 | 1% |
| Mentally Unhealthy | -0.22 | 0.46*** | 0.49*** | 6% | 5.8% ± 0.9 | 5.1% ± 1.2 | 5.0% ± 1.3 | 1% |
| Drinking | 0.12 | 0.18 | 0.19 | 5% | 5.6% ± 1.2 | 5.8% ± 1.2 | 5.7% ± 1.5 | 1% |
| Smokers | 0.15 | 0.65*** | 0.67*** | 3% | 8.7% ± 1.3 | 6.7% ± 0.5 | 6.3% ± 0.8 | 5% |
| College | 0.15 | 0.85*** | 0.87*** | 2% | 5.0% ± 1.1 | 2.8% ± 0.4 | 2.6% ± 0.4 | 6% |
| Dentist Access | 0.44 | 0.66*** | 0.67*** | 1% | 10.1% ± 0.5 | 9.0% ± 2.3 | 8.9% ± 2.7 | 1% |
| Teen Births | 0.50 | 0.86*** | 0.87*** | 1% | 15.1% ± 2.4 | 8.6% ± 2.0 | 8.4% ± 2.5 | 3% |
| Child Poverty | 0.29 | 0.93*** | 0.93*** | 0% | 15.0% ± 1.2 | 5.5% ± 1.2 | 5.4% ± 1.2 | 1% |
| Single Parent | 0.20 | 0.88*** | 0.88*** | -0% | 11.0% ± 1.9 | 5.1% ± 0.4 | 5.1% ± 0.6 | 0% |
| Chlamydia | 0.20 | 0.74*** | 0.74*** | -1% | 19.3% ± 4.5 | 13.7% ± 2.0 | 13.8% ± 1.6 | -1% |
| Mammography | 0.25 | 0.57*** | 0.56*** | -1% | 2.9% ± 0.6 | 2.5% ± 0.6 | 2.5% ± 0.5 | -1% |
| Violent Crime | 0.32* | 0.73*** | 0.72*** | -2% | 19.7% ± 3.5 | 14.0% ± 1.9 | 15.2% ± 0.9 | -9% |
| Primary Care | 0.30 | 0.68*** | 0.65*** | -4% | 11.4% ± 1.5 | 8.7% ± 1.4 | 9.0% ± 1.7 | -4% |
| Rec Facilities | 0.34 | 0.70*** | 0.67*** | -4% | 14.3% ± 3.1 | 10.7% ± 2.9 | 11.2% ± 3.0 | -5%∘ |
| HS Grad Rate | -0.10 | 0.66*** | 0.58*** | -12% | 5.2% ± 1.1 | 3.4% ± 1.0 | 3.9% ± 1.3 | -13%* |

Table 3: Held-out correlation and mean SMAPE (with standard deviation) for each outcome under three models — *T*: Twitter model using LIWC and PERMA lexicons; *C*: control variables (age, gender, race, income); *T+C*: Twitter and controls. All models use **User** normalization. Δ is the percent relative improvement (either correlation or SMAPE) from model *C* to *T+C*, an estimate of how complementary the two models are. Pearson's $r$ significance is indicated by $\circ = 0.1$, $* = 0.05$, $** = 0.01$, $*** = 0.001$ (degress of freedom = 98). The thresholds have been Bonferroni-corrected (using the 27 outcomes).

in isolation (**T**) is actually more accurate than the model that uses demographic variables in isolation (**C**).

These results appear to support the hypothesis that Twitter-derived variables complement demographic variables.

One note regarding the relatively poor performance for Violent crime and Chlamydia — according to the County Health Rankings project, the data collection methodology for these two statistics tends to vary widely across states, making inter-state comparisons difficult.[11]

### RQ4: Identifying linguistic indicators

Our fourth research question seeks to identify linguistic categories that are significantly correlated with each health statistic. In addition to providing an additional validation, this may help health researchers formulate new hypotheses about the connection between behavior, personality, and health.

We begin by computing the correlation between each independent and dependent variable in isolation, across all 160 linguistic variables, 5 control variables, and 27 health statistics. Figure 3 plots the top 10 most correlated variables for the top 12 statistics from Table 3. Significance values are again computed using spatially-adjusted $p$-values.

To disentangle those linguistic variables that are acting as surrogates for demographic variables, we perform an additional analysis which controls for these factors. For each linguistic variable, we perform regression in which the independent variables consist of one linguistic variable and the five demographic control variables and the dependent variable is one of the 27 health statistics. We then compute the statistical significance of the coefficient estimated for each linguistic variable, again using a Bonferroni correction. To the best of our knowledge, no previous work has explicitly controlled for these demographic variables when identifying significant linguistic categories. This is important to determine which variables are simply recovering demographics, and which are providing additional information.

Because of the spatial autocorrelation inherent in this geographical data, rather than using ordinary least squares regression [1], we use two stage least squares spatial regres-

[11] `http://www.countyhealthrankings.org/resources/chr-2013-data-comparability-across-states`

sion[12] (using the `pysal`[13] Python package). We use a kernel weight matrix with the default values.

This analysis yielded 33 linguistic categories that were significant predictors of 6 different health statistics after controlling for demographics. Table 4 displays the 15 categories that were found to be significant predictors of at least two different statistics. For each, we display the top five most common words found in the category and the list of health statistics for which they are predictive. Overall, we find that the user description is more predictive than the tweet itself — 80% of the significant variables come from the user description.

Caution must be taken when interpreting these results — the true context of word usage on Twitter often differs from intuition. Below, we highlight a few significant categories, including examples of the most common phrases to provide missing context. As this is a purely correlational analysis, we make no claims as to the causal mechanisms underlying these findings.

- The Family category is correlated with several negative health outcomes (limited healthy foods, lack of health insurance, teen birth rate). This category contains words such as "family" (e.g., "I love my family"), "mom" (e.g., "stay at home mom" or "single mom"), and "daddy" (e.g., "daddy's girl", "r.i.p. daddy").
- The PosFeel (positive feelings) category is correlated with increased socio-emotional support. This category contains words such as "love", "happy", and "smile"; e.g. "Seeing people smile makes me happy", and "Do what makes you happy."
- Inhibition words (e.g., "stop") appear to correlate with positive health outcomes (lower unemployment, fewer physically and mentally unhealthy days). These words often appear with ambition-oriented quotes people enter in their description field (e.g., "don't stop when you are tired; stop when you are done"; "set your goals high and don't stop until you get there").
- Job-related terms are correlated with lower unemployment — the most common word in this category is "work", often used in phrases like "going to work" or "do I have to go to work today?".
- The word "god" is the most common term in both the *Re*ligious and *Metaph*ysical categories — it appears in user descriptions as in "I love God, my family, and friends." Such profiles tends to be correlated with limited access to healthy foods, lack of health insurance, and more vehicle mortalities. This may in part be explained by increased church attendance rates for counties in the deep South, which tend to be ranked lower by many health outcomes.

## ERROR ANALYSIS

To better understand how the linguistic variables can improve accuracy, we identified counties that are similar demographically but different linguistically. To do this, we selected counties whose statistics were more accurately predicted using linguistic and control variables than using control variables alone, then identified the linguistic differences that contributed to that improved accuracy. We used the following process: For each health statistic, we compared the true value to the held-out value predicted by the controls only model (**C**) and to the Twitter plus controls model (**T + C**). We identified the county whose prediction was most improved by **T + C**. We then chose a second county that had a similar value predicted by the controls model, but a different true value (specifically, we sorted by the difference in the predicted values minus the difference in true value). Finally, we compared the linguistic variables from each of the two counties and identified those that differed the most, weighted by importance (specifically, we multiply the relative difference in the values multiplied by the absolute value of the correlation between that variable and the health statistic). In this way, we identified counties that appear similar when considering demographic variables, but exhibit different linguistic properties on Twitter.

We highlight two examples from this analysis. For obesity, we compared Kings County, NY (Brooklyn) and Wayne County, MI (which includes Detroit). (See Table 5.) Both are highly urbanized counties in the northern United States with similar demographics. However, Wayne County has a much

| | **Kings** | **Wayne** |
|---|---|---|
| **Obesity** | 25.0 | 34.0 |
| **C** | 30.2 | 28.8 |
| **T+C** | **26.8** | **30.2** |
| **65 and over** | 11.5 | 12.8 |
| **d=Sports** | .086 | .179 |
| **E-** | .017 | .033 |
| **d=School** | .133 | .232 |
| **Sleep** | .037 | .067 |
| **Swear** | .063 | .118 |

Table 5: Comparison of obesity rates, predictions, and linguistic variables for Kings County, NY and Wayne County, MI, along with the most important linguistic categories. Augmenting the control variable model (**C**) with Twitter variables (**T+C**) improves accuracy.

| | **LA** | **Jefferson** |
|---|---|---|
| **Limited Healthy Food** | 1.0 | 11.0 |
| **C** | 5.3 | 5.9 |
| **T+C** | **4.0** | **8.6** |
| **med_income** | 52k | 42k |
| **d=Relig** | .056 | .127 |
| **d=Metaph** | .068 | .139 |
| **d=TV** | .038 | .016 |
| **d=Family** | .036 | .052 |

Table 6: Comparison of rates of limited healthy food access, predictions, and linguistic variables for Los Angeles County, CA and Jefferson County, AL, along with the most important linguistic categories. Augmenting the control variable model (**C**) with Twitter variables (**T+C**) improves accuracy.

[12] We thank the anonymous reviewer for this suggestion.

[13] `http://pysal.org`

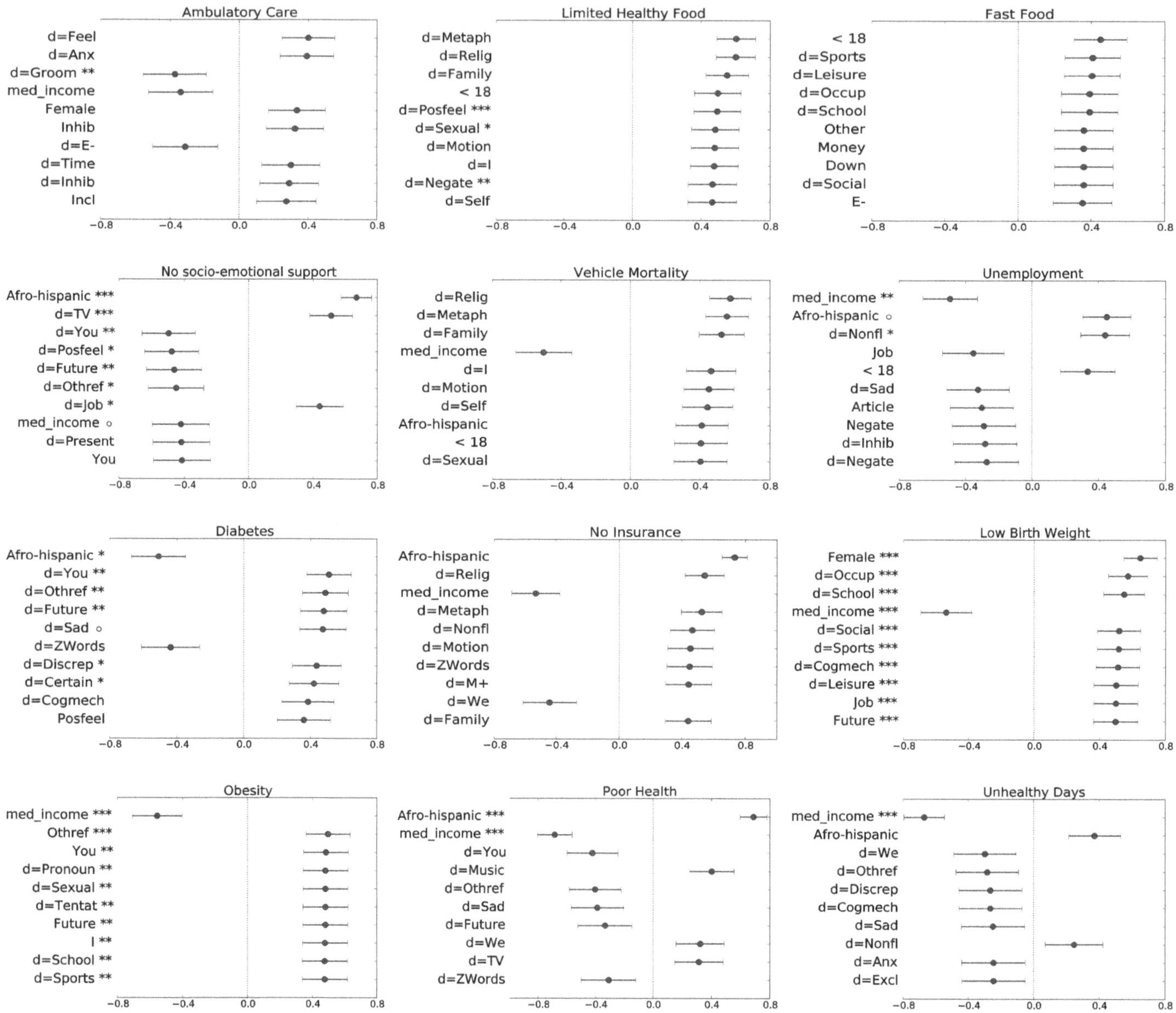


Figure 3: For the top 12 outcomes in Table 3, we plot the 10 variables with the highest correlation (error bars denote the 95% confidence interval.) Statistical significance is indicated by $\circ = 0.1$, $* = 0.05$, $** = 0.01$, $*** = 0.001$ (degress of freedom = 98). The thresholds have been Bonferroni-corrected using the total number of variables (160) times the number of outcomes (27). The prefix *d=* denotes lexical categories from the description field of a user's Twitter profile. Otherwise, the categories are derived from the tweet text. For comparison, the control variables are also included.

| Cat | Examples | Outcomes |
|---|---|---|
| Affect | love, good, best, beautiful, happy | Low Birth Weight:d+ No socio-emotional support:d- |
| Family | family, mom, son, daddy, ex | No socio-emotional support:d- Teen Births:d+ |
| Future | be, will, may, might, shall | Low Birth Weight:t+/d+ No socio-emotional support:t- |
| Metaph | god, die, jesus, blessed, christ | No socio-emotional support:t-/d- Teen Births:d+ |
| Motion | follow, go, take, going, dance | Low Birth Weight:t+ No socio-emotional support:d- |
| Negate | not, no, nothing, without, nobody | Mentally Unhealthy:d- No socio-emotional support:t-/d- Poor Health:d- Unemployment:t-/d- |
| Other | they, she, her, he, them | Low Birth Weight:d+ No socio-emotional support:d- |
| Posemo | love, good, best, beautiful, happy | Low Birth Weight:d+ No socio-emotional support:d- |
| Present | is, follow, love, like, live | Low Birth Weight:d+ No socio-emotional support:d- |
| Pronoun | i, my, you, me, it | Low Birth Weight:d+ No socio-emotional support:t-/d- |
| Relig | god, jesus, blessed, christ, soul | No socio-emotional support:t-/d- Teen Births:d+ |
| Sexual | love, loves, fu**ing, huge, gay | Low Birth Weight:d+ No socio-emotional support:d- |
| Social | you, we, who, girl, family | Low Birth Weight:d+ No socio-emotional support:d- |
| Sports | sports, football, basketball, play, teamfollowback | Low Birth Weight:t+/d+ No socio-emotional support:d- |
| TV | show, tv, movies, comedian, drama | No socio-emotional support:d+ Poor Health:d+ |

Table 4: A summary of 15 of the 80 lexical categories. These were selected by collecting all categories that are significantly correlated with at least two outcomes after controlling for demographics variables ($p < 0.05$, Bonferroni-corrected). We list the significantly correlated outcomes, the sign of correlation, and the field where the word was found: *t* for text and *d* for user description. E.g., the second row indicates that the presence of a word from the Family category in a user description is positively correlated with teen birth rates.

higher obesity rate (Wayne = 34, Kings = 25). In part because Wayne County has a higher proportion of people over 65 (1.3% higher), and this correlates with lower obesity rates, the controls-only model erroneously predicts a *lower* rate of obesity for Wayne County (Kings = 30.2, Wayne = 28.8). Including the linguistic variables improves accuracy considerably for both counties. We display the top five linguistic variables that influenced the score for **T+C**. As we can see, user descriptions from Wayne County are more likely to contain references to school and sports — the most common references are to football and basketball teams. Also, tweets from Wayne county exhibit a higher rate of negative engagement words (**E-**) (most common examples: "tired", "bored," "sleepy"), references to sleep ("bed", "tired", "wake"), and swear words ("ass", "fu**ing", "hell"). All of these lexical categories correlate with higher obesity rates. In this case, the linguistic variables provide a more nuanced distinction between two highly urbanized areas in the northern U.S.

Table 6 repeats this analysis for the Limited Healthy Food statistic (the percent of the population who live in poverty and are 1 mile from a supermarket in urban areas or 10 miles from a supermarket in rural areas). Here, we compare Los Angeles County, CA and Jefferson County, AL (which includes the major city of Birmingham). Los Angeles has much greater access to healthy foods, as predicted by both models. Income is a strong predictor of this statistic, so the smaller median income in Jefferson County has influenced the controls-only model. However, adding the Twitter variables results in a much larger (and more accurate) difference between the two counties. Jefferson County is more likely to have user descriptions containing religious and metaphysical words (e.g., "god," "jesus," "blessed"), family words ("family", "mom", "son"), and less likely to contain TV references ("show", "tv", "movies"). In this case, the linguistic categories appear to be distinguishing between two very different types of urban environments (West Coast versus Deep South). We find similar patterns with these linguistic categories for No Insurance, Vehicle Mortality, and Teen Birth Rate.

## CONCLUSION AND FUTURE WORK

The main conclusion of our analysis is that Twitter activity provides a more fine-grained representation of a community's health than demographics alone — for example, the health of counties with similar demographics can be distinguished by the prevalence of words indicating negative engagement ("tired", "bored"), television habits ("show", "tv", "movies"), and religious observance ("jesus", "blessed"). The reason for this appears to come from the insights Twitter provides into personality, attitudes, and behavior, which in turn correlate with health outcomes. We have provided a methodology to discover such predictive patterns from county-aligned Twitter data. Given the large number of variables explored, we have used very conservative estimates of significance to reduce the chance of Type 1 errors and adjust for spatial autocorrelation.

In the future, we plan to consider automatically-learned word categories (e.g., using topic models), as well as extra-linguistic attributes (e.g., graph connectivity, posting frequency).

## REFERENCES

1. Anselin, L. *Spatial econometrics: methods and models*. Kluwer Academic Publishers, Dordrecht; Boston, 1988.

2. Chen, M. K. The effect of language on economic behavior: Evidence from savings rates, health behaviors,

and retirement assets. *American Economic Review 103*, 2 (Apr. 2013), 690–731.

3. Chiswick, B. R., and Miller, P. W. *The economics of language international analyses*. Routledge, London; New York, 2007.
4. Clifford, P., Richardson, S., and Hmon, D. Assessing the significance of the correlation between two spatial processes. *Biometrics 45*, 1 (Mar. 1989), 123–134. PMID: 2720048.
5. Culotta, A. Towards detecting influenza epidemics by analyzing twitter messages. In *Proceedings of the First Workshop on Social Media Analytics*, ACM (New York, NY, USA, 2010), 115–122.
6. Culotta, A. Lightweight methods to estimate influenza rates and alcohol sales volume from twitter messages. *Lang. Resour. Eval. 47*, 1 (Mar. 2013), 217238.
7. Danner, D. D., Snowdon, D. A., and Friesen, W. V. Positive emotions in early life and longevity: findings from the nun study. *Journal of personality and social psychology 80*, 5 (May 2001), 804–813. PMID: 11374751.
8. De Choudhury, M., Gamon, M., Counts, S., and Horvitz, E. Predicting depression via social media. In *ICWSM* (2013).
9. Dredze, M. How social media will change public health. *IEEE Intelligent Systems 27*, 4 (2012), 81–84.
10. Duggan, M., and Brenner, J. The demographics of social media users – 2012. Pew Internet & American Life Project, Feb 2013.
11. Flores, B. E. A pragmatic view of accuracy measurement in forecasting. *Omega 14*, 2 (1986), 93–98.
12. Ghosh, D. D., and Guha, R. What are we tweeting about obesity? Mapping tweets with topic modeling and geographic information system. *Cartography and Geographic Information Science 40*, 2 (2013), 90–102.
13. Gottschalk, L. A., and Gleser, G. C. *The Measurement of Psychological States Through the Content Analysis of Verbal Behavior*. University of California Press, Jan. 1979.
14. Graham, L E, n., Scherwitz, L., and Brand, R. Self-reference and coronary heart disease incidence in the western collaborative group study. *Psychosomatic medicine 51*, 2 (Apr. 1989), 137–144. PMID: 2710908.
15. Hanson, C. L., Burton, S. H., Giraud-Carrier, C., West, J. H., Barnes, M. D., and Hansen, B. Tweaking and tweeting: Exploring twitter for nonmedical use of a psychostimulant drug (adderall) among college students. *Journal of Medical Internet Research 15*, 4 (Apr. 2013), e62.
16. Hecht, B., Hong, L., Suh, B., and Chi, E. H. Tweets from Justin Bieber's heart: The dynamics of the location field in user profiles. In *CHI* (New York, NY, USA, 2011), 237–246.
17. Howell, R. T., Kern, M. L., and Lyubomirsky, S. Health benefits: Meta-analytically determining the impact of well-being on objective health outcomes. *Health Psychology Review 1*, 1 (2007), 83–136.
18. James W Pennebaker, M. R. M. Psychological aspects of natural language. use: our words, our selves. *Annual review of psychology 54* (2003), 547–77.
19. Jamison-Powell, S., Linehan, C., Daley, L., Garbett, A., and Lawson, S. "I can't get no sleep": discussing #insomnia on Twitter. In *CHI*, ACM (New York, NY, USA, 2012), 1501–1510.
20. Lampos, V., De Bie, T., and Cristianini, N. Flu detector: tracking epidemics on twitter. In *ECML/PKDD* (2010), 599–602.
21. Messer, L. C. Neighborhood-level characteristics as predictors of preterm birth: Examples from wake county, north carolina. Tech. rep., North Carolina Department of Health and Human Services, 2005.
22. Paul, M. J., and Dredze, M. You are what you tweet: Analyzing Twitter for public health. In *ICWSM* (2011).
23. Pedregosa, F., et al. Scikit-learn: Machine learning in python. *Machine Learning Research 12* (2011), 28252830.
24. Pennebaker, J., Francis, J., and Booth, R. Linguistic inquiry and word count: LIWC 2001. *World Journal of the International Linguistic Association* (2001).
25. Qiu, L., Lin, H., Ramsay, J., and Yang, F. You are what you tweet: Personality expression and perception on twitter. *Journal of Research in Personality 46*, 6 (Dec. 2012), 710–718.
26. Rabi, D. M., et al. Association of socio-economic status with diabetes prevalence and utilization of diabetes care services. *BMC Health Services Research 6*, 1 (Oct. 2006), 124. PMID: 17018153.
27. Sadilek, A., Kautz, H., and Silenzio, V. Predicting disease transmission from geo-tagged micro-blog data. In *AAAI* (Dec. 2012).
28. Schwartz, H. A., et al. Characterizing geographic variation in well-being using tweets. In *Seventh International AAAI Conference on Weblogs and Social Media (ICWSM)* (2013).
29. Seligman, M. E. P. *Flourish: a visionary new understanding of happiness and well-being*. Free Press, New York, 2011.
30. Signorini, A., Segre, A. M., and Polgreen, P. M. The use of Twitter to track levels of disease activity and public concern in the U.S. during the influenza a H1N1 pandemic. *PLoS ONE 6*, 5 (May 2011), e19467.
31. Sobal, J., and Stunkard, A. J. Socioeconomic status and obesity: A review of the literature. *Psychological Bulletin 105*, 2 (1989), 260–275.
32. Stewart, A., and Diaz, E. Epidemic intelligence: For the crowd, by the crowd. In *Web Engineering*, M. Brambilla, T. Tokuda, and R. Tolksdorf, Eds., no. 7387 in Lecture Notes in Computer Science. Springer Berlin Heidelberg, Jan. 2012, 504–505.

# Unraveling Abstinence and Relapse: Smoking Cessation Reflected in Social Media

**Elizabeth L. Murnane**[1,2]
elm236@cornell.edu

**Scott Counts**[1]
counts@microsoft.com

[1]Microsoft Research, [2]Cornell University Information Science

## ABSTRACT
Analysis of smokers' posts and behaviors on Twitter reveals factors impacting abstinence and relapse during cessation attempts. Combining automatic and crowdsourced techniques, we detect users trying to quit smoking and analyze tweet and network data from a sample of 653 individuals over a two-year window of quitting. Guided by theory and practice, we derive behavioral, social, and emotional measures to compare users who abstain and relapse. We also examine the cessation process, demonstrating that Twitter can help chronicle how some people go about quitting. Among other results, we show that those who fail in their smoking cessation are far heavier posters and use relatively less positive language, while those who succeed are more social in both network ties and in directed communication. We conclude with insights on how intelligent intervention systems can harness these signals to provide tailored behavior change support.

### Author Keywords
Smoking; cessation; health; behavior; social media; Twitter

### ACM Classification Keywords
H.5.3 [Information Interfaces and Presentation]: Group and Organization Interfaces

## INTRODUCTION
Tobacco smoking is the leading cause of preventable death and the leading form of chemical dependence in the U.S, resulting in over 400,000 deaths annually [12]. According to the latest report [11] by the Centers for Disease Control and Prevention (CDC), there are nearly 44 million smokers in the U.S. alone. Importantly and encouragingly, over 68% of smokers report a desire to quit and over 50% have attempted to do so for at least one day. However, relapse is common, and only a minority of smokers are able to permanently maintain abstinence [8].

There is considerable recent evidence of the efficacy of various intervention strategies, including individual or group therapy, physician care, and self-help interventions [16, 26]. However, the former programs are not accessible, affordable, or utilized beyond a minority of smokers; and self-help strategies must be closely tailored to individual habits, circumstances, and progress to be effective [41].

Digital cessation tools, such as phone-based monitoring and assistance applications, hold tremendous potential to overcome these challenges to widespread adoption by empowering a range of users with information, strategies, and self-awareness when attempting to quit. While such tools are appearing, they have major shortcomings as well. Studies of these tools find low adherence to established clinical practice guidelines for treating tobacco use and dependence [1]. This same prior work and our own evaluation also find that these tools' support is not personalized, is not based on individual motivations, and does not adapt during the cessation process, for instance to detect or pre-empt user struggles and setbacks. Rather, their approaches are typically one size-fits all and use game-ified elements to maintain engagement instead of the customized support necessary to achieve successful cessation outcomes.

In this work, we identify the posting and network data of smokers on Twitter as a way to observe and assess key personal and social traits and behaviors relevant to providing this sort of tailored support. We aim to leverage this increasingly abundant data to develop methods for assessing and predicting a smoker's likelihood of remaining abstinent during the cessation process. Our underlying motivation is creating a new class of personalized and sustainable intervention tools for health-related behavior change that engage with a broader spectrum of users.

## BACKGROUND

### Goal Setting, Behavior Change, and Smoking Cessation
Seminal theory, recent refinements, and experimental research establish that a combination of personal, behavioral, and environmental factors influence why an individual sets a goal, performs positively or negatively during its pursuit, and ultimately reaches success or failure [6, 7, 28]. The Transtheoretical Model (TTM) [35] provides us a conceptual framework with which to evaluate an individual's readiness to embark on such a goal and monitor progress through stages of behavior change. More specifically, individuals do not have any near-term intention to quit when in *Pre-Contemplation*; begin to more fully realize the cons of the unhealthy behavior in *Contemplation*; continue evaluating the positive impacts changing could have on oneself and others as they progress


*CHI 2014*, April 26 - May 01 2014, Toronto, ON, Canada

http://dx.doi.org/10.1145/2556288.2557145

through *Preparation*; and rely on commitments, conditioning, environmental controls, and social support as they reach *Action* (i.e., modify behavior) and sustain long term *Maintenance* [34, 35]. One contribution of our current work is developing social media-based measures that capture such aspects of TTM, which can then be embedded into tools for many types of behavior change.

Numerous studies over the years have tested these models with smoking cessation interventions. Findings generally support the model and confirm that stage of change variables positively predict abstinence [15, 36], including for adolescents [38] and for smokers with varying mindsets about quitting [41]. However, some studies have met criticisms due to non-representative recruitment or lack of longitudinal follow-up beyond 1 to 24 months [4, 41].

### Text and Social Network Analysis

Advances in psycholinguistics have shown the effectiveness of using the text people write to evaluate emotional, psychological, cognitive, and behavioral attributes relevant to the aforementioned theoretical constructs. Sentiment analysis techniques and tools such as the Linguistic Inquiry Word Count (LIWC) [32] have been well validated. Through such text analysis, researchers have found strong correlations between language use and physical health, cognitive processes, and mental state [10, 31, 39]. Linguistic analysis has also been used to model emotions and affective states from text [9] such as Twitter posts [25].

Other recent work analyzes the size and structure of social networks and finds that the connections and interactions of a user can strongly influence her own health-related behaviors and goals [5, 17]. In this setting, a person is exposed to temptations as well as others' achievements, which can have negative or positive impacts on her own motivation, expectations, and effort [2, 6]. Further, the social context creates chances to seek and receive external support, with encouragement or constructive feedback improving performance [27] and negative messaging having even stronger effects in the opposite direction [6].

### Twitter and Personal Health

Data from Twitter in particular are attractive for connecting users' online generated content and social relationships with personal health. Tweets are naturally expressed in a user's own voice, permitting the kinds of linguistic analysis previously mentioned. Additionally, Twitter's social setting offers opportunity to study the accountability, exposure to success, and peer support important to goal formation, motivation, and achievement as just discussed. Finally, tweets are posted publicly, spontaneously, and over extended periods of time. This enables low-cost, large-scale, and longitudinal collection of data that exposes more realistic patterns of activity than traditional survey methods, which face challenges of low response rates and difficulty ensuring veracity of respondents' reported behavior.

With respect to the health domain, analysis of Twitter data has proved a promising way to diagnose and better understand health related behaviors and disorders such as insomnia [24], mental health [13], and fitness [40].

Regarding smoking specifically, research has very recently recognized Twitter as an ideal medium through which to promote smoking cessation programs [33]. However, the analysis of posting behavior has gone untapped as a way to identify smokers, better understand the smoking and abstinence processes, and determine signals of an attempt to quit or a need for cessation support.

## METHOD

### Identifying Smokers

Our first step was to identify Twitter users who are smokers with an intention to quit. Our qualitative examination of cessation forums, self-help materials, and tweets revealed key terms and topics relevant to smoking cessation. We used these to build queries (e.g., *+smok*/+cig* +[quit* / smoke free / cessation] [today] –ago [official*])* for the Twitter Firehose (made available to us via an agreement with Twitter) to retrieve *cessation-event* tweets posted between June 1, 2011 and June 1, 2012. This time window allowed us to collect a year's worth of a user's tweets both before and after an announcement to quit, letting us look for pre-cessation motives as well as for changes in behavior, emotion, or social dynamics following the cessation-event.

From these cessation-event tweets, we eliminated retweets (since the original message is posted by a different user), non-English tweets or those by users whose profiles do not specify language as English, tweets by users with under 100 lifetime tweets, tweets by known advertising accounts or containing defined advertisement keywords, and tweets referring to smoking-substances other than tobacco. From the resulting 33,420 posts, we sampled 2000 randomly.

We removed any personally identifiable information from the text, for example normalizing mentions to @username, and then used Mechanical Turkers to manually verify each tweet as a genuine announcement of an intention to quit. Each tweet was labeled by 3 workers required to be Masters and live in the U.S. The judgments of any annotator who did not specify a minimum familiarity level with Twitter or who did not take a minimum amount of time to complete the task were disregarded as invalid. To be conservative, we eliminated tweets not unanimously labeled as authentic announcements to quit, resulting in 733 unique users and cessation-event tweets. Fleiss kappa = 0.7613, which falls within a generally accepted range of rater agreement. The following are examples of verified cessation-event tweets:

- *Just smoked my last cigarette ever!!! I officially quit!*
- *Today I am going to quit smoking. Wish me luck*
- *Last cigarette ever today. #promiseonmylife #bestfeeling*

Having identified a set of smokers intending to quit, we collected these users' publicly available profile and network information. We also again iterated the Twitter Firehose to collect their timeline of tweets posted one year prior to their cessation-event and one year after. We identified smoking-relevant tweets using our smoking keywords originally used to retrieve cessation-events. We used Mechanical Turk to verify these tweets as relevant to smoking and the user's own habit, in which case Turkers also coded the Behavior Change Process variables described in the next section. Turkers received labels, definitions, and example tweets for all possible cessation motives, methods, and TTM stages; and like all our MTurk tasks, we disregarded tweets not coded unanimously by 3 Turkers (Fleiss kappa = 0.7615).

Finally, we eliminated any user who referenced non-tobacco smoking-substances more than a threshold amount and any user with zero smoking-relevant tweets after the cessation, leaving a sample of 653 users and 5,309,510 of their tweets (a median of 3,236 tweets per user).

### Measures

As discussed earlier, past research suggests a number of determinants that predict whether a person will successfully achieve a goal to quit smoking, and we now describe our attempt to use Twitter data to operationalize those variables plus derive new measures. While we explore a wide array of variables, it is important to note that our intention is not to simply throw any and all possible metrics at the wall but rather to carefully use prior theory and experimentation as a guide in constructing meaningful features.

#### *Response Variable*

**Outcome** represents a user's ultimate *Survival* or *Relapse*. We measure outcome as a clinician would in an offline intervention, recording whether a user is remaining abstinent as of the last available tweet (i.e., the final "assessment") or has relapsed. Recall that we used Mechanical Turk to label the stage of behavior change indicated by a smoking-relevant tweet, and we assign a survival or relapse assessment using this label. We refer to users who do and do not remain abstinent during cessation attempts as **Survivors** and **Relapsers**, respectively, and the following are examples of final assessment tweets:

| **Survivors** | **Relapsers** |
|---|---|
| • *Congratulations to me, still smoke free :)* | • *Day 26: Broke down and bought a pack of smokes last weekend. Smoked the last one today.* |
| • *@username nope i don't smoke anymore* | • *Well, tried to quit smokin tobacco but..had a fucked up day* |
| • *first few weeks were hard but I haven't craved a cig in months* | • *So day 3 of not smoking is about to get cut short..i can't do it lol* |

#### *Explanatory Variables*

We organize our predictor variables within 4 main categories: online activity, social network structure and interactions, emotional state, and behavior change process. We record measures of these variables according to all of a user's tweets as well as on smoking-relevant tweets only.

**Activity variables** assess baseline activity level as well as smoking fixation and cessation perseverance:

- Tweet Volume: Total number of tweets a user posts in the 1 year before and 1 year after his/her cessation-event
- Burstiness: Maximum number of tweets a user posts in any single hour
- Frequency: Number of hours between successive pairs of tweets a user posts

**Social variables** capture a user's support system, incoming and outgoing attention, and passive and active relationships:

- Friends: Number of other users a user follows
- Followers: Number of other users a user is followed by
- Tweets with At-Mentions: Number of tweets containing at least 1 @username mention
- Unique Mentions: Number of unique users @mentioned

**Personal and Emotional variables** collect demographic, psychological, and affective information about the user:

- Location: The location specified in the user's profile
- Sentiment Intensity Rate: A measure of how intensely positive or negative a user's emotions are, computed using ANEW [9] and LIWC [31] as (per Hutto et al. [23]) the ratio of the sum of the valence intensity of positive or negative language used in tweets to the total number of tweets in a period

**Behavior Change Process variables** are designed to model a user's cessation process in order to evaluate whether or not she is exhibiting behavioral signals known to correlate with successful outcomes. As described earlier, Mechanical Turk coders provided Motive, Treatment, and TTM stage.

- Cessation Date: Date when a user announces attempt to quit smoking (i.e., posting date of cessation-event tweet)
- Motive to Quit: The motivation triggering a user to quit
- Treatment: Any cessation strategy used to stay abstinent
- PreContemplation-, Contemplation-, Preparation-, and Abstinence-Volume: The number of tweets indicating a user is in the corresponding TTM behavior change stage

## RESULTS

We begin with comparisons to CDC statistics both in order to understand the nature of our dataset as well as to buttress our assumptions that we are working with a realistic and representative sample of the U.S. population of smokers. We then contrast our 175 Survivors and 344 Relapsers according to the measures presented in the previous section.

### Alignment with CDC Reports

We find that the locations of smokers across the country, the gender of smokers, and abstinence rates closely align with those reported by the CDC.

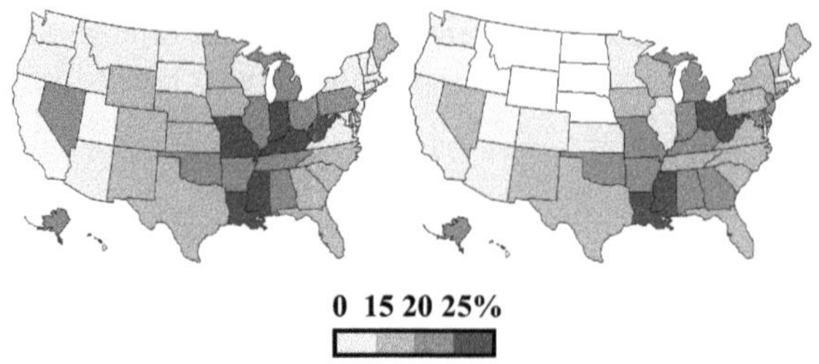


**Figure 1. Smoking prevalance according to CDC reports (left) and according to Twitter profiles (right)**

Figure 1 illustrates the concentration of smokers in US states according to the CDC [3] and according to the Location field in Twitter profiles of users in our dataset. Darker colors correspond to higher smoking prevalence, and white states are those not represented in our data.

Performing gender classification [13] on users in our dataset, Table 1 shows results very similar to national statistics of tobacco usage by men and women [3].

| | CDC | Twitter |
|---|---|---|
| Men | 54% | 59% |
| Women | 46% | 41% |

**Table 1. Proportion of smokers that are men or women according to data from CDC and from Twitter**

Finally, over time we see that trends in data on Twitter closely resemble what clinicians encounter when making longitudinal health assessments, as compared in Figure 2. On the left we see the combined abstinence rate from 17 studies of smokers [22], and on the right the same plot of the number of months users in our own dataset remain abstinent (either before relapsing for Relapsers or until the latest assessment for Survivors). An important contrast does exist here though: obtaining longitudinal data via Twitter is much less difficult than in such offline settings, where follow-ups are typically only performed at points between 1 and 12 months and rarely after 24 months [38].

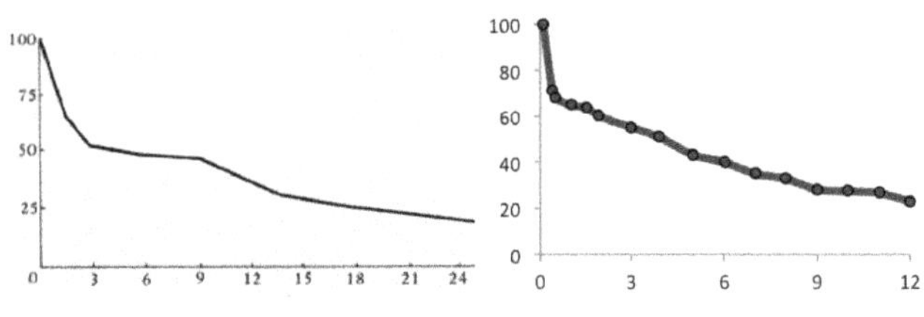


**Figure 2. Percentage of people vs. months of abstinence from 17 combined clinical studies (left) and from Twitter dataset (right)**

These alignments help verify the soundness of our data, and they also demonstrate that easily-accessible web data could substitute for or enrich data from surveys and other conventional yet burdensome methods of collection.

## Activity, Sociality, & Emotion

Next we present our analyses that explore meaningful differences in the online behaviors, social dynamics, and affective states of smokers who successfully remain abstinent (Survivors) and those who relapse and begin smoking again (Relapsers). Our later Discussion section explains how personalized and context-aware tools could capitalize on our findings. We compare these two groups by reporting on the difference in the median values of our measurements computed on the following sets of tweets:

- **All_Before; All_After**: All of a user's tweets posted up to 1 year before or 1 year after his/her cessation-event
- **Smoke_Before; Smoke_After**: Only the tweets of a user that are annotated as smoking-relevant, posted up to 1 year before or 1 year after his/her cessation-event

We removed outliers greater than 3 standard deviations above the mean posting volume, and all comparisons were done on medians using Wilcoxon sign-rank tests.

### *Activity variables*

Striking is a significantly higher activity level for Relapsers compared to Survivors across all variables, as summarized in Table 2. Specifically, Relapsers tweet over 3 times more than Survivors before cessation and nearly 5 times more after cessation, and Relapsers' posting bursts produce twice as many tweets as Survivors', both before and after cessation. Also, posting burstiness and frequency increase after quitting for Relapser yet decrease for Survivors.

| | S | R |
|---|---|---|
| **Vol_B*** ** | 412 | 1243 |
| **Vol_A*** ** | 771 | 3551 |
| **Burst_B*** ** | 4.46 | 10.12 |
| **Burst_A*** ** | 4.28 | 10.94 |
| **Freq_B*** ** | 9.91 | 3.56 |
| **Freq_A*** ** | 11.25 | 2.70 |

**Table 2. Median values of activity measures computed on tweets of (S)urvivors and (R)elapsers, (B)efore and (A)fter cessation. Significant differences in these medians indicated in the first column. (* p < 0.01, ** p < 0.001, *** p < 0.0001)**

These significantly higher levels of overall tweeting activity by Relapsers compared to Survivors may be explained by the fact that heavier Twitter use is a manifestation of the impulsiveness and sensation seeking that is characteristic of heavier smokers [33]. Looking at these measures for smoking-relevant tweets only, we see that Relapsers also mention smoking significantly more than Survivors both before and after cessation (p<0.0001). This may be a sign that Relapsers have more severe addictions that are difficult to break given that stronger addiction levels correlate with thinking about smoking more frequently during the day [19]. Tweets posted by two of the most active users in our dataset, both Relapsers, illustrate this severity of addiction (e.g., "*I had 8 cigarettes earlier in the space of 30 minutes. Whoops*") and such preoccupation with smoking (e.g., "*I'm tryna get myself to stop smoking but I know it's not gonna happen. I'm already thinking about smoking!*").

Next, looking more closely at when Relapsers and Survivors actually make these posts, we notice temporal differences in posting behavior as well, with Relapsers making more of their smoking mentions at night compared to Survivors during the day, as illustrated in Figure 3. We see at least two potential explanations for this.

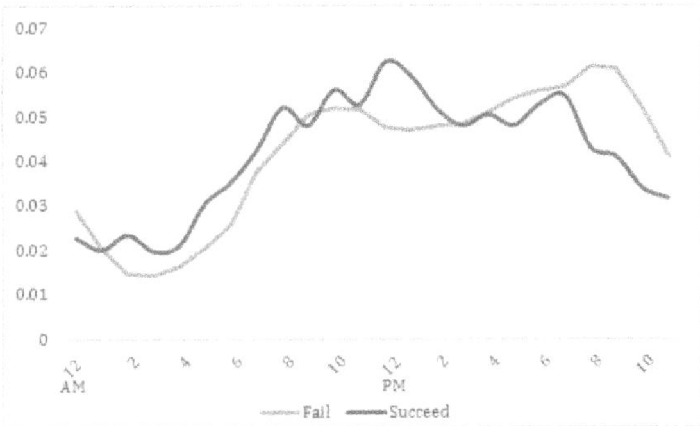


**Figure 3. Time of day at which users tweet about smoking**

First, research has shown that stress levels often peak at night and that depressed individuals are more active at night on Twitter [13]. We therefore suggest that those users suffering from stress or depression may be more prone to turn to cigarettes for coping or have more trouble resisting the relief from stress smoking provides (e.g., "*im really considering smoking tonight bcause im so stressed*").

Second, research also shows that Relapsers struggle more with temptation [14] and that living with other smokers negatively predicts successful cessation outcomes [18, 29]. We hypothesize that Relapsers encounter situations that threaten abstinence more at night. For example, we see Relapsers being tempted at social outings, especially if the individual is drinking or others nearby are smoking, (e.g., "*outside the club and guy beside me smoking makes me wanna*"), as well as when at home at the end of the day and exposed to other smokers (e.g., "*my mom smokes i stay with her she does not respect me trying to stop :*").

### *Social variables*

Next, we examine smokers' social relationships and interactions. In order to avoid Relapsers dominating the raw measures simply due to their massive posting volume, we normalize all social variables by posting volume.

Table 3 shows the differences in friends per tweet and followers per tweet between Survivors and Relapsers, with Survivors benefitting from significantly more friends and followers. These connections enable social outreach and attention, key ingredients in maintaining motivation and performance [27] and navigating the cessation process [8, 29]. Looking to the data, we find many examples of Survivors reaching out, such as "*Starting the patch today. Everyone please support me on the road to quitting smoking*" and "*Ok I started a really big challenge yesterday... I quit smoking! I may need some help from you guys in the upcoming days/weeks*".

| | S-R Before | S-R After |
|---|---|---|
| **Friends/Tweet** | 0.0948*** | 0.1340*** |
| **Followers/Tweet** | 0.0400** | 0.0608*** |

**Table 3. Differences in the median values of social network structure variables Before and After cessation for (S)urvivors and (R)elapsers. (* $p < 0.01$, ** $p < 0.001$, *** $p < 0.0001$)**

Survivors' number of connections also increases from before to after cessation, while Relapsers lose connections. We hypothesize that this is due to Relapsers becoming more socially withdrawn and hostile. For example, consider this Relapser's increasingly anti-social behavior:

- *Day 2 of not smoking #bittersweet*
- *I quit smoking yesterday and everyone is pissing me off!*
- *Day 3 without a cig. Ooo I'm about to shoot someone*

Along the same lines, it also seems the overall emotional tenor of Relapsers' conversations becomes more negative after quitting, perhaps repelling new relationships and even breaking existing ones. Consider the following examples: "*Day 2 no smoking. I hate everyone*" and "*I need a cigarette to calm down... im about to punch something #nojokes*". We discuss these kinds of affective changes further in the following sub-section on emotional variables.

Followers and friends represent more passive subscription and broadcast style relationships, so we also collect @mentions to capture active, personal interactions. Table 4 shows that Survivors have significantly more @mentions per tweet than Relapsers both before and after cessation.

| | S-R All_ Before | S-R All_ After | S-R Smoke_ Before | S-R Smoke_ After |
|---|---|---|---|---|
| **% Tweets with @Mentions** | 0.0529* | 0.0396* | -0.0007* | -0.0005* |
| **Unique @Mentions/Tweet** | 0.0675* | 0.0313* | -0.0007* | -0.0007* |

**Table 4. Differences in the median values of social interaction variables Before and After cessation for (S)urvivors and (R)elapsers in all tweets (All) and in only smoking-relevant tweets (Smoke). (* $p < 0.05$, ** $p < 0.001$, *** $p < 0.0001$)**

At the same time, we see that Survivors make significantly fewer @mentions in their smoking-relevant tweets than Relapsers. While Survivors are overall more socially engaged, one possibility is that when tweeting about smoking, they reach out more selectively, consciously targeting closer and more trusted connections for information (e.g., "*@username what is your opinion on vapor cigarettes? Do you think they make it easier to quit?*") or for emotional encouragement and camaraderie (e.g., "*I quit smoking today! A promise I made to @username & I intend on keeping this promise*").

*Emotion variables*

Research shows that high positivity and moderate negativity correlate with health [31]. Table 5 shows the differences in the intensity of positive and negative language (measured per Hutto et al. [23]) used by Survivors and Relapsers. We see Survivors speaking more positively before and after quitting and more positively when referring to smoking after quitting. We also see that Relapsers' language is only slightly more emotionally negative than that of Survivors, suggesting that Survivors manage emotional balance without repressing negative feelings, which can result in subsequent health problems [31]. Notice how this Relapser has a largely negative attitude towards cessation: "*So grouchy today, who woulda knew that quitting smoking would be so hard??*" while this Survivor expresses optimism, tempered with moderately valenced realism that acknowledges challenges: "*I quit smoking on Sunday evening. Day 3 today. I feel exhausted, annoyed, bored. But the fight must go on. Keep fighting :)*"

| | S-R All_ Before | S-R All_ After | S-R Smoke_ Before | S-R Smoke_ After |
|---|---|---|---|---|
| **Pos. Sent. Intensity** | 0.0850** | 0.0569* | 0.0009 | -0.0029** |
| **Neg. Sent. Intensity** | -0.0010 | -0.0031* | 0.0002 | 0.0003 |

**Table 5. Differences in the median values of sentiment variables Before and After cessation for (S)urvivors and (R)elapsers in all tweets (All) and in only smoking-relevant tweets (Smoke). (* p < 0.05, ** p < 0.001, *** p < 0.0001)**

Additionally, higher relapse rates are known to correspond to the strength of addiction and severity of withdrawal symptoms [37, 41]. We thus hypothesize that Relapsers' negative affect after cessation is also partly due to their more intense struggles with such negative physical and psychological feelings, which include anger, depression, and anxiety [21], as exemplified in the following tweets by three Relapsers: "*I think my body is busy detoxing, coz I have this constant headache. Must be withdrawel symptoms of the cigarettes.*"; "*Haven't smoked all day my head is killing me :(*"; "*pissed off, my back is killing me, my head is swimming with stress and I quit smoking #BadDay*".

### Cessation Motives and Setting the Goal to Quit

A long history of research has established that the motivations and orientations with which an individual forms a cessation goal highly influence subsequent commitment, performance, and outcome. Drawing on [27, 35], we perform thematic analysis of our dataset in order to identify the key motivations that trigger an attempt to quit smoking. As explained in our discussion of data preparation, Mechanical Turkers annotated whether or not a smoking-relevant tweet mentions such a motivation. For the tweets that do, we categorize them into 8 classes of "cessation motives". Table 6 presents descriptions and examples of each motive, and Figure 4 shows the proportions of users driven to quit by each. We were able to determine a motive for 224 people.

| Motive | Example Tweet |
|---|---|
| **Self-Reevaluation**: Desire to stop smoking is part of bettering oneself and improving overall life quality | *When did cigarettes do this to my life? Ending the smoking and starting a new me.* |
| **Relationships**: Realizes habit's effect on others (e.g., unborn child, family, friends) or is pressured by them to quit | *Today I quit smoking. My son came home with an ashtray he made in art class. FML* |
| **Personal-Threat**: Moderate to severe medical symptoms experienced or diagnosed, (e.g. asthma, mouth ulcers, chest pains, heart disease) | *Woke up to serious breathing problems-Mom & friend took me to the hospital for artificial breathing session. Im quitting smoking for good* |
| **Detached-Threat**: Becomes fearful for health after exposure to materials about potential dangers or after witnessing other smokers' health complications | *seeing that smoking commercial I legit plan to never have a cigarette again, scared the fuck outta me. Hope I stick with it* |
| **Financial**: Cost of cigarettes becomes burdensome or prohibitively expensive | *Just done the budget and smoking is officially unaffordable -- cold turkey here I go* |
| **Cosmetic**: Side-effects (e.g., yellow teeth & nails, feeling out of shape) that are less serious than Personal-Threat make smoking unappealing | *never smoking a ciggy again, smell like shit #notworthit* |
| **Holiday**: Quitting is a New Year's Resolution or done for a religious holiday | *I'm giving up cigarettes for Lent!!! And forever thereafter!* |
| **Whim**: Decision to quit is made casually or on a whim | *Ran out of cigarettes - going to try quitting.* |

**Table 6. Users' motives to quit smoking and example tweets**

We recognize that some motives grow from sincere desires and more permanent circumstances. These motives include Self-Reevaluation, Relationships, and Personal-Threat. Other motives are more casual and fleeting in nature, such as Holiday and Whim. We observe that the former tend to drive Survivors to abstinence (49 Survivors showed sincere motivations, 9 showed casual motivations) while the latter motivate Relapsers (47 sincere, 59 casual), yielding a significant difference between the two groups ($\chi^2 = 21.67$, df=1, p<.001). Figure 4 illustrates these differences, and the following paragraphs explore them more deeply.

**Figure 4. Motives of users who abstain (left) and relapse (right)**

First, Self-Reevaluation is a key cognitive step in changing smoking behavior [8], and this internal contemplation produces focus and better chances to meet goals [30]. Motives in our data do show Survivors envisioning their desired state of self as part of such cognitive reconditioning.

Prior work shows that people who recognize the effect of their smoking on others also have better cessation outcomes [34], and we do see Relationships motivating more Survivors than Relapsers. In addition, Personal-Threat motives, such as serious medical concerns, are also more persuasive and see better abstinence rates.

In contrast, we find Relapsers' concerns are more superficial and extrinsically oriented (Cosmetic motives, Detached-Threat), which can induce anxiety and reduce commitment [27]. Whim motives, which overwhelmingly motivate Relapsers, lack any evaluative component and lack accountability. We also see Relapsers combining quitting with more over-the-top and unrealistic fantasies often as part of Holiday resolutions, undermining willpower and causing lack of follow-through [30] (e.g., "*Quit smoking. Exercise. Eat healthier. Start a savings account. Spend less money on pointless shit. Vaycay to Vegas*").

The small numbers available for analysis are due to many users not explicitly mentioning a motive in their tweets. We believe that Holiday and Cosmetic motives are in particular under-reported since investigating when a goal to quit is undertaken (Cessation Date) reveals the pattern in Figure 5. First, we see a spike near the time of New Year's Resolutions. Also noticeable is a peak in late-spring/early summer, which inspection finds is related to users forming goals to get fitter for the summer season via dieting, exercising, and/or quitting smoking (e.g., "*So today is my last day drinking and smoking. Gotta get ma body right fa the summer time and college!*")

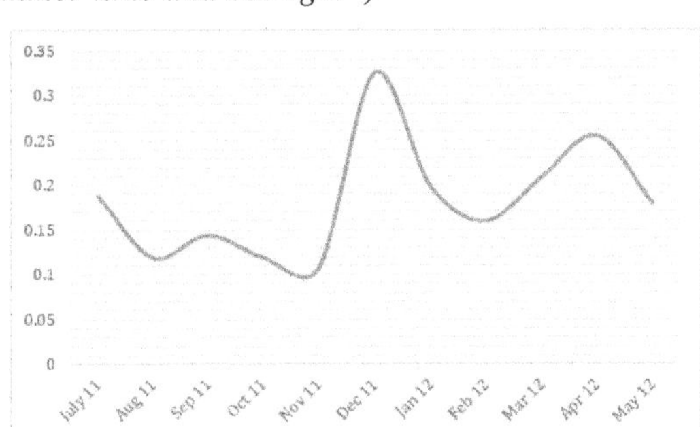


**Figure 5. Cessation-event dates throughout the year**

## The Cessation Process

### *Stages of Change*

Next we analyze whether Survivors and Relapsers demonstrate progression (or lack thereof) through the Transtheoretical Model's stages of change, known as Pre-Contemplation, Contemplation, Preparation, Action, and Maintenance [35]. Essentially, we treat each smoking tweet as an assessment of that user's stage of behavior change. We use the proportion of tweets labeled with a stage as a proxy for the amount of time spent in various stages, which research shows correlates with ultimate outcome [4, 20].

As Figure 6 shows, Relapsers linger more in a preparation phase (Pre-Contemplation, Contemplation, and Preparation combined) than Survivors ($t = 9.63$, $df = 383.30$, $p < .001$).

**Figure 6. Proportion of the cessation process spent in each stage of change for Survivors (top) and Relapsers (bottom). Pre-Contemplation, Contemplation, Preparation, Abstinence (Action & Maintenance)**

This may be due to Relapsers failing to apply the cognitive, emotional, and evaluative processes necessary to make progress; suffering from chronic procrastination and lack of motivation; and/or having little confidence in their ability to quit -- all of which have been shown to result in longer time spent in pre-abstinence stages and subsequent lower quit rates [15, 34].

We do see evidence of such flawed behaviors in our Relapsers, including procrastination (e.g., "*Quitting red bull today and smoking next week. I might just die of healthy*" and "*Quitting cigarettes cold turkey soon. Going to smoke these 5 more packs of my favorite brands and then be done*"). Relapsers also show low confidence and express pessimism from day one (e.g., "*Trying to quit cigarettes today but dunno if I can do this :-*" and "*Today is my last day smoking...This is going to be hard as hell*"), which contrasts the higher self-efficacy we see from Survivors (e.g., "*Just smoked my last ever cigarette! I know I can quit, yeah baby!*").

Overall, the consistency of our findings with clinical evidence shows that tweeted self-reports about smoking can help to diagnose stage and monitor status on a regular basis.

### *Cessation Strategies and Treatment Methods*

Continuing our analysis of the cessation process, we look more closely at individuals' use of cessation treatments, a variety of which exist and have varying levels of efficacy [16, 26]. Results of thematic analysis to evaluate the cessation strategies employed by users in our dataset are summarized in Table 7 and illustrated in Figure 7.

| Strategy | Example Tweet |
|---|---|
| **Cold Turkey**; Explicitly mention using no aid | *Hopefully yesterday would be the last time I ever touch a cigarette. Gonna go cold turkey!* |
| **Medication & E-Cigarettes**: Nicotine replacement (patch, gum, lozenge) or electronic cig, which gov. considers medicinal | *Ok tweeps, I filled my Chantix prescription today* |
| **Lifestyle Overhaul**: Quitting is combined with other positive behavior changes (e.g., with respect to diet, exercise, job) | *got myself a new, well-paid, full time job, quit smoking AND rebuilt my studio setup* |
| **Avoidance & Substitution**: Changing routine to avoid tempting situations or replacing cigarettes (e.g., with lollipops) | *Yeah. I've been avoiding smokers to avoid temptation. I'm still afraid I'll cave.* |
| **Group:** Quitting with a friend or cessation group | *Today @username and me are quitting smoking* |
| **Self-Help & Alternative Therapies**: Hypnosis, books, digital tools | *read "the easy way to stop smoking" by Allen Carr. I'm 6 months cig free with that book* |

**Table 7. Users' cessation strategies and example tweets**

**Figure 7. Cessation strategies for smokers who successfully abstain (left) and those who relapse (right)**

Clinical research finds that the majority of smokers trying to quit do so without the help of evidence-based cessation treatments, which include over-the-counter and prescription nicotine replacement products, group or individual counseling and therapy, and online programs and self-help plans [11]. Research also finds that smokers trying to quit who use medication or counseling are more successful than those who go unassisted [16]. We see both of these trends holding true in our own dataset. We are able to identify the cessation strategy of 226 people, 156 Relapsers and 70 Survivors. Both Survivors and Relapsers go unassisted more than using any other single method ($\chi^2$ = 15.08, 1 df=1, p<.001). While we see nearly 82% of Relapsers going cold turkey, less than 40% of Survivors do so and instead utilize strategies proven effective more so than Relapsers ($\chi^2$ = 6.90, 1 df=1, p<.01). We also see more Survivors using Avoidance & Substitution, a form of stimulus control important in managing abstinence [8, 34].

## DISCUSSION

### Theoretical Implications

Our primary goal for this work was to demonstrate that data from social media could bear on the nuanced process of smoking cessation. As mentioned, successful abstinence depends on a stunning range of factors. We separated our Twitter-based measures into four categories: activity, sociality, emotion, and cessation-process.

Our activity measures reflect a strong finding that Relapsers tweet far more than Survivors and are both burstier and more frequent in that tweeting. Combined with the increased likelihood of tweeting at night, these activity patterns suggest Relapsers may be more impulsive, sensation seeking, and challenged by temptation.

Despite this increased tweeting, Relapsers are not more social on a per-tweet basis in terms of friends, followers, or directed communication. This finding fits well with the known role of social support in attaining goals including abstinence from smoking. Furthermore, Relapsers are relatively more negative, aversive, and pessimistic than Survivors in terms of sentiment. As dataset examples show, this sourness may interact with social support (or lack thereof) in that Relapsers tend to appear hostile while Survivors invite and seek connectedness.

Finally, we unravel the cessation process to identify the cessation motives, preparedness, and strategy for about one third of the population studied. While a relatively small number, the results are striking. Relapsers are far more likely to procrastinate before cessation; quit for more casual, shallow, and unrealistic reasons; and chose a cold turkey strategy rather than use effective treatment methods.

### Design Implications and Technological Interventions

As mentioned, technological interventions to aid cessation efforts have not been overwhelmingly successful. That our measures differentiate Survivors and Relapsers in ways aligned with theory and experimentation suggest that incorporating social media data may legitimately enhance these interventions. We see two areas for improvement.

First, we can leverage social media to determine if a user is more or less likely to maintain abstinence from day one. For instance, even the single measure of tweeting activity prior to cessation was a strong predictor of relapse as was the amount of social connectivity and the sentiment of posted content, all of which can provide interventions such as mobile phone applications with high level direction as to the level of assistance a user needs.

Second, interventions can be tailored using the different motives, attitudes, and behaviors captured about its users. An application that provides information and reminders on the smoking cessation goal might base its content, timing, and audience on these social media based measures. As examples, users going cold turkey and tweeting frequently at night can receive an intervention designed for susceptibility to temptation, strong addiction levels, and end-of-day support. Users relatively lower in social interaction can be encouraged to reach out or can have support-seeking messages automatically posted to their feed. Those whose content signals poor mood can receive advice to reflect on positive aspects of abstinence or to broadcast more optimistic updates about their cessation attempt. Users whose cessation begins on a holiday can be guided through self re-evaluation and encouraged to consider substantive consequences of their smoking habit.

Lastly, certain activities and changes in behavior can serve as relapse warning flags. For example, context-aware applications could detect a visit to a bar and provide temptation support. A shift to noticeably higher posting activity, increasingly negative affect, a reduction in active social ties, or a lingering in certain behavior change stages can trigger a tool to intervene with therapeutic recommendations or with alerts to trusted connections.

We envision a largely, but not fully, automated intervention system that combines social media with user-provided data. User input can help fill gaps, provide labels on the social media data, and set cessation and intervention preferences and boundaries. A user's explicit contribution of detail about smoking-related behaviors and mindsets can also address activities and thoughts that may occur without a corresponding post on Twitter, which would help mitigate issues of invisible or ambiguous data and could play a role in a more holistic cessation treatment overseen by a clinician, who traditionally struggles with ensuring a patient fully reports behavior.

Finally, we recognize that for smoking cessation, individual definitions of what constitutes success can vary. One person may strive for total, permanent abstinence, whereas another may just want to cut back. Deducing and accommodating such differences in expectations will be key when personalizing intervention tools.

### Future Work

Despite its array of benefits, there are limitations to relying on Twitter data that we acknowledge to avoid making unfounded claims and to suggest compensating future plans. By focusing on Twitter users, we are drawing conclusions on people who have chosen to broadcast their smoking habits, desire to quit, and positive and negative progress towards that goal. There could be fundamental differences between these people and those who undertake goals more privately, in different online settings, or in some other manner to which we do not have access. Of course, this challenge is seen in clinical interventions as well, where participants often represent a minority of smokers [16]. Thus though we see agreement with CDC statistics that suggest our sample is aligned with the full population of smokers, an essential next step is to extend our study with data from additional online and offline sources to see how much our findings translate to broader scenarios.

Within the Twitter sample, there are potential confounds that are difficult to eliminate. For instance, age is not available in the social media data and may explain some differences observed between Survivors and Relapsers. In practice, age and other demographic details, including smoking specific information like years of smoking, may need to be entered by the user in a technological intervention. Also related to sampling, we are limited by our 2-year time window; and although this is similar to traditional clinical settings in which patients typically stop assessments after 24 months, expanding the scope of data to longer time periods is an opportunity for additional insight into complications like long-term relapse.

## CONCLUSION

In this paper, we leveraged socio-technical systems to study human behavior and inform next-generation technology designs, demonstrating the immense opportunity offered by social media to better understand, model, and predict why and how the smoking cessation behavior change process happens. We combined automatic and crowdsourced techniques to detect Twitter users trying to quit smoking; analyzed their network data, tweets, and smoking-relevant content; and explored the cessation process in the year leading up to the cessation-event as well as the year after. We illustrated that this type of data closely approximates real world data yet is much less cumbersome to obtain.

We also exhibited how the Twitter medium captures emotional expression, mediates social interaction, documents behavior, and reflects behavior change, finding clear distinctions between individuals who do and do not remain abstinent over the observation period according to such features as posting volume and frequency, social subscription and outreach, and affective intensity. Our contributions validate and advance prior work on what fine-grained aspects of these features impact and predict success and failure during smoking-related behavior change.

Finally, we provided design implications to drive forward and steps for developing systems that interpret these signals as part of tailored cessation support and intervention.

## ACKNOWLEDGEMENTS

We gratefully acknowledge guidance from Meredith Ringel Morris, Munmun De Choudhury, and other members of the Nexus research group and Microsoft Research Redmond.

## REFERENCES

1. Abroms, L., Padmanabhan, N., Thaweethai, L., Phillips, T. iPhone Apps for Smoking Cessation: A Content Analysis. *American Journal of Preventive Medicine* (2011), 279-285.
2. Alderman, M. Goals and goal setting. *Motivation for achievement* (1999), 88-111.
3. American Cancer Society. Cancer Facts and Figures. (2012).
4. Aveyard, P., Massey, L., Parsons, A., Manaseki, S., Griffin, C. The effect of Transtheoretical Model based

interventions on smoking cessation. *Social Science & Medicine 68*,3 (2009), 397-403.
5. Bahr, D. B., Browning, R. C., Wyatt, H. R., & Hill, J. O. Exploiting social networks to mitigate the obesity epidemic. *Obesity 17*,4 (2009), 723-728.
6. Bandura, A. Self-efficacy: The exercise of control. (1997).
7. Bandura, A. & Locke, E. A. Negative self-efficacy and goal effects revisited. *Applied psychology 88*,1 (2003), 87.
8. Borland, R., Partos, T., Yong, H., Cummings, K., Hyland, A. How much unsuccessful quitting activity is going on among adult smokers? *Addiction 107* (2012), 673-682.
9. Bradley, M. M. & Lang, P. J. Affective norms for English words (ANEW). *Technical Report C-1* (1999).
10. Campbell, R. S. & Pennebaker, J. W. The secret life of pronouns: flexibility in writing style and physical health. *Psychological Science 14*,1 (2003), 60-65.
11. Centers for Disease Control. Current Cigarette Smoking Among Adults - United States. (2011).
12. Chase, C. Public Policy Statement on Nicotine Dependence and Tobacco. *American Society of Addiction Medicine* (2010).
13. De Choudhury, M., Counts, S., & Horvitz, E. Major life changes and behavioral markers in social media: case of childbirth. In *Proc. CSCW* (2013), 1431-1442.
14. DiClemente, C. C., Fairhurst, S. K., & Piotrowski, N. A. Self-efficacy and addictive behaviors. (1995), 109-141.
15. DiClemente, C. C., Prochaska, J. O., Fairhurst, S. K., Velicer, W. F., Velasquez, M., & Rossi, J. The process of smoking cessation: an analysis of precontemplation, contemplation, and preparation stages of change. *Journal of consulting and clinical psychology 59*,2 (1991), 295.
16. Fiore, M. Treating tobacco use and dependence: Clinical practice guideline. (2008).
17. Fowler, J. H. & Christakis, N. A. Dynamic spread of happiness in a large social network. *BMJ: British medical journal 337* (2008).
18. Gulliver, S. B., Hughes, J. R., Solomon, L. J., & Dey, A. N. An investigation of self-efficacy, partner support and daily stresses as predictors of relapse to smoking in self-quitters. *Addiction 90*,6 (1995), 767-772.
19. Heatherton, T., Kozlowski, L., Frecker, R., Fagerstrom, K. The Fagerstrom test for nicotine dependence. *British journal of addiction 86*,9 (1991), 1119-1127.
20. Howard, K. I., Kopta, S. M., Krause, M. S., & Orlinsky, D. E. The dose-effect relationship in psychotherapy. *American Psychologist 41*,2 (1986), 159.
21. Hughes, J., Stead, L., Lancaster, T. Antidepressants for smoking cessation. *Cochrane Database Syst Rev* 1.1 (2007).
22. Hunt, W. A. & Matarazzo, J. D. Habit mechanisms in smoking. *Learning mechanisms in smoking* (1970), 65-90.
23. Hutto, C., Yardi, S., Gilbert, E. A longitudinal study of follow predictors on twitter. In *Proc. CHI* (2013), 821-830.
24. Jamison-Powell, S., Linehan, C., Daley, L., Garbett, A., & Lawson, S. I can't get no sleep: discussing #insomnia on twitter. In *Proc. CHI* (2012), 1501-1510.
25. Kouloumpis, E., Wilson, T., Moore, J. Twitter sentiment analysis: The Good the Bad and the OMG! In *ICWSM* (2011).
26. Lemmens, V., Oenema, A., Knut, I. K., & Brug, J. Effectiveness of smoking cessation interventions among adults: a systematic review of reviews. *EJCP* (2008).
27. Locke, E. A. & Latham, G. P. Building a practically useful theory of goal setting and task motivation: A 35-year odyssey. *American psychologist 57*,9 (2002), 705.
28. Locke, E. A., Shaw, K. N., Saari, L. M., & Latham, G. P. Goal setting and task performance: 1969-1980. *Psychological bulletin 90*,1 (1981), 125.
29. Manchón Walsh, P., Carrillo, P., Flores, G., Masuet, C., Morchon, S., Ramon, J. Effects of partner smoking status & gender on long term abstinence rates of patients receiving smoking cessation treatment. *Addictive behaviors* (2007).
30. Oettingen, G., Pak, H., Schnetter, K. Self-regulation of goal-setting. *Personality & social psych. 80*,5 (2001), 736.
31. Pennebaker, J. W., Chung, C. K., Ireland, M., Gonzales, A., & Booth, R. J. The development and psychometric properties of LIWC2007. (2007).
32. Pennebaker, J. W., Francis, M. E., & Booth, R. J. Linguistic inquiry and word count: LIWC 2001. (2001), 71.
33. Prochaska, J. J., Pechmann, C., Kim, R., & Leonhardt, J. M. Twitter=quitter? An analysis of Twitter quit smoking social networks. *Tobacco control 21*,4 (2012), 447-449.
34. Prochaska, J. O., DiClemente, C. C., & Norcross, J. C. In search of how people change: Applications to addictive behaviors. *Journal of Addictions Nursing 5*,1 (1993), 2-16.
35. Prochaska, J. O. & Velicer, W. F. The transtheoretical model of health behavior change. *American journal of health promotion 12*,1 (1997), 38-48.
36. Prochaska, J. O., Velicer, W. F., DiClemente, C. C., & Fava, J. Measuring processes of change: applications to the cessation of smoking. *Journal of consulting and clinical psychology 56*,4 (1988), 520.
37. Redding, C. A., Prochaska, J. O., Paiva, A., Rossi, J. S., Velicer, W., Blissmer, B. J., Greene, G. W., Robbins, M. L., & Sun, X. Baseline stage, severity, and effort effects differentiate stable smokers from maintainers and relapsers. *Substance use & misuse 46*,13 (2011), 1664-1674.
38. Robinson, L. M. & Vail, S. R. An Integrative Review of Adolescent Smoking Cessation Using the Transtheoretical Model of Change. *Journal of Pediatric Health Care 26*,5 (2012), 336-345.
39. Rude, S., Gortner, E.-M., & Pennebaker, J. Language use of depressed and depression-vulnerable college students. *Cognition & Emotion 18*,8 (2004), 1121-1133.
40. Teodoro, R. & Naaman, M. Fitter with Twitter: Understanding Personal Health and Fitness Activity in Social Media. In *ICWSM* (2013).
41. Velicer, W. F., Redding, C. A., Sun, X., & Prochaska, J. O. Demographic variables, smoking variables, and outcome across five studies. *Health Psychology 26*,3 (2007), 278.

# Weaving Clinical Expertise in Online Health Communities

**Jina Huh**
Telecommunication, Information Studies, and Media
Michigan State University
jinahuh@msu.edu

**Wanda Pratt**
The Information School
DUB
Biomedical and Health Informatics
University of Washington
wpratt@uw.edu

## ABSTRACT
Many patients visit online health communities to receive support. In face-to-face support groups, health professionals facilitate peer-patients exchanging experience while adding their clinical expertise when necessary. However, the large scale of online health communities makes it challenging for such health professional moderators' involvement to happen. To address this challenge of delivering clinical expertise to where patients need them, we explore the idea of semi-automatically providing clinical expertise in online health communities. We interviewed 14 clinicians showing them example peer-patient conversation threads. From the interviews, we examined the ideal practice of clinicians providing expertise to patients. The clinicians continuously assessed when peer-patients were providing appropriate support, what kinds of clinical help they could give online, and when to defer to patients' healthcare providers. The findings inform requirements for building a semi-automated system delivering clinical expertise in online health communities.

### Author Keywords
Online health communities; moderator; support group; health informatics

### ACM Classification Keywords
J.3. Life and Medical Sciences (Medical information systems)

## INTRODUCTION
A recent study with WebMD.com's most active online health communities [11] showed 62.1% of patient posts could benefit from clinical expertise. However, the portion of patients' posts that received replies from health professional moderators was only 4.7% (median value among 6 communities). The rest of the threads were left unmoderated, when a portion could have benefited from clinical expertise. Such moderating patterns pertain to other health communities, such as dLife.com—another popular moderated diabetes community [13]. Furthermore, according to a study conducted in 2011, only 19% of major online health communities provided health professionals as moderator staff. No non-profit online health communities provided health professional moderators, showing potential limitations in time and cost in hiring health professionals as moderators [12].


*CHI 2014,* April 26 - May 01, 2014, Toronto, ON, Canada.

http://dx.doi.org/10.1145/2556288.2557293

Although many Websites offer health information (e.g., Mayoclinic.org), patients still come to online health communities to get information that could benefit from clinical expertise. This phenomenon especially holds true because clinical issues and patients' experiential knowledge are intricately intertwined [11]. For instance, in the context of diabetes, other patients can provide recipes appropriate for diabetes based on their experience and clinicians can advise on the ideal after meal blood sugar number that patients should maintain. Accordingly, it is helpful for patients to exchange experiences and support with peers while receiving the clinical perspectives of clinicians. Realizing such benefits of weaving clinical expertise and peer-patient support, many hospitals offer moderated support groups, but such resources are scarce for all illnesses, especially in rural areas.

Delivering clinical expertise to online health communities is a much needed but unavailable feature in current online health communities. We interviewed clinicians to examine the ideal practice of providing clinical expertise to patients. The results helped to develop requirements for a new online health community paradigm, where clinical expertise is delivered semi-automatically within peer-patient conversations.

## ONLINE HEALTH COMMUNITIES: PEER-PATIENT AND CLINICAL EXPERTISE
Online health communities have been shown to provide immense social support among peer-patients in cancer [23], diabetes [10], rare diseases [19], infertility [25], and HIV/AIDS [22]. The term *peer-to-peer health care* has emerged to refer to peer patients' "pioneering new ways of pursuing health by banding together and sharing knowledge" [6].

Many hospitals have acknowledged the benefit of peer-patient interaction due to their level of social support and patients' experiential knowledge. Hartzler and Pratt [8] distinguished patient expertise from clinical expertise, highlighting the unique advantages that patients' own expertise brings to illness management. For instance, patients discuss where to find wigs or how to manage one's spousal relationship. Clinicians cannot provide such knowledge about managing the everyday experience of illness as well as peer patients can.

In hospital-led support groups, health professionals, such as dietitians, nurses, or medical doctors moderate peer-patient conversations. These clinician moderators provide clinical expertise when necessary while facilitating peer-patient exchanges of their experiences. The clinician moderators might clarify any questions requiring clinical expertise that come up, redirect potential misinformation, or add a clinician's perspective [15]. However, hospital-led support groups are scarce resources, especially to those living in rural settings where access to clinical facilities requires hours of traveling [9].

Similar to the idea of health professionals moderating peer-patient support groups in hospital settings, online health communities have also begun to incorporate health professional moderators, who can provide medical information to the community members [11]. However, only 19% of major online health communities provide health professional moderators, potentially due to monetary and time resources [11]. This study also found that no non-profit online health communities provided health professional moderators. Even though a community might provide health professional moderators, the level of moderators' participation was extremely low—health professional moderators only answered 4.7% of patient posts (Median value of the 6 most active communities on WebMD.com) [11].

Although automated medical question and answering systems have been investigated for clinicians' use [16], no studies have looked at automated ways to add clinical expertise within peer-patient online forum threads. We can learn about informal peer-patient leaders in online health communities from prior studies looking at general forums [4,18]. However, moderating with clinical expertise presents unique challenges that other expertise might not have (e.g., liability issues). Accordingly, studying the dynamics of health professional moderators and peer-patients presents unique research problems that have not been well explored before.

To facilitate delivering a combined peer-patient and clinical expertise to patients, we investigate the idea of semi-automatically weaving clinical expertise into online health communities. We ask how we can automatically insert clinical expertise into online health communities. When and how should clinical expertise be added? What clinical expertise should be added? We interviewed clinicians to understand the ideal practice in delivering clinical expertise to patients, which can then aid answering these questions and building a new online health community paradigm where both clinical and patient expertise are delivered to the patients.

## METHODS: INTERVIEWS AND EXAMPLE THREADS

Our goal was to use the ideal practice in clinicians' delivering expertise to patients as a potential gold standard in building requirements for the new online health community system, where clinical expertise is automatically weaved into peer-patient conversations. We sent emails to our social network in the northwestern U.S. and recruited 14 clinicians (Gender: 11 female, 3 male; Occupation: 8 nurses/nurse practitioners, 5 physicians, and 1 psychiatrist; Age: from mid 20s to late 60s). We interviewed the clinicians from 30 minutes to one hour.

Considering the short time (30 minutes) we can spend with each clinician, we prepared three example online health community threads for the clinicians to read and comment on how they would provide their clinical expertise. To accommodate the general expertise of the clinicians, the threads would need to cover common illnesses (e.g., diabetes) that have different causes for disease (e.g., lifestyle versus family history) and population (e.g., pediatric versus older adults). Accordingly, we chose the diabetes, ADHD (attention deficit hyperactivity disorder), and pain management communities. These three disease communities were also the most active communities at WebMD.com, a publicly available online health community, which supports over 35 disease communities. We randomly selected one thread from each community among patient-only threads (with no moderators) with at least two replies to include enough peer-patients' replies per thread but no more than four replies to keep the participant's required reading time low. We de-identified the authors of the posts before presenting the threads to the clinicians. We received approval from our institutions' Institutional Review Board for this study. The content of the example threads were typical threads of WebMD communities in terms of asking for clinical expertise, according to prior work in understanding what kinds of questions patients ask in online health communities [11].

We asked the clinicians to read one example thread at a time and think aloud as they read the threads. We then probed further on what kinds of advice they would provide to both the thread initiating patients and the repliers, if they were moderating the community. We also explained our envisioned system and asked what the system should ideally do. Below are the example threads we showed to the clinicians. Due to space constraints, we only give one full example from the diabetes thread, and we will paraphrase the other two example threads:

**Diabetes community example thread: "Blackening feet"**
Jane (the thread initiator) wrote: "*I have been trying to find anything to tell me what this means. My feet have been changing colors for about 2 years. Sometimes they are almost black. My podiatrist just shook his head. I also have pain if you just touch certain places. What can this be? :frown: Thank you, Jane (sic)*"

Hall replied: "*All kinds of things come to my mind, none of them good. You really need to get to your doctor. Neuropathy and circulatory problems could bring dire results. Get it checked out right away. (sic)*"

Amy replied: "*My feet turn really red when I stand for awhile and sometimes when I am shaving my legs and prop one foot on the side of the tub it looks darker to me until I put it back down, I guess a circulation problem with me, My dr, did not think I needed to worry,Just try to get this weight off, she said,slipper: :smile: (sic)*"

**Pain management community example thread: "Methadone side effects?"**
Jesse's thread initiating post (126 words) described taking Methadone and potential side effects that are "killing" him. Jesse asked for others who had similar experiences. To this post, Manny, also on Methadone, described (in 119 words) her experiences of becoming sick from her regular dose. She suggested that "fentanyl patches are by far the best medication for pain relief." The second replier, Eric, replied (304 words) with his experience of pain medications for the past 6 years—since he was 12. He described his significant others' experiences as well around Methadone for many years after recovering from taking Heroin. Eric noted "99% sure" that Jesse's descriptions of side effects are not those of Methadone. Eric suggested talking to the doctor about the symptoms and reassured that "Methadone is a safe, effective and proven medication."

**ADHD community example thread: "A niece with ADD help!!"**
Acary, an aunt of a girl who has ADHD, asked the community (49 words) what kinds of foods her niece needs to eat and if the pills she is taking are right for her. She says "I want her to grow up normal." To this post, Ashley responded (89 words) sharing her daughter's experience of changing diet and medications not making any difference. Ashley talked about her daughter going to college and working full-time and suggested Acary to just provide full support. Jes replied (233 words) congratulating Ashley's daughter and also shared her 4-year-old daughter's experience of having problems at home and at school. Jes described how treating children with ADHD as normal is important. She also mentioned her grandmother's quote of making an analogy between ADHD and cold medications.

We transcribed the interview data and analyzed it using open coding analysis [24]. We iteratively refined and grouped the codes using an affinity diagram to find common as well as contradicting themes that emerge across participant data [2].

Next, we present our findings in two parts. In findings 1, we describe how the clinicians would provide clinical help to the patient who initiated the thread. In findings 2, we focus on the clinicians' reaction to peer-patient interaction. These findings provide implications for how we might envision semi-automatically weaving clinical expertise in online health communities.

## FINDINGS 1: MOVING CLINICAL PRACTICES ONLINE

Clinicians used their existing clinical practices as a way to think about how they would respond to patients' posts in terms of *triaging, clinical questioning, partnering with patients, and deciding what to tell patients.*

### Triaging

*Triage* refers to a commonly used term in health settings for prioritizing treatments based on the severity of the problem. The clinicians described a similar process, attempting to first understand the severity of the problem and decide how to respond accordingly—whether to tell them not to worry at all, to try simple interventions at home, or to go see a doctor immediately:

> In medicine, [...] we always get trained [how to determine] sick or not sick. Sick you've got to deal with right away. Not sick, you can take a little bit longer to kind of figure it out. So, I think the first thing is to really categorize these posts in sick or not-sick. (P3)

The clinicians noted they would be extremely careful about overlooking severe problems. P5 said she would not come to a quick conclusion about the patient's problems, and would defer any medical opinion that does not have the expertise in (P14). Almost all clinicians mentioned that they would tell the patients to go see their doctors to ensure liability of the moderators (P14) or to help patients understand the severity (P3) and the cause of the problem (P9).

To understand severity, the clinicians focused on symptoms described in posts:

> If the [foot] color is red, you have to go to the doctor because this person already started color going dark and red—that is called Necrosis, a severe vascular injury. It can develop pressure ulcer or sometimes it can develop MRSA, a severe infection in the skin. (P1)

The clinicians considered detecting serious problems as an important task in moderating communities. Once the clinicians figured out how severe the problem was, the clinicians would then want to know further details about the patient's history and context to give better help.

### Clinical questioning

Clinicians presented the lack of information about patients' medical history as one of the biggest barriers to providing appropriate help for patients in the thread examples. In their existing clinical practices, the clinicians would ask probing questions or use documents to understand patient history, context, and specifics of the problem. Based on the context gained, they would continue to further evaluate if necessary. Below shows examples of how clinical questioning can be applied in online health communities.

**Eliciting patient history.** The following shows an example of clinical questioning to elicit patient history: "[I would ask] something more specific: How long has she been a diabetic? Is she taking insulin? What's her diet like? Because all of those things will impact the skin and the circulation and the tissue too." (P11)

**Gaining objective data.** Sometimes the clinicians wanted to further gain objective data about the person since they could not trust what the patient was reporting: "I am not very convinced of her response in general. So I would like to run a lab test again on her. I want to get more objective data from her." (P12)

**Gaining context.** While P12 considered lab tests as a potential trustful source of data, others considered asking probing questions to gain further context from the patients: "[We could assess] a simple pain level, like 0 to 10 scale … Does it change what you do during the day? How has it changed your quality of life?" (P4)

By asking what else is going on and understanding the family context, such as who are the caregivers and what is their relationships with the caregivers, would clinicians be able to assist further with informational needs that the patients might have. During this process, the clinicians noted the importance of building trust with the patients.

### Partnering with patients: Building connection and trust

The clinicians noted how patients' mistrust of clinicians can hinder the delivery of effective clinical help, especially in online settings where no personal relationships have been established. In their practice, the clinicians would attempt to first connect with patients and establish trust by attempting to *translate* what patients present into what makes sense to clinicians, *exchange* questions and answers, and *be transparent*.

#### *Translating patient posts*

Clinicians set up an analogy of moderating online communities to being on call, translating patients' words into what makes sense to clinicians, using patients' perspective: "When I'm on call, I have to just listen to what the patient is telling me over the phone and try to interpret through their eyes and their experiences." (P3)

A clinician showed how she would reinterpret patients' presented symptoms to what makes sense to her: "Opioids are known to have urinary retention, so he might be describing it as hesitant urination but it could be that he's actually experiencing some urinary retention." (P7)

Instead of disputing patients' presented symptoms, attempting to understand what really happens from a patient's perspective can help build further connections between patients and clinicians.

#### *Increased back and forth interaction*

To further build trust, the clinicians would exchange questions and answers back and forth to understand patients' knowledge and respond accordingly:

> A health professional would want to […] really find out what they (the patients) know, what they think they know, where they've learned it. (P13)

To interpret patients' situations more accurately, exchanging questions and answers will help the clinicians further understand the patients, leading to a better partnership with patients.

#### *Being transparent*

The clinicians also pointed out how being transparent about what they do not know can gain patients' trust and break boundaries:

> I am upfront about [the lack of knowledge] and I say, "So, let's look it up, if that's something that's common." I feel like it's good for my relationship with the patients, because I think it humanizes me too […] it means I drop or break boundaries... (P6)

As the clinicians establish trust and connect with patients, they would then recognize patients are dealing with difficult conditions (P14). They would then provide a supportive environment (P14) and personalized help by giving modified information based on patient types (P9) and context of knowledge (P13). This process would lead to mutually agreeable outcomes (P3). It is not just telling patients what to do (P3), but aligning expectations with the patients (P2).

### Deciding what to tell patients

Once the clinicians established an in-depth understanding about the patient's problem, the next question would be what information or help to give to patients. The clinicians would first try to give patients a *bigger picture* of what is common while highlighting *individual differences*, explain *what to expect*, *clarify* medical information, and advise how to *manage relationships*.

#### *Bigger picture, individual differences, and what to expect*

The clinicians would explain to patients in online health communities what are common treatments or side effects, and what are the unknowns and atypical situations. The clinicians would then explain the individual differences, depending on the patient type. For instance, P14 below would explain what common side effects are and what should be communicated with providers:

> I would say, "Most of these symptoms that you're describing are typical side effects of Methadone. If they

last more than a few days you might want to consider consulting your physician. [...] The foot symptoms you're experiencing are not symptoms I've typically heard as a side effect of Methadone." (P14)

Using numbers and statistics can also help patients or caregivers understand the scale of problems:

> This is something I will say—Some alarming percentage like perhaps 25% or 30% of all males under the age of 25 in jail have untreated ADHD (P8)

While showing what is common, addressing individual differences would help patients have a proper understanding of their health:

> I just get worried when I see these specific numbers this person's going to think that they're just like someone else. While they can get support from each other, each person should expect that their symptoms might be different. (P2)

The clinicians feared that not knowing patients' complete health situation could incorrectly lead patients to think their experiences were similar to each other's potentially unrelated experiences. P9 was concerned that patients would think that Jesse, the thread initiator, and Eric's situations were similar, because Eric may have had addiction problems in the past:

> We don't know if Jesse was on methadone. [...] People [like Eric] who were on methadone because they were former heroin addicts—that's just different. Their experiences are going to be probably slightly different in terms of expectations. (P9)

The clinicians considered their role to be telling patients about the unknowns and expectations for what could happen next. This way, they saw the new online health communities as a platform for prevention and additional help not provided by existing clinical care. The clinicians also noted the importance of helping patients not to be anxious about warnings but to be prepared for potential harm.

### *Clarification of medical information*

The expertise the clinicians would share with the patients included clarifying medical information, such as an overview of drugs and foods (P2, P3, P9, P10, P14), the definition of medical terms (P9), and clarifications about any information unaddressed by peer-patients (P14).

P13 emphasized that clinicians are not in the same position as a parent or caregiver who provide social support. Instead, clinicians should give evidence, medically sound facts, and reasoning. The clinicians also suggested providing other helpful medical resources online, such as WebMD.com, MayoClinic.org, MicroMedex.com, PubMed.gov, and other physician drug references.

The challenge was when there were no right answers to a patient's questions. P1 below described how existing clinical practices work when no clear solutions exit for a patient's problem:

> When there are no right answers, and when side effects are coming up, we tell patients to call back right away. When nurses cannot solve the problem, then she would ask the doctor. If the doctor is not sure either, then the doctor and the nurse would talk about notifying times, like every two weeks to call back about updates. (P1)

The anecdote helps us think about how our system might work through new problems without clear answers.

### *Managing relationships*

The clinicians also discussed how they should help patients in online health communities manage their relationships with their healthcare providers and their family members.

**With providers.** To help with patient-provider relationship, the clinicians first wanted to know the existing relationship:

> Are people really telling [the provider] when they come in? Does the provider take the time to listen? Are they too afraid to really bring it up because they're so worried that they don't really bring it up in a way that gets the attention of the healthcare provider? (P10)

Knowing existing relationships with their healthcare providers could allow clinicians to assist patients of online health communities in what to ask or include when calling their providers (P9, P14). Further, the clinicians would teach patients what to do before going into appointments with their providers—to keep a list of what is happening, how long it has been happening, and what is the intensity of the symptoms (P10). The clinicians were careful in providing such help, because they did not want to diagnose but to explain the problem the provider should examine (P3) and "just help [patients] to be able to seek appropriate help" (P10). P7 was worried that patients will print out their suggestions and bring them to their providers.

The clinicians also saw themselves as helping patients in online health communities be heard by the providers, advising patients how to describe further details (P10). Also, clinicians in online health communities could help patients make a commitment to see their providers or help figure out how the patient can be evaluated (P3, P7).

In the case of patients who have other issues that prevent them from having access to care, another clinician would volunteer other ways to give help, such as "sending them to a website that they could look at and compare with their own situation" (P13). A more common perceived challenge by the clinicians, however, was that patients "just do not go see the doctor" (P10) and might be "afraid to see the doctor because [they're] afraid of what [the doctors are] going to tell [them]" (P3). Accordingly, our system can attempt to understand where patients develop such perceptions about their providers and help patients either find an appropriate provider to talk to or advise on communication skills.

**With family.** Similar to the patient-provider relationship, the clinicians would first try to understand the patient's existing relationship with their families to help it improve. For the ADHD thread example, the clinicians wanted to understand the motivation of the aunt for being involved with care of her niece and why the aunt challenged what was prescribed to the child. A clinician described how he would suggest the poster to talk with the direct caregiver:

> Since you're the aunt, talk with the parents and go, 'How can I be supportive and how can I be helpful?' (P14)

So far we described the first part of our findings on how the clinicians applied their existing clinical practices to infer how they would moderate online health communities. This next section provides insights on how to design the semi-automated system that weaves clinical expertise into online health communities. The clinicians, however, had to expand their usual boundary—patient-provider relationship—and further think about how to work with peer-patients who are also providing help to the patients.

## FINDINGS 2: ABOUT PEER-PATIENT REPLIES

Peer-patient interaction presents a unique dynamic of online health communities distinct from regular patient-provider interaction. In response to peer-patients' replies in the example threads, the clinicians first talked about their perspectives on peer-patient sharing information in general. Furthermore, the clinicians discussed how they might work with peer-patient repliers to provide better clinical help.

### About peer-patient interaction

From the clinicians' perspective, peer-patient interaction was a double-edged sword. While they saw concerns arise around peer-patient interaction, the interaction could also provide unique support that cannot be earned from other places.

#### *Being online, misinformation, and individual differences*

When the Internet started to become widely available to the public, a series of studies examined the quality of information online with an apprehensive view toward uncensored exchange among patients [3]. Over time, researchers have shown that patients generate norms that would discourage sharing misinformation to one another [21], similar to other areas of online community activities [1]. Yet, the older, reserved view toward peer-interaction persisted in the clinicians, showing concerns about peer-patients who are 'strangers' interacting online. They were concerned with the misinformation that peer-patients might share, considering that individual differences can be unnoticed. For instance, P6 below described how unrecognized individual differences among peer patients can lead to misinformation:

> This is one of the things that's dangerous about peer discussions online. What that might mean for somebody healthy or [those with] a different set of comorbidities means something very different and the conversation doesn't include that level of complexity. (P6).

P12 further described how misinformation can be harmful, especially because "people tend to find it hard to filter out information and be objective about them" and that education is crucial in community-based settings. P1 was concerned with a random solution becoming a 'hot topic' and being misconstrued as an effective one without any evidence. P12 was also afraid that the differences in people's opinions can make people nervous and said that outdated experiences around medications have a lot of room for criticism. P5 also noted that experiences cannot simply transfer from one person to another, giving an example of Amy, who compared her red feet with Jane's black feet.

The clinicians showed stronger concerns for highly individualized regimens like medications than other topics:

> Treating of pain is not a cookie cutter thing. You have to try it, you have to check it out and see what works for you. ... it might be working just fine for [some]. And other people, you can't give them enough and it's still not working for them. (P11)

Places that the clinicians pointed out as "red flags" were when dosages were mentioned (P2), generalizing experiences that come from a small sample size, such as "my family and friends" (P3), or when other patients suggested drugs to others (P1).

Ironically, while the clinicians were concerned about sharing specific experiences, they also considered sharing specific experiences as crucial in patients relating with each other, leading to increased social support. P2 wondered what patients' expectations were—whether patients wanted just support or clinical management as well. P2 would be concerned about the latter. If it were the former, then just finding appropriate peers to exchange support would work. P5, on the other hand, considered peers' suggestions as something that he would agree with.

The prevalent perception that interacting with other patients can be harmful sometimes was not grounded on the example threads we gave them. In fact, the clinicians agreed with many replies in example threads:

> it worries me, just because... I don't know, ... But this one person says, "You really need to go to your doctor," which is reasonable. And the information they're giving is reasonable, [...] But I don't really know how that's gonna... (P2)

P2 further noted that not being familiar with online communities might have pushed her to be more concerned about misinformation online, similar to the society's early reactions toward new technology, such as the Internet [17].

#### *Uniqueness of peer-patient experience and support*

During the discussions on misinformation shared among peer-patients, the clinicians acknowledged the unique role peer-patients play in online health communities, such as providing patient expertise, social support, and personal experiences. "Patients know what they are talking about" (P10). One participant noted that online health communities should provide patients information "they cannot get through their doctors" (P3). It is uniquely helpful when peer-patients suggest other things that worked or did not work for her (P4, P9) and recommend asking the provider about the suggestion (P4). P13 below also contrasted the kinds of support that only peer-patients can give compared to clinicians:

> [patients are] supportive in a way that a health professional doesn't necessarily need to be. Health professionals need to give evidence, medically sound facts and some kind of reasoning behind that (P13).

P11 also mentioned successful cancer communities and their unique support compared to healthcare:

> The cancer people have done a good job in that whole support thing [...] But that doesn't happen in a lot of the way healthcare is delivered. So, support groups are fantastic resources (P11).

Even though the clinicians saw peer patients' reassurance as potentially harmful, they also agreed that reassurance coming from those who "actually [went] through the same thing" (P4) empowers other patients:

> That story can reassure Jesse that, gosh, you don't have to stay here. You can go and talk with physician in changing a dose. You're in charge here, and giving some ideas they might try. That's what I like about that interchange. (P4)

P5 stated that, although she has heard from lectures that peer support is important, seeing the example threads helped her further realize that family and friends can really help with the situation. Especially in situations where patients are "being blown off by providers," such as in the case of Jane in the Diabetes thread whose doctor shook his head, places like online communities could help patients feel supported (P10). Sometimes, just feeling supported by knowing that "there are other people struggling" (P9) suffices even at the cost of not getting their original questions answered. P6 also mentioned peer patients can influence each other in positive ways for interacting with their providers—letting each other know that they can contact their providers sooner, for instance. More experienced patients can also share well-known medical facts, such as side effects (P13).

### Good replies versus bad replies

During the interview, we did not ask the clinicians to evaluate the replies. However, interestingly, all clinicians categorized replies into 'good' ones and 'bad' ones based on a variety of language style and content characteristics. In this section, we discuss what the clinicians considered as "good replies" versus "bad replies" and how they would respond to these replies.

#### *"Good" replies: Balanced, focused, reassuring, and advising to go see the doctor*

What the clinicians saw as "good replies" were balanced, focused, reassuring, and suggesting to go see the provider. P9 described the post characteristics that he agreed with:

> I really liked Ashley's response, because it felt like it was (A) respectful, but (B) it was also a balanced response in saying that there is no one best medicine, and there are a variety of things that could be done. (P9)

*Balanced* responses would not emphasize any one particular piece of information but would provide wider understanding around a problem. P5 saw repliers' comparing different treatment options using evidence was a helpful reply. *Focused* responses would be those that address the patient's specific problem instead of being "derailed" or "distracted" (P2, P9) with unrelated personal experiences. Reassuring responses would validate the approaches and attitudes of the patient or the caregiver:

> In saying, "Hey, you care about your child. You're a caring aunt." I think that was something really helpful to validate what she was saying. (P10)

However, P4 was concerned about peer patients reassuring themselves, such as in the case of the diabetes thread, where severe problems get overlooked. The clinicians considered peer-patients telling the poster to go see the provider as helpful. However, in many cases, patients might already have contacted their providers [20] and they visited the community to receive peer support, not to be told to talk to their providers.

#### *"Bad" replies: Underestimating or overstating*

What the clinicians considered as "bad replies" were those that were either underestimating or overstating. The diabetes thread had a severe case of blackening feet and Amy's response that her doctor told her not to worry stood out as the underestimation problems of "bad replies" (P4, P5, P7, P8). The clinicians also considered one a 'bad' reply when they saw overstatements of a problem, such as "*mentioning his sister, brother, and being 99% sure about it*" (P12). P12 went on to explain that generalizing judgments with confidence could make people unnecessarily nervous.

#### *Working with replies: Challenge, ignore, reassure, and enrich*

As the clinicians shared their opinions about the replies, they challenged the repliers, stated they would ignore or reassure them, or said they would respond to the thread to help bring clinical expertise to enrich information shared in the thread.

P8 challenged Amy's suggestion to do weight off (to put legs higher up for blood circulation purposes), because doing weight off might not be safe depending on the poster's personal situation. P3 also challenged Manny's suggestion on trying Fentanyl patch in the Pain management thread, but could not think of the best way to identify P3's opinion that going from Methadone to Fentanyl patch is counter-productive. P1 also challenged common knowledge that people have around massaging—that massaging can be harmful for circulatory problems.

The clinicians would sometimes just ignore the replies that self-report and not address the problems of the poster, since they would not know how to respond to those. P6 said he would not know what he would respond specifically to Eric other than saying, "I agree with both Manny and Eric that if there's something that is going on, it does need to be addressed."

For good replies, the clinicians would reassure that "they have given a good reply" (P12). To further improve the conversation with better information, the clinicians would redirect, confirm, or suggest solutions:

> If I were a moderator, I might redirect them and say, "Black sounds like a big problem to me. It sounds like that's different from the darker red foot. Certainly neuropathy and circulatory problems are likely and they're common with diabetes. It will be important for you to carefully look at your feet, watch for signs of any kind of openings in your skin or problems" (P2)

Here, P2 explained that another reply about blackfoot not being a big concern was incorrect. P2 then briefly explained common background knowledge around diabetes regarding the problem and suggested the next step. P1 would add contingencies around peer-patients' suggestions, such as appropriately performing weight off (lifting the legs up high using cushions). P3 would even warn a replier about his potential danger. To enrich peer conversations, P11 saw repliers asking more patient history questions could help.

## TOWARD SEMI-AUTOMATICALLY WEAVING CLINICAL EXPERTISE IN ONLINE HEALTH COMMUNITIES

So far we described the clinicians' ideal clinical practice and their perspectives on supporting patients in online health communities. In this section, we discuss how our findings translate into thinking about semi-automatically weaving clinical expertise in online health communities. Largely, we learned (1) what clinicians would do to prioritize patient posts to respond to, (2) how to further understand the patients to give better help, and (3) what to give help and how.

### How to prioritize threads needing help

As discussed in the findings on *triaging*, to prioritize the threads that need clinical expertise, we could first go through a triage process, classifying whether a post contains any critical problems that need to be addressed directly. For instance, the clinicians often focused on numbers, biomarkers, names of medications, symptoms, and emotions. Such information can be picked up using natural language processing techniques, together with a database on medications, symptoms, and emotions. Existing work has looked at creating online patient profiles, based on detecting health-related phrases mentioned in patient posts in online community settings [7]. Using post content to predict whether the post will be moderated can also help to predict whether a post needs a clinician's attention [14]. It is an open question how much the severity of the problem can be delineated, and it might be challenging to automatically triage at greater detail as in the real world. However, detecting the "critical" or "flaggable" terms (e.g., 'urination retention', 'black feet') could help speed up the first pass at classifying whether a post is about non-medical or medical topic. A lower level triage process could be done manually by the community administrators or patients themselves (e.g., crowdsourced) or further sophisticated machine learning approach can be devised, using accumulating data produced by moderators and patients.

Similar to prior work in patientslikeme.com [26], detecting critical events of patients, such as onset of a new disease, disease progression, or recovery, can provide implications to not only patients themselves but to the healthcare infrastructure as well. Online health communities can collaborate with clinics and engage patients holistically, from prevention to after-care.

As discussed in the *peer-patient interaction* section, some repliers might present what clinicians consider as misinformation. However, what the clinicians called misinformation was often tied to lack of context—missing patient history and unnoticed individual differences, rather than the incorrectness of the information itself. The next point of discussion—how to further understand patients—will address how patients' detailed context can be further shared.

### How to further understand patients

All clinicians continuously noted that the patient posts lacked information about the patients' context and history. Disambiguating patient history helps not only in preventing potential misunderstanding of information shared among patients but also facilitating better, partnered help from moderators. Rich patient history can also lead to quality peer-patient interactions, as evident in studies attempting to match peer-patient mentors based on profiles [7]. The system should be able to respond in context to the person's knowledge as the clinicians do in their clinical practice.

The online health community system can devise methods to help patients further delineate their patient history and context related to the topic they are discussing. It could be a template that patients fill out or connect with personal health records. Privacy problems could emerge, in which case mechanisms around partial private communication features among moderators and peer-patients can be useful. Considering that patients generally find it hard to tell history and instead say, "I need help," providing a mechanism to produce probing questions for moderators and peer-patients to ask can also help, as learned from the findings around *clinical questioning*. Also, using the patients' past postings can add further context to the patient history.

### What clinical expertise to give and how

Once we know which patient threads need help and learn more about the patient history, the next problem is providing clinical expertise. The kinds of clinical expertise that the clinicians envisioned to provide to patients included: giving a bigger picture, explaining individual differences, presenting what to expect, clarifying medical information, and giving advice on relationships. Some of this information can come from databases containing statistical facts stored in open government resources such as healthdata.gov. For instance, as in the case of Jane with blackened feet, in combination with the symptoms and patient history, the system could pull up national statistics around what that symptom might imply. Such information can be either directly presented to patients or filtered through moderators, who will use the information as a tool to better support patients.

The system can also devise a mechanism with which the community administrators and peer-patients can together make sure that information shared has added references to the original source. It could be in the forms of an automated trigger, asking the patient poster to clarify where the shared medical information came from. Or it could be peer patients or administrators tagging and asking the poster to further delineate the source of information. The interface should clarify that the suggestion is not required so that it does not hinder participation. Instead, if patients supply such information, their posts can receive badges for incentives.

In hospitals, as the clinicians mentioned, many roles and specialties exist—registered nurses, nurse practitioners, interns, residents, attendees, etc, multiplied by specialties. People with these various roles collaborate and create a working, holistic care for each patient. The point is not to replicate regular healthcare to online communities—but online communities can learn from the existing practice on how roles can be divided and coordinated. At current health professional moderated forums such as WebMD.com or diabeticconnect.com, mainly three roles exist: health professional moderators, staff moderators, and peer-patients. Emerging roles of community members have been defined in prior work in online communities, such as voluntary, informal leaders [4,18]. We could utilize such unique, emerging roles in online communities such as peer-patients. More specifically, we can use various peer-patient dynamics structured around length of experience (e.g., mentor-mentee relationships [7]), degree of similarity (e.g., buddy system [10]), and community members' mini-experiences (e.g., collaging experiences [10]). These emerging social relationships, together with semi-automated clinical expertise, can extend what has been happening in regular healthcare settings to provide robust, enriched, and sustainable support for the patients coming to online health communities.

Further, for replier support, we could help repliers learn how to better compose message content to not under- or over-state their experiences, using similar mechanisms to computerized writing educational tools [5]. If the system detects any styles of language that show under- or over-statement of things, the machine can warn about it or suggest other ways of wording them. The machine can also prompt repliers to include references or sources of knowledge, or suggest helpful links to include in the content.

### Not crossing the line: Rules around "Go see your doctor"

Unsurprisingly, the clinicians were especially careful of liability issues around providing clinical help online. The clinicians continuously reminded themselves of the limitations around not being the primary care providers of the patient posters and began formulating rules for "not crossing the line."

A number of questions around 'go see your doctor' began to emerge. That is, when are moderators going to tell patients to go see their providers? Are moderators going to help what patients ask their doctors about? Should moderators help understand what to expect, such as which work-ups patients would need to do? How should moderators tell patients to go see their doctors without scaring the patients? Why not just add to every post that they need to go see their doctors?

All clinicians mentioned that they would tell the patients in the example threads to go see their providers. If we were to build an automated health professional moderator, telling the patients to go see their providers to all posts would be an easy task. However, telling patients to go see a doctor can be a conversation stopper. Rather, addressing the implications built around why one would suggest to 'go see your doctor' better tackle potential needs of the patients. Possible tasks for agents would include finding key terms relating to diet, medication, emotions (P10), triggers (P8), and critical events (P2, P13). The automated agent can then provide related online health resources (P6, P7, P14), add words of support (P10), or attempt further evaluation, going back to gaining more history of the patient. As a result, online health communities can mediate patients in ways that augment existing clinical care systems, especially if collaboration with clinics can be established. Many clinical institutions have built online communities—however, such communities are limited to their registered patients. We would still need mechanisms supporting the more spontaneous, floating forms of patient crowd, such as finding related clinics and strengthening commitment to visit clinics.

## CONCLUSION

Through interviewing clinicians, we found requirements for weaving clinical expertise into online health communities. We learned how to prioritize posts that need clinical expertise, how to further elicit patient context, what clinical expertise to provide, and how to provide that clinical expertise in online health communities. The clinicians came from a variety of academic disciplines thus sometimes perspectives differed or even contradicted. However, all clinicians considered online health communities as unique, supportive platforms from which patients can greatly benefit.

The findings help us move one step closer to improving emerging, unique peer-patient support systems, such as online health communities. Our work helps to enrich the peer-patient conversations and support by exploring a novel approach of automatically weaving clinical expertise with peer-patient conversations. By examining this research problem, we also engage studies of expert and novice relationships, machine learning, and social computing. This multi-disciplinary approach in online health communities supports patients' complex information needs that can benefit from a balanced expertise between patients and clinicians.

## ACKNOWLEDGMENTS

We thank the participants, the iMed group and the BitLab. This work has been partially funded by NIH # 5T15LM007442-10 and NSF # 1117187.

## REFERENCES

1. Berge, Z.L. and Collins, M.P. Perceptions of emoderators about their roles and functions in moderating electronic mailing lists. *Distance Education 21*, 1 (2000), 81–100.
2. Beyer, H. and Holtzblatt, K. Contextual design. *interactions 6*, 1 (1999), 32–42.
3. Eysenbach, G. and Diepgen, T. Towards quality management of medical information on the internet. *BMJ 317*, (1998), 1496.
4. Farzan, R., Kraut, R., Pal, A., and Konstan, J. Socializing volunteers in an online community: a field experiment. *CSCW*, (2012), 325–334.
5. Foltz, P.W., Laham, D., and Landauer, T.K. Automated Essay Scoring. AACE *EdMedia*, (1999), 939–944.
6. Fox, S. Peer-to-peer Healthcare. 2011. http://pewinternet.org/Reports/2011/P2PHealthcare.
7. Hartzler, A., McDonald, D., Pratt, W., Park, A., and Huh, J. Facilitating Mentoring in peer health communities through social matching. *AMIA Extended Abstracts (2012).*
8. Hartzler, A. and Pratt, W. Managing the Personal Side of Health. *J Med Internet Res 13*, 3 (2011), e62.
9. Heckman, T.G., Somlai, A.M., Peters, J., et al. Barriers to care among persons living with HIV/AIDS in urban and rural areas. *AIDS care 10*, 3 (1998), 365–75.
10. Huh, J. and Ackerman, M.S. Collaborative help in chronic disease management. *CSCW* (2012), 853–862.
11. Huh, J., Mcdonald, D.W., Hartzler, A., and Pratt, W. Patient Moderator Interaction in Online Health Communities. *AMIA*, In Press (2013).
12. Huh, J., Patel, R., and Pratt, W. Tackling Dilemmas in Supporting 'The Whole Person' in Online Patient Communities. In *CHI,* (2012), 923–926.
13. Huh, J., Yetisgen-Yildiz, M., Hartzler, A., McDonald, D., Park, A., and Pratt, W. Toward Automatic Weaving of Medical Advice with Patient Experiences Using Text Classification. *AMIA Extended Abstracts.*, (2012).
14. Huh, J., Yetisgen-Yildiz, M., and Pratt, W. Text Classification for Assisting Moderators in Online Health Communities. *J Biomed Inform*, In Press (2013).
15. Huh, J. Collaborative Help for Individualized Problems. 2011. PhD Thesis. University of Michigan.
16. Jacquemart, P. and Zweigenbaum, P. Towards a medical question-answering system: a feasibility study. *Stud Health Technol Inform 95*, (2003), 463–8.
17. Johnson, S. *Interface culture*. Basic Books, New York, 1999.
18. Lampe, C. and Resnick, P. Slash (dot) and burn. *CHI*, 2004, 543–550.
19. Lasker, J.N., Sogolow, E.D., and Sharim, R.R. The role of an online community for people with a rare disease. *Journal of medical Internet research 7*, 1 (2005), e10.
20. López, A., Detz, A., Ratanawongsa, N., and Sarkar, U. What patients say about their doctors online. *Journal of general internal medicine 27*, 6 (2012), 685–92.
21. Maloney-Krichmar, D. and Preece, J. A multilevel analysis of sociability, usability, and community dynamics in an online health community. *TOCHI 12*, 2 (2005), 201–232.
22. Mo, P.K.H. and Coulson, N.S. Living with HIV/AIDS and use of online support groups. *Journal of health psychology 15*, 3 (2010), 339–350.
23. Setoyama, Y., Nakayama, K., and Yamazaki, Y. Peer support from online community on the internet among patients with breast cancer in Japan. *Studies in health technology and informatics 146*, (2009), 886.
24. Strauss, A.L. and Corbin, J. *Basics of qualitative research*. Sage Newbury Park, CA, 1990.
25. Welbourne, J., Blanchard, A., and Boughton, M. Supportive communication, sense of virtual community and health outcomes in online infertility groups. *C&T*, (2009), 31–40.
26. Wicks, P., Vaughan, T.E., Massagli, M.P., and Heywood, J. Accelerated clinical discovery using self-reported patient data collected online and a patient-matching algorithm. *Nat biotechnol 29*, 5 (2011), 411–4.

# Seeking and Sharing Health Information Online: Comparing Search Engines and Social Media

**Munmun De Choudhury** **Meredith Ringel Morris** **Ryen W. White**
Microsoft Research, One Microsoft Way, Redmond WA 98052
{munmund, merrie, ryenw}@microsoft.com

## ABSTRACT
Search engines and social media are two of the most commonly used online services; in this paper, we examine how users appropriate these platforms for online health activities via both large-scale log analysis and a survey of 210 people. While users often turn to search engines to learn about serious or highly stigmatic conditions, a surprising amount of sensitive health information is also sought and shared via social media, in our case the public social platform Twitter. We contrast *what* health content people seek via search engines vs. share on social media, as well as *why* they choose a particular platform for online health activities. We reflect on the implications of our results for designing search engines, social media, and social search tools that better support people's health information seeking and sharing needs.

### Author Keywords
Health; social search; search engine; social media; Twitter

### ACM Classification Keywords
H.5.3. Group and Organization Interfaces; Web interaction.

## INTRODUCTION
The Internet is a popular place to learn about health matters. According to a January 2013 Pew survey [10], 59% of U.S. adults reported using online resources to obtain health information in the past year. The Web is used for a range of purposes, including seeking advice [17,32], connecting with experts and individuals with similar experiences [9,24], sharing questions and concerns around treatment options [27], or understanding professional diagnoses [4]. Online health content can enhance coping and self-efficacy [8], affect health-related decisions and behavior of users and their friends and family [11], enable better management of chronic health conditions [1], and fuel discussions with healthcare providers [15]. Besides electronic mail, the use of search engines and social media are the most common online activities of adult U.S. Internet users [27]; in this work, we compare and contrast the use of these platforms for health activities.


*CHI 2014*, April 26 - May 01 2014, Toronto, ON, Canada
Copyright 2014 ACM 978-1-4503-2473-1/14/04...$15.00.
http://dx.doi.org/10.1145/2556288.2557214

People often use general purpose search engines (e.g., Bing, Google, or Yahoo!) to find online health information [29]. Recently, social media (e.g., Twitter, Facebook) has emerged as an alternative platform for sharing, and even seeking, health information. A recent survey [11] indicated that as many as 39% of online health information seekers used social media, and a fraction of them had also followed their contacts' health experiences or updates, posted their own health-related comments, gathered health information, or joined a health-related group. Other research has shown that Twitter is used for health-oriented question-and-answer tasks [26]. Disease-specific exchanges on social sites can provide new sources of knowledge, support, and engagement, particularly important for patients with chronic conditions [12].

Such emergent practices around seeking and sharing health information online indicate a shifting landscape. Search engines and social media platforms form an important continuum in terms of how people (privately) seek health-related information, as well as (publicly) share such information, respectively. As these mechanisms for seeking and sharing health information continue to grow in accessibility and popularity, and individuals utilize them to take a more active role in managing their health, it is imperative to understand the nature of health information sought or shared via the two platforms, as well as individuals' motivations and intentions. We address this challenge in the research described in this paper, focusing on the following three research questions:

**RQ1:** What is the relative prevalence of health activity on a search engine vs. social media? (We focus on Twitter here given its public nature). What motivates people to seek and share health information via each platform?

**RQ2:** What are the characteristics of health activities on search engines and on Twitter? Are there differences in the *severity* of health conditions on which information is sought or shared, or in terms of the *social stigma* associated with the health condition? What topical contexts typically distinguish (private) health information seeking on search engines from (public) health information sharing on Twitter?

**RQ3:** How do people evaluate both: (1) the information that they seek or share via search engines and Twitter, and (2) the risks associated with health activities on these platforms?

We adopt a mixed-methods approach, combining data from a survey with 210 respondents, with 15 months of log data from a major Web search engine (anonymized for blind review) and from Twitter. Our findings indicate that there are considerable differences in health activity between the platforms. We show that people prefer search engines when seeking information on serious medical conditions, disabilities, and conditions known to bear social stigma, while Twitter is used more often to share information around symptoms of different health issues, and on conditions with benign explanations. Regardless, our finding that people use Twitter to seek or share information on *some* health concerns shows that they may underestimate the privacy implications of pursuing health content in such public channels. The differences in how people use search engines and social media suggest that they tailor their healthcare needs to the accepted norms and characteristics of the two platforms, and has implications for the design of next-generation search and social systems.

## RELATED WORK

Searching the Web for health-related information is a common pursuit [10]. Studies have examined how people find and appraise health information online [8], and its connection to healthcare utilization and health-related behaviors [1,31]. Sillence et al. [31] showed that examining online content influences health-related decision making and improves patient-physician communication. Ayers and Kronenfeld [1] found a positive correlation between online health information seeking and changes in health behavior.

A common goal in health searches is self-diagnosis. One recent study estimated that 35% of online health seekers performed this activity in particular [10]. Studies have shown that during diagnostic searches people pursue both evidence-based search (focused on symptoms) and hypothesis-based search (focused on conditions and treatments) [4]. Recent research indicated a positive correlation between the frequency and placement of serious illnesses on result pages and negative emotions, e.g., feeling overwhelmed and frightened [18].

People afflicted by medical conditions also find support via online health communities (OHCs) [9,30]. One study suggests that 30% of U.S. Web users have participated in medical or health-related groups [17]. In this light, approaches to community building have been proposed, e.g., [13,34]. In this work, we focus on how search engines and social media (two of the most heavily used online platforms [27]) are used for health activities, rather than dedicated forums and OHCs.

Recent research has demonstrated that social media provides a way for people to communicate with their contacts regarding health concerns [7,10,25]. Newman et al. [23] interviewed people with significant health concerns who participated in both OHCs and Facebook. They showed that people consider the target and the means of sharing information as they pursue social goals related to their personal health, including emotional support, motivation, accountability, and advice. Oh et al. [24] examined people's use of Facebook for health purposes and showed that the level of emotional support was a significant predictor of health self-efficacy.

New practices raise concerns about matters such as privacy. The implications of sharing health information in open fora such as social media have been examined in general [21], and specifically in the context of health [14,35]. Young et al. [35] studied factors influencing the disclosure of health information on Facebook and steps that people took to protect their privacy. Hartzler et al. [14] showed that people often made errors in determining what health information was shared with whom in their social network.

Closely related to information disclosure on online social platforms is the inherent stigma ascribed to many health conditions [5]. Social stigma describes negative feelings towards an individual or group on socially-characteristic grounds that distinguish them from others [6,20]. Berger et al. [3] showed that compared with those with non-stigmatized conditions, those with stigmatized illness were more likely to find health information online. Liu et al. [19] showed that video logs (to help people share stories, experiences, and knowledge) could support the disclosure of serious illnesses such as HIV, helping those afflicted overcome aspects of social stigma.

Our research extends prior work in several ways. We are the first to directly compare and contrast health activities on search engines and social media, two of the most-used online tools. Second, we describe how people assess the health information they encounter, including motivations for selecting a particular platform. Third, we examine the characteristics of the information sought, including social stigma and topical context. Fourth, we examine in detail the nature of health information sharing on Twitter. Finally, we complement a survey with large-scale data captured in naturalistic settings; the aforementioned prior studies mainly used only one method (e.g., surveys, focus groups, interviews), or have small sample sizes, limiting their generalizability.

## DATA AND METHODS

### Data on Health Conditions

A key challenge of this research was to identify the different health conditions on which people seek and share information via search engines and Twitter, respectively. We identified four broad categories of conditions based on their severity and types: (1) symptoms of major diseases, (2) benign explanations (non-life-threatening illnesses), (3) serious illnesses, and (4) disabilities. We also characterized each condition by the degree of perceived social stigma provided by third-party judges. Our final list contained 165 conditions.

#### *Health Condition Severity and Types*

**Symptoms:** We filtered logs based on a symptom list from the online version of the Merck medical dictionary. Starting with the Merck list, we removed duplicates (e.g., multiple references to the same condition with different cohorts), and split symptom pairs into singletons (e.g., "*Nausea and Vomiting in Adults*" and "*Nausea and Vomiting in Infants and Children*" became "nausea" and "vomiting"). The list has 58 symptoms (e.g., chest pain, headache, twitching), and has been used in prior work on health search analysis [4].

**Benign explanations:** We used a list of 43 non-life-threatening conditions, defined in a prior log-based analysis of search behavior [33]. The list comprised a range of commonly-occurring conditions selected from across the *International Classification of Diseases 10th Edition* (ICD-10: *www.who.int/classifications/icd/en/*) published by the World Health Organization. Examples of the conditions chosen include caffeine withdrawal, common cold, and pregnancy.

**Serious illnesses:** We utilized a list of 58 serious conditions defined in [33], again based on the ICD-10. Note that these are well-known conditions that were likely to appear in our data. Examples of serious illnesses chosen included "heart failure", "multiple sclerosis", and "hepatitis".

**Disabilities:** In addition to the acquired health conditions listed above, we also included six common disabilities ("autism", "attention deficit hyperactivity disorder", "deafness", "blindness", "cerebral palsy", "dyslexia"), to provide insight on the use of search and social media for seeking and sharing information related to this class of chronic health disorders.

### *Stigma of Health Conditions*

To understand how stigma impacts people's health activities on search engines and social media, we characterized each condition in terms of its level of social stigma.

We used Amazon Mechanical Turk (*www.mturk.com*) to obtain ratings on the degree of social stigma for each condition on a three-point scale: 1 = low stigma, 2 = moderate stigma, and 3 = high stigma. For each condition we obtained 10 ratings from crowdworkers and three ratings from three human factors researchers. For conditions with agreement exceeding 50% (seven or more raters agreed on a single rating), we used the majority rating as the final measure of condition stigma. 126 out of the 165 conditions (76%) met this criterion. For the other conditions, with no clear consensus, we set stigma to moderate. This resulted in 81 conditions with low stigma (e.g., headache), 72 with moderate stigma (e.g., malaria), and 12 conditions with high stigma (e.g., AIDS).

## Log Data Collection

**Twitter.** We focus on the social media platform Twitter, a popular microblogging service used by 18% of U.S. Internet users, and whose popularity continues to increase [28]. Twitter is particularly interesting to study since nearly all posts are public; the public nature of tweets provides an interesting counterpoint to the private nature of search engine activity.

We gathered a 15-month sample of Twitter's Firehose stream (which includes all public tweets) between November 1, 2011 and March 31, 2013, made available to us under contract, focusing on English-language tweets. Twitter post count and unique user count were computed for each condition, and aggregated over the full time period. Specifically, we considered a post to belong to a certain health condition if there was a regular expression match of the condition to the text of the post (this would not permit substring matches within terms). To reduce noise, we excluded posts that were retweets or contained hyperlinks, since they were likely related to general news and not a user's personal health.

Using this method, we obtained 125,166,549 tweets on the 165 health conditions from 62,269,225 users in the time period of interest. The median number of posts was 51,687 per condition, from a median of 40,152 users per condition.

**Search Engine.** We mined the logs of a popular search engine over the same 15-month period used in the Twitter analysis, focusing on English-language queries. We processed billions of queries from which the queries for the health conditions of interest were extracted. We searched for queries that were either an exact match with one of the symptoms or conditions, or those where the condition was some subset of the query terms. As with Twitter, substring matches within query terms were not permitted to reduce noise.

We also used synonyms of symptoms and conditions to increase coverage. Synonyms were identified via a two-step walk on the search engine click-graph using an approach similar to [2]. Example synonyms for "abdominal pain" included "sore stomach" and "belly ache." We applied this procedure to all of the conditions. Note that, synonyms were not used in the data collection process from Twitter to ensure efficiency by limiting the size of the substring match space (Twitter posts are considerably longer than search queries).

We observed 174,605,024 searches on health conditions from 38,676,368 users. The median number of searches was 293,505, from a median of 85,848 users, per condition.

## Health Information Seeking and Sharing Survey

To gain qualitative insight into people's health information seeking and sharing practices, we conducted an online survey during June 2013, using a recruiting service (Cint) that offers "Census representative sampling" in terms of gender and age throughout regions of the U.S. Respondents were paid approximately 4 USD to complete the survey, and were required to have a Twitter account to qualify to participate.

The survey comprised 37 questions, and took approximately 10 minutes to complete. Participants were asked if they had ever sought health information on a search engine such as Google or Bing, or on Twitter, and whether they had ever shared health information on Twitter. If they answered affirmatively, they were asked to describe the most recent occasion on which they did so, including the health condition that motivated them to search or share, and their objective in performing the activity. The survey included questions about how often participants used search engines and Twitter for various types of information seeking or sharing, views about risks associated with each platform, and basic demographics.

In total, 237 respondents completed the survey. After discarding low quality responses (as determined by nonsensical or sarcastic responses to open questions), 210 valid survey responses were analyzed. Of these respondents, 53% were female, they resided in 38 U.S. states and the District of Columbia, and 43% had a college degree or higher. Ages ranged from 18 to 70 years (median = 35 years). Respondents reported using search engines frequently (76% at least once per day, with only 7% using them less than once per week). 71% of respondents had public Twitter accounts, while the remaining 29% had "protected" accounts (i.e., only approved followers could view their postings).

## RESULTS: PREVALENCE, INTENT & MOTIVATIONS

To answer RQ1, we turn to our survey data to examine the relative prevalence of search engine and Twitter use for health activity, and users' motivations and intents in using these platforms. Note that the health activities we focus on are *seeking* health information and *sharing* health information. The *seeking* activity is relevant to both search engines (i.e., issuing health-related queries) and Twitter (i.e., asking health questions), whereas the *sharing* activity is relevant only to Twitter (i.e., posting health-related tweets). Accurately determining seeking vs. sharing distinctions from Twitter data is challenging: while presence of a question mark may provide some indication, it still captures many non-information-seeking tweets [26], requiring human labeling to accurately determine intent [16]; an approach that does not scale to our large dataset. Consequently, our log analyses considered all health-related Twitter posts to be incidents of *sharing* (since even seeking information on Twitter is a type of sharing due to the public nature of posts); however, our survey allowed us to ask users for insight on the distinction between their Twitter seeking and sharing activities.

### Prevalence

The survey is useful for understanding prevalence, because it allows us to include those who did not search or tweet (who would not be visible in the log data). Recall, however, that all survey respondents had Twitter accounts, so the perspectives of non-Twitter users are not represented in survey data.

Overall, 94% of respondents ($n$=197) reported having used a search engine to seek health-related information. 11% sought health information for themselves on search engines at least once per day, rising to 40% doing so at least once per week. 13% sought health information on behalf of family or friends at least once per day, with 34% doing so at least once a week. Many fewer respondents, 19%, reported having sought personal health information on Twitter. 23% reported having used Twitter to share information related to their health.

### Intent of Health Activities

#### *Intent of Search Engine Use*

The 197 survey respondents who reported seeking health information using a search engine were asked to recall the most recent instance, and to answer questions related to that specific incident. Respondents also described their search objective. These responses were classified using an iterative open coding process. A second rater used this scheme to rate a random sample of 30 responses; inter-rater reliability (Cohen's $\kappa$) indicated substantial agreement ($\kappa$ = .72). The same verification strategy is used in the rest of this section. We coded the intent for 183 respondents (the others had unclear intent). Some searches had multiple intents and received multiple categorizations, so the percentages sum to more than 100%.

The most common motivation for using a search engine was to identify *treatment* options (53.0%), e.g., "stretches to cure or ease [tight hamstring]." Alternative and holistic treatment was a popular sub-category, comprising 13.5% of treatment searches, e.g., "alternative treatment [hypothyroidism]."

The next most common motivation was *diagnosis of a health condition* (26.8%) (e.g., "whether or not the symptoms matched my behavior [depression]") or interpreting the symptoms that they experienced (e.g., "what may be a cause of this and if it may mean something more may be wrong [very heavy menstrual cycle]").

A third motivation was *general understanding of a health condition or procedure* (20.8%), including understanding what a medical procedure might entail (e.g., "more about the surgery process, healing time [umbilical hernia]"), understanding the causes of an illness (e.g., "the caused [sic] of it… [infertility]"), or other general learning about a condition (e.g., "prognosis [congestive heart failure]").

7.1% of recalled searches were motivated by *understanding medications*, such as understanding side effects (e.g., "to be able to learn the side effects [cholesterol medications]"), comparing and contrasting medications (e.g., "effectiveness [of cancer treatments]"), or seeking information on available medications, such as whether non-prescription options are available or learning more about how a medication worked.

6.0% sought *lifestyle information for chronic concerns*, particularly nutrition information for managing diabetes, cholesterol, or weight loss ("special diet [cholesterol]").

Beyond these broad categories, participants also described other intents behind their search activity. 2.2% sought *recent medical research findings* on conditions or their treatments, and 1.1% sought *social support* such as online support groups for people with their diagnosis.

#### *Intent of Twitter Use for Health Information Seeking*

In a similar way to engine use, the 40 respondents who indicated they had sought health information on Twitter were asked to recall the most recent event. They explained their objectives in free-text. Open coding was used to categorize responses; the same categories were used for why people used search engines, with additional categories added as needed. Once again, substantial agreement was observed with the second coder (30 ratings, $\kappa$=.77). Three responses were unclassifiable; percentages are of the remaining 37.

As with search engines, the most common objective was locating *treatment* information (56.8%), e.g., "how to help relieve the pain [numbness in the legs]". 8.1% specifically sought natural or alternative treatments, e.g., "natural remedies to headaches." 16.2% of respondents sought information about *healthy lifestyles*, such as nutrition, dieting, or fitness (e.g., "different ways to lose weight"), and 13.5% sought to gain a *general understanding of a health condition,* e.g., causes (e.g., "why it happens..." [enlarged prostate]), consequences, or general knowledge. 5.4% sought *new research* about conditions or treatments, and 5.4% looked to find others with a similar situation to offer *support or advice* (e.g., "if anyone else hsd [sic] allergy problems"). Only 2.7% reported seeking *diagnostic* information on Twitter.

#### *Intent of Sharing Health Information on Twitter*

The 48 respondents who recalled *sharing* information related to their health on Twitter were asked to consider the most recent incident, and to answer a series of questions with that specific occurrence in mind. Participants explained in free-text what their intent was behind sharing health information on Twitter (substantial agreement with second coder, $\kappa$=.65). 10 were not coded due to vagueness or missing responses.

Of the remaining 38 responses, 63.2% reported that they intended to share information about their *immediate health status or symptoms* (e.g., "I was having a few teeth removed and I may not be online for a few days"). 34.2% wanted to share information or news about a condition (e.g., "treatments that work for me [fibromyalgia and neuropathy]").

### Motivations for Health Activities

#### *Motivations for Search Engine Use*

Respondents also explained why they chose to use a search engine, rather than alternatives such as asking a family member, consulting a health professional, or using a Q&A or social networking site. Free-text responses were classified into themes using an iterative open coding method (substantial second-coder agreement, $\kappa$=.63). Percentages are reported of the 151 responses that were classifiable, and the sum may exceed 100% since respondents provided several rationales.

*Convenience* (speed, ease, availability) was the most commonly cited motivator for using a search engine to find health info (e.g., "easy to access"); routine comfort with using search engines was another factor for 6.6% (e.g., "I use google very often, and I trust it"). The next largest motivator, for 15.2%, was the *plurality of results* returned for any given inquiry (e.g., "The internet has way more answers than just 1 person, or even 10"). *Privacy of the information seeking experience* was also cited as a benefit of using a search engine to find health information by 9.9% (e.g., "because its [sic] awkward to ask someone else").

Overall, 11.9% of respondents indicated that they had consulted a health care provider and needed *more detailed info or were dissatisfied with what a health care professional had previously told them* about the issue, and turned to search in response (e.g., "I have consulted my physician and was not satisfied"). Another 9.3% indicated that they were *performing research that they intended to later share with a health care provider* (e.g., "wanted to know what kinds of questions to ask the doctor at my appointment"). Sometimes (3.3%) a search was also used when *medical care was not available* (e.g. "it was after-hours for my doctor"). For 3.3% *monetary costs* determined whether to use search versus talk to a professional (e.g., "too expensive to go to a doctor").

#### *Motivations for Twitter Use for Seeking Health Information*

Like with search, participants were asked to explain in free-text why they used Twitter rather than alternatives such as health professionals and search engines). As previously, open coding was used to categorize responses (substantial agreement was attained with the second coder, $\kappa$=.72). 14 of the 40 responses were unclassifiable due to vagueness; reported percentages are of the remaining 26 responses.

As with search engines, *convenience* (ease of use, speed) was the most common reason for seeking health information via Twitter (46.2%) (e.g., "I [already] had it opened"). The next reason, specific to Twitter but perhaps analogous to the perception that search engines return a large variety of relevant results, was the *perceived large audience* of Twitter (23.1%) (e.g., "lot of people there"). 15.4% indicated using Twitter because they were *trying something different* – they had exhausted more conventional options or were trying to corroborate information found elsewhere (e.g., "second source").

11.5% sought other people's *recommendations, advice, or opinions* on treatments or managing health conditions (e.g., "just to see what advice i could get..."), and 7.7% sought social support (e.g., "find other people who can relate").

#### *Motivations for Twitter Use for Sharing Health Information*

Participants were also asked to explain in free-text why they chose to use Twitter to share information. A total of 38 participants had codable responses. Most commonly, respondents wanted to *reach a large audience* (e.g., "because I wanted my friends to know"; "just to inform the regular crowd of a hashtag") (22%). Some specifically wanted other people to *benefit from health information* they personally had found useful (e.g., "there are other mothers out there that are looking for the same option...") (8%). A few (4%) found Twitter to be a useful platform for *complaining* (e.g., "place to vent"); some (4%) noted Twitter had some privacy benefits (e.g., "Facebook has too many of my family members").

### Summary

The findings presented in this section indicate that search engines are more extensively used for health activities than social media like Twitter. While learning about the treatment and the diagnosis process of a health condition was a common purpose of health searches, gathering knowledge about the impact of health conditions on lifestyle and deriving general understanding of a medical procedure were popular goals behind using Twitter for health activities. Respondents indicated the plurality of search engine results, perceived large social media audience for feedback, and the diversity of the information available via search engines and social media to be primary motivating factors behind these practices, beyond the obvious convenience of the two platforms.

## RESULTS: COMPARING HEALTH INFORMATION

To answer RQ2, we use log data to study the aspects of health that people engage with on search engines versus on Twitter.

### Definitions

We first introduce several measures used in our analysis.

*Relative use* – For a given health condition, its relative use on Twitter or the search engine is given by the ratio of its volume of use in that medium, to the volume of the health term that is most used in that medium. For example, the most searched condition on the search engine was "cancer" appearing in 31,443,735 queries, and the second-most queried was "pregnancy" found in 25,721,056 queries; the relative use for "cancer" on the engine=1, it was .82 for "pregnancy."

*Rank* – A relative ranking based on normalized relative mention of a health condition (on Twitter or the search engine)—lower ranks mean greater use. For example, on Twitter, the most-used term from our list is "headache", that appeared in 24,607,507 posts; it would receive a rank=1.

*Rank difference* – We compute rank difference between the search engine and Twitter for each health term – large negative values indicate that a term is searched *relatively* more than tweeted, whereas large positive values mean the reverse. For example, "cough" has rank 4 on Twitter and rank 26 on the search engine – its rank difference is 22, reflecting its relative prominence on Twitter as compared to search.

| Top rank (Twitter) | Top rank (search) | Largest pos. rank difference | Largest neg. rank difference |
|---|---|---|---|
| (1) headache | (1) **cancer** | (124) tiredness | (-98) multiple sclerosis |
| (2) stress | (2) pregnancy | (97) jet lag | (-70) pelvic pain |
| (3) **cancer** | (3) multiple sclerosis | (74) insomnia | (-68) **vaginitis** |
| (4) cough | (4) diabetes | (73) irritation | (-65) **vaginal bleeding** |
| (5) *heart attack* | (5) stress | (69) *wheezing* | (-63) liver disease |
| (6) fever | (6) *anxiety* | (68) toothache | (-62) dermatitis |
| (7) *anxiety* | (7) *acne* | (66) tonsillitis | (-61) *irritable bowel syndrome* |
| (8) insomnia | (8) arthritis | (65) *panic attack* | (-60) influenza |
| (9) **AIDS** | (9) *allergy* | (64) *twitching* | (-58) cyst |
| (10) stroke | (10) cyst | (63) sore throat | (-57) *hematuria* |
| (11) pregnancy | (11) stroke | (61) motion sickness | (-54) kidney disease |
| (12) diabetes | (12) **autism** | (58) food poisoning | (-55) balance disorder |
| (13) asthma | (13) **AIDS** | (51) indigestion | (-51) **myopathy** |
| (14) mole | (14) tumor | (48) *dysmenorrhea* | (-50) *bipolar disorder* |
| (15) tension | (15) *heart attack* | (45) laryngitis | (-48) anemia |
| (16) *diarrhea* | (16) *rash* | (45) bruise | (-46) *lymphoma* |
| (17) migraine | (17) *heart disease* | (45) amnesia | (-45) **sexually transmitted disease** |
| (18) sore throat | (18) fever | (43) narcolepsy | (-42) alopecia |
| (19) bruise | (19) influenza | (41) nasal congestion | (-41) *tuberculosis* |
| (20) *rash* | (20) constipation | (40) *heartburn* | (-39) *hepatitis* |

**Table 1. Use of health conditions on Twitter and search engine, in the light of their severity/type and social stigma rating. We show the 20 conditions of top rank (highest relative use) on Twitter and the search engine respectively, as well as top 20 conditions in terms of their most positive (more tweeted than searched) and most negative (more searched than tweeted) rank differences. Numbers in parentheses indicate ranks or rank differences. Color codes assigned to conditions indicate their severity/types: blue = benign, red = serious, green = symptom, and grey = disability. The font format indicates stigma level: bold = high stigma (level 3), italics = moderate stigma (level 2), and normal/unformatted = low stigma (level 1).**

Based on these definitions, in Table 1 we report the top 20 most searched and most shared health conditions in terms of their rank and relative use on each platform. The table also shows the top 20 most positive rank difference (relatively more tweeted than searched) and most negative rank difference (relatively more searched than tweeted) conditions, along with severity/type and stigma level of each conditions.

### Comparison: Severity and Type of Conditions

We first report on a comparison of the nature of health conditions appearing in search engine queries and Twitter posts, in the light of their severity and type. From Figure 1 we observe that search engines are used more frequently to seek information on serious conditions, compared to Twitter (per a Wilcoxon test, this difference is statistically significant: $z$=4.98, $p$<.001). Examples can be found in Table 1: in the 20 top-ranked conditions shared on Twitter and sought on the search engine respectively, there are six serious conditions in the former (e.g., "diabetes"), while nine in the latter. Benign conditions show relatively similar use on both search engines and Twitter (in Table 1, seven of 20 are benign conditions in the 20 top rank conditions for search as well as Twitter, e.g., "pregnancy", "anxiety" appear in both)—a Wilcoxon test reveals only marginal significant differences ($z$=1.42, $p$=.02).

Next, per Figure 1, relative use of symptoms suggests symptoms to be shared more on Twitter than searched (per Wilcoxon test, this is a statistically significant difference: $z$=-2.95, $p$<.01). Taking examples from Table 1, seven of 20 top ranked conditions for Twitter are symptoms while it is only three in the case of the search engine. Finally, disabilities are searched more than they are shared on Twitter (per Wilcoxon test, $z$=1.76, $p$<0.01). In Table 1, *none* of the disabilities appear in the 20 top rank conditions for Twitter; in the case of search, "autism" is found to be ranked 12. The sensitive nature of many of the disabilities studied (mean stigma rating of the six disabilities=1.83, leaning toward the higher-stigma end of the scale) means that people may be more comfortable privately searching about their treatments, diagnosis, or coping mechanisms, than discussing them publicly on Twitter.

We elaborate on these observations by analyzing rank differences (Table 1). We first observe those terms that are shared more on Twitter than searched. For the 20 most positive rank difference values, 11 are benign (e.g., "insomnia", "toothache", "sore throat", "food poisoning") and only one is serious and eight are symptoms. Supporting the observations from Figure 1, social media may be preferred for sharing benign conditions and symptoms, rather than serious illnesses.

Next, we examine which terms that are searched relatively more than shared on Twitter. For the top 20 most negative rank difference values, 12 are found to be serious conditions (e.g., "kidney disease", "bipolar disorder'", "sexually transmitted disease"), three are benign, and five are symptoms. This suggests a tendency to prefer search engines to Twitter for online activities related to serious health conditions.

### Comparison: Social Stigma of Conditions

We now focus on understanding usage of health conditions on search engines and social media, and their levels of social stigma. Comparing across the platforms, from Table 1 (columns one and two), we observe notable differences between Twitter and the search engine, e.g., conditions perceived to have higher stigma are searched more (nine of the 20 top rank conditions for search have moderate or high stigma; three of them are extremely stigmatic, e.g., "autism", "AIDS") than they are shared on Twitter (six of the 20 for Twitter have moderate or high stigma; two extremely stigmatic).

Examination of the rank differences (Table 1) reveals the same pattern more prominently. Among the top conditions searched more than tweeted, four are highly stigmatic (e.g., "vaginitis", "myopathy"), whereas there are no highly stigmatic conditions tweeted more than searched (although there are moderately stigmatic ones such as "wheezing", "dysmenorrhea"). These considerable differences regarding stigma span all 165 health conditions (not just the top 20 shown in Table 1). Wilcoxon tests reveal that the relative use of moderate or highly stigmatic conditions is higher on search engines than on Twitter (for moderate stigma: $z$=4.57, $p$<.001; for high stigma: $z$=1.89, $p$<.01). Not surprisingly, but important to show, people prefer search engines over Twitter for online activity related to health conditions that may be associated with social taboo. This is reasonable given the nature of the platforms, but it is interesting that people do use Twitter to share *some* information on stigmatic conditions.

| **Twitter** | *Benign* | *Serious* | *Symptom* | *Disability* |
|---|---|---|---|---|
| *Benign* | 0 | 0.5324*** | 0.2785 * | 0.4854*** |
| *Serious* | | 0 | 0.4574*** | 0.3785 ** |
| *Symptom* | | | 0 | 0.5469*** |
| **Search** | | | | |
| *Benign* | 0 | 0.6555*** | 0.3057 * | 0.4922*** |
| *Serious* | | 0 | 0.5491*** | 0.4218 ** |
| *Symptom* | | | 0 | 0.5061*** |

**Table 2. Jensen-Shannon divergence across the unigram category distributions of the condition types. Statistical significance tests based on paired *t*-tests (* $p$≤.05; ** $p$≤.01; *** $p$≤.001).**

| Twitter\Search | JS divergence | *t*-stat | SD | *p* |
|---|---|---|---|---|
| *Benign* | 0.3387 | 0.1426 | 0.1236 | 0.0389 |
| *Serious* | 0.4178 | 0.372 | 0.0838 | 0.0232 |
| *Symptom* | 0.5501 | 1.5679 | 0.1604 | 0.0124 |
| *Disability* | *0.6952* | *2.2325* | *0.0729* | *0.0025* |

**Table 3. Jensen-Shannon divergence between unigram category distribution on Twitter and the search engine, corresponding to the four condition types. Significance (at $p$≤.01) in italics.**

### Comparison: Context of Use

From our log data, we examined the set of all non-stopword unigrams that co-occur (≥10 times) with each of the health conditions in Twitter posts and search queries. We cluster the unigrams based on LIWC's (Linguistic Inquiry and Word Count: *www.liwc.net*) categories (style categories, e.g., pronoun use, are excluded), to obtain a general sense of the *context* of use of each term. For comparison across Twitter and search, we use a relative measure of use of each linguistic category to account for different usages in the two sources—defined in the same way as the relative use of a condition.

#### *Across Condition Severity*

We first compute the Jensen-Shannon divergences between the unigram category distributions of the condition severities/types (Table 2). Next we show differences between unigram distributions on Twitter and search (Table 3).

From Table 2 we observe that for both Twitter and the search engine, there are significant differences in the context of use of different conditions. For example, the top unigram categories for benign conditions on Twitter and the search engine are: *past* and *future* tense words, *social, work, anxiety, negative emotion*, and *anger* (example unigrams include "hate", "relieve", "tomorrow", "now", "cry", "worries", "school"). This suggests that people are referring to their benign conditions with negativity, in terms of how they are disrupting their current and future social or professional life.

On the other hand, mentions of serious conditions on Twitter and the search engine tend to include categories like: *see, hear* (perception terms), *body, family, death*, and *numbers* (e.g., "awareness", "treatment", "signs", "survival", "prognosis", "rate", "pain"). People may be seeking information related to the physical ordeals associated with serious health concerns, or specific treatment information.

Next, the context of use of symptoms Twitter and the search engine spans the categories *health, insight, cognitive mechanisms* (e.g., "pain", "hard", "remedies", "medicines", "outbreak", "bad", "sleep", "woke", "feel", "ugh", "damn"). These indicate people may be seeking information to do a self-diagnosis on their symptoms, as well as expressing frustration on the inconvenience the symptoms may be causing.

Finally, examining the context of use of disability terms, we find that on Twitter categories like *present* and *future, money, religion, social,* and *friends* are common (e.g., "god", "day", "children", "support", "month", "special", "today", "please", "money"). This indicates that through their postings, people share disability related information in the context of monetary costs and challenges, and perhaps even seek comfort through sharing religious thoughts and reaching out to their social audiences. For search these span over *motion, health, space, work* (e.g., "disorder", "school", "banned", "therapy", "treatment", "walk", "speak", "children"). Disabilities can be a personal and social challenge and impact people's life activities and work; hence through search people appear to seek coping mechanisms to deal with their condition and experiences. Thus, the context of use of disabilities is distinct from that of acute conditions. In fact, comparing the unigram category usage around disabilities for Twitter and search, we find a distinctive contrast (ref. Table 3). Perhaps individuals are less inhibited in their searches on disabilities, since search engines provide a more private experience while seeking for information on a stigmatic experience (mean stigma rating of the six disabilities=1.83).

### *Across Stigma Levels*

Next we analyze the context of use of the health conditions in the light of their level of social stigma.

We find that the context of use of high stigma conditions is considerably different from that of low stigma conditions. This is consistent for both Twitter and the search engine (Table 4). For instance, for low stigma terms, Twitter and search engine use spans context that includes categories such as *past, present*, and *future* tense, *insight, time*, and *work* (e.g., "life", "sleep", "week", "ugh", "now", "tomorrow", "people", "test", "effects", "work", "signs", "sick"). It appears that individuals are seeking or sharing information on these conditions in the light of their mundane day to day experiences and how they are affecting their lives and work conditions. However, for high stigma conditions, usage context on Twitter and search engines comprises categories such as *anger, sadness, anxiety, health, body*, and perception words like *feel* (e.g., "surgery", "HIV", "treatment", "hospital", "children", "prognosis", "die", "lost", "mad", "cure", "hate", "fight"). Highly stigmatic conditions appear to present themselves within contexts associated with mental stress and anxiety in Twitter posts and search queries; people also attempt to seek information on these high-stigma conditions for educational and treatment purposes.

However, as one would expect, Table 5 indicates that the context of use of high stigma conditions on Twitter and the search engine is statistically significantly different. For Twitter, the unigram categories for high stigma conditions span: *sadness, anxiety, social,* perception words like *see, feel* (e.g., "hope", "feel", "shit", "support", "please", "family", "suck", "mad", "fight"). In contrast, for search they include *health, body, feel, motion* (e.g., "signs", "treatment", "hospital", "children", "prognosis", "die", "surgery", "rate", "awareness"). This aligns with our prior observation: individuals are more cautious in the way they discuss highly stigmatic conditions on a public platform like Twitter, perhaps for fear of being judged by their audiences and contacts.

| Twitter | | | |
|---|---|---|---|
| | *Stigma 1* | *Stigma 2* | *Stigma 3* |
| *Stigma 1* | 0 | 0.2238* | 0.6797*** |
| *Stigma 2* | | 0 | 0.2404 * |
| **Search** | | | |
| *Stigma 1* | 0 | 0.1626* | 0.4884 ** |
| *Stigma 2* | | 0 | 0.1623 * |

**Table 4. Jensen-Shannon divergence for Twitter and the search engine respectively, across the unigram category distributions for the three stigma levels. Statistical significance of differences using paired *t*-tests is shown (* $p \leq .05$; ** $p \leq .01$; *** $p \leq .001$).**

| Twitter\Search | JS divergence | *t*-stat | SD | *p* |
|---|---|---|---|---|
| *Stigma 1* | 0.3853 | 1.8911 | 0.1093 | 0.020 |
| *Stigma 2* | 0.2760 | 0.9701 | 0.1057 | 0.037 |
| *Stigma 3* | *0.6991* | *2.1208* | *0.0784* | *0.009* |

**Table 5. Jensen-Shannon divergence between unigram category distribution on Twitter and the search engine, corresponding to the three stigma levels. Significance (at $p \leq .01$) in italics.**

### Summary

This log study comparing the nature of online health information sought and shared reveals self-censorship—serious health conditions, disabilities, and highly stigmatic conditions are generally searched considerably more than they are mentioned in Twitter postings. Symptoms of health conditions, however, were more frequently present in Twitter posts than in search queries. This perhaps indicates people's propensity to use social media as a broadcasting platform to express the ordeals and inconveniences that are caused by symptoms they face in their day to day lives.

## RESULTS: PRIVACY, QUALITY, SOCIAL SUPPORT

Turning to RQ3, we investigate how people evaluate their health information seeking or sharing experiences as manifested through their use of search engines and social media. We consider three aspects: (1) any privacy risks involved, (2) the quality of information they access, and (3) the availability of social support from others through this activity.

Respondents indicated on a seven-point Likert scale (ranging from 7 = *strongly agree* to 1 = *strongly disagree*), whether they agreed that using a search engine to seek health information was a *privacy* risk. Respondents slightly agreed (mean = 3.5, median = 3), but were more concerned about the privacy risk on Twitter (mean = 4.7, median = 5; Wilcoxon signed-rank test: $z$=7.87, $p$<.001). Similarly, in terms of health information sharing through Twitter, people slightly agreed that using Twitter to share health information is a privacy risk (mean = 4.9, median = 5) and more so than seeking on Twitter (Wilcoxon test: $z$=3.96, $p$<.001).

Respondents were in slight agreement that health information available via search engines is of *high quality* (mean = 4.8, median = 5) and moderately agreed that search engines were useful for finding sources of *social support* (mean = 5.6, median = 6). Conversely, respondents were neutral in agreement that health information available via Twitter is of high quality (mean = 3.7, median = 4). Surprisingly, people were neutral about Twitter's utility for finding social support related to health issues (mean = 4.6, median = 4).

These differences in perceptions of information quality were statistically significant, with search engines being perceived as providing higher-quality information than Twitter (median 5 vs. 4), $z$=-8.81, $p$<.001. Surprisingly, search engines were also viewed as more useful for finding social support for health issues than Twitter (median 6 vs. 4), $z$=-8.54, $p$< .001, perhaps because they are useful for surfacing forums and OHCs, which prior work has shown are seen as key venues for social support for health concerns [9,17].

Note, however, that respondents who *did* report searching for information on Twitter viewed it as less of a privacy risk (median 4) than those who had not (median 5) (Mann-Whitney test, $z$=-2.46, $p$=.01). These people also viewed health information on Twitter as of higher quality, $z$=4.12, $p$<.001, and viewed Twitter as better for finding social support on health issues (median 6 vs. 4), $z$=4.78, $p$ < .001. Similarly, respondents who reported having *shared* health information on Twitter viewed it as less of a privacy risk (median 4 vs. 5) than those who had not ($z$=-3.74, $p$< .001). It is unclear whether this view of Twitter as a higher-quality, lower-risk venue for health activity results from positive experiences in engaging in health activity on Twitter despite initial skepticism, or whether these users were more likely to engage in health tweeting because they held these positive views.

## DISCUSSION

Our results indicate that online health activity as manifested via search engine queries and tweets provides insight into users' health information needs, as well as norms of use of these two prominent online platforms with regard to this sensitive topic. The complementary nature of the two media (public vs. private, seeking vs. sharing) help develop a more complete picture of the range of online health activities.

Analyzing health trends based on public Twitter posts is an important emerging research topic [25], but our findings suggest a need for caution if using Twitter to infer health trends for high-stigma conditions—there is evidence of self-censorship. Combining Twitter data with an alternative data source (such as search logs) could give a better understanding of health information seeking and sharing practices online than using either source alone. Differential prevalence of health term use on different platforms, or differential contexts (e.g., co-occurring unigrams) might be a useful indicator of the perceived stigma associated with a given health condition.

### Design Implications

The popularity of online venues for seeking information around health issues also raises the point of developing appropriate credibility indicators. Credibility seems particularly important given the relatively high level of confidence our survey respondents reported placing in the content found online, a level of confidence health professionals consider misplaced [22]. Potentially, credibility-specific analogues of Twitter's "verified account" seal (currently used to label elite users) may be developed for health accounts (or websites, similar to healthonnet.org, but with verification of content accuracy). Systems that support easy sharing of online content with a user's healthcare provider might also be helpful.

New kinds of health information search systems maybe built that support standing queries over search and/or social media to keep users apprised of new developments related to different common health concerns, since seeking new research about conditions and diversity of health content were the goals of many respondents. Such queries might even be personalized based on a user's medical history (perhaps using data from electronic health records) to increase the likelihood that users learn about relevant health information in a timely fashion (although such personalization has serious privacy implications). Besides, users' interest in finding information about medications (e.g., drug interactions, side effects), diagnostic and treatment information for specific conditions suggest that search engines might serve users well by introducing new categories of "instant answers" that return such content directly in response to medication or illness queries.

Although our findings indicate some degree of risk-awareness (as evidenced via self-report in the survey and differential activities for high-stigma and serious conditions across the two platforms), there is need for work on educating users about the privacy risks of seeking and sharing health information online (building on some initial efforts in this area [14]). Participants' self-reporting and logged behavior suggests that they view search engines as quite private, and they may be unaware of how some search and advertising companies may collect and distribute their information. Even though less high-stigma content was shared on Twitter, the presence of any level of health information sharing in such a public venue may have serious repercussions (e.g., higher insurance rates, denial of employment, etc.). Developing interfaces to remind users of these risks (perhaps by showing an "are you sure?" dialogue upon detection of sensitive terms in a query or tweet) is an important area for further research.

### Future Directions

Finally, we outline some limitations of this work. In our survey, 94% (197) reported using a search engine to seek information related to their health. This fraction is much higher than the figure reported in the Jan 2013 Pew health survey [10], which showed that 59% of U.S. adults have looked online for health information in the past year. Possible reasons for discrepancies include a slight difference in the question (we asked "have you ever" versus "past year" in Pew) and the characteristics of individuals who volunteered for our online survey: This population may be more Internet-literate than the pool in Pew where participants are recruited via telephone, and where having a Twitter account was not a prerequisite for participation. Though popular, Twitter is only one of several key social media platforms; understanding the role of other social network sites such as Facebook, in online health activity would be a valuable complement to this work.

More research is needed to understand the characteristics of online health information seekers and those who seek such information from offline sources. Although we presented a comparison of the use of health conditions in searches and Twitter posts, in the absence of demographics (age, gender, etc.) and corresponding incidence rates of each of the 165 conditions for those populations, it is difficult to infer differences in their norms of use in searches or Twitter alone or in the prevalence of a term's use online compared to its physical manifestation. Differences in the demographics of the user base between the two platforms may introduce confounds in the cross-platform comparisons. Considering the impact of these factors are interesting extensions to our research.

## CONCLUSION

Search engines and social media are popular tools for seeking and sharing information about a range of health conditions. We presented an in-depth study around the prevalence of these practices, the nature of health information sought, and why people are increasingly choosing to use such tools for their health information needs. We demonstrated that the prevalence and characteristics of health information that are sought via search engines or shared via social media are considerably distinct. People modify their information seeking and sharing practices depending on condition type: whether it is a serious condition, a disability, or simply an issue with a benign explanation. Despite being aware of the privacy risks of search engine use or public social media use, people did in fact use both, though differentially, to seek and share information on conditions which are socially considered to be stigmatic. We believe, through the findings in this paper, we have been able to shed new light on understanding health seeking and sharing practices both on search engines and on social media, and how these findings might influence the design of future iterations of these platforms.

## REFERENCES

1. Ayers, S.L. and Kronenfeld, J.J. (2007). Chronic illness and health-seeking information on the Internet. *Health*, 11(3): 327-347.
2. Beeferman, D. and Berger, A. (2000). Agglomerative clustering of a search engine query log. *Proc. KDD*, 407-416.
3. Berger, M., Wagner, T. and Baker, L. (2005). Internet use and stigmatized illness. *Soc. Sci. Med.*, 61(8).
4. Cartright, M.A., White, R.W. and Horvitz, E. (2011). Intentions and attention in exploratory health search. *Proc. SIGIR*, 65-74.
5. Corrigan, P. (2004). How stigma interferes with mental health care. *American Psychologist*, 59(7): 614.
6. Crocker, J. and Major, B. (1989). Social stigma and self-esteem: The self-protective properties of stigma. *Psychological Review*, 96(4): 608-630.
7. De Choudhury, M., Counts, S. and Horvitz, E. (2013). Predicting postpartum changes in behavior and mood via social media. *Proc. CHI*, 3267-3276.
8. Eysenbach, G. and Köhler, C. (2002). How do consumers search for and appraise health information on the world wide web? *BMJ*, 324(7337): 573.

9. Eysenbach, G., Powell, J., Englesakis, M. et al. (2004). Health related virtual communities and electronic support groups: systematic review of the effects of online peer to peer interactions. *BMJ*, 328(7449): 1166.
10. Fox, S. (2013). Health. *Pew Internet*. 2013-01.
11. Fox, S. and Jones, S. (2009). The social life of health information. *Pew Internet*. 2009-12.
12. Greene, J.A., Choudhry, N.K., Kilabuk, E. and Shrank, W.H. (2011). Online social networking by patients with diabetes: a qualitative evaluation of communication with Facebook. *J. Gen. Int. Med.*: 26(3): 287-292.
13. Grimes, A., Landry, B.M. and Grinter, R.E. (2010). Characteristics of shared health reflections in a local community. *Proc. CSCW*, 435-444.
14. Hartzler, A., Skeels, M.M., Mukai, M., Powell, C., Klasnja, P. and Pratt, W. (2011). Sharing is caring, but not error free: transparency of granular controls for sharing personal health information in social networks. *Proc. AMIA*, 559.
15. Hawn, C. (2009). Take two aspirin and tweet me in the morning: how Twitter, Facebook, and other social media are reshaping health care. *Health Affairs*, 28(2).
16. Jeong, J-W., Morris, M.R., Teevan, J. and Liebling, D. (2013). A crowd-powered socially embedded search engine. *Proc. ICWSM*, in press.
17. Johnson, G.J. and Ambrose, P.J. (2006).Neo-tribes: the power and potential of online communities in health care, *CACM*, 49(1): 107-113.
18. Lauckner, C. and Hsieh, G. (2013). The presentation of health-related search results and its impact on negative emotional outcomes. *Proc. CHI*, 333-342.
19. Liu, L.S., Huh, J., Neogi, T., Inkpen, K. and Pratt, W. (2013). Health vlogger-viewer interaction in chronic illness management. *Proc. CHI*, 49-58.
20. Major, B. and O'Brien, L.T. (2005). The social psychology of stigma. *Ann. Rev. Psychol.*, 56: 393-421.
21. Morris, M.R., Teevan, J. and Panovich, K. (2010). What do people ask their social networks, and why?: a survey study of status message Q&A behavior. *Proc. CHI*, 1739-1748.
22. Morris, M.R. and Morris, D. (2011). Understanding the potential for collaborative search technologies in clinical settings. *Proc. CIKM Collaborative IR Workshop*.
23. Newman, M.W., Lauterbach, D., Munson, S.A., Resnick, P. and Morris, M.E. (2011). It's not that I don't have problems, I'm just not putting them on Facebook: challenges and opportunities in using online social networks for health. *Proc. CSCW*, 341-350.
24. Oh, H.J., Lauckner, C., Boehmer, J., Fewins-Bliss, R. and Li, K. (2013). Facebooking for health: an examination into the solicitation and effects of health-related social support on social networking sites. *Comp. in Human Behavior*, 29(5): 2072-2080.
25. Paul, M. and Dredze, M. (2011). You are what you tweet: analyzing Twitter for public health. *Proc. ICWSM*, 265-272.
26. Paul, S.A., Hong, L. and Chi, E.H. (2011). Is Twitter a good place for asking questions? A characterization study. *Proc. ICWSM.*
27. Pew Internet Project, Feb 2012. Online Activities: *http://www.pewinternet.org/Static-Pages/Trend-Data-(Adults)/Online-Activities-Daily.aspx*
28. Pew Internet Project, Aug 2013. Social networking site and Twitter use: *http://pewinternet.org/Reports/2013/social-networking-sites/Findings/Twitter.aspx*
29. Rice, R.E. (2006). Influences, usage, and outcomes of Internet health information searching: multivariate results from the Pew surveys. *Int. J Med. Inf.*, 75(1).
30. Rodgers, S. and Chen, Q. (2005). Internet community group participation: Psychosocial benefits for women with breast cancer. *J. Comp.-Med. Comm.*, 10(4).
31. Sillence, E., Briggs, P., Harris, P.R. and Fishwick, L. (2007). How do patients evaluate and make use of online health information? *Soc. Sci. Med.*, 64(9): 1853-1862.
32. Skeels M.M., Unruh K.T., Powell C. and Pratt W. (2010). Catalyzing social support for breast cancer patients. *Proc. CHI*, 173-182.
33. White, R.W. and Horvitz, E. (2009). Cyberchondria: studies of the escalation of medical concerns in web search. *ACM TOIS*, 27(4): 23.
34. Wicks, P., Massagli, M., Frost, J., Brownstein, C., Okun, S., Vaughan, T., Bradley, R. and Heywood, J. (2010). Sharing health data for better outcomes on PatientsLikeMe. *J. Med. Int. Res.*, 12(2).
35. Young, A.L. and Quan-Haase, A. (2009). Information revelation and internet privacy concerns on social network sites: a case study of Facebook. *Proc. Communities and Technologies*, 265-274.

# RetroDepth: 3D Silhouette Sensing for High-Precision Input On and Above Physical Surfaces

David Kim[1,3], Shahram Izadi[1], Jakub Dostal[4], Christoph Rhemann[1], Cem Keskin[1]
Christopher Zach[1], Jamie Shotton[1], Tim Large[2], Steven Bathiche[2]
Matthias Nießner[5], D. Alex Butler[1], Sean Fanello[6], Vivek Pradeep[2]

[1]Microsoft Research [2]Microsoft [3]Newcastle University
[4]University of St. Andrews [5]Stanford University [6]Italian Institute of Technology

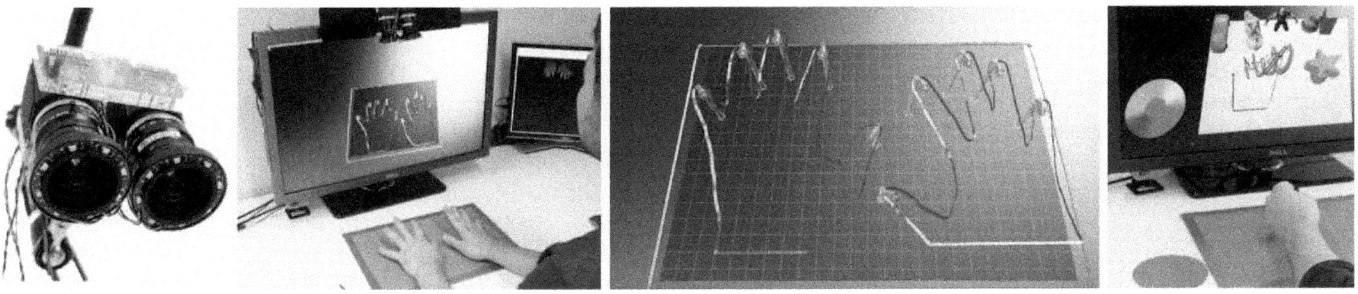

Figure 1: RetroDepth is a new 3D silhouette sensing system for high-precision interaction on and above physical surfaces.

## ABSTRACT

We present RetroDepth, a new vision-based system for accurately sensing the 3D silhouettes of hands, styluses, and other objects, as they interact on and above physical surfaces. Our setup is simple, cheap, and easily reproducible, comprising of two infrared cameras, diffuse infrared LEDs, and any off-the-shelf retro-reflective material. The retro-reflector aids image segmentation, creating a strong contrast between the surface and any object in proximity. A new highly efficient stereo matching algorithm precisely estimates the 3D contours of interacting objects and the retro-reflective surfaces. A novel pipeline enables 3D finger, hand and object tracking, as well as gesture recognition, purely using these 3D contours. We demonstrate high-precision sensing, allowing robust disambiguation between a finger or stylus touching, pressing or interacting above the surface. This allows many interactive scenarios that seamlessly mix together freehand 3D interactions with touch, pressure and stylus input. As shown, these rich modalities of input are enabled on and above *any* retro-reflective surface, including custom "physical widgets" fabricated by users. We compare our system with Kinect and Leap Motion, and conclude with limitations and future work.

### Author Keywords

NUI, 3D contours, depth sensing, 3D input, touch, stylus, vision-based UIs, stereo matching, contour classification


*CHI 2014*, April 26 - May 01 2014, Toronto, ON, Canada
Copyright 2014 ACM 978-1-4503-2473-1/14/04...$15.00.
http://dx.doi.org/10.1145/2556288.2557336

## INTRODUCTION

Natural user interfaces (NUI) have received much attention recently, as they provide rich modalities and possibilities for interaction, beyond mouse and keyboard. Whilst the term is broad and can encompass touch, gesture, gaze, voice, and tangible input, NUI often implies leveraging the dexterity and higher degrees-of-freedom (DoF) of our hands for interaction. However, even when focusing on hands, NUI has vastly different interpretations. A decade ago, the term predominately referred to emerging multi-touch interfaces. More recently, it has become more synonymous with 3D touchless input using fingers, hands or whole body interactions, popularized by products such as Kinect and Leap Motion.

This has resulted in the emergence of many underlying NUI technologies designed with very different scenarios in mind, each with strengths and weaknesses. For example, Leap Motion is only able to estimate fingertips of a hand in-air, but at a high precision, where Kinect provides more flexibility in sensing dense depth maps of arbitrary scenes and tracking a human skeleton, but at a relatively low precision.

In this paper we present RetroDepth, a system that unifies a variety of NUI modalities such as freehand touch, pressure, in-air interactions, as well as stylus and other tangible object input. Our system is designed specifically for scenarios where users interact on and above physical surfaces of different shapes and sizes, and allows seamless switching between these modes of input. RetroDepth provides a middle ground between sensors that extract high-level features such as fingertips (e.g. Leap Motion) and more flexible depth cameras (e.g. Kinect) that expose raw depth maps but at lower precision.

Our system is designed specifically to sense only the *3D silhouette* of interacting objects. The use of silhouettes greatly lowers the computation required for depth sensing, when compared to estimating a dense depth map. We present a novel vision-based approach for silhouette sensing, which leads to extremely high-precision contour estimation, and demonstrate sufficient accuracy to distinguish between touch, hover and pressure. Interestingly, most consumer depth cameras, such as stereo cameras, Kinect or even time-of-flight sensors (ToF), struggle the most at object boundaries and edges, where large depth discontinuities lead to noise and imprecise depth estimation. In this paper, we highlight the importance of precision at these object edges, as ultimately these form the main point of contact between the user and the digital/physical world.

We highlight numerous examples of how the resulting 3D silhouette information can be exploited for interactive scenarios. In particular, we demonstrate just how much information a silhouette can encode, and present a novel pipeline that identifies and tracks fingers and objects in 3D, and infers hand parts, poses and gestures, using 3D contours only. We compare the accuracy of our system with Kinect and Leap Motion, and conclude with a discussion of limitations and future work.

## RELATED WORK

Early uses of 2D silhouettes and contours in the context of interaction coincide with pioneering work on NUI, indicating their importance for enabling such experiences. Krueger's seminal work [21] and SideShow [9] enables whole-body and gestural interactions using 2D silhouettes. In recent years, 2D silhouettes and contours have been exploited in the context of vision-based tabletop systems [39, 28, 37, 20, 41]

Top-down configurations that place a 2D camera above a physical surface have proved popular as they provide more flexibility in sensing, allowing any regular desk to be transformed into an interactive one. Because these systems rely on 2D cameras, segmentation of hands and objects from the (typically cluttered) desktop is non-trivial, and touch and hover is difficult to disambiguate. These challenges have led researchers to use stereo cameras for higher precision touch sensing, combined with simple "hardware" techniques for segmentation, e.g. colored backgrounds or polarizing filters [25, 2]. Izadi et al. [16] use the same configuration as [2] to combine stereo-based touch estimation with stylus input, object recognition, and depth sensing, but the latter is used for remote feedback only.

Two recent notable products enable high-precision sensing using stereo cameras. The commercial Leap Motion sensor is a small, self-contained unit containing a pair of wide field-of-view (FoV) infrared (IR) cameras and IR LEDs pointing upwards on a desk. Whilst not published, the device provides tracking of fingertips and other strong peaks in the input signal, such as a pen, with high frame-rate and precision sensing. The device does not expose a full contour, only tracked 3D points mapping to high-level features such as fingertips. Further, segmentation is based on assuming that only freespace exists behind interacting objects. This limits the device to in-air input only, which can result in arm fatigue during prolonged interactions. Haptix [11] uses a similar small desktop unit with two IR cameras but instead points across the physical surface to detect multi-touch gestures only. Our approach combines these modalities of high-precision touch and in-air input, but also provides features such as pressure sensing, full contour-based interactions, gestures, and tracking of hands and tangible objects.

**Going beyond the tabletop** A logical next step for interactive surfaces is to explore in-air interactions, potentially in combination with touch. Systems have demonstrated stylus-based input using magnetic, inductive or vision-based systems (see [35, 40]). Many optical and non-optical techniques have been explored for freehand in-air input in the context of interactive surfaces. These include electric-field sensing techniques [30, 23], use of scanning lasers [30] and laser-line generators [36], or IR proximity sensors [29, 17, 4], either placed around the bezel or embedded behind a display. These techniques either coarsely sense 3D input, or have a limited interaction volume or are limited to 3D input only.

Other notable systems combine on-surface and in-air interactions using a variety of different hardware configurations. For example, the use of high-end (and costly) marker-based motion trackers used for 3D tabletops [26] or even 3D cardboard or foam prototypes [3]; as well as, synchronized IR cameras and switchable diffuser to image on and beyond the surface [18], where depth was coarsely estimated using diffuse IR light intensity falloff [13]; and light field imaging through an LCD to coarsely estimate depth [15]. Prior to the wide availability of depth cameras, researchers also explored ToF sensors placed behind [13] and above [43] projection surfaces. These sensors suffered from low resolution and high noise making interactions coarse and limited.

**The rise of consumer depth cameras** With the advent of consumer depth cameras, many new systems for in-air interactions coupled with surface-based interactions have appeared. Examples include situated augmented reality displays such as [14, 5], as well as augmented desktops [12, 24]. All these systems use a top-down Kinect camera to both sense touch [44] and in-air interactions. These systems inherently lack precision due to the quantization noise of the Kinect (see below) making such systems imprecise compared to other input devices [10]. 3Gear Systems [1] demonstrate tracking of specific hand gestures above a desktop, again using a top-down Kinect camera, based on early research of Wang et al. [38]. This method can be considered state-of-the-art in terms of Kinect-based hand tracking, and we provide quantitative comparisons later in this paper.

One of the main drawbacks with consumer depth cameras is high noise at object boundaries. However, for NUI, these boundaries are critical for sensing when the user's hands (or other physical tool) interacts with either digital or physical content. The original Kinect uses a method akin to stereo matching, where each small 2D patch of the reference dot pattern is matched by sweeping a window along the associated epipolar line in the observed IR image. This leads to ambiguities when matching at object boundaries, where large depth discontinuities lead to outliers, holes, and edge fattening [32, 8]. ToF sensors suffer from issues such as *multi-path* or *mixed pixels* [31], where light returns from secondary surfaces to the same pixel during a single exposure, as well as '*flying pixels*' where depth is estimated across multiple captures and scene motion results in foreground and background contributions being averaged together [31].

**Custom depth cameras** This fundamental issue of consumer depth cameras is a key motivation for RetroDepth, where we specifically design a system for real-time, high-precision depth estimation at silhouette and object boundaries. Whilst consumer depth cameras lack precision, researchers have demonstrated much higher quality sensors, in particular by using dynamic structured light patterns (see [22] for a review). There are however limitations in such systems for our interactive scenarios. Most of these systems estimate depth by projecting multiple dynamic patterns into the scene and capturing multiple images with a camera. To deal with a moving scene (which is necessary in our interactive scenarios) and therefore limit motion artifacts, these patterns need to be projected and imaged at very high frame-rates. This necessitates costly high speed camera and projector hardware that can add considerably to the system cost. There is also the computational cost associated with estimating dense depth maps, which as demonstrated in this paper is unnecessary for many interactive scenarios.

## RetroDepth

In the following sections we present the physical RetroDepth setup and demonstrate the interactive capabilities of the system. The physical configuration is shown in Fig. 1. Two off-the-shelf monochrome cameras are positioned on a metal rail at a fixed baseline (6cm apart). Currently we use Lumenera PLT-425-NIR (running at 1024x512 and 60Hz) due to their IR response and global shutter capabilities, but there is no hard restriction on manufacturer or imaging sensor. A ring of 8 diffuse IR LEDs (OSRAM CHIPLED SFH 4053) operating at 850nm are attached around the lens of each camera. This placement and number of LEDs ensures that illumination is uniform and shadows are minimized. IR bandpass filters are placed on each camera lens.

This hardware setup is easily reproducible with only off-the-shelf components. The setup is powered entirely over USB (peak power for each LED is 260mW, and average power is 35mW). The LEDs are pulsed from each camera's General Purpose Input/Output (GPIO) pins, and only active during the camera exposure (2ms). A synchronization board is used to generate a 60Hz trigger to shutter the cameras simultaneously.

Figure 2: Left: passive retro-reflective keyboard, and series of other "physical widgets". Right: IR image of scene.

### Retro-reflective segmentation

Fig. 2 also shows retro-reflective surfaces (such as the off-the-shelf 3M Scotchlite-Part 8910), which are cut in various shapes and sizes, and placed on a table. Upon shuttering, the cameras both simultaneously capture an image of the scene. All IR LEDs are switched on during this exposure time, producing a bright uniform response from all the retro-reflective materials on the table, as shown in Fig. 2 (right). This makes these reflective surfaces readily distinguishable as bright silhouettes in the captured stereo images. When objects interact on or above these surfaces, a sharp contrast is created between the background and foreground, e.g. the hand or marker pen shown in Fig. 2 (right).

In a first pass, we extract contours of any bright silhouettes observed from each camera. We then perform stereo matching across these contour images. In a second pass, we *invert* the image within the contour boundaries, creating bright silhouettes within each retro-reflective region, which correspond to objects (e.g. hands or styluses), interacting on or above the surface (Fig. 2). We again extract contours and perform stereo matching in these regions. This creates a clean separation between sensing the retro-reflective objects, and the 3D interactions occurring on or above them. Optionally, we interpolate to fill in a dense 3D silhouette of foreground objects.

### Creating and tracking physical widgets

Retro-reflective material is cheap and readily procurable. It is also easy to cut into various shapes and sizes. Fig. 2 shows a variety of simple *"physical widgets"*, made by cutting sheets of acrylic or cardboard into the desired shape and gluing the retro-reflective material on the upper-side. Additionally, a clear acetate sheet is used to print labels (most printer ink is invisible to IR) for the widget, such as keys for a 3D sensing touch keyboard (Fig. 2, left).

Our stereo matching algorithm estimates the precise metric depth of the outlines of these physical widgets. After depth estimation, a machine learning algorithm classifies the widget based on silhouette shape. This classification occurs per frame in real-time and is robust to large parts of the widget being occluded by interacting hands and objects. Once classified the widget can be tracked in 6DoF. Given that new physical widgets are easy to fabricate, our machine learning algorithm is extensible in order to add new training classes at runtime.

### Freehand 3D interactions and gestures

As the user's hand or physical tool interacts above a retro-reflective widget, a clear internal silhouette is visible (Fig. 2, right). By inverting the image, our stereo matching algorithm can precisely estimate the depth of these internal silhouettes. Even a small occluding region of the finger can be sensed accurately. This creates an *interaction volume* above each widget that allows freehand 3D input. Depending on the size of widget this can be either bimanual or single hand input, with fine-scale sensing of individual fingers (Fig. 3).

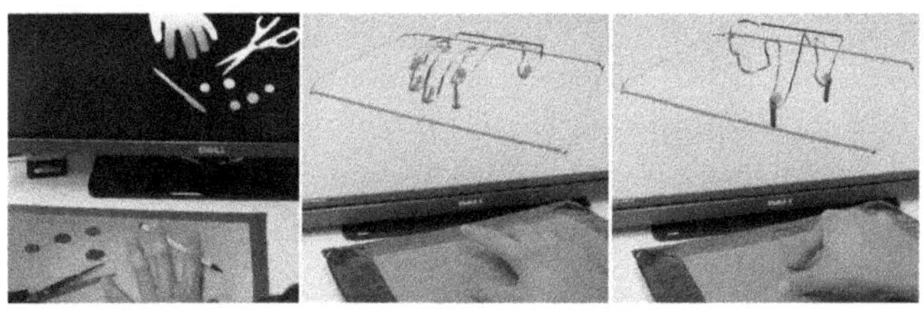

Figure 3: Left: Recovering the precise 3D contour of objects placed on the retro-reflector, including hands and other physical objects. Middle: Distinguishing between the widget (red contour) and the interacting objects (blue contour). Middle & Right: Sensing in-air (green), touch (red) and pressure (blue) input.

We repurpose the same machine learning pipeline to detect distinct hand shapes (i.e. when performing different gestures). Our system currently identifies a number of shapes including pointing, pinching, and whole hand interactions. Our approach can robustly handle variations across poses, and also estimate whether the left or right hand is observed.

After classifying the hand into distinct shapes, a machine learning classifier robustly identifies whether contour points belong to fingertips or the thumb, based on a curvature metric. These classified contour points can be clustered, and the individual fingertip peak identified. Simple line-fitting can be used to determine orientation of the fingertip in 3D. As shown in Fig. 1, Fig. 3 and accompanying video this allows for robust real-time identification of the digits of the hand.

**Stylus input and tangible tools**

As shown in Fig. 3 and Fig. 4 a variety of objects placed on top of a retro-reflective surface can be clearly identified by their contours. These objects could either invoke specific UI commands, or be used for continuous input. One example of the latter is a stylus, which can be used for fine grained manipulations in 3D as shown in Fig. 1 and accompanying video. During contour extraction, we look for very sharp peaks in the signal to identify the pen tip, and estimate the pen location and orientation in 3D (using line fitting).

**Touch & Pressure**

Beyond the 3D and tangible interactions outlined above, each retro-reflective widget has the capability of supporting touch and pressure input purely with our depth estimation method. To detect when finger or stylus touches a flat surface, a plane is estimated based on the widget's contour and intersections with any classified tips identified. One interesting possibility as shown in the accompanying video and Fig. 3 is to use a malleable material for the widget allowing users to press fingers into the substrate. Here the precision of our contour-based depth estimation method allows very small changes in the 3D location of the fingertip to be identified when the user presses the surface to approximate *pressure*.

**Example physical widgets**

Fig. 2 shows a variety of different widgets that take minutes to fabricate. As highlighted just by virtue of covering an object with retro-reflective material, a interactive volume is created above the object, where touch, pressure, in-air and stylus input can be sensed readily, without any direct computational augmentation of the widget. Widgets that allow for 3D touch pads, mice, and keyboards can be easily created. Sheets of retro-reflector can be rolled out to enable ad-hoc 3D input devices. Physical toolbars and marking menus can be mapped to specific 2D UI functions, e.g. color selection.

## SOFTWARE PIPELINE

So far we have provided a high level view of the RetroDepth system and its sensing and interactive capabilities. In the next sections, we describe the software processing pipeline that takes pairs of synchronized images and estimates depth, and classifies widgets, hand shapes and salient hand features. The pipeline is composed of fairly standard image processing tasks, followed by a new contour-based stereo and classification algorithm. We briefly discuss these initial steps before focusing on the novel components.

First an offline calibration process is performed which comprises of: 1) *intrinsic calibration* to compute the geometric parameters of each IR camera lens (focal length, principal point, radial and tangential distortion); 2) *stereo calibration* to compute the geometric relationship between the two cameras, expressed as a rotation matrix and translation vector; 3) *stereo rectification* to correct the camera image planes to ensure they are scanline-aligned to simplify disparity computation. At runtime, the synchronized input IR images are *undistorted* given intrinsic lens parameters, scanline rectified, and finally cropped to ignore non-overlapping parts.

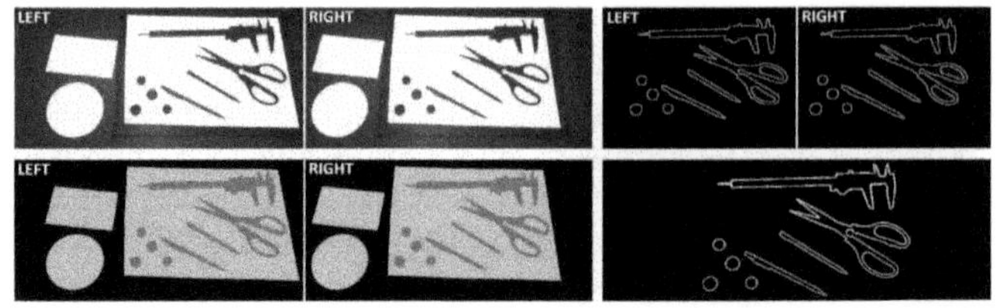


Figure 4: Early stages of processing pipeline. Top left: scanline-rectified stereo images. Bottom left: Foreground segmentation (in red) of internal objects within convex hull (blue). Note convex hull maps to each physical widget. Top right: extracted foreground contours. Bottom right: estimated depth of foreground silhouette (shown in false color).

The remainder of this online pipeline works in two steps. First, the depth for the background objects is computed, i.e. the visible widgets that are brightly lit. Second, depth is estimated for foreground objects, i.e. internal silhouettes within each widget. Because of the sparse nature of the contour-based algorithm, we can efficiently compute depth in two-passes.

To compute depth for background objects, we threshold both scanline-rectified images to remove low intensity pixels. We trace the contour of each binary image, which efficiently computes a set of 2D pixel coordinates corresponding to contour points for each connected component. At this point, stereo is computed on these background contours to estimate the 3D silhouettes of the widgets.

What remains is to compute the depth for internal foreground physical objects such as hands (the dark silhouettes inside the widget). We compute the convex hull for each background object, and generate a binary mask (1 within the convex hull, and 0 outside) for both stereo images. For each valid pixel in the mask, we invert the binary image, and repeat contour extraction on these points. This leaves us with two pairs of contour images; one corresponding to bright regions in the input images, and the other the silhouettes (of foreground objects) within these bright regions. Finally, our efficient stereo matching algorithm is computed for the foreground. (Fig. 4) shows an example of this processing pipeline.

**Efficient Contour-based Stereo**

Stereo algorithms identify corresponding points in both images that are projections from the same scene point. We refer to [32, 8] for an in-depth discussion of stereo matching approaches. Because our input images are rectified, corresponding points are known to lie on the same horizontal scanline in the left and right image (see Fig. 5), which reduces the depth estimation to a 1D search task. The horizontal displacement is known as disparity $d$ and is inversely proportional to depth. In the following, we focus on the key problem of determining the correspondences between contour points that lie on a particular scanline $S$.

A core contribution of our work is extending the standard dynamic programming dense stereo algorithms to sparse contours, which greatly reduces the amount of computation, whilst increasing precision of disparity estimation.

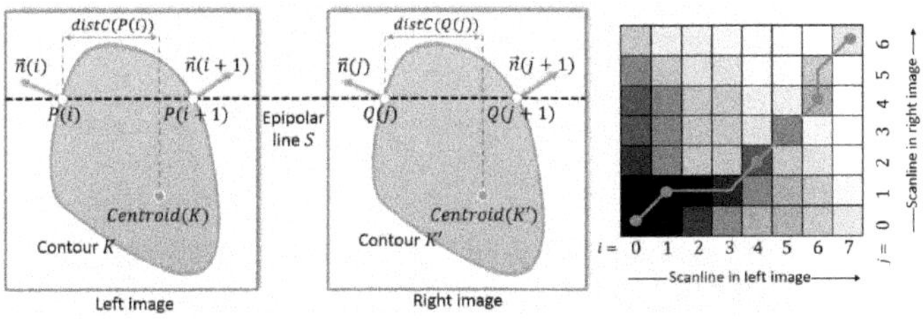


Figure 5: Left: contour-based depth estimation for rectified images. For notation please see text. Right: Cost Matrix $\mathcal{C}$. The brightness of each cell indicates the accumulated costs at $\mathcal{C}(i,j)$ (dark cells have low costs and bright ones high costs). The path of lowest costs is indicated in red. Matching pixels are marked with a red circle. All other pixels along the red path are occluded in the left or right image.

Let $p$ and $q$ be contour points in the left and right image, respectively. $P$ and $Q$ are lists of length $|P|$ and $|Q|$ that store the image $x$-coordinate of those contour points lying on scanline $S$ in the left and right image, respectively. $P(i)$ denotes the $i^{\text{th}}$ element in the list and we assume that the lists $P$ and $Q$ are sorted. For better understanding, Fig. 5 illustrates rectified stereo images that show a contour as well as lists $P$ and $Q$ for scanline $S$.

To find correspondences between the points in $P$ and $Q$, we compute the minimum-cost path through a matrix $\mathcal{C}$, illustrated in Fig. 5 (right). $\mathcal{C}$ is of size $|P| \times |Q|$ and $\mathcal{C}(i,j)$ stores the minimum accumulated cost of an optimal path from $(0,0)$ to $(i,j)$. The path of minimum cost is indicated in red in Fig. 5. Every path is restricted to start at cell $(0,0)$ and to end at cell $(|P|,|Q|)$, because we require a mapping for all contour points. Furthermore, only three moves are possible to construct a path: a diagonal $45°$ move that indicates a match, as well as horizontal and vertical moves that represent points that are only visible in the left or right image, respectively. The restrictions imposed on the path imply the following properties of the solution:

**Uniqueness property:** Every (contour) point in $P$ can only match to one point in $Q$ and vice versa. **Ordering property:** If point $P(i)$ matches $Q(j)$ than $P(i+1)$ can only match to $Q(j+\triangle)$ where $\triangle > 0$.

We enforce a third constraint, which we empirically found beneficial to improve robustness: Let $K$ be the contour that $P(i)$ belongs to and $K'$ the contour that $Q(j)$ belongs to. Then if $P(i)$ matches $Q(j)$ the height of the bounding boxes of $K$ and $K'$ must not differ by more than 50 pixels.

### Energy Function

The (accumulated) cost of a path is defined recursively (for $i > 0$ and $j > 0$) as:

$$\mathcal{C}(i,j) = \min \begin{cases} \mathcal{C}(i-1,j-1) + C_{\text{match}}(i,j) + C_{\text{smooth}}(i,j) \\ \mathcal{C}(i-1,j) + \lambda_{\text{occlusion}} \\ \mathcal{C}(i,j-1) + \lambda_{\text{occlusion}} \end{cases} \tag{1}$$

where the three different cases correspond to the three permitted moves discussed above. The boundary conditions are

$$\begin{aligned} \mathcal{C}(0,0) &= C_{\text{match}}(0,0) & \\ \mathcal{C}(i,0) &= i \cdot \lambda_{\text{occlusion}} & i > 0 \\ \mathcal{C}(0,j) &= j \cdot \lambda_{\text{occlusion}} & j > 0 \end{aligned}$$

In Eq. 1, $\lambda_{\text{occlusion}}$ is a constant occlusion penalty and the remaining terms are defined as follows.

The data term $C_{\text{match}}$ measures the compatibility of putatively matching contour points:

$$\begin{aligned} C_{\text{match}}(i,j) = &\|\vec{n(i)} - \vec{n(j)}\| \\ &+ |\text{distC}(P(i)) - \text{distC}(Q(j))| \,. \end{aligned} \tag{2}$$

Here, the first part measures the Euclidean distance of the normal vectors $\vec{n(i)}$ and $\vec{n(j)}$ at contour points indexed by $P(i)$ and $Q(j)$, respectively. The second part compares the horizontal distance of point $P(i)$ and $Q(j)$ to the centroid of their corresponding contours $K$ and $K'$, respectively: $\text{distC}(P(i)) = P(i) - \text{Centroid}(K)$.

The pairwise term $E_{\text{smooth}}$ encourages solutions where the horizontal distance between two neighboring *matching* points $P(i)$ and $P(\varphi(i))$ is similar to the distance of their matching points $Q(j)$ and $Q(l)$:

$$E_{\text{smooth}}(i,j) = \|P(i) - P(\varphi(i)) - (Q(j) - Q(\varphi(j)))\|, \tag{3}$$

where function $\varphi()$ returns the closest previous matching point for the current path.

### Optimization via Dynamic Programming

Dynamic programming is a well established technique to find the path of minimal cost through $\mathcal{C}$. The optimization consists of two consecutive steps. First, the cumulative costs $\mathcal{C}(i,j)$ are computed recursively for every pair $(i,j)$ as per Eq. 1. At each recursion we also store the best "move" (i.e. the arg min of Eq. 1) at $(i,j)$ in a matrix $\mathcal{M}$ that has the same dimensions as $\mathcal{C}$. In the second step we reconstruct the best path by tracing back the best moves stored in $\mathcal{M}$ starting from $(|P|,|Q|)$ until we reach the origin $(0,0)$ of $\mathcal{M}$. Once the best path is computed the disparity $d(i)$ (with respect to the left image) can be derived as $d(i) = P(i) - Q(j)$ for matching points $P(i)$ and $P(j)$.

### Post Processing

Although the estimated disparity map is usually of high quality, there might be outliers and contour points where no depth could be estimated (e.g. due to occlusion of this point in the other image). In the post-processing stage we aim to filter out wrong matches and assign *all* points along the contour to a depth value. In particular we apply the following steps:

**Invalidation of horizontal lines.** The depth estimation can be unreliable at contour points whose normal is almost perpendicular to the scanlines (such regions are marked in orange in Fig. 5). This is because the term $C_{\text{match}}$ is ambiguous in those regions. Therefore, we invalidate contour points whose normal vector has an angle of $\geq 85°$.

**Outlier invalidation.** The depth map obtained with dynamic programming is computed independently for each scanline. As a consequence, the depth at neighboring contour points that lie across scanlines might be inconsistent. Thus we invalidate points whose depth differs from those of the closest neighboring points along the contour by more than 3mm.

**Contour Smoothing.** We further smooth the depth values along the contour with a 1D mean filter of size 25 pixels. Note this filter can be implemented very efficiently using a sliding window technique with two operations per contour pixel.

**Filling.** Finally, we assign occluded and invalidated contour points to a depth value. This depth value is computed as a linear combination of the depth assigned to the closest valid contour points.

### Discussion

One important feature of our algorithm is the underlying computational cost. In general, the complexity of a pixel-wise stereo matching algorithm can be characterized with $O(WHD)$, where $W$ and $H$ are the width and height of the images, respectively, and $D$ is the number of tested depth hypotheses. In many scenarios $D = O(W)$, i.e. higher resolution images imply a larger set of depth hypothesis to be considered. Coarse-to-fine frameworks for stereo (e.g. [34]) and randomized stereo correspondence algorithms [6] (largely) remove the dependency of the runtime complexity on $D$. Since in our hardware setup the most discriminative regions in the image are the silhouettes, we restrict the computation of depth to pixels lying on the silhouette contours. Further, we obtain a substantial reduction in the search range $D$, since only a small set of extracted contour pixels in both images can be potential matches (~2-10 points).

## 1D HAND POSE AND FINGERTIP RECOGNITION

Once we have efficiently estimated the 3D silhouette, this high-quality contour contains valuable information about the scene objects, and in particular on the state and pose of any interacting hands – a key to enable truly interactive scenarios.

There are many options for detecting gestures and salient features of the hand. One simple approach detects points of high curvature as fingertip candidates (during contour tracing). Whilst a heuristic, these types of rules can produce convincing results [25]. However, there are often failure cases, such as complex poses where knuckles, styluses or other high curvature features confuse the peak detector. To address some of these issues, we present a novel contour (1D) based hand state and part classification algorithm, which is complimentary to more regular peak detection in specific scenarios.

For hand state classification we use a random decision forest (RDF) [7], which has been shown to be effective for both body [33] and hand [19] pose estimation using depth images. These approaches are trained to be invariant to pose and shape variations, use scale-invariant features, and achieve a robust result by averaging over multiple pixels. For RetroDepth, we adapt these approaches to silhouettes, keeping their benefits, while further reducing the complexity from 2D to 1D.

### RDF based contour classification

As a key contribution of this work, our classifiers operate on 1D contours instead of 2D images. These contours are essentially 1D sequences of 3D points in world space, sampled with a rate determined by the camera resolution and setup. For notational convenience, and without loss of generality, we will assume that the contours can be parameterized by a variable $s$, such that $X(s)$ gives the world coordinates of the point $s$ on the curve, and a unit step in $s$ on the 1D sequence corresponds to a unit step along the contour in 3D world space.

Each point on the contour is associated with two class labels $y^{\mathrm{s}}$ and $y^{\mathrm{f}}$, where $y^{\mathrm{s}}$ is a hand shape label (such as pointing, pinching, grasping or open hand) and $y^{\mathrm{f}}$ is a fingertip label (such as index, thumb, or non-fingertip). The task of the

Figure 6: Left: For a given point $s$ on the contour, we move by the offsets $u_1$ and $u_2$ to reach points $X(s+u_1)$ and $X(s+u_2)$. Middle: Hand shape class label $y^{\mathrm{s}}$ (one shared label for all pixels). Right: Fingertip class labels $y^{\mathrm{f}}$.

RDF is to classify the hand shape for the entire contour, and localize and identify the fingertips.

Decision trees use the internal split nodes to test and guide the input to one of the leaves, where class distributions of the output labels are stored. Test functions at split nodes are of the form: $f(F) < T$, where the function $f$ maps the features $F$ onto a line, and $T$ acts as a threshold. We use the following test function:

$$f(s, u_1, u_2, \vec{p}) = [X(s+u_1) - X(s+u_2)]_{\vec{p}} \quad (4)$$

where $[.]_{\vec{p}}$ is a projection onto the vector $\vec{p}$, and $\vec{p}$ is one of the primary axes $\vec{x}$, $\vec{y}$ or $\vec{z}$. This test probes two offsets on the contour, gets their world distance in the direction $\vec{p}$, and this distance is compared against the threshold $T$ (Fig. 6). Because the parameterization of $s$ is normalized, the offsets $u_1$ and $u_2$ are scale invariant. The test function splits the data into two sets and sends each to a child node. The quality of a split is determined by the information gain defined as follows:

$$G(u_1, u_2, T) = H(C) - \sum_{s \in \{\mathrm{L},\mathrm{R}\}} \frac{|C_s|}{|C|} H(C_s) \quad (5)$$

where $H(C)$ is the Shannon entropy of the class label distribution of the labels $y$ in the sample set $C$, and $C_{\mathrm{L}}$ and $C_{\mathrm{R}}$ are the two sets of examples formed by the split. At training time, multiple features and thresholds are uniformly sampled from a large range for each split node, and the one with the highest information gain is selected. Once leaves are reached, the class distribution of the remaining pixels in the node are saved. As each pixel has two labels from distinct sets in our case, we keep two histograms at each leaf: one for hand shape and one for fingertips.

At run-time, every pixel is evaluated independently with each tree in the forest and they descend into one of the leaves. For hand shape classification, the associated distributions read from the leaves are pooled across the contour to form a final set of state probabilities. The mode of this distribution is selected as the hand shape for the contour $X$. The fingertip localization algorithm is instead more akin to the part classification method of [33]. After classification, we apply a 1D running mode filter to the labeled contour to filter out the noisy labels. We finally apply connected components to give labels to the fingers. The system selects the point with the largest curvature as the fingertip.

To train a single forest that jointly handles shape classification and fingertip localization, we first disregard the $y^{\mathrm{f}}$ labels and calculate the information gain only using $y^{\mathrm{s}}$ until we reach a certain depth $m$. From then on, we switch to using $y^{\mathrm{f}}$ labels instead, and do not use $y^s$ to select features. This has the effect conditioning each subtree that starts at depth $m$ to the shape class distributions at their roots. This is similar to the idea presented in [19], in that the low level features are conditioned on the high level feature distribution. However, instead of using a multi-layered approach, we handle the classification jointly in a single forest.

We use a realistic synthetic hand model to automatically generate high-quality hand contours with labels. The hand model has 32 DoF, which can be used to automatically pose the object in a range of parameters, with added random noise on every joint angle. We generate a total of around 8000 left-hand images for each hand state class. These are then mirrored and given right hand labels. Fingertips are labeled by mapping the model with a texture that signifies different regions with separate colors. An example of the hand shape and fingertip labels for a certain pose can be seen in Fig. 6.

### Classifying other object contours

Our method for hand posture classification can also be leveraged to classify retro-reflective widgets. Even though the shapes are mostly primitive shapes e.g. rectangles and circles, applying template matching is not optimal. This is mainly because the contour of the object changes while the user is interacting with it, and also because for every type of object, a new set of heuristics or rules need to be generated. An off-the-shelf RDF on the other hand can learn all the variation of the contours for every shape. It is accurate and fast, and can learn to recognize new objects at run-time.

To reduce the variation due to occlusion, we first estimate the convex hull of the objects and evaluate this simplified contour. We use real data for training, since labeling the contours is straightforward in this case. The same features and objective function are used as in Equation 4 and 5. As the contours are much simpler in this case, much shallower forests are sufficient for online training.

### Recognizing a stylus

Pens are typically much sharper than fingers and therefore easier to recognize with heuristics. On both small objects where we have partial hand contours, as well as on larger surfaces where we have the full hand contour, finding the sharpest point on the contour (and thresholding it) is a good estimator for the pen tip location. However, the pen changes the contour of the hand shape considerably, which reduces the accuracy of the hand state classifier and causes the fingertip localizer to fail. Therefore, when a pen is detected on a large surface, the pen contour points are first removed from the contour. This can be done by following the pen contour in both directions until the gradient of the contour changes abruptly. The corresponding points are then connected to form the hand contour.

### Discussion and results

When users interact with smaller widgets, where only a few fingers or the pen is visible, hand state recognition is not desired as we have only a partial hand contour. In these cases, the pen and fingers can be found by simple peak detection. When the hand is on the large rectangular surface however, simple heuristics fail to identify or localize fingers robustly (e.g. finding peaks at knuckles). Examples that would very likely be failure cases for standard heuristic-based approaches such as detecting pinch [42] or fingertips [25] are shown in Fig. 7. Whilst these reinforce the need for a machine learning approach, our method is also complimentary to more heuristic-driven approaches.

| Class | Thumb | Index | Middle | Ring | Pinky | Reject |
|---|---|---|---|---|---|---|
| Accuracy | 0.848 | 0.754 | 0.615 | 0.594 | 0.796 | 0.882 |

Table 1: Per-pixel classification accuracy for the individual fingertip classes, before filtering.

Figure 7: Examples of results based on complex poses and visually ambiguous poses. Ground truth data shown left and test results shown right. Poses shown from left to right: two pinch gestures, a splayed hand with an occluded finger, and fused fingers on a splayed hand.

We conducted experiments with eight hand states, corresponding to left and right handed versions of four hand poses, namely "pointing", "pinching", "open hand looking down", and "open hand looking up". For each hand state we have 4000 synthetic left hand images, which are mirrored to retrieve data for the right hand. We train on half of the samples and test on the remaining ones.

We train an RDF with a single tree until depth 18 with the state labels only, and calculate the confusion matrix over all hand states. The RDF reaches perfect accuracy for both left and right handed versions of three of the command modes, and only shows confusion between the left– and right–handed pointing gestures. The success rate of left–handed pointing is 93% and right–handed pointing is 92%, and the corresponding left-right confusion is 7% for the former and 6% for the latter case. This gives us an overall command mode classification accuracy of 100% and left-right hand classification accuracy of 98% when all states are considered.

The synthetic images also have labels for the five fingertips and the reject class, corresponding to the non-fingertip areas. After the state classification training concludes at depth 18, we continue training with the fingertip labels until depth 25. The leaves are assigned the distributions of both state and fingertip labels. The success rates are given in Table 1. Even though we are operating on 1D contours, with much lower computation, the per-pixel classification rates are similar to the reported results in [33] and [19].

## CONTOUR INPAINTING

So far we have purposefully pushed the limits of what can be achieved purely based on silhouettes. However, there are certain scenarios and legacy applications that require fully dense depth maps. In this section, we show a robust and fast method for inpainting the contour of objects. The results of our contour inpainting algorithm can be found in Fig. 8.

In order to fill the interior $\Omega$ of our segmented contour $\partial\Omega$, we formulate the interpolation problem as a Laplace equation with Dirichlet boundary condition. Hence, contour depth values define a known scalar-valued boundary function $\hat{f}(x, y)|_{\partial\Omega}$ and we need to solve for the interior depth values $f(x, y)$ over $\Omega$ with:

$$\begin{aligned} \Delta f(x,y) &= 0 & (x,y) \in \Omega - \delta\Omega \\ f(x,y)|_{\partial\Omega} &= \hat{f}(x,y)|_{\partial\Omega} & \textit{otherwise} \end{aligned}$$

Then, we use a parallel Jaccobi/Gauss-Seidel solver on the GPU to solve the Laplace equation. In order to speed up convergence, we initialize the interior using a hierarchical pull-push interpolation with bi-cubic interpolation weights [27]. Note that we mark pixel values of $\partial\Omega$ with a negative sign, which allows us (except for the pull-push hierarchy) to solve the system in place. The contour inpainting results can be seen in the supplemental video.

## EXPERIMENTS

We now evaluate the performance of our system compared to three baseline measures. As a first baseline, we choose Leap Motion (**Leap**) given the widely publicized precision of the system, and its availability as a commodity sensor. The other baselines are based on another, arguably more ubiquitous depth sensor: the Kinect. With this sensor, we chose to run two conditions. The first (**KinectLight**) uses the RetroDepth hand posture and fingertip tracking pipeline described previously, and uses contour-traced Kinect depth maps as input (instead of RetroDepth stereo data). This in part evaluates our software pipeline with a commodity sensor, but also gives us an indication of the precision of the stereo matching algorithm and hardware setup that the full RetroDepth system supports. The second Kinect baseline (**3Gears**) evaluates the hand tracker from 3Gear systems [1]. This can be considered the current widely-available state-of-the-art hand tracker for Kinect with scenarios close to RetroDepth.

### 3D Target Acquisition

In our first task, we wanted to evaluate one of the core features of RetroDepth, its 3D input precision. For all conditions, the same physical setup was used as shown in Fig. 9. This provided a physical input space of 30x30x30cm. Leap was placed on the table, Kinect and RetroDepth mounted top down. All cameras were configured to share the same center of origin. A large table was used with retro-reflective material visible for the RetroDepth condition. This material was removed for the other conditions to avoid IR interference. A PC with a 6-core 2.8GHz processor and Nvidia GTX480 GPU, and large display were used for all conditions. Our pipeline ran on this hardware at 60Hz.

**Participants** Twelve participants (9 male, 3 female) between the ages of 21 and 39 were recruited for the study. Participants were daily computer users, 2 were left handed. All had normal vision. Participants had no experience of using 3D hand gesture-systems, but some had experiences playing Kinect games.

**Task** We conducted a 3D targeting task where the physical interaction volume was subdivided into 27 equally sized cells

Figure 8: Contour inpainting results in false color.

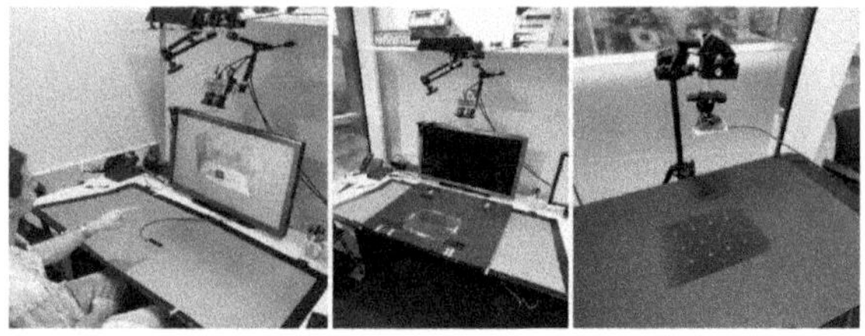

Figure 9: Study setup. Left: Kinect, Leap and RetroDepth setups for 3D acquisition task. Middle: Kinect touch evaluation. Right: Leap touch evaluation.

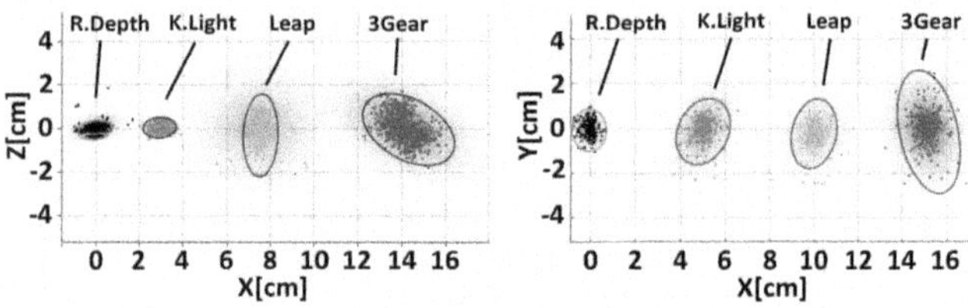


Figure 10: Left: touch targeting results, and right: 3D acquisition targeting results.

(3x3x3 grid). The user began by holding their finger in a 3D transparent box appearing centered and at the front of the 3D scene. After a fixed time, a billboarded target shown in Fig. 9 (left screen) appeared centered in one cell for users to select. 3 trials were performed per condition. Starting and target positions were coupled a priori to reduce in-condition variance. This set was used across all conditions, with the order randomized, ensuring that the total distance traveled was exactly equal across all users, and each condition. Measurement of task completion was triggered once the fingertip left the starting position and ended once the user entered the target triggering area. The targets were 5x5cm high.

**Procedure** The experiment employed a within-subject repeated measure design. The independent variable was the input type: RetroDepth, Leap, KinectLight, 3Gears. The dependent measure was the targeting accuracy (measured as a distance of the fingertip to the target center upon selection). The presentation order of the conditions was counterbalanced using a Latin Square design across users. A short training phase was first performed, after which each user was asked to perform the task as accurately as possible. The entire experiment lasted about 60 minutes. Participants filled out a post-experiment questionnaire upon completion. Users were observed at all times as the task was performed, and notes on subjective experiences were taken.

### Results

Our 12 participants produced a total of 3888 selections in this task. No effect was found between the four blocks of trails (e.g. from fatigue or learning effects). Additionally there was no significant differences between participants. This allows us to combine data to cluster per condition results as shown in Fig. 10 (right). The plot shows the average of the target hits across all participants, clustered by condition. Note we ignore the Z contribution as the targets were planar, and depth is measured along the Y axis in our 3D scene. The more compact the cluster the more accurate the result. 95% confidence ellipses are shown for each condition.

We compute the minimum target sizes required to achieve 95% accuracy for each condition. RetroDepth achieves the

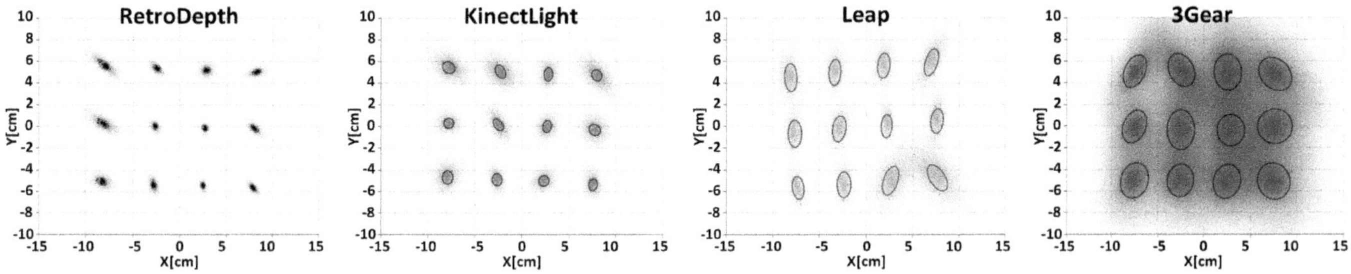


Figure 11: 2D touch results across all four conditions.

smallest minimum target size of 1.95x1.55cm with error X=7.89mm and Y=10.90mm. 3Gears achieves the largest minimum target size of 5.30x3.15cm with error X = 20.86mm and Y=29.74mm. KinectLight achieves a size of 2.89x2.08cm with error X= 15.24mm and Y=24.87mm. Leap performs similarly achieving a size of 3.18x2.00cm with error X=17.53mm and Y=22.67mm.

### Physical Touch Performance

Another important feature of RetroDepth is the ability to support touch sensing. To evaluate the performance of the system against our baseline, we ran a further experiment, where each camera (Kinect, Leap and RetroDepth) was setup in top down arrangement Fig. 9 (middle and right). For Leap this meant adding a sheet of IR absorbing film to the table. A 20cm×25cm acrylic sheet was used as a touch surface, with small laser etched targets (spaced 5cm apart), and sized for the user's fingertips. 12 participants, 3 women and 9 men, were asked to perform a physical touch task. The aim was to measure system performance in terms of touch accuracy, and overall sensor precision. Participants were asked to touch all 12 targets in turn over 5 trials. The 3D point was recorded once the user's self reported. Fig. 11 shows the X-Y 2D accuracy plots for each of the sensors. Fig. 10 (left) shows the Z-Y accuracy plots (Z axis corresponds to depth precision). Based on these statistics it is possible to define the minimum 3D target bounds to capture 95% of the touches. For RetroDepth this is 1.69x0.98x0.75cm, KinectLight is 1.49x1.29x0.85cm, Leap is 3.88x2.91x 1.63cm, 3Gear is 4.41x3.71x2.78cm.

### Discussion

We found the results extremely encouraging given the precision of RetroDepth compared to these baselines. It is however important to note that we are not comparing like-for-like necessary. In terms of fidelity, for example, Leap uses lower cost cameras, and we use more costly research cameras. Nor was the Leap designed for touch-like scenarios (i.e. pointing downwards). Although we feel that the touch accuracy of the Leap is good enough to warrant future work on this scenario, based on our IR absorbing idea. On the other hand, RetroDepth is a research prototype whilst others are engineered products. Our system also offers different data (silhouettes) than the Leap and the Kinect, and none of these elements are being measured. However, with all this in mind our results are encouraging in terms of precision and performance.

An interesting finding is how well Kinect performed in the KinectLight condition, particularly for touch sensing. This illustrates benefits of our software pipeline for improving touch and 3D acquisition. Another interesting finding is that user's perceptions and performance can be very different. Leap surprisingly did not perform as well as expected, yet it was ranked a close second to RetroDepth in terms of preference. Many users described it as fluid, which indicates that the higher frame-rate has a strong impact in terms of NUI experience, potentially even distorting views of sensor accuracy. The 3Gear performance also gives an interesting insight. Whilst the system appeared to be performing well, showing compelling 3D models fitting the Kinect data, this model fitting approach ultimately led to severe inaccuracies for touch and selection, as there will always be discrepancies between a generic model and the user's hand.

Overall we feel that RetroDepth offers an exciting new research platform for future work on NUI interfaces, leading to new applications that incorporate touch, pressure, 3D, and even tangible input. There are of course limitations with our approach. Ultimately, 3D silhouettes are a lower dimensional representation of the real world, and in that regard data can be lost. The interesting finding from our experiments is just how much information is encoded in the silhouette allowing high accuracy rates for hand pose and part classification. Another clear finding is around frame rate, where user feedback suggests that trading some precision for speed may be desirable, and where there are significant computational advantages of working with silhouettes.

## CONCLUSIONS

In this paper we have presented RetroDepth a system that allows for high-precision 3D sensing on and above physical surfaces. We have provided several key contributions: 1) A fully working real-time 3D silhouette sensing technology which combines (for the first time) the common NUI modalities of touch, pressure, stylus, objects, and 3D, into a single system. 2) a new stereo matching algorithm for computing fast and precise 3D contours. 3) a new 1D contour classification algorithm, for robustly identifying physical tools, hand poses and salient features. 4) A software pipeline with practical impact even for regular Kinect sensors.

## REFERENCES

1. 3Gear Systems Inc. http://threegear.com/, 2013.
2. Agarwal, A., Izadi, S., Chandraker, M., and Blake, A. High precision multi-touch sensing on surfaces using overhead cameras. In *Tabletop'07*, 197–200.
3. Akaoka, E., Ginn, T., and Vertegaal, R. Displayobjects: prototyping functional physical interfaces on 3d styrofoam, paper or cardboard models. In *TEI'10*, ACM (2010), 49–56.
4. Annett, M., Grossman, T., Wigdor, D., and Fitzmaurice, G. Medusa: a proximity-aware multi-touch tabletop. In *UIST'11*, ACM (2011), 337–346.

5. Benko, H., Jota, R., and Wilson, A. Miragetable: freehand interaction on a projected augmented reality tabletop. In *CHI'12*, ACM (2012), 199–208.
6. Bleyer, M., Rhemann, C., and Rother, C. Patchmatch stereo - stereo matching with slanted support windows. In *BMVC* (2011), 1–11.
7. Breiman, L. Random Forests. *Machine Learning 45*, 1 (Oct. 2001), 5–32.
8. Brown, M. Z., Burschka, D., and Hager, G. D. Advances in computational stereo. *PAMI 25*, 8 (2003), 993–1008.
9. Davis, J. W., and Bobick, A. F. Sideshow: A silhouette-based interactive dual-screen environment. Tech. rep., MIT, 1998.
10. Dippon, A., and Klinker, G. Kinecttouch: accuracy test for a very low-cost 2.5 d multitouch tracking system. In *ITS'11*, ACM (2011), 49–52.
11. Haptix. http://www.haptixtouch.com/, 2013.
12. Haubner, N., Schwanecke, U., Dörner, R., Lehmann, S., and Luderschmidt, J. Detecting interaction above digital tabletops using a single depth camera. *Machine Vision and Applications* (2013), 1–13.
13. Hilliges, O., Izadi, S., Wilson, A. D., Hodges, S., Garcia-Mendoza, A., and Butz, A. Interactions in the air: adding further depth to interactive tabletops. In *UIST'09*, ACM (2009), 139–148.
14. Hilliges, O., Kim, D., Izadi, S., Weiss, M., and Wilson, A. Holodesk: direct 3d interactions with a situated see-through display. In *CHI'12*, ACM (2012), 2421–2430.
15. Hirsch, M., Lanman, D., Holtzman, H., and Raskar, R. Bidi screen: a thin, depth-sensing lcd for 3d interaction using light fields. In *TOG*, vol. 28, ACM (2009), 159.
16. Izadi, S., Agarwal, A., Criminisi, A., Winn, J., Blake, A., and Fitzgibbon, A. C-slate: a multi-touch and object recognition system for remote collaboration using horizontal surfaces. In *Tabletop'07*, IEEE (2007), 3–10.
17. Izadi, S., Hodges, S., Butler, A., West, D., Rrustemi, A., Molloy, M., and Buxton, W. Thinsight: a thin form-factor interactive surface technology. *CACM 52*, 12, 90–98.
18. Izadi, S., Hodges, S., Taylor, S., Rosenfeld, D., Villar, N., Butler, A., and Westhues, J. Going beyond the display: a surface technology with an electronically switchable diffuser. In *UIST'08*, ACM (2008), 269–278.
19. Keskin, C., Kirac, F., Kara, Y. E., and Akarun, L. Hand Pose Estimation and Hand Shape Classification Using Multi-layered Randomized Decision Forests. In *ECCV'12* (2012).
20. Koike, H., Sato, Y., and Kobayashi, Y. Integrating paper and digital information on enhanceddesk: a method for realtime finger tracking on an augmented desk system. *TOCHI 8*, 4 (2001), 307–322.
21. Krueger, M. W. *Artificial reality II*, vol. 10. Addison-Wesley Reading (Ma), 1991.
22. Lanman, D., and Taubin, G. Build your own 3d scanner: 3d photography for beginners. In *ACM SIGGRAPH 2009 Courses*, ACM (2009), 8.
23. Lee, J., Park, K. S., and Hahn, M. The 3d sensor table for bare hand tracking and posture recognition. In *Advances in Multimedia Modeling*. Springer, 2006, 138–146.
24. Liu, Y., Weibel, N., and Hollan, J. Interactive space: A framework for prototyping multi-touch interaction on and above the desktop. In *CHI'13 EA*, ACM (2013).
25. Malik, S., and Laszlo, J. Visual touchpad: a two-handed gestural input device. In *ICMI'04*, 289–296.
26. Marquardt, N., Jota, R., Greenberg, S., and Jorge, J. A. The continuous interaction space: interaction techniques unifying touch and gesture on and above a digital surface. In *INTERACT'11*, Springer (2011), 461–476.
27. Marroquim, R., Kraus, M., and Cavalcanti, P. R. Efficient point-based rendering using image reconstruction. In *SPBG*, IEEE (2007), 101–108.
28. Matsushita, N., and Rekimoto, J. Holowall: designing a finger, hand, body, and object sensitive wall. In *UIST'97*, ACM (1997), 209–210.
29. Moeller, J., Kerne, A., and Moeller, J. Zerotouch: An optical multi-touch and free-air interaction architecture. In *CHI'12*, ACM (2012), 2165–2174.
30. Paradiso, J. A. Several sensor approaches that retrofit large surfaces for interactivity. In *UbiComp 2002* (2002).
31. Remondino, F., and Stoppa, D. *Tof range-imaging cameras*. Springer, 2013.
32. Scharstein, D., and Szeliski, R. A taxonomy and evaluation of dense two-frame stereo correspondence algorithms. In *IJCV* (2002).
33. Shotton, J., Fitzgibbon, A., Cook, M., Sharp, T., Finocchio, M., Moore, R., Kipman, A., and Blake, A. Real-time Human Pose Recognition in Parts from Single Depth Images. In *CVPR* (2011).
34. Strecha, C., and Van Gool, L. PDE-based multi-view depth estimation. In *Proc. 3DIMPVT* (2002), 416–425.
35. Subramanian, S., Aliakseyeu, D., and Lucero, A. Multi-layer interaction for digital tables. In *UIST'06*, ACM (2006), 269–272.
36. Takeoka, Y., Miyaki, T., and Rekimoto, J. Z-touch: an infrastructure for 3d gesture interaction in the proximity of tabletop surfaces. In *ITS'10*, ACM (2010), 91–94.
37. Ullmer, B., and Ishii, H. The metadesk: models and prototypes for tangible user interfaces. In *UIST'97*, ACM (1997), 223–232.
38. Wang, R., Paris, S., and Popović, J. 6d hands: markerless hand-tracking for computer aided design. In *UIST'11*, ACM (2011), 549–558.
39. Wellner, P. Interacting with paper on the digitaldesk. *CACM 36*, 7 (1993), 87–96.
40. Wesche, G., and Seidel, H.-P. Freedrawer: a free-form sketching system on the responsive workbench. In *VRST*, ACM (2001), 167–174.
41. Wilson, A. D. Playanywhere: a compact interactive tabletop projection-vision system. In *UIST'05*, ACM (2005), 83–92.
42. Wilson, A. D. Robust computer vision-based detection of pinching for one and two-handed gesture input. In *UIST'06*, ACM (2006), 255–258.
43. Wilson, A. D. Depth-sensing video cameras for 3d tangible tabletop interaction. In *Tabletop'07*, IEEE (2007), 201–204.
44. Wilson, A. D. Using a depth camera as a touch sensor. In *ITS'10*, ACM (2010), 69–72.

# SurfaceLink: Using Inertial and Acoustic Sensing to Enable Multi-Device Interaction on a Surface

Mayank Goel[1,2], Brendan Lee[1], Md. Tanvir Islam Aumi[1], Shwetak Patel[1], Gaetano Borriello[1], Stacie Hibino[2], James Begole[2]

[1]University of Washington, DUB, UbiComp Lab
Seattle, WA, USA
{mayankg, lee3, tanvir, shwetak,gaetano}@uw.edu

[2]Samsung Research America
San Jose, CA, USA
{stacie.h, james.begole}@samsung.com

## ABSTRACT

We present *SurfaceLink*, a system where users can make natural surface gestures to control association and information transfer among a set of devices placed on a mutually shared surface (*e.g.*, a table). SurfaceLink uses a combination of on-device accelerometers, vibration motors, speakers, and microphones (and, optionally, an off-device contact microphone for greater sensitivity) to sense gestures performed on the shared surface. In a controlled evaluation with 10 participants, SurfaceLink detected the presence of devices on the same surface with 97.7% accuracy, their relative arrangement with 89.4% accuracy, and a set of single- and multi-touch surface gestures with an average accuracy of 90.3%. A usability analysis showed that SurfaceLink has advantages over current multi-device interaction techniques in a number of situations.

### Author Keywords

Multi-device interaction, inertial sensing, acoustic sensing, mobile phones, surface interaction.

## INTRODUCTION

It is common to have multiple computing devices co-located in the same environment. In a number of these situations, it is useful for these devices to communicate with each other. Photo sharing is a canonical example, where a user may want to take a picture on their smartphone and share it with another smartphone, any number of computers and tablets, or even a local projector. Although the networking and data transfer aspects are largely solved using technologies such as Wi-Fi, Bluetooth, and NFC, users still need simple and natural ways to indicate the intent for creating logical connections between devices.

The radio signal strength can be used to identify proximate devices, but in today's device-dense environment, users must select which devices within wireless proximity should belong to a particular group. For instance, if the user wants to send a photo from their mobile phone to another person's


*CHI 2014,* April 26–May 1, 2014, Toronto, Ontario, Canada.

http://dx.doi.org/10.1145/2556288.2557120

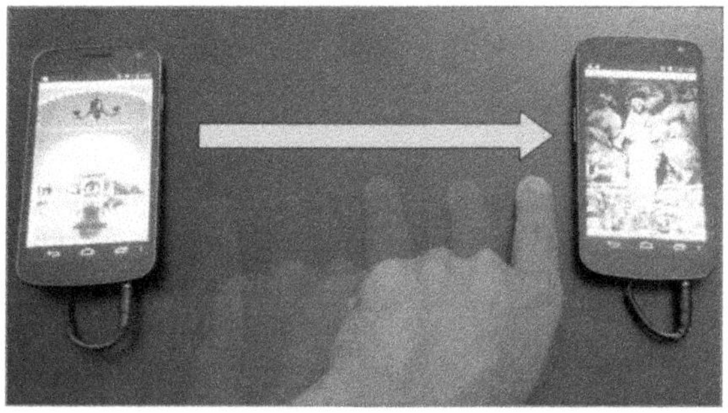

**Figure 1.** User interacting with two mobile devices on a shared table using only on-device inertial and acoustic infrastructure and inexpensive contact microphones.

computer through Bluetooth, they need to identify the computer's name from a list of nearby devices in order to pair with it.

A number of techniques [13,14,15,16,24,27,29] have been developed to establish a connection between devices based on "*context proximity*" [15], but these techniques do not scale well with increasing numbers of devices. Most of these techniques assume one or two devices per user, but it is increasingly common for users to have multiple devices for varying purposes. Thus, prior "pairing" techniques, which were suitable for a literal *pair* of devices, are inadequate for today's multi-device environments.

One common setting where devices and their users exchange information is around a table or other shared surface. For example, colleagues collaborate around a conference table, friends share photos around a coffee table, or a single user has their phone, tablet, laptop, *etc.* on a single desk. Hence, this commonly available flat surface provides an expedient medium for interacting across multiple devices within a bounded context (the shared surface). In order to enable multi-device interaction on a shared surface, three attributes need to be sensed: (1) the presence of multiple devices on the surface, (2) their relative placement on the surface, and (3) the gestures the user performs to interact between devices. Although past work has relied on hardware such as cameras and IR-LED arrays [3,5,17,23,32], similar capabilities can be enabled through simple on-device inertial and acoustic sensing.

We present *SurfaceLink* (Figure 1), a system that leverages inertial and acoustic sensing to enable multi-device interaction on a shared surface. Using only the on-device sensors plus an optional 0.20 USD contact microphone plugged directly into the microphone jack, SurfaceLink detects the presence and placement of devices and gestures between them. Using sophisticated noise cancellation, the contact microphone becomes unnecessary, and SurfaceLink can be a completely software-based solution. Although not formally evaluated, we informally tested SurfaceLink with an active noise cancellation system and the performance was comparable to using external contact microphones.

SurfaceLink detects the presence of all devices on the same surface by using the surface material's ability to conduct vibrations. To induce vibrations on the surface, the user can either knock on the surface manually or the device can vibrate using its built-in vibration motors. These vibrations are sensed through accelerometers and contact microphones. Any devices that are not on the shared surface will not be able to sense these vibration patterns, thus will not consider themselves part of the same group. The surface therefore serves as a "location limited channel" [2] for situations where users want groups that only include devices directly on the shared surface.

In addition, SurfaceLink turns most surfaces into an input medium where different types of single and multi-touch gestures can be performed to interact between devices. When a finger is dragged over a surface, it produces vibrations on the surface that can be sensed as gestures using microphones. This phenomenon has been previously demonstrated by Harrison and Hudson [8]. SurfaceLink extends prior art by adding multi-touch, directionality, speed, and length to develop a richer set of gestures. SurfaceLink also detects the relative arrangement of devices on the surface by combining a user's surface gestures with acoustic stereo positioning.

We evaluated SurfaceLink in a controlled user study with 10 participants. Our findings showed that SurfaceLink detected device presence on the same surface with 97.7% accuracy and various surface gestures with an average accuracy of 90.3%. SurfaceLink also performed the relative localization of devices with 89.4% accuracy. Lastly, we qualitatively evaluated the usefulness of SurfaceLink and showed that SurfaceLink scales better to increasing numbers of devices than current multi-device interaction techniques.

The main contributions of this paper are: (1) multiple techniques to enable rich ad-hoc multi-device interactions using the surface as an input medium; empirical results from an evaluation of SurfaceLink showing that it (2) robustly detects the *presence* of multiple devices on the same surface and establishes *connections*, (3) continuously tracks *single-* and *multi-touch gestures* between multiple devices by inferring their direction, length, speed, and touch modes, and (4) accurately detect the *relative arrangement* of devices.

## RELATED WORK

### Vision-based Surface Interaction

For over 15 years researchers have emphasized that the surfaces around us can be used for interaction [28]. HoloWall [23] is one of the first systems that allows a user to interact with a glass wall. The system leverages IR-LEDs, a camera, and a projector. Similar to HoloWall, many recent techniques have used vision for making interaction with the surface more engaging. BonFire [17] uses a camera and two projectors to improve interaction between a laptop and a table's surface. Cuypers *et al.* [5] developed a technique to determine the position of a portable device on an interactive glass surface by projecting unique visual patterns and sensing the pattern received by the portable device's camera. BlueTable [32] connects multiple devices on a shared surface using vision-based handshaking. SideSight [3] uses IR-LEDs and vision for around-the-device interaction. All these systems, whether single- or multi-device, use computer vision to detect the devices and user-interaction with the surface. A vision-based system lacks portability and requires one or more cameras in the environment. These requirements make such a system unsuitable for impromptu interactions. In contrast, SurfaceLink uses lightweight inertial and acoustic sensing to detect devices and enable user-interaction. This approach allows for much more impromptu multi-device interactions.

### Detecting Contextual Presence

Apart from the vision techniques mentioned above, others have proposed techniques for detecting the presence of multiple devices that shared some context with each other. Smart-Its-Friends [15] called this concept *"context proximity"*. The authors described how artifacts established connection with each other by detecting a shared phenomenon in their relative contexts. For example, two devices shared data when a user shook both of the devices simultaneously. This technique of detecting synchronous events has been explored by a number of researchers. Ideas such as bumping two devices together [24] or making contact with touch screens at the same time [27] provide a tangible way of initiating connections between two physically disconnected devices. PhoneTouch [29] detects co-occurrence of device vibration and surface touch to facilitate interaction between an interactive surface and a mobile device. Hutama *et al.* [16] used tilt correlations to facilitate interaction between multiple devices. All these techniques have a scalability problem as they either do not work for more than two devices, or assume a limit of about one user per device. Stitching [13] provides a very interesting way of connecting multiple devices together. The user draws a line with their finger from the touchscreen of the sending device to the touchscreen of the receiving device. This is a very intuitive action for connecting two devices, but it requires both devices to have a touchscreen and is less intuitive for connecting multiple devices. SurfaceLink avoids the scalability problem by leveraging the mutually sensed vibrations of a shared surface to allow any number of devices to be easily connected.

### Device Arrangement

Detecting where the devices are kept in the interaction environment is relatively straightforward in the earlier mentioned vision-based techniques. The main disadvantages of such techniques are their relatively demanding hardware requirements. These technologies cannot be used for impromptu interactions because it is not common to have calibrated cameras set up in the environment. Dearman *et al.* [6] developed a lightweight system where a group of mobile devices used their backside camera to infer their relative orientation. Lucero *et al.* [21,22] explored how radio tracking technology can be used to determine devices' relative positions, but this approach fails when the devices are densely packed. Similar to SurfaceLink, Kortuem *et al.* [18] used ultrasonic audio signals for relative localization of devices, but they used external hardware and were limited to only detecting whether the device is *to the left, to the right, approaching,* or *moving away* from first device. SurfaceLink, in contrast, combines surface gestures and stereo acoustic sensing to infer a multi-device arrangement on a surface in both x and y directions.

### Surface Gestures using Acoustic Sensing

Prior to SurfaceLink, others have proposed techniques for enabling interactions with a surface using acoustic sensing. Paradiso and Checka did some of the early work in this area [26]. They proposed a system that tracked a user's knock on a glass wall by measuring the time delay of arrival (TDOA) of vibrations at 4 different contact piezoelectric pickups. The work by Crevoisier and Polotti [4] was one of the earlier works that explored interaction with day-to-day physical artifacts through sensing the surface vibrations. ScratchInput [8] demonstrated that when a user drags their nails on a textured surface, the resultant vibrations could be used to convert the surface into an ad-hoc interactive surface. ScratchInput just scratched the surface of possibilities in this area, and SurfaceLink builds on this work to additionally provide single- and multi-touch gestures with varying speed and length. The gestures can be tracked in real-time and because SurfaceLink performs spectral analysis on the acoustic signal, it performs well even when the signal-to-noise ratio is low. Hence, the user no longer is limited to scratching with just the fingernails. The user can interact using any part of the hand. SurfaceLink is also first to explore how these gestures can be used in a multi-device environment and presents a set of gestures and enabling technologies for effectively interacting among multiple devices.

Seniuk and Blostein [30] explored how the surface vibrations generated by pens on a known textured surface could be used for recognizing a fixed dictionary of 26 words written by the user. Murray-Smith *et al.* [25] also used such surface vibrations to develop a handheld interaction device that could be controlled by tapping, scratching, or rubbing the surface. In a similar effort, Harrison *et al.* [11] demonstrated how structured patterns of physical notches could be used as acoustic barcodes when swiped with a hard object like a fingernail or a smartphone. TapSense [10] and similar work by Lopes *et al.* [20] leveraged the contact microphone on a touch screen to detect different touch modes while a user tapped on the screen. SurfaceLink applies this same approach, and further extends the gesture set. To the best of our knowledge, SurfaceLink is the first work to demonstrate and evaluate gesture length, speed, direction, multi-touch, and application of these gestures in a multi-device environment.

## DESIGN OF *SURFACE-LINK*

SurfaceLink enables end-to-end fluid multi-device interactions. It first detects contextually proximate devices, then enables a rich set of single- and multi-touch gestures, and combines them with stereo acoustic sensing to determine the relative positions of the devices. A contextual group of devices present on the same surface is created. Then the user can interact with these devices through gestures on the surface. SurfaceLink enables a number of on-surface gestures including single-finger directional swipes, multi-finger pinch and expand, and grouping gestures. It also enables robust detection of the length and speed of these gestures, which can be used for continuous, fluid interaction between devices. In order to provide the system with a much better understanding of the arrangement of devices, SurfaceLink combines stereo positioning with user gesture data to accurately detect the relative positions of devices in a 2-dimensional space.

SurfaceLink leverages the shared surface as a communication channel between the devices that are placed on it. It uses a combination of the on-device accelerometer, vibration motor, speakers, microphones, and off-device contact microphones for establishing connections and interactions between the devices.

### Detecting Devices on the Same Surface

SurfaceLink uses the fact that hard, flat surfaces conduct vibrations well. These vibrations can either be user-induced by knocking on the surface, or device-induced using a vibration motor. These vibrations travel through the dense material of the surface and are sensed by the device sensors. Harrison *et al.* [9] and Kunze *et al.* [19] demonstrated techniques to detect the nature of the surface on which a device is kept. In contrast, SurfaceLink detects if the devices are on the same surface, irrespective of the material. For example, SurfaceLink can distinguish between whether devices A and B are kept on the *same* or *different* tables, whereas [9] and [19] detected if a device was kept on a metal or wooden table.

#### *Using User-Induced Vibrations*

When a user knocks on a surface, it generates strong vibrations that travel through the dense material of the surface. These vibrations can be sensed by the on-device accelerometers.

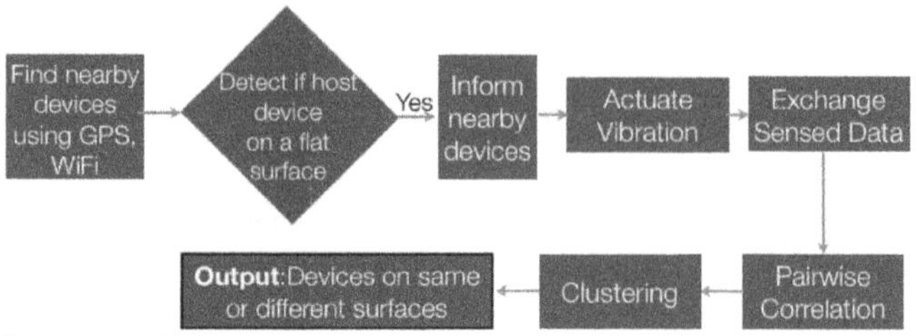


**Figure 2.** Block diagram of major components of SurfaceLink's detection of devices on the same surface. When sensing user-induced vibrations, inertial sensor data is used, and when sensing device-induced vibrations, the contact microphone data is used.

Initially, when a user wants to connect to other devices on the same surface, the user's device acts as a host device and uses GPS and Wi-Fi information to find the nearby devices. Once the device has a list of nearby devices, it instructs them to start sampling their accelerometers (Figure 2). It then instructs the user to knock on the surface in any user-defined pattern and samples its accelerometer at 100 Hz. The devices share their observed accelerometer data. A device might experience a number of vibrations in a busy environment but most of these vibrations are relatively low frequency when compared to those generated by the user's knocks. Hence, the accelerometer data of all devices is passed through a high-pass filter. Then a pairwise cross correlation is performed between these data samples. The devices are then clustered into two sets (*on same surface*, and *not*) on the basis of their cross-correlations. We use the Single Linkage algorithm that uses the smallest distance between objects in different groups to cluster them.

*Using Device-Induced Vibrations*

In a number of cases, interface designers might not want to require a user to generate the stimulus by knocking on a surface to pair devices. In such cases, we can use the built-in vibration motor to generate the stimulus. The inertial sensors on most mobile devices cannot detect device-induced vibrations because they do not have the sensitivity and resolution required. Hence we use a microphone to pick up these subtle vibrations. These vibrations are usually coupled to the air and can be heard by a microphone on some other surface as well. In order to pick up these subtle surface vibrations, it requires either noise cancellation using two microphones on the device (*i.e.*, one touching the surface and one in the opposite direction), or a low-cost external contact microphone with a resonant frequency of 6.3 kHz. The device uses on-device inertial sensors to automatically detect if it is placed on a stable, flat surface [7]. In the same way as mentioned above for the user-induced case, the device obtains a list of nearby devices. These clients are then informed to sample their microphones at 44.1 kHz. When a device vibrates on a hard, flat surface it periodically hits the surface, thereby generating a low frequency sound. The system performs noise cancellation by subtracting the audio from the microphone on the top from the microphone touching the surface. When using a contact microphone, the microphone couples strongly to the surface and only records the surface vibrations, hence no filtering is needed. The devices then share their data and a pairwise cross-correlation and clustering is done as described previously.

In some cases, where there are a number of devices on a relatively large table, the host device can be far from some potential client devices. This often leads to situations where the devices are unable to reliably experience the induced vibrations. In such a situation, the system assumes that these far-away devices would still be relatively near to some of the other devices and employs a "vibration daisy chaining" technique where identified devices induce new vibrations to extend the reach of the device network.

**Detecting Surface Gestures**

SurfaceLink uses the concept that a finger/hand dragged over most hard surfaces produces measurable vibrations. These vibrations can be detected using the on-device microphone or an off-device contact microphone.

*Gesture Class*

We observe that the vibrations generated due to dragging of finger on a surface have different characteristics in different directions. One of the differences is that in many cases they are louder when near the device and softer when far. The difference in swipe direction also results in distinctly different patterns in the frequency domain. As a user's finger comes near a device, there is a decrease in the resonant frequency (Figure 3A), and the opposite effect is observed when the finger moves away from the device (Figure 3B).

A swipe gesture may be performed between two devices, but in a number of situations, more than two devices might be present on the surface. The devices not involved in the gesture would also hear the vibrations on their

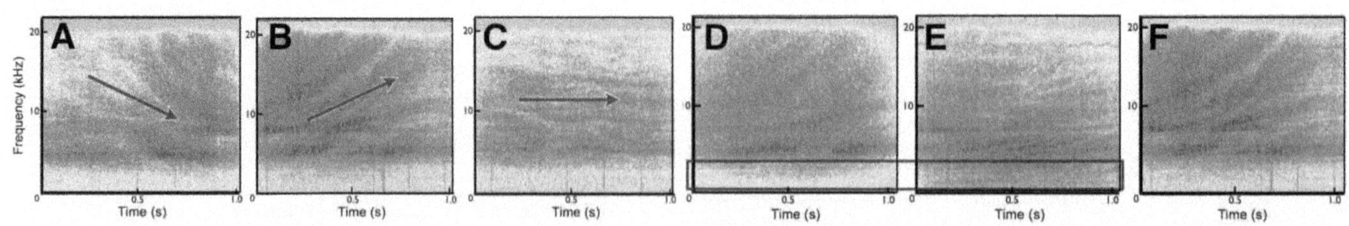


**Figure 3 (A)** Swipe towards the device. **(B)** Swipe away the device. **(C)** Vibrations experienced by the non-participating device. **(D)** Gesture performed with fingertip. **(E)** Gesture performed with fingernail. **(F)** Gesture performed with fist

microphones. Hence there is a need to disambiguate between participating and non-participating devices. In the case of a unidirectional swipe gesture between two devices, a non-participating third device can experience one of three possibilities. It will observe vibrations similar to the two participating devices (Figure 3A or 3B) if it is right next to one of the participating devices. In this case, the overall spectral energy of the vibrations will be much higher for the participating devices. If the non-participating device is not near to either of the participating devices, it might observe similar energy levels, but now the swipe is neither going towards nor away from it, and hence it will observe vibrations similar to those shown in Figure 3C (*i.e.*, no change in resonant frequency over time).

**Figure 4.** ***(Left)*** Pinch gesture, ***(Right)*** Expand gesture

SurfaceLink also supports two multi-finger gestures: *pinch* and *expand*. In the pinch gesture (Figure 4, *Left*), the user starts the swipe near each device and draws them together toward the middle. This gesture can be used to connect two devices together. In the case of such a gesture, both devices experience a swipe away from them (Figure 3B). The complimentary gesture, *expand* (Figure 4, *Right*) generates the equivalent of swiping toward both devices (Figure 3A) and can be used for disconnecting two devices.

The speed of a gesture on a surface is directly correlated to the amplitude of the resonant frequency. In addition, the duration of all gestures are bounded since they are mostly performed between two devices. Hence, if a user does a fast swipe, the gesture accelerates and decelerates quickly. Therefore, in addition to the higher amplitude, the slope of increase and decrease in amplitude is also steeper. The combination of these two phenomena can be used to differentiate between different gesture speeds. In order to make it easy for the user to discern different speed levels, SurfaceLink supports only two speeds: slow and fast.

### *Gesture Length*

Considering that SurfaceLink can estimate the speed of a gesture and the length of a gesture is bounded by the distance between two devices, we can also detect the length of a gesture. A smaller gesture can be compared to a longer gesture of same speed as both will have the same amplitude and slope but different durations. SurfaceLink supports three gesture lengths: full, half, and quarter length.

### *Touch Modes*

SurfaceLink uses the fact that different finger locations generate different vibrations when dragged across a surface. SurfaceLink employs the techniques demonstrated by Harrison *et al.* [10] to support three touch modes: fingertip, fingernail, and fist. The nail, being harder than the fingertip, produces a very different frequency profile (Figure 3D and 3E). The differentiation between fingertip and fist (Figure 3F) is slightly different. The fingertip and fist are made up of the same material, so the frequency response for the two modes is not different. However, because the area of contact is much larger in the case of the fist, it creates a higher amplitude sound.

### *Gesture Shape*

ScratchInput [8] demonstrated that analysis of peak counts and amplitude variation could be used to infer a fixed dictionary of gesture shapes, such as a line, circle, triangle, and square. We employ similar techniques, albeit using the spectral information and performing pattern matching.

### *Implementation for Detecting the Surface Gestures*

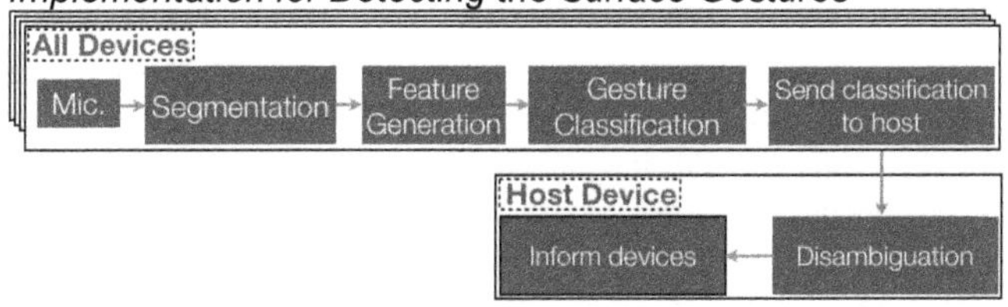


**Figure 5.** Block diagram of major components of SurfaceLink's gesture detection. Pattern matching results from all devices are sent to the host device for disambiguation.

Every device on the surface records audio data at 44.1 kHz. The data is then segmented into individual gestures. This segmentation is done by thresholding the audio data between 5 kHz and 15 kHz. We did not formally evaluate the segmentation but in our informal evaluation with 3 participants, there was virtually no segmentation error because the contact microphone couples very well to the surface and is immune to ambient noise. The segmented audio data is then used to generate machine learning features before going through gesture classification (Figure 5). Each device individually infers the gesture, and then shares the classification result with the host device. SurfaceLink classifies each gesture into four different gesture properties:

1. *Gesture Class*: Away, Towards, Non-Participating, Pinch, Expand, or Fast Swipe.
2. *Gesture Length*: Quarter, Half, or Full.
3. *Touch Mode*: Fingertip, Fingernail, or Fist.
4. *Gesture Shape*: Line, Polygon, Triangle, Circle, Semi-Circle.

In order to generate the features, we produce the magnitude spectrogram of the audio signal using a 1024-point FFT with a 100 sample Hamming window. In order to reduce the number of features, the |FFT| data over the duration of the gesture was down-sampled into 6 frequency bins and 10 time frames using median filtering. This forms a 6x10 matrix representing the first 60 features used for classification. Next, in order to capture the temporal variation for each gesture, we band-pass filtered (5 kHz to 15 kHz) the temporal data and then down-sampled into 10 time windows. Thereby providing 10 new features. The last

2 features are the total energy in the first and second half of the gesture. These 72 features are used to inform a kNN classifier ($k = 2$) on each device. We have separate kNN classifiers for each gesture property (*Gesture Class*, *Gesture Length*, *Touch Mode*, and *Gesture Shape*). It helps in keeping the number of training samples to a minimum. A detailed analysis of the effect of training size on the performance of the system is provided in the Results section.

Once each device makes a decision for each gesture, it sends the classification result, classification confidence, and the total observed energy for the gesture to the host device. The inverse of normalized distance between the observation and nearest neighbor is used as the classification confidence. For example, if the normalized kNN distance between the observation and nearest neighbor on device A is 10, and on device B is 20, then their respective classification confidences are 0.1 and 0.05. The host device then checks if all the devices agree on the classification. In case there is ambiguity, the host device checks the confidence metric for each device and selects the decision of the device with the highest confidence. In cases where multiple devices predict that they were participants in a gesture, the device with higher total observed energy is selected.

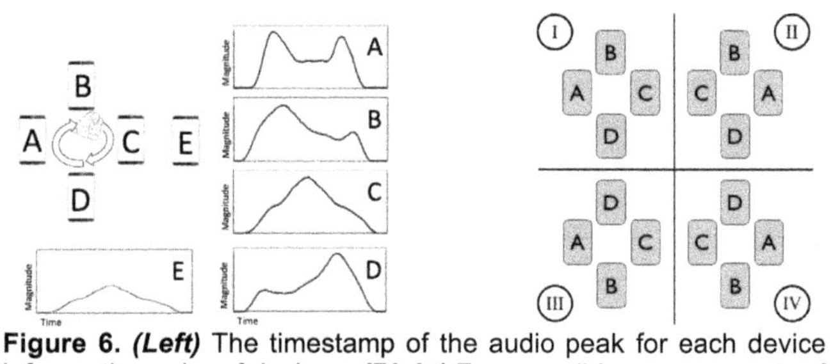


**Figure 6.** ***(Left)*** The timestamp of the audio peak for each device informs the order of devices. ***(Right)*** Four possible arrangements of devices.

### Detecting Device Arrangement

SurfaceLink also infers device arrangement that can be used to enable placement-aware interactions. It leverages the knowledge of the shape of the gesture to infer the arrangement of devices. For example, in Figure 6, *Left*, the circular gesture began and ended at Device A. As a result, different devices on the table observed a peak in the vibrations at different times and the non-participating device E, as expected, observed significantly lower vibrations. From these signals, the ordering and placement of the devices can therefore be inferred. To do so, the system places the objects on the edge of the drawn shape (*e.g.*, a circle as shown in Figure 6, *Left*). To determine the distances between the devices, the system uses the time intervals between the peaks in the audio received by each device. For example, if B receives a peak closer in time to A than C, then the system infers that B is physically closer to A on the edge of the circle. Also, if device E observes an attenuated version of the peak observed by C, but with the peak at the same time, then the system infers that C and E are at the same angle on the circle, but at different radii (*i.e.*, E is farther from the gesture).

This inference system has one limitation: the system would come back with the order of devices as A-B-C-D. The actual arrangement can be any of the four possible mirror images (Figure 6, *Right*). In order to reduce the ambiguity, SurfaceLink limits the user to perform clockwise gestures when devices are in a 2-dimensional arrangement. By adding this constraint, the system can eliminate arrangements shown in Figure 6, *Right* (III) and (IV). In order to reduce the remaining ambiguity, SurfaceLink employs an acoustic stereo positioning technique to calculate the right/left orientation of one device with respect to another. For example in Figure 6, *Left*, if Device A infers that Device C is to its right, then the only possible arrangement will be Figure 6 *Right* (I). In cases where devices are arranged in a single line (1-dimensional arrangement), there are only two mirror images. This ambiguity can be easily resolved by stereo positioning, hence there is no limitation on the user for gesture direction.

In order to determine whether a device is on the left or right side of another device, it emits two ultrasonic tones of different frequencies from both left and right speakers. Ultrasonic tones have been used for data transfer [1] and proximity detection [31] as well; however, these have never been used for relative arrangement detection. We use an 18 kHz sine wave for the left speaker and 18.5 kHz for the right speaker. If the client device is on the right side, then the observed amplitude of the 18.5 kHz tone will be higher than that of the 18 kHz tone. The frequency response for most commodity speakers is not linear at such high frequencies, hence there might be a constant offset between the magnitudes of the two frequencies. Such an offset can be easily accounted for by calibrating using the microphone of the emitting device.

In the ideal case, the amplitude of the two tones can be compared instantaneously, but we observed that the difference in amplitude could vary over time. This leads to some noisy results, hence SurfaceLink tracks the amplitude difference for 3 seconds and passes it through a low pass filter before deciding on the orientation. After this decision, the system does not re-compute the orientation until the user moves the devices.

Such placement-aware systems have been studied earlier as well. Hinckley *et al.* [13] demonstrated the utility of such a system using touchscreens and the slope of a user's swipe while connecting devices. This knowledge of relative placement of devices can be used to facilitate more natural touch-screen interactions between devices. For example, if a user swipes from left to right on the touchscreen of device A, the system detects whether device B is on right or left. If B is on left, then it means that the gesture went from B to A and so on.

## EVALUATION & RESULTS

The performance of SurfaceLink was evaluated in a controlled user study. Ten participants (6 males, 4 females) ranging in age from 21 to 32 ($\mu$=26.9, $\sigma$=3.6) were recruited. All participants had more than 10 years of experience with computers and self-rated as intermediate to expert computer and smartphone users. The evaluation was performed using a custom developed application deployed on 4 Samsung Galaxy Nexus smartphones.

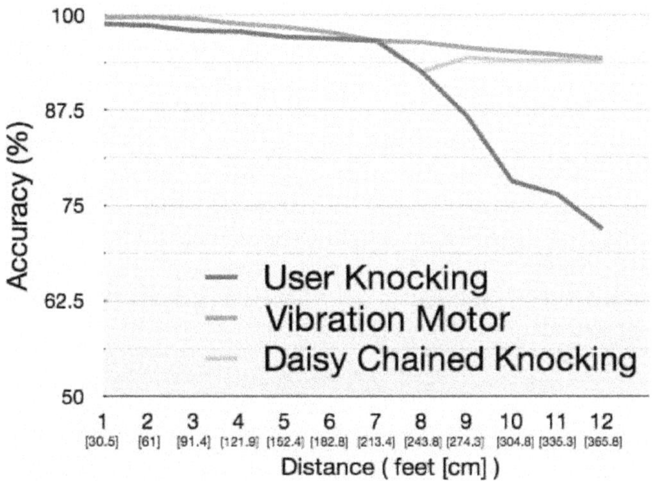


**Figure 7.** Performance of detecting devices on the same surface. User knocking performance drops significantly over larger distances, but this can be nullified using daisy chaining.

### Detecting Devices on the Same Surface

The device detection system can operate using user-induced or device-induced vibrations. In the evaluation, the order in which these two vibration sources were used was randomized. The experiments were performed on three different surfaces: wood, laminate, and metal. When using user-induced vibrations, the participants were asked to put the phone onto one of the three tables and then they were instructed to knock on the table when the application prompted them. Each table had a host device on it to detect co-presence. When using device-induced vibrations, the devices were simply placed on the table and did not require any user intervention. All the data was recorded in the application. In post processing, we checked if the system was able to classify the user's phone into respective clusters for each of the three tables.

Figure 7 shows the performance of SurfaceLink over varying distances between the client and host device. The accuracy of the system expectedly decreases as the inter-device distance increases. When using user-induced vibrations, the accuracy drops significantly around 8 feet, whereas in the device-induced vibration case, the accuracy remains above 94% even at distances more than 12 feet. In order to alleviate the accuracy drop after 8 feet while using user-induced vibrations, we used vibration daisy chaining as described previously. Daisy chaining improves accuracy from 71.9% to 93.9% at 12 feet. Overall, SurfaceLink detects devices on the same surface with 97.7% when the devices are up to 8 feet apart. The performance difference was not significant for any of the materials as the magnitude of vibrations was high in all cases.

### Detecting Surface Gestures

The data collection application for gesture classification recorded the vibrations observed by the contact microphone. We did not formally evaluate the performance with the on-device microphone because the noise cancellation capabilities of modern mobile devices are part of the hardware firmware and are not accessible to the developer. Four phones were placed on a surface in an arbitrary square with approximately 0.5 m between them.

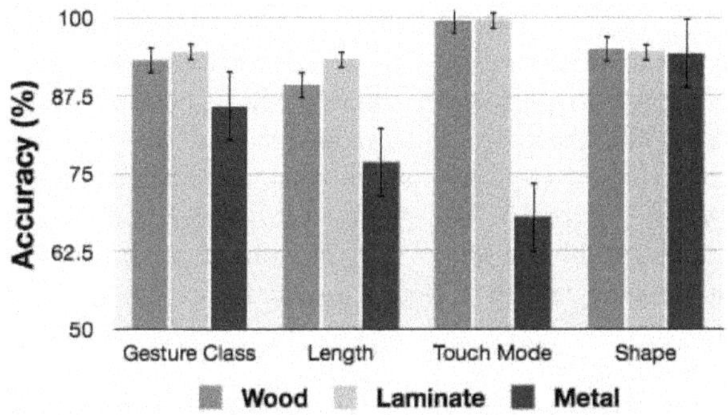


**Figure 8.** Performance of gestures on different devices (5-fold cross validation). Wood and laminate performed the best. Errorbars are standard errors.

All possible combinations of the gestures were not evaluated because it would have led to 180 different input gestures and impractically long evaluation sessions. We tested all combinations of *Gesture Shape* and *Touch Modes*. In case of *Gesture Class* and *Gesture Length,* the gestures were only performed with the fingertip. Thereby creating a vocabulary of 5*3+6+3=24 different gestures. Each gesture was repeated 10 times, and the order was randomized. Again, in order to evaluate the performance of SurfaceLink on a variety of surfaces, the data was collected on three different surfaces: wood, laminate, and metal.

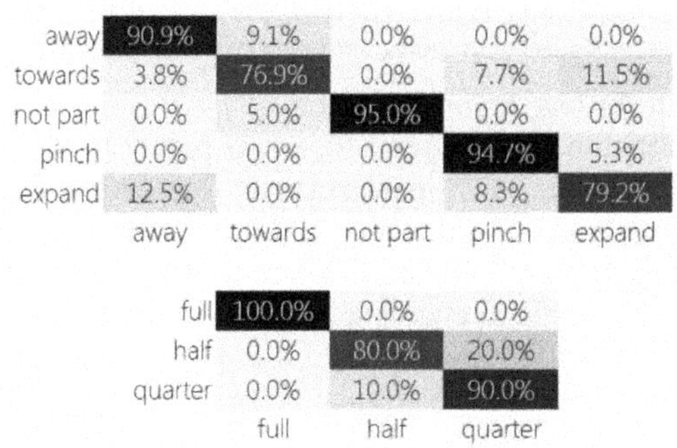


**Figure 9.** Confusion matrices for different (*Top*) Gesture Class and (*Bottom)* Gesture Length. (Note: Non-participating devices are abbreviated as *not-part*)

Figure 8 shows the performance of SurfaceLink in classifying different surface gestures using a 5-fold cross validation. The performances of wood and laminate were similar to each other (94.2% and 94.9%, respectively) and were both better than metal (81.2%). This is expected as the metal surface is not a textured surface and was used to only to test the lower bounds of SurfaceLink's performance. The mean accuracy across gesture class, length, touch mode, and shape detection was 90.3%.

The confusion matrices for *Gesture Class* and *Gesture Length* are shown in the Figure 9. It can be seen that there is no pair of gesture classes that often confused. The disambiguation of participating and non-participating devices is also very robust.

In the evaluation, each user was asked to perform each gesture 10 times, and then we used a 5-fold cross-validation in order to obtain results. In a real world setting the user would need to perform a training phase before using the system. We therefore did an analysis to see how much training data is needed to obtain reasonable performance, as shown in Figure 10. The *x*-axis shows the percentage split in training and test data. Larger values on *x*-axis signify more training data. It is clear from the figure that in the case of *Gesture Class*, *Touch Mode*, and *Shape*, SurfaceLink does not require much training data, as just a few examples would suffice. The accuracy is lowest for *Gesture Length,* but even then only 5 examples are needed to increase the accuracy to 85%.

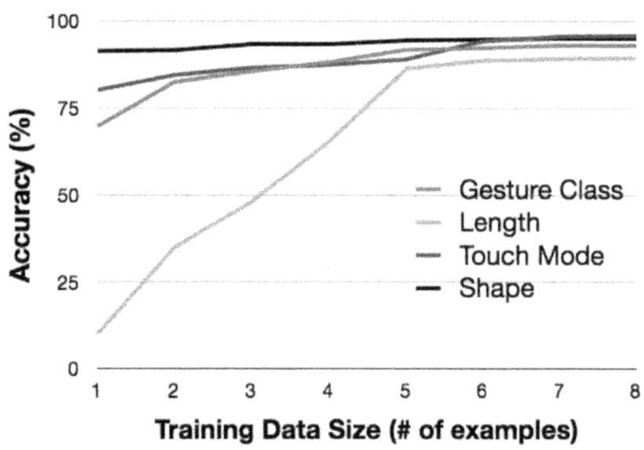


**Figure 10.** Improvement in average accuracy of gesture detection on the three surfaces with increasing size of training data.

### Detecting Device Arrangement

This evaluation was divided into two parts. The first part was to evaluate the performance of acoustic stereo positioning. A mobile device was kept at different relative locations to the host device (Motorola Xoom). The aim of this evaluation was to check the bounds of distance between the two devices where SurfaceLink is able to determine effectively determine the arrangement.

Figure 11 shows the performance of acoustic stereo positioning. The average accuracy over inter-device distances between 4 and 36 inches is 89.4%. The accuracy drops to approximately 66% when the devices are 36 inches apart. This is because the distance between the two speakers on the host device of less than 12 inches. As the inter-device distance increases, the difference in the observed tone amplitude will become negligible.

The acoustic stereo positioning detects which devices are to the left and right of each other. But in order to get the accurate arrangement of all the devices on a surface, a combination of stereo positioning and user gesture is required. The participants were asked to draw a gesture between all the devices on the table with their fist. They were presented with 10 unique device arrangements including devices in a straight line, square, triangle, *etc.* The inter-device distance was limited between 4 to 24 inches as larger distances meant devices were too far away for a single user. The participants were not informed which gesture shape to perform. They selected the gesture shape on their own from a set of triangle, square, circle, line, and arc. They were informed to select the shape keeping in mind that their gesture should try to go near all the devices. For example, when the devices were kept in a triangle arrangement, a circular or triangular gesture would be appropriate.

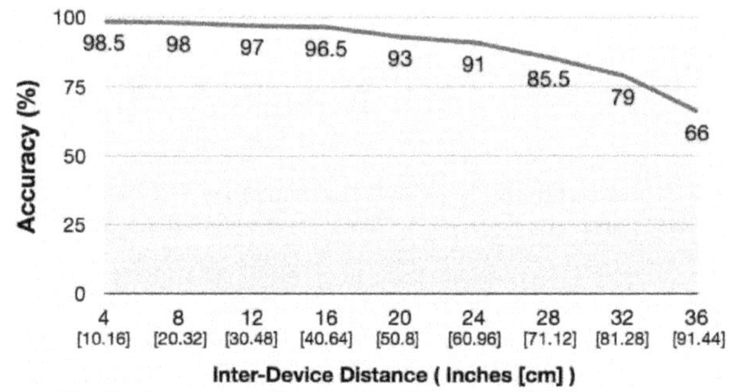


**Figure 11.** Performance of acoustic stereo positioning.

The system tried to determine the order and whether the devices were in a linear, circular, triangular, or square arrangement. The system accurately detected the device arrangement 88% of the times.

### Qualitative System Evaluation

We developed a multi-device photo-sharing application (Figure 1) in order to qualitatively evaluate the performance of interaction techniques introduced by SurfaceLink. In this application, the system first detects the devices that are present on the same surface. Then it allows the users to interact with devices through surface gestures.

The performance of this system is compared with Bump[1] and Cooperative-Stitching [14]. The purpose of this evaluation was to test how SurfaceLink performs with increasing number of users and devices. We recruited 10 users to evaluate a system in which they transferred pictures between four devices using all the three techniques (*i.e.*, Cooperative-Stitching, Bump, SurfaceLink). The participants were given a randomly generated list of 15 photo transfer tasks. An example of a task will be "Transfer

[1] Bump: http://www.bu.mp

photo from A to B". In 5 of the 15 tasks for each participant, there were multiple receiving devices. For example, "Transfer photo from A to B and C". These tasks were added to mimic a scenario where users might want to share files with multiple devices. In Cooperative-Stitching the users collaboratively drew a line with their finger from sending device to receiving device. For SurfaceLink the users used the swipe gesture to share photos between devices and drew circles with fist to create a subgroup of devices (in the case of multiple receiving devices).

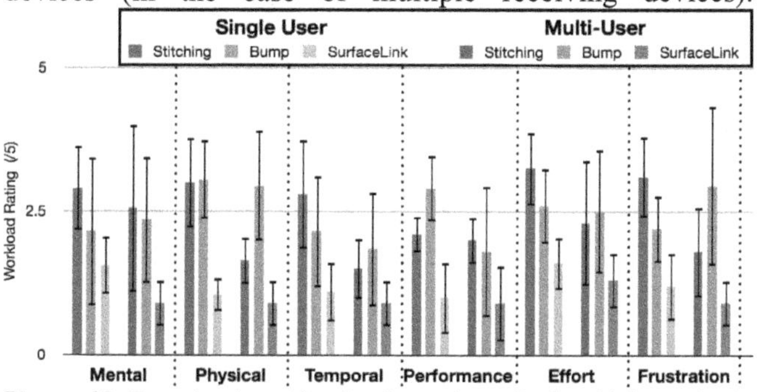


**Figure 12.** Perceived workload ratings show SurfaceLink results in significantly lower workload in the single-user scenario. Lower ratings are better.

Two experiments were conducted to test the three techniques in single- and multi-user environments. In the first experiment, a single user interacted with 4 devices. In the second experiment, a set of four users controlled one device each. We overlapped our users and each user was part of 2 separate sets. Therefore we had 5 sets of four users, each.

The participants were taught the functionality of each app and were given time to get familiarized with the interface. Once they were comfortable they were presented with the three techniques in a random order. After completion of tasks with each technique, we asked participants to make Likert-scale ratings (Figure 12) based on NASA TLX perceived workload index [12]. We also recorded the time taken by each participant to complete the tasks with each technique.

A repeated measures ANOVA revealed that, regardless of number of devices per user, participants spent significantly less time in completing the tasks while using SurfaceLink as compared to the other two techniques ($F_{2,18}$=10.94, $p$ < .05). A Friedman test showed that in the single user scenario, SurfaceLink resulted in significantly less workload in all dimensions as compared to Bump and Cooperative-Stitching. In the case of multiple users, SurfaceLink resulted in significantly less mental, temporal, and physical workload, and frustration. All Wilcoxon pairwise comparisons were protected against Type I error using a Bonferroni adjustment.

When asked which of the techniques they preferred, and all participants preferred using SurfaceLink over the other two techniques. P4 said, "The surface gestures feel very natural." P2 said, "The fact that I do not need to interact with all of the devices' touchscreens to share files can be very useful." However, 6 out of 10 participants preferred Bump or Cooperative-Stitching over SurfaceLink if they just had to send one single batch of files to a single paired device.

## DISCUSSION AND LIMITATIONS

Our results show that SurfaceLink performs better than Bump and Cooperative-Stitching when there is more than one device per user. There is no established baseline for the interaction techniques for multiple devices. We selected Bump and Cooperative-Stitching because they are very lightweight and do not require any hardware adjustment to the devices. Moreover they are good representatives of "co-occurrence" based multi-device systems. We do not aim to hypothesize that SurfaceLink is better than *all* the multi-device interaction approaches. We solely wanted to test how SurfaceLink performs with increasing number of users and devices in comparison to some of the proven techniques. The fact that all the participants preferred SurfaceLink suggests that it is an attractive interaction system as the number of devices as well as our interaction with these devices increases.

We deployed the system on a work desk for a week with almost no false positives (4 in whole week). SurfaceLink is able to use the duration of gesture to easily remove false positives. Additionally, considering it is aware of device arrangement and also classifies devices into "non-participating devices" category, accidental touches are almost always classified as "non-participating devices" for all devices.

Extended use of the microphones and accelerometer can have significant power implications. The devices do not need to be in permanent listening mode. The devices can do opportunistic sensing and would only listen when they infer they are on a flat surface [7].

Surface gestures are also useful in "around-the-device" interactions. Such interactions are becoming very popular. SideSight [3] is one example of such a system. The rich set of gestures introduced by SurfaceLink is demonstrated to be useful in a multi-device interaction scenario. But these gestures can be very useful for a single device interaction as well, and aid in "around-the-device" interaction. This paper uses the photo sharing as an example scenario but the demonstrated gesture language can be used for a variety of purposes in both single- and multi-device environments.

## CONCLUSION

It is common to have multiple computing devices in the same environment. It is also becoming increasingly common for a single user to have multiple devices. Current multi-device interaction technologies do not scale well to increasing numbers of devices per user. In this paper, we presented *SurfaceLink*, a system that uses the shared surface between devices as a bounded communication medium. It provides an end-to-end solution for impromptu, scalable interaction between devices using on-device accelerometer, vibration motor, speakers as well as an off-device contact microphone. SurfaceLink detects devices on the same surface (*Acc.*=97.7%), enables a variety of continuous multi-touch gestures (*Acc.*=90.3%), and infers relative device arrangement (*Acc.*=89.4%). Our evaluation also demonstrates that SurfaceLink scales well to increasing numbers of devices and users and can be an attractive interaction system as the number of devices or our interaction with these devices increases.

**ACKNOWLEDGEMENTS**
We thank Lilian de Greef for her help in prototyping.

**REFERENCES**

1. Arentz, W.A. and Bandara, U. Near ultrasonic directional data transfer for modern smartphones. *Proc. UbiComp'11*.
2. Balfanz, D., Smetters, D.K., Stewart, P., and Wong, H.C. Talking To Strangers : Authentication in Ad-Hoc Wireless Networks.
3. Butler, A., Izadi, S., and Hodges, S. SideSight : Multi-"touch" interaction around small devices. *Proc. UIST'08*.
4. Crevoisier, A. and Polotti, P. Tangible acoustic Interfaces and their applications for the design of new musical instruments. *Proc. Nime'05*.
5. Cuypers, T., Francken, Y., Vanaken, C., Reeth, F.V., and Bekaert, P. Smartphone localization on interactive surfaces using the built-in camera. *Proc. Procams'09*.
6. Dearman, D., Guy, R.T., and Truong, K.N. Determining the orientation of proximate mobile devices using their back facing camera. *Proc. CHI'12*.
7. Goel, M., Wobbrock, J.O., and Patel, S.N. GripSense: Using built-in sensors to detect hand posture and pressure on commodity mobile phones. *Proc. UIST'12*.
8. Harrison, C. and Hudson, S.E. Scratch Input : Creating Large, Inexpensive, Unpowered and Mobile Finger Input Surfaces. *Proc. UIST'08*.
9. Harrison, C. and Hudson, S.E. Lightweight Material Detection for Placement-Aware Mobile Computing. *Proc. UIST'08*.
10. Harrison, C., Schwarz, J., and Hudson, S.E. TapSense : Enhancing finger interaction on touch surfaces. *Proc. UIST'11*.
11. Harrison, C., Xiao, R., and Hudson, S.E. Acoustic Barcodes : Passive , Durable and Inexpensive Notched Identification Tags. *Proc. UIST'12*.
12. Hart, S.G. Nasa-Task Load Index (NASA-TLX); 20 Years Later. *Proceedings of the Human Factors and Ergonomics Society Annual Meeting 50*, 9 (2006).
13. Hinckley, K., Ramos, G., Guimbretiere, F., Baudisch, P., and Smith, M. Stitching : Pen Gestures that Span Multiple Displays. *Proc. AVI'04*.
14. Hinckley, K. and Ramos, G. Cooperative Stitching : Spontaneous Wireless Connections for Small Co-Located Groups (TECHNOTE).
15. Holmquist, L.E., Mattern, F., Schiele, B., Alahuhta, P., Beigl, M., and Gellersen, H.-w. Smart-Its Friends : A Technique for Users to Easily Establish Connections between Smart Artefacts. *Proc. UbiComp'01*.
16. Hutama, W., Song, P., Fu, C.-W., and Goh, W.B. Distinguishing multiple smart-phone interactions on a multi-touch wall display using tilt correlation. *Proc. CHI'11*.
17. Kane, S.K., Avrahami, D., Wobbrock, J.O., et al. Bonfire : A Nomadic System for Hybrid Laptop-Tabletop Interaction. *Proc. UIST'09*.
18. Kortuem, G., Kray, C., and Gellersen, H. Sensing and visualizing spatial relations of mobile devices. *Proc. UIST'05*.
19. Kunze, K. and Lukowicz, P. Symbolic Object Localization Through Active Sampling of Acceleration and Sound Signatures. *Proc. UbiComp'07*.
20. Lopes, P., Jota, R., and Jorge, J.A. Augmenting touch interaction through acoustic sensing. *Proc. ITS'11*.
21. Lucero, A., Holopainen, J., and Jokela, T. Pass-Them-Around : Collaborative Use of Mobile Phones for Photo Sharing. *Proc. CHI'11*.
22. Lucero, A., Jokela, T., Palin, A., Aaltonen, V., and Nikara, J. EasyGroups : Binding Mobile Devices for Collaborative Interactions. *Proc. CHI'12 (WIP)*.
23. Matsushita, N. and Rekimoto, J. HoloWall: Designing a Finger; Hand, Body, and Object Sensitive Wall. *Proc. UIST'97*.
24. Mayrhofer, R. and Gellersen, H. Shake Well Before Use : Authentication Based on Accelerometer Data. *Proc. Pervasive'07*.
25. Murray-Smith, R., Williamson, J., Hughes, S., and Quaade, T. Stane : Synthesized Surfaces for Tactile Input. *Proc. CHI'08*.
26. Paradiso, J.A., Leo, C.K., Checka, N., and Hsiao, K. Passive acoustic sensing for tracking knocks atop large interactive displays. *Proc. IEEE Sensors 2002*.
27. Ramos, G., Hinckley, K., Wilson, A., and Sarin, R. Synchronous Gestures in Multi-Display Environments. *Human-Computer Interaction, Special Issue: Ubiquitous Multi-Display Environments 24*, 1-2 (2009).
28. Rekimoto, J. and Saitoh, M. Augmented Surfaces : A Spatially Continuous Work Space for Hybrid Computing Environments. *Proc. CHI'99*.
29. Schmidt, D., Chehimi, F., Rukzio, E., and Gellersen, H. PhoneTouch : A Technique for Direct Phone Interaction on Surfaces. *Proc. UIST'10*.
30. Seniuk, A. and Blostein, D. Pen Acoustic Emissions for Text and Gesture Recognition. *10th Int'l Conference on Document Analysis and Recognition* (2009).
31. Thiel, B., Kloch, K., and Lukowicz, P. Sound-based proximity detection with mobile phones. *Proc. PhoneSense'12*.
32. Wilson, A.D. and Sarin, R. BlueTable : Connecting Wireless Mobile Devices on Interactive Surfaces Using Vision-Based Handshaking. *Proc. GI'07*.

# Comparing Flat and Spherical Displays in a Trust Scenario in Avatar-Mediated Interaction

**Ye Pan, William Steptoe, Anthony Steed**
Department of Computer Science, University College London, UK
y.pan, w.steptoe, a.steed@cs.ucl.ac.uk

## ABSTRACT
We report on two experiments that investigate the influence of display type and viewing angle on how people place their trust during avatar-mediated interaction. By monitoring advice seeking behavior, our first experiment demonstrates that if participants observe an avatar at an oblique viewing angle on a flat display, they are less able to discriminate between expert and non-expert advice than if they observe the avatar face-on. We then introduce a novel spherical display and a ray-traced rendering technique that can display an avatar that can be seen correctly from any viewing direction. We expect that a spherical display has advantages over a flat display because it better supports non-verbal cues, particularly gaze direction, since it presents a clear and undistorted viewing aspect at all angles. Our second experiment compares the spherical display to a flat display. Whilst participants can discriminate expert advice regardless of display, a negative bias towards the flat screen emerges at oblique viewing angles. This result emphasizes the ability of the spherical display to be viewed qualitatively similarly from all angles. Together the experiments demonstrate how trust can be altered depending on how one views the avatar.

### Author Keywords
Spherical displays; trust; telecommunication; avatars; mixed reality

### ACM Classification Keywords
H.4.3 Communications Applications: Computer conferencing, teleconferencing, and videoconferencing; H.5.1 Information Interfaces and Presentation: Multimedia Information Systems—*Artificial, augmented, and virtual realities*

### General Terms
Design, Experimentation, Human Factors.

## INTRODUCTION
In many conversations, such as advice giving or financial transactions, trust is required in order for people to work together effectively [5]. Developing trust relies on a number of nonverbal cues, of which eye contact seems to stand out [1, 19]. However, traditional video conferencing systems rely on a camera displaced relative to the image of the remote participant, which leads to an immediate misalignment and loss of eye contact [6]. Thus, it is difficult for video conferencing systems to preserve correct gaze direction to enable natural lines of sight operating within Chen's offset threshold [8]. It is even more difficult to allow distant parties to take various seating positions while reproducing correct gaze direction during conversation [35]. A variety of video conferencing systems have been developed to support gaze awareness and improve the level of trust for participants observing form multiple viewpoints (see e.g. [18, 20, 28, 32]). However, those systems usually use flat displays which are visible from only the front.

In this work, we captured a remote person's interpersonal cues and represented them as an animated avatar head on a spherical display. We developed a novel view dependent rendering method for a non-planar display. We integrated with Faceshift® enabling a remote person to drive facial expressions of the avatar in real time. We used a spherical display, as it is technically quite simple to build and can be constructed very cheaply in comparison to volumetric displays [13], robotics [10] and animatronic shader lamp avatars [16]. This display is small enough to situate almost anywhere in a room, and it is visible from all directions.

Many researchers have investigated how to maintain or increase levels of trust [19]. However, it is also crucial to ensure that users are able to place trust correctly, avoiding overestimation of the trustworthiness of others [26]. As reviewed in the next section, we have followed the previous work [26] that has conceptualised trust in terms of individuals' choice behaviour in a user-adviser relationship. We investigate two predictions regarding the effect of display type and viewing angle on trust: the spherical display may result in positive bias (i.e. more trust) because it increases social presence; or it may result in better discrimination between trustworthy and less trustworthy actors as it conveys more information. In our two experiments, participants were required to attempt to answer thirty difficult general-knowledge questions over three different viewing angles. For each question, participants could ask for advice from one of two advisers. Unknown to the participants, one was an *expert* who responded with mainly correct information, and the other was a *non-expert* who provided mainly incorrect information. We measured participants' advice seeking behavior as an indicator of their trust in the ad-


*CHI'14*, April 26–May 1, 2014, Toronto, Canada.

http://dx.doi.org/10.1145/2556288.2557276

viser. The first experiment explores how interpersonal cues of expertise presented on two identical flat displays with different viewing angle affect trust. Results demonstrate that participants were able to discriminate correct advice, but their sensitivity to correct advice decreased at off-center viewing angles. The second experiment compares two display types by investigating how people place their trust. Balanced over participants, the expert appeared either on the sphere or on the flat display. We found most participants preferred seeking advice from the expert, but we also found a tendency for seeking advice from the adviser on the spherical display instead of flat display, in particular when viewed from off-center directions.

In the following sections, we review related work and present the implementation of our spherical display teleconferencing system. This is followed by the evaluation design and two experiments. Finally, we present discussions of the results, conclusions and future work.

## RELATED WORKS

### Trust in teleconferencing

Trust can be defined as a 'willingness to be vulnerable, based on positive expectations about the actions of others' [17]. It plays an important role in interpersonal communication, sometimes even as an enabler for effective communication.

Previous research indicates that it is hard to build trust in teleconferencing, because non-verbal cues were unavailable to be 'read' [31]. To determine the effect of eye contact in video-mediated communication on trust, Bekkering and Shim [4] created a scenario in which participants indicated the trustworthiness of a message delivered by people. Results revealed that videos that did not support eye contact resulted in lower perceived trust scores, compared to videos that enabled eye contact. Voice-mail enabled just as much trust as the video that created eye contact, perhaps because lack of eye contact cannot be perceived in audio-only communication. Nguyen and Canny [19] proposed a multiView video-conferencing system and demonstrated that a video-conferencing system that affords more eye contact than the traditional video-conferencing system will create group trust levels similar to those seen in face-to-face group meetings.

As a measure of trust, a popular experimental paradigm currently employed by researchers has been social dilemma games based on the Prisoner's Dilemma, such as the Day-trader game [9]. Social dilemma games vary in how difficult they are depending on the exact rules and payoff structure, but it generally takes some amount of time and some communication in order to reach the required level of trust [7, 19, 24]. Those games are good models for synchronous and symmetric trust situations, such us two-way conversations. However, in some everyday trust situations, we can identify a trustor who decides first and a trustee who then decides to fulfil or defect, such as one-way conversation. Trust games are suitable models of such situations [25]. Many researchers have investigated the relationship between trust and advice seeking behavior [3, 30]. Riegelsberger et al. [26] investigated user's trust in advisers and effects of media bias in different representations by observing participants' advice seeking behavior. In their scenario, participants were asked to participate in a quiz and financial incentives were given for good performance. The questions included in the quiz were extremely difficult, so that good performance required seeking advice. Participants had two advisers but could only ask one for each question. Thus asking one adviser rather than the other can be understood as an indicator of trusting behavior. They found users' preference for receiving video advice led them to disregard better text-only advice.

Most of this previous work is focused on 2D planar displays. Trust formation on non-planar displays has not been evaluated yet. In pursuing this question, we adapt previous studies of trust to evaluate the advantage of a sphere display over a flat display.

### Situated displays

The 360° visibility of situated displays are interesting for teleconferencing, as observers are potentially able to understand the content from any perspective. Many situated displays have achieved accurate reproduction of nonverbal cues, including gaze and deictic gestures.

Animatronic Shader Lamps Avatars (SLA) [16] use the technique where an image is projected onto a screen whose shape physically matches the image itself. It uses cameras and projectors to capture and map the dynamic motion and appearance of a real person onto a humanoid animatronic model. It successfully delivers a dynamic, real-time representation of the user to multiple viewers. The SLA's use of front projection to texture the 3D facial geometry makes it less practical than one with internal (rear) projection, as commented by the authors. A spherical display offers flexibility compared to humanoid robotics as it isn't constrained to a single head size or shape. The SphereAvatar [21] system demonstrated a view dependent way of rendering a remote person's head as an avatar. By tracking the viewer's position, the display allows the viewer to detect the avatar's head gaze direction from any viewpoint. Similarly, a previous work used an array of cameras to capture a remote user, and then display video of that person on a spherical display, allowing observers to accurately judge where the remote user was placing their gaze [22]. TeleHuman [15] was a cylindrical 3D display portal for life-size human telepresence. It supported 360° motion parallax as the viewer moves around the cylinder and optionally, stereoscopic 3D display of the remote person. The system successfully preserved gaze and hand pointing cues. It also conveyed 3D body postural information.

Whilst the 360° and gaze preserving capabilities of these situated displays have been demonstrated by these previous works, it is not clear whether there is an effect on the observer's trust formation from different viewing directions. Our study looks at the effects of spherical display on trust formation at three different viewing angles.

### Teleconferencing, avatar-mediated communication

Video conferencing is able to represent participants' appearance across a distance. However, even minor physical movement of a user may introduce parallax between camera position and video display resulting in loss of gaze awareness.

The 2D nature of standard video constrains the rich spatial cues common to collocated interaction such as depth, resolution, and field of view [29]. In the regard to spatiality, videoconferecing has proven to be more similar to audio conferencing than to unmediated interaction [34].

Recently, avatar-mediated communication, where a remote person is represented by a graphical humanoid, has increased in prevalence and popularity as an emerging form of visual remote interaction [12]. The avatar represents the presence and activities of a remote user and can be visualized using standard displays or projection surfaces in the local room with perspective-correct graphical rendering via head tracking of the local user [27]. Avatars are capable of eliciting appropriate responses from observers (see e.g. [2], [29]). Faceshift® demonstrated a high-fidelity and real-time parametric reconstruction of facial expression method using a single depth camera [33]. We have decided to represent a remote user as an avatar instead of video in our experiment, as 3D models are simple to render from any viewing angles.

## SYSTEM DESIGN

In the *remote room*, the facial expression of the remote person, the *actor*, is captured. In the *local room*, a single PC renders an animated avatar on a spherical display which is seen by an observer. Figure 1 depicts the system design. We integrated with Faceshift® to allow an actor to control the facial expressions of the avatar. We developed a view dependent graphical representation to fully support rendering spherical display surfaces.

### Real time facial expression tracking with Faceshift

In the remote room, the actor is recorded in a natural environment using a non-intrusive, commercially available Microsoft Kinect™. The actor was seated at the same height of the sensor, about 600 mm horizontal distance from the sensor (see Figure 1). The Microsoft Kinect™ captures a 640×480 2D color image and a 3D depth map at 30 Hertz, based on invisible infrared projection. It provides a simple and low cost way for acquisition, without the use of face markers, intrusive lighting, or complex scanning hardware.

We used Faceshift® with Microsoft Kinect to obtain our actor's facial performances in realtime. Faceshift ensures robust processing given the low resolution and high noise levels of the input data. The output of the tracking optimization is a continuous stream of blendshape weight vectors that drive the avatar. With the embedded plug-in of Faceshift in Maya®, we obtain 46 blendshapes of the Rocketbox® avatar. Then, we export them as .obj format to be used in the ray tracing stage discussed below. Finally, we represent facial expressions as a weighted sum of blendshape meshes, enabling actor to control the facial expressions of the avatar.

### View dependent rendering for spherical display

In the local room, the spherical display was the commercially available Magic Planet display by Global Imagination®. The Magic Planet is a projection display device with a 16" sphere-shaped surface, a standard 1024×768 projector at 60Hz, and an internal fisheye lens to project imagery on to the inside of the sphere.

We developed a view dependent rendering method to create 3D object presenting onto spherical image surface, map from the spherical image surface into 2D image plane, and re-project onto spherical display, as if the object is situated inside the sphere display (See Figure 2). The use of a ray tracing engine should provide higher quality images with less distortion than the polygonal rendering approach that was developed for SphereAvatar [21].

We used the NVIDIA® OptiX ray tracing engine [23], to trace the path of light from observer's eye to the 3D object though pixels in the spherical image surface.

To implement the ray tracer, we translate the 3D spherical surface into 2D image plane, to represent the surface of the sphere on a flat paper map or on a computer screen. The position of each point ($Q$) on the 2D image plane (see Figure 2(c)) can be defined by a radius ($r,\ 0 \le r \le 1$) and a longitude angle ($\alpha,\ 0 \le \alpha \le 2\pi$). The corresponding position of that point ($P$) on the spherical surface (see Figure 2(a)) can be defined by a latitude angle ($\theta,\ 0 \le \theta \le \pi$) and longitude angle ($\phi,\ 0 \le \phi \le 2\pi$). The 2D image projector and the display surface are axially symmetric about the optical axis. Thus, the polar angle ($\alpha$) in 2D image plane is the same as the longitude angle ($\phi$) in the 3D spherical surface, shown the Equation 1. All the points at a given radius ($r$) in the 2D image plane are projected onto the sphere display surface at the same latitude angle ($\theta$). Because of lens distortion, there is a nonlinear relationship between latitude angle ($\theta$) of sphere display surface and the radius ($r$) of the 2D image plane. We sampled latitude angle ($\theta$) at every 15° to find out the corresponding radius ($r$) value, shown in Figure 2(b). We use the Matlab® second order polyfit to simulate a continuous function as a model to characterizing the relationship between the latitude angle ($\theta$) and the radius ($r$), presented in Equation 2. Therefore, if we want to project a certain image onto sphere display surface, the corresponding source image can be determined by applying the inverse function to that image.

$$\alpha = \phi \tag{1}$$

$$r = -0.0806 \times \theta^2 - 0.0704 \times \theta + 1.0022 \tag{2}$$

Finally, the 2D image plane that produced above would be projected through the fisheye lens of the sphere display. We could then see a corrected image presented on the spherical surface. In Figure 2(c), the red circle of the 2D image plane corresponds to the equator of the sphere; the center of the 2D image plane projects to a single point on the top of the sphere; the very outer circle in the 2D image plane projects to a single point on the bottom of the sphere. The projected result on sphere display is presented in Figure 2(d).

We use this view dependent graphic representation method discussed above to ray trace an avatar's upper body and head. Figure 3(a) to Figure 3(g) present some sampled mapping results in 2D image plane generated at different viewer's positions while the avatar is looking at the front. Once projected

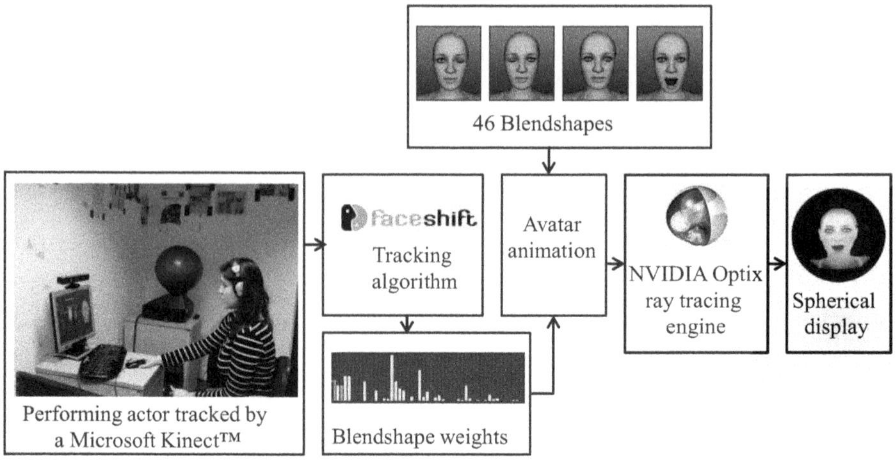


**Figure 1. Pipeline for representing an avatar with dynamic facial expressions controlled by an actor on the spherical display.**

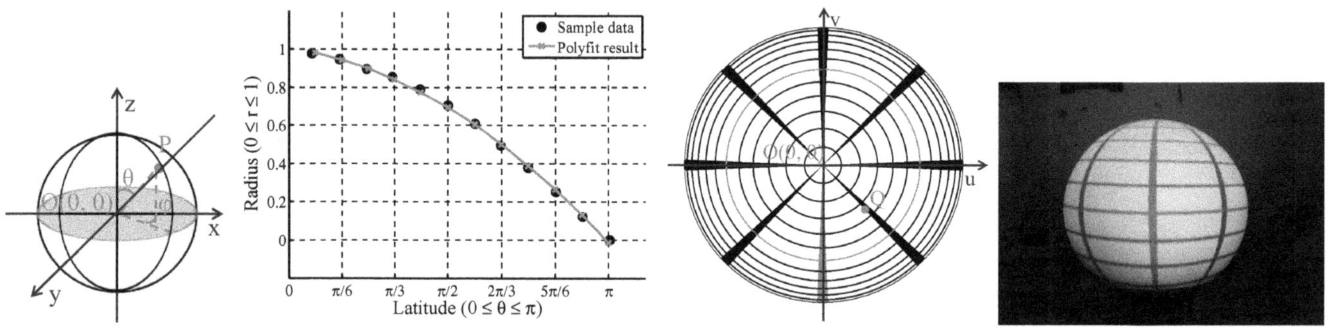


(a) 3D Sphere image surface (b) The relationship between latitude angle ($\theta$) and the radius ($r$) (c) 2D mapping image plane generated for projection (d) Photo taken in front of the sphere display

**Figure 2. The mapping relationship: each point P on the 3D spherical surface in the subfigure (a) translates into corresponding point Q on the 2D image plane in the subfigure (c), according to calibrated relationship in the subfigure (b). The subfigure (d) shows the projected result of the 2D image plane.**

(a) 0° (b) 15° (c) 30° (d) 45° (e) 60° (f) 75° (g) 90°

**Figure 3. 2D mapping image generated for projection at different viewer positions.**

(a) Neutral expression (b) Natural expression (c) Mouth open (d) Left eye close

**Figure 4. Photo taken at approximately 45° left side of sphere display. For both subfigure (a) and (b), the viewers' positions are the same as the photo taken position. The avatar head is looking at the viewer in the subfigure (a), but the avatar head is looking at the right of the viewer in the subfigure (b). For subfigure (c) and (d), each viewer's position is at right and left side of the photo taken position, respectively.**

through the fisheye lens of the display, such images would appear as correctly shaped head and upper body (see Figure 4). This method successfully avoids any seams, overlaps or registration errors in the resulting composite image in projected image on the sphere display. It is also could be extended to other display systems that have a three dimensional display surface.

## EVALUATION DESIGN: ADVICE SEEKING BEHAVIOR

Through two experiments, we investigated how display types affect trust. Our first experiment (E1) explored the effect of viewing angle on trust in traditional flat displays, and provided a benchmark by which to measure the spherical display. Our second experiment (E2) investigated the impact of the spherical display given that it could faithfully reproduce the actor's gaze at all viewing directions.

We modeled our experiments on a user-adviser relationship [26], a widely used research paradigm in social psychology. Participants were asked to answer thirty difficult general-knowledge questions and they received chocolates depending on their performance. We gave participants two advisers presented on two teleconferencing displays. Unknown to participants, the two advisers are with different levels of expertise. Additionally, the spatial arrangement of participant-to-displays was varied over the course of the experiment, thereby manipulating participants' viewing angle of the advisers. Advice was free, but only one adviser could be asked per question.

We measured participants' advice seeking behavior under risk as an indicator of trust in the adviser. People generally decide to trust others when facing situations involving risk and uncertainty [11, 17]. Uncertainty arises from the fact that the participants cannot directly observe the two advisers' ability (e.g. expertise) and motivation (e.g. desire to deceive). They need to infer those from interpersonal cues, as the questions were extremely difficult. When recording the non-expert clips, the actor exhibited less direct eye contact and less confident facial expression. When recording the expert clips, the actor exhibited confidence through more positive facial expression, such as smiles and eye contact. In our experiments, viewing angles and display types influence those interpersonal cues. Seeking advice from one adviser in preference over the other could be an indication of trust in that adviser, because receiving poor advice carried the risk of missing out better advice and therefore the participant was less likely to get the correct answer.

### Apparatus and materials

#### *Questions*

For E1 & E2, we used 30 questions and answers and a transcript of advice from previous research on trust in a human adviser [26]. Those questions are difficult general knowledge questions, to minimize effects of participants' prior knowledge. Examples of questions that were included are 'Which New York Building featured a mural depicting Lenin?' and 'Which one of these is a coastal city in North Korea?'. Based on the pre-test results, the mean probability for pre-testers giving a correct answer was .31 (SD = .11). This value was only marginally above chance (.25), indicating that very difficult questions that had been picked.

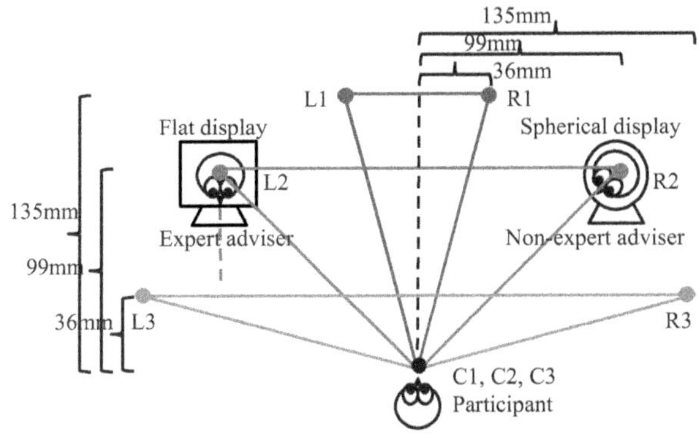


**Figure 5. Schematic layout of experiment setup. L1, R1 & C1; L2, R2 & C2 and L3, R3 & C3 are three participant-to-displays spatial arrangements. C1, C2 and C3 are participants' seating positions which are 75°, 45° and 15° relative to display, respectively. Also see Figure 6.**

#### *Expertise*

The non-expert and expert advisers were created by recording advice from the same individual before and after training, respectively. The same animations are used in both experiments. We used Faceshift to simultaneously record the actor's performance including voice and blendshape weight vectors that drive the avatar's facial expression. Then, we synchronously replayed both audio and facial expression on the display. The expert and non-expert advisers only differed in the ratio of correct to incorrect advice and in their cues to confidence about the answers. As each time the observer only had access to one of the advisers, they were unaware that both advisers were in fact the same individual recorded at different levels of expertise. For the non-expert adviser, the proportion of correct (i.e. confident) advice was 0.36. For the expert adviser, the proportion of correct (i.e. confident) advice was 0.80. Two incorrect (and less confident) pieces of advice from the untrained recording were added to the expert, in order to avoid artificial perfection.

Note that the system as designed and built is a realtime collaborative system that can connect a remote room to a local room. For the purposes of our controlled experiment we used pre-recorded clips.

#### *Display Type*

The participant observes the pre-recorded avatar video clips on two displays. We used two flat displays in E1, whereas one flat display and one sphere display in E2. For the flat display, a conventional PC screen was used with a resolution of 1024×768 pixels. For the sphere display, with perspective-correct ray traced imagery, the participant perceives the avatar to be situated inside the display and looking at him or her. We ensured the avatars' apparent sizes on sphere and flat display were the same (20 cm in height).

#### *Seat Position & viewing angle*

For both experiments, we arranged the two displays and participant's seat positions at vertices of three isosceles triangles with base angle of 75°, 45° and 15° for three different seat

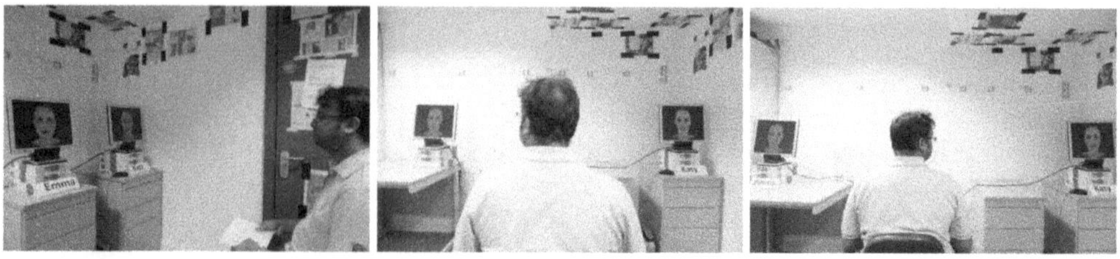

(a) E1: Photo taken at left side of participant seated at C1 (b) E1: Photo taken behind participant seated at C2 (c) E1: Photo taken slightly right behind participant seated at C3

(d) E2: Photo taken slightly right behind participant seated at C1 (e) E2: Photo taken behind participant seated at C2 (f) E2: Photo taken at right side of participant seated at C2 (g) E2: Photo taken at left side of participant seated at C2

**Figure 6. Pictures of E1 & E2 room taken from different perspective relative to the participant seated at different seat positions.**

| No. | Statement |
|---|---|
| 1 | Adviser was very friendly |
| 2 | I am please with adviser |
| 3 | I trusted adviser's advice |
| 4 | I enjoying playing with adviser |
| 5 | I would like to meet adviser face to face |
| 6 | Adviser gave good advice |
| 7 | Adviser was certain about the answer |
| 8 | I liked adviser |
| 9 | I relied mostly on adviser's advice |

**Table 1. Statements for post-experimental assessments of the adviser.**

positions (see Figure 5). The legs for all those three isosceles triangles, which is the distance between participant and display, were maintained the same at 140 cm. We ensured that the vertical alignment of the eye level of viewers and the eye level of the avatar of the actor on the two displays were the same.

#### *Incentives & risk*

For both experiments, the number of chocolates that participants received was linked to the number of correctly answered questions. The number of chocolates varied between one and six.

### Measurement Instruments

#### *Task Performance Measure*

The measure of advice seeking was defined as the proportion of one adviser being asked out of the total number of times advice was sought by a participant. As each participant had two advisers, but could only choose one of them for advice on each question, the following relationships hold: expert advice seeking = 1 − non-expert advice seeking, and one display advice seeking = 1 − the other display advice seeking.

#### *Post-Questionnaire*

Participants were presented with the post-experimental questionnaire with 9 statements (see Table 1) eliciting their subjective assessment of the two advisers, with 4 items measuring trustworthiness (Statement 3, 6, 7 & 9) and 5 items measuring enjoyment (Statement 1, 2, 4, 5 & 8). Agreement with the statements was elicited on 7-point Likert scales with the anchor 1 (Strongly disagree) - 7 (Strongly agree).

#### *Open question*

We asked each participant to write down his or her comments with a final open question: "For each round of games, please describe how you decided which adviser to rely on". The purpose of this open question was to help explain some observed events during the game and to guide future research.

## HYPOTHESES

*Hypothesis 1:* For E1 & E2, we expect participants to seek more advice from the expert adviser than the non-expert adviser. For E1, we expect that the more the seat position diverges from the central viewing position, the worse the observer will be able to discriminate between trustworthy and less trustworthy advisers. This is because the observer cannot look straight into the display and the slight visual spatial degradation will reduce observer's ability to discriminate [14]. However, by introducing the spherical display (E2), we expect that the observer's sensitivity to cues of trustworthiness to remain stable for all seat positions, as it conveys the same amount of information for all directions.

*Hypothesis 2:* For E2, we expect that the flat display will result in less trust compared to the sphere display. In other words, bias will occur when advice is preferred due to its display mode, irrespective of expertise. We further expect a negative bias towards the flat display representation will be found at off-center viewing angles, due to the loss of eye contact.

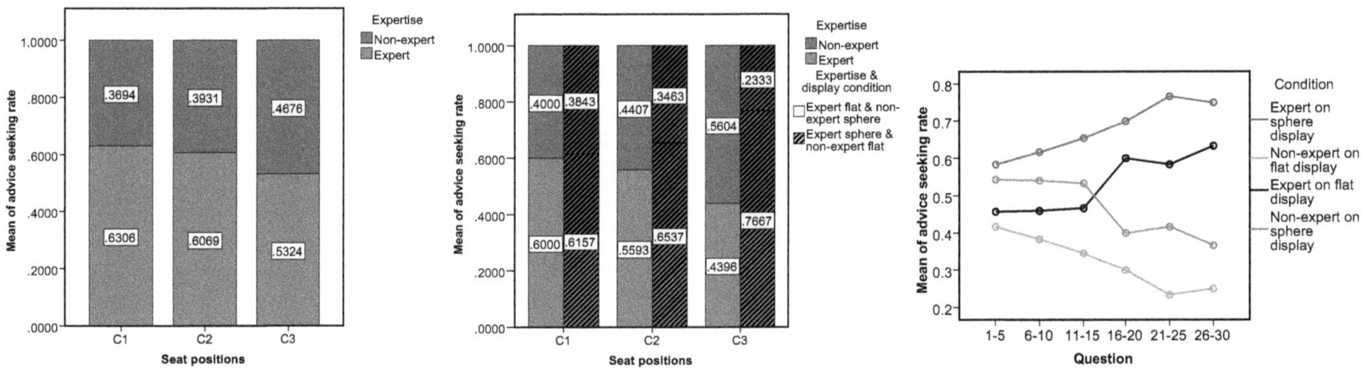


(a) E1: Advice seeking across seat positions. (b) E2: Advice seeking across seat positions. (c) E2: Advice seeking over time.

**Figure 7. Results of E1 & E2: task performance measure.**

## EXPERIMENT 1

### Method

Twelve participants (6 male), students and staff at University College London, were recruited to take part as observers in E1. The median age was 21.75 (SD = 3.20).

E1 had a one-way within-subjects design (see Figure 6(a) to Figure 6(c)). Every participant took part in the experiment at 3 different seat positions (C1, C2 and C3). The order of the answer options (A-D) of questions was randomized. The expertise and the participant's 3 different seat positions order were counterbalanced, in order to reduce any confounding influence of the experiment environment such as lighting conditions and the orderings such as learning effects or fatigue.

Prior to starting the assessed part of the experiment, each participant completed a training round that consisted of easy questions where both advisers gave identical and correct advice. Then, participants answered 10 assessed questions each round. The participant could ask for advice before answering each question. For each question, participants could ask for advice from one of two advisers without knowing of adviser's role of expertise. After each participant played one round at one seat position, the participant moved to another seat position. This process repeated for three different seat positions. Each participant has the same two advisers (Emma and Katy) for the whole study. After completing all rounds they were presented with the post-experimental questionnaire and an open question. Finally, the participants were compensated with chocolates based on their performance. The experiment took about 30 minutes.

### Results

In E1, participants sought advice on 29.33 out of 30 questions (97.78%) over 3 rounds. 7 participants (58.33%) sought advice in every question. There was no cost associated with seeking advice. Figure 7(a) shows that the experts (red bar) were chosen more often than non-experts (blue bar) for all three seat positions. However, from seat position C1 to C3, the expert advice seeking rate dropped off whereas non-expert advice seeking rate increased. We interpret this to indicate the decrement of sensitivity for cues of expertise.

A one-way repeated measures ANOVA was conducted to compare the effect of the expert advice seeking rate in 3 seat positions (C1, C2 or C3) conditions. There was a significant effect of seat positions, $F(2, 22) = 6.356, p < .01$. Three paired samples t-tests were used to make post hoc comparisons between conditions. When we did three paired samples t-tests, we increased our chances of finding a significant result when one did not exist. Instead of using the value .05 to decide if we had reached statistical significance, we would instead use the value .017 ($= .05/3$) as the cut off. A first paired samples t-test indicated that there was no significant difference between C1 ($M = 63.06\%, SD = .063$) and C2 ($M = 60.69\%, SD = .091$) conditions; $t(11) = .945, p = .365$. A second paired samples t-test indicated that there was a significant difference for C1 and C3 ($M = 53.24\%, SD = .088$) conditions; $t(11) = 3.457, p = .005$. A third paired samples t-test indicated that there was no significant difference between C2 and C3 conditions; $t(11) = 2.304, p = .042$. The expert advice seeking rate at C3 is significantly less than C1. This suggests that further the seat position aside from the central position, the more difficulty the observer had in identifying the expert. This supports our first hypothesis.

## EXPERIMENT 2

### Method

Twenty-four participants (12 male) took part in E2. The median age was 21 (SD = 2.30). Participants had not previously interacted with advisers.

E2 is similar to E1, except that instead of presenting two advisers on two identical flat displays, we presented one on sphere display, and the other on flat display. E2 had a 2 display modes (*Expert is sphere display* vs. *expert is flat display*) $\times$ 3 seat positions mixed design, resulting in 2 between-subject conditions with 12 participants each (see Figure 6(d) to Figure 6(g)). In each between-subject condition, two advisers were available. Depending on the factor display mode, either the sphere display or the flat display adviser gave expert advice, while the other gave non-expert advice. The two display positions (left-right) were counterbalanced by switching around the sphere and flat displays. To moderate the effect introduced by evaluating a novel type of display, we asked each participant to complete a practice round prior to starting the assessed part of the experiment.

### Results

*Display type & viewing angle*

In E2, participants sought advice on 29.21 out of 30 questions (97.36%) on average. 15 participants (62.5%) sought advice in every question. Figure 7(b) shows that the experts (red bar) were chosen more often than non-experts (blue bar) for all three seat positions. The overall expert advice seeking rate (expert on sphere display + expert on flat display) were 60.79%, 60.65% and 60.31% at the seat position C1, C2 and C3, respectively. This indicated that the overall expert advice seeking rate remained the same among three seat positions, which were approximately 20% higher than overall non-expert advice seeking rate. Figure 7(b) also shows that a preference for choosing sphere display increased from seat position C1 to C3, while decreased in the flat display condition. The overall sphere display seeking rate (expert on sphere + non-expert on sphere) were 50.78%, 54.72% and 66.35% at the seat position C1, C2 and C3, respectively. Sphere display advice seeking rate was higher in seat position C3. We note that for seat position C1, the flat display and sphere display were chosen equally often. This is expected as the seat position only slightly diverges from the front and the faces of two advisers can be seeing similarly on both display types.

A 2 (display: flat vs. sphere) $\times$ 3 (seat positions: C1, C2 or C3) repeated measures ANOVA was conducted on the expert advice seeking rate, with display as a between-subjects factor and seat positions as a within-subjects factor. This revealed a significant main effect of display, $F(1,22) = 13.757, p < .01$, indicating that expert advice seeking rate was significantly higher for sphere display. There was no significant main effect of seat positions, $F(2,44) = .011, p > .05$, indicating overall expert advice seeking rate at different seat positions were not statistically significant different from one another, thus further supporting our first hypothesis. However, the display $\times$ seat position interaction was significant, $F(2,44) = 11.745, p < .001$, indicating that expert advice seeking rate due to seat position was presented differently in sphere and flat display conditions. This supports the second hypothesis.

We further investigated sphere display non-expert advice seeking rate at three different seat positions (unshaded blue bar in Figure 7(b)). The non-expert advice seeking rate $< .5$ would provide evidence for users' ability to discriminate between expert and non-expert advisers, whereas the value $> .5$ would be a sign of bias outweighing discrimination. Based on a one-sample t-test, the sphere display advice seeking rate at seat position C1 is significantly below .5, $t(11) = -2.582, p < .05$. There is also some indication at seat position C2, $t(11) = -2.111, p = .058$. However, no such effect is presented at seat position C3, $t(11) = 1.781, p > .05$, indicating that a bias towards sphere display is interfering with users' ability to discriminate, thus supporting the second hypothesis.

We then analyzed how participant's advice seeking behavior changes over time. Figure 7(c) presents the mean advice seeking rate of every five questions in chronological order. The choice to seek advice from a specific adviser could be expected to depend upon the information accumulated from previous pieces of advice. It was thus assumed to be relatively arbitrary in first interactions. Participants increasingly sought advice from the expert as they gained experience with the advisers, but there is a bias towards sphere display. This gives us a further evidence for the second hypothesis.

*Post-Questionnaire*

Figure 8 shows the result of participant's self-reports. In the expert on sphere display condition, the statements measuring ability (Statement 3, 6, 7,& 9) were higher for the sphere display; and in the expert on flat display condition, those statements were higher for the flat display. This indicated that participants were able to identify the trustworthy adviser. However, statements measuring enjoyment (Statement 1, 2, 4, 5,& 8) showed similar or higher level of score for sphere display, even in the expert on flat display condition. This indicated that using the sphere display could increase social presence.

The responses to each statement item given by all the participants were averaged to create an aggregate response. We calculated Cronbach's alpha as the reliability test. The questionnaire measured four subscales: trustworthiness of the sphere display adviser (4 items, $\alpha = .893$), trustworthiness of the flat display adviser (4 items, $\alpha = .96$), enjoyment of the sphere display adviser (5 items, $\alpha = .807$), and enjoyment of the flat display adviser (5 items, $\alpha = .932$). We then analyzed the post-experimental assessments of the advisers by comparing each participant's rating of the sphere display adviser to that of the flat display adviser, irrespective of the expertise of each adviser. Significant differences in the post-experimental assessment (see Table 1) between sphere display and flat display adviser are thus indicators of bias on one subscale for one specific display type. Two paired-samples t-test were conducted to compare the ratings of the trustworthiness and enjoyment in sphere display and flat display conditions. Notable bias was found for enjoyment, sphere display rated as being friendlier than flat display, irrespective of expertise, $t(23) = -2.228, p < .05$.

## DISCUSSION

We compared the advice-seeking rate at three seat positions between E1 and E2. E1 utilized two flat displays, with results demonstrating that participants' sensitivity to correct advice decreased at the far off-center viewing positions (C3). By introducing the spherical display in E2 that was able to preserve correct gaze direction and a simple pseudo-3D experience by providing perspective-correct rendering at all viewing angles using non-planar surface, we found participants' ability to discriminate remained stable at all viewing positions.

From participants' behavioral measures, we found that participants mostly chose expert advice in both flat and sphere display representations. This indicates that participants were able to discriminate between experts and non-experts, and accordingly, distributed more trust to the expert. However, there was also evidence that display representation can interfere with participants' ability to discriminate effectively. The sphere display produced a higher rate of advice seeking

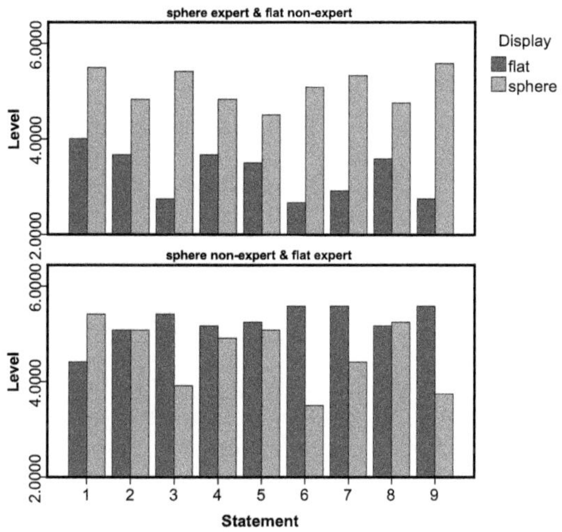


**Figure 8. Post-experimental assessments of the advisers.**

compared with the flat display. This behavioral manipulation emerged at off-center viewing positions and increased as the viewing position became more extreme. At the most extreme viewing position (C3), the rate of advice-seeking from the avatar displayed on the sphere was significantly greater than that sought from the avatar shown on the flat display. The preference for seeking advice from the avatar on the sphere display almost matched the preference for choosing expert advice, despite participants generally knowing on which display the expert was positioned. This negative bias towards the flat screen at off-center viewing angles in avatar-mediated communication parallels a similar finding by Nguyen et al. [19] in video-mediated communication. In that study, they examined the effects of spatial faithfulness on trust formation in a cooperative investment task. They found the spatial distortions of traditional flat display negatively affect trust formation patterns. The finding that trust can be easily and significantly manipulated in mediated interaction by adjusting display viewing angle has significant implications for telecommunication in general. We plan further investigation on this topic, with our next step being to quantitatively evaluate gaze of participants using eye tracking and introduce another between-subject condition (sphere display expert vs. sphere display non-expert) to further explore this finding.

Our post-experimental open question further supports our findings. Note that Katy was the adviser on flat display and Emma was the adviser on sphere display. In the expert is sphere condition, one participant stated "It is difficult to see Katy speak and look at her expressions while she answered, I could not feel good to communicate with Katy. Thus, I chose Emma more times." Regarding viewing angle, another participant stated "I was sitting facing them directly rather than an angle with Emma, the more I felt they were reliable." In the expert is flat condition, one participant expressed "Emma's eye gives a supporting feeling, but Katy's voice is more confident. Katy seems always certain about the answer, but Emma seems to tell what she knows." Participants' answers also show that there were other factors influencing their decision making, with one stating "I got a fully confident answer by myself and Katy also told me the matched answer, so I tended to ask her more.", and another stating "The longer time I spend with Katy and Emma, I figure out who knows more answers. But sometimes I still need to double check."

## CONCLUSION

We have presented a spherical display featuring a view-dependent rendering method to represent virtual avatars. We detail a method for enabling the displayed avatar to reproduce the facial expression captured from a person in real-time and with high-fidelity. The system provides observers with perspective-correct rendering and the nature of the display offers surrounding visibility whereas flat displays are only viewable from the front. This borderless spherical display can be statically situated as an interesting display for virtual avatars or other content. It could also be mounted on a robot as a mobile display for telepresence.

We investigated the display in the context of a trust scenario. We investigated the effects of display type (sphere and flat) and viewing angle for trust assessments in avatar-mediated interaction. While participants were able to discriminate trustworthy and less trustworthy advisers irrespective of display type, a negative bias for flat display can interfere with users' ability to discriminate effectively. The interference became significant at off-center viewing angles, where the flat display no longer allows an undistorted and clear view. This demonstrates that a participant's level of trust can be manipulated during avatar-mediated communication by the appearance of a remote interactant.

As the amount of our time spent in mediated interaction increases, these findings have significant implications for teleconferencing in general, and we plan to further investigate the phenomenon with classic video conferencing setups. The surrounding characteristics of spherical displays allow perspective-correct imagery to be seen from all viewing directions, and hence avoid the problems we have observed with traditional flat displays. By preserving a virtual avatar's correct appearance and gaze direction, the spherical display is able to maintain a consistently high level of trust regardless of viewing position. Trust is a fundamental part of human interaction and we intend to explore other important scenarios and natural interaction in future work.

## ACKNOWLEDGMENTS

The authors would like to acknowledge the FP7 EU collaborative project BEAMING (248620) and the China Scholarship Council. We thank the UCL VECG group members for their general support and the anonymous reviewers for their feedback.

## REFERENCES

1. Andrist, S., Pejsa, T., Mutlu, B., and Gleicher, M. Designing effective gaze mechanisms for virtual agents. In *SIGCHI*, ACM (2012), 705–714.

2. Bailenson, J. N., Yee, N., Merget, D., and Schroeder, R. The effect of behavioral realism and form realism of real-time avatar faces on verbal disclosure, nonverbal disclosure, emotion recognition, and copresence in

dyadic interaction. *Presence: Teleoperators and Virtual Environments 15*, 4 (2006), 359–372.

3. Barnett White, T. Consumer trust and advice acceptance: The moderating roles of benevolence, expertise, and negative emotions. *JCP 15*, 2 (2005), 141–148.
4. Bekkering, E., and Shim, J. Trust in videoconferencing. *Commun. ACM 49*, 7 (2006), 103–107.
5. Bickmore, T., and Cassell, J. Relational agents: a model and implementation of building user trust. In *SIGCHI*, ACM (2001), 396–403.
6. Bohannon, L. S., Herbert, A. M., Pelz, J. B., and Rantanen, E. M. Eye contact and video-mediated communication: A review. *Displays* (2012).
7. Bos, N., Olson, J., Gergle, D., Olson, G., and Wright, Z. Effects of four computer-mediated communications channels on trust development. In *SIGCHI*, ACM (2002), 135–140.
8. Chen, M. Leveraging the asymmetric sensitivity of eye contact for videoconference. In *SIGCHI*, ACM (2002).
9. Dawes, R. M. Social dilemmas. *Annual review of psychology 31*, 1 (1980), 169–193.
10. Desai, M., Tsui, K. M., Yanco, H. A., and Uhlik, C. Essential features of telepresence robots. In *TePRA*, IEEE (2011), 15–20.
11. Deutsch, M. Trust and suspicion. *The Journal of conflict resolution 2*, 4 (1958), 265–279.
12. Ducheneaut, N., Yee, N., Nickell, E., and Moore, R. J. Alone together?: exploring the social dynamics of massively multiplayer online games. In *SIGCHI*, ACM (2006), 407–416.
13. Grossman, T., and Balakrishnan, R. The design and evaluation of selection techniques for 3d volumetric displays. In *UIST*, ACM (2006), 3–12.
14. Horn, D. B., Karasik, L., and Olsen, J. S. The effects of spatial and temporal video distortion on lie detection performance. In *SIGCHI*, ACM (2002), 714–715.
15. Kim, K., Bolton, J., Girouard, A., Cooperstock, J., and Vertegaal, R. Telehuman: effects of 3d perspective on gaze and pose estimation with a life-size cylindrical telepresence pod. In *SIGCHI*, ACM (2012), 2531–2540.
16. Lincoln, P., Welch, G., Nashel, A., Ilie, A., Fuchs, H., et al. Animatronic shader lamps avatars. In *ISMAR*, IEEE (2009), 27–33.
17. Mayer, R. C., Davis, J. H., and Schoorman, F. D. An integrative model of organizational trust. *Academy of management review* (1995), 709–734.
18. Nguyen, D., and Canny, J. Multiview: spatially faithful group video conferencing. In *SIGCHI* (2005), 799–808.
19. Nguyen, D. T., and Canny, J. Multiview: improving trust in group video conferencing through spatial faithfulness. In *SIGCHI*, ACM (2007), 1465–1474.
20. Okada, K., Maeda, F., Ichikawaa, Y., and Matsushita, Y. Multiparty videoconferencing at virtual social distance: Majic design. In *CSCW* (1994), 385–393.
21. Oyekoya, O., Steptoe, W., and Steed, A. Sphereavatar: a situated display to represent a remote collaborator. In *SIGCHI*, ACM (2012), 2551–2560.
22. Pan, Y., and Steed, A. Preserving gaze direction in teleconferencing using a camera array and a spherical display. In *3DTV-CON, 2012*, IEEE (2012), 1–4.
23. Parker, S. G., Bigler, J., Dietrich, A., Friedrich, H., Hoberock, J., Luebke, D., McAllister, D., McGuire, M., Morley, K., Robison, A., et al. Optix: A general purpose ray tracing engine. *TOG 29*, 4 (2010), 66.
24. Rae, I., Takayama, L., and Mutlu, B. In-body experiences: Embodiment, control, and trust in robot-mediated communication. *interaction 15*, 28 (2013), 36.
25. Riegelsberger, J., Sasse, M. A., and McCarthy, J. D. The mechanics of trust: a framework for research and design. *IJHCS 62*, 3 (2005), 381–422.
26. Riegelsberger, J., Sasse, M. A., and McCarthy, J. D. Rich media, poor judgement? a study of media effects on users trust in expertise. In *People and Computers XIXThe Bigger Picture*. Springer, 2006, 267–284.
27. Roberts, D., Wolff, R., Rae, J., Steed, A., Aspin, R., McIntyre, M., Pena, A., Oyekoya, O., and Steptoe, W. Communicating eye-gaze across a distance: Comparing an eye-gaze enabled immersive collaborative virtual environment, aligned video conferencing, and being together. In *VR* (2009), 135–142.
28. Sellen, A., Buxton, B., and Arnott, J. Using spatial cues to improve videoconferencing. In *SIGCHI* (1992), 651–652.
29. Steptoe, W., Steed, A., Rovira, A., and Rae, J. Lie tracking: social presence, truth and deception in avatar-mediated telecommunication. In *SIGCHI*, ACM (2010), 1039–1048.
30. Swol, L. M., and Sniezek, J. A. Factors affecting the acceptance of expert advice. *British Journal of Social Psychology 44*, 3 (2005), 443–461.
31. Teoh, C., Regenbrecht, H., and O'Hare, D. Investigating factors influencing trust in video-mediated communication. In *OzCHI*, ACM (2010), 312–319.
32. Vertegaal, R., Weevers, I., Sohn, C., and Cheung, C. Gaze-2: conveying eye contact in group video conferencing using eye-controlled camera direction. In *SIGCHI* (Ft. Lauderdale, Florida, USA, 2003), 521–528.
33. Weise, T., Bouaziz, S., Li, H., and Pauly, M. Realtime performance-based facial animation. *TOG 30*, 77 (2011), 1–10.
34. Williams, E. Experimental comparisons of face-to-face and mediated communication: A review. *Psychological Bulletin 84*, 5 (1977), 963.
35. Yamashita, N., Hirata, K., Aoyagi, S., Kuzuoka, H., and Harada, Y. Impact of seating positions on group video communication. In *CSCW*, ACM (2008), 177–186.

# PrintSense: A Versatile Sensing Technique to Support Multimodal Flexible Surface Interaction

**Nan-Wei Gong[1], Jürgen Steimle[2], Simon Olberding[2], Steve Hodges[3], Nicholas Gillian[1], Yoshihiro Kawahara[1,4] and Joseph A. Paradiso[1].**

[1]MIT Media Lab, Cambridge, USA, [2] Max Plank Institute, Saarbrücken, Germany,

[3] Microsoft Research, Cambridge, UK, [4] The University of Tokyo, Japan

nanwei@media.mit.edu, {jsteimle, solberdi}@mpi-inf.mpg.de, shodges@microsoft.com, ngillian@media.mit.edu, kawahara@akg.t.u-tokyo.ac.jp, joep@media.mit.edu

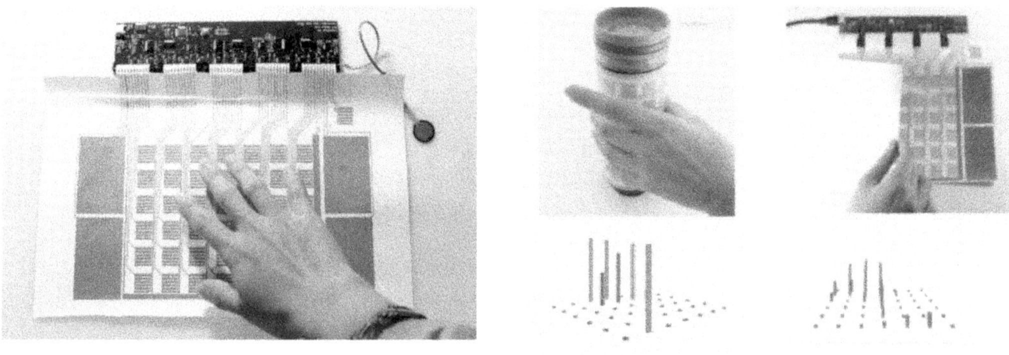

**Figure 1. The PrintSense technique supports the development of multi-modal sensing arrays, printed as a single layer onto a flexible substrate and connected to a custom hardware module (left). It supports capacitive touch and proximity sensing along with resistive pressure sensing (centre) & bend sensing of the substrate (right).**

## ABSTRACT

We present a multimodal on-surface and near-surface sensing technique for planar, curved and flexible surfaces. Our technique leverages temporal multiplexing of signals coming from a universal inter-digitated electrode design, which is printed as a single conductive layer on a flexible substrate. It supports sensing of touch and proximity input, and moreover is capable of capturing several levels of pressure and flexing. We leverage recent developments in conductive inkjet printing as a way to prototype electrode patterns, and combine this with a new hardware module for supporting the full range of sensing methods. As the technique is low-cost and easy to implement, it is particularly well-suited for prototyping touch- and hover-based user interfaces, including curved and deformable ones.

### Author Keywords

Interactive surface, touch input, multimodal input, flexible sensor, conductive inkjet, printed electronics.

### ACM Classification Keywords

H.5.2 Information interfaces and presentation: User Interfaces- Input devices and strategies.


*CHI 2014*, April 26–May 1, 2014, Toronto, Ontario, Canada.
Copyright ©ACM 978-1-4503-2473-1/14/04...$15.00.
http://dx.doi.org/10.1145/2556288.2557173

## INTRODUCTION AND RELATED WORK

While standard multi-touch sensors are now well established in a variety of HCI applications [1], flexible sensors are attracting increasing interest. For instance, prior work has contributed sensors for pressure input [7] and for deformation sensing [2]. However, these sensors are often complex to work with and modify, requiring special materials and components. Moreover, each sensor captures only limited and pre-defined modalities. Recent advances in conductive inkjet printing [3] provide an easier way to produce sensor electrodes [7] and allows an end-user to create their own electrodes with consumer grade hardware [5]. This can be highly beneficial for prototyping user interfaces [6, 8]. However, printing a single layer of passive conductive traces has to-date restricted use to basic touch sensing [6, 8].

We present PrintSense, a technique for multimodal sensing on planar, curved or flexible surfaces. In contrast to previous work, we show how a single-layer sensing electrode design may be used in conjunction with a variety of signal generation and processing techniques. This diversity supports a greater range of sensing than conventional printed touch and multi-touch sensors, including pressure, folding and proximity detection. PrintSense consists of an array of electrodes printed on a flexible substrate, and a custom-made electronic circuit that processes electrode signals. We present both components. By pairing the electronic circuit with a suitable sensor electrode design and configuring how it generates and processes sensor signals, we show that it is possible to extend sensing capabilities beyond touch input for several interactive scenarios. These scenarios include grasp detection on curved objects as well as detecting pressure and folding on flexible sheets.

Our overall aim is to highlight a spectrum of sensing techniques for flexible conductive surfaces, to illustrate usage scenarios and new opportunities for this low-cost, flexible surface interaction, and to enable other practitioners to replicate and extend our work.

## PRINTSENSE DESIGN AND IMPLEMENTATION

The primary sensing modality supported by PrintSense is capacitive. However, unlike many previous capacitive sensing systems, we support several different sensing modalities which extend basic touch interaction to include proximity and folding. Moreover, we add resistive sensing – capable of capturing different levels of contact pressure – to the same electrode design.

### Capacitive Touch Sensing

The basic operating principle of the majority of simple, single-layer electrode capacitive touch systems is to repeatedly charge up an electrode and then time how long it takes to discharge. When a finger, hand or other body-part is close to the electrode, its rate of discharge will change; this can be detected and inferred as touch [10]. PrintSense supports this mode of touch sensing which we refer to as *load sensing*. We use two interleaved sets of conductive 'inter-digitated' (IDT) fingers for each electrode, as shown on the left of Figure 2. Unfortunately, the detection range of basic capacitive sensing is limited; therefore, we include two more sensing modes for proximity sensing.

### Capacitive Proximity Sensing

Using the same sensing electrode design and layout, PrintSense also supports a completely passive capacitive sensing mode, which we call *AC hum detection*. In this condition, each electrode is connected to an analog sensing circuit, which detects any mains electricity noise coupled into it [10]. Just as touching an audio cable that is attached to an amplifier causes noise to be picked up, so proximity to a sensing electrode can be detected. More specifically, we implement a band pass filter centered at a frequency of 50 to 60 Hz to match the power line alternating current (AC). After the band pass filter, a peak detector holds the AC signal amplitude, outputting a DC voltage equal to the peak value of the AC signal. This mode provides hover detection with a ~10 cm range (Figure 2).

An alternative approach to proximity detection is an active *transmit-and-receive* scheme [10]. This active sensing approach offers a way to reference the distance (or even angle) between two electrodes, which can be not achieved with passive capacitive detection.

In this mode of operation, electrode fingers are either used to transmit or receive an electric field. When one set of electrode fingers (the 'transmitter') is stimulated with an AC signal, a second set (the 'receiver') will pick up the same signal. If part of a user's hand is in contact with the transmitting electrode, it will act as an extension to the transmitting electrode and increase the signal transfer to the receiving electrode. Conversely, when a hand is in-between the electrode pair, it tends to block the electric field, and creates a signal drop. These effects are used for proximity detection.

### Detecting Folding

In addition to capacitive proximity sensing, the active transmit-and-receive capacitive technique may be used in a slightly different way to detect folding of the array of electrodes by estimating the distance between specific pairs of electrodes. In this case one electrode acts as a transmitter and is detected by others across the sensing substrate (see Figure 6).

### Resistive (GSR) Pressure Sensing

The final sensing modality we support is resistive pressure sensing. This exploits the fact that when a fingertip comes in contact with a bare IDT electrode it will allow current to pass between the two electrode fingers. Although there is a considerable variation in baseline skin resistance between users due to a number of factors, in our experience applying an increasing pressure always decreases resistance. The advantage of resistive sensing compared with capacitive sensing is this analog force detection couple with an immunity to environmental RF noise. Note that measuring skin resistance is inherently akin to measuring conductance, i.e. galvanic skin response (GSR).

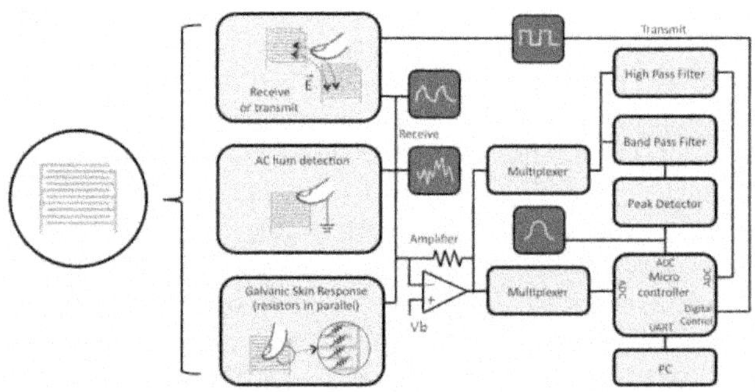


**Figure 2. Three different signal detection schemes supported by PrintSense's inter-digitated electrodes. From top to bottom: active transmit-and-receive capacitive sensing for proximity and folding detection, AC hum detection for touch and proximity detection, and resistive pressure sensing.**

### Electrode Substrate

To test and evaluate the techniques described in this paper, we designed a single pattern of conductive electrodes as shown in Figure 1, and manufactured it using Conductive Inkjet Technology [3]. As it is single-layered it is easy and inexpensive to print, even by non-experts with off-the-shelf hardware [6]. The central area contains a grid of 42 IDT electrodes. Each is around 1.5 cm$^2$ with a roughly 0.5 cm separation between adjacent electrodes designed for detecting finger presses. The size of the electrode can be easily customized depending on the application. Two larger 3 x 6 cm electrodes were included for greater transmission range in proximity detection mode.

### Hardware Implementation

The PrintSense controller is based on a 16 MHz ATmega 328 microprocessor, which can support 46 inter-digitated electrodes. The microcontroller controls a pair of three 16:1 multiplexers (MUXes, CD74HC4067) in order to switch each input between sensing modes. Each input electrode is first fed into an amplification stage for current-to-voltage conversion before the analog MUX scans through and transmits the voltage levels to a 10-bit analog-to-digital converter (ADC). A second MUX is connected to the same amplifier outputs, but feeds an analog active filter circuit with extra gain.

The geometry of the controller and the associated sensing substrate was chosen to support full-hand interactions. The connection between the flexible substrate and the controller board was made with flex circuit connectors (JST-10FDZ). For the AC hum detection, we designed a band-pass filter, 50-160 Hz with gain of 100. For the receiving electrode of each transmit-receive pair, the high pass filter has a cut-off frequency around 1.6 kHz. The ADC sampling rate of our microprocessor is approximately 10 kHz. The whole system samples 46 channels with both modalities at 84 Hz. The raw hum-detection data is envelope-detected in the hardware before being sent to the computer. The sensor board is USB powered, and a FTDI USB serial chip is used for the serial communication between the microcontroller and a PC.

## CHARACTERISATION OF OPERATION

### Resistive Sensing

Across all the sensing modalities supported by PrintSense, we were most interested to evaluate its suitability as a resistive force sensor which can distinguish more than simple touch/no-touch states because to our knowledge this has not been explored previously. Therefore our evaluation aims to distinguish between three different levels of pressure across users. We conducted a user study with 5 users in which we compared the average response and stability of two sensors: a standard force sensitive resistor (FSR, #402) and one of our IDT electrodes for GSR measurement which was glued underneath the FSR. Each unit has line width of 10 mm and spacing between lines of 0.5 mm, and roughly represents the physical footprint of a single finger. FSRs are well established for measuring pressure in interactive applications. Typically, the part-to-part repeatability tolerance is ± 15-25% of an established nominal resistance [4]. We used a voltage divider with a unity gain follower and a 10 kΩ measuring resistor [4] to determine pressure; this circuit configuration was used for GSR measurement as well, but with a 2 MΩ resistor.

Figure 3 shows the raw data output when a user was asked to tap, press gently, and press hard on the electrode. We calibrated the force with FSR resistance readings and kept samples within three force ranges: 0-200 g, 300-600 g and 700-1000 g. The user was asked to perform each gesture five times, and we took 100 samples in each gesture. Although there may be some error due to differential non-linearity, this relative pressure is effectively calibrated by the FSR measurement. The GSR measurement has less dynamic range detection, as seen in the plot. To better understand the performance of GSR over time across users, five users were recruited and asked to touch the GSR/FSR input stack 10 times for 5 seconds, each with an interval of 5 seconds between touches. To get the most stable measurement, we only used the first second of data (1000 samples) of each touch, windowed to remove the applied pressure transient. Figure 3 shows the relative pressure ratio (GSR/FSR) across users and at different times of day. The error could be improved with smaller electrode design to ensure the finger covers the same area during every touch. The GSR measurement varies between users, touches, and on different occasions, attesting to its utility mainly as a relative parameter. Long-lived implementations will need to deal with tarnishing as well; this however is less problematic in prototyping, where the ability to iterate designs rapidly is more important.

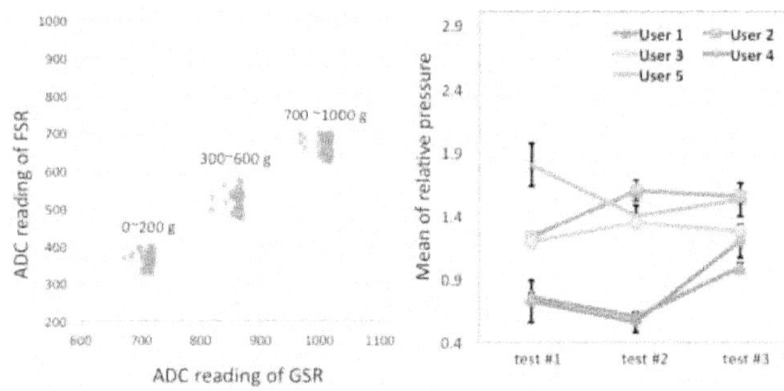


**Figure 3. Left: Raw GSR and FSR ADC data from "tapping" (0~200 g), "pressing gently" (300~600 g) and "pressing hard" (700~1000 g). Right: Mean values of the GSR/FSR ratio for each user across time.**

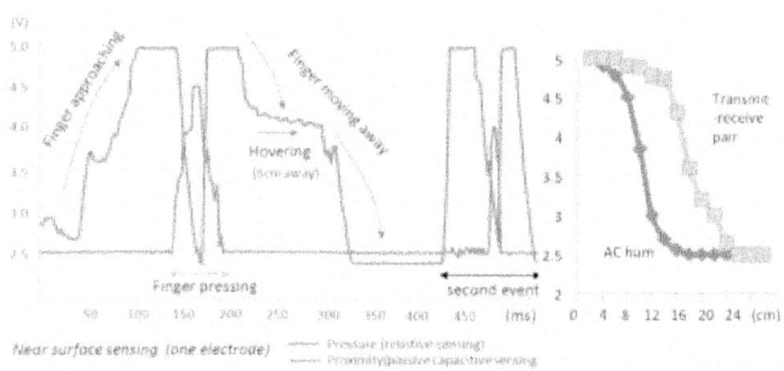


**Figure 4. Left: Near surface sensing signal responses. Right: Proximity range comparison between AC hum detection and transmit-receive pair in our design.**

### Capacitive Proximity Sensing

Figure 4 demonstrates the raw signal responses of one electrode using AC hum passive capacitive detection and also using resistive pressure sensing. The X-axis is time and Y-axis signal amplitude. The user pointed one finger at a single electrode, approached it, touched it and pressed into the electrode before slowly moving away. The blue line indicates pressure level from the resistive sensing signal; as the user presses the electrode, the signal becomes stronger.

With AC hum detection we are able to detect hands around 10 cm above the surface. The red line shows how this signal increases as the finger approaches, until the finger touches the IDT electrode and shunts the capacitive signal to ground, whereupon the signal immediately drops to the 2.5V bias voltage. We also achieved a greater dynamic range of up to 20 cm with active capacitive sensing (transmit-receive pair) as seen in Figure 4.

## EXAMPLE USE CASES

In order to demonstrate application scenarios for PrintSense, we selected two examples requiring different sensor configurations. User interaction and machine learning based gesture detection for these scenarios are demonstrated in the video that accompanies this paper.

### Grasp Detection for Curved Objects

The first use case is grasp detection for curved objects, in which the main sensing method is resistive sensing. Our test object is an insulated coffee beaker wrapped with a substrate of printed electrodes. Figure 6 shows the capture of different levels of pressure and hovering. This enables a more detailed capture of grasps than previous work, which was restricted to touch contact sensing [9].

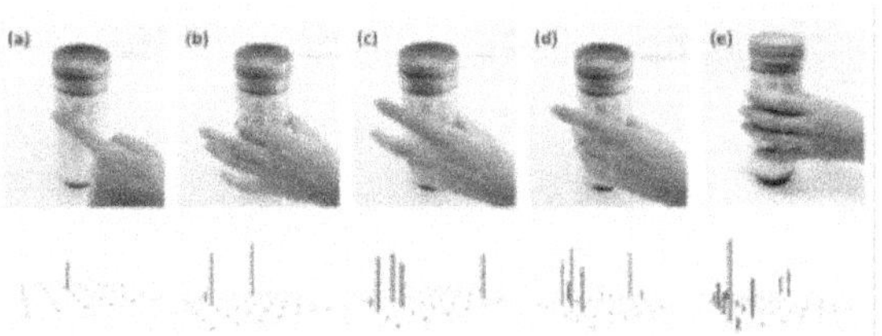

**Figure 5. Grasp detection and raw data on curved objects. (a) One finger touch. (b) Pinch – two fingers input. (c) Three fingers touch. (d) Four fingers touch. (e) Whole hand grasp. Data visualization below each image is from resistive sensing.**

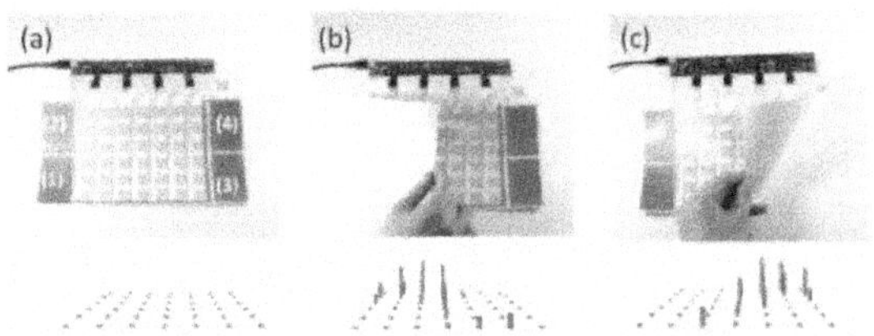


**Figure 6. Using PrintSense to detect folding. The raw data image in the bottom row shows the bigger electrodes actively transmitting signals, and signal received by the remaining IDT electrodes.**

### Manipulation of Flexible Surfaces

In our second use case (Figure 6), we demonstrate detection of the manipulation of a flexible surface, and more specifically bending and folding the corners of this surface. An example application is navigation with a flexible e-book reader. Note that two of the corner electrodes (1) and (3) are transmitting a signal in alternation, and this is picked up by nearby electrodes.

## DISCUSSION AND CONCLUSION

In this paper we presented PrintSense, a multiplexing architecture which uses flexible printed conductive electrode arrays to support a range of sensing modalities. It supports interactions such as touch, proximity, pressure and folding. The advantage of our approach over other surface sensing platforms is the multi-modal sensing using a single layer printed conductor. The size of the electrode was selected for basic finger pressing detection, and can be modified easily for different applications. The trade-off is between detection range and resolution. We characterized GSR sensing as a method for inferred force detection and tested across users and time. Although the variance among users is higher than other sensing methods, the simplicity of this method may make it a good alternative for rapid prototyping in conjunction with capacitive proximity and touch sensing. Finally, we provided two proof-of-concept examples that illustrate some of the scenarios that PrintSense can support. We hope that our work will be useful to others who need to iterate touch- and proximity-based interactive prototypes and will in turn inspire new interactive possibilities.

## ACKNOWLEDGMENT

We would like to thank our colleagues, especially Amit Zoran, Nan Zhao, Mark Feldmeier, Valentin Heun, Gershon Dublon and Brian Mayton for their help and support.

## REFERENCES

1. Buxton, B. "Multi-Touch Systems that I Have Known and Loved," 2007.
2. Balakrishnan, R. et al. "Exploring interactive curve and surface manipulation using a bend and twist sensitive input strip," In Proc. of I3D '99.
3. http://www.conductiveinkjet.com
4. http://www.interlinkelectronics.com.
5. Kawahara, Y. et al. "Instant Inkjet Circuits: Lab-based Inkjet Printing to Support Rapid Prototyping of UbiComp Devices", In Proc. of Ubicomp 13
6. Olberding, S. et al., "A Cuttable Multi-touch Sensor", In Proc. of UIST 2013
7. Rendl, C. et al. "PyzoFlex: Printed Piezoelectric Pressure Sensing Foil", UIST12
8. Savage, V. et al. "Midas: fabricating custom capacitive touch sensors to prototype interactive objects," UIST '12, pp. 579-588.
9. Taylor, B. T. and Bove, M., "The bar of soap: a grasp recognition system implemented in a multi-functional handheld device," In Proc. of *CHI EA '08*, 2008.
10. Gong, N.-W. et al. "Leveraging Conductive Inkjet Technology to Build a Scalable and Versatile Surface for Ubiquitous Sensing," In Proc. of UbiComp '11.

# Let's Kick It: How to Stop Wasting the Bottom Third of Your Large Scale Display

**Ricardo Jota**
Dept. of Computer Science
University of Toronto
Toronto, Canada
jotacosta@dgp.toronto.edu

**Pedro Lopes**
Hasso Plattner Institute
Potsdam, Germany
pedro.lopes@hpi.uni-potsdam.de

**Daniel Wigdor**
Dept. of Computer Science
University of Toronto
Toronto, Canada
dwigdor@dgp.toronto.edu

**Joaquim Jorge**
VIMMI / Inesc-ID
IST
Lisbon, Portugal
jaj@inesc-id.pt

## ABSTRACT
Large-scale touch surfaces have been widely studied in literature and adopted for public installations such as interactive billboards. However, current designs do not take into consideration that touching the interactive surface at different heights is not the same; for body-height displays, the bottom portion of the screen is within easier reach of the foot than the hand. We explore the design space of foot input on vertical surfaces, and propose three distinct interaction modalities: hand, foot tapping, and foot gesturing. Our design exploration pays particular attention to areas of the touch surface that were previously overlooked: out of hand's reach and close to the floor. We instantiate our design space with a working prototype of an interactive surface, in which we are able to distinguish between finger and foot tapping and extend the input area beyond the bottom of the display to support foot gestures.

### Author Keywords
Large-scale display, foot interaction, kick, floor input.

### ACM Classification Keywords
H.5.2. [Information interfaces and presentation]: User Interfaces. – Graphical user interfaces.

## INTRODUCTION
Researchers foresee a future in which all walls, windows, and doors – indeed, all vertical surfaces – hold the potential to serve as interactive displays. When such a future arrives, these displays will have uses far beyond the current commercial niches of telepresence [9] and advertising [7]. Several projects have explored interactions on such large-scale interactive surfaces. One area of focus has been on reaching far-away targets [16]. While useful, these techniques primarily address horizontal distance: reducing the time spent moving an object from one horizontal location to another. Largely unexplored is the issue of *vertical* position – that is, how an object's position on the large-scale display affects the types of interactions employed to use the display.


*CHI 2014,* April 26 - May 01 2014, Toronto, ON, Canada
Copyright 2014 ACM 978-1-4503-2473-1/14/04...$15.00.
http://dx.doi.org/10.1145/2556288.2557316

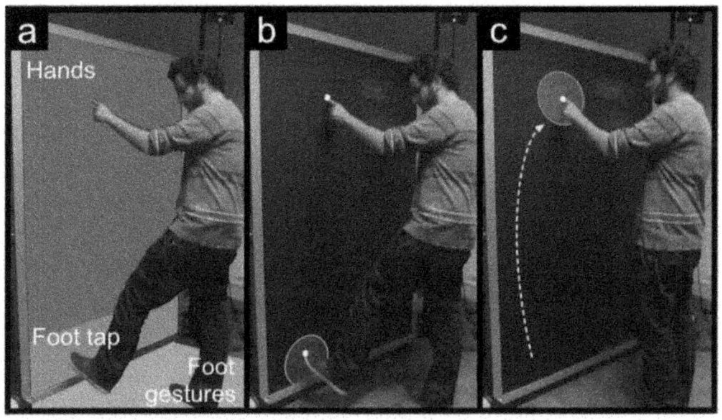


**Figure 1. (a) We propose three types of input, each ergonomically fitting one interactive region: hand interaction, foot taps, and foot gestures; (b) and (c) shows an example technique: kicking an object in the lower portion of the display causes it to pop-up to the finger position.**

In the present work, we address exactly this issue: "how to facilitate interaction with the lower region of touch displays, which is beyond hand-reach?". To explore this concern, we developed a vertical touch surface, sensitive to both feet and finger input, which is depicted in Figure 1. In our early explorations, it became immediately apparent that, for adult users, the area towards the bottom of the screen was far more easily reached with the feet than with the hands; we often found ourselves kicking at items on the display to avoid bending down to touch, as shown in Figure 1(b). This is aligned with the ergonomic literature, which regards bending down as a cause for back strain, therefore an activity that should be avoided [3]. What was also evident, though, was that traditional direct-physical manipulation techniques were not suitable for foot-based interaction. Thus, in this work, we propose an adaptation of direct manipulation techniques that takes into account the ergonomics of foot input.

As current touch-surfaces are not able to distinguish hand from feet contacts, we expanded the sensing capabilities of our prototype by adding a contact microphone, which enables us to acoustically differentiate tapping with the foot or with the hand or fingers. Furthermore, a depth-sensing camera allows us to detect foot position and orientation beneath and around the bottom of the display. Using these input streams, we developed three types of foot-based interaction methods: (1) foot tapping; (2) foot gesturing; and (3) multi-modal foot+hand combinations (as shown in Figure 1).

We condense our input techniques by proposing a design space for direct touch input on large-scale displays, taking input appendage and ergonomics into account. We review prior work with foot input, explore six interaction methods making use of foot input, and describe the prototype's technical details. Finally, we discuss findings and observations obtained during the exploration.

## DESIGNING FOR FOOT INPUT

Inspired by research in ergonomics [17], we identified three distinct interactive regions: hand, foot tapping, and foot gesturing, depicted in Figure 1(a). These regions are not used for differentiating input; our sensors do that. Instead, they guide our interaction designs, by taking into account the ergonomics of inputs closer to those areas.

***Hand:*** This region extends from the top of the display to below the user's waist, where a user close to the display can still reach down comfortably. Within this region, traditional direct touch physical manipulation can be used, along with reaching techniques described elsewhere.

***Foot Tapping:*** This region is below the knee level, which would otherwise require kneeling or crouching to operate with the hands. We note that humans are less dexterous with their feet than with their hands [4]. Our findings indicate that the rich set of gestures performed by the hands should be reduced to a small set of interactions accomplished by only *tapping* with the foot (i.e., no sliding/flicking, and so forth). It is also appropriate to limit the precision of foot-tapping gestures. Although foot tapping may occur on the screen, where finger tapping can be pixel-precise, foot gestures are only used to specify whole objects, and not specific points within those objects, as is often the case with the equivalent finger gestures.

***Foot Gesturing:*** In our prototype, we intentionally left a 10 cm gap between the floor and the display. We found that this space allows an increase in the expressiveness of input to this region since users can make gestures in front of the display, using techniques such as sliding the foot under it or pulling the foot away from it. This is possible because input to this area is made while both feet remain supported, unlike tapping, which requires a foot to be lifted. Since this region is below the display (and not actually part of it), the key challenge is how to extend the existing "direct" manipulation metaphors beyond the screen.

## RELATED WORK

Given the promise of large displays for interaction, significant efforts have been expended addressing the issue of acquiring out of reach targets on large displays. These include using indirect pointing methods and providing tools to 'pull' distant targets closer [2, 16]. While these all serve to reduce the physical distance from users to targets, their use for targets in front of but below the reach of a user would mean failing to take advantage of the pleasing directness of foot-based interaction.

In developing our design space, we built on two areas of earlier work: foot input, and appendage differentiation.

### Foot Input

Augsten et al. show how high precision foot input can be made available through FTIR-illuminated floors [1], and demonstrates how to locate the position of a foot held in mid-air above the floor. Han et al. add kicking to mobile interactions by using the device camera to detect kicks by observing leg motion from above [5]. Finally, Schoening et al. combine finger input with foot poses, using a balance board, to manipulate data on a vertical surface [8]. Our project builds on these studies by using the foot for differentiated direct-touch manipulation of the full vertical screen, thereby enabling use of the large display surface from top to bottom.

### Appendage Differentiation

We distinguish foot from hand input using acoustic sensing. Similarly, researchers have used acoustic cues to distinguish between different finger regions, but have never implemented it for foot vs. finger identification. Paradiso et al. used the frequency signature of the touch contacts to distinguish between knuckles and fingertips [13]. These acoustic cues have been used on touch surfaces to distinguish between finger pads, fingertips, knuckles, and fingernails [6,11]. Also, Touché used capacitive sensing with sweeping frequency to distinguish the electrical signatures of different poses; however, the technique is limited to direct skin contacts [14]. Additionally, shape has been used to infer input style, such as in Wu and Balakrishnan's shape sensing for multitouch surfaces [22]. We build upon these projects by distinguishing between contacts made with the screen using feet or fingers through acoustic sensing.

## INTERACTION TECHNIQUES

We propose a set of six interaction techniques, iteratively designed and implemented on our prototype, empowering users with access to the unutilized lower portion of a large-screen display using direct-touch gestures with their feet.

### Kicking & Throwing

It is common in windowing systems to provide a method to temporarily dismiss (or minimize) an application. After being dismissed, these applications are then iconified in the Task Bar (Windows), or in the Dock (OS X). Similarly, we provide a mechanism to quickly transition an object between the Hand region and the Foot Tapping region.

***1. Throw to the Bottom:*** Users "throw" objects down by flicking them with handed input towards the bottom of the display, this causes the object to transition to the feet-level region. This is similar to the gesture demonstrated by Wu and Balakrishnan to pass objects across an interactive tabletop [22]. This technique provides a fast way to lower objects using a direct physical manipulation metaphor and, at the same time, does not require the user to lean down.

*2. Kick to Eye-Level:* To interact with an object below arm reach, a user simply kicks the object. This causes the object to be moved upwards, near eye-level. The object may be returned to the bottom of the screen using the throwing gesture, or the foot+hand method described below.

*3. Relocate with Foot+Hand:* Greater expressivity is achieved by utilizing both the foot and the hand. In the previous two gestures, the horizontal location of the object was invariant: users could only change the vertical position, and even then only to a fixed value. To allow greater control, users can simultaneously touch an object and an empty space for relocation. The object and destination can be specified with either the hand or foot, allowing for greater position when throwing to the bottom of the screen, or when kicking it upward as illustrated in Figure 1.

### Extending to the Floor

The 10 cm gap beneath the display offers the user the area below the screen for foot input. A depth-sensing camera is utilized to enable the following gestures.

*4. Object Glimpse:* The user can 'lift' an object with their toes to temporarily move objects upwards to facilitate further finger gestures. The user slides a foot under the display and lifts their toes upwards, with the heel anchored, as shown in Figure 2. This action slightly raises all objects directly above the foot for the duration of the gesture. When the user removes the foot, objects slowly animate back to their original position, allowing the user an opportunity to quickly move them to eye level.

*5. Rearrange Thrown Objects:* Users affect the horizontal movement of objects on the bottom of the screen using a foot swipe. Users place their foot beneath the object on the screen, and then slide it horizontally to the desired location (as illustrated in Figure 3).

*6. Delete Objects:* To delete an object from the display, we utilized a metaphor of stepping on the image and dragging it out. To achieve this, users slide their foot under the display and then drag it backwards, as shown in Figure 3(c).

## IMPLEMENTATION

We built our prototype device, as depicted in Figure 4. It is 1.7 m tall by 1 m wide. As such, it is significantly narrower than traditional large-scale displays. Nonetheless, its size is sufficient to allow us to explore interaction methods. Multitouch input is sensed using a laser-light plane (LLP) working on the infrared spectrum and captured via a camera. A microphone mounted at one of the four corners, depicted in Figure 4(a), allows us to capture the sound of surface contacts; these are then used to classify finger or foot touches by analyzing the frequency signature of each contact, as described in previous works [6,11]. This works because the frequency distribution of the kick sound is inherently different from a finger tap. The microphone is sampled in 64 ms chunks; the sample's 11-band FFT is then compared against the database of pre-trained gestures using the algorithm described in Lopes et al. [11].

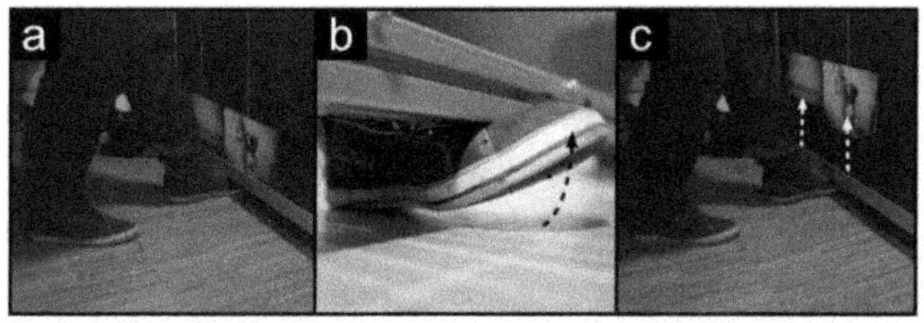


**Figure 2. Toe lift gesture: The user slides their foot under the display (a), lifts their toes (b), causing objects to rise (c).**

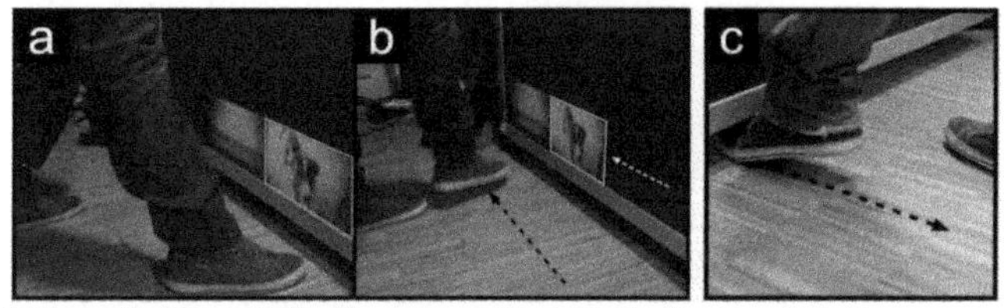


**Figure 3. Foot slide: the user places their foot under the screen (a) and slides it horizontally. The object follows (b). Foot Pull: the user removes objects by pulling them away from screen (c).**

To train the database we collected 10 x 2 (both hands) finger taps (scattered around the whole surface) and 10 x 2 (both feet) foot taps against the lower region. During informal design sessions, the recognition rate was always above 90%.

Finally, a depth-camera is mounted at the back of the frame to detect foot input beneath and in front of the display in order to provide an un-occluded view of the user's foot when gesturing. Tracking the feet is realized using a custom 3D blob tracker using real-time point cloud data from the depth camera, which reports blobs (corresponding to feet) that are within 20 cm of the display. The tracking is as follows: all data that does not reside within the defined interaction space is filtered; then, point cloud data is clustered into blobs that must exceed a radial threshold size (empirically optimized to 4 cm) to be classified as a foot; if multiple blobs are found, the closest to the display is used. Lastly, using the *mt4j* multitouch library, foot gestures (e.g., swipe, toe lift) are recognized by their unique 3D spatial pattern.

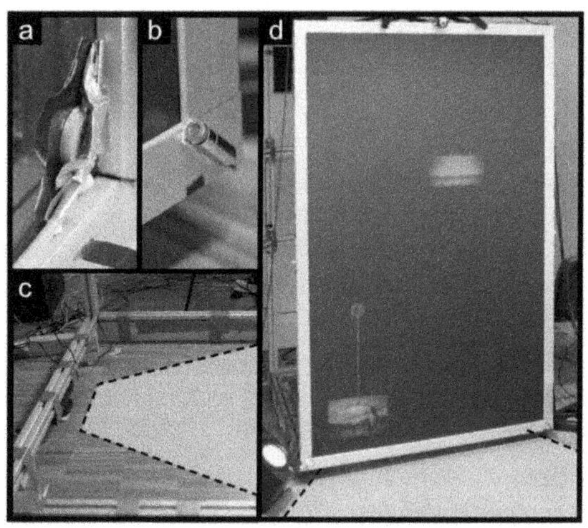


**Figure 4. The prototype (d) is comprised of: surface microphones (a) for classifying finger vs. foot input; IR light laser plane generators (b) for optical multitouch; and a depth camera (c) looking under the surface to capture foot gestures.**

## FOOT+HAND DISCUSSION

Techniques made possible with foot input have not been exhausted. Future contributions to this design space need to consider the following: it is clear that several input primitives are less suitable for fancy foot work than for direct-touch hand input. For example, dragging a finger across the display is a common input action; however, dragging a foot is difficult, since the user is required to balance on the other foot. We found that finger dragging cannot be directly mapped to its foot-equivalent, and therefore should be re-designed (e.g., using multiple kicks).

In addition, tap-based interactions need to be adjusted for foot-based input. We found, unsurprisingly, that users were less accurate when tapping with their feet than with their hands. Thus, we recommend expanding the 'iceberg' [19] targeting areas for foot interaction beyond those used for hand input. In target-dense environments, it may be necessary to limit the number of targets available for foot input, due to overlap of targeting areas.

While our interaction techniques extend direct touch input by mapping foot input on the bezel onto the adjacent pixels, alternative form factors might otherwise extend direct-touch. For example, previous projects have demonstrated the potential for non-flat displays to enhance desktop experiences [18]. A curved wall display could be integrated with a floor display to unify tapping and floor gestures into a continuous space, changing the interaction vocabulary. While such a solution would occlude the mount point for our depth camera, floor based sensors [1] and see-through displays could allow imaging of foot positions [20].

## CONCLUSIONS

We have demonstrated foot input for the bottom portion of large-scale displays. We described several interaction techniques, which improve existing direct-touch interaction with the bottom of the display. Lastly, we proposed several critical considerations necessary when designing interactive systems that take advantage of foot input.

## ACKNOWLEDGMENTS

We thank Kim Wright and Katie Barker for their revisions. Partially funded by FCT CEDAR PTDC/EIA/116070/2009.

## REFERENCES

1. Augsten, T., Kaefer, K., Meusel, R., Fetzer, C., Kanitz, D., Stoff, T., Becker, T., Holz, C., and Baudisch, P. Multitoe: high-precision interaction with back-projected floors based on high-resolution multi-touch input. *UIST '10*, 209–218.
2. Banerjee, A., Burstyn, J., Girouard, A., and Vertegaal, R. Pointable: an in-air pointing technique to manipulate out-of-reach targets on tabletops. *ITS '11,* 11–20.
3. Bridger, R. Some fundamental aspects of posture related to ergonomics, *Industrial Ergonomics 8,* 1 (1991), 3–15.
4. Chan, K., and Chan, A. Spatial stimulus–response compatibility for hand and foot controls with vertical plane visual signals. *Displays 32,* 5 (2011), 237–243.
5. Han, T., Alexander, J., Karnik, A., Irani, P., and Subramanian, S. Kick: investigating the use of kick gestures for mobile interactions. *MobileHCI '11,* 29–32.
6. Harrison, C., Schwarz, J., and Hudson, S. TapSense: enhancing finger interaction on touch surfaces. *UIST '11,* 627–636.
7. Jacucci, G., Morrison, A., Richard, G., Kleimola, J., Peltonen, P., Parisi, L., and Laitinen, T. Worlds of information: designing for engagement at a public multi-touch display. *CHI '10*, 2267–2276.
8. Schoening, J., Daiber, F., Krüger, A., and Rohs, M. Using hands and feet to navigate and manipulate spatial data. *CHI EA '09,* 4663–4668.
9. Kim, K., Bolton, J., Girouard, A., Cooperstock, J., and Vertegaal, R. TeleHuman: effects of 3D perspective on gaze and pose estimation with a life-size cylindrical telepresence pod. *CHI '12*, 2531–2540.
10. Koppel, M., Bailly, G., Müller, J., and Walter, R. Chained displays: configurations of public displays can be used to influence actor-, audience-, and passer-by behavior. *CHI '12*, 317–326.
11. Lopes, P., Jota, R., and Jorge, J. Augmenting touch interaction through acoustic sensing. *ITS '11*, 53–56.
12. Müller, J., Walter, R., Bailly, G., Nischt, M., and Alt, F. Looking glass: a field study on noticing interactivity of a shop window. *CHI '12*, 297–306.
13. Paradiso, J., Leo, C., Checka, N., and Hsiao, K. Passive acoustic sensing for tracking knocks atop large interactive displays. *IEEE ICS '02*, 11–14.
14. Sato, M., Poupyrev, I., and Harrison, C. Touché: enhancing touch interaction on humans, screens, liquids, and everyday objects. *CHI '12,* 483–492.
15. Scott, J., Dearman, D., Yatani, K., and Truong, K. Sensing foot gestures from the pocket. *UIST '10*, 199–208.
16. Schick, A., Camp, F., Ijsselmuiden, J., and Stiefelhagen, R. Extending touch: towards interaction with large-scale surfaces. *ITS '09,* 117–124.
17. Toney, A., and Thomas, B. Considering reach in tangible and table top design. *TABLETOP '06*, 57–58.
18. Weiss, M., Voelker, S., Sutter, C.,and Borchers, J. The BendDesk: dragging across the curve. *ITS '10*, 317–317.
19. Wigdor, D., and Wixon, D. *Brave NUI World: Designing natural user interfaces for touch and gesture*. Morgan Kaufmann, 2011.
20. Wilson, A. TouchLight: an imaging touch screen and display for gesture-based interaction. *ICMI '04*, 69–76.
21. Wobbrock, J., Morris, M., and Wilson, A. User-defined gestures for surface computing. *CHI '09*, 1083–1092.
22. Wu, M., and Balakrishnan, R. Multi-finger and whole hand gestural interaction techniques for multi-user tabletop displays. *UIST '03,* 193–202.

# Communiplay: A Field Study of a Public Display Media Space

**Jörg Müller**[1,2] **Dieter Eberle**[2] **Konrad Tollmar**[3]
[1]Alexander von Humboldt Institute for Internet and Society, Berlin
[2]Quality and Usability Lab, Telekom Innovation Laboratories, TU Berlin
[3]Mobile Services Lab, KTH - Royal Institute of Technology, Stockholm

## ABSTRACT
We present Communiplay, a public display media space. People passing by see their own contour mirrored on a public display and can start to play with virtual objects. At the same time, they see others playing at remote displays within the same virtual space. We are interested whether people would use such a public display media space, and if so, how and why. We evaluate Communiplay in a field study in six connected locations and find a remote honey-pot effect, i.e. people interacting at one location attract people at other locations. The conversion rate (percentage of passers-by starting to interact) rose by +136% when people saw others playing at remote locations. We also provide the first quantification of the (local) honey-pot effect (in our case it raised the conversion rate by +604% when people saw others playing at the same location). We conclude that the integration of multiple public displays into a media space is a promising direction for public displays and can make them more attractive and valuable.

### Author Keywords
Public Displays; Media Space; In-the-Wild Study

### ACM Classification Keywords
H.5.m. Information Interfaces and Presentation (e.g. HCI): Miscellaneous

## INTRODUCTION
This paper brings together the research areas of public displays, playful interaction and media spaces. Media spaces connect people in remote locations in a very casual way and are generally assumed to be effective "social catalysts" [11] by encouraging people to initiate and sustain interaction when they otherwise would not. The majority of media space research has addressed work oriented communication (e.g., [16, 19]). Some artistic media spaces have been successfully used, but less researched, in public settings (e.g., [6, 8]).

We know that public displays can be very effective social catalysts by creating a "sociable buzz" around them locally, this is known as the "honey-pot effect" [3]. For this paper we


*CHI 2014*, April 26–May 1, 2014, Toronto, Ontario, Canada.

ACM 978-1-4503-2473-1/14/04 ...$15.00.
http://dx.doi.org/10.1145/2556288.2557001

**Figure 1. In the Communiplay system, screens were connected in a public display media space. People could play with virtual objects, and people playing at one location could play with people at other locations. When others were playing at a remote location, this often attracted people to look at and play with the screens (the *remote honey-pot* effect raised the conversion rate by +136%).**

more specifically define "honey-pot effect" as (1) the increase of the conversion rate (percentage of passers-by starting to interact) [13] and (2) the increase of the interaction duration, when others are already interacting with a display. While in particular (1) has been observed qualitatively in a number of studies (e.g., [3, 14]), we are not aware of any quantification of this effect. Further, we were interested whether this effect also works remotely in public display media spaces, i.e., whether there also is a "remote honey-pot effect". To explore these ideas further we designed a public display media space, Communiplay, where people can see their own contour mirrored on a public display and can play with virtual objects. At the same time, they see others playing at remote displays illustrated by color-coded silhouettes (see Figure 1).

We describe a public deployment of Communiplay done in August 2013, where we have studied the following research questions: (1) Is there a remote honey-pot effect? (2) Can we quantitatively validate the existence of a (local) honey-pot effect? (3) Does the honey-pot effect also increase interaction durations? (4) Do more local or remote users increase the honey-pot effect?

Our main findings are:

1. We observed a remote honey-pot effect. The conversion

rate increased by +136% when passers-by saw others playing at remote locations.

2. We could quantitatively validate the (local) honey-pot effect. The conversion rate increased by +604% when passers-by saw others playing at the same location.
3. Other users and passers-by (both locally and remotely) also significantly increased the interaction durations.
4. More users (both locally and remotely) strengthened the honey-pot. The more other users (to a maximum of about 5), the higher the conversion rate and interaction duration.

We were also able to observe a multitude of interactions where people were waving, peeking and poking each other through the silhouettes. We also noted that for the short glances that Communiplay offers to passers-by it was hard to fully understand that the silhouettes on screen represented others playing at remote displays. Moreover, using different backdrops that showed the remote location or adding a location label on the silhouettes had no significant effect. However, being able to see screens in different places led to habits over time to play more regularly and show and talk about the system with friends.

One main implication from this work is that by connecting displays, conversion rate and interaction duration can be increased. Simply put, more connected screens, up to a certain limit, boosted the conversion rate even more. We believe that this generalizes to other public displays, although this needs to be validated in future studies.

We will explain the motivation and implications more concisely in the discussion but first we will talk more about related work, and then describe our study and results in detail to return to this discussion.

## RELATED WORK

### Playful Public Displays

A number of public display installations have used games as a means to attract people. For example, Flashlight Jigsaw [4] is a public display game played through controllers tracked with a Vicon system. It was designed to enable both multi user and single user play. Most players preferred to play with others than playing alone. Hence we also believe that when displays at different locations would be connected in a media space, this would give people much more opportunity to play together. Other examples are the Red Nose game [15] and Polar Defence [5].

Chained displays [18] presented a study of a space-invaders game played with full body gestures. It was shown that imitation behavior is very strong in teaching people how to play the game. Because the contour of players was shown on the screen, players also imitated what they saw the contour of others do (when both had shared focus). Connecting displays at different locations in a media space, as proposed in this paper, multiplies the opportunities for imitation and thus learning.

Within the art community public displays have been used for a long time to invoke interaction and reflection in playful ways. Starting with Myron Kruger's seminal work on VideoWall [12], many other works have also used silhouettes in a similar way as Communiplay.

### Increasing Interactions with Public Displays

Public displays are electronic displays installed in public spaces. Due to falling display prices, they are rapidly becoming ubiquitous in urban areas and soon many public surfaces may become digital and interactive. They have shown to be able to make people have a lot of fun together [18, 14, 4]. Because of their public nature, they are also available for anybody regardless of their access to technology otherwise (thus, bridging the digital divide). Finally, they can be useful for sparking discussions, reflection, and participation [17, 7].

However, in practically all deployments of interactive public displays, achieving a sufficient number of interactions with the displays was a large concern. Huang [10] investigated how many people passing by actually looked at digital displays installed in different cities. She found that the number of glances was very low, and moreover that glances were often very short.

Brignull [3] deployed Opinionizer at a party, a display where users could type in their opinions on a given topic. He observed the honey-pot effect, i.e. when somebody is already interacting with the display, this draws considerable attention and others start to interact, too. The honey-pot effect has since been noted in a large number of studies [18, 14, 20]. In all these deployments, it was observed that people already interacting with a display attract passers-by to stop, look, and also start interacting. In this paper, we investigate whether the honey-pot can be leveraged to span different locations, i.e. do people interacting at one location or time also attract people at other locations when shown on the screen?

### Media-Space

Media spaces are electronic settings in which groups of people can work together, even if they do not reside in the same place or are not present at the same time. In a media space, people can create real-time visual and acoustic environments that span physically separate areas. They can also control the recording, accessing and replaying of images and sound from those environments [16]. Media spaces are particularly good for informal communication between remote places [19].

A major focus of media spaces has been on work settings, although some examples of others, in particular in public art, exist. Hole-in-Space [8] and Bill Fontana's work on relocation of urban soundscapes [6] are among the most prominent. However, most of these art installations have not been researched from an HCI / CSCW perspective.

Other examples are Sports over a distance [1] that extended media spaces with physical exertion, and Palimpsest [1] that provided a large shared projection installed at an art festival. Telemurals [11] is also a more recent system that manipulated the video to anonymize users and overlay them within the same virtual space similar to Communiplay. The system was intended as a social catalyst to initiate and sustain interactions within and between two remote places.

### Connected Public Displays

We are aware of only two projects connecting multiple public displays into media spaces. In [9], two locations were connected with a video tunnel. Users were shown with their silhouette overlaid over frozen ice graphics. Via waving, users could melt the ice and see a color image of the other location. It was shown that a symmetric ice melting, where both sides could always see the same area, was preferred by users.

In the screens in the wild project [2], four touchscreens were connected to each other. On the bottom of the screen live video feeds from all four locations were shown. One of the applications on the screen was SoundShape, which allowed collaborative live music making. The authors observed interaction of users with people at the remote location, such as imitating movements, dancing together, or virtual sharing of food by showing it to the camera.

## COMMUNIPLAY

### Shared Interaction

Communiplay consists of a number of connected large screens. People see their own silhouette mirrored on a public display in front of them and can play with virtual objects (cubes or balls). These objects can be kicked and punched with the silhouette and behave according to simulated physics. Opposed to normal games there are no scores to collect, so the main driver is simple to bounce and juggle around with the objects.

At the same time, the players also see others playing at remote displays within the same virtual space illustrated as silhouettes (Figure 2), with the same virtual objects so the physics are shared among all screens. Each location has its own color for the silhouettes of the user to distinguish their location. Additionally a text label telling the location is shown on each silhouette. The size of the silhouette shown on the display is determined by the distance of the users to the displays, i.e. like a mirror.

On the backdrop of the screen the users will get some additional clues about the connected places in an animated banner that is rendered on top of an abstract whiteish image. We also tested to use a "live" caption as background to emphasize how the Communiplay system was connected (Figure 2, e and f) and we will soon discuss how these configurations and arrangements of the systems affected the use of the system. However, the system did not support any additional back-channeling modes such as audio feedback or speech between the remote locations since we wanted to first study how the game and silhouettes facilitate the shared interaction.

### System

At each display a depth camera is mounted to scan the environment for passers-by. The software runs under Ubuntu linux on notebooks that are attached behind the screens. The screens are connected to a server that runs the game engine and keeps track of the shared interaction of the virtual objects. The logging is done on the server-side as well.

The implementation for both client and server was done with Java with the help of some external libraries like JavaCV, a

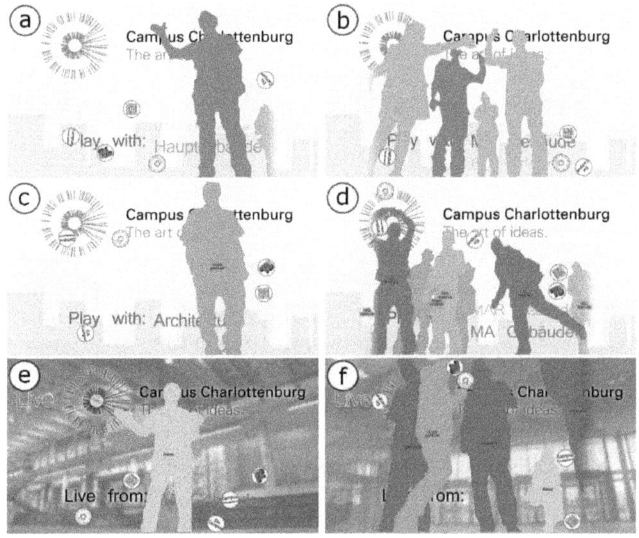


**Figure 2. Location labels: (a,b) Users were shown their silhouette without labels. (c,d) A location label was shown on each user. (e,f) A "live" caption was added and the background rotated through images of each of the locations.**

wrapper for the OpenCV implementation that focuses on real-time image processing which is needed to handle the camera input. For the access of the depth camera OpenNI and NITE were used.

All silhouettes are based on the user masks provided by OpenNI. These data are simplified with OpenCV to reduce the fine user masks to polygons. This reduces the network load to a few sets of points and Netty provided support for the networking part.

The physics simulation of the balls is realized with a simple contour collision algorithm. With the use of FFmpeg anonymous depth camera pictures are saved for analysis of logs. The whole scene is rendered with OpenGL with the LWJGL library. The physics calculation is done both on the server-side and the client side so all users interact with the same objects, but interaction continues in case of network outages.

## PRESTUDY

The objective of this study was to explore audience behavior with a public display media space and to compare different grades of anonymity (contour vs. mirror image, see Figure 3). Three displays were deployed for two days on three different floors of a research laboratory. One display was installed in the cafeteria, one in the lobby next to the reception, and the third in a hallway close to workplaces. During the first day,

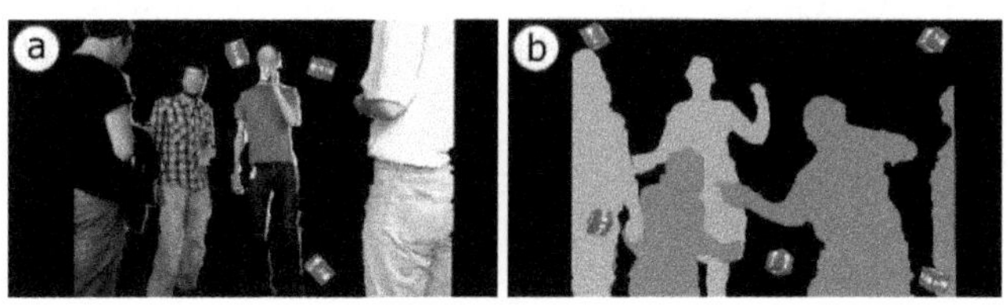


**Figure 3. Prestudy conditions. (a) Mirror condition, (b) contour condition.**

the mirror (colored rgb) image of the users was shown (image condition). On the second day, only the contour of users was shown (contour condition). We observed usage while sitting in an inconspicuous location close to the screens. We also collected anonymous depth videos of usage.

### Findings

#### *Remote Honey-pot Effect*

Although we did not quantify this, when somebody played at one of the locations, there seemed to be a higher probability that people passing by the other screens would stop and start to play. Consequently, there were often people in different locations playing simultaneously. Sometimes, this went so far as to create a kind of overcrowding. There were so many people in front of the screen that they actually could not interact with the virtual objects anymore and that not all of them were visible. It was however unclear if this overcrowding would prevent passers-by from starting to interact or make people leave the screen.

#### *Playing the game vs. playing with the mirror images*

When people interacted with the screens alone, naturally they played mostly with the virtual objects. One behavior we saw repeatedly was people trying to grab and pick up the objects. This, however, was usually unsuccessful, because the resolution of the camera was too low, and grabbing as a gesture was not supported by the application. Another common behavior was boxing objects and sometimes fighting for control over the objects with people at the other location. When there were people at other locations however, users interacted much more with the other users than with the objects. In the contour condition, people played with each others contour, e.g., by running back and forth and trying to hide each others contour and creating funny poses. Especially in the image condition, but also in the contour condition, users mostly waved towards each other and looked at each other. Some people just played with their contour, for example by dancing, even when they were alone.

#### *Ghost effect*

One funny effect occurred when people played with the screen and somebody else entered the screen at a different location. People would then turn around, apparently because they expected the other person to be behind them. When they saw that there was nobody, they would often be surprised, look at the screen again, and then apparently realize that the other person probably was at a different location.

### Discussion

The most interesting aspect for us was the remote honey-pot effect. If people interacting at one location could attract others to interact at a different location, the connection of different displays to each other could make public displays much more attractive. The flip side of the coin was the overcrowding. Especially when many screens are connected to each other, there would be a high probability that too many people would be on the screen to enable everybody to interact. It is unclear however whether such an overcrowding would be negative or positive. With the real honey-pot effect, usually the bigger the crowd the more people it attracts.

Although the mirror image has very interesting properties (users can recognize each other) we decided to continue with the contour condition. It is much easier to deploy for many public locations. The provided anonymity makes privacy issues less of a concern. In some countries (like Germany) it is also simply not legal to distribute image recordings of passers-by in public spaces without their consent. Finally, it is also more playful and technically simpler.

## FIELD STUDY

The main objective of the field study was to investigate usage of a larger public display media space in a more public setting. In particular, we wanted to confirm and quantify the honey-pot effect, and investigate the existence of a remote honey-pot effect. That is, we wanted to confirm that more people passing by would interact with the displays when 1) others interact with the display at the same location, or 2) others interact at a different location. We also wanted to confirm that the interaction duration would increase in these two conditions. Additionally, we wanted to compare the effect of real people who are streamed live from a different location to recordings of users who have interacted before. For this reason, recordings of users who interacted for more than 10s were taken and played back at random intervals when nobody else was on the screen. We conducted a two-phase deployment. In a first phase of three days, we collected observations of system and user behavior and iteratively improved the system. In the second phase of two weeks, we collected data without changing the system.

### Deployment

We deployed Communiplay in six different buildings of the Technical University of Berlin, Germany for two weeks in August 2013. The locations are close to the entrance of the main cafeteria (CAF), the main building (MAIN), in the architecture building (ARCH), in the electrical engineering building (EE), in the mathematics building (MATH) and the computer science building (CS). The chosen spots here were by the main traffic path to maximize the number of passers-by and situated so that passers-by would see them and naturally walk through the interaction area to maximize inadvertent interactions [14]. The typical passers-by are naturally students but off semesters like August the percentage of faculty are rather high. Moreover the university campus is located in the middle of Berlin and hence also visited by many others, like tourists and people just walking across the campus.

### Optimization Phase

On the technical side, we installed much stronger external WiFi antennas, considerably reducing networking problems. In the pre-study we had the cameras installed immediately below the screens to improve the perspective. This posed two kinds of problems that occurred in the fieldstudy because of the different space. First, for far away users they would hover "in the air", not being able to kick the objects. Second, patches of the floor were often recognized as false users when a user had passed by. A relocation of the cameras to the floor below the screens solved both problems. We also collected much more data than expected, causing problems with the RAM of the server. Resorting to the hard-drive for logging data helped. We also changed the physics simulation to continue simulating locally when the connection to the server was lost for more than a few milliseconds. Also, the rendering of the local silhouette was made independent of the server connection, strongly reducing latency. We noticed log data drift issues for the different logs kept locally and implemented logging on the server instead. We changed one screen to a different location because of networking issues and more people passing by in the new location. From interviews we quickly learned that people had difficulties understanding that the screens were connected. To address this, we added a hint on the screen stating which locations the screen was connected to. To lower the impact that motion alone of remote users would have compared to no users, we made the location hint move so we get one constantly moving item on the screen. We also noticed that it was considerable effort checking the state of the screens, and getting a feeling what was going on. Therefore, we installed a viewer close to our workspaces where we could permanently see what was going on on the screens, and also whether any screens were offline. We learned that it was distracting for us not to know whether users shown on the screen were real users or recorded users. We added small color pixels on the side of the screen to indicate recorded users for us.

### Design

In order to investigate the impact of other users on user behavior, we used a quasi-experimental design in the sense that we did not control the independent variables (conditions). Instead, users were assigned to conditions based on the behavior of other users and the system. We distinguish six different conditions, when a user is passing by a screen:

1. Other users play in front of the same screen (local honey-pot)
2. Other people pass by the same screen
3. Other users play in front of screens at other locations (but not at the same, remote honey-pot)
4. Other user pass by another screen
5. Recordings of users who played at different times are shown (but nobody currently plays, recorded honey-pot)
6. Nobody is shown on the screen (baseline).

Condition five (5) was generated when nobody else was on the screen. More specifically, at a random time between 30 and 90 seconds after the last passer-by, a recorded session from a past interaction was started. Throughout this paper and in the video, recorded users are highlighted (black). However, in the experiment, they were indistinguishable from real users.

In order to assign each user to one of these quasi-conditions, a time frame of 10s before the user entered the tracking area of the camera was considered. This was done because from our experience of the honey-pot effect, people are often attracted by others who played before them, but only approach the screen after the others have left.

Dependent variables were percentage of passers-by who interact (conversion rate) and duration of interactions. Our hypotheses were (1) existence of a local honey-pot effect: the conversion rate increases when people already interact at the same screen, as does the interaction duration, and (2) existence of a remote honey-pot effect: The conversion rate increases when people who interact simultaneously at other locations are shown on the screen, as does the interaction duration.

We were also interested to test how the representations of the silhouettes and background affected the interaction. The way we tested this was that we also added two additional variables. Firstly we added location labels to the silhouettes, which were toggled on and off in a interval of 15 minutes. For the second half of the deployment, we compared the location labels with a different background from an abstract design to a "live" caption background from the different locations in a interval of 15 minutes (Figure 2).

### Data Analysis

We logged the anonymous depth video from all displays during the entire duration. In addition, we logged user behavior as determined by OpenNI (entering and leaving users). Further, we logged screen capture during the entire deployment. We followed a semi-automatic video coding approach. We used the OpenNI logging to automatically determine all situations where somebody was in front of the display. We then manually decided for each person whether the detected person was passing-by, spectating, interacting, or noise.

If the person was interacting, we noted the beginning and the end of the interaction. We further categorized the interaction within the categories of playing with objects, waving / gesturing towards others, playing with contours (hiding others etc.), making funny shapes with contours, imitating others at same location, imitating others at other location, and other.

The data was annotated by four raters. A portion of the videos were annotated by all raters to determine inter-rater reliability. Inter-rater reliability was substantial (Fleiss' Kappa = 0.75 for interactions, and 0.66 for spectating). We also manually marked situations where something interesting or unusual happened. Our annotations included a pointer to the situation in the video, so we could easily go back to the original data to verify our annotations.

We also conducted semi-structured interviews with users and spectators. In particular, we asked them to describe the displays, asked whether they had communicated with people at the other location and whether the others had responded, what they thought where the people at the other location were and whether they felt connected to them. The interview data was anonymized and put into a shared form that was analyzed by two researchers.

### Results

Over the two week field test we have been able to record and analyze 30888 people by-passing the screens and 1234 interactions with the screens. The average conversion rate over all conditions was 4%. According to our experience, this is

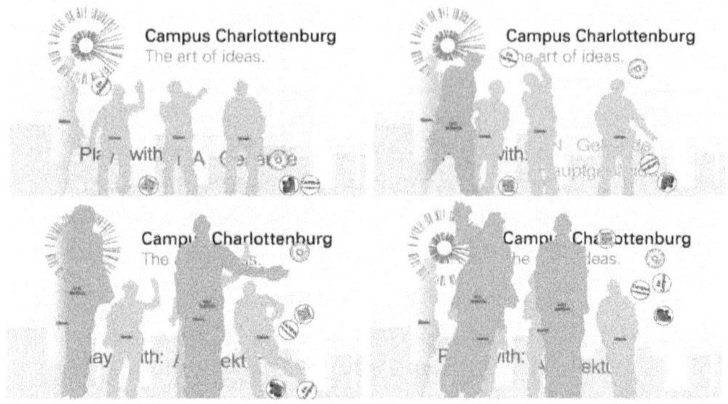


Figure 4. Remote honey-pot effect: Users attracted other users from another location.

in line with other public display deployments and industry values. We will now breakdown the data and show the key results.

*Remote and Real Honey-pot Effect*

A Kruskal-Wallis test revealed a significant effect of condition on conversion rate ($\chi^2(5) = 788.5, p < .01$). A post-hoc test using Wilcoxon tests with Bonferroni correction showed significant differences between the Baseline and all conditions except the Recorded User, between Remote Passer-by and Remote User, and between all conditions and the Local User ($p < .05$), see Figure 5.

So, we found a remote honey-pot effect. Observing people interacting at a different location (condition Remote User) increased the conversion rate by 136% compared to the baseline (see Figure 4 for an example). Recorded users increased the conversion rate only by 38% (differences to Baseline and Remote User were not significant). We also found, what we believe to be the first experimental proof, of the honey-pot effect for public displays. When others were already interacting at a screen (condition Local User) the conversion rate increased by +604% (see Figure 6 for an example).

*Honey-pot for Interaction Duration*

We found that if there were remote passers-by, interaction duration was significantly longer than if not (mean 33.3s vs. 9.3s, t-test, t(1176) = 11.4, $p < .01$). If the remote users interacted, interaction duration was even longer (mean 53.7s vs. 33.3s, t-test, t(386.5) = 3.8, $p < .05$). The same was true locally. If there were local passers-by, interaction duration was significantly longer than if not (mean 15.7s vs. 30.4s, t-test, t(817) = 5.5, $p < .01$). If the other local users interacted, interaction duration was even longer (39s vs. 30.4s, t-test, t(1098) = 2.72, $p < .01$). We also found that if local users or passers-by left, it was significantly more likely during the next 5s that another user left than otherwise ($\chi^2$ test, $\chi^2(1)$= 435.2, $p < .01$ for users, and $\chi^2(1) = 53.9$, $p < .01$ for passers-by), while this was not the case for remote or recorded users leaving.

Figure 6. Typical example of the honey-pot effect. Two users interacted with the screen, which attracted the attention of a passer-by (1). As the two previous users left (2) the passer-by approaches the screen (3) and started to interact (4).

*More Users Strengthen the Honey-pot*

Finally, we found a significant effect of the number of remote users on the remote honey-pot effect (see Figure 7). The more users were interacting remotely, the higher the conversion rate (up to about five remote users). A Kruskal Wallis test revealed a significant effect of number of remote users on whether passers-by interacted ($\chi^2(10) = 916$, $p < .01$). A post-hoc test using Wilcoxon tests with Bonferroni correction showed the significant differences between 0 and all except 10 users, 1 and all except 8 and 10, 2-5 and 3-5 remote users ($p < .05$).

This was also true for the local honey-pot effect. The more users interacted, the higher the conversion rate. A Kruskal Wallis test revealed a significant effect of number of local users on whether passers-by interacted ($\chi^2(7) = 806.7$, $p < .01$). A post-hoc test using Wilcoxon tests with Bonferroni correction showed the significant differences between all

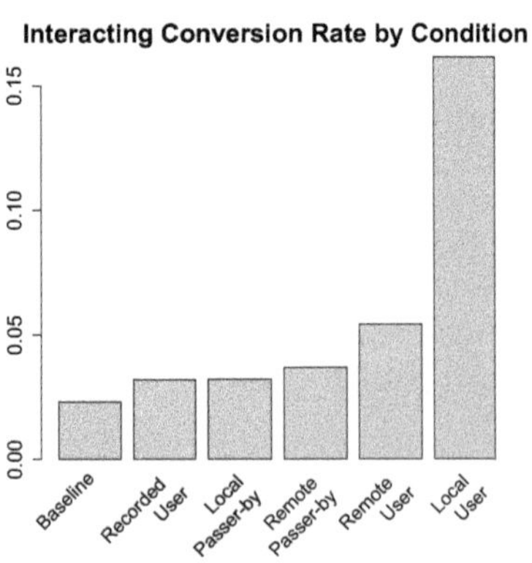


Figure 5. Conversion rate by condition. The remote honey-pot (Remote User) increased the conversion rate by +136% and the local honey-pot (Local User) by +604% compared to the baseline.

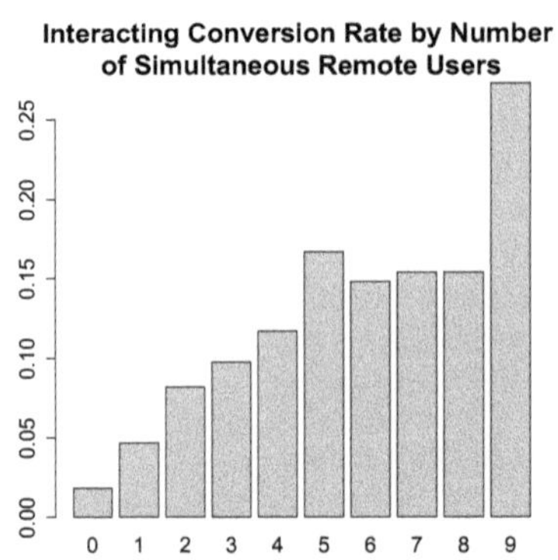


Figure 7. The remote honey-pot effect grew stronger with more remote users.

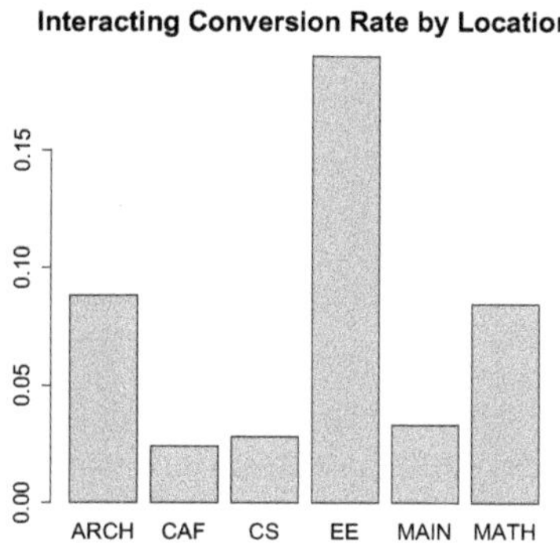


**Figure 8. Conversion rate by location.**

pairwise comparisons except 3-4, 4-7, 5-7 and 6-7 ($p < .05$).

Last, with one-way ANOVA, we found a significant effect of the number of other locally interacting users on interaction duration ($F(7,1226) = 11.7$, $p < .01$), and of other remotely interacting users on interaction duration ($F(9,1224) = 17.2$, $p < .01$). The interaction duration increased with the number of other users.

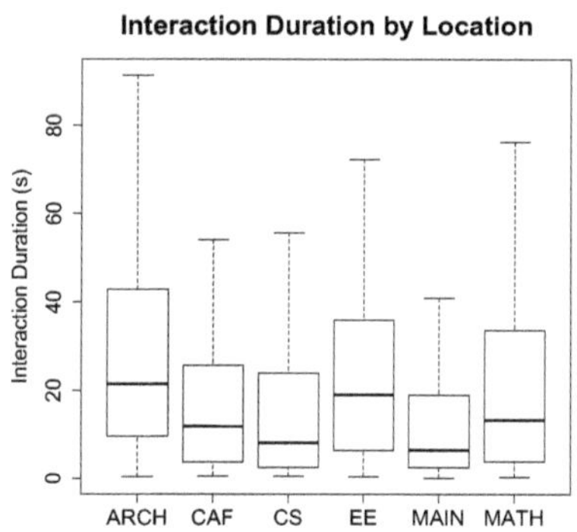


**Figure 9. Interaction duration by location.**

### *Differences between Locations*

As described above, in one of the conditions we put nametags on the silhouettes. We thought that this would make it clearer with whom you were interacting but this had no significant impact on conversion rate or interaction duration. However we found significant differences in usage between locations, both regarding conversion rate (Figure 8) and interaction duration (Figure 9). A Kruskal-Wallis test revealed a significant effect of location on conversion rate ($\chi^2(5) = 697$, $p < .01$). A post-hoc test using Wilcoxon tests with Bonferroni correction showed the significant differences between all locations comparisons except MAIN-CS, ARCH-MATH, and CS-CAF ($p < .05$). With one-way ANOVA, we found a significant effect of location on interaction duration ($F(5,1228) = 4.4$, $p < .01$). A Tukey's pairwise comparison revealed significant differences between locations ARCH-MAIN, CS-EE, and ARCH-CS ($p < .05$). Hence a strong pattern that might explain the rather large variances of duration of the interaction would be the different character of space for each screen.

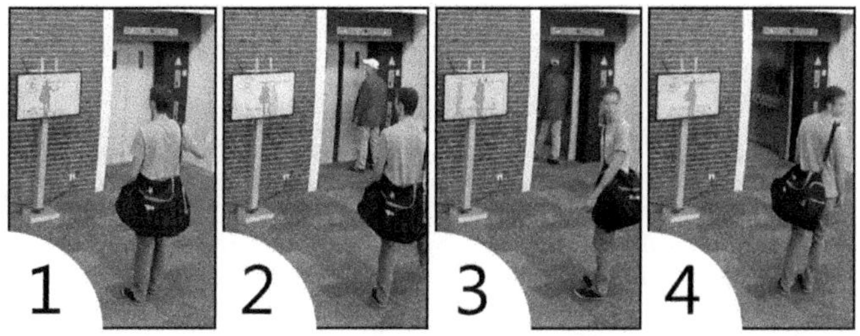


**Figure 10. Many users had difficulty understanding that the screens were connected in a media space, despite our efforts of communicating that on the screen. When they saw somebody pass at a remote location, sometimes they would turn around, apparently in the expectation that the other person would be behind them (*ghost effect*).**

Our study design did not allow us to collect quantitative data for further analysis but we will talk more about the different types of places in the discussion.

## Interaction with Communiplay

### *Video Observation*

From the analysis of the recorded depth video we have been able to observe a variety of known and also novel interaction patterns with Communiplay. People played mostly with the objects, but also communicated with remote users, e.g., by waving, making funny shapes, playing with the silhouettes, and mimicing local and also remote users. The frequency of interactions is given in Figure 11.

One recurring effect that we observed rather frequently was that when somebody passed by a remote screen, people turned around, expecting that the person was behind them. Because of the frequency of this observation, we called this the "ghost effect" (examples are shown in Figure 12 and Figure 10, and the effect was also observed in the prestudy). Although people from different locations were drawn in different colors, and had location labels drawn over their bodies, was apparently was not enough of a hint that they were at a different location. Sometimes, the shared interaction between the different locations was also experienced as annoying. In particular, when people tried to perform more complex interactions, like picking up an object, remote by-passers could

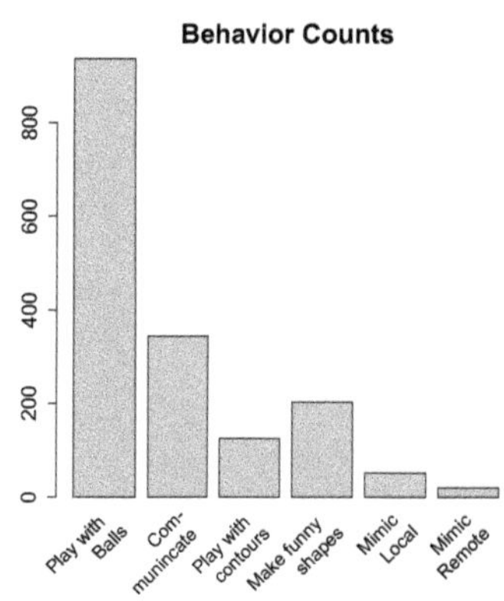


**Figure 11. Number of occurrences of different behaviors. Users spend most of the time playing with balls, followed by communicating (e.g., waving), making funny shapes, and playing with the contours.**

**Figure 12. One downside of the connection of the screens occurred sometimes when people tried to interact with the display, like this person trying to pick up a ball. Then, when a remote person walked through the screen, they would often kick the balls away (also an example of the ghost effect).**

disturb the interaction by causing all objects to fly around (see Figure 12).

When users tried to communicate with each other, this was mostly through waving (Figure 13). Users both waved to say hello as well as goodbye. We also observed a number of cases of people imitating others who interacted in the same location or remotely.

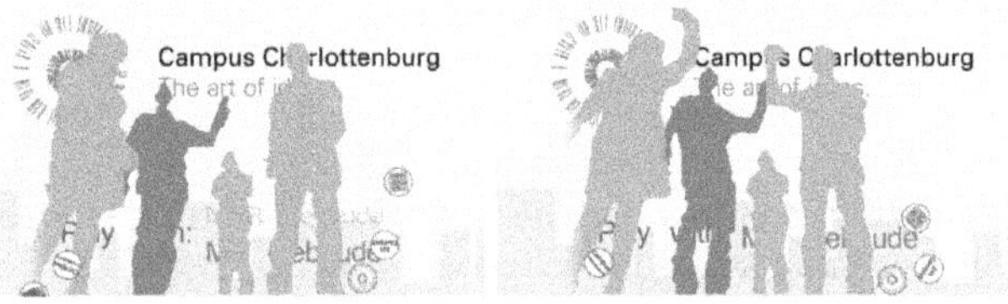

**Figure 13. People waving each other when entering the display.**

One example of playing with silhouettes is given in Figure 14. Sometimes, either because a touch was misinterpreted or because one user started punching each other, a (remote) fight broke off. People performed surprisingly acrobatic fight moves, like high kicks. Most of the playing with silhouettes was however more peaceful, like people poking each other or shaking hands.

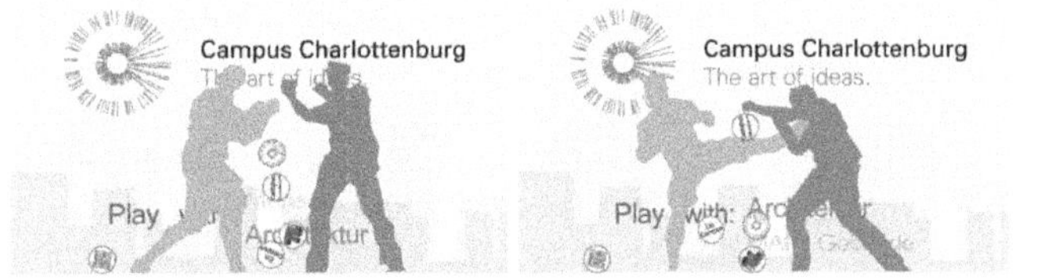


**Figure 14. Two users in different locations fighting each other.**

We also observed a number of interesting interactions with recorded users. During the deployment, the recorded users were drawn like remote users, so there was no easy way for users to distinguish between them (but in the figures, we highlighted recorded users in black). For example, Figure 15 shows a user mimicking two recorded users. Figure 16 shows a user trying to interact with a recorded user through poking, punching, and playing with balls.

*Interviews and Live Observation*

We also did live observations and semi-structured interviews with about 100 persons, and in 55 cases they also filled in a small survey. We would like to stress that it is very hard to stop people in public settings that are just passing by, so most of our respondents either stopped for looking at or interacting with the system.

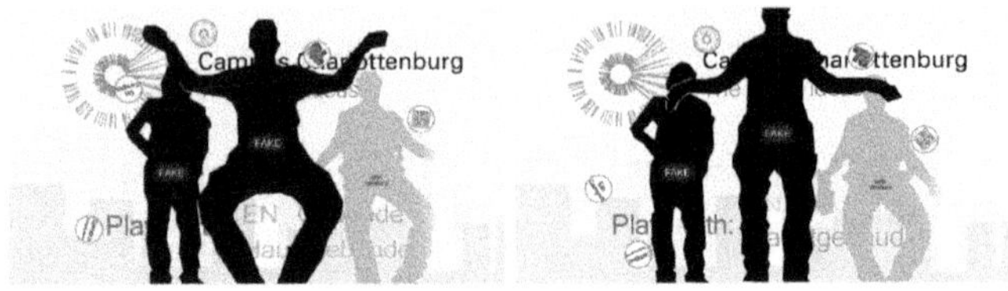

**Figure 15. A user mimics a recorded user (recorded user highlighted in black).**

We were a bit surprised that apparently it was very difficult for users to understand that the screens were connected. Probably because most existing media space research was done in relatively tight groups over prolonged time, we were not aware of reports of users having difficulty to understand that the screens are connected. 32% of the respondents noticed in forehand that it was other real persons on the screen and that the silhouettes where not just a screen decoration, but the remaining 68% did not explicitly notice this and were primarily stopping for interacting with the objects. Possibly because of the physical design of the screen stands and the placement in entrances, many users expected that the screens would be information screens. Some even expected them to be touch screens (which they were not). One interviewee said that "the balls on the ground looks like the buttons on a touch screen, you should explain the game better". When people at remote locations were passing by, they were often mistaken for video recordings or people passing behind the user locally. Some people said that "[the] connectivity sense of the other place [could be improved]", or "there should be better evidence that you can play with others", while we thought that we had already included quite explicit hints, which were apparently not noticed by many users.

Over time, more users learned that the screens were connected. Many said that they "got it" when they saw the screens in other locations, or when they saw somebody passing by remotely. Some people also reported that they developed a habit to wave every time they passed by the displays (mostly without slowing down). They stated that they hoped somebody would wave back, and sometimes somebody would. Some cafeteria employees reported that they went to the screens for each of their breaks to play a bit, and sometimes someone at another location would play with them.

**Figure 16. A user touches and tries to interact with a recorded user (recorded user highlighted in black).**

Another common pattern was that one person of a group stopped and demonstrated the system to some friends or colleagues. During the interview, the demonstrating person often took a leading role and explained that they had used it before or have seen it at some other location, and now wanted to show it to their friends.

When we asked why they stopped the most common reply was that the screens were attractive visually, like: "[I] just stopped for a short glance, saw something interesting", or "[I stopped] to look and play". Furthermore the game was experienced rather fun to play with but comments also indicated that the overall experience was rated higher than the actual game.

Many comments focused around ideas how to improve the game and how to make the communication more direct, i.e. "perhaps a score list of the sites". Also people in groups were more likely to make a quick stop than single persons especially in busy areas. Overall we noted some unease by single persons to interact in front of the display. They preferred to first spend a moment or two observing what was going on in the local proximity.

When we asked what the silhouettes represent, most find it hard to put in words what they experienced and the replies become rather vague. Many also avoided to speculate and said that they had not fully understood the interaction. However when asked what they focused on during the interaction: 36% told us the they played with the objects, 32% observed other silhouettes, 25% played with their own contour. Only 7% told us that they played with contours of remote people.

## DISCUSSION

By primarily studying the first seconds of interaction (getting people to stop and start interacting) we have learned more about the use, what attracts the usage of Communiplay and the key factors that impact these findings. We will now discuss some of the core results in more detail.

### Honey-Pot

The key finding in this study is that we could show the existence of a honey-pot effect. The strongest honey-pot effect was local presence, but also remote presence on the screens had a significant honey-pot effect.

Possible reasons may vary from quite simple, like the fact that motion attracts attention, over more complex, that people exhibit imitation behavior, or are attracted by crowds, to high level reasons, like that multiplayer games are more fun than single player games, or that playful communication is more interesting than just playing.

It has been shown that moving, especially looming, stimuli attract visual attention [13]. Remote people shown on the screen cause motion. Thus it may be that the conversion rate increases simply because this motion attracts more attention. However, we had partially addressed this by including permanent motion on the screen, and this would not explain the apparent difference between remote and recorded users.

One caveat with our study design is that the conditions are not randomly distributed over time of day. It could therefore be that the conversion rate is simply different on different times of day, e.g. higher at noon, and that some conditions (e.g., other simultaneous users) occur more frequently e.g., at noon, and that therefore it would appear as if the conversion rate would be higher with simultaneous users. As a precaution, we used the conversion rate as the dependent variable, which is much more stable over time of day than, e.g., number of users per hour. As a second precaution, we conducted the analysis separately for morning, noon, afternoon, and night, and the effects seem to be stable over these different periods.

From the interviews and observations combined with our data we can now speculate around the difference between local and remote honey-pot effect. One reason could be that people do not fully understand the remote representation and hence the effect becomes weaker. Another reason might be that handling personal space is easier done in real physical space and people feel too close to each other on screen, or do not want to disturb/interrupt others.

Interestingly, recorded users seemed to be less effective than remote users (although not significant). However, our experiment did not allow us to determine the reason for these effects so we can only speculate that the lack of shared interaction had more impact than was unrevealed in our observations and interviews. Moreover, having two people at two different locations at overlapping times is less frequent so even if we have not been able to fully demonstrate the benefit of using recorded scenes we still think this an interesting strand for further explorations.

As stated earlier, the duration of the interaction was not significantly different across the different conditions. However differences in duration of the interaction were significant between the different places and we will discuss this next.

### Type of place

We observed a clear difference in conversion rate but also interaction duration between the six different locations that were used in the fieldstudy. From conversion rates and interaction durations, it would look as three (CAF, CS and MAIN) would be the least successful locations.

However, looking at the total number of interactions, it can be seen that these locations actually have the highest number of interactions, but then lower conversion rates and shorter interaction durations.

In future work it would be interesting to look more into how the flow in a place affects the conversion rate and how to optimize the different combinations of honey-pot effects we discussed here, i.e. local and remote, due to the nature of the place.

### Playful remote interaction

People did not only interact with the shared objects in Communiplay but also used a whole range of behaviors to more playfully interact and communicate with persons on the screen, i.e. by waving, peeking and poking, and mimicing behavior.

The "ghost effect" was an example of people not understanding that other users were at a different location. It would be interesting to further explore how different levels of temporariness and abstractions affect the conversion rate and duration of the interaction, as well as the experienced interaction and the awareness of the remote persons, and how this comes together. Moreover, different forms of representations could also be further explored. As noted earlier people just passing by sometimes ruined the experience for people interacting with Communiplay and it might be a good idea to differentiate between passers-by and people interacting with Communiplay, and e.g., not letting people just passing by to interact with the objects.

## CONCLUSION

In this study we have learned that the integration of multiple public displays into a media space is a promising direction for public displays and can make them more attractive and valuable. We observed a local and a remote honey-pot effect. Further, both of these effects also increased the interaction duration. Finally, more users strengthened the honey-pot effect (both locally and remotely, and both for conversion rates and interaction durations). The over-crowding effect that showed in the pre-study was not present in the public deployment. We believe that these effects generalize to other kinds of public displays, although this needs to be validated in future studies.

We learned that the playful interaction with remote people offered by our system works even if the communication is very temporal and abstract. Moreover, people did not only play with the shared objects but also used many other means to more playfully interact and communicate, i.e. by waving, peeking and poking, and mimicing behavior.

The main implication from this project is that public displays and media spaces can be integrated effectively. The local honey-pot created by public displays translates to a remote honey-pot when displays are connected into a media space. Thus, such a public display media space can become an effective social catalyst, both locally and remotely.

## ACKNOWLEDGEMENTS

We particularly want to thank Constantin Schmidt for tremendous support during the deployment, and Tiare Feuchtner and Andreas Fender for help during annotation. This work was supported by the ICT Labs of the European Institute of Innovation and Technology.

## REFERENCES

1. Agamanolis, S. Designing displays for human connectedness. In *Public and Situated Displays*. Springer, 2003, 309–334.
2. Behrens, M., Fatah gen. Schieck, A., Kostopoulou, E., North, S., Motta, W., Ye, L., and Schnadelbach, H. Exploring the effect of spatial layout on mediated urban interactions. In *Proc. of PerDis '13*, ACM (New York, NY, USA, 2013), 79–84.
3. Brignull, H., and Rogers, Y. Enticing people to interact with large public displays in public spaces. In *Proc. of INTERACT '03*, vol. 3 (2003), 17–24.
4. Cao, X., Massimi, M., and Balakrishnan, R. Flashlight jigsaw: an exploratory study of an ad-hoc multi-player game on public displays. In *Proc. of CSCW '08*, ACM (2008), 77–86.
5. Finke, M., Tang, A., Leung, R., and Blackstock, M. Lessons learned: game design for large public displays. In *Proc. of DIMEA '08*, ACM (2008), 26–33.
6. Fontana, B. The relocation of ambient sound: Urban sound sculpture, 1987.
7. Fritsch, J., and Brynskov, M. 7 between experience, affect, and information: Experimental urban interfaces in the climate change debate. *From Social Butterfly to Engaged Citizen: Urban Informatics, Social Media, Ubiquitous Computing, and Mobile Technology to Support Citizen Engagement* (2011), 115.
8. Galloway, and Rabinowitz. Hole in space, 1980.
9. Häkkilä, J., Koskenranta, O., Posti, M., Ventä-Olkkonen, L., and Colley, A. Clearing the virtual window: connecting two locations with interactive public displays. In *Proc. of PerDis '13*, ACM (2013), 85–90.
10. Huang, E. M., and Mynatt, E. D. Semi-public displays for small, co-located groups. In *Proc. of CHI '03*, ACM (2003), 49–56.
11. Karahalios, K., and Donath, J. Telemurals: linking remote spaces with social catalysts. In *Proc. of CHI '04*, ACM (2004), 615–622.
12. Krueger, M. W., Gionfriddo, T., and Hinrichsen, K. Videoplace - an artificial reality. In *ACM SIGCHI Bulletin*, vol. 16, ACM (1985), 35–40.
13. Müller, J., Alt, F., Michelis, D., and Schmidt, A. Requirements and design space for interactive public displays. In *Proc. of MM '10*, ACM (2010), 1285–1294.
14. Müller, J., Walter, R., Bailly, G., Nischt, M., and Alt, F. Looking glass: a field study on noticing interactivity of a shop window. In *Proc. of CHI '12*, ACM (2012), 297–306.
15. O'Hara, K., Glancy, M., and Robertshaw, S. Understanding collective play in an urban screen game. In *Proc. of CSCW '08*, ACM (2008), 67–76.
16. Olson, M. H., and Bly, S. A. The portland experience: A report on a distributed research group. *International Journal of Man-Machine Studies 34*, 2 (1991), 211–228.
17. Schroeter, R. Engaging new digital locals with interactive urban screens to collaboratively improve the city. In *Proc. of CSCW '12*, ACM (2012), 227–236.
18. Ten Koppel, M., Bailly, G., Müller, J., and Walter, R. Chained displays: configurations of public displays can be used to influence actor-, audience-, and passer-by behavior. In *Proc. of CHI '12*, ACM (2012), 317–326.
19. Tollmar, K., Chincholle, D., Klasson, B., and Stephanson, T. Videocafe - exploring mediaspaces in public places within organizations. *Behaviour & Information Technology 20*, 2 (2001), 101–110.
20. Walter, R., Bailly, G., and Müller, J. Strikeapose: revealing mid-air gestures on public displays. In *Proc. of CHI '13*, CHI '13, ACM (New York, NY, USA, 2013), 841–850.

# Posting for Community and Culture: Considerations for the Design of Interactive Digital Bulletin Boards

**Claude Fortin**
Making Culture Lab (MCL)

**Carman Neustaedter**
Connections Lab (cLab)

**Kate Hennessy**
Making Culture Lab (MCL)

School of Interactive Arts & Technology (SIAT), Simon Fraser University
250 - 13450 102nd Avenue, Surrey, British Columbia, Canada, V3T 0A3
{cfortin, carman_neustaedter, hennessy_kate}@sfu.ca

## ABSTRACT

The next decade is likely to see a shift in digital public displays moving from non-interactive to interactive content. This will likely create a need for digital bulletin boards and for a better understanding of how such displays should be designed to encourage community members to interact with them. Our study addresses this by exploring community bulletin boards as a ubiquitous type of participatory non-digital display "in the wild". Our results highlight how they are used for content of local and contextual relevance, and how cultures of participation, personalization, location, the tangible character of architecture, access, control and flexibility might affect community members' level of engagement with them. Our analysis suggests entry points as design considerations intrinsically linked to the users' sense of agency within a delineated space. Overlaps with related work are identified throughout to provide further validation of previous findings in this area of research.

### Author Keywords

Large public displays; digital bulletin boards; observation; urban computing; entry points; cultures of participation.

### ACM Classification Keywords

H.5.m. Information interfaces and presentation (e.g., HCI): Miscellaneous.

## INTRODUCTION

Public digital displays can broadly be described as wall-sized video projections or digital displays using LED, LCD or plasma screens situated in public space. Such displays can provide people with contextual maps/information, announce status updates in terminals, advertise merchandise in shop windows and publicize site-specific resources. Currently, the majority of public digital displays remain non-interactive. They are mostly used for advertising or broadcast with a one-way flow of information delivery. Yet the coming decade is likely to see an increasing number of *interactive* digital displays in public settings [22].

Given this, our goal was to understand how interactive public displays, akin to *digital bulletin boards*, should be designed to meet the needs of their users and to encourage community members to interact with them as part of a *culture of participation* engaged through public usage [13]. By participation we are referring to acts such as the posting of new information, commenting on existing information, or the "taking" of content by individual community members. This contrasts with the current use of public displays, which is largely concerned with the *publication* of information, often by companies or institutions, where viewers look at the displays rather than interact with them.

To address this, we conducted an empirical study using design ethnography to investigate how communities exchange information on traditional community bulletin boards. Given that new media often borrows from existing cultural forms [5], we chose to study traditional community bulletin boards for several reasons. First, it is currently difficult to study interactive digital bulletin boards because there are few instances in which they have been deployed in public settings. Second, bulletin boards constitute one of the most ubiquitous "interactive" types of paper-based public display. Thus, they are arguably a precursor to future interactive public displays. Third, and following from this, traditional bulletin boards serve an important community-building function in public space [8]. This leads us to believe that existing practices around non-digital bulletin boards may provide a valid basis for understanding how communities might use digital bulletin boards, and possibly by extension, certain types of other public digital displays.

Our study focused on understanding what types of content people place on bulletin boards and how this ties to the boards' communities. We also sought to understand how attributes of postings and bulletin boards make them more inviting in terms of their location, context, and architectural setting. Our observational study reports on findings similar to those published in the past [3, 8, 19, 28]. We bring further validity to these findings by identifying each study in which they have been reported and by framing them in the broader context of bulletin boards and digital displays. We also extend previous work by offering a more


*CHI 2014*, April 26 - May 01 2014, Toronto, ON, Canada

http://dx.doi.org/10.1145/2556288.2556970

comprehensive classification of postings, by construing user communities as the primary stakeholder and by placing a deeper focus on entry points for action in public spaces.

To foreshadow, our results show that bulletin boards are primarily used to post information of local and of contextual relevance. Boards placed in locations with an existing culture of participation received the most postings along with boards facilitating the appropriation and personalization of content. In these spaces, tangibility, flexibility, access and control each played an important role in enabling posting. Together, these results suggest design considerations, each intrinsically linked to the users' sense of agency and discussed in relation to geographic relevance, contextual relevance and entry points that invite action.

## RELATED WORK

Most of the early prototypes for interactive digital bulletin boards were designed and deployed in research lab environments over the past decade. More recently, designers have conducted studies to evaluate their prototypes in the world, often in semi-public or public space. Some researchers have even created a permanent infrastructure of networked digital displays in an urban setting as a means to facilitate public display research [24].

### Interactive Digital Bulletin Boards for Research Labs

NOTIFICATION COLLAGE (NC) was one of the first shared display prototypes. Its UI followed the metaphor of bulletin boards with a collage aesthetic [17]. Implemented in an academic research laboratory, the simultaneous use of NC on a large digital display in the lab and on personal computers in the lab or at home was found to enhance its use and increase social interaction and communication among users inside and outside the laboratory space. Similarly, YETI was designed to simultaneously support multimedia content sharing between research labs in California and Japan to connect the two communities across time zones and space [9]. In this case, however, the importance of content was found to prevail over interaction.

CWALL also used a bulletin board format where users could place text or images on the screen; a study found that users' expectations varied in relation to the placement of the display, and that motivation and use of the display depended on how much effort was needed, and on whether users could see their postings and feel part of the display community [26]. Studies of the digital bulletin board, MESSYBOARD, showed that visibility highly impacted usage and that usage was related to the nature of the community, their projects and their collaborations [12]. Churchill et al. designed and deployed the PLASMA POSTER NETWORK in their workplace and similarly found that the culture of the workplace contributed to the boards' success [8]. Moreover, the flexibility of their display for supporting varied content was highly valued. Our study builds on this past research which highlights the importance of context and of a culture of participation in public display usage.

### Interactive Digital Bulletin Boards for Public Spaces

A second set of digital bulletin boards has been designed for public spaces, the focus of this paper. CAMPIELLO was designed for communities where people could share and read tourist guides, flyers, maps and newspapers by linking together paper and digital artifacts [15, 16]. A study of its use in schools revealed that the system helped reinforce a sense of community amongst students [1]. The E-CHANNEL system was deployed for three years on several displays within a university campus to study how users manage content when there is a clear separation between two stakeholders: display owners and content providers [11]. The study identifies several key design trade-offs between the control of content vs. access, flexibility or usability.

Churchill and her collaborators studied several prototypes that functioned as digital bulletin boards. CHIPLACE and CSCWPLACE were deployed in ACM conferences [9], while EYECANVAS was deployed in a neighborhood café/art gallery [10]. Studies of these displays found that each of the prototypes provided a context-specific means of content sharing that enhanced existing communication tools; that their strategic placement defined how often and in what ways they were used; that the prototypes were quickly adapted to users' needs, cultural norms and their physical setting; and that visual content tended to be most popular.

COCOLLAGE was designed for a large display in a café located in a university district to encourage a stronger sense of community [23]. A study found that COCOLLAGE did not instigate new interaction, but did make patrons more aware that they were sharing space. DYNAMO supported the cooperative sharing and exchange of a wide range of media in a communal setting [6]. Studied in a high school student lounge, Brignull et al.'s study found that DYNAMO lent itself to unexpected appropriation uses and different degrees of personalization; promoted a sense of collective ownership of the platform and its surroundings; and generated a social atmosphere and opportunities for people to engage with one another. CITYWALL was a large 2.5 m display that allowed users to post and interact with Flickr™ media in a downtown area [25]. Users were found to crowd around the display, learn from each other and develop social protocols surrounding interaction (e.g. turn taking).

The most recent prototype, however, is DIGIFIEDS, a digital public notice area (PNA) deployed in an urban environment in Finland for 2 months [2]. After having collected data in log files, and conducted field observations, semi-structured interviews and field trials during summer 2011, the study found that community-related information and content of local relevance rated highest amongst content providers and viewers; that privacy concerns were a major issue in using the display in public view; that there was a correlation between content posted on DIGIFIEDS and on traditional bulletin boards; and that digital natives were more likely to use the platform than people from older generations.

### Studies of Non-Interactive Bulletin Boards and Displays

Finally, other studies have examined non-digital bulletin boards and non-interactive displays "in the wild". First, Huang et al.'s study showed that to encourage interaction, displays should be placed at eye-level and at arm's reach; that although large displays tend to be more eye-catching, their ideal size is of human scale; and that physical content placed next to a digital display may attract attention [19].

Second, in their work on traditional community billboards in public areas, Churchill et al. found that boards are situated in places where people can spend time looking at them (e.g., waiting rooms, bus stops), places of leisure, and places where one looks for information (e.g., libraries) [8]. Boards allowed people to voice their viewpoints and advertise for activities and events, and also provided a sense of community. Monitoring ranged from formal to open with different levels of control being exercised over what and how content gets posted to no moderation at all. Lastly, content often had a temporal component where it may be relevant to a particular date or time period. In a follow-up study in the workplace, when comparing bulletin boards in smaller organizations with those in larger ones, they found that people in smaller groups where everyone knows one another are more likely to send emails or exchange information face-to-face. By contrast, in larger organizations, they found that "people felt that posting content to poster boards was more socially appropriate and did not risk being an unwanted intrusion" [8, p. 101].

Third, Taylor and Cheverst did a survey in North West England on the use of noticeboards in a rural community with the intention of exploring how community display practices might be digitally augmented by technology [28]. The study found that people posted notices on almost any surface which afforded noticeability; tended to put up content that advertised small, local businesses, items for sale or job openings; did not take down notices when these were "stale" (p. 3); exercised various degrees of access control over boards; and sought flexibility and ease of use.

Fourth, in their extensive study of 29 public notice areas in several towns of Switzerland and Germany, Alt et al. found that these advertising displays should provide board owner with control (while our study recommends the opposite); are mostly useful in informing people about locally relevant content; should have a flexible design to meet the needs of those who create, post or control content; and must easily support the taking away of content [3].

Although many of the observations made in these last three studies overlapped with our own, there are substantial differences in our work's methodology and focus. First, the analyses in these studies heavily rely on unstructured or semi-structured interviews with different stakeholders such as content providers, viewers and display owners/managers [3, 8, 28]. Ours is not based on interview data. Conducted without the use of extant theory, we adopted an approach that sought to generate concepts from focused observation and detailed note-taking onsite. Second, we present findings that hone in on the user rather than an analysis based on balancing the needs of different stakeholders. Third, we used a larger sampling frame collected in a different major metropolitan area, which provides a strong basis for comparison and validation with two prior studies [3, 8]. Fourth, we made a deeper analysis of posted content and organized it in fine-grained categories. Fifth, we more broadly discuss where bulletin boards should and should not be situated as a result of field observations. And sixth, our main contribution consists of proposing some new, more abstract and conceptual entry points for action.

## METHODOLOGY

Our goal was to focus our observations on traditional community bulletin boards located in public spaces to learn more about how people socially interact through and with this cultural artifact [27]. We used mixed methods to gather data and constant comparative analysis to analyze it [14].

### Data Collection

All the empirical data analyzed in this study was collected over a period of eight weeks in early 2012. Fifty-nine bulletin boards containing a total of 1297 postings were surveyed in Metro Vancouver, Canada. Because this area contains significant suburban sprawl, we were able to test whether people were posting content of urban relevance in adjacent suburbs. Locations were chosen to offer a cross-section of a broad diversity of communities.

We conducted observations in many types of environments. Each site visit lasted from 15 to 45 minutes. When possible and relevant, we conducted multiple observation sessions, varying the days, the week and the time of day during which we visited the site, especially when the bulletin boards were in more public, high traffic settings such as publicly accessible buildings or outdoors near the street.

The principal neighborhoods visited in this study included a mix of urban and suburban boroughs in five types of environments. The residential environments included a few suburban housing complexes, a remote on-campus graduate residence, and the main lobby of an urban housing co-op. The designated areas of the educational environments were rooms, hallways, and common lounges on three university campus sites. Urban and suburban municipally-run establishments such as libraries, community centers, skating rinks, public pools, and recreational centers comprised the indoor public environments. The outdoor public environments included sites where bulletin boards were located outside such establishments, on university campus sites, around store exteriors and in various bus shelters. Commercial environments included small and large retail businesses on university campus sites, in urban or suburban boroughs and in a shopping mall.

The first author (A1) was responsible for collecting and recording all of the raw data in the form of detailed field notes and photographs. A1 conducted the field study using a focused ethnographic approach that sought to carefully describe observations with detailed note-taking onsite. The visual appearance of the bulletin boards, the postings, and the context they were embedded in were recorded in 113 digital images with some boards being photographed more than once from different angles and distances. Photos were used as visual reference and for illustrative purposes only.

### Method of Analysis

The principal method of analysis used in this study is constant comparative analysis from Glaserian grounded theory (GGT) [14]. The coding techniques used were respectively open coding, core coding and selective coding applied to the field notes, to generate concepts by gradually moving from description to abstraction. In keeping with GGT's creative conceptualization principle, a single person conducted the data collection, coding and content analysis to provide an acceptable level of reliability in determining general patterns and to increase the levels of integrity and consistency [29]. In our study, the constant comparative method was also useful in collecting and analyzing data about locations where we expected to find bulletin boards, but found none. Field notes and photos were also taken at some of these locations as a reference for comparison.

Overall, we made three salient observations about how people posted content to the bulletin boards we studied. These related to the geographic relevance and contextual relevance of content (findings supported by prior research [3, 8, 28]), and to physical and aesthetic attributes of postings and bulletin boards, which could invite different degrees of engagement in terms of location, context, and architectural setting. The next sections present these results.

## GEOGRAPHIC RELEVANCE

Our analysis of bulletin board content revealed a strong correlation between content and geographic relevance. We define geographic relevance as the topographical range within which the content is pertinent. For instance, a personal ad offering babysitting services is generally geographically relevant to a neighborhood or city, but not to a whole province or country. Its scope is limited to a well-delineated zone, described in terms of geophysical distance.

Six geopolitical categories for classifying the geographic relevance of our postings emerged from our analysis: immediate local (within a neighborhood, which represented 69.5% of content), municipal (17.5%), regional (referring to the administrative state, 6%), national (5%), international (1.5%) and non-localized (i.e. web-based relevance, 0.5%). When there was overlap between categories, we made judgment calls on who was posting the content (a resident vs. the government) and the likely impact (city vs. region).

As had been previously observed in a number of studies [3, 8, 11, 28], we found that content of local relevance strongly dominated. Our results showed that 87% of content was relevant either to the neighborhood or to the city it was posted in. The other 13% of postings were on matters of regional (6%), national (5%) or international (1.5%) concern, with a mere 0.5% of content being related to the Internet and thus lacking ties with a specific place.

We often think of virtual communities as global and placeless [7]. However, our results strongly suggest that the virtual communities of digital bulletin boards would be defined by a sense of place and thus most likely use these platforms to communicate information that is either within local, municipal or regional geopolitical proximity. Given how scarce postings of relevance beyond this range were, it seems legitimate to wonder whether a digital bulletin board would be used at all for such content, as our observations showed that most postings were intended for people living in, or frequently passing by, a board's neighborhood or city.

## CONTEXTUAL RELEVANCE

Our analysis revealed that there is also a strong tie between the type of content posted and the type of environment that it was posted in. In other words, content was contextually relevant. The next two subsections outline the categories of postings according to the environments they were posted in.

### Categories of Postings

The manifest content of the 1297 postings was coded into twelve major themes forming the following categories of postings: administrative, business, recreational, educational, social/political/environmental, government-related, cultural, maintenance, health/well-being, personal ads, maintenance, and work/employment. These categories may at times overlap or present some ambiguity and although most of them are self-explanatory, a few need to be clearly defined.

Here, we briefly describe these. We defined a subject category as administrative when the subject pertained to the administrative information about the environment itself. For instance, a posting about a library's opening hours or about a housing complex's rules of conduct fell in this category. The maintenance category applied to the maintenance of the environment itself. For example, household tips in a housing complex or 'a dog scooping' ad. All content which was posted by an individual advertising a service or good was tagged as personal ads. This could include an apartment for rent, furniture for sale, tutoring services or housecleaning ads. Social/political/environmental is a catch-all category used to classify all postings with a social, political or environmental relevance. This would include postings about food banks, recycling, neighborhood events, community-supported agriculture or protests.

At a surface level, this illustrates the types of content that people already place on public bulletin boards, which suggests the types of content they may wish to place on interactive digital boards in the future. Yet more deeply, it begins to reveal interesting patterns related to the type of environment in which the content is placed, outlined next.

| RESIDENTIAL | | EDUCATIONAL | | INDOOR PUBLIC | | OUTDOOR PUBLIC | | COMMERCIAL | | TOTAL | |
|---|---|---|---|---|---|---|---|---|---|---|---|
| # of bulletin boards | 7 | # of bulletin boards | 9 | # of bulletin boards | 29 | # of bulletin boards | 8 | # of bulletin boards | 6 | # of bulletin boards | 59 |
| # of postings | 34 | # of postings | 183 | # of postings | 656 | # of postings | 272 | # of postings | 152 | # of postings | 1297 |
| CATEGORIES | % | CATEGORIES | % | CATEGORIES | % | CATEGORIES | % | CATEGORIES | % | CATEGORIES | % |
| administrative | 47.0 | cultural | 29.0 | cultural | 30.2 | personal ads | 30.0 | cultural | 22.4 | cultural | 25.4 |
| maintenance | 14.7 | educational | 25.7 | recreational | 18.3 | recreational | 23.1 | health/well-being | 15.1 | recreational | 16.0 |
| personal ads | 11.8 | social/political/env. | 16.9 | educational | 12.0 | cultural | 15.8 | personal ads | 15.1 | personal ads | 13.5 |
| social/political/env. | 11.8 | personal ads | 10.4 | social/political/env. | 11.7 | social/political/env. | 11.0 | social/political/env. | 12.5 | social/political/env. | 12.4 |
| recreational | 5.9 | administrative | 6.5 | personal ads | 7.2 | business | 8.0 | recreational | 10.5 | educational | 11.2 |
| educational | 5.9 | recreational | 3.3 | government-related | 5.9 | educational | 4.4 | fundraiser drive | 9.2 | health/well-being | 5.5 |
| cultural | 2.9 | business | 2.7 | health/well-being | 5.5 | health/well-being | 3.3 | business | 8.6 | administrative | 4.4 |
| business | 0.0 | health/well-being | 2.2 | administrative | 3.8 | fundraiser drive | 1.5 | educational | 3.9 | business | 3.6 |
| fundraiser drive | 0.0 | work/employment | 2.2 | work/employment | 2.3 | government-related | 1.1 | administrative | 2.0 | government-related | 3.2 |
| government-related | 0.0 | fundraiser drive | 1.1 | fundraiser drive | 2.0 | maintenance | 0.7 | maintenance | 0.7 | fundraiser drive | 2.6 |
| health/well-being | 0.0 | government-related | 0.0 | business | 1.1 | work/employment | 0.7 | government-related | 0.0 | work/employment | 1.6 |
| work/employment | 0.0 | maintenance | 0.0 | maintenance | 0.0 | administrative | 0.4 | work/employment | 0.0 | maintenance | 0.6 |

**Table 1. Distribution of the proportion of postings in each category by type of environment.**

### Postings by Type of Environment

Table 1 shows the distribution of postings in each subject category by type of environment. Below the total number of bulletin boards and number of postings in each type of environment is the proportion of postings in each category expressed as a percentage. Categories are organized in order of decreasing frequency. For example, column three summarizes the data collected in indoor public environments: 656 postings were surveyed on a total of 29 bulletin boards. While the majority of these postings related to cultural events (30.2%), a significant number related to recreational matters (18.3%). The proportion of social/political/environmental (11.7%) and educational (12.0%) were in a close tie, but there were few business postings (1.1%) and no maintenance related ones.

Although the exploratory nature of this study makes it difficult to generalize, some emerging patterns are sufficiently disparate to suggest distinct trends of posting in different types of environments.

The last column in Table 1 shows the data aggregated across all five types of environments. Although we can see that people posted content about a large number of things, 25.4% of content on all the bulletin boards was cultural content which means that it advertised plays, concerts, music jams, lectures, poetry readings or cultural events such as dance or music festivals. Recreational content publicizing sports and family activities, book clubs and community events of a recreational nature comprised 16.0% of overall content. Personal ads averaged 13.5% of content across the five types of environments. Social/political/environmental issues also constituted a large proportion of the overall content, namely 12.4%. At last, educational content about courses, professional training, skill acquirements, and educational workshops such as computer courses for seniors or kindergarten programs made up 11.2% of the overall content. Conversely, the overall proportion of postings related to work/employment was low at 1.6% and weak in each category.

If we consider these results in conjunction with the fact that 87% of postings were of proximate geographic relevance, this suggests that the bulletin boards are mainly used by people to communicate with members of their local community about issues that have cultural, social, political, environmental, recreational, educational and personal value. To put it otherwise, our results show that community bulletin boards do not tend to be used to publicize information related to work, business or government, which comprised only 8.4% of content overall.

At a more granular level, posting trends suggested a correlation between categories of postings and types of environment. That is, people tend to post content that they feel is relevant to the location and environment a bulletin board is situated in. Like geographic relevance, contextual relevance was an important observation made in similar studies of non-digital bulletin boards [3, 8, 28]. In addition, our results show that people tended to post personal ads more frequently in commercial and outdoor public environments than in residential, educational and indoor public ones. This seemed to be counter-intuitive; one would think that the smaller, more tightly knit community of a residential environment would foster more personal exchanges. In fact, people typically posted more personal ads in environments that could reach a wider audience.

## ENTRY POINTS FOR ACTION AND PARTICIPATION

Another significant observation made in the field was that certain postings, bulletin boards and places had features that invited people to use these bulletin boards more than others or to contribute content. By this, we mean "inviting action or user participation", which speaks to Kirsh's notion of affordance as an entry point that can provide a structure to cue or stimulate action [21]. Hornecker et al. have suggested that the concept of entry points can be useful in thinking through the design of shareable interfaces, especially in terms of motivating, facilitating and supporting action [18]. A set of *post hoc* research questions introduce the following subsections to discuss these features in relation to the postings, the bulletin boards as artifacts, the architectural setting in which they were placed, and their contextual environment and location.

### Postings

*What makes a posting more inviting?*

Like previous studies [3, 8, 19], we observed how postings could catch the eye by virtue of the diversity of their colors, sizes, and the visual patterns they produce. In particular, we noticed that different posting scenarios seemed to function as entry points which could motivate action. First, like prior research [3, 8], we saw many postings designed with tear-off strips to be ripped off or postings which users could take away such as multiple business-card-sized postings.

Second, we noticed that postings were often repeated by tiling, by fanning or by spreading in different areas across one or more boards. Two studies mention that users like to repeat postings to increase their probability of being seen [3, 11]. We found that this strategy was actually visually enticing and could attract attention, especially if postings were big, colorful and had strong graphic features.

Third, we frequently saw *blank notepaper*, *writing tools* and *empty spaces* specifically reserved for contributions and new postings. Alt et al.'s study also noted that some boards "provide support for posting" [3, p. 270]. However, our observations went beyond "tables…cards and pens", and included more playful tools that placed the emphasis on arts & crafts: cutout color construction paper, a chalkboard with color chalks, big color markers and neon-colored POST-IT™ notes randomly stuck to surfaces such as windows.

Fourth, like the lure of an empty space, postings seemed to effectively respond to a short, simple and specific question placed as a headline on a board such as "What's your favorite food?", "What makes you really happy?", "What is *your* Vancouver?" and "comments and suggestions?".

Fifth, flyers or flyer stands were often found near bulletin boards, an observation made in several other studies [3, 8, 19, 28]. We wondered if the tangible aspect of paper-based flyers might enhance the space around a digital bulletin board, an idea strongly suggested in one study which describes how people browse through them when they are placed in the vicinity of a digital display [19]. These five examples serve to illustrate how a bulletin board can be set up to draw people in and support the taking of content.

### Bulletin Boards

*What makes a bulletin board more inviting?*

Some of the bulletin boards we observed had distinct properties that inherently prevented participation by effectively limiting their function to publication. For instance, some bulletin boards were protected by glass casings which could not be removed without the gate-keepers' permission, an affordance other studies have remarked on [3, 8, 28]. Such design tends to evoke a one-way flow of information that can discourage access.

Alt et al.'s study classifies notice boards based on the degree to which they are scaffolded and curated to underscore the idea that different stakeholders may want more or less control over them [3]. Given that our study seeks to identify entry points for community, our analysis narrows down on this perspective. Thus, we were most surprised to find that this was the case with certain bulletin boards near community centers as well as with the only board of our sample located in an indoor shopping mall.

This bulletin board was located inside the entranceway of a major supermarket chain outlet. The heading of this bulletin board reads, "Community Information Centre". The word "community" seems a bit of a misnomer since the glass prevents people from posting, but the board is indeed an "information center". Although more than half of these postings had local geographic relevance, all had been professionally designed and printed by businesses or associations. A prior study remarks that non-digital boards use digital technology in their postings: they contain URLs or email addresses and are often created with desktop publishing applications [28]. Another study found that new users often tried to upload content created with Microsoft Office applications on their display network [11]. However, postings on this "Community Information Centre" lacked signs of personalization altogether. Many were from the local senior community center; a few originated from philanthropic associations or a regional fundraising initiative; and others were businesses advertising their services: a real estate agency, a pediatric dental group, a spa, and a restaurant. Almost all the content was addressed to a target audience of seniors and retirees. Unsurprisingly, no personal ads were posted on this board.

Conversely, we found other bulletin boards offered free access and thus could be said to be more inviting to post on. For example, we saw several concrete structures in the middle of university campus hallways that had been transformed into makeshift boards by students. What was particularly striking about them was that they had thick, messy layers of postings. They were seldom maintained, yet were actively used. In contrast with the "gate-keeper" model in which control is exercised over content, the postings on those unmanaged boards were often hand-written or personalized. This begs the question that one study raised in reference to similar posting practices: "how could this level of flexibility and ease of use be replicated in a digital system with today's technology?" [28, p. 3].

In the previous section, we have already mentioned that a platform can be designed with entry points that invite people to contribute a posting. Here, we suggest that open access and minimal management constitute "open" entry points that allow action to proceed, while the possibility of personalizing postings and boards could be construed as "offering a diversity of entry points...allowing for gradual adoption and appropriation of the system" [18, p. 332].

In addition to this, we observed two other factors that seemed to affect how dynamic and diverse the content of bulletin boards could be. The first was how messy (or makeshift) they were. The second was how busy they looked (i.e. the density of postings they contained). Messy boards and boards with many postings tended to attract more. We were able to assess this by observing a cross-section of bulletin boards over the full eight-week period of study. We noted that some bulletin boards had no postings at all during that period. For example, this was the case in a suburban recreation center which served as a family hub with a pool, a skating rink and a sophisticated fitness center. It had a single bulletin board located in the main hallway that led from the main lobby to the fitness center. This board remained empty for eight weeks even though it was located in an area that had a fair amount of daily traffic.

Similarly, bulletin boards that were too tidy did not seem to attract a large group of users. Their consistent appearance over the course of the study suggested that they were used by the same, small group of people, probably the gate-keepers who maintained and managed them. Our observations revealed that if a board was too neat or too clean, it did not function as a platform inviting action and instead seemed to signify a look-but-don't-touch aesthetic.

### Architectural Settings

*What makes an architectural setting more inviting?*

Our observations strongly suggest that bulletin boards should be understood as architectural elements embedded in the built environment. We noted, for example, that certain lighting conditions made bulletin boards more noticeable. This seemed to be the case especially when the lighting on the bulletin board stood out and made it more spectacular in relation to its surrounding space, the way a large outdoor digital screen appears at night compared to broad daylight.

Like Churchill et al. [8], we found that size, orientation and positioning were important considerations in the context of architectural space. We extend their findings with some statistics. Bulletin boards came in landscape (68%), portrait (25%) and square (7%) formats. While most bulletin boards were two-dimensional (93%), some were three-dimensional (7%) with several rectangular planes or a single cylindrical one in the case of a column used for posting. Content was either found within a single board frame (86%) or else it would be distributed across two (7%), three (5%) or more (2%). This suggests that bulletin boards could be designed on several screen interfaces on the same or different planes.

In fact, like [28], we found that almost any surface could be used as a bulletin board and that, in practice, it was often difficult to distinguish the boundary between the bulletin board and its architectural setting as people often posted over and beyond the bulletin board space. For instance, one bulletin board at a university campus had as many postings taped on the wall as on the board next to it. We also saw content placed on surfaces adjacent to the boards (windows, doors). Alt et al. similarly found that posting space was at times extended by attaching content next to the board [3].

Finally, we found that the larger a board was, the more dense it was with postings. Small boards were almost empty or tended to have few postings. However, this should be weighed against prior findings recommending that display interfaces be of human scale, and placed at arm's reach and eye-level [19]. This corroborates what we saw with boards.

### Contextual Environment and Locations

*What makes an environment or a location more inviting?*

We think it noteworthy that we did not find a single bulletin board or posting in areas containing mass transportation terminals, e.g. the airport, bus terminal or train station. Similarly, most museums we visited did not have a board for people to post or write, except for one large museum in the city's center which had an oversized chalkboard for visitors to write on. As we previously mentioned, only one shopping mall store contained a bulletin board. If we consider that shopping malls are the cultural hubs of certain communities of suburban dwellers (i.e. elderly and teens), this is peculiar. We believe this may relate to postmodern theory which describes such locations as "non-places" because they are branded by globalization, lack a sense of local identity and do not confer a sense of place [4].

In stark contrast, the data we collected in our commercial environments category provides evidence that people do post content on bulletin boards in certain commercial areas. Commercial Drive, one of the most diverse, grass-root neighborhoods we studied in Vancouver, contained the highest concentration of community bulletin boards inside retail stores such as bookstores, health food stores, food co-ops, cafés and restaurants. These formed a large proportion of the bulletin boards included in our commercial environment category. In this area, every retail store has its own identity, defined by the specific needs and lifestyle of the community it serves. This corroborates prior research which found that locations with a strong sense of identity will garner more bulletin boards and postings [3, 8, 28].

That said, we did notice counter examples. YMCAs are generally regarded as the flagships of community centers in North America yet we did not find a single bulletin board in a YMCA located at the outskirts of a vibrant and politically active neighborhood. Instead, the space was pristine, clean and branded with signs of corporate culture. Community bulletin boards would have clashed in these surroundings. This illustrates that even when a sense of community and identity exists in a location, the way in which the environment is constructed (e.g., overly sterile) can limit the desire of individuals to post content on bulletin boards.

What this tells us is that using principles that follow the architecture of participation of Web 2.0 would not be enough to build interactive digital bulletin boards. More important is the effervescence of a culture of participation rooted in a sense of place and identity [13]. We observed this again and again in each type of environment surveyed. Interestingly, researchers who deployed digital bulletin boards in research labs or in controlled semi-public settings made similar observations [2, 6, 9, 12, 23, 26].

## DISCUSSION AND DESIGN CONSIDERATIONS

We now summarize our results and outline our design considerations with the objective of creating conditions that will encourage participation rather than passive viewing in the design of digital bulletin boards. We present what we feel are the most pertinent lessons based on our results.

### Design for Local Content

Before the introduction of geolocation features in mobile devices, geographic relevance was less of a priority in the development of technology designed for community. In fact, one of the main affordances of social media has always been that one can exchange with members of a community regardless of where they are located in the world. In this sense, social media tends to operate with a sense of "non-place": their communities are bound by a strong sense of identity, but are placeless and in flux [4].

However, as we have seen, traditional bulletin boards are mostly used by members of place-based communities to exchange on issues and events within local range, a key finding made in every such prior study [3, 8, 11, 28]. This implies that designers may want to consider the importance of supporting and prioritizing content of local relevance. Our observations suggest that people value the locality of the boards because residents and community members can see their postings, but as we know the amount of postings on boards can easily become overwhelming. For this reason, it may be advantageous to make locally-relevant content more accessible or to place it in full view for users.

### Design for Display Placement in Areas of Identity

Our next design consideration is that the choice of location is a determinant parameter, arguably the most crucial. Based on our observations, we would suggest that institutional space, corporate space, public space and private space can invite different degrees of participation and public interaction depending on how they signify identity, access and ownership. Our results suggest that *locations in which communities already have a culture of participation, an ethic of cooperation and a sense of identity as a community* may better support digital bulletin boards. Past research also strongly supports this [3, 8, 28].

Digital bulletin boards placed in public locations that fall in the category of non-place would likely receive little participation from community members. This includes shopping malls, museums, touristic sites and mass transportation terminals. A caveat is bus shelters situated in neighborhoods serving a community; our observations showed that many people put postings up in some of these locations as well. Beyond this, public, semi-public or commercial sites that are regularly visited seem more likely to foster cultures of participation for digital bulletin boards.

### Design for Community and Culture

In reference to factors of contextual relevance, we broadly observed posting patterns that were, on the one hand, manifest across all types of environment and on the other hand, peculiar to each type of environment. In general, we found that people posted content that contributed to increasing the human, cultural or social capital of a community, rather than content providing opportunities for profit, employment, or government services. This supports Churchill et al.'s remark that identity-building may be one of the drivers of location-based bulletin boards [8]. People use them to share their political activities, their culture, their hobbies, their knowledge and their values. While Alt et al. call for the flexible design of digital bulletin boards to "allow a broad set of people using it" [3, p. 274], we also suggest that their design might be considered in terms of *how people use boards to build and share common ground.*

Our observations on the appropriation and personalization of space further suggest that digital bulletin boards *could be customized over time by the users themselves* who can adapt them to better suit the needs of their community. However, digital bulletin boards must still provide a means to reach the widest possible audience because, as the data showed in relation to personal ads posted in each type of environment, within tightly-knit communities, people prefer exchanging information face-to-face, by phone or by email. Keeping the platform both closed and open, both personal and accessible, presents a design trade-off. People should be able to choose when and where their content is placed, yet they also need to be restricted, for example, to avoid spamming locations with content that is not locally-relevant. Given that other researchers have also commented on the importance of encouraging content creation while ensuring varying degrees of access control over content [3, 8, 11, 28], this seems like one of the key design challenges.

Our results also suggest that displays *that look busy and used while still having empty areas for new content* might draw people in. Interestingly, this design feature could help make the digital board appear both closed and open. Also, as noted in our field study, *posing a short, engaging question as a headline presented in big colorful or visible font* is inviting and thus could constitute a good entry point.

### Design as a Shared Resource for Collective Ownership

Our findings showed that the degree to which bulletin boards and content were used, adapted and personalized by the public at large seemed closely related to signs of implicit or explicit ownership. Brignull et al. also remarked that "a clear sense of collective ownership of, and responsibility for, the common room" set the conditions for "the appropriation and consequent personal or shared use of resources in a very lightweight way" [6, p. 52]. In our study, boards with glass casings were implicitly understood as private property, while those with a banner headline were explicitly branded with seals of proprietorship. Our findings suggest that bulletin boards can be used as bottom-up grass-roots communication tools that enable people to find ways of acquiring knowledge about the community they belong to by exchanging human, cultural and social capital.

In keeping with this, our study suggests that digital bulletin boards *that allow for community self-regulation might be better suited when cultures of participation are taken to be the primary stakeholder*. Content moderation is a necessary feature in any community that encourages contribution, participation and collaboration. The simplest form of moderation may allow users to flag 'inappropriate' content and submit it for review to other members of the display community. More formal strategies where content needs to be pre-approved by administrative or technical staff might limit the perceived nature of the display as being "owned" by the community, and thus make it seem less accessible.

### Design for Embodied Interaction around the Display

As tempting as it is to think of displays as flat boards with two-dimensional interfaces, in reality they are tangible three-dimensional media platforms embedded in the built environment made up of palpable objects. We think it may prove useful to design digital prototypes with this in mind.

For instance, in order to optimize the appropriation of space and spread the community effect to other spaces of participation, we wonder if designs *could enable the modularization of the screen interface onto different planes and surfaces*. Could there also be a way to extend the posting space, like we saw when content was taped beyond the space of the bulletin boards (this observation was made in other studies [3, 28])? In a digital world where displays have fixed dimensions, this can be more challenging to support for one cannot extend the size of a display as easily as one can appropriate a wall surrounding a bulletin board. However, researchers may think about novel ways of providing additional digital space outside of the confines of a display through handheld projection technologies used by users themselves, or projectors permanently situated with the display (e.g., technologies such as ILLUMIROOM [20] could be used in a public setting rather than the home).

Furthermore, thinking in terms of tangibility and designing with materiality in mind would help. Indeed, we remarked that having fun tools to write and paper-based media to manipulate can attract and motivate users. This idea is also taken up by Grasso et al. [15, 16] and Huang [19] who each note that paper-based media can enhance digital ones when they are placed next to one another. What our observations suggest is that objects that have a ludic character can attract people to a board: bright colors that contrast with one another, big writing tools that feel good to grasp, lighting that has a theatrical quality, and spaces that don't feel too sterile and that might even have a playful quality to them. For instance, the lighting around a space could change as people approach a board or interfaces could better support embodied interaction such as body or hand movements.

## CONCLUSION

This paper has described how we have empirically studied traditional community bulletin boards by using an ethnographic design methodology with the objective of finding key considerations for the design and development of digital bulletin boards in public spaces. Our objects of study and units of analysis consisted mainly of postings and bulletin boards. To contextualize the data and to cast a wider net in reflecting on entry points for action, we also considered the architectural setting, the contextual environment and the contextual location in which these community bulletin boards were embedded. Our focus on content and community arguably serves to both validate and extend findings in related work in this area of research. Thus, our contribution to this area of research is twofold.

First, we validate results from prior studies that have found that bulletin boards tend to be used to: (1) post content of local and of contextual relevance; (2) negotiate the needs of its different stakeholders through design affordances related to curation, moderation, control, access, personalization and ergonomics; (3) help build a community's sense of identity or to lay claim to ownership of a space through appropriation of the board or the space around it; and (4) offer means to take away content in digital or paper form.

Second, our analysis extends these findings by proposing new entry points for digital bulletin boards in public spaces, namely a stronger focus on supporting: (1) content that can help a community exchange more cultural and social capital; (2) only locations that can confer a sense of place; (3) minimal barriers for access and moderation; (4) design strategies that place a greater emphasis on embodied interaction and visual enticement including, for instance, the use of empty space, colorful, fun props and non-digital media and tangible interfaces; and playful *mise-en-scène* which stages sensor-based interaction or a busier interface. Although our observations are about non-digital boards, we hope that some of our findings will also be applicable to other types of large interactive digital public displays and help practitioners think through the design process when the dominant stakeholders' interests are those of communities.

## ACKNOWLEDGMENTS

We thank SSHRC for funding this work. We also thank reviewers for their valuable feedback on earlier versions.

## REFERENCES

1. Agostini, A., and Divitini, M. Communityware goes to school. In *Proc. of CSCL 2002*, ACM Press (2002), 515-516.

2. Alt, F., Kubitza, T., Bial, D., Zaidan, F., Ortel, M., Zurmaar, B., Lewen, T., Shirazi, A.S. and Schmidt, A. Digifieds: Insights into deploying digital public notice areas in the wild. In *Proc. of MUM 2011*, ACM Press, (2011), 165-174.

3. Alt, F., Memarovic, N., Elhart, I., Bial, D., Schmidt, A., Langheinrich, M., Harboe, G., Huang, E. and Scipioni, M.P. Designing shared public display networks: Implications from today's paper-based notice areas. In *Proc. of PERVASIVE*, Berlin, Heidelberg (2011), 258-275.

4. Augé, M. *Non-places: Introduction to an Anthropology of Supermodernity*. Verso, London; New York (1995).

5. Bolter, J.D. and Grusin, R. *Remediation: Understanding New Media*. MIT Press, Cambridge, MA (1999).

6. Brignull, H., Izadi, S., Fitzpatrick, G., Rogers, Y. and Rodden, T. The introduction of a shared interactive surface into a communal space. In *Proc. of CSCW 2004*, ACM Press (2004), 49-58.

7. Castells, M. Museums in the information era. In *Museums in a Digital Age*, R. Parry (Ed.), Routledge, London and New York (2010), 427-437.

8. Churchill, E.F., Nelson, L. and Denoue, L. Multimedia fliers: Informal information sharing with digital community bulletin boards. In *Proc. of C&T 2003*, Kluwer Academic Publishers (2003), 97-117.

9. Churchill, E.F. and Nelson, L.D. From media spaces to emplaced media: Digital poster boards and community connectedness. *Media Spaces Workshop CSCW 2006*, Banff, Canada (November 2006).

10. Churchill, E.F., Nelson, L.D., Hsieh, G. Café life in the digital age: Augmenting information flow in a caféwork-entertainment space. In *Ext. Abstracts CHI 2006*, ACM Press (2006), 123-128.

11. Clinch, S., Davies, N., Friday, A. and Efstratiou, C. Reflections on the long-term use of an experimental digital signage system. In *Proc. of UbiComp 2011*, ACM Press (2011), 133-142.

12. Fass, A., Forlizzi, J. and Pausch, R. MessyDesk and MessyBoard: Two designs inspired by the goal of improving human memory. In *Proc. of DIS 2002*, ACM Press (2002), 303-311.

13. Fischer, G. Understanding, fostering, and supporting cultures of participation. *ACM Interactions 18*, 3 (May & June 2011), 42-53.

14. Glaser, B.G. and Strauss, A.L. *The Discovery of Grounded Theory: Strategies for Qualitative Research*. Aldine Publishing Company, Chicago, IL (1967).

15. Grasso, A., Koch, M., and Snowdon, D. Campiello : New User Interface Approaches for Community Networks, *SIGGROUP Bull. 20*, 2 (August 1999), 15-17

16. Grasso, A., Karsenty, A., and Susani, M. Augmenting Paper to Enhance Community Information Sharing. In *Proc. of DARE 2000*, ACM Press (2000), 51-62.

17. Greenberg, S. and Rounding, M. The Notification Collage: Posting information to public and personal displays. In *Proc. of CHI 2001*, ACM Press (2001), 514-521.

18. Hornecker, E., Marshall, P. and Rogers, Y. From entry to access: How shareability comes about. In *Proc. of DPPI 2007*, ACM Press (2007), 328-342.

19. Huang, E.M., Koster, A. and Borchers, J. Overcoming assumptions and uncovering practices: When does the public really look at public displays? In *Proc. of PERVASIVE 2008*, Springer, (2008), 228-243.

20. Jones, B., Benko, H., Ofek, E., and Wilson, A. IllumiRoom: Peripheral projected illusions for interactive experiences. In *Proc. of CHI 2013*, ACM Press (2013), 869-878.

21. Kirsh, D. The context of work. *Human-computer interaction 6*, 2 (2001), 306-322.

22. Kuikkaniemi, K., Jacucci, G., Turpeinen, M., Hoggan, E., and Müller, J. From space to stage: How interactive screens will change urban life. *Computer 44*, 6 (June 2011), 40-47.

23. McCarthy, J.F., Farnham, S.D., Patel, Y., Ahuja, S., Norman, D., Hazlewood, W.R. and Lind, J. Supporting community in third places with situated social software. In *Proc. of C&T 2009*, ACM Press (2009), 225-234.

24. Ojala, T., Valkama, V., Kukka, H., Heikkinen, T., Linden, T., Jurmu, M., Kruger, F., and Hoslo, S. UBI-hotspots: Sustainable ecosystem infrastructure for real world urban computing research and business. In *Proc. of MEDES 2010*, ACM Press (2010), 196-202.

25. Peltonen, P., Kurvinen, E., Salovaara, A., Jacucci, G., Ilmonen, T., Evans, J., Oulasvirta, A., and Saarikko, P. "It's Mine, Don't Touch!": Interactions at a large multi-touch display in a city centre. In *Proc. of CHI 2008*, ACM Press (2008), 1285-1294.

26. Snowdon, D. and Grasso, A. Diffusing information in organizational settings: Learning from experience. In *Proc. of CHI 2002*, ACM Press (2002), 331-338.

27. Spradley, J. P. *Participant Observation*. Holt, Rinehart and Winston, New York, NY (1980).

28. Taylor, N. and Cheverst, K. Exploring the use of non-digital situated displays in a rural community. In *Public and Situated Displays to Support Communities Workshop OZCHI 2008*, Lancaster University, (2008): http://cs-wray.lancs.ac.uk/ozchi08/programme.php

29. Van Niekerk, J.C. and Roode, J.D. Glaserian and Straussian grounded theory: Similar or completely different? In *Proc. of SAICSIT 2009*, ACM Press (2009), 96-103.

# I Can Wait a Minute: Uncovering the Optimal Delay Time for Pre-Moderated User-Generated Content on Public Displays

Miriam Greis[1], Florian Alt[1,2], Niels Henze[1], Nemanja Memarovic[3]

[1]University of Stuttgart
VIS
Pfaffenwaldring 5a
70569 Stuttgart, Germany
firstname.lastname@vis.uni-stuttgart.de

[2]University of Munich
Media Informatics Group
Amalienstraße 17
80333 München, Germany
florian.alt@ifi.lmu.de

[3]Universita della Svizzera Italiana
Via G. Buffi 13
6904 Lugano, Switzerland
nemanja.memarovic@usi.ch

## ABSTRACT
Public displays have advanced from isolated and non interactive "ad" displays which show images and videos to displays that are networked, interactive, and open to a wide variety of content and applications. Prior work has shown large potential of user-generated content on public displays. However, one of the problems with user-generated content on public displays is moderation as content may be explicit or troublesome for a particular location. In this work we explore the expectations of users with regard to content moderation on public displays. An online survey revealed that people not only think that display content should be moderated but also that a delay of up to 10 minutes is acceptable if display content is moderated. In a subsequent in the wild deployment we compared different moderation delays. We found that a moderation delay significantly decreases the number of user-generated posts while at the same time there is no significant effect on users' decision to repeatedly post on the display.

### Author Keywords
public displays, content moderation, Twitter

### ACM Classification Keywords
H.5.m. Information Interfaces and Presentation (e.g. HCI): Miscellaneous

## INTRODUCTION AND BACKGROUND
Urban spaces are getting crowded with public displays [5], from small screens showing menus in bars to large ones covering an entire building facade. Although they are mainly singular installations that show Powerpoint slides and still images it is not hard to imagine that they will soon be connected over the Internet, to form a novel communication medium open to a variety of content and applications – so-called open display networks [3].


*CHI'14*, April 26 – May 01 2014, Toronto, ON, Canada

ACM 978-1-4503-2473-1/14/04?$15.00.
http://dx.doi.org/10.1145/2556288.2557183

Previous research has shown content creation to be one of the crucial problems for public displays and this content is often expensive, both in terms of human resources and monetary value [9]. On the other hand creating content for social networking services is considered "dirt cheap", e.g., Twitter reports staggering 340 million tweets that are posted daily. Integrating user-generated content, e.g., tweets, onto open display networks is a possible solution for content creation in open display networks and has been explored in prior work [7]. It would also allow public displays to be integrated more into users' "communicative ecology" [6]. Yet, posting user-generated content on public displays comes with the problem of *content moderation* as explicit and inappropriate content could appear. In addition, posted content might be problematic in other ways for a display's particular physical location. For example, previous work reported on inadvertently posted corporate information [2].

Prior research suggests different ways of moderating public displays content, including pre-moderation [10], post moderation [2, 4], and moderation based on audience feedback [1]. However, these works only applied a certain strategy without closely investigating the effects. In our work we aim to gather an in-depth understanding of pre-moderation as we believe this to be a central prerequisite in open display networks to encourage display owners to allow user-generated content. Prior work looked at the impact of labelling content [8] whereas we focus on the delay times caused by the review process. We believe this to be a major challenge with pre-moderation. The fact that posts do not appear instantly raises the following questions: (1) What do users expect when their content appears? (2) What effect does the delay cause? (3) How can the user be notified that content is under review and when it will appear? If a system fails to address these challenges, users will wonder where the problem occurred and either resend the content or stop using the display.

To investigate pre-moderation of content on public displays we conducted two studies. First, we distributed a survey that investigated users' expectations of optimal timing for content that is pre-moderated. We found 10 minutes to be an acceptable delay for more than 70% of the users. Within this time-frame different forms of content moderation are possible, including (a) automatically, (b) by the owner, or

(c) crowdsourcing-based approaches. We then developed an application allowing people to send tweets to a public display network. We deployed the application in the wild on five connected displays and inferred an artificial delay to investigate the effect of different pre-moderation mechanisms.

The contribution of the work is twofold. First, we report on *user preferences for content upload waiting time* on public displays (a) with and (b) without moderation. Our results show that if users are aware of moderation, more than half of them is even willing to accept delays of one hour or more. For applications that do not communicate the moderation process, a delay of up to 10 minutes is still acceptable for the majority of the potential users. Second, we provide insights about the *effect of a moderation delay on users' behavior*. Through an empirical study we found that even short waiting times of 90 seconds can confuse users. Furthermore, we show that the longer the delay time the less posts appear on a display. Finally, the delay time seems to not influence a user's decision to continuously post to a display.

## STUDY I: ONLINE SURVEY

To learn about potential users' expectations towards content moderation for open display networks we distributed an online questionnaire. We were mainly interested in the expectations of people that have no previous experience with publishing user-generated content on public displays to be able to later contrast the results with the actual behavior in front of public displays.

### Method

We prepared the questionnaire using our LimeSurvey server. The questionnaire consists of three pages. After an introduction to public displays and user-generated content on the first page, the second page asks about basic demographics and if the person ever published content on a public display or even operates one. The third page asks participants if content on public displays should be moderated; if participants expect that a message they post to a display would appear instantly; if they expect a delay prior to showing the message and which delay is acceptable. Since no prior in-depth investigation on delay times exists (prior research that comes closest to investigating delay times simply classified them as "fast" or "slow" [11]), we came up with concrete values that we felt would best reflect a user's expectations.

We distributed the questionnaire through our university's mailing list, our social network, and our research projects' mailing lists. In total, 114 participants completed the questionnaire. 50 participants are female and 64 are male. On average they are 24.10 years old (SD=4.54). 89 participants are students with a variety of majors including computer science, biology, and medicine.

### Results

101 participants never posted content on a public display or operated one. 10 participants used research prototypes or installations in museums to post content on public displays and 7 participants operate, maintain, or work with public displays. We excluded the 13 participants that had previous experience with public displays from further analysis.

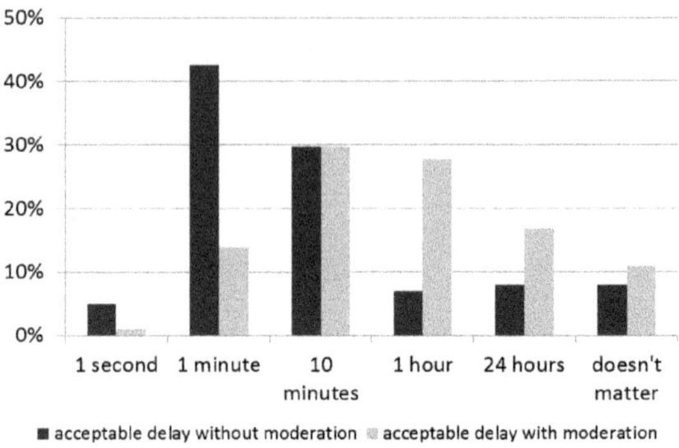


**Figure 1. The acceptable delay for messages to appear when posting messages on a public display without or with moderation.**

83% of the participants agree or strongly agree with the statement that a moderation or control process for content on public displays is necessary to avoid misuse. The average level of agreement is 4.22 (SD=1.05) on the 5-point Likert scale (1=don't agree at all, 5=totally agree). With an average of 3.89 (SD=1.08) on the 5-point Likert scale most participants agree with the statement that they expect posted messages to appear on a display instantly (81% agreed or strongly agreed). Asked about the acceptable delay (see Figure 1), 48% state that only a delay of 1 minute is acceptable if there is no content moderation. Another 30% think that a delay time of up to 10 minutes is still acceptable. If there is content moderation, 59.4% of the participants would accept a longer delay. 55.5% would even accept a delay of one hour or more.

### Discussion

The results indicate, that communicating the fact that a display is moderated overall leads to an increase of the acceptable delay. Yet, a challenge in open display networks may be the fact that moderation is handled differently across displays, even if running the same application. For example, a digital bulletin board may be globally available for use on public displays but then, supermarkets running the application may require moderation whereas universities may not. This raises the need to understand, how to employ content moderation without the user being aware of it.

We see different opportunities to enable pre-moderation of open display content within a time frame of 10 minutes. First, posts could be checked *automatically* (less than one second) by searching for explicit keywords and potentially banning the content from publication. Second, display owners may employ dedicated moderators to instantly approve or reject content by *manually* checking incoming items (i.e., within 30 seconds). Third, display or space owners may decide to outsource the reviewing task via *crowdsourcing* platforms such as Mechanical Turk. We believe that in such cases a response time of 90 seconds is feasible. In the following we explore these options by means of a real-world deployment.

## STUDY II: IN THE WILD DEPLOYMENT

We implemented a web-based app displaying tweets which mention the display network's Twitter profile. In this way people can post text and images to the display by adding the network's Twitter id to a tweet.

**Figure 2. The five display locations with the running display client. Locations included entrance areas, cafeterias, and coffee kitchens.**

The display client is depicted in Figure 2. It runs in a full screen browser and shows the 12 most recent tweets in a 3x4 grid in portrait and a 4x3 grid in landscape mode. The Twitter id to tweet to is displayed below the grid. If a tweet only contains text we just render the text and if it contains a link to a photo only the photo is shown. Each tweet is logged in a database together with a timestamp and the user's Twitter ID. If a tweet contains a link to a photo we also store the photo in the database. Hence we cannot only easily exclude explicit tweets but we can later contact the poster via his or her ID, e.g., to send an online survey.

The display client polls new tweets from the database every 1000ms. We do not provide any other interaction than showing the messages posted on Twitter to keep the application simple and concentrate on users' reactions to delays caused by moderation.

### Deployment Setting

We deployed the web-client on five displays across our campus where it ran 24/7 for the duration of 2 months (June–July 2013). All content appeared simultaneously on all five displays. Two displays were installed in the entrance area of faculty buildings and in close proximity to lecture theaters. A third display was deployed in the vicinity of a coffee kitchen shared by two research groups in one of the university building. The fourth display was deployed in a university cafeteria. The display was mounted on the wall in close proximity to tables but was visible from almost any location inside the cafeteria. The last display was located in the main canteen building of the university with a throughput of several thousand people per day. The display stood at the intersection of two aisles with tables in the vicinity. Passersby for all displays were both university employees as well as students attending lectures and courses. Figure 2 depicts the five locations.

According to the previously mentioned options for pre-moderation, we configured our display application to support a 0, 30, and 90 seconds delay. The time intervals were changed every 2 hours. Lectures on campus follow a centralized schedule which allowed us to always switch the time intervals while lectures were in progress. The reason for this is that most people were present shortly before or after the lecture as they waited for fellow students. We did not communicate the delay times to users simulating pre-moderation without informing users. During the time of deployment 518 messages were posted by 116 different users.

### Questionnaires

Each time a user posted to the display for the first time, we sent a personalized link to an online questionnaire via Twitter encoding the user ID, the tweet, and the condition in the link. To ensure that the correct user answered the questionnaire, participants had to enter their Twitter ID as they filled in the questionnaire. In the questionnaire we first asked participants about demographics, previous experience with public displays, whether they were in front of the display when posting, and whether they waited until their message appeared. In addition, we were interested in their overall experience.

Out of the 116 people who posted to the display and were asked to fill in the questionnaires, 2 female and 29 male participants replied. They were students or employees at our university in different engineering fields (avg. age = 23.71 years, SD=4.70). 9 participants interacted with a public display before using our application. 23 participants posted while being in front of the display out of which 17 waited in front of the display for their post to appear (48.6 %). 14 participants posted in the 0-seconds condition, 11 in the 30-seconds condition, and 6 in the 90-seconds condition.

Participants were asked to rate their experience with the application. Overall, participants give an average rating of 4.16 (SD=0.90) on a 5-point Likert scale (1=very low, 5=very high). The average rating after posting in the 0-seconds condition is 4.00 (SD=0.96), 4.55 (SD=0.69) after posting in the 30-seconds condition, and 3.83 (SD=0.98) after posting in the 90-seconds condition. With an average of 3.35 (SD=1.56) on the 5-point Likert scale most participants agree with the statement that they expect their message to instantly be displayed.

### Data Analysis

To understand the effect of moderation times on content behavior we analyzed the number of posts as well as how often participants posted on the display. We considered multiple consecutive posts by a user that depended on each other (e.g., a large picture) as a single post. This resulted in 349 posts that remained for the analysis. First, we found an increase in the overall *number of posts* as moderation time decreases. During the 0-seconds condition, 150 messages were posted, compared to 127 in the 30-seconds condition and only 72 in the 90-seconds condition. The difference is statistically significant ($\chi^2(2) = 27.62, p < 0.001$) and indicates a strong effect of moderation delay on number of posts. There was no significant association between the conditions and whether or not users posted again ($\chi^2(2) = 0.73, p = 0.76$). In the 0-seconds condition, 43,2% posted once, in the 30-seconds condition 51,7%, and in the 90-seconds condition 43,1%. The small difference suggests that delay times do not impact on whether people post again or not.

### Observations and Interviews

We observed users of our system during the deployment and invited seven people who filled in a questionnaire to semi-structured interviews. We were particularly interested in the first contact of the people with the display, their first message, their expectations, and why they decided to post again.

Six of the seven interviewees stated that they did not post on the first encounter but, instead, first observed the display and its mechanisms before making the decision to post themselves (*"My friends posted something first. They took a photo of themselves and waited in front of the display until the message was shown."*–P4). Interviews and observations also revealed that users often were not sure whether the display really works. They discussed with others if a moderation process was in progress, particularly because they felt 90 seconds were quite a long time for a message to be displayed. As a result, many of them spent a significant amount of time in the display vicinity. We observed that people who decided to post even sat down on the floor in front of the display to be able to post and observe the display at the same time.

Five interviewees stated that after they verified that the display is actually working they started to post remotely quite extensively, i.e. while they were not in the display vicinity. It seems that people that later frequently post 'give credit' to the display the first time, hence forgiving even longer delays. This may be an explanation why the delay time does not have any impact on whether people post or not.

Interviewees also had quite different ideas as to when they expected the posted content to appear. Whereas two did not expect any moderation, two others expected moderation and did not think that their posts would appear instantly.

We also observed a *digital honeypot effect* where posts coming in on the display as people were watching motivated them to post themselves, sometimes directly replying to the new post. This effect seems to also impact on expectations towards content moderation as new posts not only communicate what is appropriate but also that moderation is currently in progress and new posts can be expected to appear shortly.

## DISCUSSION & CONCLUSION

In this paper, we investigate the moderation of user-generated content on open public displays. We assessed users' expectation about content moderation through an online survey and used an in the wild deployment of a public display network to compare different moderation delays.

We learned that, in general, most users expect content to be moderated. Content should appear within one minute without content moderation and within 10 minutes with content moderation. The in the wild deployment revealed that delay times caused by content moderation significantly influence the number of user-generated posts on a display. Hence, for display applications that aim to maximize the number of people posting, post-moderation or automated moderation, for example through simple keyword spotting, is advisable.

At the same time we discovered no effect on the users' decision to post – neither for cases where people posted just a single piece of content nor where they posted multiple times. We believe the reason for this to be the fact that people try to compensate for the lack of information on the moderation process by observing the display prior to posting. Once they found out about moderation they posted without reservations.

In the future we plan to build upon our findings and investigate different mechanisms that convey (a) how the display is moderated and (b) what the expected delay time is.

**Acknowledgments:** This work is partly funded by the German Research Foundation within the SimTech Cluster of Excellence (EXC 310/1).

## REFERENCES

1. Alt, F., Kubitza, T., Bial, D., Zaidan, F., Ortel, M., Zurmaar, B., Lewen, T., Shirazi, A. S., and Schmidt, A. Digifieds: insights into deploying digital public notice areas in the wild. In *Proc. MUM'11*, ACM (2011).
2. Churchill, E., Nelson, L., Denoue, L., Murphy, P., and Helfman, J. The plasma poster network. In *Public and Situated Displays*. Kluwer, 2003.
3. Davies, N., Langheinrich, M., Jose, R., and Schmidt, A. Open display networks: A 21st century communications medium. *IEEE Computer* (2012).
4. Elhart, I., Memarovic, N., Langheinrich, M., and Rubegni, E. Control and scheduling interface for public displays. In *Adjunct Proc. UbiComp'13* (2013).
5. Kostakos, V., and Ojala, T. Public displays invade urban spaces. *Pervasive Computing* (2013).
6. Memarovic, N., Langheinrich, M., Rubegni, E., David, A., and Elhart, I. Designing "interacting places" for a student community using a communicative ecology approach. In *Proc. MUM'12*, ACM (2012).
7. Munson, S. A., Rosengren, E., and Resnick, P. Thanks and tweets: comparing two public displays. In *Proc. CSCW '11*, ACM (2011).
8. Schroeter, R. Engaging new digital locals with interactive urban screens to collaboratively improve the city. In *Proc. CSCW '12*, ACM (2012).
9. Storz, O., Friday, A., Davies, N., Finney, J., Sas, C., and Sheridan, J. Public ubiquitous computing systems: Lessons from the e-campus display deployments. *Pervasive Computing* (2006).
10. Taylor, N., Cheverst, K., Fitton, D., Race, N. J., Rouncefield, M., and Graham, C. Probing communities: study of a village photo display. In *Proc. OzCHI* (2007).
11. Wise, K., Hamman, B., and Thorson, K. Moderation, response rate, and message interactivity: Features of online communities and their effects on intent to participate. *Comp.-Med. Comm. 12*, 1 (2006).

# Design Patterns for Exploring and Prototyping Human-Robot Interactions

**Allison Sauppé and Bilge Mutlu**
Department of Computer Sciences, University of Wisconsin–Madison
1210 West Dayton Street, Madison, WI 53706 USA
asauppe@cs.wisc.edu, bilge@cs.wisc.edu

## ABSTRACT
Robotic products are envisioned to offer rich interactions in a range of environments. While their specific roles will vary across applications, these products will draw on fundamental building blocks of interaction, such as greeting people, narrating information, providing instructions, and asking and answering questions. In this paper, we explore how such building blocks might serve as *interaction design patterns* that enable design exploration and prototyping for human-robot interaction. To construct a pattern library, we observed human interactions across different scenarios and identified seven patterns, such as question-answer pairs. We then designed and implemented *Interaction Blocks*, a visual authoring environment that enabled prototyping of robot interactions using these patterns. Design sessions with designers and developers demonstrated the promise of using a pattern language for designing robot interactions, confirmed the usability of our authoring environment, and provided insights into future research on tools for human-robot interaction design.

## Author Keywords
Design patterns; interaction design; human-robot interaction; authoring environment; design exploration; prototyping; design sessions

## ACM Classification Keywords
H.5.2 **Information Interfaces and Presentation**: User Interfaces—*input devices and strategies, evaluation/ methodology, user-centered design*

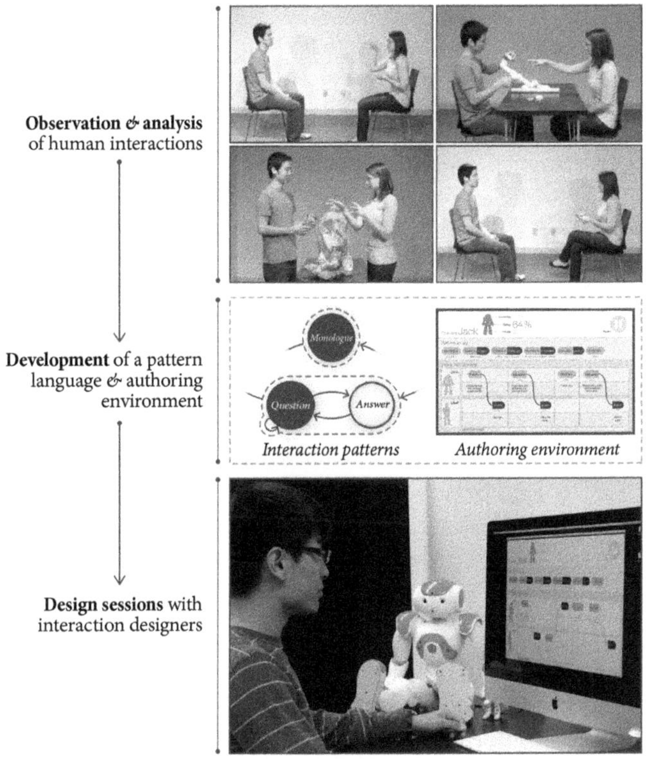


**Figure 1.** In this work, we use observations and analysis of human interactions to develop an interaction design pattern language and authoring environment called *Interaction Blocks* to enable designers to explore and prototype human-robot interactions.

## INTRODUCTION
As robots promise to become commonplace products in a range of settings, serving as receptionists, museum guides, and tutors for children, designers will need materials and tools that will enable them to explore and prototype a range of interactions that robots will offer in these settings. For example, a receptionist robot serving at a doctor's office may work with a patient to schedule an appointment, instruct a patient on how to use a medication, or inform medical staff about upcoming appointments. While interactions across settings or within a setting may take many forms, they will build on a fundamental set of communicative acts that humans draw on in communication. In this paper, we explore how these communicative acts might serve as interaction design patterns and how we might use a pattern language to enable design exploration and prototyping of human-robot interaction.

Do human interactions follow specific patterns? If so, how can we create a pattern language for human interaction? How can we enable designers to use such a language for exploration and prototyping human-robot interactions? Goffman [11] argued that human interactions follow a specific "order" and characterized a number of patterns in which people interact, such as how greetings unfold and how people leave an interaction. Research across sociology, psychology, and HCI


*CHI 2014*, April 26–May 1, 2014, Toronto, Ontario, Canada.

http://dx.doi.org/10.1145/2556288.2557057

have sought to identify similar patterns in different forms of interaction, such as interviews [19], conversations [29], and collaborations [5]. Kahn et al. [15] have proposed that the patterns observed in human interactions might serve as designing interactions for robots, describing eight patterns such as "initial interaction" and "in motion together" based on their observations of how children interacted with robots and literature on fundamental constructs in human interactions.

In this paper, we extend this concept toward building a pattern language that might serve as building blocks for human-robot interactions across different forms of interaction, focusing on five scenarios in which robots are expected to engage, including collaboration [8], conversation [12], instruction [13], interviews [9], and storytelling [20]. We present a formative study of human interactions across these five scenarios and describe seven patterns that appear across these scenarios. These patterns informed the design and implementation of *Interaction Blocks*, an authoring environment that enables users to explore and create interactions for social robots. We envision Interaction Blocks having three primary groups of users: (1) interaction designers who have little programming background, (2) designers or programmers who would like to rapidly prototype interactions, and (3) designers or programmers who might not have experience in working with human behavior as a design element. Through a qualitative evaluation with interaction designers and developers, we demonstrate the feasibility of the use of a pattern language for designing human-robot interactions and the usability of our authoring environment. Figure 1 illustrates this process.

The next section provides background on patterns in human interactions and reviews related work on interfaces for authoring robot behaviors. This section is followed by a description of the formative study that informed the development of a pattern language for human-robot interactions and the design of *Interaction Blocks*. Following sections discuss the design and implementation of Interaction Blocks, as well as its evaluation through a series of design sessions. We conclude the paper with a discussion of the findings and their implications for future research into designing human-robot interactions.

## RELATED WORK

In the paragraphs below, we review related work on patterns in human interactions, the use of patterns for designing human-robot interactions, and authoring tools and environments developed for programming robot behaviors.

### Patterns in Human Interactions

Human interactions follow an invisible structure, a shared *interaction order* [11], that signals to its participants how they should act and interact with others. For example, the openings of encounters follow a particular "routine" that involves a greeting or a summons by a participant and an in-kind response either in the form of a greeting or an answer [27]. Similarly, conversations might involve the pattern "question-answer pairs," where one participant is posing a question followed by an answer from a different participant [6]. These routines may be combined to produce a more elaborate interaction, as shown in the example below.

*Participant 1*: <upon seeing a friend at work> Oh, good morning! Are you attending the meeting this afternoon?
*Participant 2*: Yes, I was planning on going.

In this brief encounter, Participant 1 opens the interaction with a greeting and subsequently poses a question, which Participant 2 answers. The participants of this encounter employ both the greeting and question-answer pair routines to seek and provide information and coordinate activities. Research on human communication has shown that the use of such routines or "interaction patterns" facilitates effective communication, specifically processes such as fluency [29] and grounding [5]. On the other hand, breakdowns occur in communication when these patterns are violated [27].

### Patterns in Human-Robot Interactions

Research on human-robot interactions has also considered how robots might display patterned behaviors, such as gaze patterns that facilitate conversational turn-taking and joint attention [13], to enable more effective human-robot interaction. Researchers have also proposed the use of such patterned behaviors as building blocks for constructing human-robot interactions [15, 22], such as an "initial interaction" pattern proposed by Kahn et al. [15]—an interaction pattern analogous to greetings in human interactions. However, this body of work does not yet offer a pattern language that might serve as building blocks for interactions across a wide range of scenarios. Furthermore, this research has not developed tools or environments to support design exploration or prototyping for constructing human-robot interactions.

### Authoring Environments for Robot Behaviors

A complementary body of work has developed several authoring tools and environments to help expert developers and novice users better control and interact with robots [14] and to evaluate human-robot interactions [16]. Environments for developers include the Robot Operating System (ROS), which offers an architecture for abstracting and reusing specific functionalities across different robot platforms [24]. A particular ROS module, the Robot Behavior Toolkit, offers the ability to specify robot social behaviors based on a repository of "rules" or patterns [13]. However, the use of these environments requires a substantial amount of development expertise as well as effort to build suitable pattern repositories.

Authoring environments for novice users include a number of commercial and research tools for programming robot behaviors [10]. For example, Interaction Composer (IC) involves a graphical interface that enables users to coordinate multiple facets of a robot's behavior, such as dialogue and gestures, by choosing from a set of "behavior blocks" to compose the interaction [10]. RoboStudio offers an expert authoring environment to build graphical interfaces that enable novice users to customize the behaviors of the robot to their needs or preferences [7]. Finally, Lohse et al. [18] has developed a framework for iterative design and evaluation of robot behaviors [18]. While these tools and environments involve easy-to-use interfaces that are accessible to both expert and novice users, they require the designer to have knowledge of a pattern language and to map this knowledge to specific robot behaviors that can be authored using the tools.

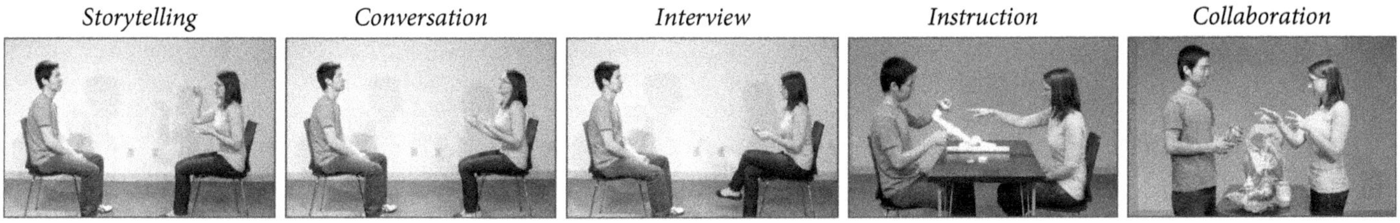


**Figure 2.** Examples of the experimental setup for all five scenarios. From left to right, participants are sharing in a storytelling experience, engaging in conversation, conducting an interview, learning how to configure a set of pipes, and collaborating on how to sort foodstuffs.

## FORMATIVE STUDY

To build a pattern language that enables design exploration and prototyping for human-robot interactions, we conducted a formative study of human interactions that involved observations of human interactions and identifying and modeling patterns in which these interactions unfolded. While a variety of behaviors and scenarios have been studied by linguists and psychologists [6,11,27], the results have not been constructed into design patterns that can be translated and implemented on a robot. To achieve natural, humanlike robot behaviors, we chose to ground our development of interaction design patterns in observations and detailed analyses of human interactions. We collected data from eight dyads performing in five social interaction scenarios that are representative of the types of interactions robots are envisioned to encounter in their future roles in society: *conversation*, *collaboration*, *instruction*, *interview*, and *storytelling*. We then followed an iterative modeling process to construct models that represented each of the scenarios. These models revealed common interaction design patterns that appeared across multiple scenarios. The paragraphs below detail and discuss the process of discovering and formalizing these patterns.

### Data Collection

#### *Participants and Data Corpus*

A total of 16 native-English-speaking participants from the University of Wisconsin–Madison took part in this study. Participants studied a diverse range of fields, and their ages ranged 19–62 ($M$ = 25.44, $SD$ = 10.39). Participants were assigned into dyads to jointly interact in the social interaction scenarios. We randomly assigned participants into dyads and conversational roles such that they were fully stratified by gender. The instructor and storyteller roles were never held by the same participant, allowing the instructor to learn the task to be instructed while the storyteller learned the story. The scenarios were executed in the same order for each dyad.

We used a single video camera equipped with a wide-angle lens to capture the entire upper body of the participants for all scenarios. The final data corpus consisted of five scenarios for each dyad, which amounted to 3 hours and 31 minutes of audio and video data. The average lengths for the collaboration, conversation, instruction, interview, and storytelling scenarios were 3:47, 4:47, 5:02, 7:32, and 3:59, respectively.

#### *Procedure*

After arrival in our laboratory, a researcher provided the participants with an overview of the interaction scenarios. Following informed consent, the participants were then led into a usability laboratory, which was initially configured for the first scenario in which they would be participating. The room was reconfigured for each scenario, as shown in Figure 2. Following the completion of all five scenarios, participants completed a demographic questionnaire. The researchers then debriefed both participants. The five scenarios and post-experiment questionnaire took approximately one hour. Participants were compensated $10 each for their time.

#### *Interaction Scenarios*

We designed five interaction scenarios that showed the characteristics of the scenarios in which robots are expected to interact with people and that followed previous modeling research, which will be discussed in more detail below. Each scenario was intended for small group interaction. For data collection, we engaged two participants in each interaction as the minimum number required to realize the scenario.

*1) Conversation:* In the conversation scenario, we aimed to observe how participants would handle a set of unstructured exchanges about a given topic. Framing, turn-taking, and recovering from errors are all important aspects of a successful conversation [29]. In particular, participants who have not yet established any level of rapport may favor question-answer pairs, rather than conversational dialogue [29].

In the scenario, the participants discussed their educational experiences and goals. They were instructed to continue this conversation until the researcher re-entered the room when the conversation naturally subsided.

*2) Collaboration:* The collaboration scenario targeted gaining a better understanding of how participants collaborate toward a common goal. Previous research has shown that joint activity requires flexibility and communication in order to effectively coordinate differing opinions from participants [5].

In our collaboration scenario, the participants worked together to sort six grocery bags of foodstuffs onto two tables. The tables were divided into three areas meant to represent common food storage locations in the home: the *pantry*, the *fridge*, and the *countertop*. These areas were further subdivided into areas based on types of food. Participants were asked to place the empty grocery bags on the table to indicate that they were done.

*3) Instruction:* In the instruction scenario, we aimed to observe how an expert conveys knowledge to a non-expert and, when that knowledge is miscommunicated, how the expert might help the non-expert to recover [28].

Our instruction scenario involved first training one of the participants (the *instructor*) in assembling a particular pipe configuration to allow two sinks to drain into a single system. The instructor was given as much time as they needed to learn how to configure the pipes. Upon learning the necessary steps to build the pipes, the instructor walked the second participant (the *student*) through each step of the assembly.

*4) Interview:* The goal of the interview scenario was to capture the process by which one participant questioned a second participant to obtain information. Interviewers may sometimes request sensitive information, requiring substantial rapport between the interviewer and interviewee. The structure and the tone of an interview can help determine the level of rapport between participants [19].

In our interview scenario, one of the participants (the *interviewer*) was told that they would be conducting a job interview for a generic position. The interviewer was given a list of 14 questions and time to review them. After reviewing the questions, the second participant (the *interviewee*) was asked all 14 questions by the interviewer. The researcher reentered the room when all the questions were answered.

*5) Storytelling:* In storytelling, we were interested in observing how one participant relayed a story to a second participant and what discourse patterns (e.g., asking questions) helped participants communicate more effectively [17].

In our storytelling scenario, one participant (the *storyteller*) watched a seven-minute video of a cartoon story. The storyteller was given as much time as they needed to feel comfortable with retelling the story, after which they had three to five minutes to retell the story to the second participant (the *listener*). After the storyteller finished, participants frequently had a conversation concerning the story. The experimenter re-entered the room when the conversation subsided.

### Analysis

For each scenario, we followed an iterative process of data coding and modeling. The coding process involved a researcher iteratively coding all video data and a second researcher annotating 10% of the videos to confirm the reliability of the coding process (81% agreement, Cohen's $\kappa$ = .76). In the coding of the data, we annotated the videos for the set of *states*—significant events in the interaction—and the *transitions* between these states, generating a *model* of the interaction scenario. From these models, we extracted what appeared as the core part of the interaction: the states that were essential to characterize the interaction. For example, in an interview, the interviewer asking a question and an interviewee answering it serve as two core states of the interaction. Finally, we examined the models from all five scenarios for states or sequences of states that frequently appeared to identify what might serve as *interaction design patterns*.

Our consideration of significant events in the interaction as states follows prior studies of social interaction [5, 19, 29]. When connected with other states, the resulting model represents the flow of the interaction from one event to the next. The idea of states translates well to social interaction, where one participant usually holds the floor and is engaged in an event (e.g., sharing a comment) [25]. For the purposes of an interaction with multiple participants, the states of all participants can be mapped to a single model. When a state that is held by only one participant is entered, all other participants implicitly wait. The use of states and transitions also fits well with a common paradigm used in robot programming where "nodes" are used to control functionalities of the robot [24]. The use of states provides a flexible representation for the flow of interaction for multiple participants.

After establishing the core states, we reviewed each video and noted any deviations from this core part of the interaction in both kind and number. An example deviation in the interview scenario is the interviewee asking for clarification regarding the interviewer's question. State models for each scenario were then constructed from the core part of the interaction, any deviations from the core part of the interaction, and notes collected from the video data. The resulting scenario models were then compared against the interactions in the videos for any mistakes or inconsistencies.

### Pattern Discovery

After constructing a model for each scenario, we identified common interaction structures, which served as *design interaction patterns*, or patterns. For example, a question being asked and answered is comprised of two separate states (a question state and an answer state). However, questions are almost always followed by answers, and thus the interaction between both states is codified into a pattern. We identified seven common patterns (Figure 3) across all five scenarios:

*1) Introductory Monologue:* The introduction that begins the interaction is often the most important indicator of how well the remainder of the interaction will play out [26]. A short introduction can be used to introduce other participants to a scenario by giving an overview of the remainder of the interaction. In the interview scenario, some participants started with a short introduction of themselves, describing the interview as part of the "hiring process." In the storytelling scenario, all participants started with a short introduction that set the stage for the story, such as identifying the primary characters and setting. An example of an introduction used in the interview scenario is shown below:

> *Interviewer*: Hi, welcome. ... So, today I'll be asking you a few questions to gauge your compatibility for this job.

Previous work on spontaneous encounters notes that these introductions can take different forms [27]. It is likely that for scenarios where we did not observe an introduction state (conversation, collaboration, and instruction), an introduction state would have occurred in a natural setting. For example, a person may pass by their friend while shopping and summon the friend with a short introduction ("Hello Jane! How are you doing?") before commencing with a conversation.

*2) Question and Answer:* The idea of a *question-answer pair* is a well-studied component of discourse management [6]. A *question* is a sentence meant to elicit information from other participants. Questions may introduce a topic of interest (e.g.,

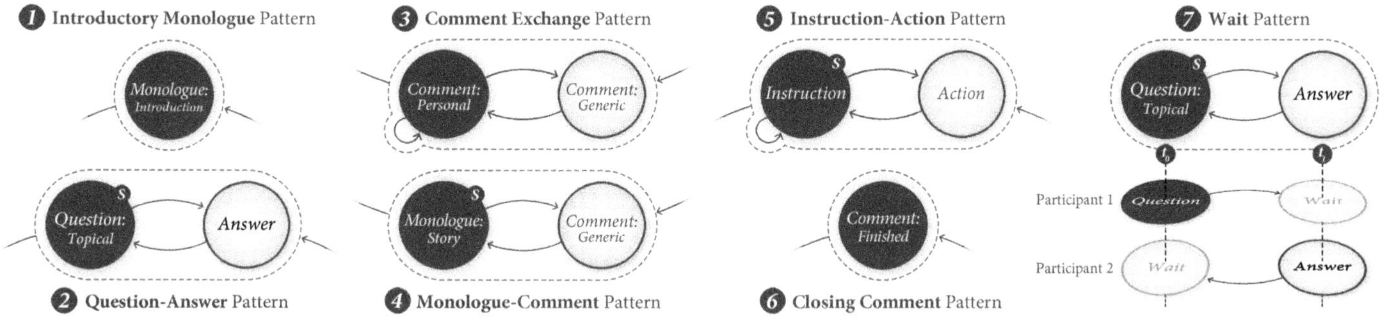


**Figure 3.** Models for the seven patterns we discovered. The dark and light-colored states indicate when one participant occupies the dark-colored state, a second participant must occupy the light-colored state. For example, for pattern 5, if one participant asks a question, the second participant gives an answer.

"What has been your most difficult job?"), request elaboration (e.g., "Could you elaborate on that?"), ask for clarification (e.g., "What do you mean by that?"), confirm understanding (e.g., "Does that make sense?"), check background (e.g., "Have you ever watched Looney Tunes?"), and request status (e.g., "How are you?"). In an archetypal question-answer pair, a question is be followed by an answer. An *answer* is the response to a question that aims to satisfy the questioning participant's curiosity [27]. The excerpt below from the storytelling scenario is an example of a question-answer pattern:

*Storyteller*: Do you know who Marvin the Martian is?
*Listener*: Oh yeah, from Looney Tunes.

*3) Generic Comment and Personal Comment:* A *comment* is a short statement offering the speaker's opinion. Comments are either generic (e.g., "Wow") or personal (e.g., "I tried that and didn't like it"). In our data, participants engaged in exchanging comments frequently move between sharing personal insights—either of their own volition or after being prompted—and offering generic comments. The following excerpt illustrates an exchange of comments from the conversation scenario:

*Participant 1*: Wow.
*Participant 2*: Yeah...I had never done anything quite like that before.
*Participant 1*: I had a similar experience once, but it wasn't nearly that exciting.
*Participant 2*: Interesting.

In this example, both participants offer both generic and personal comments, highlighting the fluidity between these two types of comments for all participants of the interaction.

*4) Monologue and Generic Comment:* A *monologue* is a longer form of speech during which no response is expected. Monologues may involve the telling of a story (e.g., "...Once Marvin had reached Bugs Bunny, he chose to..."). Although monologues expect no response, listeners may occasionally offer unsolicited commentary, as illustrated by the excerpt below from the storytelling scenario:

*Storyteller*: ...and then, all of a sudden, thousands of these aliens appear on Earth.
*Listener*: That's a lot.

*5) Instruction and Action:* An *instruction* is a command offered by one participant to direct the actions of another participant. The proper response to this instruction is often an *action*, although the action might follow the instruction with a delay depending on whether it is an appropriate time to perform that action [4]. Instruction-action pairs are commonly found in teaching scenarios where the teacher is directing the student. Below is an example of an instruction-action pair from the instruction scenario:

*Instructor*: Now connect the long pipe with the one shaped like an "S".
*Student*: <locates both the long and S-shaped pipe, and then connects them>

*6) Finished Comment:* Upon the completion of the goals of the scenario, one or more of the participants will note that the scenario is completed by offering a *finished comment.* For some scenarios (the interview, instruction, and storytelling scenarios), only one of the participants is able to end the scenario (e.g., only the storyteller knows when the story is finished). In the collaborative scenario, either participant is able to end the scenario, as illustrated in the following example:

*Participant*: I think that's it, so we should be done.

Previous work has shown that conversations frequently have a definite ending initiated by either participant, whether through an unexpected interruption (e.g., a phone call), a forced ending (e.g., a train stop forces participants to go separate ways), or an achievement of the goals of the conversation (e.g., obtaining some piece of information) [21]. However, our instantiation of a conversation scenario lacked a comment confirming the end of the interaction, due to the conversation scenario in our study providing no concrete end goal, except to converse for three to five minutes until the experimenter interrupted the conversation at a natural break.

*7) Wait:* One pattern implicit in all scenarios involving two or more participants is the *wait* pattern. The majority of states across our scenarios are intended for a single participant. When a participant transitions into a state intended for a single participant, all other participants enter a wait state, as shown in Figure 3. Data on conversations overwhelmingly supports only a single speaker at a time and other participants listening to the speaker, with multiple speakers being common but brief [25].

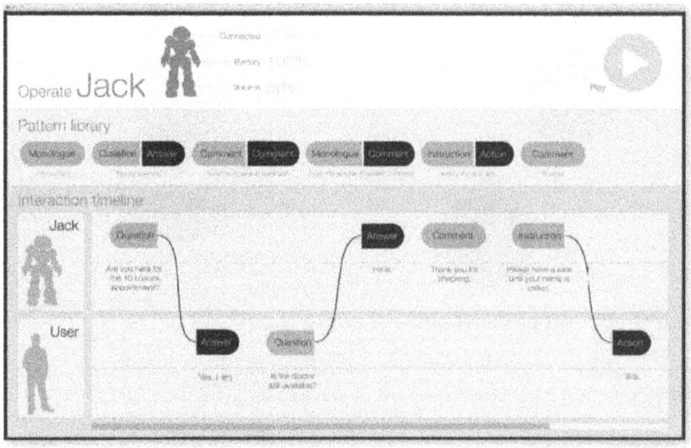


**Figure 4.** A screenshot of *Interaction Blocks*, our authoring environment for using a pattern language for synthesizing human-robot interactions.

Our analysis of five common social interactions not only provides a deeper understanding of each scenario, but also reveals the prevalence of a number of patterns across scenarios. These patterns confirmed some previous patterns (e.g., question-answer pairs [6]) as well as discovered new ones (e.g., Generic Comment and Personal Comment).

## DESIGN & IMPLEMENTATION OF INTERACTION BLOCKS

Our analysis of human interactions revealed seven core patterns that appear across the five common social scenarios. To draw on these patterns in design exploration and prototyping for human-robot social interactions, we developed *Interaction Blocks*, an authoring environment that enabled interaction designers to synthesize interactions and prototype them on a NAO humanoid robot, a robot platform commonly used in research and design for human-robot interaction.

### Authoring Environment

Our authoring environment is composed of three sections: the *control panel*, the *pattern library*, and the *interaction timeline*. An example of our tool can be seen in Figure 4.

The *control panel* displays pertinent information to the user. The silhouette of the robot provides a visual indication of connection status, with blue indicating "connected" and grey indicating "disconnected." If connected, the control panel also informs the user of which robot they are connected to, and the IP address, current battery level, and current volume of the connected robot. The "Play" button on the far right side of the interface is used to upload and execute the user's synthesized dialogue on the connected robot.

The *pattern library* contains the patterns discovered in our formative study, with each pattern represented in a capsule shape. We chose to represent our patterns in a capsule shape to accommodate dual-colored capsules for those patterns which are comprised of two states. To compose an interaction, patterns can be dragged out of the pattern library and onto the interaction timeline.

The *interaction timeline* is where the user composes the interaction. To accommodate both the user and the robot roles, the timeline is divided in half, each half assigned to one of the roles. When the user moves a pattern from the pattern library to the interaction timeline, the pattern is automatically added in place to the appropriate role. For patterns with two states, the movement of the pattern into the interaction timeline causes the pattern to divide in half, as shown in Figure 4. A Bézier curve connects the two states, indicating that no patterns can be inserted between them. When a pattern is divided into two states, the user is in control of the first state in the pattern. The second state is automatically added to the opposite role. For example, if a "question" is added to the user's timeline, an "answer" will be added to the robot's timeline.

### Implementation on the NAO Robot

To allow users to evaluate their synthesized interaction on a robot, we enabled Interaction Blocks to connect and execute the resulting dialogue on a NAO robot. All robot utterances were generated through the NAO's native text-to-speech application programming interface (API), while participant responses were recognized using the NAO's native natural language processing API.

In addition to the dialogue, socially appropriate gaze behaviors were automatically incorporated into the robot's interaction. The NAO employed its native face-tracking capabilities to enable consistent gaze with the participant. We introduced Perlin noise [23]—a technique used in animation and film to simulate randomness that appears natural—to create small head shifts in the robot and create a lifelike appearance. Additionally, we constructed socially appropriate gaze aversion behaviors for the robot, using the timings provided by Andrist et al. [1]. For instance, when the floor was passed to the robot, the robot would gaze away before returning its gaze to the participant, resuming Perlin noise, and continuing with its part of the dialogue, all of which helped the robot display natural social behaviors.

## DESIGN SESSIONS

We evaluated our tool in design sessions with local members of the design and development community from two groups: *interaction designers* and *developers*. Using a scenario for an interaction between a robot receptionist and human patient, participants were asked to construct and test an episode of interaction using our authoring environment.

### Design Task

Participants were given a scenario that described an exchange at a dentist's office between a patient (the user) and the receptionist (the robot). The scenario included a set of micro-interactions, such as "the receptionist greets the patient" or "the patient asks the receptionist when their next scheduled appointment is," that guided the participant in constructing an interaction episode. Participants took as much time as necessary, taking between 29 and 62 minutes ($M$ =45 minutes, 30 seconds, $SD$ =10 minutes, 37 seconds) to complete the design task. The setup of the study is shown in Figure 5.

### Recruitment & Selection

We recruited 10 participants—five interaction designers and five developers—from the local campus community. The interaction designers were selected from among students who

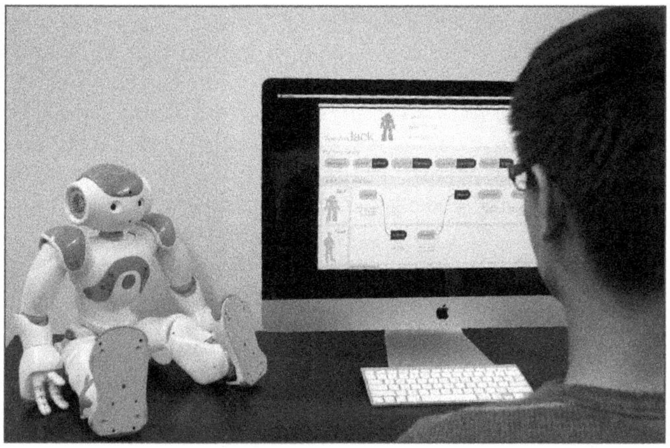

**Figure 5.** A researcher demonstrating the setup of the design sessions with the Interaction Blocks authoring environment and a NAO humanoid robot.

had completed the most advanced level interaction design course offered on campus, which taught principles and methods for user-centered interaction design and provided students with hands-on experience in design exploration and prototyping. Developers were recruited from among upper-level computer science majors with web development experience with the goal of capturing the perspectives of more technical users who might use our tool. Participants were between 19 and 26 years of age ($M$ = 22.5, $SD$ = 2.68) and were either computer science students or were employed in positions that required a computer-science background.

### Session Procedure

Following informed consent, participants were guided into a usability laboratory by a researcher. The researcher demonstrated Interaction Blocks, introducing the participant to the purpose of the tool, the layout of the interface, and the workflow necessary to explore and prototype interaction episodes and to test them with the robot. The participant was given five minutes to explore the interface independent of the researcher and was provided with the opportunity to ask questions at the end of the exploration period. At the end of this period, the researcher provided the participant with the scenario and left the room. The participant was given as much time as necessary to complete the design task. Following the completion of the task, the participant completed the System Usability Scale (SUS). The experimenter then conducted a semi-structured interview with the participant on the design of Interaction Blocks, their experience with using the authoring environment, and how it facilitated their exploration. Participants were compensated $10 USD for their time.

### Analysis

Following guidelines suggested by Bangor et al. [2], a usability score from 0 to 100 was calculated by rescaling each of the 10 items used in the SUS to range from 0 to 4, summing the scores for the 10 items, and multiplying the result by 2.5.

We used content analysis to analyze the interview data [3]. Each interview was transcribed, and pertinent responses from each participant were included in a spreadsheet. After reviewing the responses across all participants, significant responses were noted, and affinity diagramming was used to organize the responses into emerging themes, refining as necessary.

## FINDINGS

In this section, we present our findings from two different sources of data: SUS scores and interview data. The SUS scores serve as a metric of the overall usability of the authoring environment in enabling the use of a pattern language for design exploration and prototyping in creating human-robot interactions. Findings from the interview data provide insights into the designers' and developers' experiences in the design sessions and guidelines for future design and development of methods and tools for supporting human-robot interaction design.

### SUS Scores

The SUS scores for the authoring environment ranged from 75 to 95 ($M$ = 84, $SD$ = 7.38), interaction designers assigning an average score of 82, while the developers assigned an average score of 86. Based on established guidelines for interpreting SUS scores [2], a score of 80 or higher places the interface in the highest quartile when considering a survey of interfaces evaluated using the SUS.

### Interview Data

Below, we highlight themes found from the interview data. Excerpts from the interview are labeled with either ID or DE for the interaction designers and developers respectively, followed by a number.

#### *Patterns' Ease of Use*

Interaction designers and developers stated that the patterns—particularly patterns with multiple states—made it easy to quickly compose and test interactions. For patterns with multiple states, participants felt that the authoring environment's ability to automatically add the second state to the opposite role alleviated the burden of mentally planning the necessary pairings of behaviors and helped prevent creating inappropriate behaviors such as composing a question without an answer. Additionally, ID2 noted that the use of patterns—rather than a generic dialogue box used to accommodate all utterances—forced him to more carefully consider his dialogue prior to adding it. The same participant also inquired about the ability to create custom patterns. The excerpts below illustrate responses related to the ease of use of the pattern language.

> *DE1: For most people, programming is not the easiest thing, and this is a very intuitive way to design dialogues.*
>
> *ID2: I think the linkages of showing questions-answer, instruction-action show the clear delineation with that. That would really help in formalizing the structure and kind of removing the ambiguity of real conversation from what you're working on...*

However, while participants commented on the ease of use of the patterns in general, some expressed a desire for additional guidance on the nuances between some of the patterns due to their lack of domain knowledge. For example, DE2 noted that there was a "monologue" pattern, a "comment" pattern, and a "monologue-comment" pattern. The participant was initially unsure why a "monologue-comment" pattern would be different from the combination of the individual "monologue" and "comment" patterns. DE1 voiced confusion about the presence of four "comment" states across three patterns. While participants generally felt comfortable using the patterns to accomplish the task goals, many participants asked for some form of documentation. Suggestions ranged from a traditional documentation interface with examples or a walk-through (ID4) to tooltips for each pattern (ID1).

#### *Design Exploration*

Participants found the ability to compose interactions on the timeline of the authoring environment and to execute them on the robot to support their design exploration and iterative design of the behaviors and interactions that they were building toward achieving natural dialogue. These comments are best illustrated by excerpts below by ID3.

> *ID3: I think that human-human interaction can change all the time, and hearing it more and more and more would make it better in the end.*

> *ID3: I mean it seems like this kind of interface is kind of, like, to play, so you can start using questions and answers right. Change the questions and the answers, add a comment in if you want.*

#### *Approachable Interface*

All participants commented on the clean and minimalistic design of the interface for the authoring environment, discussing it as an enabling tool that gave them the confidence that the complex task of synthesizing an interaction would be doable, as highlighted by the excerpts below.

> *ID4: It's very clean in design. It seems easy to use for that reason. It doesn't have many functions, so it seems like it's easy to learn.*

> *ID3: I think everything's very easy to see, like the flow. It's not easy to get lost. It's the least amount of details for someone who's maybe not majoring computer science.*

> *DE1: For most people, programming is not the easiest thing, and this is a very intuitive way to design dialogues.*

#### *Error Prevention*

DE1 and DE3 noted that the use of the pattern language and the visual authoring environment would aid designers who may have little to no development or programming experience in building an interactive application with a robot, as illustrated in the excerpt below. Their comments also suggested that this approach would enable developers to bypass many of the bugs frequently encountered when programming, such as syntax errors and typos, and alleviate the need for them to learn a new application programming interface (API).

> *DE3: If it has the functionality to prevent me from making mistakes, then that's good too, right?*

#### *The Need to Support Free-Form Exploration*

Some designers and developers expressed that the addition of a less structured environment might better facilitate their design exploration. Examples included a whiteboard (DE1, DE3), with paper and pencil (ID1), sticky notes (ID4), and a text editor (ID1, ID2). While these participants appreciated the structure and code generation benefits provided by Interaction Blocks, they felt a need for a less-structured initial step to the exploration that allowed them to easily create, edit, and view the behavior and dialogue components that they planned to use in the more structured construction of the robot's exchange with users. Comments from DE2 and ID2 below illustrate the need to support free-form design exploration.

> *DE2: Well honestly I'd probably write out a script in a text editor, and then drag out all the parts and fill in the text.*

> *ID2: This more feels like that I know what my design is and I am going to formalize it someway rather than 'this is how I lay it out and tweak it as I go kind of thing.' I almost feel this is the last stage.*

#### *Need for Branching*

While participants appreciated the simplicity of the current interface, several participants raised the question of accommodating alternative ways in which the interaction or the dialogue between the robot and its user might unfold. Questions focused on two facets of this problem: accommodating different utterances with the same semantic meaning (e.g., "Yes" versus "Yes, please"), and accommodating utterances with different semantic meanings (e.g., "Yes" versus "No"). Participants suggested adding into the authoring environment support for a list of possible responses for accommodating utterances with the same semantic meaning. To handle multiple branches of dialogue that result from utterances with different semantic meanings, participants suggested creating multiple timelines that can be collapsed and expanded (DE5) and displaying multiple timelines at once (ID4).

In addition to these suggestions, participants commented on the possibility of additional visualizations, color coding patterns for easier identification and disambiguation, and adding additional information concerning the robot's status.

## DISCUSSION

Results from the design sessions focused on three main findings: the use of design patterns, the design of the authoring environment, and the workflow required to synthesize dialogue. These results offer many future directions for improving and expanding the pattern language and authoring environment to better support human-robot interaction design.

### Design Patterns

The use of a pattern language was reviewed favorably by interaction designers and developers alike, with many noting the ease in which they could explore and prototype exchanges for the robot and users through their use. Additionally, participants highlighted the structure that patterns afforded as an advantage, noting that patterns forced them to consider their design choices for dialogue and interaction elements and how they contributed to the overall goals of the interaction.

Although participants found patterns easy to use, what interaction elements some patterns represented was not always clear to them. Participants suggested various forms of providing help within the authoring environment, including tooltips and examples to help acclimate users to the pattern language. Documentation of the patterns would not only help interaction designers better understand the design elements, but would also inform researchers interested in using and extending the pattern library presented here.

#### Authoring Environment

The authoring environment was cited by all participants for its ease of use and approachable design, which was confirmed by the SUS scores. The requests and suggestions for improvement discussed in the previous section underline the importance of accommodating more advanced functionality, such as branching, in future versions of the authoring environment without sacrificing too much from the simplicity of the current design. Some participants suggested the use of a "superuser" mode or the ability for users to reveal or hide detailed options or functionality for patterns.

#### Workflow

Participants frequently cited the ability to rapidly modify and evaluate their design ideas as a useful feature that aided them in the iterative development of their final design. This finding confirms prior work that highlights the importance of rapid design exploration and prototyping in the development of human-robot interactions to provide designers with a better understanding of how their designs would perform in real-world settings [18]. Additionally, the use of Interaction Blocks frees the designers' workflow of debugging, enabling them to concentrate on designing interactions.

While participants expressed enthusiasm for the use of Interaction Blocks as a part of their workflow for designing and prototyping human-robot interactions, they also expressed a desire for a less formal design step prior to using Interaction Blocks. Some participants viewed using the authoring environment as a last step to formalize their work, while others suggested using Interaction Blocks earlier in the design process after brainstorming to create a basic idea of how the designed interaction may unfold. Further studies of the design practices of interaction designers might inform the design of flexible authoring environments that support informal as well as formal exploration at different stages of the design process.

Finally, designers and developers voiced a need for the ability to sketch out dialogue exchanges, see how they fit within the interaction, and easily refine individual dialogue elements. To support this need, the authoring environment might provide a view of the script of the entire dialogue, enabling users to easily gain an overview of their design and make changes at each exchange from a global perspective. Additionally, this sketching environment might allow users to draft the dialogue first and use a drag-and-drop interface to add these dialogue elements to the patterned interaction elements.

#### Interaction Designers vs. Developers

While there were many topics that interaction designers and developers agreed on, there were also differences in how these two groups evaluated the use of the pattern language and authoring interface. For instance, interaction designers were more concerned with how new visualizations might enable users to better compose and manage complex interactions, while developers focused on the reduction in errors enabled by the use of the pattern language and visual authoring, as well as the desire for more information on the robot's status, the ability to batch edit and move large portions of the interaction, and the need for incorporating branching into the development of the dialogue. These trends might reflect how interaction designers with different training, expertise, or backgrounds might have different needs for authoring human-robot interactions; those with a development background might be empowered by the ability to more precisely control the robot, while those with a design focus might want more flexibility in design exploration.

#### Limitations

The pattern language that we used in building our authoring environment relied on our observations and analysis of interactions in five scenarios. While we carefully chose these scenarios to represent many of the interactions robots will encounter, additional or more complex scenarios might reveal additional patterns. Furthermore, the evaluation of the use of the pattern language and authoring environment involved primarily student designers and developers in relatively short design sessions, due to the limited volume of interaction design practice for robotic technologies and limited number of human-robot interaction designers. Future explorations might seek to engage professional interaction designers with experience in human-robot interaction design in longer-term design sessions to better understand how the approach presented here might support design exploration and prototyping human-robot interactions. Given the difficulty and overhead involved in programming complex robot systems, design tools such as Interaction Blocks might significantly benefit such users.

#### Lessons Learned

The development of the pattern language and the authoring environment required decisions that might prove valuable for future work in this or related areas. One key challenge was selecting a diverse set of social interaction scenarios for our formative study of human interactions. While there are other roles that robots will likely fulfill, such as coaching, we needed to balance the diversity of scenarios with the workload involved in analyzing a large corpus. Another challenge was discovering an appropriate level of abstraction for our models (Figure 3) that would enable their use as design patterns. We followed an iterative process of reviewing the data from human interactions and sketching, constructing, and refining our models until no further modifications could be made.

### CONCLUSION

In this work, we explored how a design pattern language and visual authoring environment might enable designers to rapidly perform design exploration and prototyping for human-robot interaction. We observed and analyzed interactions from eight dyads engaged in five scenarios and developed seven interaction design patterns. We then built an authoring environment, *Interaction Blocks*, to enable interaction designers to use these patterns to rapidly construct, evaluate, and refine human-robot interaction. We conducted a qualitative evaluation of the use of the pattern language and authoring environment with a group of ten interaction designers and developers, as they prototyped an exchange between a robot and its user. Our results highlight the potential for the use of design patterns and the workflow that our authoring environment promotes to design, prototype, and evaluate interactions, enabling interaction designers to take advantage of patterns to synthesize complex interactions.

## ACKNOWLEDGMENTS

This work was supported by National Science Foundation award 1149970 and National Institutes of Health award 1R01HD071089-01A1. We would like to thank Brandi Hefty, Jilana Boston, Ross Luo, Jason Sauppé, Lindsay Jacobs, and Catherine Steffel for their help with our work.

## REFERENCES

1. Andrist, S., Mutlu, B., and Gleicher, M. Conversational gaze aversion for virtual agents. In *Proc. IVA* (2013), 249–262.
2. Bangor, A., Kortum, P. T., and Miller, J. T. An empirical evaluation of the system usability scale. *Intl. Journal of Human–Computer Interaction 24*, 6 (2008), 574–594.
3. Berelson, B. Content analysis in communication research.
4. Brandstätter, V., Lengfelder, A., and Gollwitzer, P. Implementation intentions and efficient action initiation. *Journal of personality and social psychology 81*, 5 (2001), 946–960.
5. Clark, H. *Using language*. Cambridge U, 1996.
6. Clark, H. H. *Arenas of language use*. U Chicago, 1992.
7. Datta, C., Jayawardena, C., Kuo, I. H., and MacDonald, B. A. Robostudio: A visual programming environment for rapid authoring and customization of complex services on a personal service robot. In *Proc. IROS* (2012), 2352–2357.
8. Fong, T., Thorpe, C., and Baur, C. Collaboration, dialogue, human-robot interaction. 255–266.
9. Fussell, S. R., Kiesler, S., Setlock, L. D., and Yew, V. How people anthropomorphize robots. In *Proc. HRI* (2008), 145–152.
10. Glas, D. F., Satake, S., Kanda, T., and Hagita, N. An interaction design framework for social robots. In *Proc. RSS* (2012).
11. Goffman, E. The interaction order. *American Sociological Review 48*, 1 (1983), 1–17.
12. Hsiao, K.-Y., Mavridis, N., and Roy, D. Coupling perception and simulation: steps towards conversational robotics. In *Proc. IROS* (2003), 928–933.
13. Huang, C.-M., and Mutlu, B. Robot behavior toolkit: generating effective social behaviors for robots. In *Proc. HRI* (2012), 25–32.
14. Humphrey, C. M., Henk, C., Sewell, G., Williams, B. W., and Adams, J. A. Assessing the scalability of a multiple robot interface. In *Proc. HRI* (2007), 239–246.
15. Kahn, P. H., Freier, N. G., Kanda, T., Ishiguro, H., Ruckert, J. H., Severson, R. L., and Kane, S. K. Design patterns for sociality in human-robot interaction. In *Proc. HRI* (2008), 97–104.
16. Kooijmans, T., Kanda, T., Bartneck, C., Ishiguro, H., and Hagita, N. Interaction debugging: an integral approach to analyze human-robot interaction. In *Proc. HRI* (2006), 64–71.
17. Langellier, K. M. Personal narratives: Perspectives on theory and research. *Text and Performance Quarterly 9*, 4 (1989), 243–276.
18. Lohse, M., Siepmann, F., and Wachsmuth, S. A modeling framework for user-driven iterative design of autonomous systems. *International Journal of Social Robotics* (2013), 1–19.
19. Matarazzo, J., and Wiens, A. *Interview: Research on Its Anatomy and Structure*. Aldine De Gruyter, 2007.
20. Mutlu, B., Forlizzi, J., and Hodgins, J. A storytelling robot: Modeling and evaluation of human-like gaze behavior. In *Proc. HUMANOIDS* (2006), 518 –523.
21. O'Leary, M. J., and Gallois, C. The last ten turns: Behavior and sequencing in friends' and strangers' conversational findings. *Journal of Nonverbal Behavior 9* (1985), 8–27.
22. Peltason, J., and Wrede, B. Modeling human-robot interaction based on generic interaction patterns. *AAAI Symposium on Dialog with Robots* (2010).
23. Perlin, K. Improving noise. *ACM Transactions on Graphics (TOG) 21*, 3 (2002), 681–682.
24. Quigley, M., Conley, K., Gerkey, B., Faust, J., Foote, T., Leibs, J., Wheeler, R., and Ng, A. Ros: an open-source robot operating system. In *ICRA Workshop on Open Source Software* (2009).
25. Sacks, H., Schegloff, E. A., and Jefferson, G. A simplest systematics for the organization of turn-taking for conversation. *Language 50*, 4 (1974), 696–735.
26. Schegloff, E. *The first five seconds: The order of conversational opening*. PhD thesis, University of California, 1967.
27. Schegloff, E. A. Sequencing in conversational openings. *American Anthropologist 70*, 6 (1968), 1075–1095.
28. Skehan, P. A framework for the implementation of task-based instruction. *Applied Linguistics 17*, 1 (1996), 38–62.
29. Tannen, D. *Talking voices: Repetition, dialogue, and imagery in conversational discourse*, vol. 6. Cambridge U, 1989.

# Improving Social Presence in Human-Agent Interaction

**André Pereira**
INESC-ID and Instituto Superior Técnico
University of Lisbon, Portugal
andre.a.pereira@ist.utl.pt

**Rui Prada**
INESC-ID and Instituto Superior Técnico
University of Lisbon, Portugal
rui.prada@inesc-id.pt

**Ana Paiva**
INESC-ID and Instituto Superior Técnico
University of Lisbon, Portugal
ana.paiva@inesc-id.pt

## ABSTRACT
Humans have a tendency to consider media devices as social beings. Social agents and artificial opponents can be examined as one instance of this effect. With today's technology it is already possible to create artificial agents that are perceived as socially present. In this paper, we start by identifying the factors that influence perceptions of social presence in human-agent interactions. By taking these factors into account and by following previously defined guidelines for building socially present artificial opponents, a case study was created in which a social robot plays the Risk board game against three human players. An experiment was performed to ascertain whether the agent created in this case study is perceived as socially present. The experiment suggested that by following the guidelines for creating socially present artificial board game opponents, the perceived social presence of users towards the artificial agent improves.

## Author Keywords
Human-Robot Interaction (HRI); social presence; board games; artificial opponents

## ACM Classification Keywords
I.2.1. Artificial Intelligence: Applications and Expert Systems - Games; I.2.9. Artificial Intelligence: Robotics - Commercial robots and applications; H.1.2. Information Systems: User/Machine Systems - Human factors

## INTRODUCTION
Techniques for representing others to evoke social presence have an ancient history that dates back to the first stone sculptures [3]. Science-fiction films or books have long included characters such as intelligent computers, robots and androids that evoke the same type of social responses from the audience or the reader [20]. With the evolution of technology, these science-fiction visions are now becoming a reality, and new interactive techniques and devices are designed to evoke social responses from users. Quasi-social relationships are beginning to be established with computers, intelligent virtual agents and robots [19]. People attribute social presence to interactive devices and treat them in social ways, even while knowing that these devices do not have real emotions or ideas [26]. Social presence can be briefly defined as the "sense of being together with another" [2]. Studying social presence can contribute to the understanding of human social behaviour while using these types of technologies. Achieving a sense of social presence is the design goal of many types of hardware and software engineering.

Creating artificial agents and robots that can interact with multiple humans is starting to become the focus of some computer entertainment and educational scenarios [17, 5]. This is a challenging task, as in multi-party interactions it is often more difficult to predict others' intentions and behaviours. The main focus of this paper is to guide researchers or engineers regarding how to design socially present agents. More specifically, we focus on intelligent agents that play board games against multiple players while still being perceived as socially present. These agents, rather than focusing on beating human players by performing millions of operations per minute, are socially aware, and their behaviours are influenced by their history with different human opponents. Board game artificial opponents are already being created both in Artificial Intelligence (AI) research and commercial applications. However, current artificial opponents still have performance and social deficits, especially in games in which they play against multiple human players. Johansson [13] stated that "bots are blind and objective, while humans may decide to eliminate the bots first, just because they are bots". This sentence shows that humans attribute a very low sense of social presence to artificial opponents. If human players do not perceive artificial opponents as socially present, their enjoyment and willingness to interact with them decreases [10].

Definitions of social presence and the factors that influence social presence in human-agent interaction are presented in the related work section of this paper. By taking these factors into account and following guidelines for creating socially present board game opponents [25], a case study was developed. This case study explores the use of today's technology to increase users' perceived social presence towards an artificial opponent. It features two main technology devices that provide an artificial opponent with the capability of playing a board game against multiple human players. First, a custom digital table was used as the interface between the human players, a robot and the game. Second, the artificial opponent is physically embodied by a robotic head with emotion rendering capabilities. We have performed an experiment in which participants played the Risk board game either against the artificial opponent described in our case study or against a control condition opponent based on a previous study [18].


*CHI 2014*, April 26–May 1, 2014, Toronto, Ontario, Canada.
Copyright © 2014 ACM 978-1-4503-2473-1/14/04..$15.00.
http://dx.doi.org/10.1145/2556288.2557180

This experiment suggested that by following the design considerations described in our case study, users' perception of the social presence of the artificial opponent improves.

## RELATED WORK

Social presence was initially proposed by Short, Williams and Christie [30] as "the degree of salience of the other person in the interaction and the consequent salience of the interpersonal relationships". The social presence theory allows researchers to guide the design, and to anticipate and measure differences of new types of social technology. Instead of using trial and error exploration, a better understanding of what social presence is can save valuable time and money, and can improve the end product in the design of new media technologies [20]. Many studies regarding social presence are found in new techniques of human-human communication such as computer conferencing. However, social presence is also used to measure an individual's perception of a particular interactive medium, be it a virtual reality environment [31] or the interaction with a social robot [18].

Several authors have discussed factors that influence social presence, but none of the authors have previously focused on artificial opponents. In the remainder of this section, we collect the factors that are deemed important for creating socially present artificial agents and opponents.

### Contributing Factors for Social Presence

There are different modes of interacting with a virtual agent, but in terms of social presence, *face-to-face interaction* is still considered the gold standard in communication against which all platforms are compared [1]. Social presence is assumed to be highest when two people are within reach of each other and are interacting on a task [4]. Therefore, virtual agents that do not use the rich set of social behaviours and cues involved in face-to-face interaction may be considered less socially present. Face-to-face interaction is generally accompanied by *verbal communication*. While interacting with virtual characters or robots, verbal communication offers the most attractive input and output alternatives. We are familiar with verbal communication, it requires minimal effort from users and it leaves their hands and eyes free [34]. Interactions should also feel natural and quick. Systems should have *quick feedback* for the user to feel immediacy of control, as delays between actions and reactions can diminish the sense of social presence [20]. In robots or on-screen characters, having a responsive real time gaze system can produce a high sense of agency and increase the agent's perceived social presence [35].

The *number of interacting entities* (be they virtual agents or humans) can also positively influence the perception of social presence in an interactive system. Having more than one entity in media interactions can be an easy way to induce a sense of social presence, regardless of the other perceptual features of the world [11]. *Knowledge and prior experience* with the medium also influences the sense of social presence. Social presence varies across individuals and across time for the same individual. When we have been exposed to artefacts of a particular medium over time, we have a higher knowledge of interacting with it, and it is possible to have an increased feeling of social presence. However, very often, continued experiences may cause the well-known habituation or novelty effect [14]. This effect causes an initially higher sense of social presence that fades away as users become more experienced with novel technology [18]. This novelty effect is present in almost all types of media, including artificial agents or robots [8]. The ability to attribute mental states to oneself and to others is fundamental to human cognition and social behaviour [32]. Biocca [4] stressed the importance that the *theory of mind* has in social presence. He defines social presence as the sense of "being together with another" and attributes this sense to the ability to relate to or to construct mental models of another's intelligence. These models can simulate minds of people, animals, agents, aliens, gods and so on. If we interact with an agent and create a mental model of it, we can anticipate the agent's behaviour and judge its consistency. The number and quality of sensory channels are important for generating a sense of social presence. More importantly, *consistency* between all of the different modalities is one of the most relevant keys for achieving social presence: "the information received through all channels should describe the same objective world" [20]. If we do not meet this criterion, we emphasise the artificial and lessen the feeling of social presence. Correlations between actions and reactions should be credible when compared to events that would be expected in reality under similar circumstances. Slater [31] notes that another important factor for social presence is the occurence of some events not directly related to the users' actions. These events show *autonomy* in the environment or character. In a study conducted in a cave-like environment, participants spent approximately five minutes in a virtual bar interacting with five virtual characters [7]. Participants were reported to automatically respond to the virtual characters present in the bar in social ways. Though these virtual characters had limited social behaviours, mutual gaze combined with lucky randomness, was perceived by participants as the characters watching and mimicking them. *Embodiment* is also important for designing a computer to achieve a higher sense of social presence. It has been reported in virtual poker environments that the simple addition of a picture personifying players made the game more likeable, engaging and comfortable [16]. We can also find examples where physically embodied agents (or robots) are used to simulate opponents. It was shown that by using a robotic embodiment instead of an on-screen character, artificial opponents have improved feedback, immersion and social interaction [23]. We use our emotions in our social world almost constantly.

Emotional responses can elicit adaptive social responses from others. For example, someone with an angry temperament can elicit a fear response from someone else, while someone distressed may elicit an empathic response from others. We also use emotional expressions for communication, signalling and for social co-ordination. These types of natural social primitives can be interpreted by humans without the need to learn something new; a human-like computer using these cues can cause social facilitation in users. Endowing agents with *emotional behaviour* can contribute to the believability of a character and thus to its perceived social presence.

Figure 1. Risk case study

## CASE STUDY

Five guidelines for designing socially present board game opponents were identified in our previous work [25]. These guidelines argue that to improve social presence, an artificial board game opponent should (1) have a physical embodiment and be able to engage in face-to-face interaction with one or multiple participants; (2) be believable and obtain players' attention by using both verbal and non-verbal behaviours; (3) have an emotion system to make better judgements and to simulate human emotions; (4) have social memory, i.e., recognise each user individually and remember its past interactions with him/her; and (5) be able to simulate social roles common in board games. We developed a case study that implements these guidelines in which an artificial opponent plays the Risk board game against three human players. The human players use a digital table as the game interface. Risk was chosen because it is a game where face-to-face interactions, social actions and strategic social reasoning are important components of the game. In the case study, the social robot is positioned on one side of a digital multi-touch table and interacts with three other players on the other sides of the table (see Figure 1). In the remainder of this section, we first present the design considerations taken in this case study. Then, we briefly describe the empirically inspired relationship variables that influence the decision process, dialogue and emotional synthesis of the robot, and finally, we describe the robot's multi-player gaze system.

### Design Considerations

By using robotic embodiments, board game computer opponents are more successful at engaging in face-to-face interaction with multiple participants [25]. For embodying the social Risk opponent we used the EMYS (EMotivc headY System) robotic head [15]. This robot was chosen for three different reasons. First, it can socially engage users face-to-face by quickly moving its head, eyes and eyelids towards the user, which makes it appropriate for our gaze system. Second, it can display idle behaviours and a wide range of emotions with different intensities. The idle behaviours and facial expressions used in this case study were developed by Ribeiro et al. [27]. These authors took inspiration from the principles and practices of animation and applied them to the development of idle behaviours and emotional expressions for the EMYS robot. Facial expressions are used in the case study for establishing turn-taking and for revealing emotional states such as sadness and pleasure. Finally, we chose this embodiment because of its fun and cartoonish appearance. While interacting with anthropomorphic robots, users have certain expectations of them, and not meeting such expectations can deteriorate the experience [22]. This consideration should also hold true when choosing an embodiment for an artificial opponent. The robot uses high quality text to speech (Brian from IVONA[1]) to vocalise its utterances. While speaking, the robot is able to accurately lip-sync with the text-to-speech system. We also upgraded the EMYS robotic head with a Kinect sensor that is used for detection of speech direction.

We designed and built a custom digital table for this case study. By using a digital table, players are able to freely communicate and still be aware of the game state. This means that they can more easily be engaged with both the game and each other [28]. In the table's design we took into account the ergonomic considerations described in [29]. The first design decision to improve ergonomics was to have edges considerable wider than those of commercial digital tables available at this writing. If the edges are not wide enough, users tend to lean their elbows or arms on the table surface, which interferes with the application. By allowing users to rest their arms, they can be more relaxed and focused on social interactions. The second ergonomic decision was interface related. When using digital tabletop hardware, users should have their interface area in a comfortable personal space [33]. We designed the game interface using this principle, and therefore, we took users' comfort into account so that they could focus solely on social interactions with their peers and the social robot. Finally, the height of the table was considered. When designing a table for casual interaction, short coffee tables are appropriate, desk-height tables are more suited for productivity or longer tasks such as long gaming sessions. Therefore, we chose the height of a normal desk table.

For implementing social memory in the artificial opponent, we simplified the user recognition process by requiring each user to login with their own private interface on the digital table. At login time, the robot acknowledges the presence and position of a user, greets that particular user, and updates its history with him/her. The artificial opponent stores basic data in memory about the results and dates of previous matches. This information is often mentioned in the initial interaction, where the robot can say for example: "One week ago you won, this time I am going to win!". More complex social variables are also used by the robot to map relationships established with particular users. These variables evolve during the game and are stored in the robot's memory for future interactions.

### Social Relationship Variables

Dialogue recordings of humans playing the traditional Risk game have been previously categorised [24]. The most relevant categories to model in a Risk artificial opponent were

[1]http://www.ivona.com/en/

extracted and that categorisation helps pinpoint the most important social behaviours to simulate in a Risk game. Additionally, in that study, a database of possible utterances was extracted from real human social behaviour. However, to understand the humans' thought process and to know when an artificial opponent should select a particular move or utterance, a protocol analysis was performed. In this analysis, participants were asked to think aloud while playing a traditional Risk game, and the most relevant variables to simulate in a social Risk opponent were extracted. In this sub-section we briefly describe the empirically extracted variables that enable the artificial opponent to establish different social relationships with different users: *Familiarity*, *Like/Dislike* and *Luck Perception*. These variables are used for generating dialogue or for choosing the next move.

Familiarity can be an important variable to model in a social agent because the number of utterances that an artificial agent can speak is often limited, and long term studies have shown that repetitive behaviours decrease social presence and believability [18]. Therefore, it is advantageous for an artificial agent to be shyer (less talkative) towards players with whom it has interacted for only a limited time and to become more familiar (talkative) with them over time. By implementing this behaviour, we are also following empirical results showing that when players already know each other outside the game or when they have played previous games before, they are more communicative and more willing to establish alliances between themselves. In our implementation, familiarity starts at a minimal value, never decreases, and increases slightly every time the robot interacts with players or every time a player interacts with the robot.

Influenced by attacks in the current and previous games, another relationship variable was simulated. This variable can be either positive (like), zero (neutral), or negative (dislike) for each of the agent's opponents. The agent can act socially according to this variable and establish different social relationships with different users. The variable changes after relevant game events; a change can be positive or negative. When players are not attacking each other, they are nicer to each other, and the opposite occurs when they attack. Thus, when a player attacks the agent, the relationship variable towards him/her decreases. The variable increases slightly when players have the opportunity to attack the robot but do not. The variable also changes when an opponent attacks a player the agent likes or dislikes. We took inspiration for this behaviour from Heider's balance theory [12]. Following the balance theory rationale, when a player is attacking one of the robot's "most hated" opponents, the Like/Dislike variable towards him/her increases. Conversely, if a player attacks one of the agent's "friends," the relationship variable will decrease. As previously reported, the Like/Dislike variable is stored, so the robot can disclose, for example, that it holds a "grudge" against a particular player because of previous games.

Luck perception is also stored in memory, so the agent can assess and comment if a player is lucky or if he/she was lucky in previous games. Risk is a game that involves lucky dice throws, and players are constantly "storing" in memory the luck that they attribute to other players. When players are lucky and constantly winning at dice throws, other players expect them to continue winning and usually comment on that fact. When the unexpected occurs and players lose after a winning or losing streak, stronger verbal and nonverbal reactions are usually elicited. Due to the frequency of verbal and emotional content commonly found in this game event [24], such behaviours seem to be important to implement in artificial agents that play games involving luck. Simple rules and statistics were used to monitor players' luck in the game. Luck events are generated by using an anticipatory mechanism [21] that assesses the mismatch between the agent's expectations of a dice throw and the actual result.

Risk is a highly social game that supports various social roles in its game play. Players can change roles throughout a game. Social roles in board games were identified by Eriksson et al. [6]. In our implementation, these roles arise because the robot's AI uses the relationship variables to influence its social behaviour. For example, when the agent "likes" another player, it often demonstrates the social role of Helper by making encouraging comments such as "It went well this turn!". Conversely, when the agent has a negative relationship with another player, it is more likely to adopt the Violator role, for example by attacking him/her without seeking any in-game benefit.

### Multiplayer Gaze System

To achieve believable face-to-face interactions, we developed a gaze system that equips our robot with the ability to simultaneously interact with multiple players in our gaming context. The gaze system uses speech direction detection, face detection, and the context of the game; it is based upon studying how humans behave in such context. We have extracted gaze patterns and created a gaze system for multi-user interaction with a social robot. The gaze system is influenced not only by the robot's own variables but also by the other players' voices and game actions. The robot also uses a camera in its "nose" for face detection and uses sound direction detection sensed from the Kinect's microphone array.

In most board games, players shift their focus between looking at different parts of the board and looking at other players. Players look at the game board when they are thinking, during their own turns and their opponents' turns or when other players make their moves on the board. When it is not a players turn, they tend to look at the active player more than any other. We noted that the factor that most influences the amount of time that participants look at the board or at other players is their concentration on the game. Inspired by this observation, we modelled these behaviours in our robot by using a *concentration* variable. This variable enables the robot to look more focused on the game during its own turn and more focused on the other players during their turns. The variable tends to be higher during the robot's turn and lower during an opponent's turn. It also decreases when other players take too long to play or when all of the events in the game are not related to the robot's game.

Once a gaze command is over or is interrupted by a relevant event for the gaze system, another gaze command is issued. When it is not the robot's turn, it performs a Concentration Test (CTest). The CTest starts by generating a random value. If that value is less than the robot's current concentration variable, the robot issues a focused gaze action. If the value is higher, it issues an unfocused gaze action. This means that if the concentration variable is low, the robot tends to be unfocused, and when the variable is high, it is more often focused. When unfocused, the robot looks at other players randomly but with a higher probability of looking at the active player. When the robot issues a focused gaze action, it looks randomly at a point on the game board, simulating that it is thinking and looking at the game action attentively.

When a user touches the interface, the robot is informed of the location of the touch, and the robot is able to gaze at it. The robot can look at points on the interface precisely. To implement this, the robot is always fixed on the same predetermined position on the digital table; parametrised gaze values were calibrated for each point on the interface. If after a touch event the robot passes a CTest, it gazes at the interface. If the CTest fails, the event is ignored. This simulates the observed behaviour that when players are thinking they are more focused on the game board.

To further improve the robot's gaze system, we found the need to implement a speech direction detection module in the robot to make it look at players when they are talking. This module was implemented by using Kinect and its beamforming algorithms from the Microsoft SDK. The Kinect microphone array reports the position of the speaking player, and we use that angle to look in the direction of the sound. However, the robot only chooses to look in the direction of speech if it fails a CTest, simulating that it only "listens" to other players when unfocused.

Finally, when the robot decides to speak to a player, the gaze system also causes the robot to look at the direction of the intended player. All gaze actions belonging to the "look at a player" group work in the following manner. First, the robot looks at a position where the player most likely is. This initial probable position was calculated by several user tests in which we fixed gaze values for looking at the three human players. Second, once the robot fixes its gaze on that position, it tries to detect a face using EmguCV[2]. If successful, it tracks the user's face and follows it for the remaining time of the gaze action. Finally, to increase accuracy, the robot stores the last position of that opponent, remembering the probable position for that user for the next time.

Every gaze action stays focused on the target, be it a player or a point on the interface, for a determined amount of time. The only exception is when speaking to a player, the robot directs its gaze to that player until it stops speaking. For every other type of gaze, we have defined a minimum and a maximum length of time, and a minimum and a maximum of gaze speed. When the robot initiates a new gaze order, it uses random values both for the speed and gaze duration between those minimum and maximum values. We fixed high speeds and shorter time spans for events in which the interface is touched or a speech direction is detected. Slower gaze speeds and longer time spans are used when the robot is inactive.

[2]http://www.emgu.com/

## EVALUATION

In this paper, we hypothesise that an agent that follows guidelines for socially present board game opponents will be perceived as more socially present than an agent that does not implement such guidelines. For testing this hypothesis, we report a study between subjects where participants played a Risk game against a robotic opponent.

### Participants

Forty five participants (12 males, 33 females) with ages ranging from 18 to 40 years old ($M$ = 24.0, $SD$ = 5.0) took part in the experiment. Participants were undergraduate and graduate students recruited via a program in which they received extra curriculum credits for their participation. The experiment was conducted at a Psychology University. Each session included three participants.

### Procedure

At the beginning of each session, participants were told that they were going to play the Risk board game against a physical robot and each other. We used a Powerpoint presentation alongside the interface of the game to explain the Risk rules and the game interface. A sequenced presentation was used so that every participant learned the rules and how to interact with the game interface in the same manner. The three participants then sat around the digital table with EMYS, our social robot, on the remaining side. EMYS acted as an artificial opponent for thirty minutes or until it was eliminated from the game. When EMYS was eliminated or the thirty minutes were over, EMYS warned participants that the interaction had ended. Finally, participants filled in a questionnaire, and the experiment was over. Each experiment lasted approximately 1 hour.

### Manipulation

The experiment had two main conditions: a socially present condition (SP) in which we used the full implementation of our social opponent, and a less social condition (¬SP) in which the behaviour of the robot was not inspired by the guidelines for creating socially present opponents. We assigned 27 participants (9 groups of 3) to the SP condition and 18 participants (6 groups of 3) to the ¬SP condition. When recruiting participants for this study, we requested good English skills as a prerequisite. However, two participants in the SP condition were removed from the study (1 male and 1 female) because they reported in the questionnaire and to the experimenters that they did not have the English skills necessary to understand EMYS.

#### *Socially Present Condition (SP)*

Our experiment had the limitation of a single 30 minute interaction with the robot. Given this time constraint, we decided to fix some of the agent's variables to have a more controlled experiment and for users to experience the same diversified behaviour that would occur in longer exposures to our artificial opponent.

We designed the familiarity variable for long term interactions with the same participants. In a single interaction, we wanted the social robot to be as interactive as possible from the beginning of the game. Therefore, we fixed this variable to its highest value, 1, for all participants.

Additionally, we randomly assigned fixed values of the Like/Dislike variable to each user. When a game started, the social robot had a *positive relationship* with one of the participants, a *negative relationship* with one of them and a *neutral relationship* with the third. By manipulating the Like/Dislike variable in this manner, we ensured that the robot displayed different social roles in each interaction and had a more diversified and constant behaviour.

#### *Not as Socially Present Condition (¬SP)*

Comparing an artificial opponent with another that has no gaze at all and no speech or non-verbal behaviour, would most certainly result in a decrease in the sense of social presence. In [18], a study was presented in which, in a similar scenario, the behaviour of a social robot was not sufficient to maintain a sense of social presence in users. This evaluation and the guidelines presented in [25] were informed by that study. We compared our SP condition with the baseline behaviour of that robot and identified the main differences between the two. As a result, in the ¬SP condition, when compared to SP, the following changes were implemented: (1) the same physical embodiment was used, but a more randomised gaze system provided less believable face to face interactions, (2) the verbal and non-verbal behaviours of our robot were limited to only non-social game events, (3) the robot exhibited fewer emotional expressions and its emotional system did not influence the moves it chose, (4) it did not store any type of social data in memory and (5) it did not display the common social roles present in board games.

To implement a randomised gaze system, the robot was always looking at random points in the interface during its turn, and during the opponent's turn, it was randomly shifting its gaze towards one of the other players. The main differences between the simplified gaze system and the complete one are the absences of speech direction detection, a face detection algorithm to more convincingly look a player in the face, and a concentration variable that informs the "randomness" of the gaze target.

Regarding the verbal and non-verbal behaviour of the robot, in this condition, our artificial opponent only commented and reacted to non-social events. To generate social events in the SP condition, we used our empirically inspired social variables such as Like/Dislike and Luck perception. These variables were set to 0 and did not change. This meant that the robot was neutral towards all users and did not comment, for example, on lucky dice throws. Familiarity was the only empirically inspired variable that we maintained in this condition. It was fixed to 1 so that there would be no differences in the speech rate across conditions. As the robot's variables did not change in this condition, the agent had no social memory and could not display social roles.

### Measures

#### *Social Presence*

The measure for social presence that we considered grounded and suited to measure social presence in human-agent interaction is the Networked Minds Questionnaire [9]. This measure was originally designed to distinguish between levels of social presence between face-to-face interactions and different levels of mediated interactions. However, we have successfully used it for measuring social presence in a human-robot interaction scenario [18]. It conceptualises social presence in the following six dimensions: (1) *co-presence*, the degree to which the observer believes s/he is not alone; (2) *attentional allocation*, the amount of attention the user allocates to and receives from an interactant; (3) *perceived message understanding*, the ability of the user to understand the message from the interactant; (4) *perceived affective understanding*, the user's ability to understand the interactant's emotional and attitudinal states; (5) *perceived affective interdependence*, the extent to which the user's emotional and attitudinal state affects and is affected by the interactant's emotional and attitudinal states; and (6) *Perceived behavioural interdependence*, the extent to which the user's behaviour affects and is affected by the interactant's behaviour.

This questionnaire uses six items for each of these dimensions; subjects were asked to express their agreement or disagreement regarding each item on a seven-point Likert scale (one means "totally disagree" and seven means "totally agree"). Two experimenters separately translated all items of the questionnaire into Portuguese. They then agreed upon the most suitable and correct translation.

#### *General Questions*

To assess whether users would like to continue interacting with the robot on a regular basis and to learn what the users liked most and least about EMYS, we asked the following general questions after the social presence questionnaire: Did you enjoy playing against EMYS? Would you like to play another game of Risk with EMYS? What would you change about EMYS? Do you think EMYS has social skills? For each of these questions we also asked why?

### Results

In this section, we first validate our translated social presence questionnaire by checking the normality and reliability of the scales. We then present a comparison between the SP and ¬SP conditions using the measures above.

#### *Reliability Analysis and Normality Tests*

For measuring social presence, we used a questionnaire that was already validated and had been used previously by the research community. However, because we had translated all of the items from English to Portuguese we started by performing reliability tests on our questionnaire. Additionally, we ran normality tests and examined the normality plots of each dimension to assess the normality of each measure. Of the six

| Social Presence Questionnaire | Mean | t(41) | p-value | r |
|---|---|---|---|---|
| Attention Allocation | SP = 4.18<br>¬SP = 3.78 | 0.99 | >0.05 | 0.15 |
| Perceived Aff. Understanding | SP = 4.34<br>¬SP = 2.57 | 5.49 | <0.01 | 0.65 |
| Emotional Interdependence | SP = 4.21<br>¬SP = 3.15 | 2.64 | <0.01 | 0.38 |
| Behaviour Interdependence | SP = 4.15<br>¬SP = 2.78 | 3.42 | <0.01 | 0.38 |
| Total | SP = 4.70<br>¬SP = 3.51 | 4.55 | <0.01 | 0.47 |

**Table 1. Mean, t-value, p-value and effect size for the parametric Social Presence questionnaire items.**

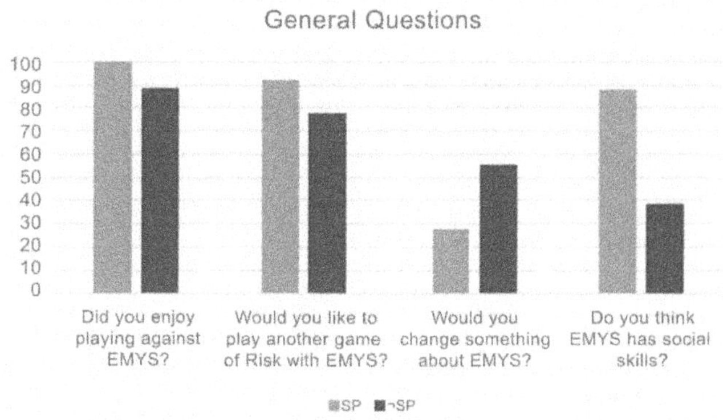


**Figure 2. Percentage of positive ("yes") answers reported.**

different dimensions of the presence questionnaire, three dimensions had unacceptable Cronbach's $\alpha$ levels. After further analysis, we found that the reliability of those scales could be greatly increased by removing two items from each of these 3 dimensions. The other items had very high reliability values and all items from the original questionnaire were used. Regarding the normality of the distribution, most measures were parametric with the exception of Co-presence and Perceived Message Understanding, which are not normally distributed. For non-parametric items, we applied the Mann-Whitney U test and report the median value between conditions. For the parametric items, we applied independent t-tests, and the mean is reported.

### *Social Presence*

Overall, participants in SP (Mdn = 6.17) experienced a significantly greater sense of co-presence than participants in ¬SP (Mdn = 5.00), U = 96.50, z = 3.17, $p < 0.001$, r = 0.48. In terms of Perceived Message Understanding there was also a significant difference between the SP condition (Mdn = 5.00) and the ¬SP condition (Mdn = 3.25), U = 102.50, z = 3.025, $p < 0.01$, r = 0.46.

The other dimensions were parametric and, with the exception of attention allocation, were similarly significantly classified as higher in SP, as we can observe in Table 1.

### *General Questions*

All participants in the SP condition claimed that they enjoyed playing against our artificial opponent, and 92% stated that they would like to play against EMYS again (see Figure 2). Enjoyment (89%) and intention to continue using the system (78%) were lower but also quite high for the ¬SP condition. When we asked participants if they would change something about EMYS, only 28% would change something in our main condition in contrast to 56% in the ¬SP condition. The Chi-Square tests did not reveal significant differences between these questions. However, when users were asked if they thought that EMYS had social skills, the difference was significant ($\chi^2(1) = 11.495$, $p < 0.001$). In the SP condition, 88% claimed that EMYS had social skills, while in the ¬SP only 39% answered affirmatively. The effect size for this finding was large ($\phi = 0.517$).

These questions had a qualitative second part asking participants to further develop their answer. Next, we report the patterns identified in the qualitative data.

### *Did you enjoy playing against EMYS?*

Many participants in the SP condition claimed that they enjoyed playing against EMYS because it was fun, interesting, challenging and the same as playing against a human player. Many participants also focused on social interactions with and the characteristics of the robot to explain their enjoyment. Empathy for, and feelings of rivalry or alliances towards the robot were the most reported social claims. One participant replied: "I felt like he was a real companion that socialised with all of us". In the ¬SP condition, participants focused more on the game being a new type of experience: "I enjoyed it because it was an experience in which I played against a robot". Enjoyment was high in both conditions, and we could not extract any relevant trend in the development of the negative answers.

### *Would you like to play another game of Risk with EMYS?*

More than half of the participants in SP responded that they would like to play another game against EMYS because it was fun. Interesting and exciting were also common words used to characterise the interaction. Some participants also said that the robot had a good sense of humour and that they enjoyed interacting socially with a robot. A common answer was: "I would like to have the opportunity of getting to know EMYS a little bit more." In the ¬SP condition, participants also mentioned the robot's sense of humour and the fact that it was a fun, novel, and interesting experience. However, they did not dwell as much on the social aspects of the robot as on the challenge that the experience provided and how well the robot played. Some participants replied that they would like to play a game until the end and not only thirty minutes. One participant said: "I would like to play until the end to determine a winner". For this question, we could also find some common negative answers. In both conditions, most participants would not like to play against EMYS again because they do not like board games. However, in ¬SP, participants also replied that it was the same as playing against a computer and that the robot should be more interactive.

### *Would you change something about EMYS?*

In the SP condition we had multiple types of suggestions to improve our artificial opponent. Some suggested changes in the embodiment, such as reducing the robot's noise or adding hands or a body to our robot. Others argued that it should recognise and speak the participants' native language, be less competitive and not so critical. Curiously, most changes suggested by participants in the ¬SP condition were already addressed in the SP condition. As expected, most participants that would not change anything about EMYS did not elaborate on their response. Typically, in both conditions we had some users saying that the "robot was already highly advanced" or that they "would not change a thing".

*Do you think EMYS has social skills?*
There were large differences in both conditions in responses to this question. In the SP condition, the most frequent positive answer was that the robot acted appropriately and according to the participants moves. Many participants also recognised the robot liking or disliking one of the players as a social act. Although the robot started with a predetermined value for the Like/Dislike variable and did not ally with other players, participants said that the robot did not like players who attacked him and made alliances with players who did not. One participant replied that "it can socialise, does not like it when we attack him and liked one of the players more, he even showed unhappiness when we attacked that player". In the ¬SP condition, players gave diverse reasons for their answers: some replied that it was able to interact socially but only in a superficial manner. One participant replied that it does interact socially but is more suited for younger people. Pressuring users to play was also regarded by two players as a social behaviour. Irony, competitive behaviour and emotional capabilities were also reported in this condition. One participant replied that "it can be a little social as it puts pressure on us when we take too long". In both conditions, negative responses were justified by the robot being programmed or simply because it is "just a robot".

### Discussion

When comparing SP versus ¬SP, only one of the social presence dimensions, attention allocation, was not significantly different across conditions. However, even in this dimension, we had a slight positive difference benefiting the socially present condition. This, alongside with the total of the social presence questionnaire being significantly higher in the SP condition, indicates that by following the guidelines for creating socially present opponents in the design of our artificial opponent, we increased participants perceived social presence. Co-presence, one of the most important factors for achieving social presence was the highest rated dimension in both conditions. Regarding attentional allocation, the difference was not significant because it was one of the highest rated dimensions in the ¬SP condition. In both conditions, participants allocated attention to the robot. We have two reasons to explain the similarity in the results between the conditions. First, the random gaze that we implemented always looked at a random player or the interface. Although it was doing it randomly, when the robot looked at participants, most thought that the robot was paying attention to them. Additionally, participants allocate their attention towards the robot because none of them had any prior experience with a robot and may have been influenced by the novelty effect. The other four dimensions, perceived message understanding, message interdependence, affective understanding and affective interdependence, were clearly more successfully achieved in our socially present condition. By implementing a gaze system that "listened" to players speaking, followed their faces, looked at where participants touched and was influenced by the game state, we successfully made users think that the robot's gaze was dependent on their behaviour. In terms of affect interdependency and understanding, the introduction of the Like/Dislike and Luck variables, which in part resulted in different social roles, seems to have contributed to this result. For example, in the qualitative questions many users noted that they thought that the robot would become angry with them if they attacked it. This means that they associated the robot's facial expressions and future behaviours with their past actions.

We also investigated differences in social presence when comparing the three different variations of the Like/Dislike variable in the SP condition. No significant differences were found. The social presence reported by participants was not significantly affected by the robot's relationship with the user. We can explain this result because within SP every participant was exposed to each variation. When replying to the qualitative questions, participants in the neutral variation also noticed the robot's social behaviour towards the other players. These players also replied that "the robot was angry with another player because that player attacked him". Some of our highest ratings for social presence were even from participants in the Negative relationship variation, which indicates that the perception of social presence does not seem to be affected by whether the relationships with the robot were positive or negative. The social presence that participants attributed to our artificial opponent seemed to be more influenced by the believability of the robot's behaviour towards the whole group.

We did not include questions in our questionnaire to directly assess if alliances were formed during the game. However, at the end of the game, we directly asked if any alliance was established. In the SP condition, only one of the 9 user groups allied against the robot, and the reported reason for doing so was that the robot was getting too strong. In the ¬SP condition, two out of six groups allied against the robot. One of the groups was even successful in eliminating our artificial opponent before the thirty minutes were over, ending the experiment at minute 27. The reasons for the alliance argued by participants were that they wanted to know what would happen if the robot lost or simply because "it was just a robot". In the introduction section, we noted that we had already predicted that users would choose to eliminate the artificial agent first. Preventing this behaviour was one of our main motivations. It seems that we had reasonable success in fighting this effect, although we would need to have a larger number of interactions to better establish it.

## CONCLUSIONS

We attempted to answer the question of how to create socially present agents that can play board games against multiple human players. Five design guidelines for increasing social presence in artificial opponents were outlined in a previous theoretical finding. To demonstrate how these guidelines can be used to create new forms of computer entertainment and to evaluate whether they indeed improve an artificial agent's social presence, we developed and evaluated a case study. An experiment was performed in which 45 participants played the Risk board game against an artificial opponent. The evaluation suggested that by following guidelines for creating socially present opponents, the users' perceived social presence towards our artificial opponent improved. We have no measure to exactly determine the success of each individual guideline. However, we can relate our results to each guideline.

*Be physically embodied and be able to engage users in face-to-face interactions.* Previous studies have shown the importance of a physical embodiment in an artificial opponent. The artificial opponent was therefore physically embodied in both of our conditions. However, when comparing both social conditions, our results suggest that the face-to-face interactions provided by the use of our gaze system contributed positively to the sense of presence. To further investigate differences in face-to-face interactions between conditions, facial videos of all the participants were retrieved during the experiment. For future work on this subject, a more detailed analysis using video annotations will be performed.

*Exhibit believable verbal and non-verbal behaviours.* By examining initial empirical studies on the target game and by carefully using those data in the implementation of the case study, we could create believable behaviour in terms of dialogue, game choices and emotional reactions. In the qualitative responses of the final user study, participants often argued that the robot's behaviour was adequate to most situations and that the behaviours were displayed in a timely manner. Additionally, there were significant differences in the dimensions of perceived message understanding and behaviour interdependence, these showed that applying data extracted from a verbal communication study and protocol analysis helped us create believable verbal and non-verbal behaviour that was displayed in a timely manner.

*Comprise an emotion system.* Our emotion system is composed of several variables that influence the artificial opponent's move selection, utterances and emotional behaviours. These variables, inspired by psychology models of appraisal, the human thought process while playing Risk and previous work on socially intelligent agents, seem to be sufficient for users to perceive the robot as an emotional/social being. Some participants claimed that the robot would become angry if they attacked him. Others said that he became sad when losing ground. These answers, along with significant differences in perceived affective understanding and emotional interdependence on the social presence questionnaire, indicate that participants believe that the robot played according to his emotional state and displayed coherent emotional behaviour throughout the game.

*Have social memory.* This guideline is of extreme importance in multiple interactions with the same participants. Although the implementation that we propose for an artificial opponent is prepared for coherently maintaining a relationship with a user throughout several interactions, our evaluation covered the span of only one interaction with each user. In the future, a longer-term evaluation should be performed. Nevertheless, participants still enjoyed and valued the robot's ability to call each participant by his/her name, and most participants in the socially present condition acknowledged that the robot established social relationships with them by remembering past actions in the game.

*Simulate social roles common in board games.* In the evaluation, more specifically in the socially present condition, the artificial opponent clearly expressed different social roles that were recognised by users. The robot expressed roles such as violator or dominator to players it did not like, for example, by threatening and attacking them more frequently. It frequently expressed the social roles of motivator and helper towards players it liked. By looking at participants' qualitative answers, we can also say that participants perceived the agent's social roles.

There is still much work to do before achieving a truly socially present artificial opponent or agent. However, by following guidelines and by taking inspiration from the case study that we have created, we believe that the next generation of artificial board game opponents or agents that are perceived as socially present can be created.

## ACKNOWLEDGMENTS

This work was partially supported by national funds through FCT–Fundação para a Ciência e a Tecnologia, under project PEst-OE/EEI/LA0021/2013 and by the EU FP7 ICT-317923 project EMOTE.

## REFERENCES

1. Adalgeirsson, S., and Breazeal, C. Mebot: a robotic platform for socially embodied presence. In *Proceeding of the ACM/IEEE international conference on Human-robot interaction* (2010), 15–22.

2. Biocca, F., Burgoon, J., Harms, C., and Stoner, M. Criteria and scope conditions for a theory and measure of social presence. *Presence: Teleoperators and virtual environments* (2001).

3. Biocca, F., Harms, C., and Burgoon, J. Toward a more robust theory and measure of social presence: Review and suggested criteria. *Presence: Teleoperators & Virtual Environments 12*, 5 (2003), 456–480.

4. Biocca, F., Harms, C., and Gregg, J. The networked minds measure of social presence: Pilot test of the factor structure and concurrent validity. In *4th annual International Workshop on Presence* (2001), 9–11.

5. Deshmukh, A., Castellano, G., Kappas, A., Barendregt, W., Nabais, F., Paiva, A., Ribeiro, T., Leite, I., and Aylett, R. Towards empathic artificial tutors. In *Proc. of the 8th ACM/IEEE int. conference on Human-robot interaction* (2013), 113–114.

6. Eriksson, D., Peitz, J., and Björk, S. Socially adaptable games. In *Proceedings of DiGRA Conference: Changing Views–Worlds in Play* (2005).

7. Garau, M., Widenfeld, H., Antley, A., Friedman, D., Brogni, A., and Slater, M. Temporal and spatial variations in presence: A qualitative analysis. In *Proc. of Int. Workshop on Presence* (2004), 232–239.

8. Gockley, R., Bruce, A., Forlizzi, J., Michalowski, M., Mundell, A., Rosenthal, S., Sellner, B., Simmons, R., Snipes, K., Schultz, A., et al. Designing robots for long-term social interaction. In *Intelligent Robots and Systems*, IEEE (2005), 1338–1343.

9. Harms, C., and Biocca, F. Internal consistency and reliability of the networked minds social presence measure. *Exploring the sense of presence* (2004), 246.

10. Heerink, M., Ben, K., Evers, V., and Wielinga, B. The influence of social presence on acceptance of a companion robot by older people. *Journal of Physical Agents 2*, 2 (2008), 33–40.

11. Heeter, C. Being there: The subjective experience of presence. *Presence: Teleoperators and virtual environments 1*, 2 (1992), 262–271.

12. Heider, F. *The Psychology of Interpersonal Relations*. Lawrence Erlbaum Associates, 1958.

13. Johansson, S. On using multi-agent systems in playing board games. In *Proceedings of the 5th International joint conference on Autonomous agents and multiagent systems*, ACM (2006), 569–576.

14. Karapanos, E., Zimmerman, J., Forlizzi, J., and Martens, J.-B. *User experience over time: an initial framework*. ACM, 2009, 729–738.

15. Kedzierski, J., Muszynski, R., Zoll, C., Oleksy, A., and Frontkiewicz, M. Emys-emotive head of a social robot. *IJ Social Robotics 5*, 2 (2013), 237–249.

16. Koda, T., and Maes, P. Agents with faces: The effect of personification. In *Robot and Human Communication*, IEEE (1996), 189–194.

17. Leite, I., Hajishirzi, H., Andrist, S., and Lehman, J. Managing chaos: models of turn-taking in character-multichild interactions. In *Proc. of the 15th ACM on Int. conference on multimodal interaction* (2013), 43–50.

18. Leite, I., Martinho, C., Pereira, A., and Paiva, A. As time goes by: Long-term evaluation of social presence in robotic companions. In *Robot and Human Interactive Communication*, IEEE (2009), 669–674.

19. Leite, I., Mascarenhas, S., Pereira, A., Martinho, C., Prada, R., and Paiva, A. "why can't we be friends?" an empathic game companion for long-term interaction. In *Intelligent Virtual Agents*, Springer (2010), 315–321.

20. Lombard, M., and Ditton, T. At the heart of it all: The concept of presence. *Journal of Computer-Mediated Communication 3*, 2 (1997), 0–0.

21. Martinho, C., and Paiva, A. Using anticipation to create believable behavior. In *Proceedings of the national conference on Artificial Intelligence*, vol. 21, Menlo Park, CA; Cambridge, MA; London; AAAI Press; MIT Press; 1999 (2006), 175.

22. Mori, M. The uncanny valley. *Energy 7*, 4 (1970), 33–35.

23. Pereira, A., Martinho, C., Leite, I., and Paiva, A. icat, the chess player: the influence of embodiment in the enjoyment of a game. In *Proceedings of the 7th international joint conference on Autonomous agents and multiagent systems - Vol 3* (2008), 1253–1256.

24. Pereira, A., Prada, R., and Paiva, A. Towards the next generation of board game opponents. In *FDG'11: Proceedings of the Sixth International Conference on Foundations of Digital Games* (June 2011).

25. Pereira, A., Prada, R., and Paiva, A. Socially present board game opponents. In *Advances in Computer Entertainment*, vol. 7624 of *Lecture Notes in Computer Science*. Springer Berlin Heidelberg, 2012, 101–116.

26. Reeves, B. *The media equation: how people treat computers, television, and new media*. Stanford, Calif.: Center for the Study of Language and Information; Cambridge, 1996.

27. Ribeiro, T., and Paiva, A. The illusion of robotic life: principles and practices of animation for robots. In *Proceeding of the ACM/IEEE international conference on Human-robot interaction* (2012), 383–390.

28. Rogers, Y., and Lindley, S. Collaborating around vertical and horizontal large interactive displays: which way is best? *Interacting with Computers 16*, 6 (2004), 1133–1152.

29. Ryall, K., Morris, M., Everitt, K., Forlines, C., and Shen, C. Experiences with and observations of directtouch tabletops. In *Proceedings of IEEE TableTop the International Workshop on Horizontal Interactive Human Computer Systems* (2006), 89–96.

30. Short, J., Williams, E., and Christie, B. The social psychology of telecommunications.

31. Slater, M. Place illusion and plausibility can lead to realistic behaviour in immersive virtual environments. *Philosophical Transactions of the Royal Society B: Biological Sciences 364*, 1535 (2009), 3549.

32. Sodian, B., and Kristen, S. Theory of mind. *Towards a theory of thinking* (2010), 189–201.

33. Toney, A., and Thomas, B. Considering reach in tangible and table top design. In *Int. Workshop on Horizontal Interactive Human-Computer Systems* (2006).

34. Yankelovich, N., Levow, G., and Marx, M. Designing speechacts: Issues in speech user interfaces. In *Proc. of the SIGCHI conference on Human factors in computing systems* (1995), 369–376.

35. Yoshikawa, Y., Shinozawa, K., Ishiguro, H., Hagita, N., and Miyamoto, T. Responsive robot gaze to interaction partner. In *Robotics: Science and systems* (2006).

# Robot Gestures Make Difficult Tasks Easier: the Impact of Gestures on Perceived Workload and Task Performance

**Manja Lohse**
Human Media Interaction
PO Box 217, 7500 AE
Enschede, The Netherlands
m.lohse@utwente.nl,
r.rothuis@student.utwente.nl

**Reinier Rothuis**
Human Media Interaction
PO Box 217, 7500 AE
Enschede, The Netherlands
r.rothuis@student.utwente.nl

**Jorge Gallego Pérez**
Human Media Interaction
PO Box 217, 7500 AE
Enschede, The Netherlands
j.gallegoperez@utwente.nl

**Daphne E. Karreman**
Human Media Interaction
PO Box 217, 7500 AE
Enschede, The Netherlands
d.e.karreman@utwente.nl

**Vanessa Evers**
Human Media Interaction
PO Box 217, 7500 AE
Enschede, The Netherlands
v.evers@utwente.nl

## ABSTRACT
Gestures are important non-verbal signals in human communication. Research with virtual agents and robots has started to add to the scientific knowledge about gestures but many questions with respect to the use of gestures in human-computer interaction are still open. This paper investigates the influence of robot gestures on the users' perceived workload and task performance (i.e. information recall) in a direction-giving task. We conducted a 2 x 2 (robot gestures vs. no robot gestures x easy vs. difficult task) experiment. The results indicate that robot gestures increased user performance and decreased perceived workload in the difficult task *but* not in the easy task. Thus, robot gestures are a promising means to improve human-robot interaction particularly in challenging tasks.

## Author Keywords
human-robot interaction; gestures; perceived workload; task performance

## ACM Classification Keywords
H.5.m. Information Interfaces and Presentation (e.g. HCI): Miscellaneous

## INTRODUCTION
Gestures are important non-verbal signals in human communication (e.g., [19, 22]). Research with virtual agents and robots has started to add to the scientific knowledge about the use of gestures in human-computer interaction (HCI). Complex gesture models for virtual agents have been developed and employed in HCI research (e.g., [1, 4, 20, 27]).


*CHI 2014*, April 26 - May 01 2014, Toronto, ON, Canada

http://dx.doi.org/10.1145/2556288.2557274

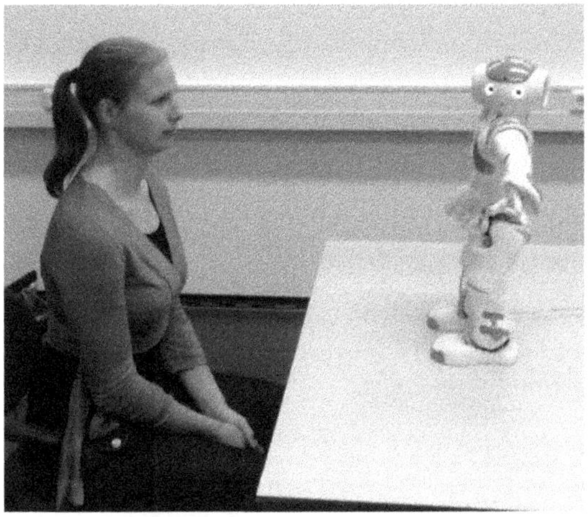

Figure 1. Nao robot providing route directions to a user.

The evaluation of these models focused, among others, on the perceived naturalness of the gestures [20], on their expressivity [27], on users' trust in the agent [4], and on gesture production depending on the cognitive load of the speaker [2]. All these studies showed that virtual agents are perceived more positively when producing co-verbal gestures.

Gesture research with agents has attracted further attention in the recent years with the increasing number of robot research platforms that cannot only produce gestures in a virtual space but in the physical world that they share with humans (e.g., [3, 25, 28]). There is quite some work on gestures in human-robot interaction (HRI), particularly with respect to gesture-speech mismatches and synchronization (e.g. [25, 28]), and persuasiveness of gestures [6]. Common findings of these studies were that, if gestures are synchronized with speech, they have positive effects on the evaluation (e.g., persuasiveness) of robots. Thus, HRI research has supported the findings from the virtual agents community.

Our research focuses on an effect of gestures that has largely been ignored in HCI in general as well as in HRI in particular: the influence of gestures produced by a system (here by a robot) on the perceived workload and task performance (here measured in terms of information recall) of the user in tasks with varying difficulty. While the impact of gesturing on objective task performance has found some attention in previous work (see Section "Related work"), perceived workload has not been taken into account. However, perceived workload is a highly important concept because it captures the users' subjective impression of the task (see Section "Related Work"). It has been shown that perceived workload affects the affective and physiological state of humans. High perceived workload can cause affective distress and increased blood pressure [8, 15] and has also been shown to influence job satisfaction [8].

To address this gap in the literature, we present an experiment on the influence of deictic (pointing) gestures that are redundant with speech in a direction-giving task. Users listen to directions provided by a robot in an easy or a difficult task. The descriptions are only accompanied by gestures for half of the participants. Based on our results, we show the importance of robot gestures particularly in difficult tasks.

Thus, our study contributes first research on the influence of robot gestures on perceived human workload and task performance. We add to the understanding of user behavior and cognitive capabilities in tasks with different levels of difficulty. In this respect, our work lays the ground for the design of future robot systems.

## RELATED WORK

In the following, we highlight related work on gestures in human interaction. Thereafter, we introduce the concept of perceived workload, before we discuss the relation between both (gestures and perceived workload) and establish the hypotheses for our experiment.

### Gestures in human interaction

There is a vast body of research on gestures in human interaction. Based on Kendon's definition [19], they are understood here as deliberate movements with sharp onsets and offsets. They are an excursion in that a part of the body (usually the arm or the head) moves away from and back to a certain position. The movement is interpreted as an addressed non-verbal utterance that conveys information.

Gesture research has resulted in categorizations of types and functions of gestures. These are described in the following sections because they help to set the frame for our experiment.

#### *Types of gestures*

Several categorizations of types of gestures that accompany speech have been introduced in the literature (see [9] for an overview). One of the best known categorizations is by McNeill [23]. He differentiates four types of gestures: *Iconic gestures* represent body movements, movements of objects or people in space, and shapes of objects or people. *Metaphoric gestures* present an abstract idea rather than a concrete object. *Deictic gestures* are used to indicate objects, people, and locations in the real world that do not necessarily have to be present. Finally, *beat gestures* are beats with the rhythm of speech regardless of content.

As has been mentioned above, our experiment focuses on a direction-giving task. In this context, deictic gestures are the most relevant type of gestures because they connect utterances to the physical setting and the physical world in which the conversation takes place is the topic of the conversation [5]. Pointing is the most obvious way to create deictic references. For the use of gestures in route direction tasks, Kita [21] found that when people utter an expression such as "turn left", they also perform gestures to describe the direction of "left". Hato et al. [14] pointed out that also in HRI such gestures are important in deictic interactions that refer to a region in space.

Kendon [19] identified different pointing gestures in interaction data, extending the index finger being the most commonly used when a speaker singles out a particular object or place. Thus, in our experiment the robot will perform pointing gestures with its index finger extended while providing the directions to the user (see Section "Independent Variables").

#### *Functions of gestures*

Most of the research on human gestures follows one of two main traditions: the one claiming that the main function of gestures is to help the speakers think and structure their speech [9], or the one stressing the communicative importance of gestures [19]. We here follow the second tradition and summarize related work on the influence of gestures on the perception of a person by others.

Gesturing has been found to strongly affect human listeners because they pay close attention to information conveyed via such non-verbal behaviors [9]. The influence of the gestures is largely determined by their relation to the information encoded in verbal utterances. This relation can be reinforcing or supplementing [16]. Especially deictic gestures such as pointing, references to objects, locations, and actions, can be reinforcing (also called "redundant" in the literature). The gestures label what is pointed at, but the referent can be understood with speech only. In contrast, when the gesture is supplementing, the referent that is pointed at is not clear without the gesture (for example, if someone says "this", a pointing gesture is needed to clarify what is referred to with the utterance). For our experiment, we use reinforcing deictic gestures. Thus, the referent is also clear without the gesture which allows us to design and compare conditions with and without the robot gesturing (see Section "Independent Variables").

### Perceived workload

Our work focuses on the effect of the reinforcing deictic gestures on the perceived workload of users. There are many definitions of the perceived workload concept in the psychology literature. One of the best known is by Hart and Staveland

[12]. They define workload as a hypothetical construct that represents the cost incurred by a human operator to achieve a certain level of performance. This view is human-centered rather than task centered and captures a subjective experience rather than an inherent property of a task. In other words, the perceived workload depends on the circumstances, skills, behaviors and perceptions of the user.

Perceived workload is a well-studied concept in HCI which is underlined by the fact that validated standard scales like the Nasa TLX exist. In [13], Hart reviews a selection of 550 papers that have used the Nasa TLX. It needs to be mentioned that the review was conducted some years ago, in 2006, and even at that time papers were selected and the overall number was higher. According to Hart's analysis, the research areas where the scale has been employed include manual control tasks such as flying (14%), driving (9%), data entry (10%) and others. However, there are much fewer studies addressing the perceived workload caused by virtual agents and robots. The Nasa TLX has mainly been used to measure human performance and workload in teleoperation scenarios (with one human teleoperating one or multiple robots) [29]. The perceived workload concept has also been mentioned in some other contexts. Gu and Badler [10] propose to research the effects of workload in studies with virtual agents by manipulating the number of agents one interacts with. However, they present no evaluation. In HRI, Yoshiike et al. [31] suggest to reduce workload by minimizing the social cues of a robot so that the user does not have to follow eye-gaze, facial expressions, life movement, etc. Again, there is no study to test the effect of this minimal design on the perceived workload of the user.

### The influence of robot gestures on users' task performance and perceived workload

In the following, we establish a connection between gestures, performance and perceived workload, and introduce our hypotheses.

For human interaction, Kendon [18] proposed that gestures along with speech make utterance units more effective. In an HRI direction-giving task (as in our experiment), Okuno et al. [26] discovered that gestures had a positive effect on recall of the information. Also McNeil, Alibali, and Evans [22] suggested that redundant gestures facilitate understanding in adult-child interaction. They assumed that indexical (deictic) gestures may facilitate comprehension most when speakers make reference to particular objects and locations. However, their findings only partially underlined these assumptions. They found that speakers' reinforcing gestures facilitated listeners comprehension of the accompanying speech when the verbal message was highly complex (in their study this was the case for younger children compared to older ones) but not when it was simple. Also for HRI, Häring et al. [11] found that additional modalities (gaze and gesture) did not help to increase performance in the simple condition of a puzzle but in the complex condition. This leads us to our first hypothesis:

| | |
|---|---|
| easy task / no gestures | easy task / gestures |
| difficult task / no gestures | difficult task / gestures |

**Table 1. Experimental conditions**

**H1**: The participants' task performance (in terms of correct recall of directions) will improve significantly when the robot produces redundant gestures in the difficult task but not in the easy task.

However, task performance is not our main interest here. In contrast to previous studies, we are also interested in the effects of gestures on the perceived workload of the users. As has been mentioned above, we are not aware of any related work addressing this relation directly. However, it has been shown that visual feedback can decrease perceived mental workload [30]. Also gestures are a visual cue which leads us to our second hypothesis:

**H2**: The participants' perceived workload will be significantly lower when the robot produces redundant gestures, both in the difficult and in the easy task.

## METHOD

We designed a 2 (gesture vs. no gesture) x2 (easy vs. difficult task) between subjects experiments (see Table 1), in which the participants played a memory game with the robot Nao. The robot told the participants a seemingly random set of directions that they were later asked to recall. The directions consisted of phrases used to navigate a building. Each direction included two pieces of information: one directional information (up, down, left or right) and a number specifying the amount of levels the participant needed to go up or down, or the number of turns the participant needed to take to left or right. The phrases we used were:

- "Take the 'nth' left"
- "Take the 'nth' right"
- "Go up 'n' levels"
- "Go down 'n' levels"

In all utterances, n was a number between one and five. The amount of directions per round was varied between difficulty levels (see Section "Independent Variables").

### Robot

The robot used in this experiment is the Nao robot by Aldebaran Robotics (see Figures 1, 2, and 3). It is a bipedal humanoid robot that measures 57.3 cm in height when in an upright, standing position. The robot has 25 degrees of freedom to move its head, arms, hands, legs, and hips. It has two speakers integrated in its head.

In our experiment, the robot was connected to a laptop from where the researcher could remote control its behavior. Scripts for the utterances and gestures were prepared beforehand and played during the interaction. All participants received the same set of directions in a randomized order.

Figure 2. Nao in the condition without gestures (static pose).

### Independent variables

The following sections describe how we manipulated the robot behavior and the task between the conditions.

#### *Gesture vs. no gesture*

We designed two different robot behaviors with respect to gesturing. In the "no gesture" condition (also referred to as "static condition" in the following), the robot stayed in one posture throughout the experiment and did not gesture (see Figure 2). For the condition with gestures (also called "animated condition" in the remainder of the paper), we developed movements that were in accordance with the directions that the robot provided to the users. Thus, all gestures were pointing (deictic) gestures redundant with speech (see "Related Work" Section). Their design was based on work by Kanda et al. [17]. However, as the Nao robot cannot rotate its torso, we replaced this motion by the rotation of the head. This should allow the participants and the robot to establish a joint perspective. We implemented the following gestures:

1. The robot points its arm and rotates its head to its right (left for the participant) or left (right for the participant).
2. The robot points its arm and tilts its head upwards.
3. The robot points its arm and tilts its head downwards.

Figure 3 depicts examples of the gestures of the robot.

#### *Easy vs. difficult task*

We chose a direction-giving task because the embodied robot could indeed be credible in such a task pointing out directions in space. Furthermore, this task allowed for manipulation of the difficulty by influencing the amount of information provided to the participants. As has been mentioned above, each direction consisted of two pieces of information. We conducted a pretest with five students of our university to determine how many directions appeared easy or difficult to them.

Figure 3. Gestures of the Nao robot (upper left: pointing to the left; upper right: pointing to the right; lower left: pointing upwards; lower right: pointing downwards).

All participants of the pretest should be able to solve the easy task. The difficult task should cause some problems to some of them but still be solvable for the majority of participants. Based on the results of the pretest, we decided for two directions (with two pieces of information each) in the easy task and four directions (with two pieces of information each) in the difficult task. This decision is in line with Miller's Law that claims that humans are able to hold $7 \pm 2$ objects in their working memory [24].

Next to the pieces of information within one direction, we also analyzed how long the participants paid attention to the task and the robot before getting bored or distracted. Based on this information, we decided for five rounds that the participants had to complete with the robot in both conditions.

### Dependent variables

Our dependent variables included measures of perceived shared reality, task performance, and perceived workload. We also collected demographic information on age, gender, and experience with robots.

#### *Perceived shared reality*

We employed a scale on perceived shared reality because it has been found that robot gestures and shared reality are closely intertwined in HRI [28]. Thus, this scale basically serves as a manipulation check to ensure that the manipulations between the static and animated conditions were actually perceived by the users and caused the potential differences in the task difficulty and perceived workload ratings.

We used the experienced shared reality scale previously employed by Salem et al. [28]. The scale contains three items:

- I feel close to the robot

- I found the interaction with the robot pleasant
- I had fun while interacting with the robot

The scale was a 5-point Likert scale (1: strongly disagree - 5: strongly agree). Its internal reliability (Cronbach's $\alpha$) was .822.

*Task performance*

The task performance was an objective measure. We counted the number of correct recalls of directions by the users based on video data that we recorded during the trials. The maximum score was 5 (minimum 0) because the users played five rounds and only if the recall of the information presented in one round was 100% correct, the recall was counted as being correct (thus, increasing the score by one point per round).

*Perceived workload*

To capture the users' subjective impression of the workload (or in other words the perceived workload), we used the Nasa TLX scale which is a standard in recording subjective task workload [12]. We included all subscales (mental demand, physical demand, temporal demand, performance, effort, and frustration) into the analysis, each of them being rated on a 10-point Likert scale ranging from "low" to "high".

We employed the weighted version of the Nasa TLX which allows to take the importance of each subscale in a specific scenario into account. Thus, the questionnaire included the scale to weigh the subscales which asked the participants to compare all individual subscales with all others and to indicate which one they found more important or relevant.

### Data analysis

Before analyzing the data, we checked for normality of distribution. If the data was normally distributed, we used two-factorial ANOVAs and we report main- and interaction effects. In case of non-normally distributed data, non-parametric tests were applied, namely Kruskall-Wallis tests followed up by post-hoc Mann-Whitney tests as proposed by Field [7].

### Procedure

At the start of the experiment, each participant was greeted by the experimenter who provided some explanation and asked the participant to fill out a consent form. Thereafter, the participant sat down in front of the table on which the Nao was standing (see Figure 1). Thus, both were facing each other (rather than having the participants look down on the small robot). The experimenter explained that when the robot would either point to the right or left, it would comply to the spatial perspective of the participants, i.e. if it used its left arm to point, it would point to the right. After providing this information, the experimenter withdrew to a laptop that was used to control the robot in a Wizard of Oz fashion. The participants could not see the experimenter from where they were sitting.

In all conditions, the interaction started with the robot uttering "Let's begin the game". As mentioned above, the robot's actions were pre-programmed and triggered by the experimenter at the correct moments. Every directional phrase was randomly separated by one of the following words: "next", "then", "following that", "subsequently", or "after that". When the participant completed the round successfully, the robot would say "That is correct". If the participant made an error, the robot said "That is not correct." Both events were triggered by the experimenter. Each new round started with the robot announcing "Let's begin a new round". After having completed five rounds, the experimenter asked the participant to fill out the questionnaire and thanked him/her.

### Sample

The experiment was conducted with 32 participants distributed equally between the conditions. All participants were students of the university (3 female, 29 male). Their age ranged between 18 and 28 years with a mean age of 21 years (standard deviation (sd) = 2 years). The participants had hardly any experience with robots: 27 had never seen a robot in real life, 3 had only seen one, and just 2 had interacted or worked with robots before the experiment.

## RESULTS

### Perceived shared reality

A Shapiro-Wilk test showed that the data for perceived shared reality were normally distributed. Thus, we conducted a two-way ANOVA to discover differences between the conditions. This ANOVA revealed that there was no statistical difference between the conditions regarding experienced shared reality, $F(3, 28) = 1.865.p = 0.159$. In fact, both the static / easy and the static / difficult conditions had a mean of 2.96 (easy: $sd = 0.81$, difficult: $sd = 0.63$). The means for the animated / easy and animated / difficult conditions were the same as well with a value of 3.58 (easy: $sd = 0.42$, difficult: $sd = 0.89$). Thus, the task difficulty did not have an impact on the perceived shared reality which is positive because only the gestures should have. There was indeed a main effect for the gestures $F(1, 29) = 5.594, p = .025$. Based on this finding, we can conclude that the manipulation was successful and the gestures led to higher perceived shared reality.

### Task performance

A Shapiro-Wilk test showed that the data on task performance were not normally distributed. Hence, we conducted a Kruskal-Wallis test to compare the conditions. The test revealed a significant difference between them (p=.001) (see Figure 4). Post-hoc Mann-Whitney tests showed that participants who completed one of the easy conditions had significantly higher scores ($m = 4.35, sd = 0.70$) than participants who completed one of the two hard conditions ($m = 3.06, sd = 1.29$), $U = 47.50, p = .002$. This finding indicates that the manipulation of the difficulty of the task was successful. Tests between the individual conditions showed that the difference was statistically significant between the static conditions ($U = 5.00, p = .003$) as well as between the animated conditions ($U = 14.00, p = .045$). Participants who completed an animated condition had significant higher scores ($m = 4.23, sd = 0.76$) than participants who completed a static condition ($m = 3.19, sd = 1.38$), $U = 68.00, p = .023$. Thus, not only the difficulty of the task, but also the gestures played an important role for task

| Subscale | Mean weight (sd) |
|---|---|
| Mental demand | 4.34 (0.90) |
| Physical demand | 0.41 (0.67) |
| Temporal demand | 2.19 (1.06) |
| Performance | 3.97 (0.93) |
| Effort | 2.81 (1.00) |
| Frustration | 1.31 (1.06) |

**Table 2. Mean weights (standard deviations) of the Nasa TLX subscales**

performance. To look at this in more detail, we compared all individual conditions. We found that the gestures had no significant influence on task performance in the easy condition but in the difficult condition ($U = 7.50, p = .007$). In other words, in the easy condition the recall of the participants did not improve if the robot gestured, but in the difficult condition it improved significantly. This finding is in line with related work and **H1** (The participants' task performance (in terms of correct recall of directions) will improve significantly when the robot produces redundant gestures in the difficult task but not in the easy task).

### Perceived workload

As has been mentioned in the "Dependent Variables" Section, we used the weighted Nasa TLX scale to assess perceived workload. The results indeed revealed that some subscales were more relevant than others to the participants, e.g., physical demand had almost no influence with a mean weight of 0.41 ($sd = 0.67$, on a scale of 0 to 5). Table 2 depicts the weights of all subscales.

Overall, the perceived workload was average ($m = 5.32$ ($sd = 1.17$) on a scale of 1:low - 10: high). Again, we conducted a Shapiro-Wilk test for normality which showed that the data for perceived workload were normally distributed. A two-way ANOVA revealed a significant difference of the perceived workload between the four conditions ($F(3, 28) = 6.905, p = .001$). We discovered main effects for animation ($F(1, 31) = 6.438, p = .017$) and for task difficulty ($F(1, 31) = 11.018, p = .003$). In other words, the perceived workload in the easy task ($m = 4.77, sd = 0.90$) was significantly lower than in the hard task ($m = 5.87, sd = 1.18$); and it was significantly lower in the animated conditions ($m = 4.90, sd = 0.83$) compared to the static conditions ($m = 5.74, sd = 1.33$). There was no interaction effect between animation and difficulty.

However, Figure 5 shows that the perceived workload decreased much more due to the gestures in the difficult task ($m_{animated} = 5.15, sd = 0.81, m_{static} = 6.58, sd = 1.07$) than it did in the easy task ($m_{animated} = 4.65, sd = 0.82; m_{static} = 4.89, sd = 1.01$). In fact, unpaired T-tests showed that the difference in the easy task was not significant, while the difference in the difficult task was ($T(14) = 3.031, p = .009$). Therefore, **H2** (The participants' perceived workload will be significantly lower when the robot produces redundant gestures, both in the difficult and in the easy task) was only supported for the difficult but not for the easy tasks.

This finding is in line with the results regarding task performance. It appears that in the case of our experiment, the task

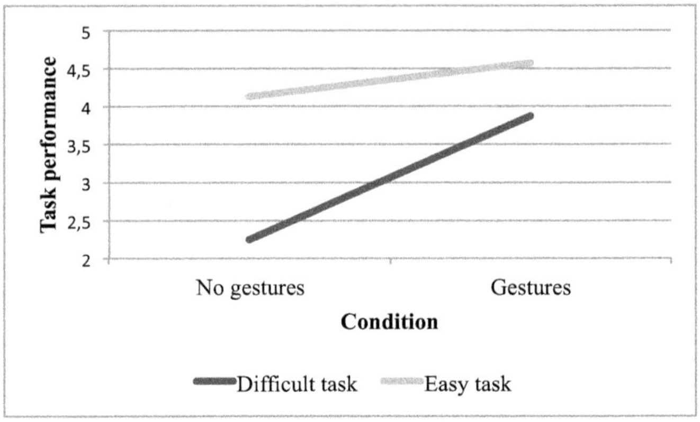


**Figure 4. Task performance (mean number of directions that the participants recalled correctly) in the conditions.**

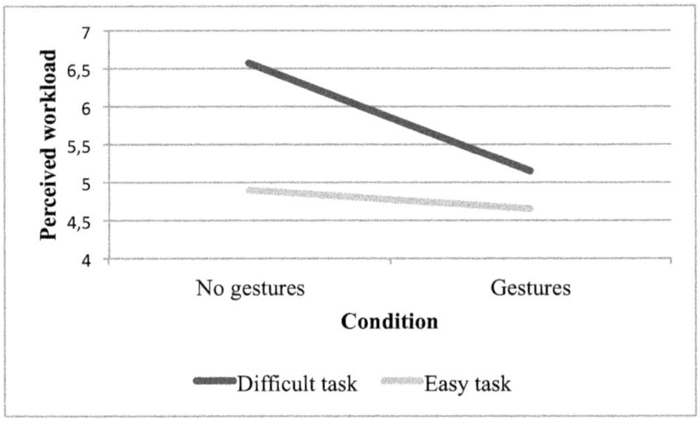


**Figure 5. Perceived workload in the conditions.**

performance was actually correlated with the perceived workload. Indeed, we discovered a significant negative correlation between the weighted Nasa TLX scores and the task performance (number of correct answers), $r(30) = -0.695, p = 0.000$. In other words, the higher the perceived workload, the less correct answers were provided by the participants.

## DISCUSSION

This paper set out to answer the question whether robot gestures can decrease the users' perceived workload and increase their performance on a task. To find an answer to this question, we conducted a direction-giving experiment in which we manipulated the gestures that a robot performed (no gestures vs. deictic gestures) and the difficulty of the task (easy vs. difficult task). Our results showed that the robot gestures did indeed support human task performance and lowered the perceived workload of the users *but* only in the difficult task. This result is in line with research on gestures in human interaction that came to the same conclusion (see "Related work", [22]). We believe that this is due to the easy task being simple enough for the participants to be completed with very little information. This little information could easily be kept in mind even if it was only presented with one modality. However, the difficult task required the participants to recall more information and multimodality was useful to convey it.

But what does this imply for the design of robots or virtual agents? As has been mentioned in the introduction, perceived high workload can have a serious negative impact on humans' psychological and physical well-being. Thus, if we are building systems, we have to strive to keep the perceived workload low enough to avoid such effects. This goal has to be achieved despite the fact that the difficulty of the task itself in many cases cannot be reduced. However, we can influence how a system and a human solve the task. Our results show that equipping systems with the capability to gesture is a promising way to reduce perceived workload while keeping the task difficulty stable.

## LIMITATIONS AND FUTURE WORK

Our work suffers from some limitations that will be addressed in future research. First of all, the impact of gesture in interaction is highly dependent on the task. Our research here is restricted to one direction-giving task and to deictic gestures. Thus, future work needs to focus on the influence of other types of gestures (iconic, metaphoric, and beat) on performance and perceived workload in a variety of tasks. Furthermore, future research would profit from larger sample sizes and samples that better capture representative user groups of robots, i.e. samples with better gender and age distribution.

Nevertheless, we believe that this work addresses a novel aspect in HRI that comes with valuable implications for the larger HCI community: it introduces the relation between robot gestures and perceived workload to the field and shows that the interaction can actually profit from robot gestures with respect to perceived workload, particularly in difficult tasks.

## ACKNOWLEDGMENTS

The research leading to these results was partially supported by the European Community's 7th Framework Programme under Grant agreements 600877 (SPENCER - Social situation-aware perception and action for cognitive robots) and 288235 (FROG - Fun Robotic Outdoor Guide).

## REFERENCES

1. Bergmann, K., Eyssel, F. A., and Kopp, S. A second chance to make a first impression? how appearance and nonverbal behavior affect perceived warmth and competence of virtual agents over time. M. Walker, M. Neff, A. Paiva, and Y. Nakano, Eds., Proceedings of the 12th International Conference on Intelligent Virtual Agents, Springer (2012), 126–138.

2. Bergmann, K., Kahl, S., and Kopp, S. Modeling the semantic coordination of speech and gesture under cognitive and linguistic constraints. In *Intelligent Virtual Agents*, R. Aylett, B. Krenn, C. Pelachaud, and H. Shimodaira, Eds., vol. 8108 of *Lecture Notes in Computer Science*. Springer Berlin Heidelberg, 2013, 203–216.

3. Breazeal, C., Kidd, C., Thomaz, A., Hoffman, G., and Berlin, M. Effects of nonverbal communication on efficiency and robustness in human-robot teamwork. In *Intelligent Robots and Systems, 2005. (IROS 2005). 2005 IEEE/RSJ International Conference on* (2005), 708–713.

4. Buisine, S., Abrilian, S., and Martin, J.-C. From brows to trust. Kluwer Academic Publishers, Norwell, MA, USA, 2004, ch. Evaluation of multimodal behaviour of embodied agents, 217–238.

5. Cassell, J. Embodied conversational agents. MIT Press, Cambridge, MA, USA, 2000, ch. Nudge nudge wink wink: elements of face-to-face conversation for embodied conversational agents, 1–27.

6. Chidambaram, V., Chiang, Y.-H., and Mutlu, B. Designing persuasive robots: how robots might persuade people using vocal and nonverbal cues. In *Proceedings of the seventh annual ACM/IEEE international conference on Human-Robot Interaction*, HRI '12, ACM (New York, NY, USA, 2012), 293–300.

7. Field, A. *Discovering statistics using SPSS*. Sage publications, 2009.

8. Fox, M. L., Dwyer, D. J., and Ganster, D. C. Effects of stressful job demands and control on physiological and attitudinal outcomes in a hospital setting. *Academy of Management Journal 36*, 2 (1993), 289–318.

9. Goldin-Meadow, S. *Hearing Gesture: How Our Hands Help Us Think*. Belknap Press of Harvard University Press, 2005.

10. Gu, E., and Badler, N. I. Visual attention and eye gaze during multiparty conversations with distractions. In *IVA*, J. Gratch, M. Young, R. Aylett, D. Ballin, and P. Olivier, Eds., vol. 4133 of *Lecture Notes in Computer Science*, Springer (2006), 193–204.

11. Häring, M., Eichberg, J., and André, E. Studies on grounding with gaze and pointing gestures in human-robot-interaction. In *Social Robotics*, S. Ge, O. Khatib, J.-J. Cabibihan, R. Simmons, and M.-A. Williams, Eds., vol. 7621 of *Lecture Notes in Computer Science*. Springer Berlin Heidelberg, 2012, 378–387.

12. Hart, S., and Staveland, L. Development of nasa-tlx (task load index): Results of empirical and theoretical research. In *Human mental workload*, P.A. Hancock and N. Meshkati (Eds.), Amsterdam: Elsevier (1988), 139–183.

13. Hart, S. G. Nasa-task load index (nasa-tlx); 20 years later. *Proceedings of the Human Factors and Ergonomics Society Annual Meeting 50*, 9 (2006), 904–908.

14. Hato, Y., Satake, S., Kanda, T., Imai, M., and Hagita, N. Pointing to space: modeling of deictic interaction referring to regions. In *Proceedings of the Conference on Human-Robot Interaction*, P. J. Hinds, H. Ishiguro, T. Kanda, and P. H. K. Jr., Eds., ACM (2010), 301–308.

15. Ilies, R., Dimotakis, N., and De Pater, I. E. Psychological and physiological reactions to high workloads: Implications for well-being. *Personnel Psychology 63*, 2 (2010), 407–436.

16. Iverson, J. M., Capirci, P., Longobardi, E., and Caselli, M. C. Gesturing in mother-child interaction. *Cognitive Development 14* (1999), 57–75.

17. Kanda, T., Shiomi, M., Miyashita, Z., Ishiguro, H., and Hagita, N. A communication robot in a shopping mall. *Robotics, IEEE Transactions on 26*, 5 (2010), 897–913.

18. Kendon, A. Gesture and speech: How they interact. In *Nonverbal Interaction (Sage Annual Reviews of Communication, Volume 11)*, J. Wiemann and R. Harrison, Eds. Sage Publications, Beverly Hills, California, 1983, 13–46.

19. Kendon, A. *Gesture – Visible Action as Utterance.* Cambridge University Press, Cambridge, 2004.

20. Kipp, M., Neff, M., Kipp, K. H., and Albrecht, I. Towards natural gesture synthesis: Evaluating gesture units in a data-driven approach to gesture synthesis. In *Proceedings of the 7th international conference on Intelligent Virtual Agents*, IVA '07, Springer-Verlag (Berlin, Heidelberg, 2007), 15–28.

21. Kita, S. *Pointing: Where Language, Culture, and Cognition Meet.* PSYCHOLOGY Press, 2003.

22. McNeil, N., Alibali, M., and Evans, J. The role of gesture in children's comprehension of spoken language:now they need it, now they don't. *Journal of Nonverbal Behavior 24*, 2 (2000), 131–150.

23. McNeill, D. *Hand and Mind: What Gestures Reveal about Thought*. University of Chicago Press, Chicago, 1992.

24. Miller, G. A. The magical number seven, plus or minus two: Some limits on our capacity for processing information. *The Psychological Review 63*, 2 (March 1956), 81–97.

25. Ng-Thow-Hing, V., Luo, P., and Okita, S. Y. Synchronized gesture and speech production for humanoid robots. In *IROS*, IEEE (2010), 4617–4624.

26. Okuno, Y., Kanda, T., Imai, M., Ishiguro, H., and Hagita, N. Providing route directions: design of robot's utterance, gesture, and timing. In *Proceedings of the 4th ACM/IEEE international conference on Human robot interaction*, HRI '09, ACM (New York, NY, USA, 2009), 53–60.

27. Pelachaud, C. Studies on gesture expressivity for a virtual agent. *Speech Commun. 51*, 7 (July 2009), 630–639.

28. Salem, M., Eyssel, F., Rohlfing, K., Kopp, S., and Joublin, F. To err is human(-like): Effects of robot gesture on perceived anthropomorphism and likability. *International Journal of Social Robotics 5*, 3 (2013), 313–323.

29. Steinfeld, A., Fong, T., Kaber, D., Lewis, M., Scholtz, J., Schultz, A., and Goodrich, M. Common metrics for human-robot interaction. In *Proceedings of the 1st ACM SIGCHI/SIGART conference on Human-robot interaction*, HRI '06, ACM (New York, NY, USA, 2006), 33–40.

30. Vitense, H. S., Jacko, J. A., and Emery, V. K. Multimodal feedback: an assessment of performance and mental workload. *Ergonomics 46*, 1-3 (2003), 68–87. PMID: 12554399.

31. Yoshiike, Y., Silva, P. R. S. D., and Okada, M. Mawari: A social interface to reduce the workload of the conversation. In *ICSR*, B. Mutlu, C. Bartneck, J. Ham, V. Evers, and T. Kanda, Eds., vol. 7072 of *Lecture Notes in Computer Science*, Springer (2011), 11–20.

# Measuring Operator Anticipatory Inputs in Response to Time-delay for Teleoperated Human-robot Interfaces

**Jonathan Bidwell**
School of Computer Science, Georgia Institute of Technology, Atlanta, GA, USA

**Alexandra Holloway**
Jet Propulsion Lab, California Institute of Technology, Pasadena, California, USA

**Scott Davidoff**
Jet Propulsion Lab, California Institute of Technology, Pasadena, California, USA

## ABSTRACT
Many tasks call for efficient user interaction under time delay—controlling space instruments, piloting remote aircraft and operating search and rescue robots. In this paper we identify an underexplored design opportunity for building robotic teleoperation user interfaces following an evaluation of operator performance during a time-delayed robotic arm block-stacking task in twenty-two participants. More delay resulted in greater operator hesitation and a decreased ratio of active to inactive input. This ratio can serve as a useful proxy for measuring an operator's ability to *anticipate* the outcome of their control inputs before receiving delayed visual feedback. High *anticipatory input ratio (AIR)* scores indicate times when robot operators enter commands before waiting for visual feedback. Low *AIR* scores highlight when operators must wait for visual feedback before continuing. We used this measurement to help us identify particular sub-tasks where operators would likely benefit from additional support.

## Author Keywords
Teleoperation; Time delay; Human-robot interface; Metric

## ACM Classification Keywords
H.5.m. Information Interfaces and Presentation (e. g. HCI): Miscellaneous

## INTRODUCTION
Human-in-the-loop user interfaces are often preferred when remote tasks call for higher-level judgment and experience, such as controlling space instruments, piloting remote drone aircraft, and operating search and rescue robots. However, in practice, time-delayed communications between the operator and remote system can make these interactions slow and error prone as operators often must *bump and wait* by nudging the controller and waiting for the robot's feedback after each input. The less the operator has to *bump and wait* the more work her or she can get done. Making telerobotic operation practical under these conditions calls for identifying and addressing challenges such as delayed feedback, increased error rates due to the unknown state of the system [3] and making difficult trade-offs between planning and action [11] throughout the design process.


*CHI 2014,* April 26–May 01, 2014, Toronto, ON, Canada.
Copyright 2014 ACM 978-1-4503-2473-1/14/04 $15.00.
http://dx.doi.org/10.1145/2556288.2557174

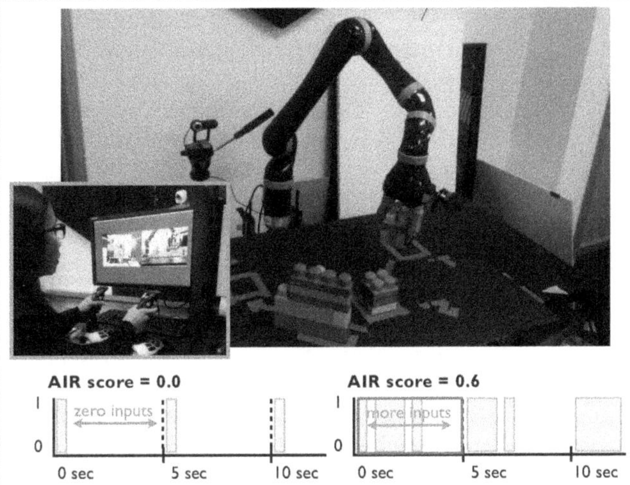


**Figure 1 - (Top) Evaluating time delay robotic manipulation using traditional joystick teleoperated controls. (Bottom) The operator's *active* inputs are logged as a time-series in yellow for calculating AIR scores. Low AIR scores highlight instances when operators *bump*, i.e., nudge controls and *wait* for visual feedback before continuing, while high AIR scores show when multiple commands are entered before receiving feedback.**

In this study, we developed a metric that we call an *anticipatory interaction ratio* (AIR) score for measuring an operator's ability to manipulate a robotic arm at a control input level. High AIR scores highlight moments when users are able to submit a series of inputs in back-to-back succession rather than waiting for visual feedback before each input. Low AIR scores indicate moments when this idle *bump and wait* behavior is prevalent (see Figure 1). By highlighting these instances we can obtain a high level idea of an operator's confidence in his or her mental model of the robot arm at any given time.

This metric was evaluated during a time-delayed telerobotic user study with 22 participants. The results showed us specific contexts where operators were able to decrease idle time under various medium-length delays and supported our intuition that sub-task level analysis is important, as the number of commands that operators sent before receiving visual feedback varied depending on the sub-task at hand.

## RELATED WORK
Often there is a cost-benefit trade off between time spent planning the next best series of actions and getting the job done earlier by taking action early and proceeding with

a less optimal plan. O'Hara et al prescribed that introducing time delayed feedback (lockout time) and high error recovery cost resulted in more planning, less action and slower overall task performance [11]. Moreover Don Norman showed that errors increase when the user does not know the state of the system [3]. Each of these factors presents an efficiency bottleneck for telerobotic operations. In our case, the more input an operator sends before receiving feedback the less he or she knows about the current state of the robot due to time delay.

Minimizing *bump and wait* becomes increasingly difficult as time delays increase. While teleoperation under minimal latencies has received considerable attention [16,17,18] notably less work has focused on higher latencies (>5 seconds) [2,20]. USAF drones are remotely piloted with between ~0.1–2.0 seconds of time delay [9,10]. Veltman et al showed an increase in situational awareness by situating camera view within a 3D map for context [8]. NASA robotic missions often face extreme time delay conditions. NASA's Ranger robot arm was evaluated under 0–3 seconds of time delay. Chorde Lane et al showed a 62% increase in task completion after introducing a *predictive,* real-time simulation of the arm during a "peg-in-hole" task [12]. NSDA teleoperated a robot arm on an Earth orbiting satellite form a ground station with 5–7 seconds of time delay [1].

Many time-delayed tasks use joysticks for input controls. The USAF Predator drone aircraft systems and numerous search and rescue robots are operated using joysticks and remote camera video feeds [8,9,10]. Interestingly while there are largely no standards governing how these systems map input to different controls commercial crane operator controls have been standardized for decades [4,5]. Most cranes are controlled with 1-2 joysticks. The rightmost joystick performs translation while the leftmost handles raising and lowering. Here we chose to model our controls after after the International Standard for Standardization (ISO)'s guidelines with the aim of providing a baseline that would be applicable for a range of applications [5].

Human Robot Interaction (HRI) evaluation metrics have traditionally been limited to reporting task completion times for pure teleoperation interfaces under time delay (akin to reporting the final score of a baseball game but not how the game was played) [12, 14]. Human Computer Interaction (HCI) researchers often ignore time delay altogether when evaluating desktop applications and assume an "infinitely fast machine" with "steady state" feedback [14].

Many times there is no one-size-fits all solution for mitigating the impacts of time delay; more detailed analysis is often required for prioritizing difficult design choices. Manual control inputs from joysticks and other devices can often afford considerable task flexibility while incurring *bump and wait* inefficiencies during feedback intensive sub-tasks such as aligning two objects. Higher-level robot automation can often reduce the need for manual input all together by automating sub-tasks at the expense of adding complexity and restricting the adaptability of the system. Finally, predictive simulations can provide operators with real-time estimates the robot without time delay at the expense of potential mismatches between the simulation and real world [7,12,18]. Multiple such strategies can be used together throughout the course of a given task [15, 16]; therefore it is important for us to also consider how people utilize control inputs at a more fine-grained sub-task level for identifying when and where teleoperation may need to be supplemented throughout the course of a task.

## STUDY DESIGN

In this study we evaluated the performance of 22 subjects during a time-delayed teleoperated robot arm block-stacking task. All 22 of the subjects performed the task with and without a 5-second time delay condition, and seven of the subjects performed the task under an additional 2.5-second time delay condition. The presentation of the time delay conditions was randomized to reduce training effects. Each study lasted approximately 20 minutes.

The subjects consisted of interns and employees at our lab, ranging from 19 and 34 years of age, with 15 males and 7 females. The subjects each had experience using joysticks for playing video games, however none of them had used a pair of joysticks for operating the particular robot arm. Subjects received no compensation for participating.

Block stacking was performed using a Kinova Jaco robotic arm with seven degrees of freedom. The arm had three cable-drive fingers for grasping objects and was controlled using a pair of joysticks with a display for visual feedback.

Joystick input was modeled after mobile crane operator controls [5]. Forward, backward, left and right inputs on the right-hand joystick mapped to translational end-effector movement in a plane parallel to the tabletop workspace. Twisting the left-hand joystick mapped to rotating the wrist of the robotic arm, while pushing forward and backward raised and lowered the end-effector relative to the table (akin to pulling back on a fishing pole). The robotic arm's fingers were opened and closed by pressing and holding the left and right triggers respectively.

The operator viewed an LCD display showing time-delayed top and side video feed views of the robot arm as video feedback for aligning blocks during the task. An examiner sat next to the operator and viewed a separate LCD display showing live feeds of the operator's face, hands and the robot arm throughout the session. The displays were each separated by a removable barrier such that the operator could not see the examiner's display.

The task consisted of three subtasks: picking up blocks, stacking blocks, and placing a block onto a target as shown in Figure 2. Blocks were reset to initial starting positions in the event that they were dropped during the task. The operators were read an introduction script, instructed to complete the task as quickly and accurately as possible and given a 1-2 minute warm-up period to familiarize themselves with the controls before beginning the task.

Joystick inputs, robot arm telemetry and display screens were logged during each session for analyzing time delay inefficiencies. Joystick input and telemetry where captured at 10 Hz and later resampled as discrete active and inactive intervals --- *active* when the robot arm was moving and *inactive* otherwise. Each display screen was recorded using screen capture software at 30 Hz. The resulting logs were used to compute AIR scores that could then be viewed alongside the screen capture recordings for evaluating instances when manual input may be inefficient under time delay (see Figure 3).

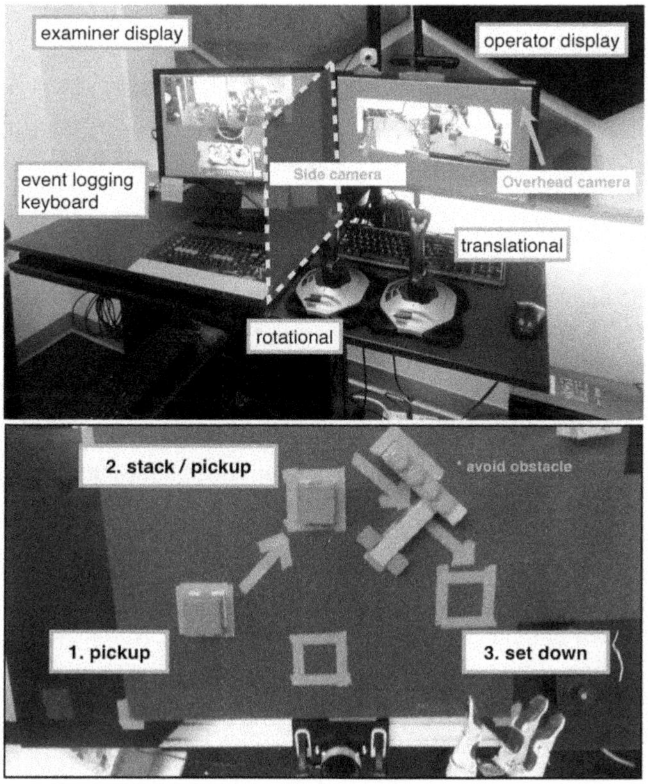


**Figure 2 - Evaluation: (Top) side-by-side operator and examiner displays; (Bottom) robot arm operators were asked to 1) pick up a block, 2) stack the block on another block, 3) lift and place the block stack on a target**

## ANTICIPATORY INPUT RATIO (AIR)

The goal of our AIR score metric is to characterize the impact of time delay on individual operator control inputs. AIR scores are evaluated at the start of each active input interval within a window. The width of the window is equal to the duration of the current time delay condition. The duration of active inputs is then summed within this window range and divided by the window length to give the percentage active to inactive inputs sent before receiving feedback from the initial input. This ratio is computed for all active inputs by jumping from the start of one control input interval to the next. Scores are only evaluated when active inputs are present; as a result operator pause intervals are skipped. The resulting scores can help to characterize a range of behaviors from a 0% score, when operators bump & wait and are uncertain about the remote robot state or environment, to a 100% score when operators can enter continuous inputs without visual feedback (see Figure 1).

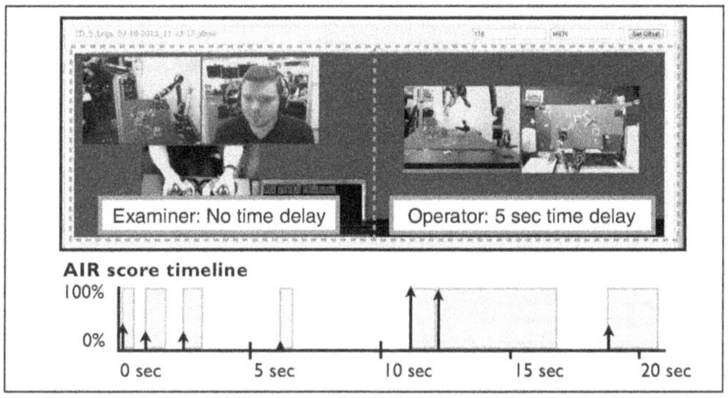


**Figure 3 - AIR scores are shown below a screencast for highlighting the context of operator inefficiencies under time delay. Input intervals are shown as yellow rectangles. AIR scores are shown as black arrows at the start of each interval where height represents a score from 0-100%. Low AIR scores reflect instances where operators *bump and wait***

## RESULTS

The average operator *AIR* scores were computed for the overall task and each sub-task under time delay—picking up a block, stacking and placing, Table 1. Logs from two participants had to be removed due to data collection issues.

**Table 1 AIR Scores vs. Time Delay Condition (N=20)**

| Time delay (sec) | 0 | 2.5 | 5 |
|---|---|---|---|
| Overall Task | 76.8% | 50.5% | 39.1% |
| Sub-task 1 | 75.7% | 54.8% | 41.1% |
| Sub-task 2 | 68.8% | 54.4% | 41.8% |
| Sub-task 3 | 70.8% | 58.4% | 48.5% |

## DISCUSSION

### *1) AIR scores decrease as time delay increases*

The results of our analysis highlighted that average AIR scores decreased as time delay increased. This trend is expected as the error recovery cost and lockout times both increase with time delay and likely contribute to *bump and wait* behaviors in the form of slower, shorter input bursts.

### *2) AIR scores can indicate sub-task challenges*

The average AIR score during block pick-up (sub-task 1) decreased by 34.6% between the 0 and 5 second time delay conditions. This findings support our intuition that our metric can reveal insights beyond sub-task completion time alone. For example three operators paused and asked clarifying questions during block stacking (sub-task 2). These pauses contributed to an average completion time of 2:12 min for sub-task 2 as compared to 1:22 min for sub-task 1. Normally we may prioritize our design efforts on the sub-task with the longest completion time (sub-task 2); however our AIR scores highlighted that users had the most input inefficiencies during the block pickup (sub-task 1) and we identified a need for supporting block alignment.

### Implications for design

The most important implication for our measure is as a video indexing design tool for HRI. Before the study our group developed software for reviewing captured operator inputs logs and screencasts on a timeline. The timeline showed the operator's face, hands, voice, live and time-delay video feeds, and was used for understanding the context surrounding operator errors. The points at which operators struggled with *bump and wait* as a result of time delay was not always clear from this timeline. By adding our metric to the timeline, our designers can more easily find and then jump to particular moments when operators were more or less *confident* in time instead of having to watch an entire session (see Figure 3). In addition the scores helped us more effectively compare and contrast specific problem contexts across operators, discuss strategies for addressing these issues.

## CONCLUSIONS & FUTURE WORK

Many human-in-the-loop tasks are subject to time-delay conditions. In this paper we proposed an anticipatory input ratio (AIR) metric for evaluating operator inputs under time delay and evaluate this measure during a telerobotic task. 22 subjects performed a block-stacking task by operating a joystick controlled robotic arm under 0, 2.5, and 5-second time delay conditions.

High AIR scores revealed moments when operators could enter commands before waiting for visual confirmation feedback while low AIR scores highlighted moments when operators waited for time-delayed feedback before continuing. By reviewing the context of these scores with video we identified specific inefficiencies under time delay that led us to explore opportunities for increasing operator feedback and decreasing operator and robot idle times.

In the future we plan to further explore how AIR scores may be useful as a video indexing design tool and a training aptitude measure for evaluating future robot arm operators.

## REFERENCES


1. Imaida, Takashi, et al. "Ground-space bilateral teleoperation of ETS-VII robot arm by direct bilateral coupling under 7-s time delay condition." Robotics and Automation, IEEE Transactions on 20.3 (2004)
2. Wilcox, Brian H. "Robotic vehicles for planetary exploration." Applied Intelligence 2.2 (1992): 181-193.
3. Norman, Donald A. "Design rules based on analyses of human error." Communications of the ACM 26.4 (1983): 254-258.
4. Sorensen, Khalid L., Joshua B. Spiers, and William E. Singhose. "Operational effects of crane interface devices." Industrial Electronics and Applications, 2007. ICIEA 2007. 2nd IEEE Conference on. IEEE, 2007.
5. International Organization for Standardization, 2011, ISO 7752/2-2011/Addendum 1 Lifting Appliances, Controls, Layout and Characteristics. Part 2: Basic Arrangement and Requirements for Mobile Cranes.
6. Sheridan, Thomas B. "Space teleoperation through time delay: review and prognosis." Robotics and Automation, IEEE Transactions on 9.5 (1993): 592-606.
7. Bejczy, Antal K., et al. "Role of computer graphics in space telerobotics: Preview and predictive displays." Fibers' 91, Boston, MA. SPIE, 1991.
8. Veltman, Hans, and Arjen Oving. Augmenting camera images for operators of unmanned aerial vehicles. No. RTO-MP-088. HUMAN FACTORS RESEARCH INST TNO SOESTERBERG (NETHERLANDS), 2003.
9. Thurling, Andrew J. Improving UAV handling qualities using time delay compensation. No. AFIT/GAB/ENY/00M-01. AIR FORCE INST OF TECH WRIGHT-PATTERSONAFB OH, 2000.
10. de Vries, S. C. UAVs and control delays. No. TNO-DV3-2005-A054. TNO DEFENCE SECURITY AND SAFETY SOESTERBERG (NETHERLANDS), 2005.
11. O'HARA, KENTON P., and Stephen J. Payne. "Planning and the user interface: The effects of lockout time and error recovery cost." International Journal of Human-Computer Studies 50.1 (1999): 41-59.
12. Lane, J. Corde, Craig R. Carignan, and David L. Akin. "Advanced operator interface design for complex space telerobots." Autonomous robots 11.1 (2001): 49-58.
13. Dix, Alan J. "The Myth of the Infinitely Fast Machine." BCS HCI. 1987.
14. Steinfeld, Aaron, et al. "Common metrics for human-robot interaction." Proceedings of the 1st ACM SIGCHI/SIGART conference on Human-robot interaction. ACM, 2006.
15. Steinfeld, Aaron. "Interface lessons for fully and semi-autonomous mobile robots." Robotics and Automation, 2004. Proceedings. ICRA'04. 2004 IEEE International Conference on. Vol. 3. IEEE, 2004.
16. Niemeyer, Günter, and Jean-Jacques E. Slotine. "Telemanipulation with time delays." The International Journal of Robotics Research 23.9 (2004): 873-890.
17. Held, Richard, and Nathaniel Durlach. "Telepresence, time delay and adaptation." Pictorial communication in virtual and real environments (1991): 232-246.
18. Chen, Jessie YC, Ellen C. Haas, and Michael J. Barnes. "Human performance issues and user interface design for teleoperated robots." Systems, Man, and Cybernetics, Part C: Applications and Reviews, IEEE Transactions on 37.6 (2007): 1231-1245.
19. Kaber, David B., et al. "Effects of visual interface design, and control mode and latency on performance, telepresence and workload in a teleoperation task." Proceedings of the Human Factors and Ergonomics Society Annual Meeting. Vol. 44. No. 5. SAGE Publications, 2000

# Stay on the Boundary: Artifact Analysis Exploring Researcher and User Framing of Robot Design

**Hee Rin Lee, Selma Šabanović, Erik Stolterman**
Indiana University
901 E. 10th Street, Bloomington, IN 47408 USA
{hrl,selmas,estolter@indiana.edu}

### ABSTRACT
In recent years, HCI researchers have increased their focus on studying the power relationships between researchers and users, and developing methodologies for eliciting design ideas that are sensitive to existing epistemic hierarchies in technology design. The differential value given to expert versus lay knowledge is a central factor in these debates. We apply Artifact Analysis, developed to help designers handle the complexity of digital artifacts, as a method to explore how experts and non-experts understand and frame robots, a technology characterized by significant complexity. Our results show that both non-expert users and expert researchers have knowledge that is significant to future robot development, but they focus on different aspects of the technology—users address mediated and interaction complexity while researchers focus on internal and external complexity. We also found that robots function as boundary objects between experts and users, and suggest that one task designers can perform is to "stay on the boundary" and mediate between the different ways in which experts and non-experts frame emerging technology to develop designs that benefit from insights from both user and researcher perspectives.

### Author Keywords
Artifact Analysis; Epistemic hierarchy; Boundary Objects

### ACM Classification Keywords
H.5.2 User Interfaces: Evaluation/Methodology.

### INTRODUCTION
HCI researchers have recently increased their reflexive awareness of [1] and interest in the power dynamics and hierarchy among experts and non-experts as stakeholders in technology design. Users are often considered to be less knowledgeable than technology experts and are placed in passive roles as informants in the design process, rather than playing more active roles as co-designers. Researchers, in contrast, are valued for their technical knowledge and positioned as being able to provide technological solutions for users' problems. The HCI community has been developing appropriate methodologies to counter such hierarchies between researchers and users, especially in the ICT4D[4] and Co-Design literature [9]. However, few studies explore how designers can approach the design process in ways that are sensitive and critical of existing hierarchies between researchers and users while also practically apply insights from critical and social studies to the development of emerging technologies.

We use Artifact Analysis as a methodology to explore and reflect critically on the ways in which expert robotics researchers and non-expert users approach everyday robot design. We focus on robotics as a historically technology-driven field, which is increasingly turning to everyday user applications and therefore requires more diverse user input in design[7]. We particularly focus on the following questions: What knowledge do researchers and users bring to bear when discussing robots for everyday use? How do they use their interpretations to frame robot design? What stance can designers take to counter existing hierarchies between users and researchers in robot design?

This paper presents an Artifact Analysis of everyday robotic technologies performed with participants who are researchers/experts in robotics and participants who are non-experts and potential users of robotic technologies. By analyzing how users and researchers critique and categorize existing robots, we can reveal how they interpret and frame these complex digital artifacts. We further suggest that digital artifacts can be understood as boundary objects [8] that have different meanings for researchers, who interpret them as research objects, and users, who see them as everyday artifacts. Based on these results, we see one of the challenges of robot design as mediating between these perspectives and suggest designers can position themselves at the boundary between researchers and users to be responsive to existing epistemological hierarchies and to incorporate the knowledge of both groups in design.


*CHI 2014,* April 26 - May 01 2014, Toronto, ON, Canada

http://dx.doi.org/10.1145/2556288.2557395

### ARTIFACT ANALYSIS OF ROBOTS

#### Artifact Analysis as Method
As a counterpart to user evaluations in the lab, researchers have been using ethnographic studies to observe how

people use technology in natural settings [2; 3] and to suggest design implications based on situated interactions (e.g., seeing a family as a group of users). However, technology designers need not only to understand the modes and contexts of technology use, but also to design objects with specific properties and shapes [5]. To address this challenge in the realm of complex digital artifacts, Janlert and Stolterman proposed Artifact Analysis as an analytical tool designers can use to contend with complexity as part of design [5]. They suggest that digital artifact complexity should be understood as composed of multiple loci of complexity. Complexity can be located and caused by internal complexity (i.e. due to the internal workings of the artifact), external complexity (i.e. due to the complexity of the interface), mediated complexity (i.e. due to the complex nature of the task or environment). The distribution of complexity between these loci, leads to an overall interaction complexity [5].

Artifact analysis was originally developed for interaction designers, but we extend it to explore how various stakeholders, namely researchers and users, frame robotics as an example of digital technology. We use the different forms of complexity[5] to categorize how our participants describe and critique robots, and to point out differences, similarities, and complementarities of their viewpoints that can inform robot design. In describing our study, we refer to participants as researchers/experts and users/non-experts, and to the broader HCI community as designers. We are specifically interested in understanding how robotics researchers with diverse backgrounds—designers, social scientists, computer scientists—and various users approach robots. While we do not generalize from our results to designers more broadly, we hope that the methodological approach will contribute to the HCI community interested in the relationship between users and researchers and in critical and collaborative methods for technology design.

### Participants

The study was conducted with 6 robotics researchers/experts (male: 3, female: 3, average age: 29) and 8 users/non-experts (male: 4, female: 4, average age: 56). Participants in both groups were chosen to represent diverse backgrounds. Users included a university student in his 20s, a 40-year-old bakery worker with no higher education experience, and a nursing home resident in her 70s with a masters in design, among others. To represent the interdisciplinarity of robotics research, we recruited researchers with backgrounds in computer science, psychology, human-robot-interaction, and mechanical engineering. Although some of our researcher participants were more sensitive to user perspectives than others as a matter of discipline, our results show that as a group their views on robots differed from those of non-expert users.

### Study Procedure

In line with the Artifact Analysis method, the interviews focused on picture cards depicting currently available industrial, research, or commercial robots. The task for each interviewee was to discuss and critique each picture of a robot (e.g., favorite and least favorite part, robot's possible function and use) and to group the pictures of robots based on criteria they found relevant. The visual materials and the procedures of critiquing and categorizing the robots enabled participants with different backgrounds to talk about the robots in their own terms.

#### *Materials: Cards with Robot Images*

The 27 6x6 inch cards mostly used full-body pictures of robots (26/27) with no additional textual information or context provided to minimize outside influence on user interpretations and allow participants to interpret the digital artifacts in their own terms. Most of the robots we chose (24/27) were designed for everyday use and were diverse in regards to design principles (e.g., uncanny valley [6], minimal design), level of humanlikeness (e.g., Geminoid (figure. 1: top left); Snackbot (figure. 1: top middle)), and function, such as assistive robots for elderly (e.g., Care-o-bot (figure.1: top left), education robots for children (e.g., Papero (figure 1: down left)), and therapeutic robots (e.g., Kaspar). We also included examples of 'social robots' designed for natural interaction with people (e.g., Kismet (figure 1: down middle)) and robots with different form factors, such as minimalist Muu (figure 1: down left), a robotic flower, an autonomous car, a robot ball, and industrial robots.

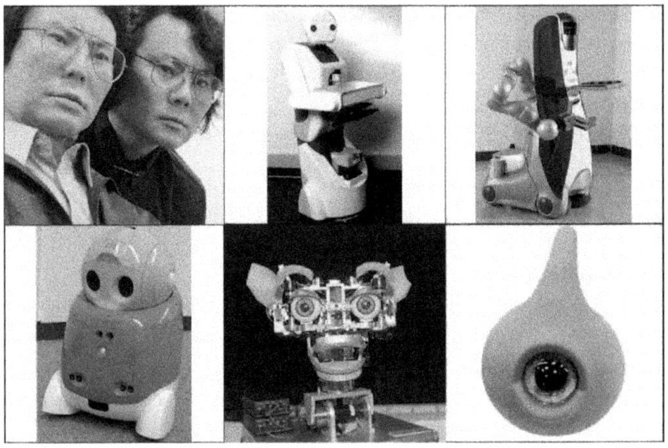

**Figure 1. Sample cards (top left: Geminoid, top middle: snackbot, top right: Care-o-robot, lower left: Papero, lower middle: Kismet, lower right: Muu)**

#### *Task: Critiquing and Categorizing Robots*

Our main elicitation strategy in the study was asking participants to critique and group the robots according to categories that made sense to them. There was no set number of groups they were asked to create. While grouping, participants compared and contrasted the robots to describe what they saw as their common properties (categories). This provided a simple yet meaningful method of understanding what participants knew about robots and how they framed them in their own mind. All participants were able to participate in and complete this task.

While we allowed the participants to discuss and categorize the robots without limitations, we did ask some questions to encourage researchers and users to think of robots in a user-centered way. We asked all participants about possible contexts of use and users for each robot as the first step in the robot critique (e.g., "Can you guess where the robot can be used, and who could use the robots?" or "What do you think the robot is for?"). Both researchers and users therefore had multiple opportunities to comment on all four forms of complexity relevant to artifact analysis, so their answers realistically would depict their framing of robots.

## RESULTS

Our results show that the two groups of participants, expert robotics researchers and non-expert potential users, had different perspectives on robots and applied different forms of knowledge to the study task. The difference in the knowledge between the groups did not come from their depth of knowledge, as might be expected in comparing experts and non-experts, but from the different ways in which the two groups epistemically situated robots. Researcher comments focused on internal and external complexity, while user comments focused on interaction complexity. Even when they were explicitly asked about users and contexts of use, researchers emphasized scientific knowledge about robots rather than developing a more use-oriented perspective.

### Epistemic Framing of Robots by Researchers

Researchers participating in our study generally approached robots as scientific objects developed through considerable efforts by their peers. Researchers were understandably knowledgeable about ways to manage internal complexity (e.g., which algorithms were used) and external complexity (e.g., degrees of freedom of arms) of robots. However, research participants focused less on addressing interaction complexity (e.g., what would be appropriate ways of interaction between users and technologies in actual context) and mediated complexity (e.g., possible applications and scenarios of technology use), even in cases when they were specifically asked to do so.

In our study, the technological knowledge of researchers sometimes restricted their imagination and critique of technology design. Researcher participants were familiar with most of the robots we presented through demo videos, articles, or personal experiences. Half of researchers tried to advocate for the intentions of researchers who were renowned in the robotics field, rather than critiquing them. Three researchers who had experience with robots in person discussed the robot not as an object for everyday life but as a research accomplishment. Two researchers considered the interview as a test to examine their knowledge in the field. The reaction of researcher participants shows how scientific knowledge can limit critique and creativity regarding the potential uses of robots.

Scientific distinctions also affected how researchers framed robots in relation to users. The robot car was an interesting example. Most (4/6) of the researchers felt uncomfortable calling autonomous cars robots. This artifact sparked researchers to discuss their definition of robots, as in this case of R2, who was majoring in cognitive science:

*R2: Uhm ... my conception of what makes a robot entirely depends on my experience. ... I am not exactly sure what is responsible my own mind to create a category (of a robot). But... obviously it's shaped in such a way that I use "robot" to describe specific things, which is cultural. (a HRI researcher majored in cognitive science)*

When categorizing the robots, researchers generally developed groupings based on their own research topics. A researcher (a HRI researcher majored in interaction design) studying a therapeutic robot for seniors with dementia divided robots depending on their ability to provide emotional support to users. A researcher (a HRI researcher majored in health informatics) studying facial expressions of a robot made groups based on the facial expressivity of each robot. Also, every researcher had a group of robots they placed in the uncanny valley[6] as entities that are almost-but-not-quite human- or animal-like and therefore "creepy." This category was not used by non-experts, and signifies an academic framing of robots.

### Epistemic Framing of Robots by Users

Non-expert participants interpreted robots in terms of their everyday potential or imagined use. Their comments focused on the mediated complexity of robots (e.g., how humanoid robots can be used for certain purposes and tasks in specific contexts) and interaction complexity (e.g., what type of interaction are appropriate and reasonable in certain circumstances), but not on internal complexity (e.g., the internal workings of the robot) and external complexity of robots (e.g., complexity of interface). Unlike the researchers, users thought the robot car was the most useful robot. The car was familiar enough for non-experts so that they could imagine using it in their everyday life. The academic definition of robots was not important to users, rather they appreciated being familiar with the modes of interaction with a robot, so they could control the robot and understand its functions without difficulties.

All non-expert participants had one group of robots that they defined as fitting into their everyday lives, such as a domestic appliance or assistant group. Non-expert participants described applying robots in everyday life in more ways than researchers (e.g., Can you guess where and how this robot is used? What is your favorite and least favorite part considering the context?). Finding applications for robotic technologies has long been a difficulty for robotics and was even mentioned by our researcher participants as a primary concern. Non-expert participants surprised us by liking Geminoid that was considered "too humanlike" by researchers and therefore likely to be rejected by users according to the uncanny valley theory. One of our participants, a 75-year-old male nursing home resident with no technology education and no previous experience with robots, explained that a humanoid shape of Geminoid (e.g., very humanlike face) allows him to feel more in control. That does not mean he would like to interact with Geminoid emotionally, but that familiar design components can decrease interaction complexity.

## DISCUSSION AND CONCLUSION

Artifact Analysis focuses on artifacts themselves with an open procedure (e.g., compare and contrast). As a method originally developed for designers, when used to explore our participants' epistemic framing of robots, it allowed them to describe technology in ways that are meaningful to them. Thus, all participants, regardless of their knowledge level, were able to actively participate in the analysis process by using their existing knowledge about technology to develop their epistemic framing. Using artifact analysis as a method, we realized that researchers' framing of robots can be somewhat restrictive in terms of dealing with interaction complexity, while users' contextual knowledge allowed them to envision creative and appropriate ways of interacting with and using robots in the context of daily life. Our finding contrasts with the dominant epistemic hierarchy in robotics, which privileges professional knowledge by researchers. While the ability of users to imagine wider everyday uses of robots can be (and has been) seen as technological naiveté, we suggest it is an opportunity for reimagining the potential for future robot design. We also suggest that these perspectives provide complementary, though sometimes conflicting, material that can be further synthesized by designers.

As a result of exploring the different epistemic framings of robots by researchers and potential users, we suggest that digital artifacts can be conceptualized as *boundary objects* [8] between different stakeholders in robot design, in our case robotics researchers and users. Researcher participants situated robots within the conceptual space of *academic inquiry* first and foremost, while non-experts treated robots as objects for *everyday use*. Both perspectives are necessary to develop practical design solutions in robotics. We suggest that, by becoming aware of this difference in framing robots and the complementary expertise of users and researchers on different aspects of robot complexity, designers can bridge the gap between these perspectives and place themselves on the boundary between researchers and users. In this process, they will also have to contend with the challenge of mediating between the contradictory visions of researchers and users of robotic technologies.

Before conducting our study, we had misgivings about using Artifact Analysis as a method for eliciting non-experts' knowledge about robots, since it is a less controlled method of study. However, all participants were capable of performing artifact analysis. Non-expert participants were in fact more open to defining appropriate interfaces for controlling robots than researcher participants, whose perceptions were sometimes limited by preconceived scientific concerns. The high possibility of miscommunication using different languages could be seen as a disadvantage of this method, but the difficulties actually helped us realize that our knowledge and ways of dealing with the complexity of robots as researchers is restricted. Consequently, we would like to suggest artifact analysis as a pragmatic way of exploring design possibilities of complex digital technologies, such as robots, in a way that shares control and responsibility in design with users and gives them a voice in conceptualizing new technologies. We also suggest that including the frameworks of users in design allow robot designers to be sensitive to and critical of existing epistemological hierarchies.

## REFERENCES


1. Bardzell, S. 2010. Feminist HCI: taking stock and outlining an agenda for design. In *Proc. of CHI 2010*, ACM Press, 1301-1310.
2. Forlizzi, J. and Disalvo, C., 2006. Service robots in the domestic environment: a study of the Roomba vacuum in the home. In *Proc. of HRI 2006*, ACM Press, 258-265.
3. Grinter, R., Edwards, W.K., Newman, M., and Ducheneaut, N., 2005. The work to make a home network work. *In ECSCW 2005*, Springer., 469-488.
4. Irani, L., Vertesi, J., Dourish, P., Philip, K., and Grinter, R.E., 2011. Postcolonial computing: a lens on design and development. *In Proc. CHI 2010*, ACM Press, 1311-1320.
5. Janlert, L.-E. and Stolterman, E., 2008. Complex interaction. ACM Trans. *Comp.-Hum. Inter.* 17, 2, 1-32.
6. Mori, M., 1970. The uncanny valley. Energy 7, 4, 33-35.
7. Šabanović, S. 2010. Robots in society, society in robots - Mutual shaping of society and technology as a framework for social robot design. *IJSR* 2, 4, 439-450.
8. Star, S.L. and Griesemer, J.R., 1989. Institutional ecology, `translations' and boundary objects: Amateurs and professionals in Berkeley's Museum of Vertebrate Zoology, 1907-39. *Soc. Studies of Sci.* 19, 3 , 387-420.
9. Vines, J., Clarke, R., Wright, P., Mccarthy, J., and Olivier, P., 2013. Configuring participation: On how we involve people in design. *In Proc.of CHI 2013*, ACM Press, 429-438.

# Help Beacons: Design and Evaluation of an Ad-Hoc Lightweight S.O.S. System for Smartphones

Amro Al-Akkad[1], Leonardo Ramirez[2], Alexander Boden[1], Dave Randall[3], Andreas Zimmermann[1]

[1]Fraunhofer FIT
Schloss Birlinghoven
53754 St. Augustin, Germany
{FN.LN}@fit.fraunhofer.de

[2]Fraunhofer Headquarters
Hardenbergstrasse 20
10623 Berlin, Germany
{FN.LN}@zv.fraunhofer.de

[3]University of Siegen
Hölderinstr. 3
57068 Siegen, Germany
{FN.LN}@uni-siegen.de

## ABSTRACT

We present the design and evaluation of a lightweight mobile S.O.S. system that facilitates ad-hoc communication between first responders and victims in emergency situations. Our approach leverages established protocols and standards in unforeseen ways to provide a platform supporting the creation of short-lived communication links. The system comprises two mobile applications: one victim application that allows the broadcasting of distress signals by a novel use of Wi-Fi SSIDs; and a responder application that allows first responders to discover and trace the people broadcasting the signals. The main difference of our system with other platforms enabling communication in crisis situations is that our system is independent from existing network infrastructure and runs on off-the-shelf, commercially available smartphones. We describe the results of our evaluation process in the context of both a design evaluation during a real world emergency response exercise and of two user workshops in preparation for an upcoming large-scale exercise.

## Author Keywords

Mobile computing; ad-hoc communication; emergency response; smartphones

## ACM Classification Keywords

H.1.2 User/Machine Systems: Human Factors,
H.5.3 Group and Organization Interfaces: CSCW.

## INTRODUCTION

The availability of broadband (3G, 4G) and wireless (Bluetooth, Wi-Fi) communication technologies as well as portable wireless devices (smartphones, tablet computers) has significantly increased over the last decade. People have become used to the omnipresence of mobile services such as map-based services, communication services, or social networks in their daily life. However, the availability of such services can be severely disrupted in crisis situations, when people are most dependent on their ability to communicate. Several studies (cf. [20, 24, 35]) have found that people immediately affected by a crisis as well as people near or far away to the affected crisis zone, are often trying to use services such as SMS, web sites, blogs, social networks or micro-blogging, to respond to the contingent needs created by a crisis. For example, Yu [35] investigated the use of texting services during the 2002-2003 SARS epidemic in China to spread information about the locality of infected persons. Also, the study of Shklovski et al. [24] examined how, in the aftermath of the 2007 Southern California wildfires, the use of blogs and web sites supported people in reconnecting geographically dispersed communities. Such incidents, however, also sometimes show that in cases of emergencies people often face intermittent or complete cut-off from their mobile platforms due to damage to or congestion in the network infrastructure. This inability to communicate also hinders emergency response personnel in finding immobilized or trapped victims, especially in cases of large-scale disasters.


*CHI 2014,* April 26–May 1, 2014, Toronto, Ontario, Canada.
Copyright ©ACM 978-1-4503-2473-1/14/04...$15.00.
http://dx.doi.org/10.1145/2556288.2557002

Research in Mobile Computing and HCI communities has striven for the design of systems that enable people in distress to communicate with each other, as well as with emergency response personnel (cf. [9, 13, 18, 22, 32]). However, most of these systems rely upon an existing network infrastructure. Other studies (cf. [11, 16, 28]) have explored the use of Bluetooth (BT) or Wi-Fi in Ad Hoc mode to provide communication platforms that are independent from existing network infrastructure, usually relying on special hardware or custom modified mobile systems. In this paper, we contribute to this stream of research by presenting an implementation of a system that runs on off-the-shelf smartphones and is independent from existing network infrastructure. Our system enables people in distress to use their smartphones to communicate their situation in the form of an ad-hoc emergency signal that can be received by professional first responders, helping them to locate victims and danger zones in emergency situations. To do so, our approach leverages established wireless network protocols and standards to create ad-hoc communication links between portable wireless devices in proximity. One device (the "Beacon") advertises an emergency message inside the Wi-Fi service identifier (SSID), i.e. the human readable network name of an access point. In turn, another device (the "Seeker") scans the environment for devices that advertise themselves as Beacons and instantiates brief connections to those in order to notify each Beacon that it has been discovered. In cases where connectivity is strong enough, both Beacon and Seeker can exchange further information that exceeds the 32 characters constraint of the SSID.

In this paper, we explore the potential uses of ad-hoc networking technology in crisis situations and how first responders and victims can benefit from the use of this technology. Using a proof-of-concept system in the context of emergency response training, we observe how our technology fits into existing practice and discuss the implications of our findings for the design of ad-hoc networking applications for emergency response. Our paper is organized as follows: We open with a description of the background of our work and the methodology we applied for our study. Then, we discuss the related work and how our approach contrasts with existing approaches. We describe in detail the design and implementation of our proof-of-concept system. In the second half of the paper, we present a design evaluation as well as results from two user workshops in the context of emergency response training. After a discussion of the limitations of our system and findings from our evaluation, we conclude the paper with implications for the design of ad-hoc communication systems for emergency situations.

## BACKGROUND AND METHODOLOGY

Our study is part of a large European research project that aims to support first responder organizations in handling large-scale emergency situations by providing a means of communication despite disruptions to existing network infrastructure. In such situations, locating and communicating with victims is an important need for first responders. Over the last two years, we have conducted several interviews with practitioners in the field of emergency response and people who have personally experienced or were otherwise affected by a crisis. A detailed account of our fieldwork and its implications for design is described in [1].

Based on our fieldwork [1] in the project, we have collected several high-level system requirements (see Table 1). In addition to those identified in the literature on dangerous and disruptive environments [15], summarized in R1-R4, we elicited five additional requirements (R5-R9). From this and following the approach of Edwards et al. [8], we have started with the design of a prototypical system, in order to test the benefits and constraints of our core ideas in an early stage. To explore the feasibility and implications of our concept, we have tested our first prototype in a fire fighting exercise in an underground tunnel, where communication was difficult and intermittent due to the high amount of steel and curves. We considered this as a very important process for identifying constraints at an early stage of our design, before making it more robust in order to provide a

| ID | Summary (The system should...) |
|---|---|
| R1 | Operate under harsh conditions in terms of temperature, vapor, or vibration. |
| R2 | Operate despite environmental impacts that weaken communication signals or hamper sensor reading. |
| R3 | Work reliably and accurately as possible. |
| R4 | Only augment users in their actions with the physical world, but not to distract them. |
| R5 | Use established technologies to exploit opportunities, e.g. everyday services as Twitter or commercial OSs. |
| R6 | Enable quick construction of networks requiring no cumbersome configuration efforts. |
| R7 | Operate fault-tolerant to cope with limitations, such as intermittent disconnections. |
| R8 | Facilitate distribution of data to co-existing networks. |
| R9 | Support dynamic re-configurations of networks as needs rapidly change in the aftermath of a crisis. |

**Table 1. Set of System Requirements.**

prototype for 'real world' end-users. We explored the potential of our technology in two ways: 1) through a design evaluation as part of a real world exercise and 2) through workshop participation with emergency response workers. We gathered feedback through semi-structured interviews. We captured all interviews in audio and video and we kept field notes along the process. Interviewees were asked to sign an informed consent form prior to the interview. All interviews were transcribed and translated into English, if necessary.

## RELATED WORK

There are a number of systems available to support people to communicate via ICT services during emergency response (cf. [9, 13, 18, 22, 32]). M-Urgency [13] enables mobile Android or iOS users to stream live audio and video reports over the cellular network to a local public-safety answering point. In order to support the dispatcher and responders in making time-critical decisions, M-Urgency provides, besides audio and video, contextual data, such as the real-time position through GPS or Wi-Fi fingerprint, disability or gender to prepare aid accordingly, or information relevant to approach the incident scene such as weather or traffic. The Federal Emergency Management Agency (FEMA) provides an application [9] that enables people in distress to receive shelter information and also to submit images with a short description to the FEMA website, which will be placed on a map for public viewing. Before images become available online, the images need to go through a basic approval process in order to guarantee privacy and ensure relevance. SafeCity [22] allows the reception of live video streams from mobile devices reporting crimes or other distress situations. Professional responders use a dedicated application to stream video along with their GPS position to the command center or to other colleagues in the field. Users can install a free application called Bambuser [3], which enables them to view and stream live video. In order to report any video to authorities, users need to register for specific "shares", such as "Crime stoppers" or "Public Officials". All these existing emergency response systems represent promising tools for communication between the public and authorities or non-governmental organizations during a crisis. However, to be of use, any of these systems require the network infrastructure to be still operable.

Other existing technologies can be utilized for building ad-hoc communication networks during a crisis. For instance, OpenGarden [19] enables people who are offline to consume online services provided that at least one device can connect to the Internet to which other devices can tether using low-power BT radio. For our research, we assumed that devices were completely disrupted from the online world, and focused on interaction among connected devices. Wi-Fi Direct also provides an interesting potential for ad-hoc communication. We considered initially using it, though our experiments with it on Android 4.0-4.1 were not promising; for iOS it is not available. We failed to implement two important operations without the need for user interaction: first, enabling Wi-Fi Direct, and second, accepting incoming connections (see also [2]), which means that Wi-Fi Direct implementations for Android does not comply with R6 from our list. Another constraint is that its key mechanisms only work between Wi-Fi Direct certified devices, but not legacy Wi-Fi devices [5], which fails to comply with R5. In general terms, Wi-Fi Direct has been designed for quick, easy and secure peering of home devices, such as connecting a camera with a printer, while our system design originated from the need to allow for serendipitous communications between devices.

Much research (cf. [14, 16, 23, 28, 30]) has been conducted around the challenge of providing communication channels in situations of disrupted network infrastructure. For instance, the Twimight [11] application enables Twitter users in proximity to communicate with each other in spite of disruptions to the fixed communication network. It runs on commercial Android devices and facilitates communication between devices in proximity via BT. Twimight builds on BT, as it operates more energy efficiently than Wi-Fi. For our research project, we decided against BT due to its range constraints and cumbersome pairing process, which fails to comply with R6 and hence makes it less suitable for our purposes. The Haggle [28] platform enables mobile users in proximity to exchange content requiring no fixed infrastructure. Through a publish-subscribe system users can express interests via keywords and receive content from other peers according to how well available content matches their interests. Haggle runs on Windows Mobile and Android, the latter being the most widespread mobile operating system (OS) [12]. However, Haggle's Android distribution requires special privileges not available to all users (so called root access) for both BT and Wi-Fi, and thus does not comply with R5. The work of [23] supports the discovery and connection of wireless devices by Wi-Fi in IEEE 802.11 Ad Hoc Mode in order to allow for opportunistic communication. A device announces its presence by broadcasting beacons filled with relevant information in the SSID field, such as the device ID, and thus allows the discovery of multiple devices at the same time as one device receives several beacons from various devices without trying to establish a connection to them. While this approach shows good results in terms of energy efficiency and satisfactory connection speed between peered devices, it does not run on commercially available smartphones (R5). This is due to the fact that it uses Wi-Fi in Ad Hoc mode (not available in mobile OSs). From a technical perspective Wifi-Opp [30] comes the closest to our system. Wifi-Opp facilitates opportunistic networking requiring no root access on Android phones. Their technology utilizes Wi-Fi in Infrastructure mode and uses the same Android API to create Wi-Fi networks. However, currently [4] there are no OpenSource distributions available for Wifi-Opp, which made it difficult for us to verify its current state functionality.

The systems and approaches, then, have certain drawbacks in relation to our work:

- Existing systems **mostly work over existing network infrastructure** (mobile broadband, Wi-Fi hotspots), which in crisis is likely to be **disrupted**, e.g. due to damage or overloading.
- Systems using BT are **inadequate for serendipitous communications between devices**, as BT initial pairing mechanism for devices requires cumbersome configuration efforts.
- Wi-Fi in Ad Hoc mode **does not run on commercially available devices, it** requires devices to be rooted (Android) or jail broken (iOs).
- Wi-Fi Direct is still an emerging standard that is either **not available for** mobile OSs such as iOS, **or it is not working properly yet** on the latest distributions, such as in Android.

Conti [6] has pointed out that novel ideas and creative uses of vulnerabilities inherent in technology are often triggered by non-mainstream communities such as the hacking community. A good example of this emergence is the Emergency S.O.S Beacon [10] system, a system similar to our system, which emits help messages through Morse codes over AM radio which is receivable in a one-mile range by search and rescue teams using simple radio transceivers. Another interesting example is the research of Starbird et al. [26, 27] which resulted in the "Tweak the Tweet" (TtT) syntax, which supports computational filtering and classification of information coming from Twitter streams. TtT specifies the use of specific hashtags before the relevant data, such as their "#loc" placed in front

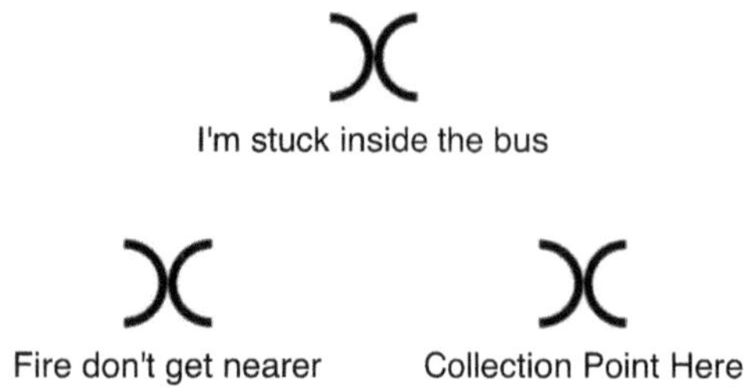


**Figure 1. Exploiting SSIDs to convey emergency needs.**

of GPS information. Analogous to these creative appropriation examples, our work leverages opportunities already existing in current standard, off-the-shelf technology, by piggybacking on the Wi-Fi connection process, exploiting Wi-Fi SSIDs to convey short emergency messages.

## THE HELP BEACONS APPROACH AND CONCEPT

The concept of our mobile S.O.S. system was inspired by how people make use of the names of Wi-Fi home networks (SSIDs) to broadcast short messages conveying simple, anonymous information. Such messages can be used for manifold purposes. For instance, some SSIDs may express political ideas (e.g. "ILoVeObAma!!") [34], requests or complains (e.g. "Turn the noise down") [25], or convey an intention or an ownership of a network (e.g. "ChrisNet") [33]. A Wi-Fi network is visible in a certain range and the advertised SSID is usually the first thing people become aware of in terms of wireless networks. Essentially, people can easily relate and understand SSID names. They represent an interesting point of contact between people and the intangible element that wireless network represent. We saw in this an interesting potential for emergency response which lead to the creation of the Help Beacons concept, illustrated in Figure 1, which explores the idea of using Wi-Fi SSIDs as beacons to ask for help, to offer resources, or to disclose locations during a disaster. The creation of an emergency beacon defines a sort of "I'm here" signal, which has the potential to support responders in finding missing persons and reestablishing communication.

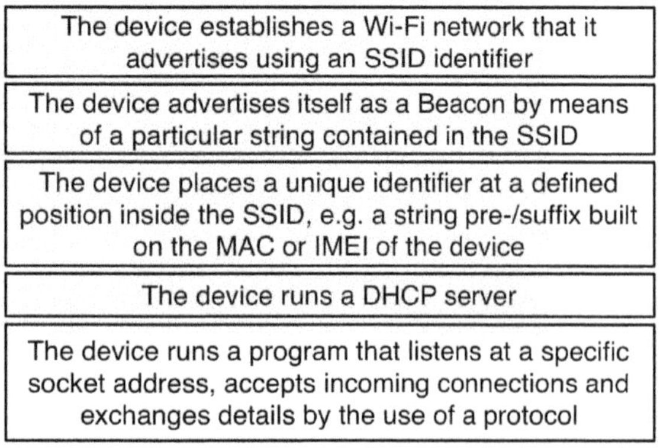


**Figure 2 Set up of Beacon.**

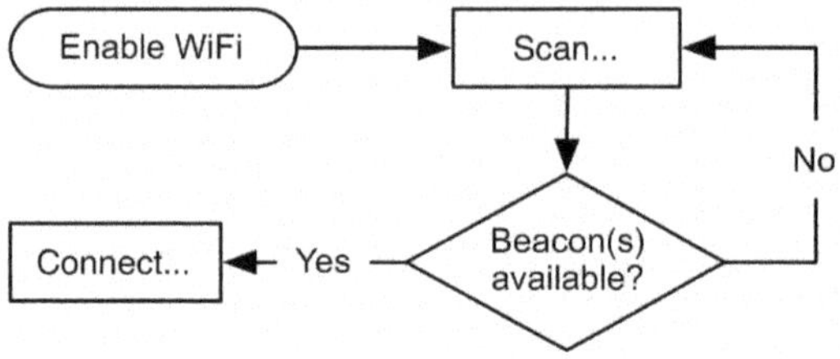


**Figure 3. Flow chart of Seeker Loop for Beacon Discovery.**

Our approach initially comprises two or more devices. Figure 2 depicts the setup process: at first, a device, i.e. a Beacon device deploys a Wi-Fi network that advertises itself as a Beacon by using a particular string of characters inside the SSID. The device runs a DHCP server for providing an IP address configuration for the Seeker, and listens to a specific socket address, i.e. the combination of an IP address and a port number, to exchange details, when the Seeker device associates to it. Figure 3 illustrates the Seeker, which enables its Wi-Fi interface, performs a scan for Wi-Fi networks, and finds the Beacon by the particular string of characters placed inside its SSID. Figure 4 illustrates how the Seeker connects to the Beacon and writes its details to the specific socket address. Subsequently, it receives details from the Beacon, and finally it disconnects.

For our system, we aimed for a design combining the networking mechanisms prevalent in smartphones and other portable wireless devices (R5) in order to allow for quick creation of networks between neighboring devices without the need for any cumbersome configuration efforts on the part of the user (R6). We decided to use Wi-Fi in Infrastructure Mode instead of BT, as the latter offers a very limited transmission range and because BT requires a

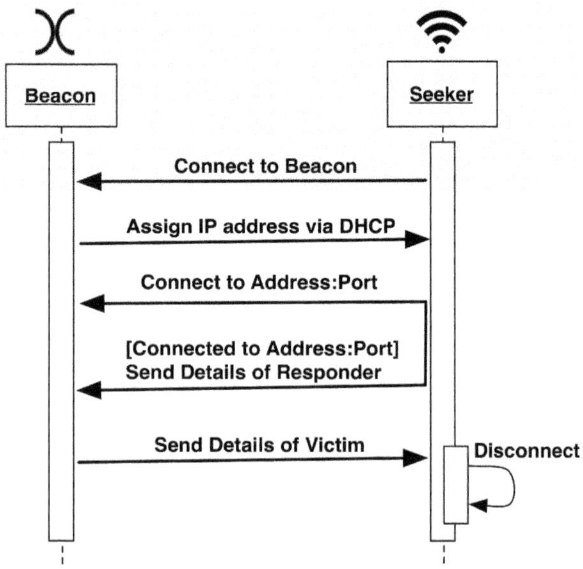


**Figure 4. Sequence Diagram of Connection Process.**

manual initial pairing of devices. This makes it less suitable for serendipitous communications between mobile devices focused on a short-lived, one time only network infrastructure. The Wi-Fi SSID sent out by a Beacon can carry useful information entered by the user, such as his or her name, health status, or other important information. Technically, the idea can be implemented by placing short messages inside the SSID, the network name of a Wi-Fi network in order to create an emergency beacon. A Seeker device uses its wireless interface to search for any Beacon devices in range, collecting the information broadcasted by the different devices calling for help. By piggybacking the handshaking process of Wi-Fi networks, i.e. by associating with an open (i.e. unencrypted) network, the Seeker can confirm that it has received the broadcast signal. Afterwards, the Seeker device can request further information or store additional information to support the logistics of the rescuing process by connecting to a network socket provided by the Beacon.

## DEVELOPMENT: HELP BEACONS

The Help Beacons system consists of two applications. The first is a victim application that enables its users to create an emergency beacon by placing short messages inside the SSID of a Wi-Fi network. The other application is a first responder application that allows professional first responders to discover the requesting Beacons. Both applications can be deployed on devices running Android (supported APIs range from `2.3.3` to `4.x`). Android is the most widespread mobile OS [12] and by supporting lower API versions, our system can be installed on a wide range of devices which complies with R5. The purpose of our system would be rather constrained if it were not linked to other emergency response systems. In our research project, the responder application, which runs on the Seeker device, sends the collected data acquired from deployed Beacons to a command center using for this a mesh network (R8), which routes the data to a publish-subscribe system that pushes the data to the command center. At the command center, people can use the data for response purposes.

### Victim Application

With regard to R4 our goal was to design this application in a very minimalistic way, requiring no complex configuration efforts from the side of the user. To create a Beacon the user only needs to push the S.O.S. button (see Figure 5). As soon as the creation of a Beacon is triggered, a Wi-Fi network is deployed. As Android provides this feature through a hidden API, we used JAVA reflection to invoke the relevant methods for creating a Wi-Fi network. To indicate that a Wi-Fi network constitutes a Beacon we prefix the SSID with an uncommon string (`*#%`). This allows a Seeker to distinguish a Beacon from other available networks. According to the 802.11 standard a SSID has a maximum of 32 bytes (which can hold up 32 ASCII chars). Our design considers a Beacon to comprise four parts inside a SSID (see Figure 5): a prefix that

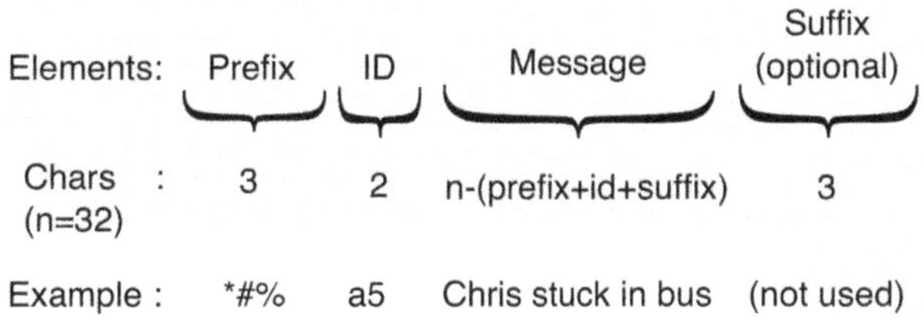


**Figure 5. Composition of Help Beacons SSID.**

indicates that this network represents a Beacon, a persistent id (2 ASCII chars), optionally a suffix (the prefix backwards) and, most importantly the emergency message. We used a "persistent" ID to be able to distinguish between equally labeled Beacons or to track devices that updated their SSID if the situation of the owner changes. Initially, we considered using the BSSID, which is automatically received when discovering a Wi-Fi network. Usually, the BSSID is the mac address of the Wi-Fi interface and hence is fixed. With Android 4.x, however, the second half of the BSSID is generated randomly. Thus, the application needs to use another static ID and puts a shortened fingerprint consisting of two ASCII chars inside the SSID. To hamper a reverse look up of a fingerprint, i.e. to prevent that attackers can derive characters of the IMEI of a Beacon, the application combines a random seed with the IMEI (a unique device ID for mobile phones) to generate an MD5 hash. Finally, the application includes inside the SSID the first two chars of the generated MD5 hash and stores this shortened device ID for later use inside the phone's cache.

In the application, users can select from predefined help messages or manually type in a new one (see Figure 6a). When their status changes, users can update their SSID broadcast accordingly (R9). Users can also select a specific entry (i.e. "I'm safe") from the list, which triggers the application to deploy the Wi-Fi network with the additional suffix mentioned above. The responder application will interpret this information automatically and will not

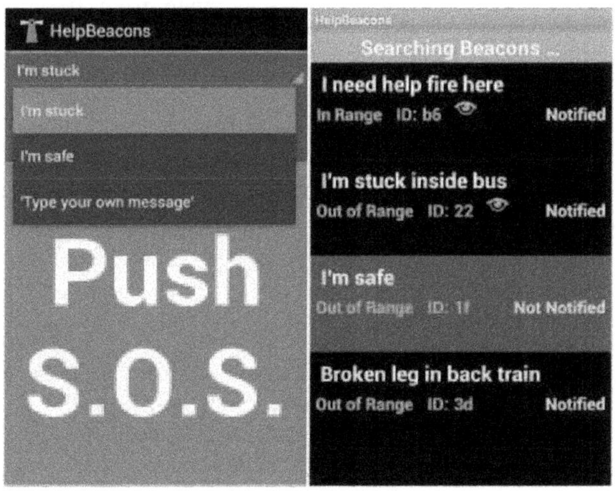


**Figure 6. a. Victim App, b. Responder App.**

connect to it (as the greyed out entry in Figure 6b shows). When a user enters a message manually, the application will provide visual feedback in form of a pop-up message.

After a Wi-Fi network has been deployed the Android OS automatically performs two internal actions that are beneficial for our application: 1) it creates a DHCP server, and 2) it flushes its cache of the address resolution protocol (ARP). The DHCP server assigns an IP address to each connecting client, enabling clients to address the Beacon. The IP address of the Wi-Fi network is always the same: `192.168.43.1`. We piggyback this static address for exchanging details that cannot be placed inside the SSID due to the 32 ASCII characters constraint. This information includes elements such as the unique ID of a device (IMEI), or the time a Beacon has been enabled. To facilitate the exchange of details, the Beacon device listens on a specific socket address (`192.168.43.1:8888`). After connecting to a Beacon, the responder application tries to establish a connection to this address in order to exchange details. A proprietary protocol has been designed for this purpose. Flushing the ARP clears the history of registered physical addresses of clients that are or which have been connected to a Beacon device. Therefore, the victim application deploys a dedicated thread that regularly checks the ARP cache for new entries in order to detect if a Seeker device (i.e. a client) has associated to the Beacon device. If a new entry appears in the ARP cache the application immediately informs its users that another device has associated to the Wi-Fi network, which was created through their device. The notification is performed by means of a short visual pop-up message and an audio cue, explaining to the users that a device carried by a first responder has associated to their device.

To avoid having other devices not taking part of our experiment connecting to one of our Beacons, the victim application configures an encrypted Wi-Fi network, although the work of [1] suggests that people in crisis situations are willing to open their private Wi-Fi networks. The time to enable a Beacon can range from 0.5 to 2 seconds. Given the transmission range capabilities available in current smartphones, the Beacon and Seeker devices can connect within a range of up to 100m. In the case that a responder cannot see or hear a victim, within this reach, s/he can at least receive a signal conveying that a victim's phone is within this range. In terms of energy consumption, the work of [30] shows acceptable values associated to the use of the same APIs used by our system.

### Responder Application

The second element of our platform is a responder application that sniffs radio signals in order to seek for Beacons. To trigger the discovery of Beacons the user needs to push the "Search" button (see Figure 6b). Then, the application enables the Wi-Fi interface of the device, i.e. the application sets up the Seeker device. The Seeker device continuously searches the environment for Beacons and the received scan results are filtered based on the particular SSID prefix set by the Beacon device. When one or more Beacons have been discovered, associations to Beacons are carried out in a pessimistic manner, i.e. the application first connects to the Beacon with the strongest signal. Typical times to associate to a Beacon, including the attempt to exchange details, are 1.5 to 4s. As soon as the Seeker device is connected to the Beacon the application plays a short sound to indicate the success of connection between Beacon and Seeker. Subsequently, a background process triggers the exchange of details via a network socket. Finally, the Seeker device disconnects in order to associate with other Beacons. The application highlights remaining Beacons with the "Not Notified" label (see Figure 6b). Where details have been exchanged, the responder application also plays another sound and visually highlights this to the user with an eye icon (see Figure 6b). To look for details the user can tap on the corresponding item. Data is not persistent on the Seeker device, i.e. the victim application removes all SSIDs from its phone cache after it disconnects from a Beacon.

In order to deal with "fake" Beacons that might interfere in the process of connecting to available Beacons, the responder application tries to connect to a Beacon with a 30s timeout. If the connection to a Beacon fails the corresponding SSID is put on a blacklist for one minute. This does not hinder the process of notifying the other Beacons in range (R7).

For evaluation purposes, we developed our application for Android, and deployed it on a commercial phone. We don't expect a professional first responder to use our application in such a configuration. A firefighter wearing heavy gloves cannot touch or type the small icons displayed in the UI, and any action that goes beyond two buttons is already problematic. For prototypical exploration, however, the common mobile phone used in our evaluations fitted our purposes nicely. To avoid problems due to such constrains, we manually initiated the action to seek for Beacons, before giving the phone to the users during the evaluation.

## EVALUATION

### Design evaluation

Evaluations of systems in "real" crisis situations is problematic [31], so we had to look for close-to-real conditions. We evaluated our design in training sessions in an underground facility used by teams of responders (ambulance, fire brigade, police and others) to train different aspects of their work. The aim was to get a better understanding on how our technology can be used in emergency situations, in a context as close to the "real world" as possible. Our evaluation consisted on the introduction of our prototype in a real exercise based on the following scenario: *Inside the middle of a tunnel, several people get stuck inside their vehicles due to an explosion in the back part of the tunnel. As some casualties lost network*

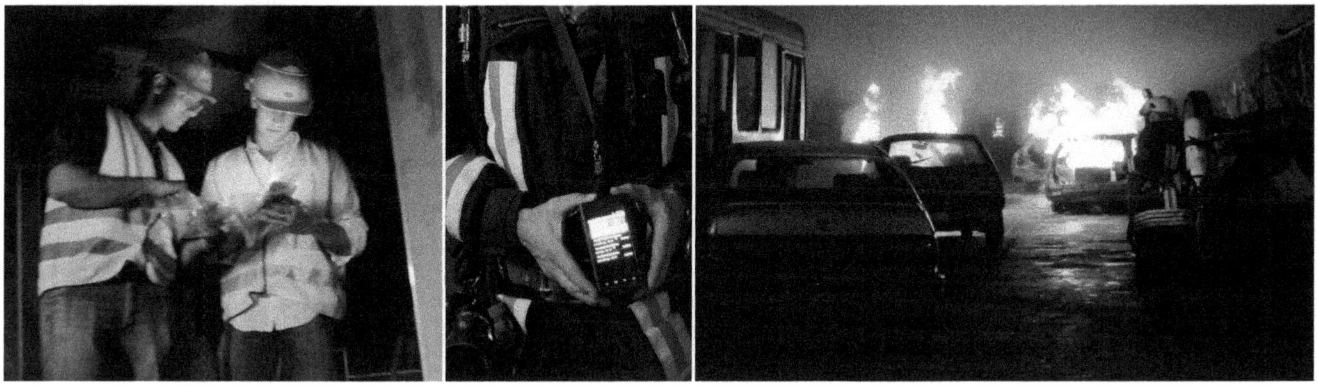

**Figure 7 a. Field tests inside tunnel, b. Boxed phone put on frontline officer, and c. System deployment in real world exercise.**

*access in their phones, they launch an application that enables them to advertise emergency beacons. After a while a phone carried by a first responder discovers those beacons and connects to them in order to notify the victims of the responder's presence. As soon as the responder is able to connect to the outside world, a report generated from the data coming from the beacons is sent to the local command center.*

During our initial field tests (see Figure 7a), we placed a set of smartphones inside some vehicles available in the facility for training purposes. We discovered that sometimes the Seeker device would connect to a Beacon, but then get stuck, instead of disconnecting from the Beacon and notifying the remaining Beacons previously discovered. The reason for this was that after the connection to a Beacon succeeded, the Seeker device tries to bind to a TCP/IP socket to exchange details. For the creation of a socket connection, a certain link speed is required—otherwise the communication may stall—which was sometimes not available as the large amount of steel inside of the tunnel weakened the signals. Also, we found out that when obtaining a scan result of a Beacon, we received a strong signal resulting in a link speed, which would normally be sufficient for establishing a socket connection. However, as we were walking or running, our position sometimes changed at the same time as the responder application tried to establish a connection. To deal with this, we revised our implementation, and introduced a connection timeout of 3s. Looking over our log files we found out that this strategy was quite helpful, as sometimes the required link speed was available right away or a bit later. After this improvement, we were able to run our tests without any technical problems in spite of the effects that the environment had on communication signals or other limitations due to the environment (R2, R3, and R7).

As our prototype proved to be robust enough, we tested it as part of a larger emergency response exercise that took place in the same underground facility. Figure 8 depicts three Beacon devices placed inside a bus and two train wagons. After a conceptual introduction, we demonstrated our prototype to the frontline officer (FO) assigned for the exercise, i.e. the firefighter who first enters the disaster scene and who provides a quick impression to the rest of the responder team. Initially, the FO expressed some reservations about the deployment of any digital technology due to bad experiences with a digital breathing device. Even so, he agreed to test our technology. We placed the Seeker phone inside a plastic box attached to a cord hanging around the neck of the FO (see Figure 7b). This way we hoped the FO would not be distracted by the device (R4), and would have the possibility to grab the smartphone when he preferred to do so. During the exercise (see Figure 7c) the FO was able to quickly receive the help calls that convey an idea of the status of trapped people despite the harsh conditions (R1). At some point the phone broke out of the box, so the FO simply put the device inside his pocket, a solution that —it turned out—for the FO worked better than our protective box.

**User Feedback**

After the design evaluation, we conducted interviews with the participants to gather feedback from end-users. The interview with the FO who used the responder application was particularly informative. From the first impression, the FO felt that using the responder application could be distracting from the actual work, especially when the first responders first enter an emergency site.

*FO: For the officer in charge at the front it is difficult, as the officer does not know what is expecting her or him. For me personally it was rather distracting. (...) You know when you stand there inside the tunnel it is really difficult to focus on the application.*

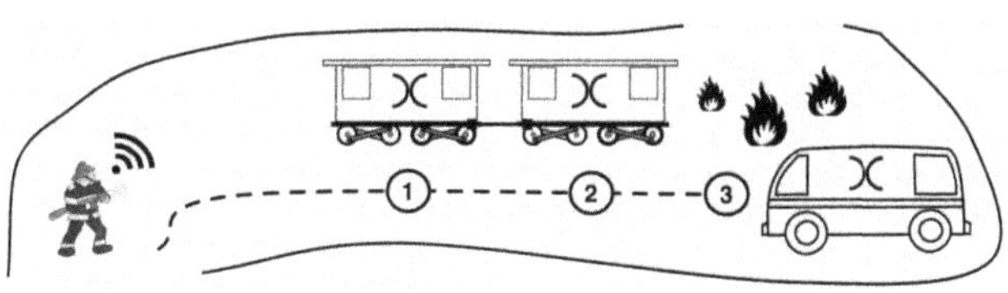


**Figure 8. Beacons put inside two train wagons and one bus.**

Apart from the possible distractions, the FO also mentioned that the initial focus of first responders would not be to find all trapped persons.

*FO: For example, if I see there is fire, I will command that the fire hoses will be rolled out, regardless of finding persons there or not. Further, if your application detects a beacon, and tells me a person is stuck inside on one of the train wagons, but I see another person over there near to the fire, I will first rescue the person next to the fire.*

The FO found the concept useful, however, for later stages of the response operation, or where the data collected in the field might be routed to the personnel working at the remote command center. The command center could then analyze the data in order to support responders in the field to find people who may have been overlooked.

*FO: But, I see the benefit of the application in its implicit use. I mean when it is linked to a rear command center. If I tell the command center we checked everything and rescued all persons, but they received a beacon call that does not match to one of the rescued persons. They can say stop, go back there and check if somebody is there.*

The FO also added that the system would be useful in larger scale emergencies, which are not as constrained as the tunnel scenario, and where the focus would be more on finding missing persons.

*FO: Inside the tunnel you usually find all people easily. I think it is rather helpful in large-scale disasters, such as a flooding or an earthquake. You could set up a beacon conveying a GPS or a message saying, "I live in the Main Street No. 15 and I'm stuck inside the debris". This could be a big advantage. You could direct upon this information a helicopter to get people from the roof. Of course, you could try to make an emergency call, but usually the dispatch center is too busy or the network is congested or damaged.*

In addition to the evaluation, we conducted user workshops to prepare for an upcoming large-scale exercise. In the first workshop, we explained our system in detail to a fire fighter (FF) and a police officer (PO). In general, the findings from the workshops provided additional evidence to support the finding that our technology would be useful for later stages of rescue missions:

*PO: I think it would help (...) later when a search and rescue team is sent to look for any overlooked persons.*

In the second workshop a professional for technical relief explained that rescue teams would follow a system of grids and sectors that they sweep systematically. The Help Beacons could be useful for making such efforts more efficient if the received information could be used to prioritize certain grids and sectors.

The participants provided also some feedback around the interaction of our system. The PO mentioned, for example, that both the responder application and victim application should not make any sounds but rather vibrate in order to avoid distraction and avoid drawing unwanted attention to the user in dangerous situations such as acts of terrorism.

## LIMITATIONS AND LESSONS LEARNED

A limitation to our user study was that no "victims" have been evaluated. This was not possible due to safety regulations within the impact zone of the exercise (people were not allowed to stay inside the vehicles). Also, we would argue that it is difficult to define what expertise or authority qualifies a "victim". Even so, we plan to conduct evaluations in which people play the role of civilians in distress. By doing so, we hope to gain further feedback on the constraints of our system.

As pointed out by Palen and Liu [20], often "first responders", in practice, are not professionals, but people from local or surrounding areas. As our system uses Wi-Fi, volunteers carrying smartphones may become aware of the messages of the Beacons and take responsive action. While this would be a positive effect, it has implications for the security of our system. In particular, we need to consider an extensible authentication protocol [17] for our system, e.g. EAP-TLS, making it more secure against malicious "Seeker" devices trying to spoof our system. How our system scales in a dense environment in which many Beacons are deployed that could cause multiple reporting of the same needs, is another broader issue we need to tackle when testing our system with more than a few devices and persons. Entangled with this are situations in which more than one victim may be present behind one Beacon.

Turoff [31] points out that a system not used on a daily basis will not be used in an emergency. We believe that our approach of designing technology in a minimalist way, leveraging established technologies, is just a first step in making the technology as open and easy to use as possible, and hopefully lessens the training curve when using our system for the first time, making it more likely to become embedded in routinely used devices. To move toward this goal, there are still some choices to be made. The means of exchanging details between Seeker and Beacon devices could be improved to use UDP instead of TCP sockets, as UDP is usually faster, or a combination of both to increase the probability of exchanging packets. Our proprietary protocol might be replaced with a standard protocol installed on every mobile device, similar to emergency localization features on phones. Another open issue is to investigate into further styles of interaction with our system, such as to use vibration feedback instead of sound, as proposed by the PO.

With regard to the design of the victim application, we have presented a first proof of concept. The technology works in contexts such as the tunnel of our design evaluation, which posed a complex environment to the operation of existing infrastructures. The field test and the user feedback hinted at some possible improvements to our design. The first open issue is how to provide positioning of the victims as envisioned by the FO. In the future, we plan to extend our system to log GPS positions for both applications. With this, even if the victim application fails to retrieve a GPS fix, at least the responder application can still provide a rough indication of the position of the Beacon device. A further issue is the question of how people can install the victim application on their devices. For our field test, we assumed that the application was already installed on the devices. As this will not be always the case in practice, and as the usual app stores cannot be accessed in the conditions we are designing for, we have begun to evaluate deployment mechanisms requiring no Internet access.

Our evaluation revealed interesting insights into the implications of our design for the practice of emergency response. The first insight is related to the design of the Seeker device. The design evaluation showed that frontline officers were skeptic towards the introduction of new technologies in general. They were considered to be potentially distracting, and that a time to appropriate the technology would be important.

*FO: A few a years ago I said that I just need a simple cell phone. I don't need to check the Internet or send emails. But, now I got used to this technology and using it to surf the Web. I think your system has a great potential. But it would need time to establish it for response work.*

The emergency workers were able to see a benefit of the technology for the command room, especially in large-scale emergencies. According to our field test, the Seeker device should be designed in a way that does not require user interaction and does not hinder the work of the emergency responder in any noticeable way. To fit these requirements, we designed our device to be carried on the person and to automatically relay discovered Beacon devices to the incident command room, so that distress signals can be processed and forwarded back to the emergency response teams. The possibility of showing collected beacons on an overview map for the incident commander or in the headquarters of the first responder organizations seems to be particularly promising in this regard.

During the user workshops, it became clear that the biggest advantage identified by the emergency personnel in our technology was the potential of providing a better overview over the incident site, allowing the discovery of people that might have been overlooked by the first responders entering the emergency site, and supporting more coordinated help efforts. In this sense, our technology fits into the discussion on the design of systems supporting coordination and knowledge sharing for emergency response [7, 21, 29]. Not least, there is definitely value in leveraging systems that exploit established technologies such as common Wi-Fi networking. With regard to our study, our system proved not to interfere with existing procedures or technologies responders used during the exercise, such as walkie-talkies using analogue radio as a communication technology.

## CONCLUSION

In this paper, we have presented a design and evaluation of a lightweight mobile S.O.S system, whose use can be helpful for situations in which existing network infrastructure has become disrupted. To enable offline communications our system facilitates the discovery of emergency beacons by exploiting the Wi-Fi SSID and allows for ad-hoc constructed, short-lived connections between neighboring devices by piggybacking on the Wi-Fi handshake. From a high-level perspective, an important aspect in the design of our system was the unforeseen exploitation of established technologies, inspired by the work in hacking and DIY communities.

Overall, we received positive feedback on the potentials of our technology for supporting the practices of emergency response, particularly in the context of large-scale disasters. Having said that, our attention was drawn to a number of contingencies that defined the use patterns of the proposed system. In our evaluations we gained a better understanding of how response staff prioritize their activities, and how new technology needs to fit within priorities. As expected, finding victims is important, but it is only one of many goals. Due to the evolving nature of emergency response work, the introduction of our system was perceived to be more useful at later stages in the process, as it needed a time for the network to emerge and stabilize.

Although systems for similar purposes [9, 18, 22] or similar technologies [14, 23, 28] have already been designed, our contribution lies in a simple and robust design that relies on established standards and provides a working solution in crisis situations. We designed our system with the specific goal of being used with commonly available Android devices, requiring no complex changes in the underlying mobile OS. This has significant advantages in situations where surviving network infrastructure is fragile or completely disrupted. We need to further evaluate our prototype in close-to-real conditions to inform our design. By solving technical limitations, we expect to enhance its value and widen its reach to further mobile platforms.

## ACKNOWLEDGEMENTS

Our special thanks go to the practitioners for providing us with thoughtful insights for emergency response. We thank the VSH Test Gallery, in particular Thomas Kulbe, for supporting us to explore our system at their premises; Wolfram Gottschlich, Erion Elmasllari and Mark Vinkovits for support on technical issues; Monika Büscher, Volker Wulf, Christian Raffelsberger and the anonymous reviewers for their valuable feedback on earlier versions. The research presented in this paper has been funded by the European Union as part of the BRIDGE project (FP7SEC-2010-1) under grant agreement n°261817.

## REFERENCES


1. Al-Akkad, A., et al. Reconstructing normality: The use of infrastructure leftovers in crisis situations as inspiration for the design of resilient technology. Proc. OzCHI'13, ACM Press (2013), 457-466.
2. Android Issue 30880: Wi-Fi Direct API for connection acceptance. http://bit.ly/ZTbwLM
3. Bambuser. http://bambuser.com/
4. Battlemesh mailing list Still no ad-hoc in Android 4.0 "Ice Cream Sandwich"? http://bit.ly/Z0pVDA
5. Camps-Mur, D., Garcia-Saavedra, A., and Serrano, P. Device-to-device communications with Wi-Fi Direct: overview and experimentation. IEEE Wireless Communications 20, 3 (2013), 96-104.
6. Conti, G. Guest Editor's Introduction. CACM 49, 6 (2006), 32-36.
7. Convertino, G., et al. Supporting common ground and awareness in emergency management planning: A design research project. ACM TOCHI 18, 4 (2011), 1-34.
8. Edwards, W.K., et al. The challenges of user-centered design and evaluation for infrastructure. Proc. CHI 2003, ACM Press (2003), 297-304.
9. Federal Emergency Management Agency (FEMA) FEMA App, USA.gov http://1.usa.gov/P8V5sf
10. HackHut Emergency S.O.S. Beacon. http://bit.ly/X2PEvE
11. Hossmann, T., et al. Twitter in disaster mode: Opportunistic Communication and Distribution of Sensor Data in Emergencies. Proc. ExtremeCom 2011, ACM Press (2011), 1-6.
12. Jones, C. Android Solidifies Smartphone Market Share, Forbes.com, 2013. http://onforb.es/X3u5wt
13. Krishnamoorthy, S. and Agrawala, A. Context-aware, technology enabled social contribution for public safety using M-Urgency. Proc. MobileHCI 2012, ACM Press (2012), 123-132.
14. Lien, Y.N., Li-Cheng, C., and Chih-Chieh, H. A Multi-hop Walkie-Talkie-Like Emergency Communication System for Catastrophic Natural Disasters. Proc. ICPPW 2010, (2010), 527-532.
15. Lukowicz, P., Baker, M.G., and Paradiso, J. Guest Editors' Introduction: Hostile Environments. IEEE Pervasive Computing 9, 4 (2010), 13-15.
16. Martin-Campillo, A., et al. Using Haggle to create an electronic triage tag. Proc. MobiOpp Workshop 2010, ACM Press (2010), 167-170.
17. Network Working Group RFC 3748 - Extensible Authentication Protocol (EAP), 2004. http://tools.ietf.org/html/rfc3748
18. NowForce Inc. http://www.nowforce.com/
19. Open Garden Inc. http://opengarden.com/
20. Palen, L. and Liu, S.B. Citizen communications in crisis: anticipating a future of ICT-supported public participation. Proc. CHI 2007, ACM Press (2007), 727-736.
21. Ramirez, L., et al. Landmarke: an ad hoc deployable ubicomp infrastructure to support indoor navigation of firefighters. PUC 16, 8 (2012), 1025-1038.
22. SafeCity Get live information from the society. http://www.safecity.nl/english/
23. Shanshan, L., et al. Device discovery and connection establishment approach using Ad-Hoc Wi-Fi for opportunistic networks. Proc. PERCOM 2011 Workshops, (2011), 461-466.
24. Shklovski, I., Palen, L., and Sutton, J. Finding community through information and communication technology in disaster response. Proc. CSCW 2008, ACM Press (2008), 127-136.
25. Simpson, P.V. Internet savvy Swedes launch 'Angry note 2.0'. The Local (Swedish News). http://bit.ly/bGnhsM
26. Starbird, K. and Stamberger, J. Tweak the Tweet: Leveraging Microblogging Proliferation with a Prescriptive Syntax to Support Citizen Reporting. Proc. ISCRAM 2010, ISCRAM Press.
27. Starbird, K. and Palen, L. "Voluntweeters": self-organizing by digital volunteers in times of crisis. Proc. CHI 2011, ACM Press (2011), 1071-1080.
28. Su, J., et al. Haggle: seamless networking for mobile applications. Proc. UbiComp 2007, Springer Press (2007), 391-408.
29. Toups, Z.O., et al. Zero-fidelity simulation of fire emergency response: improving team coordination learning. Proc. CHI 2011, ACM Press (2011), 1959-1968.
30. Trifunovic, S., et al. WiFi-Opp: ad-hoc-less opportunistic networking. Proc. CHANTS 2011, ACM Press (2011), 37-42.
31. Turoff, M. Past and future emergency response information systems. CACM 45, 4 (2002), 29-32.
32. Ushahidi Ushahidi Crowdmap. http://www.ushahidi.com/
33. Wong, M.P., A; Clement, A. Reading Service Set Identifiers (SSIDs): Marking and Locating for Public and Private Wireless Spaces. Proc. AOIR'07, (2007).
34. Yau, N. Political allegiance via wireless network SSIDs, mapped, FlowingData. http://bit.ly/LulXy2
35. Yu, H. The power of thumbs: the politics of SMS in urban China. Graduate Journal of Asia-Pacific Studies 2, 2 (2004), 30-43.

# Upvoting Hurricane Sandy: Event-Based News Production Processes on a Social News Site

**Alex Leavitt**
Annenberg School for
Communication & Journalism,
University of Southern California
aleavitt@usc.edu

**Joshua Clark**
Annenberg School for
Communication & Journalism,
University of Southern California
joshuaac@usc.edu

## ABSTRACT
This paper uses the case of Hurricane Sandy and reddit's topical community (subreddit) /r/sandy to examine the production and curation of news content around events on a social news site. Through qualitative analysis, we provide a coded topology of produced content and describe how types of networked gatekeeping impact the framing of a crisis situation. This study also examines, through quantitative modeling, what kind of information becomes negotiated and voted as relevant. We suggest that highly scored content shared in a social news setting focused more on human-interest media and perspective-based citizen journalism than professional news reports. We conclude by discussing how the mechanisms of social news sites conflict with the social norms and culture of reddit to produce differing expectations around news.

## Author Keywords
Social news site; news production; reddit; networked gatekeeping; news framing; crisis communication; mixed methods

## ACM Classification Keywords
H.5.3. Group and Organization Interfaces; Asynchronous interaction; Web-based interaction.

## INTRODUCTION
Individuals use social media for a variety of information and media sharing purposes. Personal reactions to events, sometimes called citizen journalism, have been a crucial emergent behavior on networked platforms, particularly for their role in moments of crisis or disaster (e.g., [31]). Keegan, Gergle, & Contractor [12] argue that "[s]tudies of peer production in sociotechnical systems... often presuppose that membership in and motivations to contribute to these communities are relatively stable and constant, yet such communities often self-organize and coordinate their activities under conditions of unstable and sudden collective action" (3). However, social networking platforms and microblogs (namely Twitter) have dominated the research of these situations. Another genre of social media, "social news sites," provides a unique way for participants to curate and consume information through collaborative voting processes. Not only have social news sites been rarely studied from mixed methods perspectives, but reddit and /r/sandy present a unique example of a social news site adapted for crisis communication. As sites like reddit become more popular and mainstream, it is important that we understand how technical and social features of social news site communities impact information flows. This paper examines how one social news platform, reddit.com, collected and organized information in a crisis situation. We explore the production and filtering of this information through the lens of networked gatekeeping, where a mix of average users and elite moderators work together to curate and make visible the most important content. Specifically, we examine one "subreddit" (topical community message board), /r/sandy, that was adopted in late October 2012 to curate information related to Hurricane Sandy. We then ask how a social news site can produce news around event-based topics:


CHI 2014, April 26 - May 01 2014, Toronto, ON, Canada

ACM 978-1-4503-2473-1/14/04 $15.00.
http://dx.doi.org/10.1145/2556288.2557140

**RQ1:** *How do technical and social processes work together in a social news site to determine the production, moderation, and curation of information?*

**RQ2:** *What types of content emerge around an event from a community-driven curation platform, and who contributes to its framing?*

## PLACING THE "NEWS" IN SOCIAL NEWS SITES
To explain news production in /r/sandy, we first contextualize this subreddit with other social news sites. Social news sites, like Slashdot, Digg, and reddit, allow users to submit hyperlinks to a feed of content, which other users can vote up or down (dubbed "upvotes" and "downvotes," respectively). As posts gain more upvotes, this popular content eventually reaches the top of the site's page based on a total score relative to up- and downvotes. Lerman & Ghosh [17] find that social news sites like Digg are able to disseminate information quickly. Through a combination of the platform infrastructure and underlying social networks, users continue to vote on content that had become popular through earlier voting-based moderation. Additionally, on reddit, when a user posts a hyperlink or comment, the total score it receives is added to the user's "karma" points, a measure of reputation. Users are also able

to submit "self" posts: text posts whose total score is not added to the poster's total karma.

Rather than a single main page where all users contribute, reddit is composed of subreddits: community message boards curated around a particular topic, like /r/pics for sharing pictures or /r/funny for posting jokes. Reddit as a whole is thereby founded on a network of subcommunities, where users will post across a variety of subreddits, each with their own norms and methods of evaluation. Reddit's front page displays the user-submitted hyperlinks from twenty "default" subreddits (which every viewer automatically sees), and users can create new subreddits, which other users then subscribe to in order for respective popular content to be interspersed on their personal front pages. It is important to note that content submitted to any subreddit goes through an automated detection process to see if the particular hyperlink already exists; if so, the user is forwarded to the existing page (though users are allowed to cross-post content to different subreddits). While millions of users have registered with reddit, many more merely browse the front page as viewers, resembling the structure of a mass media platform and validating reddit's slogan as "the front page of the internet."[1]

While news is shared daily on large, general subreddits like /r/news or /r/worldnews, users might try to situate information about particular events by sharing it to other topic-oriented subreddits (for example, /r/olympics becomes primarily active around its related events). Of course, users may improvise ways, outside of a particular topical subreddit, to contribute news on reddit, such as continually updating a single thread (see [6] covering an example during the Aurora, CO shootings).

Still, one of the barriers for new users to participating in reddit's extended network is discovering the variety of subreddits that exist. Subreddits that are not included in the default set must recruit users through advertising or word of mouth or rely on serendipity; therefore, newer subreddits may take some time to grow a committed collective of contributors.

## RELATED WORK

### Event-Based News Sharing in Social Media

Most work on social news sites has demonstrated the effects of their unique technical system on the potential for a large collective of users to curate relevant content in a democratic manner. Such democratic processes allow for various public spheres to form [9, 25]. However, little research has examined what kinds of content are shared in social news settings and how those types of content frame the whole of what is contributed.

[1] For statistics describing the popularity and widespread use of reddit, see [21].

The occurrence of a news event especially impacts how information sharing plays out [1, 24]. Prior research on uses of social media in crisis settings has shown at a high level that particular types of content dominate what is produced and shared, as well as what is seen as important, about breaking events. For example, Hughes & Palen [10] demonstrated that information broadcasting and brokerage were important facets of content shared during emergency situations and events with popular attendance. As far as the validity of content, Schultz, Utz, & Goritz [29] demonstrated that newspaper reports are deemed as more reputable sources in crisis communication than online media like blogs. As an exception, Chew & Eysenbach [7] showed in detail that on Twitter, in reaction to the spread of the H1N1 virus, news websites and resource-related information were the most shared type of content, and over time content like personal experiences increased while others like humor decreased. Bruns, et al. [4] also found that Twitter conversation, by looking at one coordinated hashtag, #qldfloods, during a flood situation, primarily produced information and media sharing, with fewer reactions, help, and personal experiences. Given the size and importance of news in other platforms, we then suggest that:

**H1:** *Professional news reports are more likely to be scored higher than other content.*

In addition to what kinds of content are curated around events in social news sites, we expect that more proficient users will know how to produce important and relevant information. For instance, Suh et al. [32] found that Twitter users' account ages positively affected retweetability. Burke, Marlow, & Lento [5] found that newcomers to Facebook participate less than experienced users, and increased participation on the part of newcomers depends on their experiences becoming acculturated to the platform and learning social norms early on. Similar differences in experience exist on social news sites as well [15]. While Shklovski, Palen, & Sutton [31] note that individuals in crisis situations are prone to adopt new communication technologies in order to share information, we still anticipate more experienced users to be able to produce relevant information given their experience with the community. We therefore expect that:

**H2a:** *Compared with other content, professional news reports are more likely to be contributed by more-experienced users.*

**H2b:** *Compared with other content, professional news reports are more likely to be contributed by more-active posting users.*

**H2c:** *Compared with other content, professional news reports are more likely to be contributed by more-reputed posting users.*

### News Framing & Networked Gatekeeping

Framing focuses on the way that information is presented and comprehended around a specific topic [11]. The kinds of information shared around an event frame it in a particular way as they spread inside and around the social news site. However, various gatekeepers will also affect the framing of that content by limiting its production, visibility, and access. These actors shift traditional news framing from journalism [28] into "networked gatekeeping," a distributed process where information is vetted and obstructed not by hierarchical editorship but a mix of distributed processes [2, 12, 16, 26]. On a social news site like reddit, the users negotiate information generated by the community through consensus with upvotes and downvotes. However, powerful figures that act as gatekeepers filter content too: frequently, these are elite members of online communities that take up moderation roles within the platform, through either technical or socially-mediated roles. On reddit, volunteer moderators are granted special powers to remove content (or even users) they feel conflicts with the subcommunity's rules, norms, or goals. Still, there are opportunities for more distributed moderation: for instance, Shaw [30] outlines how relational boundaries between participants in a participatory blog setting lead to a mix of centralized gatekeeping by elite users with decentralized moderation through processes like content filtering, all supported by an egalitarian ethos. In this mixed setting, moderation pushes relevant and factual information higher. Information flows directed through both moderators' decisions and the voting behaviors of users collectively mix to determine information relevancy and to produce a "networked framing" of the event [24]. On reddit, framing occurs both as an effect of the content contributed by users, what content is allowed to stay (as determined by moderators), and what content becomes visible (as voted upon by users).

Our study contributes to research on framing news events because the platform and purposes of a social news site remain distinct from microblogs and social networking sites, which have dominated the literature. The latter represents a mix of egocentric information sharing with differing audience dynamics (see [14] for the evolution of these dynamics on Facebook; for Twitter, see [22]), while social news sites particularly attract users to broadcast and share to an unknown mass audience. Just as with breaking news stories on Wikipedia [13], for a social news site like reddit, the contributions of submitters are moderated by other participants; therefore, only particular content becomes popular and visible, setting the frame and tone of how the crisis becomes transmitted in this particular space.

## METHOD & DATA

In order to analyze the impact of networked gatekeeping on the framing of news in /r/sandy, we combine qualitative observation with statistical analysis of content-coded posts. Through these observations, we identify examples of networked gatekeeping processes at work on reddit. We then use a statistical model to observe how community voting as a gatekeeping process impacts the types of content that become the most popular.

During the duration of Hurricane Sandy and its aftermath, one author conducted two months of qualitative observation, maintaining an active reddit.com account, viewing live activity in the subreddit, messaging contributors and moderators, and using a combination of field notes with archival search to structure the analysis. Both authors are also active users of reddit, having participated in the broader community for the past two years, which provides additional context to understanding behavioral norms across the site.

We later collected, using Python, MySQL, and the reddit API, a dataset of 2458 threads posted to /r/sandy during the subreddit's entire lifespan (beginning in late-October 2012). These threads consist of a population sample of all posts contributed to the subreddit up until the collection period (4 February 2013), including the 1000 highest-voted posts (with total vote scores ranging from 22 to 2724). During the hurricane, though, moderators deleted hundreds of posts, and these posts were not collected.

We also scraped user data for the 1895 distinct users that contributed each post, which includes each user's post and comment karma scores (sum of votes users receive for their own submissions and comments) and account age. Since posting, some users deleted their accounts or removed the association between their account and the post; in these cases, we removed them from the model.

From these data, we coded the top 1000 highest-voted threads (for which, along with thread authors, we provide summary statistics below in Table 1) according to content type and content format. We use the top 1000 posts because we are interested in patterns among different types of popular content (rather than differences between successful and failed content). For content type, we distinguished among four categories. We derived them using a grounded theory approach, where we took a sample of posts and coded them based on their content, using categories in line with those employed by [4] and [7]:

- Professional news reports (PROF)
- Users' perspective-centric content, commonly referred to as "citizen journalism" (PERSP)
- Content that users connected to on an emotional level or that would be of human interest related to Hurricane Sandy (INTER), and
- Conversational posts related to meta-discussions, as well as asking questions, sharing tips, and issuing corrections (CONV).[2]

[2] We further subcategorized the content into humor, tips, questions, corrections, and meta posts, though these were only used for qualitative analysis.

The content format was split among four categories:

- External textual websites (SITE)
- Internal subreddit textual self posts (REDDIT)
- Video and audio multimedia (VIDEO), and
- Images, infographics, charts, and maps (IMAGE).

Examples are shown in Table 2. Between two coders, we each labeled every post; for those we disagreed on initially, we reached consensus through discussion. The coder inter-reliability rate was calculated at Cohen's kappa = 0.72 ($p < 0.001$).

The variables we use in the statistical model are as follows:

- Score: *H1.* A measure of upvotes minus downvotes (calculated by reddit's platform).
- Comments: *Control.* The number of comments a post has garnered.
- Approximate Views: *Control.* A rounded number of logged in users viewing (and able to vote on) posts in the subreddit at the time of a post's submission.[3]
- User Experience: *H2a.* A measure of poster's account age in days (normalized to years).
- User Activity: The number of submissions (*H2b*) or comments (*Control*) of the poster (rescaled to every 100 posts).
- User Reputation: The number of submission (*H2c*) or comment (*Control*) karma points the poster has earned (rescaled to every 1000 karma points).
- Content Code: *Dependent variable.* Categorical variable of PROF, PERSP, INTER, or CONV.

| Variable | N | Min | Max | Median | Mean | Std. Dev. |
|---|---|---|---|---|---|---|
| Score[4] | 999 | 22 | 2724 | 63 | 176.7 | 332.6 |
| Comments | 999 | 0 | 514 | 9 | 21.63 | 38.5 |
| Approximate Views | 999 | 10 | 6860 | 1300 | 2516 | 2480.9 |
| User Experience (Days) | 966 | 46.9 | 2607 | 440.9 | 610.7 | 548.6 |
| User Submission Activity | 966 | 0 | 1000* | 39.5 | 131.2 | 232.8 |
| User Comment Activity | 966 | 0 | 1000* | 269 | 422.9 | 387.1 |
| User Submission Reputation | 966 | 1 | 50000** | 1031 | 5000 | 10795.2 |
| User Comment Reputation | 966 | 0 | 50000** | 921 | 3824 | 7628.2 |

* Capped at 1000. ** Capped at 50000.

**Table 1. Descriptive statistics of top 1000 /r/sandy posts and their contributors (excluding rows with NA values).**

| Type | N | Example |
|---|---|---|
| PROF | 162 | Some subway tunnels flood - CBS |
| PERSP | 331 | My moms backyard in Hatteras. That dock is usually about 3 feet above water *(sic)* |
| INTER | 282 | Sandy from space |
| CONV | 224 | Please, if you're currently without power please read |
| **Subtype** | **N** | **Example** |
| HUMOR | 81 | Horse Man Caught On Film During Live Sandy Coverage |
| TIP | 128 | Tips from a Louisiana native who lived through Katrina |
| QUEST | 76 | Is there a list of places I can volunteer in NYC? |
| CORR | 7 | 9 Viral Photos That AREN'T Hurricane Sandy |
| META | 13 | Please consider including location in the title of images you post. |
| **Format** | **N** | **Example** |
| SITE | 208 | Al Jazeera gives /r/sandy a shoutout... Thought you guys might like to know... |
| REDDIT | 211 | Update your situation here |
| IMAGE | 495 | Photo taken at 9am EST in downtown NYC |
| VIDEO | 85 | The Weather Channel Live Stream |

**Table 2. Content types, subtypes, and formats of highest scored /r/sandy submissions.**

## RESULTS

### Networked Gatekeeping in Social News Sites

A social news site, through its technical architecture, allows the community to vote on what content is important and relevant to those users. The algorithmic implementation of upvoting and downvoting only goes so far, though: social norms and processes structure those behaviors too.

/R/sandy was repurposed on October 26, 2012. All subreddits have a sidebar where the moderators can post information and rules for the subcommunity, and from the start /r/sandy's read "Information and discussion around Hurricane Sandy and the possible Frankenstorm/ Snowicane/ Noreastercane/ Floodmageddon. Post your personal experiences, photos, and video of Hurricane Sandy." Initially, users driven to the subreddit did not have much guidance regarding what would be "proper" to post, and the first few submissions included a cocktail recipe list, a joke image, and a note to stock up your fridge. As the subreddit attracted more and more viewers (in fact, viewership eclipsed the number of subscribers early on; a rare occurrence on reddit), hundreds of posts were

[3] These numbers were scraped by stattit.com.

[4] Reddit employs a vote fuzzing algorithm to prevent spam, but ultimately the score reflects the total contributions of users' voting behaviors.

contributed, and eventually users took to self posts to help shape norms around submitting, voting, and moderation.

For example, one user posted `Mods, can you please stop all the jokes? This is a serious storm and I am using /r/sandy for knowledge and safety`. This post marked one of the earliest points of conflict for the subreddit: between its use as a news and information hub versus a space for any related media, including jokes. A second user commented:

*I think we're okay making jokes and humor so long as they're clearly distinguishable from the actionable information. ... I support the humor. I support the useful information. If we don't confuse the two, we can stay safe and happy without feeling too alone.*

Less than an hour later, another user contributed a post entitled `I love you all, but can we please try and keep the jokes at a minimum?` The top voted comment in response was "You shouldn't rely on reddit for life critical information. Use your local news." Debates like these continued throughout the first few days of the hurricane, with users debating back and forth about what should and should not be allowed.

In addition to the content validity debate, other users were concerned about participatory behaviors of the community, namely that more users needed to vote so that important and relevant contributions could become visible on the top of /r/sandy's front page. These calls to action are directly in line with Gilbert's observations of underprovision on reddit [10] and the consequences this lack of participation has for users in ignoring content at the time of its first introduction to the platform. Two of the highest voted conversational meta posts were `We need to keep this subreddit fresh! View the new!` and `If you're not in the storm, one thing you can do is stroll through New to upvote life-saving posts and downvote jokes`. These related to the fact that not enough users were visiting the "new" page, which aggregates all the newest submissions, and voting up the important information and downvoting less relevant content. In the comments of these posts, we see sustained negotiation of proper content – "And please downvote the blatant karma-whoring. Idiot Redditors are trying to capitalize on an emergency situation with memes and screen caps of novelty Twitter accounts." – as well as continued suspicion around the value and purpose of the subreddit – "I see what you're trying to accomplish but I also find it hard to believe someone's gonna be in a life threatening situation and be like 'Oh lets check /r/sandy for advice on what I should do at this precise moment.'"

Of course, as different types of content were contributed over the few days, debates arose over the value of /r/sandy for posting and reading critical news content. One user complained, "You shouldn't rely on reddit for life critical information. Use your local news." Other users countered this point, given that many professional news articles had been shared, making the subreddit a helpful source of information. When a user responded "I'm pretty sure there are better sources for knowledge and safety on the internet than Reddit," another replied "[C]ould you please post them then? [I]'ve been following here and NOAA and trying to stay away from the news."

Along with these community-level debates, elite-level moderators actively helped structure much of what would be allowed in the subreddit. In an email interview with three of /r/sandy's moderators, one commented, "I was watching the news and moderating for several days with little sleep." The mods engaged in similar discussions as users about content. One responded to us:

*The goal from the beginning was to keep information flowing and accurate... to remove hearsay and things we just knew to be lies or posts from previous hurricanes just recirculating. ... We wanted this sub to be an emergency lookup location, so we wanted our information to be solid and more serious content. At one point... we were getting about 15 posts every 20 seconds posted. It was just a massive influx of data that we had to just constantly hit refresh on and delete content not deemed to be following what our mindset was.*

The moderators deleted hundreds of contributions as they were posted to the subreddit, though they were relatively permissive of what content went through. In our interview, one moderator wrote, "The only things deleted were crass, rude humor that was deemed insensitive and memes..." Everything else was allowed to be voted upon by the users. In addition, the moderators actually removed *another moderator* who they felt was conflicting with the goals of the subreddit. As one moderator recounted:

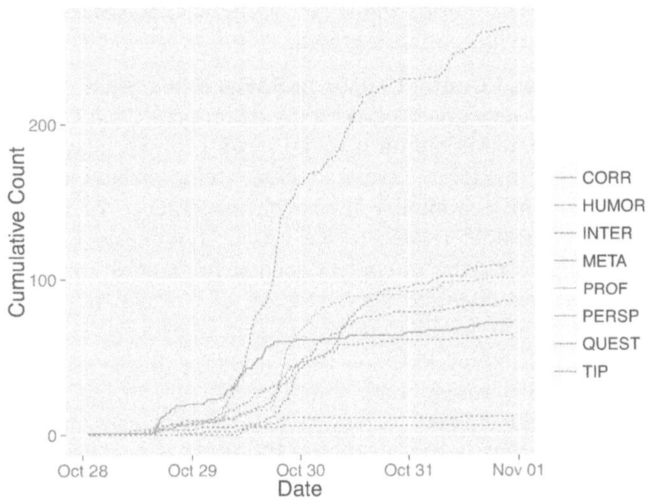


**Figure 1. Truncated timeline of content types and subtypes (subtracted from types) during first few days of activity in /r/sandy, highlighting the rise and fall of humor (solid orange line) compared to other content (dotted lines).**

| | Score | H1 | | Comments | | | Approximate Views | | | User Experience | H2a | |
|---|---|---|---|---|---|---|---|---|---|---|---|---|
| | *Exp(β)* | *p* | *z* | *Exp(β)* | *p* | *z* | *Exp(β)* | *p* | *z* | *Exp(β)* | *p* | *z* |
| **INTER** | 1.0033 | *** | 3.4169 | 1.0018 | | 0.2605 | 0.9997 | *** | -6.2783 | 0.9483 | | -0.8293 |
| **PERSP** | 1.0026 | *** | 2.6703 | 1.0034 | | 0.5092 | 0.9999 | * | -1.8345 | 0.9310 | | -1.0907 |
| **CONV** | 1.0006 | | 0.5574 | 1.0194 | *** | 2.9328 | 1.0000 | | 0.7192 | 0.8413 | ** | -2.4612 |
| | **User Submission Activity** | H2b | | **User Comment Activity** | | | **User Submission Reputation** | H2c | | **User Comment Reputation** | | |
| | *Exp(β)* | *p* | *z* | *Exp(β)* | *p* | *z* | *Exp(β)* | *p* | *z* | *Exp(β)* | *p* | *z* |
| **INTER** | 0.9189 | * | -1.5635 | 0.9755 | | -0.7353 | 1.0072 | | 0.5802 | 0.9904 | | -0.6303 |
| **PERSP** | 0.7474 | *** | -4.9703 | 0.9919 | | -0.2399 | 1.0010 | | 0.0697 | 0.9992 | | -0.0488 |
| **CONV** | 0.8644 | ** | -2.4617 | 1.0449 | | 1.2734 | 0.9870 | | -0.8619 | 1.0068 | | 0.4317 |

Baseline: PROF McFadden's Pseudo $R^2$: 0.1119 * $p < 0.05$, ** $p < 0.01$, *** $p < 0.001$

N: 967 AIC: 2455.4

**Table 3. Multinomial logistic regression for H1, H2a, H2b, and H2c (in blue; controls in grey).**

*We had a problem with one mod and I had to contact [the reddit admins] to get rid of him. I talked with three other mods who I thought also had a problem with him so we had a little vote and I wrote a letter [to the admins] with my concerns... [they] told him his services were no longer needed... [H]e was going around and undeleting things we deleted (and sent explanatory replies to), just generally undermining. Really hard to deal with...*

These top-down actions, along with the distributed moderation-through-voting of the users, represent the ecosystem of networked gatekeeping that structures what becomes (and can become) visible as important or relevant in a social news setting. In a visual example, Figure 1 demonstrates how humor, in relation to other categories, dominated the top 1000 submissions in the first few days until the social norms and actions of networked gatekeeping put a halt to its continued growth.

### Event-Based Content Types in Social News Sites

Given that networked gatekeeping determines what can and does become visible on a social news site, we next use a predictive model to examine how voting behaviors and users in the community impact the emergence of certain *types* of content related to the crisis. Hypothesis 1 and 2 examine how types of content become marked as important through the distributed gatekeeping of a social news site (upvoting and downvoting, as demarcated by a post's score) as well as what kind of users produce those types of content. To assess both hypotheses, we carried out a multinomial logistic regression with content categories as the dependent variables (using PROF as a baseline) and post, poster, and subreddit attributes as the independent variables. The results are laid out in Table 3; the exponentialized beta (Exp(β)) represents the relative risk ratio, or an increase or decrease in the relative likelihood (compared to PROF) of a post being a specific type of content per a one unit increase in the independent variable.

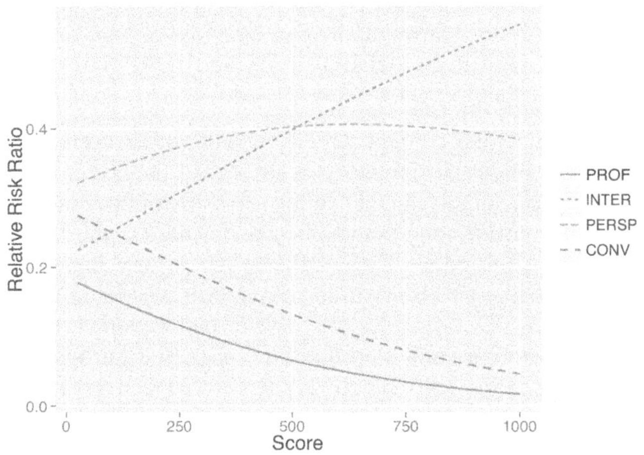


**Figure 2. Predicted relative probabilities of content types from multinomial logistic regression using post's score (H1) as x-axis (25-1000) and holding other variables at their means.**

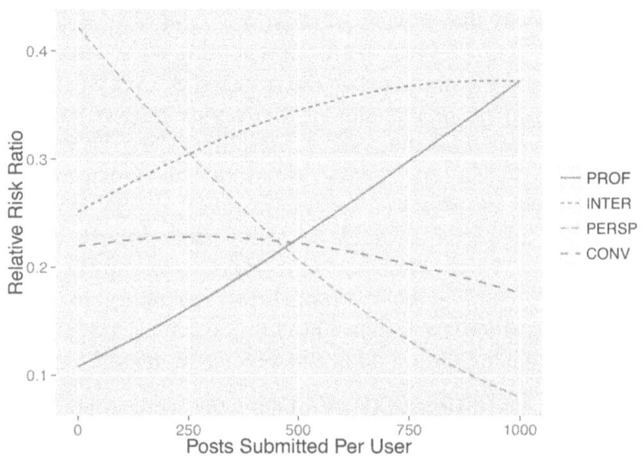


**Figure 3. Predicted relative probabilities of content types using user's submission activity (H2b) as x-axis (0-1000) and holding other variables at their means.**

Hypothesis 1 stated that professional news reports are more likely to be scored higher by the community than other content posted to /r/sandy. Conversely, the model predicted that all other types of content are relatively more likely than news content as a score increases for any particular post (the predicted relative risk ratio of each content type is visualized in Figure 2). Of these types, only human-interest posts and perspective-based citizen journalism were significant. Thus, Hypothesis 1 was not supported.

Hypothesis 2 stated that professional news reports are more likely to be contributed by a user with higher experience (2a), activity (2b), and reputation (2c). In relation to a user's experience, more experienced users were less relatively likely of posting other content compared to professional reports but only for conversational posts. Therefore, Hypothesis 2a was partially supported. Users' activity for submissions led to non-professional content being relatively less likely than news, and the effects were significant across all types of content, supporting Hypothesis 2b (like H1, summarized in Figure 3). The effects based on users' submission reputation moved in varying directions, and none were significant, suggesting Hypothesis 2c was not supported.

## DISCUSSION

This study analyzes the dynamics of event-based news production around framing and gatekeeping in a social news setting. We show that professional news reports are less likely to receive higher scores compared to other types of content. Also, we demonstrate that more experienced users are more likely to contribute professional reports than conversational posts, and users that contribute more submissions are more likely to contribute professional news reports than all other types of content.

### Who participates in "news" on a social news site?

As a massively-popular social news site, reddit occupies a particularly interesting space in terms of viewing and sharing content. While reddit boasts tens of millions of viewers on its front page, many fewer participate on the site's default subreddits. Fewer still collaborate to post and vote on content in smaller topical subcommunities. A niche, event-based subreddit like /r/sandy epitomizes a unique case of reddit subcommunities, in that it was created for a specific purpose at a very particular time period. Because of the subreddit's relevancy as a potential news source, it gained an abnormal amount of subscribers and viewers in a short duration. To attract contributors to /r/sandy, reddit administrators posted an advertisement (Figure 4) for the /r/sandy subreddit on the right-side column of the platform, making users aware of the new subreddit's existence. As stated by one /r/sandy moderator (via email interview, quoting statistics only available to mods), the subreddit received 401,675 unique visitors and 4,429,554 pageviews in October (just from the last four days of the month, with the peak occurring just after the storm), 172,102 unique viewers and 1,148,667 views in November, and 15,568 unique viewers and 28,435 views in December.

**Figure 4. Screenshot of the advertisement on reddit's front page to introduce /r/sandy to the wider community.**

We establish in Hypothesis 2 that certain types of users are relatively more likely to post professional news reports than other content: namely, users that have posted many submissions before (and older, experienced users, when comparing news and conversational contributions). However, the insignificance of most of the user attributes suggests that both inexperienced and experienced users, users of all levels of reputation, and users who post any number of comments are all relatively likely to post any type of content. This falls in line with Shklovski, Palen, & Sutton [31] who show that, in crisis situations, newer and less experienced users actively contribute alongside experienced participants in platforms oriented toward disaster communication.

From a methodological perspective, the varying utility of user attributes employed in this paper point to the necessity of understanding the platform's cultural context in its use. For example, reddit's karma points are awarded by individuals in the community but across a variety of subcommunities with differing purposes. Therefore, karma may be insignificantly related to the posting of types of content because, when the community upvotes posts and comments with karma, users will have varying reasons for awarding reputation points (e.g., upvoting for funny posts in one subreddit versus for relevant or erudite posts in another subreddit).

We do see, though, that if a user has posted more, they are more likely to post professional news content in /r/sandy than other types of content. We surmise that this effect could stem from highly-active posters being able to identify uses of subreddits well, since they have a lot of experience posting in reddit's subcommunities. For /r/sandy, then, active posters may have identified its core purpose as sharing professional news.

Conversely, less active users (who have posted fewer times in general on reddit) may have come to post on /r/sandy to contribute a one-off submission without much awareness of the point of that post. Still, users who are lurkers (who have high experience but low activity) might have come to the subreddit based on exogenous factors (like its relevancy to their local situation). With high experience, these users understand reddit's culture and context well, contributing content that they know reddit's audience appreciates (humor, interesting media, etc.), or they possibly found that they could participate in some way, such as posting a picture from their backyard – as the model suggests, posting something other than professionally-reported news content. Further qualitative research on posting behaviors could illuminate the discrepancies behind this conduct.

### How does reddit frame "news"?

The nature of reddit's technical platform mixed with its social norms allow for a unique context of networked gatekeeping to impact the framing of event-based news. In Hypothesis 1, we expected to find that, amongst the popular submissions, professional news content would likely be scored higher relative to other content. However, our model suggests that human-interest and perspective-created content would more likely appear in higher-voted submissions.

The results of Hypothesis 1 are intriguing in that they conflict with what the literature has suggested would be seen as more important by social media users (ie., professional news reports). Instead, we see that social news sites operate differently from other social media sites. We must also keep in mind that attention drives much of what is produced and mediated in social news sites: as Muchnik, Aral, and Taylor show [23], even one initial upvote in a social news platform can lead to a strong and consequential social influence bias.

But why do we see /r/sandy score other content higher more than professional news reporting? As we explored in our qualitative analysis, it is clear that some members had an idea of the subreddit's ideal use, but the technical platform and the moderators did not strictly limit what types of content could be shared. While some information was considered useful, a presumption that "news" would be produced mischaracterizes the purpose of a social news site, where instead of limiting types of information, the community makes visible through its own means content they find relevant. The /r/sandy collective still had expectations about proper content, but what resulted was in a sense engineered through networked gatekeeping: moderator actions, discursive negotiation, and bottom-up voting.

The expectations around proper content also derive from reddit's participatory culture. As Bergstrom [3] notes, participation on reddit is accompanied by a strong subculture and peculiar sets of community expectations, depending on the particular subreddit collective. Content like humor and processes like bandwagon effects permeate the behaviors of reddit's community at large. Thus, social norms become particularly important in structuring what kind of submissions and comment-driven conversations are denoted as valuable to each subreddit community. Even though we saw a drop-off in humor and a significant attempt by both moderators and users to push for helpful information, the highest voted submissions were shown to relatively less likely be traditional news reports. While news was not necessarily downvoted or removed from the subreddit, the community relatively preferred other content. Keep in mind though that some users *did* downvote this content, but more people upvoted it, resulting in positive scores.

Moderation of these social norms especially becomes important when considering the technical implementation of social news sites' core feature, voting. Reddit's "reddiquette" emphasizes upvoting if content contributes to conversation, and downvoting if it is off-topic and does not contribute to the subreddit.[5] Still, some users might upvote if they like the content and downvote if they dislike it (actions that we observed users talking about when discussing their general reddit use, albeit in subreddits other than /r/sandy). Preferential voting might then lead to the outcomes we observe in /r/sandy, where things that people like on an emotional level (like human-interest content) win out over objective (and possibly, given the context, more relevant) information.

Also, /r/sandy was not the only space on reddit for news sharing, so it is important to highlight /r/sandy's status as a small subreddit within reddit's larger culture of posting behaviors. Not all users post content only to their respective topical subreddits; usually, more general content can be found interspersed across the default subreddits. To illustrate this point, we can look at the top 50 *all-time* submissions that mention Hurricane Sandy across reddit, which were posted to /r/pics (14), /r/politics (10), /r/sandy (7), /r/funny (5), /r/gifs (3), /r/AdviceAnimals (2), and each of nine other subreddits. Therefore, some users might not even consider /r/sandy as a possible place to post content about the hurricane. But, as our analysis shows, users framed the important contributions in /r/sandy – again, through voting – as interesting tidbits about the hurricane or content that reflected the personal positions of those affected locally (as compared to news content).

## LIMITATIONS & FUTURE RESEARCH

Additional data analysis could help illuminate the dynamics underlying the production and framing of news on social news sites. For example, we did not include coded content of the population of submissions posted to /r/sandy (instead focusing solely on more-popular content), but investigation of the spectrum of posts to an event-based topical community could further illustrate the differences between content types (ie., looking at the least popular content in addition to the most popular). We also attempted, in the exploratory phase, a temporal analysis of the data to control for types of content fluctuating at different periods. However, after slicing the data into pre-, during-, and post-event periods, the samples in each set spread across our

[5] http://www.reddit.com/wiki/reddiquette

four coded categories were not sufficient for multinomial logistic regression.

Further qualitative research could also examine why social news settings – and reddit in particular – generate particular types of content and how these types flow across different subcommunities (e.g., /r/sandy appears to be filled with more personal content than the more-officially-reported /r/olympics). In particular, studying the dynamics of networked gatekeeping – especially voting behaviors – can help us understand how certain social values are translated to gatekeeping norms, as we note above.

This study contributes knowledge that has implications for the design of community-moderated platforms, as well as the design of such platforms for event-based situations like communication during crises. We especially emphasize the importance of architecting tools for determining strong social norms in a social news site context, as it becomes clear from our qualitative observation that these rules strongly influenced content production and negotiation in the subreddit. We recognize that /r/sandy represents a unique example of event-based news production processes in a social news setting, particularly in its use for crisis communication. During the writing over this paper, there were no comparable examples of a subreddit used for this purpose, though studying /r/sandy provides insight into the potential design of such platforms. However, we do believe that the social negotiations and cultural context of reddit permeate most subcommunities on the site, and thus these observations could be seen as generalizable.

Overall, this study shows in detail what kinds of content emerge in critical information moments under the moderation of networked gatekeeping. We demonstrate that information sharing is not a normative practice and differs in social news sites as compared to other social media based on the literature. Future research should consider approaches that provide nuanced details about the data that is produced and shared to further understand the dynamics behind such practices. The study also illustrates that various types of moderation crucially impact what content becomes relevant (and indeed what content can be curated to be voted on at all). Unlike other social media platforms, reddit's integration of networked gatekeeping into the norms of information production within its subcommunities ultimately changes the way that we can think about the emergence of relevant information in sociotechnical systems.

## ACKNOWLEDGMENTS

We would like to thank Kate Starbird, Brian Keegan, Peter Monge, Dennis Wixon, Dmitri Williams, fellow Annenbergers, and our anonymous reviewers from ICWSM, CSCW, and CHI for their helpful feedback. We also extend our gratitude to the /r/sandy moderators and reddit users that provided data and comments.

## REFERENCES

1. Acar, Adam, and Yuya Muraki. 2011. "Twitter for Crisis Communication: Lessons Learned from Japan's Tsunami Disaster." International Journal of Web Based Communities 7 (3): 392–402.
2. Barzilai-Nahon, Karine. 2008. "Toward a Theory of Network Gatekeeping: A Framework for Exploring Information Control." J. Am. Soc. Inf. Sci. Technol. 59 (9): 1493–1512.
3. Bergstrom, Kelly. 2011. "'Don't Feed the Troll': Shutting down Debate About Community Expectations on reddit.com." First Monday; 8(1).
4. Bruns, Axel, Jean E. Burgess, Kate Crawford, and Frances Shaw. 2012. "#qldfloods and @QPSMedia: Crisis Communication on Twitter in the 2011 South East Queensland Floods." In Brisbane QLD Australia: ARC Centre of Excellence for Creative Industries and Innovation, Queensland University of Technology.
5. Burke, Moira, Cameron Marlow, and Thomas Lento. 2009. "Feed Me: Motivating Newcomer Contribution in Social Network Sites." In Proceedings of the SIGCHI Conference on Human Factors in Computing Systems, 945–954. CHI '09. New York, NY, USA: ACM.
6. Chen, Brian. 2012. "How Reddit Scooped the Press on the Aurora Shootings." *The New York Times.* Retrieved from http://bits.blogs.nytimes.com/2012/07/23/reddit-aurora-shooter-aff/
7. Chew, Cynthia, and Gunther Eysenbach. 2010. "Pandemics in the Age of Twitter: Content Analysis of Tweets During the 2009 H1N1 Outbreak." PLoS ONE 5 (11).
8. Gilbert, Eric. 2013. "Widespread Underprovision on Reddit." In Proceedings of the 2013 ACM Conference on Computer Supported Cooperative Work, 803–808. CSCW '10. San Antonio, TX, USA: ACM.
9. Goode, Luke. 2009. "Social News, Citizen Journalism and Democracy." New Media & Society 11 (8) (December 1): 1287–1305.
10. Hughes, Amanda Lee, and Leysia Palen. 2009. "Twitter Adoption and Use in Mass Convergence and Emergency Events." International Journal of Emergency Management 6 (3): 248–260.
11. Iyengar, Shanto. 1994. Is Anyone Responsible?: How Television Frames Political Issues. Reprint. University Of Chicago Press.
12. Keegan, Brian, and Darren Gergle. 2010. "Egalitarians at the Gate: Onesided Gatekeeping Practices in Social Media." In Proceedings of the 2010 ACM Conference on Computer Supported Cooperative Work, 131–134. CSCW '10. New York, NY, USA: ACM.

13. Keegan, Brian, Darren Gergle, and Noshir Contractor. 2013. "Hot Off the Wiki: Structures and Dynamics of Wikipedia's Coverage of Breaking News Events." American Behavioral Scientist Forthcoming.
14. Lampe, Cliff, Nicole B. Ellison, and Charles Steinfield. 2008. "Changes in Use and Perception of Facebook." In Proceedings of the 2008 ACM Conference on Computer Supported Cooperative Work, 721–730. CSCW '08. New York, NY, USA: ACM.
15. Lampe, Cliff, and Erik Johnston. 2005. "Follow the (slash) Dot: Effects of Feedback on New Members in an Online Community." In Proceedings of the 2005 International ACM SIGGROUP Conference on Supporting Group Work, 11–20. GROUP '05. New York, NY, USA: ACM.
16. Lampe, Cliff, and Paul Resnick. 2004. "Slash(dot) and Burn: Distributed Moderation in a Large Online Conversation Space." In Proceedings of the SIGCHI Conference on Human Factors in Computing Systems, 543–550. CHI '04. New York, NY, USA: ACM..
17. Lerman, Kristina, and Rumi Ghosh. 2010. "Information Contagion: An Empirical Study of the Spread of News on Digg and Twitter Social Networks." Proceedings of 4th International Conference on Weblogs and Social Media (March 12).
18. Lewin, Kurt. 1943. "The Forces Behind Food Habits and Methods of Change." In The Problem of Changing Food Habits Report of the Committee on Food Habits 1941-1943. The National Academies Press.
19. Long, J. Scott, and Jeremy Freese. 2005. *Regression Models for Categorical Dependent Variables Using Stata, Second Edition*. 2nd ed. Stata Press.
20. Lotan, Gilad, Erhardt Graeff, Mike Ananny, Devin Gaffney, Ian Pearce, and danah boyd. 2011. "The Revolutions Were Tweeted: Information Flows During the 2011 Tunisian and Egyptian Revolutions." International Journal of Communication 5.
21. Martin, Erik. 2012. "2 Billion & Beyond." Blog.reddit. http://blog.reddit.com/2012/01/2-billion-beyond.html.
22. Marwick, Alice E., and danah boyd. 2011. "I Tweet Honestly, I Tweet Passionately: Twitter Users, Context Collapse, and the Imagined Audience." New Media & Society 13 (1): 114–133.
23. Muchnik, Lev, Sinan Aral, and Sean J. Taylor. 2013. "Social Influence Bias: A Randomized Experiment." Science 341 (6146): 647–651.
24. Palen, Leysia, Sarah Vieweg, Sophia B. Liu, and Amanda Lee Hughes. 2009. "Crisis in a Networked World Features of Computer-Mediated Communication in the April 16, 2007, Virginia Tech Event." Social Science Computer Review 27 (4) (November 1): 467–480.
25. Poor, Nathaniel. 2005. "Mechanisms of an Online Public Sphere: The Website Slashdot." Journal of Computer-Mediated Communication 10 (2).
26. Roberts, Chris. 2005. "Gatekeeping Theory: An Evolution." Paper presented at the Annual Meeting of the Association for Education in Journalism and Mass Communication, San Antonio, TX.
27. Scellato, Salvatore, and Cecilia Mascolo. 2011. "Measuring User Activity on an Online Location-based Social Network." In 2011 IEEE Conference on Computer Communications Workshops (INFOCOM WKSHPS), 918 –923.
28. Scheufele, Dietram A. 1999. "Framing as a Theory of Media Effects." Journal of Communication 49 (1): 103–122.
29. Schultz, Friederike, Sonja Utz, and Anja Göritz. 2011. "Is the Medium the Message? Perceptions of and Reactions to Crisis Communication via Twitter, Blogs and Traditional Media." Public Relations Review 37 (1): 20–27.
30. Shaw, Aaron. 2012. "Centralized and Decentralized Gatekeeping in an Open Online Collective." Politics & Society 40 (3): 349–388.
31. Shklovski, Irina, Leysia Palen, and Jeannette Sutton. 2008. "Finding Community Through Information and Communication Technology in Disaster Response." In Proceedings of the 2008 ACM Conference on Computer Supported Cooperative Work, 127–136. CSCW '08. New York, NY, USA: ACM.
32. Suh, Bongwon, Lichan Hong, P. Pirolli, and E.H. Chi. 2010. "Want to Be Retweeted? Large Scale Analytics on Factors Impacting Retweet in Twitter Network." In 2010 IEEE Second International Conference on Social Computing (SocialCom), 177 –184.

# Online Public Communications by Police & Fire Services during the 2012 Hurricane Sandy

**Amanda L. Hughes[1], Lise A. St. Denis[2], Leysia Palen[2], Kenneth M. Anderson[2]**

[1]Department of Computer Science
Utah State University
Logan, UT
*amanda.hughes@usu.edu*

[2]Project EPIC
University of Colorado Boulder
Boulder, CO
*{lise.st.denis, palen, kena}@colorado.edu*

## ABSTRACT

Social media and other online communication tools are a subject of great interest in mass emergency response. Members of the public are turning to these solutions to seek and offer emergency information. Emergency responders are working to determine what social media policies should be in terms of their "public information" functions. We report on the online communications from all the coastal fire and police departments within a 100 mile radius of Hurricane Sandy's US landfall. Across four types of online communication media, we collected data from 840 fire and police departments. Findings indicate that few departments used these online channels in their Sandy response efforts, and that communications differed between fire and police departments and across media type. However, among the highly engaged departments, there is evidence that they bend and adapt policies about what constitutes appropriate public communication in the face of emergency demands; therefore, we propose that flexibility is important in considering future emergency online communication policy. We conclude with design recommendations for making online communication media more "listenable" for both emergency managers and members of the public.

### Author Keywords

crisis informatics; disaster; emergency; microblogging; risk communication; social computing; social media

### ACM Classification Keywords

H.5.3 Groups & Organization Interfaces—collaborative computing, computer-supported cooperative work

## INTRODUCTION

With their need to quickly reach and engage with a diffuse target audience, emergency service workers are reportedly adopting social media and other online communication tools to connect with the public they serve [3,8,9,12,19]. Based on our ongoing research in this area, however, we see that use is uneven, and policy and practice with respect to such use are not always aligned. Studies have documented how members of the public use online communications like social media in a variety of emergency contexts [7,9,13,16,18,20,26], and emergency workers appear to be attending to that demand though seem uncertain about how to respond. The social media audience that emergency managers earnestly build and prepare in-between emergencies may find themselves frustrated when those same managers struggle to meet the online communication demand if a disaster were to happen.

What remains empirically unknown is how widespread online media use is for emergency public information communication, and what the nature of that use is. Existing studies in this area have been limited to examining emergency workers who are heavily engaged in these communications [3,12]—mostly because it is easier to find and study traces of their activity—rather than examining the absence of online communications.

This research attempts to provide a more comprehensive description of how and why much emergency services use online media to communicate with the public during mass emergencies by examining fire and police departments' use during Hurricane Sandy. In a disaster event like Hurricane Sandy—one that affected millions of people and required a massive coordinated response and recovery effort—information needs are great. We examine the activities of fire and police agencies during this event because both play significant roles in the distribution of emergency preparedness, response, and recovery information to the public during and after large-scale disasters [24].

### Background Literature

A small but growing area of crisis informatics research [6,17] examines online media use by emergency responders, and reports on their typically slow adoption of such tools [9]. Emergency responders are trained in formal command-and-control protocols for managing emergencies and it is rarely clear how to integrate social media and other online tools effectively into these existing, formal procedures [2,8]. Additionally, organizational support for online communication with the public is often lacking, with limited resources, insufficient management support, poor


*CHI 2014*, April 26 - May 01 2014, Toronto, ON, Canada
Copyright 2014 ACM 978-1-4503-2473-1/14/04...$15.00.
http://dx.doi.org/10.1145/2556288.2557227

tools, and no training [8,12]. Further, the volume of public information surrounding an event can be challenging to monitor and online sources can be difficult to identify and verify, especially in large-scale events [8].

Prior work has expounded upon some of the features of online communication by emergency personnel. Early adopters of social media in some organizations are seen as evangelists: A public information officer (the public relations representative of an emergency response organization) from the Los Angeles Fire Department [12] has influenced how his and other fire departments might use online tools like social media to retrieve intelligence and communicate with constituents. Other research examines how a wildfire response team incorporated vetted virtual volunteers to help offload the work required to deal with a fairly high volume of social media activity by the public [19]. Another study [22] examined how state and federal organizations used Twitter around the 2010 Deepwater Horizon oil spill and discovered that social structures created through Twitter affected the way information spread. More recently, Denef et al. examined Twitter use of two police departments during the 2011 London Riots, and described the different styles of public engagement that each assumed—one more formal and detached (instrumental) and the other more informal and personal (expressive) [3]. Though these studies reveal particular uses as well as uncertainty about how to incorporate social media into emergency practice, they do not provide a representative picture of how online communications like social media are used in a general emergency response context.

In this paper, we seek to fill this knowledge gap by studying fire and police public communications before, during, and directly following Hurricane Sandy. Specifically, we examine the communications across four types of online media by departments in the path of the storm.

## STUDY SITE AND DATA COLLECTION

### Hurricane Sandy

On October 29, 2012 Hurricane Sandy made landfall at Brigantine, New Jersey, in one of the most densely populated regions of the United States (US). Hurricane Sandy was the deadliest hurricane (with 72 direct deaths) to strike the east coast in over forty years, and the second-costliest hurricane (estimated at $65 Billion US dollars [15]) in US history [1]. The storm displaced approximately 776,000 people [25] and damaged or destroyed over 650,000 homes [1]. During the storm, nearly 8.5 million people lost power with outages lasting weeks in the more heavily impacted areas [1].

Several factors complicated the response to Hurricane Sandy. First, the impact of the hurricane was intensified by an existing winter storm system: a phenomenon known as the Fujiwhara effect [4] that caused the two storms to merge into one "superstorm." Second, despite dire predictions from forecasters of extreme weather and a potentially lethal storm surge, a survey conducted after the event indicates that approximately 63% of residents in coastal areas chose not to evacuate [5]. Finally, a large winter storm—termed a Nor'easter—moved into the affected area a week later, causing additional difficulty for Sandy recovery efforts, especially for those still without shelter and/or power.

### Data Collection & Analysis Methods

The data collection began with specification of a geographical boundary that included those hardest hit by the storm, with a scope that allowed for analytical breadth: we included coastal counties within a 100 mile radius of where Sandy made landfall as the target (see Figure 1). This made for a total of 26 counties located across 5 US states.

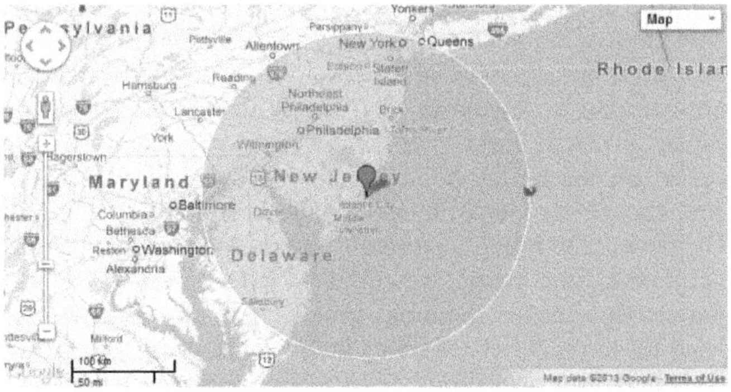


**Figure 1: 100-mile radius centered on Brigantine, NJ, where Sandy made US landfall on October 29, 2012**

*Fire and Police Department Identification*

Next, we identified all fire and police departments within the 26 counties. We extracted a list of fire departments from the National Fire Department Census Database. Unfortunately, the US Fire Administration reports that only 88% of departments participated. However, we discovered that counties sequentially assign numbers to fire departments. This rule of thumb helped identify gaps in the census data, and revealed an additional 75 departments—bringing the total sample to 568 fire departments.

The police departments exist at three levels: state, county, and municipality. Each of the 5 states has a state police department, and each of the 26 counties has a sheriff's office. Additionally, every municipality (e.g. township, city, and village) can potentially have a police department. We found online lists of all the municipalities in the 26 counties, and performed a web search for their respective departments, identifying a total of 272 police departments.

*Data Retrieval from the Four Online Communication Media*

For each fire and police department, we looked at four online communication media: a website, a subscriber-based notification service (Nixle), a microblogging service (Twitter), and a social networking service (Facebook). Though we found occasional references to other online communication tools such as Google+ and CodeRed, these were rarely used and not included in the study.

We searched for a website for each of the departments; if found, we captured the URL and then examined its content for references to social media accounts. In addition, we then looked for Nixle, Twitter, and Facebook accounts using their search interfaces. In Nixle, searching by municipality returns all accounts in that area. In Twitter and Facebook we searched using the departments' names and variations. If through due diligence we did not find an account, we assumed it either did not exist or could not be found easily by members of the public either, thus defeating any purpose of its use as a communication medium.

To narrow the scope to those online communications most likely to be about Hurricane Sandy, we restricted the data collection window to October 25-November 9, 2012. On October 25, the first online Sandy communication appeared in our datasets. By November 9, most of the immediate hurricane recovery efforts had completed and the number of online communications that were not about Hurricane Sandy began to outnumber those that were.

*Website.* Because each fire and police department website is unique and the information is presented in different ways, we were unable to collect data in a format that would allow for comparison to the other types of online communication. However, we visited and made notes for 676 websites; these sites often linked to the other media, described next.

*Nixle.* This online service offers both free and paid notification services to fire and police departments as well as other emergency management and municipal government agencies. Users can search for agencies by location and subscribe for notifications. We found 128 Nixle accounts and extracted the post information for each of these accounts using web-scraping methods. In a few cases, some of the older data for these accounts had been deleted. The *Fire & Police Nixle Collection* contains 930 posts.

*Twitter.* We found 114 Twitter accounts and retrieved the full message streams for each of these accounts using the Twitter REST API. The *Fire & Police Sandy Tweet Collection* contains 3033 tweets.

*Facebook.* We identified 556 public Facebook accounts and retrieved the full set of posts for each of these accounts using the Facebook Graph API. The *Fire & Police Sandy Facebook Collection* contains 4652 posts.

### Content Coding

We coded the data for on/off-topicness and content. The final coding scheme contains 19 categories (see Table 1) and was developed through an iterative pair-coding process. The first coding pass was done with two researchers working together to establish a consistent coding scheme on the Twitter data. After this first pass, we consolidated and refined the categories and then took a second pass on the data to correct and verify the coding scheme. Next, we divided the Facebook and Nixle coding tasks between the same two researchers. To check the validity of this independent coding process, both researchers coded a subset of 200 messages. For this subset, Cohen's kappa across the 19 coding categories averaged 0.87 (SD = 0.24).

| Category | Description |
|---|---|
| cleanup | Clearing of hurricane debris |
| closures | Closure/re-opening of public offices, transportation services, access routes, and scheduled events |
| damage | Storm damage information |
| donations | Donations of time (volunteering), money, or supplies to relief efforts |
| engagement | Invitations to engage with department on social media or direct responses to public posts/tweets |
| evacuation | Evacuation order and shelter information |
| preparation | Storm preparation information |
| protocol | Formal response protocol information (e.g. when to call 9-1-1 versus 3-1-1) |
| reassurance | Reassurance to the public that first responders are prepared for or actively monitoring the storm |
| reference | Reference to an external information source |
| relief | Storm assistance or relief information |
| response | Specific incidents or response efforts during the hurricane |
| resources | Information about supplies needed or available |
| rumor | Misinformation and rumor |
| safety | Safety precautions or conditions |
| services | Power , phone, internet, or cable services information |
| status | Changing storm condition information |
| support | Expression of gratitude or support |
| weather | Weather updates |

**Table 1: Nixle, Twitter, Facebook Content Coding Scheme**

### Level of Engagement

Lastly, we developed a coding scheme to compare engagement levels for each department across Nixle, Twitter, and Facebook (Table 2). We did not code websites for engagement because data collection occurred months after Hurricane Sandy, at which point it was difficult to know what information the website had contained during our data collection window.

| Level | Description |
|---|---|
| Inactive | No account found OR account found but not used |
| Non-Sandy Active | Account used to share information, but not used to share information about Hurricane Sandy |
| Sandy Active | Account used to communicate information about Hurricane Sandy |

**Table 2: Engagement Level Coding Scheme**

## QUANTITATIVE DESCRIPTIONS OF USE

### Overall Online Communication Use

Results indicate (Figure 2) that the majority of departments have a website (81%) and/or a Facebook account (66%). Twitter use, however, was much less common (13%) and Nixle differs greatly by type of department (police: 40%, fire: 3%, combined: 15%). In general, the percentage of departments that have a website or social media account was higher for police than fire (Figure 3), with the exception of Facebook: 70% of fire departments and 60% of police departments have Facebook accounts.

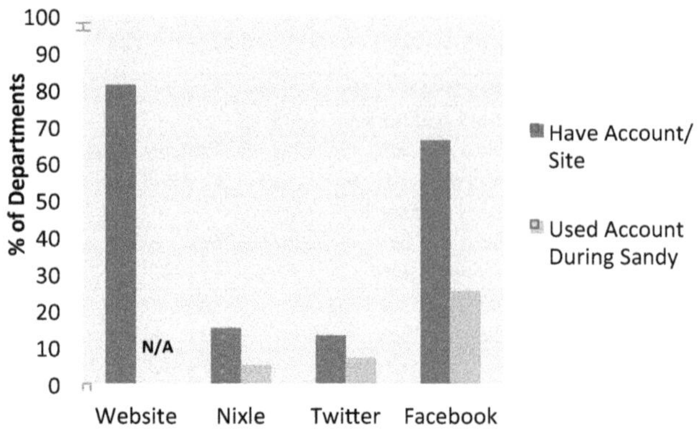


**Figure 2: % Departments with Accounts/Website versus the % That Used Their Account during Sandy**

Even though a fire or police department may have a website and/or a social media account, they did not necessarily use it to communicate during Hurricane Sandy. Figure 3 shows the smaller percentage of departments that used each communication medium to engage in storm-specific communication with the public: Facebook (25%) is the most popular, followed by Twitter (7%), and finally, Nixle (5%). We do not report website use because we could not collect reliable data around its use during Hurricane Sandy.

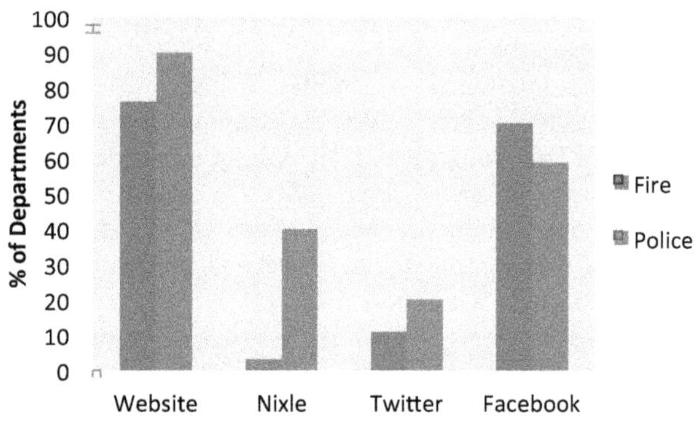


**Figure 3: % of Fire and Police Departments Using Each Communication Medium**

Figure 4 shows how frequently each content category occurs in the Facebook, Twitter, and Nixle message collections. The number of messages is averaged across the number of active accounts for each communication type. Twitter averages are higher overall for each of the categories except *reference*. The opposite is true for Facebook where the averages are mostly lower. The most frequently occurring categories are information about *closures*, *reference* to other official sources of information, *safety* instructions, and *weather* updates.

The *reference* category, which describes those cases when third party sources are discussed, is important because it shows that emergency managers operating social media accounts often play an information vetting role, sifting through available information and sharing what they think is relevant with their constituents. Usually these references point to sources from other agencies, especially those with a broad jurisdiction or scope of interest such as a state governor's office, the Federal Emergency Management Agency (FEMA), or the US National Weather Service.

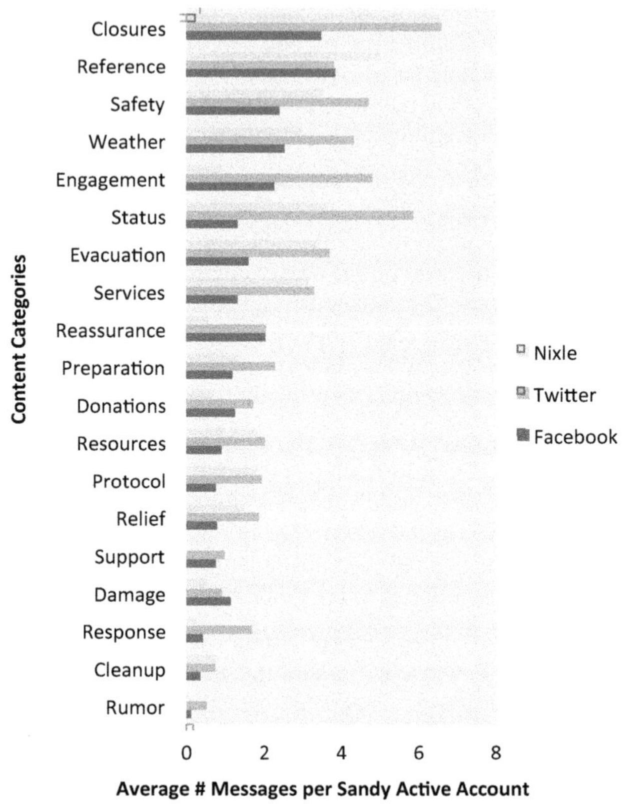


**Figure 4: Average Number of Messages per Active Account for Each Content Category for Nixle, Twitter, and Facebook**

Interestingly, we found few instances of *rumor*, where departments corrected misinformation through their online communications. A frequent concern that emergency response organizations have with the public's online communication is with the credibility and accuracy. These findings suggest that the presence of online rumor is not as much of an issue as some may fear.

Each of the four online communication media have characteristics that make them suited to different styles of communication and different ways of sharing information during an emergency. We now turn our attention to how fire and police departments used each.

### Website-Specific Communication Behavior

Fire and police departments primarily used their websites as a place to provide information about themselves and information relevant to their community, but with little to no means for two-way engagement with their constituents. The information most commonly found on fire and police department websites includes employee rosters, phone numbers, links to other local agency websites, surveys of equipment and resources, and a narrative about the department's history. Sandy-relevant information on these websites includes warnings to prepare for the storm, fundraising activities, long-term recovery information, and accountings of department response efforts (e.g. number of calls or number of rescues). One feature used for posting information about Sandy was a blog or a blog-type feature with time- and date-stamped updates. Often these updates provided a feedback mechanism where members of the public can comment, but this feature is rarely used.

### Nixle-Specific Communication Behavior

Even though Nixle is free to both fire and police departments, it was primarily used by police departments: 40% of the police departments in our sample had a Nixle account whereas only 3% of fire departments had an account. This disparity may be due to differences in role for these two organizations during an emergency event. The police communicate with the public about evacuations, closures, and safety conditions, whereas firefighters tend to focus on response to highly-localized circumstances such as administering emergency medical services or responding to a structure fire—activities that may not need to be shared with a wide audience.

Nixle provides a subscription-based, one-way channel to members of the public who want to receive notifications. Unlike a website, Facebook, or Twitter account, Nixle accounts are authenticated before creation, so members of the public have a reasonable expectation that emergency notifications they receive are from real agencies. Because Nixle can only distribute information (with no means for the public to comment or respond), the notification messages tend to read like formal press releases—carefully crafted using official and more impersonal language.

### Twitter-Specific Communication Behavior

Twitter is the least frequently occurring account type. Of the 88 Twitter accounts, we found only 58 communicated information about Hurricane Sandy. The percentage of use among police departments is higher than fire departments both for having an active Twitter account (15% for police vs. 8.3% for fire) and for using it during Hurricane Sandy (10% for police vs. 5% for fire).

The majority of tweets broadcast information to the public and 66% of these messages contain links to information sources such as National Weather Service bulletins, official disaster declarations, status updates, evacuation maps, and internally compiled information. Also appearing are retweets (17%) that originate from other official sources, such as high-ranking political officials (e.g., a governor or mayor) or emergency response organizations (e.g., FEMA). Through these (re)tweets, departments performed an information vetting role during Hurricane Sandy.

Figure 5 shows the average number of categorized Twitter messages per Sandy-active account. Here we see that police departments report far more *closures*, *status* messages, and information about *evacuations* than fire. These categories seem to speak more directly to the nature of police work, where they are expected to manage the population and maintain order during and after a disaster. The broadcast nature of Twitter can help distribute information as circumstances around an event change.

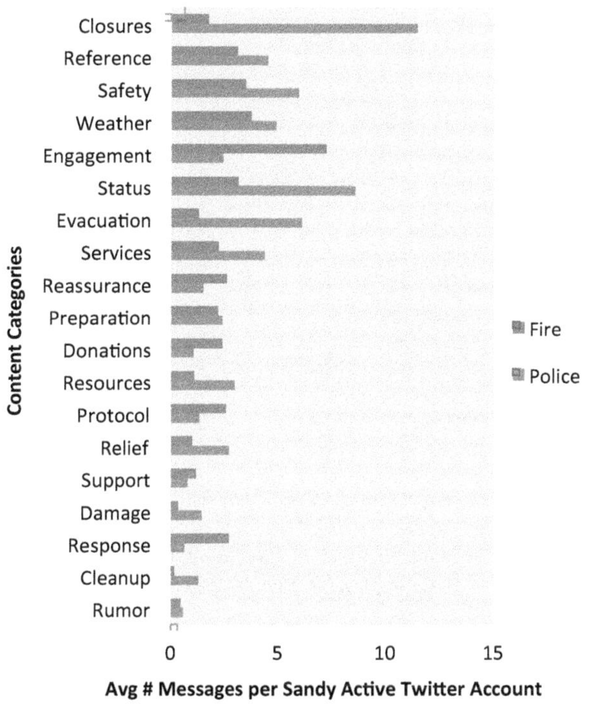


**Figure 5: Fire and Police Department Tweets by Category**

Surprisingly, only 9% of on-topic tweets in the *Fire & Police Tweet Collection* contain hashtags related to Hurricane Sandy (e.g. #Sandy, #frankenstorm, #HurricaneSandy). We expect to see heavier hashtag use as it is known to improve the searchability of tweets. This low incidence of common hashtags suggests that fire and police departments may depend more on Twitter's follower relationship to reach their constituents, rather than on providing searchable terms for a general audience.

### Facebook-Specific Communication Behavior

Facebook is the most widely used online medium to share information with the public about Sandy. Twenty-five percent of the departments in the sample used Facebook, which is 3.6 times the number of Twitter accounts, and five times the number of Nixle accounts. Facebook differs from the other tools that we studied in that it allows for direct and visible interaction with the public. People can post relevant questions, share information, and provide feedback. The format also allows for direct and readily visible replies, and it collates a lot of information in one place and over time. These qualities seem to make Facebook an effective tool for managing public conversation and maintaining a visible presence with the communities that fire and police departments serve.

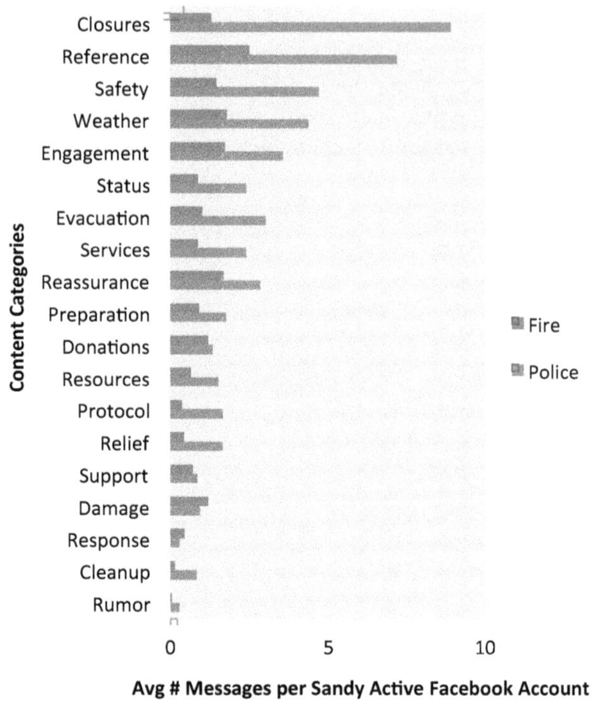


**Figure 6: Average Number of Facebook Messages for Each Category for Fire and Police**

Facebook has a similar category distribution to that of Twitter (Figure 6). The main quantitative difference is in the number of departments that replied directly to the public. With respect to the departments that used Facebook to communicate Sandy-specific information, 39% replied directly to the public whereas only 10% of the departments that used Twitter replied directly to Sandy-specific tweets and all but one of these replied sparingly (3 or less replies).

## ONLINE ENGAGEMENT

To better measure and compare the varied use of online communication during Hurricane Sandy, we assigned each department an engagement level (Inactive, Non-Sandy Active, Sandy Active) for Nixle, Twitter, and Facebook. Figure 7 shows that departments were least engaged with Nixle: 90% were *Inactive*, 6% were *Non-Sandy Active*, and only 4% were *Sandy Active*. Engagement with Twitter was only slightly higher, with 89% *Inactive*, 4% *Non-Sandy Active*, and 7% *Sandy Active*. The highest levels of online engagement were found on Facebook, with 52% *Inactive*, 23% *Non-Sandy Active*, and 25% *Sandy Active*. When we calculate the percentage of *Sandy Active* accounts in all Active accounts (*Non-Sandy Active* and *Sandy Active*), Nixle is again the lowest (40%), but Twitter (63.6%) and Facebook (47.9%) are reversed. These percentages indicate that of the departments with active accounts, those that used Twitter were most likely to use it during Hurricane Sandy.

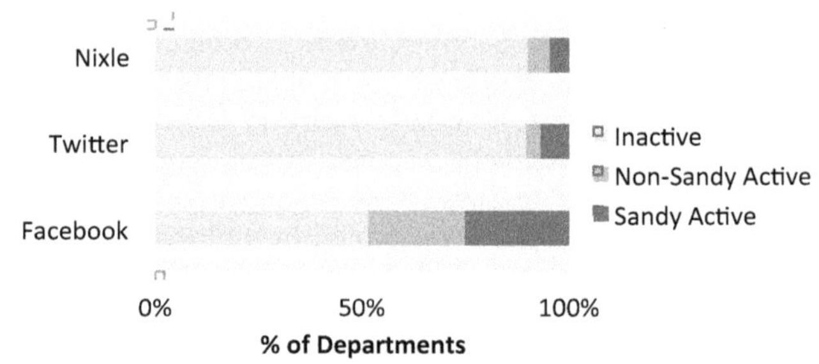


**Figure 7: Department Engagement by Media Type**

Next, we divided the departments into three groups based on the highest level of engagement each had. Departments at the lowest level, the *Inactive Group* (387 departments, 46.1%), include those that were *Inactive* across all three communication media. Departments in the *Non-Sandy Active Group* (207 departments, 24.6%) used at least one online medium, but did not use any media to share Sandy-specific information. The *Sandy Active Group* (246 departments, 29.3%) used at least one online medium to share Sandy-specific information. Figure 8 captures the number of active accounts per department within the *Non-Sandy Active* and the *Sandy Active* groups.

| Engagement Groups | Number N of Online Media | | | % of Depts |
|---|---|---|---|---|
| | N=1 | N=2 | N=3 | |
| Non-Sandy Active | 88.4% | 11.1% | 0.5% | 24.6% |
| Sandy Active | 77.6% | 19.1% | 3.3% | 29.3% |

**Figure 8: Breakdown of *Non-Sandy* and *Sandy Active Groups* by the Number of Media with that Level of Engagement**

*Inactive Group:* The majority of departments in this group (232 departments, 60%) had no Nixle, Twitter, or Facebook account. Past studies report [8] that common reasons for emergency responders not to use online media include feeling inexperienced or lacking the time, resources, and/or approval from management. Other emergency responders perceive that online media do not meet the communication needs of their organization and community [8]. We suspect these reasons explain much of the lack of activity by departments in the *Inactive Group*.

The remainder of departments in the *Inactive Group* (155 departments, 40%) had at least one online account, but the account was clearly in disuse. This lack of account activity may be explained by departments that started to use an online account only to discover that it did not meet their needs, or they found that they did not have the time or other resources to maintain it.

*Non-Sandy Active Group:* These departments showed frequent and recent activity over at least one online communication medium, but curiously this did not translate into use during Hurricane Sandy. One likely reason may be that departments were so busy responding to the disaster event that online communications were not possible given the circumstances. For instance, some of the departments most affected by the storm were incapacitated with severe flooding, power outages, and loss of vehicles, equipment, and even life. Unfortunately, the data collected in this study cannot answer questions about *why* departments did (or did not) use online communications; answers to these questions requires further data collection and study.

*Sandy Active Group:* Even though the percentage of department type in the *Sandy Active Group* is about the same (28% fire and 32% police), we saw a clear difference in the average number of messages when comparing police and fire. Police departments post more actively on average across all three platforms. This difference is the most pronounced on Facebook where the average number of Sandy-specific posts is 2.66 times higher for police compared to fire (32 posts versus 12). The average number of relevant tweets is 1.75 times higher when comparing police to fire. The results for Nixle are inconclusive because there are so few fire departments (4) using Nixle to which we could compare police departments.

All the online communications we collected come from those departments in the *Sandy Active Group*, so naturally we can report more on their activity and online communication practice. We now turn our attention to the departments in this group for insight into the adaptability of online tools to meet the needs of emergency response.

## HIGH-ENGAGEMENT IS A SITUATED PRACTICE

When examining departments in the *Sandy Active Group*, we find a mix of communication strategies and behaviors, but most interesting are those moments when we see fundamental changes in communication that show how situated practice trumps pre-planned policy and greatly affects the shaping of public information. What constitutes appropriate online interaction evolves as both emergency personnel and the public calibrate their expectations. We illustrate this point through two examples: one excerpt taken from the activity of the Long Beach Township Police Department Facebook account, and another from the @FDNY (Fire Department of New York) Twitter account.

Long Beach Island (LBI), New Jersey, is a barrier island that suffered extensive damage during Hurricane Sandy. Residents were evacuated prior to the storm surge, and the island remained closed to residents for 13 days except for a few brief periods when they were allowed to retrieve personal belongings. These circumstances produced a situation where the LBTPD was left to protect the property interests, safety, and information needs of a displaced and often frustrated population.

The LBTPD's Facebook page served as a public forum for displaced residents to comment on the response efforts. Posts from residents fell across several themes: questions and comments about re-entry details, requests for information about damage to particular neighborhoods and properties, concerns about protection of property, and expressions of gratitude. For example:

```
(November 2 13:04): Any information from on the first street Loveladies Bay side ?
```

```
(November 4 14:42): When will access to north beach be allowed?
```

```
(November 2 14:42): thank you so much for keeping us informed. Can we bring any food, water, etc to donate to those who are working on the island?
```

By posting to a public and persistent forum like Facebook, residents hold the LBTPD publically accountable—and the LBTPD allows itself to be held accountable in turn.

LBTPD answered questions in succinct messages using formal language and without referring directly to the posters, sometimes with multiple answers in one reply. For instance, LBTPD responded to residents' questions with the following post:

```
LBTPD: There is no time frame for access to north beach. Any donations would be graciously accepted! Contractors can register at WWW.LBIEOC.org
```

They did not publicly respond directly to posts that criticize evacuation procedures or that were not beneficial to the larger population. This is another behavioral feature of mutual accountability on a public stage.

Despite LBTPD's impersonal posting style and carefully crafted responses, it was clear that the LBTPD monitored comments. For example, residents post:

```
(October 29 12:22): Our home is in Loveladies 117c LBB. Are there any photos from that area or news? Thank you
```

```
(October 30 8:27): Does anyone have any information about conditions in North Beach Haven @ 18th Street? Thank you first responders!
```

In response, LBTPD provided before and after photos for each of the neighborhoods in the township and surrounding areas. Numerous requests would have been time-consuming to respond to individually, but by posting aerial photos, the LBTPD was able to respond to broad area concerns.

As recovery efforts continue, increasingly frustrated residents offered public commentary about restricted access to their homes:

```
(November 5 15:23pm): No one knows my property better than I do, so why the hell am I going to call some contractor or plumber that I don't even know to enter my house to winterize or enter my house! Plus they don't have keys! To make matters worse my house is in north beach and not allowed to enter today. I want answers! Additional damages are now the townships responsibilities!
```

Even in response to concerns like these, the LBTPD continued to communicate in highly visible and documentable ways. In these examples, we see how the responsibilities of public communication shift in response to the situation at hand and toward mutual accountability on a public stage.

Another exchange we learn from comes from FDNY's Twitter communications. The @FDNY account generated far more tweets than other accounts and responded to members of the public more as well (179 replies to 239 accounts). The disproportionately high level of public engagement found in the @FDNY Twitter account seems to be due to several factors. The @FDNY has a potential audience of 8,175,133 people [23], which is much larger than any other fire department we examined. This account is also staffed with full-time social media personnel and has a history of replying to public inquiries. In addition, at the height of the storm surge when there were widespread power and phone outages as well as a large neighborhood fire (the Breezy Point fire) the 911-dispatch system became overloaded. Members of the public began tweeting requests for emergency assistance when they were unable to reach 911 dispatch [11]. We detail these exchanges below.

On October 28, a day prior to Hurricane Sandy landfall, @FDNY sent several (re)tweets notifying the public of evacuation orders and procedures for emergency assistance:

```
@FDNY[1] (Oct 28 11:56): RT @NotifyNYC: NYC orders MANDATORY EVACUATION Zone A, Rockaways, Hamilton Bch, City Is. due to dangerous storm http://t.co/D10EV04p or 311
```

```
@FDNY (Oct 28 16:11): RT @NYCMayorsOffice: Mayor: If you can't evacuate yourself and need assistance, please call 311. #Sandy
```

The next day, on October 29 as the storm surge reaches its peak, we see the first direct response to twitterers who provided emergency information and made requests:

```
@Lochald (Oct 29 20:03): IDK address. And he's not replying right now (probably saving his cell battery). He had said others were aware & getting help. @edaro @FDNY
```

A reply from @FDNY redirected him to make a 911 call:

```
@FDNY (Oct 29 20:06pm): @Lochald @edaro Please don't tweet with emergency info. We want to help everyone as soon as we can. Please ask him to call 911.
```

A tweet about the protocol for how to request help and report other information followed soon after:

```
@FDNY (Oct 29 21:32): PLEASE NOTE: *Do not* tweet emergency calls. Please call 911. If it is not an emergency, please call 311. #NYC #Sandy
```

Shortly after this message, however, @FDNY sent numerous replies indicating that they were attempting to contact dispatchers on twitterers' behalf. In the exchange that follows, we begin to see @FDNY change its stance about what constitutes appropriate Twitter protocol under these emergency circumstances:

[1] Individual usernames are anonymized while public entities' names remain unchanged.

```
@Dynb (Oct 29 22:12): @FDNY my sis family at 78th St155-22 Howard Beach Queens NY 11414, water risinig 12 ft need help 7186745977,1st floor drowned, kids scared
```

@FDNY responded:

```
@FDNY (Oct 29 22:16): @Dynb Please keep trying to call 911. I will try to reach dispatchers now.
```

A status update from @FDNY:

```
@FDNY (Oct 29 22:32): @Dynb Please note dispatchers are aware and are trying to send help.
```

From @Dynb a few hours later the following is posted:

```
@Dynb (Oct 30 0:08): @FDNY Thank you , water resceding but help required many many kids in neighborhood very scared & stranded 155-22 78th st, Queens 11414
```

A reply from @FDNY provided reassurance:

```
@FDNY (Oct 30 0:11): @RSDynb I understand. Dispatch was notified. I know it's difficult, but please be patient. Units working to respond to all calls safely.
```

In reaction to these types of exchanges, a flurry of tweets from the public appeared with expressions of concern that @FDNY was bypassing official protocol. @FDNY replied:

```
@FDNY (Oct 30 0:23): @Bleymor @Lisar @twitter @rass Don't want NYC to rely on this as an alt to 911. But notifying dispatchers of all emergencies tweeted
```

These conversations continued throughout the storm and the Breezy Point fire. Replies went back and forth as @FDNY gathered information and relayed it to dispatchers. Numerous @FDNY tweets provided reassurance that information had been received and that help was on the way. At the same time, @FDNY keeps reinforcing the use of official channels, making it clear that Twitter as dispatch was not a permanent solution but one that had become necessary given the extenuating circumstances. This observed activity had a deeply engaging quality because of implicit admission that mass emergency response is a largely improvised [10,14], or situated [21], activity.

It is unclear how this bypass of official protocol affected dispatch work or how those who "kept to the rules" and reported their emergencies through 911 were affected. However, we believe that this *public* adaptation of online communication technology is novel, and shows how protocols in disaster response are often overruled [10,14]. Rarely are such overrides so visible to the public, which is a new contribution of the online world. It is highly doubtful that this behavior will be isolated to this one emergency and to these accounts. That such popular accounts for a populous region made these moves sets a precedent and indicates what is likely to come in future events.

## CONCLUSION

In this paper, we provide quantified evidence of both the presence and absence of online communications by fire and police departments during Hurricane Sandy. Results show that relatively few of these departments used online media in their public communications during this event, and that there was a high degree of variance across the different media under study. Among those departments that used online media during Hurricane Sandy, discursive moves signal creative adaptations and set meaningful precedents for the future of emergency management.

### Procedures & Policy

Emergency responders strive to implement common organizational structures and procedures to streamline coordination in multiagency response. However, no current standardized procedures exist for online media use and we argue that this is just as well. Given this research, we believe that implementing universal, and therefore likely restrictive, online media policies is premature and possibly even dangerous at this point of time in the socio-technical evolution of disaster response. Not only do online media support different kinds of interaction and purpose, emergency managers need to be free to improvise their practice in relation to the situations they and their constituents face. High-level policy decisions may prematurely mandate and restrict which media emergency groups use and how they use it.

Though some regularity is helpful—particularly in the case of warning messaging—the fluctuating needs of the public and the capacities that responders have as disasters then ensue must be matched by the communications media that support informational exchange—whether or not that includes online media. Future policies must provide flexibility that allows emergency organizations to employ strategies that best fit the needs of their organization, community, and response effort.

### Transparency & Public Accountability

In the data, we see regular reminders of emergency response's accountability to the public. Throughout the hurricane event, *reassurance* messages assert that response efforts are under control, and that professionals are in place to do the jobs for which they are trained. Evidence of this accountability is found in the information that departments provide about the status of the storm, recovery, and relief efforts. Cases of rumor correction appear, although not frequently, indicating that the amount of rumor that people mistakenly take seriously is not high; nevertheless, attention to rumor demonstrates a commitment to both social media as a meaningful communication venue that the public attends to, and to ensuring that its contents are accurate. Making good use of this transparency through public communication and the accountability that follows can be challenging, but has the potential to foster trust and lead to better decision-making by affected constituents.

In the past, reports of emergency response activities were not as freely available (e.g. they were filtered through the media, or reported in press releases every 12 hours). Communications enabled by online media can provide a greater sense of transparency, one where emergency service workers can directly communicate with the public and one where the communications of these workers are visible to the public in ways not previously possible. Both the LBTPD and FDNY adjusted their information strategies in response to members of the public. Yet, in the case of LBTPD, this transparency also exposed the department to increased public scrutiny and criticism.

### Design Recommendations & Future Work

Based on this research, we offer several design recommendations. First, to make online media streams more "listenable" for on-the-ground emergency managers, new features and/or tools are needed that allow emergency managers to better track, respond to, and document public information. For example, no automated means exist for tracking the status of online queries from the public (e.g. whether a reply was given, what the the reply was, how and when the reply was sent, who sent it, and to whom the reply was sent). Without tracking this kind of information, questions from the public can easily slip through the cracks, especially during a large-scale crisis event. Second, there is also a need to make online media streams more "listenable" for members of the public. In Twitter and Facebook, the data showed that replies by emergency managers to questions from the public were often buried within response threads to individual messages. Unless one knows what to search for or wades through many potentially irrelevant conversations, he or she may never find the information they seek, even though it is publically available. If emergency managers and members of the public could better "listen" to online media streams, value of the online media and therefore their use would likely increase during times of crisis.

To complement these technology design efforts, emergency management practice will need to create better capacities for departments to use online media. This involves finding a balance between a department's desire to communicate online (by virtue of establishing accounts and audience following during non-disaster times) and their (in)ability to act on those relationships when personnel resources become taxed during disaster.

Low overall use of online media by fire and police departments during Hurricane Sandy suggests that emergency management use of these media is not well understood. Indeed, little research exists around the features and affordances of online media and how each can fit into an emergency management communication strategy. The research presented here lays a foundation for future applied and basic research in this area by reporting actual online media use during a large-scale crisis event.

## ACKNOWLEDGMENTS

We thank the anonymous reviewers for their insightful critique and the US National Science Foundation for funding this research through grants IIS-0910586 and AGS-1331490.

## REFERENCES


1. Blake, E.S., Kimberlain, T.B., Berg, R.J., Cangialosi, J.P., and Beven II, J.L. *Tropical Cyclone Report - Hurricane Sandy*. National Hurricane Center, 2013.
2. Crowe, A. The Elephant in the JIC: The Fundamental Flaw of Emergency Public Information within the NIMS Framework. *Journal of Homeland Security and Emergency Management 7*, 1 (2010).
3. Denef, S., Bayerl, P.S., and Kaptein, N. Social Media and the Police-Tweeting Practices of British Police Forces during the August 2011 Riots. *Proceedings of CHI 2013*, ACM Press (2013), 3471–3480.
4. Fujiwhara, S. On the Growth and Decay of Vortical Systems. *Quarterly Journal of the Royal Meteorological Society 49*, 206 (1923), 75–104.
5. Gibbs, L.I. and Holloway, C.F. *NYC Hurricane Sandy After Action: Report and Recommendations to Mayor Michael R. Bloomberg*. New York City, 2013.
6. Hagar, C. and Haythornthwaite, C. Crisis, Farming & Community. *The Journal of Community Informatics 1*, 3 (2005), 41–52.
7. Hjorth, L. and Kim, K.-H.Y. Good Grief: The Role of Social Mobile Media in the 3.11 Earthquake Disaster in Japan. *Digital Creativity 22*, 3 (2011), 187–199.
8. Hughes, A.L. and Palen, L. The Evolving Role of the Public Information Officer: An Examination of Social Media in Emergency Management. *Journal of Homeland Security and Emergency Management 9*, 1 (2012).
9. Hughes, A.L. and Palen, L. Social Media in Emergency Management: Academic Perspective. In J.E. Trainor and T. Subbio, eds., *Issues in Disaster Science and Management: A Critical Dialogue between Scientists and Emergency Managers*. FEMA in Higher Education Program, 2014.
10. Kendra, J.M. and Wachtendorf, T. Creativity in Emergency Response After The World Trade Center Attack. In *Beyond September 11th: An Account of Post-Disaster Research*. Institute of Behavioral Science, Natural Hazards Center, University of Colorado, 2003, 121–146.
11. Khorram, Y. As Sandy Pounded NYC, Fire Department Worker was a Twitter Lifeline. *CNN*, 2012.
12. Latonero, M. and Shklovski, I. Emergency Management, Twitter, and Social Media Evangelism. *International Journal of Information Systems for Crisis Response and Management 3*, 4 (2011), 1–16.
13. Mark, G., Bagdouri, M., Palen, L., Martin, J., Al-Ani, B., and Anderson, K. Blogs as a Collective War Diary. *Proceedings of CSCW 2012*, ACM Press (2012), 37–46.
14. Mendonca, D., Beroggi, G., and Wallace, W.A. Decision Support for Improvisation during Emergency Response Operations. *International Journal of Emergency Management 1*, (2001), 30–38.
15. National Climatic Data Center. *Billion-Dollar Weather/Climate Disasters*. National Oceanic and Atmospheric Administration, 2013.
16. Palen, L. and Liu, S.B. Citizen Communications in Crisis: Anticipating a Future of ICT-supported Public Participation. *Proceedings of CHI 2007*, ACM Press (2007), 727–736.
17. Palen, L., Vieweg, S., Liu, S.B., and Hughes, A.L. Crisis in a Networked World. *Social Science Computing Review 27*, 4 (2009), 467–480.
18. Qu, Y., Wu, P.F., and Wang, X. Online Community Response to Major Disaster: A Study of Tianya Forum in the 2008 Sichuan Earthquake. *Proceedings of HICSS 2009*, IEEE Computer Society (2009), 1–11.
19. St. Denis, L.A., Hughes, A.L., and Palen, L. Trial by Fire: The Deployment of Trusted Digital Volunteers in the 2011 Shadow Lake Fire. *Proceedings of ISCRAM 2012*, (2012).
20. Starbird, K., Palen, L., Hughes, A.L., and Vieweg, S. Chatter on the Red: What Hazards Threat Reveals About the Social Life of Microblogged Information. *Proceedings of CSCW 2010*, ACM (2010), 241–250.
21. Suchman, L. *Plans and Situated Actions: The Problem of Human-Machine Communication*. Cambridge University Press, New York, NY, 1987.
22. Sutton, J.N., Spiro, E., Butts, C., Fitzhugh, S., Johnson, B., and Greczek, M. Tweeting the Spill: Online Informal Communications, Social Networks, and Conversational Microstructures during the Deepwater Horizon Oilspill. *International Journal of Information Systems for Crisis Response and Management 5*, 1 (2013), 58–76.
23. US Census Bureau, Population Division. *Table 1. Annual Estimates of the Resident Population for Counties of New York: April 1, 2010 to July 1, 2011*. 2012.
24. Wenger, D., Quarantelli, E.L., and Dynes, R.R. *Disaster Analysis: Police and Fire Departments*. The Disaster Research Center, University of Delaware, Newark, DE, 1989.
25. Yonetani, M., Holladay, S., Ginnetti, J., et al. *Global Estimates 2012: People Displaced by Disasters*. Internal Displacement Monitoring Centre & Norwegian Refugee Council, 2013.
26. Zook, M., Graham, M., Shelton, T., and Gorman, S. Volunteered Geographic Information and Crowdsourcing Disaster Relief: A Case Study of the Haitian Earthquake. *World Medical & Health Policy 2*, 2 (2010), 7.

# EmergencyMessenger: A Text based Communication Concept for Indoor Firefighting

**Matthias Betz**
Information Systems and New Media
University of Siegen, Hölderlinstr. 3,
57076 Siegen, Germany
volker.wulf@uni-siegen.de

**Volker Wulf**
Information Systems and New Media
University of Siegen, Hölderlinstr. 3,
57076 Siegen, Germany
Fraunhofer Institute for Applied Information Technology FIT, St. Augustin, Germany
volker.wulf@uni-siegen.de

## ABSTRACT
Finding and rescuing missing or injured people or fighting fire inside burning buildings is a central challenge for fire brigades. To ensure the safety of indoor work, monitoring the operations of firefighting units is crucial. As in most countries, firefighters in Germany utilize radio sets to establish voice communication between indoor operating units and the supervisory structure outside. Based on findings from a long term ethnographic study in cooperation with different German fire brigades over a time span of more than 5 years we analyzed the advantages and disadvantages of the current voice over radio communication tactics and techniques. We designed and evaluated a complementary text based communication device-the EMERGENCY-MESSENGER-to support the time critical work of indoor units working under harsh conditions, wearing Self-Contained-Breathing-Apparatus (SCBA). We conducted 13 full scale training missions including extensive debriefings to design and evaluate the communication concept and the corresponding device.

## Author Keywords
Firefighting; communication; cooperation; text; messaging; indoor; monitoring; autonomy; safety; security

## ACM Classification Keywords
H.5.m. Information interfaces and presentation (e.g., HCI): Miscellaneous.

## INTRODUCTION
Dealing proactively with fire inside a burning building is a central concept in modern firefighting tactics. Entering, reconnoitering, finding 'seats' of fire, finding affected persons and performing appropriate actions is one of the main challenges firefighters are faced with. All equipment such as fire trucks, fire engines, turnable ladders, fire hoses, protective devices and all supporting organizational hierarchies, command structures, skills, routines and practices are designed and established to support and secure the potentially life-threatening work of rescuing victims and to minimize risk to people, assets and the environment.


*CHI 2014,* April 26 - May 01 2014, Toronto, ON, Canada
Copyright © 2014 ACM 978-1-4503-2473-1/14/04...$15.00.
http://dx.doi.org/10.1145/2556288.2557188

Finding seats of fire or rescuing missing or injured people inside burning buildings is a difficult and time critical task. Firefighting tactics dictate that the time until a victim inside a burning building filled with smoke reaches her tolerance limit is limited to a maximum of 17 minutes. During this time, an incident has to be reported to the local fire brigade, firefighters have to be alarmed, and then have to travel to the incident location, equip themselves with protective clothes and devices, assess the situation on site, decide on appropriate action and accomplish the mission. The early phases of alarming, traveling and equipping have been optimized in the last decades, e.g. the design of fire stations has been optimized for equipping and departing. Most of the protective equipment is now integrated into the seats of fire trucks which allows for equipping during traveling to the incident location.

During two research projects in cooperation with different fire brigades in Germany over the last five years, we identified the crucial role of organizing *operations on site* to utilize the remaining time after arrival in an effective and efficient way. Two aspects are critical. Firstly, a division of labor which ensures disciplined and speedy working is necessary, and secondly adequate communication technologies, techniques and practices are needed. The second of these, we discovered, entails some crucial shortcomings. In this paper we describe and analyze these problems. Based on this analysis we present a complementary communication concept and a corresponding device (the EMERGENCYMESSENGER). We also provide initial findings from evaluative full scale training missions.

## STATE OF THE ART
In this section, we summarize the current state of the art in communication and coordination research. Analyzing coordination and communication practices has a long tradition especially in CSCW [1][9]. Due to the focus on computer mediated cooperation and communication 'at work' there is

a huge corpus of work on 'stationary' workplaces like offices, control rooms etc. With the advent of the Mobile and Ubiquitous Computing paradigm, the utilization of mobile and embedded systems in other domains of work has increased [19]. The use and usefulness of mobile and embedded devices in domains with special needs and constraints such as emergency response has become a focus for researchers in HCI and CSCW. In recent years, the specific requirements of emergency response have triggered critical reconsideration of concepts like awareness, context awareness, coordination and communication support.

Firefighting is one such example. However, most of the work in emergency response still focuses on command and control either on site or in control centers due to difficulties in accessing, documenting and analyzing work practices in the first line of intervention. [12] [13], for instance, provide insights into the work of leaders in firefighting during the journey to the incident site. Other research contributions focus on the education and training of emergency response forces [18]. Relatively few research contributions focus on the work of firefighters in situ. An exception is the work of our colleagues, e.g. [15], [4] and [14], who investigate the in situ navigation practices of firefighters as a cooperative activity and provide design recommendations on the basis of ethnographic enquiry. Ethnographically- grounded patterns are introduced by [3] to inform the design of interactive systems for this particular domain. Research from ubiquitous computing has provided architectural support for the development of applications for this domain as with [10]. [10], however, provides no account of the work practices and organizational structures of firefighting beyond a single scenario, nor investigate the impact of their application on firefighting practices under realistic conditions.

Our focus has to do with communication practices and we argue that communication needs in this domain have a particular character that needs to be considered while designing tools for enhancing communication practice under time-critical conditions in extreme environments.

## METHODOLOGY

In the following section we describe our approach to analysis, design and evaluation in relation to the communication and coordination aspects of the work of firefighters on-site. The research design follows the approach of design-case-studies by [21] which is theoretically grounded in [16]. The research and development process is structured as an iterative evolutionary cycle. Each cycle consists of three phases: Firstly the existing routines, organizational and social structures and the individual and cooperative practices are investigated, documented and analyzed e.g. through conducting ethnographic studies. We should point here that we, like most contemporary anthropologists, take the view that ethnography is not a method but a set of analytic practices predicated on 'taking the point of view of the actor' [7]. The results of the first phase inform the identification of problems in the investigated (social) practice. Designers utilize the ethnography and associated problem definitions to create interactive artifacts and new (cooperative) practices to meet the problem definitions. In a third phase the resulting artifacts are evaluated in the intended context of use. The usage, usefulness and usability of the introduced artifacts and the evolving new practices and social structures are observed, documented and analyzed to reframe problem definitions. The results and findings lead into refocusing the domain analysis phase in the beginning of the next iteration. The domain of first responding in general and firefighting in particular, however, has some specifics that make it necessary to complement the conventional qualitative empirical methods of ethnography (like observations and interviews). We applied three additional methods considering the addressed domain:

*Training missions:* Legal constraints and other constraints make observation of real firefighting missions-especially in the case of indoor work- impossible. Training missions provide an alternative where the tactics of firefighting in 'near real' conditions. We observed several training missions both with conventional firefighting equipment and-for evaluative purposes- with the system we developed. We documented training missions with audio/video recordings and field notes. Additionally the traffic on the on-site-radio was recorded. The material was used to analyze the application of common tactics of firefighting and to compare it with new practices induced by the new system.

*Post-mission debriefings:* To gain a deeper understanding of the existing practices and the user-experience of the introduced system, we organized group discussions right after each training-mission. By discussing the practical and tactical consequences of the introduced system, the observational data was complemented by reflections on changes to common firefighting tactics. The participating firefighters were able to assess the introduced system not only on their immediate experience of the new system but also on their long term firefighting experience.

*Map exercises:* Due to the high pace of realistic training missions and the negative impact of disruptions on the dynamics of simulations, we performed map exercises together with firefighters to gain a deeper understanding of communication practices. Equipped with floor plans of a fictional building, two groups of firefighters performed a step by step analysis of procedures utilized under the assumption of a missing person in a burning apartment. The participating designers and researchers were allowed to interrupt the ongoing exercise at any time to clarify open questions. We focused on communication practices by documenting radio messages and other communicative techniques. We identified a large amount of recurring messages and collected them on post-its and cue cards. After finishing the map exercise we structured the messages in eight categories. The map exercises have been captured with audio/video to enable a subsequent analysis.

## FIREFIGHTING PRACTICE ON SITE

Firefighting is a highly cooperative task where several actors with heterogeneous roles are involved. In the following, we describe this practice in a representative scenario in this domain. The following scenario is typical of the way firefighters are trained in German firefighting schools. The scenario is described in chronological order to give a good understanding of the dynamics of this particular practice. The given scenario is a so-called *critical apartment fire*, i.e. a fire in an apartment with one or more affected persons.

### Alerting Phase – Forming an organizational structure

The whole 'fire run' begins with a 112 call (similar to 911 in the U.S.) by e.g. a resident or neighbor. The 112 call is received in the central headquarters of the local or regional fire department. According to the category of the described incident situation the dispatcher in the headquarters alerts one or more *fire stations* geographically nearby the incident. Several vehicles including one or two *fire trucks* depart from the station. Each *fire truck* transports one *firefighting group*. Each *group* is divided into several roles: the *group leader*, the *engineer*, the *runner* and three attacking *troops*. A *troop* consists of one *troop leader* and one *troop member*. A *group* is the smallest fully operational unit. That is, if a *group* arrives on site and no *dedicated incident commander* arrived yet the *group leader* of the first arriving fire truck has the role of the incident commander. He fulfills this role until an incident commander arrives. Then, the command is passed over to this *incident commander*. That means that at least in the beginning of a fire run the group leader has to fulfill two roles: leading his group to initialize appropriate actions and to communicate with the headquarters to report the progress and state of affairs.

### Approaching Phase – Preparing and Equipping

Whilst approaching the incident site all firefighters equip themselves with appropriate tools and equipment regarding the type of fire run and their assigned role. This includes protective clothes, SCBA and mask, helmet, radio sets, etc. The fire trucks are designed in a way to allow access to the relevant equipment while driving.

### Decision Phase – Assessing, Planning, Commanding

After arriving on site the incident commander (according to the statements in our workshops usually the group leader of the first truck to arrive) starts to estimate the situation by inspecting the burning building, investigating the surrounding area and by talking to affected persons, neighbors, witnesses etc. Usually, during this phase of *situation investigation* the firefighters of the group remain on the truck. After collecting the available information, the incident commander *assesses the situation* and makes a *command decision*. The incident commander then *commands* his group to take appropriate action. For receiving the command all group members line up in front of the group leader ordered by troops. Each troop leader receives the mission assignment for his troop and has to repeat the command verbally to ensure that there are no misunderstandings.

If a group leader or the incident commander makes a decision for entering, the group leader gives order to one or at the most two troops to enter the building to search the affected areas either to find missing and potentially injured people to bring them out of the life-threatening zone or to find the seat of fire in order to put it out.

### Operation Phase –Autonomous working on a mission

After receiving orders the group enters the next phase of the incident. In this phase the group leader changes his active role of assessing, decision making and commanding to a more passive role of monitoring and steering the autonomously operating troops. One or two troops are responsible for establishing an infrastructure of water hoses connected to one or more sufficient water supplies. The other two troops are responsible for attacking the fire either indoors or from outside the affected building. In case of building entry, one water troop puts on the same SCBA equipment as building entry units after the water supply infrastructure has been established. The water troop then stands by as a backup in case of an accident of one of the building entry troops. To enable the group leader to monitor the action, the troops have to report the attainment of particular milestones.

We observed various ways in which those notifications were made, ranging from implicit notifications encoded in observable actions to explicit formal notifications face-to-face or communicated via radio. E.g. the progress of the work of the water supply troop can be observed by the group leader because he is co-located with them. Also the state of preparation of the troops with SCBA is directly observable. If there is no visual contact, troops verbally report milestones to the group leader via radio.

With the given commands in mind, troop(s) work autonomously inside the building. They explore and investigate the usually unknown environment in harsh conditions. By entering affected parts of a burning building the troops are usually faced with dense and toxic smoke, high temperatures, and potentially damaged structures like stairs and ceilings. To protect them from these dangerous conditions, the indoor troops wear and carry various pieces of protective equipment. This includes protective clothing, a self-containing breathing apparatus (SCBA) with a protective breathing mask, a fire hose connected to the pump of a truck, a rope, an axe, several smaller tools like scissors, wooden wedges to keep doors open and a radio set to keep in contact with the group leader (for more detailed description of firefighting equipment [c.f. 5]).

If conditions allow, troops try to move inside the building without connecting the SCBA to the corresponding mask to save air. The troop has to report to the group leader when and where it enters a building. If there is visual contact this usually happens implicitly. When a troop reaches an area where the breathing conditions are getting intolerable they connect their breathing mask to the SCBA. Every troop member assists his troop mate to ensure a safe and consistent fitting. From this point in time the status of the troop changes to "connected" which means from now on the available amount of air is consumed continuously. The troop leader has to notify this milestone to the group leader. This notification is usually mediated by radio.

With SCBA, one charge of air commonly lasts for about 30 minutes. To ensure a safe way back to areas were no SCBA is needed the official safety regulations prescribe indoor troops have to keep at least the double amount of air they used on the way into the life threatening zone. That is, troops working under SCBA have to follow the one-third-two-thirds-rule: The time schedule for searching and finding a victim or a seat of fire is limited to 10 minutes maximum. Double this time is reserved for the way back (20 minutes). This reserve serves as a buffer in case problems are caused on the way back by the dynamics of the ongoing fire (e.g. collapsing building structures). Another important reason for that rule is the fact of consuming significantly more air while carrying an unconscious victim.

To search for missing persons or a seat of fire indoor troops follow certain approaches of systematic search. They traverse an apartment by initially deciding to follow the walls on the right or left. If they approach a door, they enter the room, decide on the direction and proceed along the right or left side wall. This basically implements a depth-first algorithm to traverse through all rooms in a house or apartment without missing an area [c.f. 15]. The troop leader reports his initial directional decision and milestones which seem to be of relevance to enable the group leader to monitor the progress of the reconnaissance and the approximate position. During training missions we observed notifications of floor changes, entering and leaving a building, entering and leaving an apartment, or entering and leaving a room.

The discovery of a victim or a seat of fire is reported to the group leader and appropriate rescue actions are then performed or, respectively, actions to put out the fire. An indoor troop always returns along the fire hose they dragged along behind them during the search phase even if this way is not the fastest. As long as the dynamics of the incident situation does not block the way along the fire hose this direction is the most clearly defined and best known way to the entry point. After successfully leaving the danger zone the troop hands over the victim to the emergency medical service which should have arrived on site at that time. The handover has to be reported to the group leader.

### SCBA monitoring

The communication between a group leader and a troop leader is not unidirectional. The group leader is responsible for monitoring the amount of available air in the SCBA of his subordinated troops. He has to take care that troops follow the one-third-two-third-rule. There are different tools available to support this important task: Most fire departments in Germany equip their brigades with a special board [c.f. 5]. The board is equipped with three kitchen-timer-like mechanical count down clocks. Below these clocks it is possible to structure a sheet of paper in columns for each troop. When a troop leader reports the connection of the BAs, the group leader starts the kitchen timer associated with the troop at 10 minutes to apply the 10-minutes-20-minutes pattern and notes the ID of the troop and the time in the associated column. After a countdown clock expires, the group leader has to ask the corresponding troop leader via radio to report the current remaining pressure of the *least full* SCBA in his troop. The group leader notes the time and the pressure value in the corresponding column. If the SCBA is capable of carrying 300bar and the reported pressure is below 200 the group leader orders the troop to leave the danger zone. The troop then will be substituted by another.

## RESULTS AND FINDINGS

As stated in the introduction the assumed available time window on site for rescuing potential victims is very short (cf. Figure 1). The following analysis was driven by this circumstance and guided the design of the EMERGENCYMESSENGER introduced later on.

### Groups as a crucial operational units

The organization of the firefighting infrastructure in Germany can be understood as a network of very different roles and actors. The importance of a well-structured and effective coupling of all relevant factors can be demonstrated by the schedule shown in Figure 1. If a victim is exposed in a burning building and cannot move out of the life-threatening zone, even light smoke limits the time window for search and rescue to a maximum tolerance limit of 13 minutes before the victim loses consciousness. The time limit for a successful re-animation is limited to additional 4 minutes. After reaching this total limit of 17 minutes a rescue without serious consequences for the health of the victim becomes highly improbable. Extensive emergency planning and refinement over decades have optimized the first phases of a fire run until the arrival of the first group at the incident site. It turns out that effective and efficient work of the first arriving *group* is crucial for searching and rescuing victims within the given limits of the remaining 5 minutes on site. It is the group leader who has to investigate, decide and command and it is the troop leader with his troop member that has to perform actions to search and rescue the victim.

To understand what makes an effective, efficient and successful firefighting practice, focusing on the work of the smallest independent unit 'group' is crucial. The limited available time for acting on-site in relation to the complex cooperative tasks and the essential need for an adequate monitoring means effective use of time is critical.

### Autonomy: Organizational and regulatory aspects

Indoor troops work autonomously under potentially life-threatening conditions. The group leader is responsible for supporting the safety of his troops by monitoring the progress of their actions and for intervening if the operational situation requires a readjustment of the given commands or the complete abandonment of victims or affected objects. Group leaders rely on the flow of information in order to decide whether a troop is performing normally or if there are serious problems that require further actions.

Due to the high level of autonomy of indoor attacking troops, monitoring has to be framed as a communication problem: If a group leader is not able to assess the current operational state of a troop in the life-threatening danger zone, regulations assume an accident to the unreachable troop. The group leader has to report this accident to the incident commander and he has to change the mission target towards rescuing the unreachable troop. In this case the incident commander has to abort or at least interrupt the current operations and mission targets. The new orders are focused on searching and rescuing the potentially threatened troop. To support the rescue operation the incident commander has to call additional forces from other stations. These forces have to drive with several vehicles through traffic with exclusive privileges which always is a source for further accidents with other traffic participants. These additional forces are not available for other emergency cases.

After such an accident the incident commander and the responsible group leader have to give account for the decisions they made before the administration, which has been described as embarrassing especially for those cases were the troop was unreachable but turns out to be working normally and without any problems. Unburdening group leaders from these pressures can be considered as an important contribution to support the coordinative work of group

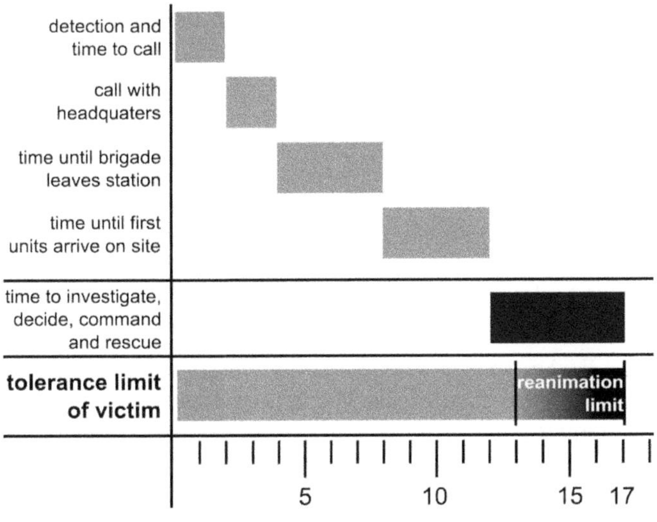


**Figure 1 Available time window for a firefighting group to rescue victims in a smoked environment** [11]

leaders and troops. This encompasses more robust communication infrastructures including the possibility to continuously monitor and assess the actual state of connectivity to troops to overcome the current practice of trial and error when estimating reachability.

### Responsibility: Dealing with uncertainty

After ordering troops into a building, the monitoring phase must not be seen as a continuous flow of information about the operating troop. Due to the autonomy of the troop operating indoors monitoring can be characterized as *periodically* reducing uncertainty. Periods are structured by an agreement evolved from regulation, education, training, experience and a mutual cultivation of trust. That is, for a group leader uncertainty begins and grows after every act of communication. The longer the indoor operations proceed without any communication, the more uncertainty about the current state of affairs inside the building grows. To fulfill his responsibility a group leader has to decide at any time during indoor work whether it is important to mitigate the uncertainty for monitoring and safety reasons or to let the troop work autonomously without disturbing the ongoing search and rescue work.

If communication breaks down, growing uncertainty cannot be mitigated. Depending on the level of experience and on current context, the group leader has to decide whether to escalate the mission from routine firefighting to a search and rescue mission to save the lives of his comrades. We discovered that experienced group leaders do not always immediately report an accident to an indoor troop after a communication breakdown. They try to balance all available and relevant factors to ground this far-reaching decision: At what point did the current communication breakdown occur? Did other break downs happen before during the current incident? How threatening may the current situation be inside the building? What is the structure of the affected building? What trust does the group leader have in the skills and experience of the affected troop leader? What self-assessment of his skills and experiences does the group leader have? Considering all these factors under tight time constraints causes high levels of stress even for the most experienced group leaders, they report. This may lead into time loss and increases the possibility of wrong decisions with far-reaching consequences.

With the currently available equipment, monitoring indoor troops is a permanent tradeoff between a growing uncertainty and the disturbance of ongoing time-critical operations of the involved troops. Decreasing the costs of communication between group leaders and troops in terms of effort, time and inconvenience would allow for saving time and would enable group leaders to intensify the monitoring of the troops if necessary. Indicators for a successful communication would enable group leaders to decide whether a conversational partner does not answer because he is too busy or because he simply has not received the radio message or because he is in serious trouble.

### Technical and practical constraints of communication technologies in use

In Germany in the domain of emergency response there are two standards of voice over radio: One standard works on a 4m wavelength (68MHz to 87.5MHz) and is used for long range communication between vehicles and the headquarters. The other standard works within the 2m band (165 MHz to 174 MHz) and is used for voice communication on site. Even with its long wavelength voice over radio communication in the 2m band suffers from problems due to limited penetrative power in large buildings and in basements, garages etc. Unfortunately, fighting fire in basements and underground garages is very difficult and dangerous and needs intensified monitoring by the group leader. As stated in several group discussions communication breakdowns in such situations are very common.

On-site, in typical fire runs, all fire fighting forces share the same channel within the 2m band, i.e. every radio message is broadcast and can be heard by everyone. The radio communication works in half duplex, therefore only one can talk at a time. To deal with constraints caused by the half duplex mode and by using a shared channel, a strict discipline is necessary to identify and address the intended sender and receiver of each radio message. In the following we present a short transcript of a typical radio message sent from a troop leader to his group leader. To illustrate the ratio between protocol and content the tactically relevant part is printed in bold.

> *Troop leader 1: Group leader 1 from troop leader 1.*
> *Group leader 1: Group leader hears.*
> ***Troop leader 1: First C-hose water on!***
> *Group leader 1: Roger.*

Firefighters with very different levels of experience and skills all agreed on the problematic combination of using radio set while working with SCBAs. Firefighters have to adapt the way they breathe under the protective mask to be understandable via radio. We also observed that troop leaders interrupt their actions, such as moving forward to search an apartment, to fully concentrate on listening and answering radio messages. In most of the observed radio communication situations, mission critical activities had to be postponed in order to answer radio requests.

Another important aspect of voice over radio is the synchronic character of communication and the ephemeral nature of the spoken word. Incoming requests have to be answered immediately to maintain the association of request and response. Both, the group leader and the troop leader have to interrupt current activities to respond on requests to prevent misconceptions. Interrupting the current flow of work is considered problematic, in particular by troop leaders. In the training missions, we observed that group leaders only make a few notes which often are related to SCBA monitoring. In case of losing contact to a troop or having an accident of a troop member group leaders have to recapitulate relevant events from memory, which is a challenge especially in stressful situations.

The efficiency of voice over radio communication can be increased significantly by reducing protocol-overhead through the automation of addressing and acknowledging. Alternatively, multi-hop capable network-topologies or ad-hoc deployed communication infrastructures could overcome these limitations by reducing radio communication breakdowns. Infrastructures should provide information about operability to enable group leaders and troop leaders to judge the uncertainty caused by malfunctions or technical constraints (c.f. [2]). The disadvantages of speaking under a protective mask shift the focus towards nonverbal forms of communication. Such a shift would open the design space for new forms of interaction and would allow for a complete reconsideration of the analyzed problems.

## DESIGNING FOR COMMUNICATION SUPPORT: THE EMERGENCY MESSENGER

Based on the results of the domain analysis, we proposed a hybrid communication concept, i.e. we decided not to adapt or completely substitute the voice over radio communication but to complement it by a text based messenger with predefined messages and categories. Such a text based messenger concept would allow group and troop leaders to send recurring status updates by selecting and sending predefined text messages. This is a situation where it is possible to delimit commonly sent requests to a troop, augmented with sets of associated answer possibilities. Thus, the receiver of such a request has not to encode an answer character by character but only has to choose from a list.

We designed two different types of devices to support the different needs of group leaders and troop leaders. We developed an application for the group leader and installed it on a ruggedized tablet-PC. For troop leaders we developed dedicated hardware, the EMERGENCYMESSENGER (c.f. Figure 2). For the interaction, we chose a form factor similar to devices firefighters are used to, e.g. the manometer of the SCBA. To minimize the disturbance of the troop leader's operations we designed the EMERGENCYMESSENGER to allow for a one-handed operation similar to mechanical stop-watches. The device has three buttons for interaction; button (1) and (2) are for scrolling up and down; button (3) is a kind of "Enter" button; pushing button (1) and (2) together is "Escape". A piezo sound generator (4) notifies incoming messages and gives acoustic feedback while pushing a button. A haptic feedback is provided by a vibration motor.

The display shows a graphical user interface structured as follows. It has three areas: The upper status bar, the categories/requests tiles and the lower status bar. The upper status bar shows a mobile phone-like Received Signal Strength Indicator (RSSI) on the right side and white dots on the left side. The dots represent the number of messages sent from the device but yet unacknowledged by the group leader.

The lower status bar shows the time since the SCBA of the troop has been connected to the protective mask. The number on the right is the remaining pressure in the SCBA in atmospheres (unit 'bar'). The categories/requests field is divided into tiles. Each tile represents a predefined message category or a received request. With the buttons (1) and (2) it is possible to scroll through the tiles. The selected tile is highlighted in black. By pushing the "Enter" button (3) the user opens the selected category/request. The opened category/request is shown in Figure 2 (right); the associated messages/responses are listed below. The user can select from this list by scrolling with buttons (1) and (2). Button (3) is to send a selected message/response. To jump back to the categories/requests tiles the user can escape the current path by pushing button (1) and (2) together.

The list of predefined categories (in Figure 2 (left) the eight tiles shown) and the associated messages can be defined by the firefighters and transferred to the device with a software application. This enables different firefighting brigades to adapt the EMERGENCYMESSENGER to their customary communication routines. Incoming requests sent by a group leader are notified by a continuously beeping sound and a notification screen. The troop leader has to push the "Enter" button (3) to stop the beeping and to close the notification. By doing this a receipt is sent to the group leader to acknowledge the recipience of the request. After that the incoming request is opened and the list of associated responses is shown (c.f. Figure 2 right). The user can select and send a response by pushing button (3) like mentioned above.

## USER EXPERIENCE EVALUATION

To evaluate the usage and appropriation of the EMERGENCYMESSENGER we conducted 14 training missions on 8 workshop days distributed over a time of 1.5 years. We benefited from the possibilities in the training center we had access to. The indoor troops in our training missions operated in real and full scale buildings where they had to deal with darkness and artificial smoke. It was possible to augment the incident scene with screaming voices coming from speakers and a fire-simulating lighting system. A fully working water supply was available for the fire engines and hoses. The firefighters were fully equipped including state of the art radio sets (cf. Figure 3). Training missions followed the minimum requirements of the educational standards in firefighting.

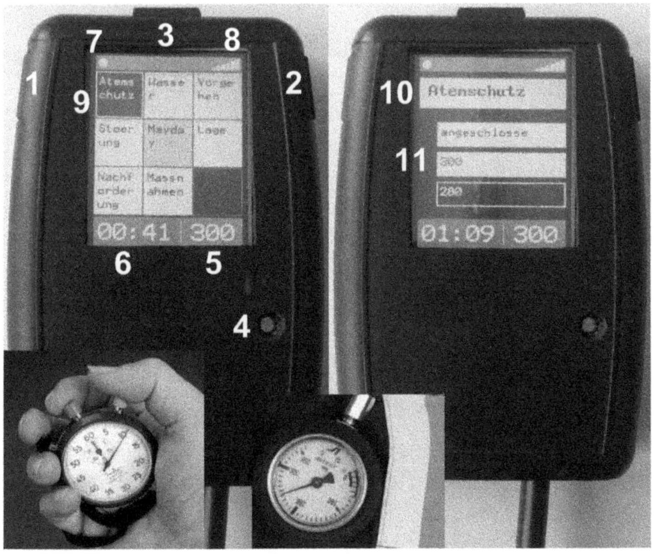


**Figure 2 (left) Main menu and (right) sub menu of the EmergencyMessenger; (lower left) one-handed stop-watch interaction scheme; (lower right) SCBA manometer**

The more realistic the missions were, the more difficult it was to document the effects of the introduced system for evaluation purposes. We decided to approach the evaluation from different perspectives. As a basis for further investigations on the impact of the EM system, we measured the actual *quantitative* benefits regarding time savings by analyzing the logs, video- and audio-recordings. As a reference we first analyzed the radio communication of the conventional training missions by counting the number of radio messages and the length of interruptions of other firefighting tasks they caused. Later, after introducing the EMERGENCYMESSENGER system, we did the same analysis of all training missions with the introduced system. A simple comparison of the data revealed significant advantages of the introduced system regarding absolute time savings.

Based on these quantitative findings we conducted further inquiry on the *qualitative* impact of the EMERGENCYMESSENGER concept on the addressed firefighting practices. For this purpose, we especially focused on the post-mission debriefings and discussions. We analyzed the data by open inductive coding: We extracted statements from the debriefings relating to the changes in practice reported by practitioners. We identified relevant categories by interpreting these statements in an iterative way. The identified categories led us to further statements and categories in the data. In the end, the categorization

**Figure 3 (left) Troop fully equipped with SCBA prepared for indoor attacking. The troop leader on the right is equipped with the EmergencyMessenger device. (right) Usage of the EmergencyMessenger device before entering the danger zone.**

process ended in saturation where no further topics, patterns and categories were found in the available data (c.f. [8]).

In the next sections we summarize the results of the analysis of the documented training missions and debriefing sessions. We limit the results to the categories *Performance*, *Standardization* and *Complementation* which are most relevant for the addressed firefighting practices.

### Interaction performance

We find evidence in the quantitative results that the EMERGENCYMESSENGER enables group and troop leaders to communicate significantly faster in relation to the established voice over radio communication:

- While using radios we observed 12 acts of communication in average between the group leader and one indoor troop.
- Even without any other traffic on the shared radio channel, we observed problems in communication such as bad link quality, no responses from the addressee or difficulties in understanding concrete information (like SCBA filling levels). Problems that needed further treatment like requests to repeat occurred in at least 3 and up to 8 cases of radio communication.
- Indoor troops needed 12-14 min. on average to find a missing person and to hand him/her over to the medical services.
- 04:33 minutes on average of this time are spent with radio communication which means 27 seconds on average for each act of radio communication.

We observed that the introduction of the EMERGENCYMESSENGER concept led into a more detailed level of reporting and monitoring:

- While using the EMERGENCYMESSENGER we counted 17 acts of communication in average between the group leader and one indoor attacking troop.
- The ad-hoc deployed ZigBee based network provided coverage of 100% in an apartment with kitchen, bath and 4 rooms on the second floor. We observed no problems in communication that needed further treatment.
- Attacking troops spent 2:37 min. in average for communication with the EMERGENCYMESSENGER which means 9 seconds in average for each act of text based communication.

The reasons for this significant decrease of communication efforts are manifold: Due to the direct addressing of messages and answers, the EMERGENCYMESSENGER approach dispenses with the need for effortful protocols as described above. The predefined messages have been perceived as unambiguous and understandable independent of the environmental conditions. Voice over radio communication, as we have seen, can be problematic in relation to audibility. Talking through a protective mask over a medium susceptible to interference to a group leader standing right beside a fire truck with a running engine and operating pump is very difficult and error prone. This way of communication regularly needs double checking and repeating to allow for unambiguous information exchange. In turn double checking and repeating blocks the shared channel and hinders others, adding to time costs. By using textual messages it is possible to keep all incoming and outgoing messages in a persistent history. In case of an incoming message, troops are able to complete the current activities before answering to an incoming request. Participating firefighters stated that the shift from synchronicity to asynchronicity of communication supports less disturbed and more efficient workflows for both the group leaders and the indoor troops.

### Standardization vs. expressiveness

Firefighting in Germany (like in many other countries) is characterized by a high quota of volunteers. Due to the establishment of effective fire safety regulations, the number of fire runs has decreased constantly in the last decades. Ironically, volunteer firefighters are less often involved in fire runs. According to the experiences of the participating group leaders and brigade leaders in our project, volunteer firefighters often struggle with communicating appropriately in stressful situations as a result of their relative inexperience. With regard to this trend, the participating firefighters in our project identified an important contribution of the EM approach especially for volunteer forces: The predefined categories and the associated messages provide a good overview of tactical needs for communication between group leaders and associated troops. The catalogue of predefined messages and categories has an educational value for firefighters to maintain their communicative skills in incidents.

Participating firefighters working at the firefighting training center identified a possibility for the standardization of heterogeneous communication practices across the large number of volunteer fire stations in Germany. With the EMERGENCYMESSENGER it is possible to share and discuss catalogues of messages and categories e.g. in responsible committees or even in online-communities of volunteering firefighters. Fire brigades then can agree on a common set of predefined messages to harmonize the communication practices for a region where stations have to cooperate to face bigger incidents. Despite the high level of confidence regarding the impact of the EMERGENCYMESSENGER for firefighting, the conventional voice over radio communication remains very important. Experienced group leaders read between the lines to decide whether a troop can continue with operations or it should be replaced by another troop. Troop leaders make use of rhetorical questions to signal their group leader their situation or constitution. During a map exercise a troop leader explained the role of rhetoric with an example:

> *"As a troop leader when I leave a burning apartment and I have enough air to receive a new order, I can ask 'I have a pressure of 260, I'll reenter the apartment now for this or that, ok?' Or I can ask: 'Are there further orders*

*for my troop? I have a remaining pressure of 260. Do I have to enter the apartment again?' An experienced group leader immediately recognizes the difference."*

The expressiveness of the EMERGENCYMESSENGER is clearly too limited to cover all possibilities and aspects of spoken language in such a social setting.

### Complementation vs. substitution

The disciplined application of trained tactics and procedures makes the necessary routine communication e.g. for monitoring and reporting operations inside the building predictable and structured. The text based communication approach implemented by the EM contributes significantly to the efficiency and effectiveness of sharing tactical information between group leaders and troops. Nevertheless, fire runs entail a high potential for unforeseen events. In such situations involved actors have to articulate the circumstances very fast and precisely. For unanticipated situations, then, the EM is inappropriate due to its limited expressiveness. Therefore, during our training missions with our prototypes and the corresponding debriefing sessions we observed a strong attachment to the conventional verbal communication techniques as a channel which enables participants to explain a complex nexus of facts and figures, assessments, estimations and even guesses. In situations where indoor troops experience disorientation or even an accident, a voice channel provides possibilities to express fears and to provide reassurance. The participating firefighters see the EM as a useful complement to and progression of an old but time-proven technique.

## DISCUSSION

### Anticipation vs. Unpredictability

One important finding of analyzing the training missions and the debriefing sessions was the self-conception of the work of firefighting and emergency response: Members of the firefighting domain have a very different understanding of the term "emergency". From the perspective of the domain, an incident like a burning apartment is not in and of itself an emergency case. Firefighters in Germany have to participate in a large number of courses in dedicated firefighting schools and must pass exams to demonstrate their knowledge and skills. Formal education complemented by regular training missions and a rigid paramilitary structure form the basis for the development of professional routines. Within the uncertainty of an incident these routines help to establish a work flow which results in efficient, target oriented actions. This means that what for an outsider might constitute an emergency can be, for them, routine. The term 'emergency' applied to the domain of firefighting means a breakdown of the routines experienced in communication breakdowns, losing orientation or having a life-threatening accident. The design of our communication concept focuses on the routines which have a high level of predictability. In CSCW there are discourses about the consequences of the introduction of predefined categories to support communication in cooperative social settings. One may be reminded to the application of speech act theory in cooperative systems by Winograd and Flores in [6] and [20] and the critique of Suchman in [17]. This raises interesting problems in relation to the 'discipline' or 'politics' of predetermined categories. The case we describe here, however, far from imposing an external discipline, supports a set of disciplines internalized through long practice. The safety, effectiveness and efficiency of the domain of firefighting are reliant on exactly those disciplining momentums and established routines. Firefighters are familiar with a structure of command and obedience and commit themselves to it, knowing and accepting the positive impact on the safety for each of them. By designing a complementary communication concept and leaving the voice channel for unpredictable non-routine situations the concept allows for both routinized and exceptional circumstance, and provides communication channels to support both.

### Overcoming technical constraints

In our participatory design workshops, firefighters considered the connectivity problem as crucial for monitoring autonomously working troops. Our communication concept fits a large range of different communication infrastructures including ad-hoc deployable mesh networks to overcome physical barriers and constraints. Research on firefighting in the first line of intervention has shown that it possible to equip firefighters with ad-hoc deployable devices to support certain tactical aspects e.g. navigation [15].

### Addressability and awareness

The design of the communication concept allows for directly addressing the sender and receiver of a message. This shift unburdens participants from vigilantly listening on the shared channel and enables senders and receivers to communicate without blocking a scarce resource. The price of this shift is a possible loss of awareness of every participant about the current state of affairs during an incident. However, the design concept allows for a circumspect and selectively distribution of communication to actors who 'need to know' while sparing others from a disruptive information overflow.

## CONCLUSIONS

In the domain of emergency response, research is often dedicated to the investigation, analysis and design of tools to support the management of critical incidents. In the domain of firefighting we identified the importance of efficient work practices at the first line of intervention. We point out the advantages and disadvantages of voice over radio communication. Radio sets are an important instrument to support the coordination between group leaders and indoor operating troops. However, we also identified shortcomings of voice over radio. Based on the identification of routines grounded in discipline and rigid structures we designed in cooperation with volunteer and career firefighters a new communication concept and evaluated it in a number of training missions. Drawing on Winograd's language/action perspective [20], we complemented the conventional radio communication with a text based messaging tool which offers a predefined set of structured message categories and requests. Based on this device, we explored new practices of routine communication which turned out to be more efficient and convenient compared to the existing practices.

## ACKNOWLEDGEMENTS

We thank all the volunteer firefighters of the fire brigade Münster and Telgte (Germany) and the Institute of Firefighting of the State North Rhine-Westphalia / Germany for participating in the 'Koordinator' project. The research project was funded by the German Federal Ministry of Education and Research contract number 13N11752.

## REFERENCES

1. Blomberg, J. and Karasti, H. Reflections on 25 Years of Ethnography in CSCW. *Computer Supported Cooperative Work (CSCW) 22*, 4-6 (2013), 373–423.
2. Chalmers, M. *Seamful design: showing the seams in wearable computing*. IEE, 2003.
3. Denef, S., Keyson, D., and Oppermann, R. Rigid structures, independent units, monitoring. *Proceedings of the 2011 annual conference on Human factors in computing systems - CHI '11*, ACM Press (2011), 1949.
4. Denef, S., Ramirez, L., Dyrks, T., and Stevens, G. Handy Navigation in Ever-Changing Spaces: An Ethnographic Study of Firefighting Practices. *Proceedings of the SIGCHI Symposium on Designing Interactive Systems*, ACM Press (2008).
5. Denef, S., Ramirez, L., and Dyrks, T. Letting tools talk: interactive technology for firefighting. *Conference on Human Factors in Computing Systems*, (2009), 4447–4452.
6. Flores, F., Graves, M., Hartfield, B., and Winograd, T. Computer systems and the design of organizational interaction. *ACM Transactions on Information Systems 6*, 2 (1988), 153–172.
7. Geertz, C. *The interpretation of cultures : selected essays*. Basic Books, New York, NY, 1973.
8. Glaser, B.G. and Strauss, A. *The Discovery of Grounded Theory: Strategies for Qualitative Research*. Aldine Transaction, New Brunswick, NJ, USA, 1999.
9. Gross, T. Supporting Effortless Coordination: 25 Years of Awareness Research. *Computer Supported Cooperative Work (CSCW) 22*, 4-6 (2013), 425–474.
10. Jiang, X., Chen, N.Y., Hong, J.I., Wang, K., Takayama, L., and Landay, J.A. Siren: Context-aware Computing for Firefighting. *Pervasive Computing - Second International Conference, PERVASIVE 2004, Linz/Vienna, Austria, April 21-23, 2004. Proceedings*, Springer Berlin Heidelberg (2004), 87–105.
11. Landesfeuerwehrschule Schleswig-Holstein. Die Aufgaben der Gruppenführung. *http://www.lfs-sh.de*, 2006. http://www.lfs-sh.de/Ausbildung/Start/PraesentationZA.php.
12. Landgren, J. and Nulden, U. A study of emergency response work: patterns of mobile phone interaction. *CHI '07: Proceedings of the SIGCHI conference on Human factors in computing systems*, ACM (2007), 1323–1332.
13. Landgren, J. Making action visible in time-critical work. *Proceedings of the SIGCHI conference on Human Factors in computing systems - CHI '06*, ACM Press (2006), 201.
14. Ramirez, L., Dyrks, T., Denef, S., and Stevens, G. Context as a resource for diagnostic work. *Proceedings of the Eurpoean Conference on Computer Supported Cooperative Work, ECSCW*, (2007).
15. Ramirez, L., Dyrks, T., Gerwinski, J., Betz, M., and Scholz, M. Landmarke: an ad hoc deployable ubicomp infrastructure to support indoor navigation of firefighters. *Personal Ubiquitous Computing*, Special Issue on Extreme Navigation (2011), 1–14.
16. Rohde, M., Stevens, G., Brödner, P., and Wulf, V. Towards a paradigmatic shift in IS. *Proceedings of the 4th International Conference on Design Science Research in Information Systems and Technology - DESRIST '09*, ACM Press (2009), 1.
17. Suchman, L. Do categories have politics? *Computer Supported Cooperative Work (CSCW) 2*, 3 (1994), 177–190.
18. Toups, Z.O. and Kerne, A. Implicit coordination in firefighting practice: design implications for teaching fire emergency responders. *CHI '07: Proceedings of the SIGCHI conference on Human factors in computing systems*, ACM (2007), 707–716.
19. Weiser, M. The Computer for the 21st Century. *Scientific American 265*, (1991), 94–104.
20. Winograd, T. A language/action perspective on the design of cooperative work. *HUMAN-COMPUTER INTERACTION 3*, December 1986 (1987), 3–30.
21. Wulf, V., Rohde, M., Pipek, V., and Stevens, G. Engaging with practices: design case studies as a research framework in CSCW. *Proceedings of the ACM 2011 conference on Computer supported cooperative work - CSCW '11*, ACM Press (2011), 505.

www.ingramcontent.com/pod-product-compliance
Ingram Content Group UK Ltd.
Pitfield, Milton Keynes, MK11 3LW, UK
UKHW051420290926
15471UKWH00009B/1697

9 781450 332873